LIBRARY

Addictive Disorders
in Medical Populations

Addictive Disorders in Medical Populations

Editors

Norman S. Miller

Clinical Professor, Department of Medicine, Michigan State University and Courtesy Professor, Department of Psychiatry, The University of Florida, USA

Mark S. Gold

College of Medicine, Chairman, Departments of Psychiatry, Neuroscience, Anesthesiology, Community Health & Family Medicine, University of Florida College of Medicine and McKnight Brain Institute, USA

A John Wiley & Sons, Ltd., Publication

This edition first published 2010, © 2010, John Wiley & Sons Ltd.

Wiley-Blackwell is an imprint of John Wiley & Sons, formed by the merger of Wiley's global Scientific, Technical and Medical business with Blackwell Publishing.

Registered office: John Wiley & Sons Ltd, The Atrium, Southern Gate, Chichester, West Sussex, PO19 8SQ, UK

Other Editorial Offices:
9600 Garsington Road, Oxford, OX4 2DQ, UK
111 River Street, Hoboken, NJ 07030-5774, USA

For details of our global editorial offices, for customer services and for information about how to apply for permission to reuse the copyright material in this book please see our website at www.wiley.com/wiley-blackwell

Library of Congress Cataloguing-in-Publication Data

Addictive disorders in medical populations / editors, Norman S. Miller, Mark S. Gold.
     p. ; cm.
  Includes bibliographical references and index.
  ISBN 978-0-470-74033-0 (cloth)
  1. Patients–Substance use. 2. Comorbidity. 3. Dual diagnosis. 4. Substance abuse. I. Miller, Norman S. II. Gold, Mark S.
  [DNLM: 1. Substance-Related Disorders–diagnosis. 2. Substance-Related Disorders–therapy. WM 270 A225 2010]
  RC564.A325 20100
  362.29–dc22

                                                                                        2010010280

ISBN: 978-0-470-74033-0

A catalogue record for this book is available from the British Library.

Set in 10.5/12.5pt Times by Thomson Digital, Noida, India
Printed in Singapore by Markono Print Media Pte Ltd

1 2010

Contents

List of Contributors

Herman S. Bagga, James Buchanan Brady Urological Institute, Johns Hopkins Medical Institutions, Baltimore, Maryland, USA

Kristen L. Barry, University of Michigan Department of Psychiatry and Department of Veterans Affairs Serious Mental Illness Treatment Research and Evaluation Center (SMITREC), Ann Arbor, MI 48109, USA

Kathleen L. Becker, John Hopkins University School of Nursing, Baltimore, MD, USA

W. Murray Bennett, Department of Psychiatry and Behavioral Sciences, University of Washington School of Medicine, Seattle, Washington, USA

Kendra Gail Bergstrom, Division of Dermatology, University of Washington, Seattle, WA 98104, USA

Andrea Bial, Department of Medicine, Section of Geriatrics, University of Chicago Medical Center, Chicago, IL, USA

Frederic C. Blow, University of Michigan Department of Psychiatry and Department of Veterans Affairs Serious Mental Illness Treatment Research and Evaluation Center (SMITREC), Ann Arbor, MI 48109, USA

Shannon K. Bolon, Department of Family and Community Medicine, University of Cincinnati College of Medicine, Cincinnati, OH 45221, USA

W. Kline Bolton, Division of Nephrology, University of Virginia Health System, Charlottesville, VA 22908, USA

Carolina F. Braga, Department of Psychiatry, College of Medicine & McKnight Brain Institute, University of Florida, Gainesville, FL 32611, USA

Steven A. Branstetter, Department of Biobehavioral Health, The Pennsylvania State University, University Park, PA 16802-6501, USA

Ashley R. Braun, University of Illinois, Chicago, IL, USA

Laurie Brockmann, University of Michigan Department of Psychiatry, Ann Arbor, MI 48109, USA

Garland A. Campbell, Division of Nephrology, University of Virginia Health System, Charlottesville, VA 22908, USA

Kendall Campbell, Department of Community Health and Family Medicine, University of Florida, Gainesville, FL 32611, USA

Lucy Chen, MGH Center for Translational Pain Research, Department of Anesthesia and Critical Care, Massachusetts General Hospital, Harvard Medical School, Boston, MA 02114, USA

James A. Cocores, Department of Psychiatry, University of Florida College of Medicine and McKnight Brain Institute, Gainesville, FL 32611, USA

Abdullah Demirkol, Drug Health Services, Sydney South West Area Health Service, Sydney, and University of Sydney, Australia

Hartmut Derendorf, Department of Pharmaceutics, University of Florida, Gainesville, FL 32611, USA

Daniel P. Evatt, University of Illinois, Chicago, IL, USA

John Finney, Veterans Affairs Palo Alto Health Care System and Stanford University School of Medicine, Menlo Park, CA 94025, USA

Marc Fishman, Mountain Manor Treatment Center, Baltimore, MD 21229, USA, and Department of Psychiatry and Behavioral Sciences, Johns Hopkins University School of Medicine, Baltimore, MD 21205, USA

Kimberly G. Blumenthal, Yale University School of Medicine, New Haven, CT 06510, USA

Mark S. Gold, College of Medicine, Chairman, Departments of Psychiatry, Neuroscience, Anesthesiology, Community Health & Family Medicine, University of Florida College of Medicine and McKnight Brain Institute, Gainesville, FL 32611, USA

Mark L. Gonzalgo, The James Buchanan Brady Urological Institute, Department of Urology, Johns Hopkins Medical Institutions, Baltimore, MD, USA

Alan H. Gradman, Division of Cardiovascular Diseases, The Western Pennsylvania Hospital, Temple University School of Medicine (Clinical Campus), Pittsburgh, Pennsylvania, USA

Noni A. Graham, Department of Psychiatry, College of Medicine and McKnight Brain Institute, University of Florida, Gainesville, FL 32611, USA

Larry Gray, University of Chicago, Pritzker School of Medicine, Department of Pediatrics, Section of Developmental Pediatrics, Comer Children's Hospital at the University of Chicago, Chicago, IL, USA

Deborah V. Gross, MD, Psychiatry and Addiction Medicine, Medical Director, Ridgeland, MS 39157, USA

K.P. Gunaga, Toxicology Testing Center, Sparrow Health System, St. Lawrence Campus, Lansing, MI 48915, USA, and Division of Human Pathology, College of Human Medicine, Michigan State University, East Lansing, MI 48824, USA

Satheesh Gunaga, Henry Ford Wyandotte Hospital, Department of Emergency Medicine and Medical Education, Wyandotte, MI 48192, USA

Thomas J. Guzzo, The James Buchanan Brady Urological Institute, Department of Urology, Johns Hopkins Medical Institutions, Baltimore, MD, USA

Paul S. Haber, Drug Health Services, Royal Prince Alfred Hospital, Sydney, Australia, and Addiction Medicine, University of Sydney, Sydney, Australia

Jason T. Hedrick, Department of Surgery, Division of Surgical Oncology, Wright State University, Dayton, OH, USA

Adrienne J. Heinz, University of Illinois, Chicago, IL, USA

Yoshimune Hiratsuka, Department of Ophthalmology, Juntendo University School of Medicine, Tokyo, Japan

Norman G. Hoffmann, Evince Clinical Assessments, Waynesville, NC, USA, and Western Carolina University, Cullowhee, NC, USA

Robert C. Hyzy, Division of Pulmonary and Critical Care Medicine, University of Michigan, Ann Arbor, MI, USA

Nosheen Javed, Division of Cardiovascular Diseases, The Western Pennsylvania Hospital, Temple University School of Medicine (Clinical Campus), Pittsburgh, Pennsylvania, USA

Jon D. Kassel, University of Illinois, Chicago, IL, USA

Kenneth L. Kirsh, The Pain Treatment Center of the Bluegrass, Lexington, KY 40503

Stephen A. Klotz, Section of Infectious Diseases, University of Arizona, Tucson, Arizona, USA

Firas H. Kobeissy, Department of Psychiatry, College of Medicine & McKnight Brain Institute, University of Florida, Gainesville, FL 32611, USA, and Center for Neuroproteomics and Biomarkers Research

Karol L. Kumpfer, Department of Health Promotion and Education, University of Utah, Salt Lake City, Utah 84112, USA

Jessica B. Leitzsch, Division of Nutrition, Department of Bioscience and Biotechnology, Drexel University, Philadelphia, PA 19104, USA

Adam W. Levinson, James Buchanan Brady Urological Institute, Johns Hopkins Medical Institutions, Baltimore, Maryland, USA

Jiang Liu, Department of Pharmaceutics, University of Florida, Gainesville, FL 32611, USA

Roberta Springer Loewy, UC Davis, University of California, Sacramento, CA 95670, USA

Sabina Low, Department of Psychology, Wichita State University, Wichita, Kansas 67260, USA

Tracy R. Luckhardt, Division of Pulmonary, Allergy, and Critical Care, University of Alabama Birmingham, Birmingham, AL, USA

John McKellar, Veterans Affairs Palo Alto Health Care System and Stanford University School of Medicine, Menlo Park, CA 94025, USA

Mary C. McCarthy, Division of Trauma/Surgical Critical Care/Emergency General Surgery, Wright State University–Boonshoft School of Medicine, Miami Valley Hospital, Dayton, OH 45409, USA

Robert Mallin, Department of Family Medicine, Medical University of South Carolina, Charleston, SC 29425, USA

Jianren Mao, MGH Center for Translational Pain Research, Department of Anesthesia and Critical Care, Massachusetts General Hospital, Harvard Medical School, Boston, MA 02114, USA

Clifford Martin, Section of Infectious Diseases, University of Arizona, Tucson, Arizona, USA

Phyllis J. Mason, John Hopkins University School of Nursing, Baltimore, MD, USA

Charles Meredith, Department of Psychiatry and Behavioral Sciences, University of Washington School of Medicine, Seattle, Washington, USA

Lisa J. Merlo, Department of Psychiatry, Division of Addiction Medicine, University of Florida, Gainesville, FL 32611, USA

Norman S. Miller, Clinical Professor, Department of Medicine, Michigan State University, East Lansing, Michigan 48824, USA, and Courtesy Professor, Department of Psychiatry, The University of Florida, Gainesville, FL 32611, USA

Rudolf Moos, Veterans Affairs Palo Alto Health Care System and Stanford University School of Medicine, Menlo Park, CA 94025, USA

Michael E. Msall, Section of Developmental and Behavioral Pediatrics, University of Chicago, Pritzker School of Medicine, Kennedy Research Center on Intellectual and Neurodevelopmental Disabilities, Institute of Molecular Pediatric Sciences, Section of Community Health, Ethics, and Policy, Comer Children's Hospital at the University of Chicago and LaRabida Children's Hospital, Chicago, IL, USA

Geetha Nampiaparampil, General Adult Psychiatry, St. Vincent's Hospital, New York Medical College, New York City, New York, USA

Jennifer A. Nasser, Division of Nutrition, Department of Bioscience and Biotechnology, Drexel University, Philadelphia, PA 19104, USA

Sara Jo Nixon, Division of Addiction Research, Department of Psychiatry, University of Florida, Gainesville, FL 32610, USA

Milap A. Nowrangi, General Adult Psychiatry, Feinberg School of Medicine, Northwestern University, Chicago, Illinois, USA

Morrow Omli, Department of Psychiatry, Division of Addiction Medicine, University of Florida, Gainesville, FL 32611, USA

James R. Ouellette, Department of Surgery, Division of Surgical Oncology, Wright State University, Dayton, OH, USA

Ellen A. Ovson, MD, Internal Medicine, Hattiesburg, MS 39402, USA

Jennifer J. Park, University of Chicago, Pritzker School of Medicine, Kennedy Research Center and Institute of Molecular Pediatric Sciences, Section of Developmental and Behavioral Pediatrics, Comer Children's Hospital at the University of Chicago and LaRabida Children's Hospital, Chicago, IL, USA

Steven D. Passik, Department of Psychiatry and Behavioral Sciences, Memorial Sloan-Kettering Cancer Center, New York, NY, USA

Kiran Patel, Division of Nutrition, Department of Bioscience and Biotechnology, Drexel University, Philadelphia, PA 19104, USA

Robert A. Prather, Department of Psychiatry, University of Florida, Gainesville, FL 32610, USA

Richard Ries, Department of Psychiatry and Behavioral Sciences, University of Washington School of Medicine, Seattle, Washington, USA

Lauren J. Rogak, Department of Psychiatry and Behavioral Sciences, Memorial Sloan-Kettering Cancer Center, New York, NY, USA, and Health Outcomes Research Group, Department of Epidemiology and Biostatistics, Memorial Sloan Kettering Cancer Center, 307 E. 63rd Street, 2nd Floor, New York, NY, USA 10065

Mitchell H. Rosner, Division of Nephrology, University of Virginia Health System, Charlottesville, VA 22908, USA

Miguel R. Sanchez, Division of Dermatology, University of Washington, Seattle, WA 98104, USA

Gabriel Sarah, Health Sciences Center, University of Arizona, Tucson, Arizona, USA

Carol Schneiderman, Section of Infectious Diseases, University of Arizona, Tucson, Arizona, USA

Joel M. Silberberg, Division of Psychiatry and Law, Feinberg School of Medicine, Northwestern University, Chicago, Illinois, USA

C. Chapman Sledge, Chief Medical Officer at Cumberland Heights, and Secretary at American Society of Addiction Medicine, Nashville, TN 37209, USA

Zili Sloboda, Institute for Health and Social Policy, The University of Akron, Akron, OH, USA

Tatiana D. Starr, Department of Psychiatry and Behavioral Sciences, Memorial Sloan-Kettering Cancer Center, New York, NY, USA

Myles Stone, Section of Infectious Diseases, University of Arizona, Tucson, Arizona, USA

Kathryn M. Tchorz, Associate Professor of Surgery, Division of Trauma/Surgical Critical Care/Emergency General Surgery, Wright State University–Boonshoft School of Medicine, Miami Valley Hospital, Dayton, OH 45409, USA

Benita J. Walton-Moss, John Hopkins University School of Nursing, Baltimore, MD, USA

Erin L. Winstanley, Lindner Center of HOPE, Mason, OH 45040, USA, and Department of Psychiatry and Behavioral Neuroscience, University of Cincinnati College of Medicine, Cincinnati, OH 45221, USA

Christine Yuodelis-Flores, Department of Psychiatry and Behavioral Sciences, University of Washington School of Medicine, Seattle, Washington, USA

Preface

Drug and alcohol addictions occur commonly in medical populations; 25–50% of patients seen by primary care physicians have alcohol and drug disorders, with even higher prevalence in certain medical specialty populations. Drug addiction, alcohol addiction, and what has been called unhealthy drinking are even more common and prevalent in trauma centers and our society. Injury due to excess and dangerous consumption of alcohol causes almost 25% of trauma center admissions. Currently, there are no authoritative addiction texts with a focus on the identification, intervention, and management of either "addictive disorders in medical populations" or "medical complications in addiction populations". This book will be useful for those seeking information to help a patient or family with a tobacco, alcohol or drug problem. We hope this book can give answers and a direction to the identification and management of addictions and their medical complications in patient populations.

The death rate for alcohol-related injury patients after discharge is almost 200% higher than that of injury patients who were not drinking. Yet it was not until 2007 that the American College of Surgeons Committee on Trauma implemented a requirement that all Level I trauma centers have a way to provide alcohol screening and intervention to patients. Additionally, the Substance Abuse and Mental Health Services Administration (SAMHSA) has established and helped get codes for the Screening, Brief Intervention, Referral and Treatment (SBIRT) initiative to expand the physician and health professional treatment support and capacity for substance use and addiction. *Addictive Disorders in Medical Populations* covers this subject in depth as far as what to say and do as well as providing additional resources for the MD.

Neurobiological progress in the field of addiction has been amazing and evidence-based treatments have developed at a phenomenal pace, with bench to office applications for tobacco, alcohol, and drugs. Pharmacological and psychosocial treatments are covered in detail in this book, in clear practical terms. The medical and mental complications of addiction are explained comprehensively throughout the text. Clinical considerations are the predominant theme; however, the standards of clinical practice described in *Addictive Disorders in Medical Populations* are grounded in the most current research. The chapters have consistent organization, which includes uniform, plentiful, and practical presentations of both clinical and research materials. The authors are leaders in their fields, selected from the respective general medical and specialty areas.

We know all too well that most, if not all, MDs in practice today did not have the benefit of learning about the neuroscience of addiction and substance addiction when they learned their basic sciences in medical school. Worse yet, if they learned addiction and misuse identification, interventions, and treatment, it was from a book. Imagine learning examinations or labor and delivery by reading a book alone, without clinical correlation and context. When we started mandatory two-week addiction medicine clerkships for all University of Florida medical school students, we hoped but did not envision how much that would change our hospitals and the College of Medicine. Knowing where we are, we hope that this book bridges the gap between what the practicing health provider or specialist needs to know and what they have learned the hard way.

Norman S. Miller and Mark S. Gold

Acknowledgements

As Editors, we would like to acknowledge the work of Rachel Griffen and Paula Edge on this project.

Rachel Griffen's contributions were vital to recruiting authors for this groundbreaking book. She devoted herself to sustained effort in liaising with the authors until delivery of the manuscripts and deserves the heartfelt thanks of the editors who relied totally on her skill and dedication as managing editor.

Paula Edge showed keen editorial abilities and dedication to her craft in managing the editorial review process and bringing the project to successful completion.

Norman S. Miller and Mark S. Gold

Part One

Addictive disorders and medicine

Part One

1

Addictive disorders as an integral part of the practice of medicine

Norman S. Miller[1] and Mark S. Gold[2]

[1] Department of Medicine, Michigan State University, East Lansing, Michigan 48824, USA and Department of Psychiatry, The University of Florida, Gainesville, FL 32611, USA

[2] Departments of Psychiatry, Neuroscience, Anesthesiology, Community Health & Family Medicine, University of Florida College of Medicine and McKnight Brain Institute, Gainesville, FL 32611, USA

1.1 OVERVIEW

The role of physician in the prevention and treatment of addictive disorders is growing in importance and magnitude. The public and managed care organizations are increasingly looking to physicians for leadership and advocacy for patients who have drug and alcohol addictions. The political climate and enormous need combine to make the role of physicians essential to prevention and treatment strategies for addictive disorders. Efforts by physicians in the past have been slow and obstructionist, partly because of moral views and lack of training in addiction problems and disorders. Physicians who were not prepared to confront patients about their addictions and nonphysicians who could treat, but not communicate with the physicians, competed for the overall care of the patients. Frequently, patients had to bridge the gap at the expensive cost of delay in prevention and diagnosis of problematic use of alcohol and drugs.

Heretofore, physicians played a supporting role, or no role at all, in fostering and developing effective prevention and treatment methods for addictive disorders. The attitude of "see no evil, hear no evil, do no evil" no longer allows physicians to ignore common alcohol and drug problems in their patients. Increasingly, generalists are called upon to screen, detect, prevent, and treat alcohol and drug disorders in their populations.

The challenge to medical schools and resident training programs to provide education and clinical experience in addiction has never been greater or more pressing. In the past, despite the presence and affects of alcohol and drug-related disorders, medical schools and residency programs failed to competently teach screening, diagnosis and treatment of such disorders to students. Increasingly, medical students and residents became aware of the need and demonstrated interest in becoming knowledgeable and skilled in the prevention and treatment of alcohol and drug addiction. Both residency directors and curriculum deans affirmatively endorsed that assessment of deficiencies in training and

Addictive Disorders in Medical Populations   Edited by Norman S. Miller and Mark S. Gold

education for alcohol disorders would lead to significant improvements in medical education for residents and medical students. As a result, medical schools and psychiatry residency programs (at least in the major university settings) are integrating addiction education and experience into their programs [1].

We have a large body of knowledge and basic skills in the prevention and treatment of addictive disorders. Considerable resources have been spent on research and development of clinic methods for prevention and treatment. The next step is to implement what is effective and useful to patients. The role of physicians will become apparent if they concentrate on what is effective in preventing and treating addictive disease [2].

After reading this chapter you will better be able to understand:

1. The clinical prevalence of addictive disorders in the general as well as special circumstance populations.

2. The role of the physician in the prevention and treatment of addictive disorders.

3. Methods to improve prevention and treatment of addictive disorders primarily through improving medical school education.

1.2 CLINICAL PREVALENCE

1.2.1 Prevalence of alcohol and drug dependence in the general population

Alcohol and drug dependence are among the most prevalent illnesses in American society. The Epidemiological Catchment Area study, which is a survey of mental health and substance-related disorders in nearly 20 000 adult Americans, found a 13.5% lifetime prevalence of alcohol addiction or dependence, and 7% of drug dependence [3]. Alcoholism and related illnesses are major causes of morbidity and mortality in patients in the United States. More than half of all accidental deaths, suicides, and homicides are alcohol or drug related [4]. A significant proportion of fetal anomalies can be attributed to the use of drugs or alcohol during pregnancy, with an estimated rate of 11% of illicit drug use among pregnant women [5]. The use of intravenous methods of administering illicit drugs has contributed to the increasing number of deaths from AIDS, according to data from the Centers for Disease Control and Prevention (CDC) [6].

1.2.2 Prevalence of multiple drug use and dependence in treatment

The use of multiple drugs and alcohol is extraordinarily common (e.g., alcohol and cocaine, heroin and cocaine, marijuana with alcohol or cocaine). The large overlap of the use of drugs and alcohol has had significant ramifications for diagnosis and treatment as they are traditionally practiced [7–11].

Research models for dependence on alcohol and drugs are affected by multiple use and dependence. In practice, one drug is frequently substituted for another, and the majority of individuals develop combined alcohol and multiple-drug dependence. The concurrent and simultaneous occurrences of multiple drug and alcohol dependence suggest a generalized susceptibility to the various types of dependence [12–15].

1.2.3 Prevalence in the medical population

Drug and alcohol addiction are among the most common disorders seen in medical practice. They are at least as common as hypertension [16]. Addiction is associated with a wide range of problems, including pancreatitis, liver disease, accidents, suicide, depression, and anxiety. 20–50% of inpatient hospitalizations may be attributed to substance use and addiction, and 25–50% of emergency room visits are alcohol use and addiction related [17–22].

Although addiction is an extremely common disorder, it remains inadequately diagnosed and treated by physicians. Of the 20% of patients seen in ambulatory care settings who are estimated to be addicted to substances, only 5% of these patients are diagnosed [23]. Physicians do not diagnose or treat substance use and addiction with the same frequency, accuracy, or effectiveness as they do other chronic medical diseases [24,25]. In a recent study, resident physicians correctly identified less than half of the patients with positive scores on a CAGE questionnaire, 22% of patients with an alcohol addiction history, and 23% of patients with a history of substance addiction [26,27].

1.2.4   Prevalence in family and workplace populations

The psychological and social costs of alcoholism and drug addiction are considerable to patients in medical practice. Alcoholism is a major cause of family dysfunction, including domestic violence and child abuse. Over 40% of adults report exposure to problem drinkers in their families [28]. Alcoholism is a major contributor to poor job performance and productivity loss. Data show that 15% of heavy alcohol users missed work because of illness or injury in the past 30 days, and 12% of heavy users skipped work because of drinking in the past 30 days [29].

1.3   CLINICAL DIAGNOSIS

Physicians must make the diagnosis of alcohol and drug dependence to develop an integrated approach to medical education about addiction. Physicians must diagnose patients who present with abnormal alcohol and drug use [30–32]. Physicians must ask routine screening questions to all patients they see and maintain a high index of suspicion for addictive diseases, especially in light of the extreme levels of denial often present in addicted patients. Physicians seeing patients in high-risk populations, such as emergency departments, prisons, and trauma units, must have an especially high index of suspicion. A family history is the best predictor of addiction in patients; therefore, questions about family history take on special importance in the detection of substance addiction or dependence. In addition, patients with chief or presenting complaints such as sleep disorders, "stress," chronic dyspepsia, recurrent peptic ulcers, or recurrent trauma should also raise a physician's index of suspicion. Physicians must be taught to listen carefully for rationalization, minimization, and denial in patient's responses while observing their affective component associated with these complaints and responses [33].

1.3.1   Risk assessment by physicians

Physicians should be able to detect patients in environments that pose a risk for the development

of substance dependence. Categories of vulnerability to the use of alcohol, tobacco, and other drugs should be learned by every physician. Family environment includes family conflict, poor discipline style, parental rejection of the child, lack of adult supervision or family rituals, poor family management or communication, sexual and physical abuse, and parental or sibling modeling for use of alcohol, tobacco, and other drugs. School environment involves lack of school bonding and opportunities for involvement and reward, unfair rules, norms conducive to use of drugs, and school failure because of poor school climate. Community environment pertains to poor community bonding; community norms that condone alcohol, tobacco, and other drug addiction; disorganized neighborhoods; lack of opportunities for positive youth involvement; high levels of crime and drug use; endemic poverty; and lack of employment opportunities. Peer factors include bonding to peer groups whose members use alcohol, tobacco and other drugs or engage in other delinquent behaviors [34].

1.3.2   Physical examination and laboratory testing

The physical examination may be helpful in detecting alcohol or drug dependence. Information about intoxication, withdrawal, or alcohol-related or drug-related organ damage and disease may yield important information about the adverse complications of addictive illness. Although no specific finding is pathognomonic of alcoholism, a physician's use of physical findings may be valuable in penetrating denial and convincing patients of the significant extent of their alcohol and drug use. Laboratory tests, such as urine toxicology screen, macrocytic red cell indices, or for serum glutamic-oxabacetic transaminase and serum glutamic-pyruvic transaminase, may also be helpful. None of these, however, is of the same degree of importance and specificity as a thorough history for addiction with every patient [33].

1.4   CLINICAL COMORBIDITY

Substance addiction disorders have been associated with serious problems including violence, injury, disease, and death. In 2006, the CDC reported 13 470 injury deaths from alcohol-impaired motor vehicle crashes in the United States; this was almost 32% of all traffic-related deaths for that year [35].

It has been estimated that one in every four deaths can be attributed to the use of alcohol, tobacco, or some other form of drug. For example, tobacco use alone has been linked to 90% of lung cancer cases, 75% of emphysema cases, and 25% of ischemic heart disease cases [36].

1.5   TREATMENT OF MEDICAL DISORDERS ASSOCIATED WITH ALCOHOL AND DRUG USE AND ADDICTION

1.5.1   Physician intervention

Physicians should know how to provide simple interventions to eliminate or decrease substance misuse before it becomes dependence or addiction. Studies have shown that brief, empathic interventions by physicians can decrease the consumption and adverse effects of addictive substances by 20–50% [34,37–39]. Physicians should be taught that messages which state that the attainment of the goal of reducing alcohol-related problems is the patients' responsibility and which encourage abstinence are powerful modifiers of patients' behavior toward alcohol and drugs.

Physicians should be well versed in using prevention strategies for those patients at risk of substance addiction or dependence. Counseling patients about the health risks and dangers of substance misuse or addiction can be extremely effective in reducing their occurrence. The education of patients about the long-term and short-term consequences of substance misuse and addiction, including the severe risks encountered by drinking and driving, is fundamental to interventions by physicians. Physicians should be aware that many patients' peers probably do not approve of substance misuse and addiction, including the severe risks encountered by drinking and driving, is fundamental to interventions by physicians. Physicians should be aware that many patients' peers probably do not approve of substance use as a healthy activity, which may prove to be an effective deterrent. Physician communication and physician availability as a source of confidential information about addictions are key to successful interventions. Open discussion between patient and physician of issues relating to the health effects of alcohol and drugs can be extremely helpful [30,32].

1.5.2   Requirements of physicians for diagnosing and treating addictive disease

A physician specialist in the treatment of alcoholism and other drug addictions must:

• Possess a current MD or DO license.

• Be able to recognize and diagnose alcoholism or other drug dependencies at both early and late stages and possess sufficient knowledge and communication skills to prescribe a full range of treatment services for alcohol and other drug addiction patients, their families, or significant others.

- Demonstrate a functionally positive attitude toward addicted patients, their families, and indicated significant others.

- Be knowledgeable in addiction treatment and be able to intervene to get patients and their families or significant others into treatment for their needs.

- Be able to provide, refer, and support standard addiction treatment methods for alcohol and drug addictions.

- Be able to recognize and manage the medical and psychiatric complications of alcohol and other drug addictions.

- Be able to recognize and manage the signs and symptoms of withdrawal from alcohol and other drugs of addiction.

- Possess sufficient knowledge and communications skills concerning alcohol and other drug addictions to provide consultation, teach lay and professional people, and provide continuing education in this field.

General physicians must possess:

- The ability to competently obtain a history and perform a physical examination on patients with addictive disorder (this presumes an ability and willingness to hospitalize patients if necessary).

- An understanding of the medical, psychiatric, and social complications of addictive disorder (this presumes a knowledge of self-help groups, such as AA, Narcotics Anonymous, and Al-Anon, and presumes a knowledge of special groups for professionals).

- A positive attitude which is essential in establishing a relationship with patients in the treatment of alcoholism and drug addiction.

- A knowledge of the spectrum of this disease and the natural progression if untreated.

- A knowledge of the medical and psychiatric effects and organ damage attributable to alcoholism or other drug addictions (this presumes a knowledge of, and ability to prescribe, treatment).

- A knowledge of the classifications of drugs of addiction and their pharmacology and biochemistry (this presumes maintenance of current knowledge in this field and knowledge and skill in one or more methods of teaching and learning).

- A knowledge and skill in standard addiction treatment to prevent relapse and recurrence of adverse consequences of addictive disorders [40].

1.5.3   Abstinence-based method

Controlled studies have found significant results in treatment outcomes in abstinence-based programs, particularly when combined with referral to Alcoholics Anonymous (AA). The first randomized clinical trial of abstinence-based treatment showed significant improvement in drinking behavior compared with that of a more traditional form of treatment [41]. A total of 141 employed alcoholics were randomized to the abstinence-based program (Hazelden type) (n = 74) or to traditional-type treatment (n = 67). The abstinence-based treatment was significantly more involving, supportive, encouraging to spontaneity, and oriented to personal problems than was the traditional-type treatment. The one-year abstinence rate was significantly greater for the abstinence-based treatment; in addition, dropout rates were 7.9% for the abstinence treatment group and 25.9% for the traditional treatment group, respectively [42].

In another controlled study, 227 workers newly identified as alcoholics and cocaine addicts were randomly assigned to one of three treatment regimens: compulsory inpatient treatment, compulsory attendance at regimens; compulsory inpatient treatment, compulsory attendance at AA meetings; and a choice of options (i.e., inpatient, outpatient, or AA meetings). Inpatient backup was provided if needed [43]. On seven measures of drinking and drug use, the hospital group had significantly greater abstinence at a one-year and two-year follow-up. Those assigned to AA had the lowest abstinence rates, and those allowed to choose either an inpatient or outpatient program or AA had intermediate results. The programs for inpatient and outpatient treatment were abstinence based with eventual referrals to AA at discharge [43].

Previous evaluation studies of large populations of patients (>9750 subjects) enrolled for abstinence-based methods have shown favorable outcomes for addiction treatment. The populations consisted of multiply-dependent patients, including those with alcohol, prescription drug, cannabis, stimulant, cocaine, and opiate dependence (DSM-III-R Substance Dependence). The overall abstinence rates at one year were 60% for inpatients and 68% for outpatients (57% of the cases were contacted for inpatients, 62% for outpatients) [44,45]. However, abstinence rates were increased to 88% for inpatients and 93% for outpatients who participated in continuing care following discharge. At one-year follow-up, only 8% were attending continuing care after discharge in the inpatient treatment programs, and 17% were attending the outpatient programs. Moreover, abstinence rates after discharge were 75% for inpatients and 82% for outpatients who were regular attendees at AA. Accordingly, 46% and 51% of those discharged from the inpatient and outpatient programs, respectively, were attending AA at least once per week. Abstinence rates at one year for nonattendees at AA were 49% and 57%, respectively. Significant outcomes on other variables were reported, such as improved psychosocial functioning and employment and legal histories for those completing the treatment programs in these studies [44–46].

According to survey results [47] (1992) conducted by AA, recovery rates achieved in the AA fellowship were:

1. Of those sober in AA less than a year, 41% remain in the AA fellowship for an additional year [47].

2. Of those sober more than one year and less than five years, 83% remain in the AA fellowship for an additional year

3. Of those sober five years or more, 91% remain in the AA fellowship for an additional year. Attendance in abstinence-based treatment programs can increase the recovery rates in AA, such as 80% from 41% with referral to AA following the treatment program [46].

1.5.4 Improving alcoholism treatment

Although treatment for alcoholism and drug addiction is clearly and significantly effective, treatment is not always as successful as physicians would wish it to be, nor is it sufficiently available to those who need it. Current data show 35–40% of alcoholics undergoing outpatient treatment relapse within three months. Improving alcoholism treatment and its availability are important priorities. The Institute of Medicine (IOM) of the National Academy of Sciences conducted a comprehensive study of the alcohol treatment process and system, entitled Broadening the Basis of Treatment for Alcohol Problems [48]. The conclusions in its report emphasized that alcohol treatment was effective but that improvement of the current alcohol treatment system in a cost-effective manner was needed. The IOM report identified several areas of treatment that needed improvement. These included: (1) the need for improvements and standardization in the diagnosis and assessment of alcoholism; (2) the need for more community-based assessment and interventions; (3) the need to base treatment referrals and level of treatment on the assessments; (4) the need for improved linkages between primary care, community-based treatment, and specialized treatment services; (5) a treatment system that provides better continuity of care; (6) the need for adequate financing for a spectrum of treatment modalities and sites to match the diversity of the population; and (7) the elimination of organizational, personal, and regulatory barriers to the diagnosis and treatment of alcohol problems.

In response to the IOM report, several groups have developed guidelines for the development of model treatment systems to meet the diverse needs of patients with substance-related disorders. In 1993, the American Society of Addiction Medicine developed core benefit requirements for addiction treatment. These include: (1) the need for and level of treatment must be a clinical judgment based on established criteria (e.g., the American Society of Addiction Medicine Patient Placement Criteria) [49], with quality of care ensured by appropriate review; (2) the concept that treatment for substance-related disorders should be included in any basic health benefit; (3) the concept that coverage should include a continuum of primary care and specialty services; (4) that ongoing treatment evaluation, case management, and outcome studies should be an integral part of the ongoing evaluation of services; (5) that eligibility should be based on competent diagnosis using objective criteria (DSM-IV, ICD-9/10) [26]; (6) that coverage should be nondiscriminatory on the same basis as other medical care; and (7) that caps or limits on treatment should be applied on the same basis as is other medical care. The need for a comprehensive treatment benefit package was also affirmed at a researcher's recent consensus conference [48].

1.6   WHY PHYSICIANS ARE UNPREPARED TO TREAT DRUG- AND ALCOHOL-RELATED DISORDERS

Physician education and training in addictions has long been ignored, although it has recently begun to increase selectively in medical schools, psychiatry residency programs, and continuing medical education. A study that examined changes in alcohol and drug education in Unites States' medical schools between 1976 and 1992 [50] found positive changes in education about drug and alcohol addictions. The number of teaching units in addictions in medical schools had doubled. More opportunities existed for required and elective experiences in addiction treatment, and more teaching activities were based in alcohol treatment and drug treatment settings. Faculty members who were teaching in this area had increased, and medical school graduates reported greater satisfaction with the medical school curriculum in substance misuse and addiction education. The number of fellowship positions in addictions had increased, and more primary care physicians were participating in advanced training. However, although promising, these results also showed that only eight medical schools had mandatory courses in substance misuse and addiction treatment. In addition, with the exception of the departments of family medicine and psychiatry, less than one third of the departments in the specialties had even a single identified faculty member teaching in this area [51]. Medical educators do not spend anywhere near the same amount of time teaching in the area of addictions as they do in other areas of chronic disease, such as hypertension or cardiac disease, although these diseases are no more common than are the addictive disorders.

Clearly, given the poor rates of diagnosis and treatment of substance misuse and addiction by physicians, significant changes must continue to be made in our medical educational and training system to combat this problem. As has been previously mentioned, training in addictions has begun to increase, but whether these new measures have been wholly successful is unclear.

1.6.1   Recommendations for improving education training

A 1996 survey concerning alcohol- and drug-related disorders showed that little change had occurred in the way of increasing curriculum coverage in this area at that time. Family medicine residency directors, internal medicine residency directors, and medical school curriculum deans from randomly selected medical programs were invited to participate in this survey. The overwhelming majority of the responding curriculum deans (96%) reported that an integrated curriculum in drug and alcohol disorders would be at least somewhat helpful.

Although programs have not seen many changes in terms of the amount of the curriculum dedicated to Substance Use Disorder education, a spotlight has been placed on the program and action plans to improve medical education in this area. In both 2004 and 2006, the Office of National Drug Control Policy had a leadership conference on Medical Education in Substance Abuse. The 2004 conference had representatives from more than 60 different federal agencies, medical groups, and certification boards in attendance to discuss ways to increase physician's motivation and ability to prevent, diagnose, and treat various substance addiction disorders [52]. The 2006 Conference's main purpose was to provide a framework to improve the education and practice of addiction medicine. During this conference, attendees divided into work groups to address improvements needed in various areas, including both undergraduate, graduate, and continuing medical education in the area.

The implementation of national conferences and Web-based educational programs has shown that the importance of addiction medicine education in the medical school curriculum has been recognized. Unfortunately, no supplemental conference or Web-based program can take the place of direct core curriculum integration on this topic. Due to the great percentage of the patient population affected by substance addiction disorders, it is imperative that medical educators make implementation of substance use education a part of their core curriculum as quickly as possible. In the following is some additional information on research studies on integration of addictive disorder information into medical school education.

1.6.2 Research studies on medical education in the area of addictive medicine

Increases in technology and online learning have greatly contributed to additional medical student exposure in this area. Distance learning by the way of online courses has been added to many university options and is increasingly shaping parts of medical school education as well. Noted as a traditionally neglected field, addiction education was tested in this format at the New York University Medical School. An interactive Web module was designed to improve students' competence in the area of alcohol addiction screening and intervention techniques. This online module was offered as an alternative choice to attending a lecture on the same topic. Traditionally, first year medical students at New York University were given three chronological sessions on this topic, a lecture, a small group seminar, and then an OSCE case. The lecture and Web module shared the same format outlines, However, researchers hypothesized that the online module would be more effective than a traditional lecture in teaching medical students how to effectively interview and screen their patients for suspected alcohol addiction. Students were assigned to the lecture or module group based upon class schedule. One to three weeks after participating in one of these sessions, both groups of students participated in seminars in which the methods of alcohol screening and interventions were reviewed. Three to five weeks following the module or lecture exposure, students were rated on their performance in dealing with an OSCE Alcohol Case. The case presented to each student was that of an adult woman with hazardous drinking tendencies in need of cutting down on her alcohol consumption or stopping all together. Student performance was assessed using the AUDIT-C, CAGE, and six brief intervention components. Those who completed the Web-based module performed better on average than their lecture-based counterparts on both performance and intervention ratings on this standardized OSCE Case [53].

Computerized learning in this area has not been limited to undergraduate medical education. A study investigating the effectiveness of a CD-ROM and Web-based training program to provide formal tobacco intervention training in pediatric residency programs was started in 2004. A study conducted prior to this at the New Jersey Medical School confirmed that formal training in addressing tobacco increased resident tobacco intervention activities [54].

More recently, a study at the University of Florida showed that an innovative addictions curriculum improved ratings on a psychiatry clerkship. The addictions curriculum included a two-week required clinical addictions experience incorporated into the six-week psychiatry clerkship. Students were all supervised by board certified addictionologists. In addition, students had eight hours of didactic lectures on addictions and completed five addiction online modules. Results indicated that overall course ratings improved, as did student ratings of their preparedness for dealing with psychiatric problems in the primary care setting [55].

Also out of the University of Florida College of Medicine was a study that showed that the addition of video clips to psychiatry lectures enhanced long-term retention and improved attitudes about learning. These results have a potential application to a number of other areas and indicate that video can be a valuable resource for maintaining attention and interest in the lecture format [56].

1.7 SUMMARY

With increasing pressure on general physicians by managed care organizations and the public to treat and advocate for drug and alcohol addicted patients, it is more necessary than ever that physicians have the knowledge and skills to appropriately address this segment of the population.

Specifically, physicians need a better understanding of the prevalence of alcohol and drug dependence in a variety of populations, along with increased awareness of the economic impact of addictive illnesses on our society. Routine screening questions should be incorporated into patient encounters, and physicians should be able to identify environments that may pose a risk for the development of addiction. Physicians need training and practice in referring patients to treatment teams, monitoring patients in recovery and providing interventions that will eliminate or reduce substance misuse before it becomes addiction.

The treatment outcomes in abstinence-based programs, particularly those combined with referral to AA, have been encouraging, demonstrating that addiction is a treatable illness and not a character defect. In addition, several studies provide evidence that addition treatment is cost-beneficial, resulting in reduced medical costs, lowered absenteeism, and increased productivity.

Despite these encouraging results, there is still room for improvement. Treatment is not always effective, and it is not sufficiently available to everyone who needs it. Addicted individuals are both stigmatized and marginalized, and many are too ill to advocate for themselves.

Widespread recognition in the medical community of addiction as a treatable illness will contribute to a greater understanding of addictive disorders and reduce the stigma attached to the diagnosis and treatment of addiction. For this to occur, better training for physicians in the recognition and management of addictive disorders, starting at the medical school level, is necessary. The approval of addiction medicine as a clinical specialty by the American Medical Association has helped also to advance the legitimacy of addiction as a treatable illness, and provides a focal point for the synthesis and integration of clinical, teaching, and research activities central to addiction medicine. The combination of knowledge, skills, and attitudes outlined will go a long way toward increasing physicians' abilities to assist their patients with recovery from addiction.

REFERENCES

1. Iannucci, R., Sanders, K., and Greenfield, S.F. (2009) A 4-year curriculum on substance use disorders for psychiatry residents. *Acad. Psychiatry*, **33** (1), 60–66.
2. Lewis, D.C. (1997) The role of the generalist in the care of substance-abusing patient. *Med. J. North Am.*, **814**, 831–844.
3. Regier, D.A., Farmer, M.E., Rae, D.S. *et al.* (1990) Comorbidity of mental disorders with alcohol and other drug abuse. *JAMA*, **268**, 1012–1014.

4. Substance Abuse and Mental Health Services Administration (SAMHSA) (1992) Highlights from the 1991 N DATUS Survey, SAMHSA, Rockville, MD.

5. Chasnoff, I.J., Griffith, D.R., MacGregor, S. *et al.* (1989) Temporal patterns of cocaine use in pregnancy: Perinatal outcome. *JAMA*, **261**, 1741–1744.

6. Miller, N.S. (1994) *Principles of Addiction Medicine*, American Society of Addiction Medicine, Washington, DC.

7. Grant, B.F. (1996) DSM-I, DSM-III R, and ICD-10 alcohol and drug abuse/harmful use and dependence, United States, 1992: A nonsociological comparison. *Alcohol Clin. Exp. Res.*, **20**, 1481–1488.

8. Kandel, D., Chen, K., Warner, L.A. *et al.* (1997) Prevalence and demographic correlates of symptoms of last year dependence on alcohol, nicotine, marijuana, and cocaine in the US population. *Drug Alcohol Depend.*, **44**, 11–29.

9. Martin, C.S., Clifford, P.R., Maisto, S.A. *et al.* (1996) Polydrug use in an inpatient treatment sample of proglem drinkers. *Alcohol Clin. Exp. Res.*, **20**, 413–417.

10. Miller, N.S. (1997) Generalized vulnerability to drug and alcohol addiction, in *The Principles and Practice of Addictions in Psychiatry* (ed. N.S. Miller), WB Saunders, Philadelphia, pp. 18–25.

11. Wiseman, E.J. and McMillan, D.E. (1996) Combined use of cocaine with alcohol or cigarettes. *Am. J. Drug Alcohol Abuse*, **22**, 577–587.

12. Denison, M.E., Parades, A., and Booth, J.B. (1997) Alcohol and cocaine interaction and aggressive behaviors. *Recent Dev. Alcohol*, **13**, 283–303.

13. Kasselbaum, G. and Chandler, S.M. (1994) Polydrugs use and self control among men and women in prisons. *J. Drug Educ.*, **24**, 333–350.

14. Miller, N.S., Gold, M.S., and Smith, D.B. (1990) *Manual of Therapeutics for Addictions*, John Wiley & Sons, Inc., New York, p. 1498.

15. Patton, L.H. (1995) Adolescent substance abuse: Risk factors and protective factors. *Pediatr Clin. North Am.*, **42**, 283–293.

16. Fleming, M.F. and Barry, K.L. (1992) *Addictive Disorders*, Mosby-Year Book, St. Louis, Missouri.

17. Beresford, T.P. (1979) Alcoholism consultation and general hospital psychiatry. *Gen. Hosp. Psychiatry*, **1**, 293–300.

18. Cherpitel, C.J.S. (1988) Alcohol consumption and casualties: A comparison of two emergency room populations. *Br. J. Addict.*, **83**, 1299–1307.

19. Hold, S., Stewart, I.C., Dixon, J.M. *et al.* (1980) Alcohol and the emergency service patient. *Br. Med. J.*, **281**, 638–640.

20. McIntosh, I.D. (1982) Alcohol-related disabilities in general hospital patients: A critical assessment of the evidence. *Int. J. Addict.*, **17**, 609–639.

21. Moore, R.D., Bone, L.R., Geller, G. *et al.* (1989) Prevalence, detection, and treatment of alcoholism in hospitalized patients. *JAMA*, **261**, 403–407.

22. Ward, R.E., Flynn, T.C., Miller, P.W. *et al.* (1982) Effects of ethanol ingestion on the severity and outcome of trauma. *Am. J. Surg.*, **144**, 153–157.

23. Cyr, M.G. and Wartman, S.A. (1988) The effectiveness of routine screening questions in the detection of alcoholism. *JAMA*, **259**, 51–54.

24. Cleary, P.D., Miller, M., Bush, B.T. *et al.* (1988) Prevalence and recognition of alcohol abuse in a primary care population. *Am. J. Med.*, **85**, 466–471.

25. Kamerow, D.B., Pincus, H.A. and MacDonald, D.I. (1986) Alcohol abuse, other drug abuse, and mental disorders in medical practice: Prevalence, costs, recognition, and treatment. *JAMA*, **255**, 2054–2057.

26. Buchsbaum, D.G., Buchanan, R.G., Lawton, M.J. *et al.* (1991) Alcohol consumption patterns in a primary care population. *Alcohol Alcohol.*, **26**, 215–220.

27. Schmidt, A., Barry, K.L. and Fleming, M.F. (1995) Detection of problem drinkers: The Alcohol Use Disorders Identification Test (AUDIT). *South Med. J.*, **88**, 52–59.

28. Schoenborn, C.A. (1988) Exposure to alcoholism in the family: U.S., Advance Data from Vital and Health Statistics. National Center for Health Statistics, No. 205.

29. NIDA (1997) Preliminary Results from the National Household Survey on Drug Abuse: 1991. US Department of Health and Human Services, Substance Abuse and Mental Heath Services Administration, Office of Applied Studies, Rockville, MD.

30. Fleming, M.F., Barry, K.L., Johnson, K. *et al.* (1997) Brief physician adice for problem alcohol and drug use: A randomized controlled study in community-based primary care practices. *JAMA*, **277**, 1039–1045.

31. Klamen, D.L. and Miller, N.S. (1997) Integration in education for addiction medicine. *J. Psychoactive Drugs*, **29**, 263–268.

32. Parish, D.C. (1997) Another indication for screening and early intervention problems. *JAMA*, **277**, 1079–1080.

33. Miller, N.S., Gold, M.S., and Smith, D.B. (1997) *Manual of Therapeutuics for Addictions*, John Wiley & Sons, Inc., New York.

34. Wmick, C. and Larson, M.J. (1997) Community action programs, in *Substance Abuse: A Comprehensive Textbook*, 3rd edn (eds J.H. Lowenson, P. Ruiz,

R.B. Millman *et al.*), Williams & Wilkins, Baltimore, pp. 755–763.

35. CDC (2004) Alcohol-Attributable Deaths and Years of Potential Life Lost – United States, 2001. *MMWR*, **53** (37), 866–870.

36. Wyatt, A. and Dekker, M. (2007) Improving physician and medical education in substance use disorders. *J. Am. Osteopath Assoc.*, **107** (9), ES27–ES28.

37. Babor, T. and Grant, M. (1990) Project on Identification and Management of Alcohol Related Problems: Report on Phase II: A Randomized Clinical Trial of Brief Interventions in Primary Health Care, World Health Organization, Geneva, Switzerland.

38. Chick, J., Lloyd, G., and Crombie, E. (1985) Counselling problem drinkers in medical wards: A controlled study. *Br. Med. J.*, **290**, 965–967.

39. Wallace, P., Cutler, S., and Haines, A. (1988) Randomised controlled trial of general practiionaer intervention in patients with excessive alcohol consumption. *Br. Med. J.*, **297**, 663–668.

40. American Society of Addiction Medicine (1991) Physicians in Addiction Medicine Policy Statement.

41. Durfee, M.F., Warren, D.G., and Sdao-Javier, K. (1994) A model for answering the stubstance abuse educational needs of health professionals: The North Carolina Govenors Institute on Alcohol and Substance abuse. *Alcohol*, **11**, 483–487.

42. Keso, L. and Salaspuro, M. (1990) Inpatient treatment of employed alcoholics: A randomized clinical trial on Hazelden-type and traditional treatment. *Alcohol Clin. Exp. Res.*, **14**, 584–589.

43. Walsh, D.C., Hingson, R.W., Merrigan, D.M. *et al.* (1991) A randomized trial of treatment options for alcohol-abusing workers. *N. Engl. J. Med.*, **325**, 775–782.

44. Harrison, P.A., Hoffmann, N.G., and Streed, S.G. (1991) Drug and alcohol addiction treatment outcome, in *Comprehensive Handbook of Drug and Alcohol Addiction* (ed. N.S. Miller), Marcel Dekker, New York, pp. 1163–1200.

45. Hoffmann, N.G. and Miller, N.S. (1992) Treatment outcomes for abstinence-based programs. *Psychiatr Ann.*, **22**, 402–408.

46. Miller, N.S. (1995) *Treatment of Addictions: Applications of Outcome Research for Clinical Management*, Haworth Press, New York.

47. Chappel, J.N. (1993) Long-term recovery from alcoholism. *Psychiatr. Clin. North Am.*, **16**, 177–187.

48. Institue of Medicine (1989) *Broadening the Base of Treatment for Alcohol Problems*, National Academy Press, Washington, DC.

49. American Society of Addiction Medicine (ASAM) (1992) ASAM Patient Placement Criteria, Psychoactie Substance Use Disorders, American Society of Addiction Medicine, Washington, DC.

50. Fleming, M.F., Barry, K.L., Davis, A. *et al.* (1994) Medical education about substance abuse: Changes in curriculum and faculty between 1976 and 1992. *Acad. Med.*, **69**, 362–369.

51. Gopalan, R., Santora, P., Stokes, E.J. *et al.* (1992) Evaluation of a model curriculum on substance abuse at the Johns Hopkins University School of Medicine. *Acad. Med.*, **67**, 260–266.

52. Wyatt, A., Vilensky, W., Manlandro, J. *et al.* (2005) Medical education in substance abuse: from student to practicing physician. *J. Am. Osteopath Assoc.*, **105.6**, S18–S24.

53. Lee, J., Triola, M., Gillespie, C. *et al.* (2008) Working with patients with alcohol problems: a controlled trial of the impact of a rich media web module on medical student performance. *J. Gen. Intern. Med.*, **23.7**, 1006–1009.

54. Hymowitz, N., Schwab, J., Haddock, C. *et al.* (2004) The pediatric residency training on tobacco project: baseline findings from the resident tobacco survey and observed structured clinical examinations. *Presse. Med.*, **39**, 507–516.

55. Averbuch, R.N. and Gold, M.S. (2008) An Innovative Addictions Curriculum Improves Ratings on a Psychiatry Clerkship. Association for Academic Psychiatry (AAP), Annual Meeting, Santa Fe, NM, 24–27 September 2008.

56. Averbuch, R., and Garvan, C., (2009) "It Works! Teaching Psychiatry with Videos Enhances Long Term Retention," Plenary Session, Research in Medical Education. 35th Annual Meeting of ADMSEP (Association of Directors of Medical Student Education in Psychiatry), Portsmouth, NH, 19 June 2009.

2

Crime, substance use, and mental illness

Joel M. Silberberg,[1] **Milap A. Nowrangi,**[2] **and Geetha Nampiaparampil**[3]

[1] *Division of Psychiatry and Law, Feinberg School of Medicine, Northwestern University, Chicago, Illinois, USA*
[2] *Feinberg School of Medicine, Northwestern University, Chicago, Illinois, USA*
[3] *St. Vincent's Hospital, New York Medical College, New York City, New York, USA*

2.1   INTRODUCTION

The connection between substance use and crime has been well documented and studied for many years. It has even become a popular notion that substance use and being behind bars go hand-in-hand. Otis Campbell, the "town drunk" from the 1960s television sitcom, *The Andy Griffith Show*, would regularly lock himself in the town jail until he was sober after a weekend-long alcohol binge. Many have estimated that the overwhelming majority of incarcerated inmates are or have been involved with the serious use of drugs or alcohol [1–3]. Those who have studied alcohol use in particular have noted strong associations to serious crimes, such as assault, robbery, rape, and murder [1,4,5]. During America's prohibition era, for example, infamous gangster Al Capone was known as the leader of a widespread and influential boot-legging operation that was involved in murder, extortion, and gambling, to name just a few. More recently, in 2008, an intoxicated off-duty Chicago police officer severely assaulted a female bartender after she refused to serve him, bringing substance use and violence into the spotlight locally.

While it has been popularized that serious mental illness and crime tend to co-occur, it is generally accepted that the rates of crime between those with a mental illness and those in the healthy general population are nearly identical [6–9]. The media's attention to such tragedies as Columbine and Virginia Tech, though, has further deepened the stigma of mental illness in society. However, when the seriously mentally ill use substances, the connection with violence and crime strengthens [10].

The movement of the chronic and severely mentally ill from large state psychiatric hospitals into the community in the 1960s was, in theory, an intelligent and compassionate reform. In effect, though, the move to nursing homes, group homes, intensive outpatient, and semi-independent living programs deprived patients of sorely needed treatment during periods of psychiatric decompensation and increased substance use. The United States' prison system and the state forensic hospitals nearly tripled in size during the 1980s and 1990s to address, in part, this lack of treatment [11]. Today, the correctional system in the United States is the largest provider of mental health services. It has

Addictive Disorders in Medical Populations   Edited by Norman S. Miller and Mark S. Gold

been pointed out that despite its efforts the prison system continues to struggle to provide rehabilitative services to inmates who suffer from substance use issues [12–14].

Much work has already been done to understand and characterize the interaction between substance use, crime, and mental illness. The purpose of this chapter is to summarize this information and equip the clinician with a basic understanding of concepts he or she would commonly encounter in general practice that pertain, primarily, to crime and substance use and, secondarily, their association to mental illness. We believe that understanding these concepts is important to the clinician for a number of reasons. Firstly, physical injury from criminal violence that was influenced by substances is a common reason for doctors' visits, whether in the emergency department, outpatient clinic, or operating suite. Secondly, prison overcrowding has resulted in the premature release of inmates, many of whom will seek medical care at general and specialty medical clinics. Thirdly, there are a growing number of primary care physicians and healthcare professionals who are seeking employment in the correctional setting and, further, will provide inmates with outpatient referrals upon their release. Finally, we believe that

competency over basic legal concepts is necessary for the clinician to master in order to understand their patients' often complex social and legal situations along with their various physical and psychiatric problems.

In this chapter we attempt to achieve four goals and objectives. Firstly, we seek to equip the clinician with salient and current empirical and epidemiological evidence. We caution, however, that epidemiological data generated from self-report surveys of such factors as drug use and violence may be biased towards under-reporting. Given this, we include data from national and independent sources. Secondly, we seek to educate the clinician on basic legal concepts that may be encountered in general medical practice. Thirdly, we describe the evaluation process for determining such things as competence, insanity, sentencing and release. Fourthly, we outline treatment issues for this population in different clinical settings.

The chapter begins with a discussion of clinical prevalence and epidemiology. Next, basic legal and forensic psychiatric concepts are introduced. Following this, common assessment principles are reviewed. Finally, the clinical course of the convicted offender is looked at starting from etiology and pathophysiology to treatment and outcomes.

2.2   EPIDEMIOLOGY

Appreciating the connection between substance use, crime, and mental illness requires a broad review of epidemiological data. In particular, incidence and prevalence statistics show the pervasiveness of substance use in incarcerated populations as well as among unincarcerated criminal offenders. There have also been interesting findings in studies of those with mental illness and other special populations, such as women and minors. It should be noted that less than 1% of offenses committed by drug users actually end up in arrest [15]. Furthermore, the number of people who admit to substance use after arrest or incarceration is significantly lower than what is deemed correct due to under-reporting bias. This underscores the fact that substance use and crime is

a larger problem than formal statistics actually present.

Statistical data over general addiction or dependence on substances among those under the criminal justice system is powerful and compelling. Of those in federal prison, 72.9% admitted to using at least one substance. Of those in state prisons the proportion was 83% and in jails it was 82.4%. Approximately 50–65% of all inmates are drug dependent at the time of their arrest [16]. Among those convicted of murder, over 50% are found to have actively used a substance at the time they committed the crime – half of these involved alcohol intoxication [17]. Of adults 18 or older who were arrested in the past year for a serious violent act or property offense, 60.1% were found to have used an illicit drug within the past year. Of adults who had been arrested for a serious offense, 46.5% had used marijuana in the past year [18].

An even stronger argument can be made for the connection between substance use and the concomitant commission of criminal acts by surveying the following data. More than 35% of state prisoners used a substance at the time the crime was committed [19]. Of those convicted for murder, housed temporarily in local jails, 43.7% were drinking alcohol at the time of committing the offense. Of those who committed property offenses, 32.8% were drinking at the time [20]. Information gathered by the Department of Justice indicates that two thirds of victims involved in intimate partner violence report alcohol as a factor and, in spousal abuse, approximately 75% note that the offender was drinking alcohol [20]. Earlier studies have theorized that drug users commit crimes to finance a drug habit. In fact, among street level drug dealers, at their time of their arrest, cocaine is found in the urine of half of them. Interestingly, most crimes committed by those within the "drug trade system" were neither substance users nor addicts – in fact, 80% of federal level drug violators are not regular substance users [15].

With respect to mental illness, bipolar disorder is associated with the highest prevalence of substance use when compared to other Axis 1 disorders. One study [21] showed a 68% criminal history rate in those with comorbid substance abuse and bipolar disorder [21]. "A psychiatric condition was diagnosed in 41% of the drug related suicide attempts treated in the emergency departments where the most frequent diagnosis was depression" [22]. Offenders diagnosed with antisocial personality disorder (ASPD) are found to use a wider range of substances than those engaged in less criminal activity. The prevalence of ASPD among substance users has been estimated to be between 20 and 50%. ASPD is found

in 45–54% of heroin addicts and 40–50% of alcoholics [15,23,24].

The prevalence of substance use among offenders who are minors is alarming. Of those between the ages of 12 and 17 who had gotten into a serious fight at school or work, 20.7% reported having used illicit drugs in the past month. Of those who carried a handgun, 34.6% admitted the use of illicit drugs in the previous month. Of those who had sold illegal drugs, 68.8% reported using illicit drugs within the past month. Of those found stealing $50 or more, 43.8% admitted past month illicit drug use [25]. These statistics argue for the need to intervene early.

When comparing between genders, similar rates of violence in alcoholic men and women were revealed [26]. Among nuisance inebriates and public disorder offenders, men were chiefly found to be the offenders. Rates of heroin/opiate use and dependence were significantly higher among female arrestees than among male arrestees [26]. One study found that 23% of female inmates were using cocaine at the time of their arrest [21]. Bipolar disorder with co-occurring substance use has a high likelihood of increasing a woman's tendency toward criminal behavior. There is an over-representation of women with bipolar disorder in the corrections system [21].

The prevalence of substance use and need for effective treatment is on the rise. State corrections officials estimate that between 70% and 85% of inmates need some level of substance addiction treatment [16]. With respect to treatment of substance addiction and other co-occurring psychiatric illnesses, the treatment of these offenders within jails is especially important as they enter and re-enter general society as perpetrators of crime. Treatment offered to those in this group is limited. Treatment offered to "pure" substance users is also limited. In fact, only 33% of jails provided onsite substance addiction treatment to inmates when it is estimated that much more is required [27].

2.3 BASIC LEGAL AND FORENSIC CONCEPTS

It is essential to discuss basic legal terms and forensic psychiatry concepts to understand the relationship between substance addiction or dependence, crime and the law, and mental health. The clinician will benefit from this review as it serves to form a conceptual foundation for understanding the nature of these problems. Furthermore, the clinician will benefit from a brief survey of general concepts that he or she may encounter in the care of patients, as well as concepts that it is believed are core to the practice of forensic psychiatry when dealing with crime and substance use.

2.3.1 Crime

The source of most definitions of crime comes from British common law. Both *Actus Rea*, the forbidden act, and *Mens Rea*, the guilty mind, are required to commit a punishable crime. *The Model Penal Code* (MPC) [28] describes the four components of *Mens Rea* as "purposefully, knowingly, recklessly and negligently." "Purposefully" is when the defendant's "conscious object [was] to engage in conduct of that nature or to cause such a result," (MPC Section 2.02(2)(a)(i)). "Knowingly" is when the defendant "is aware that it is practically certain that this conduct will cause such a result" (MPC Section 2.02(2)(b)(ii)). "Recklessly" is when the defendant "consciously disregards a substantial and unjustifiable risk," and the disregard of the risk "involves a gross deviation from the standard of conduct that a law-abiding person would observe in the actor's situation" (MPC Section 2.02(2)(c)). "Negligently" is when a defendant "should be aware of a substantial and unjustifiable risk" but inadvertently fails to act as a "reasonable person" in that situation. By common law purposefully, knowingly and recklessly involve criminal conduct. *Specific intent* includes purposefully or knowingly. *General intent* includes purposely, knowingly or recklessly. "Negligently" is not considered criminal unless designated so by statute. For example, negligent vehicular homicide is criminal in some states.

2.3.2 Punishment

The purpose of punishment is general deterrence, retribution, rehabilitation, and protection of society. A person convicted of a *misdemeanor* has a sen-tence limited to a maximum of six to twelve months and is usually confined to a jail. A jail also holds detainees who are currently in trial. A *felony* is usually a specific intent crime such as robbery, burglary or, for example, the selling of crack cocaine.

2.3.3 Insanity defense and other affirmative defenses

An *affirmative defense* is a plea to justify that an act was at least legally permissible, such as self-defense, or an excuse that admits the act was wrong but argues that the defendant should not be blamed for it in such situations as *duress*, *insanity*, *automatism*, *entrapment* or *necessity*. The *burden of production* and in many states the *burden of persuasion* is on the defendant in such cases.

Evaluation of a defendant's criminal responsibility or *sanity at the time of the act* is usually done by a forensic psychiatrist. In regard to the *Insanity Defense*, The Model Penal Code states: "A person is not responsible for his criminal conduct if at the time of such conduct as a result of mental disease or defect he lacks substantial capacity to appreciate the criminality of his conduct or to conform his conduct to the requirements of the law. The terms "mental disease or defect" do not include an abnormality manifested only by repeated criminal or otherwise antisocial conduct." The Model Penal Code, 1955 contained a cognitive [29] and volitional arm (ability to refrain or ability to conform conduct). In a similar fashion to the reaction of the jury acquitting Daniel McNaughten on the ground of insanity of the murder of Edmond Drummond (Secretary to the Prime Minister, Robert Peel, during the reign of Queen Victoria), subsequent to the attempted assassination of President Reagan by John Hinckley and the finding of him not guilty by reason of insanity, the *Federal Rule, 1984* was significantly tightened. Notably also the burden of proof was shifted to the defendant instead of on the prosecution: "It is an affirmative defense to a prosecution under any Federal Statute that, at the time of the commission of the acts constituting the offense, the defendant, as a result of a severe mental disease or defect, was unable to appreciate the nature and quality or the wrongfulness of his acts" [30]. Several states have subsequently eliminated the volitional arm of the Model Penal Code. The remaining states can, of course, provide more protection to defendants than the constitutional or federal minimum by retaining the volitional arm. How does this apply to alcohol and/or drug use or addiction? It is important to note that successful insanity defenses are raised in less than 1% of felony trials and are successful less than 25% of the time. The large majority of successful insanity defenses are for serious mental illness such as schizophrenia.

Settled insanity is defined as a permanent or "*settled*" condition caused by long-term substance addiction and differs from the temporary state of intoxication. Most jurisdictions differentiate between settled insanity and temporary intoxication. Chronic alcoholism may result in settled insanity and thus provide an insanity defense where prolonged intoxication may produce a brain syndrome characterized by a degree of confusion sufficient to lead to drastic misinterpretation of reality [31]. For example, a patient with alcohol-induced dementia murders his spouse at the time she has been devoting more attention than usual to a previous lover. Is this jealous rage and premeditated murder or an act driven by delusional jealously and the poor impulse control of settled insanity?

Voluntary intoxication alone leading to *temporary insanity* or short-lived mental changes is not considered a mental disease or defect for the insanity defense, but it may result in a diminished verdict or sentence, or in a finding of guilty but mentally ill. Defendants found guilty but mentally ill may end up in prison with limited access to care for comorbid serious mental illness and substance use or addiction. There are circumstances where *diminished responsibility* may be considered in regard to alcohol and/or drug use or addiction. This may occur in acute pathological alcoholic intoxication, where very small amounts of alcohol may precipitate impulsive aggressive behavior. This is a rare disorder that usually occurs in first time users. "The intoxication may so impair the individual's judgment that he is unable to plan his behavior rationally

or to appreciate its consequences" [31]. Diminished responsibility could occur also secondary to unwittingly ingesting a substance such as phencyclidine (PCP) in involuntary intoxication, when a person is given a drug without his knowledge leading to prolonged psychosis.

The association between alcoholic blackouts and criminal behavior is complex and may be used as a *diminished capacity defense* if an *automatism* can be linked to the amnesia. An alcoholic blackout causes a form of amnesia about events that happened during a heavy period of drinking [32]. Heavy drinking may induce a blackout, which is a type of dissociation. During the blackout, the person is awake and conscious, may be engaged in any type of activity or conversation, and may appear to the observer to be perfectly oriented [33]. The event is sometimes later recalled. The frequency and type of blackout were surveyed in two healthy samples in a Dutch study. van Oorsouw *et al.* [34] reviewed the literature and found that in the United States and the Netherlands, on average, 20–30% of offenders claim a form of amnesia after committing a crime and that, in a substantial number of these cases, defendants invoke excessive alcohol consumption as an explanation for the amnesia. The results of their study suggest that people are capable of forgetting deviant behavior after consuming large amounts of alcohol and that bona fide blackouts during criminally relevant behavior do occur. Their survey data question the reliability of those who raised blackout claims with blood alcohol levels below 250 mg/dL percent [34].

2.3.4 Competency

Competency (or *competence*) is the quality or condition of being legally qualified to perform an act and/or make decisions. It is important to note that clinicians opine on capacities relevant to competence. Evaluation of the defendant's *criminal competency* is usually done by a forensic psychiatrist. Forensic psychiatry evaluations in the criminal arena encompass a wide variety of evaluations, such as *competency to waive Miranda rights*, *competency to confess, competency to stand trial, competency to be sentenced, competency to be executed,* and the determination of mental health factors related to sentence mitigation. Substance use or addiction may play a role in these evaluations. We will devote more time in this chapter to *competency to stand trial* than the other criminal competencies or the insanity defense or other affirmative defenses because "assessment for competence to stand trial is probably the most common evaluation done by psychiatrists for the court system" [35]. Competency to stand trial is also known as *fitness to proceed* or *adjudicative competence.*

The rationale for competency to stand trial is to maintain accuracy of the adjudication and the fairness and dignity of the proceedings. The Supreme Court defined competency to stand trial in the landmark case of *Dusky vs. United States, 1960* [36] as the ability of a defendant to have a rational and factual understanding of the proceedings against him and to assist and consult with an attorney with a reasonable degree of rational understanding. Most states have since adopted a similar test of competency to stand trial. The defendant who is not able to understand the nature and objectives of the proceedings or assist in his own defense is considered incompetent to stand trial. It is clear that competence to stand trial is task specific and time specific. Many detainees have mental illness causing them to be incompetent to stand trial. It is important to recognize that symptoms of mental illness *per se* do not render a person incompetent to stand trial. The mental illness should specifically inhibit functioning at the trial to render someone incompetent [37]. Defendants who are found incompetent to stand trial most likely have serious mental disorders or mental retardation, with psychosis being the most common [37]. Thirty two states rely primarily on outpatient competency assessments and only ten primarily on inpatient evaluation [38]. In outpatient competency assessment situations, it is clear that substance use or addiction may play a critical role in rendering someone, originally found competent to stand trial, incompetent to stand trial by, for example, interference with medication adherence in a defendant with comorbid substance use and serious mental illness. These defendants

should be carefully monitored to prevent them from showing up for their day in court incompetent to stand trial. The methods to restore competence include treatment of the defendant's mental illness and education about the trial process [39]. Access to substances needs to be closely monitored even in the setting of a secure forensic hospital. These competence restoration programs involve written information and tests, and videotaped vignettes and role-playing, including mock trials to monitor improvement in competence related capacities. Restoration in a person with acute mental illness with or without substance use or addiction usually takes six to eight months. Sequelae of damage secondary to substance use or addiction, such as significant cognitive deficits, may prolong the process of restoration. A few of these defendants may never be restored to competence.

2.3.5   Reading a landmark case

Certain case precedents or landmark cases, salient case precedents designated by the American Academy of Psychiatry and the Law (AAPL), are of critical importance for the clinical and forensic psychiatrist to understand clinical, legal, ethical, patient rights and regulation of the practice of psychiatry issues. The law is formed over time by a combination of common law, statutes, and case precedents. The principle of *stare decisis,* which translates as "let the decision stand," means that courts stand by their own precedent and that an inferior court must follow a case precedent of a superior court. For example, all courts in America have to abide by *Roe vs. Wade* [40], which is a United States Supreme Court case that resulted in a landmark decision regarding abortion. According to the Roe decision, most laws against abortion in the United States violated a constitutional right to privacy under the due process clause of the Fourteenth Amendment. The state hierarchical court system consists of Trial Courts, Intermediate Appeal Courts, and State Supreme Courts. The federal hierarchical court system consists of US District Courts and US Courts of Appeals (divided into thirteen circuits nationwide). Cases from both the State Supreme Courts and the US Courts of Appeals may on rare occasion, depending on the nature and importance of the issue, be *granted certiorari* to be heard by the US Supreme Court. For example, *Bush v. Gore* [41] was a Florida Supreme Court decision, which was appealed to the US Supreme Court.

How does one read a case precedent or landmark case? It is important to pay attention to the *year of the opinion*. At the beginning of the case, there is a brief summary called the *case syllabus*. The Court to which the decision is being appealed *identifies the issue* in a two-part question in regard to the particular facts of the case and the applicable rules of law. The *Majority Opinion* contains the *summary of the facts, the procedural history, the reasoning and the holding,* which is the court's opinion on the legal questions. The *dissenting opinion* and *dicta* may indicate future thinking of the court about the issue. Many of these cases are decided on constitutional issues, such as the first Amendment right of freedom of speech, the fourth Amendment providing protection from unreasonable search and seizure, the fifth Amendment right not to incriminate oneself, the sixth Amendment right to assistance of counsel, the eighth Amendment proscription of cruel and unusual punishment, and the fourteenth Amendment (state court) and fifth Amendment (federal court) right to due process and equal protection. Equal protection requires for example that people of all races be treated similarly under the law. Due process includes *substantive due process,* which is fundamental fairness, and *procedural due process* to carefully assess competing private and government interests (*Matthews vs. Eldridge* [42]). Clinicians need to be aware of federal law which sets constitutional minimums throughout the country, but also of state and local legal statutes because that state may provide more protections on a particular issue, such as the Insanity Statute. In the interest of space, pertinent information about case precedents or landmark cases will be mentioned and described briefly in this chapter. Hopefully, readers may later explore them in more detail.

2.3.6 Review of pertinent landmark cases

You now have a basic understanding of the relationship between substance use or addiction and the law to discuss three landmark cases that specifically address important issues related to substance use and crime.

1. *Robinson vs. California* [43]: Mr Robinson was discovered to have needle marks on his arms when he was stopped by Los Angeles police. At this time, the California Health and Safety Code made it a misdemeanor to be addicted to the use of narcotics even in the absence of actual criminal behavior related to the addiction. Robinson appealed to the California Supreme Court. In the majority opinion, Justice Stewart wrote that the California statute violated the cruel and unusual punishment proscription of the eighth Amendment. The Supreme Court noted that mental illness, leprosy, and venereal diseases, which had in the past been viewed as problems with morality and hence criminal, could not be constitutionally upheld as criminal. The Court indicated that it was necessary to separate a defendant's acts from his status. This decision helped to remove other status crimes such as homelessness and vagrancy from statutes.

2. *Powell vs. Texas* [44]: Six years later this case addressed the issue of whether it was cruel and unusual punishment to convict an alcoholic for public drunkenness. Mr. Powell had been convicted in Texas for being intoxicated in public. His counsel raised the defense that alcoholism was a disease and that he was a chronic alcoholic. The Supreme Court was asked to apply the Robinson decision to prevent the state from punishing a chronic alcoholic for public drunkenness. Powell's conviction of public drunkenness was upheld because the Supreme Court did not want to open the door to a constitutional basis for an insanity defense. If Powell's claim that he did not appear in public of his own volition when he was drunk were accepted, then no one could be held accountable under a compulsion that was a "very strong influence." For

the Court to have ruled otherwise would have possibly created a constitutional basis for an insanity defense for voluntarily intoxicated persons committing a crime such as rape. The defense of drunkenness does not result in exculpation of the offender.

3. *Montana vs. Egelhoff* [45]: Mr Egelhoff was accused of shooting and killing two acquaintances after a night of heavy drinking. When arrested, his blood alcohol was 0.36%. He had amnesia for his two homicides. He was charged with deliberate homicide, which in Montana is a specific intent crime of purposefully and knowingly killing someone. He was convicted at trial after offering the defense that his extreme intoxication had rendered him mentally incapable of committing murder. Mon-

tana's criminal code, however, required that the jury be instructed that voluntary intoxication could not be considered in determining the existence of his *mens rea* or mental state at the time of the crime. He appealed to the Montana Supreme Court that his Fourteenth Amendment rights to present all relevant evidence were violated. The Montana Supreme Court overturned his conviction. The US Supreme Court agreed to review the case and held that the Montana law was constitutional and did not violate a "fundamental principle of justice" because one fifth of the states had not adopted the ruling that intoxication could be considered in the determination of specific intent formation. The court also reasoned that, historically, alcohol was viewed more as an aggravating than mitigating factor for crime.

2.4 FORENSIC ASSESSMENT

As mentioned before, few psychiatrists will perform insanity or diminished capacity evaluations, but some may perform evaluations for competence to stand trial. Some experts question whether non-forensic clinicians should accept forensic referrals at all [46]. Bearing this information in mind, the basic principles of a forensic psychiatry evaluation and then some specific details for some common forensic evaluations related to substance use and addictions are now briefly discussed.

There is no doctor–patient relationship in a forensic psychiatry evaluation. A forensic psychiatry evaluation is an extended, in-depth process that strives for honesty and objectivity. In forming his opinion, the evaluator looks for evidence of or absence of psychiatric disorders that, for example, impair competence or diminish capacity. The process often involves multiple interviews of the defendant, interview of collateral sources on a case specific basis, extensive review of collateral documents such as police and medical records, other expert witness reports, and psychological testing. The evaluator studies literature and does appropriate research about the issues of the case and then makes psycho-legal linkage between the facts of the

case and the specific jurisdictional legal standard involved.

2.4.1 Sanity

During a sanity evaluation, the evaluator creates a working alliance with the defendant in reconstructing the mental, emotional, and physical states at the time of the crime. The report must address the presence of serious mental illness or defect at the time of the crime. The report must address whether the defendant's mental state at the time of the crime satisfies the jurisdictional criteria for the insanity defense. The report must address the relationship between the mental disease or defect and the criminal behavior. In regard to substance addiction, remember that voluntary intoxication with alcohol or drugs does not qualify as serious mental illness for an insanity defense and that permanent psychosis secondary to alcohol (settled insanity) may in some jurisdictions be included as serious mental illness as a basis for an insanity defense. Intoxication, together with mental illness, may preclude specific intent. Out of policy, inability to refrain due to voluntary intoxication does not qualify in any jurisdiction for an insanity defense.

2.4.2 Competence to stand trial

In some jurisdictions or states, nonforensic evaluators with specialized training required by the legislature may carry out competence to stand trial evaluations. In some states, such as Texas, these evaluators with specialized training may also do sanity evaluations. Discussion of *Jackson vs. Indiana* [47] will assist to further understand issues in doing an evaluation for assessment of competence to stand trial, and also an evaluation for restoration of competence to stand trial. Mr Jackson was a mentally retarded, deaf mute who was charged with two robberies. He was found incompetent to stand trial based on his nonexistent communication skills, mental retardation, and lack of hearing. He was found incompetent and committed to the Indiana Department of Mental Health until his competency was restored. Jackson did not have a mental illness and his other deficiencies were not treatable. Jackson's lawyer filed an appeal saying that he would never be restored to competency citing the deprivation of due process and equal protection under the fourteenth Amendment and the proscription against cruel and unusual punishment under the eighth Amendment. The Supreme Court ruled in favor of Mr Jackson, with the finding that an incompetent defendant cannot be held more than the reasonable period necessary to determine whether there is a reasonable probability that he will regain competence in the foreseeable future. The court stated: "Due process requires that the nature and duration of confinement bear some reasonable relation to the purpose for which the individual is committed." Fortunately, 90% of defendants are restored to competency [48].

Substance use and addictions do play an important role in assessment of competence to stand trial, which is a "here and now" capacity evaluation. Alcohol or drugs may lead to dementia or other organic syndromes that may make it unlikely that competence be restored. In these situations, if it is unlikely that competence will be restored, the defendant must be released or civilly committed (*Jackson vs. Indiana* [47]). The competency assessment consists of evaluation of mental disorders, present mental status and level of functioning, past psychiatric, medical and social histories, competence to stand trial related tasks (*Dusky vs. United States* [36]), and on a case-by-case basis the use of structured competence to stand trial instruments. Should a defendant lack the capacity to perform competence-related tasks due to a disorder, such as psychosis secondary to alcohol or drugs or recurrent intoxication that precludes medication adherence for comorbid mental illness, competence restoration will need to involve use of psychotropic drugs, a competence restoration program, and substance use and addiction treatment. Once competence is restored, it is in these cases that continued hospitalization or confinement with appropriate medication monitoring will allow a speedy and fair trial to proceed before relapse. All too often detainees or offenders are restored to competency in a state forensic hospital only to relapse when accessing drugs in jail while awaiting trial. General psychiatrists may also treat patients on an outpatient or inpatient basis who are awaiting trial and should educate and support the patient about the need to adhere to treatment and abstain from drugs or alcohol in order to get a speedy trial. Crowded court dockets leading to delayed trials may make relapse – rendering the substance abusing or addicted defendant incompetent – a common event.

2.4.3 Dual agency

As the clinician aspires to provide unbiased assessment as an expert or diagnosis and treatment, the issue of dual agency frequently arises in the correctional setting. In the correctional setting the *mentally ill patient* is referred to as a *mentally ill detainee* or *offender* or *inmate*. For future reference in this chapter, the term *inmate* will be used as a general term for *detainee* (pre-trial) or *offender* (post-conviction). The correctional treating clinician may be served with a *subpoena duces tecums* to testify about competence to stand trial. This is often a cost saving effort on part of the local jurisdiction, and the treating psychiatrist should respond only to function as a *fact witness*. The treating clinician is only obligated to honor a subpoena duces tecums when it is signed by the judge or accompanied by a judge's order. In such circumstances, release of the patient's medical records alone usually suffices instead of appearance in court as a fact witness. There are several reasons that a dual relationship of *treating clinician* and *expert witness* is not advisable. Forensic consultation or testimony involves objective comment regardless of the patient's wishes or needs. This conflicts with confidentiality, which is the essential ingredient in the clinician–patient alliance. The treating clinician who agrees to testify has an intentional and unintended (counter-transference) bias toward the patient. The treating clinician has to put the patient's interests and wishes before all else. The forensic consultant's responsibilities, on the other hand, are to objectivity and the court [49].

2.5 CLINICAL COURSE

Many have argued that both drug and alcohol addiction and criminality are diagnosable and treatable conditions. Further, as previously asserted, substance use and crime share a rather strong connection, perhaps even one of causality. The medicalization of these two entities, therefore, makes them amenable to discussion in terms of their etiology, diagnosis, and treatment. While acknowledging their separateness, some time is spent here discussing the "natural history" of crime and substance use as a single reciprocating entity. Since the diagnosis of substance use or addiction has been defined elsewhere in this text, the focus is on etiology and treatment issues. While there have been outcome studies of treatment interventions, these are difficult to generalize because of the marked jurisdictional differences in drug or mental health courts and will not be discussed in this chapter. Outcomes data need to be interpreted on a jurisdiction-by-jurisdiction basis.

2.5.1 Etiology

Several theories explain the interaction between crime and substance use. One theory supports a straightforward cause-and-effect relationship of neuro-cognitive and pharmacological effects of the drug on causing violent behavior [50,51]. Another theory asserts that the costs associated with producing, transporting, and selling drugs leads to violent crime to support continued use and sustained operation of the enterprise [52]. Several studies have suggested that criminality among opiate addicts is increased during periods of higher use but decreased during periods of lower use [53,54]. It is generally accepted, though, that drugs profoundly affect the central nervous system. Pharmacologically, these psychoactive substances are known to dysregulate the relative stability of affective states, cause changes in anxiety, and even create perceptual anomalies. Amphetamines, cocaine, phencyclidine (PCP) and alcohol diminish controls, and stimulants also increase the risk of violence due to paranoia and grandiosity [55]. Alcohol intoxication, in particular, has been known to decrease inhibition, increase impulsivity and aggression. In fact, it is widely accepted that disinhibition caused by alcohol is the most important facilitator of violent behavior and, consequently, violent crimes. Dampening of the fear and stress response has been another proposed mechanism. Since alcohol essentially works as an anxiolytic, it follows that the intake of the substance disrupts the individual's threat detection, causing decreased avoidance and impaired assessment of risk leaving them open to being either victims or perpetrators of crime [51,56].

2.5.2 Treatment issues

There are some common issues in the treatment of forensic patients with substance use and addictive disorders in jail, prison, forensic institutions and community settings. Jails in particular and prisons are part of the community in which they reside. Failure to treat and link forensic patients with substance addiction alone or those with co-occurring substance addiction and mental illness (also known as *dual diagnosis*) to effective community treatment programs perpetuates the escalating problem of substance use and violence.

2.5.2.1 Jail

Screening for active substance-induced disorders (intoxication, withdrawal or other psychiatric syndromes secondary to substance use) and substance use disorders (addiction and dependence) is an important mental health task in any jail setting. The inmates with substance-induced disorders need immediate attention according to the standard of care as described in other chapters of this book. The inmates with substance use disorders need to be further evaluated in order to refer for appropriate medical consultation for high-risk comorbid medical conditions, such as HIV or hepatitis, correctional substance use programs and groups, and coordination with discharge planning regarding substance use treatment when released into the community. In addition, they need to be evaluated for sleep disorder secondary to substance use, self-medication for comorbid mental illness, malingered psychiatric illness to obtain prescribed substances, ongoing illicit substance use during incarceration, and recognition of prolonged detoxification syndromes, which may be misdiagnosed as psychiatric in etiology [57]. Factors predicting successful completion of an intensive jail-based substance user program include being age 26 or older, not having used methadone, and having already received a sentence [58]. A longitudinal study of Monroe County, New York's jail treatment drug and alcohol program [59] demonstrated that jail substance-based treatment programs have demonstrated efficacy in decreasing criminal recidivism on release into the community in a one year follow-up period when compared with an inmate control group [59].

2.5.2.2 Prison

Because the transfer of medical and mental health information between jails and prisons is far from optimal, screening for substance use disorders should occur again in the prison setting. Prison-based substance use treatment services demonstrate significant treatment efficacy [57]. The "therapeutic community model," first pioneered by the British physician Maxwell Jones at the end of World War II as described in this book, has been successfully modified for use in correctional settings and in many states is housed separately from the general prison population; it focuses on the inmate's substance use and related problems and lasts between six to twelve months [60].

2.5.2.3 The forensic setting

Contemporary movies and books tend to give the impression that not guilty by reason of insanity acquitees "get away with murder." In fact, these individuals may spend more time institutionalized for their crime than if they were sentenced to prison. The release process for these acquitees involves complex risk assessment evaluations. One very common and important assessment at the time of release is the risk for violence. There have been sophisticated, well validated instruments created for the formal assessment of violence potential [61–64]. Specific elements of these instruments were designed to address the well-established fact that substance use increases rates of violence. While mental illness alone does not increase rates of violence when compared to the general population, the concurrent use of substances (comorbid mental illness) does in fact increase rates of violence and needs to be considered in pre-release evaluations and assessments.

2.5.2.4 The community: re-entry and reintegration

Individuals with alcohol and mental illness comorbidities in general are more likely than those with mental disorder alone to show violent or suicidal behavior [65], be homeless [66], and be admitted to hospital and make greater use of emergency services [67]. Without post-release treatment referral and planning, relapse of substance use often leads to medication nonadherence or vice versa.

The process of returning to the community after incarceration/institutionalization is termed re-entry and reintegration. This period poses the inmate with formidable challenges. Obtaining gainful employment, securing housing, re-establishing social relationships, and avoiding maladaptive or problematic behaviors often seem like insurmountable tasks to them. Of particular interest is what role substance use before, during, and after institutionalization play in a successful transition. Recent studies have shown that the period immediately following release places the inmate at high risk for death. Binswanger et al. [68] reviewed prison records of 30 237 inmates release from Washington state prisons during a four-year span. They found that the leading causes of death within two weeks of release were drug over-dose, cardiovascular disease, homicide, and suicide [68].

All inmates with substance addiction or dependence should be referred for formal substance use treatment before their release [69]. Inmates who have undergone opioid detoxification should be counseled regarding the increased risk of lethal overdose following release due to loss of tolerance. To further decrease this risk of lethal overdose following release due to loss of tolerance, jails and correctional physicians should be encouraged to obtain licenses for the use of methadone and buprenorphine to provide optimal detoxification regimens, as well as to offer selected inmates the opportunity to begin medication-assisted therapy. These programs have been found to reduce rates of illicit drugs in correctional facilities and to reduce recidivism [70].

With respect to post-release drug over-doses, one theory purports that relative abstinence or lessened use of substances during incarceration, as well as the decreased purity of substances used during incarceration, physiologically diminishes tolerance so that resumption of pre-incarceration patterns of substance use after release significantly increases risk for unintentional overdose [68,71,72]. We cannot forget that in all institutional settings many inmates or acquitees learn to make their own alcohol from supplies from the commissary and/or meals provided to them, or obtain illicit drugs, or misuse or alter prescription drugs [57]. Furthermore, the use of intravenous and injection drug use (notably opiate use), places inmates at increased risk for contracting viral diseases such as HIV and hepatitis.

Finally, inmates who have undergone alcohol detoxification should be counseled that repeated alcohol withdrawal is associated with increased risk for delirium tremens and death and about medication-assisted treatment of alcoholism with naltrexone, acamprosate, and disulfiram [73]. Medication assisted treatment for opioids and alcohol are described in detail in other chapters in this book.

Even when provided with good care, some inmates are unprepared for transition back to the community. The treatment of substance use before release or on the order of mandated treatment after release lowers risk for violence. Examples of recommended mandated post-release treatment are random drug and alcohol testing, required Alcoholics and/or Narcotics Anonymous meeting attendance, and partial hospitalization programs specifically for substance addiction. Drug courts are a specific type of mandated care that integrates alcohol and other drug treatment services with justice system processing. Admission to drug courts can occur under probationary terms or diversion where records are expunged after successful treatment. Participants sign an agreement to participate with an understanding of the requirements of the program. Drug courts have been found to have a positive treatment outcome among substance abusers [74]. This may be partly due to the fact that drug court clients must meet basic admission criteria, including a history of substance use, and clients with a history of violent offences or clients who are found to be drug dealers without substance use problems are generally not eligible for admission. It takes, on average, eighteen to twenty four months for a participant to successfully graduate from a drug court program. Graduation generally means that clients have completed program requirements and have had clean results from their drug tests over a sustained period [75]. Post drug court follow-up is, of course, extremely important for continued success and further studies in this regard are needed. There are also various models of Mental Health Courts around the United States that have had a positive outcome with community-based treatment of the refractory seriously mentally ill. Most of these programs have strict admission criteria that usually exclude serious substance use disorders and a history of violence. They exclude the very individuals who desperately need comprehensive, integrated treatment.

2.6 CONCLUSIONS

The connection between substance use and crime has been studied extensively over the last three decades. Certainly these two problems have existed long before, even into antiquity, but thinking about them together has given novel ideas of how to alleviate their burden on society. We have attempted to review these topics in the context of current laws, statues, and case precedents and have made an effort to review basic concepts and ideas. The two problems share a reciprocating, multifactorial, and to some extent causal relationship. The depth and pervasiveness of the problems are undeniable, as our review of current statistical data has shown. The connection, however, is much more nuanced and varied, especially considering the presence of comorbid mental illness, involvement in minors, and when considering gender differences. The presence of mental illness alone has not been shown to increase rates of violence or crime when compared to background rates but with the addition of substances, rates do increase.

The law, driven by landmark cases, has helped us to understand how we are to legally handle crimes committed in the presence of substance use. Accountability, punishment, protection, and defense for the charged are concepts that are held as precedent today. We hope that this chapter has provided knowledge in both the assessment and treatment of criminal defendants with substance use and addiction, general systems issues within jails or prisons, and how to assist courts and attorneys on questions regarding this population. The ability to perform these assessments is a very specialized skill mastered after years of training and should not be seen as an expectation after reading this chapter. However, it is hoped that an appreciation for the nature of this complex system was garnered from this discussion. When involved with the court system or attorneys or when a patient presents you with questions pertaining to his/her legal problems, responsibilities, or prognosis, we hope this chapter has helped to empower you in handling these situations.

Finally, the authors of this chapter see the problems of crime, substance use, and mental illness as societal and multi-system issues that require a sense of ingenuity to solve. The burden of these problems socially, financially, and morally is immense. We see prevention and early intervention as major components to a solution. The treatment of substance use before release or on the order of mandated treatment after release lowers risk for violence. Examples of mandated post-release treatment recommended by drug courts and/or mental health courts may include random drug and alcohol testing, required Alcoholics and/or Narcotics Anonymous meeting attendance, and partial hospitalization programs specifically for substance addiction. Significantly more post-release community linkage beginning while institutionalized in jail, prison, or other forensic settings, to interventions such as drug use education, opiate agonist therapies such as methadone, buprenorphine and intensive case management are needed to provide better harm reduction. Mobilizing local, state, and federal resources to address this need has been and will continue to be a challenge but one that we believe is worthwhile.

As clinicians, we can do our part in shaping a culture of early intervention and prevention by screening early for mental illnesses and substance addiction disorders that may eventually lead to a life of crime. Pre- or post-adjudication diversion of these patients by entities such as drug courts or mental health courts, and referral of these substance use or dual diagnosis inmates to aggressive and comprehensive treatment is a best strategy in addressing these problems at a grass-roots level.

ACKNOWLEDGMENT

The authors would like to thank Sandra Downey for her research and technical support. Without her help the writing of this chapter would not have been possible.

REFERENCES

1. Beckson, M., Bartzokis, G., and Weinstsock, R. (2003) Substance abuse and addiction, in *Principles and Practice of Forensic Psychiatry* (ed. R. Rosner), Oxford University Press, New York, pp. 672–684.

2. Belenko, S.R. (2000) *Drugs and Drug Policy in America. A Documentary History*, Greenwood Press, Westport, CT.

3. Lamb, H.R.and Weinberger, L.E. (1998) Persons with severe mental illness in jails and prisons: A review. *Psychiatr. Serv.*, **49** (4), 483–490.

4. Haggard-Grann, U., Hallqvist, J., Langstrom, N., and Moller, J. (2006) The role of alcohol and drugs in triggering criminal violence: A case-crossover study. *Addiction*, **101**, 100–108.

5. Bradford, J.M.W., Greenberg, D.M., and Motayne, G. G. (1992) Substance abuse and criminal behavior. *Psychiat. Clin. N. Am.*, **15**, 605–622.

6. Juninger, J., Claypoole, K., Laygo, R., and Crisanti, A. (2006) Effects of serious mental illness and substance abuse on criminal offenses. *Psychiatr. Serv.*, **57**, 879–882.

7. Monahan, J., Steadman, H.J., Silver, E., and Appelbaum, P. (2001) *Rethinking Risk Assessment: The Macarthur Study of Mental Disorder and Violence*, Oxford University Press, New York.

8. Steadman, H.J., Mulvey, E.P., Monahan, J. *et al.* (1998) Violence by people discharged from acute psychiatric inpatient facilities and by others in the same neighborhoods. *Arch. Gen. Psychiatry*, **55** (5), 393–401.

9. Taylor, P.J.and Monahan, J. (1996) Commentary: Dangerous patients or dangerous diseases? *Br. Med. J.*, **312** 967–969.

10. Hodgins, S., Mednick, S.A., Brennan, P.A. *et al.* (1996) Mental disorder and crime. Evidence from a Danish birth cohort. *Arch. Gen. Psychiatry*, **53**, 489–622.

11. Harrison, P.M.and Karberg, J.C. (2004) Prison and Jail Inmates at Midyear: 2000 Bulletin. US Department of Justice, Office of Justice Programs, Bureau of Justice Statistics, Washington, DC.

12. Taxman, F.S., Perdoni, M.L., and Harrison, L.D. (2007) Drug treatment services for adult offenders: The state of the state. *J. Subst. Abuse. Treat.*, **32**, 238–254.

13. Narevic, E., Garrity, T.F., Schoenberg, N.E. *et al.* (2006) Factors predicting unmet health services needs among incarcerated substance users. *Subst. Use Misuse*, **41** (8), 1077–1094.

14. Lamb, H.R.and Weinberger, L.E. (2005) The shift of psychiatric inpatient care from hospitals to jails and prisons. *J. Am. Acad. Psychiatry*, **33** 529–534.

15. Kermani, E.J.and Casteneda, R. (1996) Psychoactive substance abuse in forensic psychiatry. *Am. J. Drug Alcohol. Ab.*, **22nl**, 1–27.

16. Drug Treatment in the Criminal Justice System (2001) Drug Policy Information Clearing House, Fact Sheet. Office of National Drug Control Policy (March 2001).

17. Lightfoot, L.O.and Hodgins, D. (1988) A survey of alcohol and drug problems in incarcerated offenders. *Int. J. Addict.*, **23**, 688–706.

18. Illicit Drug Use among Persons Arrested for Serious Crimes (2005) The National Institute on Drug Use and Health Report, Office of Applied Studies, Substance Abuse Mental Health Services Administration (16 December 2005).

19. Innes, C. (1988) Special Report: Drug Use and Crime, United States Department of Justice, Washington, DC.

20. Greenfield, L. (1998). An analysis of national data on the prevalence of alcohol involvement in crime. Prepared for the Assistant Attorney General's National Symposium on Alcohol Abuse and Crime (5–7 April 1998).

21. Friedman, S., Shelton, M., Elhaj, O. *et al.* (2005) Gender differences in criminality: Bipolar disorder with co-occurring substance abuse. *J. Am. Acad. Psychiatry*, **33**, 188–195.

22. Suicidal Thoughts, Suicide Attempts, Major Depressive Episode, and Substance Use among Adults (2006). Office of Applied Studies Report, Substance Abuse and Mental Health Services Administration, Issue 34.

23. Sakai, J.T., Stallings, M.C., Mikulich-Gilberston, S.K. *et al.* (2004) Mate similarity for substance dependence and antisocial personality disorder symptoms among parents of patients and controls. *Drug Alcohol. Depen.*, **75**, 165–175.

24. Goldstein, R.B., Powers, S.I., McCusker, J. *et al.* (1998) Antisocial behavioral syndromes among residential drug abuse treatment clients. *Drug Alcohol. Depen.*, **49**, 201–216.

25. National Survey on Drug Use and Health (2002) Office of Applied Studies, Substance Abuse and Mental Health Services Administration.

26. Sevigny, E. and Coontz, P. (2008) A gender based cluster analysis of Pennsylvania arrestees. *Int. J. Offender Ther.*, **52**, 435–453.

27. Substance Abuse Services and Staffing in Adult Correctional Facilities (2002) The Drug and Alcohol Services Information System Report, Office of Applied Studies Report, Substance Abuse and Mental Health Services Administration (4 October 2002).

28. American Law Institute, Model Penal Code, American Law Institute (ALI)Philadelphia, PA.

29. McNaughten, 8 Eng. Rep. 718, 722 (1843).

30. Criminal Resource Manual (1984) Insanity Reform Act, Federal Rule of Evidence.

31. Slovenko, R. (2002) *Psychiatry in Law, Law in Psychiatry*, Brunner Routledge, New York–London, pp. 305–322.

32. Goodwin, D.W. (1995) Alcohol amnesia. *Addiction*, **90**, 315–317.

33. Kalant, H. (1996) Intoxicated automatism: Legal concept v. scientific evidence. *Contemp. Drug Probl.*, **23**, 631–648.

34. van Oorsouw, K., Merckelbach, H., Ravelli, D. *et al.* (2000) Alcoholic blackout for criminally relevant behavior. *J. Am. Acad. Psychiatry*, **32**, 364–370.

35. Gutheil, T.G. and Appelbaum, P.S. (2000) Forensic evaluations, in *Clinical Handbook of Psychiatry and Law* (ed. T.G. Gutheiland P.S. Appelbaum), Lippincott Williams and Wilkins, Philadelphia, PA, pp. 261–316.

36. Dusky v. *United States.*, 362 U.S. 402 (1960).

37. Warren, J.I., Murrie, D.C., Stejskal, W. *et al.* (2006) Opinion formation in evaluating the adjudicative competence and restorability of criminal defendants: A review of 8,000 evaluations. *Behav. Sci. Law*, **24** (2), 113–132.

38. Grisso, T., Cocozza, J.J., Steadman, H.J. *et al.* (1996) A national survey of hospital-based and community-based approaches to pretrial mental health evaluations. *Psychiatr. Serv.*, **47**, 642–644.

39. Noffsinger, S.G. (2001) Restoration to competency practice guidelines. *Int. J. Offender Ther.*, **45** (2), 356–362.

40. Roe vs. *Wade*, 410 U.S. 113 (1973).

41. Bush vs. *Gore*, 531 U.S. 98 (2000).

42. Matthews vs. *Eldridge*, 424 U.S. 319, 335 (1976).

43. Robinson vs. *California*, 370 U.S. 660 (1962).

44. Powell vs. *Texas*, 392 U.S. 514 (1968).

45. Montana vs. *Egelhoff*, 116 S. Ct. 2013 (1996).

46. Reid, W.H. (2003) Law and Psychiatry: Why non-forensic clinicians should decline forensic referrals. *J. Psychiatric Prac.*, **9** (2), 163–166.

47. Jackson vs. *Indiana*, 406 U.S. 715 (1972).

48. Miller, R.D. (2003) Criminal competence, in *Principles and Practice of Forensic Psychiatry* (ed. R. Rosner), Oxford University Press, New York.

49. Strasburger, L.H., Gutheil, T.G., and Brodsky, A. (1997) On wearing two hats: Role conflict in serving as both psychotherapist and expert witness. *Am. J. Psychiatry*, **154** (4), 448–456.

50. Ito, T.A., Miller, N., and Pollock, V.E. (1996) Alcohol and aggression: A meta-analysis on the moderating effects of inhibitory cues, triggering events, and self-focused attention. *Psychol. Bull.*, **120**, 60–82.

51. Bushman, B.J. and Cooper, H.M. (1990) Effects of alcohol on human aggression: An integrative research review. *Psychol. Bull.*, **107**, 341–354.

52. Nurco, D.N., Ball, J.C., Schaffer, J.W., and Hanlon, T.E. (1985) The criminality of narcotic addicts. *J. Nerv. Ment. Dis.*, **173** (2), 94–102.

53. Schaeffer, J.W., Nurco, D.N., and Kinlock, T.W. (1984) A new classification of narcotic addicts based on type and extent of criminal activity. *Compr. Psychiat.*, **25**, 315–328.

54. Ball, J.C., Schaeffer, J.W., and Nurco, D.N. (1983) The day-to-day criminality of heroin addicts in Baltimore – A study in the continuity of offense rates. *Drug Alcohol. Depen.*, **12**, 119–142.

55. Brecher, M., Whang, B.W., Wong, H., and Morgan, J.P. (1988) Phencyclidine and violence: Clinical and legal issues. *J. Clin. Psychopharmacol*, **8**, 397–401.

56. Sayette, M.A. (1993) Heart rate as an index of stress response in alcohol administration research: A critical review. *Alcohol. Clin. Exp. Res.*, **17**, 802–809.

57. Scott, C.L. and Gerbasi, J.B. (2005) Assessment of mental disorders in correctional settings, in *Handbook of Correctional Mental Health*, 1st edn, American Psychiatric Publishing, Inc., Washington, DC, pp. 43–68.

58. Krebs, C.P., Brady, T., and Laird, G. (2003) Jail-based substance user treatment: An analysis of retention. *Subst. Use Misuse*, **38**, 1227–1258.

59. Turley, A., Thornton, T., Johnson, C. *et al.* (2004) Jail drug and alcohol treatment program reduces recidivism in nonviolent offenders: A longitudinal study of Monroe County, New York's jail treatment drug and alcohol program. *Int. J. Offender Ther.*, **48**, 721–728.

60. Deleon, G. (1997) Modified therapeutic communities. Emerging issues, in *Community as Method: Therapeutic Communities for Special Populations and Special Settings* (ed. G. Deleon), Greenwood Publishing, Westport, CT, pp. 261–270.

61. Monahan, J., Steadman, H.J., Appelbaum, P.S. *et al.* (2006) The classification of violence risk. *Behav. Sci. Law*, **24** (6), 721–730.

62. Elbogen, E.B. and Tomkins, A.J. (2000) From the psychiatric hospital to the community: Integrating conditional release and contingency management. *Behav. Sci. Law.*, **18** (4), 427–444.

63. Appelbaum, P.S., Robbins, P.C., and Monahan, J. (2000) Violence and delusions: Data from the MacArthur violence risk assessment study. *Am. J. Psychiatry*, **157** (4), 566–572.

64. Monahan, J., Steadman, H.J., Appelbaum, P.S. *et al.* (2000) Developing a clinically useful actuarial tool for assessing violence risk. *Brit. J. Psychiat.*, **176**, 312–319.

65. Swanson, J., Holzer, C., and Ganju, V. (1999) Violence and psychotic disorder in the community: Evidence from the Epidemiological Catchment Area Study. *Hosp. Community Psych.*, **41**, 761–770.

66. Drake, R.E. and Wallach, M.A. (1989) Substance abuse among chronically medically ill. *Hosp. Community Psych.*, **40**, 1041–1046.

67. Bartels, S.J., Teague, G.B., Drake, R.E. *et al.* (1993) Substance abuse in schizophrenia: service utilization and costs. *J. Nerv. Ment. Dis.*, **181** (4), 227–232.

68. Binswanger, I.A., Stern, M.F., Deyo, R.A. *et al.* (2007) Release from prison – A high risk of death for former inmates. *N. Engl. J. Med.*, **356** (2), 157–165.

69. McLean, R.L., Robarge, J., and Sherman, S.G. (2006) Release from jail: Moments of crisis or window of opportunity for female detainees? *J. Urban Health*, **83**, 382–393.

70. Stallwitz, A. and Stover, H. (2007) The impact of substitution treatment in prisons – A literature review. *Int. J. Drug Pol.*, **18**, 464–474.

71. Seal, D.W., Eldrige, G.D., Kacanek, D. *et al.* (2007) A longitudinal, qualitative analysis of the context of substance use and sexual behavior among 18-to 29-year-old men after their release from prison. *Soc. Sci. Med.*, **65**, 2394–2406.

72. Seaman, S.R., Brettle, R.P. and Gore, S.M. (1998) Mortality from overdose among injecting drug users recently released from prison: Database linkage study. *Br. Med. J.*, **316**, 426–428.

73. Mayo-Smith, M.F., Beecher, L.H., Fischer, T.L. *et al.* (2004) Management of alcohol withdrawal delirium. An evidence based practice guideline. *Arch. Intern. Med.*, **164**, 1405–1412.

74. Drug Courts Program Office (1997) Defining Drug Courts: The Key Components, US Department of Justice, Washington, DC.

75. Logan, T.K., Williams, K., and Leukefeld, C. (2002) A statewide drug court needs assessment: Identifying target counties, assessing readiness. *J. Offender Rehab.*, **33** (3), 1–25.

3

Ethical issues in addiction medicine

Roberta Springer Loewy

UC Davis, University of California, Sacramento, CA, 95670, USA

3.1 INTRODUCTION

This chapter ranges across at least two rapidly growing fields – addiction medicine and ethics – in both of which volumes have been written. The chore here is to provide an overview of the myriad ethical quandaries that can arise in addiction medicine, but to do so within the confines of a single chapter. Thus, I have been hard pressed to distill from such a large amount of material topics that will prove foundational, yet informative and useful to a fairly wide spectrum of medical practitioners. To that end, the chapter is divided into three broad sections. Because good ethics – like any other inquiry – begins with a basic understanding of the discipline itself, the first section contains a discussion, albeit all too brief, of what ethics is (and, perhaps more importantly, what it is not!), and how healthcare professionals can become more proficient in helping to identify and resolve existing or potential areas of ethical conflict.

In the second section, some of the more common concerns of both patients and healthcare professionals in general are reviewed – that is, confidentiality or privacy, autonomy, paternalism, beneficence, nonmaleficence, informed consent, truth-telling, professional integrity, social responsibility, justice – before turning to some of the ethical complexities that the unique context of addiction medicine presents for both healthcare professionals and patients.

The final section looks critically at the issues of spirituality and religion and how the field of addiction medicine has addressed these two aspects of the biopsychosocial elements of patients in the past, and call for the creation of and support for a wider range of therapeutic alternatives so as to provide a more comfortable fit to the particular spiritual needs of each patient.

3.2 THE DISCIPLINE OF ETHICS

One of the major difficulties encountered in any discussion, whether contentious or not, is the inevitable existence of hidden assumptions. Our everyday lives are, of course, filled with assumptions, and we would be hard-pressed if we could not rely upon

them with a fair degree of success. The problem with assumptions is that they can lull people into thinking that everyone is "on the same page" when, indeed, they may not even be close, complicating the progress of even the most elementary of

Addictive Disorders in Medical Populations   Edited by Norman S. Miller and Mark S. Gold
© 2010 John Wiley & Sons, Ltd.

discussions. A prime example: there really is no agreement as to whether ethics and morality are synonymous and how, if they are not, they ought to be distinguished. Most people – philosopher and bioethicist types included – continue to use the terms "ethics" and "morality" interchangeably, which has created interminable and, I have long argued, unnecessary confusion. To avoid such confusion it is important to recognize (and thereby, hopefully, to reduce) hidden and/or conflicting assumptions – and to discover whether they are genuinely warranted or not – as early as possible. To this end, I will (1) explain several of my own key assumptions and (2) offer some provisional definitions and criteria from which critical analysis, discussion, argument and further understanding and redefinition might more fruitfully proceed.

3.2.1 My own perspective and assumptions

My own philosophical perspective derives largely from those of the American pragmatists, most especially the work of John Dewey. Thus, I treat ethics as an empirical process of inquiry; that is, it is neither the discovery of a set of universal, unchanging, objective "truths" (somewhere out there with a capital "T") nor merely a set of subjective, relativistic human creations. Rather, I treat it as an intersubjective, progressive, cumulative and public process of inquiry – not too unlike the process of scientific inquiry – where, together, we build on the successes and (even more importantly) failures of the past while trying to understand the meaning and implications of an unsettled or, as Dewey would call it, "indeterminate" situation. We accomplish this by framing various hypotheses in light of the context of the problematic situation that presents itself to us and then by testing alternative theories, hypotheses and the wisdom of past experiences in such a way that we can better identify and measure their potential for dealing successfully with the specific problem at hand, including the respective benefits and burdens of the live alternatives that are available for those most relevantly affected [1].

Thus, ethical inquiry is prompted whenever important core values are at risk or come into conflict, where there is no answer that protects every important core value involved, and where we are forced to choose the least bad from a range of less than optimal alternatives. These, my assumptions, are foundational to understanding my commitment to the idea that good ethics, like any good science, is a process of inquiry that begins with good data – and where humans are involved that data is, necessarily, biopsychosocial [2].

3.2.2 Provisional definitions and/or criteria

3.2.2.1 What ethics is not

At the outset of any inquiry, as important as it is to discuss what something is, it is often equally important to discuss what it is not. Hence, I offer a list of things (followed by a few brief comments) that ethics decidedly is not:

- Untutored intuition

- Ungrounded opinion

- Majority opinion

- Opinion held by a powerful few

- Law

- Religion

- Personal morality.

While some forms of intuition – that is, purely subjective, unverifiable and, thus, irrational in the classic logical sense of the term – are recognized by some ethical theories, untutored intuition is little different from whimsy or gut feeling. Intuition of this kind is as likely to lead to infertile as it is to productive avenues of investigation. For example, my untutored intuition about what I must do to behave beneficently towards you might well be the least helpful thing you would want someone to do for you. I would argue that even the role of "tutored" intuition ought to be limited to the very earliest stages of ethical inquiry, where things are, as yet, so indeterminate that we are still trying to formulate the nature of the problem.

Opinion – whether ungrounded, held by a majority or held by a powerful few – offers even less in the service of ethical analysis. Ungrounded opinion, while it may prompt ethical inquiry has, by its very qualification (i.e., ungrounded), no justification, and opinion held by either a majority or a powerful few rests piggy-back on the ethically questionable assumption that "might (or a plurality) makes right" is ever justifiable. Insofar as the contradistinction between ethics and law goes, we needn't look far for enlightenment. History is filled with examples of unethical laws, for example, slavery, religious intolerance, the unequal treatment of women and minorities, and so on. And, finally, there are good reasons (which are discussed in greater detail immediately below) why ethics is not the same thing as religion or personal morality.

3.2.2.2 Morality

Contrary to what popular usage suggests, it is my contention that morality is not the same thing as ethics, and that it is essential for us to understand their similarities and differences. As far as similarities go, morality, like ethics, is concerned with human custom and behavior – "morals" having been derived from the Latin word, *mores*, and ethics from the Greek word, *ethos*. Both share the evaluative language of "right," "wrong," "good," "bad," "obligation," "responsibility," "duty," and so on, and both seek ways of justifying beliefs and claims when conflicts arise.

That being said, there remain important – arguably crucial – differences. Morality, as the sum total of a person's beliefs concerning "right," "wrong," "good," "bad," "obligation," "responsibility," "duty," and so on, is usually deeply personal, even though it – or major aspects of it – may be shared by other individuals or groups. It is often intuitive, tacit, reflexive and/or uni-perspectival, whether personal

or within a given enclave. Morality can have non-rational (i.e., transcendent, mystical or mythic) elements and, in its most extreme form, morality can exhibit absolutistic features or over-tones.

Morality is generally derived from one's psycho-social (i.e., personal, cultural, spiritual) upbringing – from one's "parent's knee," peer group, ethnic identity, culture, religion, law, personal intuitions and/or reflections. When defended, it is usually by appeal to an "authority" recognized and accepted within one's particular moral enclave (i.e., my religion, my parents, my culture, my authority figures, etc.). Such appeals rest on the presumption of certain shared core values, worldviews, interests and/or goals that often may not, in fact, be shared outside one's own particular personal morality or particular moral enclave, and it is here that most ethical problems and misunderstandings arise.

3.2.2.3 Ethics

Ethics, on the other hand, is predominately a second-order activity; namely, it is the study of moral systems, theories, values, beliefs, behaviors, and so on, and their justification. It is the study of "right," "wrong," "good," "bad," "obligation," "responsibility," "duty," and so on, concerning behavior towards others, *especially* those who may not share one's own personal morality. Central to the concept of ethics is the empirical fact of (and respect for) the existence of diverse personal, spiritual and cultural belief systems that yield conflicting worldviews, interests, values and goals (i.e., conflicting moral perspectives). Indeed, contrary to many moral points of view, one of the central assumptions in ethics is that moral conflict or difference is not a defect but, in fact, the central feature and inevitable result of the rich variety and complexity of human existence.

Thus, while the subject matter of ethical inquiry include beliefs, values and behaviors that may be nonrational, intuitive, absolutistic, transcendent, mystical or even mythic, ethical inquiry itself strives to remain an explicit, deliberate and empirically-oriented enterprise, one that aims to be logical, rational, critically reflective, and sensitive to context.

In other words, it is committed to democratic discourse and accommodation, an "all things considered" approach that celebrates a willingness (1) to listen, (2) to engage in discussion, (3) to respect differences of opinion and perspective, (4) to interpret opposing viewpoints from the most charitable perspective, and (5) to be led by the dynamic of the inquiry – rather than by predetermined assumptions or beliefs – when seeking alternatives that respect and preserve as many of the values, interests and goals of all of those relevantly affected as possible. Such a commitment requires us not only to attend to cogent argument and reasoning but also to do so with curiosity, patience, honesty, and open-mindedness. In short, ethics, as just characterized, is a process of critical, reflective, progressive inquiry, and not a set of predetermined rules and/or algorithms.

Thus, the goal of ethics is not to discover "the Truth," "the Good," or what "the Right thing to do" is. Rather, the goal of ethics is at once much more modest and much more difficult; its goal is to help all of those persons relevantly affected in a very specific problematic situation find consensus in the midst of competing claims about what the truth, the good and the right thing to do are *in this particular instance*. This entails respecting and attempting to preserve as many of those competing claims, values, and interests of those relevantly affected as possible, given that all cannot be preserved. It also entails finding a source of justification broad enough for all parties involved to recognize and to accept as reasonable for those most relevantly affected, given a thorough examination of all of the available alternatives, even though it may not be their own personal preference. Thus, the "authority" sought in ethics is not given ready-made or fully articulated by any expert, book or institution; rather it arises out of reason, logic, compassion and the pooling of our common human capacities and experiences.

Finally, I always tell my medical students – and only half jokingly – to run the other way if they are ever confronted by a bioethicist or ethics committee that tells them, the patient or the healthcare team what the "answer" is or what they are "supposed" to do. There are a number of reasons why I say this:

1. Since what is *biomedically* appropriate can only be determined by the biomedical experts involved and since only the patient (or patient's proxy and, if the patient wishes, his or her significant others) can agree to or reject the alternatives offered by the biomedical experts, the proper role of a bioethicist or ethics committee is to help discover the widest range of defensible alternatives *that are not ethically inappropriate*, given the particulars of the case and the interests, values, and goals of the patient.

2. While a bioethicist or an ethics committee may be able to help a patient or a healthcare team recognize faulty assumptions and arguments and tease out the competing claims, values, interests, and goals of a particular problematic situation, it is *not* their job to prescribe what may prove to be life-altering choices for others who must then directly bear the life-long consequences of those choices.

3. One of the hallmarks of an ethical problem or issue is that there is no "good" answer but, rather, a range of options none of which are "good" because all of the options require some "goods" to be sacrificed for others.

4. Once all of the competing claims, values, interests, and goals have been teased out, the "best" or "least bad" alternative often becomes clear enough for agreement between the patient and the appropriate biomedical experts.

3.2.3 Developing proficiency in recognizing and addressing ethical issues

Remember the old adage "an ounce of prevention is worth a pound of cure?" Well, just like all other issues in medicine, ethical issues are best addressed prospectively. Just as "rescue medicine" is costly (in both material and nonmaterial terms), so it is with *post hoc* or "rescue" ethics. However, unless we become sensitive to those things likely to trigger an issue and provide the requisite time and space for attending to them before they become full-blown problems, we are stuck – whether in medicine, ethics or any other setting – dealing with the disruptive fallout and trying to mend the patient–clinician relationship, perhaps never quite restoring the bonds of trust previously forged.

So, just as we value developing expertise in initial and ongoing physical and psychological assessments, so we should value and develop expertise in doing, as it were, initial and ongoing "ethical" assessments. By following a set of flexible guidelines (the operative word here is *flexible*), one can usually become quite adept at recognizing early warning signs of potential ethical problems, so that they can be nipped in the bud. Dr Erich H. Loewy, and I have suggested the following tentative set of guidelines, which have proved helpful to many of our students and colleagues:

1. Gather the biopsychosocial data of the case (but avoid hiding the fear of making a decision behind a never-ending quest for more).

    (a) Be sure that any biomedical data outside your own field of expertise are given and substantiated by those well-credentialed in making such judgments.

    (b) Be certain to include all of the psychosocially relevant facts about the patient.

    (c) Be sure to evaluate these data in the context in which they are embedded.

    (d) Entertain tentative options in an ongoing manner and let the options guide the search for further data.

2. Draw clear distinctions, and, as they are drawn, other options or the need for further

data may become evident and can then be pursued.

3. Scrutinize the beliefs, values, and principles motivating both the choices and those making the choices.

4. Tentatively determine (and do not simply assume!) the goals that are to be pursued – in a good 70% of the ethics cases I've seen, either all parties assumed they all had the same goal, and didn't, or else no one had, in fact, discussed goals at all!

5. When beliefs and principles clash, examine whether they do so in reality or simply because of a misunderstanding.

6. Try to establish, by consensus if possible, hierarchies of principles, duties, and obligations – the default presumption being that they must be patient-centered unless there are truly compelling reasons why they should not be.

7. Understand the unique context in which the problem plays itself out, and take differences in moral views into account – while a narrower analysis may prove useful, removing problems completely from the context in which they occur is artificial and may distort them in peculiar and unexpected ways.

8. Be aware of the tentative nature of any "goal," "solution," "answer," or series of "options" [3].

3.3 ETHICAL ISSUES AND ADDICTION

3.3.1 General ethical concepts and values

The following are intended to provide merely a provisional *starting point* for case analysis and ethical discussion:

3.3.1.1 Autonomy

Literally meaning "self-law," autonomy remains a difficult and contentiously debated concept. Broadly speaking, autonomy is both a capacity and an obligation. That is, it is the *capacity* to make deliberated and reasoned decisions for oneself and the *obligation* to respect that capacity in others. Thus, autonomy is not simply an unfettered or open-ended freedom, but an ethically weighty responsibility as well.

Autonomy is the freedom to make decisions for oneself and the freedom (when possible) to carry them out. The former is called freedom of the will, and the latter freedom of action [4]. One of the more difficult problems in all fields of medical practice – but especially in the fields related to psychology – is that these are often separated. For example, a patient may be in a state of confusion (and, therefore, have no freedom of the will) but still have freedom of action (and, therefore, may need to be restrained). Conversely, a patient may have a clear mind but, because of physical barriers, be unable to translate his or her will into action.

Autonomy presupposes a clear understanding of facts and options presented as well as the capacity to reason logically about those facts and options. Moreover, it denotes a clear understanding of the ends (or goals) desired – as well as their potential risks and benefits. Patient autonomy is what grounds such concerns as, for example, informed consent, confidentiality, truth-telling, and conscientious objection.

3.3.1.2 Beneficence

Beneficence is not the same thing as benevolence, or kindness. Beneficence (literally, "to do good") grounds the traditional Hippocratic ethical obligation of healthcare professionals to act with the good of the patient in mind. Such an action may be done because the patient:

- Is believed to lack decisional capacity.

- Is unable to understand his/her situation.

- Has decisional capacity but is acting against what the healthcare professional considers to be his or her "best interests".

Because the attempt to benefit others inevitably carries the risk of causing harm, beneficence must always be considered in the context of nonmaleficence. A wide variety of prima facie obligations flow from beneficence in the medical setting, including the individual practitioner's obligations of professional competence (e.g., sound qualifications and continuing education) and the obligations of the profession as a whole to pursue excellence in

practice, teaching, and ongoing medical research and development. While beneficence is a very important value or ideal, there are times when it can be problematic, including (1) when it conflicts with other, equally compelling ethical values or ideals, (2) when there are conflicting assessments as to benefits and harms, and (3) when there are questions about the scope of obligation (e.g., to whom is what owed?).

3.3.1.3 Coerced treatment

Unfortunately, there is considerable variation amongst experts in the field as to what is entailed by the concept, "coerced treatment," ranging anywhere from a mild "suggestion" to a legal mandate. Moreover, there is also some disagreement as to the efficacy of treatment that is not voluntarily chosen by the person undergoing it [5,6]. Good ethics begins with good facts – a point that simply cannot be stressed enough throughout this chapter. In what might be called the age of evidence-based medicine, presumably these "facts" will – sooner rather than later – eventuate in a biomedical consensus of some sort.

That being said, as far as the bioethics literature goes, it reflects the fact that there has, for the most part, been a steady exodus away from medical paternalism towards a robust patients' rights movement. According to Ronald Dworkin [7], who practically channels the classical strong antipaternalism position of John Stewart Mill: "A person has the fundamental right, well established in medical ethics and in American law, to refuse beneficial and helpful care even if such a refusal shortens his or her own life and has detrimental consequences for others."

Some of us [3] have long argued that this particular pendulum has swung too far, encouraging us to abandon patients to their own pro forma (formal, but often empty) autonomy. I would agree with Erich Loewy in his argument that an authentic, robust autonomy can only arise out of the "cradle of beneficence" – that is, that autonomy is a capacity that must be nurtured to develop and protected when vulnerable or threatened. Rather than Dworkin's position, we would be more in agreement with Art Caplan [8] who writes eloquently that:

> respect for self-determination sometimes requires mandatory treatment as a way to create or enable autonomy...People who are addicted really do not have the full capacity to be self-determining or autonomous because their addiction literally coerces their behavior. They cannot be autonomous agents precisely because they are caught up in the behavioral vice that is addiction. If that is so, then it may be possible to justify compulsory treatment for finite periods of time that could rectify this situation and restore the capacity for autonomy.

Caplan's point is, in fact, consistent with the distinction drawn earlier between freedom of the will and freedom of action [4] in Section 3.3.1.1 – the addict's freedom of the will is, so to speak, impaired, but their freedom of action, unfortunately in this case, is not. Paradoxically, if by temporarily removing their freedom of action (via coerced treatment) we might restore their freedom of the will, then we will have restored them to some semblance of their pre-addicted autonomous state. Thus, if we have good empirical evidence that a given treatment modality could disrupt the power of addiction sufficiently to restore or re-establish a patient's autonomy, then coerced or mandated treatment could presumably be ethically justifiable.

On a final note, under the concept "informed consent", I have stipulated that one of the components of a valid consent process is a reasonable lack of internal or external coercion. While it might be used to argue against me that coerced or mandatory treatment could constitute a particularly egregious form of external coercion that infringes on a patient's autonomy and, thus, precludes consent, I would argue that allowing the internal coercion of addiction to persist is an even more egregious form of coercion because, in denying coerced treatment to patients, we may well be abandoning them unnecessarily to a life of diminished – or nonexistent – "autonomy." It is difficult (naïve? cynical?) to speak of informed consent in patients who are neither able to digest the information nor in reality give consent. It would seem both prudential and respectfully

compassionate that the burden of proof here ought to rest with those who would deny that addiction impairs the ability of patients to digest information or truly give consent.

[NB: See also Sections 3.3.1.1 (Autonomy) and 3.3.1.2 (Beneficence) and the discussion in Section 3.3.2.2 (Autonomy in the Face of Addiction)].

3.3.1.4 Competence

In general parlance, competence is the ability to perform a given task. In the medical milieu, however, competence is a legal term that denotes the capacity to make decisions. All adults (conscious, unconscious, even severely demented) are legally competent *unless and until* a judge pronounces them incompetent and appoints a guardian. Moreover, one can be legally "competent" but lack the capacity to make decisions affecting one's medical care and, conversely, one can have been adjudged incompetent and yet retain decisional capacity for all or some medical decisions.

3.3.1.5 Confidentiality

Confidentiality is central to the *patient–clinician relationship* and is a crucial part of the tacit social understanding upon which it is based. It stems from the fact that the effective care of patients often requires them to divulge sensitive aspects of their personal lives that could lead to disadvantage, discrimination or stigma if known to others. Thus, the traditional presumption is that a patient's personal and/or medical information cannot be divulged to third parties without that patient's explicit consent – unless, of course, third parties are, themselves, in imminent danger of being substantially harmed by the patient's willful disregard of their safety (e.g., infectious disease, paranoid delusions, etc.). Patients who reveal that they are, in fact, about to murder a spouse or to unsafely pilot an airplane fall into this (not quite unusual) category. Patients who refuse to divulge a potentially fatal illness to their dependents likewise create severe ethical problems, as may patients who under some circumstances refuse to take their medications (e.g., a classic example would be a patient's failure/refusal to take antituberculosis medications).

3.3.1.6   Conflicts of interest

Conflicts of interest arise in clinical practice when health care professionals become involved in arrangements – often, though not solely, economic – that introduce considerations that are potentially contrary to the patient's best interests. They are especially problematic because of their potential to undermine patients' trust in the patient–clinician relationship and to weaken the standards of the profession. These conflicts are not necessarily material but also include the immaterial (e.g., the professional obligation to care for patients, the personal obligations to spend time with one's family and to pursue other outside interests).

3.3.1.7   Conscience

Conscience has often been described as an inner voice or "gut feeling" and, while some claim that conscience is a wonderful thing, it depends largely on whose it is. One would hope that our consciences differ significantly from Dr Mengele's (the chief physician at Auschwitz)! Yet, if there are no objective – or, at least, intersubjective – standards to which we can, in addition, appeal, anything can be justified – Mengele's actions as well as our own.

3.3.1.8   Conscientious objection

Conscientious objection is an objection, in principle, or a refusal, in practice, to perform an otherwise legally required or permitted practice. For example, healthcare professionals with conscientious objections to abortion may refuse to participate in medical, surgical or administrative procedures required for the termination of pregnancy. However, conscious objection does not relieve healthcare professionals from the following obligations to their patients: they still have a duty to provide *full and*

impartial counseling, speedy referral, and any required treatment incidental (as in this example) to termination or necessary to preserve/stabilize the pregnant woman's life or health.

3.3.1.9   Consent

The idea of consent is based on the ethical concept that every person has the right to bodily integrity and self-determination and, thus, the right to consent or to withhold consent to things that are done to their own person. In a life-threatening emergency when the patient lacks decisional capacity and no surrogates are available, it is both ethical and legal that treatment be instituted. The legal standard is that of the "reasonable person" – that is, the presumption that most reasonable persons would want life-saving therapy. The ethical reason is that under these circumstances the healthcare professional lacks information and, therefore, must "opt for life" – mainly so that they can "buy time" both to gather the biomedical data needed and to attempt to restore the patient's opportunity to make an informed decision.

Consent presumes a rational, fully informed patient. However, we often assume that when patients agree with us they are rational and that a refusal indicates that the patient lacks decisional capacity. (Both assumptions may, in fact, turn out to be wrong!) And, finally, there are rare cases when truth telling might be thought to be harmful to a patient who has decisional capacity. Such instances are rare indeed. To withhold such information from patients is called "therapeutic privilege," a privilege that courts have only rarely upheld. [See also Sections 3.3.1.4 (Competence) and 3.3.1.13 (Informed consent)].

3.3.1.10   Consequentialism

Consequentialism is that theory of ethics which holds that what makes an act or rule right/good or wrong/bad are the consequences it brings about. Utilitarianism is the prime example of a consequentialist approach. Act utilitarianism holds that one should always choose that act which would maximize utility (e.g., the greatest good for the greatest number); whereas rule utilitarianism holds that one should follow that rule which tends to maximize utility. The major pitfalls of such theories are the tendency to cherry-pick the consequences thought to be most efficacious and the difficulty of identifying if, when, and where we should stop measuring the consequences.

3.3.1.11 Decisional capacity

Decisional capacity is the medical term that refers to the capacity to understand one's own situation and to make decisions based on that understanding; this concept is central to informed consent, another closely related concept in biomedical ethics. Strictly speaking, decisional capacity differs from the *legal* term, competence, insofar as only a judge can render a determination as to whether a person is or is not competent. Thus, for example, a person legally declared incompetent might still have decisional capacity to make some or all of their healthcare decisions. While there is room for disagreement about the threshold of decisional capacity, the following criteria, based on the US President's Commission for the Study of Ethical Problems in Medicine and Biomedical and Behavioral Research (1982) are considered minimally necessary, however rudimentary they may be:

- Possession of a set of values, interests, life plans and goals.

- The ability to communicate and to understand information.

- The ability to reason and to deliberate about one's choices in light of one's values, interests, life plans, and goals.

It is important to remember that such a standard emphasizes *process* rather than *product* (i.e., outcome). Any standard that focuses on outcomes of decisions remains vulnerable to the charge that it is granting greater priority to the outcome than to the patient's decisional capacity, values, and goals.

3.3.1.12 Deontology

Deontology is that ethical theory which holds that following a pre-determined, universal rule regardless of outcome is praiseworthy and breaking such a rule blameworthy. In deontology what matters is the intention of the actor, not the consequences of the act. One of the weaknesses of a deontological approach is that it is often quite difficult to identify, measure or understand intentions – whether our own or others – since they are subjective, complex, and often opaque or even suppressed. Another weakness of deontological approaches is their failure to tell us what to do when such rules conflict.

3.3.1.13 Informed consent

Informed consent is the process that seeks to clarify the clinician's ethical obligation to provide biomedical data sufficient to allow a patient to make an informed and rational choice as to whether or not to consent to medical care and/or treatment. It presupposes that the patient has decisional capacity and is not being unduly coerced by either external circumstances (persons or situations) or internal conditions (e.g., pain, confusion, electrolyte imbalance, paranoia, addiction, etc.). Basically there are two main components: the information component and the consent process.

The information component requires:

- Truthful disclosure and explanation of information (diagnosis, prognosis, options, and implications of treatment/nontreatment) by the clinician (s) in language that the patient can understand and process.
  - The aim here is to provide information that is adequate (but not extraneous or overwhelming) for making a prudent choice given the context of the situation and the patient's values and goals.

- Verification that patient and/or proxy decision maker is able to comprehend and intelligently discuss the information and options presented.

The consent process requires:

- Decisional capacity.

- Reasonable lack of internal or external coercion.

- Adequate time – whenever possible – to process the implications of diagnosis, prognosis, and the range of available options.

- Authenticity – the values and goals invoked by the patient/proxy decision maker to explain choices should be reasonably consistent with that patient's past values and goals and, if not, the patient/proxy decision maker should be able to provide reasonably convincing evidence of why such a shift may have occurred.

3.3.1.14   Intuition

In ethical parlance, intuition is characterized by an immediate ("instinctive"), direct "awareness" of the truth of a proposition not proven by rational or empirical means. Such intuitions are often biased, though some thinkers claim that such intuitions are based on a perception of "Truth" or on the rapid processing of past experience and/or subconscious perceptions. By their nature, intuitions that claim to be based on a perception of "Truth" not accessible to empirical or rational proof are neither falsifiable nor verifiable (which, by the way, make disputes based on conflicting intuitions impossible to resolve). In medicine as well as healthcare ethics intuitions should by no means be discounted altogether – but neither are they alone sufficient grounds upon which to act.

3.3.1.15   Justice

While there remain a variety of conflicting conceptions of justice, there are several common features; namely (a) that justice is obligatory and not simply optional or supererogatory and (b) that justice is concerned with giving persons what is their due. Of course, what is at issue between these conflicting conceptions of justice is precisely the

substantive element of these features: namely, how to determine what constitutes "obligatory" and what constitutes "due." As a result, how persons conceive justice is qualified by how they – individually and as a society – conceive personhood, autonomy, community, and respect for persons.

In the healthcare field, concerns about justice have usually been limited to distributive aspects of justice in the public health setting. It has frequently been alleged that justice has little or no role at the individual patient's bedside because it is the professional responsibility of healthcare clinicians to benefit maximally the patient before them – but, again, this raises the question of giving persons as patients what is their due. The rise of "managed care" in the United States has tried to mount a serious challenge to both this traditional tenet of professionalism and to our understanding of what constitutes justice. It is unfortunate the degree to which it has succeeded.

3.3.1.16   Nonmaleficence

The literal translation of nonmaleficence is "to do no harm." In the healthcare context, nonmaleficence is the prima facie ethical obligation that requires us to minimize the patient's exposure to the harmful effects of our interventions [see also Section (Beneficence)]. The point here is not "to do no harm," but rather to do more good than harm, all things considered.

3.3.1.17   Paternalism

Paternalism (or, more correctly, parentalism) refers loosely to treating persons as a benevolent parent would treat his (or her) children, and is generally defined as "interfering with someone's liberty justified by reasons referring exclusively to the good, happiness, and so on of another" [7]. In medical parlance paternalism is said to be "genuine" (i.e., justified) only when invoked to restore, or to bide time for, the return of a patient's decisional capacity. This type of paternalism is called "weak" or "soft" paternalism [9]. That is, the actor in "weak paternalism" tries to prevent conduct that is largely nonvoluntary, done without adequate understanding of the consequences and at times to ascertain whether an act is truly autonomous (e.g., pulling a person from the path of an oncoming truck). "Strong" or "crass" paternalism, on the other hand, seeks to prevent "harm" or do "good" even when the other's contrary choices are informed and voluntary (e.g., transfusing a life long Jehovah's witness against his or her will).

The perennial disagreement in medicine about the benefits/burdens of nonvoluntary commitment is based as much on what view of paternalism is considered ethically (and legally) justifiable as it is on what view of patient autonomy and the effect that serious psychiatric illness, including addiction, has on it. While some have argued that patient autonomy is not impaired in addiction [10], it is a position difficult to maintain given our, as yet, dismal success rates in treating most addictions, which should come as no surprise given what little we yet understand of the biopsychosocial (including genetic) foundations and dimensions of addiction...or of autonomy, for that matter.

3.3.1.18 Patient–clinician relationship

The healing relationship follows the classic traditions of a professional, fiduciary relationship. Medicine is a profession in the classic sense; that is, a self-governing group of individuals granted exclusive rights by society to practice a service-oriented expertise, based on a special body of knowledge over which they have control (through their control of structure, admission, educational requirements, standards of practice, regulation, licensure, censure, etc.) [11]. Moreover, the practice has ethical ends or goals over and above the usual material ends or goals associated with personal reputation or private reward. Medicine is a fiduciary relationship in the sense that persons who occupy positions of such power and confidence are expected (whether by law or simply by tacit social expectation) to place the interests of those persons receiving their expertise over all else. Over-riding

this default expectation of patient priority is–and should remain – rare and rightly demands clear and convincing justification. Hence, patient–clinician relationships encompass a cluster of values that generally include, but are not limited to, beneficence, nonmaleficence, solicitousness, honesty or truth-telling, and confidentiality.

3.3.1.19 Principalism

There are many forms of principalism (deontological approaches in ethics could conceivably be called principalism because of their emphasis on rules and rule-following, as could rule-utilitarianism). However, it is perhaps best expressed today by the work of Beauchamp and Childress from Georgetown University. For this reason, principalism is often referred to as the "Georgetown mantra." These two authors hold that there are four basic principles in medical ethics: (1) Autonomy; (2) Beneficence; (3) Nonmaleficence and (4) Justice. The main weaknesses of principalism are not minor, and include determining (1) how these principles are to be interpreted, (2) how they relate to each other, (3) how they relate to the particular case at hand, and (4) what to do when they conflict. Thus, in modern Bioethics principalism tends to be much discussed, but little used.

3.3.1.20 Substituted judgment

Substituted judgment is an attempt to determine what patients who lack decisional capacity would decide had they possessed it. This is often described as the attempt to put oneself in the other's shoes, and deciding from that perspective. It is a difficult enough task if the patient at least has a previous track record to suggest what their values and interests were and how they tended make decisions. However, the task is made much more difficult when a patient has never had decisional capacity. In such cases, we must resort to a "reasonable person" standard that, while unavoidable, certainly begs the question (by presuming the very thing in question, that is, decisional capacity).

3.3.1.21   *Surrogate (proxy) decision maker*

A surrogate or proxy decision maker is a person designated to provide a substituted judgment for a patient lacking decisional capacity – preferably, it should be someone previously chosen by the patient or, at least, knowledgeable about the patient's values, interests, and goals.

3.3.1.22   *Truth-telling (honesty)*

Truth-telling is an ethical obligation for everyone, but it is especially important in the patient–clinician setting. Clinicians need to be honest with patients about their diagnoses, prognoses and the benefits and burdens of alternative treatments/nontreatments in language that is both comprehensive and meaningful for each patient. This obligation also includes disclosure of omissions or commissions on the part of the professional that may have consequences for the patient, for example, giving "bad news" or disclosing medical error, including the inevitable unexpected untoward complications that can and do occasionally occur through no one's fault.

3.3.2   Some ethical issues specific to the field of addiction medicine

Generally speaking, the goals of medicine are, essentially, to cure when possible, to comfort always, to avoid gratuitous harm, to maintain/restore function (or, at least, to minimize dysfunction), and to maintain trustworthy practices and standards of care. For the most part, the goals of addiction medicine differ little from those of medicine in general. There are, however, a number of ethical concerns fairly unique to the field of addiction medicine. I shall limit my remarks to five interrelated concerns that I consider to be of central importance.

The first is a conceptual problem that will continue to muddy the waters until the ongoing controversy about the field's basic concepts and terminology – that is, "addiction" versus "substance abuse" and "dependency" versus "substance use disorders" ("SUDs") – is resolved. The second concern was mentioned earlier, namely, the whole unresolved question of how the idea of autonomy should be construed in the face of these various forms of addiction. The third is an over-arching structural concern peculiar to the problems of addiction: that is, recognition – the fact that so many patients with some form of addiction go undiagnosed for so long, even when they are under a physician's routine care. The fourth concerns under-use, over-use and misuse of potentially addictive medications in pain therapy, which leads directly to a fifth concern that, I think, underlies all of the first four issues, is paid lip-service, but is often not taken nearly as seriously as it should be, namely, the prejudices connected with addiction. It is to these five concerns that I now turn.

3.3.2.1   *The conceptual issue*

Already discussed earlier, and at some length, is the depth of confusion that results when terms or concepts (such as "morality" and "ethics") are used interchangeably (especially when everyone assumes they are all "on the same page"). It is even more confusing in this instance, since this conceptual controversy has spawned a plethora of overlapping terms: "addiction," "substance abuse," "substance dependency," "substance use disorders" (or "SUDs"). Thus, I will be explicit: throughout this chapter, when speaking for myself, I will continue (unless specifically noted otherwise) to use the terms "addiction" or "forms of addiction" (undoubtedly less colorful than that curious acronym SUDs) inclusively to cover all of the controversial terms referring to the subject of this text. I do so for two reasons. The first reason is trivially pragmatic: to minimize the cumbersomeness and inevitable distraction that would result from having to resort to a more "politically correct," neutral, concept-inclusive phrase (like "addiction/substance abuse/dependency/SUDs") each time I wanted to make a balanced reference to the subject matter of this field. (Likewise, when I quote or paraphrase the work of others, I will retain their particular term(s) of choice.) The second reason is substantive: I personally favor the more comprehensive term, "addiction" over the others which, unfortunately, seem to be overly focused on the use/abuse of substances. It is empirically evident that persons do become addicted to things/activities – for example, sex, gambling, gangs, cults, and so on – other than substances. That being clarified, the field's conceptual issue still remains, and to this we now must turn.

So far, I have attempted to provide provisional definitions for some of the more commonly used ethical terms and concepts likely to arise in medicine in general and in addiction medicine in particular. We've come to a point where I think it might prove useful to attempt the same thing for the terms ("addiction," "substance abuse," "dependency," and "substance use disorders") that are the subject matter of addiction medicine. While the terms are often used interchangeably, I suspect (not being an addiction specialist, but a philosopher with an exceedingly remote nursing background) that, at points, they represent a significant division in philosophical viewpoints within the field concerning the relationship between self-control (autonomy) and the genesis – and, perhaps for that reason, the treatment – of addiction.

While the tendency in recent years has been to avoid the allegedly pejorative connotations of the terms, "addict" and "addiction," it is often enlightening to explore the evolution of such terms in general. The Compact Edition of the Oxford English Dictionary (OED) [12], for example, lists "addict" as originally deriving from the Latin "*addict-us*," meaning "assigned by decree, made over, bound, devoted." It defines the term variously: obliged, devoted, consecrated; given over by sentence of a judge; bound, attached, surrendered; and it describes the subject's involvement as anything from choice to habit to compulsion (though the latter has been listed as rare). Thus, today's allegedly pejorative connotation has not, in fact, come from traditional usage, which seems to suggest that the "addicted" is more often than not a passive – or, at least, semi-passive – recipient (victim?) of an addiction rather than the voluntary author or agent of it.

The online medical encyclopedia, *Answers. com* [13], provides the following definition of addiction: a dependence on a behavior or substance that a person is powerless to stop. It adds:

> Addiction has been extended, however, to include mood-altering behaviors or activities... Some researchers speak of two types of addictions: substance addictions (for example, alcoholism, drug abuse, and smoking); and process addictions (for example, gambling, spending, shopping, eating, and sexual activity). There is a growing recognition that many addicts, such as polydrug abusers, are addicted to more than one substance or process.

On the other hand, the OED's definition of the term "abuse" ranges from use up, misuse, disuse; to use improperly, pervert; to cheat, deceive, insult; to injury, violation, defilement, violence [12]), which suggests in "substance abuse" a component of some degree of voluntariness and active control on the part of the agent. *Answers.com* [13] provides the following definition of abuse: "any thing that is harmful, injurious, or offensive...[and] includes excessive and wrongful misuse of anything." Here again, there is an implicit but strong presumption of some degree of voluntary agency and active control on the part of the agent which suggests – even more strongly than does the term, "addict" – the spectre of what is often referred to as "moral failure" – hardly a nonpejorative connotation.

We come next to the notion of dependency. The OED defines it thus: (1) the condition of being dependent; the relation of a thing to that by which it is conditioned; contingent logical or causal connection and (2) the relation of a thing or person to that by which it is supported; state of subjection or subordination [12]. *Answers.com* provides the following additions: " (3) the state of being determined, influenced, or controlled by something else and (4) a compulsive or chronic need; an addiction: for example, alcohol dependence."

Here, we see a bit of retreat from voluntary agency, at least in the latter stages of the process, that is, while the person with dependency may lack an important degree of voluntary choice, there is still the tendency to blame persons for an initial choice likely to result in dependency. To complicate the issue further, *Answers.com* proceeds to describe the current practice standard of distinguishing between substance dependency and substance abuse by defining the former (dependency) in terms of physiological and behavioral symptoms of substance use, and the latter (abuse) in terms of the social consequences of substance use.

This leads us, finally, to the term, "substance use disorders" (SUDs). A relative newcomer to the scene since about the mid-90s, SUDs is a term that is intended to encompass:

> both dependence on and abuse of drugs usually taken voluntarily for the purpose of their effect on the central nervous system (usually referred to as intoxication or "high") or to prevent or reduce withdrawal symptoms. These mental disorders form a subcategory of the substance-related disorders [14].

Here, again, there appears to be an implicit tendency to conflate the mere recognition of the self-induced harms of dependency/abuse with voluntary agency. Thus, conceptual disagreement (in the minds of both lay and professional) as to whether addiction is a phenomenon that is – or is not – largely under the voluntary control of persons is what continues to drive, I would claim, the language used, the assumptions made, the attitudes towards and the treatment of those exhibiting it [15].

However, my main thrust here is not to resolve the conceptual problem – that is for the experts within the field of addiction medicine to do. Rather, my aim is to help make an indeterminate situation a bit less indeterminate; in other words, to identify more clearly what the conceptual problem is, why it remains a problem – not just for the experts but for all of us – and what the ethical benefits and burdens are of each of the alternative perspectives and solutions. Before moving to the next concern, it is important to point out that:

1. Good ethics begins with good facts – including as much conceptual clarity as we can get.

2. So long as there is such fundamental conceptual disagreement about what addiction is there is

little chance for consensus with regard to terminology.

3. Without a clear understanding of how the conceptual realm interconnects with the contextual particulars of each individual case, there will continue to be what are perceived as irresolvable difficulties and lower success rates than seen in otherwise medically comparable chronic conditions – if only because part of the process of establishing realistic goals for patients rests in ferreting out the extent of their voluntary agency in addiction.

It is to be hoped that the current revisions to what will be the fifth edition of the Diagnostic and Statistical Manual of Mental Disorders (DSM-V) will at least help to resolve some of the conceptual and terminological confusion that remains. In the interim, perhaps the following section may shed some additional light on the notion of voluntary agency in the context of addiction.

3.3.2.2 Autonomy in the face of addiction

In Section 3.3.1.1, I gave a provisional definition of autonomy, mentioning the classic philosophical distinction between freedom of the will (the freedom to make decisions for oneself) and freedom of action (the freedom to carry out one's decisions), and giving brief examples of patients capable of experiencing one of these freedoms, but not both. The problem is that each is necessary, but not alone sufficient for autonomy to exist – one simply needs both. And that is precisely the problem with the various forms of addiction that affect patients: irrespective of how robust a patient's freedom of the will (i.e., their insight and logical reasoning about their situation, choices and goals), their freedom of action is to a significant degree over-ridden by the physiologically and/or psychologically coercive context of their addiction. Thus, while a patient's goal may truly be to rid themselves of their addiction, it may be insufficient to overcome the addiction's ever-present constraints on their freedom of action.

Clearly, experts in addiction medicine have begun to recognize and appreciate this complexity, as can be seen by the following excerpts selected from the more recent literature in addiction medicine:

- The current medical consensus is that the cardinal feature of addiction is compulsive drug use despite significant negative consequences [16].

- Although we have little knowledge of the neuro-biological mechanisms at work, we know that it is very difficult – perhaps literally impossible – for agents to resist *continuously persisting* desires (no matter what the source). The evidence comes from social psychology, specifically studies on what has come to be called *ego depletion* [17,18].

- Despite somewhat different views of mechanism, all current mainstream formulations agree that addiction diminishes voluntary behavioral control. . . addictive drugs tap into and, in vulnerable individuals, usurp powerful mechanisms by which survival-relevant goals shape behavior. . . cognitive neuroscience and studies of addiction pathogenesis suggest that some apparently voluntary behaviors may not be as freely planned and executed as they first appear [20].

- . . .responsibility in many ordinary cases of loss of self control is reduced, perhaps significantly [19].

- . . .there is not yet a fully convincing theory of how addiction results from the interaction of risk factors, drugs, and the brain. Moreover, there are still disagreements at the theoretical level of what the existing data signifies for the mechanisms of addiction [20].

It's one thing to say, for example, that an otherwise autonomous person who has failed to keep a resolution to exercise is "blameworthy" for not having kept his resolution, or that a seasoned driver is "blameworthy" for having knowingly and without good reason run a red light. It is quite another thing to say that a person who has come to you for help with a serious addiction problem is "blameworthy" for knowingly continuing to exhibit "drug-seeking behavior." Since we have, as yet, little knowledge about the neurobiological changes that occur in addiction, and even less knowledge of the role that genetics plays in addiction, it seems premature simply to assume that, because a patient with an addiction problem is not totally dysfunctional they are therefore autonomous and can make responsible choices – and successfully carry them out – in the face of their addiction.

3.3.2.3 *Recognition problem*

There are many facets to what I have referred to as the recognition problem. One of the primary reasons addiction goes unrecognized is the obvious stigma associated with its being considered by many to be either a sin or a crime; one's significant others may "recognize" one's illness or disease, but not as readily if it is considered to be a sin or a crime. (The sin/crime issue itself is discussed in greater detail in Section 3.3.2.5.) The sufferer himself or herself feels stigmatized, and responds either by denial or secretiveness – a stigma, by the way, that would be greatly reduced by better public health education all around.

A second, closely related reason is that while 119 of the 125 accredited medical schools in the United States teach about "substance abuse" as part of a larger required course, only 45 offered it as a separate elective course and only 12 offered it as a separate required course [21]. Such a lack of education perpetuates biases and myths within the profession and reinforces physician discomfort in helping patients confront a dysfunctional activity before it becomes a chronic pattern that threatens autonomy, health and ability to function. Curriculum changes can help physicians in training diagnose and treat substance abuse, but there are significant barriers to implementing such changes [22].

A third, and largely unrecognized, reason is time: physicians most likely to be in a position to diagnose an addiction problem are generalists, internists, family practitioners, or pediatricians; the very ones least likely, in our current dysfunctional healthcare system, to have the time necessary to devote to it. Coerced by what is an increasingly callous and short-sighted nonmedical institutional bureaucracy that is, in turn, coerced by an equally callous and short-sighted insurance industry, these front-line diagnosticians are forced by institutional constraints to become "complaint"-oriented, seriously addressing only the patient's immediate concerns. It even takes too much time to enlighten such bureaucracies and insurance companies as to how inefficient and costly such a narrow, complaint-oriented strategy truly is... for everyone involved.

3.3.2.4   Under-use, over-use and misuse of potentially addictive medications in pain therapy

One of the most vexing problems today continues to be the inappropriate use of potentially addictive medications in patients with pain – and I mean potentially *any* patient here, but especially those with either chronic, nonmalignant pain or those with a history of substance abuse/dependency. According to one researcher: "Chronic pain and substance use disorders share a history of stigmatization, underdiagnosis, and undertreatment" [23]. Much ado is made over the now familiar refrain, "pain is what the patient says it is," but, in fact, not that much has changed. Oh, yes, nurses are now taught to ask – and they dutifully chart – whether a patient is having pain and what that pain level is, but seem genuinely surprised when asked if they actually followed through and *did* anything about it for the patient! Also, I've witnessed – on more than one occasion – patients' expression of pain not being taken seriously. I remember, in particular, one patient grimacing with pain being told by a technician to "hop up on the table" for his bone scan, and only after the technician saw the abnormal scan did he begin to show empathy for the patient, gently helping him off of the table and remarking, "Gee, you really must have a lot of pain." Apparently, for too many medical personnel it is still the case that pain is what the patient says it is *only* when it can be concretely and independently demonstrated.

Even pain specialists are not immune – it is not uncommon during pain clinic rounds to hear suspicions raised about a patient's "drug-seeking behavior." The implication is clear: this is an "ominous" sign. And yet, when a person has unrelieved pain, whatever the source, they will exhibit relief-seeking behavior – and that, most likely, will express itself in drug-seeking behavior. Ironically, on the other hand, a patient will be suspected of deception if they claim to have pain, but behave as if they did not. So how is a person having pain supposed to "behave?"

Language certainly makes a great deal of difference in the way we think about a situation. An inadequately controlled brittle diabetic will undoubtedly exhibit "water and insulin-seeking behavior" – yet we don't call it that. A thirsty patient will undoubtedly exhibit "water-seeking behavior" – but we don't call it that. We only speak of narcotics in such terms; why? Seeking drugs for pain when patients have pain, from whatever source, is a normal response to a pathological situation.

The reason why we ordinarily think that addiction to narcotics is bad and that we don't think of, for example, a diabetic as being "addicted" to insulin is largely because insulin restores normal function and narcotics usually do not. However, there are a number of chronic illnesses and terminal conditions when narcotics actually – and oftentimes dramatically – improve function. I think here not only of terminal stages of fatal cancers but also of medicine's "successes," – illnesses which, until fairly recently, were fatal but have been converted into chronic, and often painful, conditions: the arthritises (rheumatoid, osteo-arthritis and others), spondylosis, diabetic neuropathy, osteoporosis, and many others. Good and adequate pain management has given many patients months to years of prolonged function (and has, by the way, virtually eliminated "drug-seeking behavior") in such patients.

Clearly, patients who have a history of addiction can also suffer pain. This further complicates an already complex issue since, according to recent studies, addiction and pain share some common pathways in the brain to the degree that pain can influence addiction and addiction can influence pain. Thus, addicted persons may experience lower tolerance for pain and decreased relief from pain medications [24], making under-treatment of pain quite likely. Also, patients often resist taking narcotics feeling that taking such medication in adequate quantities is a weakness that must be overcome. There are still some who feel that having pain is a redemptive experience and helps to make up for some of the sins committed. These difficulties, combined with the continued existence of laws and regulations that run contrary to the effective management of pain constitute real concerns for patients and biomedical professionals alike [25].

In such cases, collaboration between attending, pain specialists and addiction medicine specialists is essential; yet, in most cases this does not occur. Also, given the difficulty we seem to have dealing with both chronic pain and addiction, it would seem appropriate that patients suffering from either or both of these conditions would receive, at minimum, a psychiatric work up. Yet, in many places this does not occur. Moreover, neither pain medicine nor addiction medicine receive much attention in either the education or the training of biomedical professionals. These are all ethical issues which ought to be taken seriously.

One really can't leave any discussion of pain without at least mentioning an important idea that we often fail to appreciate fully, namely, the idea that we can have pain without suffering, and we can suffer though we are not having pain. For example, I may undergo the pain of some minor, yet painful corrective therapy without unduly suffering, because I know that it will restore my ability to function; however, I would suffer intensely the loss of my sight even in the absence of pain. What does this imply in the face of addiction? Well, as difficult as it may be to treat pain in patients who are addiction prone, it is even more difficult to treat their suffering. As is the case with pain, addiction leads to suffering, but suffering can also lead to addiction.

Many people who take narcotics are in what they perceive to be a hopeless situation: unemployed and living in a poverty area, middle or upper class and bored, and so on. They find their reality to be unbearable and are only too glad to change it. It is obvious that only by changing their reality and providing them with some realistic hope can their situation can be addressed. Effective treatment here must be multidisciplinary and it also requires – if we *really* want to get at the source of this kind of suffering – changes in society that reduce poverty and nurture people in ways that challenge them to develop their talents and pursue their interests and goals. However, social conditions are too often treated by healthcare professionals as "givens," unfortunate "complications" in patients' lives that are beyond our ability to address. I claim that we still have an ethical responsibility to do something, if only to serve as vocal witnesses to the effects that egregious social inequities and lack of nurturing have on those we treat. There are many ways we could address this ethical responsibility – but that would, of course, be the subject of yet another chapter! My point here, though, is that if we really do consider ourselves healthcare professionals, we must recognize and take seriously this most important – and today largely ignored – ethical responsibility.

3.3.2.5 *The prejudices connected with addiction*

So, we come back to one of the foundational, yet unanswered, underlying questions of the field (alluded to in Section 3.3.2.2): Just what is addiction medicine treating anyway–a medical condition, a physical or genetic defect, a moral weakness, a crime? I cannot help being reminded here of the long evolution of our notions about masturbation and homosexuality [26]. Both of these phenomena were at some point in history considered (in both lay and professional minds) to be:

1. a "sin"

2. a "crime"

3. a "disease" (for which both, by the way, had surgical as well as medical "therapies!")

4. "normal."

We see much the same thing happening with addiction. It is still considered by some to be a "sin," a sign of "moral" weakness – witness the religious language and practices of the classic 12-step program first introduced to the public in the first edition of *Alcoholics Anonymous* in 1939 [27]. It most certainly is considered a crime if the addiction involves illicit drugs, and, increasingly, it is considered to be a disease – but, "normal?" Many might claim that addiction could never be considered "normal;" however, there are instances (and, no, I'm not thinking here of challenging our views about the evils of "recreational use") when, in a somewhat attenuated sense, that may be precisely what it could be construed as. Certainly, as I argued in Section 3.3.2.4, there are times when chronic use of addictive medications are not only justified, but essential to the maximal functioning of a patient with chronic debilitating pain – whether they are imminently dying or not. Are these patients "addicted?" It seems to me the more ethically appropriate question remains: "Is the assumption that addiction is always bad warranted?" How readers answer that question directly affects how they understand the rest of the concerns I raised in this section.

3.4   SPIRITUALITY, RELIGION AND ADDICTION

Myth: Spirituality and religion are just two different words for the same thing.

Reality: Spirituality and religion have no necessary connection. While it is true that every person is a spiritual being, and that the majority of persons – at least here in the United States – profess to be "religious" (whatever that may mean for them), not every person is or professes to be religious, despite the fact (which bears repeating) that every person is a spiritual being. According to Canda and Furman [28]:

> The term spirituality generally refers to the human longing for a sense of meaning and fulfillment through morally satisfying relationships between individuals, families, communities, cultures, and religions. Although often viewed in a religious context, spirituality is not necessarily about being religious. Spirituality is about responding to the deepest questions posed by an individual's existence with a whole heart. Religion refers to organized structures that center around particular beliefs, behaviors rituals, ceremonies, and traditions [28].

Moreover, spirituality does not entail a belief in a supreme being or god(s). It is the height of insensitivity – and, I would argue, the crassest form of majoritarian imperialism – to assume that it does. To paraphrase from an article I co-authored in 2007:

> for many individuals, religion (which The Oxford English Dictionary [29] defines as "[r]ecognition on the part of man [sic] of some higher unseen power as

being in control of his [sic] destiny, and as being entitled to obedience, reverence and worship") is but one expression of spirituality (an "attachment to or regard for things of the spiritual as opposed to material or worldly interests"). Indeed, for some of us, spiritual needs may be met by religion; but for some of us they are met by Mozart, for others by the sun glistening on fall leaves. Still others have those needs met by the presence of spouses, friends, or children. If a patient believes that religion might meet such needs – or perhaps religion in addition to Mozart and sparkling leaves – this can be of immense help in his or her care [30].

According to Miller [31], biomedical experts need what he calls "a set of proficiencies" that are sensitive not only to a patient's culture, but also to his/her spiritual needs. This set of proficiencies should include the ability and willingness to develop:

1. A nonjudgmental, accepting and empathic relationship with patients.

2. An openness and willingness to take time to understand a patient's spirituality as it relates to his/her health-related problem.

3. An understanding of culturally-related values, beliefs, and practices that are common to certain patient populations, and a willingness to seek information from appropriate professionals and coordinate care concerning patients' spiritual traditions

4. A fair degree of comfort in discussing spiritual issues with patients [31].

The problem with sets such as this one, however, is that they can too easily become meaningless algorithms. Take, for example, Miller's third proficiency: we should be cautious not to assume that a patient's cultural, religious or spiritual traditions will be determinate. I've known many patients who, for example, identify with a particular religion, but no longer practice it and most emphatically do not wish to be visited by one of its leaders (priest, minister or rabbi, as the case may be). Obviously, their seeming inconsistencies must be explored; but my point is that many people end up rejecting much of their cultural, religious or spiritual upbringing while, at the same time, they have no problem continuing to identify themselves pro forma with that culture, religion or spiritual tradition. On the other hand, for patients who do actively participate in religious, cultural and/or spiritual traditions, room for their inclusion into the patient's treatment plan would be of immense benefit for both patient and biomedical professional and should never be underestimated or devalued.

The whole problem of religious coercion – whether real or perceived – is certainly a significant ethical issue. Whether one agrees with him or not, Peele's contention [32] that "some nonreligious people will fail to thrive within the confines of Alcoholics Anonymous or any other program that demands submission to a 'higher power'," largely because they "face coerced religious indoctrination in the guise of alcohol or drug treatment" needs to be exhaustively investigated – especially in the face of court-mandated participation in Alcoholics Anonymous' 12-step program. According to Gary Pettigrew, a forensic psychologist, "The essence of the Alcoholics Anonymous approach resembles revivalistic Protestantism, with elements of ritual prayer, public confession and surrender of will to a 'higher power' ... " [33].

Pragmatically speaking, addiction medicine ignores such ethical issues at its own peril since, if they aren't recognized and addressed in a timely fashion by the profession, they most assuredly will be by the courts – and this is precisely what occurred in this instance. In September 2007, the ninth Circuit Court of Appeals determined, in *Inouye vs. Kemna* [34] – citing the precedent of three previous rulings in other (second and seventh) Circuit Court cases – that court-mandated attendance of Alcohol Anonymous/Narcotics Anonymous meetings as a condition for parole constituted an infringement of a person's First Amendment rights because it had the effect of coercing Inouye into a religious- or faith-based program. Yet another ethical – as well as biomedical – concern is that many of these and other government funded faith-based programs do not meet licensing requirements or medically-sanctioned standards of state-approved services [35].

Clearly, these are difficult ethical concerns that simply must be addressed for the fields dedicated to caring for addiction-related issues as well as for the biopsychosocial integrity – one might even say, "spiritual well-being" – of their patients. As in most other disciplines, there are rarely absolutes in ethics; however, one near-absolute is that when it comes to ethics, courts should truly be the "court of last resort." For, when courts take on ethics cases – has anyone forgotten Terri Schiavo? [36] – issues invariably become politicized and outcomes are rarely very satisfying or helpful.

REFERENCES

1. Dewey, J. (1938) *The Later Works of John Dewey, 1925–53*, vol. **12** (ed. Boydston JoAnn), Southern University Press, Carbondale, IL.

2. Loewy, R.S. (2000) *Integrity and Personhood: Looking at Patients from a Biopsychosocial Perspective*, Klüwer Academic/Plenum Publishers, NY.

3. Loewy, E.H. and Loewy, R.S. (2004) *Textbook of Healthcare Ethics*, 2nd edn, Klüwer Academic Publishers, Boston.

4. Kant, I. (1785/1959) *Foundations of the Metaphysics of Morals*, (1959; original publication 1785), (Translated by L.W. Beck), Bobbs-Merrill Educational Publishing, Indianapolis, IN.

5. Farabee, D., Prendergast, M., and Anglin, D. (1998) The effectiveness of coerced treatment for drug-abusing offenders. *Federal Probation: A Journal of Correctional Philosophy and Practice*, **62** (1), 3–11, Available at: http://

www.uscourts.gov/fedprob/1998junefp.pdf#page=5; last accessed 16 September 2009.

6. Morris, G.H. (2006) *Refusing the Right to Refuse: Coerced Treatment of Mentally Disabled Persons*, Vandeplas Publishing, Lake Mary, FL, Available at: http://works.bepress.com/gmorris/4.

7. Dworkin, R. (1994) *Life's Dominion an Argument About Abortion, Euthanasia, and Individual Freedom*, Vintage Books, NY.

8. Caplan, A.L. (2006) Ethical issues surrounding forced, mandated, or coerced treatment. *J. Subst. Abuse Treat.*, **31**, 117–120.

9. Feinberg, J. (1986) The moral limits of the criminal law, in *Harm to Self*, vol. **3**, Oxford University Press, Oxford.

10. Foddy, B. and Savulesco, J. (2006) Addiction and Autonomy: Can addicted people consent to the prescription of their drug of addiction? *Bioethics*, **20** (1), 1–15.

11. Loewy, E.H. (2007) *Textbook of Medical Ethics*, Kluwer Academic Publishers.

12. OED (1971) *The Compact Oxford English Dictionary*, Oxford University Press, Oxford.

13. *Answers.com* (2008) References: "Addiction," Available at: http://www.answers.com/addiction?cat=health; last accessed 26 February 2008. "Abuse," Available at: http://www.answers.com/abuse; last accessed 26 February 2008. "Dependence," Available at: http://www.answers.com/topic/dependence?cat=health; last accessed 26 February 2008. "Substance abuse and Dependence," Available at: http://www.answers.com/topic/substance-abuse-and-dependence?cat=health; last accessed 26 February 2008.

14. Behavenet.com (2008) http://www.behavenet.com/capsules/disorders/sud.htm; last accessed 26 February 2008.

15. O'Brien, C.P. *et al.* (2006) What's in a Word? *Am. J. Psychiatry*, **163**, 764–765, Available at: http://www.ajp.psychiatryonline.org/cgi/content/full/163/5/764; last accessed 26 February 2008.

16. American Psychiatric Association (1987) *Diagnostic and Statistical Manual of Mental Disorders*, 3rd edn, American Psychiatric Association Press, Washington, DC.

17. Baumeister, R.F., Bratslavsky, E., Muraven, M., and Tice, D.M. (1998) Ego-depletion: Is the active self a limited resource? *J. Pers. Soc. Psychol.*, **74** (5), 1252–1265.

18. Baumeister, R.F. (2002) Ego depletion and self-control failure: An energy model of the self's executive function. *Self and Identity*, **1** (2), 129–136.

19. Levy, N. (2006) Addiction, autonomy and ego-depletion: A response to Bennett Foddy and Julian Savulescu. *Bioethics*, **20** (1), 16–20.

20. Hyman, S.E. (2007) The neurobiology of addiction: implications for voluntary control of behavior. *Am. J. Bioeth.*, **7** (1), 8–11, Available at: http://www.bioethics.net/journal/j_articles.php?aid=1108; last accessed 28 February 2008.

21. Teaching about substance Abuse in Medical Schools, http://www.google.com/search?q=number + of + medical + schools + teaching + about + substance + abuse&rls=com.microsoft:*&ie=UTF-8&oe=UTF-8&startIndex=&startPage=1.

22. Yoast, RA., Filstead, WJ., Wilford, BB. *et al.* (2008) Teaching about Substance Abuse. *Virtual Mentor*, **10** (1), 21–29, Available at: http://virtualmentor.ama-assn.org/2008/01/medu1-0801.html; last accessed 26 February 2008.

23. Cohen, M.J.M., Jasser, S., Herron, P.D., and Margolis, C.G. (2002) Ethical perspectives: opioid treatment of chronic pain in the context of addiction. *The Clin. J. of Pain.*, **18**, 4.

24. Compton, P. and Gebhart, G.F. (2003) The neurophysiology of pain and interfaces with addiction, in *Principles of Addiction Medicine* (eds. A.W. Graham, T.K. Schultz, M.F. Mayo-Smith, and R.K. Ries), American Society of Addiction Medicine, Chevy Chase, MD, pp. 1385–1404.

25. Gilson, A.M. and Joranson, D.E. (2002) U.S. Policies Relevant to the Prescribing of Opioid Analgesics for the Treatment of Pain in Patients With Addictive Disease. *Clin. J. Pain*, **18** (4), (Supplement), S91–S98.

26. Engelhardt, H.T. (1974) The disease of masturbation: values and the concept of disease. *Bull. Hist. Med.*, **48**, 234–248.

27. The twelve Steps of Alcoholics Anonymous. Available at: http://www.alcoholics-anonymous.org/en_services_for_members.cfm?PageID=98&SubPage=117; last accessed: 5 March 2008.

28. Canda, E.R. and Furman, L.D. (1999) *Spiritual Diversity in Social Work Practice*, The Free Press, NY.

29. OED (1984) *The Compact Edition of the Oxford English Dictionary*, Oxford University Press, New York.

30. Loewy, E.H. and Loewy, R.S. (2007) Healthcare and the Hospital Chaplain. *Medsc. Gen. Med.*, **9** (1), 53, Available at: http://medgenmed.medscape.com/view article/552447; last accessed 7 March 2007.

31. Miller, W.R. (1999) *Integrating Spirituality into Treatment: Resources for Practitioners*, American Psychological Association, Washington, DC, p. 10.

32. Peele, S., Bufe, C., and Brodsky, A. (2000) *Resisting 12-Step Coercion: How to Fight Forced Participation in AA, NA, or 12-Step Treatment*, Sharp Press, Tucson, Arizona.

33. Franklin, K. (2008) In the News: Forensic psychology, criminology and psychology-law [e-Newsletter blog site] Available at: http://forensicpsychologist.blogspot.com/2007/09/court-strikes-down-mandated-12-step.html; last accessed 5 March 2008.

34. Inouye v. Kemna (2007) Available at: http://www.ca9.uscourts.gov/coa/newopinions.nsf/6FA63303852632AC8825734F0059D078/$file/0615474.pdf?openelement; last accessed 5 March 2008.

35. Farris, A. (2007) "Faith-Based Groups Receive One-Third of Addiction Service Vouchers." *The Roundtable on Religion and Social Welfare Policy*. Available at: http://www.religionandsocialpolicy.org/news/article.cfm?id=7145; last accessed 7 March 2008.

36. The Terri Schiavo case was a seven-year-long US legal battle to allow a bulemic woman in a persistent vegetative state to be disconnected from life support.

4

Natural history of addictive diseases

Steven A. Branstetter[1] and Sabina Low[2]

[1] *Department of Biobehavioral Health, The Pennsylvania State University, University Park, PA 16802-6501, USA*
[2] *Department of Psychology, Wichita State University, Wichita, Kansas 67260, USA*

4.1   INTRODUCTION

The natural history of infectious disease can only be understood by examining a variety of interrelated factors, including the characteristics of the pathogenic microbial agent, the defenses of the host infected by the agent, a multitude of situational and ecological variables (e.g., moisture levels, temperature), and the interaction of these elements over time. Similarly, understanding the natural history of addictive disease must consider not only the characteristics of the individual, but must also consider the characteristics of the substance of addiction, the mico- and macroenvironments in which the individual uses the substance, and how these factors interact over time. Unfortunately, elements of this integrated view have been detached from the whole and championed by different scientific disciplines. For example, the field of psychology has paid great attention to individual characteristics, such as psychopathology, familial influences, attitudes, and behavioral principals. Public health researchers have focused on policy issues, community and neighborhood standards, and other social mechanisms resulting in addictive problems. Medical science has focused on pharmacokinetics, genetics,

and other biological aspects of addiction. Whereas each of these disciplines has made important contributions to the understanding of addictive disease, there is a need to synthesize these elements [1]. Indeed, Vaillant has asserted that addiction is not well characterized by one model alone; rather it reflects equal parts of social, behavioral and biological components [2]. The lack of integration of these separate dimensions has limited our comprehensive understanding of the natural history of additive disease.

Moreover, the developmental nature of addictive disease is often overlooked. Like all human behavior, addictive disorders can be best understood in the light of a life-course perspective. That is, the true nature of a behavior is best characterized by trajectories, transitions and turning points [3]. However, decades of research have viewed addiction as an acute disorder, or have focused on specific transition points (e.g., onset, cessation). Indeed, until recently very little was known about the natural course of addictive disorders because of the lack of longitudinal studies [4]. Additionally, like any developmental phenomenon, the natural

Addictive Disorders in Medical Populations   Edited by Norman S. Miller and Mark S. Gold
© 2010 John Wiley & Sons, Ltd.

history of addictive disease is challenging to characterize; significant heterogeneity exists among individuals – even those from similar backgrounds. Moreover, even similarity within a group of individuals does not guarantee identical outcomes [5]. Furthermore, there is no "one size fits all" way in which to characterize the natural history of addictive disorders in general, as there is documented variability across substances, sex, and race/ethnicity [6].

The purpose of the current chapter is not to examine how specific factors – from the genetic to societal level – may influence the course of an individual's addictive behavior, nor to explore the multitude of potential trajectories for each addictive substance, but rather to highlight how key elements common to the majority of addictive disorders combine to influence addictive behaviors throughout an individual's substance use "career." It is hoped that by understanding the core characteristics of the natural history of addictive disease, clinicians can make informed decisions regarding assessment, selection of intervention strategies, prognosis and clinical treatment planning.

4.2   NATURAL HISTORY VERSUS "CAREER"

A traditional definition of *natural history* has been the *"sequential development of designated biological processes within the individual"* [1], p. 178. However, this view of addictive disease is somewhat limiting given the significant influence of environmental and contextual factors on the development of the disorder. To understand the development of addictive disorders over time while still accounting for the personality of the individual, the influence of peers and the broader social context, many have adopted a view of addictive disorders as a "career." Edwards [1] defined an addiction career as "...*an individual's sequential behavior within a designated role*," p. 175. With this perspective, an individual's behaviors related to their addiction "career," including their interactions with others, progression from initiation to treatment, and ultimate outcomes, can be combined to yield a more comprehensive understanding of how addiction progresses over time.

4.3   RISK AND PROTECTIVE FACTORS IN DEVELOPMENT OF ADDICTIVE DISEASE

The story of addictive disease does not begin with the onset of substance use. Instead, the foundation of addictive disease is laid well before an individual takes their first drink or uses their first illicit drug. By the time an individual uses a substance for the first time, they have a complex history of both risk and protective factors that will increase or decrease the likelihood of developing an addictive disorder. Whereas research has traditionally emphasized the identification of risk factors, it has become clear that risk factors work in concert with protective factors. For example, the presence of a cluster of risk factors and the relative absence of protective factors creates an imbalance that favors the development of problem behaviors (Figure 4.1). Although a large number of distinctive risk and protective factors have been identified, both theoretical and empirical evidence suggest most of these factors can be classified into one of five categories: (1) individual, (2) family, (3) school, (4) school, and (5) community [7,8]. Given that the typical onset of the use of substance occurs during adolescence, many of the risk and protective factors focus on early experiences, such as attachment, parenting practices, school, and peers.

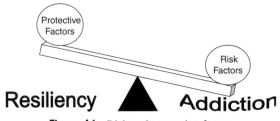

Figure 4.1   Risk and protective factors

4.4 INDIVIDUAL FACTORS

4.4.1 Genetics

Individual risk factors begin with the genetic make-up of the individual. Clinicians often warn their patients that genes do not cause addictions; genes code for proteins, and not for particular behaviors. Thus, some overlook the role that an individual's biological framework may play in their addictive disease. Indeed, it can be difficult for clinicians to acknowledge the contribution of a patients' biology in the addiction process, while emphasizing the importance of behavioral change in the recovery process. Anecdotally, some patients may use a genetic vulnerability as an "excuse" for ongoing behavior [9]. In addition to the clinical difficulty of explaining genetic influences to patients, and delineating the specific role of genes in the development of behavioral disorders like addiction and psychiatric illness, is a practical challenge for scientists [10]. This is due, in part, to the fact that addiction is a multiply determined phenomenon and any particular gene is likely to play only a small role. Nevertheless, both animal and human research has demonstrated that genetics may indeed play a vital part in the vulnerability to addiction. Genes may increase vulnerability in several ways; for example, by altering enzymes that metabolize alcohol or other substances [11] or by transforming the levels of neurotransmitters and how neurotransmitters interact with their receptors and post-receptor signaling pathways [10]. Indeed, the role of pharmacokinetics, or and individual's biological processing of substances, is a key aspect in the development of addictive disease, and is largely influenced by genetic make-up [12–14]. Regardless of the specific mechanism of influence, some research has suggested that between 40 and 60% of the vulnerability to addictive disease may be accounted for by genetics [15]. Whereas a great deal of work remains to be done in this area, it has been predicted by the Director of the National Institute on Drug Abuse that in 10 years the front-line treatment for addiction will be medication designed to address genetic/biological vulnerabilities underlying addiction [16].

4.4.2 Temperament and attachment

Infant temperament, often conceptualized as an inborn "personality" or predisposition to be *flexible*, *fearful* or *feisty*, is thought to be strongly related to adult adjustment [17]. Researchers have found links between difficult infant temperament and a range of later behavioral difficulties, including Attention Deficit/Hyperactivity Disorder [18,19], conduct disorder and psychopathy [20], and even eating behaviors and obesity [21]. Additionally, there are demonstrated links between difficult temperament and the later use of addictive substances [22–24], as well as timing of use [25] and treatment outcome. The majority of research on temperament and use of addictive substances has focused on inhibition/self-control [26–28], sensation seeking, and indirect related risk factors, such as parenting.

Infant temperament is highly associated with the development of parent–child attachment. Infants with difficult temperaments are often hard to soothe, inflexible, demanding, overly physically active, and light sleepers. It is thought that these factors may result in a disruption in the normal parental bonding that leads to secure parent–child attachment. Several social developmental theories, including the social control theory and the social development model, emphasize the importance of the attachment with parents as a critical protective factor [29–33]. Such theories suggest that individuals who have few rewarding interactions at home and who receive fewer rewards from interactions with parents are more likely to develop addictive disorders. It is thought that these individuals reject conventional values as a result of the absence of close and loving relationships with parents and reincarnate coercive interactions with peers. Subsequently, these individuals are more likely to associate with deviant peers who provide and reward unconventional behaviors, such as drug use and criminal activity.

4.4.3 Psychopathology

There is still some debate regarding the "chicken-or-the-egg" question with regard to whether addiction *causes* psychopathology or is *the result* of pre-existing psychopathology. For example, the controversial "self-medication hypothesis" of substance use first proposed by Edward Khantzian suggests that individuals use psychoactive substances to reduce negative internal states, such as depression or anxiety. Several studies have found support for the notion that psychopathology predisposes individuals to seek specific substances to "self-medicate." For example, Grant and Pickering [34] found that individuals with the most severe psychiatric comorbidity were more likely to be diagnosed as cannabis dependent. The authors concluded that this relation supports the notion that the more distressing psychiatric symptoms an individual experiences, the more likely they are to turn to the use of addictive substances. Likewise, Miranda and colleagues [35] found that females with a history of sexual abuse were significantly more likely to use alcohol at a higher rate than those who had not been abused. Gilman and Abraham [36] found similar results; depression was a significant risk factor for the development of an alcohol use disorder one year later. Conversely, however, alcohol use was a significant risk factor for the development of depression one year later.

Whereas research supports a temporal pattern in which psychopathology precedes addictive disorders, an equivalent body of literature contradicts such findings. For example, results of an international review found no predictable pattern between psychiatric disorders and addictive disorders [37]. The exception to these findings was that anxiety disorders consistently preceded addictive disorders in all countries studied. In a direct assessment of the self-medication hypothesis, Hall and Queener [38] found that no specific affective state, including depression, anxiety or hostility, predicted addiction severity. Other studies have similarly failed to support key aspects of the self-medication hypothesis [39,40].

Other evidence exists which suggests that specific psychiatric disorders precede addictive disorders for reasons other than self-medication. For example, a number of studies have linked a diagnosis of Attention Deficit/Hyperactivity Disorder (ADHD) with the later development of addictive disorders [41,42]. Whereas some believe the link between ADHD and addictive disease a direct relation, most evidence suggests the specific characteristics of ADHD are responsible of the later development of addiction, and not the ADHD diagnosis itself. For example, some research points to the strong connection between Conduct Disorder (CD), a condition highly correlated with ADHD, and addiction [41–44]. Still others think it may be the impulsivity component of ADHD that is responsible for development of later substance use [45]. Indeed, a large body of research has demonstrated how delay-discounting, a laboratory analog of impulsivity, is highly associated with addiction [46–49].

Ultimately, regardless of the cause-and-effect relations, many agree that ADHD, Conduct Disorder and Mood Disorders can be considered particularly important psychiatric risk factors for the development of addictive diseases [50] and treatment outcomes. For example, conventional wisdom held that up to 60% of psychiatric disorders, mood disorders in particular, were *secondary* to or *caused by* addictive disorders. However, data from the National Epidemiological Survey demonstrate that most addictive disorders are independent of mood disorders [51]. Therefore, clinicians are cautioned to carefully screen for comorbid conditions and take these into account in their treatment planning.

4.4.4 Attitudes and perceptions

Over the years, a number of theories have attempted to explain the cognitive processes that lead to the onset and progression of addictive behavior. One such theory, which has garnered solid empirical support, is the Theory of Planned Behavior [52]. The Theory of Planned Behavior suggests that an individual's behavior is the result of a chain of cognitions which leads the individual to engage in the behaviors. According to the theory, when an individual sees a particular behavior as positive, if they perceived that important others in their social network (e.g., peers, parents) want or support the behavior, and if the individual believes that they can easily perform the behavior, there is a resultant increase in the individual's intention to engage in the behavior.

As demonstrated in Figure 4.2, an individual holds a specific attitude, positive or negative, regarding the use of substances. This attitude is formed through interactions with parents, peers, through media portrayal of substance use, and a variety of other sources. A positive attitude towards substance use leads the individual to believe that their use of substances will be valued and result in favorable outcomes. Next, the individual perceives how substance use will be viewed and supported by other important individuals, such as peers, parents, and teachers. Traditionally, the dimension of normative beliefs is similar to the notion of peer pressure: when an individual perceives that other important persons in their life are using substances, or that those important persons want the individual to use substances, substance use becomes more likely. Next, an individual will determine how successful they can obtain and use substances. For example, if it is perceived that marijuana is readily available and easy to use (e.g., the individual has access to the materials needed, has a place to use), and that using marijuana is a behavior that can be performed with few negative outcomes (e.g., being "caught" or becoming ill), the likelihood of using is increased. Finally, each of these attitudes and perceptions come together to increase (or decrease) the intention to use substances. For some, intention

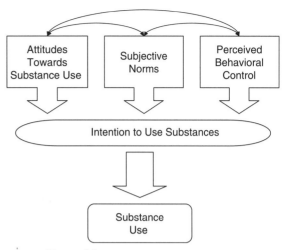

Figure 4.2   Theory of planned behavior

to use is synonymous with the concept of motivation. That is, each attitude and perception causes an individual to become more motivated to use substances; ultimately, motivation in the strongest predictor of the behavior itself.

The Theory of Planned Behavior has been used to successfully explain a range of behaviors, including increased exercise among cancer patients [53], use of dental services [54], use of multivitamins [55], binge drinking [56], cigarette smoking [57], marijuana use [58], and an array of other behaviors [59–62]. A meta-analysis found that the Theory of Planned Behavior accounted for nearly 40% of intention to perform behavior and explained over 25% of actual behavior [63]. The authors of the meta-analysis suggest that the Theory of Planned Behavior is an effective way to predict both the motivation to engage in behavior, and the behavior itself. As such, clinicians should carefully assess and consider the role of attitudes and perceptions in the onset and development of addictive disease over time.

4.5   THE ROLE OF ENVIRONMENT IN ADDICTIVE DISEASE

The individual risk factors outlined above are formed by, and expressed within, a social context. For example, genetic predispositions and temperament are only important to the extent that they influence an individual's behaviors and interactions

with others. Similarly, attitudes and perceptions result from an individual's interpretation of the environmental cues around him/her. For example, an individual cannot form an attitude favorable towards substance use if there are no data regarding the potential outcomes of substance use from family, peers, teachers, media, or other social sources.

4.5.1 Parents/family

Whereas peer substance use has been identified as the strongest proximal predictor of substance use [64], parents are thought to set the stage for many of their children's attitudes, perceptions – and for whom their children select as friends. Additionally, whereas conventional wisdom held that parental influence on their children's behavior was significantly diminished by peer influence by mid-adolescence, parents continue to play an important role in the use of substances well beyond high school graduation [65]. As such, parental behaviors and attitudes can be critical risk or protective factors for the development of addictive disorders.

4.5.1.1 Parental substance use

Research has consistently found that parents who use substances have children who use substances at higher rates. For example, children who smoke are significantly more likely to have parents who smoke [66,67]. However, many believe that the transmission of substance use from parents to children is indirect, through either genetic transmission of inhibitory control (e.g., impulsivity), poor parenting practices [27], or social modeling. For example, parents who actively use illicit substances tend to exhibit poor disciplinary skills [27], poor monitoring skills [68], and poor overall relationships [69]. Additionally, however, the social modeling of substance use and the implicit and explicit communication of positive attitudes towards substance use remain key aspects of the transmission of substance use behavior from parents to children [70,71].

4.5.1.2 Parent–child relationship/parental monitoring

The quality of the parent–child relationship, as well as the family background and structure, serve as

important risk or protective factors for the development of addictive disorder. For example, the level of parental support [72,73], the level of parental conflict [74], parental divorce, parental discord, and family disruption [50] all play a role in the development of addictive disorders. However, perhaps one of the strongest and most consistently supported elements of the family environment that serves as a risk or protective factor is parental monitoring. Parental monitoring can be conceptualized as a parent's knowledge of their child's activities, presumably garnered by attempts to track activities. Support for the importance of parental monitoring is validated by research showing that parents who know their child's whereabouts, peers, and activities have children who use fewer substances [75,76]. Parental monitoring, contrary to earlier views, is not simply a parenting behavior in which the parent gathers information from its child; rather, monitoring is the result of a dynamic relationship in which a parent solicits information from its child and where a child discloses accurate information to its parents [77]. As such, parental monitoring is the by-product of a positive, open relationship, marked by reciprocal communication. Ultimately, it is not the parent's knowledge of the child's whereabouts, peers, and activities; rather, it is the child's *perception* that the parent knows this critical information that serves as a protective factor [78]. Nevertheless, parents must actively solicit information from their children; only then does the child perceive that the parent possesses critical information.

4.5.2 Peer influences

Decades of research have demonstrated that association with delinquent peers leads to increased levels of substance use. Indeed, peers are thought to have the strongest single influence on the onset and development of substance use behavior [79]. To be sure, it is through association with substance using peers that individuals watch, imitate, and learn to use substances: virtually all initial experimentation with substance use takes place within a peer context. Peers may exert their influence on substance use in a number of ways. For example, peers may hold positive attitudes with regard to substance use, thus increasing an individual's own positive attitudes (the Theory of Planned Behavior). Likewise, peers who use increase an individual's perceptions of the acceptability or norms of substance use. Also related to the Theory of Planned Behavior is the fact that having a peer who uses substances increases an individual's perceptions that substances are easily obtained and easily used, thus increasing the perception of behavioral control. Additionally, substance use may serve as a social facilitator, increasing trust, bonding and friendships among peers. Conversely, substance use may be the result of active and direct pressure to conform along with a desire to please peers (or avoid rejection). Indeed, there is evidence that up to 84% of users of cocaine may have initiated cocaine use as the result of "pressure" [50]. Regardless of the specific mechanism, the fact remains that the association with peers who use substances is a powerful predictor for the use of substances, and warrants significant concerns for parents and clinicians.

4.5.3 Social/societal influences on addictive disease

The social context beyond the family and peer group also plays an important role in the development of addictive disorders. Environmental influences from the school setting to the state- and country-wide policies have an important impact on an individual's use of substances.

4.5.3.1 School

Because children spend a great deal of their time in schools, they provide an optimal environment for interventions. There is now mounting evidence that the social and behavioral skills that protect one from substance addiction, are also critical to academic success [80]. Therefore, schools can play an important role in targeting protective factors for substance use, while simultaneously addressing

academic pressures. However, schools, and their accompanying characteristics, can also be a source of psychological distress during key developmental transitions. As it turns out, most teenagers begin using substances at the same time that they are experiencing many school-related stressors related to the transition to middle school, including increase academic competitiveness [81], increased emphasis on discipline [82] reduction in supportive contacts with teachers, and the break-up of the peer network [83]. For these reasons, schools, particularly those with poor and inconsistent discipline and rule enforcement, can amplify risk factors. For example, poor enforcement of rules, dissatisfied teachers, fewer teacher resources, and over enrollment may all lead to disciplinary problems, lack of structure, and increased overall delinquency [84,85].

4.5.3.2 Neighborhoods

In addition to the socio-economic status of an individual's family, the economic conditions of the neighborhood in which the individual lives also have important implications for the development of addictive disease. For example, disadvantaged neighborhoods tend to have little community support, decreased willingness to intervene in delinquent behavior among residents, fewer opportunities for pro-social activities, and higher rates of mobility [86]. In such neighborhoods there also tends to be higher rates of unemployment, more "hanging around (or loitering)," and greater opportunities to witness and observe behaviors and attitudes that favor the use of substances.

4.5.3.3 Community

The laws and practices of the community in which an individual lives may also influence the use of substances. For example, large, billboard-type advertisements for alcohol and tobacco products tend to have been allowed more often in lower income neighborhoods [87]. Such advertisements influence the perceived norms and increase favorable attitudes towards smoking, thus potentially increasing the motivation to smoke. Likewise, poorer neighborhoods tend to allow more liquor licenses and have more liquor stores per capita than higher income neighborhoods [88]. Again, this not only increases the availability and perceived behavioral control, it also increases perceived norms and favorable attitudes towards drinking.

Specific community laws which may reduce the likelihood of substance use tend to be adopted more slowly by low income and disadvantaged neighborhoods. For example, curfews laws have been demonstrated to be effective in reducing a range of delinquent behavior in communities [89]. Likewise, higher rates of taxation on alcohol effectively reduce the rates of consumption in neighborhoods [90]. Additionally, community programs, such as the Drug Free Communities Program – sponsored by the Office of National Drug Control Policy's National Drug Control Strategy – assist over 700 at-risk communities to develop comprehensive prevention programs. Such efforts help promote protective factors and reduce risk factors at the community level.

4.5.3.4 Physical environment

As unlikely as it might seem, recent evidence has suggested that beyond the social environment in which an individual exists, the physical environment may increase the risk for developing addictive diseases as well. The most salient example, of course, is that of second-hand smoke. Not only does second-hand smoke increase the likelihood of negative health outcomes, it dramatically increases the chances that those exposed to it will become regular smokers themselves [91]. However, exposure need not be as overt to increase risk. For example, so-called "third-hand" smoke, or the residue from tobacco smoke, can be found in household dust, on clothing, and other surfaces. This third-hand smoke has been found to increase the presence of nicotine metabolites in infants and others exposed [92], which may in turn lead to increased susceptibility to later addiction.

There are other, less obvious, avenues for exposure to physical environmental factors that may increase the incidence of addictive diseases. One study, for example, demonstrated that workers exposed to organic solvents had a marked increase in alcohol disorders [93]. Another example is the case of anesthesiologists and other physicians and personnel experiencing second-hand exposure to anesthetic drugs administered to patients. Research has demonstrated that anesthesiologists, a group at high risk for addictive disorders, may be regularly exposed to low-levels of intravenous drugs, such as fentanyl and propofol, as these substances are released into the air via patient exhalation [94]. Such chronic exposure, even at low doses, is sufficient to lead to changes in addiction susceptibility, brain activity, and motivation, often without the individual being aware they have been exposed.

4.6 THE ONSET OF ADDICTIVE DISEASE

In 2006, over half of the population over the age of 12 had used, at least once in their lifetime, alcohol (82.7%) or tobacco (70.7%) [95]. Additionally, well over a third had tried marijuana at least once (39.8%), and over one-quarter had tried an illicit drug other than marijuana at least once (29.6%) [95]. Despite these high numbers, only a very small percentage of those who try an addictive substance go on to develop an addictive disorder. For example, in 2006 only approximately 7.6% of the population met diagnostic criteria for alcohol addiction or dependence, and only 2.9% of the population met criteria for addiction or dependence of an illicit substance [95]. There are, in fact, some controversial suggestions that those who experiment with certain substances (e.g., marijuana) are more well-adjusted than both those who never try a substance and those who develop addictive disorders [96]. Nevertheless, given that relatively high numbers of individuals try substance use, yet very few develop addictive disorders – complicated by the suggestion that some experimental use may even be socially adaptive – the question becomes "what role, if any, does the onset of substance use play in the development of addictive disorders?" That is, the act of simply trying – or initiating – substance use does not discriminate between those who use experimentally (or in moderation), and those who go on to develop addictive disorders.

The answer to this question has emerged through empirical research, which demonstrates that it is the age at which an individual initiates substance use that poses a significant risk for the development of addictive disease. Specifically, the earlier an individual first tries substance use, the greater the likelihood that the individual will develop an addictive

disorder later in life [97]. Typically, the onset of substance use before the age of 16, when experimental use becomes more normative, poses an increased risk for later addictive disorders. Some researchers have found that there is a dramatic increase in the likelihood of developing an addictive disorder among those who initiate before the age of 13, with a reduction in the likelihood if the age of onset is after the age of 14 [98]. Many clinicians, interventionists, and researchers have begun to focus efforts on delaying the onset of substance use; it has been found that there is a 4–5% reduction in the risk for the development of addictive disorders each year that onset is delayed [97].

4.7   THE PROGRESSION OF ADDICTIVE DISEASE

Currently, over 20 million Americans are active (i.e., last 30 days) users of illicit substances, and another approximately 2.8 million try an illicit substance for the first time each year [95]. A total of 3.2 million Americans are classified as misusing or being dependent upon illicit substances; another 3.8 million are classified as misusing or dependent on both illicit substances and alcohol. A staggering 15.6 million individuals misuse or are dependent upon alcohol alone [95]. Table 4.1 highlights the current prevalence and incidence rates in the use of addictive substances as well as the rates of addiction or dependence diagnoses.

Table 4.1 Incidence and prevalence of illicit substance use and addiction/dependence

	Lifetime	Last 30 Days	Initiated Past Year	Addiction or Dependence
Any Illicit Drug	45.4	8.3	1.1	2.9
Marijuana	39.8	6.0	0.8	1.7
Cocaine	14.3	1.0	0.4	0.7
Crack Cocaine	3.5	0.3	0.1	*
Heroin	1.5	0.1	0.0	0.1
Hallucinogens	14.3	0.4	0.5	0.2
Pain Relievers	13.6	2.1	0.9	0.7
OxyContin	1.7	0.1	0.2	*
Stimulants	8.2	0.2	0.3	0.2

Data Source: 2006 National Survey on Drug Use and Health [95].
Note: Numbers are percentages.
* = Data not collected.

4.7.1   Phases and transition

The progression of addictive disorders may differ dramatically depending not only on individual and environmental factors but also on the type of substances used [99]. For example, a study by Hser [100] demonstrates dramatically different trajectories of substance use depending on the drug type. As demonstrated in Figure 4.3, the weekly use of tobacco and crack cocaine increases from the mid-twenties until the mid-forties before declining. The use of marijuana, on the other hand, steadily decreases over the course of adulthood. Alcohol use, after peaking in the twenties, remains relatively stable until use begins to decrease in the mid-forties. Heroin use, however, tends to increase slightly over adulthood, until peaking in the late forties; followed by a gradual decline.

In addition to the drug of choice, the progression of addictive disorders over time is also a function of age. Following the onset or initial use of substances, which typically occurs in mid-adolescence, the use of substances and subsequent addictive disorders increases relatively rapidly. For example, as seen in Figure 4.4, trends in the use of an illicit substance in the preceding 30 days jumps dramatically for individuals between the ages of 18 and 25. This jump in the use of illicit substances is followed by dramatic declines between the ages of 26 and 34, and again

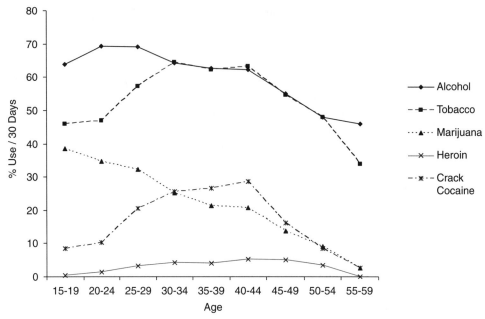

Figure 4.3 Trajectories of substance use patterns by drug type. (*Data Source: Hser, 2002 [100].*)

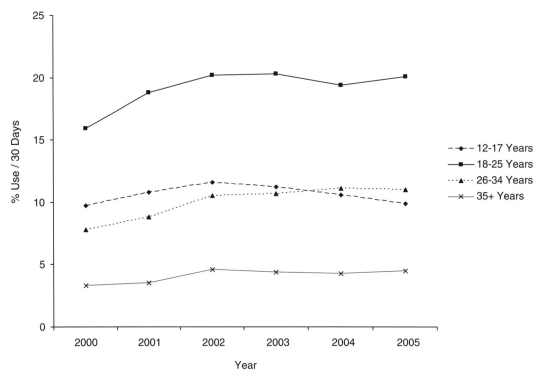

Figure 4.4 Past month use of any illicit substance by age group. (*Data Source: National Survey on Drug Abuse and Health [95].*)

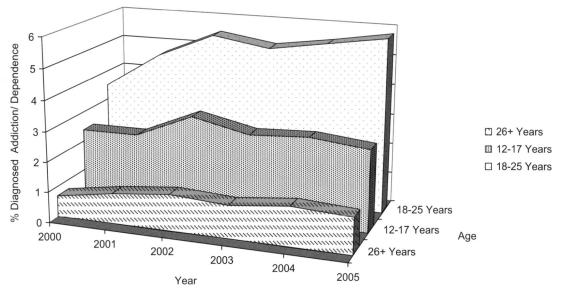

Figure 4.5 Dependence/Addiction diagnosis by age group. (*Data Source: National Survey on Drug Abuse and Health [95].*)

after the age of 35. The diagnosis of addictive disorders follows a similar pattern. As demonstrated in Figure 4.5, the diagnosis of illicit substance addiction or dependence is highest between the ages of 18–25, and proceeded by a sharp decline after the age of 26.

Many theories have been forwarded regarding why there exist such age-related shifts in the pattern of illicit substance use. One popular theory that has garnered empirical support is the maturation hypothesis of Charles Winnick [101]. According to this theory, as individuals mature, other behaviors and life options become more available and rewarding (e.g., marriage, stability, employment) than the use of substances. Bachman and colleagues [102], reflecting on trends in substance using behaviors, describe a spike in use in early adulthood, followed by a decline after the mid-twenties; according to Bachman, freedom from parental control was responsible for the spike in use between the ages of 18 and 25, which proceeds a decline that Bachman labeled the "marriage effect."

Edwards [1] noted the importance of considering not only trajectories of substance use patterns over time, but also the phases and transitions each individual passes through in their substance using

career. Whereas there are drug- and age-related differences in the patterns of substance use, there are some commonalities in the phases and transitions. For example, as shown in Figure 4.6, nearly all individuals who develop addictive disorders follow a common pathway (indicated by solid lines) from abstinence, to initiation, to casual/social use, to problematic use. Whereas it is conceivable that an individual may progress directly from initiation to problematic use, most typically pass through a phase of nonproblematic use. Once a pattern of problematic use has established itself, the duration of time the individuals remains in that phase depends on drug-of-choice, age, individual and social factors, and so forth. Indeed, an individual may remain in any of the phases depicted in Figure 4.6 indefinitely, or may transition into and out of different phases rapidly. A study conducted by Dennis and colleagues [103] found that the average duration of any addiction career has been estimated to be 27 years; however, there is considerable variation. For example, the average alcohol use career is 29 years; the average illicit drug use career is 25 years. For individuals who had an early onset of substance use, the average career is 29 years, significantly longer than those who began using after the age of 21. Additionally, males tend

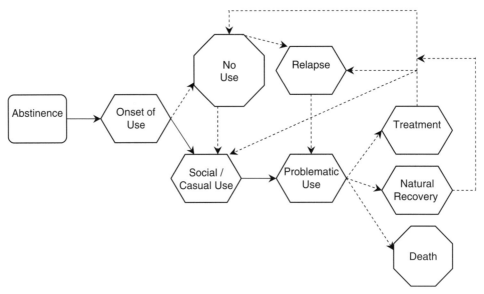

Figure 4.6   Phases/Transitions of substance use. (*Data Source: McGinnis and Foege, 1999 [114].*)

to have significantly longer careers (29 years) than do females (25 years).

Once an individual has an established addictive disorder, there are many potential pathways they can take (indicated by dashed lines in Figure 4.6). One potential pathway is entering treatment. Like addiction careers, the length of time from entry into treatment and achievement of prolonged (e.g., one year) abstinence – also known as a "treatment career" – is highly variable. The average length of a treatment career is nine years [103] – regardless of the modality of the treatment. The treatment careers of those with an early onset of substance use are longer (10 years) than those who start later (seven years). Those with more than one addictive disorder (e.g., alcohol and drug) tend to have longer treatment careers (10 years) than those with only one addictive disorder. Overall, there is evidence that 10% of those who enter treatment for an addictive disorder will recover within one year; 25% will recover within five years, and nearly 66% will recover within 12 years [104].

In addition to the individual factors listed above, the length of treatment career is also a function of the treatment itself, and treatment approaches and efficacy vary by drug-of-choice. For example, a study sponsored by the National Institutes on Alcohol Abuse and Alcoholism found that the use of

Naltrexone or specialized behavioral counseling were equally effective when combined with outpatient medical management [105]. The results demonstrated that the Combining Medications and Behavioral Interventions for Alcoholism (COMBINE) treatment intervention reduced drinking by 80%. Similarly, a recent Cochrane review demonstrated that opioid replacement therapy is significantly more effective than nonpharmaceutical interventions in the treatment of opioid dependence [106].

However, there is little overall consensus regarding specific interventions for addictive diseases. Moreover, a wide range of interventions have demonstrated empirical efficacy. For example, peer support groups, such as Alcoholics Anonymous (AA), have been among the most popular interventions for decades. Whereas little research has been conducted on AA, there is some evidence that individuals who attend AA are more likely to remain abstinent a year after treatment than those in other treatment modalities [107]. Likewise, there is strong evidence that treatments designed to enhance motivation to change addictive behaviors are effective for alcohol and drug use. A meta-analysis conducted by Burke and colleagues [108] demonstrated high rates of clinical improvement, up to 51% of motivational enhancement therapies. However, this meta-analysis found no effect of motivational enhancement on smoking behaviors. Other modalities, such as inpatient and therapeutic community treatments, family-based treatment, and cognitive and behavioral interventions each have demonstrated efficacy. Clinicians are often left to rely on judgment, client preference, and availability/practicality of interventions when faced with referral choices.

Formal treatment programs are not the only pathway out of the problematic use phase depicted in Figure 4.6. Spontaneous remission or natural recovery, that is, recovery without formal intervention, is a common pathway for many. Between 18 and 25% of all substances users are thought to quit or reduce use without any intervention [109]. The reasons behind successful spontaneous recovery include maturation [101], health concerns, pressure from family and friends, and important life events [109]. It is challenging to estimate the number of individuals who successfully undergo spontaneous recovery because of methodological flaws in the research on spontaneous recovery [110] and the fact that many of those who succeed in recovery without treatment never come to the attention of researchers or clinicians. However, it has been estimated that the number of those who recover with no formal intervention may exceed the number of individuals who recovery using structured interventions [111]. Nevertheless, it should also be noted that a large majority of those who attempt to quit without treatment fail. For example, 85% of youth smokers have attempted to quit without intervention and failed [112], and there is a low probability that these smokers will be able to quit on their own [113].

4.7.2 The role of prevention programs in curtailing addictive disorders

As previously mentioned in this chapter, the vast majority of individuals who use substances, will not go on to develop addictive disorders. For the small percentage who do, the costs (i.e., personal, relational, societal) can be significant. Thus, we have seen (justifiably) tremendous growth over the past two decades in the development and evaluation of prevention programs for substance use. These efforts

have taken several different forms, including individual-level school-based interventions, after-school programs, media campaigns, and community-wide interventions. However, by far, the vast majority of programs have been school-based [114], and typically target middle or junior high school students utilizing classroom-based interventions [115].

Meta-analyses on the effectiveness of earlier prevention efforts, which primarily focused on psycho-education, yielded mixed results, but failed to show any consistent pattern in curtailing substance use [114,115]. However, in the last decade, considerable progress has been made with regard to using theory-driven models of identifying successful components of prevention programs. To date, school-based interventions that draw from social learning theory and problem behavior theory, that address underlying psychosocial factors, have emerged as the most effective primary prevention [116]. More specifically, there is now a body of evidence that programs which target social influences (i.e., peer norms, resistance skills), and the development of cognitive-social skills (e.g., decision-making, impulse control and problem-solving skills), have the most impact in preventing or minimizing substance use [115].

Despite the promise of school-based interventions, it is likely that school-based interventions are not sufficient in targeting the broader familial and environmental risk factors for using illicit substances. Indeed, as Botvin pointed out almost twenty years ago, "in order to develop interventions comprehensive enough to reduce susceptibility to the various environmental factors promoting substance use…it will be necessary to go beyond strategies that rely solely on school-based interventions…and will be necessary to develop effective family- and community-based interventions" ([116], p. 511–512).

Because individuals are exposed to any number and/or combination of risk and protective factors, prevention programs are more likely to have an impact if they target multiple risk/protective factors, and are flexible enough to incorporate strategies that match the specific needs of the target population [117]. This framework has translated into a more recent prevention priority on comprehensive, community-based prevention. These multi-strategy, multi-level approaches target identified risk and protective factors among individuals, families, and community members (e.g., law enforcement officials, teachers), as well as community-level norms and policies (see Hawkins *et al.*, 1995). Indeed, there is growing evidence that comprehensive, community-based approaches to substance use prevention (e.g., Communities that Care, Project STAR) can be highly successful [118,119].

In sum, it is evident that great strides have been made in the last twenty years in the field of substance use prevention. But, on a larger scale, the field is still in infancy, particularly with regard to methodological rigor, testing prevention interventions on diverse populations, and determining strategies for effective adoption, implementation, and sustainability of programs in schools and communities.

4.7.3 Mortality of addictive disease

Yet another pathway from problematic use is death. It has been estimated that nearly one-quarter of the annual deaths in the United States are attributable to addictive substances [120]. The bulk of these deaths are the result of tobacco use;

however, 105 000 annual deaths are linked to alcohol use and nearly 40 000 are related to the use of illicit substances (see Figure 4.7). Vaillant [2] notes that more than a quarter of the 105 000 death attributable to alcohol may be the direct result of alcohol use itself (e.g., alcohol overdose, alcoholic cirrhosis), and 50% of these death are the result of accidents, suicides, and other factors thought to be secondary to alcohol use. Longitudinal studies by Vaillant suggest a lifetime mortality rate of 28% among alcohol users – significantly higher than would be expected of age-related individuals in the general population [2].

Unfortunately, little longitudinal data exists examining the mortality rate of users of illicit substances. Nevertheless, what data do exists suggest that annual rate of mortality among illicit substance users is approximately 1.2% [121]. In a 33-year follow-up of heroin users, nearly one-half (48%) of the original sample had died – a rate of nearly 1.5% annually [122]. Indeed, it is thought that opioid dependence – and heroin use in particular – is a particularly lethal addictive disease. By contrast, the mortality of cocaine dependent individuals is considerably less: less than 9% over a 12-year period – a rate of less than 0.75% annually [123].

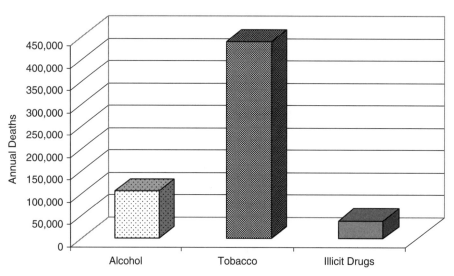

Figure 4.7 Mortality rate from addictive substances. (*Data Source: McGinnis and Foege, 1999 [116].*)

4.8 SUMMARY

This chapter demonstrates that the natural history or "career" of an addictive disorder is highly variable and depends to a great deal upon an individual's genetic make-up, parenting history, drug of choice, social context, and a range of other factors. Nevertheless, there are a number of common risk and protective factors that allow treatment providers to be alerted to high risk individuals, to make better informed predictions regarding the course of use over time, and to attend to key phases and transitions that may be possible in the course of addictive disease.

REFERENCES

1. Edwards, G. (1984) Drinking in longitudinal perspective: career and natural history. *Addiction*, **79** (2), 175–183.

2. Vaillant, G.E. (1995) *The Natural History of Alcoholism Revisited*, Harvard University Press.

3. Hser, Y.I., Longshore, D., and Anglin, M.D. (2007) The life course perspective on drug use: A conceptual framework for understanding drug use trajectories. *Evaluation Rev.*, **31** (6), 515.

4. Chen, K. (1995) The natural history of drug use from adolescence to the mid-thirties in a general population sample. *Am. J. Public Health*, **85** (1), 41–47.

5. Cicchetti, D. and Rogosch, F.A. (1996) Equifinality and multifinality in developmental psychopathology. *Dev. Psychopathol.*, **8** (4), 597–600.

6. Falck, R.S., Wang, J., and Carlson, R.G. (2007) Crack cocaine trajectories among users in a midwestern American city. *Addiction*, **102** (9), 1421.

7. Hawkins, J.D. and Weis, J.G. (1985) The social development model: An integrated approach to delinquency prevention. *J. Prim. Prev.*, **6** (2), 73–97.

8. Arthur, M.W., Hawkins, J.D., Pollard, J.A. *et al.* (2002) Measuring risk and protective factors for substance use, delinquency, and other adolescent problem behaviors: The Communities That Care Youth Survey. *Evaluation Rev.*, **26** (6), 575–601.

9. Campbell, E. and Ross, L.F. (2004) Attitudes of healthcare professionals and parents regarding genetic testing for violent traits in childhood. *Br. Med. J.*, **30** (6), 580.

10. Nestler, E.J. (2000) Genes and addiction. *Nat. Genet.*, **26** (3), 277–281.

11. Thomasson, H.R., Edenberg, H.J., Crabb, D.W. *et al.* (1991) Alcohol and aldehyde dehydrogenase genotypes and alcoholism in Chinese men. *Am. J. Hum. Genet.*, **48** (4), 677.

12. Benowitz, N.L. (2008) Clinical pharmacology of nicotine: implications for understanding, preventing, and treating tobacco addiction. *Clin. Pharmacol. Ther.*, **83** (4), 531–541.

13. Basavarajappa, B.S. (2007) Critical enzymes involved in endocannabinoid metabolism. *Protein. Pept. Lett.*, **14** (3), 237.

14. Oroszi, G. and Goldman, D. (2004) Alcoholism: genes and mechanisms. *Pharmacogenomics*, **5** (8), 1037–1048.

15. National Institute on Drug Abuse (2008) *Drugs, Brain and Behavior: The Science of Addiction*, NIH Publication No. 07-5605 ed., National Institutes of Health, Rockville, MD.

16. Interlandi, J. (2008) What Addicts Need. Newsweek.

17. Kagan, J. and Snidman, N. (2004) *The Long Shadow of Temperament*, Belknap Press.

18. Bussing, R., Gary, F.A., Mason, D.M. *et al.* (2003) Child temperament, ADHD, and caregiver strain: exploring relationships in an epidemiological sample. *J. Am. Acad. Child Adolesc. Psychiatry*, **42** (2), 184–192.

19. Nigg, J.T., Goldsmith, H.H. and Sachek, J. (2004) Temperament and attention deficit hyperactivity disorder: The development of a multiple pathway model. *J. Clin. Child Adolesc. Psychol.*, **33** (1), 42–53.

20. Saltaris, C. (2002) Psychopathy in juvenile offenders Can temperament and attachment be considered as robust developmental precursors? *Clin. Psychol. Rev.*, **22** (5), 729–752.

21. Wells, J.C.K., Stanley, M., Laidlaw, A.S. *et al.* (1997) Investigation of the relationship between infant temperament and later body composition. *Int. J. Obesity*, **21** (5), 400–406.

22. Giancola, P.R. and Mezzich, A.C. (2003) Executive functioning, temperament, and drug use involvement in adolescent females with a substance use disorder. *J. Child Psychol. Psyc.*, **44** (6), 857.

23. Wills, T.A., Sandy, J.M., and Yaeger, A. (2000) Temperament and adolescent substance use: an epigenetic approach to risk and protection. *J. Pers.*, **68** (6), 1127–1151.

24. Wills, T.A., Cleary, S., Filer, M. *et al.* (2001) Temperament related to early-onset substance use: test of a developmental model. *Prev. Sci.*, **2** (3), 145–163.

25. Gerra, G., Angioni, L., Zaimovic, A. *et al.* (2004) Substance use among high-school students: relationships with temperament, personality traits, and parental care perception. *Subst. Use Misuse*, **39** (2), 345–367.

26. King, K.M. and Chassin, L. (2004) Mediating and moderated effects of adolescent behavioral undercontrol and parenting in the prediction of drug use disorders in emerging adulthood. *Psychol. Addict. Behav.*, **18** (3), 239–249.

27. Pears, K., Capaldi, D.M., and Owen, L.D. (2007) Substance use risk across three generations: the roles of parent discipline practices and inhibitory control. *Psychol. Addict. Behav.*, **21** (3), 373–386.

28. Wills, T.A. and Dishion, T.J. (2004) Temperament and adolescent substance use: a transactional analysis of emerging self-control. *J. Clin. Child Adolesc. Psychol.*, **33** (1), 69–81.

29. Drapela, L.A. and Mosher, C. (2007) The conditional effect of parental drug use on parental attachment and adolescent drug use: social control and social development model perspectives. *J. Child Adoles. Subst.*, **16** (3), 63–87.

30. Elliott, D.S., Huizinga, D., and Ageton, S.S. (1985) *Explaining Delinquency and Drug Use*, Sage Publications.

31. Hawkins, J.D. and Weis, J.G. (1985) The social development model: An integrated approach to delinquency prevention. *J. Prim. Prev.*, **6** (2), 73–97.

32. Huebner, A.J. and Betts, S.C. (2002) Exploring the utility of social control theory for youth development: issues of attachment, involvement, and gender. *Youth Soc.*, **34** (2), 123.

33. Kierkus, C.A. and Baer, D. (2002) A social control explanation of the relationship between family structure and delinquent behaviour. *Can. J. Criminol.*, **44** (4), 425–459.

34. Grant, B.F. and Pickering, R. (1998) The relationship between cannabis use and DSM-IV cannabis abuse and dependence: results from the national longitudinal alcohol epidemiologic survey. *J. Subst. Abuse*, **10** (3), 255–264.

35. Miranda, R.Jr., Meyerson, L.A., Long, P.J. *et al.* (2002) Sexual assault and alcohol use: exploring the self-medication hypothesis. *Violence Vict.*, **17** (2), 13.

36. Gilman, S.E. and Abraham, H.D. (2001) A longitudinal study of the order of onset of alcohol dependence and major depression. *Drug Alcohol. Depen.*, **63** (3), 277–286.

37. Merikangas, K.R., Mehta, R.L., Molnar, B.E. *et al.* (1998) Comorbidity of substance use disorders with mood and anxiety disorders Results of the international consortium in psychiatric epidemiology. *Addict. Behav.*, **23** (6), 893–907.

38. Hall, D.H. and Queener, J.E. (2007) Self-medication hypothesis of substance use: testing Khantzian's updated theory. *J. Psychoactive Drugs*, **39** (2), 151–158.

39. Aharonovich, E., Nguyen, H.T., and Nunes, E.V. (2001) Anger and depressive states among treatment-seeking drug abusers: testing the psychopharmacological specificity hypothesis. *Am. J. Addiction*, **10** (4), 327–334.

40. Helzer, J.E. and Pryzbeck, T.R. (1988) The co-occurrence of alcoholism with other psychiatric disorders in the general population and its impact on treatment. *J. Stud. Alcohol*, **49** (3), 219–224.

41. Milberger, S., Biederman, J., Faraone, S.V. *et al.* (1997) Associations between ADHD and psychoactive substance use disorders: findings from a longitudinal study of high-risk siblings of ADHD children. *Am. J. Addiction*, **6** (4), 318–329.

42. Willens, T.E., Biederman, J., Mick, E. *et al.* (1997) Attention deficit hyperactivity disorder (ADHD) is associated with early onset substance use disorders. *J. Nerv. Ment. Dis.*, **185** (8), 475.

43. Biederman, J., Wilens, T., Mick, E. *et al.* (2003) Is ADHD a risk factor for psychoactive substance use disorders? Finding from a four-year prospective follow-up study. *Focus*, **1** (2), 196–204.

44. Molina, B.S.G., Smith, B.H., and Pelham, W.E. (1999) Interactive effects of attention deficit hyperactivity disorder and conduct disorder on early adolescent substance use. *Psychol. Addict. Behav.*, **13** (4), 348–358.

45. Acton, G.S. (2003) Measurement of impulsivity in a hierarchical model of personality traits: implications for substance use. *Subst. Use Misuse*, **38** (1), 67–83.

46. Bickel, W.K., Odum, A.L., and Madden, G.J. (1999) Impulsivity and cigarette smoking: delay discounting in current, never, and ex-smokers. *Psychopharmacology*, **146** (4), 447–454.

47. Madden, G.J., Bickel, W.K., and Jacobs, E.A. (1999) Discounting of delayed rewards in opioid-dependent outpatients: exponential or hyperbolic discounting functions? *Exp. Clin. Psychopharmacol.*, **7** (3), 284–293.

48. Heil, S.H., Johnson, M.W., Higgins, S.T., and Bickel, W.K. (2006) Delay discounting in currently using and currently abstinent cocaine-dependent outpatients and non-drug-using matched controls. *Addict. Behav.*, **31** (7), 1290–1294.

49. Petry, N.M. (2001) Delay discounting of money and alcohol in actively using alcoholics, currently abstinent alcoholics, and controls. *Psychopharmacology*, **154** (3), 243–250.

50. Swadi, H. (1999) Individual risk factors for adolescent substance use. *Drug Alcohol. Depen.*, **55** (3), 209–224.

51. Grant, B.F., Stinson, F.S., Dawson, D.A. *et al.* (2004) Prevalence and co-occurrence of substance use disorders and independent mood and anxiety disorders results from the national epidemiologic survey on alcohol and related conditions. *Arch. Gen. Psychiatry*, **61** (8), 807–816.

52. Ajzen, I. (1991) The theory of planned behavior. *Organ. Behav. Hum. Dec.*, **50**, 179–211.

53. Courneya, K.S. and Friedenreich, C.M. (1999) Utility of the theory of planned behavior for understanding exercise during breast cancer treatment. *Psycho-Oncology*, **8**, 112–122.

54. Liana, L. and John, S.A. (2008) Factors influencing the use of public dental services: An application of the Theory of Planned Behaviour. *BMC Health Serv. Res.*, **8**, 93.

55. Pawlak, R., Brown, D., Meyer, M.K. *et al.* (2008) Theory of planned behavior and multivitamin supplement use in caucasian college females. *J. Prim. Prev.*, **29** (1), 57–71.

56. Norman, P., Armitage, C.J., and Quigley, C. (2007) The theory of planned behavior and binge drinking: Assessing the impact of binge drinker prototypes. *Addict. Behav.*, **32** (9), 1753–1768.

57. Kosmidou, E. and Theodorakis, Y. (2007) Differences in smoking attitudes of adolescents and young adults. *Psychol. Rep.*, **101** (2), 475–481.

58. Conner, M. and Mcmillan, B. (1999) Interaction effects in the theory of planned behaviour: Studying cannabis use. *Brit J. Soc. Psychol.*, **38** (2), 195–222.

59. Dennison, C.M. and Shepherd, R. (1995) Adolescent food choice: an application of the Theory of Planned Behaviour. *J. Hum. Nutr. Diet.*, **8** (1), 9–23.

60. Furnham, A. and Lovett, J. (2001) Predicting the use of complementary medicine: A test of the theories of reasoned action and planned behavior 1. *J. Appl. Soc. Psychol.*, **31** (12), 2588–2620.

61. Godin, G. and Kok, G. (1996) The theory of planned behavior: A review of its applications to health-related behaviors. *Am. J. Health Promot.*, **11** (2), 87–98.

62. Ajzen, I. and Driver, B.L. (1992) Application of the theory of planned behavior to leisure choice. *J. Leisure. Res.*, **24** (3), 207–224.

63. Armitage, C.J. and Conner, M. (2001) Efficacy of the theory of planned behaviour: A meta-analytic review. *Brit J. Soc. Psychol.*, **40** (4), 471–499.

64. Dishion, T.J., Capaldi, D., Spracklen, K.M., and Li, F. (1995) Peer ecology of male adolescent drug use. *Dev. Psychopathol.*, **7** (4), 803–824.

65. Wood, M.D., Read, J.P., Mitchell, R.E., and Brand, N.H. (2004) Do parents still matter? Parent and peer influences on alcohol involvement among recent high school graduates. *Psychol. Addict. Behav.*, **18** (1), 19–30.

66. Isohanni, M., Moilanen, I., and Rantakallio, P. (1991) Determinants of teenage smoking, with special reference to non-standard family background. *Addiction*, **86** (4), 391–398.

67. Kandel, D.B. and Wu, P. (1995) The contributions of mothers and fathers to the intergenerational transmission of cigarette smoking in adolescence. *J. Res. Adolescence*, **5** (2), 225–252.

68. Dishion, T.J., Capaldi, D.M., and Yoerger, K. (1999) Middle childhood antecedents to progressions in male adolescent substance use: an ecological analysis of risk and protection. *J. Adolescent Res.*, **14** (2), 175.

69. Brook, J.S., Whiteman, M., Balka, E.B., and Cohen, P. (1995) Parent drug use, parent personality, and parenting. *J. Genet. Psychol.*, **156** (2), 137–151.

70. Andrews, J.A., Hops, H., and Duncan, S.C. (1997) Adolescent modeling of parent substance use: The moderating effect of the relationship with the parent. *J. Fam. Psychol.*, **11** (3), 259–270.

71. Stanton, M.D. and Todd, T.C. (1982) *The Family Therapy of Drug Abuse and Addiction*, The Guilford Press.

72. Marshal, M.P. and Chassin, L. (2000) Peer influence on adolescent alcohol use: The moderating role of parental support and discipline. *Appl. Dev. Sci.*, **4** (2), 80–88.

73. Wills, T.A., Resko, J.A., Ainette, M.G., and Mendoza, D. (2004) Role of parent support and peer support in adolescent substance use: a test of mediated effects. *Psychol. Addict. Behav.*, **18** (2), 122–134.

74. Windle, M. (2000) Parental, Sibling, and peer influences on adolescent substance use and alcohol problems. *Appl. Dev. Sci.*, **4** (2), 98–110.

75. Chilcoat, H.D. and Anthony, J.C. (1996) Impact of parent monitoring on initiation of drug use through late childhood. *J. Am. Acad. Child Psy.*, **35** (1), 91.

76. Dishion, T.J., Nelson, S.E., and Kavanagh, K. (2003) The family check-up for high-risk adolescents: motivating parenting monitoring and reducing problem behavior. *Behav. Ther.*, **34**, 553–571.

77. Stattin, H. and Kerr, M. (2000) Parental monitoring: A reinterpretation. *Child Dev.*, **71** (4), 1072–1085.

78. Li, X., Stanton, B., and Feigelman, S. (2000) Impact of perceived parental monitoring on adolescent risk behavior over 4 years. *J. Adolesc. Health*, **27** (1), 49–56.

79. Jenkins, J.E. (1996) The influence of peer affiliation and student activities on adolescent drug involvement. *Adolescence*, **31** (122), 297–306.

80. Flook, L., Repetti, R.L., and Ullman, J.B. (2005) Classroom social experiences as predictors of academic performance. *Dev. Psychol.*, **41** (2), 319–327.

81. Anderman, E.M. and Midgley, C. (1997) Changes in achievement goal orientations, perceived academic competence, and grades across the transition to middle-level schools. *Contemp. Educ. Psychol.*, **22** (3), 269–298.

82. Eccles, J.S., Lord, S.E., Roeser, R.W. *et al.* (1997) The association of school transitions in early adolescence with developmental trajectories through high school, in *Health Risks and Developmental Transitions During Adolescence* (eds J. Schulenberg, J. Maggs, and K. Hurrelmann), Cambridge University Press, pp. 283–320.

83. Feldlaufer, H., Midgley, C., and Eccles, J.S. (1988) Student, teacher, and observer perceptions of the classroom environment before and after the transition to junior high school. *J. Early Adolescence*, **8** (2), 133.

84. Gottfredson, D.C. (2001) *Schools and Delinquency*, Cambridge University Press.

85. Ostroff, C. (1992) The relationship between satisfaction, attitudes, and performance: an organizational level analysis. *J. Appl. Psychol.*, **77** (6), 963–974.

86. Sampson, R.J. and Lauritsen, J.L. (1994) *Violent Victimization and Offending: Individual-, Situational-, and Community-Level Risk Factors*, 3rd edn, National Academy Press, Washington, DC.

87. Pucci, L.G., Joseph, H.M., and Siegel, M. (1998) Outdoor tobacco advertising in six Boston neighborhoods Evaluating youth exposure. *Am. J. Prev. Med.*, **15** (2), 155–159.

88. LaVeist, T.A. and Wallace, J.M. (2000) Health risk and inequitable distribution of liquor stores in African American neighborhood. *Soc. Sci. Med.*, **51** (4), 613–617.

89. McDowall, D., Loftin, C., and Wiersema, B. (2000) The impact of youth curfew laws on juvenile crime rates. *Crime Delinquency*, **46** (1), 76.

90. Hawkins, J.D., Arthur, M.W., and Catalano, R.F. (1995) Preventing substance abuse, in *Building a Safer Society: Strategic Approaches to Crime Prevention, Crime and Justice: A Review of Research*, 19 edn (eds M. Tonry and D. Farrington), University of Chicago Press, Chicago, pp. 343–427.

91. Darling, H. and Reeder, A. (2003) Is exposure to secondhand tobacco smoke in the home related to daily smoking among youth? *Aust. NZ. J. Publ. Heal.*, **27** (6), 655–656.

92. Matt, G.E., Quintana, P.J., Hovell, M.F. *et al.* (2004) Households contaminated by environmental tobacco smoke: sources of infant exposures. *Tob. Control*, **13** (1), 29–37.

93. Moen, B.E., Sandberg, S., and Riise, T. (1992) Drinking habits and laboratory tests in seamen with and without chemical exposure. *J. Stud. Alcohol*, **53** (4), 364–368.

94. Gold, M.S., Byars, J.A., and Frost-Pineda, K. (2004) Occupational exposure and addictions for physicians: case studies and theoretical implications. *Psychiatr. Clin. N. Am.*, **27**, 745–753.

95. Substance Abuse and Mental Health Services Administration (2008) Results from the 2006 National Survey on Drug Use and Health: National Findings, Office of Applied Studies, Rockville, MD.

96. Shedler, J. and Block, J. (1990) Adolescent drug use and psychological health: A longitudinal inquiry. *Am. Psychol.*, **45** (5), 612–630.

97. Grant, B.F. and Dawson, D.A. (1997) Age at onset of alcohol use and its association with DSM-IV alcohol abuse and dependence: results from the national longitudinal alcohol epidemiologic survey. *J. Subst. Abuse*, **9**, 103–110.

98. Sung, M., Erkanli, A., Angold, A., and Costello, E.J. (2004) Effects of age at first substance use and psychiatric comorbidity on the development of substance use disorders. *Drug Alcohol. Depen.*, **75** (3), 287–299.

99. Day, E. and Best, D. (2007) Natural history of substance-related problems. *Psychiatry*, **6** (1), 12–15.

100. Hser, Y. (2002) Drug use careers: recovery and mortality, in *Substance Abuse and Mental Health Services Administration OoAS, editor. Substance use by Older Adults: Estimates of Future Impact on the Treatment System*, Department of Health and Human Services, Rockville, MD.

101. Winick, C. (1962) Maturing out of narcotic addiction. *B. Narcotics*, **14** (1), 1–7.

102. Bachman, J.G., Wadsworth, K.N., O'Malley, P.M. *et al.* (1997) *Smoking, Drinking, and Drug Use in Young Adulthood: The Impacts of New Freedoms and New Responsibilities*, Lawrence Earlbaum Associates, Mahwah, NJ.

103. Dennis, M.L., Scott, C.K., Funk, R., and Foss, M.A. (2005) The duration and correlates of addiction and treatment careers. *J. Subst. Abuse. Treat.*, **28** (2S), 51–62.

104. Best, D., Day, E., and Morgan, B. (2006) *Addiction Careers and the Natural History of Change*, National

Treatment Agency for Substance Misuse, London, UK.

105. Anton, R.F., O'Malley, S.S., Ciraulo, D.A. *et al.* (2006) Combined pharmacotherapies and behavioral interventions for alcohol dependence the COMBINE study: A randomized controlled trial. *JAMA*, **295** (17), 2003–2017.

106. Mattick, R.P., Breen, C., Kimber, J., and Davoli, M. (2003) Methadone maintenance therapy versus no opioid replacement therapy for opioid dependence. *Cochrane Database Syst. Rev.* 3 (Art. No.: CD002209). doi: 10.1002/14651858.CD002209.pub2.

107. Project MATCH (1997) Matching alcoholism treatments to client heterogeneity: Project MATCH posttreatment drinking outcomes. *J. Stud. Alcohol*, **58**, 7–29.

108. Burke, B.L., Arkowitz, H., and Menchola, M. (2003) The efficacy of motivational interviewing: a meta-analysis of controlled clinical trials. *J. Consult. Clin. Psychol.*, **71** (5), 843–861.

109. Walters, G.D. (2000) Spontaneous remission from alcohol, tobacco, and other drug abuse: seeking quantitative answers to qualitative questions*. *Am. J. Drug Alcohol Ab.*, **26** (3), 443–460.

110. Sobell, L.C., Ellingstad, T.P., and Sobell, M.B. (2000) Natural recovery from alcohol and drug problems: methodological review of the research with suggestions for future directions. *Addiction*, **95** (5), 749–764.

111. Granfield, R. and Cloud, W. (1996) The elephant that no one sees: Natural recovery among middle-class addicts. *J. Drug Issues*, **26** (1), 45–61.

112. Centers for Disease Control and Prevention (2006) Youth Tobacco Surveillance – United States, 2001–2002. *Surveillance Summaries, May 19, 2006 MMWR, 55* (No. SS-3).

113. Mermelstein, R. (2003) Teen smoking cessation. *Tob. Control*, **12** (Suppl 1), i25–i34.

114. Foxcroft, D.R., Lister-Sharp, D., and Lowe, G. (1997) Alcohol misuse prevention for young people: a systematic review reveals methodological concerns and lack of reliable evidence of effectiveness. *Addiction*, **92** (5), 531–537.

115. Botvin, G.J. (2000) Preventing drug abuse in schools Social and competence enhancement approaches targeting individual-level etiologic factors. *Addictive Behaviors*, **25** (6), 887–897.

116. Botvin, G.J. (1990) Substance Abuse Prevention: Theory, Practice, and Effectiveness. *Crime & Just*, **13**, 461.

117. Hawkins, J.D., Arthur, M.W., and Catalano, R.F. (1995) Preventing Substance Abuse. *Crime & Just*, **19**, 343.

118. Hawkins, J.D., Catalano, R.F., and Arthur, M.W. (2002) Promoting science-based prevention in communities. *Addictive Behaviors*, **27** (6), 951–976.

119. Goodman, R.M., Wandersman, A., Chinman, M., Imm, P., and Morrissey, E. (1996) An ecological assessment of community-based interventions for prevention and health promotion: Approaches to measuring community coalitions. *American Journal of Community Psychology*, **24** (1), 33–61.

120. McGinnis, J.M. and Foege, W.H. (1999) Mortality and morbidity attributable to use of addictive substances in the United States. *PAAP*, **111** (2), 109–118.

121. Gossop, M., Stewart, D., Treacy, S., and Marsden, J. (2002) A prospective study of mortality among drug misusers during a 4-year period after seeking treatment. *Addiction*, **97** (1), 39–47.

122. Hser, Y.I., Hoffman, V., Grella, C.E., and Anglin, M.D. (2001) A 33-year follow-up of narcotics addicts. *Arch. Gen. Psychiatry*, **58** (5), 503.

123. Hser, Y.I., Stark, M.E., Paredes, A. *et al.* (2006) A 12-year follow-up of a treated cocaine-dependent sample. *J. Subst. Abuse. Treat.*, **30** (3), 219–226.

5

Prevention methods: school, family, community, media and public policy approaches

Karol L. Kumpfer[1] and Paula Smith[2]

[1] *Psychologist, Program Developer and Professor, Department of Health Promotion and Education, University of Utah, 1901 E South Campus Dr. Rm 2142, Salt Lake City, Utah 84112*
[2] *Associate Professor, University of Utah, Department of Educational Leadership & Policy*

5.1 OVERVIEW

5.1.1 Significance to the clinician

An ounce of prevention is worth a pound of cure. This chapter of *Addiction in Medicine* will focus on what can be done to prevent the high cost of addictions in heath care and social services. Unfortunately, the costs of alcohol and drug abuse are increasing rapidly. Between 1995 and 2000 the estimated economic costs of substance abuse increased from $278 billion to over $450 billion [1]. These costs include health care and treatment costs as well as lost earnings because of premature death, unemployment, and impaired productivity as well as criminal justice activities such as law enforcement and incarceration costs. In 2010, the federal budget alone for substance abuse treatment, prevention, law enforcement, interdiction, and internal costs was over $15.1 billion [2]. Many of the

chapters in this book discuss diseases and increased medical complications caused or exacerbated by alcohol and drug abuse. Health care costs have been estimated to be increased by as much as 50% because of the health consequences of alcohol and drug abuse. The National Institute of Health [3] estimated that the lifetime health care costs of just one baby born with fetal alcohol syndrome in 2000 was estimated at $588,000 and the total economic cost for the U.S. was about $5.4 billion in 2003. Additionally substance abuse by parents is a major factor in child abuse and neglect contributing to the high cost of child protective services and long term foster care. In a time of economic downturn our society cannot afford this staggering loss, which is about twice as large as our current budget shortfall.

Drug abuse rates must decrease through both demand and supply reduction prevention methods.

Addictive Disorders in Medical Populations   Edited by Norman S. Miller and Mark S. Gold
© 2010 John Wiley & Sons, Ltd.

Demand reduction approaches stress getting people not to want to use drugs, whereas supply reduction approaches seek to reduce the supply of drugs. For the first time the War on Drugs is now also overlapping with the War on Terrorism. The White House Office of National Drug Control Policy (ONDCP) is currently highlighting in its national media campaign the relationship between illegal drug use and increased drug production, crime, guns, and international terrorism. The high levels of gun violence and mortality in this country (over 11,000 deaths) may also be related to drug abuse and protection of drug production or sales territory.

5.1.2 Framework of chapter content

Substance abuse is a major health problem in this country. We are a country of pill poppers and drug abusers looking for quick fixes for medical, social, and mental problems. Many of the chapters in this handbook discuss the major health care costs contributed by abuse of alcohol, tobacco, and drugs. Unfortunately most medical professionals are inadequately trained to intervene to treat or prevent substance abuse disorders. The rest of this chapter will provide an overview of the incidence and prevalence of substance abuse, the causes, the need

for physician training and education in recognizing, screening, intervening and referring for treatment or prevention services for substance abuse, evidence based prevention approaches such as the major three major types of prevention approaches (universal, selective, and indicated primary prevention), and literature reviews on what works in prevention for youth, college students, adults in workplaces, and the elderly. The chapter will end with what clinicians can do to implement and advocated for evidence-based prevention approaches that work.

5.1.3 Goals and objectives of chapter

1. *Goal and Objective #1*: To increase physician and health care specialist knowledge and awareness of the need to screen and refer for treatment and prevention services.

2. *Goal and Objective #2*: To increase knowledge of the different types of evidence-based programs (EBPs) available for prevention.

3. *Objective #3*: To increase advocacy and support for prevention of substance abuse to reduce the high cost of health care.

5.2 CLINICAL PREVALENCE

5.2.1 Need for substance abuse prevention

The recent inattention to substance abuse disorders in medicine may be about to change. Health care professionals are faced with many more patients with long-term addiction problems. Why? Although unheralded by the media, parent groups, or government agencies, the abuse of tobacco, alcohol, and illicit drugs by teenagers increased dramatically in the mid 1990s and is resulting in higher rates of addiction in adults today.

5.2.2 Incidence and prevalence of substance abuse

The good news for drug treatment provides is that for the last 12 years our country has had a slow decline in adolescent alcohol and drug use reversing the rapid rise in use from 1992 to 1997. This declining trend might be about to change to a rapid increase again because risk factors are rising. The latest Monitoring the Future survey found that youth attitudes about the risks of drug use have declined: fewer 8th and 10th graders believe smoking marijuana is dangerous; and fewer 10th and 12th graders believe that trying ecstasy is dangerous. Declines in perception of harm invariably precede increases in drug use. The 2009 National PRIDE Survey Data found increases in past 30-day use in all drug categories for all grade levels six through 12, and according to the most recent Monitoring the Future Survey, more 10th and 12th grade students are now smoking marijuana than cigarettes. Additionally the Partnership for Drug Free America survey of schools found this year a 50% increase in one year in ecstasy use, an 18% increase in 30-day alcohol use and 33% increase in marijuana use.

The decreases in actual 2010 prevention funding by 2 million (1.8 billion to 1.6 billion) and an additional proposed decrease in 2011 could not have come at a worse time. This recent upswing in alcohol and drug use by adolescents appears to be related to the use of party drugs used to reduce stress. Our country cannot afford the increased economic burden of a return to the drug epidemic of the mid 1990's when 30-day marijuana use doubled and heroin use increase by 500% [4]. The large increase in adolescent use from 1992 to 1997 was addressed by extra prevention funding to target improving parent/child relations. As the Director of the SAMHSA Center for Substance Abuse Prevention (CSAP) in Washington, D.C., the first author believes that what contributed to the slow decline in alcohol and drug use from 1998 until this year was targeting the White House Office of National Drug Control Policy (ONDCP) media campaign towards parents by launching "Parents: The Anti-drug" media campaign. Targeting youth with scare messages about consequences have been found not to be effective, but the parent media messages have been found effective. Additionally Congress funded SAMHSA an extra $15 million for evidence-based parenting and family prevention interventions to be implemented in 150 communities for five years. These family programs are *nine times more effective* than youth-only school-based approaches [5]. Funding has not been provided again for these effective parenting programs that also reduce crime, delinquency, teenage pregnancy, school failure, and dramatically reduce mental health problems. Hence, it appears that part of the

current increase is related to the economic downturn and parents spending less time with their children to support pro-social values and monitoring their activities. A 2009 study by the Annenberg Center for the Digital Future at the University of Southern California found that the time devoted to family socializing dipped from an average of 26 hours per month in 2005 to just 17.9 hours in 2008. Twenty-eight percent of Americans reported spending less time with members of their households, up from 11% in 2006. As the old saying goes: "Families that play together, stay together". Families that socialize together develop more positive relationships united by a common bond, which usually means better communication, more parental monitoring, coaching, and more meaningful interactions.

5.2.2.1 Legal drug use rates

Like illegal drugs, legal drug use has also decreased since the highs in the mid 1990s. According to recently release Youth Risk Behavior Survey (YRBS) data [6], 30 day or current use of any type of tobacco product has decreased from 43.4% in 1997 to 25.7% of 9th to 12th graders by 2007. Daily tobacco use among seniors has decreased in the last three years, from 25 to 21%, but is still higher than the low of 17% in 1992. Likewise, binge drinking (consuming five or more drinks at one setting) in the past month decreased from a high of 32.6% in 1997 to 26.0% in 2007 in 9th to 12th graders. Overall illicit drug use is at a 5 year low for 12–17 year olds, and marijuana use has dropped 18% over past 5 years. The largest increase in 2000 in regular drug use was for "club drugs" – MDMA or ecstasy – whose regular use among high school seniors more than doubled in two years, from 1.5 to 3.6%. 4.5% of seniors reported using in past year.

5.2.2.2 Over-the-counter and prescription drugs

For the most part illicit drug use has been on the decline for 12 years until this year, but over-the-counter and prescription drug use have continued to rise until this year and are a growing concern. Recent data from the National Survey on Drug Use and Health [7] reported that over 6 million Americans aged 12 and older reported using prescription drugs non-medically in the 30 days prior to the survey, including 4.4 million people using pain relievers, 1.6 million using tranquilizers, 1.2 million using stimulants, and 0.3 million using sedatives. Prescription medication abuse in youth has increased at an alarming rate [8] so that more teens are abusing prescription drugs than any illicit drug except marijuana. They report prescription drugs are easy to get and often acquired free from family or friends. In addition, teens say parents are not talking to them about the dangers of prescription and over-the-counter medications along with believing the myth that these drugs are a "safe" high. Every day, 2500 teens abuse a prescription painkiller for the first time and get addicted. Between 1995 and 2005 drug treatment admissions for prescription painkillers increased more than 300%. Among those most commonly abused by teens are painkillers, depressants such as sleeping pills are used as anti-anxiety drugs, and stimulants which are regularly used to treat disorders such as attention-deficit hyperactivity disorder (ADHD). According to the ONDCP web site, in 2006 more than 2.1 million teens abused prescription drugs. Statistics show that 4% of 8th Graders, 5% of 10th graders, and 6% of 12th graders abused over-the-counter drugs in the past year. The National Household Survey shows that although a higher *percentage* of teenagers were drug abusers during the adolescent drug epidemic that peaked in 1979, a higher *number* of youth today are abusing drugs than ever before [9].

Because of this very large increase in drug use in the middle 1990s and increased numbers of adolescents today, there is a higher number (but not percent) of young people using drugs than during the peak years of drug abuse during 1970s. At that time, concerned parents organized "The Parent's Movement" and with the help of media and government officials, increased funding for drug prevention and treatment efforts resulted in substantial decreases in drug use throughout the 1980s and early 1990s. However, our success in the "War on Drugs" ended in 1992 when eight graders

first reported substantial increases in their drug use. A booming economy, overworked parents, and neglected children resulted in a youth culture that valued alcohol and drug abuse. Drugs that could be produced in the United States in chemical laboratories, such as methamphetamine and club drugs (ecstasy and GHB) rapidly increased in use.

5.2.2.3   Gender differences in use rates

The rates of annual illicit drug use for high school seniors, while peaking in 1999 at 42.1%, had decreased by 2006 to 36.5% [10]. These decreases are notable, but marked differences in gender persist. In fact, in nearly all drug use categories girls have either increased more, decreased less, or maintained essentially the same rates of use for the past several years. By 1995, young girls exceeded boys in their use of cigarettes, methamphetamines, amphetamines, cocaine, crack, inhalants, and tranquilizers. The annual illicit substance use rates excluding marijuana for 12th grade boys and girls are converging (19.7% for boys and 18.3% for girls), and the rates in this same use category are higher for 8th and 10th grade girls than boys. That is, girls outpace boys in annual illicit substance use with 8.7% of 8th grade girls reporting use versus 6.5% of boys and 13.1% for 10th grade girls versus 12.0% of boys. By 2006 adolescent girls slightly exceeded boys in substance dependence or abuse (8.1% vs. 8.0%) as measured by regular problematic use indicative of needing treatment in the past year [11]. The use of stimulant drugs or uppers became very popular in young girls to reduce weight and self-medicate depression such that girls have continued their nearly-fixed trend of outpacing boys in the use of amphetamines and amphetamine-type substances in all secondary grade levels, with 5.7% versus 3.5% for 8th graders; 8.9% versus 6.7% for 10th graders, and 8.5% versus 7.4% versus for 12th graders for girls versus boys, respectively [10]. Young girls may have unique risk and protective factors related to the breakdown of the family, depression, and increased desire for thinness [12].

5.2.2.4 *Use rates by race and ethnicity*

Earlier studies in the 1990s found that the youth at highest risk for substance abuse were American Indian youth. The 2000 National Household Survey [9] reported that 18% of 12 to 18 year old American Indian youth used an illegal drug in the past month, compared to 10.2% of African American youth, 10% of White youth, 8.9% of Hispanic youth, and 6.7% of Asian youth. However, past year use by American Indian youth of drugs and alcohol is much higher at 58% compared to 20% among white youth, 18% among Hispanic youth, 16% among African American youth, and 12% among Asian youth.

The most recent 2008 SAMHSA National Household Survey [11] found that the past month (30-day) illicit drug use among persons aged 12 or older still varied considerably by race/ethnicity with the lowest rate among Asians (3.6%). On this survey, youth were given the opportunity to report on more than one racial category and highest use rates were for bi- or multi-racial youth. Rates were 14.7% for persons reporting two or more races, 10.1% for African Americans, 9.5% for American Indians or Alaska Natives, 8.2% for Whites, 7.3% of Native Hawaiians or Other Pacific Islanders, 6.2% for Hispanics, and 3.6% for Asians. Hence, the use rates and order of which group was more at risk had changed (see Figure 5.1) below.

5.2.3 Need for professional training in substance abuse treatment and prevention

Although preventing and treating substance abuse is considered a vital strategy for improving the nation's health (Healthy People 2010), very few health care providers identify, diagnose, refer, or treat substance abuse disorders as readily or accurately as they do other chronic diseases or illnesses [13]. For example, only 19% of physicians feel comfortable about diagnosing alcoholism and 17% diagnosing drug abuse [14]. In addition, the failure to identify addictions in parents can lead to failures to prevent future medical problems or substance abuse disorders (SUDs) in the children of substance abusers. Hence, children of alcoholics and substance abusers, who are the highest risk group of children for later developing substance abuse disorders, often go unnoticed in pediatric medical visits and unserved with needed prevention services [15].

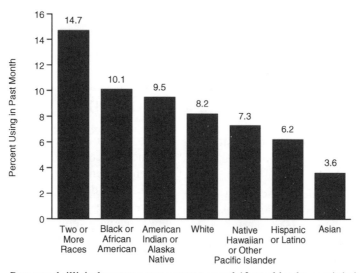

Figure 5.1 Past month illicit drug use among persons aged 12 or older, by race/ethnicity: 2008.

The training of health care and social services professionals in substance abuse is critical to broadening this approach of early identification and referral for services for children of substance abusers or the parents themselves. Most medical school or university professional training programs do not have adequate coverage of substance abuse issues and many have no courses preparing doctors, nurses, public health or health educators, social workers, psychologists, or psychiatrists in diagnosing, referring or treating substance abuse disorders [14]. Research suggests, however, that 91% of health care workers who have attended such a professional seminar report they are still using the techniques learned for early intervention even five years later. According to a survey done by the National Center on Addiction and Substance Abuse at Columbia University (CASA) 94% of primary care physicians and 40% of pediatricians who were presented with a classic description of a drug or alcohol addiction, failed to properly diagnose it [16]. In an attempt to rectify this problem, the U.S. Health Resources and Services Administration's Bureau of Health Professions collaborated with the Association for Medical Education and Research in Substance Abuse (AMERSA) to conduct a needs assessment and develop a Strategic Plan for Interdisciplinary Faculty Development [17]. They are also attempting to educate Congress on the need for funding for professional training programs for medical students in substance abuse disorders.

The Strategic Plan developed by AMERSA [17] recommends four core competencies in substance abuse disorders (SUD). All health professionals should: (1) receive education to enable them to understand SUD and accept the importance of treating SUD to improving health and wellbeing, (2) have basic knowledge of SUD and of evidence-based prevention approaches, (3) be aware of the benefits of SUD screening and appropriate intervention methods, and (4) have core knowledge of treatment methods and be able to initiate treatment or refer patients for further evaluation and treatment.

The core knowledge, skill, and attitude competencies for substance abuse specialists are also listed in the Strategic Plan ([14], p. 4). Twelve recommendations are also made to the Secretary of the Department of Health and Human Services and to the U.S. Surgeon General, including creating a Secretary's Advisory Committee on Health Professions Education in SUD, developing and disseminating a Surgeon General's Report on the State of Substance Use Disorders Prevention and Treatment in the United States, convening a National Forum on Health Professions Education on Substance Use Disorders, expanding federal support for faculty development programs in SUD including regional centers of excellence, and reviewing substance abuse specialist certification requirements to include core competencies.

5.3 CLINICAL COMORBIDITY

5.3.1 Mental health care providers and dual diagnosis

Mental health care specialists including psychiatrists, psychologists, psychiatric nurses, and social workers are rarely trained in the treatment of addictions. Although 91% of psychologists see clients with substance use disorders (SUDs) in their daily work, 75% have received no formal coursework on the subject, and 50% had no addiction training [18]. Many are trained to refer clients with SUD to substance abuse specialists, despite the high overlap of substance abuse and mental health problems. Very few specialty clinics treat clients with dual diagnoses. Providing care that is aimed at preventing substance abuse by mental health care providers is even rarer, but some community mental health clinics are beginning to offer parenting and family skills training interventions for the prevention of substance abuse in clients with conduct disorder problems.

5.4   CLINICAL COURSE OR ETIOLOGICAL PRECURSORS: RISK AND PROTECTIVE FACTORS

5.4.1   Causes of substance abuse

Research suggests that addiction is a "family disease" passed on from one generation to another. Risk of addiction appears to be high in certain types of families, primarily in certain Northern European families. Addiction is clearly not a disease of infection, but a disease of lifestyle – similar to heart disease, diabetes, skin cancer, and other chronic diseases we have not yet conquered. These diseases involve a genetic predisposition combined with environmental toxins or life stressors. Although the specific genes that increase a person's vulnerability to alcohol and drug dependency have not yet been discovered, there are enough twin, adoption, and family history studies to demonstrate a highly inheritable form of alcoholism and possibly drug dependency, called Type II Alcoholism or early-onset alcoholism [19]. This type of alcoholism affects about 25% of all alcoholics in treatment. About 75% of all addicts are suffering from a type of addiction caused primarily by environmental causes that are easier to prevent and treat. For instance, long term use or binging on alcohol or drugs can lead to neurotransmitter deficits in serotonin, dopamine, endorphins or other neurotransmitters that create a "brain disease". Primarily the prefrontal areas of the brain responsible for executive functioning such as decision making and considering consequences of actions is damaged. Even with treatment and healthy living (e.g., eating well balanced meals, sleeping at least 7 hours per night, exercising, reducing stress and staying connected to family and community) brain scans suggest it can take as long as two years for these neurotransmitters to regain their balance after quitting drug use. For this reason, psychotropic medications, particularly anti-depressants, can be an important element in the prevention of relapse or suicide during the initial treatment of substance abuse dependence and co-occurring mental health problems. Although shunned by the self-help or 12-step approach to alcohol or drug treatment, these neurotransmitters help to prevent relapse and self-medication of the withdrawal symptoms of anxiety and depression.

Because addictions are family diseases, the highest risk group for addictions are children of substance abusers – particularly those with a family history of early onset drug dependency (prior to 15 years of age). Research on phenotypes or the biological or physiological precursors of substance abuse suggest that the highest risk youth in this group are those who are: (1) over-stressed due to autonomic hyper reactivity and higher frequency brain waves resulting in self-medication using alcohol and drugs, (2) struggling in school because of verbal learning disorders from inherited pre-frontal cognitive dysfunction, and (3) thrill seeking and have poor problem solving resulting in risky choices of activities and friends [20]. Northern European boys who begin delinquent behaviors and regular use of alcohol or drugs prior to age 15 years of age are the most likely to become drug dependent. American Indian youth are also at-risk because some have inherited liver enzymes that break alcohol down rapidly and contribute to a high build-up of acetaldehyde in the blood stream that leads to loss of control. Although some Asian youth also have this genetic risk factor, the hopelessness, poverty, and breakdown of the American Indian family make them more vulnerable to alcohol and drug abuse.

5.4.2   Primary risk and protective factors for adolescents

Our understanding of the most salient risk or protective factor precursors of substance abuse has increased considerably in the last 20 years. Early in the 1980s, etiology researchers discovered using structural equation modeling or path analysis statistical methods that the final pathway or cause of substance abuse is peer influence [21]. Based on this information, the first effective prevention programs–peer resistance social skills training programs – were designed. In 1990, the primary author tested the causes of adolescent drug abuse and found that family environment was the root cause of substance abuse even if the final risk factor was drug-using peers [22]. It was not until 1998 that there was a large enough database to test a more refined model using structural equation modeling methods. This model, called the Social Ecology Model of Adolescent Substance Abuse [23] and shown in Figure 5.2, was tested with data from about 10 000 youth across CSAPs High Risk Youth programs.

The researchers discovered a more complex model of risk and protective factors that better inform prevention program selection than the earlier model. Three important family factors were found: (1) positive parent/child relationships characterized by love, care, respect, and support; (2) parent or caretaker monitoring, supervision, and discipline, and (3) communication of pro-social family values and expectations for not using tobacco, alcohol, or drugs [24]. Supervision and monitoring was even more important in preventing drug abuse in older adolescents than in preteens. Also, girls and ethnic minorities were slightly more influenced by their families than were Caucasian boys, who were more influenced by their community and neighborhood environment. Self control and school bonding and achievement were also important protective factors. A similar model with similar causal factors was tested by Ary and associates [25] and found to be good estimate of the most salient risk and protective factors for not just substance abuse, but also teen pregnancy, school failure, and delinquency. Hence, prevention programs addressing these substance abuse risk factors are also likely to be effective for multiple behavioral problems among adolescents.

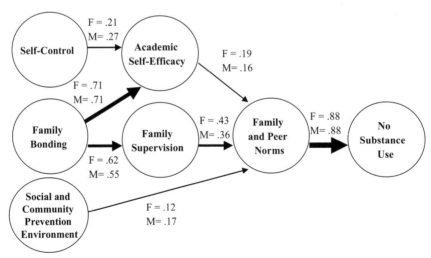

Figure 5.2 The social ecology model of adolescent substance abuse.

5.5 PREVENTION OF ALCOHOL AND DRUG USE AND ADDICTION AND ASSOCIATED MEDICAL DISORDERS

5.5.1 Evidence-based substance abuse prevention: what works

Prevention is now a science that has moved well beyond the days of "scare tactics", one shot drug prevention assemblies, and "Just Say No" Campaigns. Prevention practitioners are encouraged to use evidence-based prevention programs from lists of prevention programs determined to have multiple research studies showing effectiveness in reducing precursors of substance abuse. After collecting data on a number of local risk and protective factors in their local community or population, they are encouraged to select the most appropriate prevention programs. While there are many theories of the causes of drug abuse, the prevention field prefers to conduct their own needs assessments when designing comprehensive substance abuse prevention programs. Their purpose is to assure that the most salient risk or protective factors are known, so that the best prevention approaches can be selected to address these needs. Standardized needs assessment instruments have been recommended by the Center for Substance Abuse Prevention (CSAP) for use by states when determining how to best use their Block Grant funds for prevention. A number of communities and states also use the Communities That Care [26] student needs assessment survey and matching system to select evidence-based prevention programs.

5.5.2 Three types of primary prevention

When selecting the appropriate prevention program, it is important to be sure that one is selecting a program that is designed to meet the needs of the target population. For this reason, prevention programs are classified by the level of risks in the target population. The first designation by the Public Health Service (PHS) was to differentiate *primary* prevention, designed for lower risk non-users, from *secondary* prevention, designed for beginning initiators of drug use, from *tertiary* drug treatment, designed for addicts. A further refinement of the area of primary prevention by the Institute of Medicine in 1995 was to separate primary prevention into three types: (1) *universal prevention* targeting low risk general populations (i.e., students, families, or everyone in community through media campaigns), (2) *selective prevention* targeting at-risk groups of individuals (i.e., children of substance abusers or prisoners, American Indian children, etc.), and (3) *indicated prevention* targeting those with identified or diagnosed precursors of alcohol or drug abuse such as aggression, conduct disorders, thrill seeking, or delinquency.

The length or dosage of these prevention approaches differ for each of these three primary prevention types. Namely, *indicated* primary prevention programs are generally longer and address more risk and protective factors than do those for general populations of low risk youth in schools. Programs conducted for all youth in a school are considered *universal* prevention programs and are generally shorter in dosage, say five 1-hour sessions versus a complete summer school or after school programs lasting about 120 hours per high risk youth in an *indicated* prevention program for youth with conduct disorders.

Sometimes *indicated* prevention approaches are used to identify and prevent greater drug use in individuals who are experiencing early signs of substance use, however, technically this should be defined as secondary prevention. In 2003 ONDCP begun stressing secondary prevention approaches in its Demand Reduction Themes because non-dependent users do not perceive the negative consequences of drug use and introduce friends to drugs. This type of secondary prevention will require the adoption of effective early identification and intervention programs by school, workplace, social service, justice, and primary healthcare settings [13]. In February of 2008, President Bush released the 2008 National Drug Control Strategy of the White House Office of National Drug Control Policy, its goal being to reduce drug use in America by focusing on stopping use before it starts, healing America's drug users, and disrupting the market for illegal drugs [8]. A new 2010 national drug strategy is being created by the new ONDCP Director, Gil Kerlikowske, with broad community input.

5.5.3 Principles of effective prevention programs

There are certain characteristics of effective prevention programs, called principles of prevention, that can be used to judge the potential effectiveness of different prevention programs. Both the National Institute on Drug Abuse (NIDA) and the White House Office of National Drug Control Policy (ONDCP) have published lists of principles for substance abuse prevention programs. A broader "review of reviews" approach [27] was used to extract effectiveness principles from research articles on prevention programs in four content areas (e. g., substance abuse, risky sexual behavior, school failure, and juvenile delinquency and violence). Nine program characteristics were consistently associated with effective prevention programs: Theory-driven, comprehensive, appropriately-timed, socio-culturally relevant, sufficient dosage, varied teaching methods, positive relationships, well-trained staff, and outcome evaluation.

5.5.4 Effective substance abuse prevention programs for children and adolescents

If you consult the ONDCP web page for what they are funding in prevention, based on the 2008 National Drug Control Strategy all that is mentioned are approaches that are primarily punitive, namely, drug testing in schools and workplaces,

community coalitions (which are encouraged to conduct environmental strategies, such as increasing taxes, restrictive zoning, increasing sting operations to reduce access to minors, local regulations to restrict outlet licenses, etc.), drug courts and threats to remove children from drug using parents, brief screening interventions and referrals to treatment, and so on. What is missing is any mention of more positive youth or family skills training programs that are the primarily prevention approaches found to be effective by prevention researchers and expert review committees from different federal government offices, such as the National Institute on Drug Abuse (NIDA), National Institute on Alcohol Abuse and Alcoholism (NIAAA), Substance Abuse and Mental Health Services Administration's National Registry of Evidence-based Programs and Practices (SAMHSAs NREPP), the Centers for Disease Control and Prevention (CDC), or the Cochrane Collaboration Reviews in Medicine and Public Health.

Most of the research on the prevention of substance abuse has focused on junior high school-aged students, because students initiate substance use during this time. Less is known about the other developmental periods; however, we will discuss what is known about the most effective approaches for children and adolescents and college-aged youth or young adults in separate sections below.

From the ONDCP to individual states, funding agencies are requiring that funding be used only or primarily for evidence-based strategies. These best practices are those with research evidence in decreasing substance use, delaying age of onset of use, improving protective factors and decreasing risk factors related to later use. Fortunately, the research literature contains many evidence-based programs (EBPs) with sufficient effectiveness in Phase III Controlled Intervention Trials to warrant dissemination and adoption by schools and communities [28]. Effective EBP prevention approaches have been identified by federal review committees and are listed on these web sites (www.helpingamericasyouth.gov, www.nrepp. samhsa.gov, www.strengtheningfamilies.org). Syntheses of best practices in research-based prevention practices have been published by the Institute of Medicine [29]; CSAP [24], NIDA Preventing Drug Use Among Children and Adolescents [30] and researchers [26, 31–33].

A recent CSAP [34] cost benefit analysis of substance abuse prevention programs found that while youth-only programs have a lower cost they prevent many fewer youth from using alcohol and drugs. The highest percentages of youth are prevented from regular substance use if they are enrolled in a family intervention to change the total family system. For instance, after participation in the first author's Strengthening Families Program, 18% of youth were prevented from 30-day regular use of alcohol, 15% from marijuana, 11% from other drugs (11%), and even 7% prevented from tobacco use. Then next best program in effectiveness was also a parenting program. Hence, some youth-only programs such as All Stars has a very high cost-benefit ratio of $33, the number of youth prevented from using is less. Actually, if all the family members who attend are included in the benefits for the family interventions, the cost/benefit ratio of family programs would be equivalent to that of the youth-only programs.

The different types of approaches generally included in a comprehensive prevention plan include: child-only approaches, family-focused approaches, and community or school change approaches. Each of these are briefly reviewed below:

1. *School or Community-based, Child-only Prevention Approaches.* The most rigorously tested and effective approaches include social skills and life skills training [35] implemented in many settings (e.g., schools, community centers, churches, youth clubs, etc.). Other social competency areas include: mentoring, tutoring, alternative activities, recreation and leisure programs, wilderness challenge programs, and community service programs. School-based programs are most successful in reducing tobacco use, followed by drug use and then alcohol use. Characteristics of effective programs include involvement with positive role models or mentors, sufficient dosage or number of contact hours, interactive/coopera-

Table 5.1 Rank ordering of the effect sizes (d) of prevention programs [28]

1. Comprehensive Life Skills Training (0.30 ES)
2. "Other" Programs, peer-counseling, parent involvement, behavioral token economy, community partnerships (0.21 ES)
3. Social Influences (0.20 ES)
4. Health Education (0.18 ES)
5. DARE-type Programs (0.08 ES)
6. Knowledge-only Programs (0.07 ES)
7. Decisions, Values, and Attitudes Programs (0.06 ES)
8. Affective Education Only (0.04 ES)
9. Knowledge and Affective Education Programs (−0.05 ES)

tive learning, and booster sessions. Interventions run by mental health clinicians are two to three times more effective than programs implemented by peers, teachers, police officers, or "others". As shown in the following Table 5.1 [36], the effect size (ES) in reducing substance use varies considerably by type of child-only approach.

Comprehensive Life Skills Training Programs have the highest average effect size. These life skills training programs include refusal skills components, communication, problem solving, coping, social/dating, goal-setting, stress management, media literacy, and public commitments not to use. The average effect size for all these child-only programs (N = 206) was 0.10, which is quite small. The least effective program type which was found to produce slight negative effects is a combination of *Knowledge-only and Affective Education* Programs that were popular in the early 1980s. The recent highly publicized failure to prevent drug use of one of the most widely used school-based substance abuse prevention programs, DARE [37, 38], has highlighted the importance of enhanced dissemination of programs that work. Prevention programs using *interactive, skills training methods* to change behaviors as opposed to didactic lecture methods to change knowledge were more effective, particularly for minority youth. Donaldson and associates [39] concluded that the essential ingredient for success appears to be changing social norms or peer norms rather than refusal assertion training.

2. *Family Strengthening Approaches* The CSAP PEPS [24] review of family-focused approaches found that four approaches had sufficient research evidence to say they work for substance abuse prevention: (3) behavioral parent training, (4) family skills training, (5) family therapy, and (6) in-home family case management or support programs. Parent involvement in substance abuse prevention homework assignments with their children are recently showing promise as a cost effective approach [40, 41]. For additional reviews of effective family strengthening approaches see Kumpfer and Alvarado [42, 43], Alvarado and Kumpfer [44], Liddle *et al.* [45], Taylor and Biglan [46] or the OJJDP Strengthening America's Families web site at the University of Utah www.strengtheningfamilies.org.

The last national review of family strengthening approaches conducted in 2000 found about 35 evidence-based practices [43]. However, only 14 family programs have been tested in randomized control trials and seven independently replicated, meeting the criteria for the highest level of evidence of effectiveness or Exemplary I Programs. The Exemplary I family programs for 0–5 year old children include: Helping the Noncompliant Child and the Parent and Children's Training Series: The Incredible Years. The only Exemplary I rated program for families with 6–12 year old children is the first author's Strengthening Families Program. The only pre-teen and adolescent programs include in this category are: Functional Family Therapy, Multi-systemic Family Therapy, Preparing for the Drug Free Years, and Treatment Foster Care. Overall, family-focused approaches average effect sizes that are nine times larger than child-only prevention approaches (0.96 ES versus 0.10 ES) as shown in the Table 5.2 below.

In selecting the best family-focused program, the prevention practitioner must consider whether the target population needs a universal, selective, or indicated prevention program, the age of the child, and ethnicity or special need. A matrix of these

Table 5.2 Average effect sizes for universal school-based and family-based prevention programs ([28]; Tobler and Kumpfer, [47])

Prevention Intervention Approach	Average Effect Size
Knowledge plus Affective Education	−0.05
Affective Education	+0.04
Life or Social Skills Training	+0.30
Average Universal Child-only Approaches	+0.10
Parenting Skills Training	+0.31
Family Skills Training	+0.82
In-home Family Support	+1.62
Average Mean Family Interventions	+0.96

programs by prevention level and age is available on the www.strengtheningfamilies.org along with program descriptions and links to each of the different program developer's web sites.

The United Nations Office of Drugs and Crime [48] has developed with the first author an updated search for evidence-based parenting and family programs worldwide and identified 185 noteworthy programs. A protocol with steps for culturally adapting these EBPs was published, *Guide to Implementing Family Skills Training Programmes for Drug Abuse Prevention* [48]. This guide can be found on their web site and summarized in a recent publication by Kumpfer *et al.* [49].

1. *Community Coalition or Environmental Change Approaches.* There has been considerable political support and funding for community coalition or partnership approaches resulting in $95 million in funding for the ONDCP Drug-free Communities grants managed by CSAP. These grants provide about $125,000 per year for five years to over 750 communities [2]. Community coalition approaches typically include implementing a needs assessment and then planning and implementing multiple prevention strategies to create a comprehensive, coordinated community approach that changes the total community climate, norms, and implements multiple coordinated prevention strategies. These strategies can include individual, school, workplace, and family prevention approaches.

Examples of evidence-based community partnership or coalition approaches include the Midwestern Prevention Program [50] and the Communities That Care (CTC) model [26, 31]. Research on the Communities That Care model is being conducted on 41 matched communities in the seven states participating in their federally-funded *Diffusion Consortium Project* [51]. This project seeks to track the natural history of diffusion of risk- and protection-focused prevention planning and to assess the effectiveness of the CTC coalition model in reducing risk factors, increasing protective factors, and youth substance abuse. The CTC community coalition model is based on six phases: (1) needs assessment using standardized CTC school and community leaders surveys, (2) prioritization of risk and protective factors for intervention, (3) selection of tested interventions to address priority risk and protective factors, (4) implementation of science-based prevention interventions, (5) monitoring changes in targeted risk and protective factors, and (6) adjustment of interventions as indicated by performance monitoring data.

Most of the early evaluations of community coalitions focused primarily on process evaluations of what coalition characteristics contribute to successful implementation. These evaluations found that community coalitions were effective if they were organized in communities with a high degree of community readiness [52], progressed from planning to implementation within the first two years [50], implemented proven prevention strategies, and had strong empowering leaders who promote a shared vision, utilize members talents, and avoid or resolve conflict [53–55]. An analysis of the outcome results of a 10% sample of over 250 community coalitions funded by the Center for Substance Abuse Prevention (CSAP) found the community coalitions they funded were effective in reducing alcohol and drug abuse in 8th, 10th grade boys and adult males in communities having a coalition compared to matched communities without coalitions. The surprising effect was that community coalition efforts were not effective for girls or women and, in fact, resulted in increases in drug use in the 8th grade girls [54]. In reality, coalitions typically focus mainly on implementing environmental policy approaches that impact boys more than girls, such as their access to tobacco and alcohol. They often do not include funding for increasing school and family strengthening approaches which have more impact on reducing drug abuse in girls.

5.5.4.1   School climate change strategies

When the comprehensive community change approach is applied to schools it is called a school climate change strategy. The unique characteristic of this approach is that the prevention interventions adopted and implemented are only determined after a comprehensive needs assessment of risk and protective factors is conducted. Planning task forces within the schools, composed often of students, parents, counselors, teachers, and community leaders, use the needs assessment data to develop a strategic plan to address the most salient needs after exposure to evidence-based models. A few untested prevention approaches can be included, but most of the prevention strategies selected should be proven prevention models that are adapted to the local needs. Multiple strategies are often implemented to address multiple risk and protective factors, including the most effective social competency programs, family skills training programs, alcohol policy changes, awareness campaigns, improvements in teaching methods to include cooperative learning, tutoring, in-school suspension, recovery groups for students returning from treatment, personal growth classes for high-risk youth [30], and recreation and competency-building after school activities. Examples of effective school climate change approaches include Project PATHE [56], an adaptation of PATHE for high risk youth called Project HI PATHE [57] and the Child Development Project [58]. The goal of Safe and Drug-free Schools and the twenty first century Schools funded by the Department of Education is to modify school climate and to increase the coordination of community mental health, youth, and family treatment and prevention services. The State portion of this funding was eliminated in President Obama's budget this year in favor of a grant competition after a

Table 5.3 Prevention for FY 2010 and proposed for FY 2011: President Obama's FY 2011 budget request for drug control

	FY 2010 Appropriated	FY 2011 President's Budget Request	Net Change
Financial Services Appropriations Act			
Drug-Free Communities Act (DFCA)	$95 million	$85.5 million	−$9.5 million
Labor, HHS, Education Appropriations Act			
Substance Abuse Prevention and Treatment Block Grant	$1.799 billion	$1.799 billion	No change
Center for Substance Abuse Prevention (CSAP)	$202.2 million	$223 million	+ $20.8 million
Center for Substance Abuse Treatment (CSAT)	$454.6 million	$486.7 million	+ $32.1 million
Nat'l Institute on Drug Abuse (NIDA)	$1.060 billion	$1.094 billion	+ $34 million
Nat'l Institute on Alcohol Abuse and Alcoholism (NIAAA)	$462.3 million	$474.7 million	+ $12.4 million
State Grants portion of the SDFSC Program	—	—	No change
Successful, Safe and Healthy Students	—	$410 million	+ $410 million
State, Foreign Operations, and Related Programs Appropriations Act			
State Department's International Narcotics Control and Law Enforcement Demand Reduction Program	$14 million	$12.5 million	−$1.5 million
Commerce, Justice, Science and Related Agencies Appropriations Act			
Weed and Seed	$20 million	—	−$20 million
Byrne Criminal Justice Innovation Program	—	$40 million	+ $40 million

review of the quality of the program by the Rand Association. Unfortunately, the amount of funding was cut dramatically.

5.5.4.2 Policy change strategies

As mentioned above, community coalitions generally are most effective in mobilizing the community to advocate for changes in community policies and laws related to age of legal purchase, cost of tobacco or alcohol, availability, density of outlets, keg registration, server training, counter-advertising, warning labels, and other environmental changes [59]. Many of the alcohol misuse interventions are implemented through an overall community coalition mobilization approach [60]. Some examples of effective alcohol prevention-focused coalitions include the Community Trials Project [61] Saving Lives [62], and Project Northland [63].

Because states have less funding for substance abuse prevention services, they are turning to policy change strategies which cost less, and can generate increased tax dollars. Despite a recent upswing in the popularity of policy approaches, only a few policy approaches, such as increasing the age of purchase and the taxes and cost of tobacco or alcohol have been found to be effective in reducing substance use [64]. Attempts to reduce availability through sting operations to reduce sales of tobacco or alcohol have not been shown to reduce adolescent use, although they are effective in reducing sales to minors. For instance, Anti-drug community coalitions were mobilized by CSAP and States to implement the Syar Amendment aimed at reducing access by minors to tobacco purchases. Sting operations staffed by coalition youth when added to increased enforcement and limiting licenses resulted in a reduction in sales to minors from a average across all states of about 50 to 20% between 1997 and 2000. However, during this time tobacco use did not decreased in minors. Teens simply get adults to purchase for them or steal cigarettes.

The effects of community-based alcohol prevention policy approaches have been described as "quite modest," even though great effort and funds have been expended on them [65]. Cost-benefit studies are needed to help communities to understand how much improvement they can expect, in the light of alternative approaches. Increasing the cost of alcohol and increasing the legal drinking age or maintaining it at 21 years appears to be a very effective approach to reducing consumption among youth.

5.5.5 College aged youth substance abuse prevention

In the early 1990s, cohorts averaged greater substance use with advancing age. That is, substance use rates were lower among secondary school students than college-aged students who were lower than young adults. By 2006, these trends had reversed such that young adults (ages 19–28) reported the lowest use rates (32%), followed by college students (34%), then 12th grade students (37%). The reasons for this reversal are not clear, but if these kinds of trends continue it is clear that we may be facing another truly generational increase in substance use in the United States. The recent National Partnership youth survey that found large increases in alcohol and drug use in high school students suggests this increase in substance use is starting. In terms of college aged youth specifically, trends in annual illicit college drug use (excluding marijuana) since 1991 suggest a general upward trend with a low of 12.1% in 1994 and a high of 18.6% in 2005, with a marginal decrease of −0.1 in 2006, to 18.5% [66]. A pattern of higher rates of current alcohol use, binge alcohol use, and heavy alcohol use among full-time college students compared with rates for others aged 18 to 22 has remained consistent since 2002 [11] Among full-time college students in 2008, 61.0% were current drinkers, 40.5% binge drank, and 16.3% were heavy drinkers. Among those not enrolled full time in college, these rates were 54.2, 38.1, and 13.0%, respectively. Rates of current alcohol use and binge use for full-time college students decreased from 2007, when they were 63.7 and 43.6%, respectively.

The consequences of drinking among college students are severe. There are nearly 14,00 fatalities each year, 500,000 injuries and approximately 70,000 cases of sexual assault or date rape for students 18–24 [62]. Approximately 40% of college students binge drink, defined as five or more drinks in a row for men, four for women. In addition, it is estimated that 25% of college students have driven while impaired by alcohol [67]. According to the National Center on Addiction and Substance abuse at Columbia University in 2005, 49% of full time college students were binge drinking or abusing prescription or illegal drugs. Some colleges foster a culture where drinking is a rite of passage. Indeed, college campuses where Greek systems (fraternity and sorority) or sports teams predominate experience higher rates of alcohol misuse and associated problems [68]. Wagenaar and Toomey [64] suggested that these college campuses and their surrounding campus community encourage excessive drinking with lax enforcement of minimum age laws for use, buying or serving alcohol.

Despite the documented risk to self and others, few prevention strategies aimed at college-age drinking have been successful [67]. The Department of Education's Fund for the Improvement of Post-secondary Education (FIPSE) was very successful in funding drug prevention centers on college campuses nationwide. Many colleges continued these prevention centers when the seed funding ended. The primary prevention approaches adopted in colleges are: media campaigns, alcohol and drug policy revisions, early identification and referrals to counseling. Changing the perception that most college students are substance users through published needs assessment surveys is another effective approach [69].

Little research exists on what prevention strategies work for college students. The NIAAA Task Force [67] suggests that generalized strategies effective with adults should work (e.g., increasing taxes and cost of alcohol, increasing enforcement and consequences of minimum legal drinking age laws and driving under the influence, and instituting policies and training for servers of alcoholic beverages). Strategies recommended specific for college/university students include normative education and stress/coping strategies as well as correcting their false beliefs about the effects of alcohol and increasing their motivation to reduce drinking. Combining approaches into a comprehensive campus-wide approach should be more effective. More information on the NIAAA Task Force's report can be found at http://www.collegedrinking-prevention.gov.

5.5.6 Effective prevention strategies for adults

5.5.6.1 FAS/FDS PREVENTION FOR PREGNANT WOMEN

Because of the increasing incidence and prevalence of fetal alcohol and drug syndrome (FAS/FDS), particularly for American Indian women [70], Congress has earmarked funding in the past few years for effective detection and prevention programs. Little is known about how to prevent alcohol and drug use in pregnant women, other than to increase education and public awareness concerning the negative effects of substance use on the developing fetus. Preventing substance use altogether in girls is the most effective prevention approach, which is discussed in detail below in a separate section on Gender Specific Prevention. Most women understand that there can be negative impact on the development of the baby in utero, but many think they have to be heavy drinkers or drug users to have a noticeable negative effect. In fact, you can just be unlucky and drink on the critical day when the effect of alcohol will have a devastating impact on the baby. Hence, the best prevention of FAS/FDS is to avoid all substance use during pregnancy. Chasnoff [71] reported that since the brain of the fetus is developing the most in the last trimester, much of the damage to the prefrontal cortex and other areas of the brain can be avoided if the mother can be alcohol, tobacco and drug free by the last three months. This

is a very hopeful and motivating message for clinicians to provide to pregnant addicts.

5.5.6.2 Substance abuse prevention in workplaces

The worksite is one of the most influential settings in addition to primary health care settings where health education can take place and health behaviors can be improved [72]. Healthy People 2010 identified two specific goals for increasing health promotion programs in the worksite setting. Goal 7-5 is to "*Increase the proportion of worksites that offer a comprehensive employee health promotion program to their employees*". A target of 75% was set, and the baseline in 1999 was 33–50% of worksites having such programs [73]. Goal 7-6 is to "*Increase the proportion of employees who participate in employer-sponsored health promotion activities* [74]." Again the target was 75% and the baseline in 1999 was 61%. The Healthy People 2010 report noted that the highest risk employees are least likely to participate in worksite wellness programs and that many such programs lack comprehensive design or sufficient duration.

Workplaces are more focused on secondary substance abuse prevention rather than primary prevention. Employee assistance programs (EAPs) with early identification, screening, and referrals for treatment are the most popular approaches. Drug testing upon hire is being required by many employers today. Some employers have treatment aftercare groups, self-help groups, and also provide parent support or training groups on-site. General health and wellness employee programs can also be considered as prevention programs for substance abuse although they have generally not been evaluated this way [75].

One recent review of 24 studies on worksite health behavior interventions showed that only 8% of studies reported any maintenance data [76]. The authors suggested the need for more emphasis on the representativeness of employees, the setting of the program, and longer term results. Over 122 research studies have shown cost effectiveness in the vast majority of worksite programs [77].

5.5.6.3 Substance abuse prevention in the elderly

Substance misuse by the elderly is a growing health concern in the United States. The elderly comprise about 13% of the U.S. population ([78], p. 280) and it is estimated that by 2030 this group will nearly double in size to over 70 million individuals and will represent 20% of the U. S. population. This population increase may concomitantly double the size of the problems with substance abuse among this group. While there is currently a low prevalence of illicit drug use among the elderly, as baby boomers age we may see a continuation of the trends reported by SAMHSA of people over 50 entering treatment programs for heroin abuse alone rose from 7,000 to 27,000 between 1992 and 2002, people being treated for cocaine addiction increased from about 3,000 to 13,000 and the percent of older adults in treatment who abuse opiates, which are found in many prescription painkillers, increased from 6.8 to 12% from 1995 to 2002 [79]. While the rates of abuse of prescription drugs in the elderly is unknown, we do know that the elderly are more likely to be prescribed addictive medication for pain and poor sleep thus making them more likely to become addicted and increases the potential for prescription drug interactions.

While prescription drug abuse is rampant and problematic among the elderly, the most common drug of choice among the elderly is alcohol. When examining the overall arrest patterns, 46% of adult arrests are for drunkenness in contrast to 82% for senior citizens over 60 years old. There are fewer heavy drinkers among the elderly (9% versus 26% for 20 year-olds) but they face increased vulnerability to negative side effects (e.g., depression, sleep problems, cognitive impairment, liver disease, accidents, and injury) and harmful drug interactions. Recent data suggests that approximately 10–15% of those in treatment for alcohol

abuse are elderly who began drinking later in life and became addicted.

Because seniors seek health care more often, the most effective prevention approaches for the elderly focus on training health care professionals to monitor medication misuse and to educate seniors about alcohol and drug interactions [80, 81]. Interpersonal communication skills training for the elderly and listing or bringing in a "brown bag" all drugs (prescription, over-the-counter, and herbal drugs) being taken and asking health care professionals about possible drug interactions is also effective [82]. Seniors are willing to read extensively about the relationship between drinking, medications use and their health and act upon this information. Education and counseling have proven to be the most effective preventive measures for this population. Prevention approaches should be tailored to the unique needs, stressors, social, cognitive and physical losses, and delivery systems typical of seniors [78].

The Michigan Alcohol Screening Test-Geriatric Version (MAST-G) or Short MAST-G [83] or CAGE can be administered if alcohol misuse is a concern. It should be combined with a brief intervention, education, and referral for further assessments and treatment services, such as the Clear Horizons smoking cessation program adapted for the elderly and the Community Older Persons Alcohol (COPA) Program [84].

5.5.7 The need for better dissemination and adoption of evidence-based prevention programs

Despite the existence of a number of effective prevention programs, a gap has existed between what practitioners are doing and what works resulting in a need to improve the dissemination of effective prevention programs [85]. Only about 10% of all substance abuse prevention programs are research-based and possibly only about 25% of these are implemented with fidelity. Academically-based researchers are not trained in marketing. They need support by the federal and state governments in marketing and training. National and regional conferences have been conducted in the last few years by the Center for Substance Abuse Prevention, NIDA, NIAAA, OJJDP, and Department of Education to showcase their pick of the most effective prevention programs. CSAP hosted a symposium with written papers on how to improve dissemination of evidence-based practices [86].

Major gaps are occurring in the linkage between product research and product dissemination. In an ideal world, the proposed flow of research from basic biomedical research through the five phases of research to implementation of research-based models in nationwide prevention and health services programs [87] would be smooth. This review of the research and practice literature suggests, unfortunately, that the most commonly-used programs are synonymous with the most highly commercially marketed programs. These programs are not the same as the more effective, research-based programs. While some very popular prevention programs are based on similar principles, they are generally not of equal intensity, do not control fidelity as well, or do not have well trained implementers.

The research-based programs with effectiveness results are generally those developed and tested in federally-funded Phase III clinical trials generally by university researchers. Unfortunately, few of these university researchers have the time or the knowledge to become commercial marketers to disseminate their programs. Additional support is needed by the funding sources to support the dissemination of research-based approaches. Practitioners also have a responsibility to ask the hard questions about the effectiveness of the programs they are planning to implement and not just select a prevention program because it looks good or would be fun to implement. Even when health care practitioners are aware of the most effective programs, they should not randomly select one of them. Because there is no one best prevention approach, a major criterion in improving prevention effectiveness is matching the prevention intervention to the risk characteristics of the proposed participants.

5.5.7.1 Advocacy for prevention funding and evidence-based prevention practices

Prevention funding has not increased at the rate of the increase in drug abuse in youth. See Figure 5.3 below.

In addition, fundingfor prevention has not increased as much as drug treatment funding and actually has decreased by 25% in recent years because of the lack of advocacy by the prevention field compared to the drug treatment field [2]. Also, most of the 20% of the State Block Grant substance abuse prevention funds are controlled

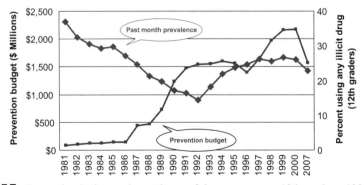

Figure 5.3 Prevention budget and prevalence of drug use among 12th graders: 1981–2007.

by more powerful drug treatment providers, who also provide drug prevention programs so as to historically maintain their funding levels. Additionally the new SPF SIG grants to states mandate the prevention funds can only be used for programs targeting youth over 12 years of age. This is a major problem because one in six "tweens" under the age of 12 are already using alcohol, tobacco, and drugs. Youth who already use alcohol are less receptive to prevention programs aimed at all students [88]. Intervening earlier in elementary school would allow for truly universal prevention that would also provide support for high-risk using students.

Prevention providers who have federal funding were warned inappropriately in the early 1990s that they could not educate or advocate for substance abuse prevention, if they received federal funding. This is not true. What is true is that a prevention agency cannot use their federal funding to lobby congressional staff or members to vote for a specific bill. However, they can use other funds to educate and advocate more generally for the importance of drug prevention in a comprehensive National Drug Control Strategy.

5.5.7.2 *Funding for substance abuse prevention and treatment*

Efforts by multiple federal agencies to reduce the supply of drugs into this country through the massive War on Drugs launched in 1989 with the new Drug Czar and White House Office of National Drug Control Policy (ONDCP) appears to have failed, at least for our nation's youth. With high demand in young people, illicit drugs are a 60 billion dollar industry costing this nation over 110 billion yearly. When the alcohol misuse cost of over $166 billion is added, the total economic cost of substance abuse is estimated at over 276 billion yearly by 1995 [1]. Health and mental health problems related to aggressive, violent, and delinquent behaviors are also on the rise and are significantly related to substance abuse [11]. The current "get tough" on drug abusers approach, which has focused on criminal penalties and incar-

ceration, is not working. The number of people incarcerated for drug problems has more than doubled, as has the number of prisons. Funding for drug treatment and prevention has not kept pace with the need. While the National Drug Control Budget rose 57% from $12.2 billion to $19.2 billion between 1994 and 2001, it has decreased to 15.1 billion in FY 2010 [2]. Prevention and treatment funding increased only 33% and 44% respectively. The only funded area to have a decrease in the FY 2010 budget was prevention decreasing from 1.8 to 1.6 billion. Hence, only about 11% of the drug control budget is spent on prevention. It is very difficult to reduce the demand for drugs, without increased funding for drug prevention.

Despite these increases in funding, the "War on Drugs" has been criticized for its failure to reduce drug use [89] or produce a consistent and fair legal policy [90]. Although demand reduction prevention approaches have been found to be more effective than supply reduction approaches, the funding for drug prevention rose only 33%. In comparison, the funding for international supply reduction increased 175% [1]. Overall, about 90% of U.S. funding for the "War on Drugs" goes for supply reduction including funding for interdiction, crop eradication, and border patrols. Despite this massive funding for supply reduction, adolescents report drugs are as available as in 1989 [10]. What emerges from this picture is an erosion of funding for prevention in this nation, which can only lead to increased substance use in the future.

It is time for health care professionals to become more vocal and involved in local and national drug policy making. They should promote increased prevention funding and support a public health approach, rather than a criminal justice and interdiction approach, to the drug problem.

5.5.7.3 *What health care professionals can do to reduce substance abuse*

First and foremost, they need to become better educated about substance abuse disorders and advocate for prevention and treatment. Because of the lack of strong advocacy groups for substance abuse prevention, prevention specialists and health care professionals are encouraged to advocate individually and in mass at the county, state, and national level. Joining CADCA, the Community Anti-drug Abuse Coalitions of America, is a good first step. This national organization in Alexandria, Virginia coordinates advocacy for substance abuse prevention with e-mail alerts. They also run a training institute for substance abuse prevention and a national conference to improve the effectiveness of community coalitions.

Over 4,000 communities in the United States have their own community substance abuse prevention coalition. Although funding only began in 1997, over 650 communities currently receive funding from the White House Office of National Drug Control Policy's Drug Free Communities Support Program administered through the SAMHSA Center for Substance Abuse Prevention. Because they only receive about $125,000 per year, these community coalitions are in need of support from the health care professionals to serve as advisors, planners, and even volunteers in implementing needs assessments or prevention programs. Local prevention providers should also advocate for more effective, evidence-based prevention in their communities. Because of the highly publicized lack of effectiveness of the DARE program, many school boards and mayors are looking for more effective approaches. Educating mayors, county commissioners, and state legislatures that substance abuse prevention programs not only work in reducing alcohol and drug misuse, but can substantially reduce crime, violence, delinquency, teen pregnancy, school failure, and health care costs is a role that prevention specialists can play. In addition these professionals, who often serve on boards of directors of private, non-profit agencies serving children and families, can advocate for the implementation of evidence-based substance abuse prevention practices.

REFERENCES

1. ONDCP (2001) Office of National Drug Control Policy, Agency Accomplishments and Significant Actions, January 1993-December 2000, White House, Executive Office of the President of the United States.

2. ONDCP (2010) National Drug Control Strategy: 2010. White House, Executive Office of the President of the United States. Retrieved from http://www.whitehouse-drugpolicy.gov/index.html.

3. National Institute of Health (2002) NICAAA and NOFAS launch awareness campaign in the District of Columbia Retrieved April 6, 2006, from www.nih.gov/news/pr/mar2002/niaaa-05.htm.

4. Johnston, L.D., O'Malley, P.M. and Bachman, J.G. (2002) Monitoring the Future national survey results on drug use, 1975-2001. Volume I: Secondary school students (NIH Publication No. 02-5106). Bethesda, MD: National Institute on Drug Abuse, c. 492 pp.

5. Tobler, N.S. and Kumpfer, K.L. (2000) Meta-analysis of Family Based Strengthening Programs. Report to CSAP/SAMHSA, Rockville, MD.

6. Centers for Disease Control and Prevention (CDC) (2008) Trends in the prevalence of tobacco use: National YRBS 1991 to 2007.Retrieved on June 5, 2008 from http://www.cdc.gov/HealthyYouth/yrbs/trends.htm.

7. OAS (2004) National Survey on Drug Use and Health, National Findings, SAMHSA, Office of Applied Studies, U.S. Department of Health and Human Services. Retrieved from http://www.oas.samhsa.gov/nsduh/2k4nsduh/2k4results/2k4results.htm.

8. ONDCP (2008) National Drug Control Strategy: 2008. White House, Executive Office of the President of the United States. Retrieved from http://www.whitehouse-drugpolicy.gov/index.html.

9. OAS (2000) National Survey on Drug Use and Health, National Findings, SAMHSA, Office of Applied Studies, Rockville, MD.

10. Johnston, L.D., O'Malley, P.M., Bachman, J.G. and Schulenberg, J.E. (2007) Monitoring the Future national survey results on drug use, 1975-2006. Volume I: Secondary school students (NIH Publication No. 07-6205). Bethesda, MD: National Institute on Drug Abuse.

11. OAS (2008) National Survey on Drug Use and Health, National Findings, SAMHSA, Office of Applied Studies, retrieved from www.oas.samhsa.gov, April 2010.

12. Kumpfer, K.L., Smith, P. and Franklin Summerhays, J. (2008) A wake -up call to the prevention field: Are prevention programs for substance use effective for girls? *Subst. Use Misuse*, **43** (8), 978–1001.

13. Fleming, M.F. (2002) Screening, assessment, and intervention for substance use disorders. *Subst. Abuse*, Supplement to vol. **23** (3), 47–66.

14. Haack, M.R. and Adger, H. (2002) Executive summary. *Subst. Abuse*, Supplement to Vol. **23** (3), 1–24.

15. Chassin, L., Carle, A., Nissim-Saat, D. and Kumpfer, K. L. (2004) Fostering resilience in children of alcoholic parents, in *Investing in Children, Youth, Families, and Communities: Strengths-based Research and Policy*, (ed. K.I. Maton), American Psychology Association Books, Washington, D.C. [PMID: 15645706].

16. AMERSA (2005) Association for Medical Education and Research in Substance Abuse. http://www.amersa. org/index.asp.

17. AMERSA (2002; 2005) Project Mainstream: Strategic Plan. AMERSA, Providence, RI or order on line.

18. Anavai, M.P., Tauge, D.O., Ja, D.Y. and Duran, E.F. (1999) The status of psychologists training about and treatment of substance-abusing clients. *J. Psychoactive Drugs*, **31**, 441–444.

19. Kumpfer, K.L. (1987) Special populations: etiology and prevention of vulnerability to chemical dependency in children of substance abusers, in *Youth at High Risk for Substance Abuse* (eds B.S. Brown and A.R. Mills), National Institute on Drug Abuse Monograph, DHHS Publication Number (ADM) 90-1537. Supt. of Doc., U.S. Government Printing Office, Washington, DC, pp. 1–71.

20. Tarter, R. and Mezzich, A. (1992) Ontogeny of substance abuse: Perspectives and findings, in *Vulnerability to Drug Abuse*, (eds M. Glantz and R. Pickens), American Psychiatric Association, Washington D.C., pp. 149–177.

21. Newcomb, M.D. and Bentler, P.M. (1989) Substance use and abuse among children and teenagers. *Am. Psychol.*, **44**, 242–248.

22. Kumpfer, K.L. and Turner, C.W. (1990–1991) The social ecology model of adolescent substance abuse: Implications for prevention. *Int. J. Addict.*, **25** (4A), 435–463.

23. Kumpfer, K.L., Alvarado, R. and Whiteside, H.O. (2003) Family-based interventions for substance abuse prevention. *Subst. Use Misuse*, **38** (11–13), 1759–1789 [PMID: 14582577].

24. Center for Substance Abuse Prevention (1998) Preventing substance abuse among children and adolescents: Family-centered approaches. Prevention Enhancement Protocols System (PEPS), DHHS Publication No. (SMA) 3223-FY'98, Superintendent of Documents, U.S. Government Printing Office, Washington, DC.

25. Ary, D.V., Duncan, T.E., Duncan, S.C. and Hops, H. (1999) Adolescent problem behavior: The influence of parents and peers. *Behav. Res. Ther.*, **37**, 217–230.

26. Hawkins, D. and Catalano, R. (1999) *Communities That Care*, 2nd edn, Jossey-Bass, San Francisco, CA.

27. Nation, M., Kumpfer, K.L., Crusto, C.A., Wandersman, A., Seybolt, D., Morrissey-Kane, E. and Davino, K.

(2003) What works in prevention: Principles of effective prevention programs. *Am. Psychol.*, **58** (6/7), 449–456 [PMID: 12971191].

28. Tobler, N. and Stratton, H. (1997) Effectiveness of school-based drug prevention programs: A meta-analysis of the research. *J. Primary Prevention*, **18** (1), 71–128.

29. IOM Institute of Medicine (IOM) (1995) *Reducing Risks for Mental Disorders: Frontiers for Preventive Intervention Research*, (eds Mrazek, P.J. and Haggerty, R.J.), Washington, DC, National Academy Press.

30. NIDA (2008) Preventing Drug Use Among Children and Adolescents: A Research-based Guide.

31. Hawkins, J. and Catalano, R. (1992) *Communities that Care: Action for Drug Abuse Prevention*, Jossey-Bass, San Francisco, CA.

32. Kumpfer, K.L. and Alder, S. (2002) Dissemination of research-based family strengthening interventions for the prevention of substance abuse, in *Handbook for Drug Abuse Prevention, Theory, Science, and Practice*, (eds Z. Sloboda and W. Bukoski), Kluwer Academic/ Plenum, New York.

33. Webster-Stratton, C. and Taylor, T. (2000) Nipping early risk factors in the bud: Preventing substance abuse, delinquency, and violence in adolescence through interventions targeted at young children 0-8 years. *Prev Sci*, **2** (3), 165–192.

34. Miller, T. and Hendrie, D. (2008) The Substance Abuse Prevention: Dollars and Sense: A Cost-benefit Analysis. retrieved from web www.samhsa.gov.

35. Botvin, G.J. (1995) Drug abuse prevention in school settings, in *Drug Abuse Prevention with Multiethnic Youth*, (eds G.J. Botvin, S. Schinke and M.A. Orlandi), Sage Publications, Thousand Oaks, CA, pp. 169–192.

36. Tobler, N.S., Roona, M.R., Ochshorn, P., *et al.* (2000) School-based adolescent drug prevention programs: 1998 meta-analysis. *J. Primary Prevention*, **20**, 275–337.

37. Ennett, S.T., Tobler, N.S., Ringwalt, C. and Flewelling, R. (1994) How effective is Drug Abuse Resistance Education? A meta-analysis of Project DARE evaluations. *Am J Health*, **84** (9), 1394–1401.

38. Harrington, N., Hoyle, R., Giles, S. and Hansen, W. (2000) The all-stars prevention program, in *Improving Prevention Effectiveness*, (eds W.B. Hansen, S.M. Giles and M.D. Fearnow-Kenney), Tanglewood Research, Inc., Greensboro, NC.

39. Donaldson, S., Sussman, S., McKinnon, D., *et al.* (1996) Drug abuse prevention programming: Do we know what content works? *Am. Behav. Sci.*, **31** (7), 868–884.

40. Bauman, K.E., Foshee, V.A., Ennett, S.T., *et al.* (2001) Family matters: A family-directed program designed to

prevent adolescent tobacco and alcohol use. *Health Promot Pract*, **2**, 81–96.

41. Bauman, K.E., Ennett, S.T., Foshee, V.A., *et al.* (2000) Influence of a family-directed program on adolescent cigarette and alcohol cessation. *Prev Sci*, **1** (4), 227–237.

42. Kumpfer, K.L. and Alvarado, R. (1998) Effective Family Strengthening Interventions. Juvenile Justice Bulletin, Family Strengthening Series. OJJDP, November, 1998.

43. Kumpfer, K.L. and Alvarado, R. (2003) Family strengthening approaches for the prevention of youth problem behaviors. *Am. Psychol.*, **58** (6/7), 457–465 [PMID: 12971192].

44. Alvarado, R. and Kumpfer, K.L. (2000) Strengthening America's families. *Juvenile Justice*, **7** (2), 8–18.

45. Liddle, H.A., Santisteban, D., Levant, R. and Bray, J. (2002) *Family Psychology: Science-Based Interventions*, American Psychological Association Press, Washington, D.C.

46. Taylor, T.K. and Biglan, A. (1998) Behavioral family interventions for improving child rearing: A review of the literature for clinicians and policy makers. *Clin Child Fam Psych*, **1**, 41–60.

47. Tobeler, N. and Kumpfer, K.L., (2001). Meta-analysis of effectiveness of family strengthening approaches. Report to CSAP CSAP/SAMHSA, Rockville, MD.

48. UNODC (2009) *Guide to Implementing Family Skills Training Programmes for Drug Abuse Prevention*, United Nations, New York, ISBN #978-92-1-148238-6.

49. Kumpfer, K.L., Pinyuchon, M., de Melo, A. and Whiteside, H. (2008) Cultural adaptation process for international dissemination of the Strengthening Families Program (SFP). *Eval Health Prof*, **33** (2), 226–239.

50. Pentz, M. (1995) Prevention research in multiethnic communities: Developing community support and collaboration, and adapting research methods, in *Drug Abuse Prevention with Multi-Ethnic Youth*, (eds G.J. Botvin, S. Schinke and M.O. Orlandi), Sage, Thousand Oaks, CA, pp. 193–214.

51. Hawkins, D., Catalano, R. and Arthur, M. (2000) *Diffusion Consortium Project Briefing for Federal Funding Agencies*, Social Development Research, Washington, D.C.

52. Kumpfer, K.L., Whiteside, H.O. and Wandersman, A. (1997) *Community Readiness for Drug Abuse Prevention: Issues, Tips, and Tools*, National Institute on Drug Abuse, Rockvillle, MD, NIH Publication No. 97-4111, pp. 1–172.

53. Kumpfer, K.L., Turner, C., Hopkins, R. and Librett, J. (1993) Leadership and team effectiveness in community partnerships for the prevention of alcohol and other drug abuse. *Health Educ Res*, **8** (3), 359–374.

54. Yin, R.K., Kaftarian, S., Yu, P. and Jansen, M. (1997) Outcomes from CSAP's Community Partnership Program: Findings from the National Cross-site Evaluation. *Eval. Program Plann.*, **20**, 345–355.

55. Yin, R. and Ware, A. (2000) Using outcome data to evaluate community drug prevention initiatives: Pushing the state-of-the-art. *Am. J. Commun. Psychol.*, **28**, 323–338.

56. Gottfredson, D. (1986) An empirical test of school-based environmental and individual interventions to reduce the risk of delinquent behavior. *Criminology*, **24**, 705–730.

57. Kumpfer, K.L., Turner, C. and Alvarado, R. (1991) A community change model for school health promotion. *J. Health Educ.*, **22**, 94–110.

58. Schaps, E., Battistich, V. and Solomon, D. (1997) School as a caring community: A key to character, in *The Construction of Children's Character. 96th Yearbook of the National Society for the Study of Education Part 2*, (ed. A. Molnar), The National Society for the Study of Education, Chicago, Il, pp. 127–139.

59. Grube, J. and Nygaard, P. (2000) Adolescent drinking and alcohol policy. Paper presented at The Alcohol Policy and the Public Good: An International Conference; February, 2000; Copenhagen, Denmark.

60. NIAAA (2000) Community-based prevention approaches, in *Prev Res.*, NIAAA, Rockville, MD, pp. 397–411.

61. Holder, H., Saltz, R., Grube, *et al.* (1997) Summing up: Lessons from a comprehensive community prevention trial. *Addiction*, **92** (Suppl. 2), S293–S301.

62. Hingson, R.W., Heeren, T., Zakocs, R.C., *et al.* (2002) Magnitude of alcohol-related mortality and morbidity among U.S. college students ages 18–24. *J. Stud. Alcohol*, **63** (2), 136–144.

63. Perry, C.L., Pirie, P., Holder, W., *et al.* (1990) Parent involvement in cigarette smoking prevention: Two pilot evaluations of the "Unpuffables Program". *J. School Health*, **60** (9), 443–447.

64. Wagenaar, A.C. and Toomey, T.L. (2000) Alcohol policy: Gaps between legislative action and current research. *Contemp. Drug Probl.*, **27**, 681–733.

65. Koepsell, T.D., Diehr, P.H., Cheadle, A. and Kristal, A. (1995) Invited commentary: symposium on community intervention trials. *Am. J. Epidemiol.*, **142**, 594–599.

66. Johnston, L.D., O'Malley, P.M., Bachman, J.G. and Schulenberg, J.E. (2006) Monitoring the Future national survey results on drug use, 1975–2005: Volume II, College students and adults ages 19–45 (NIH Publication No. 06-5884). Bethesda, MD: National Institute on Drug Abuse.

67. NIAAA (2002) A call to action: Changing the culture of drinking at U.S. colleges. Task Force Report. Co-chairs M. Goldman and E. Malloy, Rockville, MD: NIAAA, retrieved from http://www.collegedrinking-prevention.gov.

68. Knight, J.R., Wechsler, H., Kuo, M., *et al.* (2002) Alcohol abuse and dependence among U.S. college students. *J. Stud. Alcohol*, **55** (3), 425–435.

69. Perkins, H. and Berkowitz, A. (1989) Stability and contradiction in college students' drinking following a drinking age law change. *J. Alcohol Drug Educ.*, **35**, 60–77.

70. Streissguth, A. (2001) Recent advances in fetal alcohol syndrome and alcohol use in pregnancy, in *Alcohol in Health and Disease*, (eds D.P. Agarwal and H.K. Seitz), Marcel Dekker, Inc., New York, NY, US, pp. 303–324.

71. Chasnoff, I. (2009) Impact on the developing brain of fetal alcohol and drug abuse. Presentation to ACF Children's Bureau grantee conference, Crystal City, Virginia, July 2009.

72. Chapman, L.S. (2004) Expert Opinions on "best practices" in worksite health promotion. *Am. J. Health Promot.*, **18** (6), 1–6.

73. Lusk, S.L. and Raymond, D. (2002) Impacting health through the worksite, in *Nursing Clinics of North America: Lifestyle Modification*, (ed. M. Wierenga), W.B. Saunders Company, Philadelphia, pp. 247–256.

74. U.S. Department of Health and Human Services (USDHHS) (2000) *Healthy People 2010*, 2nd edn, U.S. Government Printing Office, Washington, DC, December 2003.

75. Poole, K., Kumpfer, K. and Pett, M. (2001) The impact of an incentive-based worksite health promotion program on modifiable health risk factors. *Am. J. Health Promot.*, **16** (1), 21–26.

76. Bull, S.S., Gillette, C., Glasgow, R.E. and Estabrooks, P. (2003) Work site health promotion research: To what extent can we generalize the results and what is needed to translate research to practice? *Health Educ. Behav.*, **30** (5), 537–549.

77. Pelletier, K.R. (2005) A review and analysis of the clinical and cost-effectiveness studies of comprehensiev health promotion and disease management programs at the worksite. *J. Occup. Environ. Med.*, **47** (10), 1051–1058.

78. Lisansky-Gomberg, E. (2000) Substance abuse disorders, in *Psychopathology in Later Adulthood*, (ed. K.S.

Whitbourne), Wiley series on adulthood and aging, John Wiley & Sons, Inc., New York, NY, US, pp. 277–298.

79. Menninger, J. (2002) Assessment and treatment of alcoholism and substance-related disorders in the elderly. *B Menninger Clin*, **66** (2), 166–183.

80. Barry, K.L., Blow, F.C. and Oslin, D.W. (2002) Substance abuse in older adults: Review and recommendations for education and practice in medical settings. *Subst. Abuse*, Supplement to vol. **23** (3), 105–132.

81. Fink, A., Beck, J. and Wittrock, M. (2001) Informing older adults about non-hazardous, hazardous, and harmful alcohol use. *Patient Educ. Couns.*, **45** (2), 133–141.

82. Beisecker, A. (1991) Interpersonal communication strategies to prevent drug abuse by health professionals and the elderly: Contributions of the health belief model. *Health Commun.*, **3** (4), 241–250.

83. Blow, F.C., Brower, K.J., Schulenberg, *et al.* (1992) The Michigan Screening Test-Geriatric Version (MAST-G): A new elderly specific screening instrument. *Alcohol. Clin. Exp. Res.*, **16** (2), 372.

84. Oslin, D.W. and Holden, R. (2002) Recognition and assessment of alcohol and drug dependence in the elderly, in *Treating Alcohol and Drug Abuse in the Elderly*, (eds A.M. Gurnack, R. Atkinson and N.J Osgood.), Springer Publishing Company, NY, NY, pp. 11–31.

85. Biglan, A., Mrazek, P., Carnine, D. and Flay, R. (2003) The integration of research and practice in the prevention of youth problem behaviors. (eds R. Weissberg and K. Kumpfer), Special Issue, *Am. Psychol.*, **58** (6/7), 433–440.

86. Backer, T. and Rogers, E. (1999) Dissemination Best Practices Workshop Briefing Paper: State-of-the-art Review on Dissemination Research and Dissemination Partnership. Encino, CA: NCAP.

87. Jansen, M.A., Glynn, T. and Howard, J. (1996) Prevention of alcohol, tobacco, and other drugs abuse: Federal efforts to stimulate prevention research. *Am. Behav. Sci.*, **39** (7), 790–801.

88. Pasch, K.E., Perry, C.L., Stigler, M. and Komro, K.A. (2009) Sixth grade students who use alcohol: Do we need primary prevention programs for 'tweens'. *Health Educ. Behav.*, (Sage Press online journal first edition). **36** (4), 673–695.

89. Klein, D. (2000) Ending the war on drugs: Serious challenge for the field of prevention. *J. Primary Prevention*, **21**, 147–151.

90. Battin, M., Luna, E., Gallegar, P. and Robins, J. *et al.* (2007) *Drugs and Justice: Seeking a Consistent, Coherent, Comprehensive View*, Oxford University Press, Inc.

Part Two

Assessment and diagnosis

6

Screening and diagnosis of substance use disorders

Norman G. Hoffmann[1,2]

[1]*Evince Clinical Assessments, Waynesville, NC, USA*
[2]*Western Carolina University, Cullowhee, NC, USA*

6.1 OVERVIEW

This chapter emphasizes pragmatic issues of screening and diagnostic determinations that may be implemented in a variety of settings where time is at a premium or contact time may be limited. Assessment will be used as a generic term to encompass screening, diagnosis/problem identification, and treatment planning. In most settings, other than clinics or programs specializing in the treatment of substance use disorders, screening and some level of problem identification are the only aspects of assessment undertaken.

The term substance use disorders will be used here to refer to the definitions of substance dependence and substance abuse as defined in the DSM-IV-TR [1]. Biological research and clinical distinctions between abuse and dependence for a given substance suggest that dependence is distinct from abuse [2].

The premise of this discussion is that abuse to, or misuse of, substances may be a situational or transient issue. That is not to say that abuse, or misuse, may not be harmful or in need of attention, but recognizes that in general the diagnosis of abuse is distinct from dependence. Dependence typically has a greater scope of involvement and range of consequences [2] and a more chronic course [3,4].

Given the distinctions among excessive use, abuse and dependence, one of the first decisions to be made is to determine the purpose of the screening or further assessment. If the purpose is to identify those who are using alcohol in excess or who are using illicit drugs, different screens are likely to be helpful than if the primary concern is to identify those with a serious substance use disorder such as dependence.

Brief interventions that can be implemented in medical clinics and practices are most likely to be beneficial to those in the excessive use or abuse areas. For dependent individuals, brief interventions may be most helpful in increasing motivation to access formal treatment services. For those dependent persons receptive to the prospect of treatment, referral to an appropriate treatment program may be the best disposition.

Addictive Disorders in Medical Populations   Edited by Norman S. Miller and Mark S. Gold
© 2010 John Wiley & Sons, Ltd.

6.2   SCREENING

A variety of screening instruments are currently available. Some of the best and shortest screens are free and not protected by copyright, so they can be incorporated into any standard information collection process or management information system. Longer and proprietary instruments are available, but most of these do not have great advantage over the free instruments.

6.2.1   Principles of screening

Screens for substance use disorders should be short and quickly administered by minimally trained individuals. Basic screens indicate the level of risk for a given condition. Some screens target a specific substance or group of substances while others are more generic.

Screens are most helpful for application in populations where substance use disorders are not already an identified problem. Such populations include medical patients in clinics, admissions to medical centers, and persons seeking mental health services. Various sectors of social services, such as child protection, parents of children in foster care, and welfare applicants, are other types of populations where screens can prove beneficial.

Once substance use disorders are either evident or suspected for reason, more detailed assessments are required. Screening for substance use disorders is redundant at addictions treatment programs, as the individuals presenting for services have been screened either formally or informally. Similarly, persons convicted of driving under the influence or while impaired are already at risk for substance dependence or abuse due to their offense.

Interestingly, screening is often confused with more comprehensive assessment procedures in the addictions field. The term screening is often used to refer to part of the intake process at treatment programs. This is either a misnomer or inappropriate application of instruments. An intake requires more formal and detailed diagnostic instruments. At a minimum, a detailed and comprehensive assessment of problems is required when someone presents at a treatment program for an assessment.

A number of different, but related screening instruments will be reviewed here. Similarities for at least some of the items among the screens will be noted. In point of fact, it appears that any group of four to six items covering common issues specific to substance use disorders are likely to produce reasonable accuracy in detecting substance dependence [5]. Thus, even if one screen appears to be better suited to certain applications than another, the more important issue may be that the screen is consistently used and acted upon. A less accurate screen that is always used is likely to yield more value than an excellent screen that is rarely used.

6.2.2   Recommended screening instruments

6.2.2.1   UNCOPE

As with any assessment procedure, the objective of the assessment should drive the selection of instruments and procedures. If the objective is to identify potentially harmful drinking, the screen should cover issues of quantity and frequency of consumption and possible consequences already encountered. If the objective is to identify those with a likely disorder such as dependence, the effective screen will focus on those behaviors and events likely to indicate the condition in question.

Screens for substance use disorders tend to fall into one of three categories: screens for alcohol disorders, drug disorders, or both. Many common screens are substance or substance group specific. A number of instruments used as screens are overly long and more closely resemble an initial assessment of problems. In general, a screen of no more than six items is required for screening for substance use disorders. Some have even suggested as few as two [6] but such brief instruments are not recommended, as will be seen shortly. If the screen is to encompass potentially excessive or harmful use as well as a formal substance use disorder, no more than 10–12 questions should suffice.

One of the more universal screens is the UNCOPE, which can be used as a generic screen for both alcohol and drugs or worded for a substance specific application. It has the additional advantage of being validated on both adults [5,7] and adolescents [8]. The concepts and generic wording of the UNCOPE are as follows:

U – unplanned use: Have you spent more time drinking or using than you intended?

N – neglect of responsibilities: Have you ever neglected some of your usual responsibilities because of using alcohol or drugs?

C – desire to cut down on use: Have you felt you wanted or needed to cut down on your drinking or drug use?

O – objections by others to use: Has anyone objected to your drinking or drug use?

P – preoccupation: Have you found yourself thinking a lot about drinking or using?

E – use to relieve emotional distress: Have you ever used alcohol or drugs to relieve emotional discomfort, such as sadness, anger, or boredom?

The UNCOPE lends itself to modest variations in wording for specific screening purposes. For example, the questions can be restricted to current issues by adding a timeframe to the questions, such as "Have you spent more time drinking or using than you intended in the past 12 months?" Such time specifications avoid positive findings for past but not current problems. In the application for the ADAM (Arrestee Drug Abuse Monitoring) system funded by the ONDCP (Office of National Drug Control Policy), the UNCOPE is asked once with wording specifically about alcohol and the second time about illicit drugs.

Most of the known validation of the UNCOPE has focused on correctional and juvenile justice-related populations, which are noted for caution and suspiciousness. It seems likely that the screen would be at least as effective with less guarded populations such as medical patients. The validation findings indicated that the UNCOPE is equally effective with both males and females. Among the minority populations, the screen seems adequate for African Americans, Hispanics/Latinos, and Native Americans.

Another advantage of the UNCOPE is that, although brief, it has sufficient length to adjust the cut-scores for identifying risk so as to account for differential concerns on the rate of false-positive and false-negative findings. Using three or more positive findings as the indication for dependence risk tends to produce a balance between these two types of error with both sensitivity and specificity of approximately 85%. Raising the threshold to four or more positive responses for targeting risk for dependence will cause the screen to miss a larger proportion of true-positive cases, but will drive the false-positive rate to near zero. Conversely, lowering the threshold to two or more will yield more false-positives, but will minimize false-negative findings. Such adjustments can be made depending on the importance one places on the type of errors to be minimized.

Simple scoring options or more involved algorithms can be used to indicate different levels of concern or probability of dependence versus abuse. Two of the UNCOPE items (N and O) relate to the DSM-IV-TR criteria for substance abuse. By definition, persons who endorse both of these items would appear to meet the diagnostic criteria for abuse. The items "C" and "U" correspond to two of the criteria for dependence. Individuals who are positive for dependence on a given substance also tend to be positive for the majority of the abuse criteria as well [2]. Thus, an individual positive for all of the first four items on the UNCOPE is highly likely to meet dependence criteria. The "P" and "E" items are not directly related to substance dependence, although preoccupation is infrequently endorsed in the absence of dependence. Use related to emotional distress is frequently associated with abuse.

6.2.2.2 CAGE and CAGE-AID

The CAGE is the oldest and arguably most widely used screen in medical and social service settings [9,10]. This instrument is also frequently recommended by federal agencies. The constructs and wording of the CAGE are as follows:

C – desire to cut down use: "Have you ever thought you should cut down on your drinking?"

A – annoyed by others objections: "Have you ever felt annoyed by others' criticism of your drinking?"

G – guilty about use: "Have you ever felt guilty about your drinking?"

E – having an "eye opener" to relieve withdrawal: "Have you ever had a drink first thing in the morning to steady your nerves or to get rid of a hangover?"

The CAGE-AID involves adding "or drug use" to the first three items and "or using drugs" to the fourth item. This strategy attempts to use the CAGE as a more universal screen to detect both alcohol and other drug use disorders.

A substantial number of studies have shown the CAGE to be an adequate screen for routine screening, especially in medical settings; however, some studies have indicated that it is not as accurate as other brief screens [11]. The CAGE has been found not to be as sensitive in detecting alcohol dependence among women and some ethnic groups [12].

Conceptually the CAGE has several weaknesses as a screen. The "A" and "G" items are highly subjective. Whether one is annoyed or not is not as concrete, observable, or important as whether others actually have objected. Likewise, whether or not one feels guilt is more nebulous than whether one has neglected responsibilities. Another weakness is that the eye opener (E) tends to occur later in the progression of alcohol dependence. Ideally, a screen should address those indications that occur earlier as dependence develops.

Several other brief scales have been developed in the attempt to improve on the performance of the CAGE. Two of these, TWEAK and RAPS, essentially build on the CAGE in that many of the items are similar to the CAGE items.

6.2.2.3 TWEAK

The TWEAK [13] was developed to identify risky drinking during pregnancy. The TWEAK uses similar wording for the C, A, and E items of the CAGE for its items: W (Have close friends worried or complained about your drinking in the past year?); E (Do you sometimes take a drink in the morning when you first get up?); and K (Do you sometimes feel the need to cut down on your drinking?). The "T" items refers to tolerance (How many drinks can you hold?). The "A" on the TWEAK refers to amnesia (Has a friend or family member ever told you about things you said or did while you were drinking that you could not remember?).

The suggested scoring for the TWEAK gives two points for each of the first two items and one for each of the other three. A score of two or more is considered to place an individual at risk for a problem related to alcohol.

6.2.2.4 RAPS

The RAPS (Rapid Alcohol Problems Screen) was developed to address the problems with the CAGE, AUDIT, and TWEAK associated with differential performance among ethnic groups, especially African American women [14]. Unlike the other screens, its name does not reflect an acronym for the content of the items. The five items of the RAPS are as follows:

Do you sometimes take a drink in the morning when you first get up?

During the past year, has a friend or family member ever told you about things you said or did while you were drinking that you could not remember?

During the past year, have you had a feeling of guilt or remorse after drinking?

During the past year have you failed to do what was normally expected of you because of drinking?

During the past year, have you lost friends or girlfriends or boyfriends because of drinking?

Only the last two items are substantially different from items in the CAGE or TWEAK. The first and third items are similar to the "E" and "G" items of the CAGE. The second item is similar to the "A" item of the TWEAK. Only the last item is not common to one or more of the other three screens (CAGE, TWEAK, and UNCOPE).

The scoring of the RAPS considers any positive answer to be an indication of likely problems. Such a low threshold may be appropriate for identifying possible misuse of alcohol in addition to addiction, but one would expect a high level of false-positive findings for alcohol dependence, especially among males.

6.2.2.5 AUDIT

The AUDIT (Alcohol Use Disorders Identification Test) was developed at the request of the World Health Organization for a screen to detect persons at risk for developing alcohol-related problems [15]. The AUDIT begins with three questions concerning frequency and quantity of alcohol consumption plus seven items similar to those of the previously discussed screens. All the items are scored on a five point scale from zero to four, yielding a score from 0 to 40. Two items, one for experiencing and injury to self or others as a result of drinking and the other concerning suggestions by others that the respondent cut down, do not have values of one or three. They are scored as zero if the event did not occur, two if the event occurred in the past, and four if they occurred during the past year.

A score of eight or greater is considered to suggest hazardous or harmful alcohol consumption. Thus, the AUDIT is not focused primarily on identifying an alcohol use disorder, especially dependence, as are other screens such as the CAGE and UNCOPE.

The AUDIT screen can be formatted to fit on a single page so that it can be answered and scored easily. Its length and variation in the item responses make it a bit less user friendly for applications in time-limited situations.

6.2.3 Screen selection

A variety of other screens have been developed but most simply incorporate content of the items noted in the screens discussed. As noted previously, any short list of questions that covers the type of content noted is likely to serve as a reasonable screen. The selection of a validated screen or tailoring of screening items should be based on what works best in a given setting.

Most of the screens described can be adapted in terms of the timeframe of interest. For example, the UNCOPE, CAGE, TWEAK, and RAPS can all be referenced as to whether the events or experiences covered have occurred within a given period, such as the previous 12 months. The time of interest is better referred to in terms of number of months rather than "the past year" because when the screen is conducted late in the calendar year, respondents may interpret the questing as the time since 1 January and omit occurrences during the holidays of November and December.

Regardless of the screen selected, monitoring the performance of the screen should be a standard procedure, so as to understand the sensitivity and specificity of the screen in the population on which it is used. Just because a set of items has been validated in a research study does not guarantee that it will perform well in every conceivable situation or setting. Ongoing monitoring of screen performance is the only way to verify the functionality of the screen.

6.2.4 Screens not recommended

Some commonly used screens, even those frequently recommended, should not be used due to serious deficiencies and/or issues of length. As can be seen from the recommended screens, no more than 10 items are required for reasonable screening. Longer screens tend to be a waste of time. In point of fact, screens with more than 10 items may be less accurate [5].

The most prominent of the screens that are not recommended is the MAST (Michigan Alcoholism Screening Test), initially developed by Selzer [16] as a 25 item screen and later adapted to a 10 item instrument (Brief-MAST). Both versions of the MAST have serious issues limiting the utility as a screen.

The MAST begins by asking, "Do you feel you are a normal drinker?" This is tantamount to asking the respondent for a self-diagnosis, and likely to increase defensiveness. Many people suffering from a substance use disorder will answer factual and concrete questions about events and behaviors because they do not consider the events to be of importance. The best example of this was the response, "Heck, I told you I was married," when an alcohol dependent man was asked whether anyone had objected to his drinking. Beginning with a value laden and subjective question such as whether one is a "normal" drinker is unwise.

Perhaps the greatest problem with the MAST is that it focuses on extreme and late stage problems, such as delirium tremens, being hospitalized because of one's drinking, or having sought help about drinking. These are not typically early indications of a problem. For a screen to be effective in detecting early indications of a substance use disorder, it should emphasize those indications that occur at the earliest stages of the illness.

Another problem with the MAST is the question about attending a meeting of Alcoholics Anonymous. Social work graduates at many universities will score five points on this item because attending an open AA meeting is part of required course work. The item does not ask whether the individual attended an AA meeting due to concerns about his or her own drinking, so some concerned persons attending an open meeting might also score on this item.

Finally, those without a substance use disorder tend to view the MAST as offensive and bombastic. Use of the MAST as an anonymous screen in a medical setting resulted in high rates of incomplete forms and numerous negative comments. A screen should be brief and not viewed as offensive by the respondents regardless of whether or not they are positive for the condition in question.

The DAST (Drug Abuse Screening Test) is a 28 item "yes–no" screen for drug-related problems. It is not recommended for routine screening due to its length.

6.3   DIAGNOSTIC DETERMINATIONS

The limitation of screens is that they are designed only to indicate a level of risk. They are not designed to provide definitive support for a professional to make a diagnosis. The value of a screen in many settings is in eliminating the condition in question from further consideration. Ruling out an unlikely problem may be as helpful as alerting professionals of possible problems.

Instruments for making an initial diagnostic determination are by necessity more comprehensive and more time consuming than a screen. Formal diagnostic assessment instruments will typically require about 30–45 minutes of interviewing time to appropriately cover the specific events and behaviors required to definitively document the diagnostic indications for alcohol and other drug use disorders. Such time commitments are not likely to be practical for routine use in most medical settings. Structured diagnostic instruments, such as those described here, can be administered by any staff person properly trained in the use of the tool. However, most physicians who are not experts in addiction are not likely to be sufficiently familiar with the diagnostic criteria of the DSM-IV-TR to make the diagnosis.

It should always be kept in mind that it is the professional with the appropriate expertise that determines the diagnosis based on all available information (e.g., test results, patient history, collateral informants, and observations). No instrument or tool "makes a diagnosis," and any instrument or computer program that produces a diagnostic statement should be avoided or at least used with caution. This can be particularly problematic with automated systems. Such instruments and the algorithms that drive the output are only as accurate as the data entered and the decision rules programmed in the software. Such programs are best if they simply present the findings of fact and allow the clinician with access to all information – and not just what was fed into the program – to make the determination of whether a given individual does or does not meet diagnostic criteria for the condition in question. This allows the clinician to take into account indications of falsification of information as well as other history and family input. Validity scales on an instrument are no guarantee of accurate output.

6.3.1 Diagnostic instruments

A variety of structured interviews has been developed to appropriately explore the events and behaviors that cover the four criteria of substance abuse and the seven criteria of substance dependence. Some of these instruments, such as the Structured Clinical Interview for DSM-III-R Dissociative Disorders (SCID) [17], were designed primarily as research tools and are too time consuming to be considered for routine clinical practice.

Among the more commonly used diagnostic instruments for adults are the GAIN, SUDDS-IV, and CAAPE. The GAIN (Global Assessment of Individual Needs) is actually a family of instruments designed to document diagnoses in the context of a psychosocial interview [18]. Some of the shorter versions of the GAIN can be used more as screening tools or components extracted to develop diagnostically-related documentation. The SUDDS-IV (Substance Use Disorder Diagnostic Schedule-IV) is one of the older and most widely used instruments for detailed documentation of substance use disorders [2,19]. The SUDDS-IV has one interesting advantage in that it can be used to document the age of onset for each problem indication by substance. This can be helpful for motivational enhancement. The CAAPE (Comprehensive Addiction And Psychological Evaluation) covers similar content for substance use disorders as the other instruments but also covers a number of Axis I and II psychiatric conditions [20]. A number of other similar structured interviews and questionnaires for providing diagnostic indications are available; references and descriptions can be located at http://www.niaaa.nih.gov/publications. However, as noted previously, such instruments are likely to be too time consuming for routine use in busy medical settings.

In most medical settings, the more logical approach to addressing substance use disorders is to routinely screen for such conditions and then take action for those identified as being at risk. Such action may involve monitoring or brief interventions in the medical practice or referral for an assessment by a professional or program specializing in addictions.

6.4 SUMMARY

Routine screenings using four to six questions are easy and practical to apply in virtually all medical settings, such as physician offices, ambulatory clinics, emergency rooms, and hospital admissions. The prevalence of alcohol and other drug use disorders are among the most prevalent conditions encountered in many medical settings, making such screening a high priority.

In most medical settings, a brief intervention can be used to either resolve issues of excessive use or more clearly identify a condition requiring specialized services. For those patients whose use of alcohol appears excessive, a brief intervention involving strategies for lowering consumption may be effective. In those cases where the indications for substance dependence are great or where the brief intervention is not sufficient, a referral for specialized assessment and care may be the first choice.

REFERENCES

1. American Psychiatric Association (2000) *Diagnostic and Statistical Manual of Mental Disorders*, 4th edn, American Psychiatric Association, Washington, DC.

2. Hoffmann, N.G. and Hoffmann, T.D. (2003) Construct validity for alcohol dependence as indicated by the SUDDS-IV. *J. Substance Use and Misuse*, **38** (2), 293–305.

3. Schuckit, M.A., Smith, T.L., and Landi, N.A. (2000) The 5-year clinical course of high-functioning men with DSM-IV alcohol abuse or dependence. *Am. J. Psychiatry*, **157** (12), 2028–2035.

4. Schuckit, M.A., Smith, T.L., Danko, G.P. *et al.* (2001) Five-year clinical course associated with DSM-IV alcohol abuse or dependence in a large group of men and women. *Am. J. Psychiatry*, **158** (7), 1084–1090.

5. Hoffmann, N.G., Hunt, D.E., Rhodes, W.M., and Riley, K.J. (2003) UNCOPE: A brief substance dependence screen for use with arrestees. *J. Drug Issues*, **33** (1), 29–44.

6. Brown, R.L., Leonard, T., Saunders, L.A., and Papasouliotis, O. (1997) A two-item screening test for alcohol and other drug problems. *J. Fam. Pract.*, **44** (2), 151–160.

7. Campbell, T.C., Hoffmann, N.G., Hoffmann, T.D., and Gillaspy, J.A. (2005) UNCOPE: A screen for substance dependence among state prison inmates. *J. Prison*, **85** (1), 7–17.

8. Urofsky, R.I., Seiber, E., and Hoffmann, N.G. (2007) UNCOPE: Evaluation of a brief screen for detecting substance dependence among juvenile justice populations. *J. School Counseling*, **5** (17), Retrieved 9 September 2007 from http://www.jsc.montana.edu/articles/v5n17.pd.

9. Ewing, J.A. (1984) Detecting alcoholism: the CAGE questionnaire. *JAMA*, **252**, 1905–1907.

10. Mayfield, D., McLeod, G., and Hall, P. (1974) The CAGE questionnaire: Validation of a new alcoholism instrument. *Am. J. Psychiatry*, **131**, 1121–1123.

11. Cherpitel, C.J. (1997) Brief screening instruments for alcoholism. *Alcohol Health Res. W.*, **21** (4), 348–351.

12. Cherpitel, C.J. (2002) Screening for alcohol problems in the U.S. general population: comparison of the CAGE, RAPS4, and RAPS4-QF by gender, ethnicity, and service utilization. *Alcohol. Clin. Exp. Res.*, **26** (11), 1686–1691.

13. Russell, M., Martier, S.S., Sokol, R.J. *et al.* (1994) Screening for pregnancy risk-drinking. *Alcohol. Clin. Exp. Res.*, **18**, 1156–1161.

14. Cherpitel, C.J. (1995) Ethnic differences in performance of screening instruments for identifying harmful drinking and alcohol dependence in emergency room. *Alcohol. Clin. Exp. Res.*, **19**, 628–634.

15. Saunders, J.B., Aasland, O.G., Babor, T.F. *et al.* (1993) Development of the alchol use disorders identification test (AUDIT). WHU collaborative project on early detection of prsons with harmful alcohol consumption-II. *Addiction*, **88**, 791–804.

16. Selzer, M.L. (1971) The Michigan alcoholism screening test (MAST): The quest for a new diagnostic instrument. *Am. J. Psychiatry*, **127**, 1653–1658.

17. Steinberg, M., Rounsaville, B., and Cicchetti, D.V. (1990) The structured clinical interview for DSM-III-R dissociative disorders: preliminary report on a new diagnostic instrument. *Am. J. Psychiatry*, **147**, 76–82.

18. Dennis, M., Titus, J., White, M. *et al.* (2002) Global Appraisal of Individual Needs (GAIN): Administration Guide for the GAIN and Related Measures, Chestnut Health Systems, Bloomington, IL, [Online] Available: www.chestnut.org/li/gain/gadm1299.pdf.

19. Harrison, P.A. and Hoffmann, N.G. (1995) SUDDS: Substance Use Disorder Diagnostic Schedule Administration Guide, Evince Clinical Assessments, Smithfield, RI.

20. Hoffmann, N.G. (2000) CAAPE (Comprehensive Addictions and Psychological Evaluation) Manual, Evince Clinical Assessments, Smithfield, RI.

7

Clinical pharmacology of addicting drugs

Jiang Liu and Hartmut Derendorf

Department of Pharmaceutics, University of Florida, Gainesville, FL, 32611, USA

7.1   OVERVIEW

The disorder of addiction is produced by inter-actions among individual biological organisms (*people*), specific pharmacological agents (*drugs*) and the social, cultural, historic, and geographic milieu (*environment*) [1]. Studying drugs' prop-erties in the body and their biological effects is essential for designing optimal dosing regimens to reduce the risk of addiction and developing effective therapies to treat addiction. Addiction pharmacokinetics and pharmacodynamics (PK/PD) is a novel discipline to help understand how a drug's specific PK/PD properties contri-bute to *developing or treating* of addictive disorders.

7.2   BASIC CONCEPTS OF PK/PD

7.2.1   Pharmacokinetics – concentration vs. time

The term pharmacokinetics (PK) was first intro-duced by F.H. Dost in 1953 [2]. Literally, it refers to the application of kinetics to pharmakon (the Greek word for drugs). Hence, it is a study of the change of drugs over time in the body. It studies what the body does to drugs and often describes the concentra-tion–time course of drugs and metabolites in dif-ferent bodily fluids (e.g., plasma). PK is commonly divided into several areas, including the extent and rate of drug *a*bsorption, *d*istribution, *m*etabolism, and *e*xcretion. This is often referred to as the ADME scheme.

Absorption is the process by which drug mole-cules reach the systemic circulation. In general, before a drug molecule can exert a pharmacological effect in tissues, it needs to pass through various physiologic barriers (e.g., intestinal wall and hepa-tic metabolism) before reaching the vascular system. Bioavailability (F) is the fraction of the administered dose that reaches the systemic circu-lation, and quantifies the extent of drug absorption. Commonly, the rate of absorption can be described as either first order (with absorption rate *constant* k_a) or zero order (with absorption rate R_0). The rate and extent of absorption are also frequently char-acterized by the time of the maximum concentra-tion (t_{max}) or its magnitude (C_{max}).

Addictive Disorders in Medical Populations   Edited by Norman S. Miller and Mark S. Gold
© 2010 John Wiley & Sons, Ltd.

Distribution is the dispersion of drug molecules from the bloodstream into various tissues and organs. Volume of distribution (*Vd*) is commonly used to describe the extent of distribution. It is a hypothetical volume which relates the amount of drug in the body to its plasma concentration. Drug binding to plasma proteins and binding to various tissues are the two primary factors determining the extent of distribution. Biophase distribution refers the process of carrying drug to its active site (also called effect site), most often via the bloodstream. This can be a serious problem for some drugs at barriers such as the blood–brain barrier.

Metabolism and excretion are the processes of drug elimination. Metabolism is the biotransformation process that converts the drug molecule to its metabolites. Metabolites and parent drugs may or may not have the same pharmacological effects. When metabolites are pharmacologically inert, metabolism deactivates the administered drug. Most small molecule drugs are metabolized by the redox cytochrome P450 enzymes in the liver. Excretion is the process of removing parent drugs and their metabolites from the body. It occurs primarily through the kidney (urine), biliary tract (feces), lung (respiration) or skin (sweat). Clearance (*CL*) is commonly used to quantify the extent of drug elimination. It is defined as the volume of plasma cleared of the drug per time unit. Half-life ($T_{1/2}$) is also widely used to describe the drug elimination rate for those drugs with first order elimination. It refers to the time taken for the drug concentration in the plasma to decline by 50%. It is a secondary PK parameter and depends on clearance and volume of distribution.

7.2.2   Pharmacodynamics – effect vs. concentration

Pharmacodynamics (PD) is the science of drug action on the body and the relationship between drug concentration and effect [3]. It details what the drug does to the body and characterizes the intensity of desired or undesired effects resulting from certain drug concentrations at effect sites. A drug effect can be defined as any drug-induced change in a physiological parameter when compared to the respective pre-dose or baseline value. Baseline values do not necessarily have to be constant and can change, for example, as a function of time of day or of food intake. PD is very important because the change in drug effect is usually not proportional to the change in drug concentration.

At the most fundamental level, the actions of most drugs are produced by mechanisms whereby drugs interact with specific receptive target molecules or "receptors" (in general we can call all target molecules "receptors"). There are four types of target molecule for drug binding: *receptors*, which are usually protein molecules on cell membranes, in the cytoplasm, or in the nucleus or other organelles; *enzymes*, which may be located intra- or extracellularly; *ion channels*, in cell membranes or organelles; and *transport proteins*, also in the cell membrane. Following target attachment but preceding the response, there is an ensuing linkage mechanism or transduction pathway, leading to a time lag for the response. The duration of the time lag depends on the nature of the transduction pathway; it varyies from milliseconds to hours.

The parameters which characterize the *drug receptor–response* relationship include affinity, efficacy, potency and sensitivity. Affinity describes the attraction between a drug and a "receptor" and is commonly represented as the reciprocal of the dissociation constant of the ligand "receptor" complex. Efficacy quantifies the maximal response that a drug is able to induce. Potency refers to the amount of drug required to elicit a given level of response. Sensitivity is indicated by the steepness of the change of response versus concentration and commonly determines drug selectivity *in vivo*. Combining the PK/PD parameters enable clinical drug action prediction for a given dosing regimen (Figure 7.1).

7.2.3   PK/PD modeling

Modeling in the PK/PD field uses mathematical functions to describe changes in drug concentration and changes in drug effects. PK modeling usually

Pharmacokinetic (PK)   Pharmacodynamics (PD)

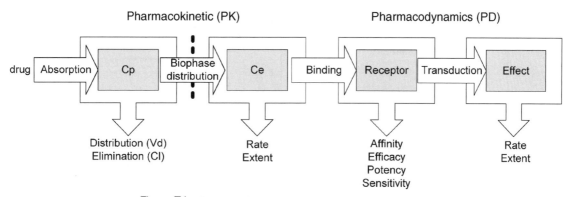

Figure 7.1   Scheme of the drug-response process in the body

describes drug plasma concentration (C) as a mathematical function of time (t):

$$C = f_1(t; \theta_1)$$

where θ_1 is the set of PK parameters (e.g., for absorption, distribution, metabolism, and elimination). Currently used PK models can be distinguished as compartmental, physiological and statistical. Compartmental models are most frequently preferred, because they provide a continuous concentration–time profile and they permit easy implementation of the popular effect compartment concept. Compartmental models assume immediate distribution in the same compartment, a first order elimination process, and linear PK. For example, Figure 7.2 shows a scheme of a classical one-compartmental PK model through oral administration, in which F and k_a are the PK parameters for absorption extent and absorption rate, V_d is the PK distribution parameter, CL is the PK elimination parameter. The concentration (C) can be characterized by a bi-exponential closed form equation

against time (t):

$$C = \frac{F \cdot Dose \cdot k_a}{V_d \cdot (k_a - CL/V_d)} \left(e^{-CL/V_d \cdot t} - e^{-k_a \cdot t} \right).$$

PD modeling describes drug effect (E) as a mathematical function of drug concentration (C):

$$E = f_2(C; \theta_2)$$

where θ_2 is the set of PD parameters (e.g., efficacy, potency, sensitivity). Ideally, concentrations should be measured at the effect site (biophase), where the interaction with the respective biological receptor system takes place. However, in most cases it is impractical to measure the effect site drug concentration. Thus, plasma drug concentrations are frequently used to establish these relationships under the assumption that the unbound (free) drug concentration in plasma reflects the unbound concentration at the effect site at steady-state condition. The most commonly used PD model is the sigmoid *Emax* model:

$$E = \frac{E_{\text{max}} \times C^n}{EC_{50}^n + C^n},$$

with E_{max} reflecting drug efficacy, the reciprocal of EC_{50} reflecting drug potency, and Hill factor n reflecting drug sensitivity.

PK/PD modeling links the change in concentration over time as assessed by PK to the intensity of the observed response, regarding to a certain concentration at the effect site, as quantified by PD. Thus, it allows descriptions of the complete time course (e.g., onset, magnitude, duration) of the

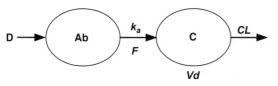

Figure 7.2   Scheme of a one-compartmental PK model through drug (D) oral administration. k_a is the absorption rate constant. F is the bioavailability. V_d is the volume of distribution. CL is the clearance

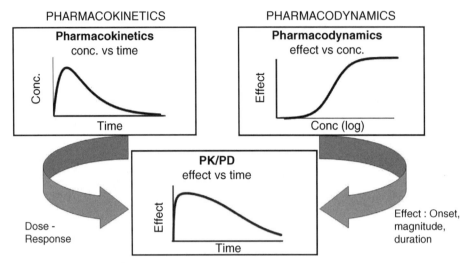

Figure 7.3   Interrelationship among PK, PD and PK/PD modeling

effects in response to a dosage regimen:

$$E = f_2(C; \theta_2) = f_2(f_1(t; \theta_1); \theta_2) = f(t; \theta)$$

where $f = (f_1, f_2)$ is the combination of PK functions and PD function and $\theta = (\theta_1, \theta_2)$ is the set of combined PK/PD parameters. This approach has proven to be effective in explaining the drug–response relatioship, and to help dose optimization

to improve drug efficiencies and reduce the risk of undesired effects (Figure 7.3) [4,5].

There are four basic attributes to characterize integrated PK/PD models (Figure 7.4): (1) the link between plasma concentration and the pharmacological response mechanism for the observed effect: direct vs. indirect link; (2) the response mechanism that mediates the observed effect: direct vs. indirect response; (3) the information used to establish the

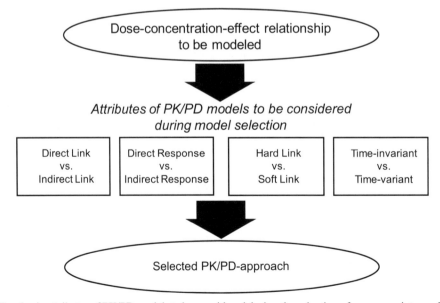

Figure 7.4   Four basic attributes of PK/PD models to be considered during the selection of an appropriate modeling approach

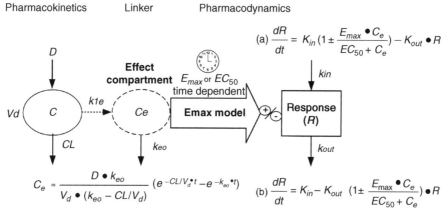

Figure 7.5 A PK/PD model example for most addictive substances that involves an indirect link, an indirect response, and a time variant procedure. PK is the arbitrarily chosen one-compartment model through i.v. administration. C_e is the drug concentration at the hypothetical effect compartment. Indirect modulation of the response is modeled by stimulating or inhibiting: (a) the production process (zero order production rate constant k_{in}) or (b) the degradation process (first order degradation rate constant k_{out})

link between plasma concentration and observed effect: hard vs. soft link; and (4) the time dependency of the involved pharmacodynamic parameters: time variant vs. time invariant [6].

An indirect link employs a hypothetical "effect compartment" to represent the effect site, which helps to explain the time dissociation between the plasma concentration and the biological response with a first order distributional delay. The effect is then a function of the concentration at the effect site. The effect compartment receives only a negligible mass of drug. Therefore, the time dependent aspects of the equilibrium between plasma concentration and the concentration at the effect site are only characterized by the effect compartment first order elimination rate constant (k_{e0}), which describes the disappearance of the drug from the effect compartment [7]. An indirect response characterizes the temporal dissociation between the plasma concentration and the biological response by describing the observed effects as a secondary result from a previous, time-consuming synthesis or degradation of an endogenous substance. Soft link models typically use both measured concentrations and effect-data sets to define the link function between PK and PD. Thus, the flow of used information is bidirectional. In contrast to the soft link approach, hard link models

use a unidirectional flow of information, in which the PK data and additional information regarding the mechanisms involved (e.g., *in vitro* receptor binding affinities) are used during the model development to predict the effect time course. Time variant models describe the effect regarding to drug concentrations as a function of exposure time. Therefore, the PD "parameters" (e.g., E_{max} and EC_{50}) mentioned previously may not stay constant over time. Tolerance and sensitization are common examples of time variant responses. In most cases, PK/PD models for addictive substances will involve indirect link, indirect response, and time variant structures (Figure 7.5).

7.2.4 Population PK/PD vs. personalized medicine

Population PK/PD was first introduced by Lewis Sheiner, the pioneer in pharmacometrics, in the 1970s [8–10] and has grown in significance since that time [11–15]. It can be defined as the study of the sources and correlates of variability in drug concentrations and drug effects among individuals who represent the target population that ultimately receive relevant doses of a drug of interest [16]. Certain patient demographical, pathophysiological, and therapeutical features, such as race, body weight, gender, age, disease status, genetic polymorphisms, excretory and metabolic functions, and the presence of other therapies, can regularly alter drug–response relationships. Population PK/PD uses nonlinear mixed effect modeling (NONMEM) to identify the population mean PK/PD parameters, as well as the measurable pathophysiological factors that cause changes in the drug–response relationship [14]. For example, the following scheme shows a classical population PK/PD model with additive error terms:

$$PK : C_{i,t} = f_1(t; \theta_{1_i}) + \epsilon_{1,t}$$

with:

$$\epsilon_{1,t} \overset{iid}{\sim} N(0, \sigma_1^2)$$
$$\theta_{1_i} = \theta_1 + \eta_{1_i} \text{ or } \theta_{1_i} = g_1(x_{1_i}) + \eta_{1_i}$$
$$\eta_{1_i} \overset{iid}{\sim} N(0, \omega_1^2) \text{ \& } \eta_{1_i} \text{ and } \epsilon_{1,t} \text{ are independent}$$

$$PD : E_{i,t} = f_2(C_{i,t}; \theta_{2_i}) + \epsilon_{2,t}$$

with:

$$\epsilon_{2,t} \overset{iid}{\sim} N(0, \sigma_2^2)$$
$$\theta_{2_i} = \theta_2 + \eta_{2_i} \text{ or } \theta_{2_i} = g_2(x_{2_i}) + \eta_{2_i}$$
$$\eta_{2_i} \overset{iid}{\sim} N(0, \omega_2^2) \text{ \& } \eta_{2_i} \text{ and } \epsilon_{2,t} \text{ are independent}$$

where $C_{i,t}$ and $E_{i,t}$ are the PK/PD dependent variables (concentration/effect at given time point t) for subject i; $\theta = (\theta_1, \theta_2)$ are the population mean PK/PD parameters; $X_i = (X_{1_i}, X_{2_i})$ are pathophysiological factors of subject i (covariates: e.g., race, body weight, age, gender, genetic polymorphisms, the presence of other therapies) that highly correlate to some of the PK/PD parameters in the set $\theta_i = (\theta_{1_i}, \theta_{2_i})$; $\omega = (\omega_1, \omega_2)$ are the between-subject variations; and $\sigma = (\sigma_1, \sigma_2)$ are the within-subject variations. Therefore, an individual drug treatment will surely be more efficient based on these pathophysiological factors, which can cause a clinically significant shift in the drug-response profile.

7.3 PK/PD FACTORS FOR DRUGS OF ADDICTION

7.3.1 Biophase distribution and the blood–brain barrier

Drugs of addiction must pass the blood–brain barrier (BBB) or the blood–spinal cord barrier to reach their targets and induce their pharmacological effects. Because of the special properties of BBB, the effect site kinetics of these drugs is often substantially different from plasma PK.

Paul Ehrlich and Edwin Goldmann first described the existence of a permeability barrier between the blood and the brain by the injection of a vital dye into the bloodstream or the cerebrospinal fluid (CSF) in the early twentieth century [17]. The BBB is primarily formed by the brain capillary endothelial cells with the presence of continuous tight junctions that seal together the margins of these cells [18]. It is a multiple regulatory brain unit with functions including: (1) providing a selective molecular sieve to maintain homeostasis in the brain; (2) serving as an active pump to take up essential substances like glucose and amino acids into the brain; and (3) working as a metabolic barrier to modify substances before entering the brain or to eliminate unwanted waste products [17].

P-gp (phosphorylated glycoprotein), a 170-kDa member of the ATP-binding cassette (ABC) superfamily of membrane transporters, is an important efflux transporter at the luminal side of the BBB. Its function is to prevent exogenous compounds from entering the brain and to excrete metabolites and transport hormones out from the brain. Many drugs of addiction, for example, fentanyl, morphine, methadone, buprenorphine, loperamide, are substrates of P-gp [19–23].

In the analysis of the PK/PD correlation for addictive substances, biophase distribution kinetics is very important since BBB transport and brain distribution are often neither instantaneous nor complete. Microdialysis has shown its promising applications in the direct brain drug concentration sampling. An indirect link with a hypothetical "effect compartment" helps to associate the plasma drug concentration to its effect in the central nervous system (CNS). Changes in BBB and P-gp expression/function caused by aging, disease, and drug applications can result in a shift in PK/PD correlations in the same subject, while differences in the BBB and P-gp expression/function in the population help to explain variations in PK/PD correlations among individuals [24–26].

7.3.2 Drug interactions

Potential drug–drug and food–drug interactions are common concerns in the drug addiction population, since this population is highly associated with increased incidence of cancer, HIV infections, and alcoholism. In this special population, drug interactions among drugs of addiction and anticancer drugs, antiretroviral agents or alcohol may cause serious clinical problems. Moreover, most opioid addiction treatments involve an interaction between the treatment drugs and addictive substances. Drug interaction is a typical PK/PD topic in which one substance affects the exposure or/and effect of another. These interactions can be predominantly of PK or PD or both in origin.

PK drug interactions result in changes in systemic or/and biophase drug concentrations. Interactions can occur in every phase of ADME, mainly by affecting intercompartmental transports, drug metabolisms, and protein bindings. For example, interactions between benzodiazepines and alcohol commonly occur at both the absorption and metabolism levels [27]. From a nutritional perspective, grapefruit juice has similarly been associated with increased absorption of CYP450 3A4 substrates (e.g., clozapine, alprazolam, and midazomam) by increasing their bioavailability [28,29]. Oral contraceptive pills have been shown to reduce the clearance of alprazolam, which may lead to increased plasma levels and accumulation of this drug [30]. Use of CNS-penetrating anticancer agents (e.g., quinidine and doxorubicin) also raised concerns regarding the biophase exposures of P-gp ligands (e.g., fentanyl, loperamide, methadone, and morphine) [31,32]. CNS depressants (e.g., pheno-

barbital and carbamazepine), anti-HIV agents (e.g., nevirapine and ritonavir), and rifampicin are CYP450 3A4 inducers; concerns that their use may decrease systemic exposure of drugs metabolized by this pathway (e.g., methadone and alfentanil) exist [31,33]. At the excretion level, opioids have been shown to have diuretic effects; hence, multiple drug interactions are theoretically possible [34]. Phenytoin was reported to induce production of $\alpha 1$-acid glycoprotein, thereby raising the possibility of increased protein binding to methadone or fentanyl analogues, with subsequent spontaneous withdrawal due to decreases of free drugs [31].

PD drug interactions can have additive, synergistic or antagonistic effects. Interactions can occur at the same or different physiological systems. Synergistic PD interactions have been observed between propofol and alfentanil with EC_{50} of alfentanil decreasing (i.e., increased potency) after propofol dosing [35]. Antagonistic PD interactions resulting in proportionally reduced sedative potency of midazolam with steady state levels of flumazenil were seen [36]. Co-administration of an ultra-low dose of the μ-opioid receptor antagonists, naloxone or naltrexone, with opioids has been shown to enhance opioid antinociception and suppress tolerance and dependence [37–40].

7.3.3 Tolerance and dependence

Drug tolerance and physical dependence are the hallmarks of addiction. Drug tolerance is described by a decreased effect with continuous/repeated drug exposure, such that a higher dose is required subsequently to maintain an equivalent effect. Drug dependence is described as a state in which a continuous drug presence is required to maintain the normal physiological or behavioral processes. Withdrawal symptoms and sensitization rebound characterize dependence in the cessation of the drug use. The potential for physical dependence can be generally thought of as the opposite effect produced by drug withdrawal (Figure 7.6).

As shown in Figure 7.6, drug tolerance and dependence are classical PK/PD topics character-

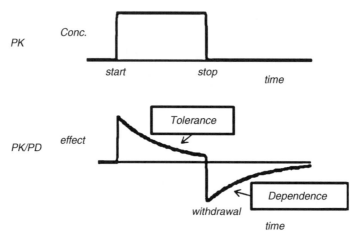

Figure 7.6 Scheme of the development of tolerance and dependence to the chronic administration of a drug

ized by a time variant dose–response pattern, and these generally have indirect link, indirect response, and time invariant attributes. Much evidence has shown that drug dose, exposure duration, frequency of dosing, previous/current use of cross dependent/tolerant drugs, and the physiological condition of the subject are the PK/PD factors that determine the severity of dependence and tolerance [42,43]. The developments of tolerance and dependence are commonly associated; hence, long-term administration of those drugs could be associated with increased risk of dependence and addiction. Theoretically, both tolerance and physical dependence are predictable pharmacological effects in response to a drug administration. However, the predictive power of current models is limited since they are commonly derived on empirical grounds, because of a lack of knowledge about the mechanisms underlying tolerance and dependence, and because of the difficulties in appropriately simplifying complex physiological processes [44].

Tolerance can be divided into "apparent tolerance" and "pharmacodynamic tolerance". Apparent tolerance may be associated with the continuous drug exposure or may be caused by the disease progress or the increased rate of metabolism (e.g., the auto-induction of carbamazepine metabolism). PD tolerance, also called functional tolerance, is typically more important for drugs of addiction. It directly links the reduction of effect

intensity to the drug exposure. The rate of the tolerance development may be rapid (acute tolerance) or slow (chronic tolerance) depending on the drug exposure situation. Acute tolerance is characterized by a clockwise hysteresis loop in a plot of effect versus concentration ordered by time (Figure 7.7). Mechanisms of drug PD tolerance have been related to neuroadaptive changes (e.g., receptor desensitization, up-regulation of cyclic adenosine monophosphate [cAMP], activation of NMDA receptors via second messengers, and down-regulation spinal glutamate transpor-

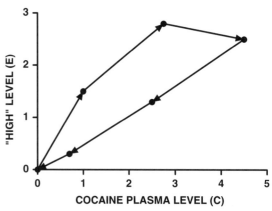

Figure 7.7 A hypothetical concentration effect plot complicated by clockwise hysteresis. Arrows indicate the direction of progressively increasing time. Note that the euphoria effect of cocaine decreased with continuous drug exposure [41]

ters) [45]. The semi-mechanistic tolerance models can be classified into four major sets:

- **Receptor desensitization:** involving a decrease of the number of receptors, and then a decrease of the efficacy and potency of drugs [47].

- **Depletion/production of endogenous modulators:** involving certain endogenous molecules (e.g., cofactors/enzymes, second messages, or certain receptor modulators) [46].

- **Counter response:** involving the opposite effects of the same drug (e.g., the biphasic effects of alfentanil, alprazolam, midazolam, and clozapinr) [48] or induction of inhibitors, antagonists, partial agonists, or inverse agonists [49].

- **Negative feedback:** homeostatic tolerance, where the measured drug response is the result of the direct drug effect and homeostatic counter-regulatory processes: for example, the down-regulation of prolactin release [50].

The detailed mechanism of tolerance involved in a specific drug situation is drug and response dependent. Differences in the tolerances to distinct drug effects during the same drug treatment suggest differences in mechanisms of tolerance and receptor subtypes involved for various drug effects [51]. Moreover, the development of tolerance for a specific effect depends on drug route, dosage, and dose regimen. Currently, all of the models are considered empirical or semi-physiological. They have proven to be useful in some specific situations, but none is general enough to describe every situation even for the same given drug [44]. Therefore, any extrapolations and prediction with a model require special caution and validation. Since most models are developed from animal data and the interspecies differences in tolerance development can be significant, the application of a tolerance model to human situations also must be verified.

Clinical and laboratory observations have converged on the hypothesis that dependence and withdrawal represent the pathological neuroadaptive changes of reward- and stress-related circuitries in the CNS (e.g., changes in the dopaminergic reward system, endogenous opioid peptides, or corticotropin-releasing factor) [52,53]. PK/PD models or dependence progression models associated with addictive substances are lacking due to the lack of reliable and quantifiable biomarkers of dependence. Intracranial self-stimulation (ICSS) procedures and drug self-administration procedures are potential animal models that may provide quantitative dependence information [54]. Lau and colleagues successfully applied PK/PD approaches to studying the effects of cocaine on reinforcement behavior [55] and later elucidated that the minimum plasma concentration (C_{min}) was the PK determinant of the frequency and pattern of intravenous cocaine self-administration in rats by PK modeling [42]. Moreover, cytokines such as IL-6, CRP and TNF-alpha may serve as potential biomarkers of stress, a known predictor of relapse and addiction, in preclinical and clinical studies.

7.4 PK/PD OF PRESCRIPTION DRUGS

Opioids (e.g., morphine, fentanyl, methadone, and codeine), CNS depressants (e.g., barbiturates and benzodiazepines), and stimulants (e.g., dextroamphetamine and methylphenidate) are the most common prescription drugs of addiction. Opioids form the mainstay for treating moderate or severe pain in neonates undergoing invasive procedures, post-operative pain populations, and cancer and AIDs pain patients. Opioid dosing is complicated in these populations because of individual differences in PK/PD (e.g., ADME, receptor expression, and pain pathways), different degrees of pain, variable illnesses, potential combination treatments with other medications, rapid changes in neonatal brain development, and potentials for tolerance and dependence.

PK/PD research has been widely conducted for these classes of drugs over the last two decades.

Quantitative information is available for most of these drugs regarding ADME and receptor binding properties such as potency, efficacy, and sensitivity. However, difficulties exist in linking the change in concentration over time as assessed by PK to the intensity of observed responses as quantified by PD because of the indirect link, indirect response, and time variant properties of the drugs. Studies that focus on drug action mechanisms, biophase distributions, drug–drug interactions, and drug tolerance will help to correctly link the drug's PK/PD information and predict drug effects throughout therapy. PK/PD studies focused on drug dependence will better inform us about the risks of prescribing these drugs, as well as on how to minimize or treat drug addiction. Altogether, these researches will help to optimize drug applications and addiction treatments.

Biophase distribution causes a temporal shift of effects versus plasma concentrations for most drugs of addiction. Biophase distributions of opioids, such as the fentanyl group, methadone, and morphine, were characterized with their PK/PD models based on EEG quantitation of narcotic effect. Alfentanil and remifentanil equilibrate very quickly with equilibration half-lives between plasma and effect site of about one minute. They are followed by fentanyl and sufentanil, each with equilibration half-lives of about six minutes. Methadone equilibrates with a half-life of about eight minutes. Morphine, in contrast, equilibrates with a half-life of two to three hours and M6G with an equilibration half-life of about seven hours. These biophase distribution parameters correlate well with Ummenhofer's microdialysis data sampled in cerebrospinal fluid (CSF) and the epidural space in pigs [56]. Hence, this quantitative information provides a rational basis for the selection of opioids in clinical circumstances [57].

As mentioned previously, potential drug–drug or drug–food interactions widely exist in the drug addiction population. Some of those interactions may cause serious clinical problems. Acceleration of methadone metabolism resulting from CYP450 3A4 induction by CNS depressants (e.g., phenobarbital and carbamazepine), anti-HIV agents (e.g., nevirapine or ritonavir) or rifampicin has

caused methadone withdrawal symptoms [58]. Inhibition of CYP450 2D6 by the anticancer agent, quinidine, has resulted in an almost complete loss of the analgesic effects of codeine due to the lack of morphine formation from codeine. Synergistic effects of systemically administered opioids with spinally or topically delivered opioids or anesthetics have been reported frequently. Antidepressants, anticonvulsants or α2-adrenoreceptor agonists have also been shown to exert additive analgesic effects when administered together with an opioid [31]. Co-administration of an ultra-low dose of naloxone or naltrexone has also been shown to enhance opioid antinociception and suppress tolerance and dependence [37–40,59]. Co-administration of a selective gamma-aminobutyric acid (GABA) receptor agonist, baclofen, produced a potentiation of opioid antinociceptive effect, whereas untoward opioid emetic and rewarding effects were completely blocked [60]. Consistent findings regarding the role of the N-methyl-d-aspartate (NMDA) receptor antagonist, ketamine, in preventing opioid-induced hyperalgesia and subsequent acute tolerance have also been reported [61,62].

PK/PD modeling of drug tolerance and dependence can provide a quantitative description of the dose effect properties over time and help understanding of the drug action under different drug exposure situations. Counting on the predictive abilities of the PK/PD models, a more efficient therapeutic design based on the administration route and dose regimen may be derived. Moreover, this quantitative information may further suggest directions for mechanistic investigation of tolerance and dependence. Clinical data pertaining to tolerance and dependence are limited with most current studies and modeling conducted in animals. Using morphine as an example, its tolerance models have been studied in detail during the last ten years. Heinzen and Pollack established the temporal relationship between morphine-induced elevations in neuronal nitric oxide (NO) and the development of antinociceptive tolerance in rats [46]. As shown in Figure 7.8, the stimulating effect of morphine on NO production was treated as an indirect response; a hypothetical effect compartment was incorpo-

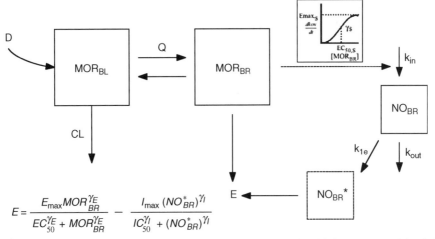

Figure 7.8 Scheme of Morphine–NO tolerance PK/PD model. A temporal relationship between morphine-induced increases in neuronal NO and loss of the antinociceptive effect is indicated [46]

rated to account for an evident delay in both NO production and the NO-associated decrease in antinociceptive effect. This model not only correctly predicted the time course of the development of tolerance at various dosages, but also helped in elucidating a strong, time-dependent relationship between morphine-induced stimulation of NO production and tolerance development. The work indicated that NO is a key mediator of antinociceptive tolerance development, which is consistent with the later investigation that NO altered in the μ-opioid receptor function [63].

Recently, population PK/PD has been adapted to drive individualized therapy. This approach is efficient in elucidating the covariates that regularly alter drug–response relationships. Bouwmeester and colleagues conducted population PK studies of morphine and its metabolites M3G and M6G in newborns and young infants and illustrated a nonlinear positive relation between PK parameters of morphine and its metabolites (e.g., V_d and CL) and postnatal age [65]. Based on the EEG model in rats,

Minto and colleagues demonstrated a negative correlation between PK/PD parameters of remifentanil on EEG (CL, k_{e0}, and EC_{50}) and age, which explained the prolonged opioid effect seen in the elderly [66]. A study of alprazolam in men showed a decrease of CL, a slower offset of effect, and a slower rate of acute tolerance development in elderly men [67]. Current knowledge is limited to qualitative data about the impact of hepatic or renal dysfunction on the effects of most misused drugs. Hepatic or renal dysfunction can cause a decreased morphine clearance or M6G accumulation. Surgery, myocardial infarction, Crohn's disease and arthritis may increase the level of α-1-acid glycoproteinand (AAG), thereby raising the possibility of decreased free concentrations of high AAG-binding opioids (methadone or fentanyl analogues) and the potential appearance of spontaneous withdrawal symptoms [68]. More population PK/PD models that quantitatively incorporate this knowledge are warranted in order to predict the clinical outcome in specific patients.

7.5 PK/PD OF NICOTINE

Although nicotine is considered to be responsible for tobacco's addictive potential, other components in tobacco smoke (e.g., tar and carbon monoxide) appear to cause lung cancer, chronic

bronchitis and emphysema. Nicotine replacement therapy (NRT) provides nicotine in a safe form to help individuals to quit smoking without enduring nicotine withdrawal. NRT is available as chewing gum, transdermal patches, nasal spray, sublingual tablet or inhaler. Understanding nicotine PK has proven very helpful in optimizing NRT.

Nicotine can cross membranes easily due to its lipophilic nature. Different administration routes (smoking, nasal spray, chewing, transdermal) may result in significantly different PK profiles and subsequent PD properties. Through cigarette smoking, it only takes about 10–20 seconds for nicotine absorbed through the pulmonary venous system to reach the brain. Plasma and brain nicotine levels reach their peaks shortly after finishing smoking. Since the likelihood that a substance will be abused depends on the time between administration and central reinforcement, tobacco smoking can easily become addictive [69]. The volume of distribution of nicotine is very large. Nicotine concentrations in various organs after smoking have been evaluated in rabbits among other species. Arterial blood and brain concentrations increase sharply after exposure, then decline over 20–30 min as nicotine redistributes to other body tissues, particularly skeletal muscle. The levels of nicotine are much higher in arterial than in venous blood during the absorption phase. In contrast to inhalation, the oral, nasal or transdermal routes of absorption result in a gradual increase in nicotine levels in the brain and a small brain–blood difference. Nicotine is extensively metabolized to a number of metabolites by the liver. About 70–80% of nicotine is converted to cotinine in two steps catalyzed by CYP450 2A6 and a cytpoplasmic aldehyde oxidase [70]. The average half-life of nicotine is two hours. The clearance of nicotine is high, ranging from 1.3–2.5 l/minute [71].

Most NRTs deliver nicotine more slowly than smoking. This enables them to relieve withdrawn symptoms, improve abstinence rates and be less addictive than smoking. The efficiency of NRT products depends, in part, on their PK properties. Nicotine delivered from nasal spray is absorbed through the nasal mucosa. Absorption is very rapid and peak arterial plasma levels are reached about five minutes after administration [72]. So it provides faster withdrawal relief than that of other NRTs. However, compared to smoking, the absorption of nasal spray is slower with lower plasma levels of

nicotine achieved at comparable doses. The transdermal nicotine patch is the most common form of NRT. The patch offers constant delivery (6–8 hours after first applying, i.e., 3–4 half-lives, to reach the steady state) and is very convenient for a subject. However, because of its slow release and passive administration, the patch does not respond to urges and craving to smoke. The relapse rate among patch treatments is an important issue. For currently available patches, the relapse rate in 16 hours/day patch treatment (4%) was lower than in 24 hours/day treatment (17%) [73]. This issue raised a concern about the development of nicotine tolerance with prolonged exposures. As shown here, the PK/PD properties of nicotine administration play an important role in nicotine addiction and NRT optimization. The PK/PD differences among NRTs may help to explain why some smokers have difficulty in quitting smoking. Combination therapy (e.g., patch + gum or patch + inhaler) or higher dosages perhaps will help more smokers to quit.

A classic PK/PD model was developed by Porchet and colleagues to characterize the development of tolerance to cardioaccelerating effects of nicotine in humans [64]. As shown in Figure 7.9, the PK model was a two-compartment structure model and the PD model $\left(E = E_0 + \frac{S \times C}{1 + C_{ant}/C_{ant50}}\right)$ was based on a hypothetic noncompetitive antagonist metabolite (ant). Meanwhile, the PD model can also be derived based on a competitive antagonist meta-

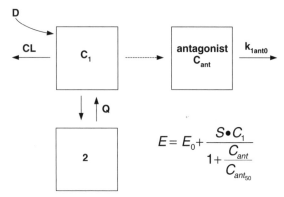

Figure 7.9 PK/PD model of nicotine tolerance. A hypothetical antagonist metabolite (ant) is proposed. The effect, E, depends on both of the drug concentration C and the hypothetical antagonist concentration Cant [64]

bolite. This PK/PD model correctly predicts the time course for drug effects in each dosing situation and the decrease of tolerance with extended interval. Similar models were further developed by Fattinger and colleagues to characterize the acute tolerance to multiple nicotinic effects in humans. In their studies, the rate of tolerance development to various effects (increases in heart rate, blood pressure, plasma epinephrine and energy expenditure) varied considerably. Their findings suggested differences in mechanisms of tolerance for various nicotinic effects [51]. Recently, a mechanistic population PK model of nicotine and its major metabolites was developed by Levi. Their model incorporated CYP450 2A6 information and

allowed more precisely prediction [74]. A population indirect-response PK/PD model that relates nicotine concentration and enforced smoking cessation craving score was developed by Gomeni. These studies suggested that the nicotine dosage regimen could influence the nicotine mechanism of action: an instantaneous delivery at an individually selected time seemed to inhibit the onset of craving (k_{in}: the production of smoking craving) while constant delivery at a pre-defined time seemed to attenuate the craving (k_{out}: the elimination of smoking craving) [75]. This type of quantitative PK/PD information will help to elucidate the PK/PD-dependent aspects of smoking behavior, understand smoking addiction, and design more efficient NRTs.

7.6 PK/PD OF ALCOHOL

The first clinical kinetic study of ethanol started in the 1930s. Alcohol absorption depends on drinking pattern, concentration of ethanol in the beverage, and the fed or fasting state of the subject [76]. Alcohol dehydrogenase (ADH) metabolizes alcohol to acetaldehyde. Gastric ADH and hepatic ADH primarily account for ethanol's bioavailability. Ethanol is transported by the bloodstream to all parts of the body with the most vascularized tissues receiving alcohol most rapidly. Ethanol is water miscible and has no plasma protein binding, so its volume of distribution is closely related to the amount of water in the body. More than 90% of ingested alcohol is metabolized by the liver, and the remainder is excreted unchanged in breath, urine, and sweat. Hepatic ADH is the primary metabolism enzyme of alcohol in the system. It has a low Michaelis–Menten constant (Km) of 0.05–0.1 g/l, leading to a saturable metabolism. The polymorphism of ADH accounts for racial and ethnic variations in PK. Alcohol also is metabolized by hepatic CYP450 2E1, which is self-inducible after chronic drinking. Therefore, the kinetics of ethanol are characterized by the parallel non-ADH first order and ADH Michaelis–Menten elimination.

Concurrent use of alcohol and other addictive substances is common. Alcohol–drug interactions can present serious healthy or social problems which

lead to bodily damage or accident. The elderly are especially likely to mix drugs and alcohol and are at particular risk for the adverse consequences of such combinations. Elderly individuals are commonly exposed to aspirin and other nonsteroidal anti-inflammatory drugs (NSAIDs) such as ibuprofen, which may cause stomach bleeding and inhibit blood clotting. Alcohol can exacerbate these effects. Even small amounts of alcohol taken with some antihistamines or CNS depressants may cause excessive dizziness and sedation in the elderly. The combination of opiates and alcohol enhances the sedative effect of both substances, increasing the risk of death from overdose. Alcohol is associated with more than half of heroin fatal overdose cases [77]. Alcoholism and depression are also frequently associated. Acute alcohol consumption increases the availability of some tricyclic antidepressants, such as amitriptyline, potentially increasing their sedative activity, but chronic alcohol consumption appears to decrease the availability of some tricyclics.

As discussed above, alcohol–drug interactions happen at all PK/PD levels. An acute dose of alcohol can alter drug absorption and distribution. It can compete with a drug for the same metabolizing enzymes to reduce the drug's metabolism. Coexistence of alcohol in the body may also alter the normal metabolism pathway of a drug. 30% of cocaine users ingest alcohol during almost every episode of cocaine use. Ethanol in the rat liver inhibits normal hydrolysis pathway of cocaine to benzoylecgonine, and simultaneously catalyzes the ethyl transesterification of cocaine to cocaethylene. Formation and accumulation of cocaethylene may account for the enhanced affective effects and worsened toxicity of cocaine, since cocaethylene may cause more euphoria and higher cardiovascular risk than the parent compound [78]. Chronic alcohol exposure may induce drug-metabolizing enzymes. This may increase the transformation of some drugs (e.g., acetaminophen) into toxic metabolites and subsequently cause organ damage. In turn, some drugs can affect the metabolism of alcohol, thus altering its potential for intoxication and the adverse effects associated with alcohol consumption [79]. At the PD level, as discussed previously, alcohol can magnify the sedation effect of some drugs [80].

Ethanol PK modeling is complex because of the parallel non-ADH first order and ADH Michaelis-Menten elimination processes, as well as its administration-dependent absorption and distribution. Two-compartment model structures with parallel saturated and first order elimination characterize systematic alcohol PK properties well. The semi-physiological three-compartment model proposed by Norberg and colleagues can further describe the nonlinear absorption of ethanol [76]. Physiological PK models have also been proposed. They are likely to have more predictive power and

allow further characterizing of the disposition of ethanol in various compartments. Alcohol tolerance may develop at the cellular or neural system levels. Berger's study in drosophila showed that neither acute nor chronic tolerance involved changes in alcohol PK. Therefore, it represents PD rather than PK tolerance. Chronic tolerance in flies is disrupted by treatment with the protein synthesis inhibitor cycloheximide, but rapid tolerance is resistant to this treatment [81]. Chronic tolerance in human may be partially attributed to the induction of hepatic CYP450 2E1, but acute tolerance is clearly not due to altered disposition of ethanol. Ethanol PD modeling is complicated by the development of tolerance and delays in biological response that may differ depending on the biomarker used. In Holford's studies, effects on motor coordination only required an additional effect compartment to account for the delay between plasma concentration and response, but the effects on cognitive testing revealed the rapid development of tolerance in addition to a delay. Similar to Porchet and colleagues' nicotine tolerance model discussed in Section 7.5, Holford's PD model $\left(E = \dfrac{E_{\max} \times \left(1 - \frac{C_m}{IC_{50} + C_m}\right) \times C_e}{EC_{50} + C_e} \right)$, based on a hypothetical inhibitory metabolite (m), fits the study data very well. However, as the author pointed out, the predictive power of this kind of empirical models needs to be further validated [82].

7.7   CONCLUSIONS

The disease of addiction is a multifactorial gene–drug–environment disorder. PK/PD studies investigate how a drug dynamically changes in the body and how the body dynamically responds to the drug over time. PK/PD modeling applies mathematical functions to describe and predict these changes. Addiction PK/PD plays an important role to elucidate drug's PK/PD factors that contribute to developing or treating of addictive diseases. With this quantitative information, it is possible to design more efficient dosage regimens to reduce the risk of

medication addiction and develop more effective therapies to treat addictive diseases.

REFERENCES

1. California Pacific Medical Center (2007) Pharmacokinetics of Addiction. In: www.cpmc.org/professionals/research/programs/addiction.html.
2. Dost, F.H. (1953) *Der Blutspiegel. Kinetik de Konzentrationsabläufe in der Kreislaufflüssigkeit*, Thieme, Leipzig.

3. Lees, P., Cunningham, F.M., and Elliott, J. (2004) Principles of pharmacodynamics and their applications in veterinary pharmacology. *J. Vet. Pharmacol. Ther.*, **27**, 397–414.

4. Derendorf, H. and Meibohm, B. (1999) Modeling of pharmacokinetic/pharmacodynamic (PK/PD) relationships: concepts and perspectives. *Pharm. Res.*, **16**, 176–185.

5. Derendorf, H., Lesko, L.J., Chaikin, P. *et al.* (2000) Pharmacokinetic/pharmacodynamic modeling in drug research and development. *J. Clin. Pharmacol.*, **40**, 1399–1418.

6. Meibohm, B. and Derendorf, H. (1997) Basic concepts of pharmacokinetic/pharmacodynamic (PK/PD) modelling. *Int. J. Clin. Pharm. Th.*, **35**, 401.

7. Holford, N.H. and Sheiner, L.B. (1981) Understanding the dose-effect relationship: clinical application of pharmacokinetic-pharmacodynamic models. *Clin. Pharmacokinet.*, **6**, 429–453.

8. Sheiner, L.B., Rosenber, B., and Melmon, K.L. (1972) Modeling of individual pharmacokinetics for computer-aided drug dosage. *Comput. Biomed. Res.*, **5**, 441.

9. Sheiner, L.B., Rosenberg, B., and Marathe, V.V. (1977) Estimation of population characteristics of pharmacokinetic parameters from routine clinical data. *J. Pharmacokinet. Biop.*, **5**, 445–479.

10. Sheiner, L.B., Beal, S., Rosenberg, B., and Marathe, V. V. (1979) Forecasting individual pharmacokinetics. *Clin. Pharmacol. Ther.*, **26**, 294–305.

11. Steimer, J.L., Mallet, A., Golmard, J.L., and Boisvieux, J.F. (1984) Alternative approaches to estimation of population pharmacokinetic parameters – comparison with the nonlinear mixed-effect model. *Drug Metab. Rev.*, **15**, 265–292.

12. Whiting, B., Kelman, A.W., and Grevel, J. (1986) Population pharmacokinetics – theory and clinical-application. *Clin. Pharmacokinet.*, **11**, 387–401.

13. Sheiner, L.B. and Ludden, T.M. (1992) Population pharmacokinetics dynamics. *Annu. Rev. Pharmacol. Toxicol.*, **32**, 185–209.

14. Ette, E.I. and Williams, P.J. (2004) Population pharmacokinetics II: Estimation methods. *Ann. Pharmacother.*, **38**, 1907–1915.

15. Pillai, G., Mentre, F., and Steimer, J.L. (2005) Nonlinear mixed effects modeling – From methodology and software development to driving implementation in drug development science. *J. Pharmacokinet. Pharmacodyn.*, **32**, 161–183.

16. US Food and Drug Administration (1999) Guidance for Industry: Population Pharmacokinetics.

17. Betz, A.L. (1992) An overview of the multiple functions of the blood–brain barrier. *NIDA Res. Monogr.*, **120**, 54–72.

18. Rubin, L.L. and Staddon, J.M. (1999) The cell biology of the blood–brain barrier. *Annu. Rev. Neurosci.*, **22**, 11–28.

19. Callaghan, R. and Riordan, J.R. (1993) Synthetic and natural opiates interact with P-glycoprotein in multidrug-resistant cells. *J. Biol. Chem.*, **268**, 16059–16064.

20. Henthorn, T.K., Liu, Y., Mahapatro, M., and Ng, K.Y. (1999) Active transport of fentanyl by the blood–brain barrier. *J. Pharmacol. Exp. Ther.*, **289**, 1084–1089.

21. Hamabe, W., Maeda, T., Fukazawa, Y. *et al.* (2006) P-glycoprotein ATPase activating effect of opioid analgesics and their P-glycoprotein-dependent antinociception in mice. *Pharmacol. Biochem. Be.*, **85**, 629–636.

22. Crettol, S., Digon, P., Golay, K.P. *et al.* (2007) *In vitro* P-glycoprotein-mediated transport of (R)-, (S)-, (R, S)-methadone, LAAM and their main metabolites. *Pharmacology*, **80**, 304–311.

23. Linnet, K. and Ejsing, T.B. (2008) A review on the impact of P-glycoprotein on the penetration of drugs into the brain. Focus on psychotropic drugs. *Eur. Neuropsychopharm.*, **18**, 157–169.

24. Shah, G.N. and Mooradian, A.D. (1997) Age-related changes in the blood–brain barrier. *Exp. Gerontol.*, **32**, 501–519.

25. de Boer, A.G. and Gaillard, P.J. (2006) Blood–brain barrier dysfunction and recovery. *J. Neural. Transm.*, **113**, 455–462.

26. Sharma, H.S., Sjoquist, P.O., and Ali, S.F. (2007) Drugs of abuse-induced hyperthermia, blood-brain barrier dysfunction and neurotoxicity: Neuroprotective effects of a new antioxidant compound H-290/51. *Curr. Pharm. Des.*, **13**, 1903–1923.

27. Abernethy, D.R., Greenblatt, D.J., Ochs, H.R., and Shader, R.I. (1984) Benzodiazepine drug-drug interactions commonly occurring in clinical-practice. *Curr. Med. Res. Opin.*, **8**, 80–93.

28. Armstrong, S.C. and Cozza, K.L. (2002) Med-psych drug-drug Interactions update. *Psychosomatics*, **43**, 169–170.

29. Kiani, J. and Imam, S.Z. (2007) Medicinal importance of grapefruit juice and its interaction with various drugs. *Nutr. J.*, **6**, 33.

30. Back, D.J. and Orme, M.L. (1990) Pharmacokinetic drug interactions with oral contraceptives. *Clin. Pharmacokinet.*, **18**, 472–484.

31. Lotsch, J., Skarke, C., Tegeder, I., and Geisslinger, G. (2002) Drug interactions with patient-controlled analgesia. *Clin. Pharmacokinet.*, **41**, 31–57.

32. Dagenais, C., Graff, C.L., and Pollack, G.M. (2004) Variable modulation of opioid brain uptake by P-glycoprotein in mice. *Biochem. Pharmacol.*, **67**, 269–276.

33. Kharasch, E.D., Russell, M., Mautz, D. *et al.* (1997) The role of cytochrome P450 3A4 in alfentanil clearance – Implications for interindividual variability in disposition and perioperative drug interactions. *Anesthesiology*, **87**, 36–50.

34. Flores, O., Camera, L.A., Hergueta, A. *et al.* (1997) Role of atrial natriuretic factor, hemodynamic changes and renal nerves in the renal effects of intraperitoneal morphine in conscious rats. *Kidney Blood Press Res.*, **20**, 18–24.

35. Vuyk, J., Engbers, F.H.M., Burm, A.G.L. *et al.* (1996) Pharmacodynamic interaction between propofol and alfentanil when given for induction of anesthesia. *Anesthesiology*, **84**, 288–299.

36. Breimer, L.T.M., Burm, A.G.L., Danhof, M. *et al.* (1991) Pharmacokinetic-pharmacodynamic modeling of the interaction between flumazenil and midazolam in volunteers by aperiodic EEG analysis. *Clin. Pharmacokinet.*, **20**, 497–508.

37. Chindalore, V.L., Craven, R.A., Yu, K.P. *et al.* (2005) Adding ultralow-dose naltrexone to oxycodone enhances and prolongs analgesia: A randomized, controlled trial of oxytrex. *J. Pain*, **6**, 392–399.

38. Leri, F. and Burns, L.H. (2005) Ultra-low-dose naltrexone reduces the rewarding potency of oxycodone and relapse vulnerability in rats. *Pharmacol. Biochem. Be.*, **82**, 252–262.

39. Olmstead, M.C. and Burns, L.H. (2005) Ultra-low-dose naltrexone suppresses rewarding effects of opiates and aversive effects of opiate withdrawal in rats. *Psychopharmacology (Berl)*, **181**, 576–581.

40. Paquette, J. and Olmstead, M. (2005) Ultra-low dose naltrexone enhances cannabinoid-induced antinociception. *Behav. Pharmacol.*, **16**, 597–603.

41. Van Dyke, C., Ungerer, J., and Jatlow, P. (1982) Intranasal cocaine: dose relationships of psychological effects and plasma levels. *Int. J. Psychiat. Med.*, **12**, 1–13.

42. Lau, C.E. and Sun, L. (2002) The pharmacokinetic determinants of the frequency and pattern of intravenous cocaine self-administration in rats by pharmacokinetic modeling. *Drug Metab. Dispos.*, **30**, 254–261.

43. Liu, J., Pan, H., Gold, M. *et al.* (2008) Effects of fentanyl dose and exposure duration on the affective and somatic signs of fentanyl withdrawal in rats, *Neuropharmacology*, **55** (5), 812–818.

44. Gårdmark, M., Brynne, L., Hammarlund-Udenaes, M., and Karlsson, M.O. (1999) Interchangeability and predictive performance of empirical tolerance models. *Clin. Pharmacokinet.*, **36**, 145.

45. Mitra, S. and Sinatra, R.S. (2004) Perioperative management of acute pain in the opioid-dependent patient. *Anesthesiology*, **101**, 212–227.

46. Heinzen, E.L. and Pollack, G.M. (2004) Pharmacodynamics of morphine-induced neuronal nitric oxide production and antinociceptive tolerance development. *Brain Res.*, **1023**, 175–184.

47. Ramakrishnan, R., DuBois, D.C., Almon, R.R. *et al.* (2002) Fifth-generation model for corticosteroid pharmacodynamics: application to steady-state receptor down-regulation and enzyme induction patterns during seven-day continuous infusion of methylprednisolone in rats. *J. Pharmacokinet. Pharmacodyn.*, **29**, 1.

48. Lau, C.E., Wang, Y., and Ma, F. (1998) Pharmacokinetic-pharmacodynamic modeling of the coexistence of stimulatory and sedative components for midazolam. *Eur. J. Pharmacol.*, **346**, 131.

49. Ihmsen, H., Albrecht, S., Hering, W. *et al.* (2004) Modelling acute tolerance to the EEG effect of two benzodiazepines. *Br. J. Clin. Pharmacol,*, **57**, 153–161.

50. Bagli, M., Suverkrup, R., Quadflieg, R. *et al.* (1999) Pharmacokinetic-pharmacodynamic modeling of tolerance to the prolactin- secreting effect of chlorprothixene after different modes of drug administration. *J. Pharmacol. Exp. Ther.*, **291**, 547.

51. Fattinger, K., Verotta, D., and Benowitz, N.L. (1997) Pharmacodynamics of acute tolerance to multiple nicotinic effects in humans. *J. Pharmacol. Exp. Ther.*, **281**, 1238–1246.

52. Bruijnzeel, A.W., Repetto, M., and Gold, M.S. (2004) Neurobiological mechanisms in addictive and psychiatric disorders. *Psychiat. Clin. N. Am.*, **27**, 661.

53. Roberts, A.J. and Koob, G.F. (2004) Alcohol: ethanol antagonists/amethystic agents in *Encyclopedia of Neuroscience*, 3rd edn (ed. G. Adelman and B.H. Smith), Elsevier BV, Amsterdam, The Netherlands.

54. Shippenberg, T.S. and Koob, G.F. (2002) Recent advances in animal models of drug addiction, in *Neuropsychopharmacology: The Fifth Generation of Progress* (eds K.L. Davis, D. Charney, J.T. Coyle, and C. Nemeroff), Lippincott Williams & Wilkins, pp. 1381.

55. Lau, C.E., Sun, L., Wang, Q. *et al.* (2000) Oral cocaine pharmacokinetics and pharmacodynamics in a cumulative-dose regimen: pharmacokinetic-

pharmacodynamic modeling of concurrent operant and spontaneous behavior within an operant context. *J. Pharmacol. Exp. Ther.*, **295**, 634–643.

56. Ummenhofer, W.C., Arends, R.H., Shen, D.D., and Bernards, C.M. (2000) Comparative spinal distribution and clearance kinetics of intrathecally administered morphine, fentanyl, alfentanil, and sufentanil. *Anesthesiology*, **92**, 739–753.

57. Lotsch, J.R. (2005) Pharmacokinetic-pharmacodynamic modeling of opioids. *J. Pain Symptom Manag.*, **29**, S90–S93.

58. Geletko, S.M. and Erickson, A.D. (2000) Decreased methadone effect after ritonavir initiation. *Pharmacotherapy*, **20**, 93–94.

59. Wang, H.Y., Friedman, E., Olmstead, M.C., and Burns, L.H. (2005) Ultra-low-dose naloxone suppresses opioid tolerance, dependence and associated changes in mu opioid receptor-G protein coupling and Gbetagamma signaling. *Neuroscience*, **135**, 247–261.

60. Suzuki, T., Nurrochmad, A., Ozaki, M. *et al.* (2005) Effect of a selective GABAB receptor agonist baclofen on the mu-opioid receptor agonist-induced antinociceptive, emetic and rewarding effects. *Neuropharmacology*, **49**, 1121–1131.

61. Laulin, J.P., Maurette, P., Corcuff, J.B. *et al.* (2002) The role of ketamine in preventing fentanyl-induced hyperalgesia and subsequent acute morphine tolerance. *Anesth. Analg.*, **94**, 1263–1269.

62. Juni, A., Klein, G., and Kest, B. (2006) Morphine hyperalgesia in mice is unrelated to opioid activity, analgesia, or tolerance: Evidence for multiple diverse hyperalgesic systems. *Brain Res.*, **1070**, 35–44.

63. Heinzen, E.L., Booth, R.G., and Pollack, G.M. (2005) Neuronal nitric oxide modulates morphine antinociceptive tolerance by enhancing constitutive activity of the μ-opioid receptor. *Biochem. Pharmacol.*, **69**, 679–688.

64. Porchet, H.C., Benowitz, N.L., and Sheiner, L.B. (1988) Pharmacodynamic model of tolerance: application to nicotine. *J. Pharmacol. Exp. Ther.*, **244**, 231–236.

65. Bouwmeester, N.J., Anderson, B.J., Tibboel, D., and Holford, N.H. (2004) Developmental pharmacokinetics of morphine and its metabolites in neonates, infants and young children. *Br. J. Anaesth.*, **92**, 208–217.

66. Minto, C.F., Schnider, T.W., Egan, T.D. *et al.* (1997) Influence of age and gender on the pharmacokinetics and pharmacodynamics of remifentanil I. Model development. *Anesthesiology*, **86**, 10–23.

67. Bertz, R.J., Kroboth, P.D., Kroboth, F.J. *et al.* (1997) Alprazolam in young and elderly men: sensitivity and tolerance to psychomotor, sedative and memory effects. *J. Pharmacol. Exp. Ther.*, **281**, 1317–1329.

68. Garrido, M.J. and Troconiz, I.F. (1999) Methadone: a review of its pharmacokinetic/pharmacodynamic properties. *J. Pharmacol. Toxicol. Methods*, **42**, 61–66.

69. Le Houezec, J. (2003) Role of nicotine pharmacokinetics in nicotine addiction and nicotine replacement therapy: a review. *Int. J. Tuberc. Lung D.*, **7**, 811–819.

70. Hukkanen, J., Jacob, P. 3rd, and Benowitz, N.L. (2005) Metabolism and disposition kinetics of nicotine. *Pharmacol. Rev.*, **57**, 79–115.

71. Kyerematen, G.A. and Vesell, E.S. (1991) Metabolism of nicotine. *Drug Metab. Rev.*, **23**, 3–41.

72. Zevin, S., Gourlay, S.G., and Benowitz, N.L. (1998) Clinical pharmacology of nicotine. *Clin. Dermatol.*, **16**, 557–564.

73. Daughton, D.M., Heatley, S.A., Prendergast, J.J. *et al.* (1991) Effect of transdermal nicotine delivery as an adjunct to low-intervention smoking cessation therapy. A randomized, placebo-controlled, double-blind study. *Arch. Intern. Med.*, **151**, 749–752.

74. Gear, R.W., Gordon, N.C., Miaskowski, C. *et al.* (2003) Dose ratio is important in maximizing naloxone enhancement of nalbuphine analgesia in humans. *Neurosci. Lett.*, **351**, 5–8.

75. Gomeni, R., Teneggi, V., Iavarone, L. *et al.* (2001) Population pharmacokinetic-pharmacodynamic model of craving in an enforced smoking cessation population: indirect response and probabilistic modeling. *Pharm. Res.*, **18**, 537–543.

76. Norberg, A., Jones, A.W., Hahn, R.G., and Gabrielsson, J.L. (2003) Role of variability in explaining ethanol pharmacokinetics: research and forensic applications. *Clin. Pharmacokinet.*, **42**, 1–31.

77. Peloso, P.M., Bellamy, N., Bensen, W. *et al.* (2000) Double blind randomized placebo control trial of controlled release codeine in the treatment of osteoarthritis of the hip or knee. *J. Rheumatol.*, **27**, 764–771.

78. Dean, R.A., Bosron, W.F., Zachman, F.M. *et al.* (1997) Effects of ethanol on cocaine metabolism and disposition in the rat, in *Pharmacokinetics, Metabolism and Pharmaceutics of Drugs of Abuse* (eds R.S. Rapaka, N. Chiang, and B.R. Martin), National Institute on Drug Abuse, pp. 35.

79. Lieber, C.S. (1990) Interaction of alcohol with other drugs and nutrients. Implication for the therapy of alcoholic liver disease. *Drugs*, **40** (Suppl. 3), 23–44.

80. Hersh, E.V., Pinto, A., and Moore, P.A. (2007) Adverse drug interactions involving common prescription and over-the-counter analgesic agents. *Clin. Ther.*, **29** (Suppl.), 2477–2497.

81. Berger, K.H., Heberlein, U., and Moore, M.S. (2004) Rapid and chronic: two distinct forms of ethanol tolerance in Drosophila. *Alcohol Clin. Exp. Res.*, **28**, 1469–1480.

82. Holford, N.H. (1997) Complex PK/PD models – an alcoholic experience. *Int. J. Clin. Pharmacol. Ther.*, **35**, 465–468.

8

Laboratory diagnosis of addicting drugs

K.P. Gunaga[1,2] and Satheesh Gunaga[3]

[1] *Toxicology Testing Center, Sparrow Health System, St. Lawrence Campus, Lansing, MI 48915, USA*
[2] *Division of Human Pathology, College of Human Medicine, Michigan State University, East Lansing, MI 48824, USA*
[3] *Henry Ford Wyandotte Hospital, Department of Emergency Medicine and Medical Education, Wyandotte, MI 48192, USA*

8.1 INTRODUCTION

Alcohol and drug addiction are responsible for precipitating a variety of acute and chronic medical and psychiatric conditions. The vast assortment of substance-induced toxidromes, which often mimic one another, creates a significant challenge for physicians to make a precise diagnosis from a history and physical exam alone. However, in today's forum of multidisciplinary medicine it is not necessary to make this diagnosis single-handedly. For many years, forensic and clinical toxicology laboratories have played a significant role in drug testing for emergency departments, drug treatment programs, pain medicine clinics, occupational medicine, law enforcement, and psychiatrists. This relationship has allowed for the use of sensitive and specific laboratory methods to help answer the complicated questions often facing a physician. The ability to use this resource depends upon a laboratories capability, one's knowledge of laboratory medicine, and the communication between the two.

8.2 DRUG TESTING

8.2.1 Clinical indications for drug testing

Physicians are repeatedly faced with clinical conditions that may be precipitated or made worse by the use of prescription medications, illicit drugs, and even poisons. The clinical exploration of these conditions often begins with a well-developed differential diagnosis, and then systematically all viable diagnoses are excluded through the use of a good history and physical, laboratory testing, and other active processes of investigation discussed by other authors in this book. The use of drug testing and, even more so, the physician's ability to interpret these results plays an important role in solving these puzzles. Knowing when and why to order a drug test is clearly the starting point. Some of the most common and highly agreed upon uses for drug testing are listed in Table 8.1.

It is evident from Table 8.1 that the indications for drug testing are highly specialty specific. Depending

Addictive Disorders in Medical Populations   Edited by Norman S. Miller and Mark S. Gold
© 2010 John Wiley & Sons, Ltd.

Table 8.1 Uses of drug abuse testing

- Evaluation of all patients with acute onset mental status changes
- Evaluation of all patients with acute onset syndromes
- Evaluation of all multisystem trauma patients
- Evaluation of a new patient
- Evaluation of all adolescents
- Monitoring response to inpatient treatment
- Monitoring abstinence in outpatients
- Occupational medicine and new employee screenings
- Pain clinic patient management
- Forensic psychiatry
- Sports medicine
- Evaluation of high-risk patients (e.g., physicians, athletes, entertainers)
- Post mortem forensic pathology
- Law enforcement

on the setting in which one practices and the specific needs of the patient, the reasoning for drug testing will vary. Nonetheless, the ultimate question remains the same. Has the patient consumed any illicit or prescribed drugs, and to what extent?

When faced with a patient who is experiencing an acute toxicological emergency, a comprehensive blood and urine toxicology screen should be done to help rule in or out pathology, as well as guide therapeutic interventions. These patients often present clinically with acute onset mental status changes (from slightly altered to completely obtunded), varying levels of distress, and with a history of recent/chronic drug and alcohol addiction. Alternatives to a full toxicology screen include testing discrete serum levels of the toxins in question, doing a urine qualitative test for drugs of addiction, or drawing specimens and holding them until it is determined that a toxicology screen is definitely indicated [1]. The laboratory has the ability to provide screening test results quickly with the use of a rapid immunoassay panel for drugs of addiction. The confirmation for presumptive positive results, while useful, often takes too long to perform and may not be readily available by most hospital laboratories. Confirmatory tests are done later on for future documentation as a protocol reflex or physician ordered test.

It is during these emergent situations that communication between the clinician and the laboratory

is most valuable. Whenever possible communicate with the laboratory about which drugs are suspected, which drugs the patient takes therapeutically, and the clinical condition of the patient. If there is a discrepancy between clinical suspicion and findings from the toxicology screen, the toxicology laboratory personnel can assist in determining if other tests are likely to be of benefit. A strong communication with the laboratory can be invaluable to the clinician by optimizing the use of screening and confirmatory tests, as well as clearly differentiating what drugs and chemicals were and were not tested for.

In pain management clinics and drug treatment programs, clinicians often want to know whether or not their patients are taking their prescription medications as ordered, in addition to any illicit drugs. Medications prescribed by pain management and drug treatment programs include morphine, oxycodone, methadone, tramadol, benzodiazepines, adderall, as well as other prescription medications used to treat concurrent medical conditions. The most common immunoassay screening methods available in clinical and toxicology laboratories cannot detect some of these drugs routinely or specifically. The opiate immunoassay assay screen may or may not pickup the legitimate use of oxycodone and will not detect tramadol. Information regarding which specific benzodiazepine has been taken also cannot be answered by the immunoassay screen alone. Toxicology and clinical laboratories have responded to these evolving challenges. One of the primary responses has been the development of custom panels suited specifically to a clinician's needs. These panels often include a high sensitivity opiate screen to pick up oxycodone, hydrocodone, and hydromorphone at about 300 ng/ml. Also included is a method to detect methadone metabolite as well as to detect tramadol. A lower cut-off value for other classes of drugs (cocaine metabolite, cannabinoids) may also be appropriate. Laboratories should work closely with the drug treatment programs and other clinical facilities to develop cost effective testing strategies that meet the specific requirements of the client. Continued follow up with program managers to evaluate the laboratory's effectiveness is highly recommended.

On occasions, patients being treated in pain management and drug treatment programs have been known to sell their prescribed drugs for monetary profit and divert to other drugs of their choice. In order to stay in these programs individuals may substitute, adulterate, or attempt to subvert the drug test using a variety of different techniques. Workplace drug testing laboratories are aware of the variety of approaches used by the subject(s) to defeat the testing process. These steps may be as simple as putting water into the collected sample to dilute it or add one of many available adulterants that may interfere with the drug testing process. An example of subversion used by pain management and drug treatment patients is to put a small amount of crushed parent methadone or oxycodone into the specimen to pass the drug test and sell the remainder for a profit. To discourage tampering with urine specimens a facilities protocol may include a witnessed collection of urine specimens, or the use of alternate specimens (blood, saliva, hair) for testing. If unwitnessed urine collection is used, the use of temperature monitoring strips or bluing toilet water is highly recommended to improve specimen validity. Beyond the on-site measures that are available, laboratories are employed with a large armamentarium to assure specimen validity.

8.3 METHODOLOGY FOR DRUG TESTING

In general, the methods used for particular drug tests and panels are well established and are available from the laboratory on request. A detailed discussion about method principle and instrumentation is beyond the scope of this text and, in most cases, beyond the scope of the physician's daily practice. However, in order to interpret drug test results effectively, the physician needs only have a rudimentary familiarity of the analytical methods employed along with their advantages and limitations. Detailed information on several methods of drug testing is readily available [2–4]. These methods vary in their sensitivity, specificity, turn around time, and cost. The test chosen depends highly on the specialty of medicine practiced, the capabilities of the laboratory, the accessibility of more elaborate toxicology facilities, as well as patient specific factors. Over the years, a variety of methods have been developed to conduct the detection of drug(s). The following is an introductory discussion of these methods.

8.3.1 Spot tests

Spot tests are the most rudimentary toxicology tests available and are generally performed on urine, blood and solid material looking for a simple color change. They are available for a number of drugs, including cocaine, opiate alkaloids, cannabis, phenothiazines, salicylates, acetaminophen, GHB, and many others. These tests are valuable indicators of drug use, and have the advantage that unskilled operators can use them as field tests in the emergency department and law enforcement settings. They are cost effective and results are often available within minutes. However, sensitivity and specificity are generally poor, thus requiring the obvious need for follow up analyses in the laboratory.

8.3.2 Ultraviolet spectroscopy

Many drugs have characteristic ultraviolet spectra that are easily measured by UV spectrophotometers. However, the specimen must be extracted in order to measure these spectra. For many drugs classes, including barbiturates, benzodiazepines, methaqualone, glutethimide and theophylline, this method offers reasonable sensitivity and specificity. This feature is now incorporated in some chromatographic (HPLC) and capillary electrophoretic methods with a diode array detector providing additional analytical sensitivity and specificity.

8.3.3 Immunoassays

Immunoassays are tests that use antibodies to identify and measure amounts of chemical substance. These assays are the most widely used in toxicology laboratories to screen for drugs in biological specimens. Antibody specificity describes the degree to which an assay correctly identifies only the compound of interest. This is a critical characteristic of immunoassays. Cross-reactivity to structurally related compounds is important to consider when identifying specific drugs in biological fluids. Table 8.2 shows quantitative cross-reactivity figures for common interfering drugs. Consequently, immunoassay presumptive positive samples must be confirmed using an alternate method of differing chemical principle, ideally gas chromatography–mass spectrometry (GC/MS).

Specific immunoassay techniques require labeled compounds. These labeled compounds must be immunologically similar to the drug being tested and will, therefore, successfully compete for the antibody. The labels must further lend themselves to sensitive detection, free from interference by common matrices. These labeled compounds are usually prepared by attaching an enzyme, micro particle, radioactive, or fluorescent molecule to the drug of interest.

Table 8.2   Cross-reactants in immunoassays

Immunoassay	Common Cross-Reacting Substances
Amphetamine/ Methamphetamine	MDA, MDMA, chloroquine, ephedrine, pseudoephedrine, phenylpropanolamine, tyramine, phentermine, phenmetrazine, fenfluramine, ranitidine
Benzodiazepines	Chlorpromazine
Benzoylecgonine/ Cocaine	Ecgonine, ecgonine methyl ester, cocaine
Cannabinoids (THC metabolites)	Ketoprofen, tolmetin, naproxen, ibuprofen, acetylsalicylic acid
LSD	Ergotamine, tricyclic antidepressants, verapamil, sertraline, fentanyl
Morphine/Opiates	Codeine, dihydrocodeine, thebaine, hydrocodone, dihydromorphine, hydromorphone
PCP	TCP, diphenhydramine, dextromethorphan

Copied from *Immunoassay in Principles of Forensic Toxicology* [5].

Table 8.3   Types of immunoassays

Heterogeneous assays	Homogeneous assays
Radio Immunoassay (RIA)	Enzyme-Multiplied Immunoassay Technique (EMIT)
Enzyme-linked Immunosorbent Assay (ELISA)	Kinetic Interaction of Microparticles in Solution (KIMS)
	Fluorescence Polarization Immunoassay (FPIA)
	Cloned Enzyme Donor Immunoassay (CEDIA)

Different manufacturers provide many of the immunoassays used for detecting drugs. The primary differences are based on the type of labeled compound used, the method of detection, and the antiserum cross-reactivity. The most common types of assays that are available in laboratories to detect and quantify drugs are of two types: homogeneous or heterogeneous (Table 8.3).

The major difference between these two types of assays is based on whether the separation of labeled drug (antigen) is required prior to analysis. Homogeneous immunoassays allow measurement of a labeled drug without separating bound and free drug. Thus the labeled drug need not be separated/washed. Hence, homogeneous assays can be easily automated on an instrument for a rapid throughput. In comparison, heterogeneous assays require bound and free drug (antigen) to be separated/washed before labeled drug (antigen) is measured.

8.3.3.1 Heterogeneous assays

Radio Immunoassay (RIA)

Strengths

- Highly sensitive.

- Useful for detection of drugs in biological specimens, especially blood and tissues because of less interference from specimen matrix.

- The combined advantage of sensitivity and low matrix interference enables this assay to detect low concentrations of drug. For example, this method can be used to detect LSD and THC in hair and saliva.

- If a subject attempts to add adulterants to their sample, this will result in a false positive result.

Limitations

- Due to radioactive decay, the kit expiration date is limited (usually ≤ 60 days).

- It cannot be easily adapted to common high-speed analyzers available in the laboratory.

- A product of this test is a radioactive waste, and creates problems for disposal.

Enzyme-Linked Immunosorbent Assay (ELISA)   The application of this technique is more recent for drug testing. Many procedures for testing oral fluid, hair, blood, and urine have been developed within the past decade.

Strengths

- ELISA has a high sensitivity.

- Like RIA, it is less subject to matrix effect.

- Compared to RIA, ELISA is much easier to automate.

- Kit shelf life is longer than RIA (usually greater than one year) because enzyme is used as the label rather than radioactive material.

Limitations

- Not easily adapted to common high-speed analyzers available in the laboratory.

- Cost per sample is generally higher than most of the homogeneous assays.

8.3.3.2 *Homogeneous assays*

Enzyme-Multiplied Immunoassay Technique (EMIT®)   EMIT assays use an enzyme-linked antigen. The label attached to drug in this assay is the enzyme glucose-6-phosphate dehydrogenase (G-6-PDH). The enzymatic activity of G-6-PDH decreases when attached drug is bound to antibody. The presence of a drug in specimen reduces the antibody available to bind to G-6-PDH and hence G-6-PDH activity is increased. G-6-PDH enzyme activity is determined by spectrophotometer measuring the NADH produced at a wavelength of 340 nm. The change in absorbance is directly related to the concentration of the drug present in biological specimen.

Strengths

- Being a homogeneous assay, it allows for easy automation of the procedure.

- Enzyme-related technology is well established, which improves troubleshooting and reduces costs.

- Many addictive drug and specialty drug assays are available.

Limitations

- Interference results from compounds that cross-react with antibody as well as due to substance(s) present in the matrix interrupting the enzyme process.

- Urinary metabolites of aspirin and tolmetin can cause false negative assay results due to interference of NADH measurement at 340 nm.

- Adulterants used to make drug test negative usually cause false negative results.

Kinetic Interaction of Microparticles in Solution (KIMS)   This patented method is marketed as an

Abuscreen online kit by Roche Diagnostic Systems. The labeled compound is a microparticle with drug molecules linked to it. In the absence of the drug of interest, microparticle–drug conjugates bind to antibody molecules forming larger aggregates that scatter transmitted light. As the aggregation reaction proceeds, the change in absorbance increases. If the specimen contains the drug of interest it will bind to antibodies, preventing the formation of microparticle–drug conjugate to antibodies aggregates. This decrease diminishes the rate of absorbance increase. The absorbance recorded is inversely proportional to drug concentration present in the biological material.

Strengths

- Inexpensive homogeneous assay.

- Microparticle–drug conjugates are more stable than enzyme drug conjugates.

- Substances that interfere with agglutination process in KIMS usually cause false positive results. This may be an advantage because false positive will be eliminated by confirmation procedure.

- The absorbance change of the solution is measured as a function. Absorbance from interfering substances does not usually change with time and hence their contribution is minimized.

Limitations

- The linear range for KIMS assay is generally smaller than EMIT and CEDIA.

- The microparticle solution coats the analyzer cuvettes and tubing, so requiring special system maintenance.

Fluorescence Polarization Immunoassay (FPIA)
The most FPIA methods are marketed by Abbott Laboratories for operation of TDX, ADX or Axsym analyzers. Fluorescein-labeled drugs are used as tracers.

Strengths

- Homogeneous immunoassay.

- Fluorescent probes provide low limits of detection.

- Specimen matrices have less effect on changes in fluorescent polarization.

- Fluorescent-labeled drug is more stable than enzyme drug conjugates.

Limitations

- The assays are generally more expensive.

- Fluorescent material present in specimen will occasionally give false positive results.

- Currently not many FPIAs are adaptable for common high-speed analyzers – must be performed on Abbott Company's own analyzers.

Cloned Enzyme Donor Immunoassay (CEDIA)
CEDIA is a trademark method marketed by Microgenic Corporation;it uses genetically engineered fragments of *E. coli* β-galactosidase as an enzyme label. The activity of the enzyme requires assembling two fragments, termed enzyme receptor (EA) and enzyme donor (ED) fragments. ED is linked to the drug and will not re-associate if bound to antibody. The concentration of the drug in biological fluid is directly proportional to enzyme activity.

Strengths

- Homogeneous immunoassay.

- The curve is linear over a wider range of drug concentration.

- The absorbance change of the solution is measured as a function of time, thus minimizing interferences.

Limitations

- CEDIA methods can be affected by urine adulterant and yield false negative result.

Recently, immunoassay techniques have also been modified for on-site testing in different settings (Emergency Room, outpatient clinics). These are usually dipstick tests that use paper strips impregnated with drug specific antibody. The specimen is applied to the dipstick causing a color development. Again, there are various commercial test kits. The presence of color or absence of color depending on the method principle will indicate a positive result.

These on-site kits can yield useful quick results. Issues of accuracy, costs, quality control, and regulatory requirements may limit their application. Clinical laboratories should be involved in decisions to establish on-site testing or provide alternatives for achieving an acceptable rapid turn around time.

8.3.4 Chromatography techniques

Prior to using a chromatography technique it is usually necessary to prepare the specimen and isolate the compound(s) of interest from the biological matrix. This process is often laborious and time consuming. The following steps are involved:

- *Hydrolysis* of specimen containing conjugated drug metabolites as to clear the conjugated bond prior to extraction for better recovery.

- *Protein precipitation* to remove proteins from specimens like blood.

- *Extraction* is used to isolate and concentrate the drug(s) of interest. The common extraction methods are liquid–liquid extraction, solid–liquid (or solid phase) extraction, solid phase micro-extraction, and supercritical fluid extraction.

8.3.4.1 Thin layer chromatography (TLC)

TLC is widely used in many hospital toxicology laboratories. The earliest technical approaches to

drug addiction screening were primarily based on this method. This ingenious technique, developed by Dole *et al.* [6], involves extraction of drug(s) from biological materials like urine and blood, onto ion-exchanged papers. Modifications were made using direct solvent extraction and absorption onto resin columns because of the need for increased analytical sensitivity. This technique does not require expensive equipment and is now also available as a commercial kit from Toxi-Lab (Marion Laboratories/Varian Inc., CA).

However, some limitations became apparent with reference to drug metabolite(s). For example, it was recognized that morphine glucuronide had to be hydrolyzed prior to chromatography to achieve an adequate sensitivity for detection of morphine. Also, after usage of certain drugs (cocaine, marijuana or diazepam), very little of the parent drug is detected in the urine. Rather, their metabolites predominate; benzyoylecgonine, 9-carboxy-THC and oxazepam. Hence, identification of characteristic metabolite patterns is a requisite for detecting drugs of abuse by TLC.

Another problem with TLC is that of interference or lack of analytical specificity. Various drugs, including such widely used agents as antihistamines, can have the same migration distance (RF) and yield the same color response to detection reagents as drugs of adiction. Therefore, definite identification on the basis of chromatographic color reaction and/or RF is impossible. Furthermore, TLC is too slow and cumbersome to be readily applied to emergency toxicology and is not quantitative. Its analytical detection limit is relatively poor.

8.3.4.2 Gas chromatography (gas–liquid chromatography-GC)

Gas chromatography is a chromatographic technique that can be used to separate volatile organic compounds by vaporizing a sample and injecting it onto the head of a chromatographic column. The volatile substances are carried by an inert gas, such as helium or nitrogen, over a stationary phase in the capillary column. The column is held at a temperature high enough to ensure that the compounds under test remain in the vapor state. A solution containing the drug compound is injected at the head of the GC column, where it is heated and vaporized. The vapor is swept over the liquid that coats the stationary phase and dissolved in liquid, returns to and re-dissolves many times during its passage along the column. Thus, through repeated process, very similar compounds can be separated and detected using different types of detectors.

8.3.4.3   High performance liquid chromatography (HPLC)

Gas chromatography requires that a compound or its chemical derivative be stable at temperatures needed to make it vaporize. This places severe limitations. In HPLC methods the compounds have to be soluble and the system usually operates at room temperature. The solvent, which is a mobile phase, is pumped under pressure through a column packed with a stationary phase. The analyte (drug) in the mobile phase emerges at the other end of the column and passes through a detector. Modern HPLC columns perform efficiently in separating the mixture of drug(s); the resolution is not as good as that of GC. Detection of drug is usually achieved by 8.3.2 Ultraviolet spectroscopy, which in its sophisticated form (diode array detection) permits spectral scanning of each eluting peak to aid in identification.

8.3.4.4   Mass spectrometry (MS)

The fundamental physical chemistry properties of a compound's mass (m) and charge (z) make ions unique and this allows for separation within one atomic mass unit. MS operates on the principle that charged particles moving through a magnetic sector or an electric field can be separated from other charged particles according to their mass-to-charge (m/z) ratios. A record of the ions formed and the relative abundance of each are used as a fingerprint to determine the identity of the compound.

All mass spectrometers include a device to introduce the samples (GC, HPLC, capillary electrophoresis), an ionization source to ionize the sample, a mass analyzer in which charged particles are separated according to their m/z ratios, an ion collector, amplifier, as well as a detection device. Contemporary MS also incorporates a computer system for control of the instrument and for the acquisition, display, manipulation, and interpretation of data.

When MS is coupled to GC, HPLC or CE, nearly foolproof drug identification is possible because substances are identified from their retention time measured by GC, HPLC, electrophoretic mobility, their characteristic fragmentation pattern by MS, and using computer-based libraries of drugs fragmentation pattern. GC/MS, LC/MS, LC/MS/MS, and CE/MS can be used to screen, confirm, and quantify a wide variety of drugs simultaneously. Advantages and limitations are listed in Table 8.4.

8.3.4.5   Capillary electrophoresis (CE)

Instrumentation for electrokinetic separations in fused silica capillaries of very small internal diameter has recently become available. The feasibility of employing CE for drug monitoring in body fluids, including plasma, serum, saliva, and urine, has been adapted successfully [7]. In electrophoresis separations, small amounts of samples are introduced by electrokinetic or hydrodynamic techniques. Upon the application of electric current, samples are transported through the capillary by the

Table 8.4   Advantages and limitations of mass spectrometry

Advantages	Limitations
• Specificity	• High cost instrumentation
• Sensitivity	• Extensive sample preparation
• Quantitation with isotope dilution	• Lengthy analysis time
• Library search for unknowns	• Requires well-trained operators

combined action of electrophoresis and electro-osmosis. Detection principles include conductivity, fluorescence (diode array detector) and MS detector.

8.4 SENSITIVITY AND SPECIFICITY

In drug testing, as in other laboratory methods, not all results are accurate. Given that the implications of a positive drug test can be far reaching, it is imperative that those interpreting the tests understand the diagnostic capability of the laboratory method used. The accuracy of a laboratory test is measured by it's sensitivity, specificity, efficiency, and predictive value [8–10]. Detailed information on the accuracy of specific drug tests is well documented and easily referenced (Table 8.5) [11,12]

8.4.1 Sensitivity

Sensitivity refers to the likelihood that a test will yield a positive result when a subject has used a drug. It is expressed as a percentage of calculated drug users. Thus a drug test with a sensitivity of 90% will correctly identify 90% of drug users (true positives), but will yield negative result for the remaining 10% (false negatives).

8.4.2 Specificity

Specificity refers to the likelihood that a test will yield a negative result when a subject has not used a drug. It is expressed as a percentage of nondrug users. Thus a test with a specificity of 90% will yield negative drug test results in 90% of people who are nondrug users (true negatives) and give positive drug test results in the remaining 10% (false positives).

8.4.3 Positive predictive value

Positive predictive value is a statistical description that describes the proportion of subjects with a positive drug test that actually used drugs. Thus a laboratory method with a 90% positive predictive value will yield a positive test result in 90% of subjects using drugs.

Table 8.5 Definition of statistical approach in test performance evaluation

	Patient used drug	Patient did not use drug
Above the cut-off value or tests positive	(A) True Positive	(B) False Positive
Below the cut-off value or tests negative	(C) False negative	(D) True Negative
Sensitivity $= \dfrac{a}{a+c}$ or $\dfrac{\text{true positive test results}}{\text{all patients with disease}}$		Proportion of persons who used drug and who test positive.
Specificity $= \dfrac{d}{d+b}$ or $\dfrac{\text{true negative test results}}{\text{all patients without disease}}$		Proportion of persons who did not use drug and who test negative.
PPV $= \dfrac{a}{a+b}$ or $\dfrac{\text{true positive}}{\text{all positive}}$		Proportion of persons with positive test who actually used drug.
NPV $= \dfrac{d}{d+c}$ or $\dfrac{\text{true negative}}{\text{all negative}}$		Proportion of persons with negative test who do not use drug.

Efficiency $= a + d/a + b + c + d \times 100$

Table 8.6   Sensitivity, specificity: false positive and false negative rates

Technique	Sensitivity	Specificity	False Positive Rate	False Negative Rate
1. Homogeneous Immunoassays (EMIT-1, EMIT-2, ADX)	61–98.5	87–99	0.6–8.4	1.5–38.8
2. RIA	55.1–98.3	92–99.7	0.3–4.7	1.7–44.9
3. On-site Kits (ONTRK, E2- Screen, (Triage)	44.4–95.3	88.7–99.4	1.7–16.4	4.7–55.6
4. TLC (Toxi-Lab)	23.3–82.1	97.4–100	0.4–3.8	17.9–76.7

Drugs analyzed: opiates, methadone, cocaine, cannabinoids, amphetamines, benzodiazepines, and barbiturates.
NOTE: The range given above represents drug assay performance for certain drugs at the lower and upper end.

8.4.4   Negative predictive value

Negative predictive value is a statistical description that describes the proportion of persons with a negative drug test result who actually did not use drugs. Thus a test with a 90% negative predictive value will yield a negative test result in 90% of subjects not using drugs.

8.4.5   Efficiency of test

The efficiency of a drug test is measured by the percentage of subjects in a population classified as drug users and nondrug users. The efficiency is an excellent demonstration of how accurate a test is. If the efficiency of a test is 90%, that means that 90% of a tests results are accurate.

8.4.6   Cut-off values

Cut-off values vary for each specific drug of interest as well as each method of testing. A drug measurement below the cut-off value is considered a negative test result while, in contrast, a drug measurement above the cut-off value is considered a positive test result. In a "perfect" test the cut-off value would easily separate drug users from nonusers, showing no overlap between the groups. In this hypothetical situation both the sensitivity and specificity of the drug test would be 100%. Unfortunately, ideal tests do not exist. Fortunately, the vast plethora of drug research has resulted in well-documented empirical cut-off values that allow laboratories to manipulate the sensitivity and specificity of any particular test. Shifting the cut-off to the left, that is, lowering the cut-off value, increases the sensitivity of the test (fewer false negatives) but reduces the specificity (more false positives). Similarly raising the cut-off value reduces the sensitivity and increases the specificity. Thus, a test with high sensitivity will reveal the majority of drug abusers. Yet, this same test will result in a greater number of false positives requiring conformation procedures at an additional cost. Alternatively, a test with lower sensitivity but higher specificity may be of limited value, since it cannot reveal many nonsymptomatic users of illicit drugs.

In an extensive study, Ferrara *et al.* [13] conducted experimental comparisons of immunochemical and chromatographic techniques with GC/MS, which is the gold standard of detection and measurement. The results are summarized in Table 8.6.

8.5   SCREENING VS. CONFIRMATION METHODS

Screening methods are generally the initial step in an investigation of drug use. Conversely, confirmatory methods are restricted to those samples that are found presumptively positive by the screening method. The screening procedure selected should be efficient, simple to perform, rapid, and comparatively inexpensive. In order to avoid false negatives, a small percentage of false positives with a first step screening are tolerable. This option is only defendable if a reliable confirmation procedure is employed. The confirmatory method should always be based on a different chemical principle than the screening method. Furthermore, it is desirable for the confirmatory method to be more specific and with a detection limit that is lower than or at least equal to that of the screening method (Table 8.7).

Table 8.7 Requirements of screening vs. confirmatory methods

Screening Methods	Confirmatory Methods
• Efficient	• Different chemical principle from screening methods
• Simple	• Greater specificity
• Relatively inexpensive	• Detection limit usually less than screening methods
• Rapid	

8.6 SPECIMENS

For many years toxicologists have detected the presence of drugs in biological materials using body fluids such as blood and urine. In recent years, remarkable advances in sensitive analytical techniques have enabled the analysis of drugs in unconventional biological samples, such as hair, nail, saliva, sweat, and meconium. In post mortem specimens, vitreous humor and various tissues have been analyzed. The disposition of drugs and abuse in each biological matrix can vary considerably compared to excretion in urine [14] is illustrated in Table 8.8.

The unique qualities of each matrix lend themselves nicely to different applications. A summary of advantages and disadvantages of sweat, saliva, and hair compared to urine is presented in Table 8.9.

Table 8.8 Relative occurrence of parent drug and metabolite(s) in urine, saliva, sweat, and hair

Drug	Urine	Saliva	Sweat	Hair
Amphetamine	Amphetamine	Amphetamine	Amphetamine	Amphetamine
Cocaine	BZE > EME > cocaine	Cocaine > BZE ≈ EME	Cocaine > EME ≈ BZE	Cocaine > BZE > EME
Marijuana	Carboxy-metabolite	THC	THC	THC > carboxy-metabolitec
Heroin	Morphine-glucuronide > morphine	Heroin ≈ 6-AM > morphine	Heroin ≈ 6-AM > morphine	6-AM > heroin ≈ morphine
Codeine	Codeine-glucuronide > codeine > norcodeine	Codeine	Codeine	Codeine > morphine
Methamphetamine	Methamphetamine > amphetamine	Methamphetamine	Methamphetamine ≫ amphetamine	Metamphetamine > amphetamine
Phencyclidine	Phencyclidine	Phencyclidine	Phencyclidine	Phencyclidine
Morphine	Morphine-glucuronide > morphine	Morphine	Morphine	Morphine

BZE, benzoylecgonine; EME, ecgonine methyl ester; THC, tetrahydroconnabinol; 6-AM, 6-acetylmorphine.
From reference [14].

Table 8.9   Comparison of urine, saliva, sweat, and hair as specimens for drug addiction testing

Biological matrix	Drug detection time	Major advantages	Major disadvantages	Primary use
Urine	2–4 d	Mature technology; on-site screening methods available; established cut-offs	Only detects recent use; specimen adulteration possible; collection procedure invasive or embarrassing	Detection of recent drug use
Saliva	1–2 d	Easily obtainable; samples "free" drug fraction; parent drug presence; commercial screening methods FDA cleared	Short detection time; oral drug contamination; collection methods influence pH and saliva/plasma ratios; only detects recent use; new emerging technology	Presence of active drug may be linked to performance or impairment
Sweat	2–10 d	Cumulative drug collection device; FDA cleared	Potential for environmental contamination during application and removal of patch	Detection of drug use during wearing of patch
Hair	Months	Detects long term or chronic drug use; similar specimen can be recollected within a few days	Potential for environmental contamination and color bias	Detection of drug use in recent past (1–3 months)

FDA, Food and Drug Administration.
From Reference [14].

8.7   ALCOHOL

8.7.1   Clinical indications for alcohol testing

The immense physiological, pathological, and psychological stigmata of alcohol consumption and dependence are well described by other authors in this textbook. Thus it is of no surprise that alcohol users account for a large proportion of healthcare visits. On a daily basis, medical professionals working in every medical specialty see the effects of alcohol consumption. As a physician taking care of these patients, one will eventually encounter a situation in which it is imperative to know whether or not a patient has consumed alcohol and to what extent. It is at this time that a basic understanding of alcohol's pharmacokinetics, metabolism, as well as the methods used to detect it, will be of the most benefit.

Ethanol (alcohol) belongs to a family of volatile alcohols, which includes methanol and isopropanol. Pharmacologically, it belongs to a family of drugs known as sedative-hypnotics. Ethanol is a central nervous system depressant, and the physiological changes it causes are dose dependant and vary per individual (Table 8.10).

Table 8.10   Dose dependent effects of ethanol

Blood Ethanol Level (% - g/dl)	Emotional and Physiological changes
0.00–02%	Considered as alcohol free.
0.02–0.05%	Most individuals experience mild euphoria with no obvious signs of fine motor dysfunction.
0.05–0.15%	Euphoria along with reduction in motor function, reaction time, and judgment.
0.15–0.30%	Visible signs of intoxication with impaired balance, speech, reaction time, emotional stability comprehension and vision.
>0.30%	Marked loss in motor function, impaired consciousness, associated with possible death in complicated adults.
>0.40%	Respiratory depression associated with most fatalities.

Once ingested, ethanol is rapidly absorbed from the upper gastrointestinal tract and makes its way to the liver via the portal vein. In the liver, hepatocytes oxidize the majority of ethanol via three major enzymatic pathways. Peak blood ethanol concentrations are attained approximately one hour after ingestion, and are influenced by a variety of factors. Height, weight, amount of ethanol consumed, duration of consumption, presence or absence of food, liver function, and gender all play a role. Women will reach consistently higher blood ethanol concentrations than men following an identical oral dose of ethanol. This occurs because women have a smaller total body water distribution than men, and thus the concentration of ethanol is greater in this smaller compartment.

The rate of ethanol elimination from the body is subjected to both zero order and first order enzyme kinetics. Zero order kinetics refers to a reaction process in which the reaction rate is independent of the concentrations of the reactants. In contrast, first order kinetics refers to a reaction process in which the reaction rate is proportional to the concentration of one of the reactants. The determinate of how ethanol will be eliminated is based on the Michaelas–Menten (M/M) constant for the alcohol dehydrogenase (ADH) isoenzyme-I (2–5 mg/dl). The majority of intoxicated individuals will have blood ethanol concentrations that are greater than the M/M constant and thus ethanol elimination is zero order. Ethanol elimination follows first order kinetics when the M/M constant is greater than the blood ethanol concentration. The studies have indicated that the average rate of elimination for ethanol is 0.015 g/dl per hour for men and 0.018 g/dl per hour for women. Several factors can affect this elimination rate. Chronic alcoholics can have increased elimination rates, whereas liver disease will impair the clearance of ethanol. Genetic factors may also be involved in the elimination process, as some ethnic groups have quicker average elimination rates.

Some of the most common and highly agreed upon uses for alcohol testing are listed in Table 8.11. The indications for alcohol testing are also very specialty specific as in the case of drug testing. In the emergency department indications for alcohol testing often include patients with altered mental status due

Table 8.11   Indications for alcohol testing

- Evaluation of all patients with acute onset mental status changes
- Evaluation of all patients with acute onset syndromes
- Evaluation of all multi-system trauma patients
- Evaluation of a patient who is known to be intoxicated or smells like alcohol
- Treating methanol and/or ethylene glycol poisoning
- Monitoring response to inpatient treatment
- Monitoring abstinence in inpatient or outpatient rehabilitation programs
- Occupational medicine
- Forensic and clinical psychiatry
- Sports medicine
- Evaluation of high-risk patients (e.g., physicians, athletes, entertainers)
- Post mortem forensic pathology
- Law enforcement and probation screenings

to poly-pharmacological drug overdoses. Often the initial management of these patients is similar regardless of the substances involved. However, rapid identification of the classes of drugs involved can be very useful in antidotal treatment and resuscitative care. In emergency departments, rapid alcohol testing is useful for diagnosis, management, and treatment of patients with altered mental status or traumatic head injury. In fact, the College of American Surgeons' Committee on Trauma recommends that alcohol testing be considered "essential" for Level I and II trauma centers [15].

8.7.2   Methodology for alcohol testing

Numerous analytical approaches have been suggested for the detection and quantification of alcohol (ethanol) in biological specimens. Generally the methods have been classified as chemical (spot tests, ADH reaction) or instrumental (GC). Comprehensive examination and descriptions of these methods are available [16–19].

8.7.2.1   The conway microdiffusion assay

This assay is a general method for measuring volatile compounds in blood samples. In this assay a blood sample and reagents are placed into a sealed diffusion unit, and any volatile substances diffuse from the sample and come into contact with the reagent. For alcohol testing, acid potassium dichromate is used as the reagent, which is reduced to a purple solution in the presence of alcohol.

A rapid alcohol test for on-site screening (microdiffusion method) of urine alcohol was developed by Toxi-lab [20]. This procedure incorporates the use of a specimen-absorbing matrix, which quickly distills or releases alcohol from the specimen. The released alcohol vapor is concentrated onto an acid dichromate reagent suspended in an inert matrix. The concentrated alcohol vapor is oxidized at this site, in turn reducing the dichromate reagent, which is evidenced by the appearance of a blue-green spot on the detection reagent pad. This procedure was modified and adapted by Gunaga [21] for the screening of volatile alcohols for whole blood, plasma, and other clinical and post mortem biological specimens. This has been the method of preference for this author's laboratory over the last ten years [22]. However, this microdiffusion assay is not specific to ethanol, and should only be used as a screening assay for volatiles.

8.7.2.2 Enzymatic assay

The alcohol dehydrogenase (ADH) assay is commonly used in clinical laboratories. This assay is based on the identical biochemical reaction that ADH catalyzes in the human liver. ADH is responsible for the reversible conversion of ethanol into acetaldehyde with the assistance of the cofactor of NAD +, which is converted into the reduced NADH, which is read at 340 nm [19].

In a secondary reaction, the NADH generated can be coupled to a diaphorase-chromagen system producing a red-colored formazan colloidal suspension that may be read spectrophotometrically at 580 nm. These methods are often automated in clinical laboratories to measure ethanol, and are thus precise and correlate well with gas chromatography procedures. Furthermore, this method exhibits little to no interference in the presence of isopropanol (to 2 g/l), methanol (to 3 g/l), acetone (to 4 g/l) and ethylene glycol (to 3 g/l).

A modification of the enzymatic method was developed for the Abbott-X series analyzers. The NADH produced by the ADH catalyzed reaction of ethanol and NAD reacts with a thiazoyl blue dye, forming a chromagen. This technique is called Radiative Energy Attenuation (REA). This is based on the principle that the measured fluorescence intensity of a solution containing fluorophore and a chromagen is related to the absorbance of the solution. This assay has been used successfully to measure ethanol in serum, fresh blood and post mortem blood specimens.

8.7.2.3 Gas chromatography (GC)

Gas chromatography is a chromatographic technique that can be used to separate volatile organic compounds by vaporizing a sample and injecting it onto the head of a chromatographic column. As describe earlier in this chapter, the organic compounds are separated due to differences in their partitioning behavior between the mobile gas phase and the stationary phase in the column.

The most common method for the analysis of ethanol in biological fluids is the GC method [16]. It can distinguish ethanol from other alcohols, aldehydes, and ketones. It has the sensitivity and precision to quantitate ethanol at a concentration as low as 0.01 g/dl.

The two common GC procedures are direct injection and headspace analysis. Carbowax or porpack columns can be used to achieve separation of volatile analytes. A thermal conductivity detector can be used but a flame ionization detector has greater sensitivity and is more commonly used today. Two commonly used internal standards for ethanol analysis are 1-propanol and 2-butanone. Unfortunately, GC procedure is time consuming and, therefore, not used for emergency determinations. For forensic purposes, GC method is used for confirmation and quantification.

8.7.2.4 Breath alcohol testing instruments

Breath alcohol instruments generally use one of five types of analytical technology. A listing of the most

Table 8.12 Detection technology employed in breath alcohol testing instruments

Primary Detection Principle	Instrument
Infrared Spectrometry	BAC DataMaster
	Intoxilyzer 5000
	Intoxilyzer 1400
	Intoxilyzer 4011A[a]
	Intoximeter 3000[a]
Electrochemical Oxidation/Fuel Cell	Alco-Sensor III, IV
	Alcolmeter S-D2
	Alcomonitor
	Breathalyzer 7410
	Intox EC/IR
	RBT III, IV
Gas Chromatography	Alco-Analyzer 2100
	Intoximeter MK IV[a]
Chemical Oxidation/ Photometry	Breathalyzer Models 900[a]/900A[a]
Taguchi Gas Sensor	A.L.E.R.T. Model J4
	Breath Alcohol Ignition Interlock Devices (BAIIDs)

[a]Instruments that are no longer manufactured.
From Ref. [23].

commonly used instruments and their detection principles are displayed in Table 8.12.

8.7.3 Specimens

Ethanol can be measured from nearly all fluid and tissues samples. The primary specimens for measurement include whole blood, serum, plasma, urine, breath, saliva, and tissue samples. The primary specimens differ for clinical (serum and plasma), law enforcement (breath and whole blood) and post mortem (whole blood, vitreous humor, urine, and tissue) applications.

Blood tubes should be filled and kept caped to prevent loss of ethanol. Blood collected under sterile conditions without preservatives should be analyzed within four hours. Addition of potassium oxalate monohydrate (5.0 mg/ml blood) plus sodium fluoride (1.5 mg/ml blood) is recommended for storage up to two days at 5 °C. Storage may be extended indefinitely if samples are maintained at temperatures $\leq 20\,^{\circ}$C. For up to two days of transport in a nonrefrigerated condition, a higher concentration of sodium fluoride (10 mg/ml of blood) is recommended. Do not use alcohol swabs or pads to prepare venipuncture site for blood collection for either clinical or forensic purposes. Use betadyne instead to cleanse the skin.

In clinical laboratories, analyses for alcohol are commonly performed on serum or plasma. Therefore, it is important to understand the relationship between whole blood alcohol and serum or plasma alcohol concentrations. Since there is about 12–18% more water in a volume of serum or plasma than the corresponding volume of whole blood, one should expect that serum and plasma would have a higher alcohol concentration than the corresponding whole blood.

8.7.3.1 Urine

Aside from blood and breath, a widely used specimen for determining alcohol has been urine. Many studies have been carried out to correlate urine alcohol concentrations with blood alcohol concentrations. The majority of these studies suggest that the average urine : blood ratio is 1 : 3. However, there is tremendous variation in the ratios determined (1.01–1.44). An individual producing dilute urine would be expected to have a lower urine : blood ratio than one producing concentrated urine. There are many additional factors to consider. To diminish these problems, the following procedure is recommended during specimen collection. The bladder is emptied and urine is discarded. After a 20–30 minute wait, a second specimen is obtained and this is used for analysis. The alcohol concentration in this second urine specimen reflects more accurately the blood concentration at that time.

8.7.3.2 Saliva

Although blood and urine are the two most popular specimens for alcohol analysis, saliva is now being used. It has the advantage of urine in being obtainable by noninvasive techniques but it has also the

Table 8.13 Distribution of ethanol in body tissue and fluid compared with blood

Specimen	Multistudy Average	Range of Averages	Number of Studies
Urine	1.29	1.01–1.44	15
Serum or plasma	1.16	1.12–1.18	4
Vitreous humor	1.14	0.99–1.34	8
Saliva	1.13	1.10–1.20	4
Cerebrospinal fluid	1.08	0.92–1.18	4
Skeletal muscle	0.90	0.89–0.91	2
Brain	0.84	0.62–1.24	9
Kidney	0.66	—	1
Liver	0.60	0.56–0.63	3

Copied from *Medico-legal aspects of alcohol* [24].

limitations that it is a highly variable specimen. In spite of these pitfalls, numerous researchers have tried to use saliva alcohol concentrations as an estimate of blood alcohol concentration. Table 8.13 shows the distribution of ethanol in body tissue and fluid compared with blood.

8.7.3.3 Breath

Whenever the patient can deliver a suitable breath sample, breath alcohol analysis is the preferred procedure for clinical purposes. It is an inherently simple, rapid, noninvasive test that reflects the alcohol content of the arterial circulation, which is physiologically, and clinically, more significant than the venous blood alcohol [19]. The desired breath specimen consists of expired alveolar air in which alcohol concentration has reached a typical plateau.

REFERENCES

1. Markovovchick, V.J., Pons, P.T., and O'Meara, O.P. (2003) *Emergency Medicine Secrets*, 3rd edn, Hanley and Belfus Inc., Philadelphia, PA, p. 360.

2. Levine, B. (ed.) (2003) *Principles of Forensic Toxicology*, 2nd edn, AACC Press, Washington, DC.

3. Moffat, A.C., Osselton, M.D. and Widdop, B. (eds) (2004) *Clarke's Analysis of Drugs and Poisons*, 3rd edn, vol. **I**, Pharmaceutical Press, London, England and Chicago, USA.

4. Baselt, R.C. (ed.) (1987) *Analytical Procedures for Therapeutic Drug Monitoring*, 2nd edn, PSG Publishing Co., Littleton, MA.

5. Smith, M.L. (2003) Chapter 8, *Immunoassay in Principles of Forensic Toxicology*, 2nd edn (ed. B. Levine) AACC Press, Washington, DC, pp. 117–137.

6. Dole, V.P., Kim, W.K., and Eglitis, I. (1966) Detection of narcotic drugs, tranquilizers, amphetamines and barbiturates in urine. *JAMA*, **198**, 349.

7. Thormann, W. (1997) Drug monitoring by capillary electrophoresis, *Handbook of Analytical Therapeutic Drug Monitoring and Toxicology* (eds S.H.Y. Wong and I. Sunshine), CRC Press, pp. 1–19.

8. Galen, R.S. and Gambino, S.R. (1975) Beyond normality, *The Predictive Value and Efficiency of Medical Diagnoses*, John Wiley and Sons, Inc.

9. Griner, P.F., Mayewski, R.J., Mashlin, A.I., and Greenland, P. (1981) Selection of interpretation of diagnostic tests and procedures: Principles and applications. *Ann. Intern. Med.*, **94** (4 Pt 2), 557–592.

10. Beck, J.R. and Shultz, E.K. (1986) The use of operating characteristic (ROC) curves in test performance evaluation. *Arch. Pathol. Lab. Med.*, **100**, 689–693.

11. Degresce, R.P., Mazura, A.C., Lifshitz, M.S. *et al.* (1989) Testing for Drugs, in *Drug Testing in the Work Place*, ASCP Press, Chicago, pp. 59–102.

12. Spiehler, V.R. (1992) Statistical approaches to accuracy in drug screening, in *Recent Developments in Therapeutic Drug Monitoring* (ed. I. Sunshine), Marcel Dekker, Inc., NY.

13. Ferrara, S.D., Tedeschi, L. *et al.* (1994) Drugs-of-abuse testing in urine: Statistical approach and experimental comparison of immunochemical and chromatographic techniques. *J. Anal. Tox.*, **18**, 278–291.

14. Cone, E.J. and Preston, K.L. (1999) Drug testing in support of drug-abuse treatment program, *Therapeutic Drug Monitoring and Toxicology*, vol. **20**, AACC, Washington, DC, pp. 175–188.

15. Committee on Trauma, American College of Surgeons (1993) *Resources for Optimal Care of the Injured Patient: 1993*, American College of Surgeons, Chicago, IL.

16. Cravey, R.H. and Jain, N.C. (1974) Current status of blood alcohol methods. *J. Chromatogr. Sci.*, **12**, 209–213.

17. Dubowski, K.M. (1977) Manual for analysis of ethanol in biological liquids. US Dept. of Transportation Report, No. DOT-TSC-NIITSA-76-4.

18. Caplan, Y.H. (1982) The determination of alcohol in blood and breath, in *The Forensic Science Handbook*

(ed. R. Saferstein), Prentice-Hall, Englewood Cliffs, NJ, pp. 592–652.

19. Dubowski, K.M. (1982) Alcohol analysis: Clinical laboratory aspects, part I. *Lab. Manage.*, **20**, 43–54.

20. Bachard, S.S., Schultheis, S.K., and O'Donell, C.M. (1992) A rapid alcohol test for onsite testing, in *Recent Developments in Therapeutic Drug Monitoring and Clinical Toxicology* (ed. I. Sunshine), Marcel Dekker, Inc., NY, pp. 483–488.

21. Gunaga, K.P. (1992) Toxi-lab alcohol screening procedure: Evaluation and adaptation for whole blood, plasma/serum. *Clin. Chem.*, **38**, 1001–1002.

22. Gunaga, K.P. and Smith, M.P. (2008) Toxi-lab alcohol screening procedure as a tool for volatile detection in biological specimens for clinical and post-mortem specimens – 15 years experience. Manuscript to be submitted for publication.

23. Harding, P. (1996) Methods for Breath Analysis, in *Medico-Legal Aspects of Alcohol*, 3rd edn (ed. J.C. Garriott), Lawyers & Judges Publishing Co., Tucson, AZ, pp. 181–217.

24. Garriott, J.C. (ed.) (1996) *Medico-Legal Aspects of Alcohol*, 3rd edn, Lawyers & Judges Publishing Co., Tucson, AZ.

9

Cutaneous manifestations of drug addiction

Kendra Gail Bergstrom and Miguel R. Sanchez

Division of Dermatology, University of Washington, Seattle, WA, 98104, USA

9.1   INTRODUCTION

Drug addiction can be suspected or diagnosed through recognition of characteristic or suggestive skin lesions. Intravenous administration of pharmacologic agents can produce a number of recognizable stigmata that may identify an individual as a misuser of drugs (Table 9.1).

In addition, parenteral drug use can lead to cutaneous and systemic infections. Because of unsafe sex practices, substance misusers have higher risks than the general population of contacting sexually transmitted diseases [1], many of which present with skin lesions. Behavior associated with drug addiction continues to be an important factor in the spread of human immunodeficiency virus [2] (HIV), hepatitis B or C, and other blood-borne infections [3] which can result in protean cutaneous findings. Drug addicts have higher incidences of depression, accidental injuries, and trauma due to criminal violence or domestic abuse. Unfortunately, drug misuse is often excluded as an underlying etiology in the evaluation of these skin lesions.

9.2   CLINICAL MANIFESTATIONS

Most of the cutaneous manifestions associated with illicit drug use can occur in other conditions, but it is their pattern, appearance, and distribution that identify persons with drug dependency. For this reason, it is the combination of dermatological signs and clinical suspicion that lead to suspicion about drug addiction.

9.2.1   Scars

The most specific sign from injectable drug use is the presence of skin tracks (Figure 9.1). Due to direct injury from needles or a reaction to the inoculated agents, punctures, ecchymoses, and crusted erosions trail along the length of the vein

---

Addictive Disorders in Medical Populations   Edited by Norman S. Miller and Mark S. Gold
© 2010 John Wiley & Sons, Ltd.

Table 9.1   Differential diagnosis of cutaneous stigmata of drug addiction

Nasal perforation
Nasal malignancies – lymphoma, carcinoma
Syphilis or yaws
Rhinosporidiosis
Hansen's Disease (leprosy)
Nasal septum trauma
Exposure to chromium solutions

Phlebitis
Livedoid vasculopathy
Mondor Disease (sclerosing thrombitis)

Linear eruptions
Sporotrichosis
Post-chemotherapy hyperpigmentation overlying veins

Abscess, Ulcerations
Atypical mycobacterial infection
Leishmaniasis
Tularemia
Actinomycosis
Ulcerative sarcoidosis

Vesciculobullous lesions
Diabetic bullae
Infections – bullous impetigo, staph scalded skin infection, Vibrio vulnificus
Porphyria cutanea tarda and other acquired blistering disorders

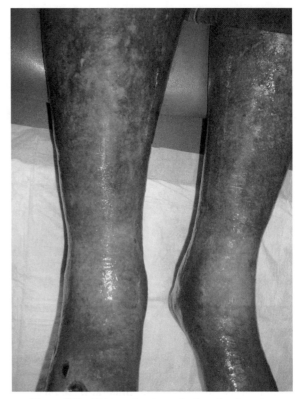

Figure 9.2   Skin tracks along the length of a vein

(Figure 9.2). With repeated injection of irritating drugs and adulterants, the veins become inflamed and fibrosed. Due to their easy access, the veins of the arms and hands are initially injected by most novice addicts. However, to avoid the presence of incriminating track marks, some addicts choose to inject the legs and feet. When the more accessible veins become scarred, drugs are injected into the

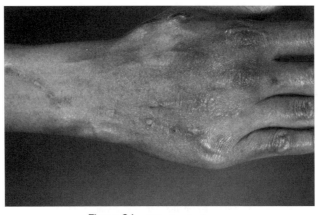

Figure 9.1   Skin tracks image

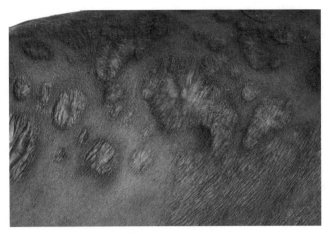

Figure 9.3 Skin popping scars

vessels of the neck, abdomen, axillae, groin, sublingual area, genitals, and any visible or palpable blood vessel, including hemorrhoids. When intact veins or arteries are no longer found, the skin may be cut superficially with razor blades or knives and powdered drugs are rubbed into the lacerations. Some young addicts actually prefer this technique. Subcutaneous and intradermal injections, whether deliberate or accidental, can cause irregular, round, leukodermic, atrophic depressions known as skin popping scars (Figure 9.3). In some cases, indurated, linear, hypertrophic, or keloidal scars form along areas of previous inflammation.

As a potent vasoconstrictor, cocaine can produce tissue ischemia, especially if extravasated into the subcutaneous tissue. Intravenously administered cocaine does not usually form tracks, but cutaneous scars on the extremities resulting from intracutaneous injection have been reported [4]. Pentazocine injection can cause brawny, fibrotic skin that may resemble localized scleroderma, and which may ulcerate [5].

9.2.2 Pigmentary changes

Post-inflammatory pigmentary changes are caused by increased melanin in the epidermis and/or dermis, after the resolution of acute inflammation from any cause. These changes are more common in persons with darkly pigmented skin. Circumferential pigmented bands due to pressure from tourniquets are common in darkly skinned intravenous drug users. Soot tattoos are black macules produced by inadvertent injection of residual carbon that remains on the needle after flaming. Persons who abuse methamphetamine develop grayish, dry, leathery skin with a strange odor.

9.2.3 Ulcerations

Intradermal injections of accidental extravasation of certain drugs and adulterants can cause tissue injury. Heroin and other powder drugs are frequently "cut" with fillers, such as lactose, mannitol, dextrose, acetaminophen, caffeine, baking soda, and flour [6]. Injection of sclerosing adulterants and drugs can produce tender and inflammatory plaques or nodules that ulcerate and heal with epidermal pigmentary changes, woody induration of the dermis and subcutaneous tissue, and retracted scars.

Even inhalation of cocaine can cause skin and muscle infarction. Extensive necrosis of the nose and upper lip accompanied by a necrotizing infection of the subcutaneous soft tissue of the cheeks, forehead, and temporal region has been caused by forced intranasal impaction of crack cocaine [7]. Because of the high alkalinity of the solution, injection of barbiturates can cause tender, edematous, indurated plaques that can ulcerate and become infected. Tripelennamine (pyribenzamine), an antihistamine usually injected in combination with pentazocine or another opioid, also induces tissue necrosis and ulceration [8]. After pentazocine injection, the skin often breaks down, resulting in irregularly shaped, deeply penetrating ulcers that may extend to fat and even muscle. Drug addicts have been known to sabotage medical wound healing efforts to maintain the very vascular granulation tissue in ulcers for heroin administration [9].

9.2.4   Burns

Burns from lit matches, cigarettes, pipes, or paraphernalia, as well as from contact with fire during cooking are common during the altered state of consciousness produced by drug intoxication. Cigarette burns, most commonly on the digits and sternum, occur from lit cigarettes that addicts were smoking before falling asleep. The "necklace sign" is produced by cigarette ashes that fall on the neck when a smoking addict dozes off. Singeing of the eyelashes and eyebrows, resulting in madarosis, may be caused by rising hot vapors during smoking of crack cocaine [10]. Individuals who use crack cocaine may also develop linear, circular, or oval blackened hyperkeratotic lesions caused by the heat of a glass pipe. The areas affected are the thenar eminences of the thumbs (crack thumbs) and the palms (crack hands) of the dominant hand [11]. More severe thermal burns may be incurred on the hands while lighting a crack cocaine pipe with a butane lighter directed downward onto the pipe.

Solvent inhalation is especially popular among adolescents. Minor, superficial burns occur as a result of flash fires caused by the ignition of lighter fluid, composed of butane and isobutene, in enclosed spaces while the fumes are being inhaled. Extensive explosion burns can occur involving the face, neck, arms, and hands as well as the trunk and/or lower extremities [12]. Severe burns also occur when other solvents, such as paint thinner or petrol, become ignited by a cigarette that the sniffer is simultaneously smoking. Widespread burns have resulted from explosions of home methamphetamine laboratories [12].

9.2.5   Pruritus

Itching, from multiple causes, is a common complaint of drug users. Chronic cocaine use coupled with marijuana inhalation may cause pruritus. Prolonged use of cocaine may lead to the development of formication, during which the individual senses that insects are crawling on or under the skin. These tactile hallucinations can be intensely vivid and associated with psychosis [13]. Foraging behavior, involving compulsive searching for pieces of crack cocaine in locations where it was once used, have been reported by some long-term users [14]. Repetitive, stereotypical skin picking leading to excoriations and skin ulcers on the face and extremities has been observed in individuals who abuse methamphetamine. The feeling of euphoria provided by heroin may be accompanied by skin flushing and itching, as well as dry mouth, watery eyes, and runny nose. Chronic heroin users often have dry skin that becomes easily irritated and pruritic.

Generalized or focal, especially genital, itching after drug administration has been named "*high*" pruritus. Conversely, hypoesthesia is a manifestation of low-dose exposure to ketamine and phencyclidine (PCP) [15].

9.2.6   Mucous membrane lesions

The misuse of drugs via an intranasal snorting or smoking has gained popularity in the addict community. Snorting cocaine causes erythema and erosion of the nasal turbinates, nasopharynx, and evental perforation of the nasal septum or even the palate (Figure 9.4) [16]. The pathogenesis is vasoconstriction with resulting ischemia and, occasionally, infection. Chronic rhinitis, epistaxis, osteolytic sinusitis, gingival retraction, and bruxism are other complications. Halitosis and frequent lip smacking are signs of cocaine addiction. Cuts from chipped glass pipes and thermal burns may be present on the

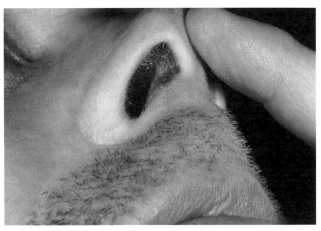

Figure 9.4 Nasal/palatal injury from intranasal cocaine use

lips of some crack cocaine users. Sniffing heroin less often causes these charges. However, invasive fungal rhinosinusitis appears to be a complication unique to intranasal narcotic abuse. A case of pemphigus vegetans, Neumann type, restricted to the intranasal tissue was reported to have been induced by inhalation of heroin [17].

Xerotic chelitis is observed commonly in methamphetamine and heroin addicts [18]. Methamphetamine users also have red, dry noses. Transient eyelid edema has been described with opiate addiction. The typical red or "bloodshot" eye frequently occurs with marijuana and sometimes with cocaine or phencyclidine use. Scleral hemorrhages in drug addicts are usually traumatic but may be caused by septic emboli due to endocarditis. There are reports of men applying cocaine powder to their glans penis to postpone ejaculation and of women rubbing cocaine on their genitals to enhance pleasure. These practices can lead to priapism, irritant dermatitis, and even ulcerations. Priapism can follow crack cocaine inhalation [19]. Penile ulcers have developed after the injection of heroin into the shaft veins.

Marked dental decay and gingival disease are common in hard-core users of opiates, as a result of the effects of opiates and of poor hygiene. Hallucinogen-induced xerostomia also predisposes to caries. Persons addicted to methamphetamine, especially snorters, have higher tooth wear caused by teeth clenching. Habitual chewing of betel palm seeds, which contain a narcotic stimulant – a practice in parts of Southeast Asia – stains the teeth a brown color.

9.2.7 Granulomas

When individuals inject foreign material into the skin, either deliberately as a narcotic or as an inert ingredient, the body may mount a granulomatous response to the foreign body. Granulomas present clinically as firm, moveable subcutaneous nodules in the superficial dermis usually without overlying epidermal change.

Pulmonary foreign body granulomas have been found in 30% of addicts on whom autopsies have been performed [20]. While not at as common as pulmonary granulomas, cutaneous granulomas can develop months to years after exposure. In particular, injection of silica can lead to silicone granulomas. This process may take years because silicone must convert into its colloidal silicate form. Most granulomas are caused by the injection of hydrous magnesium silicate (talc) and, less often, starch, into subcutaneous tissue, the deep dermis, and walls of veins. Talc granulomas also may develop in the liver, lymph nodes, spleen, and bone marrow. In addition to being a popular adulterant for powdered drugs, talc is the main ingredient in some narcotic tablets that are crushed, diluted in liquid, and injected.

Other causes of granulomatous reaction, such as sarcoidosis, tuberculosis, and atypical fungal or mycobacterial infection, should be considered in the differential diagnosis of granulomas of the skin. In fact, any of these diagnosis can occur concurrently with drug-induced granulomas in the same individual.

9.3 CELLULITIS AND SOFT TISSUE INFECTIONS

Skin and soft tissue infections are the most common disorders for which drug addicts seek care and are hospitalized [21]. In a study of 127 hospitalized intravenous drug users [22], the admitting diagnoses were cellulitis (40.9%), abscess with cellulitis (32.3%), abscess alone (16.5%), infected skin ulcers (10.2%), necrotizing fasciitis (7.1%), and septic phlebitis with cellulitis (5.5%). Lymphangitis may accompany skin infection, and the possible presence of osteomyelitis or pyogenic arthritis should be considered. Because upper extremity vessels are preferentially used, cellulitis of the hand, forearm, and arm is particularly common and should be treated aggressively. Necrotizing cellulitis and gangrene have been reported in 7% of drug addicts with upper extremity cellulitis [23].

In parenteral drug users, *Staphylococcus aureus* is the most frequently cultured bacterium from soft tissue infections, followed in successive order of prevalence by streptococcal species and by other common oral or skin flora [24]. Attempts to obtain cultures are prudent because skin infection by Gram negative bacteria, anaerobes, and unusual organisms is relatively common. Notably, in one study, the flora spectrum of street heroin had no relationship to the bacteria causing infections in intravenous drug users [23].

Combined use of tripelennamine and pentazocine, popular since the 1980s, favors selective survival of *Pseudomonas aeruginosa* [25]. These two compounds, which are usually bacteriocidal to *staphylococcus* and other skin flora, allowed the survival of a specific type of *Pseudomonas* that causes skin and soft tissue infection when injected intravenously. In patients who use these drugs, *Pseudomonas* should be considered as a source of infection.

The use of quinine and other adulterants in heroin predisposes to *Clostridium* soft tissue infection. Wound botulism due to *Clostridium botulinum* type A occurs almost exclusively in drug addicts. Several cases have been reported from California and other western states during the past decade [26]. Infection with this species can lead to systemic botulism, including transient paralysis of the diaphragm and ventilator dependence for a period of up to months. Botulism is associated with parenteral injection, especially skin popping of black tar heroin, a form that derives its color from impurities and adulterants during its manufacture. This form of heroin is highly hygroscopic and has a high water content that supports the growth of microorganisms. The spores of *C. botulinum* are not destroyed by heating the contaminated heroin and are subsequently inoculated into subcutaneous tissue, where they germinate and produce toxin. There is pain, tenderness, and swelling, but in the early stage the characteristic signs of cellulitis or an abscess may not be prominent. Other clostridia, such as *C. tetani,* have also caused outbreaks of tetanus and *C. sordellii* has been associated with outbreaks of necrotizing fasciitis [27,28].

In cocaine snorters, the intranasal septum or paranasal sinuses can become infected, leading at times to osteomyelitis [29]. Necrotizing cellulitis or Fournier's gangrene of the scrotum and penis has been reported in an addict who accidentally injected cocaine into the femoral artery instead of the vein [30].

Due to the popularity of skin popping, the incidence of cutaneous abscesses has been increasing. Abscesses from such subcutaneous drug injection are often multi-lobulated and deep, with extensive necrosis that requires exploration and debridement. Superficial abscesses may rupture spontaneously, leaving behind punched-out ulcers. In severe cases, abscesses may be contiguous with bone when osteomyelitis is present. Cervical abscesses usually occur in the anterior cervical triangle and may cause life-threatening complications, such as mediasteinitis, pneumomediasteinum, airway obstruction, internal jugular vein thrombsis, and extension into the carotid sheath. Abscesses in the groin may be deep and extensive, especially if they originate in the femoral triangle. The severity of pain usually exceeds the degree expected from clinical findings. Computed tomographic scanning is needed to determine the extent of involvement of deep abscesses and abscesses in regions such as the neck and groin [31].

In more than one-half of drug use related abscesses, only one pathogen is cultured, but in 33–45% more than one organism is present [22]. Any bacteria may be recovered from an abscess, but the more commonly cultured ones are *S. aureus* (20–60%), *Streptococcus* species (25%), and Gram negative rods (up to 25%). The rate of methicillin-resistant *Staphylococcus aureus* (MRSA) in intravenous drug users, particularly those who are HIV infected, has escalated to the point that any skin bacterial infection must be considered to be caused by this highly resistant and virulent bacteria until otherwise proven by culture [32]. MRSA soft tissue infections have also been reported to be developing with alarming frequency in methamphetamine addicts due to skin damage from repetitive skin picking. Anaerobic bacteria are also more common, particularly in polymicrobial infections [33]. In one study [34], anaerobic bacteria were recovered from two-thirds of abscesses, and in one-third of these were the only cultured organism. *Eikenella corrodens*, an oral flora bacterium, is cultured from some abscesses caused by injections of methylphenidate [35]. Fever and leukocytosis are not absolutely reliable measures of severity and are absent in about one-half of cases. Curiously, some abscesses develop months after a patient has ceased to use drugs.

Necrotizing fasciitis with or without myositis requires extensive subfascial surgical debridement. In some cases, only swelling or inconspicuous cellulitis is apparent. However, severe pain out of proportion to clinical signs is present in 94% of cases [36]. If the clinician disregards the patient's complaint merely as a request for narcotics, the outcome may be devastating [32]. For this reason, surgical exploration is mandatory in any addict with cellulitis and unexplainable severe pain. Multiple organisms are cultured in 59–85% of cases. Anaerobes are present in 12% of cases. The presence of gas is not pathognomonic for *Clostridium* infection, and can also be caused by *Staphylococcus*. The infection will progress in a majority of patients treated with intravenous antibiotics without surgical debridement. A decrease in the mortality rate from 27 to 7% was reported with a protocol consisting of early diagnosis, intravenous broad-spectrum antimicrobial therapy, supportive care, early subfascial debridement, and repeated wound debridement every 8–12 hours until no necrotic tissue is formed [32]. In this study, between two and four debridements were needed.

Infectious endocarditis is the most common systemic bacterial infection in intravenous drug users and is increasing by 40–60% annually, despite a relatively stable number of drug-using addicts during the same period [37]. Although in some reports, hospitalized addicts with skin and soft tissue infections have positive blood cultures, bacteremia from skin infection is not common [38]. Intravenous drug users with advanced HIV immunosuppression are predisposed to developing endocarditis. Cutaneous signs of endocarditis include painful red-purple, slightly raised, plaques often with a pale center often on the fingers or toes due to bacterial vasculitis (Osler nodules), nontender often hemorrhagic small nodules usually occurring on the palms and soles due to bacterial microembolism (Janeway lesions), splinter hemorrhages, necrotic ulcer arising from a bulla, surrounded by an erythematous halo caused by *P. aeruginosa* (ecthyma gangrenosum), ecchymosis, petechiae and purpura fulminans.

Sporadic cases of toxic shock syndrome related to intravenous heroin abuse have been reported [39]. Nephrotic syndrome from amyloidosis has been reported in skin poppers and intravenous drug users with chronically draining skin lesions [40].

9.4   FUNGAL INFECTION

Fungal infections can broadly be classified into superficial (dermatophytosis), deep (aggressive forms of superficial fungi, invasive fungi), and disseminated (usually in an immunocompromised host). Drug users may have an increased incidence of many of these infections due either to their drug use or increased incidence of concurrent diseases, such as HIV and HCV [2,3].

Even in the absence of HIV infection, the incidence of dermatophytosis, including onychomycosis (nail infection), tinea pedis, tinea cruris, and tinea corporis is higher among intravenous drug addicts [41]. Injections of brown heroin have caused disseminated candidiasis due to yeast overgrowth in the lemon juice used to dissolve the heroin [42]. Complications of disseminated fungal infection include ocular disease (uveitis, endophthalmitis), monoarthritis, osteochondritis, and pleuritis. Unlike HIV infection, intravenous drug use, together with diabetes mellitus, severe neutropenia, and deferoxamine therapy for iron overload, is a predisposing factor to zygomycosis, including infection, particularly with species of *Mucor* and *Rhizopus*. The characteristic lesion is a cellulitic plaque or abscess that rapidly becomes edematous and necrotic.

9.5   VASCULAR LESIONS AND VASCULITIS

The most common vascular lesions in addicts are ecchymoses and hematomas from extravasated blood along injected vessels. Petechiae, nonblanching red macules less than one centimeter in diameter, may form distal to tourniquets. Addicts who inject intra-arterially are at risk of developing vascular compromise of the hands with discoloration, edema, and cool temperature. Arterial constriction or emboli can lead to gangrene and loss of digits or a limb. Repeated vascular injury and infection of the digits may eventuate in irreversible contractures (camptodactylia) that resemble Dupuytren's disease. It is important to evaluate any patient with contractures, inflammation, or edema of the hands for soft tissue infection, as well as underlying musculoskeletal complications such as fibrous myopathy, joint restriction, muscle contractures, inflexible ankylosis, and suppurative tenosynovitis. Digital thrombosis with extensive infarctive skin lesions and associated hepatitis and glomerulonephritis may follow intravenous injection of cocaine into an arm vein. Painful discoloration with resulting ulceration of the palm also can result from injection of cocaine into the radial artery.

Cocaine may produce superficial or deep venous thrombosis. An erythematous, tender cord is the hallmark sign of superficial thrombophlebitis, which can be caused by a local pro-coagulant state after intravenous injection, or associated with a localized cellulitis secondary to infection. Rarely, mycotic infection may result in a vascular aneurysm, most frequently in the femoral artery, and require immediate surgery.

Quinine, a favored adulterant because of its bitter taste similar to heroin and its enhancement of the narcotic euphoria, is destructive to lymphatics, causing chronic, nonpitting hand or limb edema after repeated injections.

Injected propoxyphene (Darvon) produces thrombophlebitis and skin necrosis. In rare cases it has also caused disseminated intravascular coagulation.

9.5.1   Vasculitis

Necrotizing vasculitis from injected drugs usually develops on the neck or extremity as a warm, firm, tender mass that may be misdiagnosed as an abcess. Pseudovasculitis with aggressive nasal destruction, as well as oropharyngeal and cutaneous ulcers, may be misdiagnosed as Wegener's granulomatosis in cocaine addicts, especially because perinuclear antinutrophil cytoplasmic antibody (p-ANCA) levels may be falsely positive.

9.5.2 Vesiculobullous lesions

Blisters on the skin are classified in the dermatologic nomenclature as vesicles, which measure less than one centimeter in diameter or bullae, which are at least one centimeter in diameter. The causes of vesiculobullous lesions are extensive, but several patterns may be seen in drug users. Burns are one cause of vesiculobullous lesions. Traumatic vesicles or bullae at the site of injection are observed occasionally.

Comatose patients who have overdosed on barbituates or other sedative drugs often develop pressure-related erythema, bullae, and ulcerations. These so-called coma bullae are induced by chronic pressure in a particular location. Angular, irregular patterns or patterns approximating clothing may be clues to these processes. Unlike bedridden patients, who typically develop pressure-induced lesions on the sacral or ischial areas, elbows, or heels, addicts may present with bullae in unusual body areas and configurations depending on the body position in which they lost consciousness.

Vesicles or bullae can be a sign of concurrent infection. Bullous impetigo, a disease caused by local *Staphylococcus* infection, can cause bullae over sites of skin damage or trauma (from injecting, for example). In rare cases, salt water pathogens like *Vibrio vulnificus* can cause hemorrhagic bullae on the lower legs and feet of individuals who walk barefoot in salt or brakish water.

If coma bullae are suspected, a thorough evaluation should be undertaken to evaluate whether deeper damage, such as fasciitis, rhabdomyolysis, compartment syndrome, or nerve palsy, is present. The chronic pressure that causes coma bullae often leads to deeper damage as well.

9.6 ACNE AND PILOSEBACEOUS EFFECTS

Anabolic steroid use can cause acne, cysts, oily hair or skin, male or female pattern alopecia, increased hair growth in women, gynecomastia in men, coarse skin, edema, testicular atrophy, and clitoral enlargement. Papulopustular facial acneiform eruption in habitual users of 3, 4-methylenedioxymethamphetamine (MDMA, "Ecstasy") may be associated with systemic adverse effects such as hepatic damage [43]. Hyperhidrosis is a common complaint secondary to amphetamines. Piloerection, paresthesias, and percutaneous flushing are manifestations of the somatic but not the perceptual phase of lysergic acid diethylamide (LSD) intoxication. In addition to constricted pupils and runny nose, gooseflesh is a sign of opiate intoxication.

9.7 ASSOCIATED NONINFECTIOUS SKIN DISEASES

Seborrheic dermatitis – scaling on the scalp, eyebrows, nasolabial fold, and beard – may be more frequent in cocaine users. Eczema, particularly contact dermatitis, has been reported to occur more frequently in habitual users of illicit drugs. Pseudoacanthosis nigricans has been observed in heroin addicts [44]. Cocaine use has been implicated in causing or unmasking scleroderma [45] both in a local and systemic manner.

9.8 DRUG INDUCED REACTIONS

As with other medications, hypersensitivity responses can be induced by addictive drugs. These include morbiliform exanthemaous eruptions, urticaria, fixed drug reactions, leukocytoclastic vasculitis, erythema multiforme, and toxic epidermal necrolysis. Dermographism, the formation of a wheal on normal skin after firm stroking, is common. In addicts with fixed drug eruptions, one or multiple pigmented patches on the skin and mucous membranes may develop.

Narcotic addiction is a common cause of falsely reactive nontreponemal tests for syphilis, so-called biological false positive serologic tests (VDRL, rapid plasma regain tests) [46]. In these cases, treponemal test (Microhemoagglutination-Treponema Pallidum, Fluorescent Treponemal Antibody absorption tests) will be nonreactive. However, in addicts who have had syphilis, not only will both tests be positive but the titers of the treponemal tests also may not decrease after treatment.

REFERENCES

1. Fitzgerald, T., Lundgren, L., and Chassler, D. (2007) Factors associated with HIV/AIDS high-risk behaviours among female injection drug users. *AIDS Care*, **19** (1), 67–74.

2. Burt, R.D., Hagan, H., Garfein, R.S. *et al.* (2007) Trends in hepatitis B virus, hepatitis C virus, and human immunodeficiency virus prevalence, risk behaviors, and preventive measures among Seattle injection drug users aged 18–30 years, 1994–2004. *J. Urban Health*, **84** (3), 436–454.

3. Aceijas, C. and Rhodes, T. (2007) Global estimates of prevalence of HCV infection among injecting drug users. *Int. J. Drug Policy*, **18** (5), 352–358.

4. Kircik, L.H., Wirth, P., and Pincus, S.H. (1992) Scars on the legs. Cutaneous fibrosis resulting from intracutaneous injection of cocaine. *Arch. Dermatol.*, **128** (12), 1644–1647.

5. Ho, J., Rothchild, Y.H., and Sengelmann, R. (2004) Vitamin B12-associated localized scleroderma and its treatment. *Dermatol. Surg.*, **30** (9), 1252–1255.

6. Zhang, D., Shi, X., Yuan, Z. *et al.* (2004) Component analysis of illicit heroin samples with GC/MS and its application in source identification. *J. Forensic. Sci.*, **49** (1), 81–86.

7. Seyer, B.A., Grist, W., and Muller, S. (2002) Aggressive destructive midfacial lesion from cocaine abuse. *Oral Surg. Oral Med. Oral Pathol. Oral Radiol. Endod.*, **94** (4), 465–470.

8. Conde-Taboada, A., De la Torre, C., García-Doval, I. *et al.* (2006) Scalp necrosis and ulceration secondary to heroin injection. *Int. J. Dermatol.*, **45** (9), 1135–1136.

9. Williams, A.M. and Southern, S.J. (2005) Conflicts in the treatment of chronic ulcers in drug addicts – case series and discussion. *Br. J. Plast. Surg.*, **58** (7), 997–999.

10. Tames, S.M. and Goldenring, J.M. (1986) Madarosis from cocaine use. *N. Engl. J. Med.*, **314** (20), 1324.

11. Payne-James, J.J., Munro, M.H., and Rowland Payne, C.M. (2007) Pseudosclerodermatous triad of perniosis, pulp atrophy and 'parrot-beaked' clawing of the nails – a newly recognized syndrome of chronic crack cocaine use. *J. Forensic Leg. Med.*, **14** (2), 65–71.

12. Ho, W.S., To, E.W., Chan, E.S. *et al.* (1998) Burn injuries during paint thinner sniffing. *Burns*, **24** (8), 757–759; Santos, A.P., Wilson, A.K., Hornung, C.A. *et al.* (2005) Methamphetamine laboratory explosions: a new and emerging burn injury. *J. Burn Care Rehabil.*, **26** (3), 228–232.

13. Cubells, J.F., Feinn, R., Pearson, D. *et al.* (2005) Rating the severity and character of transient cocaine-induced delusions and hallucinations with a new instrument, the Scale for Assessment of Positive Symptoms for Cocaine-Induced Psychosis (SAPS-CIP). *Drug Alcohol Depend.*, **80** (1), 23–33.

14. Rosse, R.B., Fay-McCarthy, M., Collins, J.P. Jr *et al.* (1994) The relationship between cocaine-induced paranoia and compulsive foraging: a preliminary report. *Addiction*, **89** (9), 1097–1104.

15. Oye, I. (1998) Ketamine analgesia. NMDA receptors and the gates of perception. *Acta Anaesthesiol. Scand.*, **42** (7), 747–749.

16. Goodger, N.M., Wang, J., and Pogrel, M.A. (2005) Palatal and nasal necrosis resulting from cocaine misuse. *Br. Dent. J.*, **198** (6), 333–334.

17. Downie, J.B., Dicostanzo, D.P., and Cohen, S.R. (1998) Pemphigus vegetans-Neumann variant associated with intranasal heroin abuse. *J. Am. Acad. Dermatol.*, **39** (5 Pt 2), 872–875.

18. Odeh, M., Oliven, A., and Bassan, H. (1992) Morphine and severe dryness of the lips. *Postgrad. Med. J.*, **68** (798), 303–304.

19. Munarriz, R., Hwang, J., Goldstein, I. *et al.* (2003) Cocaine and ephedrine-induced priapism: case reports and investigation of potential adrenergic mechanisms. *Urology*, **62** (1), 187–192.

20. Kringsholm, B. and Christoffersen, P. (1987) Lung and heart pathology in fatal drug addiction. A consecutive autopsy study. *Forensic Sci. Int.*, **34** (1–2), 39–51.

21. Ebright, J.R. and Pieper, B. (2002) Skin and soft tissue infections in injection drug users. *Infect. Dis. Clin North Am.*, **16** (3), 697–712, Review.

22. Hasan, S.B. *et al.* (1988) Infectious complications in IV drug abusers. *Infect Surg.*, **7**, 218.

23. Smith, D.J. Jr, Busuito, M.J., Velanovich, V. *et al.* (1989) Drug injection injuries of the upper extremity. *Ann. Plast. Surg.*, **22** (1), 19–24.

24. Gonzalez, M.H., Garst, J., Nourbash, P. *et al.* (1993) Abscesses of the upper extremity from drug abuse by injection. *J. Hand Surg. [Am]*, **18** (5), 868–870.

25. Botsford, K.B., Weinstein, R.A., Nathan, C.R., and Kabins, S.A. (1985) Selective survival in pentazocine and tripelennamine of *Pseudomonas aeruginosa* serotype O11 from drug addicts. *J. Infect Dis.*, **151** (2), 209–216.

26. Cooper, J.G., Spilke, C.E., Denton, M., and Jamieson, S. (2005) Clostridium botulinum: an increasing complication of heroin misuse. *Eur. J. Emerg. Med.*, **12** (5), 251–252.

27. Brett, M.M., Hood, J., Brazier, J.S., *et al.* (2005) Soft tissue infections caused by spore-forming bacteria in injecting drug users in the United Kingdom. *Epidemiol. Infect.*, **133** (4), 575–582. Review.

28. Kimura, A.C., Higa, J.I., Levin, R.M. *et al.* (2004) Outbreak of necrotizing fasciitis due to *Clostridium sordellii* among black-tar heroin users. *Clin. Infect. Dis.*, **38** (9), e87–e91.

29. Talbott, J.F., Gorti, G.K., and Koch, R.J. (2001) Midfacial osteomyelitis in a chronic cocaine abuser: a case report. *Ear. Nose. Throat. J.*, **80** (10), 738–740, 742–743.

30. Mouraviev, V.B., Pautler, S.E., and Hayman, W.P. (2002) Fournier's gangrene following penile self-injection with cocaine. *Scand J. Urol. Nephrol.*, **36** (4), 317–318.

31. Johnston, C. and Keogan, M.T. (2004) Imaging features of soft-tissue infections and other complications in drug users after direct subcutaneous injection ("skin popping"). *Am. J. Roentgenol.*, **182** (5), 1195–1202.

32. Callahan, T.E., Schecter, W.P., and Horn, J.K. (1998) Necrotizing soft tissue infection masquerading as cutaneous abscess following illicit drug injection. *Arch. Surg.*, **133** (8), 812–817.

33. Cohen, A.L., Shuler, C., McAllister, S. *et al.* (2007) Methamphetamine use and methicillin-resistant *Staphylococcus aureus* skin infections. *Emerg. Infect. Dis.*, **13** (11), 1707–1713.

34. Henriksen, B.M., Albrektsen, S.B., Simper, L.B. *et al.* (1994) Soft tissue infections from drug abuse. A clinical and microbiological review of 145 cases. *Acta Orthop. Scand.*, **65** (6), 625–628.

35. Brooks, G.F., O'Donoghue, J.M., Rissing, J.P. *et al.* (1974) *Eikenella corrodens*, a recently recognized pathogen: infections in medical-surgical patients and in association with methylphenidate abuse. *Medicine (Baltimore)*, **53** (5), 325–342, Review.

36. Wong, C.H., Chang, H.C. *et al.* (2003) Necrotizing fasciitis: clinical presentation, microbiology, and determinants of mortality. *J. Bone Joint Surg. Am.*, **85-A** (8), 1454–1460.

37. Cooper, H.L., Brady, J.E., Ciccarone, D. *et al.* (2007) Nationwide increase in the number of hospitalizations for illicit injection drug use-related infective endocarditis. *Clin. Infect. Dis.*, **45** (9), 1200–1203.

38. Gordon, R.J. and Lowy, F.D. (2005) Bacterial infections in drug users. *N. Engl. J. Med.*, **353** (18), 1945–1954, Review.

39. Chapman, R.L., Colville, J.M., and Lauter, C.B. (1982) Toxic-shock syndrome related to intravenous heroin use. *N. Engl. J. Med.*, **307** (13), 820–821.

40. Tan, A.U. Jr, Cohen, A.H., and Levine, B.S. (1995) Renal amyloidosis in a drug abuser. *J. Am. Soc. Nephrol.*, **5** (9), 1653–1658.

41. Gaeta, G.B., Maisto, A., Sichenze, C. *et al.* (1994) Mucocutaneous diseases in drug addicts with or without HIV infection. A case-control study. *Infection*, **22** (2), 77–80.

42. Shankland, G.S. and Richardson, M.D. (1989) Possible role of preserved lemon juice in the epidemiology of candida endophthalmitis in heroin addicts. *Eur. J. Clin. Microbiol. Infect. Dis.*, **8** (1), 87–89.

43. Wollina, U., Kammler, H.J., Hesselbarth, N. *et al.* (1998) Ecstasy pimples – a new facial dermatosis. *Dermatology*, **197** (2), 171–173.

44. Young, A.W. Jr and Sweeney, E.W. (1973) Cutaneous clues to heroin addiction. *Am. Fam. Physician.*, **7** (2), 79–87.

45. Attoussi, S., Faulkner, M.L., Oso, A., and Umoru, B. (1998) Cocaine-induced scleroderma and scleroderma renal crisis. *South Med. J.*, **91** (10), 961–963.

46. Kaufman, R.E., Weiss, S., Moore, J.D. *et al.* (1974) Biological false positive serological tests for syphilis among drug addicts. *Br. J. Vener Dis.*, **50** (5), 350–353.

Part Three

Addictive disorders and clinical diseases

10

Addictive disorders in primary care medicine

Robert Mallin

Department of Family Medicine, Medical University of South Carolina, Charleston, SC 29425, USA

10.1 INTRODUCTION

The prevalence of addictive disorders in primary care outpatients varies from 7 to 28% [1,2]. Drug use including alcohol and tobacco continues to be the greatest threat to our nation's health, causing well over 600 000 deaths yearly in the United States. Although the prevalence of drug use varies within populations it remains significant for all groups seen in primary care medical practices.

50% of Americans currently drink alcohol: 23% binge drink, defined as five or more drinks on at least one occasion in the 30 days prior to the survey; 7% are heavy drinkers, defined as binge drinking on five or more days in the past month.

29% of Americans are current users of a tobacco: 25% smoke cigarettes, 6% smoke cigars, 3% use smokeless tobacco, and 1% smoke pipes.

8% of the population aged 12 years or older, are current illicit drug users. Current drug use means use of an illicit drug during the month prior to the survey interview. 6% are using marijuana, 1% are using cocaine and less than 1% are using hallucino-gens, and heroin. 6% of Americans misuse prescription medications [3].

As with other chronic medical conditions, the best hope for prevention, detection and treatment of substance use disorders begins with the primary care office visit. The primary care physician is uniquely situated to intervene in this area but often feels helpless to do so. Research reveals that primary care physicians in the United States perceive themselves as being less prepared to diagnose substance use disorders than other chronic conditions. They find it more difficult to discuss these topics with their patients, and are more skeptical about the effective-ness of available treatments [4]. Despite these concerns, 88% of primary care physicians report that they routinely screen their patients for substance use problems and 82% refer patients who screen positively for treatment. Further study reveals that although most of these physicians ask about alcohol consumption, less than 20% use a formal screening tool or ask follow-up questions important for diag-nosing substance use disorders [5].

Addictive Disorders in Medical Populations   Edited by Norman S. Miller and Mark S. Gold
© 2010 John Wiley & Sons, Ltd.

10.2   MEDICAL AND PSYCHIATRIC COMPLICATIONS OF ADDICTION

The high prevalence of addictive disease and the frequency of serious medical complications associated with addiction require that the astute primary care physician be vigilant in identifying addiction as the cause of many common medical problems, as well as looking for these common medical complications in patients identified with the disease of addiction. Because primary care physicians are often faced with the initial presentation and treatment of psychiatric illness, the high comorbidity of additive and psychiatric disease must be appreciated and considered in the evaluation of primary care patients.

10.2.1   Alcohol-related illness [6–9]

Moderate alcohol intake, defined as a daily average of two drinks or less for men and one drink or less for women, may actually improve mortality, especially for cardiovascular disease. There is, however, increased risk for those drinking over three drinks daily [10]. There is no organ system that escapes potential ruin from excessive alcohol consumption (Table 10.1). Patients with alcohol dependence may present with symptoms as benign as insomnia, or as impressive as ascities, and hepatic failure. Excessive alcohol intake has been described as the most common cause of secondary hypertension. Recent evidence suggests that this may be primarily a gender related phenomenon, with men having the greatest increase in blood pressure from excessive drinking [11]. Arrhythmias are associated with excessive alcohol use. As much as 20% of atrial fibrillation is thought to be secondary to chronic alcohol consumption [12]. Alcohol is toxic to muscle, and especially to cardiac muscle. 50% of patients with idiopathic caridomyopathy have alcohol dependence [13]. Patients that drink alcohol heavily are at greater risk for stroke as well [14].

Alcohol gastritis is a common cause of dyspepsia, and Barret's esophagus a common explanation for persistent heartburn. Mallory–Weiss tears are a frequent cause of hospitalization for alcohol dependence patients. Excessive alcohol use is the most common cause of acute and chronic pancreatitis [15]. Alcohol-related liver disease is the ninth most common cause of death in the United States. It presents in several forms. As many as 90% of alcoholics have alcoholic steatohepatitis (fatty liver

Table 10.1   Common medical complications of alcoholism [6–9]

Gastrointestinal	Cancers of the oral cavity, tongue, pharynx, esophagus, stomach, colon, pancreas, liver, bile ducts, hepatitis, steatosis, cirrhosis, portal hypertension, varices, spontaneous bacterial peritonitis, Gastritis, esophagitis, pancreatitis, gastroesophageal reflux, Barret's esophagus, Mallory weis tears, Bleeding
Cardiovascular	Hypertension, cardiomyopathy, atrial fibrillation, coronary artery disease, dysrhythmia, sudden death
Neurologic	Sedative hypnotic withdrawal, seizures, delirium tremens, hallucinosis, dementia, Korsakoffs encephalopathy, Wernicke's syndrome, cerebellar dysfunction, intreacranial bleeding, subdural hematoma, stroke, myopathy, peripheral neuropathy
Pulmonary	Aspiration, pneumonia, pneumonitis, sleep apnea, respiratory failure, tuberculosis
Renal	Acute renal failure, hepatorenal syndrome, rhabdomyolysis
Endocrine	Diabetes, hyper/hypoglycemia, alcohol ketoacidosis, testicular atrophy, gynecomastia, breast cancer, infertility, sexual dysfunction osteopenia
Hematologic	Macrocytosis, anemia, thrombocytopenia, pancytopenia, coagulopathy
Musculoskeletal	Osteonecrosis (hip), Fracture, rhabdomyolysis, gout
Neonatal	Fetal alcohol syndrome
Psychiatric	Alcohol induced delirium, dementia, amnesia, psychosis, mood disorder, anxiety, perceptual disorder, sexual disorder, sleep disorder

disease). 10–35% of patients with alcoholism will develop alcoholic hepatitis. Of that group, 70% will eventually progress to cirrhosis. Death from alcohol-related cirrhosis in 1997 was 3.8/100 000, representing 40% of all deaths from cirrhosis. Despite the fact that increased alcohol consumption (>60 to 80 g/d of alcohol in men and >20 g/d in women) increases the risk of developing cirrhosis, many patients who drink far more than this never develop cirrhosis, suggesting that there are predisposing factors other than alcohol that increase the likelihood that an individual patient will develop cirrhosis [16].

A causal association has been established between alcohol consumption and cancers of the oral cavity, pharynx, larynx, esophagus, liver, colon, rectum, and, in women, breast; an association is suspected for cancers of the pancreas and lung [17].

Aspiration pneumonitis and pneumonia are common in the intoxicated patient. Sleep apnea is more common in chronic excessive alcohol use, and acute intoxication can result in respiratory failure.

Chronic alcohol adiction has been described as one of the risk factors for acute renal failure to occur in unobstructed acute pyelonephritis. Alcohol addiction is also associated with papillary necrosis [18] Hepatorenal failure may result from alcoholic liver disease.

Alcoholism is associated with a number of endocrine abnormalities, such as ketoacidosis, diabetes, osteopenia, and sexual dysfunction. As many as 75% of male alcoholics experience erectile dysfunction [19]. Heavy-drinking women compared to moderate- and light-drinking women have the highest rates of lack of orgasm [20].

Hematologic abnormalities include red cell macrocytosis, thrombocytopenia, and pancytopenia, all the result of a direct toxic effect of alcohol on the bone marrow. Coagulpathy is common with liver disease in alcoholics.

Neuropsychiatric disorders are commonly associated with alcoholism and include: depression and anxiety disorders, delirium, dementia, hallucinosis, Korsakoffs encephalopathy, Wernicke's syndrome, cerebellar dysfunction, intreacranial bleeding, subdural hematoma, stroke, and myopathy. Peripheral neuropathy is especially common with as many as 66% of alcoholics having electromyographic findings consistent with neuropathy [21]. Recent evidence has linked depression and alcoholism genetically initially through twin studies and now gene identification [22,23]. Binge drinking in midlife is associated with increased risk of dementia [24]. Physical dependence on alcohol results in an abstinence syndrome or withdrawal of the sedative hypnotic type. This can begin within 24 hours of the last drink and is manifested by anxiety, tremulousness, nausea, diaphoresis, tachycardia, increased blood pressure, and progress to seizures and ultimately to delirum tremens.

Fetal alcohol syndrome occurs at a rate of 0.2–1.5 per 1000 live births in the United States. 11.1% of pregnant women drink alcohol and 1.9% binge drink or use alcohol frequently [25].

10.2.2 Tobacco-related illnesses

Tobacco causes over 420 000 deaths yearly in the United States. Population surveys reveal that 23.4% of the adult United States population smoke cigarettes, and these overall numbers are consistent with studies of primary care patient populations, although there are significant differences within groups in primary care patients versus population-based studies [26,27]. Tobacco causes more morbidity and mortality than any other misused substance. Atherosclerosis results in vascular disease manifesting as coronary, and carotid artery disease, cerebrovascular disease, aortic aneurysms, peripheral vascular disease, and renal disease. Smoking increases the risks of multiple cancers, including lung, bladder, larynx, esophagus, stomach, cervical, pancreatic, and oral cavity. Smoking is the leading cause of chronic obstructive pulmonary disease, chronic bronchitis, and emphysema, in addition to acute pulmonary diseases like pneumonia. Smoking is one of the leading causes of erectile dysfunction, and increases the risk of osteoporosis and Graves disease. Smoking while pregnant will result in lower birth weight, miscarriage, and increased perinatal mortality.

10.2.3 Illicit drug-related illness

Opiates, cocaine, methamphetamine, and other drugs that can be injected result in a myriad of problems that are related to the use of nonsterile needles. Infectious disorders such as HIV and Hepatitis B and C are widely spread through the sharing of infected needles. Skin abscesses, septic emboli, infectious endocarditis, and talc granulomatosis are all well known complications of injection drug use. Inhalation of these drugs through smoking crack cocaine, opium, and marijuana can result in bronchospasm, pneumothorax, pneumomediasteinum, and hemoptysis.

Opiates have a distinct withdrawal syndrome that differs from sedative hypnotic withdrawal in that it is not life threatening (except in the neonate), and is typically manifested by anxiety, mydriasis, diaphoresis, nausea, abdominal cramps, diarrhea, and rhinorrhea. Opiate overdose can result in respiratory failure, aspiration pneumonia. Chronic opiate use may lead to narcotic bowel syndrome.

Cocaine and other stimulant use may result in a multitude of cardiovascular complications, including severe hypertension, myocardial ischemia, infarction, and arrhythmias, and stroke. It can result in a dilated cardiomyopathy, pulmonary edema. Renal failure, infarction, polyarteritis nodosa, rhabdomyolysis are also seen.

10.3 TREATMENT-INDUCED REDUCTIONS IN MORTALITY AND MORBIDITY

Treatment works. Treatment for addiction substantially reduces both mortality and morbidity resulting from substance misuse. Methadone and buprenorphine maintenance therapies have been shown to reduce mortality and morbidity in heroin addicts [28]. Reductions in risk of HIV infection, violence and criminal behavior can be expected when clinical guidelines in methadone treatment

are followed [29]. Smoking cessation treatment has a dramatic effect on the reduction of death and morbidity due to lung cancer, other pulmonary disease and cardiovascular disease [30] (Table 10.2). Treatment of alcohol dependence results in reductions of all cause mortality as well as, specifically, morbidity and mortality from cirrhosis, violence, and accidents [31].

10.4 ROLE OF PRIMARY CARE PHYSICIANS IN THE IDENTIFICATION AND TREATMENT OF ADDICTIONS

Primary care physicians are at the front line of healthcare and are presented daily with opportunities to identify and treat patients with substance use disorders. Given that 8–10 of 100 patients in a primary care practice have a substance use disorder, and that 15–20 have a previous history, it is easy to appreciate the frequency with which these patients are encountered in the daily practice of primary care [32]. Given the continuity of care and personal relationship between primary care physicians and their patients the opportunity to identify and intervene in substance use disorders is unrivaled anywhere else in medicine.

Table 10.2 Health benefits of smoking cessation

Abstinence Time	Health Benefits
20 min	Decrease in heart rate and blood pressure
12 h	Carbon monoxide levels normalize
1–9 mo	Shortness of breath, cough improve
1 yr	Heart disease risk 50% of smokers
5–15 yr	Stroke risk same as nonsmoker
10 yr	Lung cancer risk 50% of smokers
10 yr	Decreased risk of cancer mouth throat, esophagus bladder, cervix, pancreas
15 yr	Heart disease risk same as nonsmokers

10.4.1 Approach to diagnosis of addictions

As with most chronic illnesses in primary care, one will not have to look far to find those patients with the most advanced disease. Patients with end stage addiction have social, family, financial, legal and health consequences that are obvious to anyone around them. Despite this, patients may have little insight into their disease because of the defense mechanism of denial. For patients with addiction the term denial refers to the inability of the patient to appreciate the connection between their drug use and their consequences. An example of rather advanced denial is the patient who when after discussing his eight arrests for driving under the influence, was asked if he thought he had a problem with alcohol. His response was "Doc, I ain't got a problem with alcohol, I got a problem with the police." As with other chronic illnesses, identification of the disease early can improve the chances of remission and prevent serious health consequences. To do this requires that the primary care physician recognize the high prevalence of substance use disorders in their practice, and screen patients effectively and identify those at greatest risk.

10.4.2 Screening tools for addiction

Assuming the patient admits to any alcohol or drug use, the CAGE questions modified to include drugs (Table 10.3) provide an excellent starting point in identifying substance use disorders in primary care. Patients that give two positive responses are correlated with a substance use disorder with a sensitivity of 0.85–0.94, and a specificity of 0.79–0.88 [33]. A longer screening tool, the AUDIT (Table 10.4) consists of ten questions and can accurately determine patients at high risk for problematic drinking as well as addiction and dependence. For busy clinicians, the two question substance abuse screen (Table 10.5) provides a way to quickly determine risk for a substance use disorder with a sensitivity and specificity of 80% [34]. Laboratory studies, such as urine drug screens, liver function tests, carbohydrate deficient transferrin levels, blood

Table 10.3 CAGE questions adapted to include drugs

1. Have you felt you ought to **C**ut down on your drinking or drug use?
2. Have people **A**nnoyed you by criticizing your drinking or drug use?
3. Have you felt **G**uilty about your drinking or drug use?
4. Have you ever had a drink or used drugs first thing in the morning to steady your nerves or to get rid of a hangover or to get the day started? (**E**ye-opener)

Two or more yes answers indicate a need for a more in-depth assessment. Even one positive response should raise a red flag about problem drinking or drug use.

Adapted from Schulz, J.E., and Parran, T., Jr. (1998) Principles of Identification and Intervention. In (eds) A.W. Graham and T.K. Shultz Principles of Addiction Medicine, second edition, American Society of Addiction Medicine, Chevy Chase, MD, p 249.

alcohol levels, and others, can support screening information but are not in and of themselves diagnostic of substance use disorders.

10.4.3 Interventions

Primary care physicians play a key role in the early intervention of problematic substance use. Many patients are surprised to hear that moderate alcohol intake is defined as an average of two drinks (12 ounces of beer, 6 ounces of wine, 1.5 ounces of liquor) daily and no more than five in any given day. The recommendations for women are one half that. Brief advice by primary care physicians results in reduction in alcohol consumption [35]. Despite this, only 23% of binge drinkers recall being advised by their physicians to reduce their alcohol intake [36]. 50–70% of smokers recall advice from their physicians to stop. Physician advice to stop smoking has also been shown to reduce smoking rates [37]. Brief interventions include asking about alcohol and drug use, looking for evidence of problematic use, and then if problems are noted, advice about reduction or abstinence. This approach might sound like this, "Jim, after hearing about your alcohol intake and looking at the elevations in your liver enzymes, I am concerned that you are drinking too much, I would like you to avoid alcohol completely for the next three months, and then we can re-evaluate your liver functions. Do you think you can

Table 10.4 The alcohol use disorders identification test: Interview version

Read questions as written. Record answers carefully. Begin the AUDIT by saying "Now I am going to ask you some questions about your use of alcoholic beverages during this past year." Explain what is meant by "alcoholic beverages" by using local examples of beer, wine, vodka, and so on. Code answers in terms of "standard drinks". Place the correct answer number in the box at the right.

1. How often do you have a drink containing alcohol?
   (0) Never [Skip to Qs 9–10]
   (1) Monthly or less
   (2) 2–4 times a month
   (3) 2–3 times a week
   (4) 4 or more times a week

2. How many drinks containing alcohol do you have on a typical day when you are drinking?
   (0) 1 or 2
   (1) 3 or 4
   (2) 5 or 6
   (3) 7, 8, or 9
   (4) 10 or more

3. How often do you have six or more drinks on one occasion?
   (0) Never
   (1) Less than monthly
   (2) Monthly
   (3) Weekly
   (4) Daily or almost daily

4. How often during the last year have you found that you were not able to stop drinking once you had started?
   (0) Never
   (1) Less than monthly
   (2) Monthly
   (3) Weekly
   (4) Daily or almost daily

5. How often during the last year have you failed to do what was normally expected from you because of drinking?
   (0) Never
   (1) Less than monthly
   (2) Monthly
   (3) Weekly
   (4) Daily or almost daily

6. How often during the last year have you needed a first drink in the morning to get yourself going after a heavy drinking session?
   (0) Never
   (1) Less than monthly
   (2) Monthly
   (3) Weekly
   (4) Daily or almost daily

7. How often during the last year have you had a feeling of guilt or remorse after drinking?
   (0) Never
   (1) Less than monthly
   (2) Monthly
   (3) Weekly
   (4) Daily or almost daily

Table 10.4 (*Continued*)

8. How often during the last year have you been unable to remember what happened the night before because you had been drinking?
   (0) Never
   (1) Less than monthly
   (2) Monthly
   (3) Weekly
   (4) Daily or almost daily

9. Have you or someone else been injured as a result of your drinking?
   (0) No
   (2) Yes, but not in the last year
   (4) Yes, during the last year

10. Has a relative or friend or a doctor or another health worker been concerned about your drinking or suggested you cut down?
    (0) No
    (2) Yes, but not in the last year
    (4) Yes, during the last year

do this on your own or should I arrange for some help for you?" For patients who are unable or unwilling to modify their drug or alcohol use, a more formal intervention may be appropriate. The primary care physician's involvement in such a procedure is varied. In some cases the primary care physician may actually prepare and orchestrate such an approach, gathering family members, employers, clergy and others that may have influence over the patient, and bringing them together, confront the patient about their concerns. In other circumstances the primary care physician may play a less central role, which can have the advantage of allowing a member of the healthcare team to not be the focus of the patient's anger at being intervened on. In these situations it may allow the primary physician to continue to work with the patient if indeed the intervention fails.

Table 10.5 Two question screening for substance abuse

1. In the past year, have you ever drunk or used drugs more than you meant to?
2. Have you felt you wanted or needed to cut down on your drinking or drug abuse in the past year?

Score Yes to both questions indicates a substance use disorder with sensitivity 0.80, specificity 0.80.

10.4.4   Referral for treatment

Given its definition, addiction will often require treatment. The nature of addiction, loss of control over the use of a substance, implies the need for assistance in getting and maintaining abstinence, which is the mainstay of recovery. Primary care physicians are often befuddled by the wide variety of treatment options available, yet typically frustrated with the roadblocks of funding and insurance limitations. The typical patient requiring treatment for addiction often will have made multiple previous failed attempts to control or stop their use on their own. Once a decision to refer for treatment is made, the next question is what type or level of treatment is most appropriate? Table 10.6 describes the American Society of Addiction Medicine's Treatment Levels [38]. Assessment of the dimensional criteria (Table 10.7) allows the clinician to determine the severity of addiction and have

Table 10.6 ASAM's basic levels of care

Level 0.5	Early Intervention
Level I	Outpatient Services
Level II	Intensive Outpatient/Partial Hospitalization
Level III	Residential/Inpatient Services
Level IV	Medically Managed Inpatient Services

Table 10.7 ASAM dimensional criteria

Dimension 1	Acute Intoxication/Withdrawal Potential
Dimension 2	Biomedical Conditions and Complications
Dimension 3	Emotional, Behavioral, or Cognitive Complications
Dimension 4	Readiness to Change
Dimension 5	Relapse, Continued Use Potential
Dimension 6	Recovery/Living Environment

the patient placed in an appropriate setting. For example, a patient who might be at risk for severe withdrawal may require a Level IV referral, even if his other dimensions are mild or moderate in intensity.

REFERENCES

1. Fleming, M.F. and Barry, K.L. (1991) The effectiveness of alcoholism screening in an ambulatory care setting. *J. Stud. Alcohol*, **52** (1), 33–36.

2. Miller, P.M., Thomas, S.E., and Mallin, R. (2006) Patient attitudes toward self-report and biomarker alcohol screening by primary care physicians. *Alcohol Alcoholism*, **41** (3), 306–310.

3. Substance Abuse and Mental Health Services Administration (2005) Results from the 2004 National Survey on Drug Use and Health: National Findings. Office of Applied Studies, NSDUH Series H-28, DHHS Publication No. SMA 05-4062, Rockville, MD.

4. Johnson, T.P., Booth, A.L., and Johnson, P. (2005) Physician beliefs about substance misuse and its treatment: findings from a U.S. survey of primary care practitioners. *Substance Use Misuse*, **40** (8), 1071–1084.

5. Friedmann, P.D., McCullough, D., Chin, M.H., and Saitz, R. (2000) Screening and intervention for alcohol problems a national survey of primary care physicians and psychiatrists. *J. Gen. Intern. Med.*, **15** (2), 84–91.

6. Flemming, M.F. and Barry, K.L. (1991) Clinical overview of alcohol and drug disorders in *Addictive Disorders* (eds M.F. Femming and K.L. Barry), Mosby, New York, pp. 1–21.

7. Novick, D.M. (1992) The medically ill *substance abuser* in *Substance Abuse*, 2nd edn (eds J.H. Lowinson, R. Pedro, and R.B. Milliman), Williams & Wilkins, Baltimore, pp. 657–664.

8. Saitz, R. (2003) Medical and surgical complications of addiction in *Principles of Addiction Medicine*, 3rd edn (eds A.W. Grahamand T.K. Schultz), American Society of Addiction Medicine, Chevy Chase, pp. 1027–1052.

9. Goldsmith, R.J. and Ries, R.K. (2003) Substance-induced mental disorders, *Principles of Addiction Medicine*, 3rd edn (eds A.W. Grahamand T.K. Schultz), American Society of Addiction Medicine, Chevy Chase, pp. 1263–1276.

10. Klatsky, A.L. and Udaltsova, N. (2007) Alcohol drinking and total mortality risk. *Ann. Epidemiol.*, **17** (5) (Suppl), S63–S67.

11. McFarlane, S.I., von Gizycki, H., Salifu, M. *et al.* (2007) Alcohol consumption and blood pressure in the adult US population: assessment of gender-related effects. *J. Hypertens.*, **25** (5), 965–970.

12. Koul, P.B., Sussmane, J.B., Cunill-De Sautu, B., and Minarik, M. (2005) Atrial fibrillation associated with alcohol ingestion in adolescence: holiday heart in pediatrics. *Pediatr. Emerg. Care*, **21**, 38–39.

13. Teragaki, M., Takeuchi, K., Toda, I. *et al.* (2000) Point mutations in mitochondrial DNA of patients with alcoholic cardiomyopathy. *Heart Vessels*, **15** (4), 172–175.

14. O'Keefe, J.H., Bybee, K.A., and Lavie, C.J. (2007) Alcohol and cardiovascular health: The razor-sharp double-edged sword. *J. Am. Coll. Cardiol.*, **50** (11), 1009–1014.

15. Munoz, A. and Katerndahl, D.A. (2000) Diagnosis and management of acute pancreatitis. *Am. Fam. Physician.*, **62** (1), 164–174.

16. Mandayam, S., Jamal, M.M., and Morgan, T.R. (2004) Epidemiology of alcoholic liver disease. *Semin. Liver Dis.*, **24**, 217–232.

17. Boffetta, P. and Hashibe, M. (2006) Alcohol and cancer. *Lancet Oncol.*, **7** (2), 149–156.

18. Camilleri, B., Wyatt, J., and Newstead, C. (2003) Acute renal failure in a patient suffering from chronic alcoholism. *Nephrol. Dial. Transpl.*, **18** (4), 840–842.

19. Fahrner, E. (1987) Sexual dysfunction in male alcohol addicts: Prevalence and treatment. *Arch. Sex. Behav.*, **16** (3) 247–257.

20. Johnson, S., Phelps, D., and Cottler, L. (2004) The association of sexual dysfunction and substance use among a community epidemiological sample. *Arch. Sex. Behav.*, **33** (1), 55–63.

21. Ammendola, A., Gemini, D., Iannaccone, S. *et al.* (2000) Gender and peripheral neuropathy in chronic alcoholism: a clinical–electroneurographic study. *Alcohol Alcohol.*, **35** (4), 368–371.

22. Prescott, C.A., Aggen, S.H., and Kendler, K.S. (2000) Sex-specific genetic influences on the comorbidity of

alcoholism and major depression in a population-based sample of US twins. *Arch. Gen. Psychiatry*, **57**, 803–811.

23. Dick, D.M., Plunkett, J., Hamlin, D. *et al.* (2007) Association analyses of the serotonin transporter gene with lifetime depression and alcohol dependence in the Collaborative Study on the Genetics of Alcoholism (COGA) sample. *Psychiatr. Genet.*, **17** (1), 35–38.

24. Jarvenpaa, T., Rinne, J., Koskenvuo, M., and Raiha, I. (2005) Binge drinking in midlife and dementia risk. *Epidemiology*, **16** (6), 766–771.

25. MMWR (2004) Alcohol use in women who are pregnant or who might become pregnant. *MMWR*, **53** (50), 1178–1181.

26. Lethbridge-Çejku, M. and Vickerie, J. (2005) Summary health statistics for US adults: National health interview survey, 2003. National center for health statistics. *Vital Health Stat*, **10** (225).

27. Ralston, S., Kellett, N., Williams, R.L. *et al.* (2007) Practice-based assessment of tobacco usage in southwestern primary care patients: A research involving outpatient settings network (RIOS Net) study. *J. Am. Board. Fam. Med.*, **20** (2), 174–180.

28. Connock, M., Juarez-Garcia, A., Jowett, S. *et al.* (2007) Methadone and buprenorphine for the management of opioid dependence: a systematic review and economic evaluation. *Health Technol. Assess.*, **11** (9), 1–171, iii–iv.

29. Trafton, J.A., Humphreys, K., Harris, A.H.S., and Oliva, E. (2007) Consistent adherence to guidelines improves opioid dependent patients' first year outcomes. *J. Behav. Health Ser. R.*, **34** (3), 260.

30. Anthonisen, N., Skeans, M.A., Wise, R.A. *et al.* (2005) The effects of a smoking cessation intervention on 14.5-year mortality. *Ann. Int. Med.*, **142** (4), 233–239; Mann, R.E., Smart, R.G., and Govoni, R. (2003) The epidemiology of alcoholic liver disease. *Alcohol Res. Health*, **27**, 209–219

31. Miller, N.S. and Gold, M.S. (1998) Comorbid cigarette and alcohol addiction: epidemiology and treatment. *J. Addict. Dis.*, **17** (1), 55–66.

32. Manwell, L.B., Fleming, M.F., Johnson, K., and Barry, K.L. (1998) Tobacco, alcohol, and drug use in a primary care sample: 90-day prevalence and associated factors. *J. Addict. Dis.*, **17** (1), 67–81.

33. Flemming, M.F. and Barry, K.L. (eds) (1992) *Addictive Disorders*, Yearbook Publishing Co., p. 28.

34. Brown, R.L. *et al.* (2001) A two-item conjoint screen for alcohol and other drug problems. *J. Am. Board Fam. Pract.*, **14**, 95–106.

35. Bertholet, N., Daeppen, J.-B., Wietlisbach, V. *et al.* (2005) Reduction of alcohol consumption by brief alcohol intervention in primary care. *Arch. Intern. Med.*, **165**, 986–995.

36. Denny, C.H., Serdula, M.K., Holtzman, D., and Nelson, D.E. (2003) Physician advice about smoking and drinking: are U.S. adults being informed? *Am. J. Prev. Med.*, **24** (1), 71–74.

37. Doescher, M.P. and Saver, B.G. (2000) Physicians' advice to quit smoking. *J. Fam. Pract.*, **49**, 543–547.

38. Graham, A.W. and Schultz, T.K. (eds) (2003) *Principles of Addiction Medicine*, 3rd edn, American Society of Addiction Medicine, Chevy Chase, p. 1591, Appendix 2.

11

Addictive disorders in the intensive care unit

Tracy R. Luckhardt[1] and Robert C. Hyzy[2]

[1]*Division of Pulmonary, Allergy, and Critical Care, University of Alabama Birmingham, Birmingham, AL, USA*
[2]*Division of Pulmonary and Critical Care Medicine, University of Michigan, Ann Arbor, MI, USA*

11.1 OVERVIEW

Alcohol and drug addictions play a prominent role in intensive care medicine. Many patients are hospitalized in the intensive care unit (ICU) as a direct result of their addictions. Alcohol and drug disorders also put patients at an increased risk of conditions commonly managed in the ICU, such as Acute Respiratory Distress Syndrome (ARDS) and pancreatitis. These addictions can also complicate management of the critically ill patient, and intensivists must consider addiction when managing sedation and withdrawal in the ICU. Finally, the long-term psychological complications in survivors of a critical illness have the potential to influence the addictive patterns of patients once they have left the ICU.

In this chapter, firstly the prevalence of addiction in the critically ill population is discussed and the difficulties in diagnosis of addiction in this patient population are explored. Some of the common critical illnesses that are directly caused by or affected by alcohol and drug disorders are then discussed. How addiction affects management of the critically ill patients is also examined.

The objectives are:

1. To explore the impact of alcohol and drug disorders on the presentation and management of critical illness.

2. To examine the difficulties that drug and alcohol addiction presents in the diagnosis and management of critically ill patients.

3. To understand the long-term psychosocial consequences of critical illness.

11.2 PREVALENCE OF ADDICTIVE DISORDERS IN THE CRITICALLY ILL

There is a high level of alcohol and drug use in the critically ill patient population. In a recent cohort study in Finland, it was found that at least 17.5% of all ICU admissions were related to alcohol use [1].

Addictive Disorders in Medical Populations   Edited by Norman S. Miller and Mark S. Gold

In Australia, 13.8% of all ICU admissions are due to acute poisoning [2], and in an urban hospital in the United States, 5% of ICU admissions were due to illicit drug use [3]. Other estimates of the prevalence of alcohol and drug misuse in critically ill patients ranges from 9–40% [3–7].

Not only is alcohol use common in ICU patients, but higher amounts of alcohol use (>72 g/day) and drinking alcohol on weekdays increases the need for ICU admission among general surgery patients [8]. In critically ill trauma patients, 71% of patients tested positive for alcohol or drug intoxication. Over half tested positive for alcohol and 42% tested positive for drugs, usually cocaine and/or opiates. African Americans were more likely to have drug intoxication whereas Hispanic patients were more likely to have consumed alcohol [9]. Alcohol use in critically ill patients is more common in younger patients and male patients [4,9]. In a recent study in an academic center in Virginia, 40% of all mechanically ventilated patients in a medical ICU had a history of alcohol or drug misuse, with alcohol misuse being more common [10]. ICU admissions with a history of alcohol misuse are less likely to have medical insurance and have a higher mean hospital cost as compared to ICU admission without alcohol misuse [3,4].

11.3 DIAGNOSING ADDICTIVE DISORDERS IN CRITICALLY ILL PATIENTS

It is important to recognize alcohol and drug misuse in critically ill patients as these behaviors have an impact on diagnosis and morbidity [5]. However, obtaining a history of addictive disorders can be difficult, as patients requiring ICU care frequently have an altered mental status due to the presenting condition or because of the presence of an endotracheal tube and the concomitant need for sedation [5]. Alcohol and drug use is underestimated in the critically ill population [11], and a high suspicion is needed to detect intoxication as a possible factor in a patient's illness. Some clinical signs and symptoms that should alert physicians to the possibility of intoxication include altered levels of consciousness, muscle rigidity, hypo- or hyperthermia, electrolyte abnormalities, hepatic or renal failure, or seizures (Table 11.1) [5,12]. However, these findings are nonspecific and are often present in critically ill patients from other causes. Questionnaires, such as the AUDIT for the detection of significant alcohol use, can be given to a patient's proxy if they are available [5].

Laboratory tests can also be useful in helping to determine if drug or alcohol intoxication is present in a critically ill patient. However, 11–45% of trauma patients admitted to the ICU will have normal serum alcohol levels even if they have a history of risky

Table 11.1 Clinical signs and symptoms of acute intoxication in unresponsive patients

History of alcohol or drug abuse
Agitation, delirium, depressed mental status
Muscle rigidity
Hypothermia or Hyperthermia
Electrolyte Abnormalities ($\downarrow$ Mg, Ca, Phos, Na, glucose)
Anion gap metabolic acidosis
Rhabdomyolysis
Hepatic or Renal dysfunction
Seizures
Positive Toxicology screen
Positive alcohol level, or elevated GGT

alcohol use [13]. An elevated gamma-glutamyltransferase (GGT) level has a sensitivity of 62.5–69%, a specificity of 69.6–100% and a negative predictive value of 97.4% in detecting alcohol misuse or dependence, although this has not been validated in an ICU population [14,15]. The presence of an unexplained anion gap acidosis, either with ketosis or high lactate, as well as electrolyte abnormalities, such as hyponatremia, hypoglycemia, hypomagnesemia, and hypophosphatemia, can also suggest alcohol intoxication [5]. Routine urine drug screens can also be used to detect the use of opiates, benzodiazepines, amphetamines, barbiturates, cannabis, phencyclidine, and propoxyphene [16]. Yet a positive result does not always mean acute ingestion, and there is sometime cross-reactivity and false positive results [16].

The decision as to when a patient with drug or alcohol addiction or intoxication needs ICU monitoring is not always clear. Table 11.2 lists the common indications for admission to ICU in intoxicated patients. In general, any patient with respiratory depression, inability to safely maintain and airway, life-threatening electrolyte abnormalities, significant organ dysfunction, or hemodynamic instability warrants admission and monitoring in the ICU setting [12].

Table 11.2 Indications for ICU admission in intoxicated patients

Altered level of consciousness with inability to protect airway
Respiratory depression with need for mechanical ventilation
Hemodynamic instability
Severe or worsening metabolic acidosis
Hypertensive emergency
Hypothermia or Hyperthermia
Arrhythmias or ECG abnormalities
Severe organ dysfunction (hepatic or renal failure, cardiac ischemia)
Need for continuous IV antagonists (i.e., naloxone, flumazenil)

11.4 CLINICAL DIAGNOSES, PATHOPHYSIOLOGY AND TREATMENT

11.4.1 Respiratory depression and mental status changes

There are very few data exploring the need for ICU monitoring and respiratory support due to acute intoxication. Nevertheless, the CNS depressive effect of alcohol and drug intoxication severe enough to require intubation for airway protection and ventilatory support is a common reason for ICU admission in patients with drug and alcohol misuse. These patients often have an inability to cough and clear their airway and a decreased respiratory drive leading to hypercarbia, acidosis, and hypoxemia [17]. Ethanol, opiates, benzodiazepines, barbiturates, and gamma-hydroxybutyrate (GHB) are all CNS depressants and intoxication can lead to both mental status changes that range from coma to violent delirium and respiratory depression [12,17,18]. However, care must be taken to not assume that mental status changes and respiratory depression are necessarily due to intoxication, as patients who misuse alcohol or other drugs (cocaine, PCP, amphetamines) are also at increased risk of stroke, intracerebral hemorrhage, and traumatic brain injury [12,19–21]. In a recent study from Poland, it was found that 3.3% of intoxicated patients required intubation and mechanical ventilation due to deep coma and respiratory failure [22]. In general, in both the surgical and medical populations, alcohol use is associated with an increased risk for need of mechanical ventilation independent of other underlying medical conditions [11]. In patients intubated for airway protection and respiratory depression, there is a very low mortality rate (2%) and, usually, only supportive care is required until the acute intoxication resolves [12].

11.4.2 Hyperthermia

3, 4-methylenedioxymethamphetamine (MDMA, "Ecstasy"), methamphetamine, and cocaine misuse can all lead to hyperthermia, which often requires ICU monitoring and care. Hyperthermia can often lead to hyponatremia, rhabdomyolysis, and renal failure, which can lead to death [23]. MDMA is a monoaminergic agonist and can inhibit the reuptake of 5HT. It also has dopaminergic stimulatory activity. MDMA is often used at raves, and the hyperthermia can be due to exertion combined with overcrowding, high room temperatures, and dehydration [24]. However, these patients can also develop serotonin syndrome, which is manifest by hyperthermia, hyperreflexia, tachycardia, myoclonus, clonus, ocular oscillations, and tremor [25]. Patients with serotonin syndrome often require ICU care with physical cooling, paralysis, and drugs to block the effects of serotonin such as chlorpromazine [25].

Methamphetamine and cocaine use can also cause hyperthermia and has been associated with neuroleptic malignant syndrome and malignant hyperthermia, both of which cause elevated temperature, hypertension, tachycardia, and mental status changes [26]. Hyperthermia is likely due to both increased agitation and locomotor activity as well as impairment in mechanisms needed for heat dissipation, such as sweating and cutaneous vasodilation [26]. Because of this, cocaine-induced hyperthermia is much more common during summer months and during high temperatures [26]. Management is mainly supportive care with fluids, cooling, sedation, and, occasionally, paralysis and mechanical ventilation [23]. Caffeine use and the increased use of stimulants allow the drinker to drink more and stay awake, but also can lead to elevated body temperature and even tachycardia.

11.4.3   Pneumonia

Substance misusers are more likely to get pneumonia than the general population. There are many factors that play into this, including adverse living conditions, malnutrition, aspiration events, comorbid illnesses, including HIV, and septic emboli in injection drug users [17]. In patients with pneumonia, those who misuse alcohol are more likely to need ICU care and to have more complications than the general population [5]. These patients have longer hospital stays and increased cost of hospitalization compared to other patients with pneumonia [27]. They are more likely to develop empyema and lung abscesses as well when compared to the general population [28,29]. Patients with a history of alcohol misuse tend to have a higher incidence of *Streptococcus pneumoniae*, gram negative enteric organisms such as *Klebsiella sp.*, and more mixed infections than other patients with pneumonia [30,31]. While some studies have not seen an increased mortality due to bacterial pneumonia in alcoholic patients as compared to nonalcoholics [27,32], others suggest that patients with a history of alcohol misuse who are admitted to the ICU with pneumonia have a mortality rate as high as 68% [33].

There are many reasons why alcohol use increases the susceptibility to pneumonia. These include increased incidence of gingivitis and colonization of the oral cavity with enteric organisms [34]. Depressed mental status and reduction in gag reflex can lead to increased risk of aspiration [35]. Alcohol use also reduces mucociliary clearance, which is vital in the initial defenses against infection in the airways [35,36]. Alcohol misuse also leads to significant immunosuppression, including suppression of neutrophil, macrophage, and T-cell function [5]. Due to immunosuppression, patients with alcohol misuse are not only more susceptible to bacterial pneumonia, but they also more susceptible to pneumocystis carinii pneumonia. In a recent case series by Faria *et al.*, pneumocystis pneumonia in patients with alcoholic hepatitis led to respiratory failure, ARDS, and death in seven patients [37].

11.4.4   Acute respiratory distress syndrome (ARDS) and multi-organ dysfunction syndrome (MODS)

Acute Respiratory Distress Syndrome (ARDS) is defined as having acute respiratory failure due to nonhydrostatic pulmonary edema. Clinically, there is an acute onset of dyspnea and a high oxygen requirement, bilateral alveolar infiltrates on radiology, and no evidence of cardiogenic causes of pulmonary edema. When the PaO2/FiO2 ratio is less than 300, it is referred to as acute lung injury (ALI) and when the PaO2/FiO2 ratio is less than 200 it is referred to as ARDS [38,39]. Risk factors for developing ALI/ARDS include pneumonia, septic shock, pancreatitis, aspiration, and trauma [38,40]. ALI/ARDS is part of a diffuse systemic inflammatory response and can be part of or lead to multi-organ dysfunction syndrome (MODS) including shock, renal failure, liver failure, and coagulation abnormalities [41]. About 10–15% of ICU admissions are due to ARDS, and the ICU mortality rate ranges from about 30–40% [40].

Multiple studies have shown that chronic alcohol misuse increases the likelihood of developing ARDS up to threefold and that alcohol abusers who develop ARDS tend to have more severe multi-organ dysfunction and higher mortality than those with no prior alcohol history [42–44]. In patients with septic shock, 70% of those with a history of alcohol addiction develop ARDS as opposed to only 31% of those with no alcohol history [45]. One possible reason for the increased risk of ARDS in this patient population is that alcohol use is a risk factor in many of the conditions leading to ARDS, such as pneumonia, acute pancreatitis, trauma, and aspiration [35]. However, even after adjusting for source of infection and severity of illness, alcohol use has been shown to be an independent risk factor for ARDS [45]. Another reason for the increase in ARDS in patients who misuse alcohol is both a systemic and an alveolar glutathione deficiency, which leads to increased oxidative stress and epithelial cell injury [35,46,47]. Chronic alcohol users also have higher protein concentrations in alveolar fluid, suggesting baseline dysfunction in the alveolar-capillary barrier, which could make these patients more susceptible to ARDS [46]. Angiotensin II levels are also increased in alcoholics, which could lead to increased alveolar epithelial cell

apoptosis and increase lung injury [35]. Cocaine and amphetamine use can also cause ARDS. The pathophysiology is not known, but some studies have implicated increased pulmonary capillary permeability from either direct injury or sympathetic induced pulmonary venous constriction as possible mechanisms [17] (Figure 11.1).

11.4.5 Severe acute pancreatitis

Alcohol use is the cause of acute pancreatitis in 20–45% of all cases [48–51]. While most cases are mild and self-limiting, 20–30% of these patients will experience severe complications that require ICU admission and management [50–52]. The overall mortality in patients with severe complications is 5–10% [53]. Complications can include pancreatic necrosis and hemorrhage, as well as sepsis, multi-organ failure, and ARDS. Pancreatitis due to alcohol consumption tends to be more severe, and these patients develop necrosis more frequently than those with pancreatitis from other causes [49,54,55]. Several studies have looked at

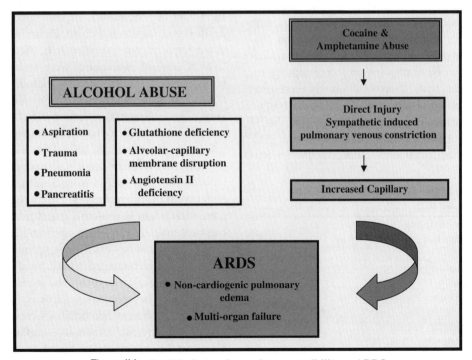

Figure 11.1 Possible factors increasing susceptibility to ARDS

Table 11.3 Ranson's Criteria: more than three Ranson's criteria is indicative of severe acute pancreatitis [100]

At Admission	Developing During First 48 Hours
Age > 55	↓ hematocrit by >10%
WBC > 16 000/µl	↑ BUN > 8 mg/dl
Blood glucose > 200 mg/dl	Serum calcium < 8 mg/dl
Serum LDH > 350 IU/dl	Arterial PaO2 < 60 mmHg
AST (SGOT) > 250 IU/dl	Base defecit > 4 meq/l
	Estimated fluid sequestration >6 liters

scoring systems that can be used to detect which patients will progress to more severe pancreatitis and to determine which patients would benefit from ICU monitoring. The Ranson criteria (Table 11.3) is the oldest and most widely used, but the APACHE score and Balthazar CT scoring system have also been shown to have good predictive value [56–59]. Dauphine *et al.*, found that an initial blood glucose level > 160 mg/dl plus a white blood cell count >17 10^3/µl had an 80% positive predictive value in predicting systemic complications, where as an initial Ranson criteria ≥3 had a 100% positive predictive value [53]. In 2004, an international consensus statement recommended that patients with hemodynamic instability, evidence for organ dysfunction, and those at high risk for severe complications (elderly, obese, ongoing resuscitation requirements, and pancreatic necrosis) should be monitored in an ICU setting (Table 11.4), and that the routine use of biomarkers such as C-reactive protein should not be used to guide clinical decision making [58]. ICU management of alcohol-induced acute pancrea-

Table 11.4 Indications for managing severe acute pancreatitis in the ICU

Hemodynamic Instability
  Organ Dysfunction
  • Hypoxia
  • Acute Renal Failure
  • Coagulopathy
  High Risk Patients
  • Elderly
  • Obesity (BMI > 30 kg/m^2)
  • Need for ongoing volume resuscation
  • >30% pancreatic necrosis by CT

titis includes supportive care with fluids, vasopressors, and mechanical ventilation. Expeditious use of antibiotics and surgical or percutaneous intervention for infected pancreatic necrosis and pseudocysts is highly recommended [58].

11.4.6   Acute hepatitis and alcoholic cirrhosis

Acute and fulminant hepatitis that requires ICU monitoring and supportive care can be caused from use of either alcohol or amphetamines, particularly MDMA. Acute alcoholic hepatitis (AAH) affects about 35% of alcoholics, and the mortality in severe hepatitis is between 40–60% [60]. Acute hepatitis is classified as severe when the total bilirubin level is > 5 mg/dl and the prothrombin time (PT) is prolonged greater than four seconds [60]. Both the Maddrey score (discriminant function) and the Glasgow Alcoholic Hepatitis Score (GAHS) (Table 11.5) can be used to assess severity, with a GAHS of ≥9 predicting a 28-day survival of only 46%, and a Maddrey score of ≥32 indicating severe disease [60–63]. If severe, hepatitis can progress to fulminant hepatic failure, hepatic encephalopathy, multi-organ failure and death. Patients with severe acute hepatitis may require ICU monitoring and liver transplant evaluation. Current therapies for severe acute alcoholic hepatitis include glucocorticoids and pentoxiphylline. TNFα inhibition has shown some potential in improving clinical severity; however its utility has been limited by mainly infectious complications [60,64,65]. Acute hepatitis from MDMA can occur with one dose or with chronic use, and ranges from a mild, self-limited hepatitis to fulminant hepatic failure requiring ICU admission. Care is supportive, and liver transplant can be considered in select cases [66].

The complications of cirrhosis secondary to alcohol use are often managed in the critical care setting. Some of these complications include variceal hemorrhage, hepatorenal syndrome, which often requires continuous hemodialysis, severe hepatic encephalopathy, and infectious complications [67]. The mortality of patients with cirrhosis who require ICU admission is quite high, ranging from

Table 11.5 Maddrey score or discriminant function (DF) and Glasgow alcoholic hepatitis score (GAHS)

Maddrey Score or Discriminant Funtion (DF)

$DF = 4.6 \times [\text{Prothrombin Time} - \text{control value (seconds)}] + \text{total serum bilirubin (mg/dl)}$

A DF $\geq$ 32 predicts a poor prognosis. Patients with DF $<$ 32 have survival of 90–100%.

Glasgow Alcoholic Hepatitis Score (GAHS)

	Score Given		
	1	2	3
Age	$<$50	$\geq$50	
WBC (10^9/l)	$<$15	$\geq$15	
Urea (mmol/l)	$<$5	$\geq$5	
Prothrombin Time ratio	$<$1.5	1.5–2.0	$>$2.0
Bilirubin (µmol/l)	$<$125	125–250	$>$250

Adapted from Ref. [60].
A GAHS of $>$ 9 predicts a 60% 3-month mortality.

36.6–76.6% [68–71]. Severe hepatic encephalopathy, shock and acute renal failure are independent predictors of mortality [68,69,72] with patients requiring dialysis and ventilatory support having a mortality rate approaching 90% [69]. If cirrhotic patients are admitted to the ICU with acute respiratory failure, sepsis, or multi-organ failure the mortality rate approaches 100% [73,74].

11.5 INFLUENCE OF DRUG AND ALCOHOL ADDICTION ON THE MANAGEMENT OF CRITICALLY ILL PATIENTS

11.5.1 Sedation management in substance disorders

Due to the severity of illness, need for multiple procedures and need for mechanical ventilation, there is a significant requirement for effective analgesia and sedation in the management of critically ill patients. The goals of analgesia and sedation in the critical care setting should be to: (1) achieve adequate levels of analgesia, anxiolysis and amnesia; (2) reduce hormonal and metabolic stress responses; (3) avoid self-extubation; (4) facilitate ventilator management; (5) reduce the need for paralysis; (6) avoid large swings in levels of consciousness; and (7) avoid elevations in intracranial pressure [75]. This is usually accomplished using a combination of continuous intravenous opiates, benzodiazepines and/or propofol. It is also important to avoid over sedation in these patients, as this can lead to prolonged mechanical ventilation [76,77]. There has been one retrospective cohort study examining the effect of a history of substance misuse on the need

for sedation in the ICU. DeWit *et al.* demonstrated that when universal sedation protocol was used for all medical ICU patients, those patients with a history of alcohol or drug use required 2.5 times more benzodiazepines and five times more opiates in order to obtain the same level of sedation and analgesia as in patients without a history of substance misuse. This increased need for sedation was independent of organ dysfunction or illness severity. Both groups of patients, those with and those without a history of substance misuse, had a similar duration of mechanical ventilation. However, the group without a history of drug misuse had an increased illness severity score, and an increased incidence of pneumonia, acute lung injury, and sepsis. Presumably the increase in sedation led to a prolonged need for mechanical ventilation in the group with a history of substance misuse that was counterbalanced out by a lower severity of illness in the group without a substance misuse history [10]. Further studies are needed to help determine the appropriate agents and protocols for sedation in patients with a history of substance misuse, since they do appear to have different needs than the general ICU population.

11.5.2 Role of addictive disorders in ICU delirium

Critically ill patients are at increased risk of developing delirium – an acute, fluctuating, confusional state with attention deficits, alterations in levels of consciousness, and/or disorganized thoughts [78]. Delirium develops in up to 50% of ICU patients with mild severity scores and up to 80% of those requiring mechanical ventilation [78]. The development of ICU delirium increases the risk of complications, such as re-intubation and prolonged hospital stay, additionally resulting in a threefold increase in mortality [78,79]. A history of alcoholism leads to a twofold increased risk in developing ICU delirium [80]. This is not surprising given that critical ill patients with a history of alcohol and substance misuse frequently have many of the common risk factors associated with ICU delirium, including chronic disease, depression, more severe critical illness, metabolic and electrolyte disturbances, withdrawal syndromes, head trauma, and increased use of sedation [78]. There are no data as to whether or not alcohol and substance misuse alter the course or management of ICU delirium, and whether or not patients with a history of misuse should be treated differently than the general critically ill population. The current mainstay of therapy for ICU delirium includes identifying and controlling risk factors, use of minimally necessary sedation, periodic interruptions in sedation, and the use of haloperidol and atypical antipsychotics to reduce sedation needs [78].

11.5.3 Management of withdrawal syndromes in the ICU

Alcohol withdrawal syndrome (AWS) is the most common diagnosis in patients who are admitted to the ICU with alcohol-related illness or it can complicate the course of patients admitted to the

ICU with other illnesses [4]. Most patients with AWS present within 24–36 hours of alcohol cessation and have symptoms of autonomic hyperactivity with tremulousness, sweating, agitation, and insomnia. In the majority of patients with AWS the symptoms will subside in 1–2 days, but 25% of patients will progress to a more severe illness. This can include hallucinations, seizures, and delirium tremens. Delirium tremens manifests as delirium, hallucinations, and autonomic hyperactivity including hypertension, fever, and tachycardia. The mortality rate associated with delirium tremens is up to 15% and all of these patients should be managed in an intensive care setting [81]. Monitoring in the ICU should be considered in any patient who has a score of >20 on the Clinical Institute Withdrawal Assessment for Alcohol Scale [81]. Some patients with seizure activity or who require large doses of benzodiazepines to control symptoms may require mechanical ventilation for respiratory support and airway protection, which can increase complications such as nosocomial pneumonia and length of stay [81,82].

Intravenous benzodiazepines are the treatment of choice for alcohol withdrawal in the ICU. Both symptom driven bolus therapy as well as continuous infusions have been shown to be beneficial in controlling symptoms [82–85]. Protocol driven treatment strategies have been shown to have advantages in diminishing symptoms, reducing complications, and improving outcomes [83,84]. In a retrospective observational trial using protocol driven intravenous lorazepam with initial boluses and escalation to continuous infusion if necessary, there was quicker symptom control, decreased duration of sedatives, and decreased total dosage of sedatives when compared to the usual ICU management [83]. Other medications that are useful in controlling the symptoms of alcohol withdrawal include phenobarbital, clonidine, haloperidol, and beta-blockers [81,82,84–88]. Clonidine, haloperidol and beta-blockers should only be used in combination with benzodiazepines, since they do not decrease the risk of seizures [81,84]. The addition of phenobarbital infusion to benzodiazepines can reduce the need for mechanical ventilation [82]. Continuous ethanol infusions have been studied but have not shown any benefit over benzodiazepines, and since they are more difficult to titrate are not commonly used [85,89]. (Table 11.6)

Patients can have withdrawal syndromes on discontinuation of addictive substances other than alcohol. Patients who chronically misuse GHB can have a withdrawal syndrome that presents with delirium, hypertension, and tachycardia. These patients are often resistant to benzodiazepines, but pentobarbital has been shown to be helpful in managing the symptoms [90]. In patients who have had difficulty with severe withdrawal from opiates, including heroin and methadone, rapid detoxification under general anesthesia can be safely done in an ICU setting using opiate receptor antagonists and clonidine [91].

Table 11.6   ICU management of alcohol withdrawal syndrome

Supportive Care
- Intravenous fluids
- Dextrose and thiamine
- Telemetry and ECG monitoring
- Monitor electrolytes
- Mechanical ventilation (significant mental status or respiratory depression)

Pharmacotherapy
  **Bolus or Continuous Infusion IV Benzodiazepines ±
  - Clonidine
  - Haloperidol
  - Beta-blockers
  - Phenobarbital

11.6   LONG-TERM PSYCHOSOCIAL EFFECTS OF CRITICAL ILLNESS AND THEIR ROLE IN ADDICTION

For many patients who survive a critical illness, not only can physical recovery be prolonged, but many patients suffer long-term psychological consequences. The "ICU syndrome" is a well described phenomenon consisting of anxiety, depression, and post-traumatic stress disorder during recovery from critical illness [92–94]. This can occur even with very short stays in the ICU. Factors that contribute to this syndrome are large amounts of sedatives, multiple procedures, and delirium, making substance misusers high risk for development of this complication. These patients often suffer from delusional memories and nightmares which can lead to chronic psychological disturbances [94]. It is well recognized that there is a high incidence of substance misuse and addiction in patients that suffer from depression, anxiety, and post-traumatic stress disorder [95–99]. There are no studies examining the incidence of substance misuse in patients who have survived critical illness, but with the high incidence of psychiatric disease in these survivors, there is potentially an increased incidence of addiction as well. There is great need for more investigation into the long-term consequences of critical illness and the role that it may play in addiction.

REFERENCES

1. Uusaro, A., Parviainen, I., Tenhunen, J.J., and Ruokonen, E. (2005) The proportion of intensive care unit admissions related to alcohol use: A prospective cohort study. *Acta Anaesthesiol. Scand.*, **49**, 1236–1240.

2. Henderson, A., Wright, M., and Pond, S.M. (1993) Experience with 732 acute overdose patients admitted to an intensive care unit over six years. *Med. J. Aust.*, **158**, 28–30.

3. Baldwin, W.A., Rosenfeld, B.A., Breslow, M.J. *et al.* (1993) Substance abuse-related admissions to adult intensive care. *Chest*, **103**, 21–25.

4. Marik, P. and Mohedin, B. (1996) Alcohol-related admissions to an inner city hospital intensive care unit. *Alcohol Alcohol.*, **31**, 393–396.

5. Moss, M. and Burnham, E.L. (2006) Alcohol abuse in the critically ill patient. *Lancet*, **368**, 2231–2242.

6. Mostafa, S.M. and Murthy, B.V. (2002) Alcohol-associated admissions to an adult intensive care unit: An audit. *Eur. J. Anaesthesiol.*, **19**, 193–196.

7. O'Brien, J.M. Jr., Lu, B., Ali, N.A. *et al.* (2007) Alcohol dependence is independently associated with sepsis, septic shock, and hospital mortality among adult intensive care unit patients. *Crit. Care Med.*, **35**, 345–350.

8. Delgado-Rodriguez, M., Gomez-Ortega, A., Mariscal-Ortiz, M. *et al.* (2003) Alcohol drinking as a predictor of intensive care and hospital mortality in general surgery: A prospective study. *Addiction*, **98**, 611–616.

9. Cornwell, E.E. 3rd, Belzberg, H., Velmahos, G. *et al.* (1998) The prevalence and effect of alcohol and drug abuse on cohort-matched critically injured patients. *Am. Surgeon*, **64**, 461–465.

10. de Wit, M., Wan, S.Y., Gill, S. *et al.* (2007) Prevalence and impact of alcohol and other drug use disorders on sedation and mechanical ventilation: A retrospective study. *BMC Anesthesiol.*, **7**, 3.

11. de Wit, M., Best, A.M., Gennings, C. *et al.* (2007) Alcohol use disorders increase the risk for mechanical ventilation in medical patients. *Alcohol. Clin. Exp. Res.*, **31**, 1224–1230.

12. Mokhlesi, B., Garimella, P.S., Joffe, A., and Velho, V. (2004) Street drug abuse leading to critical illness. *Intensive Care Med.*, **30**, 1526–1536.

13. Neumann, T. and Spies, C. (2003) Use of biomarkers for alcohol use disorders in clinical practice. *Addiction*, **98** (Suppl 2), 81–91.

14. Amaral, R.A. and Malbergier, A. (2008) Effectiveness of the cage questionnaire, gamma-glutamyltransferase and mean corpuscular volume of red blood cells as markers for alcohol-related problems in the workplace. *Addict. Behav.*, **33** (6), 772–781.

15. Gul, S., Akvardar, Y., Tas, G., and Tuncel, P. (2005) The diagnostic validity of screening tests and laboratory markers in alcohol use disorders. *Turk Psikiyatri Derg.*, **16**, 3–12.

16. Hammett-Stabler, C.A., Pesce, A.J., and Cannon, D.J. (2002) Urine drug screening in the medical setting. *Clin. Chim. Acta*, **315**, 125–135.

17. Wilson, K.C. and Saukkonen, J.J. (2004) Acute respiratory failure from abused substances. *J. Intensive Care Med.*, **19**, 183–193.

18. Yost, D.A. (2002) Acute care for alcohol intoxication. Be prepared to consider clinical dilemmas. *Postgrad. Med.*, **112**, 14–16, 21-12, 25-16.

19. Chapital, A.D., Harrigan, R.C., Davis, J. *et al.* (2007) Traumatic brain injury: Outcomes from rural and urban locations over a 5-year period (part 1). *Hawaii Med. J.*, **66**, 318–321.

20. Gururaj, G. (2004) The effect of alcohol on incidence, pattern, severity and outcome from traumatic brain injury. *J. Indian Med. Assoc.*, **102**, 157–160, 163.

21. O'Connor, A.D., Rusyniak, D.E., and Bruno, A. (2005) Cerebrovascular and cardiovascular complications of alcohol and sympathomimetic drug abuse. *Med. Clin. N. Am.*, **89**, 1343–1358.

22. Chodorowski, Z., Sein Anand, J., Kujawska, H. *et al.* (2004) Clinical aspects of acute intoxication with ethanol. *Przegl. Lek.*, **61**, 314–316.

23. Callaway, C.W. and Clark, R.F. (1994) Hyperthermia in psychostimulant overdose. *Ann. Emerg. Med.*, **24**, 68–76.

24. Parrott, A.C. (2004) MDMA (3,4-methylenedioxy-methamphetamine) or ecstasy: The neuropsychobiological implications of taking it at dances and raves. *Neuropsychobiology*, **50**, 329–335.

25. Parrott, A.C. (2002) Recreational ecstasy/MDMA, the serotonin syndrome, and serotonergic neurotoxicity. *Pharmacol. Biochem. Behav.*, **71**, 837–844.

26. Crandall, C.G., Vongpatanasin, W., and Victor, R.G. (2002) Mechanism of cocaine-induced hyperthermia in humans. *Ann. Intern. Med.*, **136**, 785–791.

27. Saitz, R., Ghali, W.A., and Moskowitz, M.A. (1997) The impact of alcohol-related diagnoses on pneumonia outcomes. *Arch. Intern. Med.*, **157**, 1446–1452.

28. Liang, S.J., Chen, W., Lin, Y.C. *et al.* (2007) Community-acquired thoracic empyema in young adults. *South Med. J.*, **100**, 1075–1080.

29. Moreira Jda, S., Camargo Jde, J., Felicetti, J.C. *et al.* (2006) Lung abscess: Analysis of 252 consecutive cases diagnosed between 1968 and 2004. *J. Bras. Pneumol.*, **32**, 136–143.

30. Jong, G.M., Hsiue, T.R., Chen, C.R. *et al.* (1995) Rapidly fatal outcome of bacteremic klebsiella pneumoniae pneumonia in alcoholics. *Chest*, **107**, 214–217.

31. Ruiz, M., Ewig, S., Marcos, M.A. *et al.* (1999) Etiology of community-acquired pneumonia: Impact of age, comorbidity, and severity. *Am. J. Respir. Crit. Care Med.*, **160**, 397–405.

32. de Roux, A., Cavalcanti, M., Marcos, M.A. *et al.* (2006) Impact of alcohol abuse in the etiology and severity of community-acquired pneumonia. *Chest*, **129**, 1219–1225.

33. Cuny, J., Chagnon, J.L., and Lambiotte, F. (2003) Prognosis of severe community-acquired pneumonia in alcoholic patients hospitalized in intensive care. *Presse. Med.*, **32**, 1162–1164.

34. Fuxench-Lopez, Z. and Ramirez-Ronda, C.H. (1978) Pharyngeal flora in ambulatory alcoholic patients: Prevalence of gram-negative bacilli. *Arch. Intern. Med.*, **138**, 1815–1816.

35. Joshi, P.C. and Guidot, D.M. (2007) The alcoholic lung: Epidemiology, pathophysiology, and potential

therapies. *Am. J. Physiol. Lung Cell Mol. Physiol.*, **292**, L813–L823.

36. Wyatt, T.A., Gentry-Nielsen, M.J., Pavlik, J.A., and Sisson, J.H. (2004) Desensitization of pka-stimulated ciliary beat frequency in an ethanol-fed rat model of cigarette smoke exposure. *Alcohol. Clin. Exp. Res.*, **28**, 998–1004.

37. Faria, L.C., Ichai, P., Saliba, F. *et al.* (2008) Pneumocystis pneumonia: An opportunistic infection occurring in patients with severe alcoholic hepatitis. *Eur. J. Gastroenterol. Hepatol.*, **20**, 26–28.

38. Atabai, K. and Matthay, M.A. (2002) The pulmonary physician in critical care. 5: Acute lung injury and the acute respiratory distress syndrome: Definitions and epidemiology. *Thorax*, **57**, 452–458.

39. Bernard, G.R., Artigas, A., Brigham, K.L. *et al.* (1994) The American-European consensus conference on ARDS. Definitions, mechanisms, relevant outcomes, and clinical trial coordination. *Am. J. Respir. Crit. Care Med*, **149**, 818–824.

40. Frutos-Vivar, F., Ferguson, N.D., and Esteban, A. (2006) Epidemiology of acute lung injury and acute respiratory distress syndrome. *Semin. Respir. Crit. Care Med.*, **27**, 327–336.

41. Vincent, J.L. and Zambon, M. (2006) Why do patients who have acute lung injury/acute respiratory distress syndrome die from multiple organ dysfunction syndrome? Implications for management. *Clin. Chest Med.*, **27**, 725–731, abstract x–xi.

42. Moss, M., Bucher, B., Moore, F.A. *et al.* (1996) The role of chronic alcohol abuse in the development of acute respiratory distress syndrome in adults. *JAMA*, **275**, 50–54.

43. Moss, M., Steinberg, K.P., Guidot, D.M. *et al.* (1999) The effect of chronic alcohol abuse on the incidence of ARDS and the severity of the multiple organ dysfunction syndrome in adults with septic shock: An interim and multivariate analysis. *Chest*, **116**, 97. S–98.

44. Wind, J., Versteegt, J., Twisk, J. *et al.* (2007) Epidemiology of acute lung injury and acute respiratory distress syndrome in The Netherlands: A survey. *Respir. Med.*, **101**, 2091–2098.

45. Moss, M., Parsons, P.E., Steinberg, K.P. *et al.* (2003) Chronic alcohol abuse is associated with an increased incidence of acute respiratory distress syndrome and severity of multiple organ dysfunction in patients with septic shock. *Crit. Care Med.*, **31**, 869–877.

46. Moss, M. and Burnham, E.L. (2003) Chronic alcohol abuse, acute respiratory distress syndrome, and multiple organ dysfunction. *Crit. Care Med.*, **31**, S207–212.

47. Moss, M., Guidot, D.M., Wong-Lambertina, M. *et al.* (2000) The effects of chronic alcohol abuse on pulmonary glutathione homeostasis. *Am. J. Respir. Crit. Care Med.*, **161**, 414–419.

48. Chang, M.C., Su, C.H., Sun, M.S. *et al.* (2003) Etiology of acute pancreatitis – a multi-center study in Taiwan. *Hepatogastroenterology*, **50**, 1655–1657.

49. Frey, C.F., Zhou, H., Harvey, D.J., and White, R.H. (2006) The incidence and case-fatality rates of acute biliary, alcoholic, and idiopathic pancreatitis in California, 1994–2001. *Pancreas*, **33**, 336–344.

50. Karsenti, D., Bourlier, P., Dorval, E. *et al.* (2002) Morbidity and mortality of acute pancreatitis. Prospective study in a French university hospital. *Presse. Med.*, **31**, 727–734.

51. Navicharern, P., Wesarachawit, W., Sriussadaporn, S. *et al.* (2006) Management and outcome of severe acute pancreatitis. *J. Med. Assoc. Thai.*, **89** (Suppl 3), S25–S32.

52. Cavallini, G., Frulloni, L., Bassi, C. *et al.* (2004) Prospective multicentre survey on acute pancreatitis in Italy (proinf-aisp): Results on 1005 patients. *Dig. Liver Dis.*, **36**, 205–211.

53. Dauphine, C., Kovar, J., Stabile, B.E. *et al.* (2004) Identification of admission values predictive of complicated acute alcoholic pancreatitis. *Arch. Surg.*, **139**, 978–982.

54. Isenmann, R., Rau, B., and Beger, H.G. (2001) Early severe acute pancreatitis: Characteristics of a new subgroup. *Pancreas*, **22**, 274–278.

55. Lankisch, P.G., Assmus, C., Pflichthofer, D. *et al.* (1999) Which etiology causes the most severe acute pancreatitis? *Int. J. Pancreatol.*, **26**, 55–57.

56. Kaya, E., Dervisoglu, A., and Polat, C. (2007) Evaluation of diagnostic findings and scoring systems in outcome prediction in acute pancreatitis. *World J. Gastroenterol.*, **13**, 3090–3094.

57. Leung, T.K., Lee, C.M., Lin, S.Y. *et al.* (2005) Balthazar computed tomography severity index is superior to Ranson criteria and Apache ii scoring system in predicting acute pancreatitis outcome. *World J. Gastroenterol.*, **11**, 6049–6052.

58. Nathens, A.B., Curtis, J.R., Beale, R.J. *et al.* (2004) Management of the critically ill patient with severe acute pancreatitis. *Crit. Care Med.*, **32**, 2524–2536.

59. Yeung, Y.P., Lam, B.Y., and Yip, A.W. (2006) Apache system is better than Ranson system in the prediction of severity of acute pancreatitis. *Hepatobiliary Pancreat. Dis. Int.*, **5**, 294–299.

60. Ceccanti, M., Attili, A., Balducci, G. *et al.* (2006) Acute alcoholic hepatitis. *J. Clin. Gastroenterol.*, **40**, 833–841.

61. Forrest, E.H., Morris, A.J., Stewart, S. *et al.* (2007) The Glasgow alcoholic hepatitis score identifies patients who may benefit from corticosteroids. *Gut*, **56**, 1743–1746.

62. Tilg, H. and Kaser, A. (2005) Predicting mortality by the Glasgow alcoholic hepatitis score: The long awaited progress? *Gut*, **54**, 1057–1059.

63. Carithers, R. and McClain, C. (2006) Alcoholic liver disease, in *Sleisenger & Fordtran's Gastrointestinal and Liver Disease* (ed. M. Feldman), Saunders Elsevier, Philadelphia, p. 1781.

64. Menon, K.V., Stadheim, L., Kamath, P.S. *et al.* (2004) A pilot study of the safety and tolerability of etanercept in patients with alcoholic hepatitis. *Am. J. Gastroenterol.*, **99**, 255–260.

65. Naveau, S., Chollet-Martin, S., Dharancy, S. *et al.* (2004) A double-blind randomized controlled trial of infliximab associated with prednisolone in acute alcoholic hepatitis. *Hepatology*, **39**, 1390–1397.

66. Brncic, N., Kraus, I., Viskovic, I. *et al.* (2006) 3,4-methylenedioxymethamphetamine (MDMA): An important cause of acute hepatitis. *Med. Sci. Monit.*, **12**, CS107–CS109.

67. Volk, M.L. and Marrero, J.A. (2006) Advances in critical care hepatology. *Minerva Anestesiol.*, **72**, 269–281.

68. Aggarwal, A., Ong, J.P., Younossi, Z.M. *et al.* (2001) Predictors of mortality and resource utilization in cirrhotic patients admitted to the medical ICU. *Chest*, **119**, 1489–1497.

69. Arabi, Y., Ahmed, Q.A., Haddad, S. *et al.* (2004) Outcome predictors of cirrhosis patients admitted to the intensive care unit. *Eur. J. Gastroenterol. Hepatol.*, **16**, 333–339.

70. Singh, N., Gayowski, T., Wagener, M.M., and Marino, I.R. (1998) Outcome of patients with cirrhosis requiring intensive care unit support: Prospective assessment of predictors of mortality. *J. Gastroenterol.*, **33**, 73–79.

71. Tsai, M.H., Chen, Y.C., Ho, Y.P. *et al.* (2003) Organ system failure scoring system can predict hospital mortality in critically ill cirrhotic patients. *J. Clin. Gastroenterol.*, **37**, 251–257.

72. du Cheyron, D., Bouchet, B., Parienti, J.J. *et al.* (2005) The attributable mortality of acute renal failure in critically ill patients with liver cirrhosis. *Intensive Care Med.*, **31**, 1693–1699.

73. Cholongitas, E., Senzolo, M., Patch, D. *et al.* (2006) Risk factors, sequential organ failure assessment and model for end-stage liver disease scores for predicting short term mortality in cirrhotic patients admitted to intensive care unit. *Aliment. Pharmacol. Ther.*, **23**, 883–893.

74. Fang, J.T., Tsai, M.H., Tian, Y.C. *et al.* (2008) Outcome predictors and new score of critically ill cirrhotic patients with acute renal failure. *Nephrol. Dial. Transplant*, **23**, 1961–1969.

75. Mattia, C., Savoia, G., Paoletti, F. *et al.* (2006) Siaarti recommendations for analgo-sedation in intensive care unit. *Minerva Anestesiol.*, **72**, 769–805.

76. Kollef, M.H., Levy, N.T., Ahrens, T.S. *et al.* (1998) The use of continuous i.v. sedation is associated with prolongation of mechanical ventilation. *Chest*, **114**, 541–548.

77. Kress, J.P. and Hall, J.B. (2006) Sedation in the mechanically ventilated patient. *Crit. Care Med.*, **34**, 2541–2546.

78. Pun, B.T. and Ely, E.W. (2007) The importance of diagnosing and managing ICU delirium. *Chest*, **132**, 624–636.

79. Ely, E.W., Shintani, A., Truman, B. *et al.* (2004) Delirium as a predictor of mortality in mechanically ventilated patients in the intensive care unit. *JAMA*, **291**, 1753–1762.

80. Ouimet, S., Kavanagh, B.P., Gottfried, S.B., and Skrobik, Y. (2007) Incidence, risk factors and consequences of ICU delirium. *Intensive Care Med.*, **33**, 66–73.

81. Al-Sanouri, I., Dikin, M., and Soubani, A.O. (2005) Critical care aspects of alcohol abuse. *South Med. J.*, **98**, 372–381.

82. Gold, J.A., Rimal, B., Nolan, A., and Nelson, L.S. (2007) A strategy of escalating doses of benzodiazepines and phenobarbital administration reduces the need for mechanical ventilation in delirium tremens. *Crit. Care Med.*, **35**, 724–730.

83. DeCarolis, D.D., Rice, K.L., Ho, L. *et al.* (2007) Symptom-driven lorazepam protocol for treatment of severe alcohol withdrawal delirium in the intensive care unit. *Pharmacotherapy*, **27**, 510–518.

84. Spies, C.D., Dubisz, N., Neumann, T. *et al.* (1996) Therapy of alcohol withdrawal syndrome in intensive care unit patients following trauma: Results of a prospective, randomized trial. *Crit. Care Med.*, **24**, 414–422.

85. Weinberg, J.A., Magnotti, L.J., Fischer, P.E. *et al.* (2008) Comparison of intravenous ethanol versus diazepam for alcohol withdrawal prophylaxis in the trauma ICU: Results of a randomized trial. *J. Trauma*, **64**, 99–104.

86. Dissanaike, S., Halldorsson, A., Frezza, E.E., and Griswold, J. (2006) An ethanol protocol to prevent alcohol withdrawal syndrome. *J. Am. Coll. Surg.*, **203**, 186–191.

87. Ip Yam, P.C., Forbes, A., and Kox, W.J. (1992) Clonidine in the treatment of alcohol withdrawal in the intensive care unit. *Br. J. Anaesth.*, **68**, 106–108.

88. Spies, C.D., Otter, H.E., Huske, B. *et al.* (2003) Alcohol withdrawal severity is decreased by symptom-orientated adjusted bolus therapy in the ICU. *Intensive Care Med.*, **29**, 2230–2238.

89. Hodges, B. and Mazur, J.E. (2004) Intravenous ethanol for the treatment of alcohol withdrawal syndrome in critically ill patients. *Pharmacotherapy*, **24**, 1578–1585.

90. Sivilotti, M.L., Burns, M.J., Aaron, C.K., and Greenberg, M.J. (2001) Pentobarbital for severe gamma-butyrolactone withdrawal. *Ann. Emerg. Med.*, **38**, 660–665.

91. Hensel, M. and Kox, W.J. (2000) Safety, efficacy, and long-term results of a modified version of rapid opiate detoxification under general anaesthesia: A prospective study in methadone, heroin, codeine and morphine addicts. *Acta Anaesthesiol. Scand.*, **44**, 326–333.

92. Scragg, P., Jones, A., and Fauvel, N. (2001) Psychological problems following ICU treatment. *Anaesthesia*, **56**, 9–14.

93. Stoll, C., Kapfhammer, H.P., Rothenhausler, H.B. *et al.* (1999) Sensitivity and specificity of a screening test to document traumatic experiences and to diagnose post-traumatic stress disorder in ards patients after intensive care treatment. *Intensive Care Med.*, **25**, 697–704.

94. Sukantarat, K., Greer, S., Brett, S., and Williamson, R. (2007) Physical and psychological sequelae of critical illness. *Br. J. Health Psychol.*, **12**, 65–74.

95. Bronson, D., Franco, K., and Budur, K. (2007) Post-traumatic stress disorder in primary care patients. *Compr. Ther.*, **33**, 208–215.

96. Griswold, K.S., Aronoff, H., Kernan, J.B., and Kahn, L.S. (2008) Adolescent substance use and abuse: Recognition and management. *Am. Fam. Physician*, **77**, 331–336.

97. Margis, R. (2003) Comorbidities in post-traumatic stress disorder: Rule or exception? *Rev. Bras. Psiquiatr.*, **25** (Suppl 1), 17–20.

98. Merikangas, K.R. and Kalaydjian, A. (2007) Magnitude and impact of comorbidity of mental disorders from epidemiologic surveys. *Curr. Opin. Psychiatry*, **20**, 353–358.

99. Schafer, I. and Najavits, L.M. (2007) Clinical challenges in the treatment of patients with posttraumatic stress disorder and substance abuse. *Curr. Opin. Psychiatry*, **20**, 614–618.

100. Steinberg, W. (2006) Acute pancreatitis, in *Sleisenger & Fordtran's Gastrointestinal and Liver Disease* (ed. M. Feldman), Saunders Elselvier, Philadelphia, p. 1241.

12

Addictive disorders in trauma center patients

Mary C. McCarthy and Kathryn M. Tchorz

Division of Trauma/Surgical Critical Care/Emergency General Surgery, Wright State University-Boonshoft School of Medicine, Miami Valley Hospital, Dayton, OH 45409, USA

12.1 OVERVIEW

The prevalence of alcohol in trauma fatalities is now well documented. The landmark US Department of Health and Human Services publication, *Healthy People 2010*, a national health promotion and disease prevention initiative directed at improving quantity and quality of life, and focusing on unintentional injuries and substance abuse, identified motor vehicle crashes (MVCs) as the most common cause of serious injury [1]. Disturbingly, serious injury from MVCs are often predictable and preventable. The reduction in driving while impaired and increased use of seat belts are two of the most effective means to reduce the risk of death and serious injury of vehicle occupants. There are more than 150 000 total trauma-related deaths every year and 40–50% of these are alcohol-related MVC fatalities [2,3].

During 2005, the most recent year for which data are available, there were 16 885 fatalities from alcohol-related crashes. This represents an average of one alcohol-related fatality every 31 minutes [3]. In 2005, an estimated 254 000 persons were injured in crashes in which police reported alcohol was present – an average of one person injured every two minutes [3]. Furthermore, half of the 414 child passengers aged 14 and younger who died in alcohol-related crashes during 2005 were riding with an alcohol-impaired driver [3]. In 2004, the FBI reported that over 1.4 million drivers were arrested for driving under the influence of alcohol or narcotics. In 2005, 85% of the drivers involved in fatal crashes had a Blood Alcohol Concentration (BAC) of 0.08 g/dl or higher [3] (Figure 12.1).

Domestic and occupational incidents, such as fires and drowning, also have a high incidence of alcohol involvement appearing in 20–70% of fatalities [2]. Over 50% of deaths attributed to intentional injuries, such as assaults and hand gun violence, are alcohol related [2]. Drugs such as marijuana and cocaine have been implicated in 18% of crash-related fatalities [2]. This enormous healthcare burden carries significant public health, financial, and societal repercussions and has spurred trauma organizations into action [4,5].

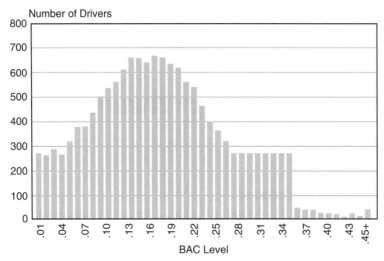

Figure 12.1 Distribution of BAC Levels for Drivers involved in Fatal Crashes with BAC .01 or Higher. Source: National Health and Transportation Safety Administration (NHTSA)

12.2 ALCOHOL USE AND INJURY

Alcohol use consists of a spectrum extending from abstinence and low-risk use to risky use, problem drinking, harmful use and alcohol addiction the spectrum continues to alcoholism and alcohol dependence, in which increasing alcohol use correlates with health-related consequences (Figure 12.2) [6]. In trauma, most injuries occur in patients who are acutely intoxicated, are chronic alcoholics or are alcohol dependent. Commonly used terms in the current trauma and addiction literature include: (1) acute intoxication which is defined by the number of alcoholic drinks ingested within a 24-hour period prior to emergency department (ED) admission [6–8]; (2) binge drinking, which is defined as five or more drinks for men (four or more drinks for women) on a single occasion, at least once per month during a 12-month span [6–8]; and (3) chronic dependence or alcoholism, which is defined as a chronic disease that has a peak onset at age 18 (Table 12.1) [9]. Not surprisingly, patients with chronic alcohol dependence usually have multiple ED visits and/or hospital admissions for alcohol-related injuries and disease-related conditions.

Binge drinking appears to be a stronger predictor of injury than average drinking and is often considered a "recurrent" disease [7–9]. This type of drinking causes risk-taking and harmful behavior, and is most commonly observed in individuals under 40 years of age. These "at risk" drinkers have been the targets of brief interventions which have been demonstrated to reduce ED recidivism among trauma patients [10]. More specifically, these "at risk" drinkers may be described as those who are not chronic alcohol users, but who are episodic heavy drinkers. The combination of alcohol and risk-taking behavior has been dubbed "The Perfect Storm" [11]. This combination of impaired judgment and recklessness due to alcohol creates a high risk for injury. Risky behaviors in trauma patients include dangerous driving, violence or aggression. These may be compounded by suicidal ideation or previous attempts associated with problem drinking [12]. Mandatory assessment of patient serum alcohol on admission, followed by a brief counseling session, is now an essential component for American College of Surgeons

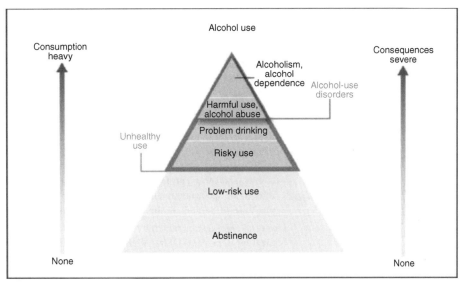

Figure 12.2 The spectrum of alcohol use. Source: Ref. [6]. Copyright © 2005 Massachusetts Medical Society. All rights reserved

(ACS)-Committee on Trauma (COT) trauma center verification [5,13].

Alcohol contributes significantly to both unintentional and intentional injuries (Figure 12.3) [14]. Although acute alcohol consumption is associated with increased rates of injury, it has not been associated with patterns of injury or specific injuries [15–20]. Co-intoxication, which is the combination of alcohol and illicit drug use, usually causes impaired reaction times and poor judgment, all predisposing factors prominently featured in MVCs, pedestrian injuries, and falls. Moreover, antisocial and disruptive behaviors caused by alcohol and illicit drug addiction have also been frequently associated with intentional injuries, such as assaults, suicide, and homicide. Finally, while wandering into unsuspected dangerous environments, acute intoxication also inhibits the inability to defend oneself.

While numerous studies have documented the characteristics of intoxicated trauma patients, some controversy exists regarding its association with higher injury severity and worse outcomes. What is not in debate, however, is the prevalence of alcohol and illicit drug addiction among trauma patients. In one cross-sectional study, after controlling for rele-vant confounders, such as drinking patterns, illicit drug use, demographics and risk-taking behaviors, the presence of alcohol was found to confer a "generic risk" to the patient [17,18]. Moreover, in a follow-up study the authors suggest that the actual "drinking setting" may be associated with a particular mechanism of injury or injury pattern [18]. Recently, one retrospective trauma center study analyzed 1049 patients who had blood alcohol and urine toxicology studies performed on admission [19]. Of these patients, 307 were BAC-positive, defined as >0.08 g/dl, and 742 were BAC-negative on admission. When compared to the BAC-negative patients, BAC-positive patients were more likely to be male, 40 years or younger in age, victims of penetrating injury, test positive for illicit drugs, and, for what it's worth, less likely to have health insurance [19]. Interestingly, the mortality rates and length of hospital stay for the BAC-positive patients were lower than the BAC-negative ones, which lead the authors to suggest that perhaps the presence of alcohol at the time of admission made these patients appear more severely injured than they really were [19]. This is in line with conclusions from other studies whereby intoxicated patients may receive a higher level of care for this appearance [20,21].

Table 12.1   Definitions of Unhealthy Alcohol Use

Category of Use	Prevalence %	Definition and Features
Risky use	30	For women and persons >65 years of age, >7 standard drinks per week or >3 drinks per occasion; for men ≤65 years of age, >14 standard drinks per week or >4 drinks per occasion; there are no alcohol-related consequences, but the risk of future physical, psychological, or social harm increases with increasing levels of consumption; risks associated with exceeding the amounts per occasion that constitute "binge" drinking in the short term include injury and trauma; risks associated with exceeding weekly amounts in the long term include cirrhosis, cancer, and other chronic illnesses; "risky use" is sometimes used to refer to the spectrum of unhealthy use but usually excludes dependence; one third of patients in this category are at risk for dependence[†]
Problem drinking	Varies[‡]	Use of alcohol accompanied by alcohol-related consequences but not meeting ICD-10 or DSM-IV criteria; sometimes used to refer to the spectrum of unhealthy use but usually excludes dependence
Alcohol abuse, harmful use	5	In DSM-IV, recurrence of the following clinically significant impairments within 12 months: failure to fulfill major role obligations, use in hazardous situations, alcohol-related legal problems, or social or interpersonal problems caused or exacerbated by alcohol; in ICD-10, physical or mental health consequences only
Alcohol dependence, alcoholism	4	In DSM-IV, clinically significant impairment or distress in the presence of three or more of the following: tolerance; withdrawal; a great deal of time spent obtaining alcohol, using alcohol, or recovering from its effects; reducing or giving up important activities because of alcohol; drinking more or longer than intended; a persistent desire or unsuccessful efforts to cut down or control use; continued use despite having a physical or psychological problem caused or exacerbated by alcohol; in ICD-10, similar definition

Data are from the Department of Health and Human Services [3], Whitlock et al. [4], the U.S. Preventive Services Task Force [5], the World Health Organization [6, 7], the American Psychiatric Association [8], and Grant et al. [9] ICD-10 denotes the *International Classification of Diseases*, 10th edition, and DSM-IV the *Diagnostic and Statistical Manual of Mental Disorders*, 4th edition.

[†]A standard drink is approximately 12 to 14 g of ethanol, which corresponds to 12 oz of beer, 5 oz of wine, or 1.5 oz of 80-proof liquor. The thresholds in the table do not apply to children, adolescents, or pregnant women; to persons taking medication that interacts with alcohol or engaging in activities that require attention, skill, or coordination (e.g., driving); or those with medical conditions that may be affected by alcohol (e.g., gastritis or hepatitis C). For all these groups, the healthiest choice is generally abstinence. The term "binge drinking" is sometimes used to mean heavy use that is prolonged (>1 day), with cessation of usual activities. It is also used to refer to consumption that exceeds the specified limits per occasion.

[‡]Because the definition of problem drinking varies among studies, estimates of the prevalence also vary.

Source: Saitz, R. Unhealthy Alcohol Use. N Engl J Med 2005; **352**: 596–607 Copyright © 2005 *Massachusetts Medical Society*.

In contrast, another study from an urban trauma center examining injuries in pedestrians and bicyclists struck by a motor vehicle, BAC-positive patients were categorized into low BAC (≥0.05 g/dl to <0.08 g/dl) and high BAC (≥0.08 g/dl) levels on admission [22]. In this study population, 42% were BAC-positive and of those, 8% had low BAC and 34% had a high BAC on admission. As with their previous work, the authors could not demonstrate a correlation between alcohol and injury severity, injury patterns or mortality [22,23]. However, there was an association of high BAC with increased length of hospital stay and major complications, such as pneumonia, sepsis, renal failure, and acute respiratory distress syndrome (ARDS) [22]. In the demonstration of a correlation

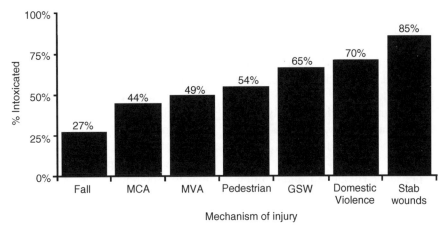

Figure 12.3 Alcohol associated injury. The incidence of alcohol associated intoxication varies for selected mechanisms of injuries. MCA = motorcycle injury; MVA = motor vehicle accident; GSW = gun shot wound. Source: Ref. [14] Copyright © 2005 Massachusetts Medical Society. All rights reserved

between substance use and injury severity over a three-year period, this same group noted that 43% of their trauma deaths screened positive for alcohol and/or illicit drugs [23]. The prevalence was higher if the victim was male, less than 50 years of age, presented with penetrating trauma, and/or was of African-American or Hispanic ancestry [23].

With regard to illicit drug use, many trauma care providers will document drug use as reported by the patient and/or test only those patients who arouse suspicion. One early study from a leading trauma center demonstrated when evaluating routine toxicology studies of 452 trauma patients, 38% of were positive for alcohol, 26% for marijuana, 12% for opiates, and 11% for cocaine [24]. Another trauma center reported that a 16-year retrospective study of a toxicology database demonstrated, in 53 000 trauma patients seen during that period, 89% of the patients were tested for alcohol and 69% for illicit drugs. The results of this study demonstrated a significant increase in opiate and cocaine use, especially in those patients presenting with intentional and/or violent injuries. Interestingly, there was a 37% overall decrease in alcohol use throughout this time period [25]. The authors suggested the decrease of BAC-positive patients over the study period (1984–1999) may have reflected changes in state and nation-wide legislative initiatives to decrease driving while intoxicated.

Subsequent work from the same group demonstrated that upon admission to the trauma center, patients who test positive for alcohol and/or illicit drugs are twice as likely to die from subsequent trauma [25]. Another study from this group demonstrated a pre-injury association with cocaine use and crash culpability in drivers, age 21–40 years old, involved in MVCs [26]. As demonstrated in previous studies, pre-injury use of alcohol was associated with crash culpability in all drivers, regardless of age or gender [26]. However, pre-injury use of marijuana was not associated with driver crash culpability in this study [26]. This result is contrary to other studies and thought to be due to small sample size and inability to determine time of impairment, since marijuana metabolites may be detected in the urine for several days [26].

In a six-month prospective study of 322 patients involved in MVCs, the same authors demonstrated that the about 60% of these patients tested positive for alcohol and/or illicit drug use [27]. Furthermore, in this study, a rapid point-of-collection assay performed on admission to the trauma center correlated with standard laboratory toxicology screening. Hence, in addition to BAC testing, the use of rapid detection for commonly misused illicit drugs may present another valuable opportunity for intervention treatments [27]. The most recent work from these authors demonstrated a higher absolute addictive risk in trauma patients when compared to the general public. In fact, this risk was likened to patients with lifetime substance dependence, such as the risk documented from patients undergoing drug addiction treatment [28]. Another group demonstrated that cocaine was independently associated with violence-related injury, and that alcohol combined with cocaine is predictive of future injures [29].

In light of the prevalence of alcohol and/or illicit drug detected among trauma patients, it is apparent that trauma centers are a prime setting for the identification and treatment of patients with substance addiction problems. Indeed, it is doubtful that any other clinical setting has a higher prevalence of patients with alcohol and drug problems than trauma centers [2]. It is postulated that the regionalization of designated trauma centers has extended the reach of alcohol awareness and injury prevention [2]. This opportunity to reduce the likelihood of further injuries has led many trauma surgeons to champion their professional associations to recommend screening and brief intervention programs as an essential component of trauma care.

12.3 CLINICAL COURSE AND PATHOPHYSIOLOGY

Acute and chronic alcohol addiction may affect many organ systems and their functioning at the cellular and molecular level. Drinking individuals are at increased risk for organ dysfunction and infection, especially during states of physiologic stress such as trauma. Various patterns of tissue and cell injury may be manifested in the critically ill and injured patient, depending on the time duration and chronic nature of alcohol exposure. Hence, even mild injury may invoke a cascade of physiologic events, such as liver dysfunction and ARDS, which may lead to multi organ dysfunction syntrome (MODS) and possibly death (Figure 12.4).

12.3.1 Traumatic brain injury

No other injury causes more mortality or life-long morbidity than Traumatic Brain Injury (TBI).

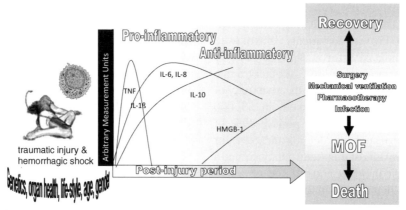

Figure 12.4 The immune counter-regulatory response to traumatic injury involves coordinated cellular and molecular events, mediated by pro- and anti-inflammatory cytokine's that contribute to the integrity of host defense mechanisms and is proportional to the magnitude of the injury. The host response to injury is determined not only by the severity of the injury but by genetic, health status, life-style, age, and gender. Alcohal abuse, through its organ-specific effects, particularly through the impairment in immune function disrupts the integrity of these responses, affecting the course of recovery during the postinjury period. The additional challenges "second-heat" that the trauma victim undergoes during the recovery phase increase the risk of tissue injury, development of multiple organ failure (MOF) and death

Alcohol is involved in 35–50% of TBIs and individuals admitted with an elevated BAC have a lower Glasgow Coma Score (GCS) on admission. This altered mental status makes physical assessment and diagnosis for additional injuries rather challenging [30]. These patients have a higher likelihood of intubation, mechanical ventilation, pneumonia, and ARDS [31]. Furthermore, these complications prolong hospital stays and delay patient recovery [30]. Computed Tomography (CT) scans of the brain in these intoxicated patients demonstrate worse injuries and increased mortality than those noted from the general population [32,33]. Intoxicated patients are also less likely to use protective devices such as seatbelts, predisposing them to a higher rate of facial fractures in conjunction with head injuries. Victims of blunt assault are also highly likely to be intoxicated, upwards of 75% in one study [34]. These data highlight the importance of early recognition of alcohol and/or substance addiction and referral for intervention.

Neuropsychological testing in patients with TBI and alcohol intoxication has demonstrated poorer cognitive outcomes than those noted in sober patients [35]. However, there is controversy over whether these differences are due to acute alcohol intoxication on the day of injury or to chronic alcohol addiction prior to the traumatic incident. The first hypothesis, that alcohol and TBI have interactive effects, states that outcomes are worse due to an increased severity of injury secondary to adverse physiologic effects on the brain in an intoxicated patient. These physiological effects include hemodynamic and respiratory depression, coagulopathy, and impaired blood–brain barrier function [35]. With the potentiation of parenchymal and vascular damage during TBI, post-injury neuronal recovery may also be impaired. An alternative hypothesis, that alcohol has a cumulative effect on the brain, states that worse outcomes in acutely intoxicated individuals are due to the high rate of pre-injury alcohol addiction, estimated to run as high as 79% [36]. Structural neuro-imaging studies have demonstrated overall brain volume loss as well as atrophic region-specific and structure-specific changes associated with chronic alcohol use [37]. Outcome measures of these two hypotheses have been equivocal, especially when compounded with illicit drug use and addictive behavior [38]. In light of these additional problems, inpatient rehabilitation for TBI represents an opportune time to intervene in substance addiction problems [39].

12.3.2 Trauma and liver disease

Recently, cellular and molecular effects of alcohol-induced tissue injury of the liver have garnished much attention in the medical literature. In particular, the (1) dysregulation of proinflammatory cytokines, such as Tumor Necrosis Factor (TNF-α), (2) oxidative stress, and (3) mitochondrial dysfunction of P-450 system have been shown to be the primary mechanisms responsible for Alcoholic Liver Disease (ALD) [40]. Peripheral blood monocytes from patients with ALD produce elevated levels of TNF-α and correlate with disease severity and mortality [40]. A perpetual cycle occurs, whereby patients with ALD readily develop endotoxemia from TNF-α induced oxidative stress of the gut mucosa [40]. While acute alcohol intoxication enhances apotosis of hepatocytes *in vitro*, chronic alcohol use is considered an independent risk factor for developing Hepatitis C (HCV) infection [40]. Moreover, viral load and genotype specificity are associated with predictable rates of hepatic fibrosis progression, leading to hepatic cirrhosis [40].

These pre-existing conditions of organ dysfunction profoundly increase morbidity and mortality in those with ALD who experience trauma, regardless of the extent of injury. In the general population, host defense mechanisms are altered in acute trauma and hemorrhagic shock (Figure 12.5) [41]. Although tissue injury may be localized, the host response is systemic and the response is reflected by host genotype, severity of injury and pre-existing organ disease.

In alcohol-intoxicated animal hemorrhage studies, the compensatory hemodynamic, proinflammatory and neuroendocrine responses are attenuated and associated with an increased susceptibility to infection [41,42]. Altered metabolic responses can be noted throughout the initial, intermediate and recovery phases of shock [41,42]. This dysregulated

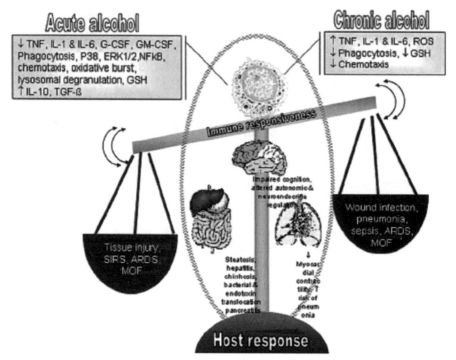

Figure 12.5   The host response to traumatic injury is affected by the acute and chronic effects of alcohol on multiple organ systems. Central to the responses during the acute phase of injury as well as during the recovery phase are the neuroendocrine, gastrointestinal, and cardiorespiratory systems, all of which show altered function resulting from acute and chronic alcohol abuse. Nevertheless, it is the immune system that play a key role in determining the course of the recovery phase through self-regulation to maintain a balance that will optimize response to pathogens and prevent tissue damage. Alcohol addiction has marked effects on multiple components of the immune response and through these effects is shown to significantly and deterimentally affect outcome from traumatic injury. Source: Ref. [41]

host response coupled with acute trauma creates a metabolic milieu ripe for MODS [41,42].

In a prospective study of intensive care unit (ICU) patients with chronic alcohol disease, admission plasma levels of proinflammatory regulators, Interleukin-6 (IL-6), Interleukin-10 (IL-10), and Soluble Endothelial Selectin (sE-selectin) were significantly elevated when compared to nonalcoholic ICU patients [43]. This was statistically significant regardless of illness, Injury Severity Scores, or transfusion requirements [43]. Peak plasma levels of IL-6 were noted at approximately 12–24 hours post-trauma while peak plasma levels of IL-10 occurred several days in the post-trauma period. Interleukin-10 inhibits IL-6 production and is associated with severity of injury [43]. Soluble endothelial selectin is expressed on endothelial cells and

mediates vascular permeability into the interstitial tissue [43]. Although the role of sE-selectin is not well elucidated, serum levels are elevated in acute inflammation [44]. In this study, there was a statistically significant association with MODS in the chronic alcoholic patients when compared to the nonalcoholics (89% vs. 50% $p < 0.01$) [43]. This study suggests that early identification and monitoring of these serum biomarkers in trauma patients with ALD and/or cirrhosis may improve resuscitative efforts.

Mortality is exceedingly high in trauma patients with ALD and/or hepatic cirrhosis. This is especially true in those requiring an emergency laparotomy for hemoperitoneum and/or peritonitis, regardless of mechanism of injury. The dismal outcomes are components of the patient's inability to control coagulopathy and/or augment oxygen delivery. In all patients, both host mechanisms are required to overcome the initial insult of trauma. Unlike elective surgery in cirrhotics, trauma presents no opportunity to optimize nutrition, ascites or coagulopathy status. The mortality exceeds 50% due to the prolonged state of hemorrhagic shock and ongoing tissue hypoperfusion. Since hepatic arterial blood flow is critical for liver perfusion in these patients, fulminant failure may readily ensue [44]. A recently described swine model of liver cirrhosis, induced with carbon tetrachloride and ethanol, may hold promise for future studies in shock and hemorrhage [45]. Although clinical studies of cirrhotic trauma patients are few, a recent five-year retrospective review of 487 trauma patients presenting with blunt splenic injuries was performed. Not surprisingly, 70% (339/487) of these patients with splenic injuries were managed nonoperatively. However, of the 74 patients who failed nonoperative management, twelve of these patients had underlying liver cirrhosis [46]. Of these twelve patients with hepatic cirrhosis, 92% failed nonoperative management of their splenic injuries whereas only 19% of the noncirrhotic patient population of this study failed nonoperative management [46]. Furthermore, the highest mortality rate was demonstrated by those cirrhotics with a severely prolonged serum Prothrombin time (PT) level on admission, regardless of splenic injury, treatment option or resuscitative efforts [46]. The authors believed that surgical management of these patients was challenging due, in part, to the anatomic and hemodynamic sequelae of portal hypertension, splenomegaly, alcohol-induced cardiomyopathy, and renal disease. However, the authors concluded that regardless of the technical challenges with surgical intervention, nonoperative management of solid organ injury in cirrhotic trauma patients is not warranted and may contribute to an exceedingly high mortality rate [46].

12.3.3 Pneumonia and ARDS

Alcohol addiction independently and significantly increases the risk of developing Acute Lung Injury (ALI), ARDS, and MODS in critically ill and injured patients [47–51]. Alcohol addiction is closely linked to pneumonia and subsequent ARDS, regardless of the diagnosis of sepsis. In addition to severe oxidant stress due to depleted glutathione reserves associated with alcohol addiction, this altered immune state contributes to a dysfunctional host response to trauma [50]. Glutathione, an antioxidant essential for DNA repair, has been extensively studied in humans and animal models. Ethanol ingestion depletes glutathione in the alveolar fluid and alveolar epithelial type II cells and, therefore, renders the lung susceptible to endotoxin-mediated ALI [50]. The deficiencies in glutathione cause abnormal surfactant synthesis and alveolar type II cell apotosis [50]. Moreover, alcohol increases alveolar capillary permeability and elevates levels of sE-Selectin [50].

In a recent five-year retrospective study of 2601 trauma patients, 837 patients were screened for the presence alcohol and/or illicit drugs on admission [47]. Of these patients, 24% (199/837) were BAC positive, 14% (118/837) were illicit drug positive and 7.3% (61/837) tested positive for both [47]. Analysis of the patients presenting with alcohol intoxication or other illicit drugs demonstrated an OR = 3.34 (95% CI: 1.19–9.34) for developing pneumonia and an OR = 2.37 (95% CI: 1.29–4.36) for requiring mechanical ventilation [47].

Likewise, in a retrospective cohort multi-center study of 26 000 medical patients with a known alcohol use disorder, a significant risk of requiring mechanical ventilation was demonstrated, OR= 1.49 (95% CI: 1.41–1.574, p < 0.0001) [52]. Interestingly, only the presence of alcohol withdrawal syndrome in these patients was predictive of a longer duration of mechanical ventilation, OR 1.48 (95% CI: 1.266–1.724, p < 0.0001) [52]. Although these were not trauma patients, the presence of a history of alcohol use strongly predicted the need for mechanical ventilation. Alcohol addiction and prolonged mechanical ventilation were independently linked as a clinical predisposition and outcome, regardless of the admitting medical diagnosis.

12.4   SCREENING AND INTERVENTION FOR ALCOHOL ADDICTION IN TRAUMA PATIENTS

Trauma center admission is an opportune time to intervene in the course of patients with alcohol and drug use problems. For many young patients, this is their only contact with a healthcare provider. Additionally, the occurrence of a traumatic injury represents a "teachable moment." As mentioned previously, most trauma patients who were alcohol-impaired drivers, are binge drinkers and not classified as alcoholics. In the surviving patients without severe cognitive deficits, trauma center brief interventions are associated with decreased ED recidivism and fewer subsequent DUI (Driving Under the Influence) or DWI (Driving While Intoxicated) arrests [10,53]. These straightforward patient interactions have validated hospitalization for injury as a critical intervention point [10,53]. Screening and brief interventions have also been demonstrated to be cost effective and every dollar spent on these two components has been shown to save $3.81 in injury-related costs [54,55]. Many other studies have demonstrated both the feasibility and effectiveness of intervention in alcohol and, to a lesser extent, screening for drug addiction disorders during trauma center admission.

Although alcohol and drug use have long been recognized to play a role in traumatic injuries, emphasis on initial hospitalization identification and treatment of these disorders in trauma has been relatively recent. This effort has been spearheaded by several trauma surgeons and mandated by the ACS-COT [5,6,10,13]. The Optimal Care of the Injured Patient is a document outlining the requirements for verification of trauma centers and the most updated version incorporates requirements for alcohol and drug use screening in trauma patients [56]. Furthermore, this document states that brief trauma patient interventions, with subsequent follow-up, must be offered to all trauma patients who screen positive for alcohol upon trauma center admission. For patients identified with more severe and/or long-term substance use disorders, referral to a treatment center is required.

To this end, the identification of patients with trauma-associated drug and/or alcohol issues may be problematic for many hospitals and third-party payers. In 1947, the Uniform Accident and Sickness Policy Provision Law (UPPL) was introduced. This allowed insurance companies to deny payment for patient hospitalization and/or medical treatment if an incident was drug and/or alcohol related [57]. At that time, this law was drafted by the National Association of Insurance Commissioners, an organization which was composed of the state insurance companies who wanted to secure uniform insurance policy and decision making practices [57]. Furthermore, the law was reflective of the presiding social belief that personal character flaws were responsible for alcohol and/or drug-related injuries. Today, this organization is known as the National Conference of Insurance Legislatures (NCOIL), and is composed of state academic, consumer, industry, and policy representatives. However, despite improved understanding of substance use disorders, many states have upheld the UPPL, thus allowing insurance companies to deny payment for alcohol- and/or drug-related hospitalization and medical care.

Fortunately, there is a national effort underway to repeal the UPPL because this law may prevent numerous trauma patients from obtaining needed treatment [57]. Since 2005, the following states have repealed the UPPL: Colorado, Connecticut, District of Columbia, Illinois, Indiana, Iowa, Maryland, Nevada, North Corelina, Oregon, Rhode Island, South Dakota, and Washington. Although attempts were made in 2007 in California, New York, and Texas, the UPPL has not been rescinded [58]. As of 2007, the following states have not attempted to repeal the UPPL: Massachusetts, Michigan, Minnesota, New Mexico, New Hampshire, Oklahoma, Utah, Vermont, and Wisconsin [58].

As presented earlier in this chapter, unhealthy alcohol use has been defined by the Department of Health and Human Services as comprising four groups: *risky use*, *problem drinking* where levels of consumption are associated with harm, *alcohol abuse* and *alcohol dependence* [6,59]. Patients in all groups are frequently seen after sustaining traumatic injuries. Trauma care providers must be able to identify these patients and refer them for intervention. Once patients screen positive, counseling should be provided to help them become aware of their problem and motivate them to change their behavior. A smaller number of patients have severe alcohol problems, a prior history of addiction, and comorbidities such as liver damage or mental illness. These patients receive brief counseling with the goal of motivation to enter specialist treatment facilities and the aim of abstinence. A public health approach has been advocated by the Institute of Medicine [59,60]. Recommendations have been made for improving treatment across the spectrum of "alcohol problems," rather than limiting the focus to alcohol dependency and addiction. Moreover, involving the healthcare community in screening, brief intervention, and referral for more severe problems, recognizes that the whole population is at risk. Extending this concept even further would be targeted at preventing excessive consumption among all drinkers.

Accurate identification of patients with risky drinking behavior is essential before treatment can be provided [60]. Unfortunately, healthcare providers are unlikely to be able to identify those patients with an alcohol or drug use disorder. In a recent study of trauma surgeons, surgical house staff, and ED nurses, those who relied on clinical suspicion to identify intoxicated and alcohol dependent trauma patients missed 23% of acutely intoxicated patients [61]. This population of patients included nearly 33% in the severely injured, chemically paralyzed, or intubated/mechanically ventilated patients and more than 50% of patients with a positive self-report screening test [61]. For these reasons, the authors concluded a more accurate assessment in the injured population may be obtained by routine alcohol and drug screening with the institution of a public-health-style screening test [61].

An ideal screening test would be one supported by research, demonstrating a high level of accuracy. It would require limited time to administer and

score. Finally, it would be applicable to the target population and appropriate for trauma centers. There are a variety of self-report screening tests that have been used and validated in clinical practice. Screening may be accomplished using the four-question CAGE questionnaire [62]. However, this questionnaire is targeted more at identification of alcohol dependence. The ten-item Alcohol Use Disorders Identification Test (AUDIT) has also been well studied and has been found to be reliable, valid, and practical to administer [54,55]. AUDIT assesses three domains – alcohol consumption, alcohol-related harm, and alcohol dependence symptoms – and evaluates the level of risk for alcohol problems. In addition, this screening tool targets a broad spectrum of alcohol problems and encourages early intervention. For example, question one (frequency) and two (drinks per day) from the AUDIT may be used to assess current alcohol use; however, in trauma patients, a lower threshold for a positive test should be used such as drinks $\geq$2–3 times per week, $\geq$3 drinks per day [63]. This shorter screening is more useful for busy trauma services and may allow prompt referral to alcohol and drug counseling services for more in depth case finding and intervention.

Several serum biomarkers have also been used in selected settings for alcohol screening: BAC, mean corpuscular volume, gamma-glutamyltransferase, and carbohydrate-deficient transferrin [64]. Although most trauma centers use BAC for screening, the optimal threshold for intervention has not been established. For example, some patients with a negative BAC may have significant problems and require intervention [65].

Drug screening tests for adults that have been validated include the Drug Abuse Screening Test, a ten-question scale, and several personality and addiction potential tests. Adolescent-specific screening instruments have also been developed and tested, but are currently too unwieldy for trauma service use. Similarly, multiple risk factor screening through tests such as the Alcohol, Smoking and Substance Involvement Screening Test (ASSIST) are valuable in strategizing counseling interventions but are too complex for routine trauma service use [69]. There is also a strong association between alcohol-related trauma and personality characteristics associated with risk taking, sociopathic, or sensation seeking behaviors [12].

The CAGE-AID (adapted to include drugs) has been tested in primary care patients [70]. Due to the lack of objectivity when using self-reported screening tests for patient assessment, trauma centers use urine drug toxicology screens to assess recent use. However, cost effectiveness and sensitivity have been brought into question. In addition, motivational, cognitive, and behavioral interventions generally employed in drug treatment are of only limited effectiveness.

Once alcohol and/or drug use disorders have been identified, the patient must be evaluated for the stages of change. But when are trauma patients truly ready to change? Five stages of change have been described as people move towards healthy behaviors: (1) pre-contemplation, (2) contemplation, (3) preparation, (4) action, and (5) maintenance [64–68]. Relapse commonly occurs during behavior change because the patients' readiness to change is important to the success of an intervention program. In one study at a Level 1 Trauma Center, 42% of patients receiving brief intervention were in the later stages of change, more than twice that seen in primary care settings [69]. Patients residing within different stages of change need different intervention strategies, early on exploring why they should change and, in the later stages, how that may be accomplished.

Hospitalization for the treatment of alcohol- and/or drug-related injuries provides a window of opportunity for intervention to reduce the likelihood of further injury [71,72]. Systematic reviews of the evidence for effectiveness of various healthcare interventions can readily be located in the Cochrane Library. Its use is invaluable when attempting to assess outcomes. According to the 2004 Cochrane Review, interventions for problem drinking reduce the incidence of suicide attempts, domestic violence, falls, and injury hospitalizations and deaths – reductions ranging from 27 to 65% [71]. Although short- term improvements in individual health are present in the majority of studies, some studies demonstrated a comparable reduction in drinking and injuries in the study and

control groups. This is most encouraging because the research results suggest that injury alone and/or monitoring alone may reduce subsequent alcohol problems [69,71,72].

Although trauma centers are uniquely positioned to intervene in alcohol problems, there are several barriers to implementation [73–75]. Firstly, the definition of the target population and a method to screen are not universally accepted in all centers. The recognition that the majority of alcohol-related trauma is caused by moderate drinkers engaged in "binge drinking", and not chronic alcoholics, may improve optimism regarding the potential for treatment. Secondly, patients may be unwilling to admit they have an alcohol-related problem. Also, operational barriers may limit the availability of patients to be counseled because treatment of injuries takes precedence. Thirdly, resistance to screening by medical practitioners may occur. If these issues can be overcome, the trauma director may also be confronted with a lack of financial and human resources to accomplish the screening and intervention program. However, regardless of the obstacles, the data are clear. In the trauma population, alcohol screening and brief interventions provide tangible benefits to the patient and society.

After screening, healthcare providers conduct brief interventions with trauma patients to relate patient alcohol and/or drug behaviors with injury. The components of brief intervention include: (1) assessment and feedback regarding current drinking patterns, (2) information on the health consequences of drinking, (3) strategies to reduce alcohol consumption, (4) negotiation of an action plan, and (5) goal setting and behavioral modification techniques. The ultimate goal of brief intervention is to help people decrease or eliminate their alcohol use.

The key elements of brief intervention can be recalled by the acronym FRAMES (Table 12.2) [76,77]. It is a focused and time-limited intervention, lasting approximately 15 minutes, designed for use by healthcare providers in their daily practice [75–77]. The three motivational elements – responsibility, empathy and self-efficacy – are enhanced by combination with the three cognitive elements, feedback based on current drinking behaviors, advice about recommended change, and

Table 12.2   Simple mnemonic for components of a brief intervention

FRAMES mnemonic
Feedback: personalized information about risk status provided by trauma-care provider
Responsibility: patient's personal or intrinsic motivation to change behavior
Advice: brief education or recommendation for change provided by trauma-care provider
Menu: choice of options for change presented by trauma-care provide
Empathy: reflective listening and understanding demonstrated by trauma-care provider
Self-Efficacy: patient's belief in ability to change behavior

menu, alternative strategies for change. Choice is the key difference between brief intervention using this decisional balance approach and the more traditional directive approaches. These directive approaches are more likely to raise defenses and lead to resistance from some trauma patients.

In order to initiate an effective program, trauma centers should study the epidemiology of alcohol and drug use in their local patient population. Next, estimates of the resources required to meet the needs and avenues explored for obtaining these resources must be determined. Also, language and cultural elements should be considered when conducting a drug and alcohol needs assessment. If available, coordination with existing alcohol and drug counseling services may provide tremendous insight and assistance. Some centers have described participation of health educators in the trauma outpatient clinic and on daily rounds [77,78]. For example, at our institution, trauma patients are automatically screened with a BAC and a urine toxicology screen. Both of these tests are included with initial trauma admission studies. Next, patients with an elevated BAC and/or positive drug screens, as well as those who did not have these markers performed but were admitted to the trauma service, undergo frequent testing and questioning by Turning Point, our alcohol and drug counseling service. Finally, appropriate ongoing interventions, follow-up plans and/or treatment center referrals are conducted prior to patient discharge. As an aside, because brief intervention services in the hospital are billable, additional financial support may be provided to the trauma center, as well.

According to the US Preventive Health Services Task Force, routine alcohol screening for all patients in medical settings is recommended. However, there is not enough evidence to recommend routine drug screening, although it should be included in the social history assessment of all adults and adolescents [75,78]. While trauma surgeons, emergency medicine physicians, and nurses who care for these patients recognize the role that alcohol and drug addiction play in injury, we will need the assistance of others to develop the optimal system to care for these patients and reduce the impact of alcohol on our patients and our communities.

12.5   CONCLUSIONS

Injury and violence prevention are relatively new entities in trauma care systems, even though the association between alcohol and injury has been noted for centuries. The recent prospective data correlating alcohol and/or illicit drug use with injury compel trauma care providers to aggressively target at-risk patients. Coupled with recent data demonstrating the benefit of brief interventions and decreased recidivism, the challenge to trauma care providers is to refine the definition of optimal care, as put forth by the ACS-COT, to include prevention efforts [79,80]. Since these interventions may be performed by non-addiction healthcare providers, the current intervention strategies should be implemented in all trauma care programs. Indeed, the ACS-COT has mandated that all trauma centers not only screen patients for alcohol and or illicit drug use on admission, but administer counseling [13].

When considering public healthcare on a global realm, trauma is surpassing infectious diseases as the most common cause of morbidity and mortality worldwide. To this end, the establishment of a cost-effective intervention in one county may be contextualized to another. Since the combination of trauma and alcohol use seems ubiquitous world-wide, the impact of essential, yet contextualized, interventions may provide a cost-effective venue to save lives and improve quality of life for all.

REFERENCES

1. US Department of Health and Human Services, Healthy People 2010 Stat Notes. http://wonder.cdc.gov/scripts/broker.exe (accessed 18 january 2010).

2. Maier, R.V. (2005) Controlling alcohol problems among hospitalized trauma patients. *J. Trauma*, **59**, S1–S2.

3. National Health and Transportation Safety Administration (NHTSA) (December 2005) Traffic Safety Facts 2005, US Department of Transportation, Washington, DC.

4. Soderstrom, C.A., Cole, F.J., Porter, J.M. (2001) Injury in America: the role of alcohol and other drugs – an EAST position paper prepared by the injury control and violence prevention committee. *J. Trauma*, **50**, 1–12.

5. Hungerford, D.W. (2005) Recommendations for trauma centers to improve screening, brief intervention, and referral to treatment for substance use disorders. *J. Trauma*, **59** (3 Suppl.) S37–S42.

6. Saitz, R. (2005) Unhealthy alcohol use. *NEJM*, **352**, 596–607.

7. Hungerford, D.W. (2005) Interventions in trauma centers for substance use disorders: new insights on an old malady. *J. Trauma*, **59**, S10–S17.

8. Gmel, G., Givel, J.C., Yesin, B. *et al.* (2007) Injury and repeated injury-what is the link with acute alcohol consumption, binge drinking and chronic heavy alcohol use? *Swiss Med. Wkly*, **137**, 642–648.

9. Li, T.K., Hewitt, B.G., and Grant, B.F. (2004) Alcohol use disorders and mood disorders: a National Institute on Alcohol Abuse and Alcoholism perspective. *Biol. Psychiatry*, **56**, 718–720.

10. Gentilello, L.M., Rivara, F.P., Donovan, D.M. *et al.* (1999) Alcohol interventions in a trauma center as a means of reducing the risk of injury recurrence. *Ann. Surg.*, **230**, 473–480.

11. Moore, E.E. (2005) Alcohol and trauma: the perfect storm. *J. Trauma*, **59**, S53–S56.

12. Field, C.A., Classen, C.A., and O'Keefe, G.O. (2001) Association of alcohol use and other high-risk behaviors among trauma patients. *J. Trauma*, **50**, 13–19.

13. Gentilello, L.M. (2007) Alcohol and injury: American College of Surgeons Committee on Trauma Require-ments for Trauma Center Intervention. *J. Trauma*, **62**, S44–S45.

14. Maier, R.V. (2001) Ethanol abuse and the trauma patient. *Surg. Infect.*, **2** (2), 133–144.

15. Sommers, M.S., Dyehouse, J.M., and Howe, S.R. (2001) Binge drinking, sensible drinking and abstinence after alcohol-related vehicular crashes: the role of intervention verses screening. *Annu. Proc. Assoc. Adv. Automot. Med.*, **45**, 317–328.

16. Watt, K., Purdie, D.M., Roche, A.M., *et al.* (2004) Risk of injury from acute alcohol consumption and the influence of cofounders. *Addiction*, **99**, 1262–1273.

17. Watt, K., Purdie, D.M., Roche, A.M., *et al.* (2005) The relationship between acute alcohol consumption and consequent injury type. *Alcohol Alcohol.*, **40**, 263–268.

18. Watt, K., Purdie, D.M., Roche, A.M., *et al.* (2006) Acute alcohol consumption and mechanism of injury. *J. Stud. Alcohol*, **67**, 14–21.

19. Blondell, R.D., Looney, S.W., Kreig, C.L. *et al.* (2002) A comparison of alcohol-positive and alcohol-negative trauma patients. *J. Stud. Alcohol*, 380–383.

20. Li, G., Keyl, P.M., Smith, G.S. *et al.* (1997) Alcohol and injury severity: reappraisal of the continuing controversy. *J. Trauma*, **42**, 562–569.

21. Cornwall, E.E., Belzberg, H., Velmahos, G. *et al.* (1998) The prevalence and effect of alcohol and drug use on cohort-matched critically ill patients. *Am. Surg.*, **64**, 461–465.

22. Plurad, D., Demetriades, D., Gruzinski, G. *et al.* (2006) Pedestrian injuries: the association of alcohol consumption with the type and severity of injuries and outcomes. *J. Am. Coll. Surg.*, **202**, 919–927.

23. Demetriades, D., Gkiokas, G., Velmahos, G.C. *et al.* (2004) Alcohol and illicit drugs in traumatic deaths: prevalence and association with type and severity injuries. *J. Am. Coll. Surg.*, **199**, 687–692.

24. Rivera, F.P., Mueller, B.A., and Fligner, C.L. (1989) Drug use in trauma patients. *J. Trauma*, **29**, 462–470.

25. Soderstrom, C.A., Dischinger, P.C., Kerns, T.J. *et al.* (2001) Epidemic increases in cocaine and opiate use by trauma center patients: documentation with a large clinical toxicology database. *J. Trauma*, **51**, 557–564.

26. Dischinger, P.C., Mitchell, K.A., Kufera, J.A. *et al.* (2001) A longitudinal study of former trauma center patients: the association between toxicology status and subsequent injury mortality. *J. Trauma*, **51**, 877–886.

27. Soderstrom, C.A., Dischinger, P.C., Kufera, J.A. *et al.* (2005) Crash culpability relating to age and sex for injured drivers using alcohol, marijuana or cocaine. *Annu. Proc. Assoc. Adv. Automot. Med.*, **49**, 327–341.

28. Martins, S.S., Copersino, M.L., Soderstrom, C.A. *et al.* (2007) Risk of psychoactive substance dependence among users in a trauma inpatient population. *J. Addict. Dis.*, **26**, 71–77.

29. Blondell, R.D., Dodds, H.N., Looney, S.W. *et al.* (2005) Toxicology screening results: injury associations among hospitalized patients. *J. Trauma*, **58**, 561–570.

30. Gururaj, G. (2004) The effect of alcohol in incidence, pattern, severity and outcome from traumatic brain injury. *J. Indian Med. Assoc.*, **102**, 157–160. 163.

31. Gourney, J.G., Rivara, F.P., Mueller, B.A. *et al.* (1992) The effects of alcohol intoxication on the initial treatment and hospital course of patients with acute brain injury. *J. Trauma*, **33**, 709–713.

32. Sparadeo, F.R. and Gill, D. (1989) Effects of prior alcohol use on head injury recovery. *J. Head Trauma Rehab.*, **4**, 75–82.

33. Ruff, R.M., Marshall, L.F., Klauber, M.R. *et al.* (1990) Alcohol abuse and neurological outcome of the severely head injured. *J. Head Trauma Rehab.*, **5**, 21–31.

34. Shapiro, A.J., Johnson, R.M., Mille, S.F. *et al.* (2001) Facial fractures in a level I trauma centre: the importance of protective devices and alcohol abuse. *Injury, Int. J. Care Injured* **32**, 353–356.

35. Wilde, E.A., Bigler, E.D., Gandh, P.V. *et al.* (2004) Alcohol abuse and traumatic brain injury: quantitative magnetic resonance imaging and neuropsychological outcome. *J. Neurotrauma*, **21**, 137–147.

36. Bodner, J.A., Corrigan, D., Mystic, W.J. *et al.* (2001) A comparison of substance abuse and violence in the prediction of long-term rehabilitation outcomes after traumatic brain injury. *Arc Phys. Med. Rehabil.*, **82**, 571–577.

37. Netrakom, P., Kruaski, J.S., Miller, N.S. *et al.* (1999) Structural and functional neuroimaging findings in substance-related disorders. *Psychiatr. Clin. North Am.*, **22**, 319–329.

38. Lange, R.T. and Iverson, G.L. (2007) Short-term neuropsychological outcome following uncomplicated mild TBI: effects of day-of-injury intoxication and pre-injury alcohol abuse. *Neuropsychology*, **21**, 590–598.

39. Bombardier, C.H., Rimmele, C.T., and Zintel, H. (2002) The magnitude and correlates of alcohol and drug use before traumatic brain injury. *Arch. Phys. Med. Rehabil.*, **83**, 1765–1773.

40. Molina, P.E., McClain, C., Valla, D. *et al.* (2002) Molecular pathology and clinical aspects of alcohol-induced tissue injury. *Alcohol. Clin. Exp. Res.*, **26**, 120–128.

41. Greiffenstein, P. and Molina, P.E. (2008) Alcohol-induced alterations on host defense after traumatic injury. *J. Trauma*, **64**, 230–240.

42. Molina, P.E., Zambell, K.L., Norenberg, K. *et al.* (2004) Consequences of alcohol-induced early dysregulation of responses to trauma/hemorrhage. *Alcohol*, **33**, 217–227.

43. Maull, K.I. and Turnage, B. (2001) Trauma in the cirrhotic patient. *South. Med. J.*, **94**, 205–207.

44. von Heymann, C., Langenkamp, J., Dubisz, N. *et al.* (2002) Posttraumatic immune modulation in chronic alcoholics is associated with multiple organ dysfunction syndrome. *J. Trauma*, **52**, 95–103.

45. Zhang, J.J., Meng, X.K., Dong, C. *et al.* (2009) Development of a new animal model of liver cirrhosis in swine. *Eur. Surg. Res.*, **42**, 35–39.

46. Fang, J.F., Chen, R.J., Lin, B.C. *et al.* (2003) Liver cirrhosis: an unfavorable factor for non-operative management of blunt splenic injury. *J. Trauma*, **54**, 1131–1136.

47. Joshi, P.C. and Guidot, D.M. (2007) The alcoholic lung: epidemiology, pathophysiology, and potential therapies. *Am. J. Physiol. Lung Cell. Mol. Physiol.*, **292**, L813–L823.

48. Rootman, D.B., Mustard, R., Kalia, V., *et al.* (2006) Increased incidence of complications in trauma patients co-intoxicated with alcohol and other drugs. *J. Trauma*, **63**, 755–758.

49. Moss, M., Bucher, B., Moore, F.A. *et al.* (1996) The role of chronic alcohol abuse in the development of acute respiratory distress syndrome in adults. *JAMA*, **270**, 50–54.

50. Moss, M., Guidot, D.M., Wong-Lambertina, M. *et al.* (2000) The effects of chronic alcohol abuse on pulmonary glutathione homeostasis. *Am. J. Respir. Crit. Care Med.*, **161**, 414–419.

51. Moss, M., Parsons, P.E., Steinburg, K.P. *et al.* (2003) Chronic alcohol abuse is associated with an increased incidence of acute respiratory distress syndrome and severity of multiple organ dysfunction in patients with septic shock. *Crit. Care Med.*, **31**, 869–877.

52. de Wit, M., Best, A.M., Gennings, C. *et al.* (2007) Alcohol use disorders increase the risk for mechanical ventilation in medical patients. *Alcohol. Clin. Exp. Res.*, **31**, 1224–1230.

53. Schermer, C.R., Moyers, T.B., Miller, W.R. *et al.* (2006) Trauma center brief interventions for alcohol disorders decrease subsequent driving under the influence arrests. *J. Trauma*, **60**, 29–34.

54. Babor, T.F. and Grant, M. (1989) From clinical research to secondary prevention: international collaboration in the development of the Alcohol Use Disorders Identification Test (AUDIT). *Alcohol Health Res. World*, **13**, 371–374.

55. Mundt, M.P. (2006) Analyzing the costs and benefits of brief intervention. *Alcohol Res. Health*, **29**, 34–36.

56. American College of Surgeons: Committee on Trauma (1999) Resources for Optimal Care of the Injured Patient, American College of Surgeons, Chicago, IL.

57. Gentilello, L.M., Donato, A., Nolan, S. *et al.* (2005) Effect of the uniform accident and sickness policy provision law on alcohol screening and intervention in trauma centers. *J. Trauma*, **59**, 624–631.

58. www.facs.org/ahp/views/uppl.pdf.

59. Institute of Medicine. http://www.nap.edu/openbook. php?record_id=1486&page=23.

60. Soderstrom, C.A., Dischinger, P.C., Kerns, T.J. *et al.* (1998) Screening trauma patients for alcoholism according to NIAAA Guidelines with alcohol use disorders identification test questions. *Alcohol. Clin. Exp. Res.*, **22**, 1470–1475.

61. Gentilello, L.M., Villaveces, A., Ries, R.R. *et al.* (1999) Detection of acute alcohol intoxication and chronic alcohol dependence of trauma center staff. *J. Trauma*, **47**, 1131–1135.

62. Mayfield, D., McLeod, G., and Hall, P. (1974) The CAGE Questionnaire: validation of a new alcoholism screening instrument. *Am. J. Psychiatry*, **131**, 1121–1123.

63. Donovan, D.M., Dunn, C.W., Rivara, F.P. *et al.* (2004) Comparison of trauma center patient self-reports and proxy reports on the Alcohol Use Identification Test (AUDIT). *J. Trauma*, **56**, 873–882.

64. Miller, P.H., Spies, C., Neumann, T. *et al.* (2006) Alcohol biomarker screening in medical and surgical settings. *Alcohol. Clin. Exp. Res.*, **30**, 185–193.

65. Neumann, T., Neuner, B., Weiss-Gerlach, E. *et al.* (2006) The effect of computerized tailored brief advice on at-risk drinking in subcritically injured trauma patients. *J. Trauma*, **61**, 805–814.

66. Prochaska, J.O., Velicer, W.F., and Rossi, J.S. *et al.* (1994) Stages of change and decisional balance for twelve problem behaviors. *Health Psychol.*, **13**, 39–46.

67. Apodaca, T.R. and Schermer, C.R. (2003) Readiness to change alcohol use after trauma. *J. Trauma*, **54**, 990–994.

68. Dunn, C., Hungerford, D.W., Field, C. *et al.* (2005) The stages of change: when are trauma patients truly ready to change? *J. Trauma*, **59**, S27–S32.

69. Cryer, H.G. (2005) Barriers to interventions for alcohol problems in trauma centers. *J. Trauma*, **59**, S104–S111.

70. Brown, R.L. and Rounds, L.A. (1995) Conjoint screening questionnaires for alcohol and other drug abuse: criterion validity in a primary care practice. *Wis. Med. J.*, **94**, 135–140.

71. Dinh-Zarr, T., Diguiseppi, C., Heitman, E. *et al.* (1999) Preventing injuries through interventions for problem drinking: a systematic review of randomized controlled trials. *Alcohol Alcohol.*, **34**, 609–621.

72. Dinh-Zarr, T., Goss, C., Heitman, E. *et al.* (2004) Interventions for preventing injuries in problem drinkers. *Cochrane Database of Systematic Reviews* 3 (Art. No.: CD001857). doi: 10.1002/14651858.CD001857.pub2.

73. Sommers, M.S., Dyehouse, J.M., Howe, S.R. *et al.* (2006) Effectiveness of brief interventions after alcohol-related vehicular injury: a randomized controlled trial. *J. Trauma*, **61**, 523–531.

74. Dauer, A.R., Rubio, E.S., Coris, M.E. *et al.* (2006) Brief intervention in alcohol-positive traffic casualties: is it worth the effort? *Alcohol Alcohol.*, **41**, 76–83.

75. Babor, T.F. and Kadden, R.M. (2005) Screening and interventions for alcohol and drug problems in medical settings: what works? *J. Trauma*, **59**, S80–S87.

76. Miller, W.R., Sarchez, V.C. (1994) Motivating Young Adults for Treatment and life style change. In: G. Howard (ed.), Issues in Alcohal use and misuse in Young Adults Notre Dame, In: University of Notre Dame Press. pp. 55–81.

77. Dyehouse, J.M. and Sommers, M.S. (1998) Brief intervention after alcohol-related injuries. *Nurs. Clin. North Am.*, **33**, 93–104.

78. Sise, M.J., Sise, C.B., Kelley, D.M. *et al.* (2005) Implementing screening, brief intervention and referral for alcohol and drug use: the trauma service perspective. *J. Trauma*, **59**, S112–S118.

79. Gentilello, L.M. (2005) Alcohol interventions in trauma centers: the opportunity and the challenge. *J. Trauma*, **59**, S18–S20.

80. Gentilello, L.M. (2005) Confronting the obstacles to screening and interventions from alcohol problems in trauma centers. *J. Trauma*, **59**, S137–S143.

13

Addictive disorders in psychiatric medicine

Christine Yuodelis-Flores, W. Murray Bennett, Charles Meredith, and Richard Ries

Department of Psychiatry and Behavioral Sciences, University of Washington School of Medicine, Seattle, Washington, USA

13.1 INTRODUCTION

Clinicians often find themselves faced with the challenge of diagnosing, treating, and managing patients with substance addiction as well as perplexing psychiatric symptoms that may or may not be associated with the substance use disorder. Evaluation of these complex patients with overlapping substance and psychiatric problems can be daunting and confusing to even the most experienced clinician. Hopefully, psychiatric consultation will be available. Ideally, an addiction psychiatrist would be consulted to assess the problem at hand.

Unfortunately, access to these specialists is far too often limited and even possibly unavailable to the clinician and patient. This chapter will serve as an overview of substance use disorders in the psychiatric population, focusing on psychiatric symptoms associated with substance misuse, epidemiology of co-occurring disorders, prognosis and complications in individuals diagnosed with dual disorders, and treatment. In addition, management of common psychiatric problems arising in patients with substance use disorders will be discussed.

13.2 ALCOHOL AND DRUG-INDUCED PSYCHIATRIC COMPLICATIONS

Psychiatric symptoms arising from primary alcohol or drug use disorders are commonly seen in clinical practice. Substance-related disorders are divided into two groups: substance use disorders (addiction and dependence) and substance-induced disorders according to DSM-IV [1], which lists nine substance-induced psychiatric disorders. Substance-induced mental disorders may be misdiagnosed as

major depression, anxiety disorders, bipolar disorder, psychosis, personality disorders, and cognitive disorders. Addictive disorders can mimic nearly every psychiatric syndrome, as psychoactive drugs and alcohol produce psychiatric symptoms as well as exacerbate psychiatric disorders. In establishing the diagnosis of a substance-induced psychiatric disorder, DSM-IV criteria specify that the psychia-

Addictive Disorders in Medical Populations Edited by Norman S. Miller and Mark S. Gold
© 2010 John Wiley & Sons, Ltd.

tric symptoms are prominent and arise within one month of substance intoxication or withdrawal. Patients will often present in crisis during acute intoxication or withdrawal with various psychiatric symptoms often characteristic of the substance of addiction.

13.2.1 Alcohol

Symptoms of alcohol intoxication include euphoria and behavioral disinhibition. Withdrawal symptoms include anxiety, depression, insomnia, agitation, tremor, sweating, tachycardia, and hypertension. Seizures can occur during severe withdrawal and a small percentage of chronic alcoholics experience delirium tremens, which can be life threatening and is characterized by delirium, hallucinations, seizures, and a hyperadrenergic state consisting of hypertension, diaphoresis, and tachycardia.

Alcohol-induced depressive disorders are commonly seen in the outpatient setting. Depressive symptoms associated with alcohol are seen with intoxication as well as withdrawal. However, it can be very difficult to determine if the depression is independent or alcohol induced. Patients, who may be in denial of their alcohol use disorder, might tend to minimize or not even recognize the role alcohol plays in causing or exacerbating their depressive symptoms. Alcohol is widely known as causing a variety of symptoms that can also be seen in depression, such as low energy, amotivation, poor concentration, sleep disorders, somatic complaints, and anxiety symptoms. Withdrawal from alcohol is associated with dysphoria, cognitive disturbances, anxiety, and insomnia. There is also a clear association of alcohol and other substances of addiction with suicidal behavior. There have been many studies documenting highly elevated rates of suicide attempts and completed suicide among those with substance use disorders [2,3]. Symptoms of anxiety as well as panic attacks are common during alcohol withdrawal. Up to 80% of alcohol dependent subjects have panic attacks during withdrawal [4]. Alcohol-induced psychotic disorders are less common and usually more indicative of serious withdrawal-associated sequelae, such as delirium tremens.

13.2.2 Stimulants

Intoxication with cocaine, amphetamine/methamphetamine, and MDMA (Ecstasy) is associated with euphoria, high energy, anorexia, and insomnia as well as anxiety and mood lability. Withdrawal symptoms include depression, anxiety, hypersomnia, increased appetite, poor concentration, low energy, and anhedonia. Stimulant-induced mood disorder is common and diagnosed when the depressive symptoms are substantially in excess of what would normally be seen during withdrawal.

Stimulant-induced psychotic disorder is very common during intoxication and withdrawal. The presence and duration of psychotic symptoms in chronic methamphetamine users increase with severity and length of dependence, and are particularly associated with long-term intravenous methamphetamine use. A small percentage of chronic intravenous methamphetamine-dependent patients can present with long-term psychotic symptoms that appear almost identical to paranoid schizophrenia, as studied in the Japanese population where an "epidemic" of intravenous methamphetamine use has occurred over a long period [5,6]. In the United States population, the misuse of smokable methamphetamine, also known as "crank" or "ice," is more common than intravenous methamphetamine use. Chronic use of this drug seems to be associated with longer duration of psychotic symptoms (up to months), as compared to smokers of crack cocaine.

13.2.3 Benzodiazepine/sedative hypnotics

Benzodiazepines are widely prescribed in the United States for anxiety disorders, and sedative hypnotics are commonly prescribed for sleep disorders. Intoxication with these agents causes euphoria, disinhibition, and sedation. Chronic users of these agents will develop physical dependence and experience withdrawal syndromes characterized by anxiety, dysphoria, insomnia, tremors, diaphoresis, tachycardia, hypertension, agitation, and nausea and vomiting. Severe withdrawal syndromes are life threatening and necessitate hospitalization for treatment of seizures, hallucinosis, delirium, and autonomic hyperactivity.

13.2.4 Hallucinogens

This group of substances includes Phencyclidine (PCP), LSD, mescaline, psylocybin, and dimethyltryptamine (DMT). As the name suggests, hallucinogens produce auditory, visual, and other perceptual distortions and frank hallucinations during intoxication. The experience of intoxication with hallucinogens can also produce panic reactions and paranoid or delusional states accompanying the hallucinations. PCP intoxication is associated with violent dissociative behavior and amnesia for the event. The hallucinations and behavioral disturbances should resolve over several hours. A small percentage of hallucinogen users will have prolonged psychotic reactions, which may represent an exacerbation of pre-existing psychiatric illness or possibly suggest the presence of underlying emerging psychotic illness. Hallucinogen dependence is rare, and hallucinogen withdrawal syndromes are not known to exist. Hallucinogen Persisting Perception Disorder, commonly referred to as "flashbacks," is defined in DSM-IV as the re-experiencing of one or more perceptual disturbances (after cessation of use) that were experienced during intoxication. Common perceptual disturbances include geometric hallucinations, perceptions of movement in the peripheral visual fields, flashes of color, trails of images of moving objects, positive afterimages, and halos around objects.

13.2.5 Cannabis

Dependence on cannabis, the most commonly used illicit drug in the United States, occurs in about 10% of users. Frequent use is associated with a gradual increase in tolerance to the effects. Symptoms of intoxication include short-term memory loss, perceptual distortions, anxiety, difficulties in concentration, and sedation. Hashish and cannabis products with higher concentrations of tetrahydrocannabinol (THC) could cause an overt hallucinogen experience similar to LSD. A withdrawal syndrome, usually mild and self-limiting, is reported by about half of those seeking treatment for marijuana dependence [7]. Symptoms of withdrawal may mimic a mood or anxiety disorder and include anxiety, irritability, restlessness, anorexia, and insomnia. Although marijuana use does not usually cause psychiatric illness, recent studies have linked the use of cannabis to an increased risk of psychosis and psychotic relapse in later life [8,9].

13.2.6 Gamma-hydroxy butyrate (GHB)

The intoxicating effects of this drug commonly used in the "rave scene" and among body builders include relaxation, euphoria, sedation, and disinhibition. Dependence on Gamma-Hydroxy Butyrate (GHB) is rare, but severe withdrawal symptoms are reported in chronic users. Withdrawal symptoms mimic alcohol, benzodiazepine, or sedative hypnotic withdrawal and include anxiety, tremor, and insomnia that can last for up to several weeks. Severe withdrawal resembles delirium tremens and is marked by seizures, psychosis, bizarre behavior, delirium, and agitation [10].

13.3 COMORBID ADDICTIVE AND PSYCHIATRIC DISORDERS

13.3.1 Prevalence

The co-occurrence of a substance use disorder with another psychiatric disorder is referred to as dual diagnosis or co-occurring disorder. The term may also refer to substance-induced psychiatric disorders that occur in the context of substance addiction or dependence. Judging from epidemiological studies, co-occurring disorders are very common in the general population. Results from the Epidemiological Catchment Area (ECA) Survey [11] showed a 61% lifetime prevalence rate for substance use disorders in those diagnosed with bipolar disorder. Among those diagnosed with schizophrenia, there is a 34% prevalence rate of alcohol use disorders. The ECA study reported that individuals with affective disorder had a 32% prevalence of comorbid substance use disorder. A more recent study, the National Epidemiological Survey on Alcohol and Related Conditions (NESARC) reported that the 12-month prevalence of substance use disorder among those with mood disorders is 20%. Among those with anxiety disorders, the 12-month prevalence of substance use disorders is 15% [12]. There is also a significant association of substance use disorders with personality disorders. Among those in the NESARC study with a personality disorder, 16.4% reported a current alcohol use disorder and 6.5% had a drug use disorder. Conversely, those diagnosed with a current alcohol use disorder had a 28.6% prevalence rate of a personality disorder and among those with a drug use disorder, 47.7% had a personality disorder [13].

13.3.2   Identification and diagnosis of co-occurring psychiatric and addictive disorders

When evaluating an individual with substance addiction and psychiatric symptoms, the clinician's primary concern is to determine the relationship between the two. The symptoms may be caused by the substance use disorder or they may represent a primary psychiatric disorder co-occurring with a substance use disorder. To clarify this relationship, it is important to conduct a full substance use history in order to determine what substances are used, how often, and in what quantity. This history should be elicited by asking direct and detailed questions in a nonjudgmental and respectful manner. When was the last time the patient used a particular substance? Has the patient had medical illness or physical complications related to the substance use? This includes a history of injuries while intoxicated and any infections, neurological, cardiovascular, hepatic or gastrointestinal problems. Does the patient have a history of tolerance or withdrawal symptoms? Does the patient have social, legal or occupational problems related to the substance use? Has the patient ever received any treatment for chemical dependency? Several screening instruments such as the CAGE questionnaire [14] and the Alcohol Use Disorders Identification Test (AUDIT) [15] can also be used to assess substance use disorders.

It can be very difficult to determine if the psychiatric symptoms are substance induced or represent an independent mental disorder co-occurring with the substance use disorder. To assess whether a patient's depressive symptoms are independent or substance induced, it is first necessary to establish if the depressive symptoms were present prior to the onset of a substance use disorder, or if the depressive disorder was present during a period of abstinence greater than one month. Predictive of the disorder being an independent depression include: less severe substance dependence, less heavy substance addiction, a family history of major depression, and a history of depression prior to onset of substance addiction/dependence [16].

As the patient with psychiatric symptoms and addiction can often be an inaccurate historian, it is also important to obtain additional information from laboratory examination and outside sources, such as family, past providers, and previous hospitalizations. Substance-induced psychiatric illness is more likely to exist if the patient has prolonged heavy substance use or dependence, if the substance use disorder preceded the psychiatric symptoms, or if the symptoms resolve during periods of abstinence. Individuals with co-occurring disorders are more likely to have a history of psychiatric illness prior to developing a substance use disorder or during prolonged abstinence, have a family history of the psychiatric illness, and have less severe substance dependence.

13.3.3   Prognosis and complications of comorbid disorders

13.3.3.1   Depression and addiction

Depression is a common mental illness affecting one in six Americans during their lifetime. Almost a third of these patients have a co-occurring substance use disorder [11]. Patients with addictive disorders are at two to fourfold increased lifetime risk for mood disorder [11,17], which has a significant adverse effect on the course of substance dependence, predicting poor treatment response, increased risk of suicide, and higher rates of relapse [18–24]. In patients treated for Major Depression and alcohol use disorders, sustained remission from alcohol significantly improved depression outcomes and protected against recurrence of depression [25]. One year of sobriety from alcohol is associated with a threefold reduction in risk of depression [2].

Substance use should not be a barrier to treating depression, as early diagnosis and treatment can improve outcomes [26]. Accurate diagnosis of depression in a patient just starting to recover from substance dependence is difficult and can delay efforts to begin potentially effective antidepressant treatment. After 12 months, one third of substance-dependent patients initially diagnosed with substance-induced depression are reclassified to have Major Depression [27].

13.3.3.2 Anxiety and addiction

Anxiety disorders, including panic, generalized anxiety, social anxiety and post-traumatic stress, are strongly associated with substance use disorders. For panic and generalized anxiety disorders, symptoms overlap with those of acute intoxication, withdrawal, and recovery from alcohol, making a clear diagnosis challenging. The social lubrication that alcohol provides for socially anxious patients, consistent with a self-medication hypothesis, often precedes problems with substance dependence [28]. More than a third of panic disorder patients have addictive disorders [11], with their risk of comorbid substance use disorder being 2.4 times higher than that of the general population. Uniquely, patients with post-traumatic stress disorder (PTSD) have increased risk for drug as well as alcohol use disorder, 2–4 times greater than non-PTSD patients [29]. Rates of PTSD among female opiate and cocaine dependent patients were increased

10-fold using ECA data [30]. Less is known about how co-occurring anxiety disorders affect treatment of substance use disorders, but they are theorized to have a negative impact [31–33].

13.3.3.3 Bipolar disorder and addiction

Bipolar Type I is a severe and persistent mental illness found in roughly 1–3% of Americans [34,35]. Bipolar Type II is a more common mental disorder but perhaps less severe, found in about 3–6% of the United States population [36,37]. Lifetime prevalence of substance use disorders is at least 40% in Bipolar Type I patients [11,38,39]. Substance use disorders are found in roughly 20% of Bipolar Type II or Bipolar spectrum (including Cyclothymia and Bipolar NOS) [40]. Illness course is adversely affected, as with other psychiatric illnesses co-occurring with substance use disorders. Bipolar patients with addictive disorders are less adherent to treatment [41], have more, and more prolonged, affective episodes [42], more suicidal behavior [43,44], and lower overall quality of life [45] in comparison to nonsubstance using bipolar patients.

13.3.3.4 Attention deficit and hyperactivity disorder (ADHD) and addiction

Significant controversy follows the accurate diagnosis of Attention Deficit and Hyperactivity Disorder (ADHD) in adults, as it requires considerable retrospective collection of history and is found to have significant psychiatric comorbidity of major depression, bipolar disorder, and anxiety disorders [46]. ADHD has childhood onset with symptoms of inattention and hyperactivity noted prior to the age of seven years. Roughly half of children diagnosed with ADHD will experience some persistent symptoms into adulthood, affecting 7.5–8.7% of children [47,48] and less than 4% of adults [1]. Prospective studies of children and adolescents with ADHD predict increase risk for addictive disorders and earlier age of onset [49]. A number of studies of substance misusing adults have established an over representation of ADHD patients [46,50–52]. Research has established that among ADHD patients comorbid for substance use disorders, the addiction is of greater severity [53,54] and has an earlier age of onset [55]. Addiction treatment will take longer for patients with ADHD [56], and the patients are more likely to relapse [57]. Research has suggested that children receiving adequate treatment for ADHD are less likely than their untreated cohort to develop addictive disorders [58,59]. However, no such data exists for adults with persistent ADHD symptoms. Current treatment guidelines recommend that patients reach sobriety of 30 days from substances of addiction prior to initiating treatment of co-occurring psychiatric disorder. A recent literature review summarizes that none of the four adult double blind studies of ADHD treatment in patients with comorbid substance use disorder found overall improvement of substance addiction symptoms [60]. When treating persistent ADHD symptoms in adult patients comorbid for addictive disorders, emphasis is on use of nonstimulant medications such as buproprion or atomoxetine [61,62]. Diversion of prescribed stimulants is worrisome in this group [63], particularly among college students [64–66].

13.3.3.5 Psychotic disorders and addiction

Almost half of schizophrenic patients are either alcohol or illicit drug dependent [11], and the majority are dependent on nicotine [11,67]. This has profound negative impact, reflected in medication noncompliance, poor social function, increased hospitalizations, earlier onset, and poor treatment response [68]. Diagnostic challenges arise in stimulant misusing patients presenting with psychosis and result in under-detection or under-reporting of substance use among schizophrenic patients [69]. Comorbid addiction and schizophrenia increases likelihood of homelessness, legal problems, verbal threats, violence, treatment noncompliance, multiple medical problems, frequent emergency visits, frequent hospitalizations, and suicidal behavior [68,70,71]. Comorbidity predicts poor prognosis [72], vulnerability to social dysfunction, suicide attempts, and more problems with housing, finances, and nutritional deficiencies [73–76]. Denial and minimization are often observed in patients with comorbid schizophrenia and addiction [77], indicating traditional recovery principles may not be accepted.

13.3.3.6 Personality disorders and addiction

Antisocial personality disorder holds the distinction of being the most comorbid psychiatric illness in patients with addictive disorders. Prevalence of personality disorder diagnoses is estimated at 44% of patients with alcohol use disorders and almost 80% of opiate users [78]. Personality disorders present significant challenges to addiction treatment [79]; these patients are at greater risk of relapse [80–82] and are associated with more severe treatment problems [83].

Integrated treatments show the most promise, using dialectical behavioral therapy or dual focus schema therapy adapted for addiction treatment [84–86].

13.4 INTERVENTION AND TREATMENT

13.4.1 Brief interventions

Providers will find it helpful to conduct a brief intervention when patients present with psychiatric symptoms that appear to be exacerbated or caused by substance use. A brief intervention may simply consist of presenting the evidence of substance misuse and consequences in a nonjudgmental manner, expressing concern and educating the patient about the effects of the substance on psychiatric illness. After this, the provider should ask if the patient has a desire to make a change and how the provider can best assist the patient in doing so. Further follow up on a discussion of substance use is important and should occur regularly with subsequent visits even if the provider can only briefly address the issue. This process will go well if the provider and patient have an established therapeutic relationship and treatment alliance. It will not proceed as smoothly if the provider has not first engaged the patient by taking a history of substance use, psychiatric illness, and complications or consequences. Harm reduction is crucial and may be the only step that a patient will accept initially. Successful treatment for addictive disorders depends largely on an individual's desire to change and belief that change is possible. Motivational interviewing is a therapeutic style developed by Miller and Rollnick [87,88] and designed to increase an individual's motivation to change behavior by helping to explore and resolve ambivalence. Chemical dependency counselors and therapists use motivational interviewing techniques to help patients develop insight into their addictions and resolve ambivalence regarding treatment. Once a patient has decided to accept addiction treatment, it is up to the physician to provide support for the decision and assist the patient in making the next step: referral to an addiction inpatient or outpatient program to do a chemical dependency assessment and make recommendations as to treatment.

13.4.2 Pharmacological management of psychiatric and co-occurring addictive disorder

Patients with co-occurring disorder, their families, supportive peers, and treatment providers can all have strong feelings regarding the use of psychotropic medication during their recovery. Family members and peers active in 12-step programs may pressure patients into discontinuing, avoiding, or feeling the need to hide necessary treatment with psychotropic medication. For many, recovery is a model of self-reliance, defined as living a life free of all psychoactive compounds [89]. Prescribing a medication for symptom control deviates from this model and can be interpreted as validating patients' past attempts at self-medication and invalidating current attempts to avoid this behavior [90]. This

may stem in part from patients' past difficulties limiting use of controlled substances that can be immediately reinforcing, such as medically indicated opioids or psychiatrically indicated benzodiazepines. When initiating pharmacotherapy in patients with co-occurring disorders, it is recommended to have a threshold similar to that one might use with nondually diagnosed mental health patients. Pharmacotherapy is both safe and effective in these patients, although it is best to minimize medications that may be reinforcing, have addiction potential or can lead to dependence, or have lethal interactions with the substance of addiction in actively using patients [90]. For example, tricyclic antidepressants and benzodiazepines can increase risk of overdose with alcohol, and benzodiazepines can increase risk of overdose with misused opioids or opioid-substitution treatment with buprenorphine and methadone. Risk of misuse can be limited if patients with comorbid anxiety can be adequately controlled with scheduled prophylactic medications, such as serotonergic antidepressants, rather than abortive (and thus reinforcing) "prn" medications. Patients who need "prn" anxiolytics may do better with uncontrolled substances, such as hydroxyzine, noradrenergic β blockers, or low-dose atypical antipsychotics.

Pharmacological management of psychiatric illness in patients with addictive disorders is often complicated by the difficulty of correct diagnosis. In the absence of significant suicidality or clearly disabling symptoms, it is reasonable to withhold pharmacological treatment of mood or anxiety symptoms until the diagnosis can be further elucidated. A common strategy is to wait and see if psychiatric symptoms resolve without pharmacological intervention after an unspecified period of abstinence. It is thought that alcohol induced depression should remit after 2–3 weeks and cocaine-induced depression may be even shorter [91]. However, untreated depression in the setting of alcohol dependence [19], and the presence of depression in opioid dependence [21] and cocaine dependence [92], have been shown to lead to treatment-resistant substance dependence.

Significant psychiatric symptoms prior to development of an addictive disorder or psychiatric symptoms atypical for a psychiatric disorder secondary to the patients' addictive substance (i.e., long-standing psychotic symptoms in the setting of opioid dependence), are suggestive of a free-standing psychiatric condition rather than one that is substance-induced. Early pharmacological treatment is warranted in these cases, as well as when life threatening or severely disabling symptoms such as active suicidal ideation or acute psychosis occur. Without such an intervention, treatment retention and improvement in substance use are unlikely to occur.

13.4.3 Pharmacotherapy for mood and anxiety disorders with co-occurring addiction

Both tricyclic [93,94] and selective serotonin reuptake inhibitor antidepressants [95–98] have been shown to be effective in major depressive disorder in the setting of comorbid alcohol dependence, as has nefazodone [99]. However, neither class of medication significantly impacts alcohol consumption. While opioid substitution treatment for opioid dependence has been shown to improve depression [100–102] in 80–90% of patients entering treatment, most studies of antidepressants for residual depression in this population have been negative [97]. Early studies of doxepin [103,104] showed efficacy for depression in this population, but the initial success of tricyclics was not replicated in this group [100,105–107], save for one study of imipramine [108]. Nor has bupropion shown efficacy [109]. Nonetheless, the recommendation for treatment of persistent depression in opioid dependence is to consider a serotonin reuptake inhibitor or tricyclic trial in addition to psychosocial treatment, given the presence of several positive clinical medication trials in the literature and the consistent pattern of tolerability of these agents in this population [110]. Serotonin reuptake inhibitors have not been shown to reduce depressive symptoms with comorbid cocaine dependence [111,112], although tricyclics have shown some promise [113]. Even so, the serotonin

reuptake inhibitors are often a clinician's first choice in this population. This is likely due to their improved tolerability compared to tricyclic antidepressants, as well as the increased risk of cardiotoxicity of tricyclics in combination with cocaine [114] in the event of relapse.

Rigorous data on pharmacological treatment of bipolar illness with co-occurring disorders are sparse. However, carbamazepine, valproic acid, and lithium are all commonly accepted treatments for acute mania as well as prophylaxis of mania in patients with addictive and bipolar disorders [115], although patients with substance use disorders may have a less optimal response to lithium than those without [116,117]. Brady and colleagues [115] propose this is due to lithium's well-known limited efficacy in rapid-cycling or mixed bipolar disorder, common in patients with addiction and co-occurring bipolar disorder [118]. Given the reinforcing nature and high misuse potential of benzodiazepines in patients with co-occurring disorders, these are not recommended as first line treatments for mania.

Similarly, benzodiazpines are discouraged as a regular treatment for anxiety disorders in patients with addictive disorders [119,120]. Buspirone has no significant addiction potential and was initially shown to have some success in patients with alcohol dependence [121]. Although not well studied in this population, tricyclics, monoamine oxidase inhibitors, and serotonin reuptake inhibitors [119] are treatments of choice for anxiety disorders such as post-traumatic stress disorder, generalized anxiety disorder, obsessive-compulsive disorder, social phobia, and panic disorder in general psychiatric populations. Given their more advantageous side effect profile, serotonin reuptake inhibitors are first line treatments for those with co-occurring addiction and anxiety disorders. It is recommended that providers use very low starting doses and slow titrations to increase the chance of tolerability in patients with anxiety disorders. To provide quicker anxiolytic effect during this slow titration, many providers will often prescribe beta-blockers such as propranolol three times daily until an antidepressant trial takes effect [119,120].

13.4.4 Pharmacotherapy for psychotic disorders

Emerging literature suggests that treatment with atypical antipsychotic medications may be associated with decreases in substance use [122] and improve chances of smoking cessation in patients with schizophrenia [123]. Early and potentially sustained remission is seen in 30–50% of patients with schizophrenia and comorbid addiction [124], with alcohol more likely than cocaine or cannabis [125]. Integrated treatments combining medications, psychosocial treatments, active case management, contingency management and social supports have shown best results [126–129].

13.4.5 Use of addiction pharmacotherapy in patients with psychiatric illness

In general, medications for relapse prevention and detoxification are frequently used similarly in patients without psychiatric conditions as well as patients with co-occurring disorders. Patients with co-occurring disorders may be more open to psychoactive medication and thus more open to consider medications for relapse prevention. Opioid-dependent patients with co-occurring psychiatric illness may have increased access to psychiatric care in an opioid substitution program rather than those seeking buprenorphine treatment for opioid dependence in a primary care clinic setting. As disulfiram has been reported in rare cases to alter mental status or worsen psychosis, it may be wise to delay initiation of this agent in thought-disordered patients in the midst of a psychiatric decompensation and to monitor such patients frequently.

13.4.6 Pharmacotherapy for alcohol and opioid dependence

There are currently four FDA approved medications for the treatment of chronic alcohol dependence. These are discussed in detail below. Disulfiram was approved in 1951 and has long been available in generic form. The μ-opioid antagonist naltrexone received US Food and Drug Administration (FDA) approval for daily oral use in 1994 and then again as a long-acting intramuscular medication in 2006. Finally, after many years of use in Europe, acamprosate was approved by the FDA in 2004 for the treatment of alcohol dependence. There are also three FDA approved medications for opioid dependence: naltrexone, methadone, and buprenorphine.

13.4.6.1 Disulfiram

By inhibiting aldehyde dehydrogenase, a key enzyme in the major metabolic pathway for ethanol, disulfiram causes accumulation of acetaldehyde after alcohol ingestion. Within minutes of alcohol ingestion, the buildup of acetaldehyde usually causes an "alcohol-disulfiram reaction," characterized by diaphoresis, flushing, nausea and vomiting, tachycardia, and headache. This aversive reaction can motivate patients to abstain from alcohol but can also lead to hesitation to adhere with pharmacotherapy. Disulfiram has greater benefit with monitoring of medication administration. Although the largest study to date demonstrated that disulfiram dosed at 250 mg per day over one year did not lead to increased abstinence rates or longer time to first drink compared to placebo, it did lead to significantly fewer drinking days over the study year [130].

Though rare, psychotic symptoms and delirium have been reported with the use of disulfiram and necessitate immediate discontinuation. So as not to mask the rare development of medication-induced mental status changes, most practitioners do not start this agent in patients with a history of psychotic disorders.

13.4.6.2 Naltrexone

Originally developed to treat opioid dependence, the μ-opioid antagonist naltrexone decreases the reinforcing effects of alcohol [131–133] and has been shown to delay relapse to alcohol and to delay the percentage of drinking days [134–136]. Naltrexone will precipitate withdrawal in patients with physiologic dependence on opioids and should not be started until such patients have been opioid free for 5–10 days. Because naltrexone blocks μ-opioid receptors, opioid medications will be much less effective in the situation in which an injury or serious medical condition calls for acute pain control (although higher than normal doses of opioid analgesics can be given under close medical monitoring to over-ride this blockade).

Naltrexone is also FDA approved for treatment of opioid dependence and works by blocking the euphoric effects of misused opioids. With a higher affinity for the μ receptor than heroin, a 50 mg dose of naltrexone blocks the effects of 25 mg of heroin for up to 24 hours [137]. Although shown across multiple studies to be efficacious for the treatment of opioid dependence, a disadvantage to naltrexone is poor compliance compared to opioid agonist therapy, as naltrexone does little to block cravings which can be prominent in opioid dependence and drive the patient to relapse. In addition, chronic treatment with naltrexone leads to down-regulation of the μ receptor, significantly decreasing a patient's tolerance to misused opioids. Thus, a patient needs to be forewarned that they are quite susceptible to unintentional overdose should they relapse and immediately start using the high doses of opioids they were able tolerate during past episodes of chronic use. Furthermore, introduction of naltrexone can precipitate an unpleasant withdrawal unless the clinician ensures the patient with chronic opioid use has been free of short-acting opioids for at least five days and long-acting opioids for 10 days.

Naltrexone can be ideal for patients who have had a successful detoxification from opioids, have not had extensive periods of opioid dependence, are highly motivated to comply with treatment, and are reluctant to consider opioid-substitution treatment and its implications of being on an anticraving medication for an extended period. Patients with limited coping skills to tolerate the challenges of abstinence-based treatment, high cravings, notable psychosocial instability, failed attempts at abstinence-based treatment or prolonged periods of

opioid dependence may have higher chances of success with opioid-substitution treatment. Patients with history of severe co-occurring disorders are likely to fall into the latter category.

13.4.6.3 Long-acting injectable naltrexone

Although oral naltrexone generally appears efficacious compared to placebo in reducing relapse to heavy drinking [138–140], it did not perform well in several studies [141,142]. However, when patients found to be nonadherent for oral naltrexone were factored out in several other studies, naltrexone demonstrated efficacy for treatment of alcohol dependence compared to placebo [143,144]. Administered in a 360 mg monthly gluteal injection, long-acting intramuscular naltrexone alleviates the problem of nonadherence and has been shown to be effective compared to placebo in reducing heavy drinking [145]. Additional advantages of long-acting intramuscular naltrexone include much lower rates of first-pass hepatic metabolism, exposing the liver to significantly lower peak dosages than daily oral dosing (and thus potentially less risk of dose-dependent hepatotoxicity) and exposing the patient to lower levels of the active metabolite 6β-hydroxynaltrexol, which has been correlated with side effects such as nausea.

13.4.6.4 Acamprosate

Because it is a central nervous system (CNS) depressant, chronic alcohol use leads to compensatory up-regulation of the brain's major excitatory system (glutamate) and down-regulation of its major inhibitory system (GABA) as the CNS attempts to maintain homeostasis. Stopping chronic alcohol use leads to severe withdrawal, characterized by glutamatergic activity and GABA hypoactivity. This imbalance can take many months to dissipate, leading to prolonged subsyndromal symptoms of alcohol withdrawal such as insomnia, anxiety and restlessness. Extensively studied and in clinical use in Europe for nearly 20 years, acamprosate is believed to help restore the balance between the glutamate and GABA systems, decreasing subsequent cravings and risk of relapse in early recovery [146,147]. Acamprosate may diminish reinforcement derived from alcohol ingestion [147], diminishes the amount of alcohol consumed by patients in treatment who do experience relapse [148], and leads to higher total abstinence rates and longer time to relapse for acamprosate in multiple randomized controlled trials, mainly in Europe. For reasons that remain unclear, acamprosate failed to show efficacy in two recent large clinical trials conducted in the Unite States [138,149], although it has been proposed that subjects in these trials may not have been experiencing enough prolonged subsyndromal withdrawal to benefit from acamprosate [150].

Labeling indicates that acamprosate should be started after a modicum of abstinence has been achieved, but there are no safety issues if acamprosate is taken concomitantly with alcohol and acamprosate should be continued if a patient relapses to alcohol use. Although this should not limit use in patients with co-occurring disorders, all patients started on acamprosate should be monitored for suicidal thoughts, since such thoughts occurred more frequently among acamprosate-treated patients than among placebo-treated patients in clinical trials.

13.4.6.5 Methadone

The first agent the FDA approved for maintenance treatment of opioid dependence, methadone, has been an effective life saving treatment [151–153] with much better retention and clinical outcomes than psychosocial treatment alone. The objective of opioid substitution treatment is to reduce illicit opioid use and the negative effects of this activity on patients' physical health, mental health, and interpersonal and occupational functioning. Methadone is a long-acting orally active, μ-opioid agonist that allows for once daily dosing without serious withdrawal discomfort during that interval, treating subjective cravings from opioid dependence. Opioid substitution with methadone is closely regulated under federal law, and only physicians working in federally-regulated methadone programs can legally prescribe methadone for treatment of opioid dependence. Methadone programs are required to provide at least weekly counseling, to monitor patients' urine samples frequently for illicit drug use, and to administer methadone in a supervised setting six days per week, permitting the patient a "carry" dose to take home for Sundays. After three months, such programs can permit patients additional "carry" doses during the week, requiring less frequent observed dosing in the clinic. In fact, most programs use a contingency management system in which patients earn additional "carries" by turning in urine samples documenting their continued abstinence. Patients who cannot remain abstinent can be mandated to attend increased counseling sessions, should they wish to stay in treatment. Consequently, treatment with methadone (or buprenorphine) in a methadone maintenance program provides significantly increased support, structure, and monitoring of patients than does treatment with buprenorphine in an office-based setting. Patients with limited coping skills, increased psychosocial instability, or increased psychiatric comorbidity, such as severe co-occurring disorders, are likely to do better with this more intensive level of treatment.

Federal law mandates that patients have severe opioid dependence to be eligible for treatment. Admission criteria are stringent and, with few exceptions, patients need to demonstrate evidence of 12 months of dependence prior to treatment entry [154]. Tapering off of methadone into abstinence-based treatment without relapse is difficult but possible. It is recommended to limit such attempts to times of high stability in the patient's clinical course; thus, co-occurring disorder patients should be in remission from their psychiatric illness for the prior 12 months before initiating a voluntary taper [154].

13.4.6.6 Buprenorphine

FDA approved in 2002 for the treatment of opioid dependence, buprenorphine is a partial μ agonist with extremely high affinity for the μ receptor.

Thus, it blocks the euphoric affects of misused opioids while relieving cravings for opioids through moderate stimulation of the receptor. Due to its partial agonism, it has a ceiling effect for CNS respiratory depression – making it far safer than other opioids in overdose attempts. However, its partial agonism can be overcome by co-administration with large doses of benzodiazepines, which is thought to have led to several isolated reports of patient deaths in Europe. Under the Drug Addiction Treatment Act of 2000, buprenorphine can be used for opioid substitution treatment in an office setting, which appeals to patients turned off by the restrictive nature of daily dosing in a federally-regulated methadone program.

Poorly absorbed orally, buprenorphine is administered sublingually, and most often as a combination agent with naloxone in a ratio of 4 mg buprenorphine: 1 mg naloxone. Naloxone is not absorbed sublingually, and is an aversion to addiction as it will induce withdrawal if patients try to dissolve and inject the medication. (Single agent buprenorphine can be quite reinforcing and has high addiction potential if used in this fashion). Of note, the high affinity and partial μ agonism of buprenorphine can precipitate withdrawal in opioid dependent patients by acutely "knocking" full μ agonists off of the μ receptor and immediately decreasing stimulation of the receptor. Thus patients should not be started on this agent unless they are visibly in moderate withdrawal and have been off short-acting opioids for at least 12 hours. Buprenorphine can be administered daily or even every 48 hours, due to its long half-life.

As efficacious as methadone for maintenance treatment of opioid dependence [155], buprenorphine can be offered through a primary care model, although providers are required to have the ability to refer interested patients for psychosocial treatment. Patients with severe co-occurring disorders may have more severe and longer periods of opioid dependence, more psychosocial instability, lower coping skills, and higher rates of polysubstance dependence or medical comorbidity. Such patients may ultimately have higher success rates in a regulated methadone program, where they will have access to more intensive psychosocial treatment services, more support, and more structure to their treatment. Opioid substitution programs can administer buprenorphine in place of methadone in select cases, particularly in cases where oral administration of methadone is difficult or buprenorphine would have fewer medications interactions (such as patients on antiretroviral therapy for HIV).

13.5 ADDICTION TREATMENT FOR CO-OCCURING DISORDER PATIENTS

13.5.1 Detoxification and treatment settings

Success of detoxification can be measured in several ways, including linkage to and retention in a long-term substance addiction rehabilitation program following the detoxification phase [156]. Entry into treatment is often precipitated by crisis, including decompensation of a co-occurring psychiatric disorder in already fragile patients. Furthermore, the detoxification process can further worsen co-occurring disorders. As discussed earlier in this chapter, depression is more common in patients presenting for detoxification than in the general public, perhaps highest in patients who misuse combinations of opioids and alcohol or benzodiazepines. Up to 30% of such patients report suicidal ideation in the prior three months [157], although ongoing cocaine use and withdrawal are risk factors for suicide as well [158–160]. Patients at significant risk for suicide warrant management of their detoxification in an acute care inpatient psychiatric facility where their clinical safety can be intensively monitored. Indicators of such risk include active suicidal ideation, hopelessness, ongoing depression, and past suicide attempts.

Using six dimensions, the American Society of Addiction Medicine (ASAM) has designed patient placement criteria [161] to guide clinicians in determining a patient's level of need and matching

Table 13.1 ASAM placement criteria: levels of care

Level 0.5	Early Intervention
Level 1	Outpatient Services
Level 2	Intensive Outpatient/Partial Hospitalization
Level 3	Residential/Inpatient Hospitalization
Level 4	Medically Managed Intensive Inpatient Services

Source: Ref. [161].
Issues specific to COD populations in substance addiction treatment settings.

them to an appropriate treatment setting. Dimension 3 includes emotional, behavioral, or cognitive conditions such as co-occurring psychiatric disorders. The placement criteria distinguish five levels of care (Table 13.1), and patients are expected to move appropriately between levels as their addictive disorder stabilizes. Patients presenting with severe disorders, such as thought disorders, severe mood disorders with psychotic features, severe anxiety disorders or severely disabling personality disorders, are thought to be most appropriate for dual diagnosis specialty programs that can seamlessly integrate mental health treatment with substance addiction treatment [162]. Patients presenting with previously stabilized mood or anxiety disorders, or subthreshold symptoms of a co-occurring disorder can possibly be managed in a primary substance use program, although that program should provide on-site psychiatric consultation, and at least some staff should be competent to understand and identify signs and symptoms of psychiatric disorders [161].

Substance use disorder patients with co-occurring disorders are hospitalized twenty times as frequently as those without co-occurring psychiatric illness, and five times as frequently as mental health patients without a substance use disorder [163]. This provides a significant opportunity to engage these patients in the treatment process, but unless these patients are accurately assessed and referred to an appropriate level and acceptable form of outpatient treatment, they may not make much long-term change or clinical improvement. Acceptable treatment opportunities exist for motivated patients, as roughly half of substance addiction treatment programs in the United States offer specialized services for co-occurring disorder patients [164].

Previously, treatment providers had attempted to treat addicted psychiatric patients in a sequential or parallel fashion. In a sequential model, patients are directed to postpone treatment of one facet of their disorder (often mental illness) until their other disorder (usually substance dependence) has been stabilized for some time. In a parallel model, patients seek and receive simultaneous treatment for both facets of their co-occurring disorders, but in separate programs using separate philosophies. Unfortunately, in severe co-occurring disorders it can be nearly impossible to prioritize which condition needs to be treated first in sequence, or to retain a patient long enough in treatment to resolve one condition to resolution while not addressing the other [90]. Furthermore, severe co-occurring disorder patients have been shown to do poorly in traditional addiction treatment without some emphasis on their comorbid psychiatric conditions [165]. Subsequently, there has been a concerted administrative effort nationally to transition toward a model of integrated treatment, in which both mental illness and substance use disorders are treated concurrently in the same program by treatment providers who are knowledgeable about both conditions [90]. The goal of integrated treatment is to coordinate addiction and mental health interventions so as to treat the whole person more effectively, addressing all aspects of a patient's struggle [166].

13.5.2 Intensive outpatient treatment

Also known as partial hospitalization, intensive outpatient treatment is often an appropriate starting level of treatment intensity for addicted patients who do not require inpatient detoxification or residential treatment. Given their comorbidity, co-occurring disorder patients may have more need for structure and support than do patients without comorbid psychiatric disorders. Thus, intensive outpatient treatment is an important phase in their treatment as they transition from residential treatment or an acute psychiatric hospitalization. Co-occurring disorder patients frequently enter treatment in response to crisis from psychosocial stressors and exacerbations in their psychiatric condition that have resulted in part from their substance use. They may be suffering from significant social isolation and stressors that are overwhelming their coping skill repertoire, and they are at particularly high risk for poor outcomes in unstructured environments [166]. Intensive outpatient treatment can provide frequent monitoring of psychiatric functioning and access to a consulting psychiatrist for med management, frequent contact with staff who reinforce medication compliance, access to a supportive peer group in a time of need and isolation, a high degree of structure, and the opportunity to operationalize and to experiment with applying learned coping strategies outside of a restricted environment when the patient goes home at the end of the day [162,167].

13.5.3   Residential programs

Long-term residential programs provide the most intense level of treatment and have been shown to be significantly effective in treatment of substance use disorders [168]. To successfully engage and retain patients with co-occurring disorders, long-term residential programs must successfully meet their wide level of needs and stabilize their psychiatric functioning [166]. Services directed at these goals can be far-reaching and extensive. They include a mental health intake with appropriate diagnosis at admission, psychoeducation on prognosis, and prescription of appropriate pharmacotherapy for both psychiatric disorders and substance dependence. Such programs provide regular medication monitoring with a psychiatrist for efficacy and tolerability and monitoring of medication adherence by support staff.

13.5.4   Mutual self-help groups

Twelve-step groups such as Alcoholics Anonymous (AA) are nearly impossible to study in a controlled, randomized fashion, in part due to the anonymous nature of treatment participation. However, significant evidence, such as their widespread dissemination by members throughout North America, suggests they are efficacious for many patients [169]. Intensity of involvement in AA has been consistently shown to be correlated positively with abstinence [170–172]. Unfortunately, many patients with co-occurring disorders have felt that traditional twelve-step treatment groups are inaccessible to them due to stereotypes of traditional twelve-step groups being "antimedication" and stigmatization by some twelve-step members of mental illness. In fact, nearly 30% of AA members report being encouraged to stop psychiatric or addiction medications by fellow AA members, and 12% report they would actively give peers such advice [173,174]. Subsequently, mutual self-help programs have arisen, providing co-occurring disorder patients a more tolerant alternative to traditional 12-step groups. Such groups combine a focus on taking personal responsibility for one's substance use as well as peer support group principles and structured change by working the twelve steps [166]. Several mutual self-help organizations have become popular, including "Double Trouble in Recovery," "Dual Disorders Anonymous," "Dual Recovery Anonymous," and "Dual Diagnosis Anonymous." Experienced members are encouraged to sponsor junior members in working the steps and members' anonymity is preserved by their peers. Double Trouble in Recovery participation has been correlated with improved mental health outcomes, such as decreased hospitalization and improved medication adherence, and improved substance use outcomes, such as greater utilization of traditional twelve-step groups and decreased drug and alcohol use [175–179].

13.6   CONCLUSIONS

As mentioned in the introduction, the task of evaluation and management of co-occurring addiction and psychiatric illness is challenging to a clinician. In perplexing cases, obtaining consultation from an addiction psychiatry specialist would be advisable, although it is recognized that availability may be limited. Without appropriate consultation, referral to an addiction treatment program specializing in co-occurring disorder treatment is essential, and assistance should be available from local county social service agencies.

REFERENCES

1. American Psychiatric Association (APA) (1994) *Diagnostic and Statistical Manual of Mental Disorders*, American Psychiatric Press.

2. Agosti, V. and Levin, F.R. (2006) One-year follow-up study of suicide attempters treated for drug dependence. *Am. J. Addiction*, **15** (4), 293–296.

3. Hesselbrock, M., Hesselbrock, V., Syzmanski, K. *et al.* (1988) Suicide attempts and alcoholism. *J. Stud. Alcohol*, **49** (5), 436–442.

4. Schuckit, M.A. and Hesselbrock, V. (1994) Alcohol dependence and anxiety disorders: what is the relationship? *Am. J. Psychiatry*, **151** (12), 1723–1734.

5. Akiyama, K. (2006) Longitudinal clinical course following pharmacological treatment of methamphetamine psychosis which persists after long-term abstinence. *Ann. N. Y. Acad. Sci.*, **1074**, 125–134.

6. Ujike, H. and Sato, M. (2004) Clinical features of sensitization to methamphetamine observed in patients with methamphetamine dependence and psychosis. *Ann. N. Y. Acad. Sci.*, **1025**, 279–287.

7. Budney, A.J., Novy, P.L., and Hughes, J.R. (1999) Marijuana withdrawal among adults seeking treatment for marijuana dependence. *Addiction*, **94** (9), 1311–1322.

8. Semple, D.M., McIntosh, A.M., and Lawrie, S.M. (2005) Cannabis as a risk factor for psychosis: systematic review. *J. Psychopharmacol.*, **19** (2), 187–194.

9. van Os, J., Bak, M., Hanssen, M. *et al.* (2002) Cannabis use and psychosis: a longitudinal population-based study. *Am. J. Epidemiol.*, **156** (4), 319–327.

10. Galloway, G.P., Frederick, S.L., Staggers, F.E. Jr. *et al.* (1997) Gamma-hydroxybutyrate: an emerging drug of abuse that causes physical dependence. *Addiction*, **92** (1), 89–96.

11. Regier, D.A., Farmer, M.E., Rae, D.S. *et al.* (1990) Comorbidity of mental disorders with alcohol and other drug abuse. Results from the Epidemiologic Catchment Area (ECA) Study. *JAMA*, **264** (19), 2511–2518.

12. Grant, B.F., Stinson, F.S., Dawson, D.A. *et al.* (2004) Prevalence and co-occurrence of substance use disorders and independent mood and anxiety disorders: results from the National Epidemiologic Survey on Alcohol and Related Conditions. *Arch. Gen. Psychiatry*, **61** (8), 807–816.

13. Grant, B.F., Stinson, F.S., Dawson, D.A. *et al.* (2005) Co-occurrence of DSM-IV personality disorders in the United States: results from the National Epidemiologic Survey on Alcohol and Related Conditions. *Compr. Psychiat.*, **46** (1), 1–5.

14. Ewing, J.A. (1984) Detecting alcoholism. The CAGE questionnaire. *JAMA*, **252** (14), 1905–1907.

15. Babor, T.F., de la Fuente, J., and Saunders, J. (1992) AUDIT – The alcohol use disorders identification test: Guidelines for use in primary health care. World Health Organization.

16. Schuckit, M.A., Tipp, J.E., Bergman, M. *et al.* (1997) Comparison of induced and independent major depressive disorders in 2,945 alcoholics. *Am. J. Psychiatry*, **154** (7), 948–957.

17. Kessler, R.C., Nelson, C.B., McGonagle, K.A. *et al.* (1996) The epidemiology of co-occurring addictive and mental disorders: implications for prevention and service utilization. *Am. J. Orthopsychiat.*, **66** (1), 17–31.

18. Compton, W.M. 3rd, Cottler, L.B., Ben Abdallah, A. *et al.* (2000) Substance dependence and other psychiatric disorders among drug dependent subjects: race and gender correlates. *Am. J. Addiction*, **9** (2), 113–125.

19. Greenfield, S.F., Weiss, R.D., Muenz, L.R. *et al.* (1998) The effect of depression on return to drinking: a prospective study. *Arch. Gen. Psychiatry*, **55** (3), 259–265.

20. Hasin, D., Liu, X., Nunes, E. *et al.* (2002) Effects of major depression on remission and relapse of substance dependence. *Arch. Gen. Psychiatry*, **59** (4), 375–380.

21. Kosten, T.R., Rounsaville, B.J., and Kleber, H.D. (1986) A 2.5-year follow-up of depression, life crises, and treatment effects on abstinence among opioid addicts. *Arch. Gen. Psychiatry*, **43** (8), 733–738.

22. Murphy, G.E., Wetzel, R.D., Robins, E. *et al.* (1992) Multiple risk factors predict suicide in alcoholism. *Arch. Gen. Psychiatry*, **49** (6), 459–463.

23. Rounsaville, B.J., Kosten, T.R., Weissman, M.M. *et al.* (1986) Prognostic significance of psychopathology in treated opiate addicts. A 2.5-year follow-up study. *Arch. Gen. Psychiatry*, **43** (8), 739–745.

24. Rounsaville, B.J., Weissman, M.M., Crits-Christoph, K. *et al.* (1982) Diagnosis and symptoms of depression

in opiate addicts. Course and relationship to treatment outcome. *Arch. Gen. Psychiatry*, **39** (2), 151–156.

25. Hasin, D.S., Tsai, W.Y., Endicott, J. *et al.* (1996) Five-year course of major depression: effects of comorbid alcoholism. *J. Affect. Disord.*, **41** (1), 63–70.

26. Brady, K.T. and Verduin, M.L. (2005) Pharmacotherapy of comorbid mood, anxiety, and substance use disorders. *Subst. Use Misuse*, **40** (13–14), 2021–2041; 2043–2048.

27. Nunes, E.V., Liu, X., Samet, S. *et al.* (2006) Independent versus substance-induced major depressive disorder in substance-dependent patients: observational study of course during follow-up. *J. Clin. Psychiat.*, **67** (10), 1561–1567.

28. Marshall, J.R. (1994) The diagnosis and treatment of social phobia and alcohol abuse. *Bull. Menninger Clin.*, **58** (2 Suppl A), A58–A66.

29. Kessler, R.C., Sonnega, A., Bromet, E. *et al.* (1995) Posttraumatic stress disorder in the National Comorbidity Survey. *Arch. Gen. Psychiatry*, **52** (12), 1048–1060.

30. Cottler, L.B., Compton, W.M. 3rd, Mager, D. *et al.* (1992) Posttraumatic stress disorder among substance users from the general population. *Am. J. Psychiatry*, **149** (5), 664–670.

31. Kushner, M.G., Abrams, K., Thuras, P. *et al.* (2005) Follow-up study of anxiety disorder and alcohol dependence in comorbid alcoholism treatment patients. *Alcohol. Clin. Exp. Res.*, **29** (8), 1432–1443.

32. Randall, C.L., Johnson, M.R., Thevos, A.K. *et al.* (2001) Paroxetine for social anxiety and alcohol use in dual-diagnosed patients. *Depress. Anxiety.*, **14** (4), 255–262.

33. Schade, A., Marquenie, L.A., van Balkom, A.J. *et al.* (2005) The effectiveness of anxiety treatment on alcohol-dependent patients with a comorbid phobic disorder: a randomized controlled trial. *Alcohol. Clin. Exp. Res.*, **29** (5), 794–800.

34. Grant, B.F., Stinson, F.S., Hasin, D.S. *et al.* (2005) Prevalence, correlates, and comorbidity of bipolar I disorder and axis I and II disorders: results from the National Epidemiologic Survey on Alcohol and Related Conditions. *J. Clin. Psychiat.*, **66** (10), 1205–1215.

35. Narrow, W.E., Rae, D.S., Robins, L.N. *et al.* (2002) Revised prevalence estimates of mental disorders in the United States: using a clinical significance criterion to reconcile 2 surveys' estimates. *Arch. Gen. Psychiatry*, **59** (2), 115–123.

36. Akiskal, H.S., Bourgeois, M.L., Angst, J. *et al.* (2000) Re-evaluating the prevalence of and diagnostic composition within the broad clinical spectrum of bipolar disorders. *J. Affect. Disord.*, **59** (Suppl 1), S5–S30.

37. Berk, M. and Dodd, S. (2005) Bipolar II disorder: a review. *Bipolar. Disord.*, **7** (1), 11–21.

38. Baethge, C., Baldessarini, R.J., Khalsa, H.M. *et al.* (2005) Substance abuse in first-episode bipolar I disorder: indications for early intervention. *Am. J. Psychiatry*, **162** (5), 1008–1010.

39. McElroy, S.L., Altshuler, L.L., Suppes, T. *et al.* (2001) Axis I psychiatric comorbidity and its relationship to historical illness variables in 288 patients with bipolar disorder. *Am. J. Psychiatry*, **158** (3), 420–426.

40. Chengappa, K.N., Levine, J., Gershon, S. *et al.* (2000) Lifetime prevalence of substance or alcohol abuse and dependence among subjects with bipolar I and II disorders in a voluntary registry. *Bipolar. Disord.*, **2** (3 Pt 1), 191–195.

41. Strakowski, S.M., Keck, P.E. Jr., McElroy, S.L. *et al.* (1998) Twelve-month outcome after a first hospitalization for affective psychosis. *Arch. Gen. Psychiatry*, **55** (1), 49–55.

42. Tohen, M., Zarate, C.A. Jr., Hennen, J. *et al.* (2003) The McLean-Harvard First-Episode Mania Study: prediction of recovery and first recurrence. *Am. J. Psychiatry*, **160** (12), 2099–2107.

43. Dalton, E.J., Cate-Carter, T.D., Mundo, E. *et al.* (2003) Suicide risk in bipolar patients: the role of co-morbid substance use disorders. *Bipolar. Disord.*, **5** (1), 58–61.

44. Goldberg, J.F., Garno, J.L., Leon, A.C. *et al.* (1999) A history of substance abuse complicates remission from acute mania in bipolar disorder. *J. Clin. Psychiat.*, **60** (11), 733–740.

45. Weiss, R.D., Ostacher, M.J., Otto, M.W. *et al.* (2005) Does recovery from substance use disorder matter in patients with bipolar disorder? *J. Clin. Psychiat.*, **66** (6), 730–735. quiz 808–809.

46. Kessler, R.C., Adler, L., Barkley, R. *et al.* (2006) The prevalence and correlates of adult ADHD in the United States: results from the National Comorbidity Survey Replication. *Am. J. Psychiatry*, **163** (4), 716–723.

47. Barbaresi, W., Katusic, S., Colligan, R. *et al.* (2004) How common is attention-deficit/hyperactivity disorder? Towards resolution of the controversy: results from a population-based study. *Acta Paediatr Suppl*, **93** (445), 55–59.

48. Froehlich, T.E., Lanphear, B.P., Epstein, J.N. *et al.* (2007) Prevalence, recognition, and treatment of attention-deficit/hyperactivity disorder in a national sample of US children. *Arch. Pediatr. Adolesc. Med.*, **161** (9), 857–864.

49. Molina, B.S. and Pelham, W.E. Jr. (2003) Childhood predictors of adolescent substance use in a longitudinal study of children with ADHD. *J. Abnorm. Psychol.*, **112** (3), 497–507.

50. Biederman, J., Faraone, S.V., Spencer, T. *et al.* (1993) Patterns of psychiatric comorbidity, cognition, and psychosocial functioning in adults with attention deficit hyperactivity disorder. *Am. J. Psychiatry*, **150** (12), 1792–1798.

51. Levin, F.R., Evans, S.M., and Kleber, H.D. (1998) Prevalence of adult attention-deficit hyperactivity disorder among cocaine abusers seeking treatment. *Drug Alcohol Depen.*, **52** (1), 15–25.

52. McGough, J.J., Smalley, S.L., McCracken, J.T. *et al.* (2005) Psychiatric comorbidity in adult attention deficit hyperactivity disorder: findings from multiplex families. *Am. J. Psychiatry*, **162** (9), 1621–1627.

53. Biederman, J., Wilens, T., Mick, E. *et al.* (1995) Psychoactive substance use disorders in adults with attention deficit hyperactivity disorder (ADHD): effects of ADHD and psychiatric comorbidity. *Am. J. Psychiatry*, **152** (11), 1652–1658.

54. Carroll, K.M. and Rounsaville, B.J. (1993) History and significance of childhood attention deficit disorder in treatment-seeking cocaine abusers. *Compr. Psychiat.*, **34** (2), 75–82.

55. Wilens, T.E., Biederman, J., Mick, E. *et al.* (1997) Attention deficit hyperactivity disorder (ADHD) is associated with early onset substance use disorders. *J. Nerv. Ment. Dis.*, **185** (8), 475–482.

56. Wilens, T.E., Biederman, J., and Mick, E. (1998) Does ADHD affect the course of substance abuse? Findings from a sample of adults with and without ADHD. *Am. J. Addiction*, **7** (2), 156–163.

57. Schubiner, H., Tzelepis, A., Milberger, S. *et al.* (2000) Prevalence of attention-deficit/hyperactivity disorder and conduct disorder among substance abusers. *J. Clin. Psychiat.*, **61** (4), 244–251.

58. Katusic, S.K., Barbaresi, W.J., Colligan, R.C. *et al.* (2005) Psychostimulant treatment and risk for substance abuse among young adults with a history of attention-deficit/hyperactivity disorder: a population-based, birth cohort study. J Child. *Adolesc. Psychopharmacol.*, **15** (5), 764–776.

59. Wilens, T.E., Faraone, S.V., Biederman, J. *et al.* (2003) Does stimulant therapy of attention-deficit/hyperactivity disorder beget later substance abuse? A meta-analytic review of the literature. *Pediatrics*, **111** (1), 179–185.

60. Upadhyaya, H.P. (2007) Managing ADHD in the presence of comorbid substance use disorder. *J. Clin. Psychiat.*, **68** (6), e15.

61. Riggs, P.D. (1998) Clinical approach to treatment of ADHD in adolescents with substance use disorders and conduct disorder. *J. Am. Acad. Child Adolesc. Psychiatry*, **37** (3), 331–332.

62. Schubiner, H. (2005) Substance abuse in patients with attention-deficit hyperactivity disorder: therapeutic implications. *CNS Drugs*, **19** (8), 643–655.

63. Wilens, T.E., Gignac, M., Swezey, A. *et al.* (2006) Characteristics of adolescents and young adults with ADHD who divert or misuse their prescribed medications. *J. Am. Acad. Child Adolesc. Psychiatry*, **45** (4), 408–414.

64. McCabe, S.E., Teter, C.J., and Boyd, C.J. (2006) Medical use, illicit use and diversion of prescription stimulant medication. *J. Psychoactive Drugs*, **38** (1), 43–56.

65. Teter, C.J., McCabe, S.E., LaGrange, K. *et al.* (2006) Illicit use of specific prescription stimulants among college students: prevalence, motives, and routes of administration. *Pharmacotherapy*, **26** (10), 1501–1510.

66. Upadhyaya, H.P., Rose, K., Wang, W. *et al.* (2005) Attention-deficit/hyperactivity disorder, medication treatment, and substance use patterns among adolescents and young adults. *J. Child Adolesc. Psychopharmacol.*, **15** (5), 799–809.

67. Ziedonis, D.M., Kosten, T.R., Glazer, W.M. *et al.* (1994) Nicotine dependence and schizophrenia. *Hosp. Community Psych.*, **45** (3), 204–206.

68. Ziedonis, D.M., Steinberg, M.L., D'Avanzo, K. *et al.* (2004) Co-occurring schizophrenia and addiction, in *Dual Diagnosis and Psychiatric Treatment: Substance Abuse and Comorbid Disorders* (eds H.R. Kranzler and B. Rounsaville), Marcel Dekker.

69. Shaner, A., Khalsa, M.E., Roberts, L. *et al.* (1993) Unrecognized cocaine use among schizophrenic patients. *Am. J. Psychiatry*, **150** (5), 758–762.

70. Bartels, S.J., Teague, G.B., Drake, R.E. *et al.* (1993) Substance abuse in schizophrenia: service utilization and costs. *J. Nerv. Ment. Dis.*, **181** (4), 227–232.

71. Mueser, K.T., Bellack, A.S., and Blanchard, J.J. (1992) Comorbidity of schizophrenia and substance abuse: implications for treatment. *J. Consult. Clin. Psychol.*, **60** (6), 845–856.

72. Dixon, L. (1999) Dual diagnosis of substance abuse in schizophrenia: prevalence and impact on outcomes. *Schizophr. Res.*, **35** (Suppl), S93–S100.

73. Alterman, A.I., Ayre, F.R., and Williford, W.O. (1984) Diagnostic validation of conjoint schizophrenia and alcoholism. *J. Clin. Psychiat.*, **45** (7), 300–303.

74. Drake, R.E., Osher, F.C., Noordsy, D.L. *et al.* (1990) Diagnosis of alcohol use disorders in schizophrenia. *Schizophr. Bull.*, **16** (1), 57–67.

75. Mueser, K.T., Gingerich, S.L., and Rosenthal, C.K. (1994) Educational Family Therapy for schizophrenia: a new treatment model for clinical service and research. *Schizophr. Res.*, **13** (2), 99–107.

76. Westermeyer, J., Neider, J., and Westermeyer, M. (1992) Substance use and other psychiatric disorders among 100 American Indian patients. *Cult. Med. Psychiatry*, **16** (4), 519–529.

77. Jordan, L.C., Davidson, W.S., Herman, S.E. *et al.* (2002) Involvement in 12-step programs among persons with dual diagnoses. *Psychiatr. Serv.*, **53** (7), 894–896.

78. Verheul, R., Van den Brink, W., and Hartgers, C. (1995) Prevalence of personality disorders among alcoholics and drug addicts: an overview. *Eur. Addict. Res.*, **1**, 166–177.

79. van den Bosch, L.M. and Verheul, R. (2007) Patients with addiction and personality disorder: Treatment outcomes and clinical implications. *Curr. Opin. Psychiatry*, **20** (1), 67–71.

80. Krampe, H., Wagner, T., Stawicki, S. *et al.* (2006) Personality disorder and chronicity of addiction as independent outcome predictors in alcoholism treatment. *Psychiatr. Serv.*, **57** (5), 708–712.

81. Thomas, V.H., Melchert, T.P., and Banken, J.A. (1999) Substance dependence and personality disorders: comorbidity and treatment outcome in an inpatient treatment population. *J. Stud. Alcohol*, **60** (2), 271–277.

82. Verheul, R., van den Brink, W., and Hartgers, C. (1998) Personality disorders predict relapse in alcoholic patients. *Addict. Behav.*, **23** (6), 869–882.

83. Westermeyer, J. and Thuras, P. (2005) Association of antisocial personality disorder and substance disorder morbidity in a clinical sample. *Am. J. Drug Alcohol Abuse*, **31** (1), 93–110.

84. Ball, S.A., Cobb-Richardson, P., Connolly, A.J. *et al.* (2005) Substance abuse and personality disorders in homeless drop-in center clients: symptom severity and psychotherapy retention in a randomized clinical trial. *Compr. Psychiat.*, **46** (5), 371–379.

85. Linehan, M.M., Dimeff, L.A., Reynolds, S.K. *et al.* (2002) Dialectical behavior therapy versus comprehensive validation therapy plus 12-step for the treatment of opioid dependent women meeting criteria for borderline personality disorder. *Drug Alcohol Depen.*, **67** (1), 13–26.

86. Linehan, M.M., Schmidt, H. 3rd, Dimeff, L.A. *et al.* (1999) Dialectical behavior therapy for patients with borderline personality disorder and drug-dependence. *Am. J. Addiction*, **8** (4), 279–292.

87. Miller, W.R. and Rollnick, S. (2002) *Motivational Interviewing: Preparing People for Change*, Guilford Press.

88. Rollnick, S. and Miller, W.R. (1995) What is Motivational Interviewing? *Behav Cogn Psychother*, **23**, 325–334.

89. Zweben, J.E. (2003) Integrating psychosocial services with pharmacotherapies in the treatment of co-occurring disorders, in *Principles of Addiction Medicine* (eds A.W. Graham, T.K. Schultz, M.F. Mayo-Smith *et al.*), American Society of Addiction Medicine, Inc., Chevy Chase, MD.

90. Dennison, S.J. (2005) Substance use disorders in individuals with co-occuring psychiatric disorders, in *Substance Abuse Treatment. A Comprehensive Textbook* (eds J.H. Lowinson, P. Ruiz, R.B. Millman *et al.*), Lippincott, Williams & Wilkins.

91. Goldsmith, R.J. and Ries, R.K. (2003) Substance-induced mental disorders, in *Principles of Addiction Medicine* (eds A.W. Graham, T.K. Schultz, M.F. Mayo-Smith *et al.*), American Society of Addiction Medicine, Inc.

92. McKay, J.R., Pettinati, H.M., Morrison, R. *et al.* (2002) Relation of depression diagnoses to 2-year outcomes in cocaine-dependent patients in a randomized continuing care study. *Psychol. Addict. Behav.*, **16** (3), 225–235.

93. Mason, B.J., Kocsis, J.H., Ritvo, E.C. *et al.* (1996) A double-blind, placebo-controlled trial of desipramine for primary alcohol dependence stratified on the presence or absence of major depression. *JAMA*, **275** (10), 761–767.

94. McGrath, P.J., Nunes, E.V., Stewart, J.W. *et al.* (1996) Imipramine treatment of alcoholics with primary depression: A placebo-controlled clinical trial. *Arch. Gen. Psychiatry*, **53** (3), 232–240.

95. Carpenter, K.M., Brooks, A.C., Vosburg, S.K. *et al.* (2004) The effect of sertraline and environmental context on treating depression and illicit substance use among methadone maintained opiate dependent patients: a controlled clinical trial. *Drug Alcohol Depen.*, **74** (2), 123–134.

96. Cornelius, J.R., Salloum, I.M., Ehler, J.G. *et al.* (1997) Fluoxetine in depressed alcoholics. A double-blind, placebo-controlled trial. *Arch. Gen. Psychiatry*, **54** (8), 700–705.

97. Nunes, E.V. and Levin, F.R. (2004) Treatment of depression in patients with alcohol or other drug dependence: a meta-analysis. *JAMA*, **291** (15), 1887–1896.

98. Pettinati, H.M. (2004) Antidepressant treatment of co-occurring depression and alcohol dependence. *Biol. Psychiatry.*, **56** (10), 785–792.

99. Roy-Byrne, P.P., Pages, K.P., Russo, J.E. *et al.* (2000) Nefazodone treatment of major depression in alcohol-dependent patients: a double-blind, placebo-controlled trial. *J. Clin. Psychopharmacol.*, **20** (2), 129–136.

100. Kosten, T., Oliveto, A., Feingold, A. *et al.* (2003) Desipramine and contingency management for cocaine and opiate dependence in buprenorphine maintained patients. *Drug Alcohol Depen.*, **70** (3), 315–325.

101. Kosten, T.R., Morgan, C., and Kosten, T.A. (1990) Depressive symptoms during buprenorphine treatment of opioid abusers. *J. Subst. Abuse Treat.*, **7** (1), 51–54.

102. Rounsaville, B.J., Kosten, T.R., and Kleber, H.D. (1986) Long-term changes in current psychiatric diagnoses of treated opiate addicts. *Compr. Psychiat.*, **27** (5), 480–498.

103. Titievsky, J., Seco, G., Barranco, M. *et al.* (1982) Doxepin as adjunctive therapy for depressed methadone maintenance patients: a double-blind study. *J. Clin. Psychiat.*, **43** (11), 454–456.

104. Woody, G.E., O'Brien, C.P., and Rickels, K. (1975) Depression and anxiety in heroin addicts: a placebo-controlled study of doxepin in combination with methadone. *Am. J. Psychiatry*, **132** (4), 447–450.

105. Arndt, I.O., Dorozynsky, L., Woody, G.E. *et al.* (1992) Desipramine treatment of cocaine dependence in methadone-maintained patients. *Arch. Gen. Psychiatry*, **49** (11), 888–893.

106. Kleber, H.D., Weissman, M.M., Rounsaville, B.J. *et al.* (1983) Imipramine as treatment for depression in addicts. *Arch. Gen. Psychiatry*, **40** (6), 649–653.

107. Ziedonis, D.M. and Kosten, T.R. (1991) Depression as a prognostic factor for pharmacological treatment of cocaine dependence. *Psychopharmacol. Bull.*, **27** (3), 337–343.

108. Nunes, E.V., Quitkin, F.M., Donovan, S.J. *et al.* (1998) Imipramine treatment of opiate-dependent patients with depressive disorders. A placebo-controlled trial. *Arch. Gen. Psychiatry*, **55** (2), 153–160.

109. Margolin, A., Kosten, T.R., Avants, S.K. *et al.* (1995) A multicenter trial of bupropion for cocaine dependence in methadone-maintained patients. *Drug Alcohol Depen.*, **40** (2), 125–131.

110. Nunes, E.V., Sullivan, M.A., and Levin, F.R. (2004) Treatment of depression in patients with opiate dependence. *Biol. Psychiatry.*, **56** (10), 793–802.

111. Cornelius, J.R., Salloum, I.M., Thase, M.E. *et al.* (1998) Fluoxetine versus placebo in depressed alcoholic cocaine abusers. *Psychopharmacol. Bull.*, **34** (1), 117–121.

112. Schmitz, J.M., Averill, P., Stotts, A.L. *et al.* (2001) Fluoxetine treatment of cocaine-dependent patients with major depressive disorder. *Drug Alcohol Depen.*, **63** (3), 207–214.

113. McDowell, D., Nunes, E.V., Seracini, A.M. *et al.* (2005) Desipramine treatment of cocaine-dependent patients with depression: a placebo-controlled trial. *Drug Alcohol Depen.*, **80** (2), 209–221.

114. Weiss, R.D. and Mirin, S.M. (1989) Tricyclic antidepressants in the treatment of alcoholism and drug abuse. *J. Clin. Psychiat.*, **50** (Suppl), 4–9; discussion 9–11.

115. Brady, K.T., Myrick, H., and Sonne, S.C. (2003) Co-occurring addictie and affective disorders, in *Principles of Addiction Medicine* (eds A.W. Graham, T.K. Schultz, M.F. Mayo-Smith *et al.*), American Society of Addiction Medicine, Inc., Chevy Chase, MD.

116. Bowden, C.L. (1995) Predictors of response to divalproex and lithium. *J. Clin. Psychiat.*, **56** (Suppl 3), 25–30.

117. Tohen, M., Waternaux, C.M., Tsuang, M.T. *et al.* (1990) Four-year follow-up of twenty-four first-episode manic patients. *J. Affect. Disord.*, **19** (2), 79–86.

118. Keller, M.B., Lavori, P.W., Rice, J. *et al.* (1986) The persistent risk of chronicity in recurrent episodes of nonbipolar major depressive disorder: a prospective follow-up. *Am. J. Psychiatry*, **143** (1), 24–28.

119. Nitenson, N. and Gastfried, D.R. (2003) Co-occurring addictive and anxiety disorders, in *Principles of Addiction Medicine* (eds A.W. Graham, T.K. Schultz, M.F. Mayo-Smith *et al.*), American Society of Addiction Medicine, Inc.

120. Center for Substance Abuse Treatment (1994) Assessment and Treatment of Patients with Coexisting Mental Illness and Alcohol and Other Drug Abuse, Treatment Improvement Protocol (TIP) Series 9, DHHS Publication No. (SMA) 95-3061. Substance Abuse and Mental Health Services Administration, Rockville, MD.

121. Modesto-Lowe, V. and Kranzler, H.R. (1999) Diagnosis and treatment of alcohol-dependent patients with comorbid psychiatric disorders. *Alcohol Res. Health*, **23** (2), 144–149.

122. Brady, K.T. and Sinha, R. (2005) Co-occurring mental and substance use disorders: the neurobiological effects of chronic stress. *Am. J. Psychiatry*, **162** (8), 1483–1493.

123. George, T.P., Ziedonis, D.M., Feingold, A. *et al.* (2000) Nicotine transdermal patch and atypical antipsychotic medications for smoking cessation in schizophrenia. *Am. J. Psychiatry*, **157** (11), 1835–1842.

124. Bell, M., Greig, T., Gill, P. *et al.* (2002) Work rehabilitation and patterns of substance use among persons with schizophrenia. *Psychiatr. Serv.*, **53** (1), 63–69.

125. Drake, R.E., McHugo, G.J., and Noordsy, D.L. (1993) Treatment of alcoholism among schizophrenic outpatients: 4-year outcomes. *Am. J. Psychiatry*, **150** (2), 328–329.

126. Drake, R.E. and Mueser, K.T. (2000) Psychosocial approaches to dual diagnosis. *Schizophr. Bull.*, **26** (1), 105–118.

127. Mueser, K.T., Torrey, W.C., Lynde, D. *et al.* (2003) Implementing evidence-based practices for people with severe mental illness. *Behav. Modif.*, **27** (3), 387–411.

128. Ridgely, M.S., Goldman, H.H., and Willenbring, M. (1990) Barriers to the care of persons with dual diagnoses: organizational and financing issues. *Schizophr. Bull.*, **16** (1), 123–132.

129. Ries, R.K. and Ellingson, T. (1990) A pilot assessment at one month of 17 dual diagnosis patients. *Hosp. Community Psych.*, **41** (11), 1230–1233.

130. Fuller, R.K., Branchey, L., Brightwell, D.R. *et al.* (1986) Disulfiram treatment of alcoholism. A Veterans Administration cooperative study. *JAMA*, **256** (11), 1449–1455.

131. King, A.C., Volpicelli, J.R., Frazer, A. *et al.* (1997) Effect of naltrexone on subjective alcohol response in subjects at high and low risk for future alcohol dependence. *Psychopharmacology*, **129** (1), 15–22.

132. McCaul, M.E., Wand, G.S., Eissenberg, T. *et al.* (2000) Naltrexone alters subjective and psychomotor responses to alcohol in heavy drinking subjects. *Neuropsychopharmacology*, **22** (5), 480–492.

133. Swift, R.M., Whelihan, W., Kuznetsov, O. *et al.* (1994) Naltrexone-induced alterations in human ethanol intoxication. *Am. J. Psychiatry*, **151** (10), 1463–1467.

134. Kranzler, H.R. and Van Kirk, J. (2001) Efficacy of naltrexone and acamprosate for alcoholism treatment: a meta-analysis. *Alcohol. Clin. Exp. Res.*, **25** (9), 1335–1341.

135. O'Brien, C.P. (2001) Naltrexone for alcohol dependence: compliance is a key issue. *Addiction*, **96** (12), 1857.

136. Srisurapanont, M. and Jarusuraisin, N. (2002) Opioid antagonists for alcohol dependence. *Cochrane Database of Systematic Reviews* 1 (Art. No.: CD001867). doi: 10.1002/14651858.CD001867.pub2.

137. Tucker, T.K. and Ritter, A.J. (2000) Naltrexone in the treatment of heroin dependence: a literature review. *Drug Alcohol Rev.*, **19** (1), 73–78.

138. Anton, R.F., O'Malley, S.S., Ciraulo, D.A. *et al.* (2006) Combined pharmacotherapies and behavioral interventions for alcohol dependence: the COMBINE study: a randomized controlled trial. *JAMA*, **295** (17), 2003–2017.

139. Bouza, C., Angeles, M., Munoz, A. *et al.* (2004) Efficacy and safety of naltrexone and acamprosate in the treatment of alcohol dependence: a systematic review. *Addiction*, **99** (7), 811–828.

140. Mann, K. (2004) Pharmacotherapy of alcohol dependence: a review of the clinical data. *CNS Drugs*, **18** (8), 485–504.

141. Kranzler, H.R., Modesto-Lowe, V., and Van Kirk, J. (2000) Naltrexone vs. nefazodone for treatment of alcohol dependence. A placebo-controlled trial. *Neuropsychopharmacology*, **22** (5), 493–503.

142. Krystal, J.H., Cramer, J.A. Krol, W.F. *et al.* (2001) Naltrexone in the treatment of alcohol dependence. *N. Engl. J. Med.*, **345** (24), 1734–1739.

143. Chick, J., Anton, R., Checinski, K. *et al.* (2000) A multicentre, randomized, double-blind, placebo-controlled trial of naltrexone in the treatment of alcohol dependence or abuse. *Alcohol Alcohol.*, **35** (6), 587–593.

144. Volpicelli, J.R., Rhines, K.C., Rhines, J.S. *et al.* (1997) Naltrexone and alcohol dependence. Role of subject compliance. *Arch. Gen. Psychiatry*, **54** (8), 737–742.

145. Garbutt, J.C., Kranzler, H.R., O'Malley, S.S. *et al.* (2005) Efficacy and tolerability of long-acting injectable naltrexone for alcohol dependence: a randomized controlled trial. *JAMA*, **293** (13), 1617–1625.

146. Litten, R.Z., Fertig, J., Mattson, M. *et al.* (2005) Development of medications for alcohol use disorders: recent advances and ongoing challenges. *Expert Opin. Emerg. Drugs*, **10** (2), 323–343.

147. Myrick, H. and Anton, R. (2004) Recent advances in the pharmacotherapy of alcoholism. *Curr. Psychiatry Rep.*, **6** (5), 332–338.

148. Chick, J., Lehert, P., and Landron, F. (2003) Does acamprosate improve reduction of drinking as well as aiding abstinence? *J. Psychopharmacol.*, **17** (4), 397–402.

149. Mason, B.J., Goodman, A.M., Chabac, S. *et al.* (2006) Effect of oral acamprosate on abstinence in patients with alcohol dependence in a double-blind, placebo-controlled trial: the role of patient motivation. *J. Psychiatr. Res.*, **40** (5), 383–393.

150. Kiefer, F. and Mann, K. (2006) Pharmacotherapy and behavioral intervention for alcohol dependence. *JAMA*, **296** (14), 1727–1728. author reply 1728-9.

151. Caplehorn, J.R., Dalton, M.S., Haldar, F. *et al.* (1996) Methadone maintenance and addicts' risk of fatal heroin overdose. *Subst. Use Misuse*, **31** (2), 177–196.

152. Gronbladh, L., Ohlund, L.S., and Gunne, L.M. (1990) Mortality in heroin addiction: impact of methadone treatment. *Acta Psychiatr. Scand.*, **82** (3), 223–227.

153. Mattick, R.P., Breen, C., Kimber, J., and Davioli, M. (2003) Methadone maintenance therapy versus no opioid replacement therapy for opioid dependence. *Cochrane Database of Systematic Reviews* 3 (Art. No.: CD002209). doi: 10.1002/14651858.CD002209.pub2.

154. Center for Substance Abuse Treatment (2005) Medication-Assisted Treatment for Opioid Addiction in Opioid Treatment Programs, Treatment Improvement Protocol (TIP) Series 43, DHHS Publication No. (SMA) 05-4048. Substance Abuse and Mental Health Services Administration, Rockville, MD.

155. Mattick, R.P., Kimber, J., Breen, C., and Davioli, M. (2002) Buprenorphine maintenance versus placebo or methadone maintenance for opioid dependence. *Cochrane Database of Systematic Reviews* 2 (Art. No.: CD002207). doi: 10.1002/14651858.CD002207.pub3.

156. Center for Substance Abuse Treatment (2006) Detoxification and Substance Abuse Treatment, Treatment Improvement Protocol (TIP) Series 45, DHHS Publication No. (SMA) 06-4131, Substance Abuse and Mental Health Services Administration, Rockville, MD.

157. Marsden, J., Gossop, M., Stewart, D. *et al.* (2000) Psychiatric symptoms among clients seeking treatment for drug dependence. Intake data from the National Treatment Outcome Research Study. *Brit. J. Psychiat.*, **176**, 285–289.

158. Marzuk, P.M., Tardiff, K., Leon, A.C. *et al.* (1992) Prevalence of cocaine use among residents of New York City who committed suicide during a one-year period. *Am. J. Psychiatry*, **149** (3), 371–375.

159. Marzuk, P.M., Tardiff, K., Smyth, D. *et al.* (1992) Cocaine use, risk taking, and fatal Russian roulette. *JAMA*, **267** (19), 2635–2637.

160. Roy, A. (2001) Characteristics of cocaine-dependent patients who attempt suicide. *Am. J. Psychiatry*, **158** (8), 1215–1219.

161. Mee-Lee, D., Schulman, G.D., and Fishman, M. *et al.* (2001) *ASAM Patient Placement Criteria for the Treatment of Substance-Related Disorders*, Second Edition-Revised (ASAM PPC-2R), American Society of Addiction Medicine, Inc., Chevy Chase, MD.

162. Mee-Lee, D. and Shulman, G.D. (2003) The ASAM placement criteria and matching patients to treatment, in *Principles of Addiction Medicine* (eds A.W. Graham, T.K. Schultz, M.F. Mayo-Smith *et al.*), American Society of Addiction Medicine, Inc.

163. Coffey, R., Graver, L., Schroeder, D. *et al.* (2001) Mental Health and Substance Abuse Treatment: Results from a Study Integrating Data from State Mental Health, Substance Abuse, and Medicaid Agencies. Substance Abuse and Mental Health Services Administration.

164. Office of Applied Studies (2003) National Survey of Substance Abuse Treatment Services (N-SSATS): 2002 – Data on Substance Abuse Treatment Facilities, DASIS Series S-19, DHHS Publication No. (SMA) 03-3777. Substance Abuse and Mental Health Services Administration, Rockville, MD.

165. Sciacca, K. (1996) On co-occurring addictive and mental disorders. *Am. J. Orthopsychiat.*, **66** (3), 474.

166. Center for Substance Abuse Treatment (2005) Substance Abuse Treatment for Persons With Co-Occurring Disorders, Treatment Improvement Protocol (TIP) Series 42, DHHS Publication No. (SMA) 05-3922, Substance Abuse and Mental Health Services Administration, Rockville, MD.

167. Finney, J.W. and Moos, R.H. (2003) Effects of setting, duration and amount on treatment outcomes, in *Principles of Addiction Medicine* (eds A.W. Graham, T.K. Schultz, M.F. Mayo-Smith *et al.*), American Society of Addiction Medicine, Inc., Chevy Chase, MD.

168. Hubbard, R.L., Craddock, S.G., Flynn, P.M. *et al.* (1997) Overview of 1-year follow-up outcomes in the Drug Abuse Treatment Outcome Study (DATOS). *Psychol. Addict. Behav.*, **11** (4), 261–278.

169. McCrady, B.S. and Share, D. (2003) Recent research into twelve step programs, in *Principles of Addiction Medicine* (eds A.W. Graham, T.K. Schultz, M.F. Mayo-Smith *et al.*), American Society of Addiction Medicine, Inc., Chevy Chase, MD.

170. Fortney, J., Booth, B., Zhang, M. *et al.* (1998) Controlling for selection bias in the evaluation of Alcoholics Anonymous as aftercare treatment. *J. Stud. Alcohol*, **59** (6), 690–697.

171. Johnsen, E. and Herringer, L.G. (1993) A note on the utilization of common support activities and relapse following substance abuse treatment. *J. Psychol.*, **127** (1), 73–77.

172. Schuckit, M.A., Tipp, J.E., Smith, T.L. *et al.* (1997) Periods of abstinence following the onset of alcohol dependence in 1,853 men and women. *J. Stud. Alcohol*, **58** (6), 581–589.

173. Emrick, C.D. (1987) Alcoholics Anonymous: affiliation processes and effectiveness as treatment. *Alcohol. Clin. Exp. Res.*, **11** (5), 416–423.

174. Rychtarik, R.G., Connors, G.J., Dermen, K.H. *et al.* (2000) Alcoholics Anonymous and the use of medications to prevent relapse: an anonymous survey of member attitudes. *J. Stud. Alcohol*, **61** (1), 134–138.

175. Laudet, A.B., Cleland, C.M., Magura, S. *et al.* (2004) Social support mediates the effects of dual-focus mutual aid groups on abstinence from substance use. *Am. J. Commun. Psychol.*, **34** (3–4), 175–185.

176. Laudet, A.B., Magura, S., Cleland, C.M. *et al.* (2004) The effect of 12-step based fellowship participation on abstinence among dually diagnosed persons:

a two-year longitudinal study. *J. Psychoactive Drugs*, **36** (2), 207–216.

177. Magura, S., Laudet, A.B., Mahmood, D. *et al.* (2002) Adherence to medication regimens and participation in dual-focus self-help groups. *Psychiatr. Serv.*, **53** (3), 310–316.

178. Magura, S., Laudet, A.B., Mahmood, D. *et al.* (2003) Role of self-help processes in achieving abstinence among dually diagnosed persons. *Addict. Behav.*, **28** (3), 399–413.

179. Magura, S., Rosenblum, A., Villano, C.L. *et al.* (2008) Dual-focus mutual aid for co-occurring disorders: a quasi-experimental outcome evaluation study. *Am. J. Drug. Alcohol Abuse*, **34** (1), 61–74.

14

Addiction and short-term pain management

Steven D. Passik,[1] **Lauren J. Rogak,**[1,3] **Tatiana D. Starr,**[1] **and Kenneth L. Kirsh**[2]

[1] Department of Psychiatry and Behavioral Sciences, Memorial Sloan-Kettering Cancer Center, New York, NY, USA
[2] The Pain Treatment Center of the Bluegrass, Lexington, KY 40503
[3] Health Outcomes Research Group, Department of Epidemiology and Biostatistics, Memorial Sloan Kettering Cancer Center, 307 E. 63rd Street, 2nd Floor, New York, NY, USA 10065

14.1   DEVELOPING A THERAPEUTIC APPROACH

As in any therapeutic approach, a comprehensive assessment and strategy must be based on a solid diagnostic foundation. When a clinician chooses to use opioid therapy for pain management, it is necessary to be able to employ the current tenets for prescribing these medications. Additionally, all patients should be evaluated for the risks associated with misuse, addiction, and diversion, along with the added responsibility of managing these risks over time. Patients' within the chronic pain population who have a history of substance addiction require the prescribing clinician and the comprehensive treatment team to be proficient in these aspects of treatment [1].

Chronic pain is a multifaceted phenomenon that is often correlated with additional symptoms and functional disturbances. Chronic pain is true to its name in its perpetual and unremitting nature. Hence, searching for a cure is not the standard treatment result, rather the goal is management. Consequently, the goals of treatment for pain center about comfort, functional restoration, and improved quality of life [2].

14.2   GENERAL GUIDELINES

The basis for recommendations for the long-term administration of potentially addictive drugs, such as opioids, to patients with a history of substance addiction, is clinical experience and consensus from pain experts, rather than from randomized controlled clinical trials. Further research is a necessity in order to identify the level of responsiveness in each patient subgroup to each of the strategies. The following guidelines are a broad reflection of a variety of interventions that might be considered in this clinical context [3,4].

Addictive Disorders in Medical Populations   Edited by Norman S. Miller and Mark S. Gold

14.2.1 Multidisciplinary approach

The idea behind a multidisciplinary approach focuses on collaboration as an effective way to work with patients from a multitude of perspectives. An illustration of the most effective version of this collaboration would include a physician with expertise in pain and palliative care, nurses, social workers, and, if possible, a mental healthcare provider, preferably with expertise in the area of addiction medicine [3,4]. The primary goals of the mental health professional would include management of the multiple comorbidities associated with addiction, helping assess the patient's behavior with medications, addressing addiction, and helping manage the team's countertransference reactions to the patient.

14.2.2 Assessment of substance use history

A comprehensive assessment is necessary when medications with the potential for addiction are being considered. This includes a history focused on pain complaints, the associated consequences, prior treatments (e.g., prescribed and nonprescribed medications), relevant comorbidities, and other elements in a routine history. In regard to the actual pain, intensity, temporal features (e.g., onset, course), location, quality, and aggravating or relieving factors should all be considered. Physical and psychosocial aspects of the pain experience are also important elements in determining the impact of the pain on patients' overall functioning and quality of life (Table 14.1) [2].

This comprehensive pain assessment would be remiss without a detailed history of any drug addiction, focusing on duration and frequency of use, as well as the desired effect from the patient. When assessing patients with a known history of substance addiction, information regarding the specific pattern of addictive behaviors should be obtained. This includes but is not limited to the patients' choice of drug(s), routes and frequency of administration, means of acquisition, and means of financing. The perceived relationship between these behaviors and the pain experience is an important

piece of information and should be elucidated during the assessment [2]. The optimal strategy to obtain a complete, accurate, and truthful history is to adopt a nonjudgmental attitude and use empathic and honest communication [3,5,6]. It is important to keep in mind the possibility that patients may have a tendency towards misrepresenting their drug taking behaviors for a number of logical reasons, including stigmatization, mistrust of the interviewer, or concerns regarding fears of under-treatment. Thus, it is important that the clinician explains to the patient that an accurate account of their drug taking behaviors is necessary to prevent any withdrawal during treatment [4,6,7].

14.2.3 Set realistic goals for therapy

Outside of the terminal illness population, there is a high rate of recurrence for drug use and addiction. It has been shown, for example, that nearly 80% of patients relapse within one year [9]. When factoring in the stress associated with advanced illness coupled with the easy availability of centrally acting drugs, this risk is increased. As a result, complete prevention of relapse may not be a practical goal in this type of setting.

There is a subgroup of patients that lacks the ability to act in accordance with conventional therapeutic standards. This may be due to the presence of severe substance use disorders and comorbid psychiatric diagnoses. When this is the case, clinicians must adapt by amending limits and modifying the supportive services, such as frequency of team meetings and consultations with additional clinicians on a case-by-case basis. When therapeutic strategies are being modified, the respective expectations must be clarified. These strategies should be watched carefully and when unsuccessful ones come about, should be adjusted [4,6].

14.2.4 Evaluate and treat comorbid psychiatric disorders

There is an extremely high comorbidity of personality disorders, depression, and anxiety disorders

Table 14.1 Suggestions and sample questions for approaching patients about potentially aberrant drug taking behaviors [8]

Take a nonjudgmental stance

We think of this process as a fact-finding mission and not an inquisition of our patient. If we are successful with our approach, patients likely will be much more forthcoming, because they do not feel that they are being judged.

Start with sweeping questions

Jumping right in with tough questions about possible abuse of medications is difficult to initiate and undoubtedly will put the patient in a defensive posture from the beginning. Sweeping questions allow us to discover general attitudes toward medications and what they mean to our patients. Here are a few examples:

- What do your medications mean to you?
- How helpful have they been for you?
- Have you ever had any bad outcomes with your medications (either from side effects, your social life, or legally)?

Avoid "yes/no" style questions

Again, the goal is to help the patient open up and share their perspective. Questions that may be answered with either a "yes" or "no" create the sense of a cross-examination and do not allow an opportunity for exposition. These types of questions can be used later in the conversation when necessary.

Remember, the patient is the expert in these matters

We try to take a curious and interested stance in what our patient has to say. Using the tips mentioned previously, we sometimes find patients revealing a great deal about how they use their medications and what these medications mean to them in their daily lives (i.e., if the medications are a form of coping when under stress, instead of a routine medicine used solely for pain).

Close in on possible problems with detailed questions about warning signs

When appropriate avenues open, we make our questions more specific as we look for signs of self-medication and chemical coping. Here are a few examples:

- Have you ever taken your pain medications for other reasons?
- Have you ever taken them to help you sleep? When under stress? After a fight with a spouse or loved one?

Examine the patient for signs of flexibility

Building on the previous step, we try to determine how central the medications are to the patient's life. It is important to determine how open he or she is to alternate forms of pain therapy (i.e., relaxation training, interventional procedures, adjuvants, etc.). A patient who lives life "by the bottle" and cannot see other possibilities is likely someone how is chemical coping.

Use existing questionnaires

We use measures such as the Screener and Opioid Assessment for Patients in Pain (SOAPP) and the CAGE questionnaire to augment our discussions with our patients. These measurements can be found at sites such as: http://www.painedu.org or http://www.npecweb.org

---

among alcoholics and other patients with substance addiction histories [10]. Treating a patient's depression and/or anxiety has been shown to increase patient comfort and decrease the risk of relapse or aberrant drug taking [4,6].

14.2.5 Consider the therapeutic impact of tolerance

Pain management can be further hindered by patients who are actively misusing substances and who, therefore, may be tolerant to drugs administered for therapy. Since the exact degree of toler-

ance is unknown, it is best to begin with a conservative dose of the therapeutic drug and then titrate the dose with frequent reassessments until the patient has reached an adequate level of comfort [5,11]. This phase is crucial and is one that must be adhered to with this subgroup of patients, but is also useful with the entire patient population.

14.2.6 Apply pharmacological principles to treating pain

Employing the widely accepted guidelines for cancer pain management will optimize long-term opioid therapy [12,13]. In order to identify a complementary balance between efficacy and side effects, these guidelines stress patient self-reporting as the foundation for dosing, consistent monitoring, and the individualization of therapy [4]. These principles are also applicable to the concurrent treatment of side effects as the basis for enhancing the balance between both palliative and adverse effects (Table 14.2) [7].

Following the guidelines for long-term opioid therapy among patients with histories of substance use can be complex and involved, specifically in determining the actual dose required for a therapeutic response . Extra care and consideration should be used when prescribing to this specific population, while staying within the guidelines pertaining to dose individualization. If this guideline is relinquished, the clinician runs the risk of under-treatment [14]. In response to this risk of under-treatment, and further unrelieved pain, aberrant drug-related behaviors may develop. Regardless of the understanding that these behaviors are considered pseudo-addiction, their presence should be taken into serious consideration when prescribing medication [4]. Based on clinical experience, pseudo-addiction can lead patients with a history of substance addiction to genuinely become out of control [15].

It is imperative to understand the pharmacology of methadone in its dual role as a treatment for opioid addiction and as an analgesic [16,17]. A

Table 14.2 Basic principles for prescribing controlled substances to patients with advanced illness and issues of addiction [15]

Choose an opioid based on around-the-clock dosing

Choose long-acting agents when possible

As much as possible, limit or eliminate the use of short-acting or "breakthrough" doses

Use nonopioid adjuvants when possible and monitor for compliance with those medications

Use nondrug adjuvants whenever possible (i.e., relaxation techniques, distraction, biofeedback, TNS, communication about thoughts and feelings about pain)

If necessary, limit the amount of medication given at any one time (i.e., write prescriptions for a few days worth or a weeks worth of medication at a time)

Utilize pill counts and urine toxicology screens as necessary

If compliance is suspect or poor, refer to an addictions specialist

significant characteristic of methadone is that it has been shown to hinder withdrawal for significantly longer periods than it alleviates pain. As a result, abstinence can be averted and a single dose will lessen opioid cravings. However, most patients appear to require a minimum of three daily doses in order to obtain a prolonged analgesic result. Therapeutic modifications, that is, dose escalation and multiple daily doses, may become necessary when patients who are receiving methadone maintenance for treatment for opioid addiction are receiving methadone as an analgesic [4,6,18]. A major misconception in the use of methadone is in regard to the need for a special license; such a license is needed to use methadone to treat addiction, but not when using it to treat pain.

14.2.7   Recognizing specific drug addiction behaviors

Maintaining open lines of communication between the clinician and patient will aid in the preservation of the therapeutic environment. Upholding this constant dialog will aid in monitoring the development of any aberrant drug taking behaviors. Evaluating patients who are prescribed drugs with the potential for addiction and monitoring their behaviors regularly is a necessity [6]. This is particularly true for those patients with a remote or current history of drug addiction and alcohol addiction. If there is a substantial level of concern regarding such behaviors, it may be necessary to increase the frequency of visits and, additionally, to seek out additional historical information from significant others regarding the patient's drug use [15].

14.2.8   Use written agreements

Written agreements are helpful tools in structuring outpatient treatment. These agreements should clearly state the roles of each member of the team and the rules and expectations for the patient (Table 14.3). Patient's behaviors should be used as the basis for the level of restrictions, and graded agreements that clearly state the consequences of aberrant drug use should be

Table 14.3 Key elements of an opioid agreement [8]

Understand that there is no universally accepted agreement
   Many examples can be found via the Internet, but no definitive version exists. However, the following features are some that an agreement should contain.

Explain the expectations of the patient
   In clear and concise language, we make it known that the patient has a stake in his or her own care and is not simply a passive participant. The agreement should be written with flexibility and avoid ultimatums if transgressions occur. Ultimatums serve only to limit the choices the physician can use in light of problematic behaviors. If an ultimatum is listed, and not followed through for an "exception", the agreement will lose all meaning and forever be subject to having its boundaries tested by the patient.

Explain the role of the physician
   This is a relationship, and the document should explain the role of the physician and healthcare team. The agreement can spell out important issues, such as:
   • Medications will be provided by a single provider
   • Medications will be prescribed on a "round-the-clock" schedule
   • Lost or stolen medications will not be replaced.

Lists risks and benefits of the proposed therapy
   We list issues with the medications, such as their ability to create physical dependence and tolerance, the potential for addiction, and the warning signs of addiction.

Designate a single pharmacy
   It is important to keep the treatment as streamlined as possible to eliminate both intentional and unintentional sources of confusion on the part of the patient. The patient should be able to pick the pharmacy of his or her choice, but must stick with it to maintain a consistent relationship.

Provide a rationale for your policies
   We try to be flexible in setting policies, but we recognize the importance of explaining why certain policies exist (i.e., "if we see you engaging in certain behaviors – such as consistently requesting early renewals – it is a warning sign to us that might indicate you are having a problem controlling your medication usage.")

Get consent for the treatment and testing
   In our practice, both the physician and patient must sign the document. It is also necessary to have a consent in the document that clearly spells out the types of testing that might be done (i.e., random urine toxicology screens, pill counts, etc.) in the course of treatment.

enforced [4,6,19]. This may need to be modified as the patient becomes more imminently terminal, and the threat of dismissal from care less tenable. This agreement template can be amended and structured to fit individual practices and clinics. To date, there are no definitive studies that show any benefit from using this type of template [15].

14.2.9 Guidelines for prescribing

All patients who present with a history of misuse and addiction should be monitored with extra consideration. Those patients who are actively misusing substances should be seen on a more frequent basis than those who are not. Weekly sessions may be needed in order to build a good rapport with staff and provide an evaluation of symptom control and addiction-related concerns. Rather than being stilted by missed appointments, frequent home or nursing visits allow the opportunity to prescribe small quantities of drugs, which may decrease the temptation to divert from the regimen.

Procedures regarding prescription loss or replacement should be explicitly outlined to the patient, with the stipulation that no renewals will be given if appointments are missed or if home supplies are not accounted for. It should also be clarified that any dose changes require prior communication with the clinician. In the event that the primary care provider employs a covering clinician, they must be also advised of the explicit guidelines that have been established, in order to avoid conflict and disruption of the treatment plan [4,20].

14.2.10 Use 12-step programs

When working with patients in an outpatient setting, a clinician may choose to refer patients to a 12-step program as an addendum to their treatment plan. This referral must stipulate that documented attendance is a condition for ongoing drug prescriptions. As part of this referral, clinicians may decide to communicate with the patient's sponsor in an effort to disclose the patient's illness and treatment-based medication requirements. Establishing this contact will also limit any ostracism the patient may experience because of perceptions of not being compliant with the ideals of the twelve-step program [4,6]. Twelve-step programs pose a risk, because the liberal use of opioids may not be supported and the side effects misunderstood despite the patient's terminal status.

14.2.11 Urine toxicology screens

In an effort to support compliance and reveal any concurrent use of illicit substances or unprescribed licit drugs, patients with a history of aberrant drug use should be asked to submit to periodic urine toxicology screens. This will determine the early recognition of any aberrant drug-related behaviors. Patients should be provided with a detailed explanation that this is a method of monitoring, which can both reassure the clinician and provide a foundation for aggressive symptom-oriented treatment, thereby enhancing the therapeutic alliance [6,21]. Additionally, clinicians should ensure that the patient has an understanding of how positive screens will be managed, and related procedures should be clearly defined and explained at the beginning of outpatient treatment. In the event that there is a positive screen, a predetermined response should involve tightening the guidelines for continued treatment, such as more frequent visits and smaller quantities of prescribed drugs [4,6,22]. When using urine toxicology screens, it is important that providers understand that false positive tests can occur (Table 14.4).

14.2.12 Family sessions and meetings

The clinician may choose to involve family members and friends in the treatment plan as an effort to increase and strengthen a patient's support system. These family meetings serve a multitude of purposes. One is to familiarize the clinician with the

Table 14.4 Tips for ordering urine toxicology screens [8]

Get a detailed history on the medications prescribed to the patient
  We ensure that our records are current on all of our patient's medications before sending a urine toxicology screen. Up-to-date records help to prepare for the expected results and to order any specific test we might desire.

Know your laboratory
  It is worthwhile to establish a relationship with the laboratory where the specimens are sent. This facility can be an invaluable source for helping us determine what tests are needed and the cut-off levels used for various substances.

Be careful with your false negatives
  We find it disturbing to order a urine screen and find a negative result for a particular opioid we are prescribing to the patient. However, as mentioned previously, it is important to know the cut-off levels employed by the laboratory as well as whether they even can test for the drug of interest (e.g., fentanyl is not commonly found in urine).

Be careful with your false positives
  Our knowledge of the laboratory's cut-off values helps us determine which drugs might show up as metabolites of others in testing.

Talk with the patient
  We ask the patient if any illicit or other substances will be in his or her urine. Aberrant findings in urine should not be used to dismiss patients outright, but are useful as a check of the honestly and level of communication the patient has with us. We engage them around the topic of urine drug screens as an opportunity to work on any problems he or she might be having with loss of control or addiction of their treatment.

patients' support system, which has the potential to help the clinician understand a patient's history of aberrant drug taking behaviors. Another purpose of these meetings is to identify any family members who are using illicit drugs. The team may then choose to refer these family members to drug treatment, in order to get them help and to gather support for the patient [6]. Clinical experience has shown that encouraging family members to make changes in deference to the patient, and to support them with specific referrals, can be useful [15]. The

patient should be made aware of the possibility that family members or friends may attempt to buy or sell the patient's medications and, further, to be prepared to cope with this. In the case that a family member is identified as untrustworthy, clinicians can recommend the use of lock boxes with access limited to the patient and perhaps one caregiver. Dependable individuals will be easily identified in these meetings. They will serve as an integral source of strength and support for the patient during treatment [6,23].

14.3 CONCLUSIONS

All practitioners involved in pain management have the dual responsibility of relieving suffering while avoiding contributing to drug addiction and diversion. In general, successful pain management is dependent on a mutual relationship and open communication between doctor and patient. The goal of chronic pain management is to enable people with pain to live a full and rewarding life in the face of chronic illness.

A greater understanding of the principles of addiction medicine has clinical utility in the world of pain management. The assessment of aberrant behaviors in patients with chronic pain is one key aspect of mastering these principles [1].

REFERENCES

1. Passik, S.D. and Kirsh, K.L. (2004) Assessing aberrant drug-taking behaviors in the patient with chronic pain. *Curr. Pain Headache Rep.*, **8** (4), 289–294.

2. Portenoy, R.K., Lussier, D., Kirsh, K.L., and Passik, S. D. (2005) *Pain and addiction*, in *Clinical Textbook of Addictive Disorders*, 3rd edn (eds R.J. Frances, S.I. Miller, and A.H. Mack), Guilford Press, New York, pp. 367–395.

3. Passik, S.D., Portenoy, R.K., and Ricketts, P.L. (1998) Substance abuse issues in cancer patients. Part 1: Prevalence and diagnosis. *Oncology (Williston Park)*, **12** (4), 517–521, 524.

4. Passik, S.D., Portenoy, R.K., and Ricketts, P.L. (1998) Substance abuse issues in cancer patients. Part 2: Evaluation and treatment. *Oncology (Williston Park)*, **12** (5), 729–734; discussion 736, 741–722.

5. Passik, S.D.and Portenoy, R.K. (eds) (1998) *Substance Abuse Issues in Palliative Care*, Lippincott-Raven Publishers, Philadelphia, PA; Berger, A., Portenoy, R.,and Weissman, D. (eds) (1998) *Principles and Practice of Supportive Oncology*, Lippincott-Raven Publishers, Philadelphia, PA.

6. Passik, S.D. and Portenoy, R.K. (1998) Substance abuse disorders, in *Psycho-Oncology* (ed. J.C. Holland), Oxford University Press, New York, NY, pp. 576–586.

7. Portenoy, R.K. (1994) Management of common opioid side effects during long-term therapy of cancer pain. *Ann. Acad. Med. Singapore*, **23** (2), 160–170.

8. Passik, S.D. and Kirsh, K.L. (2005) Managing pain in patients with aberrant drug-taking behaviors. *J Support Oncol*, **3** (1), 83–86.

9. Hser, Y.I., Anglin, D., and Powers, K. (1993) A 24-year follow-up of California narcotics addicts. *Arch. Gen. Psychiatry*, **50** (7), 577–584.

10. Khantzian, E.J. and Treece, C. (1985) DSM-III psychiatric diagnosis of narcotic addicts. Recent findings. *Arch. Gen. Psychiatry*, **42** (11), 1067–1071.

11. Macaluso, C., Weinberg, D., and Foley, K.M. (1988) Opioid abuse and misuse in a cancer pain population. *J. Pain Symptom. Manag.*, **3** (3), S24–S31.

12. Agency for Health Care Policy and Research (1994) Clinical Practice Guideline 9: Management of Cancer Pain, US Department of Health and Human Services, Washington, DC.

13. American Pain Society (2003) *Principles of Analgesic Use in the Treatment of Acute Pain and Cancer Pain*, 5th edn, American Pain Society, Glenview, IL.

14. Breitbart, W., Rosenfeld, B.D., Passik, S.D. *et al.* (1996) The undertreatment of pain in ambulatory AIDS patients. *Pain*, **65** (2–3), 243–249.

15. Kirsh, K.L. and Passik, S.D. (2006) Palliative care of the terminally ill drug addict. *Cancer Invest.*, **24**, 425–431.

16. Fainsinger, R., Schoeller, T., and Bruera, E. (1993) Methadone in the management of cancer pain: a review. *Pain*, **52** (2), 137–147.

17. Lowinson, J.H., Marin, I.J., Joseph, H., and Dole, V.P. (1992) Methadone maintenance, in *Substance Abuse: A Comprehensive Textbook* (eds J.H. Lowinson, P. Ruiz, and R.B. Millman), Williams & Wilkins, Baltimore, MD, pp. 550–571.

18. Toombs, J.D. and Kral, L.A. (2005) Methadone treatment for pain states. *Am. Fam. Physician*, **71** (7), 1353–1358.

19. Fishman, S.M. and Kreis, P.G. (2002) The opioid contract. *Clin. J. Pain*, **18** (4 Suppl.), S70–S75.

20. Auret, K. and Schug, S.A. (2005) Underutilisation of opioids in elderly patients with chronic pain: approaches to correcting the problem. *Drugs Aging*, **22** (8), 641–654.

21. Weaver, M.F. and Schnoll, S.H. (2002) Opioid treatment of chronic pain in patients with addiction. *J. Pain Palliat. Care Pharmacother.*, **16** (3), 5–26.

22. Katz, N.P., Sherburne, S., and Beach, M. *et al.* (2003) Behavioral monitoring and urine toxicology testing in patients receiving long-term opioid therapy. *Anesth. Analg.*, **97** (4), 1097–1102, table of contents.

23. Farber, S., Andersen, W., Branden, C. *et al.* (1998) Improving cancer pain management through a system wide commitment. *J. Palliat. Med.*, **1** (4), 377–385.

15

Prescription opiate medications: clinical assessment and treatment of tolerance and dependence

Norman S. Miller,[1] Lucy Chen,[2] and Jianren Mao[2]

[1] Department of Medicine, Michigan State University, East Lansing, Michigan 48824, and Department of Psychiatry, The University of Florida, Gainesville, FL 32611, USA
[2] MGH Center for Translational Pain Research, Department of Anesthesia and Critical Care, Massachusetts General Hospital, Harvard Medical School, Boston, MA 02114, USA

15.1   EXTENT OF DEPENDENCE ON OPIATE MEDICATIONS

The National Household Survey on Drug Abuse demonstrates that 2.6 million people misused pain relievers, including hydrocodone and oxycodone. The misuse of prescription medicines affects a broad range of users, particularly older adults, adolescents, and women. There has been a sharp increase in new users of prescription drugs for nonmedical purposes, particularly painkillers, among teenagers and young adults 12–17 years old (2.9% increase), and 18–25 years old (3.7% increase) [1].

A fivefold increase in the incidence of narcotic medication use for nonmedical purposes was seen from the 1980s to the late 1990s and 2000. In 1999, approximately four million people were using prescription drugs nonmedically, which is about double the 2.1 million people who use heroin and cocaine [1].

In 2003, an estimated 6.3 million persons, or 2.7% of the population aged 12 or older had used prescription psychopharmacologic therapeutic medications nonmedically in the month prior to being surveyed. This number included 4.7 million persons using pain relievers, predominately prescription opiate medications, whose sources for the prescriptions were physicians [2].

In addition, the Drug Abuse Warning Network (DAWN) narcotic analgesic mentions in the Emergency Room increased 153% in the nation (from 42 857 to 108 320 emergency room visits) between 1995 and 2002. Dependence was the most frequently mentioned motive underlying drug addiction related to opioid mentions (47%), followed by suicide (22%), and psychic effects (15%). Disposition involving opioid analgesics was 53% admitted for treatment, 44% admitted and released from the hospital, and 3% left Against Medical Advice (AMA) [3].

To underscore the growing magnitude of addiction and dependence to opioid analgesics, an estimated 415 000 Americans received treatment for pain medication misuse and addiction in the past year in 2003. Correspondingly, the number of new "pain reliever" (opioid analgesics) users increased from 573 000 in 1990 to 2.5 million in 2000 (55% were females) [2].

In two clinical studies, significant rates of addiction and dependence to opioid analgesics were found in clinical populations. For 579 admissions to an Addictive Diseases Unit from October 2000 to March 2002, 298 admissions were for the treatment of opioid addiction or dependence. One hundred and eighty-seven patients were on OxyContin, using an average does of 184 mg of OxyContin a day [4]. In another study of 534 admissions to an Addiction Detoxification Unit in 2000, 27% of the admissions were for opioid prescription dependence; 53% for Vicoden (hydrocodone) dependence and 19% for OxyContin (oxycodone) dependence [5].

15.2   SIGNS AND SYMPTOMS OF DEPENDENCE ON OPIATE MEDICATIONS

The principle behavior manifestation of the presence of addiction is loss of control over the use of the medications, which results in excessive and continuous use in the presence or absence of pain from other sources. Addiction is a compulsion to use opiate medications that is not necessarily linked to a pain state from an identifiable cause, for example, neurological pain. Paradoxically, pain from addictive use develops because opiate medications become of central importance to one's life, despite development of adverse consequences. The pattern of addictive use becomes evident in the behavioral constellation beginning with preoccupation with acquiring followed by compulsive use and finally a pattern of relapse [6].

The five criteria in DSM-IV that reflect this definition of addiction are (1) using larger doses for longer period than intended, (2) persistent desire or unsuccessful attempts to cut down or control substance use, (3) preoccupation with acquiring opioid medications (e.g., multiple doctors, trips to the emergency room), (4) important social, occupational, or recreational activities abandoned or reduced because of opiate use, and (5) opioid use despite knowledge (being informed) of adverse physical or psychological problems caused by or exacerbated by opioids (e.g., depression, anxiety, muscle and back pain, restricted options in daily living, pursuit of drugs to exclusion of social, occupational, and normal interpersonal relationships, poor motivation to solve pain problems through evaluation and treatment, and resistance to alternative treatments of pain conditions to opioids [6,7]).

Identifying these behaviors is often obscured by the diffuse, vague and intractable complaint of pain persistently coupled with requests or demands for more opioid medications. In addition, the clinician's concern with relieving pain without a critical, medical judgment of etiology of pain, and an objective and skilled assessment of addiction, tolerance, and dependence perpetuated the prescribing and compulsive use of the prescription opioid medications. Predictably, aberrant opioid-seeking behavior may complicate the clinical picture of failed opioid therapy [8]. Although occasionally aberrant behavior (drug seeking) is a manifestation of inadequate analgesia and will revert to normal behavior when pain is adequately treated, more commonly it is a manifestation of addiction or noncompliance [8].

The relationship between addiction and noncompliance is complex and poorly understood. In general, noncompliance should arouse the physician's concern about possible addiction or diversion and embrace careful control and monitoring of opioid therapy [9,10]. The physician should continuously reassess such drug seeking behavior and opioid therapy should be discontinued if the aberrant (drug seeking) behavior persists and conduct evaluations for detoxification and addiction treatment [8–10]. Importantly, addiction can be masked when physicians comply with the patient's unreasonable demands for opioids. In this case, the addictive behavior is not reported by the patient, and is in fact denied, and the physician must authenticate and confirm addiction to the opioid medications. Importantly, the physician should consider detoxification and treatment of opioid addiction or refer for such services [6–8,11].

15.3   PSYCHOLOGICAL CONSEQUENCES (CHEMICALLY INDUCED)

- Anxiety

- Insomnia

- Depressed mood with suicidal ideation

- Fatigue

- Anhedonia

- Problems with concentration.

Medical problems can be aggravated by the misuse of opiate medications, which can mask important pain pathways. Because addictive opiate use is not linked to a pain source, the usual protective signal, that is, pain to refrain from behaviors that aggravate the underlying source of pain, is dulled or absent because of effects of the narcotic medications on the perception of pain. As a result, the pain source can become worse, with further destruction of tissue and increased neurological damage [12].

Given the sources of painful symptoms from opioid use itself, namely, addiction, tolerance, increased sensitivity, dependence, intoxication and withdrawal, it should not be surprising that effects of detoxification and abstinence would improve on pain perceptions and self-reports. This study confirmed that patients experienced less pain after completion of withdrawal and reaching the abstinent state free from the intoxicating effects. These findings strongly suggested that regular use and high doses of prescription opioid medications led to heightened pain perceptions and increased self-reports of pain from opioid analgesics [12].

15.4   OCCUPATIONAL DIFFICULTIES AS A RESULT OF ADDICTION

- Decreased productivity

- Increase in number of missed workdays

- This can lead to loss of employment and subsequent financial problems.

Patients with drug addictions may allocate their income for drugs at the expense of required items.

These patients' relationships may suffer because they are preoccupied with getting and maintaining their addiction at the expense of their family and friends. Being "unavailable" and not invested in the relationship is common, as is physical and mental abuse. They may also lie or do illegal activities to obtain their drugs.

15.5   BIOLOGICAL MECHANISMS UNDERLYING ADDICTION AND DEPENDENCE

The major opiates include natural substances, such as opium, morphine, and codeine (extracted from opium). Additional opiates include semi-synthetic and synthetic drugs produced by alteration in the chemical structure of the basic poppy products, such as semi-synthetic drugs for example, heroin, hydromorphone (Dilaudid), and oxycodone (OxyContin); synthetic drugs include propoxphene (Darvon), meperidine (Demerol), hydrocodone (Vicodin), and others. These opiate medications are metabolized similarly but differ according to their absorption (low for heroin and high for propoxyphene) and their half-life.

All prescription opiates act primarily on the mu receptor (named after morphine) with much less action at the other receptors. The sites with mu receptors where opiates act are distributed widely in the central nervous system (CNS), including brain and spinal cord, the peripheral nervous system, and the gastrointestinal tract. Activation of the mu receptor results in analgesia, euphoria, miosis, decreased breathing rate and muscle tone, decreased motility in the digestive tract and hormonal changes. Addiction is directly linked to the mu receptor, as it is responsible for "the rush" or "thrill" as well as the urge and drive to use more opiates (reinforcement of use).

The pharmacological basis of withdrawal includes firing of the neurons in the locus coeruleus (LC) and release of exaggerated levels of norepi- nephrine (NE) as in seen in other drug withdrawals. Clonidine acts to lessen withdrawal symptoms by suppressing presynaptic release of NE by inducing inhibition at the alpha-receptor on the presynaptic NE neurons (LC). Diazepam may act similarly at the benzodiazepine chloride ionophore channel by diffusely reducing sympathetic nervous system discharge of catecholamines in general by acting to suppress central nervous excitability during opioid withdrawal [13].

15.6   PHYSIOLOGICAL RESPONSES TO INTOXICATION

In addition, intoxication from opioid analgesics includes psychological effects of brief if any euphoria, followed by apathy, dsyphoria, depressed mood and affect, impaired social and occupational functioning, drowsiness, impaired attention and concentration, faulty memory, and poor insight and judgment. Physiological responses include papillary constriction, hypotension, constipation, slurred speech, psychomotor agitation or retardation, anxiety, depression, respiratory depression, and cardiovascular collapse. During intoxication, pharmacological tolerance and dependence will develop selectively to various psychological and physiological parameters with continued, repeated administration of opioids over time. However, the pharmacological tolerance is often not sufficient to overcome intoxication effects of larger doses of opioid medications, rather to an extent allow the use of larger doses without toxic or lethal effects on the central nervous system [12,13].

Tolerance will develop selectively to various psychological and physiological parameters with combined use over time.

15.7   TOLERANCE AND DEPENDENCE

Tolerance is the decreasing effect from the dose of the drug, or the need to increase the dose to maintain an effect. Intracellular changes occur, which account for tolerance and withdrawal. Tolerance develops to most addicting drugs, for example, 20 to 100-fold increase in dosage for opiates compared to 2–4 fold increase in dosage for alcohol, and can be expected as a neuroadaptation to drugs and alcohol with repetitive use and in higher doses [13].

Currently, a fundamental principle in pain management is to increase the dose until maximal analgesia is achieved with minimal side effects. However, doses used to reach these goals are often large and prescribing by physician is liberal [8]. Clinical experience suggest that patients receiving high doses of opioid medications rarely report satisfactory analgesia or improved function [8,9]. In fact, the patient-reported pain scale rarely reflects decremental changes, rather remains the same or augmental increases in response to elevated doses of opioid analgesics as a result of pharmacological tolerance [8,14].

The development of tolerance with chronic administration of opioid analgesics is expected and predictable, and large in comparison to other drugs, including other medications and alcohol. The pharmacological basis of tolerance pertains in part to changes or down-regulation in mu receptors, mu1 and mu2 (a reduction in the turnover rate and number of receptors), where opioid drugs act to exert their clinical effects. In addition, desensitization of opioid receptors may be linked to N-methyl-D-aspartate (NMDA) receptor cascade [8,14]. Also, increased expression of dynorphin has been noted in the spinal cord dorsal horn in associated with enhanced pain sensitivity [8,14].

15.8 INCREASED SENSITIVITY TO CHRONIC ADMINISTRATION OF OPIOID MEDICATIONS

Increased pain sensitivity rather than lowered pain sensitivity, can result from chronic administration of opioid analgesic medications in humans. In one study, patients treated chronically with opioids reported more pain than the matched nonopioid controls [15]. In addition, there was an increased demand for opioids from patients who had received opioids as compared to the matched patients without intraoperative opioid infusion [15].

These phenomena are different and are distinguished from traditional pharmacological toler-ance (reduced analgesic effect) as increased sensitivity to pain caused by chronic use of opioid medications. Increased sensitivities are described as allodynia, which is a painful response to normally non-noxious stimuli, and hyperalgesia, which is an exaggerated painful response to normally noxious stimuli [14,15]. Chronic opiate use induces hyperalgesia or increased pain sensitivity. Those actively maintained on methadone experience enhanced or increased levels of sensitivity to pain [16].

15.9 SYMPTOMS OF PHARMACOLOGICAL DEPENDENCE AND WITHDRAWAL FROM OPIATES

Symptoms of opioid withdrawal include but are not limited to dsyphoria, depression, nausea, vomiting, muscle aches, back pain, joint pain, rhinnorhea, piloerection, lacrimation, diaphoresis, anxiety, yawning, fever, insomnia, and an intense drive or desire to use more drugs [17]. The peak period and duration of withdrawal after cessation of opioids depends on the elimination (half-life) of the parent compound and any active opioid metabolite. In general, the shorter the half-life of the opioid, the earlier the onset and shorter the duration of withdrawal. Also, the longer the duration of opioid use and the higher the dose of opioids, the more severe and protracted the withdrawal characteristics [17]. For example, withdrawal from short-acting opiates, such as morphine, will start 6–8 hours after the last dose, peak in 7–10 days, and last up to 21 days. A post-acute withdrawal syndrome (p.a.w.s.) also occurs in most opiate addicts. This post-acute withdrawal can last months and includes the following symptoms: insomnia, irritability, fatigue, drug craving, sweating, and dysphoria [6,17].

Importantly, withdrawal is manifested regularly and daily in chronic opioid administration because it is difficult or impossible to maintain a constant blood level through the day, particularly during sleep. Typically, opioid withdrawal begins within an hour after the last opioid dose, as the peak blood levels begin to fall despite dosage forms. Frequently, patients experience intermittent and frequent withdrawal symptoms throughout the day, and thus report painful symptoms (confused with pain from medical sources) from the opioid withdrawal itself [17]. However, usually neither the patient nor the physician realizes the pain is from the withdrawal, and confusion occurs with increased patient subjective reports of pain with some underlying pain conditions inadequately treated, for example, back pain [6,17].

15.10 TREATMENT OF WITHDRAWAL

Clonidine, a nonopiate alpha-2 agonist, decreases sympathetic outflow to the body. This can often reduce the symptoms of opiate withdrawal, particularly when given in an outpatient setting, by 50–75%, if given in adequate dosages. Generally, oral Clonidine 0.1 mg qid and 0.1 mg qid as needed are given daily and a Clonidine patch 0.2 mg is used weekly for 1–2 weeks. Doses should be held if the patient is too sedated or if they experience orthostatic hypotension or if the blood pressure drops below 90 systolic/60 diastolic [17,18].

Benzodiazepines, such as diazepam, work at the GABA A receptor and are used to help with agitation, insomnia, muscle aches, and cravings. Doses are typically as follows: diazepam 5 mg qid as needed for 48–72 hours, although this can be given for longer periods, depending on the severity of the withdrawal [17,18].

Other medications used for helping with opiate withdrawal are hydroxyzine 50 mg, or trimethobenzamide 250 mg po or 200 mg rectally for nausea and vomiting. Loperamide 4 mg is used for abdominal cramping while acetaminophen or ibuprofen are used for headaches and other pains [17,18].

Naltrexone is a mu antagonist and has been used in conjunction with the above medications for an accelerated detoxification. The advantage to this is shorter withdrawal time with less cost. Typically 12.5 mg are used the first day, with an increase to 25 mg on the second day and 50 mg on day 3. Some motivated patients may also want to be maintained on naltrexone 50 mg daily to help maintain abstinence from opiates. This seems to be especially helpful for addicted healthcare workers under direct supervision (someone who ensures the patient is taking the medication). Side effects of naltrexone include abdominal pain, headache, insomnia, anxiety, nausea, and vomiting. A more serious problem is potential hepatotoxicity, especially as the dose is increased above 50 mg. Liver enzymes should be monitored monthly for at least the first six months and every 2–3 months thereafter if the enzymes are normal. Naltrexone is contraindicated in patients with severe liver disease, hepatitis, and those taking opiate agonists [17,18].

Opiate medications, such as methadone, which is a long-acting opiate, can be used for detoxification from opiate medications. They are effective in reducing symptoms of opiate withdrawal, especially for intravenous opiate users, and can be used instead of the above medications. Generally 15–20 mg of methadone is given on the first day. If the person experiences withdrawal, the dose will be increased by 10 mg increments [17,18].

Once the patient no longer experiences withdrawal, the dose is decreased by 10% per day. However, there can be problems in withdrawing from methadone, for example, a decrease in addicts' subsequent motivation to become drug free. Another challenge is that methadone can only be dispensed by FDA and DEA-licensed clinics, which severely limits its use by most physicians. Buprenorphine, which is a partial agonist-antagonist at the mu receptor is also being used for opiate withdrawal and maintenance and appears to be effective. Advantages to buprenorphine are its limited analgesia and respiratory depression at higher doses. It also has a milder withdrawal syndrome compared to other opiates [17,18].

15.11   CONTINUED TREATMENT OF ADDICTION

Supporting and treating opiate addicts through acute withdrawal is only the first step in sobriety. Next, patients should be referred to substance addiction treatment centers, either inpatient or outpatient depending on their drug history. Here, they can gain a greater understanding of addiction, learn new coping skills, and receive help in making the personal and behavioral changes needed for recovery. This is accomplished through didactics, group, family, and individual therapies, and treatment of any comorbid medical or psychiatric conditions [19].

Also of great importance is the patient's early involvement in a 12-step group, such as Narcotics Anonymous, for further support of their recovery. Studies show that patients' chances of remaining drug free are much greater if they complete a treatment program and then continue in a 12-step program on a regular basis for an extended period [19].

15.12   PREVENTION AND LONG-TERM INTERVENTIONS

Importantly, alcoholism and other drug addiction are accepted as contraindication to the use of opiate medications in patients with chronic, noncancer pain. However, clinicians must always consider the potential for addiction during treatment. The patients at risk for the development of addiction, tolerance, and dependence to opiate medications include patients with idiopathic pain (no clear etiology) and high levels of psychological distress or disability [6,7,20].

There is general agreement that those at substantial and significant risk for the development of overuse and addiction are patients who have a prior or current history of alcohol and drug addiction. Patients should be screened for high risk problematic opiate use if they have any previous history of alcohol or drug misuse or addiction [6,7,20].

15.12.1   Opioid-induced hyperalgesia

Opioid-induced hyperalgesia is a phenomenon in which opioids may induce a paradoxical increase in pain, such as hypersensitivity to noxious stimuli (hyperalgesia) and non-noxious stimuli (allodynia). A number of studies have shown that opioid administration can unexpectedly cause hyperalgesia (enhanced painful response to noxious stimuli) and allodynia (pain elicited by innocuous stimuli). This phenomenon has been observed following either acute or chronic opioid administration in both preclinical and clinical settings.

A large dose of intrathecal morphine administration (ten to hundred times more than a therapeutic dose) can induce nonspecific excitatory responses in rats, such as biting and scratching at dermatomes corresponding to the injection site, and aggressive behaviors in response to light brushing of the flanks [21,22]. Recent studies, however, have shown that repeated opioid administration, at a clinically relevant dose range, can lead to a progressive and lasting reduction of baseline nociceptive thresholds, resulting in an increase in pain sensitivity [23]. Rats receiving repeated intrathecal morphine administration (10 or 20 μg) over a seven-day period showed

a progressive reduction of baseline nociceptive thresholds [24–26]. This reduction is also seen in animals after subcutaneous fentanyl boluses using the Randall-Sellitto test, in which a constantly increasing pressure is applied to a rat's hind paw [27,28]. The decreased baseline nociceptive thresholds lasted for as long as five days after the cessation of four fentanyl bolus injections. A similar phenomenon has been observed in animals with repeated heroin administration as well [29].

Since hyperalgesia is an accompanying sign of opioid withdrawal, it is possible that decreased baseline nociceptive thresholds observed in animals treated with opioid boluses may reflect a subliminal withdrawal in which changes in baseline nociceptive thresholds might precede other withdrawal signs, such as wet-dog shaking and jumping. However, a progressive reduction of baseline nociceptive thresholds has also been demonstrated in animals receiving continuous intrathecal opioid infusion via osmotic pumps [25,26,30]. Moreover, opioid-induced pain sensitivity including thermal hyperalgesia and tactile allodynia is observed in these animals even when an opioid infusion continues, suggesting the involvement of active cellular mechanisms in the process of developing opioid-induced hyperalgesia [25,26,30].

While changes in baseline nociceptive thresholds can be measured in a controlled setting in animal studies, it is difficult to determine in human subjects whether the lack of the analgesic effect following opioid administration is from pharmacological tolerance and/or hyperalgesia, since the efficacy of opioid analgesia is usually assessed based on subjective pain scores. Several clinical reports appear to support the notion that opioid-induced hyperalgesia may be present in the clinical setting. For example, those patients receiving intraoperative remifentanil infusion reported more postoperative pain and more opioid consumption than the matched controls without receiving intraoperative remifentanil infusion [31,32]. Had there been only the development of pharmacological tolerance without opioid-induced hyperalgesia, the level of postoperative pain would have been comparable between these two groups. Recently, it has been reported that pain sensitivity to experimental pain stimulation is increased in opioid addicts. Furthermore, opioid addicts enrolled in a methadone maintenance program showed the increased pain sensitivity as compared to those matched former opioid addicts without methadone maintenance [33–36]. These data suggest that a prolonged methadone maintenance program may further worsen abnormal pain sensitivity in former opioid addicts. Several recent case reports have also suggested that opioid dose reductions may improve pain in patients with cancer-related pain or chronic nonmalignant pain on opioid therapy [37–40].

15.12.1.1 Proposed mechanisms of opioid-induced hyperalgesia

Studies suggest that opioid-induced hyperalgesia and antinociceptive tolerance may have mechanisms in common with neuropathic pain after peripheral nerve injury [14,41]. Both are associated with the reduced analgesic effect of morphine and are reversible by NMDA antagonists. Recent evidence also suggests that prolonged exposure to opioids induces neuroplastic changes, resulting in the enhanced ability of the neuropeptide cholecystokinin (CCK) to excite pathways arising from the rostroventromedial medulla (RVM). This mechanism enhances morphine-induced pain and tolerance by an up-regulation of spinal dynorphin content, which promotes the release of excitatory neurotransmitters [30]. While the exact cellular mechanisms of opioid-induced hyperalgesia remain to be elucidated, it is possible chronic opioid administration may lead to a pronociceptive process manifesting as the decreased clinical opioid analgesic efficacy.

15.12.2 Clinical implications of opioid-induced hyperalgesia

A decreased opioid analgesic effect during a course of opioid treatment (apparent opioid tolerance) is often considered an indication of pharmacological tolerance. Besides pharmacological tolerance, changes in the disease status and psychological process may be considered as well [42]. For example, there may be an increased activity in nociceptive pathways, including peripheral (tumor growth, inflammation, neuroma formation, etc.) and central sensitization (shift in receptive fields and changes in modulating process). Escalation of opioid doses has been a common clinical approach in order to improve analgesia. However, this conventional practice may need to be revisited in light of paradoxical opioid-induced hyperalgesia in both animal and human studies. Thus, apparent opioid tolerance is not synonymous with pharmacological tolerance and/or disease progression, which calls for an increase in opioid dose, but may be a sign of opioid-induced hyperalgesia. There are several issues related to opioid-induced hyperalgesia, which would be relevant to clinical opioid therapy.

- *Opioid-induced hyperalgesia versus pre-existing pain*. Several features of opioid-induced pain observed in animal and human studies may help make distinctions between opioid-induced hyperalgesia and pre-existing pain. Firstly, since opioid-induced hyperalgesia would conceivably exacerbate a pre-existing pain condition, pain intensity would be increased above the level of pre-existing pain following opioid treatment in the absence of apparent disease progression. Secondly, opioid-induced hyperalgesia would be diffuse, less defined in quality, and beyond the distribution of a pre-existing pain state, given that the underlying mechanisms of opioid-induced hyperalgesia involve neural circuits and extensive cellular and molecular changes. Thirdly, quantitative sensory testing may reveal changes in pain threshold, pain tolerance, and distribution patterns associated with the development of hyperalgesia. These parameters may also help make distinctions between the exacerbation of pre-existing pain and opioid-induced pain. Fourthly, under-treatment of pre-existing pain or the development of pharmacological tolerance may be overcome by a trial of opioid dose escalation, but opioid-induced hyperalgesia may be worsened following an opioid dose increase.

- *Opioid regimens and opioid-induced hyperalgesia.* Several factors may influence the development of opioid-induced hyperalgesia, although it remains unclear as to what opioid dose may lead to opioid-induced hyperalgesia. Firstly, there may be differences between different categories of opioid analgesics (e.g., morphine versus methadone) in terms of their ability to induce hyperalgesia. Some evidence suggests that the development of opioid-induced hyperalgesia may differ between individual opioid medications [36]. Secondly, it remains to be seen whether there is cross pain sensitivity to other opioids following the development of hyperalgesia induced by one opioid? Thirdly, administration of opioid through a neuraxial or systemic route may differentially contribute to the development of opioid-induced hyperalgesia. Fourthly, the temporal correlation between opioid therapy and the development of opioid-induced hyperalgesia remains unclear. Although opioid-induced hyperalgesia has been demonstrated in patients receiving a short intraoperative course of opioids, it remains to seen how long it takes to develop opioid-induced hyperalgesia in a clinical setting. Conceivably, opioid-induced hyperalgesia would be more likely to develop in patients receiving high opioid doses with a sustained treatment course.

- *Opioids and pre-emptive analgesia.* The clinical relevance and effectiveness of pre-emptive analgesia still is an issue in debate. A large dose of intraoperative opioids may activate a pronociceptive system leading to the development of hyperalgesia postoperatively, as discussed earlier. This may confound the assessment of postoperative pain and counteract the opioid analgesic effect. The idea of pre-emptive analgesia calls for pre-emptive inhibition of neural plastic changes largely mediated through the activation of the central glutamatergic system. Although opioid inhibits the nociceptive input that could activate the central glutamatergic system, opioid may also active a pronociceptive process mediated by the activation of glutamatergic mechanisms [43]. Therefore, the use of opioid as the main agent for pre-emptive analgesia may be counter-effective in certain cases.

15.12.3 Clinical management of opioid therapy

In approaching a patient receiving opioid treatment who has demonstrated the increased pain, it is essential to differentiate various causes of the increased pain (i.e., differential diagnosis of increased pain). If disease progression and/or psychological processes are unlikely to be the primary contributor to the patient's worsened pain, the focus should be concentrated on differentiating between pharmacologic tolerance and opioid-induced hyperalgesia. It would be reasonable to give a trial of opioid dose escalation at this point. If the patient's pain improves, the cause of the increased pain is more likely to be pharmacological tolerance. However, if the patient's pain worsens or does not consistently respond to the dose escalation, the presence of opioid-induced hyperalgesia should be seriously considered. The presence of those features of opioid-induced hyperalgesia as described previously can help make this diagnosis.

When opioid-induced hyperalgesia is being considered as a diagnosis, the opioid dose may be decreased or even weaned off as a diagnostic and therapeutic measure. Opioid rotation may be another option given that patients might get better pain relief often at lower equi-analgesic dosages. Moreover, combining adjuvant pain medication with the opioid therapy may minimize the amount of opioid and reduce the risk of tolerance and hyperalgesia. Finally, the history of a patient's pain treatment regimen and his/her response to opioids may assist the differential diagnosis as well. For example, a patient who was previously on a stable opioid regimen and now complains of a lack of pain relief would be different from a patient whose pain has never responded to opioids. In the latter case, opioid therapy should be weaned off and a nonopioid regimen should be pursued instead of opioid dose escalation. Clinicians should be familiar with various aspects of apparent opioid tolerance, including pharmacological opioid tolerance, opioid-induced hyperalgesia, and/or disease progression and make appropriate adjustment of opioid therapy under each condition [44].

In summary, opioids are effective analgesics for treating severe acute and chronic pain. Exposure to opioids, however, may lead to two seemingly unrelated cellular processes, the development of pharmacological tolerance and opioid-induced hyperalgesia. The converging effects of these two processes can significantly reduce the opioid analgesic efficacy. Moreover, pharmacological tolerance and opioid-induced hyperalgesia should be differentiated from physical dependence, addiction, pseudoaddiction, and substance (opioid) use disorders. In clinical practice, a systematic approach should be taken to diagnose and manage patients with a decreased opioid responsiveness. In many cases, increasing opioid dose may not always be the answer to this clinical challenge. Under certain circumstances, less opioid may be more effective in pain reduction. This approach may be combined with opioid rotation and/or addition of nonopioid adjuvant medications.

REFERENCES

1. National Institutes of Drug Abuse NIDA Info Facts: Prescription Pain and Other Medications. NIDA Info-Facts, Revised 2/05, http://www.drugabuse.gov/Infofacts/PainMed.html (Accessed 13 May 2005).

2. National Survey on Drug Use and Health (NSDUH) (2003) Prescription Psychotropic Medications. http://oas.samhsa.gov/nsduh.htm#NHSDAinfo (Accessed 13 May 2005).

3. Drug Abuse Warning Network, funded by Substance Abuse and Mental Health Services Administration, DHHS (2002) http://www.samhsa.gov (Accessed 13 May 2005).

4. Hays, L.R. (2004) A profile of OxyContin addiction. *J. Addict. Dis.*, **23** (4), 1–9.

5. Miller, N.S. and Greenfeld, A. (2004) Patient characteristics and risks factors for development of dependence on hydrocodone and oxycodone. *Am. J. Ther.*, **11** (1), 26–32.

6. Miller, N.S. and Lyon, D. (2003) Biology of opiates: affects, prevalence of addiction, options for treatment. *Psychiat. Ann.*, **33** (9), 559–564.

7. American Psychiatric Association (1994) *Diagnostic and Statistical Manual of Mental Disorders*, 4th edn, American Psychiatric Association, Washington, DC.

8. Ballantyne, J.C. and Mao, J.M. (2003) Opioid therapy for chronic pain. *N. Engl. J. Med.*, **349**, 1943–1953.

9. Compton, W.M. and Volkow, N.D. (2005) Major increases in opioid analgesic abuse in the United States: Concerns and strategies. *Drug Alcohol Depend.*, **81**, 103–107

10. Cicero, T.J., Inciardi, J.A., and Munoz, A. (2005) Trends in abuse of OxyContin® and other opioid analgesics in the United States (2002-2004). *J. Pain*, **6** (10), 662–672.

11. Miller, N.S. and Kipnis, S.(2006) Detoxification and Substance Abuse Treatment. Treatment Improvement Protocol (TIP) 45. Substance Abuse & Mental Health Services Administration/Center for Substance Abuse Treatment (SAMHSA/CSAT), DHSS, Rockville, MD.

12. Miller, N.S., Swiney, T., and Barkin, R. (2006) Effects of opiate prescription medication dependence and detoxification on pain perceptions and self-reports. *Am. J. Ther*, **13** (5), 436–444.

13. Gold, M.S. and Johnson, C.R. (1998) Psychological and psychiatry consequences of opiates, in *Handbook of Substance Abuse: Neurobehavioral Pharmacology* (eds R.E. Tarter, R.T. Ammerman, and P.J. Ott), Plenum Press, New York.

14. Mao, J. (2002) Opioid-induced abnormal pain sensitivity: implications in clinical opioid therapy. *Pain*, **100**, 213–217.

15. Guignard, B., Bossard, A.E., Coste, C. *et al.* (2000) Acute opioid tolerance: intraoperative remifentanil increases postoperative pain and morphine requirement. *Anesthesiology*, **93**, 409–417.

16. Inturrisi, C.E. (2002) Clinical pharmacology of opioids for pain. *Clin. J. Pain*, **18** (4 Suppl.), S3–S13.

17. Miller, N.S. (2002) Drug abuse, in *Conn's Current Therapy*, 54th edn (eds R.E. Rakeland E.T. Bope), W.B. Saunders, pp. 1117–1123.

18. Miller, N.S., Gold, M.S., and Smith, D.E. (1997) *Manual of Addiction Therapeutics*, John Wiley and Sons, Inc., New York.

19. Miller, N.S., Ninonuevo, F., Hoffman, N.G., and Astrachan, B.M. (1999) Prediction of treatment outcomes: lifetime depression versus the continuum of care. *Am. J. Addict.*, **8** (3), 243–253.

20. Przewlocki, R. (2004) Opioid abuse and brain gene expression. *Eur. J. Pharmacol.*, **500** (1–3), 331–349.

21. Woolf, C.J. (1981) Intrathecal high dose morphine produces hyperalgesia in the rat. *Brain Res.*, **209** (2), 491–495.

22. Yaksh, T.L., Harty, G.J., and Onofrio, B.M. (1986) High dose of spinal morphine produce a nonopiate receptor-mediated hyperesthesia: Clinical and theoretic implications. *Anesthesiology*, **64** (5), 590–597.

23. Mao, J. (2006) Opioid-induced abnormal pain sensitivity: Is it clinically relevant? *Curr. Pain Headache Rep.*, **10** (1), 67–70.

24. Mao, J., Price, D.D., and Mayer, D.J. (1994) Thermal hyperalgesia in association with the development of morphine tolerance in rats: roles of excitatory amino acids receptors and protein kinase C. *J. Neurosci.*, **14**, 2301–2312.

25. Mao, J., Sung, B., Ji, R.R., and Lim, G. (2002) Chronic morphine induces downregulation of spinal glutamate transporters: implication sin morphine tolerance and abnormal pain sensitivity. *J. Neurosci.*, **22**, 8312–8223.

26. Mao, J., Sung, B., Ji, R.R., and Lim, G. (2002) Neuronal apoptosis associated with morphine tolerance: evidence for an opioid-induced neurotoxic mechanism. *J. Neurosci.*, **22**, 7650–7661.

27. Celerier, E., Rivat, C., Jun, Y. *et al.* (2000) Long lasting hyperalgesia induced by fentanyl in rats: preventive effect of ketamine. *Anesthesiology*, **92**, 465–472.

28. Laulin, J.P., Maurette, P., Corcuff, J.B. *et al.* (2002) The role of ketamine in preventing fentanyl-induced hyperalgesia and subsequent acute morphine tolerance. *Anesth. Analg.*, **94**, 1263–1269.

29. Celerier, E., Laulin, J.P., Corcuff, J.B. *et al.* (2001) Progressive enhancement of delayed hyperalgesia induced by repeated heroin administration: a sensitization process. *J. Neurosci.*, **21**, 4074–4080.

30. Vanderah, T.W., Ossipov, M.H., Lai, J. *et al.* (2001) Mechanisms of opioid induced pain and antinociceptive tolerance: descending facilitation and spinal dynorphin. *Pain*, **92**, 5–9.

31. Vinik, H.R. and Igor, K. (1998) Rapid development of tolerance to analgesia during remifentanil infusion in humans. *Anesth. Analg.*, **86**, 307–311.

32. Crawford, M.W., Hickey, C., Zaarour, C. *et al.* (2006) Development of acute opioid tolerance during infusion of remifentanil for pediatric scoliosis surgery. *Anesth. Analg.*, **102** (6), 1662–1667. 22–24.

33. Ho, A. and Dole, V.P. (1979) Pain perception in drug-free and in methadone-maintained human ex-addicts. *Proc. Soc. Exp. Biol. Med.*, **162**, 392–395.

34. Compton, P., Charuvastra, V.C., Kintaudi, K., and Ling, W. (2000) Pain responses in methadone-maintained opioid abusers. *J. Pain Symptom. Manag.*, **20**, 237–245.

35. Doverty, M., White, J.M., Somogyi, A.A. *et al.* (2001) Hyperalgesic responses in methadone maintenance patients. *Pain*, **90**, 91–96.

36. Compton, P., Charuvastra, V.C., and Ling, W. (2001) Pain intolerance in opioid-maintained former opiate addicts: effect of long-acting maintenance agent. *Drug and Alcohol Depen.*, **63**, 139–146.

37. Wilson, G.R. and Reisfield, G.M. (2003) Morphine hyperalgesia: a case report. *Am. J. Hosp. Palliat. Care*, **20** (6), 459–461.

38. Mercadante, S., Ferrera, P., Villari, P., and Arcuri, E. (2003) Hyperalgesia: an emerging iatrogenic syndrome. *J. Pain Symptom. Manag.*, **26** (2), 769–775.

39. Heger, S., Maier, C., Otter, K. *et al.* (1999) Morphine induced allodynia in a child with brain tumor. *Br. Med. J.*, **319** (7210), 627–629.

40. Sjogren, P., Jensen, N.H., and Jensen, T.S. (1994) Disappearance of morphine-induced hyperalgesia after discontinuing or substituting morphine with opioid agonists. *Pain*, **59**, 313–316.

41. Ossipov, M.H., Lai, J., Vanderah, T.W., and Porreca, F. (2003) Induction of pain facilitation by sustained opioid exposure: relationship to opioid antinociceptive tolerance. *Life Sci.*, **73**, 783–800.

42. Portenoy, R.K. (1994) Tolerance to opioid analgesics: clinical aspects. *Cancer Surv.*, **21**, 49–65.

43. Mao, J., Price, D.D., and Mayer, D.J. (1995) Mechanisms of hyperalgesia and opioid tolerance: a current view of their possible interactions. *Pain*, **62**, 259–274.

44. Chang, G., Chen, L., and Mao, J. (2007) Opioid tolerance and hyperalgesia. *Med. Clin. North Am.*, **91** (2), 199–211.

16

Substance addiction and HIV infection: scope of the problem and management

Gabriel Sarah,[1] **Clifford Martin,**[2] **Myles Stone,**[2] **Carol Schneiderman,**[2] and **Stephen A. Klotz**[2]

[1] *Health Sciences Center, University of Arizona, Tucson, Arizona, USA*
[2] *Section of Infectious Diseases, University of Arizona, Tucson, Arizona, USA*

16.1   INTRODUCTION

HIV-infected individuals typically face a host of complex medical issues involving the diagnosis of HIV infection, treatment of opportunistic infections, and the implementation of Highly Active Antiretroviral Therapy (HAART) for most patients. Many patients have other serious medical problems that are separate from those related to immune destruction caused by HIV infection. In addition, complex social issues surrounding social acceptance and stigma attached to the HIV-positive status have major impacts on patient's lives. A special subset of HIV-positive individuals, that is, HIV-positive individuals with substance use, addiction and/or dependency, have distinct behavioral and possibly, biological components. The HIV-positive substance misuser is the topic of this chapter with particular attention to substance addiction among older HIV-positive patients, a rapidly growing patient population.

Three important aspects of HIV infection and substance addiction will be addressed: the contribution of substance addiction to "at-risk" behaviors for HIV infection; the contribution of substance addiction to failure of adherence to antiretroviral regimens; and the potential direct effect of addicting substances on patients' immunity. In addition, management strategies of HIV-infected substance addicts and the experience of an urban HIV clinic are discussed. Substance addiction is defined as a maladaptive pattern with recurrent and significant adverse consequences related to the use of substances for a 12-month period. Substance addicts often do not fulfill obligations at work, school, or home and continue substance use despite recurrent social or inter-personal problems caused by the effects of the substance. This is consistent with the definition in DSM-IV. Other terminology in this chapter includes the use of HIV infection for HIV-1 and HAART for antiretroviral regimens.

Addictive Disorders in Medical Populations   Edited by Norman S. Miller and Mark S. Gold

16.2 SCOPE OF THE PROBLEM

Substance addiction is common, with estimates of 25–40% of hospital admissions and 10–15% of outpatient visits being associated with substance addiction [1]. Substance addicted HIV-infected patients interact with the medical and social realms often unpredictably, but frequently with deleterious effects to themselves and possibly to others by transmission of wildtype or resistant HIV to sexual or intravenous drug user (IVDU) partners. Substances commonly used by HIV-infected patients include tobacco, alcohol, heroin, cocaine, poppers (alkyl nitrites), methamphetamine, marijuana, methadone, and oxycodone. To a lesser extent, occasional patients are encountered who are dependent upon morphine and benzodiazepines. Infrequently, rare patients use phosphodiesterase-5 enzyme inhibitors commonly prescribed for erectile dysfunction and fentanyl. One uncommon "street drug" is actually an antiretroviral drug, efavirenz (Sustiva), which penetrates the central nervous system (CNS) and can be associated with dysphoria, delusions, hallucinations, and *pavor nocturnis*. We have not, however, encountered its use among HIV-positive patients as a recreational agent. The following cases illustrate some of the complex issues surrounding the addicted HIV-infected patient in the typical outpatient setting specializing in the care of HIV-infected patients.

16.2.1 Case history 1

A. is a 44-year old heterosexual male infected with HIV for over twenty years. He acquired HIV by intravenous heroin use along with hepatitis C. Although he no longer uses intravenous drugs, he occasionally uses methamphetamine, marijuana, and cocaine, all of which have been documented by screening for urinary metabolites. He is a heavy smoker, but does not drink. He is married, but separated and has two children. He does not work because of disability (due to AIDS), lives alone, and has Medicaid only.

He is currently experiencing major immunosuppression and is categorized as having AIDS: the CD4+ cell count is 42/μl and his viral load is 90 000 copies of RNA/μl. He intermittently comes to clinic, unscheduled, with various complaints ranging from abdominal pain related to a urinary tract infection to painful mouth due to thrush. In the past he has been on multiple antiretroviral regimens (over 15 drugs) with demonstrated resistance to many of them. He claims to take 100% of his antiretroviral medications, yet a recent HIV genotype demonstrated no mutations, instead it was "pan-sensitive," thus confirming that he is not taking his antiretroviral medications. Due to the marked immunosuppression, the patient will be started on two new classes of antiretroviral drugs as well as several nucleoside drugs that he has received in the past.

16.2.1.1 Comment

This vignette illustrates several points. The patient is actively misusing illicit drugs and comes to clinic *ad hoc,* not as scheduled, resulting in disruption of clinic flow and the care of other patients. Laboratory and radiology resources are often ordered that are unnecessary. Major blocks of time are needed from the physician, nurse, and pharmacist to determine the problem and its solution. The finding of a wildtype virus on the genotype proves that the patient is not taking his antiretroviral drugs because, if he were taking the medications, mutations would have been found on the genotype. The likelihood of the new HAART regimen achieving success is minimal based upon the patient's history.

16.2.2 Case history 2

B. is a 55-year old man who practices Men who have Sex with Men (MSM) and has been infected with HIV for 25 years. He is self-employed, has health insurance and for years his HIV infection has been excellently controlled with antiretroviral medications with CD4 + cell counts consistently over 700/µl and nondetectable viral loads. He suffers from several side effects of antiretroviral therapy including lipodystrophy with a distended abdomen secondary to fatty infiltration of the mesentery and painful neuropathy of the lower limbs that has been present for over 15 years. (Distal symmetric, painful neuropathy may affect upwards of 30% of patients on HAART.) He makes his regular appointments at the clinic and obtains laboratory values as requested.

B. has been refilling a morphine prescription on a monthly basis for years. The drug was prescribed for neuropathic pain and he is loath to do without the medication or attempt other medications.

16.2.2.1 Comment

Variations of this patient's story of dependency upon morphine are fairly common in HIV clinics. Patients use many different strategies to cope with peripheral neuropathy, including the use of marijuana, intravenous drug use, amphetamines, and alcohol [2]. Opiates were commonly prescribed by physicians for neuropathic pain associated with the use of nucleoside drugs although this treatment was judged to be unsuccessful. Many patients like B. are reluctant to stop the opiates, but otherwise are model patients with complete suppression of the HIV virus and excellent drug adherence. The neuropathy is a side effect of the use of nucleoside drugs, in particular ddC and D4T, and is due to mitochondrial damage caused by the binding of the antiretroviral nucleoside to mitochondrial γ-DNA polymerase. This injury is not entirely reversible upon cessation of the offending drug.

16.2.3 Case history 3

C. is a 44-year old male with a history of documented cocaine use. He comes to the clinic because he is feeling unwell. One month previously his CD4 + cell count was 33 cells/µl and his viral load was over 100 000 copies/µl. He has documented drug-resistant HIV virus and was prescribed a regimen of two protease inhibitors and two nucleoside inhibitors. Laboratory specimens were ordered and the patient went to an outside laboratory to have blood drawn. The phlebotomist after removing the syringe from C. tried to recap the needle and stuck her forefinger. The needle stick site began to bleed.

16.2.3.1 Comment

This injury to the healthcare worker is serious and without post-exposure prophylactic treatment would carry a risk of transmission of HIV of three in 1000 incidences. The phlebotomist was begun on three antiretroviral drugs for one month and had a negative serology for HIV at one, three and six months.

Although the post-exposure prophylaxis was successful, the risk in this incident was heightened by the presence of multi-resistant virus in the source. Substance addicts are not the only patients harboring resistant virus, but substance addiction directly impacts the ability of individuals to remain adherent to antiretroviral regimens. Cocaine use, in particular, is associated with nonadherence to HAART [3].

16.3 MATRIX OF HIV AND SUBSTANCE ADDICTION

Individuals with substance dependence, addiction, or intoxication may be at high risk for acquisition of HIV. Contraction of HIV by sexual contact and IVDU account for the majority of HIV infections worldwide. Patients using intoxicating substances are consistently less likely to engage in safe sex when under the influence of substances such as alcohol [4] or amphetamines [5] or if the sex involves more than one partner [6]. Furthermore, a loss of inhibition under the influence of an intoxicating substance can lead to the sharing of intravenous needles. Substance addiction is a primary cause of the spread of HIV in individuals who are sharing needles, engaging in prostitution, and

Table 16.1 Risk for acquisition of HIV for certain behaviors

Behavior	Estimated Average Per Contact Transmission Risk (%)
Receptive anal sex	1
Shared needles	0.7
Occupational needle stick	0.3
Male to female, vaginal sex	0.2
Female to male, vaginal sex	0.1
Insertive anal sex	0.1
Receptive oral sex with male	0.03

having sexual contact with IVDU. "At-risk" behavior is particularly a crisis among young people aged 15–24, who are most likely to indulge in binge drinking and initiate the use of illegal drugs. Not surprisingly, AIDS is the leading cause of death by illness among people in this age group. The risks for contraction of HIV from various behaviors is found in Table 16.1.

Particularly noteworthy is the high rate of methamphetamine use in MSM. MSM use methamphetamine at a rate ten times higher than the general population, with 10–20% of MSM having used methamphetamine in the past month [7]. Both heavy use (once a week or more) and light use (less than once a week) of methamphetamine have been associated with increased high-risk sexual behaviors that transmit HIV/AIDS, syphilis, and other sexually transmitted infections (STIs). Methamphetamine users have more sexual partners, many of whom are anonymous. They are less likely to practice safer sex, less likely to use a condom, have more anal sex, and are more likely to engage in sex with a discordant HIV-status partner. MSM using methamphetamine were three times as likely as other gay men to have syphilis, and twice as likely to have infection with *Chlamydia* or gonorrhea [8]. The use of methamphetamine has been found to be associated with HIV seroconversion, even after controlling for other behavioral risk factors (such as having a high number of partners or engaging in unprotected receptive anal intercourse) [7]. It is noteworthy that receptive anal sex and IVDU are the two most "at-risk" behaviors when performed with an HIV-positive partner (Table 16.1).

16.4 SUBSTANCE ADDICTION AND HIV RISK IN OLDER ADULTS

As the prevalence of HIV in the United States has increased over the past 25 years, the demographics of the disease have changed dramatically, with minority populations being infected disproportionately. In addition, while HIV has historically been considered a disease of young adults, it is now estimated that approximately 25% of patients infected with HIV in the United States are 50 years of age or older, up from 19% in 2001 [9–11]. The cumulative number of AIDS cases in this age group increased fourfold between 1990 and 2001 [12]. The incidence of AIDS cases in older adults has also grown steadily. Prior to 1995, patients over the age of 50 comprised 10% of new cases; in 1999, the number rose to 14% [12]. In addition, the number of persons aging into this age bracket accounts for a significant proportion of HIV-positive older adults.

Despite the fact that older adults, defined in the HIV literature as patients 50 years of age and older, make up an ever-growing proportion of HIV/AIDS cases in the United States, misconceptions about HIV risk factors in older adults persist [13]. Early in the HIV epidemic, a small but significant proportion of older adults were infected with HIV through blood transfusion [14,15]. After routine HIV screening of blood donors was implemented in 1985, this trend changed [16], and by the mid-1990s similar percentages of older and younger HIV-infected men were reportedly infected through MSM behavior. Compared to younger men, however, men 50 years of age and older were still generally more likely to be infected via heterosexual than MSM behavior (11% vs. 9%) and less likely through intravenous drug use (16% vs. 26%) (14). Among men, MSM behavior, intravenous drug use, and heterosexual transmission has accounted for 36%, 19%, and 15%, respectively, of HIV cases in older patients, with transfusion accounting for only 2% [17]. Data such as these highlight intravenous drug use as a primary risk factor for HIV acquisition in roughly 20% of older male patients. Data directly linking other risk factors, such as alcohol addiction and the use of noninjected illicit substances, to HIV risk specifically in older adults is lacking in the medical literature.

The overall impact of substance addiction in older adults is much more complicated, however, than these data preliminarily suggest. Significant differences between younger and older adults have emerged in the literature, particularly at the intersection of age, race (particularly minority status), sex, and substance addiction. A close look at the published data on HIV in older adults reveals that substance addiction is a major issue in this age group, particularly for minority women.

It is well documented that HIV disproportionately affects minority populations in the United States, and this trend is equally pronounced in older adults [18]. While African Americans comprise only 13% of the US population, they accounted for 49% of HIV infections in 2005, with a rate of 71.3 per 1 000 000; rates in Hispanics, Native American, Caucasian, and Asian/Pacific Islander were 27.8, 10.4, 8.8, and 7.4 per 100 000, respectively [10,11,19,20]. For both men and women, African Americans account for approximately 50% of all HIV infections in older adults, and among older HIV-infected women, over two-thirds are in minorities [19]. Women tend to make up a larger percentage of older adults with HIV (22.2% of patients over age 60 were women in one study, compared to 12.6% in the 30–49 age group) [21].

Approximately, 92% of older Caucasian MSM had health insurance, compared to 83% of younger Caucasians, 63% of younger intravenous drug users, and 44% of older intravenous drug users. Older injection drug users were more likely to be African American, be unemployed, and have low annual incomes. Older intravenous drug users were much more likely to have physical disabilities than younger users, but older and younger MSM did not differ in rates of physical disability [22]. It is not surprising, therefore, that additional studies have reported alarming rates of HIV infection,

particularly in older adult MSM. In two studies of MSM in four large urban centers in the United States, HIV prevalence was reported as 19%; African American MSM and MSM/injection drug users had rates of 29% and 40%, respectively. Incidence rates were reported at 1–2%, with most patients aging into the disease (i.e., diagnosed at ages younger than 50 but surviving into older adulthood). Prevalence was attenuated by a remarkably high 69% mortality rate [18,22].

Another study that compared younger drug users to older users found that older users were less risky with shared needles and have fewer sexual encounters. However, older drug users who do engage in sex are equally likely to do so in exchange for drugs or money, and equally unlikely to use condoms. Older crack cocaine users were found to be more risky than older adults who used other substances [23]. While crack cocaine use in older adults is less common than in younger adults, it has been studied, and previous and current older addicts of intravenous drugs and alcohol should be considered at high risk for crack cocaine-related HIV risk behavior [23].

Several studies have highlighted issues of drug and alcohol addiction, lack of knowledge about partner risk behaviors, sexism, ageism, physical or sexual abuse, and ethnicity as risks for HIV infection on older women [24–26]. Very little research has focused on the prevalence of injection drug use in older minority women, but lack of effective prevention knowledge, racism, drug use, poverty, and sexism have been cited as reasons for increased prevalence in this population [18,19,24–26]. In at least one study, older adults were one-sixth as likely to report condom usage compared to younger adults; they were also significantly less likely to have been tested for HIV (24% vs. 44%) (9).

Synthesis of these data on older adults reveals that substance addiction is a major risk factor for HIV acquisition and transmission in older adults. Rates of substance addiction in older HIV patients are high, particularly in minority men. Older substance addicts are less likely to have health insurance and more likely to have limited financial resources, limiting their access to prevention and treatment services. Combined with low perception of risk, low levels of effective prevention knowledge, and lack of empowerment of women, it is not difficult to see how substance addiction has lead to alarming rates of HIV infection on older minority adults. Culturally appropriate prevention efforts targeting older adults are rare [13,27], as is evidence-based research focused on this group.

Failure of physicians to screen for HIV in older adults is widespread, as highlighted in the Boston Globe in 2001 [28]. Even when appropriate screening questions are asked in the clinical setting, responses are often less reliable than in younger populations, which leads to false assumptions regarding risk behavior [29]. Putting these assump-tions aside, astute clinicians need to be aware of potential risk behaviors in older patients in order to prevent delay in timely testing and treatment for HIV. Failure to do so can easily lead to inaccurate diagnosis in elderly patients. Until evidence-based prevention and education programs targeting older adults are implemented, the responsibility for aggressive screening for substance addiction in older adults, particularly in ethnic minorities, falls to the individual medical provider. Indeed, the intersection of race, poverty, age, and drug use should not be underestimated, and until it is recognized and addressed substance addiction will continue to be a major risk factor for the spread of HIV in vulnerable populations.

16.5 BIOLOGY OF THE SUBSTANCE MISUSING HIV-INFECTED INDIVIDUAL

Patient's suffering from substance misuse are also, in general, more prone to infection following exposure to HIV. Several mechanisms can account for the increased risk of infection, including possibly reduced immunity. This is particularly true of IVDU, where sharing of needles is involved and compounded with poor hygiene and colonization with pathogenic microorganisms [30].

The prevalence of smoking among HIV-positive individuals is high and may increasingly impact their lives as they age. Associations have been found between smoking and alteration of the immune system, specifically a reduction in absolute CD4 + cell numbers and increased viral loads in female heavy smokers [31]. Although it is unlikely that tobacco directly increases risk behavior, it appears that smokers have a high rate of depression [32] and, in conjunction with alcohol, tobacco may adversely affect brain neurobiology and neurocognition [33] possibly leading to "at-risk" behavior.

Alcohol consumption prior to sex increases the rate of unsafe sex in HIV-positive adults [4], particularly among MSM [34], but does not appear to impact directly the number of CD4 + cells [35]. However, alcohol consumption does correlate with poorer adherence to antiretroviral regimens [36,37], which ultimately may translate into HIV treatment failure. It is claimed that the association of alcohol use and depression correlates with HIV treatment adherence failure, more so than other substance addiction [38]. Alcohol increases susceptibility to some infections that can occur as a complication of AIDS. Infections associated with both alcohol and AIDS include tuberculosis, pneumonia, and especially Hepatitis C (HCV). HCV, which is commonly spread through injection drug use, infects about 14% of all people with HIV/AIDS (with much higher rates in many cities) and is a leading cause of death among HIV-positive individuals. Alcohol may also increase the severity of AIDS-related brain damage, which can cause profound dementia and death [39].

A longitudinal study of HIV-negative and HIV-positive MSM users of marijuana, cocaine, poppers and amphetamines demonstrated that the addiction of those drugs did not adversely affect either the CD4 + or CD8 + cell numbers [40]. It is interesting to recall that before HIV was shown to be the cause of AIDS, strong consideration was given to inhaled alkyl nitrites (poppers) as a cause for the immune suppression seen in AIDS [41]. Although the nitrites cause profound smooth muscle relaxation they do not cause immunosuppression. Table 16.2 lists some illicit substances and their putative biological/social implications. Cocaine use is correlated with nonadherence to HAART [3] and, therefore, with harboring resistant virus. Heroin,

Table 16.2 Drugs of addiction: possible biological and social impact

Substance	Effects
Cocaine	Current and past users likely to be nonadherent with HAART [3]
Heroin	Elevated amounts of cytokines in plasma of HCV-infected "speedball" users [42]
Methamphetamine	Increases percentage of CD4 + cells and decreases CD8 + cells in mice [43]
"Hard" drug use	No relationship between CD4 + cell count or viral load; more infectious diseases were correlated with drug use [50]
Methadone and HAART clinics	Direct observation of ingestion of methadone and HAART confers benefit on HAART adherence with more patients with undetectable viral loads [46]

among its many properties, is associated with elevated cytokine levels [42], which may account, in part, for the emaciated body habitus of users. Methamphetamines may actually increase CD4 + cell numbers [43] (Table 16.2) but, in general, it appears that the behaviors associated with drug use, that is, "at-risk" behaviors and the inability to sustain healthy practices, are the most important characteristics in drug addicts that lead to a decline in their health rather than any profound immunomodulary properties of the addicting substances.

A recent Gay and Lesbian Medical Association focus group project found the underlying cause of much of the drug use in the gay community to be social in nature, and included such issues as homophobia, lack of positive self-esteem, lack of a strong and healthy sense of community, and lack of healthy role models. Drug use, and especially "club drug" use in MSM, appears to have a "pain prevention" function as well: a way of preventing or decreasing the potential discomfort associated with certain sex acts (e.g., anal receptive) [8].

Many physical symptoms of HIV infection overlap with those of substance misuse (e.g., patients in drug withdrawal, may have complaints of malaise, fatigue, weight loss, fever, diarrhea, and night sweats that can be easily confused with symptoms of opportunistic infections). Neurological symptoms due to HIV and substance addiction also can overlap. For instance, both AIDS dementia and drug intoxication can present with apathy, disorientation, aggression, and an altered level of consciousness.

The major concerns of physicians caring for addicted HIV-positive patients are the patients' compliance with the antiretroviral regimen and the adverse effects a substance addiction lifestyle may have on adherence to the antiretroviral drug regimen and, thus, markers of disease progression, such as the viral load and the CD4 + cell count. Substance addiciton is often confounded with comorbid psychiatric illness that increases the incidence of noncompliance with antiretroviral medications.

16.6 MANAGEMENT OF ADDICTION OR DEPENDENCY ON MEDICALLY INDICATED AGENTS

Providers must be aware of the unique difficulties of living with HIV. Ideally, proper rehabilitation treatment must be achieved for all patients suffering from substance misuse. A variety of programs exist for the HIV-positive patient who misuses substances. Modalities of care that can be offered to the HIV-infected IVDU are enrollment in a methadone maintenance program, which can be successful provided the patient stays in the program long enough. Other

patients may benefit by treatment with buprenorphine [44]. Needle exchange programs may help reduce the incidence rate of the disease [45].

These programs have a high success rate, surpassing that of rehabilitation facilities not dedicated solely to HIV-positive patients by combining methadone and HAART observed ingestion resulting in more HIV-positive drug users achieving nondetectable viral loads [46]. Patients currently in treatment programs should be supported in this effort. Communication and coordination of adherence interventions should be developed between medical and substance addiction treatment providers. All providers should give a clear adherence message in an optimistic framework.

In some studies substance addiction is related to decreased adherence to antiretroviral (ARV) medications [47,48]. These patients often present late in the course of disease and have complex medical and social comorbidities, such as hepatitis, depression, and lack of access to adequate housing, food, and social support. Depression should be addressed before starting antiretroviral therapy, as depression can be a predictor of nonadherence [47]. Support systems should be identified for each patient and medication, adherence, and resistance education provided. Visual aids can be particularly useful as educational tools in this population. Some HAART regimens may need to be altered in patients on methadone therapy [49]. Also, education efforts directed to the patient should be performed to explain to patients the risks they expose themselves to, even with casual substance use. Antiretroviral therapy should not be withheld from patients actively using substances if medically indicated. However, it can be challenging for these patients to adhere to ARV therapy. A harm reduction model may be used and substance addiction treatment discussed at each visit.

HIV-infected substance addicts frequently request (or are prescribed) controlled substances for legitimate and occasionally for erroneous reasons. HIV-positive patients with a history of substance addiction should be managed closely, so as not to encourage or enable further addiction. If these patients require narcotic analgesics for pain control or other controlled substances there are several techniques that can be used to help the patient and protect the provider. The first step is to implement a pain contract agreed to by both provider and patient. The pain contract is a preprinted form with statements that commit the patient to certain positive behaviors and describe the consequences of breaking the contract. Both provider and patient sign the contract and it is maintained in the patient's chart with a copy given to the patient. The pain contract includes statements that commit the patient to an honest dialogue with the provider, preclude the patient from using illicit drugs, limit the patient to filling prescriptions to one pharmacy, and prevent the patient from obtaining prescriptions from outside providers. Patients must agree to submit a urine or blood specimen to test for illicit substances when requested by the provider. If the patient breaks any part of the contract, the provider may stop writing prescriptions for controlled substances and taper the patient off of the medications over several days. The patient may then be referred to a substance addiction treatment program. Initially, frequent face-to-face meetings may be required to establish trust between the provider and patient. Clinic staff such as nurses and pharmacists should be involved in this process.

Another essential management element in the care of such patients is to record the history of all prescriptions written for controlled substances. Anytime a prescription is written for a controlled substance the date, medication name, strength, quantity, and instructions are recorded in a database that all clinic staff can access. This allows any clinic staff to know if the patient is eligible to have a new prescription written for the medication. Clinic staff can monitor patient requests and advise providers on the progress of patient adherence to the contract. Other techniques sometimes useful for controlling substance using patient's behavior include writing prescriptions for one or two weeks rather than for an entire month, requiring the patient to bring prescription bottles when picking up each new prescription, and contacting pharmacies to ensure compliance.

16.7   EXPERIENCE OF AN URBAN HIV CLINIC AND SUBSTANCE ADDICTS

Data from our HIV clinic is consistent with published reports on the role and impact of substance addiction among HIV-positive patients. The University of Arizona Ryan White Early Intervention

Table 16.3 Relative risk for HIV-positive substance addict in the University of Arizona Ryan White Early Intervention Services Clinic. Relative Risk of >2 or <0.5 is significant. HAART: antiretroviral therapy. They are compared against HIV-positive patients on HAART who do not have a history of substance addiction

Characteristic	Relative Risk: HIV + Patients with Substance Addiction History Compared to HIV +, No Substance Addiction. (All Patients on HAART.)
History of attempted suicide	4.78
Comorbid depression	2.4
Co-infected with HCV	2
Nonadherence to HAART	2
Detectable HIV viral load	2
Lower CD4 cell count (cells/μl)	1.6

Services Clinic in Tucson, Arizona serves over 300 HIV-infected persons. 39% of the patients are of a minority status, 26% being Hispanic and 11% African American. (African Americans constitute <5% of the population of Tucson).

Roughly seven out of ten patients (67%) in our clinic are taking an antiretroviral regimen. Of those patients on antiretroviral medications, 33 (17%), have a history of substance addiction, of which 18 (9%) have a history of IVDU. Of patients who attempt suicide in our clinic, half of them have a history of substance addiction (Relative Risk of 4.78, Table 16.3). In addition, substance addicts are more likely to have a history of depression, co-infected with HCV, and nonadherent with HAART. There is a trend to lower CD4 + cell counts and detectable viral loads as well (Table 16.3). 25% of substance adicts had <250 CD4 + cells/μl, whereas 16% of nonaddicts had CD4 + cells <250/ml.

A looming problem in our clinic and nationwide is the number of older HIV-positive patients and, thus, the growing number of older HIV-positive substance addicts. Patients older than 45 years of age constitute 53% of our entire clinic population. As was noted earlier in this chapter, knowledge to act in an evidence-based manner involving older HIV-positive patients (and, hence, older HIV-positive substance addicts) is lacking.

16.8 CONCLUSIONS

In summary, our experience in an HIV clinic as well as the review of the literature supports several generalities concerning HIV-positive substance addicts.

1. HIV-positive patients who are intoxicated with a substance or have a history of active substance addiction more often engage in "at-risk" behavior with the potential for the transmission of HIV, such as IVDU or unprotected sex. This may result in contraction or transmission of HIV, HCV or other STIs.

2. The HIV-positive substance addict has a high rate of noncompliance or failure with HAART regimens resulting in acquisition of resistance

to medications through mutation of the infecting virus.

3. The HIV-positive substance addict who is noncompliant with the HAART regimen will eventually manifest lower CD4 + cell counts, increasing viral loads, and increasing numbers of opportunistic infections.

4. The HIV-positive substance addict who fails HAART may transmit wildtype or resistant HIV to sexual and IVDU partners.

5. What effect, or to what extent, the drugs of addiction directly affect the HIV virus or host immunity is unknown at present.

REFERENCES

1. Kissen, B. (1997) Medical management of alcoholic patients, in *Treatment and Rehabilitation of the Chronic Alcoholic* (eds B. Kissenand H. Besleiter), Plenum Publishing Co., New York.

2. Nicholas, P. *et al.* (2007) Unhealthy behaviours for self-management of HIV-related peripheral neuropathy. *AIDS Care*, **19**, 1266–1273.

3. Cofrancesco, J. *et al.* (2008) Illicit drug use and HIV treatment outcomes in a US cohort. *AIDS*, **30**, 357–365.

4. Barta, W. *et al.* (2008) A daily process investigation of alcohol-involved sexual risk behavior among economically disadvantaged problem drinkers living with HIV/AIDS. *AIDS Behav.*, **12**, 729–740

5. Koblin, B. *et al.* (2007) Amphetamine use and sexual risk among men who have sex with men: results from the National HIV Behavioral Surveillance study – New York City. *Subst. Use Misuse*, **42**, 1613–1628.

6. Courtenay-Quirk, C. *et al.* (2007) Factors associated with sexual risk behavior among persons living with HIV: gender and sexual identity group differences. *AIDS Behav.*, **12**, 685–694.

7. Gay and Lesbian Medical Association (2006) Breaking the grip: treating crystal meth addiction among gay and bisexual men.

8. Adrian, M. (2006) Addiction and sexually transmitted disease (STD), human immunodeficiency virus (HIV), and acquired immune deficiency syndrome (AIDS): their mutual interactions. *Subst. Use Misuse*, **41**, 1337–1348.

9. Rezza, G. (1998) Determinants of progression to AIDS in HIV-infected individuals: an update from the Italian seroconversion study. *JAIDS and Human Retrovirol.*, **17**, S13–S16.

10. Operskalski, E. (1997) Influences of age, viral load and CD4+ count on the rate of progression of HIV-1 infection to AIDS. *JAIDS*, **15** (3), 243–244.

11. Casado, J. *et al.* (1998) Predictors of long-term response to protease inhibitor therapy in a cohort of HIV-infected patients. *AIDS*, **12**, F131–F135.

12. Mack, K.A. and Ory, M.G. (2003) AIDS and older Americans at the end of the Twentieth Century. *JAIDS*, **33**, S68–S75.

13. Lieberman, R. (2000) HIV in older americans: an epidemiologic perspective. *J. Midwifery & Women's Health*, **45** (2), 176–182.

14. Gupta, S. *et al.* (2005) Guidelines for the management of chronic kidney disease in HIV-infected patients: recommendations of the HIV Medicine Association of the Infectious Diseases Society of America. *Clin. Infect. Dis.*, **40**, 1559–1585.

15. Dube, M. *et al.* (2000) Preliminary guidelines for the evaluation and management of dyslipidemia in adults infected with Human Immunodeficiency Virus and receiving antiretroviral therapy: recommendations of the Adult AIDS Clinical Trial Group Cardiovascular Disease Focus Group. *Clin. Infect. Dis.*, **31**, 1216–1224.

16. Chiao, E., Ries, K., and Sande, M. (1999) AIDS and the elderly. *Clin. Infect. Dis.*, **28**, 740–745.

17. Capili, B. and Anastasi, J. (1998) Assess for HIV, too. *RN*, **61**, 28.

18. Montoya, I.D. and Whitsett, D.D. (2003) New frontiers and challenges in HIV research among older minority populations. *JAIDS*, **33**, S218–S221.

19. Brown, D. and Sankar, A. (1998) HIV/AIDS and aging minority populations. *Res. Ageing*, **20**, 865.

20. Jimenez, A. (2003) Triple jeopardy: targeting older men of color who have sex with men. *JAIDS*, **33**, S222–S225.

21. Emlet, C. and Farkas, K. (2002) Correlates of service utilization among midlife and older adults with HIV/AIDS. *J. Ageing and Health*, **14**, 315–335.

22. Crystal, S. *et al.* (2003) The diverse older HIV-positive population: A national profile of economic circumstances, social support, and quality of life. *JAIDS*, **33**, S76–S83.

23. Johnson, W. and Sterk, C. (2003) Late-onset crack users: an emergent HIV risk group. *JAIDS*, **33**, S229–S232.

24. Neundorfer, M. *et al.* (2005) HIV-Risk Factors for Midlife and Older Women *The Gerontologist*, **45**, 617–625.

25. Zablotsky, D. and Kennedy, M. (2003) Risk factors and HIV transmission to midlife and older women: knowledge, options, and the initiation of safer sexual practices. *JAIDS*, **33**, S122–S130.

26. Zablotsky, D. (1998) Overlooked, ignored, and forgotten: older women at risk for HIV infection and AIDS. *Res. Ageing*, **20**, 760.

27. Linsk, N., Fowler, J., and Klein, S. (2003) HIV/AIDS prevention and care services and services for the aging: bridging the gap between service systems to assist older people. *JAIDS*, **33**, S243–S250.

28. (2001) Doctors often fail to warn elderly of AIDS risk. Boston Globe.

29. Gribble, J. *et al.* (1998) Measuring AIDS-related behaviors in older populations: methodological issues. *Res. Ageing*, **20**, 798–821.

30. Gordon, R. and Lowy, F. (2005) Bacterial infections in drug users. *NEJM*, **353**, 1945–1954.

31. Wojna, V. *et al.* (2007) Associations of cigarette smoking with viral immune and cognitive function in human immunodeficiency virus-seropositive women. *J. Neurovirol.*, **13**, 561–568.

32. Benard, A. *et al.* (2007) Tobacco addiction and HIV infection: toward the implementation of cessation programs. ANRS CO3 Aquitaine Cohort. *AIDS Patient Care and STDs*, **21**, 458–468.

33. Durazzo, T. *et al.* (2007) Chronic cigarette smoking and havy drinking in human immunodeficiency virus: consequences for neurocognition and brain morphology. *Alcohol*, **41**, 489–501.

34. Woolf, S. and Maisto, S. (2009) Alcohol use and risk of HIV infection among men who have sex with men. *AIDS Behav.*, **13** (4), 757–782.

35. Parsons, J., Rosof, E. and Mustanski, B. (2008) Medication adherence mediates the relationship between adherence self-efficacy and biological assessments of HIV heath among those with alcohol use disorders. *AIDS Behav.*, **12**, 95–103.

36. Finucane, M., Samet, J., and Horton, N. (2007) Translational methods in biostatistics: linear mixed effect regression models of alcohol consumption and HIV disease progression over time. *Epidemiol Perspect Innov.*, **4**, 8.

37. Lazo, M. *et al.* (2007) Patterns and predictors of changes in adherence to highly active antiretroviral therapy: longitudingal study of men and women. *Clin. Infect. Dis.*, **45**, 1377–1385.

38. Kim, T. *et al.* (2007) Factors associated with discontinuation of antiretroviral therapy in HIV-infected patients with alcohol problems. *AIDS Care*, **19**, 1039–1047.

39. Professionals, N.A.f.A., Issue brief: the importance of addiction prevention, intervention, and treatment in addressing the nation's HIV/AIDS epidemic. amfAR The Foundation for AIDS Research.

40. Chao, C. *et al.* (2008) Recreational drug use and T lymphocyte subpopulations in HIV-uninfected and HIV-infected men. *Drug Alcohol Depend*, **94**, 165–171.

41. Goedert, J. (1984) Recreational drugs: relationship to AIDS. *Ann. N.Y. Acad. Sci.*, **437**, 192–199.

42. Rios-Olivares, E. *et al.* (2006) Impaired cytokine production and suppressed lymphocyte proliferation activity in HCV-infected cocaine and heroin ("speedball") users. *Drug Alcohol Depend*, **85**, 236–243.

43. In, S. *et al.* (2005) Methamphetamine administration produces immunomodulation in mice. *J. Toxicol. Environ. Health A*, **68**, 2133–2145.

44. Mattick, R. *et al.* (2003) Buprenorphine veresus methadone maintenance therapy: a randomized double-blind trial with 405 opoid-dependent patients. *Addiction*, **98**, 441–452.

45. Laufer, F. (2001) Cost-effectiveness of syringe exchange as an HIV prevention strategy. *J. Acquir. Immune Defic. Syndr.*, **28**, 273–278.

46. Lucas, G. *et al.* (2006) Directly administered antiretroviral therapy in methadone clinics is associated with improved HIV treatment outcomes, compared with outcomes among concurrent comparison groups. *Clin. Infect. Dis.*, **42**, 1628–1635.

47. Arnsten, J. *et al.* (2002) Impact of active drug use on antiretroviral therapy adherence and viral suppression in drug users. *J. Gen. Intern. Med.*, **17**, 377–381.

48. Golin, C. *et al.* (2002) A prospective study of predictors of adherence to combination antiretroviral medications. *J. Gen. Intern. Med.*, **17**, 756–765.

49. PoAGfAA. (2008) Guidelines for the use of antiretroviral agents in HIV-1-infected adults and adolescents. Department of Health and Human Services.

50. Thorpe, L. *et al.* (2004) Effect of hard-drug use on CD4 cell percentage, HIV RNA level, and progression to AIDS-defining classs C events among HIV-infected women. *J. Acquir Immune Defic. Syndr.*, **37**, 1423–1430.

17

Addictive disorders in cardiovascular medicine

Alan H. Gradman and Nosheen Javed

Division of Cardiovascular Diseases, The Western Pennsylvania Hospital, Temple University School of Medicine (Clinical Campus), Pittsburgh, Pennsylvania, USA

17.1 INTRODUCTION

Addiction to drugs and alcohol constitutes an important factor in the development and progression of a variety of cardiovascular conditions. Because addictive behavior is compulsive, the cardiovascular system of an addicted individual is exposed to high doses of a particular chemical entity on a regular and recurring basis. Many drugs have a neutral or even beneficial effect on the cardiovascular system when taken in moderation, but produce toxic effects when administered at high dosage over prolonged periods. The impact of substance addiction is, therefore, a function not only of the addictive substance but of addiction itself, which leads to exaggerated drug exposure.

Addictive drugs may contribute to the manifestations of cardiovascular diseases in two fundamental ways. A drug may promote the *development* of disease by contributing to its pathogenesis. An example is the adverse impact of cigarette smoking on vascular biology promoting the development of atherosclerosis. Alternatively, addiction may *exacerbate* an existing condition, becoming operative only after end organ disease is established. The patient with underlying coronary artery disease who develops a myocardial infarction after exposure to cocaine illustrates this phenomenon. In some conditions, such as alcoholic cardiomyopathy, the toxic substance may contribute both to disease development and to its progression. In all cases, the severity of addiction and the subjective barrier to drug cessation constitute major factors determining long term outcome. In this chapter, relevant aspects of the epidemiology, pharmacology, clinical presentation, and treatment of specific addictions are presented. Emphasis is placed on information useful in informing the practitioner and guiding medical practice.

17.2 TOBACCO

17.2.1 Prevalence

Among the addictions discussed in this chapter, tobacco accounts for the vast preponderance of adverse cardiovascular outcomes. According to the World Health Organization (WHO), approximately five million deaths worldwide were attributable to cigarette smoking in 2002 [1]. According to data from Framingham, smoking reduces average life expectancy in men and women by 8.7 and 7.6 years, respectively [2]. Although tobacco exerts adverse effects on multiple organs, it takes its greatest toll on cardiovascular health. Epidemiologic studies demonstrate that smoking increases the risk of myocardial infarction (MI), fatal coronary artery disease (CAD), stroke, and peripheral vascular disease in both men and women. In the United States, approximately 138 000 deaths annually are related to the use of tobacco, accounting for approximately 20% of all cardiovascular deaths [3].

The prevalence of tobacco use in patients with established cardiovascular disease exceeds that seen in the general population, particularly in men. Khot analyzed data from 122 458 patients enrolled in 14 international trials involving CAD patients. It was found that 29.5% of women and 41.6% of men were current cigarette smokers, and that smoking was the most common coronary risk factor in males [4].

17.2.2 Pathophysiology

Cigarette smoking exerts its deleterious effects primarily on the vasculature; most of its cardiovascular consequences are linked to the development of atherosclerosis and its complications [5]. The severity of angiographically determined coronary atherosclerosis and the number of new atherosclerotic lesions is related directly to cigarette smoking [6,7]. Smoking has been linked to progression of atherosclerosis in the thoracic aorta and to carotid intimal media thickness (IMT) assessed by ultrasound techniques [8,9]. In the presence of established atherosclerosis, smoking promotes thrombosis, which is usually the proximate cause of acute MI and stroke [10,11].

The effects of smoking on atherosclerosis development appear to be related primarily to free radical formation producing *oxidative stress* (Figure 17.1). There are two phases of cigarette smoke, the tar or particulate phase which makes up 8% of inhaled smoke, and the gaseous phase that constitutes the remaining 92%. Nicotine appears in the particulate phase and is the addictive component of cigarette smoke. Both phases contain very high concentrations of free radicals [5,12].

Free radicals exert their harmful effects by reducing the availability of nitric oxide (NO) leading to endothelial dysfunction, the initiating step in atherosclerosis development. Nitric oxide is a vasodilator released by the endothelium, and also responsible for maintaining multiple aspects of vascular health. Nitric oxide regulates vascular tone, platelet activation, leucocyte adhesion, inflammation, and the balance between thrombosis and thrombolysis. These cellular processes are directly involved in the development of atherosclerosis and its thromboembolic complications [13–15]. Nicotine also causes transient elevation in blood pressure (BP) and heart rate (HR) through sympathetic stimulation leading to increased myocardial oxygen demand [16]. Cigarette smoke has also been shown to increase lipid peroxidation leading to the formation of foam cells, an integral event in the progression of atherosclerosis [17].

17.2.3 Cardiovascular risk

17.2.3.1 Coronary heart disease

The link between cigarette smoking and myocardial infarction (MI) has been documented for all ethnic groups and both sexes [18]. This association was first reported in the 1950s, was highlighted by the Framingham Heart Study in 1960 [19], and has been

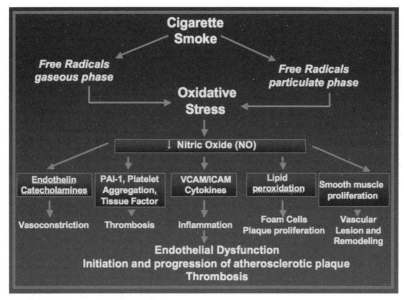

Figure 17.1   Pathogenesis of cardiovascular dysfunction related to cigarette smoking

confirmed in subsequent epidemiologic investigations. The INTERHEART study was a recent global case-control study that enrolled 27 089 patients from 52 countries and investigated the association of various risk factors with MI occurrence. Current smoking was associated with an increased risk of nonfatal MI with an odds ratio (OR) of 2.95 compared to nonsmokers. The relationship was dose dependent and risk increased by 5.6% for every cigarette smoked per day. Chewing tobacco was also associated with an increased MI risk (OR 2.23), and smokers who also chewed tobacco exhibited a greater than fourfold increase in risk. In young smokers <50 years of age, tobacco use was associated with the majority (58%) of acute infarctions [20].

Several studies have emphasized the risks of smoking in women, a group which is relatively resistant to the development of coronary artery disease (CAD) prior to menopause. In one study, MI incidence increased threefold in men and sixfold in women who smoked ≥20 cigarettes a day compared to nonsmokers [21]. A recent study evaluated the age of presentation of first myocardial infarction in Norwegian patients. Male smokers presented eight years earlier than nonsmoking counterparts, whereas women who smoked presented an average of 14 years earlier [22]. Whether these differences

reflect the generally lower incidence of CAD in women or true sex-related differences in the effects of smoking is unclear.

Smoking is unique among addictions in its ability to confer cardiovascular risk on individuals who do not themselves smoke but who are exposed to tobacco through the actions of others. Second-hand smoke is associated with a graded increase in risk related to duration of exposure. In the INTERHEART Study OR for MI was 1.24 in individuals who were least exposed (1–7 h per week) and 1.62 in people who were most exposed (>21 h per week). It was estimated that exposure to second-hand smoke for more than one hour per week accounted for 15.4% of MIs in individuals who had never smoked [20].

Patients with established coronary heart disease (CHD) who continue to smoke have a higher risk of cardiovascular mortality, recurrent MI, and sudden cardiac death compared to nonsmokers and former smokers. In one study, the risk of a recurrent coronary events increased by 51% in patients who continued to smoke after a first MI [23]. In a cohort of 3000 CAD patients, the hazard ratio for sudden death in patients who continue to smoke was 2.47 [24]. In a 20-year follow-up of 985 patients following coronary by-pass surgery, persistent smokers had a 75% increase in the risk of cardio-vascular death compared with patients who stopped smoking for at least one year. Quitters were also less likely to undergo repeat coronary artery bypass graft (CABG) or percutaneous coronary interven-tion (PCI) [25]. In a study of 2000 patients who underwent successful percutaneous coronary inter-vention at the Mayo Clinic, a 16-year follow-up showed that persistent smokers had a greater rela-tive risk of death, 1.76, and of Q-wave infarction, 2.08, than nonsmokers [26].

Smoking cessation reduces mortality risk after MI. In a meta-analysis which included 5878 patients derived from 12 studies, the risk of death was reduced by 46% in quitters compared to patients who continued to smoke. Only 13 patients would have to stop smoking to prevent one unne-cessary death [27].

17.2.3.2 Stroke

Cigarette smoking is associated with ischemic and hemorrhagic stroke as well as subarachnoid hemorrhage. Among the various types of stroke, the association is strongest for subarachnoid hemorrhage with a reported RR of 2.14. For ischemic and hemorrhagic stroke – which constitute the vast majority of clinical events – the risk was increased by 31% and 37% respectively [28]. In the Framingham database, the RR of stroke in heavy smokers (>40 cigarettes/day) was twice that in light smokers (<10 cigarettes/d) [29]. In a Kaiser Per-manente Study that followed >1 million American women of reproductive age, those who smoked and took oral contraceptives exhibited a greater than threefold increase in the risk of hemorrhagic stroke [30].

Smoking cessation reduces stroke risk with the lowest risk levels observed after five years. The risk returns to the same level as nonsmokers in light smokers (<20 cigarettes/d) but remains elevated in heavy smokers (RR = 2.2). In the British Regional Heart Study, risk of recurrent stroke in patients who quit smoking within five years of an index event was reduced by more than half compared to those who continued to smoke [31].

17.2.3.3 Peripheral vascular disease

There is a strong association between smoking and peripheral atherosclerotic vascular disease and aor-tic aneurysm. There is a dose-response relationship between cigarette smoking and aortic aneurysm. The OR for development of an abdominal aortic aneurysm (AAA) increases from 2.75 for indivi-duals with a 1–19 pack/year smoking history to 9.55 for those with >50 pack/year [32]. The risk of AAA related mortality increases by fourfold in current smokers and twofold in former smokers compared to nonsmokers [28].

One of the most devastating vascular diseases associated with smoking is Buerger's Disease or Thromboangitis Obliterans. This inflammatory arteritis is a segmental vasoocclusive disease which is not atherosclerotic and is thought to be an immu-nologic reaction to tobacco. Buerger's Disease usually presents before the age of 45 with rest pain in the extremities and often leads to gangrene and amputations. The disease is extremely rare in non-smokers and has an overall prevalence in smokers of approximately 12/100 000 cases. The only treat-ment is complete discontinuation of all tobacco products. In patients who continue to smoke, ampu-tations are required in nearly 50% [33].

17.2.3.4 Cor pulmonale

Cigarette smoking is the leading cause of chronic obstructive pulmonary disease (COPD) which affects ∼15 million people in the United States. Of these, 5–7% will develop the syndrome of *cor pulmonale,* a type of right-sided heart failure sec-ondary to lung disease and pulmonary hyperten-sion. Cor pulmonale typically presents with symp-toms of dyspnea and signs of pulmonary disease such as increased chest diameter and bronchos-pasm. On physical examination, jugular venous distention, lower extremity edema, a right paraster-nal heave, and the pansystolic murmur of tricuspid regurgitation are often present [34]. Patients with cor pulmonale are prone to the development of cardiac arrhythmias especially atrial arrhythmias such as paroxysmal atrial tachycardia, atrial flutter, atrial fibrillation, and multifocal atrial tachycardia. The five-year survival is approximately 30%.

17.2.3.5   *Congenital heart defects*

Congenital heart defects occur in 8–10/1000 live births and are the most prevalent congenital birth defects found in the United States population [35]. Smoking increases the risk of heart defects in infants whose mothers smoke during pregnancy. In a case-control study, smoking one month prior to conception and during the first trimester of pregnancy was linked to atrial and ventricular septal defects and right-sided obstructive abnormalities such as pulmonic stenosis. Second-hand smoke has not been convincingly associated with birth defects [36].

17.2.4   Smoking cessation

Smoking cessation is a valuable, cost-effective strategy for both primary and secondary prevention of cardiovascular disease. In addition to direct benefits to smokers, smoking cessation reduces cardiovascular risk for family members by reducing exposure to second-hand smoke and, in females, by eliminating risk to unborn children. However, nicotine is addictive and smoking cessation is a difficult task. To maximize results, a comprehensive behavioral and pharmacological approach is required.

It is important for the clinician to take advantage of critical life events to increase the patient's commitment to stop using tobacco. Patients are especially receptive to advice regarding smoking cessation at the time of an acute coronary event. The concern of a pregnant woman for her unborn child and the dangers which second-hand smoke pose to the child after delivery can be a powerful inducement to smoking cessation. The thoughtful clinician should remain alert for other psychological openings which may be operative in individual patients.

Behavioral approaches include a concerted counseling effort by the physician with careful follow-up preferably through a specialized smoking cessation clinic or support group. It is important to encourage the patient to choose a quit date and to assist him/her through counseling and pharmacological replacement therapies. Group therapy involving lectures, interaction with other people, and role playing are of considerable value in assisting smokers in coping with nicotine withdrawal and adopting strategies to prevent relapse. One year quit rates of about 20% have been reported after completion of such programs [37,38].

17.2.5   Pharmacological approaches to smoking cessation

Drug treatment may be used to suppress the symptoms of nicotine withdrawal which include anxiety, irritability, depressed mood, and weight gain. Nicotine-containing gums, lozenges, nasal sprays, inhalers, and transdermal patches are widely available. These agents provide 40–50% of the nicotine levels achieved with smoking and greatly decrease withdrawal symptoms [39]. The highest quit rates are seen with those transdermal preparations which deliver a high nicotine replacement dose and stable steady state nicotine concentrations. When combined with behavioral interventions, quit rates are doubled. Studies have reported smoking cessation rates of 12–25% over a period of 1–3 years. Full dose therapy with the 21 mg patch is recommended for 4–6 weeks. Most studies show no additional benefit of extending treatment beyond eight weeks [40–42].

There have been concerns regarding the safety of nicotine replacement therapy in CAD patients. Nicotine in cigarettes increases myocardial oxygen demand by increasing heart rate and blood pressure [43]. It also causes the release of neurotransmitters and may induce coronary vasoconstriction [44]. Nevertheless, nicotine replacement therapy has been shown to be safe in a large number of studies in patients without [45,46] as well as with CAD [47,48]. However, in a retrospective study of critically ill ICU patients, Lee *et al* found that nicotine replacement was independently associated with increased mortality [49]. In a larger study, though, 374 patients presenting with acute coronary syndrome were randomized to receive nicotine replacement therapy beginning during hospitalization and followed for a one-year period. There was no difference in mortality between treatment groups [50]. The consensus of opinion is that nicotine replacement therapy is safe in patients with CAD who are not critically ill.

Other pharmacologic approaches to smoking cessation are available. Quit rates of 25–30% have been reported with the antidepressant bupropion given at a dose of 150 mg twice daily [51,52].

Veranicline, a partial nicotinic receptor agonist, is the newest agent approved for smoking cessation. In a comparative study, veranicline was more effective than bupropion or placebo when given at a dose of 1 mg bid for 12 weeks. Using this regimen, one study reported quit rates of 44% for veranicline compared to 29.5% for bupropion and 17.7% for placebo after 12 weeks of therapy. After 52 weeks of follow-up, however, only 23% of participants in the varanicline group remained abstinent compared with 14.6% treated with bupropion and 10.3% who received placebo [52,53].

17.3 ALCOHOL

17.3.1 Pathophysiology

The effect of alcohol consumption on cardiovascular health is best explained by a J-shaped curve (Figure 17.2). Low-to-moderate alcohol consumption (1–2 drinks per day) is associated with lower cardiovascular mortality compared to complete abstention [54]. [A standard alcoholic drink contains 0.5 ounces – approximately 11–14 g – of alcohol, the amount found in 1.5 fl oz of spirit,

5 fl oz of wine, or 12 fl oz of beer.] Despite the hypothesis that certain types of alcoholic beverage (notably red wine) might be more beneficial than others, available evidence indicates that it is the amount of alcohol consumed and not the particular beverage chosen that is responsible for cardiovascular protective effects [55].

There are inherent differences in alcohol metabolism between men and women. Women have lower alcohol dehydogenase levels in the stomach

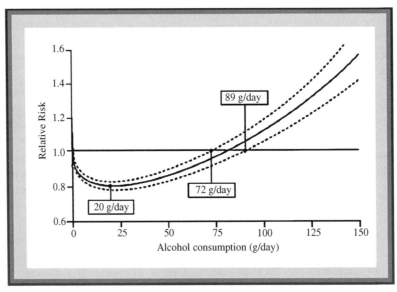

Figure 17.2 J-Shaped curve representing the relationship between alcohol consumption and coronary heart disease. Middle line represents the results of meta-analysis. Upper and lower lines represent confidence intervals. Source: Ref. [10]

and develop higher blood alcohol levels compared to men after consuming identical amounts of alcohol [56]. The safe drinking threshold is therefore lower in women than in men.

Higher consumption levels or binge drinking is associated with an increased incidence of hypertension, dilated cardiomyopathy, atrial fibrillation, stroke, and sudden cardiac death. Not surprisingly, it is common to see high levels of alcohol consumption in patients presenting with these conditions. The prevalence of excessive alcohol consumption in patients with dilated cardiomyopathy ranges from 3–40% [57–59].

17.3.2   Cardiovascular risk

17.3.2.1   Coronary heart disease

Low-to-moderate alcohol consumption significantly reduces CHD risk. There is an inverse relationship between low-to-moderate alcohol consumption and cardiovascular mortality in both men and women, mostly related to lower risk of myocardial infarction [60–62]. One study reported RR for CHD incidence and mortality of 0.62 and 0.73 respectively for men and 0.51 and 0.55 for women who consumed 2–7 drinks per week [63]. In patients with known CHD, mortality is reduced by ~20% with these levels of alcohol consumption [64].

Several mechanisms may explain the cardioprotective effects of alcohol. A meta-analysis evaluating the effects of alcohol on lipid parameters concluded that 30 g of ethanol a day increased HDL by 4 mg/dl, apolipoprotein A I by 8.8 mg/dl, and triglycerides by 5.7 mg/dl. Hemostatic factors such as fibrinogen and tissue type plasminogen activator (tPA) were favorably affected. Based upon the associations between these biomarkers and CHD risk, it was estimated that 30 g of alcohol/day would reduce CHD risk by 25% [65].

Binge drinking and heavy drinking are associated with adverse cardiovascular outcomes. The British Regional Heart Study followed 7735 men for eight years and reported a twofold increase in sudden death risk in individuals consuming >6 drinks/

day [66]. Heavy alcohol consumption affects cardiac electrophysiologic properties, increasing vulnerability for potentially fatal ventricular arrhythmias [67–69]. In patients who have sustained an MI, binge drinking is also associated with a higher risk of recurrent infarction and a doubling of mortality [70].

17.3.2.2   Hypertension

Heavy alcohol consumption is correlated with the development of hypertension in observational studies. The effect is dose related and risk rises with >3 drinks/day in both sexes and all racial groups [71–73]. Klatsky demonstrated in his landmark study that subjects who consumed >3 drinks per day had twice the prevalence of hypertension compared to abstainers [71]. The worldwide INTERSALT study reported that men who drank 3–5 drinks per day had systolic/diastolic blood pressure on average 2.7/1.6 mm Hg higher than nondrinkers; men who drank ≥5 drinks per day had pressures of 4.6/3.0 mmHg higher. For women, heavy drinkers (≥3 drinks per d) had blood pressures that were 3.9/3.1 mmHg higher than nondrinkers [74]. Multiple mechanisms have been implicated in the pathogenesis of alcohol-related hypertension including sympathetic stimulation, increased renal sodium sensitivity, impaired endothelial function, and increased corticosteroid levels.

In patients with hypertension, heavy alcohol consumption may increase cardiovascular morbidity and mortality by further increasing BP. Low-to-moderate alcohol consumption, however, decreases MI risk and mortality in hypertensive men [55,75]. Heavy drinkers with hypertension should be advised to decrease alcohol intake to <3 drinks per day. In alcoholics, abstinence clearly reduces BP [76]. In one study involving 42 alcoholic men consuming >100 g/day of alcohol, one month of abstinence led to a reduction of 7.2 mm Hg for 24-hour systolic BP and 6.6 mm Hg for diastolic BP [77]. However, as noted earlier, moderate alcohol consumption is beneficial in hypertensive patients and the decision to recommend complete abstention should be individualized.

17.3.2.3 Stroke

The relationship of alcohol consumption and stroke is complex. It varies with geographic location and the prevalent type of stroke seen in different ethnic populations. In the United States and most Western countries, ischemic stroke outnumbers hemorrhagic stroke by 4 : 1. In these regions, light-to-moderate alcohol consumption up to two drinks per day leads to a decrease in both total and ischemic stroke [78]. In contrast, in countries like Japan where hemorrhagic stroke is much more common, even moderate drinking is associated with a higher stroke incidence [79].

Hemorrhagic stroke exhibits a linear relationship to alcohol consumption. Several pathophysiologic mechanisms have been proposed. As noted earlier, alcohol reduces fibrinogen and increases t-PA levels and can also impair platelet function. Alcoholic liver disease can lead to reduced production of clotting factors. Increasing amounts of alcohol are also associated with fibrinoid necrosis of cerebral vessels resulting in microaneurysms, a common source of intracerebral bleeding [80]. Heavy alcohol intake is associated with an increase in all types of stroke. In a large meta-analysis, a RR of 1.64 was observed for total stroke, 1.69 for ischemic stroke, and 2.18 for hemorrhagic stroke in patients consuming >60 g/d [78].

17.3.2.4 Cardiomyopathy

Alcohol, when consumed in large amounts on a chronic basis causes cardiomyopathy. Alcohol and its metabolite, acetaldehyde, have direct myocardial depressant effects in animal models and in man [81,82]. These effects are both acute and chronic. Acute cellular changes include dilation of the sarcoplasmic reticulum of cardiomyocytes. Chronically, myofibrillar degeneration, mitochondrial swelling and cellular edema are seen. There is altered calcium flux across the sarcoplasmic reticulum, decreased protein synthesis, and alteration in myocardial energy stores [83]. Nutritional deficiencies seen in alcoholics – particularly thiamine deficiency (beriberi) – can also lead to heart failure.

Unlike alcoholic cardiomyopathy, heart failure associated with beriberi is a high output state induced by widespread vasodilation.

Patients with heavy chronic alcohol consumption are more likely to exhibit reduced ejection fraction, histological changes of cardiomyopathy, higher left ventricular mass, and symptomatic heart failure. One third of patients entering a rehabilitation program after consuming a mean of 243 g of alcohol per day for 16 years had an LVEF <55% [83]. Another study noted an 18% prevalence of subclinical LV dysfunction in 162 alcoholics entering a rehab program [84]. Conversely, low-to-moderate alcohol consumption protects against the development of heart failure [85,86]. The hazard ratio for heart failure among men consuming 8–14 drinks per week was 0.41 compared with those who consumed <1 drink per week in the Framingham Heart Study [87].

In patients with ischemic cardiomyopathy, data from Studies Of Left Ventricular Dysfunction (SOLVD) showed that light-to-moderate drinking reduced both overall mortality and mortality related to myocardial infarction. This effect was not seen in patients with nonischemic cardiomyopathy [88]. However, continued alcohol use in large amounts reduces survival in patients with alcoholic cardiomyopathy (Figure 17.3). Abstinence leads to improvement in ejection fraction over a period of several months with a mean increase from 29% to 36% in one study [89]. In general, treatment of alcoholic cardiomyopathy should follow the same principles as other dilated cardiomyopathies. In patients who continue to drink, thiamine supplementation is indicated. Abstinence from alcohol is the cornerstone of treatment.

17.3.2.5 Arrhythmias

Binge drinking is associated with acute cardiac arrhythmias, a phenomenon which has been termed the holiday heart syndrome. This was defined as a cardiac rhythm and/or conduction disturbance, most commonly a supraventricular tachyarrhythmia, associated with acute ingestion of large quantities of alcohol in a person without other evidence

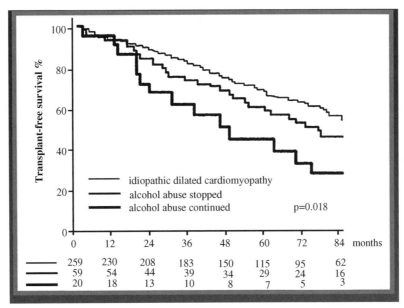

Figure 17.3 Seven year transplant free survival in patients with idiopathic dilated cardiomyopathy. Numbers below X-axis indicate the patients at risk at each time. Source: Ref. [89]

of heart disease. Ettinger, who first described *holiday heart syndrome*, reported 32 cases of supraventricular and ventricular arrhythmias seen after binge drinking. The most common arrhythmia was atrial fibrillation [90]. Compared to patients who experience arrhythmias in the absence of alcohol consumption, ECGs performed after acute alcohol consumption may demonstrate prolongation of the PR, QRS, and QT intervals. These findings can be used as helpful clues in making a diagnosis of alcohol-related arrhythmias.

17.3.2.6   Congenital heart defects

In most but not all studies, maternal alcohol consumption during pregnancy has been linked to conotruncal defects such as transposition of great arteries and other outflow tract defects in the fetus [91,92]. Ingestion of more than one drink per week has been shown to result in a nearly twofold increase in these defects [93]. The weight of the evidence dictates that alcohol intake during pregnancy should be completely avoided.

17.3.3   Treating patients with alcohol addiction and cardiovascular disease

Once patients with problem drinking patterns and/ or alcohol dependence are identified, efforts should be made to reduce alcohol intake. The approach to treatment in patients with cardiovascular diseases is more complex because of the beneficial effect of moderate drinking. Patients who are not alcohol addicted but demonstrate high risk drinking patterns should be advised to decrease their consumption. If possible, light-to-moderate drinking can be maintained. Once alcohol dependence develops, the amount of alcohol consumed far exceeds the level of any health benefit and alcohol becomes a cardiovascular risk factor. It is, therefore, important to recommend abstinence. Both behavioral and pharmacological approaches should be employed. None of the pharmacological agents used to treat alcohol addiction, including naltrexone, acamprosate or nalmafene, have adverse cardiovascular effects. These agents can be used safely in patients with any cardiovascular condition.

17.4   COCAINE

17.4.1   Pathophysiology

Cocaine is derived from coca leaves and has been used by the Indians of South America for medicinal purposes since ancient times. Coca leaves are still chewed in the Andes as a remedy for mountain sickness. When ingested in this fashion, coca suppresses fatigue and hunger and increases energy and endurance. The beneficial effects of coca were reluctantly acknowledged by the Spanish who conquered the Inca Empire in the sixteenth century. They initially banned coca, but soon discovered that the natives could barely work the fields and gold mines without it; later it was distributed to the workers three or four times daily. Although physiologic studies are lacking, this history suggests that low dose cocaine (about a ton of coca leaves are required to make a kilogram of cocaine) may have salutary cardiovascular effects.

Although reliable figures are difficult to obtain, a national household survey conducted in the United States in 2002 and 2003 found that 14.4% of adults (aged 12 years or older) reported lifetime experience of cocaine use. Use within the past 12 months was reported by 2.5%. Among males age 18–25 years, the lifetime prevalence of cocaine use was 18.1% and recent use was reported in 8.4% [94]. The higher rate of cocaine use in young men accounts, in large measure, for the demographics of many of the cocaine-induced cardiovascular disorders discussed below.

Most of the toxicity associated with cocaine is acute and cardiovascular complaints are the most frequent cause for emergency room (ER) visits in cocaine abusers [95]. In urban medical centers, 5–10% of ER visits are related to cardiovascular complications of cocaine [96]. In the acute setting, cocaine is associated with myocardial ischemia and infarction, cardiac arrhythmias, uncontrolled hypertension, stroke, and aortic dissection. In a study of 359 patients presenting to suburban emergency departments with chest pain, 17% tested positive for cocaine [97]. A survey from Dallas noted a 13%

prevalence of cocaine use as determined by urine screening among ER patients with diastolic BP $\geq$120 mm Hg [98]. In 248 young Americans between the ages of 15 and 44 who developed a stroke, there was a 27% prevalence of cocaine addiction among African Americans and 38% among Caucasians [99]. A review of 38 cases of acute aortic dissection presenting over a 20-year period to an inner city hospital in San Francisco revealed that 14 (37%) were associated with cocaine use [100]. These high figures may reflect the largely inner city populations from which they are derived, and may not be representative of the general population. Nevertheless, physicians should include cocaine toxicity in the differential diagnosis of acute cardiovascular conditions, particularly in younger individuals.

17.4.2   Pharmacology

The primary pharmacologic effect of cocaine and its active metabolite, norcocaine, is to inhibit the synaptic reuptake of norepinephrine by sympathetic neurons. Reuptake of dopamine and serotonin by dopaminergic and serotonergic nerve endings is also inhibited. The result is enhancement of sympathetic stimulation and activation of both alpha- and beta-adrenergic receptors [101]. This leads to an acute increase in HR of 17 ± 16 beats per minute and mean BP of 8 ± 7 mm Hg [102]. Myocardial contractility and cardiac output are also augmented. These effects increase myocardial oxygen demand. Cocaine also increases the release of endothelin [103], a powerful vasoconstrictor, and decreases the release of nitric oxide, a powerful vasodilator. These latter effects contribute to the vasospasm induced by cocaine in different vascular beds and to its hypertensive effects [104]. There are some animal and human data to suggest that cocaine may also promote progression of atherosclerosis, presumably as a result of sympathetic activation [105]. Figure 17.4.

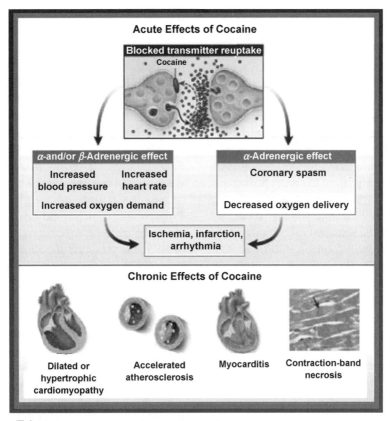

Figure 17.4   Selected acute and chronic effects of cocaine on the heart. Source: Ref. [106]

17.4.3   Cardiovascular risk

17.4.3.1   Coronary heart disease

Acute myocardial ischemia and infarction are the most common adverse cardiovascular consequences of cocaine. In cocaine users presenting to the ER with chest pain, the incidence of MI has been found to be 0.7–8% [107–109]. In one study, the estimated risk of myocardial infarction was increased 24 times over baseline in the 60 minutes following cocaine self-administration [110]. The timing of MI after cocaine use varies from minutes to four days, and its occurrence does not appear to be dose related [111]. The majority of MIs in cocaine users is non-Q wave (68%), but Q-wave infarctions are also seen [112]. Most patients who develop cocaine-induced MI are young, non-Cauacasian cigarette smokers with no previous history of CAD [110,112]. In a study involving younger patients (18–45 years) with acute

myocardial infarction, fully 25% were associated with use of cocaine [113].

There are several mechanisms by which cocaine contributes to the development of myocardial ischemia and infarction. Mismatch between myocardial oxygen supply and demand may be important, particularly in patients with pre-existing coronary atherosclerosis. Coronary thrombosis may be precipitated by activation of platelets and the coagulation cascade. A critical pathophysiologic mechanism appears to be coronary vasospasm mediated by alpha-adrenergic receptor stimulation. In studies performed in the cardiac catheterization laboratory, coronary artery diameter decreases significantly in diseased as well as nondiseased segments in response to cocaine administration [114,115].

Patients presenting with cocaine-induced chest pain have an abnormal ECG in 56–84% of cases. ECG abnormalities include ST segment elevation, ST segment depression, increased QRS voltage [116], and a Brugada-like pattern consisting of right bundle branch block with ST-segment elevation in leads V_1 through V_3 [117]. These abnormalities include normal variants and other ECG findings often seen in young individuals, such as early repolarization syndrome and left ventricular hypertrophy. Particularly confusing is the early repolarization pattern consisting of concave upward ST elevation (Figure 17.5). Patients with this finding may present with atypical chest pain and ST elevation in the absence of myocardial ischemia or infarction. Coronary vasospasm may also result in ST segment elevation, reflecting transient transmural ischemia without infarction. Overall, the diagnostic sensitivity/specificity of the ECG for detecting a true MI lare only 36% and 90%, respectively [108]. Cardiac biomarkers, especially troponins, are more specific for the diagnosis of MI in cocaine users. Troponin measurement is preferred over creatinine kinase (CPK-MB) that can be elevated even in the absence of MI from factors such as muscle injury and rhabdomyolysis [118]. In cases of diagnostic uncertainty, echocardiography may be useful in detecting new cardiac wall motion abnormalities resulting from ischemia.

17.4.3.2 Clinical management

Because it influences treatment, it is important to make the association between cocaine use and myocardial ischemia/infarction in individual patients. Intravenous benzodiazepines should be administered early as they have beneficial effects on cardiac hemodynamics and on the neuropsychiatric manifestations of cocaine addiction [119]. Beta-blockers are contraindicated in acute coronary syndromes related to cocaine use, including acute myocardial infarction. In experimental animal models, beta-blockers decrease coronary blood flow and increase seizure activity and mortality in the setting of cocaine administration, related in part to unopposed alpha-adrenergic stimulation [120]. Propranolol, esmolol and labetalol have all been shown to increase either coronary vasoconstriction or BP in the presence of cocaine. Labetalol, despite its alpha-blocking properties, does not reduce coronary vasospasm induced by cocaine [121–125]. Non-dihydropyridine calcium channel blockers (verapamil and diltiazem) reduce HR and relieve coronary spasm [126]. These agents may be used in this setting but should be avoided in patients with LV dysfunction or hypotension. Nitroglycerin is also useful in treating coronary vasospasm.

Revascularization should be considered in patients with acute myocardial infarction related to cocaine. Because a significant fraction of cocaine users with ST elevation do not have an acute infarction, thrombolytics should generally be avoided. Another reason to avoid thrombolytics is the increased risk of intracranial bleeding seen in

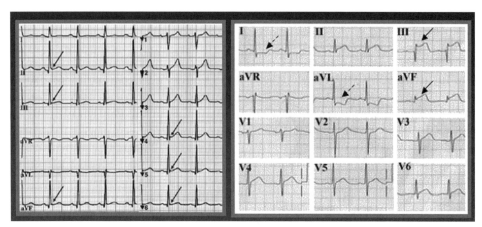

Figure 17.5 Twelve-lead electrocardiogram showing early repolarization pattern on the left and inferior wall ST elevation myocardial infarction on the right. Note the subtle concave ST elevation on the left compared to marked ST elevation accompanied by reciprocal ST depressions (dashed arrows) on the right

these patients [127,128]. The preferred method of revascularization is percutaneous coronary intervention [129–131]. In cases where transmural MI is suspected due to clinical presentation, ECG, and/or troponin elevation, early catheterization is indicated to verify the diagnosis and restore blood flow to the infarct-related artery if coronary occlusion is present.

The immediate prognosis in patients with cocaine-associated MI is favorable. Hospital mortality is quite low; this is generally attributed to the younger age of these patients. Once the acute phase is over, cocaine cessation should be a primary focus of management. The outlook in patients who stop using cocaine is good and the incidence of recurrent coronary events or death is low [112,132]. Unfortunately, a majority of patients with cocaine-associated ischemia or infarction continue to misuse cocaine. In one study, 60% of patients presenting with cocaine-induced chest pain reported continued use [133]. It is, therefore, not surprising that many patients with cocaine-induced MI have another ischemic event; one small study reported an incidence of 58% [111].

17.4.3.3   Hypertension

Cocaine causes acute hypertension predominantly through its adrenergic effects; there is no association with chronic hypertension [134]. True hypertensive emergencies imply the presence of end organ dysfunction, such as myocardial ischemia or a dissecting aortic aneurysm, and mandate immediate and aggressive BP reduction. Hypertensive urgencies in which BP is markedly elevated without evidence of acute organ dysfunction may be treated in a more relaxed manner keeping in mind that the BP elevation associated with cocaine use is usually transient. A major goal should be sedation with drugs such as benzodiazepines, which usually helps to control BP in this setting. If drug treatment is still needed after benzodiazepine use, calcium antagonists, nitroglycerin, or alpha-blockers such as phentolamine should be used. Nicardipine is a dihydropyridine calcium channel blocker available for intravenous administration. This agent can be used

to rapidly reduce BP in hypertensive emergencies related to cocaine. In patients with myocardial ischemia or infarction, non-dihydropyridine calcium blockers which reduce HR are preferred. Beta-blockers including labetalol should be avoided [124,135,136].

17.4.3.4   Stroke

Cocaine is a major cause of stroke, especially in young people. The risk of stroke is 14 times higher in a cocaine user compared to an age-matched nonuser [137]. Many cocaine users have additional risk factors for stroke, including tobacco use and heavy alcohol intake. The incidence of hemorrhagic stroke is higher than ischemic stroke in most studies [138]. Cerebral artery aneurysms are commonly seen when autopsies are performed in patients dying of cocaine-associated stroke [138,139]. The precise mechanism of stroke is unclear, but clearly cocaine can cause transient BP elevation and rupture of pre-existent aneurysms. Cocaine may also induce cerebral vasospasm, thrombus formation, and vasculitis, all of which may precipitate an ischemic stroke [140].

Management of cocaine-associated stroke uses the general principles of stroke management. Dihydropyridine calcium channel blockers have shown promise in the management of cerebral artery vasospasm associated with cocaine use [141]. Caution should be exercised before using thrombolytics in these patients due to the higher risk of intracranial bleeding and the fact that these patients may have cerebral artery vasospasm rather than thrombosis as the etiology of ischemic stroke [142]. Long term use of antiplatelet agents after an acute event may risk bleeding complications in patients who continue high risk behaviors. Every effort should be made to encourage cessation of cocaine use.

17.4.3.5   Cardiomyopathy

Chronic cocaine use has been associated with the development of a diffuse cardiomyopathy characterized by systolic ventricular dysfunction. In a study evaluating the frequency of asymptomatic left ventricular dysfunction in chronic cocaine users, the prevalence was 7% [84]. The number of patients who develop signs and symptoms of heart failure is considerably less. The proposed mechanisms for cocaine-induced cardiomyopathy include direct toxicity to cardiac muscle cells similar to that seen secondary to catecholamines in patients with pheochromocytoma. Repeated exposure to high catecholamine levels results in intracellular calcium overload and contraction band necrosis on histopathological specimens [143,144]. Another mechanism by which cocaine produces LV dysfunction is via the development of autoimmune myocarditis [145]. Myocarditis has been observed in autopsy specimens obtained from up to 30% of patients dying from cocaine toxicity [146,147]. Myocardial dysfunction may also result from cocaine-induced MI.

Management of asymptomatic LV dysfunction and overt heart failure involves complete abstinence from cocaine. Reversal of cardiomyopathy has been shown to occur with this approach although the exact frequency is unknown [148]. Although chronic beta-blocker therapy is indicated in most patients with dilated cardiomyopathy, these agents should be used with caution if continued cocaine use is suspected. When a beta-blocker is used, the vasodilating beta-blocker carvedilol is preferred.

17.4.3.6   Arrhythmias

Cocaine may precipitate supraventricular and ventricular *arrhythmias* as well as sudden cardiac death [95,101,149]. Occasionally, bradyarrhythmias are seen [150]. Multiple mechanisms have been implicated. As discussed above, cocaine can induce coronary ischemia/infarction and can also cause reperfusion arrhythmias as a consequence of transient coronary occlusion due to vasospasm. Its catecholinergic and vagolytic effects can trigger cardiac arrhythmias. In addition, cocaine has sodium channel blocking properties and can prolong the action potential, widen the QRS, and increase the QT interval. These changes predispose

to the development of potentially fatal ventricular arrhythmias [95].

Management of cocaine-induced arrhythmias involves correcting any underlying cause, such as metabolic acidosis or myocardial ischemia/ infarction. Type 1A antiarrhythmic drugs, such as quinidine, disopyramide and procainamide, should be avoided due to their QT and QRS prolonging effects. Sodium bicarbonate and lidocaine have been shown to be effective for the treatment of ventricular tachycardia and fibrillation [151,152]. Temporary pacing should be undertaken for symptomatic bradyarrhythmias.

17.4.3.7   Aortic dissection

Aortic dissection should be considered as a cause of chest pain in any patient presenting with cocaine use. The incidence of cocaine-associated dissection varies from 1 to 37% of all cases of aortic dissection and depends upon the prevalence of cocaine use in the population studied [100,153]. Acute BP elevation mandates aggressive management as a prelude to emergency corrective surgery. The use of labetalol is controversial and is best avoided, particularly if there is evidence of myocardial ischemia. Intravenous calcium channel blockers, preferably non-dihydropyridines which reduce HR, BP and contractility or IV nitroglycerin, would appear to be agents of choice in this setting [154]. However, controlled studies are lacking.

17.4.3.8   Congenital heart disease

Cocaine use during pregnancy has been linked to congenital heart defects including atrial septal defect, ventricular septal defect, hypoplastic left or right heart syndromes, absent ventricle, coarctation of aorta, aortic valve prolapse, patent ductus arteriosus, and pulmonary stenosis. Cocaine use has also been related to the occurrence of fetal arrhythmias [154,155]. Even patients not committed to permanent cessation of cocaine should be strongly counseled to avoid exposure to the fetus *in utero*.

17.5 AMPHETAMINES

17.5.1 Pathophysiology

Amphetamines are the most widely used stimulant drugs in the United States and the most frequently abused drugs worldwide other than marijuana. They share many characteristics with cocaine. Like cocaine, they are sympathomimetic agents and are responsible for acute cardiovascular events, including myocardial ischemia/infarction, stroke, acute hypertension, and cardiac arrhythmias. In studies of methamphetamine-related fatalities in Australia and the United States, autopsies reveal a high prevalence of coronary atherosclerosis, cardiac enlargement, intracranial and subarachnoid hemorrhage [156,157]. Chronic exposure may lead to cardiomyopathy. Amphetamine use has also been identified as a risk factor for idiopathic pulmonary hypertension. In one series of subjects with this diagnosis, 27% had used amphetamine or methamphetamine, alone or in combination with cocaine [158].

17.5.2 Pharmacology

Amphetamines are synthetic amines that act as indirect neurotransmitters. Methamphetamine can be administered via several routes, including oral, intravenous, intramuscular, pulmonary, nasal, rectal and vaginal. Once in the blood stream, it is incorporated into the cytoplasmic vesicles that normally contain the neurotransmitters epinephrine, norepinephrine, dopamine, and serotonin. As a result, these neurotransmitters are displaced into the neuronal synapses where they activate post-synaptic receptors. The result is adrenergic, dopaminergic, and serotonergic stimulation. Methamphetamine also blocks the reuptake of these neurotransmitters. The only pathway through which they can then be destroyed involves the slow degradation pathway, catechol-o-methyl transferase. This explains the relatively sustained effects of methamphetamine following a single dose [159].

17.5.3 Cardiovascular risk

17.5.3.1 Acute effects

Adrenergic stimulation produced by amphetamines leads to acute elevation in BP and HR [160] and may precipitate cardiac arrhythmias [161]. When taken in large doses, methamphetamine can produce hypotension and acute cardiovascular collapse. The pathogenesis of this syndrome is complex and includes depletion of neurotransmitters, metabolic acidosis, and dehydration. Management of acute cardiovascular collapse requires general cardiopulmonary support, fluid resuscitation, correction of metabolic acidosis, and the use of intravenous norepinephrine for hemodynamic support.

17.5.3.2 Coronary heart disease

Myocardial ischemia and infarction can occur from acute or chronic use of amphetamines [162,163]. In a small study of 33 patients presenting to the ER with chest pain after methamphetamine use, an acute coronary syndrome was diagnosed in nine (25%) [164]. Most were in the fourth decade of life. The pathogenesis appears to be similar to that of cocaine-induced ischemia although far fewer studies have been reported. Patient management should follow the treatment guidelines discussed in the cocaine section.

17.5.3.3 Cardiomyopathy

Amphetamine-induced cardiomyopathy has been reported in the literature [165]. A case-control study of patients <45 years of age concluded that methamphetamine increased the risk of cardiomyopathy by a factor of 3.7 compared to nonusers [166]. The pathogenesis of cardiomyopathy is attributed to the hyperadrenergic state induced by amphetamines. Urinary testing for amphetamines should be considered in younger patients presenting with otherwise unexplained cardiomyopathy.

17.5.3.4 Pulmonary hypertension

Amphetamine use has been associated with idiopathic pulmonary hypertension (PAH) through a number of case reports [167]. More recently, a retrospective review looking at patients with idiopathic PAH found that these patients were 10 times more likely to have used amphetamines alone or in combination with cocaine compared to patients with other risk factor for PAH [158]. The proposed pathophysiology invokes vasospastic and growth modulating effects of norepinephrine and serotonin on smooth muscle cells, the receptors for which are found in the pulmonary vasculature.

17.5.3.5 Miscellaneous

There are reports of aortic dissection, berry aneurysm rupture, and sudden cardiac death associated with amphetamine use [168]. In a series of 413 deaths related to methamphetamine use in San Francisco, there were 10 cases of subarachnoid or intracranial hemorrhage found at autopsy [157]. It is estimated that the mortality rate is four times higher in amphetamine users compared to the general population and is comparable to that of alcoholics and heroin addicts [169].

17.6   PHENCYCLIDINE (PCP)

Phencyclidine is a commonly misused stimulant and hallucinogen that was developed in the 1950s as an anesthetic. It is cheaply and easily synthesized in home laboratories and is available on the street by the names of "Angel dust," "Super Weed," and "Peace pill." It can be administered intravenously, orally or through inhalation.

17.6.1   Pharmacology

PCP has multiple pharmacologic effects. It inhibits norepinephrine, dopamine, and serotonin reuptake, and hence produces adrenergic stimulation. It acts as an antagonist of N methyl D aspartate (NMDA) complex receptor and inhibits the release of excitatory neurotransmitters. It also acts on the opiate receptors.

17.6.2   Cardiac risk

Through its adrenergic effects PCP causes acute tachycardia and hypertension. Blood pressure becomes elevated in >50% of the patients who take the drug and usually resolves in 4–24 hours [170]. Subarachnoid hemorrhage has also been reported and should be suspected in patients presenting with neurological deficits and sustained hypertension. The incidence of sudden death has been reported to be 0.3% [170]. The management of tachycardia and hypertension are similar to cocaine.

17.7   MARIJUANA

Marijuana is the most commonly misused drug in United States. It is derived from the hemp plant, *cannabis*. Marijuana has been used in religious ceremonies on the Indian subcontinent since antiquity. It has been used for its medicinal value as an anesthetic, analgesic, antiemetic and as an appetite stimulant for centuries by the Chinese, Egyptians, Muslims, and Indians. A synthetic cannabinoid, dronabinol, is currently approved in the United States for the treatment of nausea and vomiting associated with cancer chemotherapy and to counteract weight loss in AIDS patients.

17.7.1   Pharmacology

The primary active ingredient of cannabis is tetrahydrocannabinol (THC), which acts on various pharmacologic pathways. It stimulates endogenous cannabinoid receptors in the CNS that are involved in regulation of mood, appetite, cognition, memory, and pain perception. It also affects the immune system. When given acutely, the cardiovascular effects of THC include increased heart rate, blood pressure, cardiac output, and myocardial oxygen demand. It also facilitates AV nodal conduction. THC reduces vascular resistance and may occasionally cause orthostatic hypotension.

17.7.2 Cardiovascular risk

Case reports have described the occurrence of myocardial infarction after marijuana use. In a study that evaluated 124 patients presenting with an MI who had recently used marijuana, the risk of MI within an hour of consumption was estimated to be increased fivefold [171]. In one study of 1913 adults who presented with an MI, the calculated hazard ratio for mortality in weekly marijuana users was 4.2 compared to nonusers. This study suggested that marijuana might worsen outcomes following myocardial infarction [172]. Marijuana use has also been linked to atrial fibrillation and ventricular tachycardia in isolated case reports. The fragmentary evidence of cardiovascular toxicity despite widespread use in the population suggests, however, that any cardiovascular risks associated with marijuana are minimal.

17.8 OPIATES

Although opiates occupy an important place in the study of addiction, their cardiovascular effects are few. The only major cardiovascular complication of long-term opiate use is infective endocarditis in IV heroin users. This complication is discussed in the following section.

17.9 INFECTIVE ENDOCARDITIS

Infective endocarditis (IE) is a life-threatening complication of IV drug addiction, regardless of the drug administered. Whenever a drug is introduced into the bloodstream via the intravenous route, bacteremia may result. Depending upon the virulence of the organism and the susceptibility of the host, valvular structures may become infected. The result is bacteremia accompanied by variable destruction of valvular structures, heart failure, and systemic or pulmonary embolization. Infective endocarditis may be fatal despite aggressive medical and surgical therapies.

The incidence of IE in IV drug abusers is variably estimated at 1–20 per 10 000 injection drug users/year. Individuals with pre-existent congenital or acquired valvular abnormalities are at considerably higher risk. Infective endocarditis is responsible for 5–8% of hospital admissions among injection drug users [173]. A male-to-female ratio between 2 : 1 and 5 : 1 has been reported, and patients tend to be younger than IE patients who are not drug abusers [174,175]. Cocaine use and HIV infection are independent risk factors for the development of IE [176,177].

The risk of endocarditis is attributed to the nonsterile techniques frequently employed by drug addicts and recreational drug users. Trauma to the tricuspid valve and valvular endothelium from particulate matter found in injected material has also been implicated as a pathophysiologic mechanism [178]. IV drug addicts exhibit higher rates of nasal colonization with S. aureus, and this virulent organism is the most common infectious agent seen. The incidence of methicillin-resistant S. aureus is also higher in this population. Streptococcus and enterococcus are the other two common organisms found in these patients. Gram negative rod infections with pseudomonas and serratia are also seen when nonsterile water is used for injections.

Polymicrobial and fungal infections, though uncommon, are also reported [174].

Right-sided valves are affected much more commonly in IV drug users compared to nondrug users, and tricuspid endocarditis is classic. Overall, left-sided valvular involvement is more frequent, however. In a series from Cook County Hospital, right-sided (predominantly tricuspid valve) involvement was seen in 34% of patients and left-sided involvement in 46% (mitral valve 32%, aortic 19%); infection of multiple valves occurred in 13% [175].

Fever is the most common initial complaint, and IE should be considered whenever an IV drug addict presents to the ER with fever. Most patients develop acute as opposed to subacute endocarditis and do not exhibit classic signs, such as splinter hemorrhages, Osler's nodes, Janeway lesions, splenomegaly, and so on. Septic pulmonary emboli from right-sided vegetations are common and patients may present with chest pain and/or hemoptysis. Multiple blood cultures should be obtained and, if positive, transthoracic and/or transesophageal echocardiography performed to visualize vegetations, evaluate valvular function, and establish a definitive diagnosis. Culture-negative endocarditis is occasionally seen. The modified Duke Criteria (Table 17.1) may be helpful in establishing the diagnosis.

Mortality from IE in IV drug users ranges from 7 to 12% in various series [174,175,180]. Left-sided involvement portends a worse prognosis. *P. aeruginosa* infection has a poor prognosis and is associated with mortality of approximately 30%. Outcome is also dependent on vegetation size. Vegetations <1 cm are associated with a better prognosis in terms of cure and survival compared to larger vegetations [180].

Treatment is based on the microbiological sensitivity of organisms. Combinations of IV antibiotics are generally required for 4–6 weeks. Very rarely, patients with uncomplicated tricuspid valve endocarditis in whom IV antibiotic treatment is impossible for psychosocial reasons may be given oral therapy with agents to which the microorganism is sensitive. Close outpatient follow-up is required. Indications for surgery are similar to

Table 17.1 Modified Duke Criteria for diagnosis of infective endocarditis (IE)

Definite IE

Pathological Criteria

- *Microorganism*: demonstrated by culture or histology in a vegetation or in a vegetation that has embolized or in an intracardiac abscess
- *Pathologic lesions*: vegetation or intracardiac abscess confirmed by histology showing active endocarditis

Clinical criteria

- 2 major criteria *or* 1 major and 3 minor criteria *or* 5 minor criteria

Possible IE

1 major criterion and 1 minor criterion *or* 3 minor criteria

Rejected IE

- Firm alternate diagnosis for manifestations of endocarditis
- Resolution of manifestations of IE, with antibiotic therapy for ≤4 d
- No pathologic evidence of IE at surgery or autopsy after antibiotic therapy for ≤4 days
- Does not meet criteria for possible IE, as above

Major criteria

1. Positive blood cultures for IE:
   - Typical microorganism for infective endocarditis from 2 separate blood cultures (*Strep viridans, S. bovis, S. aureus, enterococcus*, HACEK group)
   - Persistently positive blood culture, defined as recovery of a microorganism consistent with IE from: blood cultures drawn >12 h apart OR all of 3 or a majority of ≥4 separate blood cultures, with first and last drawn at least one hour apart
   - Single positive blood culture for Coxiella burnetii or antiphase I IgG antibody titer >1 : 800
2. Evidence of endocardial involvement:
   - Positive echocardiogram for IE (Oscillating intracardiac mass on valve or supporting structures, or in the path of regurgitant jets, or on implanted material, in the absence of an alternative anatomic explanation or abscess or new partial dehiscence of prosthetic valve
   - New valvular regurgitation

Minor criteria

1. *Fever*: 38.0 °C (100.4 °F)
2. *Immunologic phenomena*: glomerulonephritis, Osler's nodes, Roth spots, RF
3. *Vascular phenomena*: major arterial or pulmonary emboli, mycotic aneurysm, intracranial hemorrhage, conjunctival hemorrhages, Janeway lesions
4. *Microbiologic evidence*: Positive culture but not meeting major criterion or serologic evidence of active infection with organism consistent with IE
5. Predisposing heart condition or intravenous drug use

Modified from Ref. [179] and up to Date Online.

other cases of IE and include persistent infection, heart failure, and recurrent embolization. Every effort should be made to discourage future IV drug addiction. Patients who survive but continue to use IV drugs have recurrence rates as high as 20–40% [181].

17.10 CONCLUSIONS

Addictive drugs vary greatly in their cardiovascular toxicity. Opiates and marijuana pose little cardiovascular risk. Alcohol is protective at low-to-moderate consumption rates but leads to strokes, hypertension, and cardiomyopathy with exaggerated exposure. Cocaine may have a beneficial effect at very low dosage when chewed in the Andes but poses major risks of myocardial infarction, stroke, cardiomyopathy, and sudden death when taken in the high dose preparations sold illegally around the world. Tobacco is harmful at almost any dose regardless of the route of administration. Intravenous drug use carries with it a risk of infective endocarditis irrespective of the administered agent.

Prevention and treatment of cardiovascular disease may be directly affected by the presence of addiction. Thus, calcium antagonists rather than beta-blockers should be used to treat myocardial ischemia in cocaine users. The use of anticoagulants should be approached with caution in alcoholics at increased risk of trauma. Providing a source of sterile needles to an intravenous drug addict may constitute the most important available avenue for cardiovascular protection despite an understandable reluctance of physicians to facilitate or enable self-destructive behavior. Achieving cessation of drug use may be directly life saving.

The role of the physician in treating addicted individuals is complex and rarely straightforward. Clearly, it is important to provide accurate information regarding the risks associated with addictive behavior, and to recommend a realistic course of action designed to protect the individual from harm. Frequently, however, individuals are painfully aware of the dangers associated with their actions but remain unwilling or unable to modify them. Attachment to immediate enjoyment despite future risk is a characteristic common to much of mankind. Addiction to drugs and alcohol is an ancient phenomenon and will, no doubt, remain a prominent feature of human behavior. In circumstances in which addiction is ongoing despite medical advice, the physician's responsibility is to use evidence-based approaches to manage the consequences of addiction. In addition, the physician should remain alert to psychological openings which may aid the patient in developing the extremely high level of motivation required to make fundamental lifestyle changes.

REFERENCES

1. Guilbert, J.J. (2003) The world health report 2002 – reducing risks, promoting healthy life. *Educ. Health (Abingdon)*, **16** (2), 230.

2. Mamun, A.A. *et al.* (2004) Smoking decreases the duration of life lived with and without cardiovascular disease: a life course analysis of the Framingham Heart Study. *Eur. Heart J.*, **25** (5), 409–415.

3. Centers for Disease Control and Prevention (2005) Annual smoking-attributable mortality, years of potential life lost, and productivity losses – United States, 1997–2001. *MMWR Morb. Mortal Wkly Rep.*, **54** (25), 625–628.

4. Khot, U.N. *et al.* (2003) Prevalence of conventional risk factors in patients with coronary heart disease. *JAMA*, **290** (7), 898–904.

5. Ambrose, J.A. and Barua, R.S. (2004) The pathophysiology of cigarette smoking and cardiovascular disease: an update. *J. Am. Coll. Cardiol.*, **43** (10), 1731–1737.

6. Ramsdale, D.R. *et al.* (1985) Smoking and coronary artery disease assessed by routine coronary arteriography. *Br. Med. J. (Clin. Res. ed.)*: **290** (6463), 197–200.

7. Waters, D. *et al.* (1996) Effects of cigarette smoking on the angiographic evolution of coronary atherosclerosis. A Canadian Coronary Atherosclerosis Intervention Trial (CCAIT) Substudy. CCAIT Study Group. *Circulation*, **94** (4), 614–621.

8. Inoue, T. *et al.* (1995) Relationship of cigarette smoking to the severity of coronary and thoracic aortic atherosclerosis. *Cardiology*, **86** (5), 374–379.

9. Howard, G. *et al.* (1994) Active and passive smoking are associated with increased carotid wall thickness. The Atherosclerosis Risk in Communities Study. *Arch. Intern. Med.*, **154** (11), 1277–1282.

10. Fusegawa, Y. *et al.* (1999) Platelet spontaneous aggregation in platelet-rich plasma is increased in habitual smokers. *Thromb. Res.*, **93** (6), 271–278.

11. Rival, J., Riddle, J.M., and Stein, P.D. (1987) Effects of chronic smoking on platelet function. *Thromb. Res.*, **45** (1), 75–85.

12. Pryor, W.A. and Stone, K. (1993) Oxidants in cigarette smoke. Radicals, hydrogen peroxide, peroxynitrate, and peroxynitrite. *Ann. NY Acad. Sci.*, **686** 12–27, discussion 27–8.

13. Napoli, C. and Ignarro, L.J. (2001) Nitric oxide and atherosclerosis. *Nitric Oxide*, **5** (2), 88–97.

14. Celermajer, D.S. *et al.* (1993) Cigarette smoking is associated with dose-related and potentially reversible impairment of endothelium-dependent dilation in healthy young adults. *Circulation*, **88** (5 Pt 1), 2149–2155.

15. Mazzone, A. *et al.* (2001) Cigarette smoking and hypertension influence nitric oxide release and plasma levels of adhesion molecules. *Clin. Chem. Lab. Med.*, **39** (9), 822–826.

16. Cryer, P.E. *et al.* (1976) Norepinephrine and epinephrine release and adrenergic mediation of smoking-associated hemodynamic and metabolic events. *N. Engl. J. Med.*, **295** (11), 573–577.

17. Yokode, M. *et al.* (1988) Cholesteryl ester accumulation in macrophages incubated with low density lipoprotein pretreated with cigarette smoke extract. *Proc. Natl. Acad. Sci. USA*, **85** (7), 2344–2348.

18. (2004) The Health Consequences of Smoking: A Report of the Surgeon General. US Department of Health and Human Services.

19. Kannel, W.B., Castelli, W.P., and McNamara, P.M. (1968) Cigarette smoking and risk of coronary heart disease. Epidemiologic clues to pathogensis. The Framingham Study. *Natl. Cancer Inst. Monogr.*, **28**, 9–20.

20. Teo, K.K. *et al.* (2006) Tobacco use and risk of myocardial infarction in 52 countries in the INTER-HEART study: a case-control study. *Lancet*, **368** (9536), 647–658.

21. Njolstad, I., Arnesen, E., and Lund-Larsen, P.G. (1996) Smoking, serum lipids, blood pressure, and sex differences in myocardial infarction. A 12-year follow-up of the Finnmark Study. *Circulation*, **93** (3), 450–456.

22. Grundtvig, M. (2008) Myocardial Infarction Occurs More Frequently in Females than in Male Smokers. ESC Congress 2007. Munich, Germany.

23. Rea, T.D. *et al.* (2002) Smoking status and risk for recurrent coronary events after myocardial infarction. *Ann. Intern. Med.*, **137** (6), 494–500.

24. Goldenberg, I. *et al.* (2003) Current smoking, smoking cessation, and the risk of sudden cardiac death in patients with coronary artery disease. *Arch. Intern. Med.*, **163** (19), 2301–2305.

25. van Domburg, R.T. *et al.* (2000) Smoking cessation reduces mortality after coronary artery bypass surgery: a 20-year follow-up study. *J. Am. Coll. Cardiol.*, **36** (3), 878–883.

26. Hasdai, D. *et al.* (1997) Effect of smoking status on the long-term outcome after successful percutaneous coronary revascularization. *N. Engl. J. Med.*, **336** (11), 755–761.

27. Wilson, K. *et al.* (2000) Effect of smoking cessation on mortality after myocardial infarction: meta-analysis of cohort studies. *Arch. Intern. Med.*, **160** (7), 939–944.

28. Doll, R. *et al.* (1994) Mortality in relation to smoking: 40 years' observations on male British doctors. *BMJ*, **309** (6959), 901–911.

29. Wolf, P.A. *et al.* (1988) Cigarette smoking as a risk factor for stroke. The Framingham Study. *JAMA*, **259** (7), 1025–1029.

30. Petitti, D.B. *et al.* (1996) Stroke in users of low-dose oral contraceptives. *N. Engl. J. Med.*, **335** (1), 8–15.

31. Wannamethee, S.G. *et al.* (1995) Smoking cessation and the risk of stroke in middle-aged men. *JAMA*, **274** (2), 155–160.

32. Blanchard, J.F., Armenian, H.K., and Friesen, P.P. (2000) Risk factors for abdominal aortic aneurysm: results of a case-control study. *Am. J. Epidemiol.*, **151** (6), 575–583.

33. Olin, J.W. and Shih, A. (2006) Thromboangiitis obliterans (Buerger's disease). *Curr. Opin. Rheumatol.*, **18** (1), 18–24.

34. Han, M.K. *et al.* (2007) Pulmonary diseases and the heart. *Circulation*, **116** (25), 2992–3005.

35. Moller, J.H. *et al.* (1993) Report of the task force on children and youth. American Heart Association. *Circulation*, **88** (5 Pt 1), 2479–2486.

36. Malik, S. *et al.* (2008) Maternal smoking and congenital heart defects. *Pediatrics*, **121** (4), e810–e816.

37. Spice, P. (2004) Setting up a cessation service. *BMJ*, **328** (7441), 699–701.

38. Jamrozik, K. (2004) Population strategies to prevent smoking. *BMJ*, **328** (7442), 759–762.

39. Transdermal Nicotine Study Group (1991) Transdermal nicotine for smoking cessation. Six-month results from two multicenter controlled clinical trials. Transdermal Nicotine Study Group. *JAMA*, **266** (22), 3133–3138.

40. Richmond, R.L., Kehoe, L., and de Almeida Neto, A. C. (1997) Three year continuous abstinence in a smoking cessation study using the nicotine transdermal patch. *Heart*, **78** (6), 617–618.

41. Perkins, K.A. and Scott, J. (2008) Sex differences in long-term smoking cessation rates due to nicotine patch. *Nicotine Tob. Res.*, **10** (7), 1245–1250.

42. Hurt, R.D. *et al.* (1994) Nicotine patch therapy for smoking cessation combined with physician advice and nurse follow-up. One-year outcome and percentage of nicotine replacement. *JAMA*, **271** (8), 595–600.

43. Smith, C.J. and Fischer, T.H. (2001) Particulate and vapor phase constituents of cigarette mainstream smoke and risk of myocardial infarction. *Atherosclerosis*, **158** (2), 257–267.

44. Kool, M.J. *et al.* (1993) Short- and long-term effects of smoking on arterial wall properties in habitual smokers. *J. Am. Coll. Cardiol.*, **22** (7), 1881–1886.

45. Greenland, S., Satterfield, M.H., and Lanes, S.F. (1998) A meta-analysis to assess the incidence of adverse effects associated with the transdermal nicotine patch. *Drug Saf.*, **18** (4), 297–308.

46. Kimmel, S.E. *et al.* (2001) Risk of acute first myocardial infarction and use of nicotine patches in a general population. *J. Am. Coll. Cardiol.*, **37** (5), 1297–1302.

47. Working Group for the Study of Transdermal Nicotine in Patients With Coronary Artery Disease (1994) Nicotine replacement therapy for patients with coronary artery disease. Working Group for the Study of Transdermal Nicotine in Patients with Coronary artery disease. *Arch. Intern. Med.*, **154** (9), 989–995.

48. Joseph, A.M. *et al.* (1996) The safety of transdermal nicotine as an aid to smoking cessation in patients with cardiac disease. *N. Engl. J. Med.*, **335** (24), 1792–1798.

49. Lee, A.H. and Afessa, B. (2007) The association of nicotine replacement therapy with mortality in a medical intensive care unit. *Crit. Care Med.*, **35** (6), 1517–1521.

50. Meine, T.J. *et al.* (2005) Safety and effectiveness of transdermal nicotine patch in smokers admitted with acute coronary syndromes. *Am. J. Cardiol.*, **95** (8), 976–978.

51. Hughes, J., Stead, L., and Lancaster, T. (2007) Antidepressants for smoking cessation. *Cochrane Database Syst. Rev.*1, (Art. No.: CD000031). doi: 10.1002/14651858.CD000031.pub3.

52. Gonzales, D. *et al.* (2006) Varenicline, an alpha4beta2 nicotinic acetylcholine receptor partial agonist, vs sustained-release bupropion and placebo for smoking cessation: a randomized controlled trial. *JAMA*, **296** (1), 47–55.

53. Jorenby, D.E. *et al.* (2006) Efficacy of varenicline, an alpha4beta2 nicotinic acetylcholine receptor partial agonist, vs placebo or sustained-release bupropion for smoking cessation: a randomized controlled trial. *JAMA*, **296** (1), 56–63.

54. Corrao, G. *et al.* (2000) Alcohol and coronary heart disease: a meta-analysis. *Addiction*, **95** (10), 1505–1523.

55. Beulens, J.W. *et al.* (2007) Alcohol consumption and risk for coronary heart disease among men with hypertension. *Ann. Intern. Med.*, **146** (1), 10–19.

56. Frezza, M. *et al.* (1990) High blood alcohol levels in women. The role of decreased gastric alcohol dehydrogenase activity and first-pass metabolism. *N. Engl. J. Med.*, **322** (2), 95–99.

57. Fuster, V. *et al.* (1981) The natural history of idiopathic dilated cardiomyopathy. *Am. J. Cardiol.*, **47** (3), 525–531.

58. Prazak, P. *et al.* (1996) Differences of disease progression in congestive heart failure due to alcoholic as compared to idiopathic dilated cardiomyopathy. *Eur. Heart J.*, **17** (2), 251–257.

59. McKenna, C.J. *et al.* (1998) Alcohol consumption and idiopathic dilated cardiomyopathy: a case control study. *Am. Heart J.*, **135** (5 Pt 1), 833–837.

60. Rimm, E.B. *et al.* (1991) Prospective study of alcohol consumption and risk of coronary disease in men. *Lancet*, **338** (8765), 464–468.

61. Klatsky, A.L., Armstrong, M.A., and Friedman, G.D. (1992) Alcohol and mortality. *Ann. Intern. Med.*, **117** (8), 646–654.

62. Gaziano, J.M. *et al.* (2000) Light-to-moderate alcohol consumption and mortality in the Physicians' Health Study enrollment cohort. *J. Am. Coll. Cardiol.*, **35** (1), 96–105.

63. Rehm, J.T. *et al.* (1997) Alcohol consumption and coronary heart disease morbidity and mortality. *Am. J. Epidemiol.*, **146** (6), 495–501.

64. Iestra, J.A. *et al.* (2005) Effect size estimates of lifestyle and dietary changes on all-cause mortality in coronary artery disease patients: a systematic review. *Circulation*, **112** (6), 924–934.

65. Rimm, E.B. *et al.* (1999) Moderate alcohol intake and lower risk of coronary heart disease: meta-analysis of effects on lipids and haemostatic factors. *BMJ*, **319** (7224), 1523–1528.

66. Wannamethee, G. and Shaper, A.G. (1992) Alcohol and sudden cardiac death. *Br. Heart J.*, **68** (5), 443–448.

67. Patel, R., McArdle, J.J., and Regan, T.J. (1991) Increased ventricular vulnerability in a chronic ethanol model despite reduced electrophysiologic responses to catecholamines. *Alcohol Clin. Exp. Res.*, **15** (5), 785–789.

68. Day, C.P. *et al.* (1993) QT prolongation and sudden cardiac death in patients with alcoholic liver disease. *Lancet*, **341** (8858), 1423–1428.

69. Greenspon, A.J. *et al.* (1979) Provocation of ventricular tachycardia after consumption of alcohol. *N. Engl. J. Med.*, **301** (19), 1049–1050.

70. Mukamal, K.J. *et al.* (2005) Binge drinking and mortality after acute myocardial infarction. *Circulation*, **112** (25), 3839–3845.

71. Klatsky, A.L. *et al.* (1977) Alcohol consumption and blood pressure Kaiser-Permanente Multiphasic Health Examination data. *N. Engl. J. Med.*, **296** (21), 1194–1200.

72. Stamler, J., Caggiula, A.W., and Grandits, G.A. (1997) Relation of body mass and alcohol, nutrient, fiber, and caffeine intakes to blood pressure in the special intervention and usual care groups in the Multiple Risk Factor Intervention Trial. *Am. J. Clin. Nutr.*, **65** (1Suppl), 338S–365S.

73. Klatsky, A.L., Friedman, G.D., and Armstrong, M.A. (1986) The relationships between alcoholic beverage use and other traits to blood pressure: a new Kaiser Permanente study. *Circulation*, **73** (4), 628–636.

74. Marmot, M.G. *et al.* (1994) Alcohol and blood pressure: the INTERSALT study. *BMJ*, **308** (6939), 1263–1267.

75. Malinski, M.K. *et al.* (2004) Alcohol consumption and cardiovascular disease mortality in hypertensive men. *Arch. Intern. Med.*, **164** (6), 623–628.

76. Potter, J.F. and Beevers, D.G. (1984) Pressor effect of alcohol in hypertension. *Lancet*, **1** (8369), 119–122.

77. Aguilera, M.T. *et al.* (1999) Effect of alcohol abstinence on blood pressure: assessment by 24-hour ambulatory blood pressure monitoring. *Hypertension*, **33** (2), 653–657.

78. Reynolds, K. *et al.* (2003) Alcohol consumption and risk of stroke: a meta-analysis. *JAMA*, **289** (5), 579–588.

79. Kiyohara, Y. *et al.* (1995) The impact of alcohol and hypertension on stroke incidence in a general Japanese population. The Hisayama study. *Stroke*, **26** (3), 368–372.

80. Weisberg, L.A. (1988) Alcoholic intracerebral hemorrhage. *Stroke*, **19** (12), 1565–1569.

81. Cheng, C.P., Shihabi, Z., and Little, W.C. (1990) Acute effects of mildly intoxicating levels of alcohol on left ventricular function in conscious dogs. *J. Clin. Invest.*, **85** (6), 1858–1865.

82. Lang, R.M. *et al.* (1985) Adverse cardiac effects of acute alcohol ingestion in young adults. *Ann. Intern. Med.*, **102** (6), 742–747.

83. Urbano-Marquez, A. *et al.* (1989) The effects of alcoholism on skeletal and cardiac muscle. *N. Engl. J. Med.*, **320** (7), 409–415.

84. Bertolet, B.D. *et al.* (1990) Unrecognized left ventricular dysfunction in an apparently healthy cocaine abuse population. *Clin. Cardiol.*, **13** (5), 323–328.

85. Abramson, J.L. *et al.* (2001) Moderate alcohol consumption and risk of heart failure among older persons. *JAMA*, **285** (15), 1971–1977.

86. Bryson, C.L. *et al.* (2006) The association of alcohol consumption and incident heart failure: the Cardiovascular Health Study. *J. Am. Coll. Cardiol.*, **48** (2), 305–311.

87. Walsh, C.R. *et al.* (2002) Alcohol consumption and risk for congestive heart failure in the Framingham Heart Study. *Ann. Intern. Med.*, **136** (3), 181–191.

88. Cooper, H.A., Exner, D.V., and Domanski, M.J. (2000) Light-to-moderate alcohol consumption and prognosis in patients with left ventricular systolic dysfunction. *J. Am. Coll. Cardiol.*, **35** (7), 1753–1759.

89. Gavazzi, A. *et al.* (2000) Alcohol abuse and dilated cardiomyopathy in men. *Am. J. Cardiol.*, **85** (9), 1114–1118.

90. Ettinger, P.O. *et al.* (1978) Arrhythmias and the "Holiday Heart": alcohol-associated cardiac rhythm disorders. *Am. Heart J.*, **95** (5), 555–562.

91. Shaw, G.M. *et al.* (1992) Congenital cardiac anomalies relative to selected maternal exposures and conditions during early pregnancy. *Eur. J. Epidemiol.*, **8** (5), 757–760.

92. Grewal, J. *et al.* (2008) Maternal periconceptional smoking and alcohol consumption and risk for select congenital anomalies. *Birth Defects Res. A Clin. Mol. Teratol.*, **82** (7), 519–526.

93. Carmichael, S.L. *et al.* (2003) Maternal periconceptional alcohol consumption and risk for conotruncal

heart defects. *Birth Defects Res. A Clin. Mol. Teratol.*, **67** (10), 875–878.

94. (2005) National Survey on Drug Use and Health: Cocaine Use 2002 and 2003. THE NSDUH Report. 2005, Office of Applied Studies (OAS), SAMHSA, RTI International.

95. Lange, R.A. and Hillis, L.D. (2001) Cardiovascular complications of cocaine use. *N. Engl. J. Med.*, **345** (5), 351–358.

96. Cregler, L.L. (1991) Cocaine: the newest risk factor for cardiovascular disease. *Clin. Cardiol.*, **14** (6), 449–456.

97. Hollander, J.E. *et al.* (1995) Chest pain associated with cocaine: an assessment of prevalence in suburban and urban emergency departments. *Ann. Emerg. Med.*, **26** (6), 671–676.

98. Givens, M.L. *et al.* (2007) Prevalence of cocaine use in ED patients with severe hypertension. *Am. J. Emerg. Med.*, **25** (6), 612–615.

99. Qureshi, A.I. *et al.* (1995) Stroke in young black patients. Risk factors, subtypes, and prognosis. *Stroke*, **26** (11), 1995–1998.

100. Hsue, P.Y. *et al.* (2002) Acute aortic dissection related to crack cocaine. *Circulation*, **105** (13), 1592–1595.

101. Kloner, R.A. *et al.* (1992) The effects of acute and chronic cocaine use on the heart. *Circulation*, **85** (2), 407–419.

102. Boehrer, J.D. *et al.* (1992) Hemodynamic effects of intranasal cocaine in humans. *J. Am. Coll. Cardiol.*, **20** (1), 90–93.

103. Wilbert-Lampen, U. *et al.* (1998) Cocaine increases the endothelial release of immunoreactive endothelin and its concentrations in human plasma and urine: reversal by coincubation with sigma-receptor antagonists. *Circulation*, **98** (5), 385–390.

104. Mo, W. *et al.* (1998) Role of nitric oxide in cocaine-induced acute hypertension. *Am. J. Hypertens*, **11** (6 Pt 1), 708–714.

105. Dressler, F.A., Malekzadeh, S., and Roberts, W.C. (1990) Quantitative analysis of amounts of coronary arterial narrowing in cocaine addicts. *Am. J. Cardiol.*, **65** (5), 303–308.

106. Kloner, R.A. and Rezkalla, S.H. (2003) Cocaine and the heart. *N. Engl. J. Med.*, **348** (6), 487–488.

107. Weber, J.E. *et al.* (2000) Cocaine-associated chest pain: how common is myocardial infarction? *Acad. Emerg. Med.*, **7** (8), 873–877.

108. Hollander, J.E. *et al.* (1994) Prospective multicenter evaluation of cocaine-associated chest pain. Cocaine Associated Chest Pain (COCHPA) Study Group. *Acad. Emerg. Med.*, **1** (4), 330–339.

109. Feldman, J.A. *et al.* (2000) Acute cardiac ischemia in patients with cocaine-associated complaints: results of a multicenter trial. *Ann. Emerg. Med.*, **36** (5), 469–476.

110. Mittleman, M.A. *et al.* (1999) Triggering of myocardial infarction by cocaine. *Circulation*, **99** (21), 2737–2741.

111. Hollander, J.E. and Hoffman, R.S. (1992) Cocaine-induced myocardial infarction: an analysis and review of the literature. *J. Emerg. Med.*, **10** (2), 169–177.

112. Hollander, J.E. *et al.* (1995) Cocaine-associated myocardial infarction. Mortality and complications. Cocaine-Associated Myocardial Infarction Study Group. *Arch. Intern. Med.*, **155** (10), 1081–1086.

113. Qureshi, A.I. *et al.* (2001) Cocaine use and the likelihood of nonfatal myocardial infarction and stroke: data from the Third National Health and Nutrition Examination Survey. *Circulation*, **103** (4), 502–506.

114. Moliterno, D.J. *et al.* (1994) Coronary-artery vasoconstriction induced by cocaine, cigarette smoking, or both. *N. Engl. J. Med.*, **330** (7), 454–459.

115. Flores, E.D. *et al.* (1990) Effect of cocaine on coronary artery dimensions in atherosclerotic coronary artery disease: enhanced vasoconstriction at sites of significant stenoses. *J. Am. Coll. Cardiol.*, **16** (1), 74–79.

116. Hollander, J.E. *et al.* (1994) "Abnormal" electrocardiograms in patients with cocaine-associated chest pain are due to "normal" variants. *J. Emerg. Med.*, **12** (2), 199–205.

117. Littmann, L., Monroe, M.H., and Svenson, R.H. (2000) Brugada-type electrocardiographic pattern induced by cocaine. *Mayo. Clin. Proc.*, **75** (8), 845–849.

118. Hollander, J.E. *et al.* (1998) Effect of recent cocaine use on the specificity of cardiac markers for diagnosis of acute myocardial infarction. *Am. Heart. J.*, **135** (2 Pt 1), 245–252.

119. Baumann, B.M. *et al.* (2000) Randomized, double-blind, placebo-controlled trial of diazepam, nitroglycerin, or both for treatment of patients with potential cocaine-associated acute coronary syndromes. *Acad. Emerg. Med.*, **7** (8), 878–885.

120. Smith, M., Garner, D., and Niemann, J.T. (1991) Pharmacologic interventions after an LD50 cocaine insult in a chronically instrumented rat model: are beta-blockers contraindicated? *Ann. Emerg. Med.*, **20** (7), 768–771.

121. Lange, R.A. *et al.* (1990) Potentiation of cocaine-induced coronary vasoconstriction by beta-adrenergic blockade. *Ann. Intern. Med.*, **112** (12), 897–903.

122. Ramoska, E. and Sacchetti, A.D. (1985) Propranolol-induced hypertension in treatment of cocaine intoxication. *Ann. Emerg. Med.*, **14** (11), 1112–1113.

123. Pollan, S. and Tadjziechy, M. (1989) Esmolol in the management of epinephrine- and cocaine-induced cardiovascular toxicity. *Anesth. Analg.*, **69** (5), 663–664.

124. Sybertz, E.J. *et al.* (1981) Alpha and beta adrenoceptor blocking properties of labetalol and its R,R-isomer, SCH 19927. *J. Pharmacol. Exp. Ther.*, **218** (2), 435–443.

125. Boehrer, J.D. *et al.* (1993) Influence of labetalol on cocaine-induced coronary vasoconstriction in humans. *Am. J. Med.*, **94** (6), 608–610.

126. Negus, B.H. *et al.* (1994) Alleviation of cocaine-induced coronary vasoconstriction with intravenous verapamil. *Am. J. Cardiol.*, **73** (7), 510–513.

127. Bush, H.S. (1988) Cocaine-associated myocardial infarction. A word of caution about thrombolytic therapy. *Chest*, **94** (4), 878.

128. Hollander, J.E. *et al.* (1996) Complications from the use of thrombolytic agents in patients with cocaine associated chest pain. *J. Emerg. Med.*, **14** (6), 731–736.

129. Hollander, J.E. (1995) The management of cocaine-associated myocardial ischemia. *N. Engl. J. Med.*, **333** (19), 1267–1272.

130. Hollander, J.E. *et al.* (1995) Cocaine-associated myocardial infarction. Clinical safety of thrombolytic therapy. Cocaine Associated Myocardial Infarction (CAMI) Study Group. *Chest*, **107** (5), 1237–1241.

131. Sharma, A.K. *et al.* (2002) Percutaneous interventions in patients with cocaine-associated myocardial infarction: a case series and review. *Catheter Cardiovasc Interv.*, **56** (3), 346–352.

132. McCord, J. *et al.* (2008) Management of cocaine-associated chest pain and myocardial infarction: a scientific statement from the American Heart Association Acute Cardiac Care Committee of the Council on Clinical Cardiology. *Circulation*, **117** (14), 1897–1907.

133. Hollander, J.E. *et al.* (1995) Cocaine-associated chest pain: one-year follow-up. *Acad. Emerg. Med.*, **2** (3), 179–184.

134. Brecklin, C.S. and Bauman, J.L. (1999) Cardiovascular effects of cocaine: focus on hypertension. *J. Clin. Hypertens (Greenwich)*, **1** (3), 212–217.

135. Gay, G.R. and Loper, K.A. (1988) The use of labetalol in the management of cocaine crisis. *Ann. Emerg. Med.*, **17** (3), 282–283.

136. Gay, G.R. and Loper, K.A. (1988) Control of cocaine-induced hypertension with labetalol. *Anesth. Analg.*, **67** (1), 92.

137. Petitti, D.B. *et al.* (1998) Stroke and cocaine or amphetamine use. *Epidemiology*, **9** (6), 596–600.

138. Klonoff, D.C., Andrews, B.T., and Obana, W.G. (1989) Stroke associated with cocaine use. *Arch. Neurol.*, **46** (9), 989–993.

139. Kibayashi, K., Mastri, A.R., and Hirsch, C.S. (1995) Cocaine induced intracerebral hemorrhage: analysis of predisposing factors and mechanisms causing hemorrhagic strokes. *Hum. Pathol.*, **26** (6), 659–663.

140. Treadwell, S.D. and Robinson, T.G. (2007) Cocaine use and stroke. *Postgrad Med. J.*, **83** (980), 389–394.

141. Johnson, B.A. *et al.* (2001) Treatment advances for cocaine-induced ischemic stroke: focus on dihydropyridine-class calcium channel antagonists. *Am. J. Psychiatry*, **158** (8), 1191–1198.

142. Konzen, J.P., Levine, S.R., and Garcia, J.H. (1995) Vasospasm and thrombus formation as possible mechanisms of stroke related to alkaloidal cocaine. *Stroke*, **26** (6), 1114–1118.

143. Pitts, W.R. *et al.* (1998) Effects of the intracoronary infusion of cocaine on left ventricular systolic and diastolic function in humans. *Circulation*, **97** (13), 1270–1273.

144. Tazelaar, H.D. *et al.* (1987) Cocaine and the heart. *Hum. Pathol.*, **18** (2), 195–199.

145. Isner, J.M. and Chokshi, S.K. (1991) Cardiovascular complications of cocaine. *Curr. Probl. Cardiol.*, **16** (2), 89–123.

146. Virmani, R. *et al.* (1988) Cardiovascular effects of cocaine: an autopsy study of 40 patients. *Am. Heart J.*, **115** (5), 1068–1076.

147. Om, A., Ellahham, S., and Ornato, J.P. (1992) Reversibility of cocaine-induced cardiomyopathy. *Am. Heart J.*, **124** (6), 1639–1641.

148. Henzlova, M.J. *et al.* (1991) Apparent reversibility of cocaine-induced congestive cardiomyopathy. *Am. Heart J.*, **122** (2), 577–579.

149. Nanji, A.A. and Filipenko, J.D. (1984) Asystole and ventricular fibrillation associated with cocaine intoxication. *Chest*, **85** (1), 132–133.

150. Castro, V.J. and Nacht, R. (2000) Cocaine-induced bradyarrhythmia: an unsuspected cause of syncope. *Chest*, **117** (1), 275–277.

151. Parker, R.B. *et al.* (1999) Comparative effects of sodium bicarbonate and sodium chloride on reversing cocaine-induced changes in the electrocardiogram. *J. Cardiovasc. Pharmacol.*, **34** (6), 864–869.

152. Shih, R.D. *et al.* (1995) Clinical safety of lidocaine in patients with cocaine-associated myocardial infarction. *Ann. Emerg. Med.*, **26** (6), 702–706.

153. Eagle, K.A., Isselbacher, E.M., and DeSanctis, R.W. (2002) Cocaine-related aortic dissection in perspective. *Circulation*, **105** (13), 1529–1530.

154. Plessinger, M.A. and Woods, J.R. Jr. (1998) Cocaine in pregnancy. Recent data on maternal and fetal risks. *Obstet. Gynecol. Clin. North Am.*, **25** (1), 99–118.

155. Lipshultz, S.E., Frassica, J.J., and Orav, E.J. (1991) Cardiovascular abnormalities in infants prenatally exposed to cocaine. *J. Pediatr.*, **118** (1), 44–51.

156. Kaye, S. *et al.* (2008) Methamphetamine-related fatalities in Australia: demographics, circumstances, toxicology and major organ pathology. *Addiction*, **103** (8), 1353–1360.

157. Karch, S.B., Stephens, B.G., and Ho, C.H. (1999) Methamphetamine-related deaths in San Francisco: demographic, pathologic, and toxicologic profiles. *J. Forensic. Sci.*, **44** (2), 359–368.

158. Chin, K.M., Channick, R.N., and Rubin, L.J. (2006) Is methamphetamine use associated with idiopathic pulmonary arterial hypertension? *Chest*, **130** (6), 1657–1663.

159. Katzung, B. (2000) *Basic and Clinical Pharmacology*, 8th edn, Appleton and Lange, Norwalk.

160. Derlet, R.W. *et al.* (1989) Amphetamine toxicity: experience with 127 cases. *J. Emerg. Med.*, **7** (2), 157–161.

161. Lucas, P.B. *et al.* (1986) Methylphenidate-induced cardiac arrhythmias. *N. Engl. J. Med.*, **315** (23), 1485.

162. Ragland, A.S., Ismail, Y., and Arsura, E.L. (1993) Myocardial infarction after amphetamine use. *Am. Heart J.*, **125** (1), 247–249.

163. Carson, P., Oldroyd, K., and Phadke, K. (1987) Myocardial infarction due to amphetamine. *Br. Med. J. (Clin. Res. ed.)*: **294** (6586), 1525–1526.

164. Turnipseed, S.D. *et al.* (2003) Frequency of acute coronary syndrome in patients presenting to the emergency department with chest pain after methamphetamine use. *J. Emerg. Med.*, **24** (4), 369–373.

165. Smith, H.J. *et al.* (1976) Cardiomyopathy associated with amphetamine administration. *Am. Heart J.*, **91** (6), 792–797.

166. Yeo, K.K. *et al.* (2007) The association of methamphetamine use and cardiomyopathy in young patients. *Am. J. Med.*, **120** (2), 165–171.

167. Schaiberger, P.H. *et al.* (1993) Pulmonary hypertension associated with long-term inhalation of "crank" methamphetamine. *Chest*, **104** (2), 614–616.

168. Davis, G.G. and Swalwell, C.I. (1994) Acute aortic dissections and ruptured berry aneurysms associated with methamphetamine abuse. *J. Forensic Sci.*, **39** (6), 1481–1485.

169. Kalant, H. and Kalant, O.J. (1975) Death in amphetamine users: causes and rates. *Can. Med. Assoc. J.*, **112** (3), 299–304.

170. McCarron, M.M. *et al.* (1981) Acute phencyclidine intoxication: clinical patterns, complications, and treatment. *Ann. Emerg. Med.*, **10** (6), 290–297.

171. Mittleman, M.A. *et al.* (2001) Triggering myocardial infarction by marijuana. *Circulation*, **103** (23), 2805–2809.

172. Mukamal, K.J. *et al.* (2008) An exploratory prospective study of marijuana use and mortality following acute myocardial infarction. *Am. Heart J.*, **155** (3), 465–470.

173. Brown, P.D. and Levine, D.P. (2002) Infective endocarditis in the injection drug user. *Infect. Dis. Clin. North Am.*, **16** (3), 645–665, viii–ix.

174. Levine, D.P., Crane, L.R., and Zervos, M.J. (1986) Bacteremia in narcotic addicts at the Detroit Medical Center. II. Infectious endocarditis: a prospective comparative study. *Rev. Infect. Dis.*, **8** (3), 374–396.

175. Mathew, J. *et al.* (1995) Clinical features, site of involvement, bacteriologic findings, and outcome of infective endocarditis in intravenous drug users. *Arch. Intern. Med.*, **155** (15), 1641–1648.

176. Chambers, H.F. *et al.* (1987) Cocaine use and the risk for endocarditis in intravenous drug users. *Ann. Intern. Med.*, **106** (6), 833–836.

177. Manoff, S.B. *et al.* (1996) Human immunodeficiency virus infection and infective endocarditis among injecting drug users. *Epidemiology*, **7** (6), 566–570.

178. Frontera, J.A. and Gradon, J.D. (2000) Right-side endocarditis in injection drug users: review of proposed mechanisms of pathogenesis. *Clin. Infect. Dis.*, **30** (2), 374–379.

179. Li, J.S., Sexton, D.J., Mick, N. *et al.*. (2000) Proposed modifications to the Duke criteria for the diagnosis of infective endocarditis. *Clin. Infect. Dis.*, **30**, 633–638.

180. Hecht, S.R. and Berger, M. (1992) Right-sided endocarditis in intravenous drug users. Prognostic features in 102 episodes. *Ann. Intern. Med.*, **117** (7), 560–566.

181. Welton, D.E. *et al.* (1979) Recurrent infective endocarditis: analysis of predisposing factors and clinical features. *Am. J. Med.*, **66** (6), 932–938.

18

Alcohol use and diseases of the eye

Yoshimune Hiratsuka

Department of Ophthalmology, Juntendo University School of Medicine, Tokyo, Japan

18.1   INTRODUCTION

Alcohol has been widely consumed through the ages because of its perceived benefits as a social lubricant and for relaxation. Although alcohol has long been recognized to be causally associated with a number of medical conditions, such as liver cirrhosis, pancreatitis, and cardiomyopathy, it is unclear whether alcohol plays a significant role in eye diseases. In this chapter, relevant epidemiologic and clinical studies are reviewed to synthesize the empirical evidence for the relations between alcohol use and eye diseases.

18.2   OCULAR PROBLEMS IN CHILDREN WITH FETAL ALCOHOL SYNDROME (FAS)

Fetal alcohol exposure can lead to a wide spectrum of systemic defects and vision deficits. Characterized by growth retardation, cognitive impairment, and facial dysmorphism, Fetal Alcohol Syndrome (FAS) is the most severe birth defect produced by *in utero* alcohol exposure. Abel [1] estimated that FAS occurs at a rate of 1 per 1000 live births in the general obstetric population. For children born to heavy drinking women, the incidence rate of FAS is 43 per 1000 [1]. It has been suggested that FAS is the third most common cause of birth defects (behind Down syndrome and spina bifida) and the most common cause of mental retardation in the United States [2]. Children with FAS often have problems with visual processes. Ocular anomalies may result from the toxic effects of alcohol on neural crest cells, which give rise to sensory neurons [3]. Experimental evidence indicates that the developing sensory systems of the central nervous system are susceptible to the effects of alcohol [4]. Despite the established diagnostic criteria, clinicians continue to experience considerable difficulty in diagnosing FAS, because none of the characteristic abnormalities is specific to FAS. As ocular signs, such as small palpebral fissure, microcornea, corneal clouding, strabismus, myopia, astigmatism, cataract, increased tortuosity of retinal vessels, and optic nerve hypoplasia, are prevalent among children with FAS [5], consultation with ophthalmologists may assist pediatricians in diagnosing FAS. Visual function may be reduced to a moderate or severe degree in children of FAS [6]. Needless to add, the early detection of visual loss and ocular abnormalities in affected children is important in the management of FAS.

Addictive Disorders in Medical Populations   Edited by Norman S. Miller and Mark S. Gold
© 2010 John Wiley & Sons, Ltd.

18.3 CATARACT

Cataract is the clouding of the natural lens of the eye that can lead to vision loss, and the most important factor in cataract formation is increasing age. Cataract is the leading cause of blindness in the world [7], and the leading cause of low vision in the United States [8]. So, cataract surgery has become the most frequent surgical procedure in people aged 65 years or older in the Western world, occasionally causing a considerable financial burden to the national healthcare system. Now, more than 1.3 million cataract operations are yearly performed in the United States and approximately 60% of Medicare spending in the 1990s was devoted to cataract surgery and associated costs [9]. As the world's population ages, visual impairment due to cataract is on the increase. This is a significant global problem. The stimulating challenges are to prevent or delay cataract formation.

There are mainly three types of cataract, each defined by the location of the opacities on the lens. A nuclear cataract occurs in the center of the lens. This type is the most common form of cataract and usually the result of the natural aging process. The cortical cataract begins at the outer rim of the lens, which is called cortex of the lens, and develops into the center. A subcapsular cataract starts at the back of the lens in the capsule, which is the thin membrane wrapping the lens. This type of cataract is often found in patients with diabetes, retinitis pigmentosa, high myopia, and patients who use steroids for extended periods. It is quite usual to have more than one type of cataract at the same time.

Are there any relationships between cataract and alcohol consumption? The answer is "Yes." There are some epidemiologic studies to investigate the relationship between alcohol drinking and cataract. However, the findings on the association between cataract and alcohol consumption are inconsistent. Ritter and colleagues [10] examined the relationship between alcohol use and lens opacities in a population-based cross-sectional study of adults aged 43–86 years in Beaver Dam, Wisconsin (n = 4926). Based on a standardized questionnaire, the amount of pure ethanol consumed in one week was determined for each study subject. Those who consumed, on average, four or more drinks per day were considered current "heavy" drinkers. A history of heavy drinking was related to nuclear, cortical, and posterior capsular opacities (odds ratios (OR) 1.34, 95% confidence interval (CI) 1.12–1.59; OR 1.36, 95% CI 1.04–1.77; and OR 1.57, 95% CI 1.10–2.25; respectively) [10]. In addition, also in a population-based cross-sectional study of adults aged 49–97 years in Blue Mountains, Australia (n = 3654), heavy alcohol consumption (four or more drinks a day) was associated with nuclear cataract in current smokers (adjusted OR compared with nondrinkers, 3.9; 95% CI, 0.9–16.6). However, the association was not found in nonsmokers [11].

Smoking and alcohol use are often correlated. Estimates of smoking prevalence among alcoholics range from 75 to 90%, a rate approximately three-fold higher than among the general population [12–14]. Smoking has been linked primarily to nuclear opacities [15]. However, in the Ritter *et al.* study [10], the reported relation between alcohol use and lens opacities remained significant after adjusting for smoking and other risk factors.

Munoz *et al.* [16] evaluated the association of alcohol use with posterior subcapsular opacities. Posterior subcapsular cataract, albeit less common than nuclear opacity, is visually disabling, accounting for 40%–60% of cataract surgical cases in the United States [17]. In the Munoz *et al.* study [16], 119 cases and 120 controls were interviewed, and current alcohol use and usual and maximum weekly alcohol consumption were assessed. After adjusted for smoking, heavy drinking, defined as consuming an average of 91 g of pure ethanol per week, was associated with a significantly increased risk of posterior subcapsular opacities (OR 4.6, 95% CI 1.4–15.1) relative to nondrinkers [16].

There are some prospective cohort studies of alcohol intake and risk of cataract. Retrospective and cross-sectional studies may be limited by the potential for recall bias in reporting of alcohol consumption and the inability to ascertain the temporal association between exposures (alcohol consumption) and disease outcomes (cataract). In this kind of study, usually, cataract extraction is used as the disease outcome. Cataract extraction is defined as the surgical removal of an incident cataract. Strictly speaking, however, cataract extraction is not as same as incidence of cataract. Because, the standardized eye examination by only one ophthalmologist is impossible in a population-based cohort. The indication of cataract surgery is not always the same in any ophthalmologists and cataract patients. The only prospective study of the relationship of alcohol consumption and cataract extraction among men is the Physicians' Health Study, which followed 22 071 men for an average of five years. Comparing daily drinkers with those who consumed alcohol less frequently, the relative risk (RR) of posterior subcapsular cataract extraction among daily drinkers was 1.65 (95%CI 0.99–2.72), after adjustment for some possible variables, such as smoking and diabetes [18]. In the Nurses Health Study (n = 77 466), which followed women for 12 years, among nonsmokers, multivariate relative risk for the women who take more than 25 g alcohol increased and became statistically significant for posterior subcapsular cataract (RR = 2.46; 95%CI 1.09–5.55) [19] In another prospective study in women in Sweden (n = 34 713, seven year follow up), an increment of 13 g alcohol intake per day (corresponding to one drink = 330 ml of beer, 150 ml of wine, or 45 ml of liquor) was associated with a 7% increased risk of cataract extraction (RR = 1.07; 95%CI 1.02–1.12). The risk increased with increasing total alcohol intake. No information on cataract subtypes was shown in this study [20].

Since heavy drinking is more prevalent among people of lower socioeconomic status [21], other correlates of low socioeconomic status may confound the alcohol–cataract association. Heavy drinking has been linked to poor nutrition status, because alcohol suppresses appetite and interferes with digestive processes and the absorption of nutrients [22]. Many alcoholics suffer from vitamin deficiency. The antioxidant vitamins A and E are normally present in the liver, but their levels can be lowered with chronic alcohol consumption [23,24]. Diet has been considered as one of the risk factors for cataract. The main impact of diet seems to be on the intake of Vitamins A, C, and E [25]. Numerous studies have been published regarding the effect of nutritional supplementation on cataract progression. However, the results of the studies are still controversial. Therefore, it is hard to affirm that the reported association of cataract with heavy alcohol consumption may be due to poor nutrition rather than alcohol *per se*. However, in the absence of dietary assessment, it is unclear what the etiologic pathways linking alcohol to cataract are. It has been suggested that heavy drinkers develop opacities through acetoaldehyde (a product of alcohol metabolism) reaction with lens protein and associated protein modification [26]. Further work is needed to evaluate the effect of alcohol and its metabolites on the lens.

The clinical implication of these findings is clear: adult patients with posterior subcapsular cataract should be screened for alcoholism. Drews [27] has suggested that posterior subcapsular cataracts among alcoholics may progress to maturity in only a few months. But if the opacities are incipient and if the consumption of alcohol is stopped completely, the posterior subcapsular changes may reverse and even disappear [27].

18.4 KERATITIS

Keratitis is an inflammation of the cornea, the superficial part of the eye. It is usually caused by bacteria, herpes virus, and fungi. The infection usually begins by affecting the outer layer of the cornea, but it can go deeper into the cornea, increasing the risk of visual loss. The symptoms of keratitis are red eye, severe eye pain, watering eye, and blurred vision. Untreated cases can cause permanent eye damage, such as corneal opacity, and keratitis is the most common infectious cause of corneal blindness in the United States.

Nutritional disorders usually arise from malabsorption, gastrointestinal surgery, and alcohol addiction. Deficiencies in vitamins A, B1(thiamine),

B12, and C may be manifest in the eye. It has been documented in a case report that bilateral corneal melting in an alcoholic patient with no improvement following antibiotic therapy was completely healed by 20 days of treatment with vitamin A [28]. Recently, a case report of bilateral corneal ulcer as a consequence of caloric-protein malnutrition and vitamin A deficit in a patient with chronic alcoholism has been reported from Spain [29]. Most of the keratitis cases are of infectious etiology. However, in the case of no improvement following antibiotic therapy, to detect the cause of keratitis is quite difficult. Pathogens such as viruses, fungus, and some systemic diseases have to be considered. When confronted with corneal ulceration and melting in alcoholic patients, it is important to consider the possibility of vitamin A deficiency as a possible cause.

It is well documented that chronic alcoholics are at heightened risk for several systemic infectious diseases [30]. Ormerod et al. [31] reported that of 227 patients with microbial keratitis, one-third were associated with chronic alcoholism. Moreover, chronic alcoholism may be a major unsuspected risk factor for microbial keratitis [31]. The prevalence of alcohol dependence is higher in blue-collar occupations than in white-collar occupations [32]. Since the former, such as construction workers, laborers, and farmers, are at a higher risk of trauma, the lack of information on occupation in the Ormerod et al. study [31] can be source of bias for the reported association between alcoholics and keratitis. The microbial pathogenesis in cases reported by Ormerod et al. [31] was distinctive, coagulase negative staphylococci, alpha- and beta-streptococci, moraxellae, enteric Gram negative bacilli. In general, microbial keratitis is mainly associated with *staphylococcus aureus, streptococcus peumoniae*, and *pseudomonas aeruginosa* [33]. However, these usual causative organisms accounted for only 30% of the cases in the Ormerod et al. study [31]. It was suggested that while trauma and self-neglect are the major recognized predisposing causes, the nutritional, toxic, and immunological sequelae of alcoholism may also have been contributory [31]. When confronted with microbial keratitis, it is imperative to consider chronic alcoholism as a possible cause of the disease.

18.5   OPTIC NEUROPATHY

Nutritional optic atrophy or amblyopia may develop in patients with chronic alcoholism or malnutrition. The clinical sign of optic neuropathy is temporal optic paleness. Deprivation of essential nutrients is considered to be more likely to play an important role in optic nerve damage than direct toxic effect of alcohol. As a result of the extensive destruction of myelinated nerve fibers in the temporal portion of the optic nerve in the papillo-macular budle area, visual loss, color vision defects, and central visual-field loss may be observed. The visual acuity may range from 20/20 to worse than 20/200. Brain examination such as MRI and CT scans should be obtained to rule out other etiologies of bilateral optic atrophy. Treatment may include medications, a balanced diet, as well as thiamine and folic acid vitamin supplementation [34].

18.6   COLOR VISION DEFICIENCIES

It is well known that chronic alcoholism can cause color vision deficiencies [35,36]. Kapitany et al. [37] found that out of 36 chronic alcoholics, 47.2% manifested acquired color vision deficiencies. With the withdrawal of alcohol, a marked improvement of these disturbances was observed [37]. Early in the disease process, tritan color defects that become deutranomalous when it gets severe may be observed [34]. It is also suggested that the combination of alcohol intake and occupational exposure to solvents, such as toluene, xylene, trichloroethylene, and tetrachloroethylene, can cause acquired subclinical color vision defects [38]. Recently, the abnormal visual field change in chronic alcohol tobacco smoking consumers by using blue-on-yellow perimatry was reported [39]. This may reflect a higher number of alterations in the cells of the parvocellular system, which is responsible for color function. Abstinence of alcohol should be encouraged for these cases.

18.7   CORNEAL OPACITY

Corneal arcus is the most common corneal opacity. It appears as a white ring in the peripheral cornea without magnification. It is frequently associated with abnormal serum lipid levels [40]. Corneal arcus could also be a sign of alcoholism [41–43]. Ewing and Rouse [44] reported that among the people with alcoholism, the prevalence of corneal arcus is five times higher than that among those without alcoholism. The association between arcus and alcoholism might be due to the fact that alcohol ingestion may induce the mobilization of free fatty acids and an increase in plasma levels of free fatty acids [40].

In the cornea eye bank for keratoplasty, grafts from donors with alcoholism seemed to be of lower quality than grafts from other donors. The vitro study from Germany suggested that high concentrations of ethanol and its metabolites in vitreous and aqueous humor in chronic alcoholism have a direct toxic effect on cornea [45]. This may cause the quality of corneas from donors with alcoholism to be lower.

18.8   ACUTE VISUAL LOSS AND ALCOHOLIC PANCREATITIS

Alcohol addiction can lead to chronic pancreatic inflammation, atrophy, and fibrosis. Pancreatitis is characterized as inflammation of the pancreas, typically caused by surgery of the stomach and biliary tract occlusion or alcoholism. The mechanisms leading to alcoholic pancreatitis are poorly understood. A period of 6–12 years of alcohol consumption may be necessary before initial symptoms occur [46]. There are some case reports that describe acute visual loss associated with alcoholic pancreatitis [34,47–51]. The typical signs of fundus are cotton-wool patches located primarily within the temporal retinal vascular arcades and macula, retinal edema, and occasionally striate and blot hemorrhages. Visual loss and visual field deficits are the patient's primary subjective complains. The retinal manifestations are almost the same as those in Purtscher's retinopathy, which is a retinal lesion associated with diseases such as cardiac aneurism, thoracic compression, bone fracture, post-trauma, and pancreatitis. Acute alcohol intoxication and loss of vision can be indicative of methanol poisoning and fat emboli are believed to be responsible for the retinal change [49].

While the incidence of visual loss resulting from alcoholic pancreatitis is rare, fundus examination is necessary for all patients with alcoholic pancreatitis, especially for those who complain of visual disturbance.

18.9   EFFECTS ON SENSORY PROCESSING

The critical flicker fusion frequency (CFF) refers to the highest frequency at which a light can be flashed on and off before an observer reports it to be continuous. CFF is a quantitative index which indicates the function of the optic nerve. One of the most reliable effects of alcohol on sensory processing is the reduction of the CFF. The mechanism by which alcohol may cause such changes is unknown. However, some authors have suggested that alcohol may act in ways analogous to dark adaptation [52,53]. Pearson and Timney [54] reported that there is a different effect of alcohol on rod and cone CFF. They concluded that the cone system, with its extensive inhibitory interactions, is likely to be much more influenced by alcohol than the rod system, in which neural inhibition play a less important role [54].

Alcohol induces changes in the performance of the oculomotor system, with a marked decrease in the peak velocity of saccades [55–57]. During the acute alcohol intoxication, nystagmus can be occurred. It has also been reported that alcohol consumption reduces cerebellar control of the vestibulo-ocular reflex [58]. In Wernicke–Korsakoff syndrome, sixth nerve palsies, diplopia, ophthalmoplegia, ptosis, esotropia, and nystagmus (horizontal and vertical) may be observed. In later stages, miotic nonreacting pupils may develop [34].

18.10   GLAUCOMA

Glaucoma is a group of eye diseases in which the optic nerve at the back of the eye is slowly destroyed, and gradually steals the visual field of the patients. In most people this damage is due to an increased pressure inside the eyeball – a result of blockage of the circulation of aqueous, or its drainage. In other patients the damage may be caused by poor blood supply to the vital optic nerve fibers, and a weakness in the structure of the nerve. Many studies showed no association between alcohol consumption and glaucoma [59–63]. However, in terms of the intra-ocular pressure (IOP), the association is reported in some studies. Buckingham and

Young [64] investigated the change of the IOP after drinking alcohol. They reported that the IOP decreases with alcohol consumption by a maximum of 3.7 mm Hg, regaining pre-test values in all subjects after 65 minutes [64]. Two epidemiologic studies [61,65], however, reported that alcohol consumption is associated with an increased risk of IOP. To date, the epidemiologic studies on the relation between glaucoma, IOP and alcohol drinking have yielded inconsistent results. According to the latest large prospective cohort study there was no association between alcohol consumption and risk of glaucoma [66].

18.11   OCULAR BENEFITS OF MODERATE ALCOHOL CONSUMPTION

Several studies suggest that moderate drinking has beneficial health and societal outcomes. How about in eye conditions? While heavy drinking is associated with a variety of eye diseases as reviewed above, moderate consumption of alcohol has been reported to be possibly protective against age-related macular degeneration (AMD), cataract, and diabetic retinopathy.

AMD is a disease associated with aging that gradually destroys central vision. Central vision is needed for seeing objects clearly and for common daily tasks, such as reading, writing, and driving. AMD affects the macula, the part of the eye that allows you to see fine detail. In some cases, AMD advances so slowly that people notice little change in their vision. In others, the disease progresses faster and may lead to a loss of vision in both eyes.

AMD is the leading cause of blindness in older adults after 65 years of age [67,68]. With the world population aging, AMD is a public health problem of increasing importance. However, data concerning alcohol consumption and AMD are limited with mostly null findings [69–72]. In a case control study based on the first National Health Nutrition and Examination Survey data, Obisesan et al. [73] reported a statistically significant association between moderate wine consumption and decreased AMD after adjusting for age, gender, income, history of congestive heart failure, and hypertension (OR 0.81, 95% CI 0.67–0.99). Among the different types of alcohol consumed (beer, wine, and liquor), the effect of wine, either alone (OR 0.66, 95% CI 0.55–0.79) or in combination with beer (OR 0.66; 95% CI 0.55–0.79) or liquor

(OR 0.74, 95% CI 0.63–0.86), exhibited a significant beneficial effect on AMD [73]. The decreased risk of AMD associated with moderate alcohol consumption could result from increased total cholesterol levels. It has been suggested that the risk of neovascular AMD increases as the level of total cholesterol rises [69]. Alcohol intake raises the levels of high-density lipoprotein (HDL) [74,75]. It is noteworthy that smoking is an established risk factor for AMD [60,69,76], but was not taken into account in these studies [69,73]. The recent prospective study by Knudtson et al. [77] reported that increased wine drinking among women showed a reduction in the risk of incident early AMD after adjusting for smoking. The antioxidant and antiplatelet aggregation properties in wine have been hypothesized to explain this relationship. However, this relationship was not consistent among men or for other AMD types. The other prospective studies by Cho et al. [78] (n = 62 252), and Ajani et al. [79] (n = 278) did not support an inverse relationship between alcohol consumption and risk of AMD.

In the Blue Mountain Eye Study, Cumming et al. found that alcohol consumption was associated with a reduced prevalence of cortical cataract: compared with people who did not drink, the adjusted OR for cortical cataract among people who drank 1–3 drinks per day was 0.7 (95% Ci: 0.6–0.9). They also found significant inverse relations between both moderate drinking (1–3 drinks per day) of wine and spirits, and cortical opacity. Moreover, in the sub cohort of Nurses Health Study, wine was found to be inversely related to cortical opacity. The lenses of regular wine drinkers were 0.5 (95%CI: 0.3–0.8) times as likely as the lenses of nonwine drinkers to have cortical opacity. Furthermore, results of modeling wine drinking as a continuously scaled term indicated that the odds of higher cortical opacity decreased by 12%

(OR = 0.88, 95%CI: 0.79–0.98) for every two additional glasses of wine consumed per week [80] Cumming et al. hypothesized that alcohol could protect against cortical cataracts by contributing to reduction in the degree of atherosclerosis in the uveal vessels that supply oxygen and nutrients to the metabolically active lens cortex. A Maryland study of posterior subcapsular cataract [16] also found a J-shaped dose-response relationship that is similar to that reported for cardiovascular disease. For those who consumed more than one drink per day, the adjusted odds ratio was 4.6, whereas a nonsignificant protective effect was observed for light drinkers (OR 0.51, 95% CI 0.24–1.56) [16].

According to the systematic review on effect of alcohol consumption on Diabetes Mellitus, moderate drinking is associated with a decreased incidence of diabetes mellitus and decreased incidence of heart disease in persons with diabetes [81]. How about in Diabetic retinopathy? Diabetic retinopathy remains a leading cause of blindness in industrialized countries. It is the most common cause of blindness in people of working age [82]. Much of the information about the epidemiology of diabetic retinopathy has come from the Wisconsin Epidemiologic Study of Diabetic Retinopathy [83], which involved 996 persons whose onset of diabetes occurred before age 30 years, and 1370 persons whose onset of diabetes was after age 30. The study found no association between alcohol consumption and incidence or progression of diabetic retinopathy in general. However, alcohol consumption was found to be associated cross-sectionally with lower frequency of proliferative retinopathy in only younger-onset diabetics at baseline, but not with the incidence or progression of retinopathy six years later (P = 0.28) [84]. Moss et al. [84] concluded that in the moderate range of consumption, alcohol does not appear to be a risk factor for the incidence or progression of retinopathy.

18.12 CONCLUSIONS

There is a small yet growing body of literature on alcohol use and eye diseases. In addition to alcohol-induced ocular anomalies among children with

FAS, epidemiologic studies in the past three decades have demonstrated that chronic alcoholism is associated with a significantly increased risk of cataract, keratitis, optic neuropathy, color vision deficiencies, and corneal arcus. Although the pathophysiologic mechanisms for these alcohol-related eye diseases have not been adequately understood, it is evident that there exist multiple pathways linking alcohol to these diseases, including alcohol's various biologic effects and effects on nutrient deficits. Information on patient's drinking history can be valuable to general physicians in the diagnosis and treatment of a variety of eye diseases and should be collected on a routine basis.

REFERENCES

1. Abel, E.L. (1995) An update on incidence of FAS: FAS is not an equal opportunity birth defect. *Neurotoxicol. Teratol.*, **17**, 437–443.

2. Bratton, R.L. (1995) Fetal Alcohol syndrome. How you can help prevent it. *Postgrad. Med.*, **98**, 197–200.

3. Carones, F., Brancato, R., Venturi, E. *et al.* (1992) Corneal endothelial anomalies in the fatal alcohol syndrome. *Arch. Ophthalmol.*, **110**, 1128–1131.

4. Miller, M.W. and Dow-Edwards, D.L. (1993) Vibrissal stimulation affects glucose utilization in the trigeminal/somatosensory system of normal rats and rats prenatally exposed to ethanol. *J. Comp. Neurol.*, **335**, 284–294.

5. Chan, D.Q. (1999) Fetal alcohol syndrome. *Optom. Vis. Sci.*, **76**, 678–685.

6. Strömland, K. (2004) Visual impairment and ocular abnormalities in children with fetal alcohol syndrome. *Addict. Biol.*, **9**, 153–157.

7. Resnikoff, S., Pascolini, D., Etya'ale, D. *et al.* (2004) Global data on visual impairment in the year 2002. *Bull. World Health Organ.*, **82**, 844–851.

8. Eye Disease Prevalence Research Group (2004) Cause of prevalence of visual impairment among adults in the United States. *Arch. Ophthalmol.*, **122**, 477–485.

9. Ellwein, L.B. and Urato, C.J. (2002) Use of eye care and associated charges among the Medicare population: 1991–1998. *Arch. Ophthalmol.*, **120**, 804–811.

10. Ritter, L.L., Klein, B.E.K., Klein, R., and Mares-Perlman, J.A. (1993) Alcohol use and lens opacities in the Beaver Dam Eye Study. *Arch. Ophthalmol.*, **111**, 113–117.

11. Cumming, R.G. and Mitchell, P. (1997) Alcohol, smoking, and cataracts: the Blue Mountains Eye Study. *Arch. Ophthalmol.*, **115**, 1296–1303.

12. Burling, T.A. and Ziff, D.C. (1988) Tobacco smoking: A comparison between alcohol and drug abuse inpatients. *Addict. Behav.*, **13**, 185–190.

13. Istvan, J. and Matarazzo, J. (1984) Tobacco, alcohol, and caffeine use: A review of their interrelationships. *Psychol. Bull.*, **55**, 543–548.

14. Toneatto, A., Sobell, L.C., Miller, C. *et al.* (1995) The effect of cigarette smoking on alcohol treatment outcome. *J. Subst. Abuse*, **7**, 245–252.

15. West, S.K., Munoz, B., Emmett, E.A. and Taylor, H.R. (1989) Cigarette smoking and risk of nuclear cataracts. *Arch. Ophthalmol.*, **107**, 1166–1169.

16. Munoz, B., Tajchman, U., Bochow, T., and West, S. (1993) Alcohol use and risk of posterior subcapsular opacities. *Arch. Ophthalmol.*, **111**, 110–112.

17. Adamsons, I., Munoz, B., Enger, C., and Taylor, H.R. (1991) Prevalence of lens opacities in surgical and general populations. *Arch. Ophthalmol.*, **109**, 993–997.

18. Manson, J.E., Christen, W.G., Seddon, J.M. *et al.* (1994) A prospective study of alcohol consumption and risk of cataract. *Am. J. Prev. Med.*, **10**, 156–161.

19. Chasan-Taber, L., Willett, W.C., Seddon, J.M. *et al.* (2000) A prospective study of alcohol consumption and cataract extraction among U.S. women. *Ann. Epidemiol.*, **10**, 347–353.

20. Lindblad, B.E., Håkansson, N., Philipson, B., and Wolk, A. (2007) Alcohol consumption and risk of cataract extraction: a prospective cohort study of women. *Ophthalmology*, **114**, 680–685.

21. Ames, G.M. and Janes, C.R. (1987) Heavy and problem drinking in an American blue-collar population: implications for prevention. *Soc. Sci. Med.*, **8**, 949–960.

22. Lieber, C.S. (1989) Alcohol and nutrition: An overview. *Alcohol. Health Res. World*, **13**, 197–205.

23. Hagen, B.F., Bjorneboe, A., Bjoreneboe, G.E., and Drevon, C.A. (1989) Effect of chronic ethanol consumption on the content of alpha-tocopherol in subcellular fractions of rat liver. *Alcohol. Clin. Exp. Res.*, **13**, 246–251.

24. Leo, M.A., Rosman, A.S., and Lieber, C.S. (1993) Differential depletion of carotenoids and tocopherol in liver disease. *Hepatology.*, **17**, 977–986.

25. Taylor, A., Jacques, P.F., and Epstein, E.M. (1995) Relations among aging, antioxidant status, and cataract. *Am. J. Clin. Nutr.*, **62**, 1439–1447.

26. Harding, J.J. (1991) Physiology, biochemical pathogenesis, and epidemiology of cataract. *Cur. Opinion Ophthalmol.*, **2**, 3–15.

27. Drews, R.C. (1993) Alcohol and cataract. *Arch. Ophthalmol.*, **111**, 1312.

28. Reisin, I., Reisin, L.H., and Aviel, E. (1996) Corneal melting in a chronic alcoholic contact lens wearer. *CLAO J.*, **22**, 146–147.

29. Benítez Cruz, S., Gómez Candela, C., Ruiz Martín, M., and Cos Blanco, A.I. (2005) Bilateral corneal ulceration as a result of caloric-protein malnutrition and vitamin A deficit in a patient with chronic alcoholism, chronic pancreatitis and cholecystostomy. *Nutr. Hosp.*, **20**, 308–310.

30. Adams, H.G. and Jordan, C. (1984) Infections in the alcoholic. *Med. Clin. North Am.*, **68**, 179–200.

31. Ormerod, L.D., Gomez, D.S., Schanzlin, D.J., and Smith, R.E. (1988) Chronic alcoholism and microbial keratitis. *Br. J. Ophthalmol.*, **72**, 155–159.

32. Harford, T.C., Parker, D.A., Grant, B.F., and Dawson, D.A. (1992) Alcohol use and dependence among employed men and women in the United States in 1988. *Alcohol. Clin. Exp. Res.*, **16**, 146–148.

33. Asbell, P. and Stenson, R. (1982) Ulcerative keratitis. Survey of 30 years laboratory experience. *Arch. Ophthalmol.*, **100**, 77–80.

34. Shimozono, M., Townsend, J.C., Ilsen, P.F., and Bright, D.C. (1998) Acute vision loss resulting from complications of ethanol abuse. *J. Am. Optom. Assoc.*, **69**, 293–303.

35. Sakuma, Y. (1971) Studies on color vision defects in alcoholics. *Nippon. Ganka. Kiyo.*, **22**, 438–450.

36. Smith, J.W. and Layden, T.A. (1971) Color vision defects in alcoholism. II. *Br. J. Addict. Alcohol Other Drugs*, **66**, 31–37.

37. Kapitany, T., Dietzel, M., Grunberger, J. *et al.* (1993) Color vision deficiencies in the course of acute alcohol withdrawal. *Biol. Psychiatry.*, **33**, 415–422.

38. Valic, E., Waldhor, T., Konnaris, C. *et al.* (1997) Acquired dyschromatopsia in combined exposure to solvents and alcohol. *Aust. N. Z. J. Ophthalmol.*, **25**, 225–230.

39. de Carvalho, J.F., Danda, D., Dantas, H. *et al.* (2006) Blue-on-yellow perimetry in tobacco and alcohol consumers. *Arq. Bras. Oftalmol.*, **69**, 675–678.

40. Barchiesi, B.J., Eckel, R.H., and Ellis, P.P. (1991) The cornea and disorders of lipid metabolism. *Surv. Ophthalmol.*, **36**, 1–22.

41. Hirano, K., Matsuzawa, Y., Sakai, N. *et al.* (1992) Polydisperse low-density lipoproteins in hyperalphalipoproteinemic chronic alcohol drinkers in association with marked reduction of cholesteryl ester transfer protein activity. *Metabolism.*, **41**, 1313–1318.

42. Matsuzawa, Y., Yamashita, S., Kameda, K. *et al.* (1984) Marked hyper-HDL2- cholesterolemia associated with premature corneal opacity. A case report. *Atherosclerosis.*, **52**, 207–212.

43. Thomas, J.V., Ewing, J.A., and Desrosiers, N.A. (1972) Alcohol consumption and arcus senilis: a search for a significant relationship. *Br. J. Addict. Alcohol. Other Drugs*, **67**, 177–179.

44. Ewing, J.A. and Rouse, B.A. (1980) Corneal arcus as a sign of possible alcoholism. *Alcohol. Clin. Exp. Res.*, **4**, 104–106.

45. Grütters, G. Ritz (2002) Alcohol-induced morphologic and biochemical corneal changes. *Ophthalmologe*, **99**, 266–269.

46. Van Thiel, D.H., Lipsitz, H.D., Porter, L.E. *et al.* (1981) Gastrointestinal and hepatic manifestations of chronic alcoholism. *Gastroenterology*, **81**, 596–615.

47. Carrera, C.R., Pierre, L.M., Medina, F.M., and Pierre-Filho Pde, T. (2006) Purtscher-like retinopathy associated with acute pancreatitis. *Sao. Paulo Med. J.*, **123**, 289–291.

48. Cohen, S.Y., Gaudric, A., and Chaine, G. (1989) Retinopathy in pancreatitis. *J. Fr. Ophthalmol.*, **12**, 261–265.

49. Kincaid, M.C., Green, W.R., Knox, D.L., and Mohler, C. (1982) A clinicopathological case report of retinopathy of pancreatitis. *Br. J. Ophthalmol.*, **66**, 219–226.

50. Snady-McCoy, L. and Morse, P.H. (1985) Retinopathy associated with acute pancreatitis. *Am. J. Ophthalmol.*, **100**, 246–251.

51. Steel, J.R., Cockcroft, J.R., and Ritter, J.M. (1993) Blind drunk: alcoholic pancreatitis and loss of vision. *Postgrad Med. J.*, **69**, 151–152.

52. Ikeda, H. (1963) Effects of ethyl alcohol on the evoked potential of the human eye. *Vision Res.*, **3**, 155–169.

53. Wallgren, H. and Barry, H. (1970) Actions of alcohol, in *Biochemical, Physiological and Psychological Aspects: Chronic and Clinical Aspects*, vol. **1**, Elsevier Science Publishing Co., Inc., New York.

54. Pearson, P. and Timney, B. (1999) Differential effects of alcohol on rod and cone temporal processing. *J. Stud. Alcohol.*, **60**, 879–883.

55. Holdstock, L. and de Wit, H. (1999) Ethanol impairs saccadic and smooth pursuit eye movements without producing self-reports of sedation. *Alcohol Clin. Exp. Res.*, **23**, 664–672.

56. Lehtinen, I., Lang, L.H., Jantti, V., and Keskinen, E. (1979) Acute effects of alcohol on saccadic eye movements. *Psychopharmacology (Berl)*, **63**, 17–23.

57. Moser, A., Heide, W., and Kompf, D. (1998) The effect of oral ethanol consumption on eye movements in healthy volunteers. *J. Neurol.*, **245**, 542–550.

58. Tomizawa, I., Takahashi, M., Okada, Y. *et al.* (1991) Effect of alcohol on VOR compensation after unilateral labyrinthine loss. *Acta Laryngol.*, **481**, 99–105.

59. Klein, B.E., Klein, R., and Ritter, L.L. (1993) Relationship of drinking alcohol and smoking to prevalence of open-angle glaucoma. The Beaver Dam Eye Study. *Ophthalmology*, **100**, 1609–1613.

60. Klein, R., Klein, B.E., Linton, K.L., and Franke, T. (1993) The Beaver Dam Eye Study: the relation of age-related maculopathy to smoking. *Am. J. Epidemiol.*, **137**, 190–200.

61. Leske, M.C., Warheit-Roberts, L., and Wu, S.Y. (1996) Open-angle glaucoma and ocular hypertension: the Long Island Glaucoma Case-control Study. *Ophthalmic Epidemiol.*, **3**, 85–96.

62. Quigley, H.A., Enger, C., Katz, J. *et al.* (1994) Risk factors for the development of glaucomatous visual field loss in ocular hypertension. *Arch. Ophthalmol.*, **112**, 644–649.

63. Doshi, V., Ying-Lai, M., Azen, S.P. for the Los Angeles Latino Eye Study Group (2008) Sociodemographic, family history, and lifestyle risk factors for open-angle glaucoma and ocular hypertension the Los Angeles Latino Eye Study. *Ophthalmology*, **115** (4), 639–647.

64. Buckingham, T. and Young, R. (1986) The rise and fall of intra-ocular pressure: the influence of physiological factors. *Ophthalmic Physiol. Opt.*, **6**, 95–99.

65. Wu, S.Y. and Leske, M.C. (1997) Associations with intraocular pressure in the Barbados Eye Study. *Arch. Ophthalmol.*, **115**, 1572–1576.

66. Kang, J.H., Willett, W.C., Rosner, B.A. *et al.* (2007) Prospective study of alcohol consumption and the risk of primary open-angle glaucoma. *Ophthalmic Epidemiol.*, **14**, 141–147.

67. Green, W.R. and Enger, C. (1993) Age-related macular degeneration histopathologic studies. The 1992 Lorenz E. Zimmerman Lecture. *Ophthalmology*, **100**, 1519–1535.

68. Whitemore, W.G. (1989) Eye disease in a geriatric nursing home population. *Ophthalmology*, **96**, 393–398.

69. Eye Disease Case-Control Study Group (1992) Risk factors for neovascular age-related macular degeneration. *Arch Ophthalmol.*, **110**, 1701–1708.

70. Kahn, H.A., Leibowitz, H.M., Ganley, J.P. *et al.* (1977) The Framingham Eye Study. Association ophthalmic pathology with single variable previously measured in the Framingham Health Study. *Am. J. Epidemiol.*, **106**, 33–41.

71. Maltzman, B.A., Mulvihill, M.N., and Greenbaum, A. (1979) Senile macular degeneration and risk factors: a case study. *Am. J. Ophthalmol.*, **11**, 1701–1708.

72. Smith, E. and Mitchel, P. (1996) Alcohol intake and age-related maculopathy. *Am. J. Ophthalmol.*, **122**, 743–745.

73. Obisesan, T.O., Hirsch, R., Kosoko, O. *et al.* (1998) Moderate wine consumption is associated with decreased odds of developing age-related macular degeneration in NHANES-1. *J. Am. Geriatr. Soc.*, **46**, 1–7.

74. Gordon, T., Ernst, N., Fisher, M., and Rifkind, B.M. (1988) Alcohol and high density lipoprotein cholesterol. *Circulation.*, **8**, 737–741.

75. Pietinen, P.D.S.C. and Huttunen, J.K. (1987) Dietary determinants of plasma high-density lipoprotein cholesterol. *Am. Heart J.*, **113**, 620–625.

76. Vingerling, J.R., Hofman, A., Grobbee, D.E., and de Jong, P.T. (1996) Age-related macular degeneration and smoking: the Rotterdam Study. *Arch. Ophthalmol.*, **114**, 1193–1196.

77. Knudtson, M.D., Klein, R., and Klein, B.E. (2007) Alcohol consumption and the 15-year cumulative incidence of age-related macular degeneration. *Am. J. Ophthalmol.*, **143**, 1026–1029.

78. Cho, E., Hankinson, S.E., Willett, W.C. *et al.* (2000) Prospective study of alcohol consumption and the risk of age-related macular degeneration. *Arch. Ophthalmol.*, **118**, 681–688.

79. Ajani, U.A., Christen, W.G., Manson, J.E. *et al.* (1999) A prospective study of alcohol consumption and the risk of age-related macular degeneration. *Ann. Epidemiol.*, **9**, 172–177.

80. Morris, M.S., Jacques, P.F., Hankinson, S.E. *et al.* (2004) Moderate alcoholic beverage intake and early nuclear and cortical lens opacities. *Ophthalmic Epidemiol.*, **11**, 53–65.

81. Howard, A.A., Arnsten, J.H., and Gourevitch, M.N. (2004) Effect of alcohol consumption on diabetes mellitus: a systematic review. *Ann. Intern. Med.*, **140**, 211–219.

82. Johnson, G.J., Minassian, D.C., and Weale, W. (1998) *The Epidemiology of Eye Diesase*, Chapman & Hall Medical, London, UK.

83. Klein, R., Klein, B.E.K., and Moss, S.E. (1984) Prevalence of diabetes mellitus in SouthWisconsin. *Am. J. Epidemiol.*, **119**, 54–61.

84. Moss, S.E., Klein, R., and Klein, B.E.K. (1994) The association of alcohol consumption with the incidence and progression of diabetic retinopathy. *Ophthalmology*, **101**, 1962–1968.

19

Addictive disorders in nutritional diseases – from an addictions viewpoint

James A. Cocores,[1] Noni A. Graham,[1] and Mark S. Gold[2]

[1] Department of Psychiatry, University of Florida College of Medicine and McKnight Brain Institute, Gainesville, FL 32611, USA

[2] Departments of Psychiatry, Neuroscience, Anesthesiology, Community Health & Family Medicine, University of Florida College of Medicine and McKnight Brain Institute, Gainesville, FL 32611, USA

19.1 INTRODUCTION

Medical nutrition is a re-burgeoning discipline which focuses on the assimilation of both traditional and more contemporary macronutrients and anti-nutrients into the body. There are two fundamental types of malnutrition syndrome that result in severe epidemiological consequences as it relates to addiction: overeating foods sparse in nutrients and under consumption of nutritionally dense foods. Keeping up with the protean landscapes of addiction and medical nutrition harvests an ever-expanding perspective on how body organs function and become subject to disease. Addiction and malnutrition with dysfunctional lifestyle, collectively referred to as "nutritional diseases" from this point forward, often lurk in patients seeking nutritional consultations and go unnoticed among other specialized clinical practices. It has been taught that if a medical student knows syphilis, the student knows medicine. The same can be said about medical nutrition and addiction medicine because together they serve as a window of insight into many other specialties.

A phenomenological link between consummatory and drug addictive behavior has been suspected for decades [1–3]. Recent studies show that over-eating and drug addictions share common neuronal pathways [4] and emerging research suggests that overeating nutritionally sparse food is a type of drug addiction [5–7]. The overlap in behavioral patterns between pathological eating and drug addiction underscores the necessity of a keen differential diagnostic eye among medical nutritionists. The reverse is also true for addictionologists.

Nutritional diseases frequently coexist with addictive disorders. Substance dependent individuals are often in denial, minimize or eliminate their substance use history during an initial evaluation, like those that suffer from nutritional diseases. Hence, it may be wise to reassure patients about Federal confidentiality laws, obtain a brief substance use history and comprehensive urine drug screen as part of the initial assessment. Where there is prevailing drug dependence, there are often one or

Addictive Disorders in Medical Populations   Edited by Norman S. Miller and Mark S. Gold

more companion addictive and addictive psychiatric disorders [8]. For example, an oxycodone addict may also be dependent on benzodiazepines and nicotine, and engage in compulsive internet spending sprees. Poly drug addiction and malnutrition often begin during the early teens and usually vary over the life cycle. For example, a young teen experimenting with five different drugs along with low end fast food, sodas (carbonated drinks), energy drinks, and chips over the course of several years, settles on beer, amphetamine, nicotine, and caffeine along with fast foods, soda, energy bars, and problematic gambling throughout college. The same person may engage in weekend cannabis and wine addiction during early adulthood with a decline in food consumption during the weekdays and a surge throughout the evening and while watching late night television programs. A different pattern may prevail later on in the late forties consisting of benzodiazepine and nicotine use along with essentially daytime starvation (i.e., a hand-full of supplements, diet soda, black coffee with sucralose, and a nutrition bar), a "healthy" low calorie and fat dinner, and sporadic evening and night mini-binges.

The purpose of this chapter is to assist medical nutritionists in gaining better insight about how addiction is, at least in part, responsible for nutritional disease. Researchers have known for decades about the alcohol dependence–malnutrition interface. Diseases such as liver cirrhosis, pancreatitis, and Wernickes encephalopathy [9] are most often the product of an ethanol and malnutrition blend. Today, the list of addictions and related medical illnesses has grown substantially. Although a comprehensive review of old and new macronutrients and antinutrients, and how they interplay with each of the drug categories to participate in scores of diseases across medical specialties, is beyond the scope of this chapter, an attempt will be made to touch on some of the more prevalent nutritional diseases as they relate to specific addictions. Emphasis is placed on the clinical management of drug addiction related nutritional diseases with whole foods rather than processed supplements, a practice recommended in the management of nutritionally-based diseases such as cancer [10]. A beginning is made with a brief overview of the most studied addiction, alcohol.

19.2   ALCOHOL

Alcoholism is a common cause of vitamin, trace element, macronutrient and antioxidant deficiencies, and disease in adult Americans. Alcohol addiction is one of the leading causes of nutritional diseases in the United States [9] and admissions to hospitals [11]. Nutrition and alcohol interact at many different levels and alcohol-containing beverages can contribute to nutritional disease in three fundamental ways by providing nutritionally scarce calories and functioning as an *antinutrient*, influencing the absorption and *bioavailability* of nutrients, and promoting *oxidative stress* and tissue toxicity.

19.2.1   Antinutrient

Ethanol-containing beverages contribute significantly to overall calorie consumption. An imbiber of 600 ml of 86-proof alcohol produces 1500 calories

of energy. Alcohol provides 7.1 kcal/g of energy but contains almost no other useful ingredients [12]. Calories derived from alcohol are essentially void of vitamins, minerals, amino acids, and fatty acids. Nutrients such as calcium, iron, fiber, Vitamins A and C, and thiamine are displaced and produce malnutrition when more than 30% of total calories are ingested as alcohol [13,14]. The presence of these empty calories is one reason appetite and consummatory behavior can be suppressed, and why regular and heavy alcohol ingestion contributes to or produces a variety of nutritional diseases [15] (Table 19.1). However, the displacement of nutrients with nutritionally void calories is not the only mechanism influencing changes in appetite and weight. Research suggests that alcohol-induced appetite suppression may be due to shared common reward mechanisms. Food moderated reward may be satiated by alcohol, and

Table 19.1 Nutritional diseases associated with alcohol addiction

Disease	Causes	Medicinal Foods
Bleeding Disorders	Steatorrhea, decreased intake and altered colonic microflora may produce vitamin K deficiency	Asparagus, broccoli, celery, collards, cucumber, kale, peas, spinach, turnip greens
Megaloblastic Anemia	Decreased intake and malabsorption of Folic Acid	Asparagus, avocados, black-eyed peas, chickpeas, collards, lentils, okra, pineapple juice, pinto beans, sunflower seeds
Night blindness, Hypogonadism	Malabsorption, impaired storage, increased degradation and decreased activation of Vitamin A	Apples, broccoli, carrots, fresh apricots, kale, lemons, peas, rolled oats, peaches, sweet potatoes, tomato juice, winter squash
Night blindness (possibly associated)	Deficiency of zinc, a cofactor of Vitamin A dehydrogenase	Beans, brown rice, meats (lean), peanuts (unsalted), potatoes, poultry, pumpkin seeds, wild salmon
Osteoporosis, Osteopenia, Aseptic Necrosis	Decreased intake and absorption, and altered metabolism of Vitamin D	Calcium: Beet greens, broccoli, collard greens, kale, rhubarb, white beans and wild salmon Vitamin D: Cod, herring, mushrooms, potatoes, wild salmon
Systemic Oxidative Stress	Pancreatic insufficiency may increase iron absorption and contribute to iron overload	Antioxidants: Blackberries, cherries, oranges, plums, raisins and red grapes; beets, corn, kale, onions, red peppers Limit: Red meats
Sideroblastic Anemia Neurological and Dermatologic Disorders	Ethanol and reduced intake of pyridoxine	Avocados, bananas, Mahi Mahi, pears, peas, potatoes, walnuts, wild salmon
Wernicke–Korsakoff Syndrome	Malabsorption and possibly defective activation of thiamine	Asparagus, brown rice, cauliflower, eggs, kale, oranges, potatoes and rolled oats

female overeaters have lower rates of alcohol use [16]. Compounds that inhibit alcohol consumption attenuate the reward produced by palatable food [17]. Another reason alcohol acts like an antinutrient is because of its reduced energy value, an inefficiency brought about by its ability to augment metabolic rate. Additional energy wastage is propagated by the microsomal ethanol oxidizing system in chronic alcoholism [18] and during its conversion to acetaldehyde.

The addition of calories from alcohol results in less weight gain than an equivalent amount of calories from carbohydrate and fat [12]. No additional weight was gained when 1800 calories from alcohol was added to a 2600 calorie diet [19], and a 50% isocaloric replacement of carbohydrate from alcohol to a balanced diet results in weight loss [20]. Alcoholics often have lower body weights compared to nondrinkers. This finding is especially apparent in women [21]. However, weight loss is not the rule and changes in weight are subject to several variables. Alcohol's ability to maintain body weight may vary depending on the quality of carbohydrate consumed [22]. For the purpose of this chapter, "quality carbohydrate" refers to those with low Glycemic Index (GI) and Glycemic Load (GL), as there is substantial evidence suggesting that postprandial glycemia is a universal mechanism for disease progression [23]. GI and GL are preferred to the essentially meaningless term "complex carbohydrate," taking into consideration that a few researchers find the Indices controversial [24], and the Fructose Index may be more relevant to cardiovascular disease [25]. In addition to high GI/GL foods, such as no fat added instant mashed potatoes – with a GI higher than Skittles manufactured in Australia [26] – alcohol-containing beverages have been scored with a high (GI greater than 70) to moderate (GI 56–69) GI/GL. Beer has a GI of 95 [27], making the beverage equivalent to jelly beans [26], and wine and mixed drinks 61 [27], a GI similar to that of a Mars Bar [26]. Beer, wine, and mixed drinks may have even higher GL values as is often the case relative to GI. A high GI/GL from ethanol-containing drinks links alcohol addiction to hyperglycemia

and, ultimately, insulin resistance and sensitivity, an anomaly that not only compromises pancreatic function, but also impairs neuronal and cognitive function [28]. This may be especially true when a person drinks more alcohol relative to the consumption of balanced meals. High GI/GL meals accompanied by drinks before, during and after eating, can contribute significantly to chronic hyperglycemia and insulin resistance. Low fat meals high in processed carbohydrate, such as foods made of cylinder or hammer milled flour, tend to raise the total GI/GL of the alcoholic's dinner, while an acidic meal and one high in fat lowers the overall GI/GL of the meal. However, coupling chronic alcoholism with high lipid intake (i.e., cheese – the new beef fat) and a sedentary lifestyle [29] increases the incidence of truncal obesity, especially in women [30].

19.2.2 Bioavailability

Alcohol and food interact at almost every portion of the gastrointestinal tract and alter the mobilization, digestion, absorption, metabolism, use and storage of nutrients. Mobilization, digestion, and absorption are disrupted by alcohol's direct influence on the wall of the small intestine, interfering with peristalsis, pancreatic function and at several other levels. Alterations in saliva, esophageal peristalsis and the direct toxic effect of alcohol can cause esophagitis and stricture, which significantly reduces food intake in alcoholics. Ethanol-containing beverages have the ability to prompt acute gastritis and duodenitis [31], additional deterrents to consummatory behavior. Upper areas of the gastrointestinal tract tend to be exposed to alcohol for long periods. However, absorption of alcohol and food essentially does not begin until the duodenum. This is validated by post-bariatric surgery studies that show these patients absorb alcohol and certain nutrients (i.e., moderate to high GI/GL foods) substantially faster. One drink can feel like three and moderate GI carbohydrates bypass the stomach and are absorbed sooner after consumption, transforming into high GI foods. It is for this reason that one component of our post-bariatric recommendations is to primarily consume low GI carbohydrates like in diabetes. Under normal circumstances the stomach, especially in the presence of acidic or fatty food, essentially turns into a time released pouch, which serves like a slow intra-duodenal drip of alcohol and food. The gastric mucosa becomes susceptible to alcohol's direct toxic effects. Nonerosive hemorrhagic gastritis can occur [32]. Gastritis in either form significantly influences appetite, motility, and absorption of nutrients. Toxicity continues in the intestines, frequently resulting in diarrhea and malabsorption of nutrients. One of the acute effects includes alterations of motility, while chronic exposure to alcohol directly affects the mucosa. Preexisting nutritional deficits, such as folate and antioxidant deficiency, also contribute to mucosal changes. Alcohol decreases impeding peristaltic waves in the jejunum, increases propulsive waves in the ileum, and increases the absorption of glucose.

Alcoholism influences the activation and inactivation of nutrients. An example of the latter is that it reduces the synthesis of pyridoxal phosphate from pyridoxine, which has been associated with the oxidation of alcohol and may be linked with the displacement and degradation of pyridoxal-5-phosphate from its cytosol-binding protein by phosphatase, yielding a net decrease in activation.

19.2.3 Oxidative stress

Alcohol is directly toxic to tissue throughout the body. Coexisting malnutrition compounds the damage and dysfunction among organs, particularly in the brain, liver, heart, pancreas, and bone [33,34]. The genesis of diseases within these and other organs has, at least in part, reactive oxygen species (ROS) or free radical (FR) production as a common causative denominator [35–39]. Alcoholics have lower serum Vitamin E and Vitamin C levels than nonalcoholics [40], and some may have a thiamine, niacin, pyridoxine or Vitamin B12 deficiency. These vitamins are important in the preservation and functioning of nervous tissue [41]. Although most of the

research at the nutritional disease/alcohol addiction interface has focused on cirrhosis, Wernickes and vitamin deficiencies, more recent efforts include investigating alcohol's impact on insulin sensitivity and oxidative stress in many other organs and association with other diseases. Alcohol-related oxidative stress is thought to play a central role in cirrhosis and numerous other forms of pathogenesis [42,43]. Emerging research suggests this also applies to neurological disorders such as Alzheimer's disease [44] and numerous forms of cancer [45,46]. Breast cancer risk is increased among women who imbibe less than 1–2 ethanol-containing beverages daily and is thought to come about by means of a hormone-related mechanism [47]. It is conceivable that prescription and dietary hormones, such as those found in conventional dairy and phytoestrogens in processed soy products, immune system status, and genetics may also factor into risk. Reports of minor cardio-protection associated with drinking small amounts of beer and wine, and not especially red wine [48], might be viewed with caution in nutritional diseases/addictions as the potential liability of relapse, stroke, ongoing malnutrition and accruing oxidative stress outweigh the few controversial benefits.

19.2.4 Central effects

Alcohol stimulates γ-aminobutyric acid (GABA) receptors and chronic drinking has the capacity to reduce brain plasticity and GABA receptor availability. Baclofen, a GABA-B receptor agonist, has found utility in the clinical management of stimulant, opiate, nicotine, and alcohol addiction [49]. It has also been found to be effective in treating binge eating disorder. [50] The mesoaccumbens dopamine system, originating from the ventral tegmental area (VTA) and projecting to the nucleus accumbens (NAc), also presides over the actions of alcohol. The ventral pallidum (VP) and the dorsal striatum (dSTR) may also be involved [51]. It is largely held that both alcohol and food increase the activity of the mesoaccumbens dopamine system.

19.3 OTHER DRUG ADDICTIONS

Drug addiction leads to the composite syndrome of multiple nutrient deficiencies popularly known as malnutrition [52,53]. There is also evidence that drug addicts have immunonutritional deficiency tendencies [54] as a direct result of their substance addiction. Drug addicts have significantly lower Body Mass Index (BMI), hemoglobin, serum total protein, and albumin levels, and a higher incidence of nutritional disease [55]. Combining this data, more than 60% of drug addicts suffer from multiple-malnutrition.

Drug addicts consume less fruits and vegetables than the general population and they are more likely to eat nutrient-depleted food [56]. Drug addicts have deficiencies in Vitamins E, C, A, and other antioxidants [57]. Chronic use leads to progressive systemic oxidative stress and an inadequate antioxidant defense. Addicts are subject to compromised lifestyle factors, which also significantly influence corporal antioxidant tone [57]. Nutrients play an important role in immunity and drug addiction sets the stage for the development of an immunodeficiency.

19.3.1 Benzodiazepines

Benzodiazepines modulate GABA-mediated conductance increases. They have the capacity to increase GABA receptor desensitization and increase peak response to GABA. Benzodiazepines have the capacity to increase food intake. This is in sharp contrast to alcohol's influence on appetite. Benzodiazepine agonists can be divided into full and partial agonists. Inverse agonists have also been identified and exhibit anorectic properties. Benzodiazepine receptors constitute a part of the GABA (A) receptor complexes [58]. Neuropsychiatric evidence indicates that the benzodiazepine-induced hyperphagic response is not secondary to the anxiolytic, sedative, and muscle relaxant properties of this drug family, but rather from interactions with specific recognition sites in the brain. Benzodiazepine-related hyperphagia may be mediated by $\alpha 2/\alpha 3$ subtype and not the $\alpha 1$ subtype. They probably influence palatability by working in the caudal brainstem.

19.3.2 Cannabinoids

Cannabis addiction is associated with appetite changes and malnutrition. Typically it leads to overeating high calorie foods sparse in nutrients and under consumption of nutritionally dense foods. One of the primary ways cannabis addiction is associated with systemic oxidative stress and malnutrition is by virtue of its interaction with the endocannabinoid system. Overactivation of the endocannabinoid system can lead to obesity and there is hyperactivation of endocannabinoid tone in obesity. The endocannabinoid system consists of cannabinoid receptors, numerous endocannabinoids and endocannabinoid synthesizing and degrading enzymes [59]. It is believed that an association exists between endocannabinoid overactivity and obesity. Exogenous cannabinoids interact with receptors, such as those of the CB1 type, distributed in regions of the brain that regulate appetite [60]. The CB1 receptor antagonist rimonabant has been used to treat overeating and obesity-related metabolic variants: it is of interest to note that the administration of rimonabant produced an increase in high-density lipoprotein cholesterol and a reduction in triglyceride levels. The endocannabinoids and Δ^9-tetrahydrocannabinol (THC), the main psychoactive ingredient in marijuana, are orexigenic and trigger the motivation to eat. Endocannabinoid levels surge in response to a fasted state and are proposed to result in food intake by stimulating mesolimbic dopaminergic pathways within the brain. The hypothalamus receives hormonal and neural signals regarding metabolic changes and nutrition status at any given point in time. Information collected from these two central regions is continuously integrated and used to adjust calorie intake and energy storage in peripheral areas accordingly.

Food palatability may increase further when both THC and opiate are used concurrently, as strong functional interactions exist between these two endogenous substrates. The hyperphagic effects of THC and morphine are blocked by naloxone and rimonabant, respectively. This demonstrates that μ-opioid receptors are likely to be involved in the food reinforcing effects of THC and CB1 receptors in the food reinforcing effects of morphine [61]. Salted food is also believed to stimulate μ-opioid receptors [7].

19.3.3 Opioids

Opioid receptor agonists augment food intake and receptor blockers decrease food intake. It is believed that opioids are involved in meal maintenance, orosensory reward and functional diversity regarding consummatory behavior [62]. However, opiate addicts tend to consume foods containing spare nutritional value. More than three-fourths show evidence of hypovitaminemia, almost half are deficient in Vitamin B_6 and folate, and 13–19% show deficiencies of thiamine, Vitamin B_{12}, riboflavin and nicotinate [63].

Nutritional status and corresponding physiological states can influence sensitivity to, and dependence on, opiates and their effects. Diabetes reduces sensitivity to morphine and Vitamin D deficiency slows the progression of morphine addiction. Heroin addiction has been associated with hyperkalemia and morphine can cause calcium inhibition, impaired gastrin release, hypercholesterolemia, hypothermia, and hyperthermia [64]. It is widely believed among opiate addicts on buprenorphine maintenance that methadone is associated with a relatively high incidence of osteopenia and osteoporosis [65]. However, studies show that methadone maintenance patients often carry several other risk factors for osteopenia and osteoporosis, such as tobacco dependence, alcohol addiction, being HIV positive, hypogonadism, and malnutrition. Opiates,

such as oxycodone, methadone, and buprenorphine, can contribute to oxidative stress and also have a direct effect on bone mineral density (BMD) [66]. Hyperoxidant stress secondary to opiate-related malnutrition can also lead to bone fracture [66]. The use of opiates as a street drug, in pain management, opiate detoxification and maintenance is on the rise. Patients with a history of opiate addiction or that take opiates on a regular basis should increase their consumption of calcium-containing foods (Table 19.2), expose their hands and face to the sun for 10–15 minutes a few times per week, make a concerted effort to improve diet and lifestyle in addition to the recommendations of their physician if low BMD is a concern. In addition, addicts should consider curtailing their consumption of excess protein, spinach, sodium, and wheat bran, as these are also risk factors for osteoporosis.

19.3.4 Stimulants

Stimulants such as cocaine affect food and liquid intake, taste preference, and BMI. Major behavioral changes occur regarding food selection and consumption during cocaine use and withdrawal, which lead to weight gain or loss. Cocaine, amphetamine, and 3,4-N-methylenedioxymethamphetamine (MDMA or Ecstasy) reduce food consumption [67,68]. Abnormal inhibitions of food intake are thought to be multifactorial, but largely due to altered signaling events within the nucleus accumbens (NAc) [69], a brain reward center influencing the drive to eat [70]. Stimulation of serotonin (5-hydroxytryptamine, 5-HT) 4 receptors in the NAc reduces the drive to eat and increases the satiety factor, cocaine- and amphetamine-regulated transcript (CART) and the administration of $5-HT_4R$ antagonist induces hyperphagia. It is believed that CART peptides are involved in stress,

Table 19.2 Calcium-containing foods

Acorn Squash	Carob	Legumes	Turnip Greens
Almonds	Dried Figs	Okra	Walnuts
Broccoli	Fish (see Table 19.4)	Rolled Oats	Watercress
Butternut Squash	Kale	Sesame Seeds/Tahini	

cardiovascular function, and bone remodeling, and interfere with eating and drug reward. Neuropsychiatric studies strongly support an anorectic action of CART in consummatory behavior and mutations in the CART gene are associated with anorexia and obesity. CART is yet another common denominator shared by food and drug-related rewards [71].

19.3.5   Tobacco

Cigarette smoking and malnutrition are among the leading public health problems of our times. Tobacco addiction directly and indirectly causes nutritional deficiencies [72]. Smokers generate an extraordinary amount of ROS or free radicals, which essentially target all living cells and organ systems in the body, contributing to progressive oxidative stress. Hence, the antioxidant capacity of

smokers is markedly reduced. Ascorbic acid deficiency and hypercholesterolaemia are mediated by both smoking and dietary factors. It has been suggested that smokers supplement their diets with Vitamin C, a potent water soluble antioxidant, in order to fractionally offset the pathogenic effect of smoking caused by the bombardment of free radicals on the organism [73]. Both active and passive tobacco smoke inhalation is associated with decreased folate levels [74], and folic acid deficiencies can lead to elevated homocysteine levels. There is some evidence that cigarette smoking affects homocysteine levels, which has been associated with artherogenesis, thrombogenesis, coronary disease, cerebrovascular disease, and peripheral vascular disease [75]. In addition, hemoglobin is lower as well as the incidence of anemia (unrelated to folate deficiency) and elevated white blood cell count in smokers compared to nonsmokers [76].

19.4   TREATMENT OF NUTRITIONAL DISEASES IN ADDICTED PATIENTS

It is important that drug addicts adhere to a recovery program that includes modest stress management exercise such as yoga, physical exercise such as a forty minute walk several times weekly, and healthier eating habits. Convenience foods and supplements are no substitute for a sound lifestyle correction plan, especially during the first year of recovery.

19.4.1   Antioxidant and fiber-containing and low glycemic index foods

There is evidence that aging [77], the pathogenesis of anxiety [78], cancer [79,80], cardiovascular disease [81,82], diabetes [83], mild cognitive impairment [84], learning and memory disabilities [85], neurodegenerative diseases [86] such as Alzheimer's disease [87], and skin carcinogenesis [88] are associated with the generation of ROS and depletion of antioxidants. Evidence also exists for creation of ROS, pathogenesis by oxidative stress, depletion of antioxidants and disease

prevention by antioxidants for the various addicting drugs [89,90]. Increased oxidative stress associated with drug addiction is thought to be the product of both drug metabolism and malnutrition in the form of antioxidant-deficient consummatory behavior.

Cooking practices can significantly contribute to the production of free radicals and oxidative stress. Meats cooked at high temperatures contain mutagenic heterocyclic amines [91]. Increased production of heterocyclic amines can result from excessive baking, broiling, barbecuing or frying meats, fish, dairy products, and vegetables. While frying produces the greatest amounts of free radical-based carcinogens, this method has the added disadvantage of general loss of *cis* double bonds (i.e., Omega 3, 6 and 9) and an increase in *trans* formation [92]. Progressive degradation occurs when frying oil discard times are improperly monitored [93]. Charbroiled meat forms similar carcinogenic combustion products [94]. Acrylamide is yet another carcinogen formed in heated protein-rich foods and carbohydrate-rich foods, such as certain potato products and crispbread [95]. For example, potato chips and whole potato-based fried snacks can contain more than $1000\,\mu g/kg$ of acrylamide [96]. However, it may be aversive to advise an addict to abruptly refrain from eating fried or deep-browned foods; responses similar to "what am I supposed to eat!" are not unusual. Instead, lifestyle planning might include gradual reduction in the frequency with which oxidative stress-producing fried or over-heated meat [97] is consumed and mitigate risk by consuming larger portions of antioxidant-containing foods [98] (Table 19.3), taking 1000 mgs of buffered Vitamin C plus recommending a piece of fresh produce before and after the entrée. Consumption of a fresh fruit or vegetable approximately every two hours between meals until bedtime and before eating oxidant-generating foods is purported to be associated with enhanced systemic antioxidant tone, reduced oxidative stress, and reduce risk for disease [99–102]. Seasoning meals with modest amounts of cinnamon, black pepper, curcumin and cold pressed olive oil further reduces oxidative stress and augments the antioxidant value of the meal or snack [103].

Most antioxidant-containing foods progressively oxidize depending on the amount of processing they undergo. Supplements can oxidize even more during processing. Raw produce usually has the highest antioxidant value. The antioxidant value progressively diminishes with one minute compared to four minute steaming, boiling al dente, and well done. Canned and extract versions can have the lowest relative antioxidant value. The GI/GL values often follow similar fates. There are few exceptions, such as low sodium tomato juice, sauce and paste, which gains antioxidant strength and maintains its bioavailability with processing. Recovering addicts should strive towards eating about 60% of their total calories from foods such as those listed in Table 19.3.

Table 19.3 Antioxidant- and fiber-containing, and low Glycemic Index foods

Fruit	Vegetables	Grain
Apple	Asparagus	Bulgar
Banana (New)	Avocado	Barley (non-instant)
Cherry	Broccoli	Converted Rice (C)
Grape, green	Carrot	Fettuccine (A, C, M)
Mango	Cauliflower	Koshikari Rice
Orange	Celery	Linguini (A, C, M)
Peach	Corn	Macaroni (A, C, M)
Pear	Cucumber	Rice Bran
Juice (Unsweetened)	Garlic	Spaghetti (A, C, M)
Apple	Green Bean	Spirali (A, C, M)
Carrot	Pea	Wild Rice
Pineapple	Pepper	*Bread*
Tomato (Low sodium)	Smashed Potato (C)	Buckwheat
Soup (Low NaCl and KCl)	Squash	Cracked Wheat
Lentil	Sweet Potato	9 Grain or greater (C)
Minestrone	*Legumes*	Oat Bran
Tomato	Chickpeas	Pumpernickle
Nuts (Unsalted)	Kidney Beans	Sourdough
Brazil	Lentil Beans	Sourdough Rye
Cashew	Navy Beans	*Cereal*
Pecan	Peanuts (Unsalted)	Kellogg's Complete Oat
Walnut	Split Peas	Old Fashioned Oatmeal (A, C)

A: Cooked al dente; C: Cold press olive oil added; M: Multigrain.
Table from [104].

19.4.2 Minimally processed protein

Meats contain essentially no antioxidant potential, which marks one possible mechanism underlying the association between high protein diets and pathogenesis. Their ability to generate more free radicals relative to most other foods underscores the importance of balancing the 25–30% of total calories from protein with 60% of foods high in antioxidants and fiber, but having a low GI. Minimally processed lean protein, such as poultry and hypo-toxic species of fish (Table 19.4), with infrequent consumption of red meat is preferred during early recovery. Vegans can meet their daily protein requirements by keeping track of protein sources, such as legumes, unsalted nuts and seeds, and tahini; these also contain antioxidants.

Controversy over the toxicity and benefits of fish continues. Primary concerns include mercury [105], and polychlorinated biphenyls and related free radical producers. Mercury content varies greatly from species to species [106] and dioxin level is more a function of whether or not a particular species is fatty, or farm raised [107]. It has been suggested that the consumption of large quantities of certain species could significantly increase health risks due to the lipophilic organic compounds [108]. The consumption of farm raised salmon at relatively low frequencies can increase exposure to dioxins and dioxin-like compounds sufficiently to increase the risk of disease [109]. On a more optimistic note, levels of dioxin-like compounds and PCBs appear to be decreasing in Mississippi catfish [110].

Processed proteins, such as cheese, delicatessen meats, hydrolyzed plant protein (soy), and albumin and whey powder, should be avoided during recovery as they can have higher relative percentages of denatured protein. The controversy over processed soy continues with signs that it is behaving like an antinutrient [111,112] and its levels of concentrated phytoestrogens are of concern to a few researchers studying cancer [113]. Brief reports link processed soy with allergies, fluorosis [114], and increased exposure to manganese [115] and aluminum [116,117].

19.4.3 Omegas

Although fish oil supplements may be more healthful than the consumption of organochlorines-containing fish [118], minimally processed and unheated omegas, such as those found in cold pressed olive oil, are preserved by several other antioxidants. The omegas in cold pressed olive oil may also be a more bioavailable source of omega-3 compared with fish oil supplements. Omega 3 and omega 6 need to be ingested in a certain ratio, preferably in the presence of omega 9, or bioavailability is likely to be affected [119,120]. Topping each meal with two tablespoons of cold pressed olive oil helps provide a bioavailable ratio of omega 3, 6, and 9 without contributing to adipose storage nearly as readily as from saturated fat sources such as cheese.

19.4.4 Sodium chloride

Sodium chloride appears to act as a food consumption accelerant and may be an addictive substance. Salted food stimulates appetite, increases calorie consumption and the incidence of overeating, obesity and related illnesses. Individuals consume fewer calories from a low sodium meal, eat less and often initially struggle with a low sodium eating plan. The Salted Food Addition Hypothesis proposes that

Table 19.4 Lower mercury (Hg) and polychlorinated biphenyls (PCBs) containing fish and shellfish

Butterfish	Haddock	Ocean Perch	Snapper
Clam[a]	Hake	Oyster[a]	Sole
Cod	Lobster, Spiny[a]	Perch, Freshwater	Squid[a]
Crab[a]	Mahi Mahi	Salmon, Wild	Tilefish, Atlantic
Crawfish[a]	Monkfish	Scallop[a]	Trout
Flounder	Mackerel, Spanish	Shrimp[a]	Tuna, Canned, Light (not albacore)

[a]Not recommended in hypercholesterolaemia.

salted food acts in the brain like an opiate agonist, producing a hedonic reward which has been perceived as being only peripherally "flavorful", "tasty" or "delicious" [7]. Impulses originating primarily from the posterior aspect of the tongue and palate travel into the mesolimbic opioid system, yielding reward and continued salted food consumption even while satiated [121]. The Salted Food Addiction Hypothesis also proposes that mesolimbic opiate receptor withdrawal has been perceived as "appetite," "craving" or "hunger" for salted food. Regardless of the underlying mechanism, patients may want to begin the transition by beginning with a moderately salted (which in most cases translates into a reduction in processed convenience food) eating plan for approximately two weeks prior to beginning a low sodium diet. "Light salt" or potassium chloride should also be avoided. Popular salted foods, such as cheese, may require more extended and gradual step-down plans.

19.4.5   Non-nutritive sweeteners

Cylamate and saccharin were the forerunners to today's artificial, non-nutritive and low-energy sweeteners. Safety issues surrounding these sweeteners have been controversial since their inception and have focused primarily on the question of carcinogenesis, essentially to the exclusion of their possible role in the development of other diseases. They are found in numerous foods with the purpose of lowering the number of total calories from carbohydrate.

Low-energy sweeteners have only been sanctioned noncarcinogenic and acceptable for dental hygiene. The controversies lie outside these realms. Anecdotal reports include the relationships between sweeteners and anxiety attacks, diarrhea and altered bioavailability of nutrients and medicines, eczema, immune response, irritability, insomnia, light sensitivity, migraine headaches, nausea, pain perception, tachycardia, and wheezing. Investigators continue to disagree about the relationships between non-nutritive sweeteners and lymphomas, leukemias, cancers of the bladder and brain, chronic fatigue syndrome, Parkinson's disease, Alzheimer's disease, multiple sclerosis, autism, and systemic lupus [122]. They also have not been adequately brain-tested or linked to weight reduction in adult or pediatric populations to warrant their large presence within the food chain. Non-nutritive sugars are chemical concoctions that substitute for low GI foods essential to sustained energy; they are not sources of minimally processed protein or omega 3, 6, and 9, and, most importantly, have essentially no antioxidant properties. Sugar substitutes are best classified as macro-antinutrients and have no place in a recovering addict's food plan. Healthier alternatives include natural cane sugar, crystalline fructose, and agave nectar. Recovering addicts, especially those with metabolic syndrome, may benefit greatly by avoiding foods made of hammer and cylinder milled flours, including whole wheat. Products made of flour can often have a GI higher than that of granular sugar.

19.5   CONCLUSIONS

Drug addicts are elusive historians and are often difficult to diagnose when they present for nutritional consultation. Supplementing the nutritional evaluation with a mini substance addiction evaluation and comprehensive urine drug screen is essential. Substance addiction and the associated lifestyle are directly linked to nutritional diseases. Patients can be directed to AlcoholDetoxDiet.com or OpiateRecoveryDiet.com for quick reference regarding lifestyle guidelines.

REFERENCES

1. Collins, G.B., Kotz, M., Janesz, J.W. *et al.* (1985) Alcoholism in the families of bulimic anorexics. *Cleveland Clin. Q.*, **52**, 65–67.

2. Jonas, J.M., Gold, M.S., Sweeney, D., and Pottash, A.L.C. (1987) Eating disorders and cocaine abuse: A survey of 259 cocaine abusers. *J. Clin. Psych.*, **48**, 47–50.

3. Holderness, C.C., Brooks-Gunn, J., and Warren, M.P. (1994) Co-morbidity of eating disorders and substance

abuse review of the literature. *Int. J. Eat. Disord.*, **16** (1), 1–34.

4. Volkow, N.D., Wang, G.J., Fowler, J.S. *et al.* (2008) Overlapping neuronal circuits in addiction and obesity: evidence of systems pathology. *Philos. Trans. R. Soc. Lond. B Biol. Sci.*, **363** (1507), 3191–3200.

5. Avena, N.M., Rada, P., and Hoebel, B.G. (2008) Evidence for sugar addiction: Behavioral and neurochemical effects of intermittent, excessive sugar intake. *Neurosci. Biobehav. Rev.*, **32** (1), 20–39.

6. Gold, M.S., Graham, N.A., Cocores, J., and Nixon, S.J. (2009) Food addiction? *J. Addiction Med.*, **3**, 42–45.

7. Cocores, J.A. and Gold, M.S. (2009) The salted food addiction hypothesis may explain overeating and the obesity epidemic. *Medical Hypotheses*, **73** (6), 892–899.

8. Cocores, J. (1994) Addictive psychiatric disorders, in *Treating Coexisting Psychiatric and Addictive Disorders* (ed. N.S. Miller), Hazelden, Center City, MN.

9. Feinman, L. and Lieber, C.S. (1999) Nutrition and diet in alcoholism, in *Modern Nutrition in Health and Disease* (eds M.E. Shils, J.A. Olson, M., Shike, and A.C. Ross), Lippincott Williams & Wilkins, pp. 1523–1542.

10. American Cancer Society (2006) Cancer Facts & Figures 2006, American Cancer Society, Atlanta.

11. Vlahcevic, Z.R., Buhac, I., Farrar, J.T. *et al.* (1971) Bile acid metabolism of cholic acid metabolism. I. Kinetic aspects of cholic acid metabolism. *Gastroenterology*, **60**, 491–498.

12. Feinman, L. and Lieber, C.S. (1988) Toxicity of ethanol and other components of alcoholic beverages. *Alcohol Clin. Exp. Res.*, **12** (1), 2–6.

13. Gruchow, H.W., Sobocinski, K.A., and Barboriak, J.J. (1985) Alcohol, nutrient intake, and hypertension in US adults. *JAMA*, **253** (11), 1567–1570.

14. Hillers, V.N. and Massey, L.K. (1985) Interrelationships of moderate and high alcohol consumption with diet and health status. *Am. J. Clin. Nutr.*, **41** (2), 356–362.

15. Miller, N.S. and Gold, M.S. (1991) *Alcohol*, Plenum Medical Book Company, NY, pp. 53–56.

16. Kleiner, K.D., Gold, M.S., Frost-Pineda, K. *et al.* (2004) Body mass index and alcohol use. *J. Addict. Dis.*, **23** (3), 105–118.

17. Ottani, A., Leone, S., Vergara, F.B. *et al.* (2007) Preference for palatable food is reduced by the gamma-hydroxybutyrate analogue GET73, in rats. *Pharmacol Res.*, **55** (4), 271–279.

18. Lieber, C.S. (1991) Perspectives: do alcohol calories count? *Am. J. Clin. Nutr.*, **54** (6), 976–982.

19. Mezey, E. and Fallance, L.A. (1971) Metabolic impairment and recovery time in acute ethanol intoxication. *J. Nerv. Ment. Dis.*, **153** (6), 445–452.

20. Pirola, R.C. and Leiber, C.S. (1972) The energy cost of the metabolism of drugs, including alcohol. *Pharmacology*, **7** (3), 185–196.

21. Williamson, D.F., Forman, M.R., Binkin, N.J. *et al.* (1987) Alcohol and body weight in United States adults. *Am. J. Public Health*, **77** (10), 1324–1330.

22. Guthrie, G.D., Myers, K.J., Gesser, E.J. *et al.* (1990) Alcohol as a nutrient: interactions between ethanol and carbohydrate. *Alcohol Clin. Exp. Res.*, **14** (1), 17–22.

23. Barclay, A.W., Petocz, P., McMillan-Price, J. *et al.* (2008) Glycemic index, glycemic load, and chronic disease risk-a meta-analysis of observational studies. *Am. J. Clin. Nutr.*, **87** (3), 627–637.

24. Arteaga Liona, A. (2006) The Glycemic index. A Current controversy. *Nutr. Hosp.*, **21** (Suppl. 2), 53–59.

25. Segal, M.S., Gollub, E., and Johnson, R.J. (2007) Is the fructose index more relevant with regards to cardiovascular disease than the Glycemic index? *Eur. J. Nutr.*, **46** (7), 406–417.

26. Foster-Powell, K., Holt, S.H., and Brand-Miller, J.C. (2002) International table of glycemic index and glycemic load values. *Am. J. Clin. Nutr.*, **76** (1), 5–56.

27. Schultz, M., Liese, A.D., Mayer-Davis, E.J. *et al.* (2005) Nutritional correlates of dietary glycaemic index: new aspects from a population perspective. *Br. J. Nutr.*, **94** (3), 397–406.

28. Neumann, K.F., Rojo, L., Navarrete, L.P. *et al.* (2008) Insulin resistance and Alzheimer's disease: molecular links & clinical implications. *Curr. Alzheimer Res.*, **5** (5), 438–447.

29. Armellini, F., Zamboni, M., Mandragona, R. *et al.* (1993) Alcohol consumption, smoking habits and body fat distribution in Italian men and women aged 20–60 years. *Eur. J. Clin. Nutr.*, **47** (1), 52–60.

30. Tremblay, A., Buemann, B., Theriault, G. *et al.* (1995) Body fatness in active individuals reporting low lipid and alcohol intake. *Eur. J. Clin. Nutr.*, **49** (11), 824–831.

31. Gottfried, E.B., Kosten, M.A., and Lieber, C.S. (1978) Alcohol-induced gastric and duodenal lesions in man. *Am. J. Gastroenterol.*, **70** (6), 587–592.

32. Laine, L., and Weinstein, W.M. (1988) Histology of alcoholic hemorrhagic "gastritis": a prospective evaluation. *Gastroenterology*, **94** (6), 1254–1262.

33. Baran, D.T., Teitelbaum, S.L., Bergfeld, M.A. *et al.* (1980) Effect of alcohol ingestion on bone and mineral

metabolism in rats. *Am. J. Physiol.*, **238** (6), E507–E510.

34. Garcia-Sanchez, A., Gonzalez-Calvin, J.L., Diez-Ruiz, A. *et al.* (1995) Effect of acute alcohol ingestion on mineral metabolism and osteoblastic function. *Alcohol*, **30** (4), 449–453.

35. Tabet, N., Mantle, D., Walker, Z. *et al.* (2005) Higher fat and carbohydrate intake in dementia patients is associated with increased blood glutathione peroxidase activity. *Int. Psychogeriatr.*, **17** (1), 91–98.

36. Zakhari, S. (2006) Overview: how is alcohol metabolized by the body? *Alcohol Res. Health*, **29** (4), 245–254.

37. Seitz, H.K. and Becker, P. (2007) Alcohol metabolism and cancer risk. *Alcohol Res. Health*, **30** (1), 38–41.

38. Das, S.K. and Vasudevan, D.M. (2007) Alcohol-induced oxidative stress. *Life Sci.*, **81** (3), 177–187.

39. Haorah, J., Ramirez, S.H., Floreani, N. *et al.* (2008) Mechanisms of alcohol-induced oxidative stress and neuronal injury. *Free Radic. Biol. Med.*, **45** (11), 1542–1550.

40. Bonjour, J.P. (1979) Vitamins and alcoholism. I. Ascorbic acid. *Int. J. Vitam. Nutr. Res.*, **49** (4), 434–441.

41. Clark, L.T. and Friedman, H.S. (1985) Hypertension associated with alcohol withdrawal: Assessment of mechanisms and complications. *Alcoholism*, **9**, 125–130.

42. Zima, T. and Kalousova, M. (2005) Oxidative stress and signal transduction pathways in alcoholic liver disease. *Alcohol Clin. Exp. Res.*, **29** (11 Suppl.), 110S–115.

43. De Minicis, S. and Brenner, D.A. (2008) Oxidative stress in alcoholic liver disease: role of NADPH oxidase complex. *J. Gastroenterol Hepatol.*, **23** (Suppl. 1), S98–S103.

44. Marlatt, M.W., Lucassen, P.J., Perry, G. *et al.* (2008) Alzheimer's disease: cerebrovascular dysfunction, oxidative stress, and advanced clinical therapies. *J. Alzheimers Dis.*, **15** (2), 199–210.

45. Seifried, H.E., Anderson, D.E., Fisher, E.I. *et al.* (2007) A review of the interaction among dietary antioxidants and reactive oxygen species. *J. Nutr. Biochem.*, **18** (9), 567–579.

46. Galanis, A., Pappa, A., Giannakakis, A. *et al.* (2008) Reactive oxygen species and HIF-1 signaling in cancer. *Cancer Lett.*, **18** (1), 12–20.

47. Li, Y., Baer, D., Friedman, G.D. *et al.* (2008) Wine, liquor, beer and risk of breast cancer in a large population. *Eur. J. Cancer*, **45** (5), 843–850.

48. Klatsky, A.L., Armstrong, M.A., and Friedman, G.D. (1997) Red wine, white wine, liquor, beer, and risk for coronary artery disease hospitalization. *Am. J. Cardiol.*, **80** (4), 416–420.

49. Colombo, G., Addolorato, G., Agabio, R. *et al.* (2004) Role of GABA(B) receptor in alcohol dependence: reducing effect of baclofen on alcohol intake and alcohol motivational properties in rats and amelioration of alcohol withdrawal syndrome and alcohol craving in human alcoholics. *Neurotox Res.*, **6** (5), 403–414.

50. Broft, A.I., Spanos, A., Corwin, R.L. *et al.* (2007) Baclofen for binge eating: an open-label trial. *Int. J. Eat. Disord.*, **40** (8), 687–691.

51. Melendez, R.I., Rodd-Hendricks, Z.A., McBride, W.J. *et al.* (2003) Alcohol stimulates the release of dopamine in the ventral pallidum but not in the globus pallidus: a dual-probe microdialysis study. *Neuropsychopharmacology*, **28**, 939–946.

52. Chandra, R.K. (1997) Nutrition and the immune system: an introduction. *Am. J. Clin. Nutr.*, **66**, 460–463.

53. Valerla, P., Marcos, A., Ripoll, S. *et al.* (1997) Effects of HIV infection and detoxification time on anthropometric measurements and dietary intake of male drug addicts. *Am. J. Clin. Nutr.*, **66**, 509S–514.

54. Valera, P., Marcos, A., Santacruz, I. *et al.* (1997) Human immunodeficiency virus infection and nutritional status in female drug addicts undergoing detoxification: anthropometric and immunologic assessments. *Am. J. Clin. Nutr.*, **66** (2), 504S–508.

55. Nazrul, I.S.K., Jahangir, H.K., Ahmed, A. *et al.* (2002) Nutritional status of drug addicts undergoing detoxification: prevalence of malnutrition and influence of illicit drugs and lifestyle. *Br. J. Nutr.*, **88** (5), 507–513.

56. Himmelgreen, D.A., Perez-Escamilla, R., Segura-Millan, S. *et al.* (1998) A comparison of the nutritional status and energy security of drug-using and non-drug using Hispanic women in Hartford. *Connecticut. Am. J. Phys. Anthropol.*, **107**, 351–361.

57. Nazrul Islam, S.K., Jahangir Hossain, K., and Ahsan, M. (2001) Serum vitamin E, C and A status of the drug addicts undergoing detoxification: influence of drug habit, sexual practice and lifestyle factors. *EJCN*, **55** (11), 1022–1027.

58. Cooper, S.J. (2005) Palatability-dependent appetite and benzodiazepines: new directions from the pharmacology of GABA(A) receptor subtypes. *Appetite*, **44** (2), 133–150.

59. Piomelli, D. (2003) The molecular logic of endocannabinoid signaling. *Nat. Rev. Neurosci.*, **4**, 873–884.

60. Bellocchio, L., Mancini, G., Vicennati, V. *et al.* (2006) Cannabinoid receptors as therapeutic targets for

obesity and metabolic diseases. *Curr. Opin. Pharmacol.*, **6** (6), 586–591.

61. Solinas, M. and Goldberg, S.R. (2005) Motivational effects of cannabinoids and opioids on food reinforcement depend on simultaneous activation of cannabinoid and opioid Systems. *Neuropsychopharmacology*, **30**, 2035–2045.

62. Glass, M.J., Billington, C.J., and Levine, A.S. (1999) Opioids and food intake: distributed functional neural pathways. *Neuropeptides*, **13** (5), 360–368.

63. Nakah, A.E.L., Frank, O., Louria, D.B. *et al.* (1979) A vitamin profile of heroin addiction. *AJPH*, **69** (10), 1058–1060.

64. Mohs, M.E., Watson, R.R., and Leonard-Green, T. (1990) Nutritional effects of marijuana, heroin, cocaine, and nicotine. *J. Am. Diet. Assoc.*, **90** (9), 1261–1267.

65. Kim, T.W., Alford, D.P., Malabanan, A. *et al.* (2006) Low bone density in patients receiving methadone maintenance treatment. *Drug Alcohol Depend.*, **85** (3), 258–262.

66. Sheweita, S.A. and Khoshhal, K.I. (2007) Calcium metabolism and oxidative stress in bone fractures: role of antioxidants. *Curr. Drug Metab.*, **8** (5), 519–525.

67. Cohen, R.S. and Cocores, J.A. (1997) Neuropsychiatric manifestations following the use of 3,4-methylenediozymethamphetamine (MDMA; ECSTASY). *Pro. Neuro-Psychophamacol & Biol. Psychiat.*, **21**, 727–734.

68. Rochester, J.A. and Kirchner, J.T. (1999) Ecstasy (3,4-methylenedioxymethamphetamine): history, neurochemistry, and toxicology. *J. Am. Board Fam. Pract.*, **12** (2), 137–142.

69. Jean, A., Conductier, G., Manrique, C. *et al.* (2007) Anorexia induced by activation of serotonin 5-HT$_4$ receptors is mediated by increases in CART in the nucleus accumbens. *PNAS*, **104** (41), 16335–16340.

70. Stratford, T.R. and Kelley, A.E. (1997) GABA in the nucleus accumbens shell participates in central regulation of feeding behavior. *J. Neurosci.*, **17** (11), 4434–4440.

71. Vicentic, A. and Jones, D.C. (2007) The CART (cocaine- and amphetamine-regulated transcript) system in appetite and drug addiction. *J. Pharmacol. Exp. Ther.*, **320** (2), 499–506.

72. Marangon, K., Herbeth, B., Lecomete, E. *et al.* (1998) Diet, antioxidant status and smoking habits in French men. *Am. J. Clin. Nutr.*, **67**, 231–239.

73. Hijova, E., Kuchta, M., and Petrasova, D. (2002) Smokers-vitamin C-hypercholesterolaemia. *Cent. Eur. J. Public Health*, **10** (1–2), 29–31.

74. Mannino, D.M., Mulinare, J., Ford, E.S. *et al.* (2003) Tobacco smoke exposure and decreased serum and red blood folate levels: data from the Third National Health and Nutrition Examination Survey. *Nicotine Tob. Res.*, **5** (3), 357–362.

75. Sobczak, A.J. (2003) The effects of tobacco smoke on the homocysteine level – a risk factor of atherosclerosis. *Addict. Biol.*, **8** (2), 147–158.

76. Tungtrongchitr, R., Pongpaew, P., Soonthornruengyot, M. *et al.* (2003) Relationship of tobacco smoking and serum vitamin B12, folic acid and haematological indices in healthy adults. *Public Health Nutr.*, **7**, 675–681.

77. Calabrese, V., Guagliano, E., Sapienza, M. *et al.* (2007) Redox regulation of cellular stress response in aging and neurodegenerative disorders: role of vitagenes. *Neurochem. Res.*, **32** (4–5), 757–773.

78. Ramirez, M.R., Izquierdo, I., do Carmo Bassols Raseira, M. *et al.* (2005) Effect of lyophilised Vaccinium berries on memory, anxiety and locomotion in adult rats. *Pharmacol. Res.*, **52** (6), 457–462.

79. La Vecchia, C. (2004) Mediterranean diet and cancer. *Public Health Nutr.*, **7** (7), 965–968.

80. Loft, S., Hogh Danielson, P., Mikkelsen, L. *et al.* (2008) Biomarkers of oxidative damage to DNA and repair. *Biochem. Soc. Trans.*, **36** (5), 1071–1076.

81. Van Wagoner, D.R. (2008) Oxidative stress and inflammation in atrial fibrillation: role in pathogenesis and potential as a therapeutic target. *J. Cardiovasc. Pharmacol.*, **52** (4), 306–313.

82. Mariani, E., Polidori, M.C., Cherubini, A. *et al.* (2005) Oxidative stress in brain aging, neurodegenerative and vascular diseases: an overview. *J. Chromatogr. B Analyt. Technol. Biomed. Life Sci.*, **827** (1), 65–75.

83. Osawa, T. and Kato, Y. (2005) Protective role of antioxidative food factors in oxidative stress caused by hyperglycemia. *Ann. NY Acad. Sci.*, **1043**, 440–451.

84. Keller, J.N., Schmitt, F.A., Scheff, S.W. *et al.* (2005) Evidence of increased oxidative damage in subjects with mild cognitive impairment. *Neurology*, **64** (7), 1152–1156.

85. Head, E. and Zicker, S.C. (2004) Nutraceuticals, aging, and cognitive dysfunction. *Vet. Clin. North Am. Small Anim. Pract.*, **34** (1), 217–228.

86. Calabrese, V., Lodi, R., Tonon, C. *et al.* (2005) Oxidative stress, mitochondrial dysfunction and cellular stress response in Friedreich's ataxia. *J. Neurol. Sci.*, **233** (1–2), 145–162.

87. Reddy, P.H. (2006) Amyloid precursor protein-mediated free radicals and oxidative damage: implica-

tions for the development and progression of Alzheimer's disease. *J. Neurochem.*, **96** (1), 1–13.

88. Nishigori, C., Hattori, Y., and Toyokuni, S. (2004) Role of reactive oxygen species in skin carcinogenesis. *Antioxid Redox Signal.*, **6** (3), 561–570.

89. Kovacic, P. (2005) Role of oxidative metabolites of cocaine in toxicity and addiction: oxidative stress and electron transfer. *Med. Hypothesis*, **64** (2), 350–356.

90. Kovacic, P. and Cooksy, A.L. (2005) Unifying mechanism for toxicity and addiction by abused drugs: electron transfer and reactive oxygen species. *Med. Hypothesis*, **64** (2), 357–366.

91. Knize, M.G. and Felton, J.S. (2005) Formation and human risk of carcinogenic heterocyclic amines formed from natural precursors in meat. *Nutr. Rev.*, **63** (5), 158–165.

92. Goburdhun, D., Jhaumeer-Laulloo, S.B., and Musruck, R. (2001) Evaluation of soybean oil quality during conventional frying by FTIR and some chemical indexes. *Int. J. Food Sci. Nutr.*, **52** (1), 31–42.

93. Paul, S. and Mittal, G.S. (1997) Regulating the use of degraded oil/fat in deep-fat/oil food frying. *Crit. Rev. Food Sci. Nutr.*, **37** (7), 635–662.

94. Strickland, P.T., Qian, Z., and Friesen, M.D. (2002) Metabolites of 2-amino-1-methyl-6-phenylimidazo (4,5-b)pyridine (PhIP) in human urine after consumption of charbroiled or fried beef. *Mutat. Res.*, **30** (506–507), 163–173.

95. Tareke, E., Rydberg, P., Karlsson, P. *et al.* (2002) - Analysis of acrylamide, a carcinogen formed in heated foodstuffs. *J. Agric. Food Chem.*, **50** (17), 4998–5006.

96. Yoshida, M., Ono, H., Chuda, Y. *et al.* (2005) Acrylamide in Japanese processed foods and factors affecting acrylamide level in potato chips and tea. *Adv. Med. Exp. Biol.*, **561**, 405–413.

97. Yousef, M.I. and El-Demerdash, F.M. (2006) Acrylamide-induced oxidative stress and biochemical perturbations in rats. *Toxicology*, **219** (1–3), 133–141.

98. Rabin, B.M., Shukitt-Hale, B., Joseph, J. *et al.* (2005) Diet as a factor in behavioral radiation protection following exposure to heavy particles. *Gravit Space Biol. Bull.*, **18** (2), 71–77.

99. Feskanich, D., Ziegler, R.G., Michaud, D. *et al.* (2000) Prospective study of fruit and vegetable consumption and risk of lung cancer among men and women. *J. Natl. Cancer Inst.*, **92** (22), 1812–1823.

100. Riboli, E. and Norat, T. (2001) Cancer prevention and diet: opportunities in Europe. *Public Health Nutr.*, **4** (2B), 475–484.

101. He, F.J., Nowson, C.A., and MacGregor, G.A. (2006) Fruit and vegetable consumption and stroke: meta-analysis of cohort studies. *Lancet*, **367** (9507), 320–326.

102. Ray, A.L., Semba, R.D., Walston, J. *et al.* (2006) Low serum selenium and total carotenoids predict mortality among older women living in the community: the women's health and aging studies. *J. Nutr.*, **136** (1), 172–176.

103. Wu, A., Ying, Z., and Gomez-Pinilla, F. (2006) Dietary curcumin counteracts the outcome of traumatic brain injury on oxidative stress, synaptic plasticity, and cognition. *Exp. Neurol.*, **197** (2), 309–317.

104. Cocores, J. (2006) *BrightFoods: Discover the Surprising Link Between Food and Learning, Memory, Mood, and Performance*, Emmaus Publishing LLC, Boca Raton, FL, p. 155.

105. Valko, M., Rhodes, C.J., Moncol, J. *et al.* (2006) Free radicals, metals and antioxidants in oxidative stress-induced cancer. *Chem. Biol. Interact.*, **160** (1), 1–40.

106. US Department of Health and Human Services and the US Environmental Protection Agency (2006) Mercury Levels in Commercial Fish and Shellfish, http://www.cfsan.fda.gov/~frf/sea-mehg.html.

107. Hayward, D., Wong, J., and Krynitsky, A.J. (2007) Polybrominated diphenyl ethers and polychlorinated biphenyls in commercially wild caught and farm-raised fish fillets in the United States. *Environ. Res.*, **103** (1), 46–54.

108. Domingo, J.L. and Bocio, A. (2007) Levels of PCDD/PCDFs and PCBs in edible marine species and human intake: a literature review. *Environ. Int.*, **33** (3), 397–405.

109. Foran, J.A., Carpenter, D.O., Hamilton, M.C. *et al.* (2005) Risk-based consumption advice for farmed Atlantic and wild Pacific salmon contaminated with dioxins and dioxin-like compounds. *Environ. Health Perspect.*, **113** (5), 552–556.

110. Scott, L.L., Staskal, D.F., Williams, E.S. *et al.* (2009) Levels of polychlorinated dibenzo-p-dioxins, dibenzofurans, and biphenyls in southern Mississippi catfish and estimation of potential health risks. *Chemosphere*, **74** (7), 1002–1010.

111. Grant, G. (1989) Anti-nutritional effects of soyabean: a review. *Prog. Food Nutr. Sci.*, **13**, 317–348.

112. Li, Z., Li, D., Qiao, S. *et al.* (2003) Anti-nutritional effects of moderate dose soybean agglutinin in the rat. *Arch. Tierernahr.*, **57** (4), 267–277.

113. Levison, D.A., Morgan, R.G., Brimacombe, J.S. *et al.* (1979) Carcinogenic effects of Di(2-hydroxypropyl)

nitrosamine (DHPN) in male Wistar rats: promotion of pancreatic cancer by a raw soya flour diet. *Scand. J. Gastroenterol.*, **14** (2), 217–224.

114. Buzlaf, M.A., Damante, C.A., Trevizani, L.M. *et al.* (2004) Risk of fluorosis associated with infant formulas prepared with bottled water. *J. Dent. Child (Chic)*, **7** (2), 110–113.

115. Cockell, K.A., Bonacci, G., and Belonje, B. (2004) Manganese content of soy or rice beverages is high in comparison to infant formulas. *J. Am. Coll. Nutr.*, **23** (2), 124–130.

116. Greger, J.L. (1992) Dietary and other sources of aluminum intake. *Ciba Found. Symp.*, **169**, 26–35.

117. Fernandez-Lorenzo, J.R., Cocho, J.A., Rey-Goldar, M.L. *et al.* (1999) Aluminum contents of human milk, cow's milk, and infant formulas. *J. Pediatr. Gastroenterol. Nutr.*, **28** (3), 270–275.

118. Melanson, S.F., Lewandrowski, E.L., Flood, J.G. *et al.* (2005) Measurement of organochlorines in commercial over-the-counter fish oil preparations: implications for dietary and therapeutic recommendations for omega-3 fatty acids and a review of the literature. *Arch. Pathol. Lab Med.*, **129** (1), 74–77.

119. Bezard, J., Blond, J.P., Bernard, A. *et al.* (1994) The metabolism and availability of essential fatty acids in animal and human tissues. *Reprod. Nutr. Dev.*, **34** (6), 539–568.

120. Gibson, R.A., Makrides, M., Neumann, M.A. *et al.* (1994) Ratios of linoleic acid alpha-linolenic acid in formulas for term infants. *J. Pediatr.*, **125** (5 Pt 2), S48–S55.

121. Lucas, L.R., Grillo, C.A., and McEwens, B.S. (2007) Salt appetite in sodium-depleted or sodium-replete conditions: possible role of opioid receptors. *Neuroendocrinology*, **85** (3), 139–147.

122. Whitehouse, C.R., Boullata, J., and McCauley, L.A. (2008) The potential toxicity of artificial sweeteners. *AAOHN J.*, **56** (6), 251–259.

20

Addictive disorders in nutritional diseases – from a nutritional viewpoint

Jennifer A. Nasser, Jessica B. Leitzsch, and Kiran Patel

Division of Nutrition, Department of Bioscience and Biotechnology, Drexel University, Philadelphia, PA 19104, USA

20.1 INTRODUCTION

20.1.1 Definition of nutritional disorders

Nutritional disorders can be defined from a number of perspectives. One method of classification is based on the use of nutrients as therapeutic modalities in situations of disordered organ function. In this regard the Center for Medicare Services defines reimbursable medical nutrition therapy for diabetes, renal disease, and comorbid hypertension and hyperlipidemia. Another classification system is based on the effect of nutrient excess or deficiency on the functioning of organ systems. In this regard, illnesses such as osteoporosis, anemia, thyroiditis, obesity, marasmus, and kwashiorkor would be considered nutritional disorders. A third method of classification involves the behavioral relationship between nutrients and the regulation of their intake. In this regard, eating disorders such as anorexia nervosa, bulimia nervosa, binge eating disorder, night eating syndrome, and obesity could be considered nutritional disorders.

This chapter addresses the interaction of substance addiction and nutritional disorders classified by all three methods described above. It provides an overview of currently accepted nutrition therapy methods and discusses the pathophysiology of aberrant intake regulation.

20.1.2 Interaction of addictive disorders with medical nutritional therapy

Substance addictions involve the use of various classes of drugs that affect a range of bodily organ systems. Since all classes of misused drugs – alcohol, tobacco, stimulants, pain killers, tranquilizers – are believed to usurp the naturally occurring reward pathways meant to help control food (and thus nutrient/energy) intake [1], substance addiction has the potential to induce clinical and subclinical malnutrition states. In addition, psychological desire for food is altered in individuals misusing substances. This can be especially dangerous in diseases such as diabetes and renal disease in which acute nutrient intake plays a major role in treating the organ dysfunction.

Addictive Disorders in Medical Populations   Edited by Norman S. Miller and Mark S. Gold
© 2010 John Wiley & Sons, Ltd.

20.1.3 Interaction of addictive disorders and food intake regulation

Food intake regulation involves interactions between peripheral sensory signals, intestinal hormonal signals, and central neurotransmitter signals. Oral stimulation with food through taste and smell as well as drugs of addiction directly causes release of brain dopamine that promotes pleasure and continued motivation to acquire more food or drug. Volkow *et al.* [1] reviewed the similarities in neural circuitries underlying motivation to acquire and ingest food and drugs. Common neurotransmitters involved in these processes include mesolimbic dopamine and opioid circuits. These neurotransmitter circuits are modulated by peptide hormones [2] which originate in the gastrointestinal tract, such as ghrelin, insulin, leptin, cholecystokinin (CCK), and glucagon-like-peptide-1 (GLP-1), as well as centrally derived peptides, such as neuropeptide Y (NPY), melanin concentrating hormone (MCH), and cocaine-amphetamine-related transcript (CART). Some data exist suggesting that overeating and obesity are protective against drug addiction [3,4] and Carr [5] reports that, in animals, chronic food restriction increases the sensitivity to addictive drugs.

20.1.4 Prevalence of nutritional disorders in chronic alcohol and drug use

Chronic alcoholics and drug addicts have distorted eating behavior that predisposes them to eating disorders [6], malnutrition disorders, and hematological disorders. There are high rates of co-occurrence of eating disorders and substance addiction [7]. Jonas *et al.* [8] found 32% of 259 surveyed cocaine users met the DSM-III criteria for anorexia, bulimia or both. Santolaria-Fernández *et al.* [9] found 66.4% of hospitalized drug addicts exhibited anorexia at the time of admission. When compared to the general population, those with eating disorders have higher frequencies of positive family history for substance addiction [10]. The development of de novo alcohol addiction and dependence after bariatric surgery for severe obesity is a topic of

recent concern. Estimated incidence rates range from a low of less than 3% to a high of 30% [11]. Possible hypotheses explaining these findings are (1) the presence of a common mechanism for over-use of rewarding substances that is expressed differentially in different individuals, and (2) an interaction between food and substance addiction that increases the susceptibility to the other [10].

Drug addicts tend to lose interest in everything other than drugs, including food. Santolaria-Fernández *et al.* [9] reported that 92.4% of drug addicts without organic pathology were under the mean weight for the population. Of the 140 studied, 54 (39%) met the criteria for marasmus and/or Kwashiorkor-like malnutrition. Himmelgreen *et al.* [12] found significantly lower measures of body weight and anthropometric measures in drug users when compared to nondrug users.

In several studies of hospitalization due to diabetic ketoacidosis (DKA), a considerable percentage of patients admitted with DKA were found to have either alcohol or drugs in their system. Pedersen-Bjergaard *et al.* [13] found that 31% of diabetics admitted with severe hypoglycemia had a psychoactive substance in their blood sample, and 17% had alcohol in their system. Warner *et al.* [14] found that 14% of admissions of DKA were cocaine users. Hart and Frier [15] found 19% of diabetics were admitted with severe hypoglycemia due to alcohol intake.

Substance addiction and dependence can exacerbate the consequences of reduced nutrient intake and its concomitant diseases. It seems prudent then to screen for substance addiction/dependence in those with eating disorders, diabetes, malnutrition and those who have undergone bariatric surgery. Criteria for eating disorders and substance addiction/dependence can be found in the DSM-IV of the American Psychiatric Association. Simple anthropometric measurements of weight, waist circumference, and percentage body fat, as well as blood test indicating nutritional status (albumin, prealbumin, liver function tests, fasting glucose, hematocrit, hemoglobin, red and white blood cell counts, and platelet counts), can suggest the presence of malnutrition that can then be probed further for substance use.

20.2 INTERACTION OF ADDICTIVE DISORDERS WITH DISEASE-SPECIFIC MEDICAL NUTRITION THERAPY

20.2.1 Diabetes, metabolic syndrome and addictive disorders

Drug and alcohol use are major risk factors for complications in diabetic patients, whether due to changes in behavioral patterns, decreased awareness of symptoms, interference with self-care, or direct effects on carbohydrate metabolism. In addition, at least two separate studies have documented increased risk of developing metabolic syndrome, itself a risk factor for cardiovascular disease, with increasing over-consumption of alcohol. Freiberg *et al.* [16] and Fan *et al.* [17] both analyzed National Health and Nutrition Examination Survey (NHANES) data from 1990s and concluded that alcohol consumption in excess of daily recommend guidelines (one drink for women, two drinks for men) causes a significant increase in waist circumference, blood pressure, glucose intolerance, insulin resistance, and serum triglycerides.

20.2.1.1 Alcohol and carbohydrate metabolism

Alcohol is metabolized in preference to other energy sources in the body, thus reducing glucose disposal and causing insulin resistance. Higher levels may reduce insulin binding and inhibit intracellular signaling related to insulin. Alcohol also inhibits gluconeogenesis and, when used in moderation, may be related to enhanced insulin sensitivity, resulting in glycemic control [18]. In chronic alcoholics, whose liver stores of glycogen are often depleted, this inhibition of gluconeogenesis may lead to hypoglycemia [19].

20.2.1.2 Stimulant drugs and carbohydrate metabolism

Use of dopamine-related stimulants (cocaine and amphetamine, etc.) can interfere with certain aspects of glucose metabolism. Amphetamines have been found to have a counter-regulatory effect to insulin. In a study by Baudrie and Chaouloff [20] in rats, administration of amphetamine elicited a rapid rise in plasma glucose that was associated with a decreased insulin response to a glucose bolus. They found that the hyperglycemic effect was mediated by centrally located 5-HT2 receptors and, in turn, adrenal epinephrine release. Cocaine addicts are at high risk for DKA, mainly due to the omission of insulin therapy. Another possible reason is the effect of cocaine on counter-regulatory hormones. Cocaine increases the levels of catecholamines, which greatly affects carbohydrate metabolism in the following ways: inhibiting pancreatic insulin secretion, increasing glucagon production, stimulating glycogenolysis and gluconeogensis in the liver, activating lipolysis in the skeletal muscle, impairing the peripheral use of glucose, as well as stimulating ketogensis. This increased production of ketoacids combined with omission of insulin therapy greatly increases the chance of DKA [14].

20.2.1.3 Cannabis and nicotine and carbohydrate metabolism

Cannabis has been found to have little or no effect on diabetics, although it is known to cause food cravings, which could in effect cause hyperglycemia. A survey on young adult diabetics by Ng *et al.* [21] found that several subjects were admitted to the hospital for DKA after using cannabis. A study by Pedersen-Bjergaard *et al.* [13] found 5% of patients admitted with severe hyperglycemia had marijuana in their system.

Some people believe that smoking opium can reduce serum glucose and lipids in diabetes. To test this theory, Azod *et al.* [22] compared blood glucose and lipids in opium addicts and nonaddicts with individuals with Type 2 diabetes. They found a significant difference between the fasting blood glucose and two-hour post prandial glucose between the two groups, but no difference in hemoglobin A1C

(HbA1C) levels. This indicates that opium decreases blood glucose levels temporarily, but has no long-lasting effects on blood glucose [22].

Studies on the relationship of nicotine and diabetes have reported mixed results. Nicotine use has been shown to cause insulin resistance, increase the risk of developing Type 2 diabetes, and increase the risks of micro- and macrovascular complications in both Type 1 and Type 2 diabetics [23]. Smoking increases the circulating levels of insulin-antagonistic hormones such as epinephrine and norepinephrine [24]. A study by Facchini *et al.* [25] reported chronic cigarette smokers to be insulin resistant, hyperinsulinemic, and dyslipidemic when compared with nonsmokers. Chiolero *et al.* [26] analyzed the tolerability of a nicotine lozenge or gum and found that the conditions in a majority of the diabetic patients were unaffected. A large cross-sectional study by Henkin *et al.* [27] found that smoking status did not influence insulin sensitivity. However, since smoking and diabetes are independent risk factors for cardiovascular disease, there is wide support for recommending smoking cessation in those with diabetes.

20.2.1.4 Diabetes control and substance addiction

There is a definite lack of awareness about the effects of drug and alcohol use on diabetes in chronic drug users. A survey done by Ng in London of young adults with Type 1 diabetes found that 72% of street drug users were unaware of the adverse effects of diabetes. Diabetic patients with either a drug or alcohol addiction are at high risk for poor diabetes control [21]. Physicians are encouraged to assess for substance addiction in diabetics, and counsel their patients about the adverse effects of drug and alcohol use on diabetes course and outcome.

20.2.2 Renal disease and addictive disorders

Drug and alcohol addictions have been associated with causing and exacerbating renal disorders.

Chronic exposure to inhalants has been associated with various kidney abnormalities including acute and chronic renal failure [28]. Ecstasy and cocaine have both been associated with acute renal failure [29,30]. Several forms of renal disease and progression of chronic renal failure to end-stage renal disease have been associated with cocaine addiction. The mechanisms include the hemodynamics of cocaine and its effect on matrix synthesis, glomerular inflammation, and glomerulosclerosis [28]. Heroin has been associated with renal damage, though the current reduced incidence suggests that earlier impure heroin contained nephrotoxic substances [31].

Smoking has been found to hasten the progression of renal disease. It has been associated with decreased filtration rate, though the underlying mechanisms are not yet understood. Smoking is one of the most important remediable risk factors – cessation of smoking has been shown to improve both renal and cardiovascular prognosis and should be recommended to all renal patients [32].

Medical nutrition therapy for renal disease typically involves a high carbohydrate, low protein diet, with restrictions in sodium and potassium depending on the particular type of renal disease present [33]. As discussed previously, chronic alcoholics and drug addicts typically have poor diets with low carbohydrate intake, and little interest in eating or self-care processes. Consequently, diet therapy compliance is often difficult and needs to be carefully monitored. The kidney is involved in maintenance of calcium–phosphorus homeostasis through production of the active form of Vitamin D and elimination of calcium and phosphorus [33]. Activated Vitamin D regulates absorption of calcium and phosphorus from the gut [34]. This is complicated further in chronic alcoholics, as alcoholism commonly leads to hypocalcemia and hypophosphatemia, and Vitamin D deficiency is not uncommon [35]. Calcium and phosphorus control is crucial in maintaining bone composition, and should be closely regulated [34].

Some water soluble vitamins have been found to be in increased demand in those with chronic kidney disease [34]. This should be taken into consideration for chronic alcoholics and drug addicts who are already prone to vitamin deficiencies as well as smokers, who have been found to be deficient in Vitamin C as well as carotenes [36].

A higher body mass index (BMI) of 25–28 is correlated with increased survival rates compared to lower BMI in normal kidney function [34]. Chronic alcoholics and drug users typically have lower anthropometric measures when compared to the general population [9]. This is secondary to protein deficiencies, which are common in chronic alcoholics [9,12]. A heart healthy diet of limited saturated fat and increased "good" fats is recommended, as cardiovascular disease is accelerated in patients with chronic kidney disease [34].

20.2.3 Obesity and malnutrition

20.2.3.1 Caloric excess

Obesity is a multifactorial disease caused by an interaction of genetics, caloric over-consumption, and a sedentary lifestyle. Incidence of obesity has risen sharply since the 1990s and currently stands at ~30% of the adult United States population [37]. By definition, people are classified as obese if they have a body mass index of 30 or greater, with those who have a body mass index of 40 or greater considered severely obese. Although behavior therapy coupled with a low calorie diet can promote weight loss in obese individuals, those who are severely obese tend not to benefit very much from this intervention [38]. Currently, the most effective treatment for severe obesity is bariatric surgery.

Two types of bariatric surgery are common – the vertical gastric banding (VGB) and the Rouen Y gastric bypass. Both these procedures physically reduce stomach capacity, thereby creating a de facto state of caloric restriction. Since those individuals who qualify for surgery (those with BMI of 40 or greater) also have problems controlling food intake, the reduction in stomach capacity can present a major obstacle to successful weight loss if the individual has not learned to adjust food intake prior to surgery. Bariatric surgery reduces mortality rates due to diabetes, cardiovascular disease, hypertension, and stroke [39] in severely obese individuals. Although the benefits of bariatric surgery are impressive with respect to reductions in mortality, a new "concern" with respect to substance addiction in post-bariatric surgery patients has developed, specifically alcohol addiction. [11,40] reports that 28.4% of post-bariatric surgery patients have a difficult time controlling alcohol consumption, resulting in post-surgery alcohol consumption greater than that seen before surgery, while also reporting that in their own study (of post-surgery patients queried 6–10 years post surgery) incidence of alcohol addiction and dependence was less than 3%. There have been articles in the popular press [41] and stories on magazine news shows such as ABC's Good Morning America that suggest that occurrence of de novo addictions following bariatric surgery may partly be due to "addiction transfer," since there is overlap in reward circuitry between food and drugs. Another possible mechanism for de novo addiction post bariatric surgery may be related to the enhancement of drug reinforcement through food restriction that results as a consequence of bariatric surgery. No prospective study has addressed this hypothesis; however, animal studies on the effect of food restriction on substance use show increased substance use with caloric restriction and weight loss; and increased substance use is reversed after weight regain [5,42].

The increase in alcohol consumption also has an effect on weight loss and maintenance after bariatric surgery, as alcohol contributes calories as well as modulation of the reward circuitry [39]. Alcohol consumption also causes a shift in macronutrient preference, as those who consume more alcohol after bariatric surgery also tend to increase intake of lipids and proteins, and decrease intake of carbohydrates [39]. In addition, alcohol metabolism is altered in bariatric patients with intoxication occurring at lower levels of alcohol intake than before surgery [40,43]. It seems prudent to monitor alcohol consumption after bariatric surgery both to prevent negating of the positive effects of bariatric surgery and to intervene early in the potential development of de novo alcohol addiction and dependence.

20.2.3.2 Alcoholism and macronutrient deficiency

Malnutrition in alcoholics can be primary or secondary – alcohol can replace other nutrients in the diet or it can interfere with the absorption and use of nutrients [44]. Alcohol intake up to 23% of total kilocalories is typically associated with slightly increased total energy intake, while intake greater than 30% is associated with a decrease in total kilocalorie and, thus, nutrient intake [44]. Patients with chronic liver failure experience deficits in protein metabolism, possibly leading to ascites, internal bleeding, or hepatic encephalopathy [44]. Acute and chronic alcohol intake impairs amino acid uptake and synthesis into proteins, reduced protein synthesis and secretion from the liver, and increased catabolism in the gut [45].

20.2.3.3 Alcoholism and micronutrient deficiency

There is limited research on the nutritional effects of recreational drug use. Most research comes from patients who are beginning drug treatment programs. Malnutrition in drug users results from drug induced anorexia, poor self-care, and irregular eating behavior [12]. Drug users tend to lose interest in everything except drugs [46]. They are more likely to be food insecure and to consume lesser amounts of fruits and vegetables [12].

Heavy alcohol consumption can lead to reduced Vitamin A levels in the liver. The primary reason may be inadequate intake, but decreased hepatic storage may also play a role [47]. Normal levels of beta-carotene suggest an impaired ability of the liver to take up beta-carotene and/or convert it to Vitamin A [44]. The enzymes involved in the conversion of retinol to its active form are the same as those used to metabolize ethanol, suggesting a possible disruption in Vitamin A metabolism with chronic alcoholics. Deficiency can result in eye disorders, such as night blindness, and impaired immune function [48]. Excess Vitamin A can also have harmful consequences for chronic alcoholics. When taken with alcohol, excess Vitamin A causes

a significant leakage of the mitochondrial enzyme glutamine dehydrogenase into the bloodstream, which may promote hepatic fibrosis. Both Vitamin A deficiency and excess have been associated with promoting carcinogenesis [49]. Due to the hepatotoxic effects of Vitamin A in conjunction with alcohol use, supplementation with Vitamin A should be carried out with caution and only used in those who are capable of modifying their alcohol intake [44].

Thiamin deficiency is the most common vitamin deficiency seen in chronic alcoholics, and may be the most important cause of tissue damage [48]. It occurs as a result of decreased intake, reduced absorption, and malutilization [50] and affects the cardiovascular (wet beriberi) and nervous (dry beriberi and Wernicke–Korsakoff syndrome) systems.

Deficiencies of Vitamin B6 and riboflavin may be seen in alcoholics due to a general low intake of B vitamins or the adverse effects of alcohol on hepatic storage of these vitamins. Vitamin B6 deficiency can be partly responsible for neurologic, hematologic, and dermatologic disorders in alcoholics. Alcoholics may be deficient in Vitamin B6 but not exhibit hematological or abnormal liver function [48].

Niacin deficiency is frequently seen among chronic alcoholics. It may result in pellagra, which presents with various mental, neurological, and gastrointestinal symptoms, with or without skin lesions. Pellagra can lead to death by bronchopneumonia if not recognized and treated [51].

Folate and Vitamin B12 deficiencies can lead to megaloblastic anemia. Levels of Vitamin B12 are often normal in chronic alcoholics until development of pancreatic insufficiency and/or liver disease due to the large body stores of the vitamin [48]. Folate deficiency usually appears first, as a result of poor intake, impaired absorption, accelerated excretion and altered storage and metabolism [45]. Folate deficiency can usually be treated with proper diet, but supplementation may be necessary due to poor diet compliance in active alcoholics [44]. Vitamin C deficiency tends to be more frequent among alcoholics than nonalcholics [48], and occurs in those with and without liver disease [49]. When alcohol intake exceeds 30% of total calories, intake usually falls below the recommended daily allowance (RDA [52]).

Depressed Vitamin E levels have been seen in patients with alcoholic liver cirrhosis [48] and with chronic alcohol induced pancreatitis [53]. Pancreatic insufficiency may cause Vitamin K deficiency due to a disruption of fat absorption [49].

Vitamin D deficiency may result from insufficient intake, malabsorption due to cholestasis, inadequate sunlight exposure, as well as pancreatic insufficiency [48]. Low Vitamin D status may contribute significantly to calcium and phosphorus deficiencies [35]. Hypocalcemia may also be caused by hypoalbuminemia, insufficient intake, hypomagnesemia, or excessive renal loss. Hypomagnesemia is very common among hospitalized alcoholics, along with hypophosphatemia, and results from deficient intake, malabsorption, excessive renal losses, and cellular uptake [35].

Chronic alcoholics occasionally present with zinc deficiency, most often in those with alcoholic cirrhosis, due to decreased intake and absorption as well as increased urinary excretion [49]. Iron may either be in excess or deficient in chronic alcoholics. Deficiency may result from gastrointestinal lesions [48]. Elevated hepatic stores of iron have been found in chronic alcoholics with liver disease. The mechanisms of iron accumulation and the source of excess iron remain unclear. These increased iron levels may contribute to liver injury, as both alcohol and iron cause oxidative stress and lipid peroxidation [54].

20.2.3.4 Smoking and malnutrition

Cigarette smoking has been found to be associated with poorer eating habits. Smokers tend to eat more white bread, meat, sugar, and potatoes and less fruits, vegetables, and whole grain and high fiber products [36,55]. They are more likely to have an imbalance between metabolic demand for antioxidants and dietary intake of antioxidant nutrients. For similar levels of nutrient intake, smokers were found to have lower circulating levels of beta-carotene, alpha-carotene, cryptoxanthin, and

lycopene than nonsmokers [56]. Smoking is known to cause decreases in serum levels of Vitamin C. Marangon *et al.* [55] found an inverse association between serum Vitamin C levels and smoking, independent of dietary intake, suggesting that smoking may have a direct influence on Vitamin C metabolism.

20.2.4 Hematological disorders

20.2.4.1 Alcoholism and folate deficiency anemia

Chronic alcoholism is often associated with anemia, resulting from nutritional deficiencies, chronic gastrointestinal bleeding, hepatic dysfunction, or direct toxic effects of alcohol on erythropoiesis [57]. Macrocytosis is commonly seen among chronic alcoholics, particularly those with poor eating habits, and is associated with megaloblastic anemia due to folate deficiency [57,58].

Studies in folate-deficient alcoholics suggest that ethanol interferes with the recovery of folate status and the hematopoietic response to folate. Halsted *et al.* [59] reviewed the interactions of folate with alcohol intake and reported decreased intestinal folate absorption, increased renal excretion, and decreased expression of the reduced folate carrier in hepatic tissue. These disruptions in folate metabolism result in the development of megaloblastic anemia, a condition marked by elevated mean corpuscular volume of erythrocytes in the presence of reduced erythrocyte number. Since megaloblastic anemia is common to both folate and Vitamin B 12 deficiencies, it is important to determine the exact deficiency before providing supplement treatment. Supplementation with folate will correct the morphological symptons but can mask Vitamin B12 deficiency which is associated with irreversible neurological damage [33]. Vitamin B12 deficiency is not common in chronic alcoholism as alcohol induced liver damage usually results is release of Vitamin B12 and concomitant increase blood Vitamin B12 levels.

20.3 FUTURE DIRECTIONS

The presence of common neuro circuits underpinning both over-eating and substance addiction, coupled with the current obesity epidemic suggests that greater attention must be directed at determining the interactions between substance addiction, food over-consumption, weight gain and loss. What are the common risk factors? Why is it that some individuals misuse drugs, while others abuse food? Recent data suggests the possibility that bariatric surgery can potentiate de novo addictions in susceptible individuals. While the risk factors for this phenomenon have not been identified, it is possible that there is a common neuro substrate that links the two behaviors.

More information is needed on the effects of nutrients as they interact with genetic risk factors for choice of addicted substance, promotion of relapse and "transfer of addiction". The field of epigenetics is relatively new but holds promise for determining the effects of nutrients on human disease [60]. Recent work (in rats) has demonstrated a role for nutrient exposure in the prenatal period to shape offspring preferences not only for food but also for alcohol [61], and Gomez-Pinilla [62] reviews data suggesting a role for nutrients in modulating brain cognitive functions. He states that, "Understanding the molecular basis of the effects of food on cognition will help us to determine how best to manipulate diet in order to increase the resistance of neurons to insults and promote mental fitness". Since it is known that substance addiction can damage neurons as well as affect neuro-plasticity, the ability to identify those at genetic risk for these events (through their response to various nutrients) may provide additional options for treatment and prevention interventions.

REFERENCES

1. Volkow, N.D., Wang, G.J., Fowler, J.S., and Telang, F. (2008) Overlapping neuronal circuits in addiction and obesity: evidence of systems pathology. *Philos. Trans. R. Soc. Lond. B Biol. Sci.*, **363**, 3191–3200.

2. Lattemann, D.F. (2008) Motivation to Eat: neural control and modulation, *Appetite and Food Intake* (eds R.B.S. Harris and R.D. Mattes), CRC Press, New York, pp. 81–94.

3. Kleiner, K.D., Gold, M.S., Frost-Pineda, K. *et al.* (2004) Body Mass Index and Alcohol Use. *J. Addict. Dis.*, **23**, 105–118.

4. McIntyre, R.S., McElroy, S.L., Konarski, J.Z. *et al.* (2007) Substance use disorders and overweight/obesity in bipolar I disorder: preliminary evidence for competing addictions. *J. Clin. Psychiatry.*, **68**, 1352–1357.

5. Carr, K.D. (2007) Chronic food restriction: enhancing effects on drug reward and striatal cell signaling. *Physiol. Behav.*, **91**, 459–472.

6. Virmani, A., Binienda, Z., Ali, S., and Gaetani, F. (2006) Links between nutrition, drug abuse, and the metabolic syndrome. *Ann. NY Acad. Sci.*, **1074**, 303–314.

7. Varner, L.M. (1995) Dual diagnosis: patients with eating and substance-related disorders. *J. Am. Diet. Assoc.*, **95**, 224–225.

8. Jonas, J.M., Gold, M.S., Sweeney, D., and Pottash, A.L. (1987) Eating disorders and cocaine abuse: a survey of 259 cocaine abusers. *J. Clin. Psychiatry*, **48**, 47–50.

9. Santolaria-Fernández, F.J., Gómez-Sirvent, J.L., González-Reimers, C.E. *et al.* (1995) Nutritional assessment of drug addicts. *Drug Alcohol Depend.*, **38**, 11–18.

10. Krahn, D.D. (1991) The relationship of eating disorders and substance abuse. *J. Subst. Abuse.*, **3**, 239–253.

11. Ertelt, T.W., Mitchell, J.E., Lancaster, K. *et al.* (2008) Alcohol abuse and dependence before and after bariatric surgery: a review of the literature and report of a new data set. *Surg. Obes. Relat. Dis.*, **4**, 647–650.

12. Himmelgreen, D.A., Perez-Escamilla, R., Segura-Millan, S. *et al.* (1998) A comparison of the nutritional status and food security of drug-using and non-drug-using Hispanic women in Hartford. *Connecticut. Am. J. Phys. Anthropol.*, **107**, 351–361.

13. Pedersen-Bjergaard, U., Reubsaet, J.L.E., Nielsen, S.L. *et al.* (2005) Psychoactive drugs, alcohol, and severe hypoglycemia in insulin-treated diabetes: analysis of 141 cases. *Am. J. Med.*, **118**, 307–310.

14. Warner, E.A., Greene, G.S., Buchsbaum, M.S. *et al.* (1998) Diabetic ketoacidosis associated with cocaine use. *Arch. Intern. Med.*, **158**, 1799–1802.

15. Hart, S.P. and Frier, B.M. (1998) Causes, management and morbidity of acute hypoglycaemia in adults requiring hospital admission. *Q. J. Med.*, **91**, 505–510.

16. Freiberg, M.S., Cabral, H.J., Heeren, T.C. *et al.* (2004) Alcohol consumption and the prevalence of the Metabolic Syndrome in the US. *Diabetes Care*, **27**, 2954–2959.

17. Fan, A.Z., Russell, M., Naimi, T. *et al.* (2008) Patterns of alcohol consumption and the metabolic syndrome. *J. Clin. Endo. Metab.*, **93**, 3833–3838.

18. Meyer, K.A., Conigrave, K.M., Nain-Feng, C. *et al.* (2003) Alcohol consumption patterns and HbA1c, C-peptide, and insulin concentrations in men. *J. Am. Coll. Nutr.*, **22** (3), 185–194.

19. Christiansen, C., Thomsen, C., Rasmussen, O. *et al.* (1994) Effect of alcohol on glucose, insulin, free fatty acid and triacylglycerol responses to a light meal in non-insulin-dependent diabetic subject. *Br. J. Nutr.*, **71**, 449–454.

20. Baudrie, V. and Chaouloff, F. (1992) Mechanisms involved in the hyperglycemic effect of the 5-HT1C/5HT2 receptor agonist. *Eur. J. Pharmacol.*, **213**, 41–46.

21. Ng, R.S., Darko, D.A., and Hillson, R.M. (2004) Street drug use among young patients with type 1 diabetes in the UK. *Diabetes Med.*, **21**, 295–296.

22. Azod, L., Rashidi, M., Afkhami-Ardekani, M. *et al.* (2008) Effect of opium addiction on diabetes. *Am. J. Drug. Alcohol Ab.*, **34** (4), 383–388.

23. Eliasson, B. (2003) Cigarette smoking and diabetes. *Prog. Cardiovasc. Dis.*, **45** (5), 405–413.

24. Cryer, P.E., Haymond, M.W., Santiago, J.V., and Shah, S.D. (1976) Norepinephrine and epinephrine release and adrenergic mediation of smoking-associated hemodynamic and metabolic events. *NEJM*, **295**, 573–577.

25. Facchini, F.S., Hollenbeck, C.B., Jeppersen, J. *et al.* (1992) Insulin resistance and smoking. *Lancet*, **339**, 1128–1130.

26. Chiolero, A., Faeh, D., Paccaud, F., and Cornuz, J. (2008) Consequences of smoking for body weight, body fat distribution, and insulin resistance. *Am. J. Clin. Nutr.*, **87**, 801–809.

27. Henkin, L., Zaccaro, D., Haffner, S. *et al.* (1999) Cigarette smoking, environmental tobacco smoke exposure and insulin sensitivity: the insulin resistance atherosclerosis study. *Ann. Epidemiol.*, **9** (5), 290–296.

28. Nzerue, C.M., Hewan-Lowe, K., and Riley, L.J. Jr (2000) Cocaine and the kidney: a synthesis of pathophysiologic and clinical perspectives. *Am. J. Kid Dis.*, **35**, 783–795.

29. Henry, J.A., Jeffreys, K.J., and Dawling, S. (1992) Toxicity and deaths from 3,4-methylenedioxymethamphetamine ("ecstasy"). *Lancet*, **340**, 384–387.

30. Blowey, D.L. (2005) Nephrotoxicity of over-the-counter analgesics, natural medicines, and illicit drugs. *Adolesc. Med.*, **16**, 31–43.

31. Friedman, E.A. and Tao, T.K. (1995) Disappearance of uremia due to heroin-associated nephropathy. *Am. J. Kidney Dis.*, **25** (5), 689–693.

32. Orth, S.R. and Ritz, E. (2002) The renal risks of smoking: an update. *Curr. Opin. Nephrol. Hypertens.*, **11**, 483–488.

33. Kathleen Mahan, L. and Escott-Stump, S. (eds) (2007) *Krause's Food & Nutrition Therapy*, 12th edn, Elsevier Health Science Publishing, Philadelphia, PA.

34. Beto, J.A. and Bansal, V.K. (2004) Medical nutrition therapy in chronic kidney failure: integrating clinical practice guidelines. *J. Am. Diet. Assoc.*, **104**, 404–409.

35. Pitts, T.O. and Thiel, D.H. (1986) Disorders of divalent ions and vitamin D metabolism in chronic alcoholism. *Recent Dev. Alcohol*, **4**, 357–377.

36. Margetts, B.M. and Jackson, A.A. (1993) Interactions between people's diet and their smoking habits: the dietary and nutritional survey of British adults. *BMJ*, **307**, 1381–1384.

37. Flegal, K.M., Carroll, M.D., Ogden, C.L., and Johnson, C.L. (2002) Prevalence and trends in obesity among US adults, 1999–2000. *J. Am. Med. Assoc.*, **288**, 1723–1727.

38. Hsu, G., Benoth, P.N., Dwyer, J. *et al.* (1998) Non-surgical factors that influence the outcome of bariatric surgery: a review. *Psychosom. Med.*, **60**, 338–346.

39. Hagedorn, J.C., Encarnacion, B., Brat, G.A., and Morton, J.M. (2007) Does gastric bypass alter alcohol metabolism? *Surg. Obes. Relat. Dis.*, **3**, 543–548.

40. Buffington, C.K., Daley, D.L., Worthen, M., and Marema, R.T. (2006) Changes in alcohol sensitivity and effects with gastric bypass. Abstract presented at the Annual Meeting of the American Society for Bariatric Surgery, San Francisco.

41. Spencer, J. (2006) Alcoholism in People Who Had Weight-Loss Surgery Offers Clues to Roots of Dependency. *Wall Street Journal* July 18, D1.

42. Comer, S.D., Turner, D.M., and Carroll, M.E. (1995) Effects of food deprivation on cocaine base smoking in rhesus monkeys. *Psychopharmacology (Berl)*, **119** (2), 127–132.

43. Klockhoff, H., Naslund, I., and Jones, A.W. (2002) Faster absorption of ethanol and higher peak concentration in women after gastric bypass surgery. *Br. J. Clin. Pharm.*, **54**, 587–591.

44. Lieber, C.S. (2003) Relationships between nutrition, alcohol use, and liver disease. *Alcohol Res. Health*, **27**, 220–231.

45. Stickel, F., Hoehn, B., Schuppan, D., and Seitz, H.K. (2003) Review article: nutrition therapy in alcoholic liver disease. *Aliment. Pharmacol. Ther.*, **18**, 357–373.

46. Gambera, S.E. and Clarke, J.A. (1976) Comments on dietary intake of drug-dependent persons. *J. Am. Diet. Assoc.*, **68**, 155–157.

47. Majumdar, S.K., Shaw, G.K., and Thompson, A.D. (1983) Vitamin A utilization status in chronic alcoholic patients. *Int. J. Vit. Nutr. Res.*, **53**, 273–279.

48. Leevy, C.M. and Moroianu, S.A. (2005) Nutritional aspects of alcoholic liver disease. *Clin. Liver Dis.*, **9**, 67–81.

49. Lieber, C.S. (2000) Alcohol: Its metabolism and interaction with nutrients. *Annu. Rev. Nutr.*, **20**, 395–430.

50. Leevy, C.M. (1982) Thiamin deficiency and alcoholism. *Ann. NY Acad. Sci.*, **378**, 316–324.

51. Ishii, N. and Nishihara, Y. (1981) Pellagra among chronic alcoholics: clinical and pathological study of 20 necropsy cases. *J. Neurol. Neurosurg. Psychiatry*, **44**, 209–215.

52. Gruchow, H.W., Sobocinski, K.A., Barboriak, J.J., and Scheller, J.G. (1985) Alcohol consumption, nutrient intake and relative body weight among US adults. *Am. J. Clin. Nutr.*, **42**, 289–295.

53. Marotta, F., Labadarios, D., Frazer, L. *et al.* (1994) Fat-soluble vitamin concentration in chronic alcohol-induced pancreatitis. Relationship with steatorrhea. *Dig. Dis. Sci.*, **39** (5), 993–998.

54. Harrison-Findik, D.D. (2007) Role of alcohol in the regulation of iron metabolism. *World J. Gastroenterology*, **13**, 4925–4930.

55. Marangon, K., Herbeth, B., Lecomte, E. *et al.* (1998) Diet, antioxidant status, and smoking habits in French men. *Am. J. Clin. Nutr.*, **67**, 231–239.

56. Pamuk, E.R., Byers, T., Coates, R.J. *et al.* (1994) Effect of smoking on serum nutrient concentration in African-American women. *Am. J. Clin. Nutr.*, **59**, 891–895.

57. Beutler, E. (2006) Anemia Resulting from Other Nutritional Deficiencies, in *Williams Hematology*, 7th edn (eds M.A. Lichtman, E. Beutler, T.J. Kipps, *et al.*), McGraw-Hill, New York.

58. Fernando, O.V. and Grimsley, E.W. (1998) Prevalence of folate deficiency and macrocytosis in patients with and without alcohol-related illness. *South Med. J.*, **91**, 721.

59. Halsted, C.H., Villanueva, J.A., Devlin, A.M., and Chandler, C.J. (2002) Metabolic interactions of alcohol and folate. *J. Nutr.*, **132** (8 Suppl), 2367S–2372.

60. Hirst, M. and Marra, M.A. (2009) Epigenetics and human disease. *Int. J. Biochem. and Cell Biol.*, **41** (1), 136–146.

61. Nicolaidis, S. (2008) Prenatal imprinting of postnatal specific appetites and feeding behavior. *Metabolism*, **57**, S22–S26.

62. Gomez-Pinilla, F. (2008) Brain foods: effects of nutrients on brain function. *Nat. Rev. Neurosci.*, **9**, 568–578.

21

Gastrointestinal diseases associated with substance addiction

Paul S. Haber[1] and Abdullah Demirkol[2]

[1] Sydney, and University of Sydney, Royal Prince Alfred Hospital, Sydney, and University of Sydney, Sydney, Australia
[2] Sydney, Sydney South West Area Health Service, Sydney, and University of Sydney, Sydney, Australia

21.1 INTRODUCTION

The gastrointestinal system and liver are major targets for most commonly used licit and illicit substances. This chapter describes the more common gastrointestinal diseases associated with addiction to alcohol and other drugs. The emphasis is on the clinical manifestations, diagnosis, and management.

21.2 ALCOHOL CONSUMPTION AND THE GASTROINTESTINAL SYSTEM

Alcohol addiction is associated with injury to all parts of the gastrointestinal tract [1–3]. The impact of alcoholic liver disease in particular is more severe than that of many cancers, yet it attracts much less concern among both the public and the medical profession. The prevailing nihilism about treatment may contribute to this attitude. However, new insights into the pathophysiology of alcohol use disorders now allow for prospects of earlier recognition and more successful efforts at prevention and treatment prior to the medical and social disintegration of the patient.

21.2.1 Parotids

Painless symmetrical enlargement of the parotid glands, termed as sialosis or sialadenosis, is common in patients with alcoholic liver injury. Sialosis is characterized by the triad of acinar cell hypertrophy, myoepithelial degeneration, and neural degeneration. Salivary secretion is reduced in experimental animals given alcohol. These effects may contribute to progressive dental caries and poor oral mucosal health. The effect of alcohol addiction on salivary function in humans is controversial, with

Addictive Disorders in Medical Populations   Edited by Norman S. Miller and Mark S. Gold
© 2010 John Wiley & Sons, Ltd.

reports of both increased, unaltered [4], and decreased salivary flow [5].

21.2.2 Esophagus

Both acute and chronic alcohol consumption are associated with symptomatic gastro-esophageal reflux disease (GERD). Reflux episodes were increased by 60 g of ethanol given to healthy non-alcoholic subjects with a meal [6]. A number of mechanisms have been identified that may contribute to these effects of alcohol [1]. Direct application of 30% ethanol to the esophageal mucosa led to mucosal injury but lower concentrations were less toxic. An acute dose of alcohol reduced both lower esophageal sphincter pressure (LESP) and reduced maximal LESP stimulated by a meal. Chronic alcohol addiction was also associated with manometric abnormalities relevant to GERD that recovered with a month of abstinence [4]. These abnormalities were found regardless of the presence or absence of peripheral neuropathy. These studies support the time-honored advice to reduce alcohol consumption in the presence of symptomatic GERD.

Alcohol addiction was found in most cases of Barretts' Esophagus in an early series [7]. More recently, alcohol addiction was not often found in asymptomatic Barretts' [8], but was strongly associated with carcinoma [9].

21.2.3 Gastrointestinal bleeding including mallory–weiss syndrome

Upper gastrointestinal bleeding is common amongst alcoholics. The most common cause is hemorrhagic gastritis, an acute mucosal lesion. Variceal hemorrhage is an uncommon and life-threatening event with approximately 50% mortality for the first episode and about 25% for subsequent episodes.

Mallory–Weiss syndrome comprises vomiting following by hematemesis associated with a tear at the cardio-esophageal junction. Most cases of Mallory–Weiss syndrome are seen in alcoholics.

The amount of blood lost is usually minor, typically without a fall in hemoglobin or hemodynamic compromise but life-threatening hemorrhage can occur. The lesion usually heals within 72 hours without specific treatment.

The management of upper gastrointestinal bleeding depends on the etiology and severity. Patients are referred to the emergency department without delay. The initial assessment focuses on hemodynamic stability (BP, pulse, circulation, hemoglobin level) and etiology (evidence is particularly sought for the presence of liver disease with signs of portal hypertension such as splenomegaly). A large-bore intravenous catheter is placed and fluids and blood given as required. Immediate administration of acid suppression drugs has not been consistently shown to benefit clinical outcomes but one report suggests a role in bleeding peptic ulcers requiring endoscopic treatment [10]. Endoscopy is performed as soon as practicable, as the findings direct management and indicate the prognosis. Endoscopic signs of recent bleeding (adherent clot, visible vessel, and active bleeding, respectively) are associated with an increased risk of recurrent bleeding. There is now evidence from several controlled trials that endoscopic therapy for actively bleeding lesions reduces recurrent bleeding, transfusion requirement, and the need for surgery. Mortality is increased in the elderly, those with shock on presentation, those requiring large volume transfusion, and those with serious intercurrent illness. Surgery is indicated for bleeding uncontrollable by endoscopic treatment, recurrent hemorrhage or where endoscopic treatment is not available.

21.2.4 Alcoholic gastritis

The gastric mucosa is a target for alcohol-related toxicity but also contributes to the oxidation of alcohol. Exposure of the gastric mucosa to 20% alcohol induces gastric mucosal injury. Lower concentrations are not toxic, whereas higher concentrations lead to extensive hemorrhagic injury. These lesions are characterized by subepithelial haemorrhages and epithelial erosions. Inflammatory cell infiltration is not a consistent feature.

The clinical syndrome of alcoholic gastritis has been surprisingly controversial despite considerable study [11,12]. Brown *et al.* [13] found that gastritis was not more common in patients with cirrhosis than healthy controls. It was shown that gastritis in the alcoholic was strongly associated with *H. pylori* infection, with histological and symptomatic relief after eradication of the organism but no improvement with abstinence from alcohol [14,15]. The presence of alcohol dehydrogenase (ADH) activity in *H. pylori* organisms may tend to protect the alcohol drinking host from infection, as exposure to alcohol leads to generation of acetaldehyde that may be bactericidal. Healing of established ulcers is not retarded by moderate alcohol consumption. More severe alcohol addiction is associated with reduced medication compliance and delayed healing.

The clinical term 'alcoholic gastritis' is nonspecific and is often used to refer to a broad range of upper gastrointestinal symptoms experienced by alcoholics, such as gastro-esophageal reflux, peptic ulceration, fatty liver, alcoholic hepatitis or alcoholic pancreatitis to name a few. Given the uncertainty surrounding the etiologic role of alcohol addiction in gastritis and the broad range of potential explanations for these symptoms, it is appropriate to evaluate patients on an individual basis.

21.2.5   Alcoholic pancreatitis

Alcoholic pancreatitis remains a major cause of morbidity amongst alcoholics. The incidence appears to have risen in the United States and internationally through the twentieth century [16]. United Kingdom data confirm this trend and reveal a correlation between rising total community alcohol consumption and the number of hospital admissions for chronic pancreatitis [17].

21.2.5.1   Definitions

The term acute pancreatitis refers to an acute inflammatory process of the pancreas, with variable involvement of other regional tissues or remote organ systems [18]. Chronic pancreatitis is characterized by chronic inflammation, glandular atrophy, and fibrosis. Clinically, it manifests with abdominal pain and/or exocrine or endocrine insufficiency.

21.2.5.2   Predisposing factors

Only a minority (less than 5%) of heavy drinkers develops clinically evident pancreatic disease, although a post-mortem study has shown that pathological changes in the pancreas are common amongst alcoholics [19]. Numerous investigators have attempted to account for this individual susceptibility by studying associations between alcoholic pancreatitis and potential risk factors [20,21]. These studies have focused on the amount, type and pattern of alcohol consumption, genetic markers, diet, hypertriglyceridemia [22], tobacco consumption [23], and pancreatic ischemia. A number of these studies are difficult to interpret due to small study sizes, inappropriate controls, and inconsistent findings between studies, so there remains insufficient evidence to consider that any of the above factors well established. As a result, individual susceptibility to this disease remains largely unexplained.

21.2.5.3   Etiology

The most common associations of acute pancreatitis in Western societies are gall stones and alcohol addiction, which together account for approximately 75% cases. Alcoholic pancreatitis typically occurs in subjects who have consumed greater than 100 g alcohol per day for at least 5–10 years and rarely, if ever, follows an isolated alcoholic debauch. Once the disease is established, episodic heavy drinking often precipitates relapses. Relapses have been described after only one day of recurrent drinking. The causative link between alcohol addiction and pancreatitis for an individual patient is made on clinical grounds by a compatible history and exclusion of other etiologic factors. Pancreatitis is common amongst people with HIV, particularly in association with alcohol addiction [24].

Other relatively common causes for pancreatitis that should be considered include gall stones, hypercalcemia of any cause, and severe hypertriglyceridemia. Hypertriglyceridemia (greater than 10 mmol/l) of any cause is associated with recurrent attacks of pancreatitis. Although alcohol addiction is a known cause of hypertriglyceridemia, the majority of cases of alcoholic pancreatitis are not associated with marked hyperlipidemi [22].

21.2.5.4 Pathogenesis

Two important factors leading to tissue injury in pancreatitis are *autodigestion* and *oxidant stress.* Alcohol administration has been reported to increase the tone of the sphincter of Oddi [25] and inhibit pancreatic secretion [26]. In experimental animals, alcohol intake impairs the stability of critical acinar cell organelles, zymogen granules, and lysosomes. This may allow their contents containing digestive enzymes and lysosomal enzymes to become co-located. Lysosomal enzymes (particularly cathepsin B) are capable of activating trypsinogen to trypsin, which in turn can activate other digestive enzyme precursors resulting in a cascade of autodigestion. Ethanol consumption has been shown to increase the pancreatic content of the major alcohol metabolizing isoform of cytochrome P450 (CYP2E1) and increase tissue markers of oxidant stress [27]. The progression of the disease involves local inflammation and, when severe, systemic inflammation. A range of cytokines are involved and these may be detected in blood and pancreatic tissue. These mediators of inflammation include chemokines that act at CCR1, platelet activating factor (PAF), and substance P. Inhibition of these mediators of inflammation has the potential to limit the progression of pancreatitis and prevent serious complications or death but cannot prevent the initial attack of pancreatitis. None has found a clinical role to date.

21.2.5.5 Diagnosis

A confident diagnosis of pancreatitis can often be made on the basis of an attack of severe abdominal pain and tenderness with elevation of the serum amylase more than three times the upper limit of normal and with imaging studies suggestive of inflammation in and around the pancreas. Gall stones should be excluded by ultrasound examination. In cases with a negative ultrasound, serum alkaline phosphatase or transaminase levels raised at least twofold suggest associated gall stones, which may be detected by repeat ultrasonography or endoscopic retrograde cholangiopancreatography (ERCP). Magnetic resonance cholangiography is increasingly performed to diagnose gall stones.

The diagnosis of alcoholic pancreatitis is occasionally difficult. Amylase testing is useful in establishing the presence of acute pancreatitis, but peak levels do not correlate well with the severity of the disease. Moreover, the amylase level does not rise significantly in approximately 10% of cases of acute pancreatitis, including many with alcoholic pancreatitis or those in whom the presentation is delayed. Determination of serum lipase, which remains elevated longer than the serum amylase, may be helpful. Amylase levels in the range found in acute pancreatitis may occur in other gastrointestinal disorders, including perforated peptic ulcer and ischemic bowel. Estimation of serum lipase levels does not help distinguish these disorders from pancreatitis because the source of the amylase (intestinal fluid) also contains lipase. In renal failure, serum amylase levels may occasionally be strikingly elevated. Salivary gland disease with hyperamylasemia occurs in alcoholics and may be differentiated by fractionation of serum amylase and investigation of the salivary glands. Macroamylasemia is a condition in which amylase forms large complexes with an abnormal serum protein. The disorder is usually found co-incidentally in a patient with very high amylase levels but without abdominal pain and is differentiated from pancreatitis by a normal serum lipase and the absence of amylase in the urine. Minor elevations of the serum amylase (less than threefold) may be due to many disorders, including administration of morphine with secondary spasm of the sphincter of Oddi. Painless pancreatitis can occur, usually in the setting of a comatose or post-operative patient where pain is not appreciated. The diagnosis rests on other clinical and laboratory features.

21.2.5.6 Assessment of severity

A number of clinical and laboratory criteria have been developed to identify patients at risk of complications so that they may be treated more intensively at an earlier stage. These objective criteria add little to careful clinical assessment [28], are cumbersome, and not often used clinically.

The contrast-enhanced CT scan is now widely performed to detect pancreatic necrosis and complications of severe pancreatitis, such as fluid collections, pseudocysts, and abscesses. Caution in the unrestricted use of contrast-enhanced CT scans appears warranted at present. CT scanning without contrast can detect most diagnostic features of pancreatitis and is often performed first.

21.2.5.7 Treatment

Severe cases, particularly those associated with respiratory or renal failure, require treatment in an intensive care unit. Initially, patients are treated with bed rest, analgesics, intravenous fluids, and fasting. The preferred analgesic is pethidine, since morphine has a greater tendency to contract the sphincter of Oddi [29], which may exacerbate pancreatitis. Intravenous fluids are given to restore vascular volume and renal perfusion.

Various specific therapies have been evaluated. Treatments to reduce pancreatic secretion aim to reduce pressure in the pancreatic duct and, consequently, reduce the block in exocytosis from pancreatic acinar cells. However, the inflamed pancreas already secretes very little [30] and no beneficial effect has been found for measures designed to reduce pancreatic secretion. However, patients are initially fasted, partly for symptomatic reasons, but also because early re-feeding seems to cause clinical relapse. Protease inhibitors may limit the damage done by activated digestive enzymes. In clinical practice, it may be impossible to commence treatment early enough in the attack of pancreatitis for

protease inhibitors to be effective. Peritoneal lavage might improve the outcome by removing toxic inflammatory products from the peritoneum but the results of controlled studies have been conflicting [31,32]. New approaches that may prove more effective include extended lavage for seven days and retroperitoneal lavage using operatively placed cannulae. Antibiotics have not been shown to be beneficial for unselected cases of acute pancreatitis for which the prognosis is already excellent. However, in severe pancreatitis two controlled trials of prophylactic antibiotic therapy with imipenem [33] or a combination of ceftazidine, amikacin, and metronidazole [34] demonstrated a significant reduction in septic episodes. Nonetheless, mortality and the need for surgery were not altered.

21.2.5.8 Treatment of chronic pancreatitis

The main problem is usually pain and this may be a very difficult management problem. Complete abstinence from alcohol is essential to minimize progression of the disease and this may help to control pain. Reassurance that the disorder is benign with a tendency to slowly remit is helpful. Nonnarcotic analgesia may suffice, but opioids are often required and should not be unreasonably withheld. Antidepressants should be tried. Celiac plexus injection helps about 60% of patients but pain may recur. The procedure is not often performed due to limited efficacy, frequent recurrence, and significant complications. Pancreatic enzyme supplements have been evaluated for the treatment of pain but the evidence is mixed. A trial of one month is sufficient to determine whether this works in practice. Octreotide is not effective. Endoscopic approaches to dilate pancreatic duct strictures and remove calculi are widely available but the relationship between pancreatic duct obstruction and pain is not clear. Surgery has been employed for refractory cases, and two controlled trials have shown better results than endoscopic therapy. The Whipples procedure or modified Whipples procedures are the most commonly performed procedure. The Puestow procedure (lateral pancreatico-jejunostomy) involves decompression of a dilated pancreatic duct and side-to-side anastomosis onto a roux-en-Y loop of jejunum. Distal pancreatectomy is not often performed now.

Exocrine failure is treated by dietary modification and pancreatic enzyme replacement. Reduction of dietary fat intake reduces steatorrhea. Pancreatic enzymes are required with each meal and snack. The newer preparations are more potent and are preferred. Enteric coated microsphere preparations release enzymes only in the duodenum and this reduces inactivation of lipase by gastric acid. Histamine-2 receptor antagonists or proton pump inhibitors also limit lipase inactivation. Fecal fat levels typically fall but are not usually normalized. Diabetes mellitus is treated with dietary modification, treatment of malabsorption, and specific therapy. Some patients respond to oral hypoglycaemic agents but most require insulin. The diabetes is "brittle" in that the patient is susceptible to hypoglyemia due to loss of both insulin and glucagon secretion. Despite earlier reports, long-term surviving patients with this form of diabetes are prone to diabetic complications.

21.2.6 Alcoholic liver disease

Cirrhosis of the liver is the fifth most common cause of death amongst middle aged American men and accounts for more than 26 000 deaths per annum in the United States [35]. Alcohol is the most common cause for cirrhosis in developed nations, typically accounting for about 50% of all cases. End-stage alcoholic liver disease ranked as the leading primary indication for liver transplantation in the United States for more than a decade, and is now second to chronic hepatitis C, which commonly co-exists with alcohol addiction.

The population risk of cirrhosis is related to the population level of alcohol consumption. This phenomenon has been demonstrated by comparing rising or falling levels of alcohol consumption in several populations across time and by comparing different populations [1]. Recent reductions in population alcohol consumption in France and Australia can, therefore, be expected to lead to reduced prevalence of this disease. By contrast, alcohol use

and cirrhosis rates have substantially increased in the United Kingdom over the last decade.

21.2.6.1 Pathogenesis

The pathogenesis of alcoholic hepatitis is complex and is still subject to debate [36]. Recent studies suggest that alcohol addiction leads to liver injury via oxidative stress, endotoxin and cytokine activation leading to progressive fibrogenesis. These broadly described processes interact with each other. Ethanol metabolism within the liver is thought to lead to the generation of toxic metabolites which mediate alcoholic liver damage. Ethanol itself also contributes to liver injury. Ethanol has been shown to affect intracellular signaling pathways [37] by its effects on lipid membranes and its interaction with several cellular proteins, including phospholipases and adenylate cyclase. Ethanol is metabolized to acetaldehyde and to acetate mainly via ADH and ALDH enzymes, respectively. Acetaldehyde has been shown to affect many aspects of normal cellular functioning, including DNA repair, microtubule assembly, mitochondrial respiration, fatty acid oxidation, and activation of fibrinogenesis. High levels of acetaldehyde have been measured in patients with alcoholic liver disease, in part due to impaired mitochondrial ALDH function. A second pathway involving cytochrome P450 2E1 is part of the microsomal ethanol-oxidizing system (MEOS), and is induced by chronic ethanol consumption A third system involving catalase is generally thought to play a minor role under most circumstances [38].

21.2.6.2 Risk factors for alcoholic liver disease

These include the amount of alcohol consumed, gender, genetic factors, obesity, chronic viral hepatitis, ingestion of hepatotoxins, and nutrition.

Amount of Alcohol Consumed Fatty liver may be observed after a single binge, but more advanced liver disease is typically seen after more than 10 years consumption at average levels greater than 100 g/day. The risk of liver disease increases above

60 g/day for men. Amongst very heavy drinkers, the risk rises to approximately 50%, but does not reach 100% even at the highest level of alcohol consumption.

Gender   Women appear to be at greater risk of alcoholic liver disease with a risk rising for alcohol consumption greater than 20–40 g/day.

Genetic Factors   A classic twin study showed that the concordance rate for alcoholic liver disease (ALD) is threefold higher in monozygotic twins compared to dizygotic twins [39], suggesting that genetic factors contribute to the risk of liver disease amongst those that misuse alcohol.

Obesity   The prevalence of obesity is continuing to rise and the disorder now affects almost 34% of adult Americans. Liver disease is one of its manifestations and nonalcoholic steatohepatitis (NASH) is now recognized as a very common and potentially progressive liver disease. NASH resembles alcoholic liver disease with respect to the pathological appearance of liver tissue and certain mechanisms of injury. There is both experimental and clinical evidence of an alcohol–obesity interaction in the liver [40,41]. The effect of weight reduction on alcoholic liver disease has not been documented, but continuing NASH may explain failure to normalize liver tests in patients who attain abstinence from alcohol.

Chronic Viral Hepatitis B and C   Alcohol addiction is widely recognized as a factor that is associated with advanced liver fibrosis in patients with chronic viral hepatitis, particularly hepatitis C (discussed further in Section 21.5.2.3).

A similar, but less marked interaction has been ascribed to chronic hepatitis B infection in alcoholics but this interaction is not supported by all studies. One possible explanation for this controversy is that the older hepatitis B studies antedated recognition of hepatitis C virus. The studies may have been confounded by unrecognized co-infection with hepatitis C [42].

Other Hepatotoxins Including Acetaminophen
Chronic alcohol consumption is associated with a range of drug interactions which may alter drug effects or increase the risk of liver injury. Chronic ethanol consumption increases the hepatotoxicity of a number of compounds, including paracetamol, industrial solvents, anesthetic gases, isoniazid, phenylbutazone, and illicit drugs (e.g., cocaine). The induction of cytochrome P450 2E1 (CYP2E1) by chronic alcohol consumption explains the increased vulnerability of the heavy drinker to these substances. CYP2E1 oxidizes ethanol but also has an extraordinary capacity to activate many xenobiotics to highly toxic metabolites.

Among alcoholic patients, hepatic injury associated with acetaminophen has been described following repetitive intake such as for headaches (including those associated with withdrawal symptoms). Amounts well within the accepted rate for the general community (2.5–4 g) have been incriminated as the cause of hepatic injury in alcoholic patients [43]. It is likely that the enhanced hepatotoxicity of acetaminophen after chronic ethanol consumption is caused, at least in part, by an increased microsomal production of reactive metabolite(s) of acetaminophen. Consistent with this view is the observation that, in animals fed ethanol chronically, the potentiation of acetaminophen hepatotoxicity occurs after ethanol withdrawal [44], at which time production of the toxic metabolite may be at its peak, since at that time competition by ethanol for a common microsomal pathway has been withdrawn. At this time, there may be the greatest need for analgesia because of the headaches and other symptoms associated with withdrawal. This also explains the synergistic effect between acetaminophen, ethanol, and fasting, since all three deplete reduced glutathione (GSH), thereby contributing to the toxicity of each compound because GSH provides a fundamental cellular mechanism for the scavenging of toxic free radicals. Furthermore, CYP2E1 promotes the generation of active oxygen species that are toxic in their own right and may overwhelm the antioxidant system of the liver and other tissues with striking consequences. A similar effect may also be produced by the free hydroxy ethyl radical generated from ethanol by CYP2E1.

Nutrition For many years, alcohol *per se* was not thought to be hepatotoxic and alcoholic liver disease was thought to result from poor nutrition. Nutritional impairment is universally present in patients with alcoholic liver disease and correlates with the severity of the disease. In addition, nutritional supplementation may play a therapeutic role in established cases. However, Lieber *et al.* [45] have clearly shown in the baboon model that experimental alcohol administration can lead to progressive liver injury, including cirrhosis, in the presence of an otherwise nutritionally adequate diet Short-term administration of ethanol produces fatty liver with striking ultrastructural lesions [46] both in rats and in humans, an effect that is accelerated by co-administration of a high-fat diet.

Nutritional disorders may accelerate progression of alcoholic liver disease. Protein deficiency is a recognized cause for fatty liver due to impaired apoprotein synthesis required to export lipid from hepatocytes. Choline deficiency is associated with hepatic fibrosis. Vitamin A excess also leads to hepatic fibrosis. Alcohol addiction is associated with low serum levels of Vitamin A and, if supplements are inappropriately given, Vitamin A toxicity may result, even with normal serum levels [1].

21.2.6.3 Clinical features

Symptoms and signs are not reliable indicators of the presence or severity of alcoholic liver disease. There may be no symptoms, even in the presence of cirrhosis. This paucity of symptoms may facilitate denial of an alcohol problem until end-stage complications occur. However, in some cases, florid clinical features do allow a confident clinical diagnosis.

Alcoholic liver disease comprises three clinicopathological entities that frequently co-exist: alcoholic fatty liver, alcoholic hepatitis, and alcoholic cirrhosis. Alcoholic fatty liver may be observed after several days of heavy drinking or in long-term drinkers and manifests anorexia, nausea, and right upper quadrant discomfort. The liver is enlarged, firm, and may be tender. There are typically no other signs. Alcoholic hepatitis is classically defined by symptoms and signs of hepatitis in association with alcohol addiction. Mild cases are common and typically resolve quickly with abstinence. Severe alcoholic hepatitis is rare and carries a short-term mortality of approximately 50%. These cases present with anorexia, nausea and abdominal pain, impaired liver function with jaundice, bruising and encephalopathy. Ascites may be present. Systemic disturbances include fever and neutrophilic leukocytosis. Alcoholic cirrhosis may present with nausea or weight loss but typically presents with complications such as portal hypertension leading to variceal bleeding and/or ascites, liver failure, and hepatocellular carcinoma. Alcoholic cirrhosis is a recognized risk factor for hepatocellular carcinoma but it is not clear that there is an association between alcohol addiction and hepatocellular carcinoma in the absence of cirrhosis [47].

21.2.6.4 Diagnosis of alcoholic liver disease

Many cases of alcoholic liver disease are detected only by results of liver tests. The liver tests are a sensitive marker for alcoholic liver disease but similar findings may be observed in nonalcoholic steatohepatitis (NASH) and in patients treated with medications such as anticonvulsants. The γ-glutamyl transpeptidase (γGT) level is almost always raised and often exceeds 1000 U/l. The transaminases are only moderately elevated. Levels above 500 U/l suggest an additional disorder, such as acetaminophen ingestion, viral hepatitis or liver ischemia. The aspartate aminotransferase (AST) exceeds the alanine aminotransferase (ALT) level in most cases. Possible explanations for this observation are that AST is a mitochondrial enzyme and alcoholic injury selectively injures mitochondria. In addition, AST is also found in other tissues subject to alcohol injury, including skeletal muscle and heart. If the ALT exceeds the AST, chronic hepatitis C, acetaminophen ingestion or other causes for hepatocellular injury should be considered. Neutrophilia is found in severe cases but may reflect concomitant sepsis.

The diagnosis of alcoholic liver disease rests on the history of prolonged alcohol addiction with a compatible clinical and laboratory picture. Other contributing factors that should be routinely considered are ingestion of hepatoxic drugs including herbal preparations and acetaminophen, diabetes mellitus, hepatitis B and C infection, and iron overload. Additional investigations are restricted to atypical cases or those that fail to resolve with abstinence from alcohol. Other explanations for liver disease, including autoimmune hepatitis, Wilson's Disease, alpha-1-antitrypsin deficiency, cholestatic liver disease including primary biliary cirrhosis, may need to be considered in specific cases.

The severity of alcoholic hepatitis can be assessed using several objective rating scales. The Maddrey Discriminant Function (MDF) is the most widely used as it is the simplest and correlates well with the Mayo end-stage liver disease score (MELD score).

Role of Liver Biopsy   There is insufficient evidence to offer clear guidelines for the use of liver biopsy in alcoholic liver disease [48]. The risks of liver biopsy may outweigh the limited benefit. Outside research settings, liver biopsies are generally reserved for atypical cases where the history of alcohol consumption is unclear, or where other liver diseases co-exist, such as hepatitis C. In life-threatening cases where transplantation is being considered pending accurate diagnosis, Vitamin K, fresh frozen plasma may be required, to reverse coagulopathy to accomplish biopsies. Transjugular biopsy is a safe procedure in coagulopathic patients to obtain sufficient tissue for diagnosis, but the procedure is not widely available.

21.2.6.5 Management of alcoholic liver disease

The management of alcoholic liver disease rests upon avoidance of further alcohol consumption. Other interventions are reserved for those with particularly severe disease or who are unable to maintain abstinence. There is considerable evidence that survival is increased by maintaining abstinence. The improvement with abstinence is so consistent that the γGT falls with an apparent half-life of 26 days [49]. Failure to do so suggests continuing alcohol consumption or occasionally another co-existing liver disease, such as obesity-related liver disease or drug toxicity. Advanced cirrhosis does not resolve with abstinence as it is an irreversible lesion, but the activity is reduced and many very ill patients make striking improvements, often returning to compensated cirrhosis.

The first issue is to define what level of alcohol consumption to recommend for the patient with liver disease. Those with alcohol dependence or severe liver disease should be given clear advice to remain abstinent long term. However, many patients have only minor abnormalities in liver function tests without clinical evidence of cirrhosis. A typical recommendation is a six-week period of abstinence followed by repeat liver tests. If these normalize and the patient wishes to resume drinking, consumption within recommended levels may be resumed provided follow-up liver tests remain normal. Continuing follow-up in a primary care setting is important, as the major causes of death in mild alcoholic liver disease are nonhepatic problems related to alcohol misuse, such as trauma and suicide.

Several management problems commonly arise. Many patients with alcohol-induced disorders decline referral to an alcohol treatment service. In these cases, internists and primary care physicians can readily develop the skills to perform motivational interviewing, maintain regular follow-up, and monitor progress. Discussion with addiction or psychiatric specialists may provide additional management suggestions. Another issue is the safety of acamprosate and naltrexone in patients with significant liver disease. Acamprosate does not accumulate even in severe liver disease, as the drug is excreted unchanged in the urine and is not metabolized. Acamprosate is listed as contra-indicated in severe decompensated (Childs C) liver disease but, even in that setting, the risks of treatment should be balanced against the risks of continuing alcohol consumption and there are no published reports of an adverse effect on liver function. Naltrexone is associated with dose-dependent hepatotoxicity (typically at doses of 300 mg/day), but reactions are most unusual at the standard dose of 50 mg/day. In two studies, liver function tests improved in naltrexone-treated alcoholics with no cases of clinically evident hepatotoxicity, indicating the therapeutic effect to reduce alcohol consumption exceeded the potential hepatotoxic effect [50]. Nonetheless, because of the above concerns, there is little experience with naltrexone in patients with advanced alcoholic liver disease. Nalmefene is a second generation orally active opiate receptor antagonist that has been reported to have similar efficacy to naltrexone in the treatment of alcohol dependence [51] without reported hepatotoxicity, but the drug is not currently registered for unrestricted use. A recent report has found that baclofen was particularly useful in reducing alcohol consumption in patients with alcoholic liver disease and was free of toxicity [52].

Selected cases of alcoholic hepatitis may respond to corticosteroids, but this remains controversial despite a number of controlled trials. Prednisolone (40 mg/day for 28 days) has been shown to improve survival of patients with spontaneous hepatic encephalopathy or a high Maddrey discriminant function (MDF >32). Widespread use of corticosteroids has been limited by the knowledge that they may exacerbate sepsis, a common complication of severe liver disease. The management of the complications of cirrhosis, such as ascites and bleeding, lies outside the scope of this chapter. Patients who present with signs of hepatocellular insufficiency or portal hypertension should be evaluated by a gastroenterologist or hepatologist.

Liver transplantation is now an accepted treatment option for individuals with advanced liver disease who have stopped drinking, but only 5% of patients with end-stage alcoholic liver disease are transplanted in the United States. The procedure has been controversial because of ethical concerns about allocation of precious donor livers to individuals with a self-induced disease, concerns about the chance of a successful outcome in this cohort, and concerns about resumption of drinking after a successful transplant. It is unreasonably simplistic to regard alcoholic liver disease as just a "self-induced disorder". External factors such as family,

peers, and society as a whole encourage the availability and use of alcohol. Genetic factors also contribute to the risk of alcohol addiction and alcohol dependence is now considered a chronic relapsing brain disease. The five-year survival after transplantation for alcoholic liver disease is comparable to that of nonalcoholics in series from the United States, Europe, and Australia [53,54]. Whereas alcoholics may be at higher risk of some post-transplant problems, there is evidence that the rate of rejection may be lower than for nonalcoholic liver disease [55]. Resumption of alcohol consumption remains the major concern and occurs in approximately one-third of survivors. Of those that return to drinking, many develop life-threatening alcohol-related morbidity, such as pancreatitis, recurrent alcoholic liver disease, and noncompliance with immunosuppression resulting in graft rejection. These outcomes are comparable to the post-transplant recurrence rate of other liver diseases. This low rate of recurrent alcohol consumption is better than that observed after other treatments for alcohol dependence. This may be due to careful case selection for transplantation, or the appreciation of the intensity of treatment by the transplant team.

The ideal candidate for transplantation accepts the etiological role of alcohol in his/her liver disease and has ceased drinking, has strong family supports with a stable home, employment, no psychiatric comorbidity, does not smoke, and has enthusiasm to resume interests [56].

21.2.7 Alcohol and the small intestine

Diarrhea is common among those who abuse alcohol, both acutely and chronically. Multiple factors contribute to this complaint including altered motility, permeability, malabsorption, and nutritional disorders. Small intestinal mucosal injury can occur after acute or chronic administration of alcohol.

Acute administration of alcohol leads to increased gut permeability, resulting both in abnormal absorption of luminal content such as endotoxin, which contributes to the pathogenesis of alcoholic liver disease, and abnormal leakage of mucosal contents such as albumin. Ethanol also inhibits absorption of actively transported sugars, dipeptides, and amino acids. Many defects in absorption have been reported in alcoholics, including water carbohydrate, lipid, vitamins (notably thiamine, folate), and minerals (calcium, iron, zinc, and selenium). Ethanol may exacerbate lactase deficiency, especially in non-Caucasians [57]. Folate deficiency, common among alcoholics, causes intestinal injury leading to malabsorption and diarrhoea and further loss of folate.

21.2.8   Alcohol and the colon

Portal hypertension may manifest uncommonly with hemorrhoids and rarely with colonic varices. Colonic varices appear as filling defects on barium enema and may occur in any part of the colon, most commonly in rectum. Alcohol has also been reported to cause nonulcerative inflammatory changes in human colonic epithelium which resolve with abstinence.

Inappropriate alcohol enema has been reported to cause a chemical colitis [58] and this may result from a toxic effect similar to the direct toxicity of alcohol on the gastric mucosa. Alcohol addiction is a recognized association of colorectal cancer, as indicated below. Finally, alcohol consumption may have at least one beneficial effect on the colon in that it has been linked to a reduced incidence of ulcerative colitis in one study [59].

21.2.9   Alcohol and gastrointestinal cancer

Alcohol addiction is a recognized risk factor for several gastrointestinal neoplasms, including tumors of the tongue, mouth, pharynx, larynx, esophagus, stomach, pancreas, colon, and liver. Alcohol addiction has been repeatedly associated with an increased incidence of esophageal and oropharyngeal cancer, especially in those who also smoke. For examples, Blot *et al.* [60] reported a 5.8-fold increased risk among drinkers, a 7.4-fold increased risk among smokers, and a 38-fold increased risk among those that both drank and smoked.

In general, the experimental studies have not shown that alcohol is itself a complete carcinogen. Rather ethanol is a co-carcinogen that increases the cancer risk after exposure to another compound. The effect of ethanol may occur at the initiation, induction or progression stages of tumor development.

With respect to hepatocellular carcinoma (HCC), alcohol addiction has been long recognized as a predisposing factor. Alcohol might contribute to carcinogenesis via mechanisms considered for other tissues and listed above, but there is insufficient experimental evidence to conclude that alcohol is a complete hepatic carcinogen. Most patients are cirrhotic, itself known to predispose to HCC. Many patients also have other risk factors for HCC, such as chronic hepatitis B, C or exposure to chemical carcinogens such as aflatoxins [61].

21.3   TOBACCO AND THE GASTROINTESTINAL SYSTEM

Although recent public health interventions have contributed significantly to the reduction of tobacco consumption, tobacco is still a major public health problem which is currently responsible for the death of five million people annually. There is a wide range of tobacco related diseases, some of which impact on the gastrointestinal system.

21.3.1   Effects of tobacco on gastrointestinal function

21.3.1.1   *Gastro-esophageal reflux*

Smoking has been linked to exacerbations of reflux symptoms and cessation of smoking is one of the lifestyle changes traditionally recommended in the treatment of reflux [62]. At a practical level, smoking cessation is difficult to achieve and has not been shown to induce remission of reflux or healing of esophagitis. Nicotine has been shown to reduce lower esophageal sphincter pressure and promote gastro-esophageal reflux in response to straining during coughing and deep breathing. Smokers have also been shown to have delayed acid clearance from the esophagus. It is accordingly appropriate to advise patients with GERD to quit smoking, particularly in view of the potential benefits from reducing the risk of the many other adverse effects of smoking.

21.3.1.2   Peptic ulceration

There is considerable evidence that smoking is involved with peptic ulcer. Smokers are at an increased risk of ulcer according to the number of cigarettes smoked. Heavy smoking is associated with delayed ulcer healing and the risk of recurrence is increased in smokers [63]. Smoking increases the risk of complications from peptic ulcer. Finally, the overall ulcer-related mortality is increased in smokers compared to nonsmokers. The mechanism by which smoking exacerbates peptic ulcer disease remains unclear.

21.3.1.3   Pancreatic disease

There have been inconsistent findings concerning the relationship between smoking and pancreatitis [64]. In general, most alcoholics smoke, so it is difficult to segregate these two variables, particularly since both are difficult to measure and rely heavily on self-report. The most appropriate comparison is between a group with alcoholic pancreatitis and a control group who drank at least as much alcohol, did not develop pancreatitis, and who were clinically well. The only study using this methodology found no association with smoking [23].

Evidence from a number of countries provides a clear link between smoking and pancreatic cancer. Several studies have consistently found a moderately increased risk (about threefold) of pancreatic cancer among smokers [64].

21.3.1.4   Inflammatory bowel disease

A curious relationship exists between smoking and inflammatory bowel disease. Smoking has been consistently been shown to increase the risk of Crohn's disease and to decrease the risk of ulcerative colitis [65]. Somewhat provocatively, smoking may also reduce the severity of established ulcerative colitis, leading to investigation of nicotine-based approaches to treatment.

21.3.1.5   Tobacco and gastrointestinal malignancy

Smoking has been strongly linked to cancers of the upper aero-digestive tract, and pancreas as discussed above. The link between smoking and stomach cancer is weaker but is present in most studies [66].

21.4   OPIATE USE AND THE GASTROINTESTINAL SYSTEM

Opiates act on gut function in a complex fashion via all three receptor classes in the brain, spinal cord, and enteric nervous systems. Low doses act at enteric nervous system sites and higher doses also act within the CNS. Opiates alter both motility and electrolyte absorption leading to constipation that may be severe, particularly in the elderly. Opiates increase absorption of chloride by both increasing chloride transport and reducing chloride secretion in response to various secretogogues [67]. These effects in turn increase passive water absorption and reduce colonic volume, exacerbating the tendency to constipation. The motility effects are more prominent for the clinically available opioids. Opioids decrease the frequency of contractions in, and propulsion along, the small bowel and colon. Classically, chronic opiate use was thought not to induce tolerance to gut motility, but tolerance and withdrawal have been demonstrated in an experimental animal model [68]. Tolerance to the gastrointestinal motility effects took longer to develop than to the nociceptive effects and tolerance to the inhibitory effects developed more slowly than that to the excitatory effects. The mechanism(s) by which tissues become tolerant to the effects of opioids have been extensively studied within the CNS but much less is known about the gut effects, which are determined by both central and peripheral opioid actions.

Amongst methadone maintenance patients, constipation is common and tends to be worse early in treatment [69]. The high prevalence of persisting constipation suggests that tolerance to the gut effects of opiates occurs to only a limited extent. Fecal impaction and even stercoral perforation have been described. Opiate-related constipation usually responds to increased fluid intake and fiber supplementation to correct for poor dietary intake. Laxatives are not often required but lactulose is the laxative of choice. The narcotic bowel syndrome is characterized by a picture similar to intestinal pseudo-obstruction, with worsening abdominal pain associated with increasing opioid doses. This syndrome responds to withdrawal of opioids and administration of the α_2-agonist clonidine [70]. Methylnaltrexone is a parenterally active peripheral opioid receptor antagonist that has been reported to relieve constipation without crossing the blood–brain barrier and precipitating opioid withdrawal [71].

21.5 INJECTING DRUG USE AND THE GASTROINTESTINAL SYSTEM

21.5.1 Toxicity from co-injected materials

It is often suspected that other materials may contribute substantially to toxicity after injection of illicit drugs, but this problem appears to be most uncommon. Injection of drugs intended for oral ingestion may lead to accumulation of talc in a dose-dependent fashion at several sites, particularly the lung and liver. There is a striking difference between the toxicity of talc in the lung compared to other tissues that may be simply a dose effect [72]. Talc is strongly fibrogenic in the lung, leading to pulmonary granulomatous disease with a progressive or fatal outcome. Talc liver is inconsequential clinically. A series of 70 liver biopsies from injecting drug users with chronic hepatitis was examined under polarizing microscopy, revealing talc particles in two-thirds with no granulomas [73]. Another series reviewed the liver biopsy appearances in chronic hepatitis C with and without known injecting drug use (IDU). Talc was found in nine of 109 biopsies, of which only two had reported IDU before biopsy. Of the five patients in whom follow-up interview was possible, three admitted to prior IDU after being confronted with the liver biopsy evidence. Thus, the presence of intrahepatic talc was a useful marker of previous IDU, but is not sensitive for those with a minimal IDU history.

Lead poisoning has been reported in several patients after amphetamine injection [74]. Lead acetate used in the synthesis of methamphetamine may contaminate the final product. The effects of acute lead poisoning include hepatitis, encephalopathy, and renal impairment. A survey of blood lead levels in 92 amphetamine users presenting to the emergency department found no cases of lead toxicity, indicating that this problem is sporadic [27].

21.5.2 Infections associated with injecting drug use and the gastointestinal system

A wide array of bacterial, fungal, and viral infections may occur in the IDU and these may involve the liver. This section focuses on viral hepatitis related to injecting drug use. Other infections related to IDU are described elsewhere in this book.

21.5.2.1 Hepatitis A

Hepatitis A virus (HAV) is an RNA virus that is transmitted by fecal-oral contamination. HAV causes acute hepatitis but does not persist as a chronic infection. With improving hygiene, hepatitis A is now less common but, because it is increasingly severe with advancing age, its severity is rising as the population ages. Parenteral infection is rare due to the short period of viremia, but has been described [75].

The prevalence of hepatitis A IgG antibodies is high among IDUs and prison inmates in California [76] and Australia [77]. Hepatitis A correlated more closely with institutionalization than sharing of injecting equipment and vaccination of seronegative prison entrants has been suggested.

Prevention measures include hygiene precautions to prevent fecal-oral contamination, passive immunoglobulin to household contacts of cases, and active immunization to those at risk. Accepted indications for vaccination include those at occupational risk, travelers, men who have sex with men, and those with chronic liver disease. While agreeing IDUs are at increased risk of hepatitis A, difficulties of accessing IDUs and the high cost of vaccine limit the usefulness of this strategy.

21.5.2.2 Hepatitis B

Hepatitis B virus (HBV) is the most prevalent chronic viral infection of humans. It is readily transmitted among injecting drug users. Serological evidence of past hepatitis B infection increases in prevalence with the duration of injecting drug use, which is now the commonest association of hepatitis B infection acquired in adults. Other risk groups include people who have more than one sexual partner (heterosexual and sexual contact between men), people from certain ethnic groups (e.g., Asia, Southern European, Mediterranean countries), indigenous people, children of infected parents, and healthcare workers. The incubation period is six weeks to six months.

Acute hepatitis B may be preceded by a transient serum-sickness prodrome, with polyarthralgia, fever, malaise, urticaria, and proteinuria. The acute illness is characterized by anorexia, nausea and sometimes vomiting with malaise, jaundice pale stools, and dark urine. The infection is frequently subclinical. Hepatitis B persists as chronic hepatitis B infection in about 5% of adults, much less often than does hepatitis C (Section 21.5.2.3). Acute and chronic hepatitis B are diagnosed by serological tests. People who remain HBsAg positive for six months or more are designated chronic carriers. Chronic hepatitis B is associated with chronic hepatitis, cirrhosis, and hepatocellular carcinoma in a significant minority.

Progression of HBV has been associated with heavy alcohol consumption, co-infection with HIV/ HCV/HDV, pre-core and other mutant viruses, male sex, ethnic group, and duration of infection. Liver injury results from the cell-mediated immune response to infected hepatocytes. In chronic disease, a series of hepatitis flares may precede viral clearance and recovery. These flares vary in severity from subclinical through to life threatening. Patients with chronic HBV should be initially assessed by determining HBeAg status, the hepatitis B viral load, assessing the severity of liver disease, and screening to exclude hepatocellular carcinoma. Patients with persistently abnormal alanine aminotransferase (ALT) levels or clinical evidence of liver disease should be referred for consideration of antiviral therapy. Patients with chronic HBV may be offered regular screening for HCC via α-fetoprotein and liver imaging by ultrasound or CT, measured annually for less active disease or more frequently if cirrhotic.

Treatment with interferon-α (IFNα) has been promising in chronic hepatitis B, with a high success rate in clearing the virus and decreasing hepatic inflammation [78] and with demonstrated cost effectiveness [79]. IFNα can induce HBeAg seroconversion in 30–40% of selected patients after a 4–6 month course compared to spontaneous seroconversion rates of 15% in controls. These patients become anti-HBe positive. Some eventually lose HBsAg and only a very small proportion will relapse. Loss of HBeAg has been associated with improvements in liver histology and clinical outcome. Side effects related to IFNα are common

(Section 21.5.2.3). The best response to IFNα is seen in Caucasian patients who have had the disease for a short time, who have biochemical hepatitis and a low viral load (low HBV-DNA). More recent studies have focused on the pegylated interferons which are given once weekly [10]. IFNα should be used with extreme caution in patients with HBV-related cirrhosis, as it may induce a flare of hepatitis and lead to hepatic decompensation. Such patients should be assessed for liver transplantation in an appropriate center.

Lamivudine (3-TC) is a cytosine nucleoside analogue with potent inhibitory activity against HBV as well as HIV. It is very well tolerated and induces rapid and dramatic reductions in serum HBV-DNA. Treatment with oral lamivudine (100 mg per day for one year) has resulted in HBeAg seroconversion in 30% with a significant reduction in hepatic necro-inflammatory activity and progression of fibrosis [80]. Therapy is continued until HBeAg seroconversion occurs. One of the major problems with lamivudine is viral resistance, associated with the YMDD mutation in the virus, which occurs in up to 25% of patients by one year and in up to 50% of patients by two years. Patients may develop a flare of hepatitis that may lead to hepatic decompensation. It is important to continue lamivudine therapy despite the emergence of a resistant variant. Adefovir is a novel antiviral that appears to be effective, even in patients with lamivudine resistance, but it may lead to renal impairment [81]. Currently, the most effective oral antiviral agent is entecavir, which is now the drug of choice for treatment naïve patients [82].

21.5.2.3 Hepatitis C

Hepatitis C virus (HCV) is now recognized by health authorities as a major public health problem worldwide. Approximately 3.9 million people are infected in the United States [83]. HCV is already the leading indication for liver transplantation but it is projected that the number of people with advanced liver disease and associated hepatocellular carcinoma (HCC) doubled between 1999 and 2010. HCV is transmitted by blood-to-blood contact. The most common risk factor is injecting drug use (IDU).

Virology   HCV is an RNA virus, with seven major genotypes. The most common genotypes in the Unied States are Types 1 and 3. Reinfection after clearance and co-infection with more than one genotype can occur if the patient is re-exposed to virus. Patients with genotypes 2 or 3 respond better to current antiviral therapies than those with other genotypes. The virus alters its genetic structure over time by mutation leading to the presence of multiple species of virus with similar genetic sequence (quasi-species). This process is thought to allow HCV to evade immune clearance leading to chronic infection. The continual alteration in genetic structure makes the development of a preventative vaccine difficult. Antibodies in the blood reliably indicate infection, but are not protective.

Transmission

Injecting Drug Use: In the United States, Europe, and Australia the most common risk factor for transmission of hepatitis C infection is IDU, which now accounts for the bulk of incident cases, 91% in Australia [84]. HCV prevalence is strongly associated with duration of injecting with an incidence of approximately 20% for each year of IDU [85]. Most regular Injecting Drug Users (IDUs) are infected with HCV. Measures to limit the spread of this infection appear to be making only a modest impact [86,87]. The continuing high incidence appears to be related to the continuing high prevalence of sharing any component of injecting equipment, including mixing spoons, filters, swabs or tourniquets or even on the hands. The continuing epidemic of hepatitis C among IDUs has given rise to calls for wider implementation of infection control procedures, such as needle-syringe programs. Distribution of needles is associated with falling HCV transmission in some settings [87], but not all [88]. The negative findings may be attributed to a study design with low sensitivity (small number of incident infections; contamination of study groups) compared to larger studies. Nonetheless, needle-syringe programs remain controversial, particularly among the general community.

Sexual transmission: Rates are generally thought to be very low. An Italian study of the male partners of women infected with contaminated anti-D immunoglobln showed no evidence of transmission over a combined follow-up period of 862 years [89]. Recent studies have demonstrated sexual transmission between men who have sex with men [90].

The vertical transmission: The rate from mother to baby is approximately 5%. The risk is increased if the mother is also HIV positive, unless she is taking Highly Active Antiretroviral Therapy (HAART). One study showed a transmission rate of 9.5% from mothers with viremia, but no transmission if the mother was hepatitis C RNA negative at time of delivery [91]. Hepatitis C RNA has been found in breast milk but there is no evidence for transmission. Antibody testing of infants should be deferred for 18 months until transmitted antibody has disappeared.

Blood products: The risk of hepatitis C infection in recipients of blood and blood products before 1990 was related to the volume of blood products transfused. The majority of severe hemophiliacs became infected. After screening of blood products for hepatitis C antibody was introduced, the number of people with post transfusional non-A, non-B hepatitis has reduced markedly. The risk of hepatitis C infection following blood transfusion in Australia was estimated at 1 in 250 000 units transfused [92].

Occupational and nosocomial transmission: Healthcare and laboratory staff handling blood and blood products are at risk of contracting hepatitis C. Estimates for the risk of transmission from a needlestick injury range from 0–10% [91].

Tattooing: Several studies have demonstrated an association between tattooing and hepatitis C infection. In an Australian study of blood donors the independent relative risk associated with a history of tattooing was 27 [84]. Although infection control guidelines for tattooists have been introduced in

recent years, the possibility of hepatitis C transmission continues where these guidelines are not followed.

Primary Infection   Primary infection with HCV is typically subclinical, but mild hepatitis may occur. Fulminant hepatitis is almost unknown. Peak viremia occurs in the pre-acute or early in the acute phase and antibodies appear as early as four weeks (average 6–8 weeks) using third-generation testing. Clinically evident hepatitis reflects a significant immune response to the virus and may be associated with a higher rate of viral clearance than subclinical infection.

Chronic Infection   As many as 75% of patients infected with hepatitis C will develop persistent chronic infection. After an average of 20 years, approximately 8% of people will develop cirrhosis, rising to 20% after 40 years. Progression to cirrhosis is associated with duration of disease, age >40 at the time of infection, average alcohol consumption >50 g/day, co-infection with HBV and HIV. The route of transmission or viral factors such as genotype or viral titre do not appear to play a role [93].

Symptoms of chronic hepatitis C without cirrhosis do not correlate well with disease activity or severity and tend to be nonspecific, mild, and intermittent. The most common is fatigue, with nausea, muscle aches, right upper quadrant pain, and weight loss. These symptoms are rarely incapacitating but they can have a detrimental effect on quality of life.

Diagnosis   The third-generation enzyme immunoassay for antibodies to hepatitis C is the most practical screening test for hepatitis C infection. This assay suffers from a high rate of false positives when used in populations with a low prevalence of hepatitis C, so screening of the general population is not recommended. The antibody tests do not differentiate between current and resolved infection, as the antibody typically takes more than 10 years to disappear after viral clearance.

A positive hepatitis C RNA test via polymerase chain reaction (PCR) indicates viremia, the presence of active infection, while a negative test in people with risk factors and positive antibody, indicates probable spontaneous clearance of HCV infection. HCV RNA analysis is particularly useful to assess the status of HCV antibody positive patients with normal liver function tests. Approximately 50% of these patients are PCR negative. The test should be repeated 3–6 months later and, if again negative, the patient can be reassured the virus has been cleared. Almost all hepatitis C antibody positive patients with abnormal liver function tests (LFTs) have detectable levels of hepatitis C RNA in their blood. Therefore, if a patient has a risk factor for HCV with abnormal LFTs (without another reason for abnormal LFTs), hepatitis C PCR is unlikely to be diagnostically helpful. Patients with another explanation for abnormal LFTs, such as alcohol addiction, are exceptions to this principle.

Hepatitis C genotyping can be performed to aid decision making about treatment. Genotyping may also be used to analyze cases of hepatitis C transmission by identifying the same genotype in the source patient and the recipient. Quantification of HCV RNA (or viral load) may be useful when considering antiviral therapy and transmission risk. Individuals with a very high viral load are less likely to benefit from therapy and may be more infectious compared to those with low viral load.

Management Issues IDUs infected with hepatitis C may be marginalized, indigent, homeless, and frequently experience discrimination. As a consequence, they may lack access to healthcare and health information [94]. It is important to provide culturally appropriate written material that matches the educational level of the patient, as many cannot discuss their illness with others. Outreach clinics have been established in needle-syringe services and prisons. These provide diagnostic evaluation and build a therapeutic relationship to facilitate referral for antiviral therapy along with other substance addiction treatment. Primary care physicians or other healthcare workers can also engage HCV infected patients and clinical guidelines can assist them to provide appropriate management.

Pre- and Post-Test Counseling Issues A diagnosis of hepatitis C often engenders a high level of anxiety that can be exacerbated by misinformation. Adequate time should be set aside for pre-test counseling in private. The results of hepatitis C testing should be given in person. Post-test counseling issues include the natural history of the disease, the symptomatology, and privacy issues. Accurate, nonjudgmental language combined with a sincere concern for the patient's welfare helps to build the patient's trust. Clarify the meaning of any colloquial, subcultural terms. Patients are fearful of transmitting hepatitis C to their partners, household contacts, and their children. They can be reassured that the risks are minimal but contact testing should be offered. Full explanations about the advantages, and limitations, of antiviral therapy allow the patient to make an informed choice about treatment options.

Assessing the Severity of the Disease Symptoms, including lethargy, do not correlate with the severity of liver disease. Spider nevi are commonly seen, but the physical signs are nonspecific unless advanced cirrhosis is present. Plasma alanine aminotransferase (ALT) is the best laboratory indicator of active viral hepatitis, but the level commonly fluctuates and does not correlate well with the stage of liver disease. A normal ALT level does not exclude cirrhosis. Patients with normal ALT levels and those who decline treatment may be monitored in primary care settings 2–3 times per year and referred if the ALT levels rise. Numerous noninvasive markers of liver fibrosis have been studied to reduce the need for liver biopsy. Among them are FibroScan® and FibroTest®, techniques to measure liver elasticity, which have recently been validated alone and in combination with serum markers for HCV infection. They have a good capacity to detect HCV-related cirrhosis or advanced fibrosis but lesser accuracy in early fibrosis [95].

LIVER BIOPSY In view of the limitations of noninvasive assessment, liver biopsy remains the "gold standard" for assessment of disease stage and prognosis. The biopsy appearances are ranked according to the stage (extent of fibrosis ranging from normal to cirrhosis) and grade (activity of hepatitis) using Scheuer or Ishak scoring systems. Significant fibrosis indicates a risk of progression to cirrhosis and is the major indication for antiviral therapy. The risk of a major complication after liver biopsy is in the order of 1/500. Biopsy is inappropriate in the presence of coagulopathy and thrombocytopenia due to increased risk of haemorrhage. Although still a controversial issue, liver biopsy is now less often performed prior to antiviral therapy.

Hepatitis A and B Vaccination   When there is no evidence of immunity, vaccination is indicated to reduce the risk of further liver injury. Chronic co-infection with other hepatitis viruses is associated with accelerated progression to cirrhosis [96]. Hepatitis B vaccination should be offered and patients with hepatitis C respond well, albeit with lower titres, compared to uninfected controls. An early report of high mortality from hepatitis A in patients with chronic HCV has not been replicated, but vaccination for hepatitis A is appropriate if available.

Alcohol   Alcohol addiction interacts adversely with chronic hepatitis C in several ways [97]. There is now a consensus that daily consumption of alcohol above 40 g has an additive effect on liver inflammation, and accelerates the progression of hepatic fibrosis. Alcohol addiction is also associated with increased viral load [98], reduced response to therapy, increased risk of progression to HCC, and exacerbation of the skin lesions of porphyria cutanea tarda.

There is no clear evidence concerning adverse effects of moderate levels of alcohol consumption on people with chronic hepatitis C. A practical recommendation is to limit alcohol consumption to 20 g per day for those without chronic hepatitis, 10 g per day for those with chronic hepatitis, and nil for those with advanced liver disease. A recent study has shown that continuing moderate use of alcohol was associated with reduced completion rates of antiviral HCV treatment but did not reduce the rates of viral clearance among those who completed treatment [99].

Dietary Guidelines   There is no published evidence to support any specific diet in unselected people with hepatitis C. Hepatic steatosis is a feature of hepatitis C and obesity and Type 2 diabetes mellitus are associated with hepatitis C and accelerated progression of fibrosis [100,101]. The potential for dietary interventions in selected subjects to control the activity of hepatitis is under investigation.

Management of Risk Factors   The presence of HCV infection may increase motivation to participate in treatment, particularly if the patient is seeking antiviral therapy. Avoidance of injecting drug use is the preferred option but it may not be the choice of the patient. Evidence-based harm minimization and abstinence-based treatments should be offered, as described elsewhere in this volume.

Antiviral Treatment   The main indication for treatment is chronic active hepatitis C with persisting viremia. The main goal of antiviral therapy is sustained virological response (SVR), defined by a continued normal ALT level and negative hepatitis C PCR at least six months following completion of treatment. Individuals with SVR generally remain PCR negative long term. Several studies have found significant improvements in general health and specific hepatitis C related symptoms in patients who achieve a sustained response to antiviral therapy [102,103]. In previously untreated patients, IFNα alone leads to a sustained response of only 10%. Ribavirin is a guanosine analogue that is absorbed orally and well tolerated. The combination of IFN and ribavirin substantially increases SVR rates [104]. The duration of treatment varies from six months for those with genotype 2 or 3 to 12 months for those with genotypes 1, 4, 5 or 6. A modified form of IFN, peginterferon, has a polyethylene glycol side chain and leads to sustained IFN levels for a week and results in higher response rates than unmodified IFN without increased side effects [105]. Combination peginterferon and ribavirin trials is now the standard treatment that is offered to those without contraindications. Consensus interferon links the most common occurring amino acid sequences at each position of available natural alpha interferons into one "consensus" protein with a 10-fold higher *in vitro* biological activity compared to single recombinant IFN-alpha-2a or -2b.

Patients on combination therapy experience more significant side effects compared to IFN monotherapy and require more medical and psychological support. Support groups or individual counseling may help patients manage side effects and other consequences of their treatment and reduce drop-out rates.

Treatment of Special Groups

HIV co-infection: The progression of chronic hepatitis C is accelerated in co-infected patients. Treatment of hepatitis C may be indicated in patients with early HIV infection and those stable on HAART. Consideration must be given to possible drug interactions and to additive blood abnormalities when treating co-infected patients.

Patients with compensated cirrhosis: Patients with compensated cirrhosis may be treated [105]. There is some evidence that treatment reduces the risk of hepatocellular carcinoma and decompensation, but these are subject to ongoing trials.

Persistently normal aminotransferases: Patients who are hepatitis C RNA positive and have persistently normal aminotransferase levels generally have mild disease [106] and an uncertain response to treatment [107]. It is recommended that these patients not undergo treatment, but they should be followed up every 4–6 months and treated if ALT becomes abnormal.

Patients with ongoing substance addiction: Compliance with treatment is likely to be poor in patients with active drug or alcohol dependence and may lead to exacerbation of hepatitis and drug resistance. The initial NIH

consensus meeting recommended against treating such individuals until substance addiction stabilized [108]. Subsequent opinion papers have reconsidered these issues and agreed that treatment should be made available, on an individualized basis, to recent drug injectors who enter substance addiction treatment and who are likely to comply with therapy [109,110].

Patients on opioid treatment programs: Several case series have demonstrated good completion rates and viral clearance rates in this group [111]. There is no evidence that methadone maintenance therapy impairs treatment response and methadone is encouraged, when indicated, if hepatitis C treatment is contemplated [112]. In the author's experience, patients who meet these criteria have completed treatment successfully, but have high comorbidity rates and require close and sympathetic management.

Side Effects of Therapy

Interferon: Flu-like symptoms occur within four to six hours of the injections, tend to subside within the first month of treatment, and respond to phenacetin. More persistent side effects are fatigue, alteration in mood, sleep disturbance, moderate suppression of white cell count and platelet count, skin rash, reduction in appetite and weight, dryness of the mucous membranes, and hair loss. Dose reduction or cessation of treatment may be required. Major side effects include stimulation of autoimmunity leading to retinopathy, interstitial fibrosis of the lung and thyroid disease.

Ribavirin: The most common side effect is hemolytic anemia. Other side effects are pruritus, cough, and myalgia. Dose reduction is commonly required. Significant teratogenic effects have been associated with ribavirin. Both women of child-bearing potential and men on treatment must use two forms of effective contraception during treatment and for six months thereafter (15 half lives for clearance of ribavirin).

Contraindications for Treatment Decompensated cirrhosis, pregnancy, lactation, active psychiatric illness and those who drink more than seven standard drinks a week are at higher risk of side-effects and lower chance of response and are generally not treated. Depression may worsen during therapy and suicide has been reported. Careful psychiatric assessment and ongoing care may be required. Contraindications to ribavirin include end-stage renal failure due to drug accumulation, chronic anemias, a history of cardiovascular dysfunction and inadequate contraception.

OTHER TREATMENTS An intense search for new antiviral agents is underway. Phase II trials involving VX-950 are in progress but, to date, the successful regimens have used these new drugs in combination with Peg-interferon and ribavirin. [113] An Interferon-free treatment regimen is still to be developed. A variety of drugs including rimantadine, ursodeoxycholic acid (UDCA), nonsteroidal anti-inflammatory drugs (NSAIDs), and venesection have been investigated alone or in combination with alpha interferons. Available studies do not support the use of alternative therapies such as Chinese herbs [114,115].

Advanced Hepatitis C Cirrhotic patients are at increased risk of hepatocellular carcinoma (HCC), and hepatitis C is among the commonest underlying associations of HCC. Once hepatic decompensation occurs, the five-year survival falls to 50% and transplantation should be considered rather than antiviral treatment.

HEPATOCELLULAR CARCINOMA (HCC) Small primary liver cancers can be resected or treated by local therapies. Cirrhotic patients with HCC are considered for transplantation if there are fewer than three tumour nodules smaller than 3 cm or a single nodule less than 5 cm with no extrahepatic spread or vascular invasion. It is currently recommended that such patients undergo six-monthly screening with upper abdominal ultrasound and serum alphafoetoprotein. If abnormalities are found, more extensive evaluation should be undertaken in a specialist liver center.

LIVER TRANSPLANTATION Hepatitis C is now the leading indication for liver transplantation and the numbers are expected to rise further during the next decade. Patients with cirrhosis should be considered for transplantation if they develop major complications of their cirrhosis indicating a life expectancy of 1–2 years without transplantation. The three-year survival is 84%, which is equivalent to survival in patients transplanted with other forms of liver disease [116]. Before transplantation, patients should be informed of the high risk of hepatitis C recurrence and its potential consequences including a 10% risk of cirrhosis at five years. Methadone maintenance is no longer considered a contraindication for transplantation [117–119].

21.5.2.4 Hepatitis D

The delta agent is a RNA particle coated with HBsAg. The virus cannot replicate without co-infection with hepatitis B. Outbreaks of delta virus co-infection with hepatitis B have occurred among IDUs and were associated with high mortality [116]. Control of hepatitis B by vaccination will limit the spread of HDV. The diagnosis of HDV is by rising titres of IgG antibody or IgM antibody. Delta infection should be considered in any HBV positive patient with relapse. Delta hepatitis responds poorly to interferon unless high doses are given for long periods.

21.6   COCAINE AND THE GASTROINTESTINAL SYSTEM

Cocaine is an illicit substance that can be used orally, nasally, and parenterally. It has a powerful vasoconstrictor effect related to inhibition reuptake of neurotransmitters (norepinephrine and epinephrine and dopamine) in addition to a direct effect. Its use may result in abdominal pain accompanied with vomiting, possibly due to its vasoconstrictor effects on mesenteric vessels. Severe intestinal ischemia with gangrene was reported in illicit drug couriers whose ingested packages of cocaine ruptured in the body leading to massive overdose [120].

Hepatic injury appears to be uncommon in humans [74]. Most cases occur in association with other systemic features of cocaine toxicity, such as hyperthermia, rhabdomyolysis, hypoxia, and hypotension [121]. In some other cases, other drugs, particularly alcohol, have been involved. In experimental animals, cocaine hepatotoxicity is readily demonstrated and is both time and dose dependent [122].

The clinical presentation is characterised by a marked increase in serum aminotransferase activities beginning within a few hours of drug ingestion associated with the systemic features of cocaine toxicity listed above. Rhabdomyolysis may account for some of the increase in transaminases, as AST and ALT are both present in muscle. The liver biopsy shows coagulative hepatic necrosis typically in a centrilobular distribution, extending to panlobular necrosis in extreme cases. Micro- and macrovesicular steatosis may be present, consistent with involvement of mitochondria in hepatic injury.

The mechanism of hepatic injury is thought to involve hepatic ischemia and/or toxic oxidative metabolites. Hepatic ischemia is a likely mechanism, as cocaine is a powerful vasoconstrictor and this action accounts for many of the toxic effects of the drug characterized by impaired systemic perfusion.

Pre-treatment of experimental animals with cimetidine or cysteine protects against cocaine toxicity and provides additional evidence in support of the metabolic theory of toxicity, but pre-treatment is not a clinically feasible approach to therapy in humans. No specific therapy has been shown to be effective.

21.7   ECSTASY (MDMA) AND THE GASTROINTESTINAL SYSTEM

An increasing number of cases of severe liver failure are being reported [74] leading to fatalities and liver transplantation [123]. Two clinical syndromes are emerging [122]: heat-shock like syndrome presenting early and toxic hepatitis, which has a more delayed presentation. The heat-shock like syndrome is similar to cocaine hepatitis and presents shortly after ingestion with systemic toxicity accompanied by severe liver injury. The other presents days to weeks after ingestion with jaundice and pruritus and may proceed to fulminant liver failure. The diagnosis of delayed presentations may be difficult unless MDMA use is suspected and specific enquiries are made. Biochemically, marked hyperbilirubinemia is noted with a disproportionate increase in AST as compared to ALT. The severity of hepatic dysfunction does not appear to be dose related [124].

Severe liver injury is a rare event, whereas MDMA use is extremely common, suggesting that other factors may contribute to liver injury. The drug is often taken at "rave" parties where participants dance for hours, predisposing to hyperthermia and volume depletion. Those who suffer from hepatic dysfunction with rhabdomyolysis and hyperprexia may have an abnormality of muscle metabolism similar to that seen in malignant hyperpyrexia syndrome. Other individuals may be susceptible on the basis of delayed drug elimination. The cytochrome P450 isoenzyme CYP2D6 metabolizes MDMA and approximately 5% of the population has low activity mutations of this isoenzyme with reduced hydroxylation of MDMA *in vitro* [125]. Increased susceptibility to MDMA toxicity *in vivo* has been demonstrated in CYP2D6 deficient mice [126]. An immunological mode of liver injury has been proposed on the basis that re-challenge with ecstasy has produced greater liver damage in the absence of hyperthermia and liver biopsy features on one patient suggested an auto-immune hepatitis-like injury which resolved spontaneously on withdrawal of the drug [127]. In some cases, corticosteroids have been successfully used but there are no controlled studies to support this approach to treatment.

The differential diagnosis of a patient with grossly elevated transaminases includes acute viral hepatitis, toxin ingestion, and ischemia. Unexplained liver test abnormalities in a young adult with hepatomegaly should prompt inquiry into illicit drug use and a urinary drug screen. A negative drug screen may result from delayed presentation or consumption of "ecstasy" tablets not containing MDMA, as approximately one in three ecstasy tablets does not contain MDMA [128]. Meticulous supportive care should be employed, with vigorous rehydration and active cooling measures [127]. The benefit/risk ratio of orthotopic liver transplantation for fulminant hepatic failure remains in question but there have been survivors of transplantation and early discussion of cases in liver failure with a liver transplant unit is advised.

REFERENCES

1. Lieber, C.S. and Leo, M.A. (1992) Alcohol and the liver, in *Medical and Nutritional Complications of Alcoholism* (ed. C.S. Lieber), Plenum, New York, pp. 185–239.

2. Preedy, V.R. and Watson, R.R. (eds) (1996) *Alcohol and the Gastrontestinal Tract*, CRC Press, Boca Raton, FL.

3. Bujanda, L. (2000) The effects of alcohol consumption upon the gastrointestinal tract. *Am. J. Gastroenterol.*, **95** (12), 3374–3382.

4. Silver, L.S., Worner, T.M. *et al.* (1986) Esophageal function in chronic alcoholics. *Am. J. Gastroenterol.*, **81** (6), 423–427.

5. Proctor, G.B. and Shori, D.K. (1996) The effects of ethanol on salivary glands, in *Alcohol and the Gastrontestinal Tract* (eds V.R. Preedy and R.R. Watson), CRC Press, Boca Raton, FL, p. 347.

6. Kaufman, S.E. and Kaye, M.D. (1978) Induction of gastro-oesophageal reflux by alcohol. *Gut*, **19** (4), 336–338.

7. Messian, R.A., Hermos, J.A. *et al.* (1978) Barrett's esophagus. Clinical review of 26 cases. *Am. J. Gastroenterol.*, **69** (4), 458–466.

8. Robertson, C.S., Mayberry, J.F. *et al.* (1988) Value of endoscopic surveillance in the detection of neoplastic change in Barrett's oesophagus. *Br. J. Surg.*, **75** (8), 760–763.

9. Gray, M.R., Donnelly, R.J. *et al.* (1993) The role of smoking and alcohol in metaplasia and cancer risk in Barrett's columnar lined oesophagus. *Gut*, **34** (6), 727–731.

10. Lau, G.K., Piratvisuth, T., Luo, K.X. *et al.* (2005) Peginterferon Alfa-2a, lamivudine, and the combination for HBeAg-positive chronic hepatitis B. *N. Engl. J. Med.*, **352** (26), 2682–2695.

11. Feinman, L., Korsten, M.A. *et al.* (1992) Alcohol and the digestive tract, in *Medical and Nutritional Complications of Alcoholism* (ed. C.S. Lieber), Plenum, New York, pp. 307–340.

12. Konturek, S.J., Stachura, J. *et al.* (1996) Gastric cytoprotection and adaptation to ethanol, in *Alcohol and the Gastrontestinal Tract* (eds V.R. Preedy and R.R. Watson), CRC Press, Boca Raton, FL, pp. 123–141.

13. Brown, R.C., Hardy, G.J. *et al.* (1981) Gastritis and cirrhosis – no association. *J. Clin. Pathol.*, **34** (7), 744–748.

14. Uppal, R., Rosman, A. *et al.* (1991) Effects of liver disease on red blood cell acetaldehyde in alcoholics and non-alcoholics. *Alcohol Alcohol Suppl.*, **1**, 323–326.

15. Hauge, T., Persson, J. *et al.* (1994) Helicobacter pylori, active chronic antral gastritis, and gastrointestinal symptoms in alcoholics. *Alcohol Clin. Exp. Res.*, **18** (4), 886–888.

16. Go, V.L.W. and Everhart, J.E. (1994) Pancreatitis, in *Digestive Diseases in the United States: Epidemiology and Impact* (ed. J.E. Everhart), NIH, NIDDK, Washington, DC, pp. 615–646.

17. Johnson, C.D. and Hosking, S. (1991) National statistics for diet, alcohol consumption, and chronic pancreatitis in England and Wales, 1960–88. *Gut*, **32** (11), 1401–1405.

18. Bradley, E.L. 3rd (1993) A clinically based classification system for acute pancreatitis. Summary of the international symposium on acute pancreatitis (Atlanta, GA, 11–13 September 1992). *Arch. Surg.*, **128** (5), 586–590.

19. Pitchumoni, C.S., Glasser, M. *et al.* (1984) Pancreatic fibrosis in chronic alcoholics and nonalcoholics without clinical pancreatitis. *Am. J. Gastroenterol.*, **79** (5), 382–388.

20. Haber, P.S., Wilson, J.S. *et al.* (1995) Individual susceptibility to alcoholic pancreatitis: still an enigma. *J. Lab. Clin. Med.*, **125**, 305–312.

21. Witt, H., Apte, M.V., Keim, V. *et al.* (2007) Chronic pancreatitis: challenges and advances in pathogenesis, genetics, diagnosis, and therapy. *Gastroenterology*, **132** (4), 1557–1573.

22. Haber, P.S., Wilson, J.S. *et al.* (1994) Lipid intolerance does not account for susceptibility to alcoholic and gallstone pancreatitis. *Gastroenterology*, **106** (3), 742–748.

23. Haber, P.S., Wilson, J.S. *et al.* (1993) Smoking and alcoholic pancreatitis. *Pancreas*, **8** (5), 568–572.

24. Dutta, S.K., Ting, C.D. *et al.* (1997) Study of prevalence, severity, and etiological factors associated with acute pancreatitis in patients infected with human immunodeficiency virus. *Am. J. Gastroenterol.*, **92** (11), 2044–2048.

25. Pirola, R.C. (1966) Effects of ethyl alcohol on sphincteric resistance at the choledochoduodenal junction in man. *Gut*, **9**, 557–560.

26. Hajnal, F., Flores, M.C. *et al.* (1990) Effect of alcohol and alcoholic beverages on meal-stimulated pancreatic secretion in humans. *Gastroenterology*, **98** (1), 191–196.

27. Norton, I., Apte, M.V., Haber, P.S. *et al.* (1996) Cytochrome P-450 2E1 is present in rat pancreas and induced by chronic ethanol administration. *Gastroenterology*, **110** (Abstract), A1280.

28. Steinberg, W.M. (1990) Predictors of severity of acute pancreatitis. *Gastroenterol. Clin. North Am.*, **19** (4), 849–861.

29. Thune, A., Baker, R.A. *et al.* (1990) Differing effects of pethidine and morphine on human sphincter of Oddi motility. *Br. J. Surg.*, **77** (9), 992–995.

30. Mitchell, C.J., Playforth, M.J. *et al.* (1983) Functional recovery of the exocrine pancreas after acute pancreatitis. *Scand. J. Gastroenterol.*, **18** (1), 5–8.

31. Stone, H.H. and Fabian, T.C. (1980) Peritoneal dialysis in the treatment of acute alcoholic pancreatitis. *Surg. Gynecol. Obstet.*, **150** (6), 878–882.

32. Mayer, A.D., McMahon, M.J. *et al.* (1985) Controlled clinical trial of peritoneal lavage for the treatment of severe acute pancreatitis. *N. Engl. J. Med.*, **312** (7), 399–404.

33. Pederzoli, P., Bassi, C. *et al.* (1993) A randomized multicenter clinical trial of antibiotic prophylaxis of septic complications in acute necrotizing pancreatitis with imipenem. *Surg. Gynecol. Obstet.*, **176** (5), 480–483.

34. Delcenserie, R., Yzet, T. *et al.* (1996) Prophylactic antibiotics in treatment of severe acute alcoholic pancreatitis. *Pancreas*, **13** (2), 198–201.

35. Dufour, M.C. (1994) Chronic liver disease and cirrhosis, in *Digestive Diseases in the United States: Epidemiology and Impact* (ed. J.E. Everhart) NIH, NIDDK, Washington, DC, pp. 615–646.

36. Hill, D.B., Deaciuc, I.V. *et al.* (1998) Mechanisms of hepatic injury in alcoholic liver disease. *Clinics in Liver Dis.*, **3**, 703–721.

37. Hoek, J.B. and Kholodenko, B.N. (1998) The intracellular signaling network as a target for ethanol. *Alcohol Clin. Exp. Res.*, **22**, 224S–230.

38. Lieber, C.S. and Leo, M.A. (1998) Metabolism of ethanol and some associated adverse effects on the liver and the stomach. *Recent Dev. Alcohol*, **14**, 7–40.

39. Hrubec, Z. and Omenn, G.S. (1981) Evidence of genetic predisposition to alcoholic cirrhosis and psychosis: twin concordances for alcoholism and its biological end points by zygosity among male veterans. *Alcohol Clin. Exp. Res.*, **5**, 207–215.

40. Tsukamoto, H., Towner, S.J. *et al.* (1986) Ethanol-induced liver fibrosis in rats fed high fat diet. *Hepatology*, **6**, 814–822.

41. Naveau, S., Giraud, V. *et al.* (1997) Excess weight risk factor for alcoholic liver disease. *Hepatology*, **25**, 108–111.

42. Younossi, Z.M. (1998) Epidemiology of alcohol-induced liver disease. *Clin. Liver Dis.*, **2**, 661–671.

43. Black, M. (1984) Acetaminophen hepatotoxicity. *Annu. Rev. Med.*, **35**, 577–593.

44. Sato, C., Matsuda, Y. *et al.* (1981) Increased hepatotoxicity of acetaminophen after chronic ethanol consumption in the rat. *Gastroenterology*, **80**, 140–148.

45. Lieber, C.S., DeCarli, L.M. *et al.* (1975) Sequential production of fatty liver, hepatitis, and cirrhosis in subhuman primates fed ethanol with adequate diets. *Proc. Natl. Acad. Sci. USA*, **72**, 437–441.

46. Lane, B.P. and Lieber, C.S. (1966) Ultrastructural alterations in human hepatocytes following ingestion

of ethanol with adequate diets. *Am. J. Pathol.*, **49**, 593–603.

47. Bassendine, M.F. (1986) Alcohol – a major risk factor for hepatocellular carcinoma? *J. Hepatol.*, **2**, 513–519.

48. Poynard, T., Ratziu, V. *et al.* (2000) Appropriateness of liver biopsy. *Can. J. Gastroenterol.*, **14**, 543–548.

49. Orrego, H., Blake, J.E. *et al.* (1985) Relationship between gamma-glutamyl transpeptidase and mean urinary alcohol levels in alcoholics while drinking and after alcohol withdrawal. *Alcohol Clin. Exp. Res.*, **9**, 10–13.

50. Croop, R.S., Faulkner, E.B. *et al.* (1997) The safety profile of naltrexone in the treatment of alcoholism. Results from a multicenter usage study. The Naltrexone Usage Study Group. *Arch. Gen. Psychiatry*, **54**, 1130–1135.

51. Mason, B.J., Ritvo, E.C. *et al.* (1994) A double-blind, placebo-controlled pilot study to evaluate the efficacy and safety of oral nalmefene HCl for alcohol dependence. *Alcohol Clin. Exp. Res.*, **18**, 1162–1167.

52. Addolorato, G., Leggio, A.F., Cardone, S. *et al.* (2007) Effectiveness and safety of baclofen for maintenance of alcohol abstinence in alcohol-dependent patients with liver cirrhosis: randomised, double-blind controlled study. *Lancet*, **370**, 1915–1922.

53. Wiesner, R.H., Lombardero, M. *et al.* (1997) Liver transplantation for end-stage alcoholic liver disease: an assessment of outcomes. *Liver Transpl. Surg.*, **3**, 231–239.

54. Haber, P.S., Koorey, D.J. *et al.* (1999) Clinical outcomes of liver transplantation for alcoholic liver disease. *J. Gastroenterol. Hepatol.*, **14**, A34.

55. Van Thiel, D.H., Bonet, H. *et al.* (1995) Effect of alcohol use on allograft rejection rates after liver transplantation for alcoholic liver disease. *Alcohol Clin. Exp. Res.*, **19**, 1151–1155.

56. Kelly, M., Chick, J., Gribble, R. *et al.* (2006) Predictors of relapse to harmful alcohol after orthotopic liver transplantation. *Alcohol Alcohol.*, **41**, 278–283.

57. Perlow, W., Baraona, E. *et al.* (1977) Symptomatic intestinal disaccharidase deficiency in alcoholics. *Gastroenterology*, **72** (4 Pt 1), 680–684.

58. Herrerias, J.M., Muniain, M.A. *et al.* (1983) Alcohol-induced colitis. *Endoscopy*, **15** (3), 121–122.

59. Boyko, E.J., Perera, D.R. *et al.* (1989) Coffee and alcohol use and the risk of ulcerative colitis. *Am. J. Gastroenterol.*, **84** (5), 530–534.

60. Blot, W.J., McLaughlin, J.K. *et al.* (1988) Smoking and drinking in relation to oral and pharyngeal cancer. *Cancer Res.*, **48** (11), 3282–3287.

61. Farber, E. (1996) Alcohol and other chemicals in the development of hepatocellular carcinoma. *Clin. Lab. Med.*, **16** (2), 377–394.

62. Pandolfino, J.E. and Kahrilas, P.J. (2000) Smoking and gastro-oesophageal reflux disease. *Eur. J. Gastroenterol. Hepatol.*, **12** (8), 837–842.

63. Korman, M.G., Hansky, J. *et al.* (1983) Influence of cigarette smoking on healing and relapse in duodenal ulcer disease. *Gastroenterology*, **85** (4), 871–874.

64. Chowdhury, P. and Rayford, P.L. (2000) Smoking and pancreatic disorders. *Eur. J. Gastroenterol. Hepatol.*, **12** (8), 869–877.

65. Rubin, D.T. and Hanauer, S.B. (2000) Smoking and inflammatory bowel disease. *Eur. J. Gastroenterol. Hepatol.*, **12** (8), 855–862.

66. Neugut, A.I., Hayek, M. *et al.* (1996) Epidemiology of gastric cancer. *Semin. Oncol.*, **23** (3), 281–291.

67. McKay, J.S., Linaker, B.D. *et al.* (1982) Studies of the antisecretory activity of morphine in rabbit ileum in vitro. *Gastroenterology*, **82** (2), 243–247.

68. Williams, C.L., Bihm, C.C. *et al.* (1997) Morphine tolerance and dependence in the rat intestine in vivo. *J. Pharmacol. Exp. Ther.*, **280** (2), 656–663.

69. Langrod, J., Lowinson, J. *et al.* (1981) Methadone treatment and physical complaints: a clinical analysis. *Int. J. Addict.*, **16** (5), 947–952.

70. Sandgren, J.E., McPhee, M.S. *et al.* (1984) Narcotic bowel syndrome treated with clonidine. Resolution of abdominal pain and intestinal pseudo-obstruction. *Ann. Intern. Med.*, **101** (3), 331–334.

71. Yuan, C.S., Foss, J.F. *et al.* (2000) Methylnaltrexone for reversal of constipation due to chronic methadone use: a randomized controlled trial. *JAMA*, **283** (3), 367–372.

72. Kringsholm, B. and Christoffersen, P. (1987) The nature and the occurrence of birefringent material in different organs in fatal drug addiction. *Forensic Sci. Int.*, **34**, 53–62.

73. Allaire, G.S., Goodman, Z.D. *et al.* (1989) Talc in liver tissue of intravenous drug abusers with chronic hepatitis. A comparative study. *Am. J. Clin. Pathol.*, **92**, 583–588.

74. Riordan, S.M., Skouteris, G.G. *et al.* (1998) Metabolic activity and clinical efficacy of animal and human hepatocytes in bioartificial support systems for acute liver failure [editorial]. *Int. J. Artif. Organs.*, **21**, 312–318.

75. Hollinger, F.B., Khan, N.C. *et al.* (1983) Posttransfusion hepatitis type A. *JAMA*, **250**, 2313–2317.

76. Tennant, F. and Moll, D. (1995) Seroprevalence of hepatitis A, B, C, and D markers and liver function abnormalities in intravenous heroin addicts. *J. Addict. Dis.*, **14**, 35–49.

77. Crofts, N., Cooper, G. *et al.* (1997) Exposure to hepatitis A virus among blood donors, injecting drug users and prison entrants in Victoria. *J. Viral. Hepat.*, **4**, 333–338.

78. Korenman, J., Baker, B. *et al.* (1991) Long-term remission of chronic hepatitis B after alpha-interferon therapy. *Ann. Intern. Med.*, **114**, 629–634.

79. Dusheiko, G.M. and Roberts, J.A. (1995) Treatment of chronic type B and C hepatitis with interferon alfa: an economic appraisal [see comments]. *Hepatology*, **22**, 1863–1873.

80. Dienstag, J.L., Schiff, E.R. *et al.* (1999) Lamivudine as initial treatment for chronic hepatitis B in the United States. *N. Engl. J. Med.*, **341**, 1256–1263.

81. Perrillo, R., Schiff, E. *et al.* (2000) Adefovir dipivoxil for the treatment of lamivudine-resistant hepatitis B mutants. *Hepatology*, **32**, 129–134.

82. Chang, T.T., Gish, R.G., de Man, R. *et al.* (2006) A comparison of entecavir and lamivudine for HBeAg-positive chronic hepatitis B. *N. Engl. J. Med.*, **354** (10), 1001–1010.

83. Alter, M.J. (1997) Epidemiology of hepatitis C. *Hepatology*, **26**, 62S–65.

84. Kaldor, J.M., Archer, G.T. *et al.* (1992) Risk factors for hepatitis C virus infection in blood donors: a case-control study. *Med. J. Aust.*, **157**, 227–230.

85. van Beek, I., Dwyer, R. *et al.* (1998) Infection with HIV and hepatitis C virus among injecting drug users in a prevention setting: retrospective cohort study [see comments]. *BMJ*, **317**, 433–437.

86. Alter, H.J. and Seeff, L.B. (2000) Recovery, persistence, and sequelae in hepatitis C virus infection: a perspective on long-term outcome. *Semin. Liver Dis.*, **20**, 17–35.

87. MacDonald, M.A., Wodak, A.D. *et al.* (2000) Hepatitis C virus antibody prevalence among injecting drug users at selected needle and syringe programs in Australia, 1995–1997. Collaboration of Australian NSPs. *Med. J. Aust.*, **172**, 57–61.

88. Hagan, H., McGough, J.P. *et al.* (1999) Syringe exchange and risk of infection with hepatitis B and C viruses. *Am. J. Epidemiol.*, **149**, 203–213.

89. Sachithanandan, S. and Fielding, J.F. (1997) Low rate of HCV transmission from women infected with contaminated anti-D immunoglobulin to their family contacts. *Ital. J. Gastroenterol. Hepatol.*, **29**, 47–50.

90. Danta, M., Brown, D., Bhagani, S. *et al.* (2007) Recent epidemic of acute hepatitis C virus in HIV-positive men who have sex with men linked to high-risk sexual behaviours. *AIDS*, **21** (8), 983–991.

91. Dore, G.J., Kaldor, J.M. *et al.* (1997) Systematic review of role of polymerase chain reaction in defining infectiousness among people infected with hepatitis C virus. *BMJ*, **315**, 333–337.

92. Whyte, G.S. and Savoia, H.F. (1997) The risk of transmitting HCV, HBV or HIV by blood transfusion in Victoria. *Med. J. Aust.*, **166**, 584–586.

93. Poynard, T., Ratziu, V. *et al.* (2001) Rates and risk factors of liver fibrosis progression in patients with chronic hepatitis c. *J. Hepatol.*, **34**, 730–739.

94. Stephenson, J. (2001) Former addicts face barriers to treatment for HCV. *JAMA*, **285**, 1003–1005.

95. Shaheen, A.A., Wan, A.F., and Myers, P.P. (2007) FibroTest and FibroScan for the prediction of hepatitis C-related fibrosis: a systematic review of diagnostic test accuracy. *Am. J. Gastroenterol.*, **102** (11), 2589–2600.

96. Weltman, M.D., Brotodihardjo, A. *et al.* (1995) Coinfection with hepatitis B and C or B, C and delta viruses results in severe chronic liver disease and responds poorly to interferon-alpha treatment. *J. Viral Hepat.*, **2**, 39–45.

97. Degos, F. (1999) Hepatitis C and alcohol. *J. Hepatol.*, **31** (Suppl 1), 113–118.

98. Cromie, S.L., Jenkins, P.J. *et al.* (1996) Chronic hepatitis C: effect of alcohol on hepatitic activity and viral titre. *J. Hepatol.*, **25**, 821–826.

99. Anand, B.S., Currie, S., Dieperink, E. *et al.* (2006) Alcohol use and treatment of hepatitis C virus: results of a national multicenter study. *Gastroenterology*, **130** (6), 1607–1616.

100. Adinolfi, L.E., Gambardella, M. *et al.* (2001) Steatosis accelerates the progression of liver damage of chronic hepatitis C patients and correlates with specific HCV genotype and visceral obesity. *Hepatology*, **33**, 1358–1364.

101. Clouston, A.D., Jonsson, J.R. *et al.* (2001) Steatosis and chronic hepatitis C: analysis of fibrosis and stellate cell activation. *J. Hepatol.*, **34**, 314–320.

102. Neary, M.P., Cort, S. *et al.* (1999) Sustained virologic response is associated with improved health-related quality of life in relapsed chronic hepatitis C patients. *Semin. Liver Dis.*, **19**, 77–85.

103. Ware, J.E. Jr, Bayliss, M.S. *et al.* (1999) Health-related quality of life in chronic hepatitis C: impact of disease and treatment response. The Interventional Therapy Group. *Hepatology*, **30**, 550–555.

104. Poynard, T., Marcellin, P. *et al.* (1998) Randomised trial of interferon alpha2b plus ribavirin for 48 weeks or for 24 weeks versus interferon alpha2b plus placebo for 48 weeks for treatment of chronic infection with hepatitis C virus. International Hepatitis Interventional Therapy Group (IHIT). *Lancet*, **352**, 1426–1432.

105. Heathcote, E.J., Shiffman, M.L. *et al.* (2000) Peginterferon Alfa-2a in Patients with Chronic Hepatitis C and Cirrhosis. *N. Engl. J. Med.*, **343**, 1673–1680.

106. Persico, M., Persico, E. *et al.* (2000) Natural history of hepatitis C virus carriers with persistently normal aminotransferase levels. *Gastroenterology*, **118**, 760–764.

107. Sangiovanni, A., Morales, R. *et al.* (1998) Interferon alfa treatment of HCV RNA carriers with persistently normal transaminase levels: a pilot randomized controlled study. *Hepatology*, **27**, 853–856.

108. NIH (1997) National Institutes of Health consensus development conference panel statement: management of hepatitis C. *Hepatology*, **26**, 2S–10S.

109. Davis, G.L. and Rodrigue, J.R. (2001) Treatment of chronic hepatitis C in active drug users. *N. Engl. J. Med.*, **345**, 215–217.

110. Edlin, B.R., Seal, K.H. *et al.* (2001) Is it justifiable to withhold treatment for hepatitis C from illicit-drug users? *N. Engl. J. Med.*, **345**, 211–215.

111. Hallinan, R., Byrne, A., Amin, J., and Dore, G.J. (2005) Hepatitis C virus prevalence and outcomes among injecting drug users on opioid replacement therapy. *J. Gastroenterol. Hepatol.*, **20** (7), 1082–1086.

112. Novick, D.M. (2000) The impact of hepatitis C virus infection on methadone maintenance treatment. *Mt. Sinai. J. Med.*, **67**, 437–443.

113. Davis, G.L. (2006) New therapies: oral inhibitors and immune modulators. *Clin. Liver Dis.*, **10** (4), 867–880.

114. Batey, R.G., Bensoussan, A. *et al.* (1998) Preliminary report of a randomized, double-blind placebo-controlled trial of a Chinese herbal medicine preparation CH-100 in the treatment of chronic hepatitis C. *J. Gastroenterol. Hepatol.*, **13**, 244–247.

115. Batey, R.G., Salmond, S.J., and Bensoussan, A. (2005) Complementary and alternative medicine in the treatment of chronic liver disease. *Curr. Gastroenterol. Rep.*, **7** (1), 63–70.

116. Levy, M.T., Chen, J.J. *et al.* (1997) Liver transplantation for hepatitis C-associated cirrhosis in a single Australian centre: referral patterns and transplant outcomes. *J. Gastroenterol. Hepatol.*, **12**, 453–459.

117. Lau, N., Schiano, T.D. *et al.* (2000) Survival and recidivism risk in methadone-dependent patients undergoing liver transplantation. *Hepatology*, **32**, 245.

118. Rothstein, K.D., Kanchana, T.P. *et al.* (2000) Is liver transplantation appropriate in patients on methadone maintenance? *Hepatology*, **32**, 245.

119. Koch, M. and Banys, P. (2001) Liver transplantation and opioid dependence. *JAMA*, **285**, 1056–1058.

120. Schrank, K.S. (1993) Cocaine-related emergency department presentations, in *Acute Cocaine Intoxication: Current Methods of Treatment, NIDA Research Monograph Series, Number 123* (ed H. Sorer), National Institute on Drug Abuse, Rockville, MD, pp. 110–128.

121. Silva, M.O., Roth, D. *et al.* (1991) Hepatic dysfunction accompanying acute cocaine intoxication. *J. Hepatol.*, **12**, 312–315.

122. Selim, K. and Kaplowitz, N. (1999) Hepatotoxicity of psychotropic drugs. *Hepatology*, **29**, 1347–1351.

123. Brauer, R.B., Heidecke, C.D. *et al.* (1997) Liver transplantation for the treatment of fulminant hepatic failure induced by the ingestion of Ecstasy. *Transpl. Int.*, **10**, 229–233.

124. Ellis, A.J., Wendon, J.A. *et al.* (1996) Acute liver damage and Ecstasy ingestion. *Gut*, **38**, 454–458.

125. Tucker, G.T., Lennard, M.S. *et al.* (1994) The demethylenation of methylenedioxymethamphetamine ("Ecstasy") by debrisoquine hydroxylase (CYP2D6). *Biochem. Pharmacol.*, **47**, 1151–1156.

126. Colado, M.I., Williams, J.L. *et al.* (1995) The hyperthermic and neurotoxic effects of 'Ecstasy' (MDMA) and 3,4 methylenedioxyamphetamine (MDA) in the Dark Agouti (DA) rat, a model of the CYP2D6 poor metabolizer phenotype. *Br. J. Pharmacol.*, **115**, 1281–1289.

127. Jones, A.L. and Simpson, K.J. (1999) Review article: mechanisms and management of hepatotoxicity in Ecstasy (MDMA) and amphetamine intoxications. *Aliment. Pharmacol. Ther.*, **13**, 129–133.

128. Baggott, M., Heifets, B. *et al.* (2000) Chemical analysis of Ecstasy pills. *JAMA*, **284**, 2190.

22

Addictive disorders in malignant diseases

Thomas J. Guzzo and Mark L. Gonzalgo

The James Buchanan Brady Urological Institute, Department of Urology, Johns Hopkins Medical Institutions, Baltimore, MD, USA

22.1   INTRODUCTION

Cancer continues to be a major public health problem in the United States. Cancer is the second leading cause of death among men and women in the United States, surpassed only by heart disease [1]. The American Cancer Society estimates that 1 399 790 million new cancer cases will be diagnosed in 2006 (excluding basal and squamous cell skin cancers) [1]. It is also estimated that 564 830 Americans will die of cancer in 2006. This includes an estimated 720 280 men and 679 510 women [1]. The impact of cancer does not stop with the morbidity and mortality in the individuals that it afflicts, since the economic burden for cancer treatment is immense. The National Institutes of Health estimated the overall cost for cancer treatment in 2005 to be US$ 209.9 billion [1]. Given that the prevalence of cancer increases with increasing age, this amount of money spent on cancer treatment will be even greater as the United States population continues to age [2].

The lifetime prevalence of alcohol addiction and dependence has been estimated to be 17.8% and 12.5% respectively [3]. In 2005, an estimated 19.7 million Americans over the age of 12 were illicit

drug users. Furthermore, according to the National Survey on Drug Use and Health, 3.6 million Americans over the age of 12 were classified with substance addiction or dependence on illicit drugs in 2005 [4]. Given the high prevalence of malignancy and substance addiction in America, it becomes readily apparent that there is a high probability that a large number of people will be affected by both conditions.

The treatment of malignancy is labor intensive for the patient with cancer and the healthcare providers administering treatment. Very often, treatment entails a multimodal approach using all or a combination of chemotherapy, surgery, and radiation. Cancer patients must face issues regarding pain management either in the post-operative setting or in the palliative setting often requiring potent narcotic pain medications. Chemotherapeutic and radiation regimens often require several visits to a healthcare provider each week during treatment. Furthermore, rigorous follow up in the post-treatment phase is often necessary to monitor for disease response and recurrence. The psychological and physical strains an individual

Addictive Disorders in Medical Populations   Edited by Norman S. Miller and Mark S. Gold
© 2010 John Wiley & Sons, Ltd.

encounters at the time of diagnosis, during treatment, and post-treatment can be immense. Even in the best of circumstances the intensive therapeutic regimens and follow up protocols can be extremely difficult for cancer patients. These healthcare demands can prove to be even more challenging for active substance addicts or patients with a prior history of alcohol or drug addiction.

22.2 ROLE OF ALCOHOL AND DRUGS IN MALIGNANCY

Alcohol use and addiction has been associated with an elevated risk for certain cancers in both men and women. Worldwide chronic alcohol consumption has been estimated to account for approximately 389 000 cancers or 3.6% of all cancers [5]. Although it is difficult to control for confounding factors in large epidemiologic studies, several well designed meta-analyses in the last decade have shed more light on the role of alcohol consumption in the development of malignant diseases. It appears that there is a direct dose-response relationship between amount of alcohol consumption and the risk of certain types of cancer. In a meta-analysis of 235 studies comprising 117 471 cases, Bagnardi *et al.* found alcohol use to be associated with significantly elevated risks for cancers of the oral cavity and pharynx (RR = 6.0), esophagus (RR = 4.2), larynx (RR = 3.9), stomach (RR = 1.32), colorectal (RR = 1.38), liver (RR = 1.86), breast (RR = 2.7), and ovary (RR = 1.53). For most cancers, increased risk was associated with 25 grams (approximately two drinks) per day [6]. Multiple studies have clearly shown that alcohol consumption is a risk factor for cancers of the upper GI tract and oral cavity, even when controlled for tobacco exposure [7–9]. Ellison *et al.* also found an elevated risk for breast cancer in women who consumed alcohol. In their meta-analysis of 42 studies comprising 41 477 cases, women who consumed 6, 12 and 24 grams of alcohol per day had 4.9%, 10% and 21% increased risk of breast cancer compared to women with no alcohol intake, respectively [10]. The causal association between alcohol consumption and breast cancer has been documented in both premenopausal and postmenopausal women and the exact relevance of the timing of exposure is unknown [11–16]. There is little or no evidence to support an increased risk of stomach, pancreatic, lung, endometrial, bladder or prostate cancer associated with alcohol consumption [17–22].

There is mounting evidence that genetic susceptibility plays a role in alcohol-induced carcinogenesis. Variability in genes for alcohol metabolism, folate metabolism, and DNA repair have been implicated for possible roles in alcohol-induced cancers [23].

Genetic polymorphisms within the genes that encode the alcohol dehydrogenase and aldehyde dehydrogenase enzymes responsible for the metabolism of alcohol have been identified as risk factors for alcohol-induced carcinogenesis [23–25]. A genetic polymorphism for reduced activity in the methylenetetrahydrofolate reductase enzyme that is active in DNA synthesis and methylation has been found to have a protective effect with regard to carcinogenesis in individuals with modest alcohol consumption [26]. Smaller associations have also been noted with various DNA repair genes with regard to alcohol consumption and malignancy [27]. A comprehensive review of genetic polymorphisms and their association with carcinogenesis and alcohol intake is beyond the scope of this chapter. A more thorough review of this subject is available elsewhere [23].

It is unclear exactly how alcohol consumption causes a carcinogenic effect in humans. Early studies in animal models concluded that ethanol itself was not directly carcinogenic [28,29]. More contemporary animal studies have found alcohol to be directly carcinogenic [30–32]. Several different mechanisms for carcinogenesis have been proposed and different mechanisms or combinations may be at work for different cancer sites. The carcinogenic pathways for ethanol-induced breast cancer have been some of the most extensively studied. Increased estrogen production in alcohol consumers is thought to play a role in breast cancer carcinogenesis. Alcohol is known to interfere with estrogen pathways on multiple levels, including by menstrual cycle variability, increasing the frequency and length of cycles, increasing serum estrogen metabolites, decreasing sex binding globulin, follicle stimulating hormone, and luteinizing hormone [33].

Alcoholic drinks may act as a solvent to allow for easier penetration of other carcinogens in the oral cavity and GI tract [34]. Production of reactive oxygen species, which are known carcinogens, may also play a role in alcohol-associated malignancy [5,35,36]. Acetaldehyde, the primary metabolite of alcohol, is carcinogenic in animal models [37]. Although the evidence is less convincing than in animal models, increased acetaldehyde salvia levels have been noted in alcoholic patients with head and neck cancer [38]. Nutritional deficiencies related to alcohol addiction may also predispose individuals to certain types of cancer. Furthermore, chronic malnourishment, which is often present in alcoholics, may predispose individuals to more aggressive cancers and increase the chances of developing metastatic disease [39].

The causal relationship between alcohol and carcinogenesis is obvious in the literature. Future studies are needed to further define the role of alcohol as a carcinogen both epidemiologically and on a molecular level. As alcohol usage increases worldwide with continued industrialization of the world, a greater burden related to alcohol-induced malignancy can be anticipated.

There is little direct evidence for a causal association between illicit substance addiction and the development of malignancy. The carcinogenesis of illicit drugs has been far less studied than alcohol and tobacco, but *in vitro* studies have been performed for most drugs, including cocaine, LSD, marijuana, heroin, and methamphetamines. *In vitro* data have shown that all of these drugs have the ability to induce genotoxicity, but their exact carcinogenic risk to humans is not well established [40–44]. There is conflicting evidence that marijuana addiction may predispose individuals to an increased risk of several types of cancer [45]. This has obvious public health implications, as marijuana is the most commonly used illegal drug in the United States [46]. Suspicion for an association between marijuana use and malignancy has been fostered by the fact that marijuana contains many of the same known carcinogens as tobacco [47]. Due to difficulty with study design and data collection, a clear-cut association has been difficult to demonstrate [45].

22.3   TREATMENT OF MALIGNANCY IN PATIENTS WITH ADDICTIVE DISORDERS

Cancer treatment in patients with a history of or active substance addiction poses unique challenges to healthcare providers. Specific challenges encountered by both the patient and the healthcare provider include the psychological impact of a new diagnosis of cancer, maintenance of treatment regiments, potential for drug and alcohol withdrawal during hospitalization, and pain management.

The psychological impact for the individual who is newly diagnosed with cancer can be immense. For individuals with a history of substance addiction, this can be an obvious time for relapse or increased substance misuse. At the time of diagnosis, early referral to appropriate psychological council and substance addiction specialists is imperative. Frank discussion with the individual with regard to the meaning of the diagnosis, prognosis, treatment options, and expectation of treatment can help to alleviate stress and anxiety. If possible a "point person" should be identified in the individual's life that can help with coordination of treatment appointments, medications, and can serve as a contact person with healthcare providers in the event of emergency or relapse.

Cancer treatment often involves surgical treatment requiring inpatient hospitalization. It is important to identify individuals with a substance addiction history in order to minimize potential complications during hospitalization. Substance dependence needs to be identified pre-operatively in order to decrease the risk of a withdrawal syndrome. Alcohol dependence is the most commonly encountered dependence disorder in hospitalized patients [48]. Unfortunately, it is often unrecognized at the time of admission and can be life threatening if not appropriately diagnosed and treated. There are several validated questionnaires that can be administered to patients at the time of admission to identify potential alcohol dependence, including the alcohol use disorders identification test (AUDIT) and CAGE questionnaire [49,50]. Unfortunately, less than 25% of chronic alcohol addicts are identified pre-operatively in the surgical setting [51,52]. If appropriately identified, patients with current alcohol dependence should be managed with early attention to the identification and treatment of any alcohol-related health issues. Chronic alcohol use can result in malnutrition, vitamin deficiency, liver dysfunction, metabolic acidosis, bleeding disorders, cardiac dysfunction, pancreatitis, and numerous electrolyte disorders [53–58]. Early recognition and treatment of any of these disorders can significantly impact surgical outcomes. Particularly germane to surgical oncology patients are the pulmonary, hemotologic, and cardiac manifestations of chronic alcohol addiction. Chronic alcohol users are more likely to develop pneumonia in the post-operative setting than nonalcohol users [59]. Furthermore, critically ill patients with a history of alcohol addiction have a higher likelihood of developing acute respirtory distress syndrome [60]. The cardiac effects of alcohol addiction, including dilated cardiomyopathy, high output cardiac failure, and atrial fibrillation, place individuals at increased risk for surgical procedures [61]. Platelet dysfunction in chronic alcoholics resulting in increased bleeding risk in the peri-operative period also needs to be considered [62]. Patients with alcohol addiction are three times more likely to have a complication in the post-operative period [63].

The most feared complication in alcohol dependent post-surgical patients is acute withdrawal. If unrecognized, acute alcohol withdrawal syndromes can lead to significant morbidity and even mortality in the peri-operative period. The initial signs of alcohol withdrawal can appear within hours of the last drink [51]. Early symptoms reach their height 24–48 hours after the last drink and most commonly consist of tremulousness, sweating, nausea, vomiting, anxiety, and agitation. If not recognized and treated, early progression to life-threatening delirium tremens can result with hallucinations, confusion, autonomic hyperactivity, and seizures [51]. Although the exact mechanisms are unclear, severe electrolyte imbalances can occur, including hypomagnesaemia, hypokalemia, and hypoglycemia [64]. The potential for death from either respiratory or cardiovascular collapse is high at this point [51].

Treatment of alcohol withdrawal syndrome ideally should be prophylactic, but if it is unrecognized until symptoms develop then prompt treatment is essential. Prophylactic treatment with benzodiazepines should be used to combat agitation and prevent the development of seizures [65,66]. Beta-blockers or carbamazepine can be used in conjunction to reduce the benzodiazepine dosage, but should not be used as single agents because they are not effective in preventing seizures associated with withdrawal [67–70]. If acute alcohol withdrawal syndrome is diagnosed in the post-operative period, management is tailored to its severity and symptoms. Intravenous benzodiazepines should be used to treat seizures. Hallucinations, agitation, and acute psychosis can be treated with haloperidol [64].

22.4 PAIN MANAGEMENT IN CANCER PATIENTS WITH PREVIOUS OR PRESENT ADDICTION

Opioid analgesics are currently the standard of care for the treatment of moderate to severe cancer pain [71,72]. There are well documented treatment algorithms for the management of pain in cancer patients. Generally a long-acting oral opioid is the most preferable initial form of treatment combined with a short-acting opioid for breakthrough pain [72]. It is important to remember that any patient who requires long-term opioid therapy for chronic pain will develop tolerance and physical dependence. These are expected outcomes and should not be considered signs of addiction or misuse [73]. Although studies vary by their criteria and definition of addiction or misuse, most demonstrate that the risk of opioid addiction in cancer and chronic pain patients is rare [74–76]. Unfortunately, due to both physician and patient bias cancer pain is often grossly under-treated [77–79].

Cancer patients who have had a history of substance addiction in the past or current substance addicts present a unique and difficult problem with respect to pain management. Although a cancer patient may have an active or prior history of substance addiction, it must be remembered that they will experience the same pain as an individual without a prior history of addiction if they are not adequately treated. A prior history of substance addiction is not a contraindication to opiate use to manage cancer pain, but it should alert the physician to carefully monitor the patient for relapse. Careful management of this subset of patients is important because treatment and prevention of addiction will aid in adherence to medical therapy. The goal in treating cancer pain in patients with an active or prior history of substance addiction should be to adequately treat their current pain while preventing relapse or limiting any ongoing illicit drug use. The appropriate treatment of pain in this setting is crucial. If a patient's pain is under treated the risk of misusing prescription medications or other substances increases [80].

As with other aspects of care, a multidisciplinary approach is crucial to both appropriately treat these patients' pain and, at the same time, avoid the potential for fostering addictive behavior. Ideally, in addition to the patient's oncologist, a substance addiction team or chronic pain expert, social work staff, and nurses should all be involved in the treatment of these patients. A mental health professional with experience in addiction is also key in helping to address behaviors associated with addiction. Open communication between the entire team and the patient will help to define expectations for treatment. A detailed history of prior drug use should be obtained prior to starting therapy. A written contract at the beginning of treatment is paramount to define exactly how and when drugs will be available and under what conditions, if any, additional prescriptions will be provided. Within the written contract, a clear treatment goal should be defined and also how any aberrant drug taking behavior will be dealt with [81]. It is also useful to identify one member of the healthcare team as the prescription writer to avoid the possibility of a patient receiving multiple prescriptions from differing providers.

Pain control in the palliative setting also warrants special attention for patients with a history of substance addiction. Multiple studies have shown that even in patients with advanced malignancy, pain is often under-treated [82–84]. Several groups are more at risk for their pain being under-treated, including ethnic minorities, females, elderly, children, and patients with a history of prior substance addiction [85–88]. As in nonterminal patients the use of a long-acting opioid is preferable to shorter acting agents.

22.5   CONCLUSIONS

Alcohol and illicit drugs cause significant morbidity and mortality in the United States. Well designed studies have shown a association between alcohol use and the subsequent development of certain types of malignancy. The treatment of cancer in patients with an active or prior history of substance addiction is challenging and a multidisciplinary approach is needed to adequately treat the medical, behavioral, psychological, and social issues in this difficult subset of patients.

REFERENCES

1. American Cancer Society Facts and Figures 2006. Available at http://www.cancer.org/downloads/STT/CAFF2006WSecured.pdf (accessed 15 October 2007).

2. Meropol, N.J. and Schulman, K.A. (2007) Cost of cancer care: Issues and implications. *J. Clin. Oncol.*, **25**, 180–186.

3. Hasin, D.S., Stinson, F.S., Ogburn, E. *et al.* (2007) Prevalence, correlates, disability, and comorbidity of DSM-IV alcohol abuse and dependence in the United States. *Arch. Gen. Psychiatry*, **64**, 830–842.

4. 2005 National Survey on Drug Use and Health: National Findings. Available at http://www.oas.samhsa.gov/NSDUHlatest.htm (accessed 15 October 2007).

5. Seitz, H.K. and Stickel, F. (2007) Molecular mechanisms of alcohol-mediated carcinogenesis. *Nat. Rev. Cancer*, **7**, 599–612.

6. Bagnardi, V., Blangiardo, M., Vecchia, C.L. *et al.* (2001) A meta-analysis of alcohol drinking and cancer risk. *Br. J. Cancer*, **85**, 1700–1705.

7. Ng, S.K., Kabat, G.C., and Wynder, E.L. (1993) Oral cavity cancer in non-users of tobacco. *J. Natl. Cancer Inst.*, **85**, 743–745.

8. Kabat, G.C., Ng, S.K., and Wynder, E.L. (1993) Tobacco, alcohol intake, and diet in relation to adeno-carcinoma of the esophagus and gastric cardia. *Cancer Causes Control*, **4**, 123–132.

9. Fioretti, F., Bosetti, C., Tavani, A. *et al.* (1999) Risk factors for oral and pharyngeal cancer in never smokers. *Oral Oncol.*, **35**, 375–378.

10. Ellison, R.C., Zhang, Y., McLennan, C.E. *et al.* (2001) Exploring the relation of alcohol consumption to risk of breast cancer. *Am. J. Epidemiol.*, **154**, 740–747.

11. Singletary, K.W. and Gapstur, S.M. (2001) Alcohol and breast cancer: Review of epidemiologic and experimental evidence and potential mechanisms. *JAMA*, **286**, 2143–2151.

12. Friedenreich, C., Howe, G., Miller, A. *et al.* (1993) A cohort study of alcohol consumption and risk of breast cancer. *Am. J. Epidemiol.*, **137**, 512–520.

13. Longnecker, M., Newcomb, P., Mittendorf, R. *et al.* (1995) Risk of breast cancer in relation to lifetime alcohol consumption. *J. Natl. Cancer Inst.*, **87**, 923–929.

14. Gapstur, S., Potter, J., Sellers, T. *et al.* (1992) Increased risk of breast cancer with alcohol consumption in postmenopausal women. *Am. J. Epidemiol.*, **136**, 1221–1231.

15. Van den Brandt, P.A., Goldbohm, R.A., and Van't Veer, P. (1995) Alcohol and breast cancer: Results from the Netherlands cohort study. *Am. J. Epidemiol.*, **141**, 907–915.

16. Holmberg, L., Baron, J., Byers, T. *et al.* (1995) Alcohol risk and breast cancer risk: effect of exposure from 15 years of age. *Cancer Epidemiol. Biomarkers Prev.*, **4**, 843–847.

17. Franceschi, S. and La Vecchia, C. (1994) Alcohol and the risk of cancers of the stomach and colon-rectum. *Dig. Dis.*, **12**, 276–289.

18. Zheng, W., Mclaughlin, J.K., Gridley, G. *et al.* (1993) A cohort study of smoking, alcohol consumption, and dietary factors for pancreatic cancer (United States). *Cancer Causes Control*, **4**, 477–482.

19. Korte, J.E., Brennan, P., Henley, S.J. *et al.* (2002) Dose-specific meta-analysis and sensitivity analysis of the relation between alcohol consumption and lung cancer risk. *Am. J. Epidemiol.*, **155**, 496–506.

20. Bandera, E.V., Kushi, L.H., Olson, S.H. *et al.* (2003) Alcohol consumption and endometrial cancer: some unresolved issues. *Nutr. Cancer*, **45**, 24–29.

21. Kogevinas, M. and Trichopoulos, D. (2002) Urinary bladder cancer, in *Textbook of Cancer Epidemiology* (eds H.O. Adami, D., Hunter, and D. Trichopoulos), Oxford University Press, New York, pp. 446–466.

22. Dennis, L.K. (2000) Meta-analysis for combining relative risks of alcohol consumption and prostate cancer. *Prostate*, **42**, 56–66.

23. Boffetta, P. and Hashibe, M. (2006) Alcohol and cancer. *Lancet Oncol.*, **7**, 149–156.

24. Brennan, P., Lewis, S., Hashibe, M. *et al.* (2004) Pooled analysis of alcohol dehydrogenase genotypes and head and neck cancer: a HuGE review. *Am. J. Epidemiol.*, **159**, 1–16.

25. Bosron, W.F., Crabb, D.W., and Li, T.K. (1983) Relationship between kinetics of liver alcohol dehydrogenase and alcohol metabolism. *Pharmacol. Biochem. Behav.*, **18**, 223–227.

26. Sharp, L. and Little, J. (2004) Polymorphisms in genes involved in folate metabolism and colorectal neoplasia: a HuGE review. *Am. J. Epidemiol.*, **159**, 423–443.

27. Hung, R.J., Van der Hel, O., Tavtigian, S.V. *et al.* (2005) Perspectives on the molecular epidemiology of aerodigestive tract cancers. *Mutat. Res.*, **592**, 102–118.

28. Boyle, P., Autier, P., Bartelink, H. *et al.* (2003) European code against cancer and scientific justification: third version (2003). *Ann. Oncol.*, **14**, 973–1005.

29. World Health Organization (1999) Global Status Report on Alcohol, World Health Organization, Geneva.

30. Beland, F.A., Benson, R.W., Mellick, P.W. *et al.* (2005) Effect of ethanol on the tumorgenicity of urethane(ethyl carbamate) in B6C3F1 mice. *Food Chem. Toxicol.*, **43**, 1–19.

31. Soffritti, M., Belpoggi, F., Cevolani, D. *et al.* (2002) Results of long-term experimental studies on carcinogenicity of methyl alcohol and ethyl alcohol in rats. *Ann. N Y Acad. Sci.*, **982**, 46–69.

32. Watabiki, T., Okii, Y., Tokiyasu, T. *et al.* (2000) Long-term ethanol consumption in ICR mice causes mammary tumor in females and liver fibrosis in males. *Alcohol Clin. Exp. Res.*, **24**, 117S–122.

33. Dumitrescu, R. and Shields, P.G. (2005) The etiology of alcohol induced breast cancer. *Alcohol*, **35**, 213–225.

34. Wight, A.J. and Ogden, G.R. (1998) Possible mechanisms by which alcohol may influence the development of oral cancer-a review. *Oral Oncol.*, **34**, 441–447.

35. Chamulitrat, W. and Spitzer, J.J. (1996) Nitric oxide and liver injury in alcohol fed rats after lipopolysaccharide administration. *Alcohol Clin. Exp. Res.*, **20**, 1065–1070.

36. Albano, E. (2006) Alcohol, oxidative stress and free radical damage. *Proc. Nutr. Soc.*, **65**, 278–290.

37. IARC (1999) Re-evaluation of some organic chemical, hydrazine and hydrogen peroxide, in *Monographs on the Evaluation of the Carcinogenic Risk of Chemicals to Humans. Acetaldehyde 77*, International Agency for Research on Cancer, Lyon.

38. Jokelainen, K., Heikkonen, E., Roine, R. *et al.* (1996) Increased acetaldehyde production by mouth washings from patients with oral cavity, laryngeal or pharyngeal cancer. *Alcohol Clin. Exp. Res.*, **20**, 1206–1210.

39. Cook, R.T. (1998) Alcohol abuse, alcoholism, and damage to the immune system-a review. *Alcohol Clin. Exp. Res.*, **22**, 1927–1942.

40. Yu, R.C., Lee, T.C., Wang, T.C. *et al.* (1999) Genetic toxicity of cocaine. *Carcinogenesis*, **20**, 1193–1199.

41. Li, J.H., Hu, H.C., Chen, W.B. *et al.* (2003) Genetic toxicity of methamphetamine in vitro and in human abusers. *Environ. Mol. Mutagen.*, **42**, 233–242.

42. Cohen, M.M., Maronello, M.J., and Back, N. (1967) Chromosome damage in human leukocytes induced by lysergic acid diethylamide. *Science*, **155**, 1417–1419.

43. Falek, A., Jordan, R.B., King, B.J. *et al.* (1972) Humane chromosomes and opiates. *Arch Gen. Psychiat.*, **27**, 511–515.

44. Li, J.H. and Lin, L.F. (1998) Genetic toxicology of abused drugs: a brief review. *Mutagenesis*, **13**, 557–565.

45. Hashibe, M., Straif, K., Tashkin, D.P. *et al.* (2005) Epidemiologic review of marijuana use and cancer risk. *Alcohol*, **35**, 265–275.

46. Johnston, L.D., O'Malley, P.M., Bachman, J.G. *et al.* (1975–2003) Monitoring the future national survey results on drug use, Volume I, secondary school students (NIH publication No. 04-5507). Bethesda, MD: National Institute on Drug abuse. Available at http://monitoringthefuture.org/pubs/mongraphs/voll2003.pdf (accessed 20 December 2007).

47. Hoffmann, D., Brunneman, D.K., Gori, G.B. *et al.* (1975) On the carcinogenicity of marijuana smoke. *Recent Adv. Phytochem.*, **9**, 63–81.

48. Saitz, R., Freedner, N., Palfai, T. *et al.* (2006) The severity of unhealthy alcohol use in hospitalized medical patients. The spectrum is narrow. *J. Gen. Intern. Med.*, **21**, 381–385.

49. Soderstrom, C.A., Smith, G.S., Kufera, J.A. *et al.* (1997) The accuracy of CAGE, the Brief Michigan Alcoholism Screening Test, and the Alcohol Use Disorders Identification Test in screening trauma patients for alcoholism. *J. Trauma*, **43**, 962–969.

50. Reinert, D.F. and Allen, J.P. (2002) The alcohol use disorders identification test (AUDIT): a review of recent research. *Alcohol Clin. Exp. Res.*, **26**, 272–279.

51. Spies, C.D. and Rommelspacher, H. (1999) Alcohol withdrawal in the surgical patient: prevention and treatment. *Anesth. Analg.*, **88**, 946–954.

52. Moore, R.D., Bone, L.R., Geller, G. *et al.* (1989) Prevalence, detection and treatment of alcoholism in hospitalized patients. *JAMA*, **261**, 403–407.

53. Lieber, C.S. (2003) Relationships between nutrition, alcohol, and liver disease. *Alcohol Res. Health*, **27**, 220–231.

54. Zakhari, S. and Li, T.K. (2007) Determinants of alcohol use and abuse: Impact of quantity and frequency patterns on liver disease. *Hepatology*, **46**, 2032–2039.

55. Vamvakas, S., Teschner, M., and Bahner, U. (1998) Alcohol abuse: potential role in electrolyte disturbances and kidney diseases. *Clin. Nephrol.*, **49**, 205–213.

56. Tonnesen, H. and Kehlet, H. (1999) Preoperative alcoholism and postoperative morbidity. *Br. J. Surg.*, **86**, 869–874.

57. O'Connor, A.D., Rusyniak, D.E., and Bruno, A. (2005) Cerbrovascular and cardiovascular complications of

alcohol and sympathomimetic drug abuse. *Med. Clin. North Am.*, **89**, 1343–1358.

58. Pandol, S.J. and Raraty, M. (2007) Pathobiology of alcoholic pancreatitis. *Pancreatology*, **7**, 105–114.

59. Spies, C.D., Nordmann, A., Brummer, G. *et al.* (1996) Intensive care unit stay is prolonged in chronic alcoholic men following tumor resection of the upper digestive tract. *Acta Anaesthesiol. Scand.*, **40**, 649–656.

60. Guidot, D.M. and Hart, C.M. (2005) Alcohol abuse and acute lung injury: epidemiology and pathophysiology of a recently recognized association. *J. Investig. Med.*, **53**, 235–245.

61. Spies, C.D., Sander, M., Stangl, K. *et al.* (2001) Effects of alcohol on the heart. *Curr. Opin. Crit. Care*, **7**, 337–343.

62. Scharf, R.E. and Anul, C. (1988) Alcohol-induced disorders of the hematopoietic system. *Z. Gastroenterol.*, **3**, 75–83.

63. Tonnesen, H. (1999) The alcohol patient and surgery. *Alcohol Alcohol*, **34**, 148–152.

64. Morris, P.R., Mosby, E.L., and Fergusen, B.L. (1997) Alcohol withdrawal syndrome: current management strategies for the surgery patient. *J. Oral Maxillofac. Surg.*, **55**, 1452–1455.

65. Mayo-Smith, M.F., Beecher, L.H., Fischer, T.L. *et al.* (2004) Management of alcohol withdrawal delirium. An evidence-based practice guideline. *Arch. Intern. Med.*, **164**, 1405–1412.

66. Jenkins, D.H. (2000) Substance abuse and withdrawal in the intensive care unit. Contemporary issues. *Surg. Clin. North Am.*, **80**, 1033–1053.

67. Worner, T.M. (1994) Propranolol versus diazepam in the management of the alcohol withdrawal syndrome: Double-blind controlled trial. *Am. J. Drug Alcohol Abuse*, **20**, 115–124.

68. Kraus, M.L., Gottlieb, L.D., Horwitz, R.I. *et al.* (1985) Randomized clinical trial of atenolol in patients with alcohol withdrawal. *N. Engl. J. Med.*, **313**, 905–909.

69. Neff, D.A. (1991) Beta-blockers in alcohol withdrawal. *DICP*, **25**, 31–32.

70. Gallant, D.M. (1992) One more look at carbamazepine in the treatment of alcohol withdrawal. *Alcohol Clin. Exp. Res.*, **16**, 1174–1175.

71. McQuay, H. (1999) Opioids in pain management. *Lancet*, **353**, 2229–2232.

72. WHO (1990) Cancer Pain and Palliative Care. Report of WHO Expert Committee, Technical Report Series 804, World Health Organization, Geneva.

73. Penson, R.T., Nunn, C., Younger, J. *et al.* (2003) Trust violated: Analgesics for addicts. *Oncologist*, **8**, 199–209.

74. Fountain, J., Strang, J., Gossop, M. *et al.* (2000) Diversion of prescribed drugs by drug users in treatment: analysis of the UK market and new data from London. *Addiction*, **95**, 393–406.

75. Porter, J. and Jick, H. (1980) Addiction rare in patients treated with narcotics. *N. Engl. J. Med.*, **302**, 123.

76. Aronoff, G.M. (2000) Opioids in chronic pain management: is there a significant risk of addiction? *Curr. Rev. Pain*, **4**, 112–121.

77. Fitzgibbon, D.R. (2007) Clinical use of opioids for cancer pain. *Curr. Pain Headache Rep.*, **11**, 251–258.

78. Zenz, M., Zenz, T., Tryba, M. *et al.* (1995) Severe undertreatment of cancer pain: a 3-year survey of the German situation. *J. Pain Symptom Mange*, **10**, 187–191.

79. Noyes, R. Jr (1981) Treatment of cancer pain. *Psychosom. Med.*, **43**, 57–70.

80. Schnoll, S.H. and Weaver, M.F. (2003) Addiction and pain. *Am. J. Addict.*, **12**, S27–S35.

81. Fishman, S.M. and Kreis, P.G. (2002) The opioid contract. *Clin. J. Pain*, **18**, S70–S75.

82. Bitros, B.S. (2007) Advocating for management of cancer pain. *J. Am. Osteopath. Assoc.*, **107**, ES4–ES8.

83. Grossman, S.A. (1993) Undertreatment of cancer pain: barriers and remedies. *Support Care Cancer*, **1**, 74–78.

84. Cleeland, C.S. (1987) Barriers to the management of cancer pain. *Oncology (Williston Park)*, **1**, 19–26.

85. Seale, J.P. and Muramoto, M.L. (1993) Substance abuse among minority populations. *Substance Abuse*, **20**, 167–180.

86. Ward, S.E., Goldberg, N., Miller-McCauley, V. *et al.* (1993) Patient-related barriers to management of cancer pain. *Pain*, **52**, 319–324.

87. Anderson, K.O., Mendoza, T.R., Valero, V. *et al.* (2000) Minority cancer patients and their providers. *Cancer*, **88**, 1929–1983.

88. Glajchen, M., Fitzmartin, R.D., Blum, D. *et al.* (1995) Psychosocial barriers to cancer pain relief. *Cancer Pract.*, **3**, 76–82.

23

Substance addiction and gastrointestinal malignancy

Jason T. Hedrick and James R. Ouellette
Department of Surgery, Division of Surgical Oncology, Wright State University, Dayton, OH, USA

23.1 INTRODUCTION

Malignant disease and addiction are challenging diagnoses for both patients and physicians. When they coexist, management of both can be increasingly difficult. The reported incidence of substance addiction in cancer patients is lower than in the general population although this may be due to underreporting or referral patterns [1].

Patients can generally be divided into three groups with regards to smoking, alcohol, and substance addiction: never users, former users, and current users. Each of these groups is unique in treating malignant disease and requires different follow up and attention. Never users rarely develop a new substance addiction problem during their cancer management, and prescriptions for opioids and other medications can be given without a high suspicion for misuse [1–4].

Past users are at risk for resuming addiction. Often patients with substance addiction histories have poor coping skills and the stress of a cancer diagnosis may increase the chance of recidivism. Drug use must be monitored. Also, these patients are more likely than never users to have stressed their support networks in the past and to need more support from their treatment team.

Current users are even more challenging. This group of patients is less likely to comply with treatment of both their cancer as well as their addiction. The compliance may be so poor that it may shorten the patients' life [1]. Physicians may have their own ideas of the patients' drug use and may hold their feelings back from the patient, which may further the mistrust in the doctor–patient relationship. The relationship between surgeon and cancer patient is often a very close one, as well as with the patients' family, but even these strong bonds can be severed by drug addiction and mistrust.

23.1.1 Identifying substance addiction

Taking a thorough substance addiction history often is avoided in patients due to fears of offending the

Addictive Disorders in Medical Populations Edited by Norman S. Miller and Mark S. Gold
© 2010 John Wiley & Sons, Ltd.

patient and assumptions that the patient will not be truthful. These feelings need to be put aside as a complete substance history is vital in the subgroup of patients that will require pain medications either for post-operative pain control or for palliation. Physicians should reassure the patient that accuracy in the substance history will aid the physician in adequately treating the patient's pain. Occasionally, including family members in the interview is helpful.

It is also important to recognize aberrant drug-related behavior. This may involve increasing the frequency of office visits, drug screening, and including family members in the patients' interviews. It is vital to inform the patient of all of these activities so they are not surprised by their family members' involvement or by a positive drug screen they did not realize was performed.

Unfortunately, the treating physician often must prioritize treatment plans. Considering cancer the more proximate life-threatening entity, treatment usually takes precedence. This frequently places substance addiction as a secondary problem, to be addressed after treatment or not at all.

23.1.2 Treating cancer pain

Every patient feels pain differently, though there are similarities based on tumor location and type. Inexperienced physicians and cancer patients themselves that have no history of addiction often will fear addiction inappropriately. Several studies have documented the low rate of addiction in patients treated with opioids that were never users [5,6]. One such survey included 11 882 patients and only four cases of addiction were identified subsequently [7].

Other misconceptions that exist in pain management in never users are that patients get a euphoria from medication administered for pain and that short-acting medications and intravenous formulations are more risky for the development of addiction. This is simply not true in the never user. Chronic pain studies have shown that these medications are safe and that there is no need to resort to the agonist/antagonist medications that are used in addicts [1,8–10].

Treating cancer pain in former and current addicts is challenging for many physicians. Recent evidence suggests that pain is under-treated in patients with cancer or AIDS [11,12] and, as a result, some patients may exhibit drug seeking behaviors because of this under-treatment [13]. Finding a balance of pain control to allow daily function without potentiating addiction is the goal. This is even more difficult in patients who have developed tolerance to opioid medications, either from long-term use or previous addiction. Long-term administration of potentially addictive medications is currently based on clinical experience. Generally, care for this patient subgroup involves a multidisciplinary team with physicians and nurses skilled in the medical illness, addiction, and, often, psychiatric care. Realistic goals are important. Instead of perfect compliance, perhaps identifying new addiction patterns and incorporating them into the treatment plan would be a goal. Setting limits is important also. As mentioned earlier, addicted patients require psychiatric evaluation due to the fact that up to 93% of addicts have a DSM IV diagnosis other than addiction (77% of the sample met criteria for one or more diagnoses on axis I, and 65% met criteria for a personality disorder on axis II [14]).

It is also important to consider dosing. Patients with a history of addiction often require larger doses to achieve pain control and neglect of this fact will lead to under treatment [15]. Tolerance allows these patients to overcome the concerning neurologic and respiratory depressive effects that concern prescribing physicians, especially when large doses are required.

23.2 ROLE OF ADDICTION IN SPECIFIC GI MALIGNANCIES

Risk factors for gastrointestinal malignancies are many and varied. A large volume of recent research has been directed at identifying genetic factors or hereditary predispositions to certain cancers [16–18].

Here the focus is on environmental factors or, more specifically, factors that either result from exposure to addictive materials or from the lifestyle that results in exposures. Most common tumors in the GI tract will be either Squamous Cell Carcinoma (SCC) or Adenocarcinoma (AC) and will often have similar patterns of disease. In the following sections, the discussion has been simplified to bring out commonalities and special conditions amongst the (1) solid organ and (2) nonsolid organ malignancies of the GI tract.

23.2.1 Nonsolid organ malignancies (esophagus, stomach, colorectal)

23.2.1.1 Esophagus and gastric cardia

Esophageal carcinoma is the sixth leading cause of death from cancer. In 2007 the estimated incidence was 15 560 cases in the United States and 13 940 deaths from esophageal carcinoma [19]. Squamous cell carcinoma and adenocarcinoma make-up the overwhelming majority of esophageal cancers. Incidence rates for adenocarcinoma are higher in white males while squamous cell is higher in African-American males. Risk increases with age and the mean age of diagnosis is 67 years [20]. The incidence of adenocarcinoma of the esophagus and gastric cardia is increasing in the United States [21].

The pathogenesis of esophageal carcinoma is uncertain but some data suggest that oxidative damage to the esophageal mucosa causes carcinogenesis [22]. This is reinforced by findings that diets rich in antioxidants, such as vitamin-C and beta-carotene, lend a 40–50% risk reduction across both main histologic types of esophageal cancer [22,23]. Smoking and alcohol addiction have long been established as risk factors for squamous cell carcinoma (SCC) of the esophagus. Hard liquor does appear to have more of a causative effect than beer, but the amount of alcohol abused seems to be more important than the type. In case control studies, smoking does appear to increase the risk of esophageal and gastric cardia adenocarcinomas by 140%, albeit this is not nearly as strong an association as with SCC [21]. Cessation does not have the

same protective effect in adenocarcinoma as it does in SCC [24]. There is a steady decline in risk of SCC with smoking cessation, but a protective effect may not be seen in adenocarcinoma for 20–30 years. Gammon *et al.* postulate that this may be due to smoking playing a role very early in the pathogenesis of adenocarcinoma and later for SCC. None of these studies could correlate the increasing rate of adenocarcinoma with smoking and alcohol however [24]. It has been estimated that combined, smoking and alcohol may account for 90% of all squamous cell carcinomas of the esophagus. SCC has also been linked to low socio-ecomomic status, achalasia, caustic injury, Plummer–Vinson syndrome, history of head and neck cancer, and radiation exposure. Risk factors are summarized in Table 23.1.

Screening for esophageal carcinoma is only undertaken in high risk areas, typically Asian countries [25]. Patients with long standing gastroesophageal reflux disease (GERD) who are candidates for intervention may undergo screening endoscopy. Barrett's esophagus is a risk factor for developing esophageal carcinoma and should be followed closely. Patients with documented Barrett's esophagus should have surveillance endoscopy and biopsy every 2–3 years, regardless how the underlying GERD is treated. Because inflammation can be confused with dysplasia, patients with pathologic low-grade dysplasia should be treated with complete acid suppression and rebiopsied at approximately 3–6 months. If low-grade dysplasia is confirmed, surveillance should be performed annually to rule out progression to high-grade dysplasia and/or cancer. If high-grade dysplasia is detected and confirmed by two expert pathologists, a patient should be referred for surgical consultation [20], and may elect to undergo esophagectomy vs. intensive endoscopic surveillance (e.g., every three months) [20,26,27]. The risk of frank malignancy in high-grade dysplasia patients is so great, surgical candidates are typically recommended for resection.

Esophageal cancer often presents late in patients not undergoing screening. Approximately 50% of patients have cancer beyond locoregional confines, less than 60% of those with locoregional disease can undergo resection, and nearly 70–80% of these

Table 23.1   Risk factors for esophageal carcinoma

Risk Factor	Squamous Cell Carcinoma	Adenocarcinoma
Tobacco	Increased	Increased
Alcohol	Increased	No proven increase in risk
Barrett's esophagus	No proven increased risk	>8
Obesity	No proven increased risk	2–4
Esophageal webs	>8	No proven increase in risk
Tylosis	>8	No proven increase in risk
Achalasia	4–8	No proven increase in risk
Very hot liquids	<2	No proven increase in risk
Low Socio-economic Status	<2	<2
Mediastinal Radiation	4–8	4–8
Caustic injury	>8	No proven increase in risk
History of head and neck cancer	>8	No proven increase in risk

Adapted from Enzinger and Mayer [20].

have positive lymph nodes [28]. The overall five-year survival for esophageal carcinoma is 14% [29], which is due to the advanced stage at presentation in most patients. Patients must be evaluated for their physical ability to tolerate surgery as the treatment plan is being determined. Also, the patient must have the tumor staged as part of the work-up. Endoscopic ultrasound, chest CT, PET, and CT-PET may be used for staging [30,31]. Staging is summarized in Table 23.2.

Patients with stage I, II, III tumors are generally considered resectable. Patients who are medically fit with noncervical T1 tumor generally undergo resection. Patients with more advanced resectable disease (Other T1, T2–T4, N0, N1, Nx or stage IVa) may first undergo preoperative or neoadjuvant chemo/radiotherapy before resection [32]. There are multiple approaches to esophageal resection and the best approach is controversial. Minimally invasive esophagectomy has been shown to be safe but any survival difference has not yet been shown [33]. Patients with distant metastases or who are unfit surgical candidates are recommended chemoradiation or best supportive care. The combination of cisplatin and 5FU are the most investigated and most commonly used chemotherapeutic agents in esophageal cancer. Multiple other agents such as irinotecan, gemcitabine, docetaxel, and

Table 23.2   TMN Staging of esophageal carcinoma with associated survival

Primary Tumor (T)	Nodal Status (N)	Metastasis (M)	Stage	5-yr survival (%)
Tis (Carcinoma *in situ*)	N0 (No regional nodal metastasis)	M0 (No distant metastasis)	0	95
T1	N0	M0	I	50–80
T2	N0	M0	IIA	30–40
T3	N0	M0	IIA	30–40
T1	N1	M0	IIB	30–40
T2	N1	M0	IIB	30–40
T3	N1	M0	III	10–30
T4	Any N	M0	III	10–30
Any T	Any N	M1a	IVA	0–1
Any T	Any N	M1b	IVB	0–1

Tumors of lower esophagus: M1a – Metastasis to celiac lymph nodes; M1b –other metastasis. Tumors of the midesophagus: M1a – not applicable; M1b – nonregional lymph node or other metastasis. Tumors of upper esophagus: M1a – metastasis to cervical nodes; M1b – other metastasis.
Staging from NCCN [32]. Survival data from Enzinger and Mayer [20].

many others have been and are being evaluated [20,32]. Best supportive care entails stent placement in the case of esophageal obstruction, aggressive pain control, esophageal dilations, or nutritional support. Surgery or radiotherapy may be indicated for brisk bleeding of the tumor.

Addiction plays a role in many aspects of esophageal carcinoma besides its etiology and prevention. Do *et al.* showed that continued smoking doubled the risk of a second primary tumor of the upper aerodigestive tract. Smoking decreases response to radiation in head and neck cancer, but has not been studied in esophageal cancer [34]. One study, comparing patients who continued to smoke with those that quit 12 weeks before diagnosis, showed a mortality risk reduction of 40%. Those who quit smoking one year before diagnosis had a reduction in mortality of 70%. An argument can be made that this data be extrapolated to SCC of the esophagus.

Surgery is a mainstay of treatment for many malignancies, both solid organ and nonsolid organ. Smoking increases the risk of many post-operative complications, such as pneumonia, myocardial infarction, wound infection, and anastamotic breakdown [35].

There currently is no specific body of literature that addresses surgical complication risk for alcohol and drug addicted patients. However, substance addiction can indicate a poor general standard of health for an individual. For surgeons, this raises concerns for post-operative recovery and compliance with follow-up treatment.

23.2.1.2   Colorectal

Colorectal cancer is the second leading cause of cancer deaths worldwide. The age-adjusted death rate was 4.4 per 100,000 men and women per year between 2002–2006. Colon cancer generally presents on a screening examination or with bleeding, obstruction,and, less commonly, perforation or symptoms due to metastasis. Screening is imperative and is based on risk factors including genetic predisposition and family history. Screening recommendations are summarized in Table 23.3.

Table 23.3   Colorectal cancer screening recommendations

Average Risk	Patients over the age of 50, no history of Inflammatory bowel disease (IBD) or adenomas and a negative family history	Begin at age 50	Colonoscopy every 10 years or FOBT annually with Flexible Sigmoidoscopy every 5 yr or Double contrast barium enema every 5 yr. (Colonoscopy preferred)
Increased Risk	History of adenomas, colorectal cancer (CRC), endometrial or ovarian cancer before age 60, inflammatory bowel disease (IBD), or a positive family history	• Begin at age 40 or at age of diagnosis of endometrial/ ovarian cancer • Begin 8–10 years after onset of IBD symptoms • Begin at age 40 or 10 yr earlier than diagnosis of cancer	Colonoscopy • 3–5 yr for adenoma • 1–3 yr for CRC • Every 5 yr for endometrial/ ovarian cancer • Every 1–2 yr for IBD • Repeat every 1–5 yr depending on level of family history
Hereditary High Risk	Patients who have had colorectal cancer before age 50, family history of clustering or hereditary nonpolyposis colorectal cancer (HNPCC), personal and familial polyposis syndromes	Colonoscopy • HNPCC: begin at age 25 or 10 yr before youngest age of diagnosis • Familial adenomatous polyposis (FAP): begin at age 10–15 • MYH associated begin at age 25–30	Genetic Testing • HNPCC: repeat colonoscopy every 1–2 yr • FAP: flexible sigmoidoscopy or colonoscopy yearly • MYH: every 3–5 yr

Data summarized from www.NCCN.org [36].

Risk factors for colon cancer include obesity, high fat diet, family history, hereditary syndromes, alcohol, and tobacco. The pathophysiology of colon cancer is that of a progression from normal epithelium to adenoma to carcinoma. The first step in the sequence is thought to be the loss of the APC gene on chromosome 5q. This sets the stage for future gene losses that allow the progression of polyp to carcinoma generally over a time frame of 5–10 years. This is the so-called "adenoma to carcinoma sequence" [37].

Once the diagnosis of colon cancer is made, appropriate treatment should be instituted. Localized colon cancer is typically treated with resection of the involved section of colon along with the vascular arcade and associated lymph nodes. Depending on the stage of the tumor the patient may require adjuvant therapy. Rectal cancer requires special consideration with regard to neoadjuvant therapy with chemotherapy and radiation in appropriate candidates. Surgery must include a mesorectal excision and determination of sphincter preservation versus permanent colostomy. Patients who present with metastatic disease often have a different treatment plan involving a multidisciplinary team approach. Surgery may be indicated before or after chemotherapy depending on the site of disease and resectability of metastases. A complete discussion is beyond the scope of this chapter [38]. Staging is summarized in Table 23.4.

Smoking and alcohol addiction clearly increase the risk of colon cancer. Studies have shown that smoking alone has a twofold increase in colorectal cancer risk and is implicated in 12% of colorectal caner deaths, with alcohol having similar statistics [40–42]. Most patients without a history of a hereditary component of colon cancer begin screening with colonoscopy or flexible sigmoidoscopy, barium enema, and annual fecal occult blood testing (FOBT). A recent retrospective analysis [42] of 161 172 colorectal cancer patients found that current drinking, smoking, or smoking plus drinking were associated with an earlier age of colorectal cancer diagnosis at 5.2, 5.2, and 7.8 years, respectively. To further put this into perspective, the mean age of diagnosis of current drinkers and smokers was 62.6 years, which approaches the mean age

Table 23.4 TMN staging of colon cancer

Stage	Tumor (T)	Node Status (N)	Metastasis (M)	5-yr Survival (%)
0	Tis	N0		>94
I	T1	N0		93.2
	T2	N0		
IIA	T3	N0		84.7
IIB	T4	N0		72.2
IIIA	T1–T2	N1		84.4
IIIB	T3–T4	N1	M0	64.1
IIIC	Any T	N2	M0	44.3
IV	Any T	Any N	M1	8.1

Tis – carcinoma *in situ*; T1 – tumor invades submucosa; T2 – tumor invades muscularis propria; T3 – tumorinvades muscularis propria into subserosa or into no peritonealized structures; T4 – tumor invades other organs or structures directly or is perforated; N0 – no nodal metastasis; N1 – metastasis to 1–3 regional nodes; N2 – metastasis to 4 or more regional nodes; M0 – no distant metastasis; M1 – distant metastasis.
Staging from NCCN [39].
Survival Data from O'Connell *et al.* [38].

for hereditary nonpolyposis colon cancer, which requires screening at age 20–25 compared to age 50 (Figure 23.1).

The change in age at diagnosis from current users to past users suggests that cessation will decrease risk. Based on these findings, one can make a case for earlier screening for patients who use alcohol and smoke.

23.2.2 Effect of smoking and alcohol on chemotherapy

The effect of addiction on specific chemotherapy and outcomes has not been well studied. One study

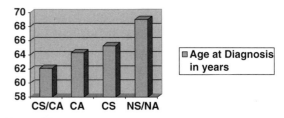

Figure 23.1 Age at diagnosis of colorectal cancer in men. CS/CA – current smoker/current alcohol use; CS – current smoker; CA – current alcohol use; NS/NS – never smoker/never alcohol user [16]

found a decreased level of the active metabolite of irinotecan in smokers. The study was too small to detect an outcome difference, but this may suggest that some chemotherapeutic agents may need to be dosed specifically for the patient [43,44]. Further research is necessary.

At times, motivation and an ability to follow the appropriate treatment plan can be the difference between successful and unsuccessful cancer treatment. Patients with a history of substance addiction are less likely to have adequate coping skills and their addiction may interfere with treatment in the form of missed appointments and so on. The goal for these patients may be reduction in mind altering or sedating substances instead of immediate abstinence [18].

23.2.3   Solid organ GI malignancy (liver, pancreas)

23.2.3.1   Hepatobiliary

Hepatocellular carcinoma (HCC) is the most common form of hepatobiliary tumor. The incidence of hepatocellular carcinoma depends on geographic location. High incidence areas, such as Sub-Saharan Africa, the People's Republic of China, Hong Kong, and Taiwan, see many more cases compared to the United States. China reported an annual incidence of 137 000 cases [45] while 25 000 cases were estimated in the United States in 2005 [46]. The incidence of HCC has been increasing in the United States over the past two decades. Studies among United States hospitalized veterans, as well as those conducted in large single centers, indicated that a large portion of the observed increase was attributable to hepatitis C virus (HCV) infection, whereas the incidence of hepatocellular carcinoma related to hepatitis B virus (HBV), alcoholic liver disease, or idiopathic cirrhosis remained relatively stable [47,48].

A study from the Centers for Disease Control and Prevention that used mathematical modeling estimated that the HCV epidemic started in the 1960s and peaked in the 1980s [49]. Risk factors for transmitting HCV were rampant during this period,

for example, injection drug use, needle sharing, and transfusion of unscreened blood and blood products.

Males are more commonly affected than females and this disparity is greater in high incidence areas, up to 5.7 times more frequently [50]. Chronic hepatitis B viral infection, aflatoxin, betel nut chewing, chronic HCV infection, cirrhosis, tobacco and alcohol addiction, and hemochromatosis are risk factors for HCC [51,52]. Of the 3–4 million patients in the United States with hepatitis C, 5–30% of these with develop chronic liver disease and 30% of those will develop cirrhosis. Cirrhosis carries a 12% chance of HCC per year [53]. The latency period between hepatitis exposure and diagnosis of HCC is 30–50 years [54].

Given that the increase in HCC now being seen is due to hepatitis exposures decades ago, it is concerning that the incidence of intravenous drug addiction (IVDA) is again on the rise. Emergency room records show an increase of heroin and morphine use up 51% from 1997 to 1999 [55]. This problem is present in patients presenting for surgery as well. Weiss *et al.* screened 2876 patients at one urban center for IVDA [56]. In patients reporting a current or past history of IVDA, 85% had serologic evidence of hepatitis C (Figure 23.2). In this study, to prevent one case of hepatitis C, only 1.5 patients needed to stop using [56].

This underscores the importance of screening surgical patients for IVDA and, if given a positive history, screening for hepatitis as well. Another interesting interaction is the role of alcohol

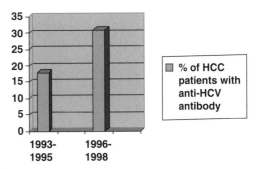

Figure 23.2   Increasing rate of anti-HCV in HCC patients at a single institution [48]

addiction on risk of HCC and age of presentation. Tagger *et al.* showed that alcohol increased the risk of HCC conferred by hepatitis C twofold for consumption of 41–80 g/day and fourfold for intake of >80 g/day [54,57]. Not all studies investigating the increasing rate of HCC evaluated for alcohol [48], and so this interaction is not consistently reported.

Hepatocellular cancer typically presents with nonspecific symptoms. For example, previously compensated cirrhotics can decompensate in the form of ascites, encephalopathy, jaundice, and so on. Abdominal pain may be the presenting symptom and a palpable mass may or may not be present. Weight loss, early satiety, and diarrhea are common; however, bone pain or dyspnea due to metastases are late presenting signs [58].

The work-up of HCC generally includes laboratory investigations that include a serum alpha fetoprotein (AFP) as well as C-reactive protein (CRP), as CRP has been shown to be a predictor of early recurrence [59]. Patients also undergo arterial and venous phase imaging by CT or MRI. Biopsy may be considered in hepatitis B negative patients if the AFP is less than 400, or less than 4000 in hepatitis B positive patients.

Cure is obtained only with removal of the tumor, whether by resection or transplant. The treatment for noncirrhotic patients is resection whenever possible. In unresectable noncirrhotics treatment options include ablation of the tumor, transarterial chemoembolization (TACE), systemic chemotherapy, or transplantation. Noncirrhotic patients must have an adequate functional hepatic reserve once resected and many times lack of adequate reserve makes the tumor unresectable [54]. In cirrhotic patients, resection is generally limited to Childs–Pugh Class A patients and some Class B. Childs–Pugh Class C is generally a contraindication for resection and will require transplantation in appropriate candidates (Table 23.5). Patients that require transplantation must have single tumor less than 5 cm, or 2–3 nodules less than 3 cm to be candidates. This is based on the Milan Criteria developed by Mazzaferro [60]. Recent evidence has suggested extended criteria for transplant, including single tumors up to 6.5 cm or ≤3 nodules with the largest lesion ≤4.5 cm and total tumor

Table 23.5 Unadjusted graft survival, deceased donor liver transplants 1999–2004

	One year survival (%)	Five year survival (%)
Alcoholic liver disease	81.9	67.6
Autoimmune hepatitis	83.5	77.2
Chronic viral hepatitis	80.3	65.3
Hepatoma	68.1	34.5
Primary biliary cirrhosis	85.8	79.4
Primary Sclerosing cholangitis	87.0	76.2
All diagnoses	81.3	68.4

Data from UNOS [23,62].

diameter ≤8 cm [61]. Patients who are not surgical candidates or who decline surgery may enroll in a clinical trial, undergo ablative therapy, TACE, selective internal radiation therapy (SIRT), chemotherapy plus radiation, supportive care or other modalities [54].

Addiction plays a significant role in the treatment of HCC. Survival has been shown to decrease for smokers and heavy alcohol users independently [49,56,63,64]. Since alcoholic liver disease (ALD) is the second most common indication for transplantation [64], post-transplant alcohol addiction is an important concept. Many transplant programs require six months of abstinence before patients can be considered for transplant as well as participation in alcohol addiction rehabilitation. This may also entail random urine and blood testing. One year and five year survival has been shown to be similar in transplants for ALD as well as other disease processes.

Many retrospective studies have evaluated post-transplant alcohol use and were summarized by Lim and colleagues [64]. Post-transplant alcohol use has been reported to interfere with immunosuppressive medications as well as medical and laboratory visits. The amount and frequency of interference is difficult to quantify. If patients are asked about "any" alcohol use after transplantation, approximately 20% (7–95%) report use. This is significantly limited by self-reporting. Self-reporting and limited periodic urine and blood alcohol levels still fail to accurately quantify the frequency and amount of use. Frequent and systematic screening may help detect recidivism earlier and allow prompt action. Furthermore, there have been no long-term prospective studies evaluating relapse and its effect on outcomes. However, there are no existing data to suggest that relapse has led to worse outcomes. In the largest study to date on this subject, all rejection episodes associated with heavy drinking were related to poor compliance with immunosuppressive drugs [65]. Not addressed in this study, but of even more concern, is recidivism in patients with coexisting hepatitis B or C virus infection. This may lead to rapid progression of recurrent viral infection [66].

Studies have failed to identify factors that reliably predict recidivism. There exist multiple studies that have failed to correlate six months of pretransplant sobriety with decreased risk of recidivism [64]. Although the six-month sobriety periods did not correlate recidivism, without models that can predict relapse, the period allows physicians to assess the patients commitment to their health as well as compliance with the rigorous demand of the post-transplant regimen.

Noncompliance in organ transplantation ranges from 20–50% when all forms of noncompliance are accounted for, including medication, office visits, exercise, diet, and abstinence from substance misuse. Predictors of these patients much like those for recidivism are lacking. One literature review cites alcohol addiction and psychiatric disorder as the only two predictive factors. It does note, however, that 60% of noncompliant patients have no predictive factor [67].

Hepatitis C virus recurrence after transplant is universal. Fibrosis develops faster in this cohort of transplant patients and as many as 20–30% will progress to cirrhosis in the first five years post-transplant [68]. Retransplantation in this group is controversial and studies are ongoing. Significant alcohol use in this population could be devastating although is not well defined.

Other hepatobiliary malignancies have less association with addiction than hepatocellular carcinoma. However, cholangiocarcinoma and less common tumors of the liver and biliary tract can be just as devastating.

23.2.3.2 Pancreas

Pancreatic adenocarcinoma is the fourth most common cause of cancer death in the United States. The age-adjusted death rate was 10.7 per 100,000 men and women per year between 2002–2006. The incidence is roughly equal in the two sexes and is slightly higher in the African-American population than in White Americans [69,70]. Risk factors for pancreatic adenocarcinoma include smoking, increased BMI, occupational exposures such as beta-naphthylamine, and benzidine. Familial forms are rare and associated with less than 5% of cases. True familial forms are associated with P16 and patients are at increased risk as well with BRCA-2 [70]. The role of alcohol and chronic pancreatitis in pancreatic cancer has been debated and a recent study suggests that the role of chronic pancreatitis in increasing the risk of pancreatic adenocarcinoma is likely due to alcohol, smoking, and selection bias [71].

Presenting symptoms include weight loss, pain, floating stools, depression, jaundice, and nausea. The sudden onset of adult Type 2 diabetes in patients over 50 should also alert the clinician to the possibility of pancreatic cancer. The diagnosis of pancreatic cancer is usually made by CT or U/S of the abdomen for the above nonspecific symptoms. Only 50% of patients diagnosed with pancreatic cancer are free of distant metastases, and only 20% of these patients have localized disease amenable to curative resection [72]. Palliation of obstructive symptoms and pain is important in unresectable patients. Staging is summarized in Table 23.6.

The only curative therapy for pancreatic adenocarcinoma is surgical resection. If the patient has a resectable tumor, he or she will undergo a pancreaticoduodenectomy known as the Whipple procedure or other pancreatic resection. Unresectable patients, patients with metastatic disease, or patients that have a resectable tumor but are medically unfit to undergo surgery are offered chemotherapy with gemcitabine, chemoradiation or combination therapy, or best supportive care. Even with maximal therapy long-term survival from pancreatic cancer is dismal (5%) [73]. Survival by stage is summarized in Table 23.6.

Table 23.6 TMN staging of pancreatic adenocarcinoma

Stage	Primary Tumor (T)	Nodal Status (N)	Metastasis (M)	5 Year Survival (%)
Stage 0	Tis	N0	M0	20.3
Stage IA	T1	N0	M0	20.3
Stage IB	T2	N0	M0	20.3
Stage IIA	T3	N0	M0	8
Stage IIB	T1, T2, T3	N1	M0	8
Stage III	T4	Any N	M0	8
Stage IV	Any T	Any N	M1	1.7

Tis – carcinoma *in situ*; T1 – <2 cm tumor limited to pancreas; T2 – >2 cm tumor limited to pancreas; T3 – tumor extends beyond pancreas but does not involve celiac axis or superior mesenteric artery; T4 – tumor involves celiac axis or superior mesenteric artery; N0 – no nodal metastasis; N1 – regionalnodal metastasis; M0 – no distant metastasis; M1 – distant metastasis.

5 year survival statistics from SEER database [73].

Treatment of pancreatic cancer in addicts can be challenging in that pain is often a major problem and the most debilitating symptom in patients with locally advanced and metastatic disease. More than 80% of patients with advanced cancer experience severe pain before death [17,74]. Aggressive pain control with opioid medications can be augmented with regional neurolysis. Advanced tumors infiltrate the retroperitoneal nerves that have sympathetic afferent nerve fibers which transmit nociceptive information from the pancreas [71]. The addition of celiac plexus nerve block has been shown to increase quality of life [74]. Neurolysis can be performed with laparoscopic, open, and thoracoscopic approaches, or with minimally invasive procedures such as endoscopic ultrasound guidance, CT-guided, and percutaneous fluoroscopically guided neurolysis [70]. Since its introduction in 1978, chemical splanchniectomy has been used to palliate pain in patients found to be unresectable at the time of exploratory laparotomy. Celiac block can be performed simultaneously with other palliative care procedures, such as biliary and gastrointestinal bypass. Chemical splanchniectomy can achieve acute pain relief in more than

80% of patients and can prevent the subsequent onset of pain for up to six months post-operatively [74]. Patients who underwent celiac plexus block had a significant increase in survival and, therefore, should be considered at surgery for any patient deemed intraoperatively to be unresectable [71,74].

Pancreatic cancer can be especially challenging for addicts as pain can be a large part of the symptomatology. Emphasis must be put on a treatment plan that is agreed to by the patient and the treatment team. The plan should focus on decreasing addiction and focus on pain control and compliance with the medical treatment plan. Previous studies have not investigated the role of neurolysis in substance addicted patients with pancreatic cancer, but it is likely that they would benefit increasingly as it is another modality and opioid addicts are likely already tolerant to medication effects. Some evidence suggests that chronic pancreatitis may increase the risk of pancreatic cancer [73]. Alcohol is widely known as a common cause of pancreatitis. Numerous studies have shown that the amount consumed in patients with alcoholic pancreatitis is significantly higher than controls and may be over eight drinks per day for a 5–10 year period [75,76]. Once chronic pancreatitis develops, pain can become a significant symptom. There is a role for neurolysis, as well as lateral pancreaticojejunostomy (Peustow procedure), pancreatic head resection, and Whipple procedure, for pain secondary to chronic pancreatitis. In one study, quality of life in alcoholic pancreatitis was impaired in the vitality domain and ongoing alcohol use or alcoholic etiology was associated with unemployed or retiree status [77].

Generally, alcoholism and drug addiction lead to worse overall outcomes in cancer patients, although this relationship has not been well studied in pancreatic cancer specifically. Interaction of smoking or alcohol with gemcitabine (current the most effective chemotherapy) has also not been well studied similar to many chemotherapeutic agents. Irinotecan, as discussed earlier, is an exception and since gemcitabine is also a prodrug, studies of potential interactions are needed.

23.3 PALLIATIVE CARE ISSUES

Addiction is an important topic in patients with advanced cancer. There are many misconceptions with regard to terminally ill cancer patients and substance addiction. Some people believe that removing an addicting substance from a terminally ill patient removes the patient's only source of enjoyment, or adds to the stress he or she is currently dealing with [18]. Often, chemically dependent patients have negative emotions associated with their addiction and their use may be driven to alter their mood rather than being driven by attaining euphoria. Removing these negative feelings and encouraging healthy coping mechanisms leads to an improved quality of life. Alcoholism also leads to a decreased quality of life in advanced cancer patients. The incidence may be as high as 30% and is often undiagnosed [78].

Patients with advanced cancer often have pain. Patients with a history of substance addiction are often under-treated with their pain regimen due to clinicians' fears of fueling the patient's addiction. Most often there is an under-treatment of pain due to the patient's tolerance after long-term use or addiction of opioid medications or drugs. This can lead to mistrust between the patient and clinician and disrupt the palliative care plan. The key lies in realistic goals for the addiction pattern that instead of abstinence my include reduction in the mind altering drugs, such that the patient can comply with other forms of treatment or maintain an adequate quality of life. Even small improvements can give patients who suffer from addiction a sense of accomplishment.

Untreated substance addiction and alcoholism can have deleterious effects on the family of the advanced cancer patient. Family members are often involved in the patient's treatment, both that of the addiction and cancer. Failure to comply with one or both of the regimens can lead to frustration. Educating the family members as to the goals of treatment as well as an understanding of the difference between dependence and addiction may help family members better assist with aggressive pain management.

Diagnosis of addiction in the palliative care setting is paramount as patients often will under-report their histories [1]. The CAGE questionnaire has been shown to be effective in this setting when compared to an experienced multidisciplinary team in the diagnosis of alcoholism. Similarly, screening for other substance addiction with thorough history taking and drug screening is important. These populations of patients often have a psychiatric comorbidity that when untreated can impede treatment of other symptoms. Up to 85% of chemically dependent or alcoholic patients will have a psychiatric comorbidity, which makes screening all patients and especially those with addiction histories vital. This allows the most appropriate and beneficial care each patient with an incurable and likely terminal malignancy.

Addiction increases cancer risk, increases recurrence, decreases the effectiveness of administered treatments, interferes with treatments being administered, decreases patients' quality of life, and affect patients in so many other ways. Many of these impacts are not well studied. Many patients are not well screened and, therefore, opportunities are being missed. Physicians and healthcare teams need to understand the impact of addiction on GI malignancy to adequately and appropriately educate and treat their patients.

REFERENCES

1. National Cancer Institute, Substance Abuse Issues in Cancer. Available from: http://www.cancer.gov/cancertopics/pdq/supportivecare/substanceabuse/HealthProfessional/page1 (accessed 23 January 2010).
2. Schug, S.A., Zech, D., and Dorr, U. (1990) Cancer pain management according to WHO analgesic guidelines. *J. Pain Symptom Manage*, **5** (1), 27–32.
3. Ventafridda, V., Tamburini, M., Caraceni, A. *et al.* (1987) A validation study of the WHO method for cancer pain relief. *Cancer*, **59** (4), 850–856.
4. Zech, D.F., Grond, S., Lynch, J. *et al.* (1995) Validation of world health organization guidelines for cancer pain relief: A 10-year prospective study. *Pain*, **63** (1), 65–76.

5. Perry, S. and Heidrich, G. (1982) Management of pain during debridement: A survey of U.S. burn units. *Pain*, **13** (3), 267–280.

6. Medina, J.L. and Diamond, S. (1977) Drug dependency in patients with chronic headaches. *Headache*, **17** (1), 12–14.

7. Porter, J. and Jick, H. (1980) Addiction rare in patients treated with narcotics. *N. Engl. J. Med.*, **302** (2), 123.

8. Gardner-Nix, J.S. (1996) Oral methadone for managing chronic nonmalignant pain. *J. Pain Symptom Manage*, **11** (5), 321–328.

9. France, R.D., Urban, B.J., and Keefe, F.J. (1984) Long-term use of narcotic analgesics in chronic pain. *Soc. Sci. Med.*, **19** (12), 1379–1382.

10. Portenoy, R.K. and Foley, K.M. (1986) Chronic use of opioid analgesics in non-malignant pain: Report of 38 cases. *Pain*, **25** (2), 171–186.

11. Breitbart, W., Rosenfeld, B.D., Passik, S.D. *et al.* (1996) The undertreatment of pain in ambulatory AIDS patients. *Pain*, **65** (2–3), 243–249.

12. Cleeland, C.S., Gonin, R., Hatfield, A.K. *et al.* (1994) Pain and its treatment in outpatients with metastatic cancer. *N. Engl. J. Med.*, **330** (9), 592–596.

13. Weissman, D.E., Haddox, J.D., and Haddox, J.D. (1989) Opioid pseudoaddiction – an iatrogenic syndrome. *Pain*, **36** (3), 363–366.

14. Khantzianh, E.J. and Treece, C. (1985) DSM III psychiatric diagnosis of narcotic addicts. *Arch. Gen. Psychiatry*, **42** 1067.

15. Kaplan, R., Slywka, J., Slagle, S. and Ries, K. (2000) A titrated morphine analgesic regimen comparing substance users and non-users with AIDS-related pain. *J. Pain Symptom Manage*, **19** (4), 265–273.

16. Anna, L.Z., Nickolov, A., Brand, R.E. *et al.* (2006) Associations between the age at diagnosis and location of colorectal cancer and the use of alcohol and tobacco: Implications for screening. *Arch. Intern. Med.*, **166** (166), 1669–1670.

17. Fasanella, K.E., Davis, B., Lyons, J. *et al.* (2007) Pain in chronic pancreatitis and pancreatic cancer. *Gastroenterol. Clin.*, **36** (2), 335–364.

18. Passik, S.D. and Theobald, D.E. (2000) Managing addiction in advanced cancer patients. *J. Pain Symptom Manage*, **19** (3), 229–234.

19. American Cancer Society (2007) Cancer facts & figures 2007.

20. Enzinger, P. and Mayer, R. (2003) Esophageal cancer. *N. Engl. J. Med*, **349** (23), 2241.

21. Gammon, M.D., Schoenberg, J.B., Ahsan, H. *et al.* (1997) Tobacco, alcohol, and socioeconomic status and adenocarcinomas of the esophagus and gastric cardia. *J. Natl. Cancer Inst*, **89** (17), 1277–1284.

22. Terry, P., Lagergren, J., Ye, W. *et al.* (2000) Antioxidants and cancers of the esophagus and gastric cardia. *Int. J. Cancer*, **87** (5), 750–754.

23. Ghardirian, P., Ekoe, J.M., and Thouez, J.P. (1992) Food habits and esophageal cancer: An overview. *Cancer Detect. Prev.*, **16** 163.

24. Lagergren, J., Bergström, R., Lindgren, A., and Nyrén, O. (2000) The role of tobacco, snuff and alcohol use in the aetiology of cancer of the oesophagus and gastric cardia. *Int. J. Cancer*, **85** (3), 340–346.

25. Yang, H., Berner, A., Mei, Q. *et al.* (2002) Cytologic screening for esophageal carcinoma in a high-risk population in anyang county, china. *Acta Cytol.*, **46**, 445.

26. Society for Surgery of the Alimentary Tract (SSAT) (2002) Management of Barrett's Esophagus. Available from: http://www.guideline.gov/summary/summary. aspx?ss=15&doc_id=5594&nbr=3780#s23 (March 2010).

27. Hirota, W.K., Zuckerman, M.J., Adler, D.G. *et al.* (2006) ASGE guideline: The role of endoscopy in the surveillance of premalignant conditions of the upper GI tract. *Gastrointest. Endosc.*, **63** 570.

28. Jemal, A., Siegel, R., Ward, E. *et al.* (2007) Cancer statistics, 2007. *CA Cancer J. Clin.*, **57** (1), 43–66.

29. National Cancer Institute (2002) Surveillance Epidemiology and End Results (SEER) cancer statistics review c1973–1999. Available from: http://seer.cancer. gov/csr/1973_1999/esoph.pdf (Dec 2007).

30. Vazquez-Sequeiros, E., Norton, I.D., Clain, J.E. *et al.* (2001) Impact of EUS-guidedfine needle aspiration on lymph node staging in patients with esophageal carcioma. *Gastrointest. Endosc.*, **53** 751.

31. Flamen, P., Lerut, A., Van Custem, E. *et al.* (2000) Utility of posiitron emission tomography for the staging of patients with potentially operable esophogeal carcioma. *J. Clin. Oncol.*, **18** 3202.

32. National Comprehensive Cancer Network (NCCN) (2007) Esophageal Cancer. Available from: www .NCCN.org (Dec 2007).

33. Luketich, J.D., Alvelo-Rivera, M., Buenaventura, P.O. *et al.* (2000) Minimally invasice esophagectomy. *Ann. Thorac. Surg.*, **70**, 906.

34. Browman, G.P., Wong, G., Hodson, I. *et al.* (1993) Influence of cigarette smoking on the efficacy of radiation therapy in head and neck cancer. *N. Engl. J. Med.*, **328** (3), 159–163.

35. Moller, A., Pedersen, T., Villebro, N. *et al.* (2003) A study of the impact of long-term tobacco smoking on postoperative intensive care admission. *Anaesthesia*, **58** 55–59.

36. Esophageal Cancer [Internet]. Available from: www .NCCN.org (Dec 2007).

37. Townsend, C., Beauchamp, R., Evers, B., and Mattox, K. (2004) Colon and rectum, in *Sabiston Textbook of Surgery Online*, 17th edn (eds C.M. Townsend, B.M. Evers,and R.D. Beauchamp), Barnes & Noble.

38. O'Connell, J.B., Maggard, M.A., and Ko, C.Y. (2004) Colon cancer survival rates with the new american joint committee on cancer sixth edition staging. *J. Natl. Cancer Inst.*, **96** (19), 1420–1425.

39. National Comprehensive Cancer Network (NCCN) Colon Cancer. Available from: www.NCCN.org (Dec 2007).

40. Cho, E., Smith-Warner, S., Ritz, J. *et al.* (2004) Alcohol intake and colorectal cancer: A pooled analysis of 8 cohort studies. *Ann. Intern. Med.*, **140** (8), 603–613.

41. Chao, A., Thun, M.J., Jacobs, E.J. *et al.* (2000) Cigarette smoking and colorectal cancer mortality in the cancer prevention study II. *J. Natl. Cancer Inst.*, **92** (23), 1888–1896.

42. Zisman, A.L., Nickolov, A., Brand, R.E. *et al.* (2006) Associations between the age at diagnosis and location of colorectal cancer and the use of alcohol and tobacco: Implications for screening. *Arch. Intern. Med.*, **166** (6), 629–634.

43. Benowitz, N. (2007) Cigarette smoking and the personalization of irinotecan therapy. *J. Clin. Oncol.*, **25** (19), 2646–2647.

44. vanderBol, J., Mathijssen, R.J., Loos, W. *et al.* (2007) Cigarette smoking and irinotecan treatment: Pharmacokinetic interaction and effects on neutropenia. *J. Clin. Oncol.*, **25** (19), 2719–2726.

45. Skolnick, A. (1996) Armed with epidemiologic research, china launches program to prevent liver cancer. *JAMA*, **276** (18), 1458–1459

46. Jemal, A., Murray, T., Ward, E. *et al.* (2005) Cancer statistics, 2005. *Cancer J. Clin.*, **55**, 10–30.

47. El-Serag, H.B., Davila, J.A., Petersen, N.J., and McGlynn, K.A. (2003) The continuing increase in the incidence of hepatocellular carcinoma in the United States: An update. *Ann. Intern. Med.*, **139** (10), 817–823.

48. Hassan, M.M., Frome, A., Patt, Y.Z., and El-Serag, H.B. (2002) Rising prevalence of hepatitis C virus infection among patients recently diagnosed with hepatocellular carcinoma in the united states. *J. Clin. Gastroenterol.*, **35** (3), 266–269.

49. Armstrong, G.L., Alter, M.J., McQuillan, G.M., and Margolis, H.S. (2000) The past incidence of hepatitis C virus infection: Implications for the future burden of chronic liver disease in the united states. *Hepatology*, **31** (3), 777–782.

50. Okuda, K. (ed.) (1992) *Epidemiology of Primary Liver Cancer*, Springer-Verlag, Tokyo.

51. Davila, J.A., Morgan, R.O., Shaib, Y. *et al.* (2004) Hepatitis C infection and the increasing incidence of hepatocellular carcinoma: A population-based study. *Gastroenterology*, **127** (5), 1372.

52. Tsai, J.F., Chuang, L.Y., Jeng, J.E. *et al.* (2001) Betel quid chewing as a risk factor for hepatocellular carcinoma: A case-control study. *Br. J. Cancer*, **84** (5), 709.

53. Izzo, F., Cremona, F., Ruffolo, F. *et al.* (1998) Outcome of 67 patients with hepatocellular cancer detected during screening of 1125 patients with chronic hepatitis. *Ann. Surg.*, **227**, 513.

54. National Comprehensive Cancer Network (NCCN) (2008) Clinical Practice Guidelines in Oncology: Hepatobiliary Cancers V.2. Available from: www.NCCN .org (Dec 2007).

55. Lemberg, B. and Shaw-Stiffel, T. (2002) Hepatic disease in injection drug users. *Infect. Dis. Clin. N. Am.*, **16**, 667.

56. Weiss, E.S., Cornwell, E.E., Wang, T. *et al.* (2007) Human immunodeficiency virus and hepatitis testing and prevalence among surgical patients in an urban university hospital. *Am. J. Surg.*, **193** (1), 55–60.

57. Tagger, A., Donato, F., Ribero, M.L. *et al.* (1999) Case-control study on hepatitis C virus (HCV) as a risk factor for hepatocellular carcinoma: The role of HCV genotypes and the synergism with hepatitis B virus and alcohol. *Int. J. Cancer*, **81** (5), 695–699.

58. Kew, M.C. (2006) Hepatic tumors and cysts, in *Feldman: Sleisenger & Fordtran's Gastrointestinal and Liver Disease*, 8th edn, Saunders.

59. Hashimoto, K., Ikeda, Y., Korenaga, D. *et al.* (2005) The impact of preoperative serum C-reactive protein on the prognosis of patients with hepatocellular carcinoma. *Cancer*, **103** (9), 1856–1864.

60. Mazzaferro, V. (1994) Milan multicenter experience in liver transplantation for hepatocellular carcinoma. *Transplant Proc.*, **26** (6), 557.

61. Yao, F.Y., Ferrell, L., Bass, N.M. *et al.* (2001) Liver transplantation for hepatocellular carcinoma: Expansion of the tumor size limits does not adversely impact survival. *Hepatology*, **33** (6), 1394–1403.

62. Health Resources and Services Administration (1998) 1997 annual report of the US scientific registry for organ transplantation and the organ procurement and

transplantation network: Transplant data 1988–1997, Bureau of Health Resources and Service Administration, US Dept of Health and Human Services, Rockville, MD.

63. Park, S.M., Lim, M.K., Shin, S.A., and Yun, Y.H. (2006) Impact of prediagnosis smoking, alcohol, obesity, and insulin resistance on survival in male cancer patients: National health insurance corporation study. *J. Clin. Oncol.*, **24** (31), 5017–5024.

64. Lim, J.K. and Keeffe, E.B. (2004) Liver transplantation for alcoholic liver disease: Current concepts and length of sobriety. *Liver Transpl.*, **10**, S31–S38.

65. Pageaux, G.P., Bismuth, M., Perney, P. *et al.* (2003) Alcohol relapse after liver transplantation for alcoholic liver disease: Does it matter? *J. Hepatol.*, **38** (5), 629–634.

66. Jauhar, S., Talwalkar, J.A., Schneekloth, T. *et al.* (2004) Analysis of factors that predict alcohol relapse following liver transplantation. *Liver Transpl.*, **10** (3), 408–411.

67. Laederach-Hofmann, K. and Bunzel, B. (2000) Non-compliance in organ transplant recipients: A literature review. *Gen. Hosp. Psychiat*, **22** (6), 412–424.

68. Neff, G.W., O'Brien, C.B., Nery, J. *et al.* (2004) Factors that identify survival after liver retransplantation for allograft failure caused by recurrent hepatitis C infection. *Liver Transpl.*, **10** (12), 1497–1503.

69. Silverman, D.T., Dunn, J.A., Hoover, R.N. *et al.* (1994) Swanson GM. Cigarette smoking and pancreas cancer: A case-control study based on direct interviews. *J. Natl. Cancer Inst.*, **86** (20), 1510–1516.

70. National Comprehensive Cancer Network (NCCN), Clinical Practice Guidelines in Oncology: Pancreatic Adenocarcinoma. Available from: www.NCCN.org (Dec 2007).

71. Karlson, B.M., Ekbom, A., Josefsson, S. *et al.* (1997) The risk of pancreatic cancer following pancreatitis: An association due to confounding? *Gastroenterology*, **113** (2), 587–592.

72. House, M. and Choti, M. (2005) Palliative therapy for Pancreatic/Biliary cancer. *Sur. Clin. North Am.*, **85** (2), 287–302.

73. National Cancer Institute (2007) Surveillance Epidemiology and End Results (SEER) Cancer of the Pancreas. Available from: http://seer.cancer.gov/statfacts/htm/pancreas.html (Dec 2007).

74. Lillemoe, K.D. (1993) Chemical splanchniectomy in patients with unresectable pancreatic cancer. A prospective randomized trail. *Ann. Surg.*, **217** (5), 447.

75. Haber, P.S. (1993) Smoking and alcoholic pancreatitis. *Pancreas*, **8** (5), 568.

76. Yadav, D. (2007) Alcohol-associated pancreatitis. *Gastroenterol. Clin.*, **36** (2), 219–238.

77. Wehler, M. *et al.* (2004) Factors associated with health-related quality of life in chronic pancreatitis. *Am. J. Gastroenterol.*, **99** (1), 138.

78. Bruera, E., Moyano, J., Seifert, L. *et al.* (1995) The frequency of alcoholism among patients with pain due to terminal cancer. *J. Pain Symptom Manage*, **10** (8), 599–603.

24

Renal manifestations of recreational drug use

Garland A. Campbell, W. Kline Bolton, and Mitchell H. Rosner

Division of Nephrology, University of Virginia Health System, Charlottesville, VA 22908, USA

24.1 INTRODUCTION

Drug addiction is a common etiological and complicating factor in many medical conditions. Renal disease is no exception. Drugs of addiction with the most frequent renal effects include cocaine, heroin, and ecstasy. Other drugs with renal manifestations include amphetamines, inhalants, alcohol, and hallucinogenic mushrooms. Many of these drugs have been linked to acute kidney injury (AKI), as well as chronic kidney disease (CKD) and glomerular disease that can progress to end-stage renal disease (ESRD). Several of these compounds can cause electrolyte abnormalities with serious and, rarely, fatal complications. Many drugs (amphetamines, cocaine, heroin, ethanol, barbiturates, and phencyclidine) can also lead to nontraumatic rhabdomyolysis with secondary AKI due to pigment (myoglobin) toxicity (Table 24.1). Other issues in addiction medicine that are pertinent to renal medicine include the risk of chronic addiction in patients with polycystic kidney disease (PKD) and nephrolithiasis. Finally, as many of these compounds are cleared via renal excretion, drug addiction in patients with advanced CKD and ESRD can have increased risk secondary to this altered metabolism with greater sensitivity to lower doses of drugs (especially narcotics) as renal function worsens.

24.2 COCAINE

Cocaine is an ergot alkaloid, benzoyl methylecgonine, extracted from the leaf of *Erythroxylon* plant [1]. It is most commonly available in two forms, a hydrochloride salt and a "freebase" form which is not acidified to form salt. The hydrochloride salt is most commonly taken intravenously, intranasally, or subcutaneously. "Freebase" cocaine is most often smoked. Both forms can be taken orally [2,3]. Cocaine is generally sold as white powder and often diluted with other substances, such as talc or cornstarch, or with other drugs, such as procaine or amphetamines [1]. Diluting substances are present either to increase the yield during processing or to increase potency.

Addictive Disorders in Medical Populations   Edited by Norman S. Miller and Mark S. Gold
© 2010 John Wiley & Sons, Ltd.

Table 24.1 Drugs of addiction associated with rhabdomyolysis

Drug	Mechanism
Amphetamines	Coma (crush syndrome)
	Hyperthermia
	Serotonin syndrome
Cocaine	Direct myotoxicity
	Hyperthermia
	Increased muscle activity
	Neuroleptic malignant syndrome
Heroin	Coma (crush syndrome)
Ethanol	Coma (crush syndrome)
	Direct myotoxicity
	Hypophosphatemia
Barbiturates	Coma (crush syndrome)
Phencyclidine	Coma (crush syndrome)
	Seizures
Ecstasy	Hyperthermia
	Increased muscle activity

There are several pharmacological and toxicological issues related to cocaine which manifest in the potential to cause both acute and chronic changes in renal function (Table 24.2). Many of these effects are mediated via the vasoconstrictive effects of cocaine [1,2,4]. These effects are due to a combination of a direct effect of cocaine on vascular smooth

Table 24.2 Renal effects of cocaine

Acute effects	
-Hypertension	
-Acute renal failure due to rhabdomyolysis	
-Acute renal failure due to ischemia (intense vasoconstriction)	
-Rare (case reports):	Henoch–Schonlein purpura
	Hemolytic–Uremic Syndrome
	Scleroderma crisis
Chronic effects	
-Hypertensive nephrosclerosis	
-Premature arteriosclerosis	
Congenital urinary tract abnormalities	

muscle as well as cocaine-induced stimulation of endothelin. Furthermore, cocaine has been shown to affect the kidney through stimulation of the renin-angiotensin system. This effect leads to vasoconstriction as well as stimulation of the pro-fibrotic growth factor TGF-β [2]. In animal studies, the angiotensin-converting enzyme inhibitor (ACEI) captopril has been shown to improve survival to a lethal dose of cocaine in rats [1,5]. Cocaine also has effects on the vascular nitric oxide pathway and this leads to enhanced vasoconstriction with the potential for tissue ischemia [5]. Furthermore, cocaine has also been shown to increase platelet aggregation and thromboxane synthesis [6]. In total, these profound vasoconstrictive and pro-thrombotic effects lead to decreased renal blood flow and potentially a fall in glomerular filtration rate (GFR) as well as a risk for ischemia and tubular injury [7].

For chronic cocaine addicts, accelerated arteriosclerosis becomes an issue. This has been documented in numerous organ systems including the kidney [1,6,8]. Over time, the development of atherosclerosis will lead to accelerated vascular hypertension and malignant hypertension as well as a risk for the development of CKD [9].

24.2.1 Cocaine and AKI

Cocaine can present with multiple forms of AKI, the most common of which is nontraumatic rhabdomyolysis [1,10,11]. In fact, up to 53% of patients presenting to the hospital with a cocaine-related admission have elevated creatine kinase (CK) levels [12]: This can occur with either of the forms of cocaine and with any route of administration. Rhabdomyolysis is due to multiple interacting factors. As mentioned above, cocaine leads to marked vasoconstriction with concomitant tissue ischemia [10,12]. Also, cocaine can be associated with seizures, hyperthermia and extended periods of unconsciousness (all significant risk factors for rhabdomyolysis). Finally, there are data to suggest that cocaine use can have direct toxicity to muscle cells *in vitro* [10]. Furthermore, adulterants such as arsenic, strychnine, amphetamine, and phencyclidine are potentially myotoxic [12]. As opposed to other causes of rhabdomyolysis, cocaine-associated rhabdomyolysis does not present with muscle pain and the rhabdomyolysis is generalized. Thus, a high degree of suspicion is required and laboratory investigation, including serum creatine kinase levels and urine myoglobin, should be requeated in those patients presenting with AKI and a history of cocaine ingestion. AKI is due to direct tubular toxicity of the myoglobin pigment.

There are other, less common causes of AKI associated with cocaine usage. This includes a potential link with scleroderma and scleroderma renal crisis [10]. It is unclear if cocaine use induces scleroderma renal crisis, or merely exacerbates an already present medical condition [10,13]. Due to the intense vasoconstriction caused by cocaine it is not surprising that there have been several case reports documenting renal infarction following use of cocaine [7]. Other cases have documented renal diseases, including antiglomerular basement membrane disease, Henoch–Schonlein purpura [13], hemolytic-uremic syndrome [14], and necrotizing vasculitis associated with cocaine use [10]. Causality in these case reports should be viewed with caution.

24.2.2 Cocaine and CKD

Cocaine use and the potential for cocaine-associated accelerated hypertension are significant risk factors, in susceptible subjects, for the development of CKD and ESRD [9,12]. Epidemiologic data in both urban and African American populations has documented that a significant number of patients with the diagnosis of hypertensive ESRD have a history of substance addiction, notably cocaine [12,14]. In a cross-sectional study of 163 ESRD patients, the

clinical diagnosis of hypertensive nephrosclerosis was strongly associated with cocaine use [14,15]. These patients also had a shorter duration of diagnosis of hypertension prior to the onset of ESRD than those patients without a history of cocaine use [14]. Despite these epidemiological associations, there are confounding factors (socioeconomic factors, genetic propensity to kidney disease, concomitant other drug use and environmental exposures) that limit the causal nature of this link. More convincingly, in a rat model, cocaine has been shown to stimulate mesangial cell proliferation, induce release of macrophage secretory products (IL-6, TGF-β), and lead to chronic glomerular sclerosis and tubulointerstitial damage [16]. Although limited, human renal pathology findings in cocaine users also support the theory of chronic cocaine nephropathy as a distinct pathological entity. DiPaolo *et al.*, in autopsy studies of 40 patients with cocaine-associated death, found increased vascular damage (extensive arteriosclerosis with medial thickening, luminal narrowing and vessels obstruction) when compared to control subjects [8]. The patients with a history of cocaine had an 18-fold increase in the ratio of sclerotic glomeruli. There were also significant increases in the amount of periglomerular fibrosis, degree of cellular inflammatory infiltrates in the interstitium, as well as an increase in hyperplastic arteriolosclerosis [8]. All of these findings support a causal role of cocaine addiction in the pathogenesis of chronic kidney fibrosis.

In utero exposure to cocaine due to maternal use is also associated with significant congenital urinary tract abnormalities, including: hydronephrosis, horseshoe kidney, prune belly syndrome, renal agenesis, prominent renal pelvis, nephromegaly, unilateral small kidney, and renal vascular disease [17].

24.3 HEROIN

Heroin, diacetylmorphine or diamorphine, is a naturally occurring substance processed from the poppy plant. It has similar pharmacological actions to other opiates and is rapidly metabolized to

morphine [1,12]. It is most commonly used by injection, either intravenously or subcutaneously in a practice termed "skin popping." Heroin can also be smoked, snorted or swallowed. Street heroin

Table 24.3 Renal effects of heroin addiction

Acute effects
  -Acute renal failure due to rhabdomyolysis
Chronic effects
  -Glomerular diseases directly associated with heroin
   addiction
    -Heroin-associated nephropathy (focal segmental
     glomerulosclerosis)
    -Membranoproliferative glomerulonephritis (usually
     with HCV infection)
    -Mesangial proliferative glomerulonephritis
    -Amyloidosis (AA variant)
  -Glomerular diseases indirectly associated with heroin
   addiction
    -Infectious glomerulonephritis due to endocarditis
    -HIV-associated nephropathy
  -End-stage renal disease

often has contaminants, including sugars, powdered milk, caffeine, procaine, and strychnine. US Drug Enforcement Agency (DEA) analysis of confiscated heroin put the frequency of containments at 5% [1]. Heroin can lead to protean renal manifestations (Table 24.3).

24.3.1 Heroin and AKI

Acute kidney injury is seen with heroin addiction and most commonly presents as nontraumatic rhabdomyolysis. Often this is associated with prolonged pressure on dependent areas during periods of decreased level of consciousness [10,12]. Other associated symptoms, such as hypotension, hypoxia, acidosis, and dehydration, can worsen the severity of the rhabdomyolysis [12]. There are several documented case reports in the literature, however, with nontraumatic rhabdomyolysis following heroin use without evidence of diminished consciousness or compression of muscles and vascular structures [10]. This has been felt to be due to a direct myotoxic effect of heroin or possibly secondary to an adulterant compound [10,12,18]. In these cases, the rhabdomyolysis is generalized and not restricted to the dependent areas. Unlike cocaine, there are no reports of acute vasculopathy associated with heroin use.

24.3.2 Heroin-associated nephropathy

Heroin-associated nephropathy (HAN, also referred to as heroin-associated focal segmental glomerulosclerosis) is an entity which was first described in the literature in 1970s [19,20]. There are, however, references to patients with chronic opium addiction presenting with clinical findings of nephrotic syndrome as early as the nineteenth century, but these reports may have little relevance to the renal disease now described in heroin addicts [10]. HAN typically presents as the nephrotic syndrome (>3 g/day of proteinuria, edema, and hyperlipidemia) and rapidly progresses to ESRD. HAN is primarily a diagnosis of young (mean age 29 years) African American populations (>90% of cases), although it has been rarely documented in Caucasians and other ethnic groups [19,20]. The majority of patients present with edema and up to 10–15% may present with uremic symptoms [19,21–24]. Hypertension is a common finding on presentation. Over 75% of presentations are associated with significant impairments in renal function. Average urinary protein excretion is 9.3 g/day [19,21–24]. Unfortunately, the renal prognosis is dismal with inexorable progression to ESRD over a relatively short period (for those with baseline GFRs >50 ml/min, the mean time to ESRD was 43 months) [19,21–24].

Renal biopsy in these patients reveals focal segmental glomerular sclerosis (FSGS).

Typically, there is segmental glomerulosclerosis, hyalinosis, and foam cells similar to the idiopathic variant of FSGS. The degree of globally sclerotic glomeruli is often variable and may not correlate with renal function [1,10,19]. Immunoglobulin M (IgM) and C3 deposits have been seen with immunofluoresence on biopsy, which suggests that there may be an immunological mechanism. This led to speculation that the renal lesion was a reaction to a viral or bacterial innoculum from intravenous delivery of heroin, a contaminant in the heroin, or the drug itself. However, a more likely explanation is that these immune deposits represent nonspecific localization [10]. This interpretation is supported by the fact that these deposits are only seen in sclerotic regions and not in uninvolved capillary tufts and that this pattern of IgM and C3 deposition is seen in other forms of FSGS.

The exact pathogenesis of this renal lesion in not known. As mentioned above, the likelihood of an immunologically-mediated etiology is unlikely. One possibility is that morphine, as a metabolite of heroin, may mediate direct nephrotoxicity to mesangial cells. Morphine can stimulate production of fibrogenic and proliferative cytokines and suppress collagenase activity. Also, morphine can increase fibroblast proliferation, with increased release of pro-inflammatory compounds secreted from macrophages [10,16,17]. However, other animal studies have not seen the development of glomerular lesions secondary to morphine exposure but instead the development of tubulo-interstitial lesions [25]. In any case, the applicability of these studies to human HAN is suspect, as administration of morphine is not analogous to nonsterile injection of heroin. Whether the deposition of additives such as talc granules, which have been observed in arterioles and glomeruli on biopsy, can play a role in the pathogenesis of HAN is unknown but certainly possible [10].

Other renal lesions have been described in heroin addicts. This spectrum includes minimal change disease, mesangial proliferative glomerulonephritis, membranoproliferative glomerulonephritis (MPGN), dysproteinurias, diabetic nephropathy, and interstitial nephritis [1]. The exact link between these presentations and heroin addiction is not known. Unlike HAN, the epidemiological link in these cases is weak.

An important issue is why there is a predominance of HAN in African Americans that is not accounted for by the demographics of heroin addiction. One possible explanation for this is the association of HAN with an increased frequency of HLA-B53 genotypes, suggesting a genetic link [1,26]. Furthermore, in the general population African Americans are four times more likely than Caucasians to develop FSGS [1,18]. This brings to light the question whether heroin or other associated factors lead directly to the development of FSGS or merely activate or hasten an already present genetic predisoposition for FSGS [10].

In Caucasian patients, the renal pathology associated with heroin addiction has been more commonly MPGN [20]. This is a lesion now commonly associated with hepatitis C (HCV) infection and many of the older series documenting MPGN did not or could not assess infection with HCV [27]. Thus, whether heroin itself leads to MPGN is questionable.

In 2001, Perneger *et al.* assessed the risk of developing ESRD based upon recreational drug use [28]. In this case control series of 716 drug addicts, the risk for ESRD of those who had ever used heroin or opiates was 19.1 times higher than the control group of nondrug addicts. Based upon this analysis, the authors estimated that up to 5.6% of prevalent ESRD patients aged 20–64 years was associated with heroin addiction. Given the nature of this study, HIV or HCV-renal disease could not be distinguished from HAN. However, the United States Renal Data System (USRDS) lists heroin-related renal disease as a cause of 0.1% of new ESRD cases over the period 1998–2002, with a median age of 45 years [29].

HAN is most often refractory to treatment even with aggressive courses of steroid and other immunosuppressants [1,20]. Whether abstinence from continued heroin use can halt progression is unknown. There are cases where HAN progressed to ESRD despite abstinence, as well as case reports of either stabilization or remission of nephropathy with drug use cessation [30].

24.3.3 Heroin-associated amyloidosis

In the 1970s, amyloidosis as a cause of nephropathy due to heroin use was described [10,31]. In some patients who chronically misuse heroin, the intravenous route becomes too difficult to use secondary to chronic vascular scarring. These patients will often turn to subcutaneous administration of heroin, termed "skin popping." This subcutaneous administration of heroin predisposes patients to chronic suppurative skin infections. These infections can either be bacterial or fungal, and can eventually lead to secondary (AA) amyloidosis due to the chronic inflammatory state [10,21]. Menchel *et al.*, in a series of 150 patients, documented that the vast majority of patients with documented renal amyloidosis had chronic skin infections due to "skin popping" [1,22]. These skin infections are usually extensive and can involve up to 20% of the body surface area [1,22]. In the 1980s, this condition was so prevalent that up to 50% of heroin addicts who underwent renal biopsy for nephrotic syndrome demonstrated findings consistent with amyloidosis [1,21,22]. In most cases, these addicts have been misusing heroin for extended periods (average duration in one series was 18 years [22]). In patients who have prolonged subcutaneous exposure, continued addiction can cause further deterioration in GFR and lead to ESRD [1,10]. However, several case reports have shown improvement in renal function with drug abstinence. This includes a study by Crowley which documented a decrease in proteinuria from 6.8 g to 170 mg/day with stable renal function following cessation of "skin popping" and treatment of chronic skin infections [21].

The clinical features of heroin-associated amyloidosis have been well documented in the literature. A review of data from 60 cases published in the literature by Neugarten *et al.* showed a preponderance of male gender and African American race [10]. As noted above, there was also a longer time of addictin prior to presentation of the nephrotic syndrome (averaging 18 years) with an average of three years of subcutaneous misuse. This contrasts with previously referenced studies of HAN where the average duration of misuse was 6.3 yrs [1]. Patients typically present with nephrotic range proteinuria and a lower incidence of hypertension than seen with HAN. Dubrow *et al.* described hypertension in less than 20% of heroin-associated amyloidosis cases, as contrasted by the hypertension in two-thirds of patients with FSGS associated with heroin addiction [23]. Kidney size was increased in the majority of patients consistent with the infiltrative nature of amyloidosis [23]. Limited follow-up was available in this data set, but progression to uremia occurred within 2–3 years with continued subcutaneous use of heroin [10].

"Skin poppers" amyloidosis has not been found to be pathologically or biochemically different from amyloidosis seen in other chronic infections or chronic inflammatory states [1,10]. There is prominent renal deposition of AA-type amyloid fibrils in all segments of the kidney. There are findings of mesangial expansion with Congo-red positive amyloid material as well prominent thickening of tubular basement membranes. Tubular atrophy correlates with the amount of amyloid deposits [10]. The majority of patients with amyloidosis progress to ESRD over a relatively short period [32]. However, there are some reports of either disease stabilization or improvement with cessation of drug misuse [33]. There is one case report of treatment with colchicine with stabilization of renal function and nephrotic syndrome but no improvement in the amount of amyloid deposition on repeat biopsy [34].

24.3.4 Infectious glomerulonephritis associated with endocarditis in heroin addicts

Heroin addicts are at high-risk for the development of endocarditis due to bloodstream infections induced by the use of nonsterile techniques. In a small subset of patients, especially those with *Staphylococcus aureus* infections, diffuse proliferative glomerulonephritis has been described [35,36]. The mechanism is usually secondary to immune complex formation and deposition in the glomerulus with complement activation and inflammation. These patients usually present with impaired renal function, microscopic hematuria, and non-nephrotic range proteinuria. Occasionally, gross hematuria accompanied by flank pain due to renal infarction (septic emboli) can be seen. Renal biopsy reveals diffuse proliferative and inflammatory exudates with subepithelial electron dense immune deposits [35–37]. Most patients show significant improvement in renal function and urinary abnormalities with appropriate antibiotic therapy [35]. However, those patients who present with advanced renal failure may not improve and may be at higher risk for therapy failure with antibiotics [36].

24.3.5 Other renal diseases associated with infections seen in heroin addicts

Hepatitis B and C-related renal disease is common in heroin addicts given the high rate of infection with these viruses. A review of the literature by Jaffe and Kimmel referenced infection rates of 85, 77–84 and 24–28% of Hepatitis C, Hepatitis A and B, and HIV respectively in heroin addicts [1]. Viral hepatitis B and C can predispose patients to not only MPGN as discussed above, but also cryoglobulinemic glomerulonephritis (Hepatitis C), polyarteritis nodosa (Hepatitis B), and membranous glomerulonephritis (Hepatitis B and C) [38,39]. These renal diseases are uncommon but present in manners similar to the more common HIV-associated nephropathy (HIVAN) and HAN: nephrotic-range proteinuria, hypertension, and renal insufficiency. This highlights the importance of performing a renal biopsy in those patients who present with renal findings and a history of heroin addiction, as the differential diagnosis is wide.

24.3.6 Changing demographics of kidney disease in heroin addicts: the rise of HIV nephropathy

Since the early 1980s, there has been a dramatic decrease in the number of cases of HAN with a concomitant rise in the cases of HIV-associated nephropathy in this population [1]. There have been several theories relating to this. One of which has been that presence of toxic additives in street heroin has decreased and that this "purer" heroin supply has led to less chronic damage from contaminants and additives. One report had documented an increase in the purity of street heroin in New York from approximately 8% in 1981 to 61% in 1992 [10,24]. Most importantly, there has been a rise in HIV infection in IV drug users and an increased incidence of HIV-associated nephropathy (HIVAN) [40,41]. The drop in HAN has been met with an almost corresponding rise in incidence of HIVAN [1]. There has also been a decrease in

Table 24.4 Characteristics of HIV-associated nephropathy versus heroin-associated nephropathy

	HIVAN	HAN
Age	20–40	20–40
Race	African American predominance	African American predominance
Proteinuria	>3 g/day	>3 g/day
Hematuria	Minimal or none	Minimal or none
Hypertension	Unusual	Common
Risk of ESRD	High	High
Renal size	Large to normal	Normal to small
Pathology	FSGS-collapsing Tubuloreticular inclusions Microcystic dilation	FSGS-typical
Treatment	Antiretroviral therapy	Cessation of drug abuse

HIVAN: HIV-associated nephropathy; HAN: Heroin-associated nephropathy; FSGS: focal segmental glomerulosclerosis.

"skin poppers" amyloidosis seen during this same period [10].

Similar to heroin-associated nephropathy, HIVAN presents as focal segmental glomerulosclerosis (FSGS). HIVAN, however, has some unique pathological characteristics that allow differentiation from HAN (Table 24.4). Typically, HIVAN is a collapsing variant of FSGS (the glomerular tufts collapses on itself) [42]. Clinically, HIVAN generally presents as more severe nephrotic syndrome than HAN [43]. Also, hypertension, seen often in HAN, is not as prevalent in HIVAN. This collapsing variant does not respond well to treatment and renal function can deteriorate rapidly culminating in ESRD [43]. Treatment of HIVAN focuses on control of HIV disease with antiviral therapy [25,40].

Overall, even in its changing demographics, heroin addiction may predispose patients for risk for further progression of both CKD and ESRD. One study of 647 hypertensive men showed a threefold increase in relative risk of a mild decline in renal function; however, when assessed by multivariate analysis the difference was not statistically significant [44]. Strong associations between heroin use and progression to ESRD have been shown when assessing by gender, race or other demographics by subgroup analysis [1,28].

24.4 ECSTASY

Ecstasy (3,4-methylenedioxymethamphetamine, MDMA) is a newer synthetic drug that has found widespread use in young adult populations [12,30,32,33,45]. It is most commonly used in night-club environments or "rave" parties. Ecstasy is most often taken for mood enhancing properties, which have been described as causing energy, empathy, and euphoria. Ecstasy can also cause significant hyper-pyrexia and an increased thirst sensation. This has lead to education regarding the risks of the drug and even development of "chill out" areas in many clubs and parties where patrons can hydrate and rest with either reduced cost or free beverages and water [12]. Unfortunately, the significant potential side effects of ecstasy include rhabdomyolysis, hyponatremia, hepatic failure, serotonin syndrome, and sudden death either from cardiac or cerebral edema [12,30,32,33,45]. Risk of death in first time users is cited at between 1 in 2000 and 1 in 50 000 [30].

24.4.1 Acute kidney injury associated with Ecstasy

As with other previously mentioned drugs of addiction, nontraumatic rhabdomyolysis is seen with ecstasy use as well [12,30,45]. Rhabdomyolysis can be due to two possible major etiologies. Firstly, is secondary to hyperpyrexia, muscle rigidity, and hyper-reflexia likely due to activation of 5-HT receptors and dopamine receptor systems [30]. Secondly, there also has been some suggestion of direct muscle toxicity [30]. However, the validity of these *in vitro* studies has been questioned. In these studies, markedly elevated concentrations of drug have been used, up to 2000 times the dose seen physiologically [30].

Other etiologies of acute kidney injury include rare cases of necrotizing vasculitis [34] and prox-imal tubule dysfunction with a Fanconi's like syn-drome (wasting of phosphate, glucose, amino acids in the urine) [35]. Finally, acute kidney injury may be seen as a secondary event in those cases where ecstasy use has been linked with malignant hyper-tension and fulminant liver failure [12,30].

24.4.2 Hyponatremia and Ecstasy

One of the most serious medical complications of ecstasy addiction is related to symptomatic hypona-tremia (usually associated with a serum sodium less than 130 meq/l) [30,45]. The etiology of hypo-natremia seen with ecstasy is likely due to several interacting effects. Firstly, is dilutional hyponatremia associated with significant ingestion of free water. This occurs as a response to the hyperpyrexia and increased activity induced by the drug and also due to the stimulation to ingest liquids when taking ecstasy. Whether ecstasy leads to a primary drive to drink secondary to its central nervous system effects is not known but has been hypothesized. Secondly, there is likely to be a component of the syndrome of inap-proapriate antidiuretic hormone secretion (SIADH) induced by ecstasy use [30,32]. Henry and colleagues administered small doses of ecstasy to eight patients and documented a significant increase in ADH levels in the serum associated with a rise in urine osmolality and a decrease in free water excretion [30,36]. This combination of increased fluid intake associated with a concomitant rise in ADH levels will lead to reten-tion of free water and a fall in serum sodium levels. Acutely, this fall in serum sodium leads to the osmotic shift of water in the brain and resulting risk for cerebral edema and its associated complications, such as mental status changes, seizures, coma, and brain stem herniation resulting in death.

In ecstasy users, the female gender has been associated with increased odds of developing sig-nificant hyponatremic symptoms. This has been documented in multiple case series, including a case review of emergency room admissions in the state of California over a span of five years. This study documented that women had a significantly higher incidence of symptomatic hyponatremia, coma, and death when seeking medical attention with complications of ecstasy use [32]. This gender susceptibility to the effects of hyponatremia may be secondary to the effects of estrogen to inhibit the membrane Na-K ATPase [37]. Normally, the Na-K ATPase is the primary defense against the osmotic shifts caused by severe hyponatremia, and inhibition by estrogen makes the development of cerebral edema more likely. This may explain the increased incidence of adverse outcomes seen in female patients.

Treatment of severe, symptomatic hyponatremia requires intensive unit care with nephrological or endocrinological consultation and may require the use of hypertonic 3% saline to rapidly increase the serum sodium to safe levels.

24.5   INHALANTS

Inhalants are a class of substances or solvents which can be breathed in to cause psychotrophic effects. The most common of these substances include: toluene (found in spray paints, glues, lacquer, and paint thinners), nitrates, benzene, butane, propane, or methylene. These are common chemicals found in gasoline, paints and paint thinners, sprays, and cleaners. The most common side effects include neurotoxic complications, pulmonary, hepatic and renal damage. Of these common inhalants, toluene is most commonly associated with renal damage and electrolyte changes [10,12].

24.5.1   AKI with inhalants

Reports vary on frequency, but some studies site between 4 and 38% rates of AKI with toluene exposure [46–48]. Etiologies include nontraumatic rhabdomyolysis and hypotension with acute tubular necrosis (ATN) due to renal ischemia. The finding of nontraumatic rhabdomyolysis may be related to direct toxicity of the inhalant and its metabolites, or due to profound hypophosphatemia or hypokalemia which can be induced by these agents. Fulminant hepatic failure with inhalant use or addiction can also occur. This can present with secondary AKI due to hepatorenal syndrome or multi-organ failure [10].

As described later, toluene addiction can lead to a distal renal tubular acidosis and hypercalciuria with a propensity to form kidney stones [49]. These calculi can lead to urinary tract obstruction and AKI.

Interestingly, Streicher and colleagues have described a very high incidence of urinary sediment abnormalities in chronic toluene addicts [50]. In this series, 18 of 21 patients had hematuria, pyuria, and proteinuria (ranging up to 1 g/day) indicative of chronic renal injury induced by toluene. Others have also described pyuria as a relatively common finding, followed by hematuria and proteinuria in fewer subjects [51,52].

24.5.2   Electrolyte disturbances with inhalants

A variety of electrolyte and acid–base abnormalities are associated with inhalant addiction. The vast majority of these are associated with toluene and only these are reviewed here. A syndrome of a nonanion gap metabolic acidosis, hypokalemia, and an elevated urinary pH has been most commonly described [53,54]. This picture is similar in many respects to a distal renal tubular acidosis. It is hypothesized that toluene leads to a defect in distal tubular acidification secondary to impaired active hydrogen ion secretion [55]. Patients may present with extreme muscle weakness or even flaccid quadriparesis due to the hypokalemia.

In patients with renal insufficiency, the metabolites of toluene (benzoic acid and hippuric acid) cannot be rapidly excreted and lead to an anion gap metabolic acidosis [56]. However, if renal function is normal, these anions are rapidly excreted but consume bicarbonate leading to a nonanion gap acidosis.

Finally, there have been case reports of proximal tubule dysfunction associated with toluene addiction [57]. Patients develop a hyperchloremic nonanion gap acidosis, hypokalemia, hypouricemia, hypophosphatemia, and hypocalcemia. These defects persist despite abstinence from toluene.

24.6 AMPHETAMINES

Amphetamine use has been associated with AKI secondary to nontraumatic rhabdomyolysis as well as acute glomerulonephritis [10,58]. Parenteral use of amphetamines has been reported to be associated with the development of a systemic necrotizing vasculitis [10,11]. However, causality in these case reports is questionable, as several of these cases had concomitant positive viral hepatitis serologies (either B or C) as well as the presence of cryoglobulins.

24.7 ETHANOL

Ethanol is one of the most commonly misused substances in the world. While direct acute kidney injury is uncommon with ethanol (as opposed to other toxic alcohols like methanol and ethylene glycol), electrolyte abnormalities are commonly seen in chronic ethanol addicts. As with other substances that alter the level of consciousness, nontraumatic rhabdomyolysis leading to AKI can be seen with ethanol intoxication.

24.7.1 Common electrolyte issues with chronic ethanol addiction

Chronic addiction of ethanol can lead to numerous electrolyte abnormalities. One of the more common electrolyte disorders is termed "beer drinker's potomania," which is manifested by severe and sometimes life-threatening hyponatremia (serum sodium <130 mmol/l) [59,60]. This condition is due to the increased intake of low solute fluids (beer or other ethanol-containing fluids) and protein-calorie malnutrition over an extended period [61]. Other electrolyte disorders seen in chronic ethanol addiction include hypophosphatemia, hypocalcemia, and hypomagnesemia [62]. Although there may be a component of nutritional deficiency in severe alcoholics leading to these electrolyte disturbances, there is also evidence of renal tubule dysfunction due to direct ethanol toxicity. This has been shown by assessing fractional excretion of these electrolytes, and ethanol-induced changes are consistent with decreased tubular reabsorptive capacity [63]. In many cases, as little as four weeks abstinence led to reversal of these tubular abnormalities [63]. The importance of these electrolyte abnormalities is that they can lead to seizures, muscle weakness, rhabdomyolysis, and cardiac arrhythmias.

24.7.2 Chronic renal changes with ethanol addiction

Chronic alcohol addiction (usually with associated cirrhosis) has been associated with changes in renal histology [64]. Post-mortem studies have shown a greater than a 50% incidence of structural changes in the glomeruli of patients with alcoholic cirrhosis [64]. Pathologically these findings are similar to IgA nephropathy with deposition of IgA in the mesangium of the glomeruli [64]. Patients present with clinical findings of microscopic hematuria and mild proteinuria with normal renal function. Macroscopic hematuria and renal insufficiency are rarely seen without other glomerular pathology. The pathogenesis of this condition is thought to be secondary to increased levels of serum IgA and circulating immune complexes brought on by portocaval shunting from alcoholic cirrhosis (with decreased clearance of IgA and immune complexes from the blood).

Another renal complication of chronic alcohol addiction and alcoholic cirrhosis is the hepatorenal syndrome associated with end-stage liver disease. Patients present with oliguria (urine output less than 400 ml/day) and progressively worsening renal function [65]. This is a devastating complication of end-stage liver disease and responds poorly to treatment without liver transplant. If there is no significant primary renal pathology, renal function can return to normal in patients with hepatorenal syndrome who receive liver transplantation [66].

24.7.3 Toxic alcohol ingestions

Many chronic alcoholics exhibit indiscriminate drinking behavior and are thus at risk from either accidentally or intentionally ingesting toxic alcohols such as ethylene glycol, methanol, or isopropyl alcohol. Although ethanol itself rarely causes AKI, toxic alcohols can often present with AKI and other toxic effects which can routinely require dialysis for emergent removal of either the alcohol or toxic metabolites.

24.8 HALLUCINOGENIC MUSHROOMS

Several mushroom species are hallucinogenic when taken orally. These species include *Panaeolus muscari* and *Psilocybe* species. Although these mushrooms are themselves not renal toxic, they can be mistaken for other poisonous species. Case reports exist in the literature regarding mistaken ingestion of *Cortinarius* species of mushrooms, which contain the nephrotoxic compound orellanine. Ingestion of this species leads to oliguric renal failure. Case reports vary on the prognosis of the AKI, but in some cases the complication was irreversible [15,67].

24.9 BENZODIAZEPINES

Benzodiazepines (such as temazepam and diazepam) are commonly misused both for their sedative and euphoric properties. When accidentally injected intra-arterially, these drugs can cause limb ischemia and nontraumatic rhabdomyolysis [10,15,68]. Previous formulations of temazepam which were available in hard gel or capsule formulations could also cause AKI and rhabdomyolysis due to particulate embolization when injected [10]. This formulation is no longer available and has decreased the risk for some complications seen in misuse of benzodiazepines [10,15]. Otherwise, these drugs have no direct nephrotoxic properties.

24.10 TOBACCO AND MARIJUANA

Tobacco addiction has minimal direct effects on the kidney. However, numerous recent studies have demonstrated that tobacco smoking can worsen the progression of many forms of CKD [15,69]. Tobacco addiction is an independent risk factor for the development of microalbuminuria [15,69]. Tobacco addiction can also worsen hypertension, diabetes, and vascular disease, all of which can have secondary effects to further progression of CKD. Other forms of CKD which have been documented to progress more rapidly in smokers include lupus nephritis, renal artery stenosis, renal tubular dysfunction, and pulmonary hemorrhage seen in antiglomerular basement membrane disease [15].

Cannabis addiction is generally free of nephrotoxic side effects. A review of the literature cited one case of renal infarction related to heavy cannaibas addiction [15,70].

24.11 CHRONIC NARCOTIC ADDICTION IN THE RENAL DISEASE PATIENT POPULATION

As with all specialties of medicine, there are certain renal diseases associated with chronic pain syndromes that can lead to narcotic addiction. The most common is nephrolithiasis, where kidney stone formation and/or passage can lead to severe pain requiring therapy with narcotics. In a small subset of patients, this can lead to narcotic addiction and misuse. In these patients, it can be very difficult to determine if they are actually suffering from an acute episode of nephrolithiasis or simply malingering in an effort to obtain narcotics [71]. This can manifest not only as malingering, but also in some cases as Munchausen's syndrome [72]. Other kidney diseases associated with chronic pain and prone to narcotic addiction and misuse are polycystic kidney disease [73] and the loin pain hematuria syndrome [74].

24.12 DRUG CLEARANCE IN CKD AND ESRD

Certain drugs of addiction are extensively metabolized and cleared from the body by the kidney. If a drug is extensively excreted unchanged into urine, alteration of renal function will alter the drug elimination rate. This increases the likelihood of toxicity in the setting of impaired renal function. Fortunately, creatinine clearance or glomerular filtration rate (GFR) calculated from the Modification of Diet in Renal Risease (MDRD) formula can be used as a measure of renal function [75]. For most drugs which are excreted extensively unchanged in the urine it has been found that there is a good correlation between creatinine clearance or estimated GFR and drug clearance or observed elimination rate. A dosage regimen may be adjusted either by lowering the dose or prolonging the dosage interval. The dosage reduction method is recommended for those drugs for which a relatively constant blood level is desired, for example, beta-lactam antibiotics. The interval extension method is recommended for those drugs whose efficacy is related to the peak level, for example, fluoroquinolone antibiotics. For narcotic drugs, both a lowering of dosage and an extension of the dosing interval is recommended. Furthermore, for some narcotics, such as meperidine, toxic metabolites (normeperidine) are renally cleared [76,77]. Numerous case examples of inadvertent overdosing of narcotics secondary to impaired renal clearance have been documented. Table 24.5 lists dosing recommendations for common drugs of addiction [77].

Table 24.5 Renal dosing adjustment of selected drugs of addiction

Drug	Half-life in Hours (Normal/ESRD)	GFR		
		>50	10–50	<10
Fentanyl	2–7/no data	100%	75%	50%
Meperidine[a]	2–7/7–32	100%	75%	50%
Methadone	13–58/no data	100%	100%	50–75%
Morphine[b]	1–4/unchanged	100%	75%	50%
Codeine	2.5–3.5/no data	100%	75%	50%
Alprazolam[c]	9.5–19/unchanged	100%	100%	100%
Clonazepam[c]	18–50/no data	100%	100%	100%
Diazepam[c]	20–90/unchanged	100%	100%	100%
Lorazepam[c]	5–10/32–70	100%	100%	100%
Temazepam[c]	4–10/no data	100%	100%	100%

[a] Normeperidine, an active metabolite, accumulates in ESRD. Can cause seizures. 20–25% of Meperidine excreted unchanged in acidic urine.
[b] Increased sensitivity to drug effect in ESRD.
[c] Benzodiazepines can cause excess sedation and encephalopathy in ESRD.
  From Aronott et al. [77].

24.13 CONCLUSIONS

Drugs of addiction can affect the kidney in numerous manners. These range from indirect effects, such as nontraumatic rhabdomyolysis, to direct toxic effects, such as with heroin. Knowledge of these renal effects is critical in the care of these patients as end-stage renal disease can be the net result of addiction. Whether individual patient counseling on the renal toxicity of these drugs is likely to change behavior is doubtful, in some cases fear of renal disease may be a motivating factor in leading patients to seek assistance. Finally, knowledge of renal clearance of these medications is critical to avoid over-dosage and side effects.

REFERENCES

1. Jaffe, J.A. and Kimmel, P.L. (2006) Chronic nephropathies of cocaine and heroin abuse: a critical review. *Clin. J. Am. Soc. Nephrol.*, **1**, 655–667.

2. Nzerue, C.M., Hewan-Lowe, K., and Riley, L.J. (2000) Cocaine and the kidney: A synthesis of pathophysiologic and clinical perspectives. *Am. J. Kidney Dis.*, **35**, 783–795.

3. Hollister, L.E. (1992) Drugs of abuse, in *Basic and Clinical Pharmacology* (ed. B.G. Katzung), Appleton and Lange, Norwalk, pp. 437–449.

4. Creger, L.L. and Mark, H. (1986) Medical complications of cocaine abuse. *N. Engl. J. Med.*, **315**, 1495–1500.

5. Mo, W., Singh, A.K., Arruda, J.A., and Dunea, G. (1998) Role of Nitric Oxide in cocaine associated acute hypertension. *Am. J. Hypertension*, **11**, 708–714.

6. Lange, R.A. and Hillis, L.D. (2001) Cardiovascular complications of cocaine use. *N. Engl. J. Med.*, **345**, 351–358.

7. Bemanian, S., Motallebi, M., and Nosrati, S.M. (2005) Cocaine-induced renal infarction: report of a case and review of the literature. *BMC Nephrology*, **6**, 10.

8. Dipalo, N., Fineschi, V., Dipaol, M. *et al.* (1997) Kidney vascular damage and cocaine. *Clin. Nephrol.*, **47**, 298–303.

9. Dunea, G., Arruda, J., Bakir, A. *et al.* (1995) Role of cocaine in end stage renal disease in some hypertensive African Americans. *Am. J. Nephrol.*, **15**, 5–9.

10. Neugarten, J., Gallo, G.R., and Baldwin, D.S. (2007) Nephrotoxicity secondary to drug abuse and lithium use, in *Diseases of the Kidney and Urinary Tract*, 8th edn (ed. R.W. Shrier), LWW, pp. 1121–1139.

11. Richards, J.R. (2000) Rhadbomyolysis and drugs of abuse. *J. Emerg. Med.*, **19** (1), 51–56.

12. Counselman, F.L., McLaughlin, E.W., Kardon, E.M. *et al.* (1997) Creatine phosphokinase elevation in patients presenting to the emergency department with cocaine-related complaints. *Am. J. Emerg. Med.*, **15**, 221–223.

13. Chevalier, X., Rostoker, G., Larget-Piet, B. *et al.* (1995) Henoch–Schonlein purpura with necrotizing vasculitis after cocaine snorting. *Clin. Nephrol.*, **43**, 348–349.

14. Tumlin, J.A., Sands, J.M., and Someren, A. (1990) Hemolytic–uremic syndrome following "crack" cocaine inhalation. *Am. J. Med. Sci.*, **299**, 366–371.

15. Crowe, A.V., House, M., Bell, G.M. *et al.* (2000) Substance abuse and the kidney. *Q. J. Med.*, **93**, 147–152.

16. Mantana, J., Gibbons, N., and Singhal, P.C. (1994) Cocaine interacts with macrophages to modulate mesangial cell proliferation. *J. Pharmacol. Exp. Ther.*, **271**, 311.

17. Greenfield, S.P., Rutigliano, E., Steinhardt, G. *et al.* (1991) Genitourinary tract malformations and maternal cocaine abuse. *Urology*, **37**, 455.

18. Grossman, R.A., Hamilton, R.W., Morse, B.W. *et al.* (1974) Nontraumatic rhabdomyolysis and acute renal failure. *N. Engl. J. Med.*, **291**, 807–811.

19. Norris, K.C., Thornhill-Joynes, M., Robinson, C. *et al.* (2001) Cocaine use, hypertension, and end-stage renal disease. *AJKD*, **38** (3), 523–528.

20. Thornhill-Joynes, M., Norris, K.C., Witana, S.C. *et al.* (1994) The impact of substance abuse on hypertensive end-stage renal disease in inner city African Americans. *J. Am. Soc. Nephrol.*, **5**, 342 (abstract).

21. Cunningham, E.E., Brentjens, J.R., Zielensky, M.A. *et al.* (1980) Heroin nephropathy – a clinicopathologic and epidemiologic study. *Am. J. Med.*, **68**, 47.

22. Cunningham, E.E., Zielezny, M.A., and Venuto, R.C. (1983) Heroin-associated nephropathy – a nationwide problem. *JAMA*, **250**, 2935.

23. McGinn, J.T., McGinn, T.G., Cherubin, C.E. *et al.* (1974) Nephrotic syndrome in drug addicts. *NY State J. Med.*, **74**, 92.

24. Uzan, M., Volochine, L., Rondeau, E. *et al.* (1988) Renal disease associated with heroin abuse. *Nephrologie*, **9**, 217.

25. Marchand, C., Cantin, M., and Core, M. (1969) Evidence for the nephrotoxicity of morphine sulfate in rats. *Can. J. Physiol. Pharmacol.*, **47**, 6–49.

26. Perneger, T.V., Whelton, P.K., Klag, M.J. *et al.* (1995) Diagnosis of hypertensive end-stage renal disease: Effect of the patient's race. *Am. J. Epidemiol.*, **41**, 10–15.

27. Rao, T.K., Nicastri, A.D., and Friedman, E.A. (1974) Natural history of heroin associated nephropathy. *N. Eng. J. Med.*, **290**, 19–23.

28. Perneger, T.V., Klag, M.J., and Whelton, P.K. (2001) Recreational drug use: a neglected risk factor for end-stage renal disease. *AJKD*, **38** (1), 49–56.

29. United States Renal Data System (USRDS) (2004) Annual Data Report, National Institutes of Health, National Institutes of Diabetes, and Digestive and Kidney Diseases, Bethesda, MD.

30. Llach, F., Descoeudres, C., and Massry, S.G. (1979) Heroin associated nephropathy: clinical and histological studies in 19 patients. *Clin. Nephrol.*, **11**, 7–14.

31. do Samerio Faria, M., Sampoa, S., Faria, V. *et al.* (2003) Nephropathy associated with heroin abuse in caucasian patients. *Nephrol. Dial. Transplant.*, **18**, 2308–2313.

32. Scholes, J., Derosena, R., Appel, G.B. *et al.* (1979) Amyloidosis in chronic heroin addicts with the nephrotic syndrome. *Ann. Intern. Med.*, **91**, 26–29.

33. Crowley, S., Feinfeld, D.A., and Janis, R. (1989) Resolution of nephrotic syndrome and lack of progression of heroin associated renal amyloidosis. *Am. J. Kidney Dis.*, **35**, 1358–1370.

34. Tan, A.U., Cohen, A.H., and Levine, B.S. (1995) Renal amyloidosis in a drug abuser. *J. Am. Soc. Nephrol.*, **5**, 1633.

35. Neugarten, J. and Baldwin, D.S. (1984) Glomerulonephritis in bacterial endocarditis. *Am. J. Med.*, **77**, 297.

36. Neugarten, J., Gallo, G.R., and Baldwin, D.S. (1984) Glomerulonephritis in bacterial endocarditis. *Am. J. Kidney Dis.*, **5**, 371.

37. Freeman, B.G., Kreps, E.M., Ronsheim, N.J. *et al.* (1974) Poststaphylococcal glomerulonephritis in heroin addicts. *NY State J. Med.*, **74**, 2241–2243.

38. Haskell, L.P., Glicklich, G., and Senitzer, D. (1988) HLA associations in heroin-associated nephropathy. *Am. J. Kidney Dis.*, **12**, 45–50.

39. Rose, B., Renal disease with Hepatitis C virus infection. In: Up To Date. www.uptodate.com (accessed 5 December 2007).

40. Singhal, P.C., Sharma, P., Sanwal, V. *et al.* (1998) Morphine modulates proliferation of kidney fibroblasts. *Kidney Int.*, **53**, 350.

41. Dubrow, A., Mittman, N., Ghali, V. *et al.* (1985) The changing spectrum of heroin-associated nephropathy. *Am. J. Kidney Dis.*, **5**, 36.

42. D'Agati, V., Suh, J.I., Carbone, L. *et al.* (1989) The pathology of HIV nephropathy: a detailed morphologic and comparative study. *Kidney Int.*, **35**, 1358–1370.

43. Carbone, L., D'Agati, V., Cheng, J.T. *et al.* (1989) Course and progression of human immunodeficiency virus-associated nephropathy. *Am. J. Med.*, **87**, 389–395.

44. Diamantis, I., Bassetti, S., Erb, P. *et al.* (1997) High prevalence and coinfection rate of hepatitis G and C infection in intravenous drug addicts. *J. Hepatol.*, **25**, 794–797.

45. Neugarten, J., Gallo, G.R., Buxbaum, J. *et al.* (1986) Amyloidosis in subcutaneous heroin abusers ("skin poppers amyloidosis"). *Am. J. Med.*, **81**, 635.

46. Knight, A.T., Pawsey, C.G., Aroney, R.S. *et al.* (1991) Upholsterers' glue associated with myocarditis, hepatitis, acute renal failure and lymphoma. *Med. J. Aust.*, **154**, 360–365.

47. Russ, G., Clarkson, A.R., Woodroffe, A.J. *et al.* (1981) Renal failure from glue sniffing. *Med. J. Aust.*, **2**, 121–125.

48. Will, A.M. and McLaren, E.H. (1981) Reversible renal damage due to glue sniffing. *Br. Med. J.*, **283**, 525–526.

49. Kaneko, T., Koizumi, T., Takezaki, T., and Sato, A. (1992) Urinary calculi associated with solvent abuse. *J. Urol.*, **147**, 1365.

50. Streicher, H.Z., Gabow, P.A., Moss, A.H. *et al.* (1981) Syndromes of toluene sniffing in adults. *Ann. Intern. Med.*, **94**, 758–762.

51. Hamilton, D.V., Thiru, S., and Evans, D.B. (1982) Renal damage and glue sniffing. *Br. Med. J.*, **284**, 117.

52. Ehrenreich, T. (1977) Renal disease from exposure to solvents. *Ann. Clin. Lab. Sci.*, **7**, 6–16.

53. Fischman, C.M. and Oster, J.R. (1979) Toxic effects of toluene – a new cause of high anion gap metabolic acidosis. *JAMA*, **241**, 1713.

54. Taher, S.M., Anderson, R.J., McCartney, R. *et al.* (1974) Renal tubular acidosis associated with toluene "sniffing". *New Engl. J. Med.*, **290**, 765–768.

55. Batlle, D.C., Sabatini, S., and Kurtzman, N.A. (1988) On the mechanism of toluene-induced renal tubular acidosis. *Nephron.*, **49**, 210–218.

56. Sarmiento Martinez, J., Guardiola Sala, J.J., Martinez Vea, A. *et al.* (1989) Renal tubular acidosis with an elevated anion gap in a "glue sniffer". *Hum. Toxicol.*, **8**, 139–140.

57. Moss, A.H., Gabow, P.A., Kaehny, W.D. *et al.* (1980) Fanconi's syndrome and distal renal tubular acidosis after glue sniffing. *Ann. Intern. Med.*, **92**, 69–70.

58. Citron, B.P., Halpern, M., McCarron, M. *et al.* (1970) Necrotizing angiitis associated with drug abuse. *N. Engl. J. Med.*, **283**, 1003–1011.

59. Rose, B., Causes of hyponatremia. UptoDate. www.uptodate.com (accessed 23 January 2008).

60. Hilden, T. and Svendsen, T.L. (1975) Electrolyte disturbances in beer drinkers. *Lancet*, **2**, 245.

61. Vamvakas, S., Teschner, M., Bahner, U. *et al.* (1998) Alcohol abuse: potential role in electrolyte disturbances and kidney diseases. *Clin. Nephrol.*, **49**, 205–213.

62. Rodrigo, R., Thielemann, L., Olea, M. *et al.* (1998) Effect of ethanol ingestion on renal regulation of water and electrolytes. *Arch. Med. Res.*, **29**, 209–218.

63. DeMarchi, S., Cecchin, E., Basile, A. *et al.* (1993) Renal tubular dysfunction in chronic alcohol abuse – effect of abstinence. *N. Engl. J. Med.*, **329**, 1927–1934.

64. Pouria, S. and Feehally, J. (1999) Glomerular IgA deposition in liver disease. *Nerphol. Dial. Transplant.*, **14**, 2279–2282.

65. Gines, P. and Arroyo, V. (1999) Hepatorenal syndrome. *J. Am. Soc. Nephrol.*, **10** (8), 1833–1839.

66. Badalamenti, S., Graziani, G., Salerno, F., and Ponticelli, C. (1993) Hepatorenal syndrome. New perspectives in pathogenesis and treatment. *Arch. Intern. Med.*, **153** (17), 1957–1967.

67. Short, A.I., Watling, R., MacDonald, M.K. *et al.* (1980) Poisoning by Cortinarius speciosissmus. *Lancet*, **2**, 942–944.

68. Jenkinson, D.F. and Pussey, C.D. (1994) Rhabdomyolysis and renal failure after intra-aterial tempazepam. *Nephrol. Dial. Transplant.*, **9**, 1334–1335.

69. Orth, S.R., Ritz, E., and Schrier, R.W. (1997) The renal risks of smoking. *Kidney Int.*, **51**, 1669–1677.

70. Lambrecht, G.L., Malbrain, M.L., Coremans, P. *et al.* (1995) Acute renal infarction and heavy marijuana smoking. *Nephron.*, **70**, 494–496.

71. Reich, J.D. and Hanno, P.M. (1997) Factitious renal colic. *Urology*, **50** (6), 858–862.

72. Gluckman, G.R. and Stoller, M. (1993) Munchausen's syndrome: manifestation as renal colic. *Urology*, **42** (3), 347–350.

73. Bajwa, Z.H., Sial, K.A., Malik, A.B. *et al.* (2004) Pain patterns in patients with polycystic kidney disease. *Kidney Int.*, **66**, 1561–1569.

74. Bass, C.M., Parrott, H., Jack, T. *et al.* (2007) Severe unexplained loin pain (loin pain haematuria syndrome): management and long-term outcome. *QJM*, **100** (6), 369–381.

75. Levey, A.S., Greene, T., Schluchter, M.D. *et al.* (1993) Glomerular filtration rate measurements in clinical trials. Modification of Diet in Renal Disease Study Group and the Diabetes Control and Complications Trial Research Group. *J. Am. Soc. Nephrol.*, **4** (5), 1159–1171.

76. Kurella, M. (2003) Analgesia in patients with ESRD: a review of available evidence. *Am. J. Kidney Dis.*, **42**, 217–228.

77. Aronott, G.R., Berns, J.S., Brier, M.E. et al. (1999) *Drug Prescribing in Renal Failure: Dosing Guidelines for Adults*, 4th edn, ACP.

25

Addictive disorder in urological diseases

Herman S. Bagga and Adam W. Levinson

James Buchanan Brady Urological Institute, Johns Hopkins Medical Institutions, Baltimore, Maryland, USA

25.1 INTRODUCTION

In the United States, the burden of urological disease is estimated to annually result in over 35 million visits to office-based physicians and hospital outpatient clinics, over 2.5 million visits to emergency rooms, and nearly one million hospital stays. The economic impact of such disease in the United States is equally as impressive, resulting in medical expenditures approaching $11 billion annually, approximately half of which is financed by Medicare [1]. With current statistics estimating nearly 17% of Americans to be daily smokers [2] and 9.2% of the United States population to meet the criteria for addiction and dependence of substances including alcohol and illicit drugs [3], it is not unexpected that urological diseases and substance addictions coexist frequently. Such associations are worthy of discussion, as substance addiction is a powerful phenomenon that can directly affect the health and care of the urological patient. In particular, the addiction of substances such as alcohol, tobacco products, cocaine, and opiate narcotics can result in a wide variety of urological sequelae, including organ and tissue damage, sexual dysfunction, infertility, and cancer. It is hoped that the exploration of such associations will prove useful to the clinical evaluation and understanding of patients with both substance use disorders and urological illnesses.

25.2 ALCOHOL ADDICTION

Most individuals are familiar with the effects of reasonable amounts of alcohol on the urinary system. True alcohol addiction, however, is associated with more dire consequences than awkward, impatient dances while waiting in line to use the restroom. Rather, such behavior is linked with many serious urological illnesses and disease processes.

25.2.1 Prostatic disease

Alcohol's known effects on estrogen, progesterone, and testosterone levels, as well as the antioxidant activity of certain wines, has motivated multiple studies exploring the connections between alcohol use and prostatic disease.

Addictive Disorders in Medical Populations Edited by Norman S. Miller and Mark S. Gold

Prostate cancer has been the disease process most enthusiastically studied, given the entity's few established modifiable risk factors. Studies exploring the association of alcohol consumption and prostate cancer have shown mixed and often conflicting results, even when comparing studies which investigate similar volumes and/or categories of alcohol (beer, white/red wine, hard liquor, etc.) consumed. A striking example of the potentially negative effects of alcohol addiction in regards to prostate cancer development was presented by Sesso in 2001, who described a dose-dependent increased risk of prostate cancer of up to 1.85 times for those who consume more than three hard liquor drinks per day [4]. This data has been contested, however, most notably by a recent large prospective cohort study of over 45 000 patients conducted to investigate the associations of alcohol consumption with risk of prostate cancer diagnosis. Generally, this study found no increased risk of prostate cancer diagnosis for patients at any level of beer, liquor, or total alcohol consumption. In terms of the effects of red wine (originally explored due to its known antioxidant activity), the study found that regular wine drinkers (defined as men who consumed 1–4 glasses of red wine a week) under the age of 65 had slightly lower rates of prostate cancer diagnosis than abstainers. In contrast, men who consumed more than this amount had perhaps a slightly increased risk of prostate cancer diagnosis. This study was in contrast to other studies which have found a more striking protective effect of moderate red wine consumption [5].

Alcohol consumption is known to increase testosterone clearance, and therefore lower circulating testosterone levels. This phenomenon has led researchers to investigate the potential for such activity to inhibit the development of benign prostatic hyperplasia (BPH). Indeed, multiple studies have found that those who misuse alcohol tend to have lower rates of surgery for BPH. The validity of this finding has been questioned, however, as it is possible that those individuals who misuse alcohol have other medical or social comorbidities which prevent them from being operated upon [6].

Nevertheless, multiple studies have revealed that moderate intake of alcohol may lower overall rates of BPH. Data from the over 29 000 patients in the Health Professionals Follow-up Study revealed that patients who consumed 30–50 g of alcohol per day had a dose-dependent decrease in of BPH symptoms. This effect was attenuated with alcohol consumption greater than 50 g, but the effect was still present [7]. Furthermore, although results have been conflicting, multiple studies investigating patients with liver cirrhosis have found that these patients often have a lower incidence of clinical BPH and have smaller prostate gland size at autopsy in comparison to the general population. These effects are likely due to the higher circulating levels of estrogens relative to androgens in cirrhotic patients [6]. Of course, while we certainly do not advocate the utilization of excessive amounts of alcohol as a medicinal, anti-BPH therapy, the associations are nonetheless noted.

25.2.2 Fournier's gangrene

There are a variety of rare genitourinary infections that alcoholics are more susceptible to than the general population [8]. Fournier's gangrene is likely the most deadly. Fournier's gangrene is a form of necrotizing infeciitis of the perineum that targets the male genitalia. Polymicrobial infection of both anaerobes and aerobes is implicated as the inciting entity of this rapidly progressive and potentially lethal condition. In addition to diabetes, a primary causative association is alcoholism. The incidence of alcoholism in patients with Fournier's gangrene is quite high, likely higher than 60% [9–11]. A combination of immunosuppression and poor personal hygiene in this population is likely to be of primary importance in the etiology of the disease. Prompt diagnosis followed by immediate debridement, broad spectrum antimicrobial therapy, and supportive care is the standard of care, but despite these interventions, mortality still approaches 26% [12].

25.2.3 Infertility/sexual dysfunction

Alcohol addiction has been shown to result in testicular atrophy via peritubular fibrosis and a reduction in the overall number of germ cells. In the extreme, this process can, theoretically, progress to male infertility. However, studies investigating infertility and its links to alcohol consumption have been conflicting. In studies investigating alcohol consumption in groups of infertile men, there has been no significant association of decreased sperm count or motility directly attributable to alcohol intake. Nevertheless, associations have been found linking a decreased chance of conceiving with increased alcohol consumption in men [6]. This association may be due to direct effects on fertility, but also due to changes in male sexual function.

Alcohol impairs the metabolism of estrogen by the liver. This phenomenon coupled with decreased testosterone production secondary to atrophied testes, and increased testosterone clearance lead to a disruption of the balance of androgens in the male, and can have multiple effects on sexual function. These effects include a decreased libido, erectile dysfunction, decreased virilization, and gynecomastia. In addition, the use of alcohol has been known to contribute to autonomic and peripheral neuropathy, both phenomena which can impair sexual function due to decreased ability to stimulate the sexual gland to function appropriately [6].

25.2.4 Erectile dysfunction

The development of a male erection is attributed to an increased inflow of blood into the erectile tissue of the penis with decreased outflow. Essential to this process is the relaxation of the corporal muscles of the penis, which allows space to be created for the blood to flow and also stimulates the occlusion of the venous outflow. The use of alcohol has been shown to not only decrease arterial blood flow to the penis, but also block smooth muscle relation of the corporeal muscles, effectively decreasing a man's chance at creating or sustaining an erection [6]. Whereas moderate quantities of alcohol may have

protective cardiovascular effects, excessive alcohol use can lead to hypertension, increased obesity, and a higher risk of developing diabetes – all of which can lead to vasculogenic erectile dysfunction [13]. Heavy alcohol use has also been associated with the development of priapism, or a potentially hazardous prolonged erection in the absence of sexual stimulation. This dangerous condition can result in permanent erectile dysfunction or even organ loss if not treated [14]. This association may be due to the association of heavy drinking with misuse of other substances, such as cigarettes, prescription sedatives, and cocaine (see below).

25.2.5 Spontaneous bladder perforation

Bladder perforations generally occur due to pelvic fractures secondary to external trauma, as the attachments of the bladder to the pelvic inlet are sheared, which can result in bladder rupture. Perforations of this type are generally extraperitoneal, as opposed to intraperitoneal, or combination intra-extraperitoneal. Extraperitoneal perforations are the most common and are estimated to occur in up to 80–90% of cases. The more dangerous intraperitoneal ruptures are less common, estimated to represent about 15–20%, and roughly 10% of bladder perforations may be combination intra-extraperitoneal. Intraperitoneal bladder perforations occur when there is an increase in intravesicular pressure due to an overfilled bladder, and are often the result of blunt trauma applying pressure to the overdistended bladder, creating a rupture. The rupture usually occurs at the dome of the bladder, which is the weakest and most mobile aspect of the bladder. Whereas many extraperitoneal bladder ruptures may be managed conservatively with catheter drainage, most intraperitoneal ruptures require prompt surgical repair. 3–4% of bladder ruptures are nontraumatic, or "spontaneous," and these are usually intraperitoneal in nature. The majority of these "spontaneous" ruptures are associated with alcohol intoxication. Diuresis as a result of alcohol consumption results in an overdistended bladder if the inebriated individual ignores signals to urinate, particularly if 'passed out' or asleep. The ballooned bladder then becomes exquisitely susceptible to rupture from increased intra-abdominal pressure and even a cough can result in rupture of the organ. Given the late diagnosis that occurs in such described situations, morbidity and mortality is said to reach 50% in these cases [6,15–17].

25.2.6 Incontinence

Increased urinary output during times of drinking can exacerbate the symptoms of incontinence experienced by patients suffering from overactive bladder or other etiologies. As such, patients with such diagnoses are counseled to limit their alcohol intake.

25.2.7 Renal calculi

The associations between diuretics such as alcohol and the development of kidney stones have been investigated in multiple studies. A Finnish study of over 300 patients diagnosed with kidney stones found an inverse relationship between beer consumption and the development of the stones after controlling for other variables. Specifically, in this study each additional bottle of beer consumed reduced the risk of stone development by 40%. Interestingly, this association was not found to be significant with the consumption of other forms of alcohol, suggesting the effect may be associated with other components of beer than the ethanol [18]. American studies have also supported this contention, with one study suggesting that in certain areas of the country, increased beer consumption could be a contributing factor to decreased incidence of kidney stones in that region [19]. Data from the Health Professionals Follow-up Study has also corroborated the association, finding a 21% decreased chance of developing stones with each eight ounces of beer consumed daily. The study also found an association with wine, with each daily eight ounces consumption associated with a 39% decrease in the likelihood of stone formation [20]. Despite these favorable associations, it is important to note that use of alcohol is not encouraged as a protective behavior for renal stone formation. Though beer and wine consumption are associated with a likely nephrolithiasis protective diuresis to some degree, those who misuse alcohol are unlikely to replace lost fluids appropriately. Subsequent dehydration could actually then encourage the formation of stones.

25.3 TOBACCO ADDICTION

25.3.1 Neoplasia

According to the National Cancer Institute and the American Cancer Society, tobacco use, particularly cigarette smoking, is the single most preventable cause of death in the United States. Cigarette smoking is directly responsible for over 440 000 deaths annually, and approximately one out of every five deaths in the United States. 30% of all cancer deaths may be directly attributed to tobacco usage. Likewise, smoking is one of the strongest risk factors for the development of cancers of the urinary tract, primarily bladder cancers, and also of kidney, penile, and ureteral cancers. A recent meta-analysis of over forty studies found that, compared to non-smokers, smokers had more than three times the risk of developing urinary tract cancers – even after adjusting for age and gender. For those who were successful in smoking cessation, over time, their risk dropped to approximately twice the level of people who had never smoked [21]. Cigarette smoke contains both DNA-reactive bladder carcinogens as well as aromatic amines, both of which have been implicated as pro-neoplastic agents. Recent evidence from mouse-model studies and anecdotal evidence of urothelial hyperplasia in human patients has suggested that increased proliferation of the urinary bladder epithelium secondary to these tobacco toxins plays a significant role in the development of bladder cancer specifically. This is believed to be due to either direct mitogenesis or due to cytotoxicity of the smoke elements [22].

Bladder cancer is an exposure-driven disease, with little influence of genetics on the incidence. The overwhelmingly most common inciting or associated exposure in Western countries is cigarette smoke. Indeed, cigarette smoking has been found to increase the risk of bladder cancer in smokers by over 2.5 times compared to nonsmokers [23] and, in European studies, has been implicated as the causative factor in over half of all cases of bladder cancer in men and about one-third of all cases in women [24,25]. The exposure usually predates the disease by as many as 15–20 years, and the increase in the incidence of female bladder cancer in the United States is felt to be secondary to the increase of smoking in women over the past several decades. The incidence does fall over time though after cessation of smoking. For bladder cancer, the risk falls over 30% after over one year of smoking cessation and over 60% after 25 years of abstinence [23–25].

Tobacco smoke has also been implicated as a risk factor for the development of certain types of kidney cancer. Renal cortical cancer, previously known as renal cell carcinoma (RCC), is the most common form of kidney cancer and claims 3% of all adult cancer-related deaths. Although there has been debate of the exact amount of risk attributable to tobacco products, a recent meta-analysis of 24 studies found that the extent of the increased risk approached 1.4 times for those who had ever smoked compared to those who had never done so. The risk was described to be dose-dependent, with those who smoked from half to a full pack daily (with a typical pack containing 20 cigarettes) increasing their risk by 1.8 times and those exceeding one pack at least doubling their risk to develop renal cortical cancer. Again, cessation of smoking was found to significantly lower the increased risk of RCC development, especially after 10 years of abstinence [26].

Men who smoke or use any form of tobacco are also at increased risk of the development of penile cancer. In addition to the primary risk factor of being uncircumcised, the risk of developing penile

cancer has been found to significantly increase with the amount and duration of tobacco addiction. Procarcinogenic risks are increased not only with the smoking of tobacco, but also with chewing and snuffing [27]. The mechanism has been suspected to be the promotion of malignant transformation of normal tissue by chronic inflammation, especially when tobacco is consumed in the presence of other irritative factors such as HPV or bacterial infection [6].

Unlike the clear associations of smoking with the previously mentioned urinary cancers, tobacco addiction has not been clearly implicated to be involved in the pathogenesis of prostate cancer. This is despite speculation that the increase of circulating androgen levels and cellular oxidative stress of the agent could promote such disease [6]. In contrast, data from the Health Professionals Follow-up Study revealed that heavy smokers consuming 35 or more cigarettes per day had increased risk of developing BPH, by as much as 50% when compared to those individuals who had never smoked [7].

25.3.2 Incontinence

Smoking can also exacerbate the symptom of urine loss for patients suffering from urinary incontinence. Increased intra-abdominal pressures from a "smoker's cough" may upset the delicate balance of continence in patients, usually women, who may suffer from borderline symptoms of stress incontinence. In addition, patients with symptoms of over-active bladders may suffer from additional incontinence-producing bladder spasms, incited by the same coughs. These patients may often "squirt" urine with the cough, as opposed to the patients with pure stress incontinence who will usually just "drip" urine in association with the cough.

25.3.3 Infertility/sexual dysfunction/ erectile dysfunction

Tobacco smoking is a significant and independent risk factor for cardiovascular disease and concomitant endothelial damage. This phenomenon has also been implicated in the development of erectile dysfunction [28,29]. The identical causative pathophysiologic mechanism between smoking with peripheral vascular disease in the extremities leads to vasculogenic erectile dysfunction in the male. Furthermore, toxins within tobacco smoke have been suspected to exert a constrictive effect on the cavernous muscle of the penis, which may induce vasoconstriction and penile venous leakage, effectively decreasing blood engorgement of the penis, a necessary prerequisite for erection [30]. In addition to the direct effects of tobacco smoke toxins on the vasculature of the penis, smoking is a risk factor for cardiovascular disease and hypertension, which are, along with diabetes, the other major risk factors for the development of erectile dysfunction [6]. Many studies have explored and defined the association between smoking and erectile dysfunction, including one study of over 7500 smokers without clinical vascular disease which concluded that up to 22% of its cases of erectile

dysfunction could be independently attributed to smoking [31].

It is also strongly suspected that smoking creates a direct danger for male fertility as well, with a belief that smoking may affect spermatogenesis. Although the exact mechanism of tobacco's damage to spermatogenesis is as of yet undefined, the habit has been found to have adverse effects on many semen parameters, including volume, as well as, sperm count, motility, and morphology. The evidence, while inconclusive, has been strong enough to lead most infertility experts to consider smoking a risk factor for male infertility. Further evidence of smoking adversely affecting male fertility include decreased success rates for patients undergoing *in vitro* fertilization when the male was a smoker, and reports that exposure to prenatal smoke is associated with decreased rates of fertility in male offspring [6,32,33]. There are other effects of smoking to the fetus and to women as well, but these are covered in more depth in another chapter.

25.4 ILLICIT DRUG ADDICTION

25.4.1 Cocaine-induced priapism

To achieve erection, the penis is engorged with blood, which is trapped within the smooth muscles of the organ (as described above). Priapism is a persistent, painful erection which lasts for more than four hours in the absence of sexual stimulation. It results when blood is unable to drain from the penis, preventing detumescence. There are many causes of priapism, and it is sometimes induced in association with usage or misuse of prescription medications, such as trazadone, diazepam, or thorazine, or with illicit drug use, such as with marijuana, ecstasy or cocaine addiction. Cocaine is the most common illicit drug associated, and has been implicated in the development of priapism when taken in all forms, including the rare patient who injects it directly into the penis. Although the mechanism is not completely understood, it is speculated that the pathophysiology is the result of

cocaine's known effect of blocking reuptake of norepinephrine at the presynaptic neuron. As this neurotransmitter is depleted, there is reduced ability to signal the penile smooth muscle to contract, which is mechanically necessary to allow for the outflow of blood, as described earlier [34,35]. The result can be a persistently erect penis, which is a medical emergency as it can result in scarring and even permanent erectile dysfunction or organ loss.

25.4.2 Falsified illness

As described elsewhere, the desire to attain opiates by the heroin, morphine, or codeine addict coupled with the ability of the physician to provide opiate narcotics can create a very delicate relationship between the two parties. The development of renal calculi and their subsequent irritation of the urinary tract is known by the general population to be a very painful phenomenon, for which no caring physician would refuse his patient often ample narcotics. As a result, opiate addicts will sometimes approach their healthcare providers with falsified complaints of kidney stones or their symptoms in an effort to attain these drugs. As such, it is always appropriate for the physician to confirm the existence of renal calculi by CT scan before prescribing narcotics for pain relief, even if a recent diagnosis is claimed by the patient. Any patient suspected of falsifying illnesses should be counseled, and referred to an appropriate addiction medicine specialist.

Challenging, is the patient with a chronic pain syndrome. In urology, one such syndrome is the chronic pelvic pain syndrome. Painful bladder/interstitial cystitis are diagnoses often offered to patients with chronic, functionally impairing pain of the pelvic region. For this disease, as for many chronic pain syndromes, the long-term use of opiate medications is often the most effective if not only form of effectual treatment. The subjective nature of pain assessment along with liberal prescription of opiate-based pain control medications for these patients, can leave room for opiate addiction and can influence patients to falsify the severity of symptoms in order to attain more narcotics for misuse. Though it must be stressed that the overwhelming majority of patients with this painful condition are honest about their levels of pain, it is not surprising that a 2005 study found that chronic pain patients were more likely to misuse prescribed opiates if they had a history of substance addiction. Furthermore, this can be difficult to detect as patients with a history of substance addiction, even if they are not misusing the medications, require a greater quantity of opiates than patients without a history of misuse. Interestingly, those who misused also openly expressed stronger beliefs regarding the addiction potential of opiates. These reports certainly add a level of complexity to the traditional education-based approach for deterring opiate addiction [36]. Appropriate consultation with addiction medicine specialists will help in the management of these complex patients.

25.4.3 Opiates and sexual dysfunction

Opiates are well known to reduce libido in heroin addicts and methadone-maintained patients. Additionally, orgasm dysfunction (delayed or unattainable orgasm) and menstrual irregularity (chiefly oligomenorrhea and amenorrhea) are known adverse sexual effects [37–39]. Although the exact mechanisms are not known, the knowledge that opiates play a role in endocrine regulation has led to the theory that these effects could be due to reduction of lutenizing hormone levels centrally, thereby reducing testosterone and upsetting the natural balance of body androgen and sex steroids [40,41]. Examination of patients receiving chronic opiates for pain syndromes has found that such therapy indeed affects the hypothalamic-pituitary axis, with long-term administration of opiates causing decreased libido and changed sexual function, notably men with impotence and women with menstrual cycle changes and/or anovulation. Efforts to supplement the lowered levels of gonadal steroids in affected patients have been found to restore sexual function in many of these cases [39,42–44].

REFERENCES

1. Litwin, M.S. and Saigal, C.S. (eds) (2007) Urologic Diseases in America. US Department of Health and Human Services, Public Health Service, National Institutes of Health, National Institute of Diabetes and Digestive and Kidney Diseases, US Government Printing Office, Washington, DC, NIH Publication No. 07–5512.

2. Centers for Disease Control and Prevention (2005) Cigarette Smoking Among Adults – United States, 2003. *MMWR*, **54**, 509–513.

3. Substance Abuse, Mental Health Services Administration (2007) Results from the 2006 National Survey on Drug Use and Health: National Findings, (Office of Applied Studies, NSDUH Series H-32, DHHS Publication No. SMA 07-4293). Rockville, MD.

4. Sesso, H.D., Paffenberger, R.S., and Lee, I.-M. (2001) Alcohol consumption and risk of prostate cancer: the Harvard Alumni Health Study. *Int. J. Epidemiol.*, **30**, 749–755.

5. Sutcliffe, S., Giovannucci, E., Leitzmann, M.F. *et al.* (2007) A prospective cohort study of red wine

consumption and risk of prostate cancer. *Int. J. Cancer*, **120** (7), 1529–1535.

6. Wein, A.J., Kavoussi, L.R., Novick, A.C. *et al.* (2007) *Campbell-Walsh Urology*, 9th edn, Saunders.

7. Platz, E.A., Rimm, E.B., Kawachi, I. *et al.* (1999) Alcohol consumption, cigarette smoking, and risk of benign prostatic hyperplasia. *Am. J. Epidemiol.*, **149** (2), 106–115.

8. Hinchey, W.W. and Someren, A. (1981) Cryptococcal prostatitis. *Am. J. Clin. Pathol.*, **75**, 257–260.

9. Clayton, M.D., Fowler, J.E. Jr., Sharifi, R. *et al.* (1990) Causes, presentation and survival of 57 patients with necrotizing fasciitis of the male genitalia. *Surg. Gynaecol. Obstet.*, **170**, 49–55.

10. Hejase, M.J., Simonin, J.E., Bihrle, R. *et al.* (1996) Genital Fournier's gangrene: Experience with 38 patients. *Urology*, **47**, 734–739.

11. Smith, G.L., Bunker, C.B., and Dinneen, M.D. (1998) Fournier's gangrene. *Br. J. Urol.*, **81**, 347–355.

12. Vick, R. and Carson, C.C. 3rd (1999) Fournier's disease. *Urol. Clin. North Am.*, **26** (4), 841–849.

13. American Heart Association (2008) Alcohol, Wine, and Cardiovascular Disease. http://www.american-heart.org/presenter.jhtml?identifier=4422 (accessed 25 January 2010).

14. Kulmala, R., Lehtonen, T., Nieminen, P., and Tammela, T. (1995) Aetiology of priapism in 207 patients. *Eur. Urol.*, **28**, 241–245.

15. Gomez, R., Ceballos, L., Coburn, M. *et al.* (2004) Consensus statement on bladder injuries. *BJU Int.*, **94**, 27–32.

16. Corriere, J.N. Jr. (2002) Trauma to the lower urinary tract, in *Adult and Pediatric Urology*, 4th edn (eds J.Y. Gillenwater, J.T. Grayhack, S.S. Howards, and M.E. Mitchell, Lippincott, Williams & Wilkins, Philadelphia, pp. 507–530.

17. Lynn, S.J., Mark, S.D., and Searle, M. (2003) Idiopathic spontaneous bladder rupture in an intoxicated patient. *Clinical Nephrol.*, **6**, 430–432.

18. Hirvonen, T., Pietinen, P., Virtanen, M. *et al.* (1999) Nutrient Intake and use of beverages and the risk of kidney stones among male smokers. *Am J Epidemiol*, **150** (2), 187–194.

19. Soucie, J.M., Coates R.J., McClellan, W. *et al.* (1996) Relation between geographic variability in kidney stones prevalence and risk factors for stones. *Am. J. Epidemiol.*, **143** (5), 487–495.

20. Curhan, G.C., Willett, W.C., Rimm, E.B. *et al.* (1996) Prospective study of beverage use and the risk of kidney stones. *Am. J. Epidemiol.*, **143** (3), 240–247.

21. Zeegers, M.P., Tan, F.E., Dorant, E., and van Den Brandt, P.A. (2000) The impact of characteristics of cigarette smoking on urinary tract cancer risk: a meta-analysis of epidemiologic studies. *Cancer*, **89** (3), 630–639.

22. Ohnishi, T., Arnold, L.L., He, J. *et al.* (2007) Inhalation of tobacco smoke induces increased proliferation of urinary bladder epithelium and endothelium in female C57BL/6 mice. *Toxicology*, **241**(1–2), 58–65.

23. Silverman, D.T., Devesa, S.S., Moore, L.E., and Rothman N. (2006) Bladder cancer, in *Cancer Epidemiology and Prevention*, 3rd edn (eds D. Schottenfeld and J. Fraumeni), Oxford University Press, New York.

24. Brennan, P., Bogillot, O., Cordier, S. *et al.* (2000) Cigarette smoking and bladder cancer in men: a pooled analysis of 11 case-control studies. *Int. J. Cancer*, **86** (2), 289–294.

25. Brennan, P., Bogillot, O., Cordier, S. *et al.* (2001) The contribution of cigarette smoking to bladder cancer in women (pooled European data). *Cancer Causes Control*, **12** (5), 411–417.

26. Hunt, J.D., van der Hel, O.L., McMillan, G.P. *et al.* (2005) Renal cell carcinoma in relation to cigarette smoking: meta-analysis of 24 studies. *Int. J. Cancer*, **114** (1), 101–108.

27. Harish, K. and Ravi, R. (1995) The role of tobacco in penile carcinoma. *Br. J. Urol.*, **75**, 375–377.

28. Müller, A. and Mulhall, J.P. (2006) Cardiovascular disease, metabolic syndrome and erectile dysfunction. *Curr. Opin. Urol.*, **16** (6), 435–443.

29. Juenemann, K.P., Lue, T.F., Luo, J.A. *et al.* (1987) The effect of cigarette smoking on penile erection. *J. Urol.*, **138**, 438–441.

30. Rahman, M.M. and Laher, I. (2007) Structural and functional alteration of blood vessels caused by cigarette smoking: an overview of molecular mechanisms. *Curr. Vasc. Pharmacol.*, **5** (4), 276–292.

31. He, J., Reynolds, K., Chen, J. *et al.* (2007) Cigarette smoking and erectile dysfunction among Chinese men without clinical vascular disease. *Am. J. Epidemiol.*, **166** (7), 803–809.

32. Zitzmann, M., Rolf, C., Nordhoff, V. *et al.* (2003) Male smokers have a decreased success rate for in vitro fertilization and intracytoplasmic sperm injection. *Fertil Steril*, **79** (Suppl 3), 1550–1554.

33. Jensen, T.K., Henriksen, T.B., Hjollund, N.H. *et al.* (1998) Adult and prenatal exposures to tobacco smoke as risk indicators of fertility among 430 Danish couples. *Am. J. Epidemiol.*, **148**, 992–997.

34. Altman, A.L., Seftel, A.D., Brown, S.L., and Hampel, N. (1999) Cocaine associated priapism. *J. Urol.*, **161** (6), 1817–1818.

35. Munarriz, R., Hwang, J., Goldstein, I. *et al.* (2003) Cocaine and ephedrine-induced priapism: case reports and investigation of potential adrenergic mechanisms. *Urology*, **62** (1), 187–192.

36. Schieffer, B.M., Pham, Q., Labus, J. *et al.* (2005) Pain medication beliefs and medication misuse in chronic pain. *J. Pain.*, **6** (9), 620–629.

37. Deglon, J.J., Martin, J.L., and Imer, R. (2004) Methadone patients' sexual dysfunctions: Clinical and treatment issues. *Heroin Add. Rel. Clin. Probl.*, **6**, 17–26.

38. Dyer, K.R. and White, J.M. (1997) Patterns of symptom complaints in methadone maintenance patients. *Addiction*, **92**, 1445–1455.

39. Abs, R., Verhelst, J., Maeyaert, J. *et al.* (2000) Endocrine consequences of long-term intrathecal administration of opioids. *J. Clin. Endocrinol. Metab.*, **85** (6), 2215–2222.

40. Gulliford, S.M. (1998) Opioid-induced sexual dysfunction. *Journal of Pharmaceutical Care in Pain and Symptom Control*, **6** (2), 67–74.

41. Mirin, S.M., Meyer, R.E., Mendelson, J.H. *et al.* (1980) Opiate use and sexual function. *Am. J. Psychiatry*, **137** (8), 909–915.

42. Paice, J.A., Penn, R.D., and Ryan, W.G. (1994) Altered sexual function and decreased testosterone in patients receiving intraspinal opioids. *J. Pain Symptom Manage*, **9** (2), 126–131.

43. Paice, J.A. and Penn, R.D. (1995) Amenorrhea associated with intraspinal morphine. *J. Pain Symptom Manage*, **10** (8), 582–583.

44. Rajagopal, A., Vassilopoulou-Sellin, R., Palmer, J.L. *et al.* (2004) Symptomatic hypogonadism in male survivors of cancer with chronic exposure to opioids. *Cancer*, **100** (4), 851–858.

Part Four

Management of addictive disorders in selected populations

26

Management of addictive disorders in medical nursing care populations

Kathleen L. Becker and Benita J. Walton-Moss

John Hopkins University School of Nursing, Baltimore, MD, USA

26.1   INTRODUCTION

The prevalence of addictive disorders in hospitalized medical patients is significant and recognition, referral, and treatment are of paramount importance. Early recognition of tobacco, problematic alcohol, and illegal drug use "provides the opportunity to influence consumption, modify drinking habits, and assist with the management of withdrawal" [1–5]. Measures of addictive disorders in the hospitalized medical patient vary widely depending on the: (1) type of screening method used (blood/urine tests or self-report assessment tools); (2) specific drug of addiction; (3) patient population and geographic location; and (4) gender, ethnicity, and socio-economic status. Hospitals, in particular medical units, have large numbers of alcohol- and drug-related admissions. "It is estimated that up to 20% of patients admitted to general hospitals during an acute medical intake are drinking above safe limits" [6,7].

Compounding this problem is chronic drug use. The prevalence rate of illegal drug use is estimated to be 5–13% of hospital admissions [8,9]. A recent study by Mordal *et al.* [8], which involved blood and urine testing on admitted medical patients in a major public hospital in Norway, found that 14% had illegal drugs detected. According to the National Survey on Drug Use and Health [10], an estimated 20.4 million people aged 12 and older were projected to be using illegal drugs. This does not include tobacco or alcohol. More than 6.3 million Americans reported current use of prescription drugs for non-medical purposes in 2003. Three types of drugs are commonly misused: opioids (prescribed for pain relief), CNS depressants-barbiturates and benzodiazepines (prescribed for anxiety or sleep problems), and stimulants (prescribed for attention-deficit hyperactivity disorder, narcolepsy or obesity).

With the exception of tobacco, recognition of the primary substance use disorders diagnosis is often overlooked in the diagnosis and treatment of the presenting comorbid condition. These comorbid conditions often present as acute and chronic

Addictive Disorders in Medical Populations   Edited by Norman S. Miller and Mark S. Gold
© 2010 John Wiley & Sons, Ltd.

cardiac, respiratory, gastrointestinal, neurological, and musculoskeletal conditions [11]. Compounding the low detection rates of substance use disorders in the hospitalized patient is the persistent lack of referral and treatment offered to those inpatients once identified. Referral and treatment intervention rates for identified substance use disorders patients have remained static over the past 20 years and are less than 50% [9,12,13].

The most common addictive substance worldwide is nicotine. In the United States, the prevalence rates of cigarette smoking are 23.4% among men and 18.5% in women, with nicotine dependence commonly occurring before the age of 20 [14]. Alcohol is the second most commonly used substance worldwide. The National Institute of Alcohol and Alcohol Abuse [15] estimates that about three in ten adults in the United States drink at levels that increase their risk for physical, mental health, and social problems. Of these heavy drinkers, about one in four meets the American Psychiatric Association's DSMR-IV criteria for alcohol addiction or dependence [16]. The National Survey on Drug Use and Health [10] estimated that 8.3% of the population age 12 years or greater used illegal drugs in the past month, not including alcohol or tobacco. According to the survey, the most commonly addicted drug was marijuana, followed by prescription drugs for nonmedical use, cocaine, hallucinogens, and methamphetamine.

26.2   ROLE OF THE MEDICAL NURSE

An acute care medical hospitalization represents a unique opportunity to identify an addictive disorder. Screening all medical patients for problematic substance use identifies those most at risk. An acute care hospitalization often highlights the patients' perceived vulnerability to the health risks associated with substance addiction, making the hospitalization a "teachable moment" [17]. The experience of an acute illness has the potential to increase a patient's motivation to change and modify risky or substance-dependent behaviors [18].

Every hospital in the United States is now smoke free as well as drug and, in general, alcohol free. Therefore, upon admission, all patients with substance use disorders become acutely abstinent. The medical nurse is in the unique position to identify those most at risk and promote healthy lifestyle behaviors. By employing the skills of brief interventions (which are discussed later in this chapter) as well as timely referral and treatment, the quality and safety of patient care is enhanced. Screening for addictive disorders also identifies the patient who is at risk for toxicity and/or withdrawal symptoms. Prevention of these withdrawal symptoms significantly decreases the morbidity and mortality. In 2005, for the first time, alcoholic psychoses became the largest group of principal alcohol-related hospital discharges in the United States (36%), surpassing alcohol dependence syndrome (30%) and cirrhosis of the liver (26%) [19].

The medical nurse must be cognizant of his or her own personal views on risky behaviors and substance use. The role of the nurse is to recognize the problem through screening, prevent and treat complications related to withdrawal, use the acute care hospitalization as an opportunity to motivate the patient to change their behavior, and facilitate referral for treatment of the substance use disorders. Unfortunately, evidence suggests that healthcare providers, specifically nurses and physicians, project on to the patient their own negative perceptions of drug and alcohol use [20,21]. A judgmental attitude on behalf of the nurse may influence and impair the quality of care the patient receives. This is particularly true of opiate addicts who require pain management medications. Healthcare providers often fear being deceived by the drug addicted patient, fearing that the request for pain medication is drug seeking behavior. As a result, these patients are often under-medicated and under-treated and suffer needlessly. Opiate addicted patients often perceive the attitudes of the nurses and physicians as punitive [20].

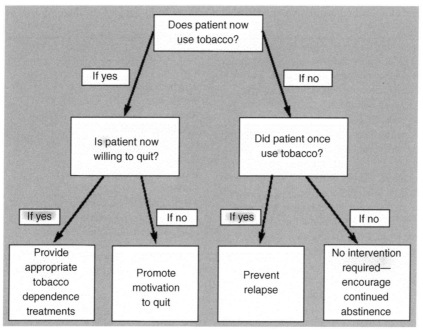

Figure 26.1   Treating tobacco use and dependence: PHS clinical practice guideline screen for tobacco use status.

26.3   COMPLICATIONS

Medical complications can directly occur from tobacco, alcohol, and other drugs of addiction in one or more of the following ways: (1) in the substance's original form, (2) through the drug's metabolites, and (3) through the substance's interactions with other drugs or alcohol. Such complications may arise regardless of the drug's dose or whether it is from the patient's first use or in the context of a long history of substance addiction. These medical disorders primarily originate in the cardiovascular, respiratory, gastrointestinal, neurologic, and renal systems (see relevant chapters in this book).

26.4   CUES OF ADDICTION

The medical nurse may note signs and symptoms suspicious of either a substance use disorder or withdrawal. There are several findings on physical examination that may be suggestive of addiction or its complications (Table 26.1). These physical findings, combined with drug and alcohol screening questions (which are discussed elsewhere in this book), increase the likelihood of identification of a substance use disorder. Identification of specific withdrawal syndromes can be challenging because while users tend to have a preferred substance of addiction, they also tend to use multiple drugs. A common combination is tobacco, alcohol, benzodiazepine, and barbiturates. Signs and symptoms of recent substance use may be evident upon admission to the unit for a diagnosis that may or may not be related to a substance use disorder. Alternatively, signs and symptoms suggestive of withdrawal may

Table 26.1 Examination findings suggestive of addiction or its complications

- General: Odor of alcohol on breath, odor of marijuana on clothing, odor of nicotine or smoke on breath or clothing, poor nutritional status, poor personal hygiene
- Behavior: Intoxicated behavior during exam, slurred speech, staggering gait, scratching
- Skin: Signs of physical injury, bruises, lacerations, scratches, burns, needle marks, skin abscesses, cellulitis, jaundice, palmar erythema, hair loss, diaphoresis, rash. puffy hands
- Head, Eyes, Ears, Nose, Throat (HEENT): Conjunctival irritation or injection, inflamed nasal mucosa, perforated nasal septum, blanched nasal septum, sinus tenderness, gum disease, gingivitis, gingival ulceration, rhinitis, sinusitis, pale mucosae, burns in oral cavity
- Gastrointestinal: Hepatomegaly, liver tenderness, positive stool hemoccult
- Immune: Lymphadenopathy
- Cardiovascular: Hypertension, tachycardia, cardiac arrhythmia, heart murmurs, clicks, edema, swelling
- Pulmonary: Wheezing, rales, rhonchi, cough, respiratory depression
- Female reproductive/endocrine: Pelvic tenderness, vaginal discharge
- Male reproductive/endocrine: Testicular atrophy, penile discharge, gynecomastia
- Neurologic: Sensory impairment, memory impairment, motor impairment, ophthalmoplegia, myopathy, neuropathy, tremor, cognitive deficits, ataxia, pupillary dilation or constriction

Ref. [22].

Table 26.2 Upper limit detection times for common drugs for urine

Drug	Urine
Alcohol	12 h
Amphetamines	2 d
Barbiturates – short acting	1 d
Barbiturates – long acting	3 wk
Benzodiazepine	1–14 d
Cannabinoids	4 wk
Cocaine metabolites	4 d
Heroin metabolite (morphine)	4 d
Codeine	2 d
Methamphetamine Gamma hydroxybutyrate (GHB)	5 d
Lysergic acid diethylamide (LSD)	8 h

Sources: Martin [23]. Drug Detection Laboratories, Inc. www. drugdetectionnet/drug.htm (accessed 22 July 2008).

be evident at some time post-admission, with the timing dependent upon the specific substance. Prompt recognition of these signs is needed to provide timely appropriate care. If signs are observed and laboratory work is being considered, it needs to be done promptly because many substances have short half-lives (Table 26.2).

26.4.1 Tobacco

Nicotine is a highly addictive substance that is readily absorbed by the brain, spleen, and liver. The immediate "kick" from nicotine inhalation causes the release of epinephrine (adrenaline) from the adrenal cortex and stimulates the central nervous system (CNS) and other endocrine glands, which causes release of glucose [24]. The nicotine molecule rapidly binds to the acetylcholine receptors while also increasing the level of the neurotransmitter dopamine. Dopamine affects the brain pathways, which influence mood, reward, pleasure, and motivation.

Within seconds of cigarette inhalation, the smoker experiences symptoms of pleasure and increased energy. A typical smoker will take 10 puffs on a cigarette over a period of five minutes, in an attempt to continue the drug's pleasurable side effects and prevent withdrawal. The smoker will repeat this behavior through out the day in the continued pursuit of reward and pleasure and to stave off the symptoms of withdrawal.

The initial feeling of pleasure and increased energy that occurs after smoking, caused by the increased levels of dopamine, is followed by feelings of depression and fatigue. The evidence suggests that chronic smokers who abstain from nicotine for 24 hours experience increased anger, hostility, aggression, loss of cooperation, and impaired psychomotor and cognitive functions [25]. This is termed nicotine abstinence syndrome, more commonly referred to as nicotine withdrawal. Nicotine dependence is characterized by any two of the following: (1) tolerance; (2) withdrawal; (3) substance is used in larger amounts or over a longer period than intended;

(4) persistent desire or unsuccessful efforts to cut down; (5) a great deal of time spent in activities to obtain the substance; (6) giving up or reducing important social, occupational or recreational activities because of substance use; and (7) continued use despite knowledge of having persistent or recurrent health problems that are likely due to the substance use [16]. The most common three criteria of nicotine dependence, noted in both adult and adolescent tobacco users, are tolerance, withdrawal, and impaired control [16].

26.4.2   Alcohol

Alcoholism is characterized by a cycle of denial, minimization, and multiple failed quit attempts that result in negative consequences that affect every aspect of a person's life. Alcoholics involuntarily and unintentionally acquire an inconsistent inability to control alcohol intake, coupled with a persistent urge to drink. This intermittently controlled drinking produces personality changes. The negative consequences affect the individual's personal, professional, emotional, physical, and economic life.

Alcohol is considered to be a central nervous system depressant with both protective and harmful qualities. According to the World Health Organization [26], the link between alcohol consumption and consequences depends on: (1) the amount consumed and patterns of drinking, and (2) toxic and beneficial biochemical effects. Alcohol is metabolized primarily by alcohol dehydrogenase (ADH) and aldehyde dehydrogenase (ALDH). ADH metabolizes alcohol to acetaldehyde, a highly toxic and known carcinogen. Acetaldehyde is then metabolized into acetate, which is metabolized into water and carbon dioxide for elimination [27]. Alcohol is a water-soluble molecule that diffuses uniformly into all body water, both inside and outside of cells. Men have a total body water content of $65 \pm 2\%$ and women of a comparable size have total body water content $51 \pm 2\%$ [28,29]. Women therefore achieve higher blood alcohol concentrations than men after drinking equivalent amounts of alcohol. As a result, women exhibit a "telescoped" or more rapid development to alcoholism, with fewer drink-

ing years, than men [28,29]. The morbidity and mortality data on alcoholism reflect these phenomena. Female alcoholics have death rates 50–100% higher than those of male alcoholics. Fifty percent to 60% of the risk for alcoholism is genetically determined. Identical twins are twice as likely as fraternal twins, who share only 50% of their genes, to resemble each other in terms of the presence of alcoholism.

Alcohol readily crosses the blood–brain barrier, profoundly affecting the central nervous system; it crosses the placenta to affect fetal development and affects every organ in the body. It is primarily absorbed from the stomach (approximately 20%) and the small intestine (approximately 80%) [30].

Alcohol increases the release of the excitatory neurotransmitters, dopamine, serotonin, and glutamate, which results in a positive reinforcement of the drug and can change the neurobiology of the brain [31]. The initial pleasurable sensation of drinking alcohol is attributed to an immediate and large release of dopamine. Over time, the brain responds to this large dopamine release by reducing normal dopamine activity. Eventually, the alcohol-dependent patient becomes incapable of feeling pleasure [31,32]. Chronic alcohol exposure also increases the release of the inhibitory neurotransmitter GABA, and similarly reduces the number of GABA receptors in the brain. When the patient is no longer exposed to alcohol (abstinent) it is believed that "the body suddenly has too few GABA receptors to balance the actions of the excitatory neurotransmitters, dopamine, serotonin and glutamate. As a result, the brain experiences an excess of excitatory nerve signals. This phenomenon, known as rebound hyperexcitability, may contribute to the physical and psychological manifestations of alcohol withdrawal and addiction" [33].

Alcohol withdrawal syndromes vary from minor symptoms, such as insominia, tremulousness, anxiety, gastrointestinal upset, diaphoresis, palpitations, headache, and anorexia, which generally occur within six hours of abstinence and abate within 24–48 hours, to major symptoms, such as seizures, hallucinosis and delirum tremens. Withdrawal seizures are usually tonic-clonic and occur within 2–48 hours after abstinence. Approximately 3% of chronic alcoholics have withdrawal-associated seizures and 3% of those develop status epilepticus [34,35].

Alcoholic hallucinosis refers to hallucinations that are primarily visual, although both auditory and tactile hallucinations do occur. They usually begin within 12–24 hours and resolve within 24–28 hours. Delirium Tremens (DTs) are associated with hallucinations, disorientation, tachycardia, hypertension, a low grade fever, agitation, and diaphoresis. They usually begin within 48–96 hours after abstinence and last 1–5 days [34,35]. It is important to remember that withdrawal may also affect fluid and electrolyte status. Patients who have experienced previous DTs, have a history of sustained and chronic drinking, have a comorbid condition, and are over 30 years old are at increased risk for recurrent DTs.

The revised Clinical Institue Withdrawal Assessment for Alcohol Scale (Table 26.3) is a resource for the medical nurse to assess the severity of risk for alcohol withdrawal symptoms.

26.4.3 Opioids

Opioids include heroin, morphine, codeine, and oxycodone, most of which have legal prescribed uses. Their mode of action, effects, tolerance and dependence are described elsewhere in this book.

26.4.4 Stimulants

Stimulants include cocaine, methamphetamines, and other amphetamines such as methylphenidate. In the United States cocaine is the second most commonly used illicit drug [10]. Cocaine and other amphetamines act as vasoconstrictors and prevent reuptake of the brain's neurotransmitter's including dopamine, norepinephrine, and serotonin in the brain. Dopamine is involved in the brain's "reward" system and is the key transmitter responsible for cocaine's effects. Norepinephrine is integral to the body's regulation of arousal and serotonin has a central role in the regulation of hunger. The buildup of excess neurotransmitters leads to receptor cell over-activity and the intense feelings of pleasure,

drug cravings, and compulsive drug seeking behaviors reported by cocaine users. At the same time, prevention of norepinephrine reuptake and vasoconstriction are the primary contributors to the observed adverse effects and complications.

It is the short-term effects of cocaine that are frequently sought after, including euphoria, heightened alertness and libido, and less need for food and sleep. The duration of effect can range from approximately 15 to 30 minutes for the intravenous or inhalation route [37]. Although increasing cocaine doses are needed to obtain the same level of euphoria, unlike opioids, there is no physical tolerance because an associated classic abstinence syndrome does not exist. However, there is a definite withdrawal syndrome that occurs a few hours to a few days from the last cocaine use persisting for at least 24 hours.

This syndrome is characterized by dysphoric mood and two or more of the following: insomnia or hypersomnia, unpleasant dreams, fatigue, increased appetite, psychomotor retardation or agitation or hypervigilance. These symptoms are often accompanied by tachycardia, diaphoresis, pupillary dilation, high blood pressure, tremor, fever, nystagmus, confusion, loss of rapid eye movement (REM) or muscular weakness. These effects manifest within minutes to one hour. "Crack lung" is a syndrome uniquely attributed to cocaine inhalation that occurs within one to 48 hours and characterized by fever, eosinophilia, and alveolar infiltrates [38]. Cocaine and other amphetamine toxicity can also cause psychosis associated with include delusions, auditory and visual hallucinations, preoccupation with their own thoughts, and violent, erratic behavior, a presentation similar to schizophrenia. The likelihood of psychosis is greater for other amphetamines than cocaine, perhaps due to longer drug duration and observed persistence of these neurotoxic symptoms for months or years.

26.4.5 Sedatives-hypnotics

Like alcohol, sedative-hypnotics (comprising benzodiazepines and barbiturates) are central nervous system depressants that affect the body in a dose-dependent manner. Often these drugs are added by

Table 26.3 The revised Clinical Institute withdrawal assessment for alcohol scale (CIWA-Ar)

Patient:_____ Date: ____ Time: _____ (24 h clock, midnight = 00:00)

Pulse or heart rate, taken for one minute:_____ Blood pressure:___

NAUSEA AND VOMITING – Ask "Do you feel sick to your stomach? Have you vomited?" Observation.
0. no nausea and no vomiting
1. mild nausea with no vomiting
2.
3.
4. intermittent nausea with dry heaves
5.
6.
7. constant nausea, frequent dry heaves and vomiting

TACTILE DISTURBANCES – Ask "Have you any itching, pins and needles sensations, any burning, any numbness, or do you feel bugs crawling on or under your skin?" Observation.
0. none
1. very mild itching, pins and needles, burning or numbness
2. mild itching, pins and needles, burning or numbness
3. moderate itching, pins and needles, burning or numbness
4. moderately severe hallucinations
5. severe hallucinations
6. extremely severe hallucinations
7. continuous hallucinations

TREMOR – Arms extended and fingers spread apart. Observation.
0. no tremor
1. not visible, but can be felt fingertip to fingertip
2.
3.
4. moderate, with patient's arms extended
5.
6.
7. severe, even with arms not extended

AUDITORY DISTURBANCES – Ask "Are you more aware of sounds around you? Are they harsh? Do they frighten you? Are you hearing anything that is disturbing to you? Are you hearing things you know are not there?" Observation.
0. not present
1. very mild harshness or ability to frighten
2. mild harshness or ability to frighten
3. moderate harshness or ability to frighten
4. moderately severe hallucinations
5. severe hallucinations
6. extremely severe hallucinations
7. continuous hallucinations

PAROXYSMAL SWEATS – Observation.
0. no sweat visible
1. barely perceptible sweating, palms moist
2.
3.
4. beads of sweat obvious on forehead
5.
6.
7. drenching sweats

VISUAL DISTURBANCES – Ask "Does the light appear to be too bright? Is its color different? Does it hurt your eyes? Are you seeing anything that is disturbing to you? Are you seeing things you know are not there?" Observation.
0. not present
1. very mild sensitivity
2. mild sensitivity
3. moderate sensitivity
4. moderately severe hallucinations
5. severe hallucinations
6. extremely severe hallucinations
7. continuous hallucinations

ANXIETY – Ask "Do you feel nervous?" Observation.
0. no anxiety, at ease
1. mild anxious
2.
3.
4. moderately anxious, or guarded, so anxiety is inferred
5.
6.
7. equivalent to acute panic states as seen in severe delirium or acute schizophrenic reactions

HEADACHE, FULLNESS IN HEAD – Ask "Does your head feel different? Does it feel like there is a band around your head?" Do not rate for dizziness or lightheadedness. Otherwise, rate severity.
0. not present
1. very mild
2. mild
3. moderate
4. moderately severe
5. severe
6. very severe
7. extremely severe

AGITATION – Observation.
0. normal activity
1. somewhat more than normal activity
2.
3.
4. moderately fidgety and restless
5.
6.
7. paces back and forth during most of the interview, or constantly thrashes about

ORIENTATION AND CLOUDING OF SENSORIUM – Ask "What day is this? Where are you? Who am I?"
0. orientated and can do serial additions
1. cannot do serial additions or is uncertain about date
2. disoriented for date by no more than 2 calendar days
3. disoriented for date by more than 2 calendar days
4. disoriented for place/person
Total CIWA-Ar Score ___
Rater's Initials ___
Maximum Possible Score 67

The **CIWA-Ar** is not copyrighted and may be reproduced freely. This assessment for monitoring withdrawal symptoms requires approximately 5 minutes to administer. The maximum score is 67 (see instrument). Patients scoring less than 10 do not usually need additional medication for withdrawal.
Ref. Sullivan et al. [36].

users to counteract effects of cocaine withdrawal or to increase the effect of heroin, marijuana or alcohol. Similar to opioids, tolerance can develop, so requiring increasingly larger doses for the same effect, except for the anxiolytic effects of benzodiazepines for which tolerance is essentially nonexistent [39]. For example, sedation usually deceases within the initial days of treatment while the drug's beneficial effects on anxiety may remain unchanged at the same dose [23]. Tolerance is rapid and may be present after only a few days [40]. The cross-tolerance evident for concomitant alcohol use magnifies the risk of a fatal overdose [39].

Withdrawal from sedative-hypnotics differs from opioid withdrawal in that it lasts longer and is usually perceived as more unpleasant. Withdrawal from sedative-hypnotics, often requiring hospitalization, is potentially life threatening with death occurring in as many as 5% [41]. Seizures can be precipitated with abrupt discontinuation of this drug group. Drugs in this class are also used as antiepileptics because they raise the seizure threshold. When abruptly discontinued, a rebound drop in the seizure threshold is produced that may cause seizures even in patients without a history of prior seizures [39]. Clinically significant withdrawal signs and symptoms can occur when consumed at amounts as low as twice the maximum recommended dose for more than one month [42]. Symptoms of adverse effects include altered consciousness ranging from somnolence to coma, amnesia, anxiety, irritability, decreased concentration, and disturbing dreams. Horizontal nystagmus is the cardinal sign differentiating adverse effects from intoxication. Other signs include disinhibition, slurred speech, loss of motor coordination, and impaired judgment.

Withdrawal tends to be most severe for drugs that are quickly eliminated, such as amobarbital, methyprylon, and triazolam [23]. Symptoms are delayed or prolonged if the person has liver disease. Similar signs and symptoms seen with adverse effects are also observed for withdrawal reflecting CNS hyperactivity. Withdrawal usually begins with anxiety, irritability, anorexia, nausea and vomiting, apprehension, restlessness, insomnia, tremor and hyperreflexia. Withdrawal then extends to fever, diaphoresis, tachycardia, hypertension, and muscle fasciculations. After moderate or high doses withdrawal can include delirium, agitation, sensory distortions, and seizures [43]. The signs and symptoms are virtually identical to that from alcohol. These individuals become increasingly drowsy until unconsciousness, associated with cold and clammy skin, decreased heart rate, and have shallow respirations.

Short-acting medications, such as pentobarbital and secobarbital, have withdrawal symptoms that usually start 12 to 24 hours after the last dose, peaking in intensity between one and three days after the last dose. Long-acting medications, such as phenobarbital, diazepam and chlordiazepoxide, have a withdrawal syndrome that usually commences between one and two days after the last dose, peaking in intensity on the fifth to eighth day [42]. A few individuals may also have a protracted withdrawal characterized by mild to severe signs and symptoms that can be present intermittently over many months. Clinical features of protracted withdrawal include mild to moderate anxiety, mood instability, sleep disturbances, increased sensitivity to light and sound, and psychosis.

26.4.6 Cannabinoids, hallucinogens, and inhalants

Cannabinoids (principally marijuana) are the most commonly used illicit drugs in the United States [10]. Effects include initial euphoria often followed by drowsiness or sedation. Perception of time usually slows down, while hearing and vision are distorted, effects that are enhanced by also consuming alcohol. The most common physical signs include conjunctival injection and tachycardia [44]. At high doses there can also be anxiety, agitation, paranoia, or psychosis [23]. Cardiopulmonary effects may be considerably potent as evidenced by exercise-induced angina that may be more pronounced after marijuana use compared to tobacco cigarette smoking [44]. Impaired cognitive and performance functioning lasts several hours, substantially beyond the user's perceived high lasting two hours [43]. Tolerance can rapidly develop for tachycardia among regular marijuana users [44]; however, there is no widely agreed upon withdrawal syndrome [23]. For example, the popular notion of increased appetite is not a consistent symptom [23].

Hallucinogens include the following drug groups: (1) indoalkylamines (e.g., D-lysergic acid diethylamide, also known as LSD); (2) phenylethylamines (such as methamphetamines, also known as Ectasy); and (3) all others such as arylcyclohexylamines (e.g., phencycline, also known as PCP). Primary effects seen with hallucinogen intoxication are visual hallucinations and disturbed thoughts, cognitive impairment, amnesia, personality changes, delusions and paranoia that can last from eight to 18 hours. Other signs and symptoms include euphoria or dysphoria, impaired motor coordination, diaphoresis, altered time perception, nausea and vomiting, and dizziness. Classic anticholinergic effects can also present, including dry mouth, constipation, tachycardia, bronchodilation, urinary retention, pupil dilation and photophobia, or blurred vision. Dementia can occur with long term or heavy use [23]. Flashbacks may occur after cessation of LSD use. Although tolerance rapidly develops for psychological changes precipitated by LSD, there is no withdrawal syndrome [43].

Effects from PCP include hypersalivation, fever, catalepsy, rigidity, myoclonus, diaphoresis, hyperreflexia, cardiac dysrrhythmias, hypertension, and seizures that can progress to coma [23,44]. PCP users may also display agitation, violence, analgesia, anorexia, increased blood pressure, horizontal or vertical nystagmus, and hyperacusis. Chronic PCP use has also been noted to induce marked social and behavioral changes, sometimes also diagnosed as chronic schizophrenia [44].

Inhalants are comprised of aromatic, aliphatic, and halogenated compounds such as glues. Effects from intoxication generally only last several minutes and may include euphoria but also "confusion, sedation, cardiac dysrrhythmias, dizziness, syncope, and dementia. Physical signs noted include hypotension, impaired motor coordination, and respiratory depression. Similar to hallucinogens, there is no withdrawal syndrome [23].

26.5   EARLY INTERVENTIONS FOR PROBLEM USE OF ALCOHOL AND OTHER DRUGS

The medical nurse can address treatment of addictive disorders by screening, which can increase the patient's awareness. If the user has a significant problem, the nurse can make appropriate referrals. Motivational interviewing can be employed for both screening and referral and, if more time is available, a brief intervention can be implemented.

26.5.1   Overview of treatment for addictive disorders

Generally, users are treated in the following "stages": detoxification, continued treatment, and rehabilitation and continuing care. Detoxification is often conceptualized as the first step in alcohol and drug treatment and involves withdrawing patients from substances safely and effectively. This approach can vary with the substance(s) of addiction but is basically similar. Detoxification is typically completed in the inpatient setting but may also occur in the outpatient setting.

Continued treatment and rehabilitation should occur in either an outpatient department specializing in substance addiction treatment or in community-based clinics. There are generally three approaches to continued treatment: abstinence based (also known as drug free), pharmacotherapy, or a combination of the two. Behavioral therapy (e.g., cognitive behavioral treatment) is the mainstay for abstinence-based treatment. It also usually supplements pharmacotherapy. Factors related to the approach selected include: duration of substance addiction problems, presence of coexisting medical and psychiatric problems, prior treatment experience, and patient preferences for treatment [45]. Whatever approach is selected, patients are encouraged to participate in 12-Step self-help groups such as Alcoholics Anonymous. These groups emphasize the abstinence approach and most do not support the use of pharmacotherapy. The goal is to encourage abstinence by helping patients to learn and master effective coping skills that can help them to resist relapsing to substance addiction. One exception however, is Methadone Anonymous (www.methadone-anonymous.org)

Continuing care, also known as aftercare, is the last stage that emphasizes relapse prevention. Patients are taught the skills needed to prevent a return to substance addiction. Generally it is agreed that treatment with comorbid medical and psychiatric problems should be simultaneously addressed throughout all stages. Continuing care may be lifelong, as substance use disorders dependence is a chronic condition requiring on-going treatment similar to diabetes or hypertension.

26.5.2 Motivational interviewing

Motivational interviewing is based on the Transtheoretical Model of Change and refers to the stages of precontemplation, contemplation, preparation, action, maintenance, and termination [46,47]. The stages of change are outlined in Table 26.4. Motiva-

Table 26.4 Stages of change

Precontemplation	Patients deny that their substance use is a problem.
Contemplation	Patients recognize that their substance use is a problem and believe they should stop its use but have not made definitive plans to do so.
Preparation	Patients have a plan to change their substance use behavior (e.g., entering a treatment program) usually in the next month.
Action	Patients implement specific changes in their behavior.
Maintenance	Existence of sustained changes in patients' behavior.
Termination	Patients are no longer enticed by substance use. Few patients reach this phase.

tional interviewing strategies are adapted to the stage patients are currently in rather than simply presenting treatment options without considering the patient's current readiness to change. These strategies are premised on the concept that motivation is the key to changing patients' behavior. Motivation used to be interpreted as the patient who was not motivated to change. In the motivational interviewing context, motivation is dynamic and potentially modifiable by the nurse's interviewing style.

FRAMES is the mnemonic often used to adapt the treatment approach to the patient's stage of change to implement motivational interviewing. FRAMES stands for:

- *Feedback* – after completing a comprehensive assessment, the nurse shares with the patient his or her problems compared to the general population.

- *Responsibility* – patients are explicitly given the choice whether or not to change their behavior.

- *Advice* – the nurse *suggests* rather than directs ways in which the client can change.

- *Menu* – the nurse offers various options for treatment.

- *Empathy* – the essential component in counseling.

- *Self-efficacy* – the nurse helps the patient to feel he or she is capable of making the change.

26.5.3 Brief intervention

A brief intervention may be all that is needed if patients appear to only have mild substance use problems. Spontaneous remission of problematic substance use is not uncommon and a short intervention may be all that is required. The inpatient setting is less likely to be socially stigmatizing compared to drug treatment settings and it may also be the ideal location to integrate drug treatment with other comorbid health problems. Timing can be particularly useful if the medical problem currently under treatment is negatively impacted by substance use – a teachable moment. Components of brief interventions include: (1) giving feedback, (2) informing about safe consumption, (3) assessing the patient's readiness for change, (4) negotiating goals and strategies, and (5) arranging for follow-up treatment.

Treatment can be limited to a single 10-to-15-minute session, although this approach can accommodate several such sessions. Evidence suggests that even interventions lasting less than three minutes increase overall tobacco abstinence rates. The recommendation of the 2008 update, Treating for Tobacco Use and Dependence [17], states that every tobacco user should be offered at least a minimal intervention. The evidence further suggests that there is a strong dose-response relation between

the length of the session and successful treatment outcomes. Person to person treatment provided in four or more session appears especially effective in increasing abstinence rates.

Brief interventions have been effective in reducing alcohol consumption by up to 50% [47]. The focus might be limited to encouraging persons to recognize that they have a substance use problem similar to the "screen only" approach. For patients with moderate to severe substance use problems, encouragement could be given to obtain care in a specialty treatment setting. For many individuals, a brief intervention serves as a good transition to specialist care where more comprehensive assessment and treatment can occur. Content may be as simple as supplying patient with a self-help booklet.

26.6   INTERVENTIONS FOR ADDICTIONS

26.6.1   Nicotine

Once a patient has been screened and identified as a tobacco user and the medical nurse has assessed the patient's willingness to stop all tobacco products, the nurse should coordinate tobacco cessation care with other healthcare team members. The patient is acutely abstinent because of his or her hospitalization; the goal is to maintain this abstinence post-hospitalization. The nurse should begin by employing counseling based on motivational interviewing and brief interventions to enhance the likelihood of continued abstinence. Common elements of practical counseling and supportive interventions are given in Tables 26.5 and 26.6.

The evidence demonstrates that the "combination of counseling and medication is more effective for smoking cessation than either medication or counseling alone. Therefore, wherever feasible and appropriate, both counseling and medication should be provided to patients trying to quit smoking" [17]. Suggestions for the clinical use of pharmacotherapies for tobacco cessation are shown in Table 26.7. The evidence in Treating Tobacco Use and Dependence; 2008 Update [17] found that specific

combinations of first line agents were effective. These were:

- Long-term (>14 weeks) nicotine patch + other NRT (gum and spray)

- The nicotine patch + the nicotine inhaler

- The nicotine patch + bupropion SR

Upon discharge from the medical unit, it is very important that the patient has established a follow up plan for continued tobacco cessation. A referral for an outpatient appointment in one to two weeks post-discharge that addresses tobacco cessation, telephone follow-up or self-help groups all have been found to be effective in promoting continued abstinence.

26.6.2   Alcohol

The initial treatment goal for the patient with alcohol addiction or dependence is to prevent harm from acute intoxication and/or the complications

Table 26.5 Common elements of practical counseling (problem solving/skills training)

Practical counseling (problem solving/skills training) treatment component	Examples
Recognize danger situations – Identify events, internal states, or activities that increase the risk of smoking or relapse.	• Negative affect and stress • Being around other tobacco users • Drinking alcohol • Experiencing urges • Smoking cues and availability of cigarettes
Develop coping skills – Identify and practice coping or problem solving skills. Typically, these skills are intended to cope with danger situations.	• Learning to anticipate and avoid temptation and trigger situations • Learning cognitive strategies that will reduce negative moods • Accomplishing lifestyle changes that reduce stress, improve quality of life, and reduce exposure to smoking cues • Learning cognitive and behavioral activities to cope with smoking urges (e.g., distracting attention; changing routines)
Provide basic information – Provide basic information about smoking and successful quitting.	• The fact that any smoking (even a single puff) increases the likelihood of a full relapse • Withdrawal symptoms typically peak within 1–2 weeks after quitting but may persist for months. These symptoms include negative mood, urges to smoke, and difficulty concentrating. • The addictive nature of smoking

Public Health Service Clinical Practice Guideline, *Treating Tobacco Use and Dependence*, www.ahrq.gov/path/tobacco.htm.

Table 26.6 Common elements of intratreatment supportive interventions

Supportive treatment component	Examples
Encourage the patient in the quit attempt	Note that effective tobacco dependence treatments are now available Note that one-half of all people who have ever smoked have now quit Communicate belief in patient's ability to quit
Communicate caring and concern.	Ask how patient feels about quitting Directly express concern and willingness to help as often as needed Ask about the patient's fears and ambivalence regarding quitting
Encourage the patient to talk about the quitting process	Ask about: Reasons the patient wants to quit Concerns or worries about quitting Success the patient has achieved Difficulties encountered while quitting

Public Health Service Clinical Practice Guideline, *Treating Tobacco Use and Dependence*, www.ahrq.gov/path/tobacco.htm.

associated with withdrawal. Once the patient has stabilized medically, it is important that the nurse, in conjunction with other healthcare team members, evaluates the patient for comorbid psychiatric problems and other conditions. Employing the communication skills of motivational interviewing and brief interventions throughout the hospitalization will enhance motivation to change and abstinence behavior. Referral to appropriate addictions specialists, *while the patient is still hospitalized,* is critical. It is important to remember that evidence suggests that referral and treatment intervention rates for identified substance use disorders patients have remained static over the past 20 years and are less than 50% [9,12,13].

Management of alcohol-dependent patients and associated withdrawal symptoms is often guided by the severity of the condition, the patient's previous history of withdrawal, and associated comorbid psychiatric or medical conditions. It is critically important that the nurse frequently evaluates the patient with alcohol withdrawal and avoids

Table 26.7   Suggestions for the Clinical Use of Medications for Tobacco Dependence Treatment[a]

Pharmacotherapy	Precautions/ contraindications	Side effects	Dosage	Duration	Availability
Nicotine patch		Local skin reaction Insomnia	21 mg/24 hours 14 mg/24 hours 7 mg/24 hours	4 weeks then 2 weeks then 2 weeks	Prescription and OTC[b]
Nicotine gum		Mouth soreness Dyspepsia	1–24 cigs/day-2 mg gum (up to 24 pcs/day) 25 + cigs/day-4 mg gum (up to 24 pcs/day)	Up to 12 weeks	OTC[b] only
Nicotine nasal spray		Nasal irritation	8–40 doses/day	3–6 months	Prescription only
Nicotine inhaler		Local irritation of mouth and throat	6–16 cartridges/day	Up to 6 months	Prescription only
Nicotine lozenge		Local irritation of throat Hiccups Heartburn/ Indigestion Nausea	First a.m. cigarette after 30 minutes from waking: 2 mg (up to 20 pcs/day) First a.m. cigarette before 30 minutes from waking: 4 mg (up to 20 pcs/day)	12 weeks	OTC[b] only
Bupropion SR	History of seizure History of eating disorders Use of MAO inhibitors in past 14 days	Insomnia Dry mouth	150 mg every morning for 3 days then 150 mg twice daily (Begin treatment 1–2 weeks pre-quit)	7–12 weeks mainte- nance up to 6 months	Prescription only
Varenicline	Monitor for changes in mood, behavior, psychiatric symptoms, maintenance up to and suicidal ideation	Nausea Trouble sleeping	0.5 mg once daily for days 5–7 before quit date 0.5 mg twice daily for days 1–4 before quit date 1 mg twice daily starting on quit date	3 months mainte- nance up to 6 months	Prescription only

[a]The information contained within this table is not comprehensive. Please see medication package inserts for additional information.
[b]OTC refers to over the counter.
Public Health Service Clinical Practice Guideline, *Treating Tobacco Use and Dependence*. http://www.ahrq.gov/clinic/tobacco/medsmoktab. htm

complacency. The revised Clinical Institute Withdrawal Assessment Scale (CIWA-Ar, Table 26.3) provides a quantitative measure of the patient's withdrawal symptoms and is a benchmark for treatment intervention. The goal in the treatment of alcohol withdrawal is twofold; firstly, to alleviate the symptoms associated with withdrawal; and, secondly, to identify and correct fluid and electrolyte imbalances [34].

Patient's who are experiencing withdrawal symptoms should be placed is a quiet environment. Oral benzodiazepines are considered first-line treatment and are used to minimize the psychomotor agitation experienced by withdrawal and to prevent progression from minor withdrawal symptoms to major ones [34]. In the patient with a history of significant long-standing alcohol consumption, DTs, or seizures, chlordiazepoxide PO 50–100 mg every six hours for one day followed by 25–50 mg every six hours for an additional two days should be administered. Clearly, these patients need to be assessed by the nurse frequently. If the patient has a score of eight on the CIWA-Ar, the patient should be give an additional 25–50 mg doses of chlordiazepoxide [34].

In patients who are experiencing DTs, the nurse may have to provide mechanical restraint in the lateral decubitis position for the protection of the patient and the healthcare team. DTs should be treated with intravenous diazepam, 5–10 mg IV every five minutes until the patient is calm but alert. According to Winehose [34], refractory DTs that have been unsuccessfully managed by benzodiazepines should be managed with the addition of phenobarbital or propofol. The patient who requires this treatment should be managed in the ICU with mechanical ventilation.

Antipsychotics, including haldol, should not be used in the management of alcohol withdrawal because they lower the seizure threshold and interfere with heat dissipation. The use of anticonvulsants for withdrawal-associated seizures is controversial. The evidence is inconclusive and this approach is not recommended [34]. However, if the patient experiences status epilepticus, phenytoin may be used in conjunction with benzodiazepines for short-term management.

26.6.3 Opioids

Management of opioid-dependent individuals hospitalized for medical reasons is contentious. Overall, it is accepted that detoxification from opioids during the acute stage of a medical illness is not often successful [48]. The medical nurse may care for the patient who misuses opioids in one or more of the following scenarios: (1) opioid overdose, (2) opioid withdrawal suppression, (3) opioid detoxification, and (4) opioid maintenance.

26.6.3.1 Opioid overdose

Opioids are listed as the most frequent cause of drug overdoses [49]. It may be unlikely that a patient is admitted to the medical floor with a diagnosis of opioid intoxication; however, this may be a yet-to-be-diagnosed underlying problem to the presenting medical diagnoses. Opioid intoxication and subsequent risk of overdose may not begin to manifest until after admission to the unit. The most rapid removal of opioid from its receptor site is accomplished by the opioid antagonists, which selectively compete for the site but have no agonist properties.

Patients who have overdosed on opioids usually have severe respiratory depression and may become comatose. In the beginning bag-valve-mask support or endotracheal intubation may be required to assist with adequate oxygenation. The next priority in this situation is to re-establish adequate respiration by immediately giving an opioid antagonist such as naloxone, preferably intravenously.

Naloxone is a pure antagonist that competitively binds to the receptors, decreasing the effects of the opioid agonists but without producing any additional effects on the receptor. Naloxone can fully reverse the opioid-induced respiratory depression. Duration of action for naloxone, shorter than that of most opioids, is 20 to 60 minutes. When administered intravenously, a rapid response should be observed within one to two minutes. The amount of naloxone needed is largely dependent on the dose of opioid. To avoid precipitating withdrawal, the dose required is much smaller than with an identical clinical scenario in a nonopioid-dependent individual. Consequently, close patient monitoring must continue because additional doses may be required, particularly for long-acting opioids such as propoxyphene. If a maximum of 10 mg IV has been administered and respiratory depression is not reversed, etiologies other than opioid toxicity should be considered.

26.6.3.2   Opioid detoxification and withdrawal suppression

Ordinarily, physicians may only treat opioid-dependent patients in the clinic setting if they have either received a waiver from special registration requirements as specified in the Narcotic Addict Treatment Act. This is the process that enables buprenorphine treatment. However, when an opioid-dependent patient is admitted for a medical problem other than substance dependence, no such limitations exist [49], allowing opioids to be administered to prevent withdrawal and avoiding complicating the medical problem under treatment.

Detoxification seeks to achieve safe withdrawal from opioids with a minimum of withdrawal symptoms. Naturally-occurring withdrawal is not ordinarily life threatening; however, some persons may not be as tolerant of iatrogenic withdrawal (e.g., naloxone) because of the hemodynamic instability that may occur [50]. How a client is withdrawn depends in part upon:

1. the degree of withdrawal symptoms they are willing to tolerate,

2. any coexisting medical problems that may complicate the withdrawal process, and the available treatment setting in which withdrawal can occur.

Since natural withdrawal is not inherently dangerous among healthy users, they may opt to withdraw without the support of medications. Otherwise, withdrawal can be treated by substituting another opioid drug (then slowly tapering its dose) or a nonopioid drug.

An example of use of a nonopioid drug is clonidine, a central acting alpha-2 agonist used to treat high blood pressure that requires baseline blood pressure and regular monitoring of blood pressure. Clonidine acts by dampening parts of the sympathetic system made hyperactive by opioid withdrawal. It suppresses many of the autonomic signs and symptoms of withdrawal (e.g., nausea, vomiting, perspiration, intestinal cramps, and diarrhea). Clonidine may not provide as smooth a withdrawal compared to an opioid because it does not significantly improve the muscle aches, back pain, insomnia, and craving for opioids. Further, use of clonidine is limited by its own side effects of sedation and low blood pressure. Other nonopioid drugs useful for selected withdrawal symptoms include promethazine for nausea, ibuprofen for muscle cramps, and loperamide for diarrhea [23]. Sedatives can help to deal with the restless sleep and insomnia that occur as part of withdrawal. However, sedative use is not recommended as first-line treatment, since patients may then develop physical dependence to sedatives.

Methadone is a common drug used to detoxify the opioid-dependent hospitalized patient through its substitution for shorter-acting opioids. Generally, patients are given small doses based on the severity of withdrawal until the patient is stabilized, then the dose is reduced by about 20% each day. A standard approach to evaluating withdrawal is the Clinical Institute Narcotic Assessment (CINA) to estimate the severity of 11 signs and symptoms including: pupil dilation, rhinorrhea, watery eyes, piloerection, nausea or vomiting, diarrhea, yawning, cramps, restlessness, voiced complaints, and increased vital signs. Each symptom is graded from 0 = absent to 2 = severe. Patients are thus evaluated every six hours and medicated based on the result. Traditionally, 1 mg of methadone is given for each point after a minimum of five points. With this schedule, the user experiences mild withdrawal symptoms beginning about the third or fourth day. These symptoms often continue for some time after hospital discharge when methadone is totally withdrawn unless it is re-established in another treatment setting. If the CINA is not used, patients can be given by mouth intramuscularly 20 mg methadone or 10 mg. These dosages should inhibit withdrawal symptoms for most patients but not induce euphoria. No methadone should be administered until the appearance of withdrawal symptoms [48].

Alternatively, for use in the hospital setting, ultrarapid detoxification approaches have been developed that entail antagonists such as naloxone to precipitate opioid withdrawal while the patient is heavily sedated with short-acting benzodiazepines. This approach, which takes 48 hours, has been demonstrated to be successful in the short term, as few or no withdrawal symptoms are observed when the sedation wears off [51]. The patient may then be transitioned to naltrexone. This is an available treatment for opioid dependence for individuals who desire a long-acting antagonist versus a drug substitute. Persons taking naltrexone who attempt to use opioids for their euphoric effects are blocked from doing so, reinforcing abstinence. Ordinarily, prior to induction it is vital that individuals be free of opioid for a minimum of five days to avoid precipitating severe withdrawal. However, in this scenario some patients continue to have minimal withdrawal symptoms with naltrexone and many stop taking it. Naltrexone is a treatment option most successful for highly motivated patients. Depot formulations are currently being explored which thus far has been well tolerated [49].

Another approach is to premedicate clients with buprenorphine before they undergo ultrarapid detoxification, which may diminish the occurrence of some side effects such as nausea and vomiting that may otherwise occur following the detoxification procedure [52].

Inpatient programs, especially ultrarapid detoxification, are subject to high monetary costs and the likelihood of rapid relapse to opioid use is substantial, especially given the continued presence of withdrawal symptoms, [51]. Currently, there is little evidence to justify continued use of this method [53].

26.6.3.3 Opioid maintenance

Opioid maintenance is also known as drug substitution. The rationale for drug substitution is that, for some individuals, prolonged exposure to opioids induced long-lasting adaptive changes. Goals of drug substitution include: (1) minimizing the abstinence syndrome, (2) blocking the euphoric effects of the addicted opioid, and (3) relieving opioid craving. These patients are physically dependent but because opioid craving is alleviated, they are able to fully participate in work and other social activities. Continued administration of an opioid is then necessary to maintain normal mood states and normal responses to stress. Methadone and buprenorphine are available for drug substitution.

Methadone Methadone is a full opioid agonist that is the oldest and most commonly used drug in the treatment setting. It is a strictly regulated drug for use in licensed opioid treatment programs or licensed inpatient hospital detoxification units. Both settings are required to provide counseling and social services along with methadone dispensing. Eligibility criteria for methadone maintenance are listed in Table 26.8.

Methadone is absorbed well when given orally and, at appropriate doses, is neither intoxicating nor significantly sedating; its effects last 24 hours, permitting once a day dosing. When consumed in larger than prescribed doses, opioid side effects may increase but euphoria does not occur. Side effects for methadone maintenance include mild sedation, constipation, decreased sexual drive, diaphoresis, and peripheral edema. High doses of methadone use can prolong the QT_c interval and cause torsades de pointes; patients who report palpitations should have further evaluation with an

Table 26.8 Criteria for methadone maintenance

- At least 18 yr of age (exception: if less than 18 yr, must have current physical dependence and at least two prior detoxification attempts or abstinence-based treatment)
- Physical opioid dependence for a minimum of 1 yr continuous use or longer for intermittent use
- Physical signs of opioid withdrawal or of chronic use on physical exam (e.g., needle tracks on skin)
- Recent release from incarceration where criteria for physical dependence were met prior to incarceration
- On methadone maintenance within past two years

If pregnant – can be dependent for less than one year or opioid dependent in the past and likely to return to use during pregnancy.

ECG. Further, the risk of QT_c prolongation among patient on high methadone doses increases if the patient is hypokalemic, has abnormal liver function or is taking P450 inhibitors [45].

If an opioid dependent person is hospitalized for another medical condition and is already participating in a licensed methadone treatment program, the same methadone regimen can be continued provided the maintenance dose is confirmed by the prescribing physician (i.e., addiction treatment provider). When a patient has been stabilized on a specified methadone dose, it is just adequate to prevent withdrawal and additional analgesia is not provided with the same dose. Therefore, if pain control is required during hospitalization, additional medications should be prescribed. Ideally, nonopioid drugs should be given but if pain relief requires opioids, short-acting opioid analgesics should be administered. These should be prescribed on a specific schedule versus as-needed [45]. If the patient cannot take oral methadone, the intramuscular or subcutaneous route can be used at half to two-thirds of the maintenance dose, because methadone is absorbed in these circumstances twice as efficiently as oral doses. Mixed agonist and antagonist opioid analgesics, such as pentazocine (Talwin), nalbuphine (Nubain), and butorphanol (Stadol), should not be administered to methadone-maintained patients and others on agonist-only drugs, because these drugs can compete with methadone at the μ receptor, thereby precipitating withdrawal. Additionally, opioid formulations that include acetaminophen should be avoided, since higher opioid doses required due to cross-tolerance require concomitant high and potentially hepatotoxic doses of acetaminophen.

Buprenorphine Buprenorphine is also used for treatment of opioid addiction. It has been used for the phases of detoxification as well as the maintenance. Unlike methadone, buprenorphine can be provided to outpatients outside of formal drug treatment settings. It is a mixed agonist-antagonist that is a partial μ-agonist and a κ-antagonist with a high affinity for its receptors. Partial agonist effects mean the euphoric effects of other opioids are blocked and drug craving is suppressed. Since there are ceiling effects, similar effects of full agonists are produced but at reduced intensity. Moreover, in large part due to its high affinity and slow dissociation, buprenorphine's antagonistic character is evident when withdrawal is precipitated among users on high doses of full-agonist opioids. These antagonist effects are evident with increasing doses of buprenorphine whereby analgesic effects at lower doses are also reversed [49]. Additionally, antagonist effects at the κ-receptor mean some of the dysphoric effects experienced as part of withdrawal may be inhibited. These properties provide advantages over methadone, including substantially less respiratory depression, less physical dependence, and fewer and less intense withdrawal symptoms. The high affinity means that greater doses of naloxone are often needed in the event of buprenorphine overdose. In such a scenario, naloxone infusions may be more appropriate than bolus doses.

Buprenorphine is administered sublingually due to poor absorption by mouth. Buprenorphine has a long duration of action when used for maintenance due to its slow dissociation from its receptors; this makes it particularly beneficial in the outpatient setting because it may be used only three times a week [51]. The formulation recommended for drug addiction treatment is a combination of buprenorphine and naloxone. Naloxone is included to deter addiction because if the tablet is crushed, the naloxone component precipitates withdrawal. However, naloxone has minimal activity when consumed sublingually. Due to its potential antagonist effects, buprenorphine should only be initiated (whether for detoxification or maintenance) if the patient is already in acute withdrawal or after detoxification is complete.

Similar to methadone, if patients are hospitalized on maintenance buprenorphine doses and require no additional opioid analgesia, they should be continued on their usual dose after dose verification from their drug treatment provider. If opioid analgesia is needed, there are three basic management options:

1. Continue the maintenance dose of buprenorphine and add a short-acting opioid

2. Temporarily discontinue buprenorphine to give an intermediate or long-acting opioid analgesic or

3. Substitute low-dose methadone for buprenorphine and add a short-acting opioid.

Naloxone should be available at the bedside in the event that buprenorphine is displaced from its receptor, thereby increasing the risk for opioid overdose [45]. Similar to methadone maintenance, other mixed agonist-antagonist opioids should not be administered. Discontinuation of buprenorphine may be preferred because it can attenuate or block the effect of opioids. Although buprenorphine is discontinued, its slow dissociation from its receptors still elevates the risk of opioid overdose, necessitating appropriate monitoring.

26.6.4   Stimulants

Detoxification from cocaine is supportive and requires no specific treatment other than stopping its use. However, many patients find the symptoms of withdrawal so uncomfortable that they are driven to continue using cocaine in order to delay symptoms of withdrawal. Any medical treatment, such as anxiolytics, can be administered to help relieve withdrawal symptoms. Detoxification can also be facilitated by the addition of ammonium chloride to acidify the urine to increase excretion of cocaine [23]. Any medications used though, should not include phenothiazines, especially chlorpromazine or haloperidol, because these drugs may lower the seizure threshold. Since there is no effective drug-substitute, treatment must emphasize avoiding conditions that precipitate drug use.

26.6.5   Sedative-hypnotics

Treatment for sedative-hypnotic withdrawal is required since the symptoms can be life threatening. Medical observation is required for several days as these drugs have extremely long half-lives and are metabolized slowly. Generally, withdrawal is treated with a CNS depressant with a longer half-life than the drug from which the patient is being withdrawn. Three basic treatment strategies include: (a) use of gradually decreasing doses of the sedative-hypnotic; (b) substitution of a long-active barbiturate followed by gradual withdrawal of the substituted long-acting sedative-hypnotic; and (c) substitution of an anticonvulsant such as tegretol or depakote [40,42]. The occurrence of seizures indicates the necessity of a more gradual withdrawal [40].

Phenobarbital is often used for treatment for sedative-hypnotic withdrawal because of its multiple benefits: (1) as a long-acting drug, any withdrawal symptoms that may occur are milder; (2) it maintains a relatively stable blood level with appropriate dosing; (3) its margin for safety is much wider than the shorter-acting drugs, therefore only extremely high doses will be lethal; (4) if toxicity does occur with phenobarbital, the signs of slurred speech, sustained nystagmus, and ataxia are easily recognized [42]; and (5) even if the individual does become intoxicated, effects of high doses do not include disinhibition, a desired state for many individuals who misuse the drug. Phenobarbital is administered hourly until the withdrawal symptoms are suppressed (for treatment of alcohol withdrawal) or until the patient manifests signs of mild intoxication (for other CNS depressant withdrawal) [23]. Patients must be carefully evaluated before administration of the next dose. If signs of sedative-hypnotic intoxication occur the dose is reduced; if symptoms of withdrawal occur (e.g., intense nightmares, muscle twitching, and psychosis) the dose is increased. After stabilization (meaning no signs of intoxication or withdrawal), phenobarbital can be gradually withdrawn, typically by 30 mg each day.

The use of an anticonvulsant as a substitute for sedative-hypnotic withdrawal is also effective. Tegretol and depakote are both effective in suppressing the withdrawal symptoms because they increase gamma aminobutyric acid (GABA) (i.e., how benzodiazepines exert their effects) function. Patients with pre-existing seizure disorders readily tolerate the use of tegretol [40]. Perhaps most importantly, neither of these drugs has effects that are sought after by individuals misusing sedative-hypnotics.

Benzodiazepine overdose is most dangerous when combined with other sedative-hypnotic drugs. A benzodiazepine antagonist, flumazenil is available for the treatment of acute intoxication, but this drug must be used with caution since it may not reverse respiratory depression completely and can provoke withdrawal seizures in persons with benzodiazepine dependence [54]. Similar to cocaine toxicity, patients can be treated with urine alkalinization to increase drug excretion of benzodiazepines. The goal is to maintain a urine pH of 7.5. Sodium bicarbonate can be given intravenously but severely ill persons may require dialysis.

26.6.6 Hallucinogens and inhalants

Supportive care is used to treat hallucinogens or inhalant intoxication; this can also include anxiolytics. Particularly for PCP, this means removing sources of sensory stimulation and possible treatment with neuroleptics [23]. Phenothiazines should be avoided because they potentiate PCPs anticholinergic effects. Haloperidol has also been successfully administered on an hourly basis to suppress the patient's psychotic behavior [44].

KEY POINTS

- All patients' admitted to the medical unit should be screened for substance use. The AUDIT is recommended for alcohol screening.

- If it is not possible to screen each patient admitted to the medical unit, the nurse should consider the following upon patient admission:
  - Does the patient have a medical condition that may be drug or alcohol related?
  - Is the patient male or female (>4 : 1 ratio)
  - Is the patient between the ages or 30–50 years old?

- If only one question is asked this question should be:
  - *"On any single occasion during the past three months, have you had more than five drinks containing alcohol?"* or
  - *"Have you used street drugs more than five times in your life?"*

- Hospitalization represents a unique opportunity to modify health behaviors. Hospitalized patients are acutely abstinent. The medical nurse is in the unique position to identify those most at risk and promote healthy lifestyle behaviors.

- Employ the strategies of brief interventions and motivational interviewing to enhance behavior change. Remember, *Ask, Assess, Advise, Assist, and Arrange.*

- Early identification of patients with alcohol and drug withdrawal symptoms decreases morbidity and mortality.

- Refer the patient to a substance addiction specialist while the patient is hospitalized.

- Arrange follow up for the patient with in two weeks post-discharge to enhance abstinence.

REFERENCES

1. Roche, A.M., Freeman, T., and Skinner, N. (2006) From data to evidence, to action: findings from a systematic review of hospital screening studies for high risk alcohol consumption. *Drug Alcohol Depen.*, **83**, 1–14.

2. Brown, R.L., Leonard, T., Saunders, L.A., and Papasouliotis, O. (1998) The prevalence and detection of substance use disorders among inpatients ages 18 to 49: an opportunity for prevention. *Prev. Med.*, **27**, 101–110.

3. Conigliaro, J., Lofgren, R.P., and Hanusa, B.H. (1998) Screening for problem drinking: impact on physician behavior and patient drinking habits. *J. Gen. Intern. Med.*, **13**, 251–256.

4. Dinh-Zarr, T., Goss, T.W., Heitman, E., *et al.* (2004) Interventions for preventing injuries in problem

drinkers. *Cochrane Database of Systematic Reviews* 3 (Art. No.: CD001857). doi: 10.1002/14651858. CD001857.pub2.

5. Foy, A. (1999) Alcohol problems in a general hospital. *Addict. Biol.*, **4**, 23–24.

6. Dolman, J.M. and Hawkes, N.D. (2005) Combining the audit questionnaire and biochemical markers to assess alcohol use and risk of alcohol withdrawal in medical inpatients. *Alcohol Alcohol.*, **40**, 515–519.

7. Taylor, C.L., Passmore, N., Kilbane, P., and Davies, R. (1986) Prospective study of alcohol-related admissions to an inner-city hospital. *Lancet*, **328**, 265–268.

8. Mordal, J., Bramnes, J.G., Holm, B., and Morland, J. (2008) Drugs of abuse among acute psychiatric and medical admissions: laboratory based identification of prevalence and drug influence. *Gen. Hosp. Psychiat.*, **30**, 55–60.

9. Smothers, B.A. and Yahr, H.T. (2005) Alcohol use disorder and illicit drug use in admissions to general hospitals in the United States. *Am. J. Addiction.*, **14**, 256–267.

10. United States Department of Health and Human Services (2007) Results from the 2006 National Survey on Drug Use and Health: National Findings. Substance Abuse and Mental Health Services Administration, Office of Applied Studies. http://www.oas.samhsa.gov/NSDUH/2k6NSDUH/2k6results.pdf (accessed 21 July 2008).

11. Canning, U.P., Kennell-Webb, S.A., Marshall, E.J. *et al.* (1999) Substance misuse in acute general medical admissions. *QJM*, **92**, 319–326.

12. Schneekloth, T.D., Morse, R.M., Herrick, L.M. *et al.* (2001) Point prevalence of alcoholism in hospitalized patients: continuing challenges of detection, assessment and diagnosis. *Mayo Clin. Proc.*, **76**, 460–466.

13. Smothers, B.A., Yahr, H.T., and Sinclair, M.D. (2003) Prevalence of current DSM-IV alcohol use disorders in short-stay, general hospital admissions, United States 1994. *Arch. Intern. Med.*, **163**, 713–719.

14. Centers for Disease Control (2005) Cigarette Smoking Among Adults – United States, 2004. *Morb. Mortal Wkly. Rep.*, **54**, 1121–1124.

15. National Institute on Alcohol Abuse and Alcoholism (2005) Helping patients who drink too much. A clinician's guide. http://pubs.niaaa.gov/publications/Practitioner/CliniciansGuide2005/clinicians_guide.htm (accessed 21 July 2008).

16. American Psychiatric Association (2000) *Diagnostic and Statistical Manual of Mental Disorders (DSM-IV)*, 4th edn, American Psychiatric Association, Washington, DC.

17. Fiore, M.C., Jaén, C.R., Baker, TB. *et al.* (2008) Treating Tobacco Use and Dependence: 2008 Update, Clinical Practice Guideline, U.S. Department of Health and Human Services. Public Health, Service, Rockville, MD.

18. Stewart, S.H. and Connors, G.J. (2007) Perceived health status, alcohol-related problems, and readiness to change among medically hospitalized, alcohol-dependent patients. *J. Hosp. Med.*, **2**, 372–377.

19. Chen, M.C. and Yi, H. (2007) Trends in alcohol-related morbidity among short-stay community hospital discharges, United States, 1979–2005. Surveillance Report #80. National Institute on Alcohol Abuse and Alcoholism, Division of Epidemiology and Prevention Research, Alcohol Epidemiologic Data System. http://pubs.niaaa.nih.gov/publications/surveillance80/HDS05.htm (accessed 5 July 2008).

20. Merrill, J.O., Rhodes, L.A., Deyo, R.D. *et al.* (2002) Mutual mistrust in the medical care of drug users: The keys to the "narc" cabinet. *J. Gen. Intern. Med.*, **17**, 327–333.

21. McLaughlin, D. and Long, A. (1996) Review: an extended literature review of health professionals' perceptions of illicit drugs and their clients who use them. *J. Psychiatr. Ment. Health Nurs.*, **3**, 283–288.

22. SAMHSA/CSAT (2008) Clinical Guidelines for the Use of Buprenorphine in the Treatment of Opioid Addiction. Treatment Improvement Protocols (TIP) Series 40. Chapter 3. Substance Abuse and Mental Health Services Administration/Center for Substance Abuse Treatment (SAMHSA/CSAT), Rockville, MD. http://www.ncbi.nlm.nih.gov/books/bv.fcgi?rid=hstat5.section.72374 (accessed 24 June 2008).

23. Martin, P.R. (2008) Substance-related disorders, in *Current Diagnosis & Treatment: Psychiatry*, 2nd edn (eds M.H. Ebert, P.T. Loosen, B. Nurcome, and J.F. Leckman), McGraw-Hill, USA.

24. National Institute on Drug Abuse (2005) Heroin abuse and addiction. Research report.

25. National Institute of Drug Abuse (2006) Nicotine Addiction. Research Report. *NIH Publication No. 01-4342, Revised*, http://www.drugabuse.gov/ResearchReports/Nicotine/Nicotine.html (accessed 16 August 2008).

26. World Health Organization (2004) Global Status Report on Alcohol 2004. Department of Mental Health and Substance Abuse, Geneva. http://www.who.int/substance_abuse/publications/alcohol/en/ (accessed 12 August 2008).

27. National Institute on Alcohol Abuse and Alcoholism (2007) Alcohol Metabolism: An Update. Alcohol

Alert 72. http://pubs.niaaa.nih.gov/publications/AA72/AA72.htm (accessed July 2008).

28. Randall, C., Roberts, J., DelBoca, F. *et al.* (1999) Telescoping of landmark events associated with drinking: a gender comparison. *J. Stud. Alcohol*, **2**, 252–260.

29. National Institute of Alcohol Abuse and Alcoholism (2004) Alcohol an important women's health issue. Alcohol Alert 62: http://pubs.niaaa.nih.gov/publications/aa62/aa62.htm (accessed 12 August 2008).

30. Boggan, B. (2003) Alcohol, chemistry and you. Absorption of ethyl alcohol http://www.chemcases.com/alcohol/alc-04.htm (accessed July 2008).

31. Weed, C.M. (2008) The biology of addiction. *Alcohol Anwsers/* www.alcoholanswers.com (accessed 12 August 2008).

32. Volkow N.D. (2007) Addiction and the Brain's Pleasure Pathway: Beyond Willpower. HBO, http://www.hbo.com/addiction/understanding_addiction/12_pleasure_pathway.html (accessed 16 August 2008).

33. Wong, D.F. *et al.* (2003) Positron Emission Tomography: A tool for identifying the effects of alcohol dependence on the brain. *Alcohol Res. Health*, **27** (2), 161–173, http://pubs.niaaa.nih.gov/publications/arh27-2/161-173.pdf (accessed 12 August 2008).

34. Winehose, G.L. (2008) Alcohol withdrawal syndromes. *UpToDate.* www.uptodate.com (accessed 12 August 2008).

35. Schuckit, M.A., Tipp, J.E., Reich, T. *et al.* (1995) The histories of withdrawal convulsions and delirium tremens in 1648 alcohol dependent subjects. *Addiction*, **90**, 1335.

36. Sullivan, J.T., Sykora, K., Schneiderman, J., *et al.* (1989) Assessment of alcohol withdrawal: The revised Clinical Institute Withdrawal Assessment for Alcohol scale (CIWA-Ar). *Br. J. Addict.*, **84**, 1353–1357.

37. Morgan, J.P. (2008) Cardiovascular complications of cocaine abuse. *UpToDate.* www.uptodate.com (accessed 21 July 2008).

38. Mechem, C.C. (2007) Pulmonary complications of cocaine abuse. *UpToDate.* www.uptodate.com (accessed 28 April 2008).

39. DuPont, R.L., Greene, W., and Lydiard, R.B. (2007) Sedatives and hypnotics: Pharmacology and epidemiology. *UpToDate*, www.uptodate.com (accessed 28 April 2008).

40. DuPont, R.L. and DuPont, C.M. (2005) Sedatives/hypnotics and benzodiazepines, in *Clinical Textbook of Addictive Disorders*, 3rd edn (eds R.J. Frances, S.I.

Miller, and A.H. Mack), Guilford Press, New York, pp. 219–242.

41. Ray, O. and Ksir, C. (2002) Opiates, in *Drugs, Society, and Human Behavior*, 9th edn, McGraw-Hill, Boston, pp. 376–411.

42. Wesson, D.R., Smith, D.E., Ling, W., and Seymour, R. B. (2005) Sedative-hypnotics, in *Substance Abuse. A Comprehensive Textbook*, 4th edn (eds J.H. Lowinson, P. Ruiz, R.B. Millman, and J.G. Langrod), Lippincott, Williams, & Wilkins, Philadelphia, pp. 302–312.

43. O'Brien, C.P. (2006) Drug addiction and drug abuse, in *Goodman and Gilman's: The Pharmacological Basis of Therapeutics*, 11th edn, Online edition (eds L.L. Brenton, J.S. Lazo, and K.L. Parker), McGraw-Hill, USA.

44. Mendelson, J.H. and Mello, N.K. (2008) Cocaine and other commonly abused drugs, in *Harrison's Online* (eds A.S. Fauci, E. Braunwald, D.L. Kasper, *et al.*), McGraw-Hill (accessed 21 July 2008).

45. Weaver, M.F. and Hopper, J.A. (2008) Heroin and other opioids: Management of chronic use. *UpToDate.* www.uptodate.com (accessed 28 April 2008).

46. Miller, W.R. and Rollnick, S. (1991) *Motivational Interviewing: Preparing People to Change Addictive Behavior*, Guilford Press, New York.

47. United States Department of Health and Human Services (1999) Brief Interventions and Brief Therapies for Substance Abuse. Center for Substance Abuse Treatment/Substance Abuse and Mental Health Services Administration (SAMHSA/CSAT), Rockville, MD, DHHS Publication Number 99-3353.

48. Doyon, S. (2004) Chapter 167, Opioids, in *Tintinalli's Emergency Medicine. A Comprehensive Study Guide* (eds Tintinalli, J., Kelen, G.D. *et al.*), McGraw-Hill, USA, Online edition (accessed 28 April 2008).

49. Boothby, L.A. and Doering, P.L. (2007) Buprenorphine for the treatment of opioid dependence. *Am. J. Health-Syst. Ph.*, **64**, 266–272.

50. Stolbach, A. and Hoffman, R.S. (2006) Opioid withdrawal in the emergency setting. *UpToDate.* www.uptodate.com (accessed 28 April 2008).

51. Knapp, C.M., Ciraulo, D.A. and Jaffe, J. (2005) Opiates: Clinical aspects, in *Substance Abuse. A Comprehensive Textbook*, 4th edn (eds J.H. Lowinson, P. Ruiz, R.B. Millman, and J.G. Langrod), Lippincott, Williams, & Wilkins, Philadelphia, pp. 180–195.

52. Dilts, S.L., Jr., and Dilts, S.L. (2005) Opioids, in *Clinical Textbook of Addictive Disorders*, 3rd edn

(eds R.J. Frances, S.I. Miller, and A.H. Mack), Guilford Press, New York, pp. 138–156.

53. Gowing, L.R. and Alli, R.L. (2006) The place of detoxification in treatment of opioids dependence. *Curr. Opin. Psychiatry*, **19**, 266–270.

54. Charney, D.S., Minic, S.J., and Harris, R.A. (2006) Hypnotics and sedatives, in *Goodman and Gilman's: The Pharmacological Basis of Therapeutics*, 11th edn, Online edition (eds L.L. Brenton, J.S. Lazo, and K.L. Parker), McGraw-Hill, USA.

27

Management of addictive disorders in surgical nursing care practice

Phyllis J. Mason

John Hopkins University School of Nursing, Baltimore, MD, USA

27.1 INTRODUCTION

Drug use has increased to a point where it impinges on society in general and on many aspects of medical practice, so that every practitioner needs to be "streetwise" concerning illicit drugs and their medical and surgical implications [1]. Clinicians need to have a basic understanding of the different short- and long-term complications of illicit drug use because many users end up as patients. There is an increase of trauma related to fights, automobile accidents, and impaired mental states in this population. Addictive disorders are common in the United States at 3.8% for alcoholics and 0.6% for drug dependence [2]. Addiction occurs with legal drugs such as alcohol, tobacco, and prescription medications, as well as illegal drugs purchased on the street and prescription medications sold on the street. Alcohol is the most commonly used legal drug, and cocaine, heroin, and marijuana are the most commonly used illegal drugs [3]. Alcohol, tobacco, and illicit drugs are associated with more than 80 recognized disease and injury conditions and with substantial costs, both personal and societal [4]. Tobacco is responsible for the greatest portion of

mortality, in terms of years lost (Table 27.1); alcohol and illicit drug use both have substantial impacts [5]. Patients have different levels of consumption, they may be at risk of addiction or dependent on a substance. Cocaine dependence can lead to medical complications related to the heart, the respiratory, nervous, and digestive system (Table 27.2). Heroin, a powerful opioid, produces euphoria, a feeling of relaxation, and slows respirations while intravenous use increases the risk of infection (Table 27.3). Perioperative nurses need to recognize symptoms of drug addiction and be prepared to manage the effects on the body systems. In surgical settings, chronic excessive alcohol consumption is associated with a two to fivefold increased risk of perioperative complications (Table 27.4).

Pain is an integral part of the post-operative recovery process, and ineffective pain management is common. Today it is known that ineffective analgesia and/or untreated pain have negative psychological and physiological consequences for the patient and are associated with higher morbidity and mortality when compared to patients whose

Addictive Disorders in Medical Populations   Edited by Norman S. Miller and Mark S. Gold
© 2010 John Wiley & Sons, Ltd.

Table 27.1 Complications/effects of nicotine

Increased pain threshold
Coronary artery disease
Wound infection
Pneumonia
Ateletasis
Thromboembolism

Table 27.2 Effects of cocaine

Blood pressure elevation
Cardiac acceleration
Vasoconstriction
Impairment of cardiac electoral activity
Arrhythmias
Cardiac standstill
Gastric ulceration
Cerebral ischemia
Hemorrhagic stroke
Cerebral vasculitis
Seizures
Cardiomyopathy
Myocarditis

Table 27.3 Effects of heroin

Drowsiness
Constipation
Mood changes
Peripheral and venous dilatation
Decreased gastric motility
Bacterial infections
Endocarditis
Soft tissue abscess
Scarred, sclerosed veins

Table 27.4 Effects of alcohol addiction

Gastric hemorrhage	Cirrhosis
Gastritis	Gastric Ulcer
Portal hypertension	Nutritional deficiencies
Alcoholic hepatitis	Alcoholic psychosis
Anemia	Dysrhythmias
Cardiomyopathy	Hypertension
Stroke	Neuropathies

post-operative pain is effectively controlled with analgesics [6,7]. Addiction causes neurophysiologic, behavioral, and social responses that worsen the pain experience and complicate provision of adequate analgesia [8,9]. In the perioperative setting, opioid tolerance can manifest as increased sensitivity to otherwise non-noxious stimuli, lower threshold for pain, intolerance to pain, and the need for higher doses of opioids to provide plasma levels adequate for analgesia [10]. Acute post-operative pain is usually treated with opioids, non-steroidal anti-inflammatory drugs (NSAID) or mild oral analgesics on a demand basis, which is not effective for moderate to severe post-operative pain. The chronic opioid consuming patient can experience significant post-operative pain given that healthcare professionals are not accustomed to their increased opioid requirements. Assessment and management of pain is outlined as a standard of care in many treatment guidelines. Inadequate pain management is common among all patients. To care for patients with chemical dependency, analgesic therapy using opioid drugs requires a high level of knowledge and skill on the part of the clinician. Identifying the opioid-dependent and alcohol-dependent consumer pre-operatively avoids problems with withdrawal symptoms and uncontrolled pain intra-operatively and post-operatively.

Patients taking methadone are often "opioid tolerant" but they also may be pain intolerant. Opioid hyperalgesia represents increased sensitivity to pain, whereas tolerance may reflect decreased sensitivity to opioids [9]. Hyperanalgesia should be suspected when repeated opioid dose increases fail to provide the expected analgesic effect or when there is unexplained pain exacerbation after an upward titration of opioid. A reduction in the opioid dose with or without adding a replacement opioid or a gradual rotation to an alternative opioid would decrease the pain level in these patients [9].

Patients on methadone develop some tolerance to all opioids although cross-tolerance is variable. Nonopioid analgesics should be combined with opioids to increase the efficacy of treatment and reduce adverse effects, such as nausea and vomiting, or respiratory depression.

For patients on methadone maintenance therapy (MMT) care must be taken during the perioperative period not to add or discontinue medications that may interact adversely with methadone. Patients on methadone for MMT or pain management should continue the dose before and on the day of surgery to avoid unnecessary fluctuations of drug levels, which could lead to withdrawal and potential complications in medical, surgical, and pain treatment. A history of dose, frequency of dosing, time of last dose, the location and number of the MMT program should be obtained. The time and date of the last methadone dose and prescription should be confirmed with the methadone dispensary. Opioids produce a characteristic withdrawal syndrome, distressing but not life threatening within 24 hours of last drug use [1]. Some of these patients may have ingested illicit drugs prior to coming to the hospital, and thus a pre-operative urine toxicology screen, complete blood count, liver and renal function test, and electrocardiogram should be performed.

The depressant effect of methadone can be increased by sedative classes of drugs. The patient should be monitored closely for respiratory depression. In the opioid consuming patient, doses of opioids causing respiratory depression and analgesia may vary compared to opioid naïve patients. Opioid consuming patients are not immune to the catastrophic consequences of opioids, such as respiratory depression; respiratory rate and level of sedation take precedence over trying to achieve an arbitrary value on the pain scale [11].

27.2   PREVALENCE OF ADDICTIVE DISEASE IN SURGICAL NURSING POPULATIONS

The prevalence of licit and illicit opioid use is growing, and a greater percentage of chronic opioid consuming patients are presenting for surgery [12]. Today, with the extension of opioid treatment for nonterminally ill patients, and chronic conditions being treated with opioids, every anesthesiologist will likely be confronted with acute pain management issues in these patients. The prevalence of chronic pain in patients with addictions appears to be much higher than the prevalence of chronic pain in the general population [13]. Alcohol, tobacco, and illicit drugs are associated with over 80 recognized disease and injury conditions, and have been associated with considerable health and social costs [14].

Persons with alcohol addiction and dependence can have significant withdrawal complications in the perioperative period. The same holds true for those with dependence on tobacco or caffeine. The time course for development of withdrawal symptoms is variable, based on the drug of choice. Symptoms can range from mild to severe. Patients who experience severe withdrawal symptoms will require intervention, whereas patients with mild to moderate symptoms may not require pharmacological treatment. The stress of surgery may exacerbate existing withdrawal symptoms.

The use of tobacco is a worldwide epidemic. By 2030 it is estimated that one in six deaths will be directly attributable to tobacco [15]. While nicotine replacement is possible for post-surgical patients, the actual tobacco addiction (cravings for the inhalation of smoke, taste in the back of the throat, anxiety relief) also needs to be treated.

Consumed by 80% of Americans on a daily basis, caffeine is the most widely used stimulant in the world. Caffeine has been shown to exacerbate both medical disorders and psychiatric disorders; in addition, it can interfere with the metabolism of medications. Caffeine withdrawal headaches have been described post-surgery if patients are deprived of caffeine for longer than eight hours. The risk of these headaches can be reduced through perioperative ingestion of caffeine [16].

27.3   COMPLICATIONS FROM ADDICTIVE DISORDERS IN SURGICAL NURSING CARE

Patients who use or are addicted to substances are more likely to experience difficulties with treatment/medication adherence, administrative discharges, compromised functional status, difficult community adjustment, reduced quality of life, and worse outcomes [17]. Many patients experiencing opioid addiction have cross-addiction to nicotine, cocaine, benzodiazepine, marijuana, and alcohol, and may have communicable blood-borne infections that should be brought to the attention of the medical team [18]. Abstinence from drinking and using illicit drugs imposed by hospitalization puts the substance user or addicted patient at risk for withdrawal. Patients who smoke and/or drink may have more complications than nonsmokers and light or nondrinkers [19]. Tobacco smoke contains over 3000 pharmacologically active substances and chronic exposure to smoke produces multiple physiologic effects. Smoking-related comorbidities, such as cardiac and pulmonary diseases, increase anesthetic risk for complications such as those related to the respiratory system and surgical wounds [15]. Tobacco is linked mainly to chronic diseases with a high risk of mortality; alcohol is linked to acute diseases such as intentional and unintentional injuries as well as chronic diseases [14].

Surgical patients should be screened for tobacco and alcohol use and alcohol withdrawal. Alcohol withdrawal may cause other symptoms such as behavioral problems, noncompliance, and verbal abuse post-surgery. Chronic exposure to smoke affects the metabolism of several drugs, including those used in anesthesia such as muscle relaxants [15].

Patients identified at risk for alcohol withdrawal pre-operatively should be given withdrawal prophylaxis prior to surgery. Shourie *et al.* [20] suggest patients for nonurgent surgical cases should be assessed for alcohol consumption at least 3–4 weeks in advance of surgery and disulfiram controlled pre-operative abstinence implemented one month before elective surgery.

Management of pain after surgery continues to be a challenge in clinical practice. Pain is an unpleasant subjective sensation that results from a physiologic response of noxious, thermal, or chemical stimuli [21,22]. Opioid analgesics continue to be the mainstay of pharmacologic treatment of moderate to severe pain [9,23]. Opioid analgesics are used extensively in the management of all types of pain – acute, chronic, neuropathic, and non-neuropathic.

Untreated pain is associated with significant physiologic, emotional, mental, and economic consequences; uncontrolled pain is reported by approximately 50% of patients [23,24]. Patients who have a substance addiction problem report high levels of pain and need higher amounts of pain medication for pain relief as well as to prevent withdrawal [9,11,25]. Opioid-induced tolerance and hyperalgesia have been documented in animal and human studies [9]. Patients receiving opioids to control their pain may become more sensitive to pain as a direct result of opioid therapy [26]. Underdosing can provoke drug-seeking behaviors as the patient obtains partial relief from medications, but experiences break-through pain. Requesting more medication or higher doses gives the false impression of addiction or "pseudoaddiction". Effective opioid analgesia across all patient populations may not be prescribed because of fear of cognitive, respiratory, and psychomotor side effects, iatrogenic drug addiction, and prescription drug diversion. These fears are exaggerated when treating patients with a known history of substance addiction. There is concern among care-givers that the use of opioids to treat pain may cause the patient to relapse to drug use again. There is no evidence that exposure to opioid analgesics in the presence of acute pain increases rates of relapse [8].

Rhabdomyolysis and cardiac muscle involvement should be suspected in cases of heroin use. Heroin-associated cardiomyopathy was reported for the first time in 1976, since then additional cases have been described [27].

27.4 THE REDUCTION IN MORBIDITY AND MORTALITY FROM TREATMENT

The level of mortality in a given population is influenced by gender, age, drug administration, personality, general health status, and treatment availability [28]. Opioid dependence is associated with mortality rates approximately 13 times higher than the general population of the same age and sex [29]. Opioid replacement therapy has been demonstrated to reduce mortality risk in opioid-dependent individuals. It is imperative that drug addiction is seen as a major challenge facing researchers and practitioners of clinical pharmacology. Increasing knowledge about the neurobiology and genetics of addictions will increase our ability to match them to the correct populations [5].

The recognition and diagnosis of substance addiction/dependence allows the clinician the opportunity to anticipate operative and post-operative complications and offer pre-operative interventions to reduce perioperative morbidity and problems such as break-through pain, tolerance, and withdrawal. Alcohol addiction is a leading cause of preventable morbidity and mortality in the United States. Alcohol and drug dependence increase the risk of death in substance addicts. Tobacco is linked to chronic diseases with a high risk of mortality; alcohol is linked to acute disease categories, such as intentional and unintentional injuries, and also chronic diseases, both with and without high risk of mortality [14]. A large portion of the substance-attributable burden of disease would be avoided if known effective interventions were implemented [14]. Referral of illicit drug users to outpatient treatment programs reduces morbidity and mortality.

Tobacco is related to mortality and morbidity later in life, whereas morbidity and mortality from alcohol and illicit drugs tend to occur in the younger years.

As a result of substance dependence many suffer from HIV infection, chronic liver disease, infections, cardiovascular, digestive, respiratory, metabolic, head and neck cancers, and hematological disorders that contribute to death [2,14].

Opioid-dependant patients particularly substance addicts, may present with comorbid conditions, and drug-specific adaptations such as tolerance, physical dependence, and withdrawal; these variables alone or in combination may diminish opioid analgesic effectiveness in the perioperative setting [30].

It has been found that abstinence from smoking will reduce the risk of perioperative complications, though duration of abstinence necessary to reduce the risk is unclear [15]. Encouraging smokers to quit is the single most important thing smokers can do to improve their health.

27.5   THE ROLE OF THE SURGICAL NURSE IN DIAGNOSIS AND TREATMENT OF ADDICTIONS

There are a number of issues to be considered in a patient with a history of previous or ongoing opioid use; there are those taking opioids for a legitimate medical indication and those who are or have a history of misusing opioids. These patients may present problems that require special support in areas such as psychiatric disorders, polysubstance addiction, infections, and legal issues. To identify these patients, it is important that the pre-operative assessment includes a thorough history about chronic pain, treatment with opioids, and previous substance use to include ethanol, tobacco, and all prescribed and illicit drugs [10]. To treat patients with substance addiction the nurse must develop skills to screen patients for substance use, learn how to treat these patients for their pain complaints, and locate support and referral ser-vices [25]. There are few outward signs of drug addiction making it difficult to identify people who misuse drugs. Some physical clues that may be visible include "track-marks", phlebitis, abscesses and scarring, atrophied or perforated nasal septum. Diseases that may be associated with drug addiction include cirrhosis, HIV, AIDS, and hepatitis.

Signs of acute intoxication will depend on the substance used and may include meiosis/mydriasis, hypo/hypertension, sweating, tremor, pyrexia, an abnormal affect or bizarre behavior, respiratory depression (characteristic of opioids), and a reduced level of consciousness [1]. Nurses should take a through drug history as part of the pre-operative assessment, asking about tobacco, alcohol, prescription medications, and street drugs. Some patients will deny using drugs because they do not want the healthcare provider to think badly of them or they may fear they will report them to the authorities. The patient may admit to drug use if they understand the effect of their drug use and the reaction it may have when mixed with anesthetic agents. The nurse must be alert to complications that can occur before, during, and after surgery.

Assessment of the patient suspected of alcohol addiction should include screening strategies to identify addiction, detect end-organ damage related to alcohol consumption, and provide prompt intervention prior to surgery. Patients at risk for developing alcohol withdrawal should undergo medical detoxification prior to operative intervention. The urgency of surgery will determine the feasibility of pre-operative detoxification. These patients should receive multivitamins and high doses of thiamine and receive oral or parenteral thiamine during the pre-operative and perioperative periods to prevent stress induced Wernicke–Korsakoff syndrome.

The best strategies for prevention and treatment of nonmedical use of prescription opioids, especially among patients with painful disorders, are not known [7]. Individualized pain management, vigilant clinical monitoring, and appropriate pain consult are essential in managing the substance addicted patient.

27.6   APPROACH TO DIAGNOSIS OF ADDICTIONS

Healthcare providers must rely on self-report: no questionnaire will uncover drug use unless the person is truthful or information is provided by a family member. Patients may present with strange behavior or abnormal vital signs raising suspension of substance addiction. A through review of the patient's medical history and medications may provide valuable clues. The most important step is identifying the opioid-dependent patient. Chronic pain patients tend to underestimate and under report their medication use [18,31]. Abuse, misuse and addiction risk in the chronic pain patient varies with the medical setting, the patient population served and the presence of a history of addiction or misuse [31].

All individuals seeking healthcare should be asked about substance use so that appropriate health interventions can be implemented [3]. The perioperative period affords an opportunity to identify patients with an addiction but with the increase in the number of same day surgeries the patient often presents to close to the time of the scheduled procedure making diagnosis difficult.

27.7   SCREENING INSTRUMENTS FOR ADDICTION

In order to manage surgical patients with addictions, in the perioperative period it is essential to identify patients with addictions effectively and efficiently. Because addiction is a common problem in the general population, patients should be screened for addiction just as patients are screened for hypertension and diabetes. Screening distinguishes between those who could benefit from a minimal intervention and others who may require further diagnostic assessment or possible treatment [32]. The appropriate way to assess a substance use disorder depends on the objective [33]. While there are numerous screening instruments for addiction, the perioperative period does not allow time for formal, time-consuming screening. Some screening tests can be administered as part of the general health interview or while performing the physical examination. To be practical they must be brief, easy to score and remember. Sensitivity and specificity are important, but if a less sensitive instrument is more acceptable to the clinician and is used with more patients a larger number of substance dependent patients could be identified. Patient comfort may affect clinician acceptance; a screening tool that is uncomfortable for the patient might provoke resistance on their part, leading clinicians to be less likely to use it [34]. Simple yes/no questions that lend themselves to oral administration and mnemonic acronyms are ideal [35]. The most effective tool is a short validated screening instrument that would screen for alcohol and illicit drugs (Chapter 6).

If substance addiction is suspected, one or more positive answers using the CAGE questionnaire may indicate a problem with substance addiction [25] (Chapter 6).

Another quick assessment for substance addiction with two or more positive answers indicating the patient has a problem is the Trauma Test [25]. Has the patient:

1. Had any fracture/dislocation of bones or joints (excluding sports injuries)?

2. Been injured in a traffic accident?

3. Injured their head (excluding sports injuries)?

4. Been in a fight or assaulted while intoxicated?

5. Been injured while intoxicated?

Smoking behavior can be assessed in a few minutes using the CAGE questionnaire modified from the familiar CAGE questionnaire for alcoholism [36].

The Criteria ('Four Cs' Test) from the Diagnostic and Statistical Manual of Mental Disorders, 4th ed. (DSM-IV) is used by addiction counselors, social workers, psychiatrists and psychotherapists to diagnose all addictive substances (e.g., alcohol, opioids, cannabis, amphetamines) [36]. The criteria are grouped into four categories that begin with C:

1. **Compulsion** – the intensity with which the desire to use a chemical overwhelms the patient's thoughts, feelings, and judgement.

2. **Control** – the degree to which patients can (or cannot) control their chemical use once they have started using.

3. **Cutting down** – the effects of reducing chemical intake; withdrawal symptoms.

4. **Consequences** – denial or acceptance of the damage caused by the chemical.

The Alcohol Use Disorder Identification Test (AUDIT) was developed by the World Health Organization as a screening tool for hazardous alcohol consumption. The AUDIT is a 10 item multiple-choice questionnaire that requires approximately two minutes to administer and another three minutes to score. A total score of eight or more indicates a strong likelihood of harmful alcohol consumption [37].

27.8 EARLY INTERVENTIONS FOR PROBLEM USE OF ALCOHOL AND DRUGS

Primary care physicians and other healthcare providers can play an important role in preventing the harm associated with alcohol and illicit drug use by recognizing problems early and providing appropriate intervention. In the perioperative period it is important to identify substance misuse/addiction in order to tailor treatment and identify and prevent complications at might arise as a result.

To obtain an optimal effect of a pre-operative intervention, pre-operative screening for excessive drinking needs to take place at least 3–4 weeks prior to surgery when possible [20].

In primary care or acute care, the focus for treating pain in a patient with a history of substance addiction should be aimed at treating the pain, not the addiction [25]. The initial dose of pain medication should be an appropriate dose to relieve pain adequately for the patient's condition [22]. For patients having same day surgery or resuming oral intake the methadone dose should be started post-operatively. NSAIDs are effective for low to moderate intensity pain, they are not as effective as opioids, but they lack the adverse effects of opioids. NSAIDs do not cause physical dependence or respiratory depression.

Treating patients with addictions for pain requires an understanding of the terms, "addiction", "dependency," and "tolerance". A perioperative pain consult may be necessary for patients on methadone for chronic pain or MMT [38].

27.9   INTERVENTIONS FOR ADDICTIVE DISORDERS

Rehabilitation-detoxification should not be considered in the immediate perioperative period [18]. Current evidence suggests nicotine replacement therapy is safe to use in the perioperative period, but more data are needed. Interventions for pre-operative smokers continue to be developed: organized efforts to systematically intervene in smokers requiring surgery are few and far between in actual clinical practice; there is a need to devise simple interventions that can be applied by busy surgical practitioners [15]. Pharmacologic agents, such as nicotine patches, nasal spray, nicotine gum, inhaled nicotine, lozenges, and bupropion, are effective agents to increase the chance of quitting. Efforts are under way to develop a nicotine vaccine.

Pre-operative intervention for excessive alcohol consumption among elective surgery patients has been shown to reduce complications of surgery. Successful intervention depends on an effective and practical screening procedure [20]. Patients most often present for surgery too close to the time of surgery to reverse any alcohol effects. In the surgical setting, intervention for alcohol use is aided by defining the level of alcohol use: is the patient at risk, alcohol addicted or dependent. Patients with addiction and dependent history are at risk for alcohol withdrawal syndrome if they reduce or eliminate alcohol consumption. Alcohol withdrawal symptoms can range from mild to severe. If the level of alcohol use is determined prior to surgery, interventions can be tailored to prevent withdrawal during the recovery period.

Effective substance dependence treatment requires both pharmacologic and psychosocial treatment. Opioid agonist therapy with methadone is an accepted medical treatment for opioid addiction with documented efficacy [39]. Patients should be referred to an addiction specialist for long-term treatment with methadone or buprenorphine in conjunction with appropriate counseling for substance misuse or addiction. Stable maintenance programs have been shown to reduce mortality risk. Addiction is a difficult disorder to treat; definitive treatment is a long process taking months to years, with the level of treatment based on level and substance of misuse and/or addiction.

Methadone maintenance is one form of treatment for opioid addiction that can only be administered in a licensed methadone clinic. These treatment centers provide ongoing counseling and referral for primary medical services. Treatment must be tailored to address individual drug addiction pattern and drug-related medical, psychiatric, and social problems.

Providing pain control is an essential part of surgical nursing, the nurse has the responsibility to understand pharmacotherapies used for controlling pain from surgery, appropriate perioperative monitoring, and to be able to implement the best approaches without compromising patient safety.

REFERENCES

1. Hall, A.P. and Henry, J.A. (2007) Illicit drugs and surgery. *Int. J. Surg.*, **5** (5), 365–370.

2. Saitz, R., Gaeta, J., Cheng, D. *et al.* (2007) Risk of mortality during four years after substance detoxification in urban adults. *J. Urban Health*, **84** (2), 272–282.

3. Bailes, B. (1969) What perioperative nurses need to know about substance abuse. *AORN*, **68** (4), 617–622, 625–626.

4. Rehm, J., Taylor, B., and Room, R. (2006) Global Burden of Disease from Alcohol, Illicit Drugs and Tobacco. *Drug Alcohol Rev.*, **25** (6), 503–513.

5. Tyndale, R. (2008) Drug addiction: a critical problem calling for novel solutions. *Clin. Pharmacol. Ther.*, **83** (4), 503–506.

6. Barak, M., Poppa, E., Tansky, A., and Drenger, B. (2006) The activity of an acute pain service in a

teaching hospital: five years experience. *Acute Pain*, **8** (4), 155–159.

7. Becker, W.C., Sullivan, L.E., Tetrault, J.M. *et al.* (2008) Non-medical use, abuse and dependence on prescription opioids among U.S. adults: psychiatric, medical and substance use correlates. *Drug Alcohol Depen.*, **94** (1–3), 38–41.

8. Alford, D., Compton, P., and Samet, J. (2006) Acute pain management for patients receiving maintenance methadone or buprenorphine therapy. *Ann. Intern. Med.*, **144** (3), 127–134.

9. DuPen, A., Shen, D., and Ersek, M. (2007) Mechanisma of opioid-induced tolerance and hyperalgesia. *Pain Manag. Nurs.*, **8** (3), 113–121.

10. Krenzischek, D.A., Dunwoody, C.J., Polomano, R.C., and Rathmell, J.P. (2008) Pharmacology for acute pain: implications for practice. *Pain Manag. Nurs.*, **9** (1), S22–S32.

11. Swenson, J., Davis, J., and Johnson, K. (2005) Postoperative care of the chronic opioid-consuming patient. *Anesthesiol. Clin. of North America*, **23** (1), 37–48.

12. Carroll, I., Angst, M., and Clark, J. (2004) Management of Perioperative Pain in Patients Chronically Consuming Opioids. *Reg Anesth Pain Med.*, **29** (6), 576–591.

13. Strain, E.C. and Stitzer, M.L. (2006) *The Treatment of Opioid Dependence*, The Johns Hopkins University Press.

14. Rehm, J., Taylor, B., Patra, J., and Gmel, G. (2006) Avoidable Burden of Disease: Conceptual and Methodological Issues in Substance Abuse Epidemiology. *Int. J. Methods Psychiatr. Res.*, **15** (4), 181–191.

15. Warner, D. (2007) Tobacco dependence in surgical patients. *Curr. Opin. Anaesthesiol.*, **80** (2), 253–258.

16. Weber, J.G., Ereth, M.H., and Danielson, D.R. (1993) Perioperative ingestion of caffeine and postoperative headache. *Mayo Clin. Proc.*, **68** (9), 842–845.

17. Dennis, M. and Scott, C. (2007) Managing Addiction as a Chronic Condition. *Addict. Sci. Clin. Pract.*, **4** (1), 45–55.

18. Brill, S., Ginosar, Y., and Davidson, E. (2006) Perioperative management of chronic pain patients with opioid dependency. *Curr. Opin. Anaesthesiol.*, **19** (3), 325–331.

19. Williams, G., Daly Proude, E., Kemode, S., *et al.* (2008) The influence of alcohol and tobacco use in orthopaedic inpatients on complications of surgery. *Drug Alcohol Rev.*, **27** (1), 55–64.

20. Shourie, S., Conigrave, K.M., Proude, E.M. *et al.* (2007) Pre-operative screening for excessive alcohol consumption among patients scheduled for elective surgery. *Drug Alcohol Rev.*, **26** (2), 119–125.

21. Carr, D.B. and Goudas, L.G. (1999) Acute pain. *Lancet*, **353** (9169), 2051–2058.

22. Schnoll, S.H. and Weaver, M.F. (2003) Addiction and pain. *Am. J. Addiction.*, **12** (Suppl. 2), S27–S35.

23. Dunwoody, C.J., Krenzischek, D.A., Pasero, C. *et al.* (2008) Assessment, physiological monitoring, and consequences of inadequately treated acute pain. *J. Perianesth. Nurs.*, **23** (1A), S15–S27.

24. Polomano, R., Rathmell, J., Krenzischek, D., and Dunwoody, C. (2008) Emerging Trends and New Approaches to Acute Pain Management. *Pain Manag. Nurs.*, **9** (1), S33–S41.

25. D'Arcy, Y., and McCarberg, B. (2007) Pain management of patients with a substance use disorder. *Nurse Pract.*, **32** (9), 36–44.

26. Angst, M. and Clark, J. (2006) Opioid-induced hyperalgesia. *Anesthesiology*, **104** (3), 570–587.

27. Routsi, C., Kolias, S., Kaskarellis, P. *et al.* (2007) Acute cardiomyopathy and cardiogenic pulmonary edema after inhaled heroin use. *Acta Anaesthesiol. Scand.*, **51** (2), 262–264.

28. Clausen, T., Anchersen, K., and Waal, H. (2008) Mortality Prior to, During and After Opioid Maintenance Treatment (OMT): A National Prospective Cross-Registry Study. *Drug Alcohol Depend.*, **94** (1–3), 151–157.

29. Gibson, A., Degenhardt, L., Mattick, R.P. *et al.* (2008) Exposure to opioid maintenance treatment reduces long-term mortality. *Addiction*, **103** (3), 462–468.

30. Mitra, S. and Sinatra, R. (2004) Perioperative management of acute pain in the opioid-dependent patient. *Anesthesiology*, **101** (1), 212–227.

31. Gallagher, R. and Rosenthal, L. (2008) Chronic pain and opiates: balancing pain control and risks in long-term opioid treatment. *Arch. Phys. Med. Rehabil.*, **89** (1), S77–S82.

32. Babor, T.F. and Kadden, R.M. (2005) Screening and interventions for alcohol and drug problems in medical settings: what works? *J. Trauma*, **59** (Suppl. 1), S80–S87.

33. Samet, S., Waxman, R., Hatzenbuehler, M., and Hasin, D. (2007) Assessing Addiction: Concepts and Instruments. *Addict. Sci. Clin. Pract.*, **4** (1), 19–31.

34. Vinson, D.C., Galliher, J.M., Reidinger, C., and Kappus, J.A. (2004) Comfortably engaging: which approach to alcohol screening should we use? *Ann. Fam. Med.*, **2** (5), 398–404.

35. Knight, J.R., Sherritt, L., Harris, S.K. *et al.* (2003) Validity of brief alcohol screening tests among adolescents:

a comparison of the AUDIT, POSIT, CAGE, and CRAFFT. *Alcohol. Clin. Exp. Res.*, **27** (1), 67–73.

36. Rustin, T. (2000) Assessing Nicotine Dependence. *Am. Fam. Physician*, **62 (3)**, 579–584, 591–592.

37. Allen, J., Litten, R., Fertig, J., and Babor, T. (1997) A review of research on the Alcohol Use Disorders Identification Test (AUDIT). *Alcohol. Clin. Exp. Res.*, **21** (4), 613–619.

38. Peng, P., Tumber, P., and Gourlay, D. (2005) Review article: perioperative pain management of patients on methadone therapy. *Can. J. Anaestheology*, **52** (5), 513–523.

39. Scimeca, M., Savage, S., Portenoy, R., and Loweinson, J. (2002) Treatment of pain in methadone-maintained patients. *Mt. Sinai J. Med.*, **67** (5–6), 412–417.

28

Addictive disorders in psychology practice

Lisa J. Merlo

Department of Psychiatry, Division of Addiction Medicine, University of Florida, USA

28.1 OVERVIEW

Addictive [i.e., substance use disorders (SUDs)] represent a major public health concern, affecting nearly one in seven Americans. Addiction can lead to the development of acute and chronic illnesses, as well as the exacerbation of existing conditions, including mental illness. Substance use is associated with increased mortality due to medical complications, accidents, and suicide. In addition, criminal involvement, incarceration, unemployment, poverty, and homelessness are associated with substance use, abuse, and dependence. When considering this increased morbidity and mortality, as well as lost productivity, the estimated national cost of addictive disorders in the United States is approximately $500 billion per year [1]. Given the significance of these findings, psychologists have long been interested in the assessment, prevention, and treatment of these disorders. However, theory, research, and clinical application of knowledge related to addictive disorders have generally developed independently of efforts related to mental illness [2]. Many psychologists do not routinely include comprehensive screening and assessment for addictive disorders in their practice. However, undiagnosed substance use disorders can negatively affect treatment success by interfering with the patient's ability to understand psychoeducational efforts, participate effectively in sessions, complete therapy-related assignments, and implement lasting changes. In addition, continued substance use may exacerbate underlying psychological symptoms. As a result, more work is needed to help psychologists recognize, understand, and respond to patients with addictive disorders who are being treated within the practice of psychology.

This chapter focuses on the impact of substance use disorders in the field of applied psychology (e.g., clinical and counseling psychology). It will review the estimated prevalence of these disorders among populations served by psychologists, as well as common complications of addiction in the practice of psychology. Information relating to the screening and identification of addictive disorders in psychology patients will be reviewed, including various instruments to assist with this endeavor. In addition, the typical progression of these disorders among populations seen

Addictive Disorders in Medical Populations   Edited by Norman S. Miller and Mark S. Gold
© 2010 John Wiley & Sons, Ltd.

in psychology practice will be highlighted, along with the role of the psychologist in their assessment and treatment. Current research on empirically-supported treatment options will be reviewed and discussed.

The major goal of the chapter is to help the psychology practitioner become aware of the importance of discussing substance use with all patients, screening for substance use disorders, and following up with appropriate referrals for further assessment, treatment, and/or observation when indicated. It is hoped that the reader will become familiar with the major addiction-related issues in the practice of psychology and, specifically, will:

1. Be aware of the prevalence of substance use disorders in psychology populations, as well as common comorbidities within these groups.

2. Understand the complications from substance use disorders as related to increased morbidity and mortality in psychology populations.

3. Recognize commonly used screening instruments that can be used to assist with identification and diagnosis of substance use disorders.

4. Obtain basic familiarity with psychological interventions for substance use disorders and their efficacy.

28.2 CLINICAL PREVALENCE

Within the general population, there are relatively high rates of alcohol abuse and dependence, with lifetime prevalence rates of approximately 17.8% and 12.5%, respectively [3]. However, rates of substance use disorders are generally higher among patients encountered in psychological practice. For example, alcohol use disorders are strongly associated with mood and anxiety disorders, personality disorders, and other drug use disorders [3]. Similarly, drug use, abuse, and dependence are relatively common in the general population. Up to 12% of individuals exhibit a lifetime drug use disorder [4]. However, drug addiction is also strongly associated with mood and anxiety disorders, severe mental illness, eating disorders, personality disorders, and other conditions [5].

Given the high prevalence of substance use disorders in the general population and the association between substance use disorders and other mental illness, it is important for psychologists to be vigilant to signs of addiction among their patients. Though substance use disorders are prevalent in most populations served by psychologists, there are some populations that warrant special attention due to increased risk and prevalence of substance use disorders. Descriptions of such populations and prevalence rates for substance use disorders within each specific group are reviewed below.

28.2.1 Adolescents

Adolescents may be introduced to psychological care for a variety of reasons, including learning difficulties, mental illness, behavior problems, parent–child relational difficulties, adjustment to life stressors, or a primary substance use disorder. Indeed, high rates of past-month cigarette smoking (22%), alcohol consumption (45%), and marijuana use (22%) have been reported by adolescents [6], and data suggest that rates of other substance use (e.g., sedatives, stimulants, barbiturates, and prescription medications such as opioid painkillers) are on the rise. Careful screening for substance use is a vital component of care for adolescent patients, as the co-occurrence of psychological disturbance and substance use among this population is particularly common. For example, research suggests that adolescent girls with depression are almost three times more likely to misuse substances than girls without depression, and girls who misuse substances are twice as likely to develop major depressive disorder within three years of graduation from high school [7]. As noted by Star and colleagues [8], this can present a diagnostic challenge, as psychological symptoms and side effects of substance addiction can overlap. For example, irritable mood, violent/aggressive behavior, disturbed sleep, decreased school performance, and so on are common in both conditions. In addition, adolescents served in a psychology practice may be secretive regarding their substance use, particularly if they do not want their parents to learn about their use. Psychologists should consider initiating a discussion with adolescent patients and their parents at the onset of care regarding the importance of allowing the adolescent privacy in his/her therapy sessions. Though the legal limits of confidentiality must be enforced, it is frequently helpful for adolescent patients to feel that they can "open up" to the psychologist without fear of negative reprisal. In the event that the adolescent discloses dangerous behavior, the psychologist may consider negotiating a plan with the patient whereby they can tell the parent together, during session, in order that the psychologist can help to manage any inappropriate responses from the parent.

28.2.2 Couples counseling populations

Marital and other relationship difficulties represent a common reason for referral to a psychologist or other mental healthcare provider. Problems in the primary relationship can lead to increased stress and exacerbation of difficulties in other areas of life; in addition, mental health issues and substance use can lead to increased relationship distress. Indeed, although men with alcohol use disorders marry at rates similar to other men, rates of divorce are much higher in this group [9]. Across marital relationships, alcohol abuse/dependence predicts divorce and the use of illicit drugs may further increase the likelihood that the marriage will end in divorce [10]. Maintaining a loving relationship with an individual who is misusing substances can be extremely difficult and stressful. Some spouses may experience psychological distress due to their inability to cope effectively with the situation. For example, wives of substance addicted men may seek individual therapy to cope with the consequences of their husbands' substance use [11]. Unfortunately, many such women report that their husbands refuse to attend treatment, despite frequent marital conflict surrounding the substance

use [12]. Indeed, even among men in treatment for alcohol use disorders, only about half will agree to couples counseling [13]. This can present a significant strain on the relationship that may exacerbate substance use in the addict as well as psychological symptoms in the addict's spouse. As a result, psychologists may wish to include a brief family substance use assessment when meeting with new patients, particularly married individuals who present with significant relationship conflict and distress.

28.2.3 Pregnant and postpartum women

Pregnancy and the postpartum period can be particularly difficult for women and their families due to physical discomfort, hormonal changes, body image concerns, decreased sleep quality, and the increased stress associated with such a major life event. The development or recurrence of a psychological disorder (e.g., depression, anxiety, obsessive-compulsive tendencies, and even psychosis) and adjustment difficulties have been linked to pregnancy and the postpartum period. As a result, this population has gained increased attention from the field of psychology, and more women are seeking psychological care. Substance use during pregnancy and the postpartum period can have serious detrimental effects on the fetus or infant, as well as the mother [14]. For example, congenital birth defects, premature birth, delayed development, learning difficulties, and behavior problems have been linked to maternal substance use during pregnancy or while breast-feeding. Unfortunately, research suggests that 18% of pregnant women continue to smoke cigarettes, 10% drink alcohol, and 4.3% use illicit drugs during pregnancy [15], putting many children at risk for these negative outcomes. Fortunately, many women are motivated to deliver a healthy baby, and pregnancy represents a major life event that also helps encourage some women to discontinue their substance use [16]. Psychologists can sometimes encourage women to abstain from or cut down on substance use during pregnancy for the sake of their unborn child. After this period of abstinence, some women feel prepared to quit "for good." As a result, pregnancy may represent a critical period during which substance addiction treatment may be particularly effective.

28.2.4 Geriatric populations

For many, the transition to retirement is a very positive experience; however, for some older individuals, the additional stresses associated with aging can become overwhelming. Health concerns may be more prominent, financial difficulties may cause increased stress, loss of role function may lead to depressed mood, death of loved ones may result in bereavement, and remitted mental illness may recur. As a result, more elderly individuals are seeking mental healthcare [17]. In addition, recent research has demonstrated that substance addiction is a growing problem in this group. Though illicit drug use is relatively uncommon among older adults, rates of both illicit and prescription drug addiction are increasing among elderly individuals with psychiatric conditions and without. Among older adults with a substance use disorder, the most commonly-used illicit drugs include marijuana (42%), cocaine (36%), pain relievers (25%), stimulants (18%), and sedatives (17%) [18]. In addition, prescription medication addiction may be widespread. A study conducted in 2001 demonstrated that approximately 300 000 individuals over the age of 55 had misused more than one prescription medication within the previous month [19], and a later study suggested that each year up to 11% of women over the age of 60 misuse psychoactive prescription drugs [20]. Finally, alcohol use disorders remain the most common substance use disorder among elderly individuals. Approximately 86% of older adult with a substance use disorder use alcohol only, and an additional 4% use both alcohol and other drugs [18]. Thus, screening for alcohol use disorders may be particularly important for this population and is recommended as part of the initial clinical interview. Although most would not expect substance use disorders to be particularly problematic in elderly populations, psychologists must refrain from neglecting to inquire about substance use, abuse, and dependence in this population.

28.2.5 Victims and perpetrators of abuse

Individuals who were victims of physical, sexual, or emotional abuse in childhood are at risk for a variety of psychological disturbances throughout childhood and later life. Similarly, individuals who experience domestic abuse and their children also show higher rates of physical and psychological problems compared to others without an abuse history. Unfortunately, these individuals may turn to substance use in an effort to manage their distress and cope with difficult memories or experiences. Indeed, experiencing childhood physical or sexual abuse is associated with alcohol use throughout adolescence and into adulthood [21]. Female victims of domestic abuse demonstrate a similar pattern, and the rate of substance use disorders is increased in this population as well [22]. In addition, the link between domestic violence and substance use disorders extends to perpetrators of abuse [23]. Up to 92% of perpetrators arrested for domestic violence used alcohol or drugs the day of the attack [24], and approximately 70% of battered women report that their partner has an alcohol use disorder [25]. It appears that some perpetrators may purposely use alcohol or drugs in order to provide an excuse or justification for their violent behavior [23]. Thus, psychologists working with patients due to experiences in an abusive relationship or environment should be vigilant to symptoms of substance use and reassess throughout the treatment process. Substance use in this population may interfere with treatment goals by allowing the patient to avoid dealing with difficult issues, or providing an excuse for inappropriate behavior.

28.2.6 Homeless populations

Homelessness is a significant problem, particularly in the United States, with 1994 estimates indicating that up to 9.32 million Americans were homeless [26]. Census-based estimates suggest that about

1% of the general population, and 6.3% of Americans living in poverty, are homeless [27]. Given that many homeless individuals have mental illness and/or substance use disorders, psychologists frequently become involved in their care through services offered through community mental health clinics, substance addiction treatment centers, VA hospitals, emergency departments, and so on. Among homeless adults, the prevalence of substance use disorders is estimated to be between 20 and 75% across different countries [26], and homeless individuals are almost two times more likely to have a past history of substance use disorders than housed individuals [28]. Unfortunately, substance use is associated with increased morbidity and mortality in this population. Homeless individuals may be less likely to access social services if they are misusing substances and are less likely to return to gainful employment. For psychologists working with homeless individuals, helping the person attain sobriety and initiate the recovery lifestyle may be the most important first step in helping them return to successful functioning.

28.2.7 Criminal justice populations

Individuals who become involved in the criminal justice system are generally introduced to the field of psychology though a jail-alternative program, as a contingency of their parole, or during their period of incarceration. Some may be mandated to psychological care through the decision of a drug court. Indeed, the link between substance use and criminal activity has been well established. About half of prison inmates meet DSM criteria for a substance use disorder, and up to 70% meet criteria for a lifetime substance use disorder [29]. In addition, between 67 and 80% of individuals involved in the criminal justice system (i.e., inmates, parolees, and those on probation) have some involvement with drugs or alcohol [30–32]. For example, these individuals may have been convicted of a drug-related crime, they may have committed a crime to support their drug habit, they may have been drunk or high at the time of the crime, or they may have a history of substance addiction. Unfortunately, despite efforts at substance addiction treatment for this population, the overwhelming majority of offenders return to substance misuse within a few years after release from prison [33]. It is clear that alternative rehabilitation options are needed to improve outcomes for this group. Psychologists are currently involved in designing and evaluating treatment options to be used as an adjunct or alternative to incarceration. For example, some contingency-based prison alternative treatments have demonstrated good outcomes [34]. However, more research is needed to determine the most appropriate method and level of care for this group.

28.3 CLINICAL DIAGNOSIS

Within the field of psychology, the importance of screening and brief intervention for substance use disorders has been understood for decades. Substance use may represent an individual's attempt to mask other problems or self-medicate for psychological disturbance. In addition, there can be significant overlap among symptoms of psychological disorders and consequences of substance use. Indeed, diagnostic criteria for virtually all disorders in the DSM-IV note that the diagnosis should not be given if the symptoms can be accounted for by the direct physiological consequences of a substance. Thus, a careful assessment of substance use, abuse, or dependence is necessary to determine the patient's clinical diagnosis and recommended course of care. Substance use disorders may pre-empt or exacerbate mental health problems or interfere with treatment for other conditions. As a result, the psychologist should be aware of all substance use, as it may present a barrier to treatment success and may need to be addressed before other issues can be targeted in treatment.

Unfortunately, most individuals with substance use disorders will not spontaneously discuss their substance use, and most will attempt to minimize or deny their symptoms. As many clinicians fail to adequately inquire about substance use at the patient's initial visit and, generally, do not follow-up with additional questions if the patient does not spontaneously report problematic levels of substance use, substance use disorders frequently remain undiagnosed. Thus, more effort is needed on the part of psychologists to conduct a sufficient substance use assessment with every patient. In order to assist the psychologist with this task, many high-quality screening instruments have been developed. These measures may facilitate the identification of substance use disorders by providing sensitive, standardized questions that can be completed independently or in collaboration with the psychologist. In general, substance use disorder diagnoses should not be based exclusively on a patient's responses to the screening questionnaires. The measures are most useful as a supplement to a comprehensive clinical interview with collateral information. A brief review of some commonly used instruments follows.

- *Addiction Severity Index (ASI)* [35]. The ASI is a comprehensive measure that assesses symptoms of addiction, as well as seven life domains that may contribute to or be affected by substance use, including: Medical status, Employment and support, Drug use, Alcohol use, Legal Status, Family/social status, and Psychiatric status. It is administered in interview format by a trained clinician who provides severity ratings on a 10-point scale. The measure and instructions for administration are offered free-of-charge in the public domain. The ASI contains 142 items and takes about 60 minutes to administer. Validity ratings have been well established.

- *Alcohol Use Disorders Identification Test (AUDIT)* [36]. The AUDIT core measure consists of 10-items used to identify harmful patterns of alcohol use. Items are scored on a scale from zero to four, with higher scores indicating greater problem. Scores of eight or above are suggestive of problematic alcohol use and indicate that further assessment is needed. Additional items comprise a basic clinical screening procedure.

The AUDIT has good psychometric properties and can be completed in a few minutes.

- *Michigan Alcohol Screening Test (MAST)* [37]. The MAST is a brief measure of alcohol consumption habits and consequences. It was developed to be sensitive to the under-reporting of problems that is often exhibited by individuals with alcohol abuse/dependence. The MAST contains 24 yes/no items. Respondents may complete it independently or it may be administered by a clinician. The MAST has excellent reliability and validity.

- *Drug Abuse Screening Test (DAST)* [38]. The DAST is a 28-item measure of drug-taking behavior and associated consequences. Items are scored in a yes = 1, no = 0 format, yielding a possible range of 0–28. A cut-off score of six is recommended to distinguish individuals with drug addiction. The DAST has good psychometric properties and can be administered by a clinician or through self-report.

- *CAGE Questionnaire* [39]. The CAGE is the most commonly used screen for alcohol use disorders. It consists of four questions scored as yes = 1, no = 0, including: (C) Have you ever felt you ought to Cut down on your drinking? (A) Have people Annoyed you by criticizing your drinking? (G) Have you ever felt bad or Guilty about your drinking? (E) Have you ever had a drink first thing in the morning to steady your nerves or to get rid of a hangover (Eye opener)? A score of one detects approximately 90% of alcohol addicts, but results in a 48% false positive rate. A score of two or more can be used as a strong indicator of an alcohol use disorder.

- *CRAFFT Questionnaire* [40]. The CAGE questionnaire is a sensitive measure and easy to administer; however, its utility with younger populations is questionable. The CRAFFT questionnaire was developed to be a more sensitive brief screener for drug and alcohol addiction in adolescents. It consists of six items scored as yes = 1, no = 0, including: (C) Have you ever ridden in a Car driven by someone (including yourself) who was high or had been using alcohol or drugs? (R) Do you ever use alcohol/drugs to Relax, feel better about yourself, or fit in? (A) Do you ever use alcohol/drugs while you are by yourself or Alone? (F) Do you ever Forget things that you did while you are using alcohol/drugs? (F) Do your Family or Friends ever tell you that you should cut down on your drinking or drug use? (T) Have you ever gotten into Trouble while you were using drugs or alcohol? A score of two or higher indicates a potential problem that should be evaluated further.

- *Rutgers Alcohol Problem Index (RAPI)* [41]. The RAPI is a self-report measure of alcohol use and related consequences for adolescent patients. It consists of 23 items, with higher scores indicating a more severe problematic alcohol use. The RAPI has good psychometric properties and can be used effectively as a screening measure.

28.4   CLINICAL COMORBIDITY

Substance use disorders and other mental illnesses are frequently comorbid [4]. In fact, this occurs so commonly that the term "dual diagnosis" was developed to describe the population of individuals who are dealing with both mental illness and a substance use disorder. Research has estimated that, among individuals with a lifetime history of mental illness, 29% also have a lifetime history of a substance use disorder. Among individuals with a serious mental illness (SMI) such as schizophrenia, almost half (47%) have a history of addiction; these rates are compared to the 13.2% of individuals without a history of mental illness who have a substance use disorder [4,5]. In addition, patients who present with "other conditions that may be the focus of clinical attention" (such as relational difficulties, a history of addiction, bereavement, or academic/occupational difficulties, etc.) frequently display increased rates of substance use. In these cases, substance use is often closely tied to the presenting problem. For example, the substance use may contribute to relational difficulties or may represent the individual's maladaptive attempts to cope with the stressor.

However, even within the population of individuals with mental illness, substance addiction is more common among individuals with certain conditions than others. For example, individuals with bipolar disorder have the highest rates of substance use, with about 60% exhibiting a lifetime history of abuse or dependence [5]. On the other hand, Grant and colleagues [42] demonstrated that individuals with other mood disorders generally exhibit significant, but much lower, rates of substance use disorders. In their study, 18–28% of individuals who met criteria for a mood disorder diagnosis within the past year had a concurrent substance use disorder. Similarly, they found that 14–24% of individuals with past-year anxiety disorders also met criteria for drug or alcohol abuse/dependence. Among anxiety and mood disorder patients, those with panic disorder with agoraphobia and generalized anxiety disorder had the highest rates of substance use disorders. Substance use is also very common among individuals with personality disorders, with rates of substance use disorders reaching approximately 50% [42]. However, individuals with somatoform disorders generally display significantly lower rates of substance abuse and dependence. Prevalence in this group ranges from about 2 to 7% for drug and alcohol use disorders, respectively [43].

Other disorders with impulsive/compulsive qualities display high rates of comorbidity with substance use disorders as well. For example, disruptive behavior disorders (e.g., ADHD, conduct disorder, and antisocial personality disorder) are associated with substance use. Hyperactive/impulsive symptoms may be particularly important to the prediction of substance use initiation, even when controlling for conduct disorder [44]. Substance use disorders are quite prevalent among individuals with eating disorders as well. In fact, about 17% of women with eating disorders also have a lifetime history of a substance use disorder [45]. There appear to be many similarities between these disorders, and clinical evidence suggests that some patients may replace disordered eating behaviors with substance misuse and vice versa. Similarly, other "behavioral addictions" such as sexual addiction [46] and pathological gambling [47], show high rates of comorbidity with substance use disorders, particularly in men.

When a patient presents with both mental illness and a substance use disorder, an important step in the diagnostic process is the attempt to determine the sequence whereby the conditions developed.

For example, it is possible that the mental illness led to the development of the substance use disorder (e.g., through attempts at self-medication), the substance use disorder led to the development of the mental illness (e.g., mood disorder symptoms may result from reaction to the consequences of substance use), or the two disorders developed independently [48]. In some cases, this process may help to determine whether the individual actually suffers from two (or more) distinct disorders, or whether the mental illness symptoms can be attributed to the substance use, particularly in the case of polysubstance abuse/dependence, where this may be particularly problematic.

28.5   CLINICAL COURSE

28.5.1   Natural course of substance use disorders

Treatment of substance use disorders can be very challenging, whether comorbid psychopathology is present or not. Indeed, relapse is the rule, rather than the exception among individuals with substance use disorders. As demonstrated by Jellinek [49], the general progression of the substance addict follows a downward curve through a crucial phase during which use increases, into a chronic usage phase. For many, this progression includes deterioration with regard to personal relationships, academic/occupational functioning, financial stability, and more. Unfortunately, for those with an underlying or comorbid psychological disturbance, the consequences of substance use can be even more devastating. After hitting "rock bottom," the substance user generally must choose between maintaining the status quo until death or honestly admitting defeat, expressing a desire for help, and beginning their recovery (which frequently involves entering a treatment/rehabilitation program). Indeed, research has consistently demonstrated that untreated drug and alcohol use disorders are associated with premature death [50,51]. These fatalities may occur due to accidents, illness, or suicide. On the other hand, treatment entry generally marks the beginning of the substance

addict's progressive ascent to the maintenance of stable sobriety and recovery.

28.5.2   Clinical course of treated substance use disorders

Outcomes for individuals who undergo treatment for substance use disorders can vary greatly, with some achieving stable recovery and returning to productivity, and others continuing a chronic cycle of relapse to substance use across their lifespan. Thus far, research has not identified specific patient variables that are associated with treatment failure or success. Rather, treatment retention has emerged as the strongest predictor of outcome. On a related note, the length of sustained abstinence the patient achieves during treatment is associated with improved post-treatment outcome. Those who achieve longer periods of abstinence tend to display shorter and less frequent relapse episodes [52]. Abstinence from other mind-altering substances (e.g., alcohol) can be important as well, because any substance use can lead to relapse to the drug of choice or development of a new addiction [53]. Adjunctive services to improve marital and family relationships, occupational functioning, housing difficulties, social support, and psychological well-being may also help to decrease the likelihood of relapse, because difficulties in these areas may precipitate substance use. These interventions are frequently included as part of a comprehensive treatment program. Unfortunately, most individuals drop out of treatment before discharge is recommended, often within the first few days or sessions. However, the likelihood that a patient will drop out decreases over time. In addition, interventions to improve patient motivation and readiness to change may help to improve treatment retention and decrease drop-out rates.

28.5.3 Role of alcohol and drugs in the course of psychological disturbance

Alcohol and other drugs can have a significant effect on the course of mental illness and other psychological disturbances. For example, substance addiction may precipitate the onset of severe mental illness (e.g., schizophrenia) among individuals with a genetic vulnerability. Similarly, patients with bipolar disorder may find that substance use triggers more rapid cycling between manic and depressive episodes. In some cases, this may result from decreased compliance with mood stabilizing pharmacotherapy while actively using substances. Among individuals with depressive disorders, substance use (particularly alcohol and other depressants) can exacerbate depressive symptoms. The vegetative symptoms of depression (e.g., appetite suppression, reduced libido, fatigue/lack of energy, and sleep problems) are particularly sensitive to the effects of substance use. In fact, alcohol dependence frequently precedes the onset of depression in men. In women, depression more frequently leads to alcohol abuse/dependence [54]. Among eating disorder patients, and particularly those with anorexia nervosa, substance use is associated with worse treatment outcome. Patients who misuse drugs or alcohol may also misuse diet pills or diuretics/laxatives as well. Comorbid anorexia nervosa with a substance use disorder strongly predicts the likelihood of a fatal outcome [55,56]. Anxiety disorders can also be influenced by substance use disorders. For example, substance use (especially stimulants)

and withdrawal can both lead to increased anxiety symptoms. Whereas for some, substance use may reflect an attempt to self-manage anxiety symptoms, for others, drug or alcohol use may ultimately lead to the identification of an underlying anxiety disorder [57]. Unfortunately, mood disorders, eating disorders, and anxiety disorders are associated with increased risk for suicide. Substance addiction contributes an additional risk factor for suicidal ideation, attempts, and completion [58,59] and should be taken very seriously.

Among patients suffering from a personality disorder or other focus of clinical attention, substance use may have a significant impact on the development, treatment, and remission of problems. Patients with "cluster B" personality disorders (e.g., Borderline, Narcissistic, Histrionic, and Antisocial) are particularly likely to exhibit a comorbid substance use disorder, and substance use may exaggerate or exacerbate their personality disorder symptoms. Relational problems (e.g., marital conflict, parent-child conflict, etc.) can also be worsened by substance abuse or dependence. And, as described previously, substance use may interfere with recovery from traumatic experiences such as history of child abuse. As suggested by Miller [60], patients may attempt to self-medicate with substances in order to avoid experiencing the negative symptoms; however, this substance use typically results in increased distress. Psychologists should be aware of this and work with the patient to develop alternative methods of coping.

28.5.4 Biological and behavioral mechanisms in the clinical course of SUDs with comorbid psychological disturbances

Drugs and alcohol have a substantial negative impact on virtually every organ in the human body; however, it can be argued that the brain is most sensitive to the effects of these substances. Given the well-established link between the brain and behavior, it is obvious that substance abuse and dependence would have behavioral consequences that influence the course of psychological disturbances. For example, substance use negatively affects the functioning of the frontal lobe [61], which is important for impulse control, decision making, planning, and delay-of-gratification. These deficits are associated with many psychological problems including mood disorders, conduct disorders, eating disorders, impulse control disorders, relational problems, academic/occupational difficulties, abusive behavior, and so on. Thus, substance use can cause or exacerbate these problems by contributing to functional neurological deficits. And, because substance use affects cognitive processes (i.e., thinking), it can interfere with individuals' ability to face their fears, learn/use adaptive coping strategies, evaluate situations rationally, and effectively problem-solve. This may cause everyday stressors to escalate out of control and contribute to psychological distress, particularly depressive and anxiety symptoms.

In addition, research has demonstrated that drugs and alcohol have such reinforcing effects because they use the same "reward system" in the brain as natural reinforcers, but with a much stronger effect. Thus, substance abuse and dependence reflect the consequences of an acquired drive, which is similar to and competes with natural drives for food, drink, and sex [62]. Unfortunately, due to the magnitude of reinforcement resulting from substance use, the "competition" is relatively one-sided. Individuals with substance use disorders have difficulty choosing alternate activities when the opportunity for substance use presents itself. In addition, previously rewarding activities (e.g., eating palatable foods, building relationships, successfully accomplishing

tasks at work/school, etc.) may seem less desirable by comparison. This can contribute to the development or exacerbation of eating disorders, sexual disorders, marital problems/family conflict, academic/occupational failure, and other problems.

Given its association with behavioral reinforcement, a person's social context (e.g., family, peer network, neighborhood contacts, religious/spiritual community, work colleagues, therapeutic relationship, treatment community, 12-step group, etc.) can serve as both a risk factor and a protective factor for substance use [63]. For example, positive experiences using drugs with peers may contribute to the initiation and escalation of substance use. It may also provide an impetus for relapse. On the other hand, concerns about negative evaluation from friends, family, colleagues, and/or a religious/spiritual community may be important to the prevention of substance use disorders. Individuals suffering from a substance use disorder may eventually enter treatment in order to salvage their relationships with family, and the camaraderie and support they experience during treatment (e.g., in the therapeutic relationship, group therapy, or 12-step meetings) is frequently noted as an important factor in helping recovery. Enlisting the support of a patient's social networks may assist them in being more successful in their recovery. As a result, the psychologist may want to consider conducting couples therapy or family sessions along with individual therapy. Similarly, the psychologist may consider referral to group therapy, special support groups, and/or 12-step meetings.

28.6 PSYCHOLOGICAL TREATMENT OF ALCOHOL AND DRUG USE DISORDERS

For the last several decades, psychologists have been centrally involved in the development of assessment and treatment methods for patients with substance use disorders, as well as the evaluation of these methods [63]. Many case series, open trials, and randomized controlled trials have been conducted in order to evaluate the efficacy of various interventions. Results have indicated that a number of approaches have utility in the treatment of substance use disorders.

28.6.1 Early interventions for problematic drug or alcohol use

As mentioned previously, screening and brief intervention are important to the identification of problematic substance use, substance abuse, and substance dependence, and their treatment. However, many practitioners express concern that they do not have enough time with patients to address these concerns. Compared to other healthcare professionals, psychologists are often afforded more frequent contact (e.g., weekly therapy sessions) of a longer duration (e.g., sessions typically last 45–60 minutes) with their patients. As a result, they are in a unique position to intervene with patients who endorse concerning substance use patterns. Several methods for early intervention with these individuals have been developed and have demonstrated efficacy.

28.6.1.1 Promoting self-change

Though many patients with substance use disorders need formal substance addiction treatment in order to achieve abstinence and stable recovery, the vast majority of individuals who have demonstrated problematic substance use, but who do not meet criteria for substance dependence, actually choose to change their substance use behavior on their own [64]. Self-change has been documented among individuals recovering from problematic drinking, smoking, and drug use, as well as other addiction-like behaviors such as gambling, binge eating, and so on. Thus, psychologists have opportunities to help encourage this progression to "natural recovery" by promoting self-change. Psychologists may use methods including psychoeducation, examining substance use patterns during therapy focused on another condition, and/or through community-based public health interventions. The goal of such interventions is to help raise the salience of the issue to the patient by bringing attention to it, providing information about the negative effects of continued substance use, offering the patient a choice to change their behavior, and assuring the patient that the psychologist is available to support and assist them through this change.

28.6.1.2 Motivational interviewing

Traditional approaches to substance addiction treatment involve the psychologist assuming an "expert" role, confronting the patient's denial, explicitly labeling the problem (e.g., "addiction"), and responding to patient resistance with argumentation and correction. Though this approach can be effective with some patients, it is frequently experienced as unpleasant and punitive, potentially contributing to high rates of patient drop out from substance addiction treatment programs. In order to address this problem, Miller and Rollnick [65,66] developed a new approach, which they termed "motivational interviewing" (MI). Motivational interviewing is a brief, patient-centered, directive approach to substance addiction treatment. The approach emphasizes personal choice and responsibility on the part of the patient. Labeling of the problem is not considered an important part of the change process; rather, the clinician attempts to meet the patient where they are with regard to the stages of change. The focus is on helping the patient to move from precontemplation/contemplation to action/maintenance. In addition, the therapeutic relationship is conceptualized as balanced and collaborative; the patient is viewed as the "expert" on his/her own experience. As a result, the clinician works with the patient to elicit his or her own personal reasons for change and helps the patient to develop a change plan. Resistance is conceptualized as an interpersonal process that is influenced by the clinician's behavior. The major goals of motivational interviewing are to decrease the patient's ambivalence about the importance of making a change in their substance use, support the patient's self-efficacy in making the change, and assist the patient in developing reasonable goals to increase the likelihood of success. Motivational interviewing sessions are individually tailored to the patient's problem severity and readiness to change. For example, the goal of motivational interviewing for some patients might be to help prepare them for more intensive treatment in a specialized program. For others, motivational interviewing sessions might focus on achieving and maintaining abstinence. Motivational interviewing interventions are generally brief and may range from one 15-minute encounter to several full-length sessions. Results of over 100 clinical trials have demonstrated the efficacy of motivational interviewing in helping people change their behavior.

28.6.1.3   12-Step facilitation

For many individuals who suffer from a substance use disorder, participation in 12-step programs (e.g., Alcoholics Anonymous, Narcotics Anonymous) is beneficial in helping them to achieve and maintain stable sobriety [67]. Research has demonstrated that 12-step group participation is well accepted and beneficial for individuals with dual diagnosis as well [68]. Unfortunately, some individuals with substance use disorders are hesitant to participate in 12-step programs due to pre-existing attitudes or beliefs, anxiety, embarrassment, or other reasons. As a result, psychologists can have a positive influence on patients with substance use disorders by providing psychoeducation about 12-step programs and encouraging the patient to participate. This intervention, described as "12-step facilitation" [69] has emerged as a useful psychological intervention for individuals with substance use disorders. Psychologists who provide 12-step facilitation meet with the patient on a weekly basis (typically for 12 weeks) and focus on three "core topics" as well as some elective topics. The primary foci include: (1) introducing the patient to the 12-step philosophy, (2) working with the patient to complete the first three steps, and (3) encouraging the patient to become actively involved in a 12-step program such as Alcoholics Anonymous, Narcotics Anonymous, or Double Trouble in Recovery (for dual diagnosis patients). Patients are encouraged to attend meetings, connect with other group members, and identify a sponsor. Throughout 12-step facilitation therapy, the clinician may assign the patient readings from 12-step publications.

28.6.1.4   Contingency management

For some, initiation of abstinence can be particularly difficult. However, certain interventions, such as voucher-based reinforcement therapy (VBRT), can be particularly helpful at this crucial point [70]. VBRT is a contingency management intervention in which the substance user earns rewards for abstinence. Typically, abstinence is verified by urine screening (or sometimes breathalyzer screening for alcohol use). Upon provision of a substance-negative sample, the patient is given a voucher with preset value that can be used to "purchase" desired items and prizes. Most VBRT interventions use an escalating value schedule, in which the patient receives increasingly larger rewards for consecutive substance-negative samples. In addition, provision of a substance-positive sample generally results in a reset of the vouchers to the entry-level value. Patients can generally earn the right to resume their previous value level after submitting a predetermined number of consecutive negative samples. VBRT has demonstrated efficacy in helping individuals achieve abstinence from cocaine and other stimulants, opioids, marijuana, tobacco, and alcohol. In addition, it has been effective in increasing patient's compliance with medications to limit substance use, such as disulfiram [70].

28.6.2   Psychological interventions for substance use disorders

Psychological interventions represent an important component of substance addiction treatment. Substance use disorders are chronic disorders with both physiological and behavioral components. Treatment of such a condition involves changing deeply-embedded behaviors and requires a great deal of effort. As a result, development of positive skills to cope with challenges and stressors is crucial. In addition, many individuals with substance use disorders have damaged relationships due to their substance use. They may require assistance in the reparation of these relationships and development of goals for future interpersonal interactions. Thus, psychosocial treatments are generally designed to help the patient understand the nature of addiction, achieve sobriety, improve functioning across lifestyle domains, repair relationships, and return to a productive lifestyle. Finally, prevention of relapse is an important task, as this is a very common concern among this population. Patients should be prepared for the challenges they will face in maintaining a sober lifestyle, and they should be taught ways to resume recovery in the event of a relapse to substance use.

28.6.2.1 Cognitive behavioral therapy

In most treatment programs, cognitive behavioral therapy (CBT) serves as the foundation for psychosocial intervention with substance use disorder patients. This approach may combine psychoeducation, functional analysis, skill building, environmental modification and contingency management, examination of dysfunctional thinking, coping skills training, and other techniques. Efforts at psychoeducation may include in-session teaching, bibliotherapy, and/or attendance at specialized lectures, programs, or support groups. Next, the psychologist and patient will likely complete a comprehensive evaluation of factors contributing to the patient's substance use (e.g., dysfunctional beliefs, environmental triggers, lack of confidence, and internal and external reinforcers). After doing so, the psychologist can engage the patient in more adaptive thinking, work to address barriers to sobriety, teach alternative coping strategies, and assist the patient in identifying and eliciting social support. For some patients, group CBT may be beneficial in confronting denial, providing the patients with opportunities to share success stories and strategies, allowing patients to learn from other's experiences, and helping patients to develop a support network.

28.6.2.2 Marital/family therapy

Substance use by one family member can have a profound negative effect on other members of the family. Relationships are damaged, trust is broken, family resources may be strained, and structure is frequently replaced by chaos. These problems can lead to the development of psychological disturbance among spouses, parents, and children of the addict. As a result, marital and/or family therapy can be a useful component of care. Research has repeatedly demonstrated the efficacy of this approach in improving treatment retention and helping individuals to attain the recovery lifestyle [71]. When the family is involved, there is generally a higher level of commitment to treatment participation and support of the patient in learning

to manage their substance use disorder. Marital therapy often focuses on improving communication between the individuals, restoring trust, teaching the spouse how to support the patient in his/her recovery, and helping the spouse to work through feelings of anger, guilt, anxiety, and depression related to the current situation. Family therapy is particularly helpful when children are involved and affected by the individual's substance use. Children are likely to experience emotional distress due to increased family conflict and chaos when either a parent or sibling is misusing substances. In addition, the patient may feel isolated and ostracized from the family. Given that social support can be so important to the outcome of treatment for substance use disorders, family therapy provides a structured setting in which family members can express their support and learn ways to cope with difficult situations and assist the patient's efforts at recovery.

28.6.2.3 Relapse prevention

Finally, given that relapse is the rule, rather than the exception, for substance use disorder patients, efforts to decrease the likelihood and frequency of relapse comprise a crucial part of the psychological intervention. Marlatt and Gordon [72] developed a model termed "relapse prevention" to help patients prepare for the recovery lifestyle. This model includes an assessment of both immediate determinants and covert antecedents that contribute to relapse [73]. For example, the clinician provides psychoeducation regarding relapse (i.e., abstinence violation) and explains that one slip does not equal complete failure, as such feelings of guilt may be associated with resumed substance use. Slips are generally referred to as a "lapse" rather than a "relapse" to highlight the fact that such an event does not signal a complete return to the devastating situation that the patient likely experienced before first attempting sobriety. Similarly, the clinician works to support the patient's feelings of self-efficacy related to refusing substance use and maintaining sobriety. They work together to review which situations are associated with a high risk for substance use and ways to avoid or minimize exposure to these situations. Next, the clinician teaches coping skills to use in place of substance use, and helps the patients to adjust expectancies regarding life without their substance of choice. In relapse prevention, the clinician also works with the patient regarding ways to manage urges and cravings to use. Research has repeatedly supported the use of relapse prevention techniques in helping individuals to maintain recovery.

28.6.3 Management of psychological disturbance in patients with SUDs

When treating individuals in psychological practice, clinicians should consider the following five suggestions offered by Nace and Tinsley [48] for clinicians treating patients with a dual diagnosis. Firstly, be sure to screen all patients for dual diagnosis, as this is a common concern for individuals seeking treatment. Secondly, be aware that, even if the two seem related, both the substance use disorder and psychological disturbance represent distinct conditions that will require specialized treatment. Symptoms of one condition should not be excused as secondary to the other condition. Thirdly, allow flexibility in the treatment plan in order to address the more severe condition first. The goal should be to minimize risk to the patient while maximizing the likelihood of treatment retention and success. Fourthly, remember that relapse is likely to occur. Most patients are better served by responding with empathy and encouraging open communication, rather than exhibiting a critical or punitive response. Finally, psychologists should encourage patients with a dual diagnosis to continue regular appointments with their psychiatrist if they are taking psychotropic medications. This may be particularly important in the case of a relapse, as maintaining psychiatric stability is crucial to the reestablishment of sobriety.

28.7 CONCLUSIONS

Substance use disorders (SUDs) can cause devastating consequences and are very common among patients seen in psychology practice. Comorbidity of psychological disturbance with substance use disorders is extremely high in some populations and among individuals with certain psychiatric conditions. However, many patients with substance use disorders go undiagnosed and are not offered appropriate intervention. Inclusion of screening instruments for substance use disorders in the general intake assessment process may help psychologists to identify individuals who would benefit from substance use disorder treatment. In addition, assessment for substance misuse should be repeated throughout the course of treatment, as patients may be less likely to deny substance use once they have established rapport with the clinician. It is noteworthy that substance use disorders are treatable. Both psychosocial and pharmacological interventions have demonstrated efficacy in helping individuals achieve sobriety, maintain a recovery lifestyle, and return to adaptive functioning and productivity.

REFERENCES

1. ONDCP (2004) The economic costs of drug abuse in the United States, 1992–2002 (No. 207303). Washington DC, Executive Office of the President.
2. Rawson, R. (1990–1991) Chemical dependency treatment: the integration of the alcoholism and drug abuse/use treatment system. *Int. J. Addict.* (Special Anniversary Edition), **25**, 1515–1536.
3. Hasin, D.S., Stinson, F.S., Ogburn, E., and Grant, B.F. (2007) Prevalence, correlates, disability, and comorbidity of DSM-IV alcohol abuse and dependence in the United States. *Arch. Gen. Psychiatry*, **64** (7), 830–842.
4. Regier, D.A., Narrow, W.E., Rae, D.S. *et al.* (1993) The defacto U.S. mental and addictive disorders service system: Epidemiologic Catchment Area prospective one-year prevalence rates of disorders and services. *Arch. Gen. Psychiatry*, **50**, 85–94.
5. Regier, C.A., Farmer, M.E., and Rae, D.S. (1990) Comorbidity of mental disorders with alcohol and other drug abuse results from the Epidemiologic Catchment Area (ECA) Study. *JAMA*, **264**, 2511–2518.

6. Grunbaum, J.A., Kann, L., Kinchen, S. *et al.* (2003) Youth risk behavior surveillance – United States. *Morb. Mortal. Wkly. Rep.*, **53** (2), 1–96.

7. Rao, U., Daley, S.E., and Hammen, C. (2000) Relationship between depression and substance use disorders in adolescent women during the transition to adulthood. *J. Am. Acad. Child Psy.*, **39** (2), 215–222.

8. Star, J.E., Bober, D., and Gold, M.S. (2005) Double trouble: depression and alcohol abuse in the adolescent patient. *Psych. Annals*, **35** (6), 496–502.

9. Reich, J. and Thompson, W.D. (1985) Marital status of schizophrenic and alcoholic patients. *J. Nerv. Ment. Dis.*, **173**, 499–502.

10. Collins, R.L., Ellickson, P.L., and Klein, D.J. (2007) The role of substance use in young adult divorce. *Addiction*, **102**, 786–794.

11. Thomas, E.J., and Ager, R.D. (1993) Unilateral family therapy with spouses of uncooperative alcohol drinkers, in *Treating Alcohol Problems: Marital and Family Interventions* (ed. T.J. O'Farrell), Guilford Press, New York, pp. 3–33.

12. Halford, W.K. and Osgarby, S.M. (1993) Alcohol abuse in individuals presenting for marital therapy. *J. Fam. Psychol.*, **11**, 1–13.

13. O' Farrell, T.J., Kleinke, C., and Cutter, H.S.G. (1986) Differences between alcoholic couples accepting and rejecting an offer of outpatient marital therapy. *Am. J. Drug Alcohol Abuse*, **12**, 301–310.

14. Young, N. (1997) Alcohol and other drugs: The scope of the problem among pregnant and parenting women in California. *J. Psychoactive Drugs*, **29**, 3–22.

15. SAMHSA (2005) Substance Use During Pregnancy: 2002 and 2003 Update, SAMHSA, Rockville, MD.

16. Daley, M., Argeriou, M., and McCarty, D. (1998) Substance abuse treatment for pregnant women: A window of opportunity? *Addict. Behav.*, **23**, 239–249.

17. Phillips, M.A. and Murrell, S.A. (1994) Impact of psychological and physical health, stressful events, and social support on subsequent mental health help seeking among older adults. *J. Consult. Clin. Psychol.*, **62** (2), 270–275.

18. Gffoerer, J.C. and Epstein, I.F. (1999) Marijuana initiates and their impact on future drug abuse treatment need. *Drug Alcohol Depend.*, **54**, 229–237.

19. SAMHSA (2004) Results from the 2003 National Survey on Drug Use and Health: National findings. Office of Applied Studies, NSDUH Series H-25 2004, Rockville, MD.

20. Simoni-Wastila, L. and KeriYang, H. (2006) Psychoactive drug abuse in older adults. *Am. J. Geriatr. Pharmacother.*, **4**, 380–394.

21. Clark, D.B., DeBellis, M.D., Lynch, K.G. *et al.* (2003) Physical and sexual abuse, depression and alcohol use disorders in adolescents: onsets and outcomes. *Drug Alcohol Depend.*, **69** (1), 51–60.

22. Miller, R. and Downs, W. (1993) The impact of family violence on the use of alcohol by women. *Alcohol and Health Research World*, **17**, 137–143.

23. Jacobson, N. and Gottman, J. (1998) *When Men Batter Women: New Insights into Ending Abusive Relationships*, Simon and Schuster, New York.

24. Brookoff, D., O'Brien, K., Cook, C. *et al.* (1997) Characteristics of participants in domestic violence: assessment at the scene of domestic assault. *JAMA*, **277**, 1369–1373.

25. Fagan, J., Stewart, D., and Hansen, K. (1983) Violent men or violent husbands: background factors and situational correlates, in *The Dark Side of Families* (D. Finkelhor, R.J. Gelles, G.T. Hotaling, and M.A. Straus), Sage, Beverly Hills, CA, pp. 49–67.

26. Martens, W.H. (2001) Homelessness and mental disorders: A comparative review of populations in various countries. *Int. J. Mental Health*, **30** (4), 79–96.

27. Burt, M.R. and Aron, L.Y. (2001) *Helping America's Homeless*, Urban Institute, Washington, DC.

28. Toro, P.A., Bellavia, C.W., Daeschler, C.V., *et al.* (1995) Distinguishing homelessness from poverty: A comparative study. *J. Consult. Clin. Psychol.*, **63**, 280–289.

29. Peters, R.H., Greenbaum, P.E., Edens, J.F. *et al.* (1998) Prevalence of DSM-IV substance abuse and dependence disorders among prison inmates. *Am. J. Drug Alcohol Abuse*, **24**, 573–587.

30. Belenko, S. and Peugh, J. (1998) Behind Bars: Substance Abuse and America's Prison Population, National Center on Addiction and Substance Abuse at Columbia University, New York.

31. Bureau of Justice Statistics (2001) Trends in State Parole, 1990–2000, US Department of Justice, Washington, DC.

32. Bureau of Justice Statistics (1998) Substance Abuse and Treatment of Adults on Probation 1995, US Department of Justice, Washington, DC.

33. Martin, S.S., Butzin, C.C.A., Saum, S.A., and Inciardi, J.A. (1999) Three-year outcomes of therapeutic community treatment for drug-involved offenders in Delaware. *Prison Journal*, **79**, 294–320.

34. Marlowe, D.B. and Wong, C.J. (2008) Contingency management in adult criminal drug courts, in *Contingency Management in Substance Abuse Treatment* (eds S.T. Higgins and S.H. Heil), Guilford, New York.

35. McLellan, A., Luborsky, L., Woody, G., and O'Brien, C. (1980) An improved diagnostic evaluation instrument for substance abuse patients: the Addiction Severity Index. *J. Nerv. Ment. Dis.*, **168**, 26–33.

36. Bohn, M.J., Babor, T.F., and Kranzler, H.R. (1995) The Alcohol Use Disorders Identification Test: Validation of a screening instrument for use in medical settings. *J. Stud. Alcohol*, **56**, 423–432.

37. Selzer, M.L. (1971) The Michigan Alcohol Screening Test: the quest for a new diagnostic instrument. *Am. J. Psychiatry*, **127** (12), 1653–1658.

38. Skinner, H.A. (1982) The Drug Abuse Screening Test. *Addict. Behav.*, **7**, 363–371.

39. Ewing, J.A. (1984) Detecting alcoholism: the CAGE questionnaire. *JAMA*, **252** (14), 1905–1907.

40. Knight, J.R., Shrier, L.A., Bravender, T.D. *et al.* (1999) A new brief screen for adolescent substance abuse. *Arch. Pediatr. Adolesc. Med.*, **153** (6), 591–596.

41. White, H.R., and Labouvie, E.W. (1989) Towards the assessment of adolescent problem drinking. *J. Stud. Alcohol*, **50** (1), 30–37.

42. Grant, B.F., Stinson, F.S., Dawson, D.A. *et al.* (2004) Prevalence and co-occurance of substance use disorders and independent mood and anxiety disorders: results from the National Epidemiologic Survey on Alcohol and Related Conditions. *Arch. Gen. Psychiatry*, **61** (8), 807–816.

43. Simon, G.E. and Von Korff, M. (1991) Somatization and psychiatric disorder in the NIMH epidemiologic catchment area study. *Am. J. Psychiatry*, **148**, 1494–1500.

44. Elkins, I.J., McGue, M., and Iacono, W. (2007) Prospective effects of attention deficit/hyperactivity disorder, conduct disorder, and sex on adolescent substance use and abuse. *Arch. Gen. Psychiatry*, **64** (10), 1145–1152.

45. Herzog, D.B., Franko, D.L., Dorer, D.J. *et al.* (2006) Drug abuse in women with eating disorders. *Int. J. Eat. Disord.*, **39**, 364–368.

46. Black, D.W. (2000) The epidemiology and phenomenology of compulsive sexual behavior. *CNS Spectrums*, **5**, 26–72.

47. Dannon, P.N., Lowengrub, K., Shalgi, B. *et al.* (2006) Dual psychiatric diagnosis and substance abuse in pathological gamblers: a preliminary gender comparison study. *J. Addict. Dis.*, **25** (3), 49–54.

48. Nace, E.P., Birkmayer, F., Sullivan, M.A. *et al.* (2007) Socially sanctioned coercion mechanisms for addiction treatment. *Am. J. Addict.*, **16**, 15–23. doi: 10.1080/10550490601077783

49. Jellinek, E.M. (1960) *The Disease Concept of Alcoholism*, Hillhouse, Oxford.

50. Price, R.P., Risk, N.K., Murray, K.S. *et al.* (2001) Twenty-five year mortality of US servicemen deployed in Vietnam: predictive utility of early drug use. *Drug Alcohol Depend.*, **64**, 309–318.

51. Timko, C., DeBenedetti, A., Moos, B.S., and Moos, R. H. (2006) Predictors of 16-year mortality among individuals initiating help-seeking for an alcoholic use disorder. *Alcohol. Clin. Exp. Res.*, **30**, 1711–1720.

52. Higgins, S.T., Badger, G.J., and Budney, A.J. (2000) Initial abstinence and success in achieving longer term cocaine abstinence. *Exp. Clin. Psychopharmacol.*, **8**, 377–386.

53. DeLeon, G. (1993) What psychologists can learn from addiction treatment research. *Psychol. Addict. Behav.*, **7** (2), 103–109.

54. Helzer, J. and Pryzbeck, T. (1988) The co-occurence of alcoholism with other psychiatric disorders in the general population and its impact on treatment. *J. Stud. Alcohol*, **49**, 210–224.

55. Herzog, D.B., Greenwood, D.N., Dorer, D.J. *et al.* (2000) Mortality in eating disorders: a descriptive study. *Int. J. Eat. Disord.*, **28**, 20–26.

56. Keel, P.K. and Klump, K.L. (2003) Are eating disorders culture-bound syndromes? Implications for conceptualizing their etiology. *Psychol. Bull.*, **129**, 747–769.

57. Brady, K.T. (2004) Substance dependence and anxiety disorders, in *Dual Diagnosis and Psychiatric Treatment*, 2nd edn (eds H.R. Kranzlerand J.A. Tinsley), Mercel Dekker, New York.

58. Garrison, C.Z., McKeown, R.E., Valois, R.F., and Vincent, M.L. (1993) Aggression, substance use, and suicidal behaviors in high school students. *Am. J. Public Health*, **83** (2), 179–184.

59. Woods, E.R., Lin, Y.G., Middleman, A. *et al.* (1997) The associations of suicide attempts in adolescents. *Pediatrics*, **99** (6), 791–796.

60. Miller, D. (2002) Addictions and trauma recovery: an integrated approach. *Psychiatric Quarterly*, **73** (2), 157–170.

61. Goldstein, R.Z. and Volkow, N.D. (2002) Drug addiction and its underlying neurobiological basis: neuroimaging evidence for the involvement of the frontal cortex. *Am. J. Psychiatry*, **159**, 1642–1652.

62. Kreek, M.J. and Koob, G.F. (1998) Drug dependence: stress and dysregulation of brain reward pathways. *Drug Alcohol Depend.*, **51**, 230–247.

63. Gifford, E. and Humphreys, K. (2007) The psychological science of addiction. *Addiction*, **102**, 352–361.

64. Klingemann, H.and Sobell, L.C. (eds) (2007) *Promoting Self-Change from Addictive Behaviors: Practical Implications for Policy, Prevention, and Treatment*, Springer, New York.

65. Miller, W.R. and Rollnick, S. (1991) *Motivational Interviewing: Preparing People to Change Addictive Behavior*, Guilford Press, New York.

66. Miller, W.R. and Rollnick, S. (2002) *Motivational Interviewing: Preparing People for Change*, Guilford Press, New York.

67. Chappel, J.N. and DuPont, R.L. (1999) Twelve-step and mutual-help programs for addictive disorders. *Psych. Clin. North Am.*, **22** (2), 425–446.

68. Bogenschutz, M.P., Geppert, C.M.A., and George, J. (2006) The role of twelve-step approaches in dual diagnosis treatment and recovery. *Am. J. Addict.*, **15**, 50–60. doi: 10.1080/10550490500419060

69. Nowinski, J. and Baker, S. (1992) *The Twelve-Step Facilitation Handbook: A Systematic Approach to Early Recovery from Alcoholism and Addiction*, Lexington Books, New York.

70. Higgins, S.T., Silverman, K.,and Heil, S.H. (eds) (2008) *Contingency Management in Substance Abuse Treatment*, Guildford Press, New York.

71. Stanton, M.D. and Shandish, W.R. (1997) Outcome, attrition, and family couples treatment for drug abuse: A meta-analysis and review of the controlled comparative studies. *Psychol. Bull.*, **22** (2), 170–191.

72. Marlatt, G.A.and Gordon, J.R. (eds) (1985) *Relapse Prevention: Maintenance Strategies in the Treatment of Addictive Behaviors*, Guilford Press, New York.

73. Larimer, M.E., Palmer, R.S., and Marlatt, G.A. (1999) Relapse prevention. An overview of Marlatt's cognitive-behavioral model. *Alcohol Res. Health*, **23** (2), 151–160.

29

Addictive disorders in diseases of women

Deborah V. Gross,[1] C. Chapman Sledge,[2] and Ellen A. Ovson[3]

[1] Medical Director, A Bridge to Recovery, 361 Towne Center Blvd. Suite 1300, Ridgeland, MS 39157, USA
[2] Chief Medical Officer, Cumberland Heights, P.O. Box 90727, Nashville, TN 37209
[3] 2255 Broadway Drive, Hattiesburg, MS 39402

29.1 INTRODUCTION

Ms Addy is a 42-year old mother of three whom you've been seeing for several months for new onset hypertension. She has no obvious risk factors and no family history of the disease, nor has she responded very well to the medication you've prescribed. She has a stressful professional job and she missed her last appointment with you. Today she comes in crying, complaining of headaches, depression, anxiety, insomnia, and problems with her husband. She tells you that she is up against a deadline at work and is also having difficulties with her boss. She would like something for sleep and maybe for anxiety and depression as well. What she doesn't say is that she is drinking herself to sleep every night and has been for more than a year.

Women are different from men. Research has begun to take this into account, but much more work is needed, especially with addicted women. In an excellent review [1], Zilberman et al. point out the documented differences in screening, physiological effects of substances, medical consequences, psychiatric comorbidity, craving, family issues, and developmental perspectives. Covington [2,3] has outlined characteristics of "gender responsive treatment." Addicted women who are pregnant present special challenges [4].

A woman generally thinks and views her problems in emotional and relational terms. She presents for help accordingly. She is much more likely to come to you with complaints of depression, insomnia, and/or life stresses than to say she has a problem with drugs or alcohol. Some of this relates to the denial inherent to the addictive disorders but it's also a function of the way she sees the world. She will tend to think that her relationship problems cause the drinking, for example, and that the solution is to work on the relationship. She may continue to believe this long after the addiction has taken on a life of its own.

Addicted women present to primary treatment centers less often than men and tend to access healthcare systems through family doctors, internists, obstetricians and gynecologists, psychiatrists, or therapists [5]. Screening and intervention in these settings thus becomes especially important. You may be her only chance at early diagnosis and treatment.

Addictive Disorders in Medical Populations Edited by Norman S. Miller and Mark S. Gold

29.2   PREVALENCE OF ADDICTIVE DISORDERS IN WOMEN

The history of the American woman and addiction, with links to social inequality and dependence on men (including their doctors) has been well summarized [6]. Early studies of addiction involved only men. Recognizing the gap and concerned about the rapidly increasing number of AIDS cases in women, the National Institute on Drug Abuse (NIDA) sponsored a conference in 1994 to present findings, issues, and challenges regarding women with addictive disorder. Summaries and discussions from this meeting were published in 1998 [7].

Greenfield [8] has pointed out the gender bias still present in research on alcohol dependence in the early 1990s. Male populations were used, with findings generalized to both genders, though women are more sensitive to alcohol, have faster onset of medical morbidity and have greater mortality associated with accidents and violence which are alcohol related [9].

Greenfield's [10] review of the English language literature from 1975 to 2005 found that 90% of the studies investigating gender differences in substance addiction treatment outcomes were published since 1990 and 40% of those were published since the year 2000. Only 11.8% of these studies were randomized clinical trials.

Throughout history, society has held women to a double standard with regard to alcohol and drug use, which has been more socially acceptable for men. Woman's role in society dictated these

standards [11], and women who drink or use drugs have traditionally been more stigmatized. Until recently, women used less alcohol and illicit drugs than men. This relative epidemiological "advantage" is disappearing [12].

Prescription drugs are another story. During the nineteenth century, women were prescribed addictive drugs, particularly opium, for a variety of ailments. By the end of the century, the majority of opium and morphine addicts in the United States were women [13]. This socially acceptable pattern of prescription drug use continued through the twentieth century with amphetamines and sedatives [14]. Women remain more likely than men to be prescribed medications with addiction liability, including sedatives, stimulants, and opioids [15].

The so-called "gender gap" is closing, as more and more girls and women are using and becoming addicted to alcohol and drugs relative to men. In the 2006 National Survey on Drug Use and Health (NSDUH) [16], 45.2% of females aged 12 and over reported current use of alcohol (defined as any use in the past thirty days) compared to 57.0% of men (Figure 29.1). However, current alcohol use among youths between the ages of 12 and 17 is nearly identical: 17.0% for females and 16.3% for males. For women between the ages of 18 and 25, 57.9% reported current alcohol use, compared to 65.9% of men the same age (Figure 29.2).

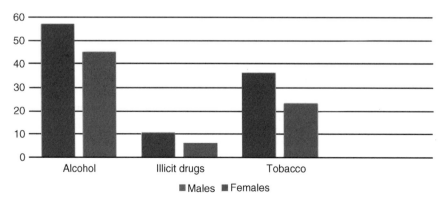

Figure 29.1   Current substance use: age 12 and over (Compiled by Dr Sledge from NSDUH data in Ref. [16].)

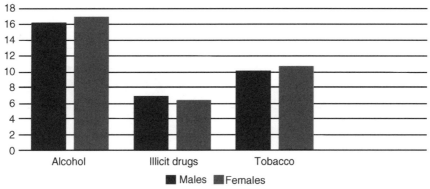

Figure 29.2 Current substance use: ages 12–17 (Compiled by Dr Sledge from NSDUH data in Ref. [16].)

Females over age 12 were less likely to report current illicit drug use than males: 6.2% of women compared to 10.5% of men. Current marijuana use was about half that of men (4.1 vs. 8.1%). Rates of current use of stimulants (0.5%), MDMA (0.2%), oxycodone (0.1%), and LSD (0.1%) were virtually identical.

As with alcohol use, the rates of illicit drug use in girls and boys aged 12–17 is very similar: 6.4% for girls and 6.8% for boys. Women over age 12 reported current nonmedical use of prescription drugs at 2.5%; 3.2% of men in this age group were current users. For adolescents, though, the rate of current nonmedical use of prescription drugs was 3.5% for girls and 3.1% for boys [16].

Current use of tobacco was reported by 23.3% of women over age 12 compared to 36.4% of men. Among adolescents, however, current tobacco use is nearly the same for girls (10.7%) as for boys (10.0%) [16]. Women have been getting lung cancer and other diseases from smoking cigarettes at increasing rates as we see the end result of coming "a long way, baby."

Among pregnant women, 11.8% reported current alcohol use, 2.9% reported binge alcohol use, and 0.7% reported heavy alcohol use. These rates were much lower than nonpregnant women in the same age group (53.0, 23.6, and 5.4%, respectively).

Binge drinking has decreased significantly in pregnant women compared to data from recent years. 4% of pregnant women reported current illicit drug use compared to 10.0% in the same age group of nonpregnant women [16].

The rate of drug use during pregnancy has been constant in recent years: 16.5% of pregnant women reported current cigarette use compared to 29.5% of nonpregnant women in the same age group. Though older pregnant women were less likely to smoke cigarettes than a matched sample of nonpregnant women, pregnant adolescents smoked at higher rates than their nonpregnant peers [16].

The overall rate of substance addiction or dependence in women is about half that of men. In 2006, NSDUH data [16] indicated that 6.3% of women received a diagnosis of substance addiction or dependence in the previous year compared to 12.3% of men. For the age group 12–17, however, the rate of substance addiction or dependence was 8.1% for females and 8.0% for males (Figure 29.3). For this younger cohort, the gender gap is closed.

Remember!

Current teenaged girls and boys have the same rate of Substance Use Disorder!

29.3 ROLE OF ALCOHOL AND DRUGS IN THE DISEASES OF WOMEN

You screened Ms Addy and determined that she was drinking excessively. You talked to her about it

(intervened), set a goal for reducing her drinking and referred her and her husband for couples'

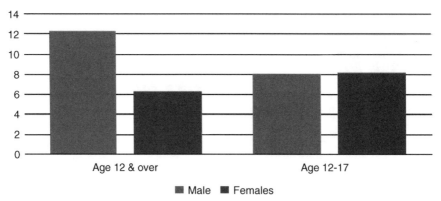

Figure 29.3   Substance addiction or dependence in previous year (Compiled by Dr Sledge from NSDUH data in Ref. [16].)

therapy. She looks much better at her next visit and reports that she was able to stick with the drinking goals you and she had set. Her blood pressure is normal.

There are physical (sexual) differences between men and women which affect the development of addiction and its health toll. There are also social and environmental (gender) differences which strongly influence the woman's response to intervention and treatment [2].

Alcohol has been studied more than any other substance both in women and in men. Women start drinking later than men, start drinking addictively later than men and drink quantitatively less than men. However, women progress to serious alcohol-related problems faster and go into treatment sooner, a phenomenon first named telescoping by Piazza *et al.*, in 1989 [17] and later replicated in Project MATCH [18] and by others [19,20].

Women have a lower percentage of body water. Alcohol is thus less diluted in women than in men and is transported to the organs (all of them) at a higher concentration. Alcohol is first pass metabolized in the gastric mucosa via alcohol dehydrogenase. Women have less of this enzyme, so more pure ethanol circulates in the system before getting to the liver. Alcohol dehydrogenase decreases in anyone with alcohol dependence but in alcohol-dependent women it virtually disappears, so much of the alcohol an alcohol-dependent woman consumes is absorbed from the gastrointestinal mucosa as ethanol. These differences, in addition to hormo-

nal influences, estrogen in particular, may account for the telescoping effects of alcohol in women [21,22].

Remember!

Women Get Sicker Quicker!

"Telescoping" is the process by which the effect of excessive alcohol is magnified in women compared to men. Despite consumption of lower quantities of alcohol, medical consequences in women are more severe and occur earlier in the course of the addictive disorder.

In both men and women, failure to recognize the presence of addictive disorder can result in progression of the disease and further damage to mind and body [23]. End-stage alcoholism looks similar in men and women, but telescoping sets the clock ticking for women and makes early diagnosis and intervention even more imperative [24].

HIV and AIDS, other sexually transmitted diseases, domestic violence, and every common psychiatric disorder with the exception of Antisocial Personality Disorder are all strongly comorbid with addictive disorders in women [25–28].

Psychiatric comorbidity is addressed elsewhere in this book, but for women, psychiatric disorders more often precede substance use disorder (opposite for men). This is especially true for Major Depressive Disorder and appears to relate to distinct genetic and environmental risk factors across genders [1,29]. Among depressed alcoholics, depression tends to be more severe in women, whereas alcoholism is more severe in men. Treating the comorbid psychiatric condition is crucial for recovery in either gender, and the presence of addictive disease hampers recovery from any psychiatric condition.

In a prospective study using a clinical sample of men and women with alcohol dependence, Greenfield *et al.* [30] found remarkably little difference by gender in response to inpatient treatment. They hypothesized that perhaps alcohol exerts its most gender specific effects in physiological responses to alcohol (greater vulnerability for women), onset of adverse medical consequences (faster for women), and barriers to treatment (more for women), so that by the time women actually get to inpatient treatment, the gender differences are not so marked.

29.4 MORBIDITY FROM ALCOHOL AND DRUGS, INCLUDING GENDER SPECIFICITY

Progression from the casual use of alcohol and drugs to dependence is accelerated in women compared to men. Women move from first use to dependence on cocaine, heroin, and marijuana more rapidly than men and their risk of cocaine-induced cognitive impairment and strokes is greater [31].

Women are more vulnerable to alcohol-related cognitive impairments and liver disease, which occur after a woman drinks less for a shorter time than her male counterpart. The prevalence of alcohol-related medical problems seems to be similar between women and men but problems occur sooner for women, especially fatty liver, hypertension, malnutrition, and gastrointestinal hemorrhage [32]. Even correcting for blood alcohol levels, women progress to cirrhosis much more rapidly and the risk of progression continues despite abstinence [33]. Estrogen may be a factor in the increased susceptibility of women to alcoholic liver disease [34].

The incidence of alcoholic cardiomyopathy is higher for women at any given dose of alcohol. The risk of hemorrhagic stroke is increased in women who consume over two drinks per day [33].

Breast cancer is more frequent in alcoholic women, with an estimated 9% increased risk for each 10-gram (standard drink = 14 grams) increase in alcohol consumption up to total intake of 60 grams per day [33]. Even in middle-aged and elderly women who consume one drink per day, the risk compared to nondrinkers is 30% higher [35].

Remember!

Addicted Women Have Greater Health Risks!

Older women may be even more vulnerable to the effects of alcohol and drugs. Heavy drinking in this population correlates with increased risk of osteoporosis, impaired activities of daily living, and poorer psychosocial functioning. Older women who drink heavily (perhaps unknown to their doctors) may be prescribed sedatives or pain medication which can further increase their risk of substance-related morbidity [24].

The tendency for women with addictive disorders to drink or use drugs in response to loss and crisis may be magnified in the older population because loss is so common in this phase of life. The increasing use and abuse of prescription narcotics by the older woman is of particular concern. Her cognitive impairment and traumatic injuries may be assumed to be age-related when they are actually caused by a treatable addictive disorder.

29.5 MORTALITY FROM ALCOHOL AND DRUGS, INCLUDING GENDER SPECIFICITY

Gender specific mortality data for women are limited, but over the past three decades in England alcohol-related death rates for women have almost doubled and death by alcoholic cirrhosis in women has increased eightfold. Death rates for women aged 25–44 have tripled and substance misuse is a very strong predictor for completed suicide [36]. A Swedish study showed risk of death increased fivefold in alcohol-addicted women and threefold in addicted men [37]. In the United Kingdom in 2000–2002, 8% of all maternal deaths up to one year from delivery were caused by substance misuse [38].

Remember!

Substance misuse, especially of alcohol, may be more deadly in women.

29.6 APPROACH TO THE DIAGNOSIS OF ADDICTION IN WOMEN

The stereotypical alcoholic is male, middle-aged, and derelict. Anyone who doesn't fit this profile is less likely to be diagnosed [39], which means that women, in whom the disease progresses more rapidly, are frequently not diagnosed until later in the disease.

If there were a female stereotype for addiction, it would likely be a young woman – single, no kids, sexually promiscuous, HIV positive, living on welfare or on the street. However, women of all ages, from all walks of life, and at all education levels develop addictive disorders. Women are nearly 50% more likely than men to be prescribed drugs of addiction and the largest substance addiction problem in older women is the addiction of prescription drugs [1]. Women seek medical care more readily than men but are less likely to be screened for or identified as having addictive disorder and are under-represented in alcohol treatment services [5,40].

Remember!

Don't Assume! Screen Everyone!

Addiction Is An Equal Opportunity Disease!

To reduce misery, morbidity, and mortality, intervention must be early. To intervene early, diagnosis must be early. To diagnose early, everyone must be screened. To screen everyone, there must be both the knowledge and the willingness to use it. In women, this life saving process depends almost entirely on primary care physicians, obstetricians and gynecologists, psychiatrists, and therapists.

Choose a screening method you will use. In busy practices, this is best incorporated into your usual health information gathering format and delegated to your staff. They can be trained to notify you when someone shows a positive result, just as they do when blood pressure is elevated. Screen everyone, and repeat the screen yearly.

Multiple randomized controlled trials have substantiated the benefit of screening patients in the primary care setting, not only for alcohol addiction and dependence, but also for levels of alcohol use which increase health risks [41]. This is called "at-risk" drinking. Questions about frequency and amounts of substances used should be asked after initial screening to avoid increasing defensiveness and decreasing the reliability of your screen. Addiction is not a disease of how much or how many, but a disease of loss of control and continued use despite adverse consequences.

Because women experience complications of alcohol use at lower consumption, alcohol screening tests are less sensitive in women [42], and lower cut-off scores are generally required. An excellent review of screening tools by Bradley and associates [43] includes three questionnaires effective in women: CAGE, TWEAK, and AUDIT.

CAGE performs adequately in African American populations but is less sensitive for detecting alcohol addiction or dependence in Caucasian women. AUDIT and TWEAK are sensitive in African American women, but since both CAGE and AUDIT miss 41–62% of alcohol use disorders in Caucasian women, TWEAK is preferred as an overall screen for women.

Each of these instruments may be used to screen for drug use with equal efficacy.

Table 29.1 Historical clues to possible substance use issues in women

Anxiety	Family history of addiction
Depression	Psychological abuse/trauma
Insomnia	Physical or sexual abuse
Gastrointestinal complaints	Past history of addictive disorder
Gynecological complaints	Smoking cigarettes
Severe premenstrual syndrome	Family problems
Sexual dysfunction	Job/school problems
Psychological abuse/trauma	Legal problems

Compiled by Dr Gross from Refs. [33,44–46].

Basic information, from a thorough history and physical, can alert you to more subtle clues that a woman's presenting problem may at least partly be related to substance use [33,44,45] (Table 29.1). For example, a history of sexual assault in women in one general population study increased the risk for a lifetime diagnosis of addiction by a factor of 3.5–4 [46].

Early laboratory abnormalities discussed elsewhere may herald addictive disorder and are not known to be different in men and women. Although this has been little-studied [47], we have observed that alcohol-dependent women admitted for treatment frequently have an elevated TSH, commonly in conjunction with a low-normal free T4, and opioid-dependent women may have a low thyroid-stimulating hormone (TSH). These correct with abstinence.

29.7 ASSESSMENT OF THE ROLE OF DRUGS AND ALCOHOL IN DISEASES OF WOMEN

Women tend to use drugs and alcohol for different reasons than men and have different patterns of use, different needs in recovery and different triggers for relapse. For example, men report misusing drugs and alcohol for the sensation whereas women do it to increase confidence, decrease tension, and/or lose weight [47]. Much more work is needed to elucidate these factors and incorporate knowledge gained into treatment given.

Though less prevalent than in men, addictive disease is prevalent in women and the gap is narrowing [48]. Women get every psychiatric disorder except Antisocial Personality Disorder more often than men, are beaten, raped, and abused (in all walks of life) more often than men and more often turn to drugs and alcohol to relieve the associated negative affect. Women more often than men turn to drugs in response to social pressure to be thin (Table 29.2).

Psychological trauma and eating disorders carry particularly strong associations for women. Treatment centers without psychiatric staffing often maintain that the trauma will be addressed after the addiction is stabilized. Unfortunately, the addiction often cannot be adequately addressed in the first place unless the trauma (and any other psychiatric diagnosis) is also managed, because many women addicts react to

Table 29.2 Issues in addicted women compared to men

Screened	Less often
Diagnosed	Less often
Treated	Less often
Social consequences	More severe
Medical consequences	Earlier and more severe
Researched	Less thoroughly
Response to treatment	At least as good if completed
Likelihood of leaving treatment early	Greater
Barriers to treatment	Greater
Family support for treatment	Less
Use and relapse triggers	Loss and crisis
Psychiatric comorbidity	Greater
Domestic violence	Greater
Trauma/abuse	More likely
Living with an addict	More likely
Specific treatment resources available	Less
Prevalence of addictive disorder	Less but equalizing
Seek specialized addiction treatment	Less often
Seek help at primary care level	More often

Source Note: This table was compiled by Dr. Gross as a summary of data referenced throughout this chapter.

trauma triggers by turning or returning to drug or alcohol use. This results in women leaving treatment prematurely, a well-known risk factor for relapse.

Personality disorders, especially Borderline Personality Disorder, share many characteristics with active addictive disorder. The diagnosis of Borderline Personality Disorder is sometimes overused in women and should be reviewed periodically throughout the patient's clinical course, since a woman in solid recovery often thinks, feels, and behaves very differently.

Women are using and misusing drugs and alcohol at ever-increasing rates relative to men. Doctors have been prescribing addictive medication more often for women than men in this country for 200 years, starting with laudanum and alcohol in the early days and continuing into the present with benzodiaze-

pines and pain pills. Women move from casual use to dependence faster and are more vulnerable to physical, emotional and social consequences of addiction. Women are less likely than men to be diagnosed and treated and more likely to be prescribed controlled substances. In addition to untold misery for women and their families, we are looking at a public health disaster in the making.

However, women do seek general medical care more than men, and this represents an opportunity. Doctors can learn the skills and information necessary to screen and intervene early and thus prevent progression. Careful prescription practices can be developed and taught to prevent inappropriate prescribing and diversion, and funding for research on both addictive disorders and women's health issues has been increasing.

29.8 TREATMENT OF DISEASES IN ADDICTED WOMEN

When you treat addicted women, the relationship you develop with her is paramount. The stigma that exists for all people with the disease of addiction is magnified for women, especially if there are children involved. Women of color, lesbian women, incarcerated women, and women in different cultures face similar, but magnified, challenges [2]. Women think and assess problems relationally, tend to be self-critical, and often have been abused or mistreated by men, which may lead to lack of trust and thus lack of openness. The entire recovery concept of powerlessness and surrender is particularly difficult for a woman who has been victimized, as have most women with addictions. She must trust you before she will confide in you.

We offer the R-E-S-P-E-C-T model as a mnemonic for important issues in treating women, especially women with addictive disorder (Table 29.3).

Childhood sexual abuse is common in women with addiction and women with childhood sexual abuse have a substantially increased risk for a wide range of psychopathology. The association is especially strong for bulimia, alcohol dependence, and drug dependence [49]. Pay particular attention to asking about drugs and alcohol in any woman with past or present history of trauma or abuse [50].

Table 29.3 R-E-S-P-E-C-T: Important issues in treating women

R	Relationship	Build it and gain her trust.
E	Emotions	Listen and validate her feelings.
S	Sanctuary	Make your physical space inviting.
P	Psychiatry	Assess and address any issues.
E	Empathy	Enter her world and see her reality.
C	Connections	Find out who's in her life to help or hinder.
T	Trauma	Ask about abuse, loss, violence, and trauma.

Mnemonic was developed by Dr Gross.

She may still be in the abusive relationship, which she may or may not reveal to you right away. Don't take it personally. A woman who has been abused usually has trouble trusting anyone. This is an injury caused by the trauma and not a reflection on you. Care and mindfulness with personal boundaries and physical touch are important. Ask the questions about drinking, drug use, and trauma up front, and she may come back later and tell you the whole story once she trusts you.

Women with untreated addictive disorders sometimes fail to protect themselves and are re-traumatized, increasing the risk of relapse. The use of substances mitigates the affective storms and flashbacks of Post-traumatic Stress Disorder, and these symptoms may surge forth once the patient is clean and sober. She often doesn't have the resources to cope if the trauma hasn't been treated, which increases the risk of relapse. The use of substances then increases the risk of re-victimization, creating a vicious cycle.

Women with substance use disorders who have been labeled as treatment failures frequently have untreated psychiatric disorders and and/or psychological trauma which account for the so-called "failure." Simultaneous, integrated treatment of trauma and other psychiatric issues in women improves retention and recovery rates [50].

Depressed patients cannot make full use of addiction treatment or enter into full recovery because their cognitions and energy are impaired. Traumatized patients may be too fearful to open up. Women with eating disorders frequently report escalation of symptoms in recovery. Addiction treatment programs may not screen for eating disorder and eating disorder programs may not screen for addiction, despite frequent co-occurrence in women. The connection between these disorders is usually easily acknowledged by patients but remains controversial in some treatment circles.

Treat depressive disorders and other psychiatric issues aggressively. Do not wait for abstinence, since depression in addicted women usually precedes addiction and impedes recovery. Psychotherapy is often needed, sometimes for extended periods, to address cognitive distortions and teach new, healthier coping skills. Women with alcoholism and cocaine addiction are more likely than men to be living with an addicted significant other [51,52]. A good family therapist may help support her recovery efforts.

Be extremely careful when prescribing controlled substances in women with addictive disorders. Only prescribe when there is no alternative and set up office procedures to track refills and promptly address any patterns that might indicate addiction.

Women with the disease of addiction face terrible odds. Rates of psychological trauma for addicted women are 75–95%. There is much interpersonal difficulty and little social support [53]. Drug addicted women are more likely than drug addicted men to report psychiatric symptoms and suicide attempts, to live in an unsafe place, to have a history of physical abuse, and to report serious conflicts with the people in their lives.

Covington [2] has enumerated challenges for women with addiction. Women addicts are shamed and stigmatized more severely than men with the same disease. Women addicts have higher rates of physical and sexual abuse than men addicts or than nonaddicted women. There are relational issues – fear of losing children or a partner, for instance. Some women have to have a partner's permission to get treated. Treatment issues include lack of services for women, lack of understanding of women's needs in treatment in what services do exist, long waiting lists, and lack of child care resources. Broader social issues include lack of financial resources, lack of clean and sober housing, and poorly coordinated services.

The woman in your office today may face all of these problems. You may be the only person she ever turns to for help and today may be the only day she tries. If not you, who? If not now, when?

29.9   INTERVENTION AND REFERRAL FOR WOMEN WITH THE DISEASE OF ADDICTION

Remember!

Women with addiction are more likely to seek help from family doctors, internists, therapists and psychiatrists than from any specialist or specialty treatment program.

Despite having more severe alcohol-related symptoms than men, women tend to seek treatment from less specialized sources – for example, family doctors, internists, obstetricians/gynecologists, therapists, or psychiatrists [5,29].

Unfortunately, most primary care physicians neither want nor like to treat patients with addictions, nor have they been taught the skills to do so. The average medical school provides an average curriculum of only 12 hours on this deadly and highly prevalent disorder of body and brain. The average primary care physician doesn't consider addiction a disorder and/or doesn't consider it treatable [54].

So a woman with addictive disorder is most likely to show up for help where she may be less likely to get it. Up to half of patients admitted to general hospitals have an addictive disorder. Up to 75% of those admitted to general psychiatric units are addicted [54]. The question is not whether you will treat women with addictive disorders. The only question is how well and with what level of awareness you will do so.

You do not have to be an addiction specialist to be effective. Screening and brief intervention at the primary care level is effective for patients with addictive disorders, perhaps even more so for women than men [55]. Brief interventions can bring about significant, lasting decreases in at-risk drinking in people who are not alcohol dependent [56], thus potentially preventing full-blown substance dependence.

Not knowing that your patient is using and/or misusing substances can have dire ramifications [23]. Because of telescoping, women with alcohol use disorders are at particular risk. Screening is only the first step toward more in-depth evaluation of drinking and drug use, exploration of adverse consequences of substance use, and assessment of motivation to change.

We have been in private practice (psychiatry, family medicine, and internal medicine) and we understand what primary care physicians are up against in today's managed care world. In this real world where addicted women will seek help from you despite the pressures and constraints of medicine today, you need a system that is efficient and streamlined.

The National Institute on Alcohol Abuse and Alcoholism (NIAAA) has put together an excellent set of integrated tools [57,58] for both men and women. We recommend that you set up your office procedures to include them. They are comprehensive, carefully designed, user-friendly and free (Table 29.4).

Table 29.4   Resources available free online

- Tutorial on the use of the tools, with case studies
- Training materials
- CME for screening and brief intervention
- Downloadable screening instruments
- Preformatted progress notes and templates for patient charts
- Information on evidence-based use of medications for alcoholism
- Medication management support templates
- Patient education information in English and Spanish
- Information about what constitutes a standard drink
- Recommended drinking limits for different patient groups

Source: www.niaaa.nih.gov/guide.

The NIAAA guide [57] and the pocket guide [58] are available online and provide a simplified process for screening, diagnosis, and brief intervention for both at-risk drinking and alcohol addiction and dependence. The tools are easy to use within personalized charting and information systems. The flow chart format allows you to add questions about the use of other drugs so that you can screen and intervene for both at the same time.

Remember!

Choose a screening method.

Make it part of your practice routine.

Screen everyone.

Educate everyone.

Assess and diagnose anyone with a positive screen.

Advise and assist those who need it.

Follow up routinely.

Health risk increases for women who drink more than three drinks in a day and for women who drink more than seven drinks in a week [59]. Using the NIAAA system [58], a woman who drinks four or more standard drinks in a day one or more times in a year would be considered an at-risk drinker. By comparison, a man is considered an at-risk drinker if he drinks five or more standard drinks in a day, one or more times in a year.

Educate your women patients (and men over age 65) to stay within maximum drinking limits of no more than three drinks in a day and no more than seven drinks in a week. Advise abstinence for women who are pregnant or trying to become pregnant. Recommend lower limits or abstinence for anyone on medications that could interact with alcohol and those who have a medical problem that could be worsened by alcohol. Talking routinely and nonjudgmentally about these matters sends the message of concern and sets the stage for your patients to come to you later even if they do not open up right away.

Continued maladaptive use despite consequences but without signs of physical dependence indicates substance addiction. Signs of withdrawal, tolerance, and inability to stop indicate dependence, and you will need to assess for risk of withdrawal and possible need for detoxification. Because they do not depend on amounts consumed, these basic diagnostic assessments for substance addiction and dependence are not substantially different in women.

Women respond to medications for alcohol use disorders. Naltrexone may be somewhat less effective in women, though the response is better (as in men) when there is a lead-in period of abstinence. Updated information is available in the NIAAA guide [57].

Alcoholics Anonymous, Narcotics Anonymous and other 12-step programs are not treatment *per se*, so they are sometimes referred to as "mutual help groups." The meetings are organized, attended, and led by people who have the disease of addiction, not by professional therapists. Each group may have a different feel. Recommend that your patient attend several different groups to find one that suits her.

Your staff can call the Alcoholics Anonymous number in the blue pages of your local telephone book and get a list of meetings, some of which may be women-only. Ask if anyone is willing to be a contact. Helping others is part of 12-step work, and sometimes you can find someone to talk to

your patient on the phone or help her get to a meeting.

Alcoholics Anonymous was originally developed by and for men. Some elements, particularly those involving the issue of powerlessness and surrender, are difficult for women, especially the many who have been abused. However, many women have had success in these groups and they remain important for anyone with the disease of addiction. Covington's book, "A Woman's Way through the 12 Steps," can be very helpful [60].

Your emotional tone matters greatly in the treatment of addicted women. Be caring. Be direct. Don't judge. Acknowledge that change is hard, link your concerns about her drinking and/or drug use to her medical problems, and let her know you can and want to help her. Keep the lines of communication open.

Patients who have more severe disease or do not respond to your interventions may need more specialized treatment. Addiction services are provided at many levels, from office-based outpatient treatment to inpatient or long-term residential care. Referral to specialized gender-specific treatment may improve outcomes [59].

Keep a list of local resources in your office, and update it regularly. Hospital social workers usually have lists of addiction treatment facilities, some of which may provide free evaluation services. The help of an Addiction Medicine specialist can be invaluable. You may be able to enlist the help of an "interventionist," who specializes in helping families and businesses get patients into treatment. Some interventionists provide monitoring services after treatment, which improves outcomes.

When you refer to specialized treatment, continue your concerned, nonjudgmental stance. As with any chronic disease, treatment of addiction must continue and the patient must be compliant to achieve and sustain recovery. Longer addiction treatment and successful treatment completion are associated with positive outcomes in both men and women [61]. With women, this is more likely to occur in an atmosphere of nonjudgmental concern in which the whole picture of her needs and life situation is considered.

A survey in the late 1980s [62] found little evidence that women needed to be treated separately but then, as now, much of the research was done entirely with men and the results then extrapolated to women. An expert panel in 1999 [63] reported serious gaps in research, services, access, and outcomes in the treatment of alcoholism in women, and the problem is even more profound for addiction to other drugs, since alcohol remains far more studied.

There is mounting evidence that treatment which addresses certain specific gender-related issues is better tolerated, more often completed, and more effective in the long run than the "one size fits all" approach, which is still prevalent even in programs in which men and women are treated separately [10,64–67]. Treatment involving strong confrontation may worsen depression and shame in already stigmatized women and women with trauma histories may decompensate or leave treatment prematurely. Women in mixed gender groups may fall into caretaking roles with men. Models for "gender-responsive" treatment have been set forth [2] but are not yet widely available, especially in the public sector where the need is very great.

Women are more likely than men to face barriers to accessing substance addiction treatment and are less likely to enter specialized treatment. When they do, when they complete treatment, and when gender differences are reported in mixed gender studies, they may have slightly better outcomes than men. Some women will not enter mixed gender programs and further health services research has been recommended [68]. It is not clear whether older research findings still apply to women today due to rapid social, demographic, and epidemiological changes.

Women may be reluctant to seek treatment, especially in mixed gender facilities, because of lack of money and family support, increased social stigma compared to men, history of sexual or physical abuse or assault, living with a significant other who uses or is addicted, living with an addict who is abusive, tendency to attribute substance use to depression or anxiety and seek help for that [69–71]. Women may leave treatment prematurely for the same reasons.

Green has reviewed much of the literature on gender differences in treatment services [40]. Women may leave treatment prematurely more often than men but when they complete treatment their recovery rates are at least as good. Women suffer greater psychiatric comorbidity, which tends to predict a poorer prognosis. There is some evidence that providing child care may greatly improve treatment completion rates for women but programs that do so are rare [50,72].

Appropriate, affordable treatment resources are in short supply for everyone, but the data suggest that over the lifetime, women with substance use disorders are less likely than men to enter treatment. In 1990 among people with alcohol-related problems, almost four times as many men (8.3%) as women (2%) reported ever seeking help [73].

Women with substance use disorders perceive women-only treatment groups to be safer and more comfortable for them [67]. Differences in risk factors, presenting problems, co-occurring disorders, medical consequences, and reasons for relapse may not be adequately addressed in mixed-gender settings. Differences in interactive styles may negatively affect women in mixed-gender groups [10].

Relapse prevention and better outcomes have been linked to accepting addiction as a disease (thus decreasing denial, ambivalence, and stigma), learning gender-specific triggers and strategies for coping, strengthening attachment to treatment (and attachments in general), and increasing social support [74–76].

Covington has described the needs of addicted women in treatment [2]. These women need a sense of sanctuary in a safe, respectful environment that is not shaming or harsh. Gender must be acknowledged as important and the addicted woman needs to learn to view herself and her problems within this social context. Healthy relationship skills must be taught, modeled, and promoted. Integrated, comprehensive services must be available to address substance addiction, trauma, and mental health issues. Socioeconomic issues should be acknowledged and help provided to improve and to access appropriate community services, many of which do not exist yet and need to be developed.

Addiction is a chronic disease just like the many others you already treat. By definition, "chronic" means care over the long haul, rather than cure.

The addicted women may require many "doses" of time and connection with you before she trusts you enough to take your advice. However, we have seen many patients come to treatment and achieve life saving remission because a caring doctor gently addressed the issue over and over. Successful treatment of addiction is as frequent and happens the same way as with any other chronic illness [77].

Even if the addicted woman in your office doesn't respond at first, maintain the connection and keep trying. Say this a lot: "You can do it. I will help you." She will remember and she may come to you one day for help she refuses at first. You can save her life and change for the better the lives of all who depend on her.

REFERENCES

1. Zilberman, M.L., Taveres, H., Blume, S.B., and el-Guebaly, N. (2002) Towards best practices in the treatment of women with addictive disorders. *Addict. Disord. Their Treat.*, **1**, 39–46.

2. Covington, S. (2007) Women and Addiction. Hazelden Foundation Clinical Innovators Series.

3. Covington, S.S. (2002) Helping women recover: Creating gender-responsive treatment, in *The Handbook of Addiction Treatment for Women: Theory and Practice* (eds S.L.A. Straussner and S. Brown), Jossey-Bass, San Francisco, pp. 52–72.

4. Helmbrecht, G.D. and Thiagarajah, S. (2008) Management of addiction disorders in pregnancy. *J. Addict. Med.*, **2** (1), 1–16.

5. Schober, R., and Annis, H.M. (1996) Barriers to help-seeking for change in drinking: a gender focused review of the literature. *Addict. Behav.*, **2**, 81–92.

6. Staussner, S.L.A. and Attia, P.R. (2002) Women's Addiction and treatment through a historical lens, in *The Handbook of Addiction Treatment for Women: Theory and Practice*, (eds S.L.A. Straussner and S. Brown), Jossey-Bass, San Francisco, pp. 3–25.

7. Wetherington, C.L. and Roman, A.B. (eds) (1998) Drug Addiction Research and the Health of Women: Executive Summary, US Dept of Health and Human Services, NIH, NIDA, Rockville, MD.

8. Greenfield, S.F. (2002) Women and alcohol use disorders. *Harvard Rev. Psychiat.*, **10** (2), 76–85.

9. Anonymous (1996) Substance Abuse and the American Woman, National Center on Addictive Substance Abuse at Columbia University, New York.

10. Greenfield, S.F., Brooks, A.J., Gordon, S.M. *et al.* (2007) Substance abuse treatment entry, retention, and outcome in women: a review of the literature. *Drug Alcohol Depend.*, **86**, 1–21.

11. Blume, S.B. (1991) Sexuality and stigma: the alcoholic woman. *Alcohol. Health Res. World*, **15**, 139–146.

12. Grucza, R.A. (2008) Secular trends in the lifetime prevalence of alcohol dependence in the United States: a re-evaluation. *Alcohol. Clin. Exp. Res.*, **32** (5), 763–770.

13. Kandall, S.R. (1996) *Substance and Shadow*, Harvard University Press, Cambridge, MA.

14. Abadinsky, H. (1997) *Drug Abuse: An Introduction*, Nelson-Hall, Chicago.

15. NIDA (2005) Prescription drug abuse and addiction. Research Reports, No 05-4881. Bethesda, MD.

16. Substance Abuse Mental Health Services Administration (2007) Results from the 2006 National Survey on Drug Use and Health: National Findings. Office of Applied Studies, NSDUH Series H-32, DHHS Publication No. SMA 07-4293, Rockville, MD.

17. Piazza, N.J., Vrbka, J.L., and Yeager, R.D. (1989) Telescoping of alcoholism in women alcoholics. *Int. J. Addict.*, **24**, 19–28.

18. Anonymous (1997) Matching Alcoholism Treatments to Client Heterogeneity: Project MATCH posttreatment drinking outcomes. *J. Stud. Alcohol*, **58**, 7–29.

19. Johnson, P.B., Richter, L., Kleber, H.D. *et al.* (2005) Telescoping of drinking-related behaviors: gender, racial/ethnic, and age comparisons. *Subst. Use Misuse*, **40**, 1139–1151.

20. Edens, E.L., Glowinski, A.L., Grazier, K.L., and Bucholz, K.K. (2008) The 14-year course of alcoholism in a community sample: Do men and women differ? *Drug Alcohol Depen.*, **93**, 1–11.

21. Freeza, M., di Padova, C., and Pozzato, G. *et al.* (1990) High blood alcohol level in women: the role of decreased alcohol dehydrogenase activity and first-pass metabolism. *N. Eng. J. Med.*, **322** (2), 95–99.

22. Randall, C.L., Roberts, J.S., and Del Boca, F.K. *et al.* (1999) Telescoping of landmark events associated with drinking: a gender comparison. *J. Stud. Alcohol.*, **60** (2), 252–260.

23. Saltz, R., Mulvey, K.P., Plough, A., and Samet, J.H. (1997) Physician Unawareness of serious substance abuse. *Am. J. Drug Alcohol. Abuse*, **23** (3), 343–354.

24. McGarry, K.A. (2005) Women and alcohol. *Comp. Ther.*, **31** (1), 83–93.

25. Hudson, J., Hiripi, E., Pope, H., and Kessler, R. (2007) The prevalence and correlates of eating disorders in the national comorbidity survey replication. *Biol. Psychiatry*, **61**, 348–358.

26. Bulik, C.M., Klump, K.L., Thornton, L. *et al.* (2004) Alcohol use disorder comorbidity in eating disorders: A multicenter study. *J. Clin. Psychiatry*, **65**, 1000–1006.

27. Herzog, D., Franko, D., Dorer, D. *et al.* (2006) Drug abuse in women with eating disorders. *Int. J. Eat Disord.*, **39**, 364–368.

28. Gold, M.S. (ed.) (2004) *Eating Disorders, Overeating, and Pathological Attachment to Food: Independent or Addictive Disorders*, Haworth Inc.

29. Grant, B.F., Stinson, F.S., and Dawson, D.A. *et al.* (2004) Prevalence and co-occurrence of substance use disorders and independent mood and anxiety disorders: results from the national epidemiologic survey on alcohol and related conditions. *Arch. Gen. Psychiat.*, **61** (8), 807–816.

30. Greenfield, S.F., Weiss, R.D., Muenz, L.R. *et al.* (1998) The effect of depression on return to drinking: a prospective study. *Arch. Gen. Psychiat.*, **55**, 259–265.

31. Hanson, G.R. (2002) In Drug Abuse, Gender Matters, NIDA Notes 17 (2), National Institute on Drug Abuse.

32. Lindberg, S. and Agren, G. (1988) Mortality among male and female hospitalized alcoholics in Stockholm 1962–1983. *Br. J. Addict.*, **83**, 1193–1200.

33. Cyr, M.G. and McGarry, K.A. (2002) Alcohol use disorders in women. *Postgrad. Med.*, **112** (6), 31–47.

34. Day, C.P. (2000) Who gets alcoholic liver disease: nature or nurture? *J. R. Coll. Phys. Lond.*, **34**, 557–562.

35. The National Council on Alcoholism and Drug Dependence (NCADD) (1999) Use of Alcohol and Other Drugs Among Women – Consumption Rates, Patterns, and Trends. NCADD Facts and Information.

36. Appleby, L., Shaw, J., Amos, T. *et al.* (1999) Safer services: report of the National Confidential Enquiry into suicide and homicide by people with mental illness. The Stationary Office, London.

37. Lindberg, S. and Agren, G. (1988) Mortality among male and female hospitalized alcoholics in Stockholm 1962–1983. *Br. J. Addict.*, **83**, 1193–1200.

38. Lewis, G.(ed.) (2004) Why mothers die 2000–2002: confidential enquiry into maternal and child health (CEMACH) – the sixth report, CEMACH, London.

39. Moore, R.D. (1989) Prevalence, detection and treatment of alcoholism in hospitalized patients. *JAMA*, **261**, 403–408.

40. Brienza, R.S. and Stein, M.D. (2002) Alcohol use disorders in primary care: Do gender-specific differences exist? *J. Gen. Int. Med.*, **17**, 387–397.

41. Dawson, D.A. (2005) Quantifying the risks associated with exceeding recommended drinking limits. *Alcohol. Clin. Exp. Res.*, **29** (5), 902–908.

42. Fiellin, D.A. (2000) Screening for alcohol Problems in primary care: a systematic review. *Arch. Int. Med.*, **160**, 1977–1989.

43. Bradley, K.A., Boyd-Wickizer, J., Powell, S.H. *et al.* (1998) Alcohol screening questionnaires in women: a critical review. *JAMA*, **280** (2), 166–171.

44. Perper, J.A. and Van Thiel, D.H. (1992) Cardiovascular complications of cocaine abuse. *Recent Dev. Alcohol*, **10**, 343–361.

45. Felitti, V.J., Anda, R.F., Nordenburg, D. *et al.* (1998) Relationship of childhood abuse and household dysfunction to many of the leading causes of death in adults: The Adverse Childhood Experiences (ACE) Study. *Am. J. Prev. Med.*, **14** (4), 245–258.

46. Winfield, I. (1990) Sexual assault and psychiatric disorders among a community sample of women. *Am. J. Psychiatry*, **147**, 335–341.

47. White House Office of National Drug Control to the Boston Globe, 4/30/07.

48. McPherson, M., Casswell, S., and Pledger, M. (2004) Gender convergence in alcohol consumption and related problems: Issues and outcomes from comparisons of New Zealand survey data. *Addiction*, **99**, 738–748.

49. Kendler, K.S., Bulik, C.M., Silberg, J. *et al.* (2000) Childhood Sexual Abuse and Adult Psychiatric and Substance Use Disorders in Women. *Arch. Gen. Psychiatry*, **57**, 953–959.

50. Root, M.P.P. (1989) Treatment failures: The role of sexual victimization in women's addictive behavior. *Am. J. Orthopsychiat.*, **59** (4), 542–549.

51. Griffin, M.L. (1989) A comparison of male and female cocaine abusers. *Arch. Gen. Psychiatry*, **46**, 122–126.

52. Jacob, T. and Bremer, D.A. (1986) Assortative mating among men and women alcoholics. *J. Stud. Alcohol.*, **47**, 219–222.

53. Curtis, C.E., Jason, L.A., Olson, B.D., and Ferrari, J.R. (2005) Disordered Eating, Trauma, and Sense of Community: Examining Women in Substance Abuse Recovery Homes. *Women Health*, **41** (4), 87–100. Available online at http://www.haworthpress.com/web/WH.

54. Miller, N.S., Sheppard, L.M., Colenda, C.C., and Magen, J. (2001) Why physicians are unprepared to

treat patients who have alcohol- and drug-related disorders. *Acad. Med.*, **76** (5), 410–418.

55. Anton, R.F., O'Malley, S.S., and Ciraulo, D.A. *et al.* (2006) Combined pharmacotherapies and behavioral interventions for alcohol dependence: The COMBINE study: A randomized controlled trial. *JAMA*, **295** (17), 2003–2017.

56. Fleming, M.F., Mundt, M.P., French, M.T. *et al.* (2002) Brief physician advice for problem drinkers: Long-term efficacy and cost-benefit analysis. *Alcohol. Clin. Exp. Res.*, **26** (1), 36–43.

57. National Institute on Alcohol Abuse and Alcoholism (NIAAA) (2007) Helping Patients Who Drink Too Much: A Clinician's Guide. Updated 2005 edition (contains supporting information on medications updated to 2007). US Dept of Health and Human Services, NIH, and NIAAA.

58. National Institute on Alcohol Abuse and Alcoholism (NIAAA) (2005, updated) A Pocket Guide for Alcohol Screening and Brief Intervention. NIAAA, Rockville, MD. Also available at www.niaaa.nih.gov.

59. Bradley, K.A. (2003) Two brief alcohol-screening tests from the alcohol use disorders identification test (AUDIT): validation in a female veterans affairs patient population. *Arch. Int. Med.*, **163**, 821–829.

60. Covington, S.S. (1994) *A Woman's Way Through the Twelve Steps*, Hazelden Information and Education Services, Center City.

61. Stark, M.J. (1992) Dropping out of substance abuse treatment: a clinically oriented review. *Clin. Psychol. Rev.*, **12**, 93–116.

62. Vannicelli, M. and Nash, L. (1984) Effect of sex bias on women's studies on alcoholism. *Alcohol. Clin. Exp. Res.*, **8**, 334–336.

63. Smith, W.B. and Weisner, C. (2000) women and alcohol problems: a critical analysis of the literature and unanswered questions. *Alcohol. Clin. Exp. Res.*, **24**, 1320–1321.

64. Najavits, L.M., Rosier, M., Nolan, A.L., and Freeman, M.C. (2007) A new gender-based model for women's recovery from substance abuse: Results of a pilot study. *Am. J. Drug Alcohol Abuse*, **33** (1), 5–11.

65. Greenfield, S.F., Trucco, E.M., McHugh, K. *et al.* (2007) The Women's Recovery Group Study: A Stage I trial of women-focused group therapy for substance use disorders versus mixed-gender group drug counseling. *Drug Alcohol Depen.*, **90**, 39–47.

66. Hien, D.A., Cohen, L.R., Miele, G.M. *et al.* (2004) Promising treatments for women with comorbid PTSD and substance use disorders. *Am. J. Psychiatry*, **161**, 1426–1432.

67. Kauffman, E., Dore, M., and Nelson-Zlupko, L. (1995) The role of women's therapy groups in the treatment chemical dependence. *Am. J. Orthopsychiat.*, **65** (3), 355–363.

68. Green, C.A. Gender and use of substance abuse treatment services. Available at http://pubs.niaaa.nih.gov/publications/arh291/55-62.htm (accessed 14 April 2008).

69. Greenfield, S.F. and O'Leary, G. (2002) Sex differences in substance use disorders, in *Psychiatric illness in women: emerging treatments and research* (eds F. Lewis-Hall, T.S. Williams, J.A. Panetta, and J.M. Herrera), American Psychiatric Press, Washington, DC, pp. 547–610.

70. Lex, B.W. (1992) Alcohol problems in special populations, in *Medical Diagnosis and Treatment of Alcoholism* (eds J.H. Mendelson and N.K. Mello), McGraw-Hill, New York, pp. 71–154.

71. Greenfield, S.F. (1996) Women and substance use disorders, in *Psychopharmacology and Women: Sex, Gender, and Hormones* (eds M.F. Jensvold, U. Halbreich, and J.A. Hamilton), American Psychiatric Press, Washington, DC, pp. 299–321.

72. Hurley, D.L. (1991) Women, alcohol and incest: an analytical review. *J. Stud. Alcohol.*, **52**, 253–268.

73. Weisner, C., Greenfield, T., and Room, R. (1995) Trends in the treatment of alcohol problems in the US general population, 1979 through 1990. *Am. J. Publ. Health*, **85**, 55–60.

74. Hser, Y., Evans, E., Huang, D., and Anglin, D. (2004) Relationship between drug treatment services, retention, and outcomes. *Psychiatr. Serv.*, **55** (7), 767–774.

75. Irvin, J., Bowers, C., Dunn, M., and Want, M. (1999) Efficacy of relapse prevention: a meta-analytic review. *J. Consult. Clin. Psych.*, **67** (4), 563–570.

76. Blume, S. (1990) Chemical dependency in women: important issues. *Am. J. Drug Alcohol Abuse*, **16** (3), 297–307.

77. Miller, M.M. (2007) Addictive disorders and their treatment. **6** (3), 101–106.

30

Children and adolescents with ADHD: risk and protective factors for addictive disorders

Larry Gray,[1] Jennifer J. Park,[2] and Michael E. Msall[3]

[1] University of Chicago, Pritzker School of Medicine, Department of Pediatrics, Section of Developmental Pediatrics, Comer Children's Hospital at the University of Chicago, Chicago, IL, USA
[2] University of Chicago, Pritzker School of Medicine, Kennedy Research Center and Institute of Molecular Pediatric Sciences, Section of Developmental and Behavioral Pediatrics, Comer Children's Hospital at the University of Chicago and LaRabida Children's Hospital, Chicago, IL, USA
[3] University of Chicago, Pritzker School of Medicine, Kennedy Research Center on Intellectual and Neurodevelopmental Disabilities, Institute of Molecular Pediatric Sciences, Section of Community Health, Ethics, and Policy, Comer Children's Hospital at the University of Chicago and LaRabida Children's Hospital, Chicago, IL, USA

30.1 INTRODUCTION

In the past decade, attention deficit hyperactivity disorder (ADHD) has received unprecedented interest from the media, the public, as well as the medical community. The diagnostic criteria of ADHD has broadened considerably since the American Psychiatric Association defined "attention deficit disorder" and "attention deficit disorder with hyperactivity" in the 1980s, and currently ADHD is one of the most prevalent mental health disorders affecting children and adolescents in North America [1,2]. Approximately 2–7% of children and adolescents in the United States are estimated to have ADHD, with an annual cost of more than $50 billion in treatment and management [3,4]. With increased diagnosis of ADHD and the increased

recognition of the importance of ADHD treatment among the child population, the United States witnessed a sharp increase in the production of stimulant medication (methylphenidate (MPH) and amphetamine (AMP)). Annual rates of stimulant production rose 740% from 1991 to 2000, with methylphenidate now being the most common behavioral medication prescribed to children in both the United States and Australia [5,6].

Despite the tremendous increase in patient population and public attention, the research on ADHD is still in its early stages, and controversy and speculation surrounding ADHD remains rampant. Critics question the effectiveness of drug therapy in treating conduct and behavioral issues, while some

Addictive Disorders in Medical Populations   Edited by Norman S. Miller and Mark S. Gold
© 2010 John Wiley & Sons, Ltd.

Internet websites and alternative religions doubt that ADHD is an actual disorder despite robust scientific evidence [7]. One issue that has received considerable amount of interest in recent years from both the public and the medical community is the relationship between children with ADHD and the risk for substance addiction later in life [8]. Several researches have addressed this issue, yet the debate and fears regarding ADHD and its treatment have not ceased. In this chapter, our current knowledge of the epidemiology, diagnosis, etiology, and treatment of ADHD is reviewed, as well as the relationships between ADHD and comorbidities of oppositional defiant disorder (ODD), conduct disorder (CD), mood and learning disorders, and their relationship to substance use disorder (SUD). Also discussed are the role of alcohol and illicit drugs in the ADHD population and current gaps in our knowledge of managing ADHD. In addition, we will also examine the impact of current ADHD treatment on SUD among children and adolescents with ADHD.

30.2   BACKGROUND ON ADHD

Attention deficit hyperactivity disorder (ADHD) represents a significant impairment in an individual's ability to inhibit behaviors that are seen as unsafe, impair learning, or are perceived as socially inappropriate. Such behaviors include disruptiveness, excessive activity, impulsiveness, and inattention. If not managed properly, ADHD can result in adverse outcomes such as severe disruptions in familial and social relationships (e.g., parents, teachers, peers, and siblings), academic problems during school years, as well as delinquency, substance addiction, and poor money management in adolescence and adulthood [9,10].

There is no biomedical test for ADHD, nor is there a vaccine that will prevent it. Diagnosis is based solely on "the presence of 'developmentally inappropriate' levels of attention, concentration, activity, distractibility and impulsivity" as observed and described by the child's parents, teachers, social workers, and by the physician [5]. Since many typical young children demonstrate these behaviors at developmentally appropriate times, caution must be used when diagnosing ADHD in preschool children (five years and younger). Determining the prevalence of ADHD is not an easy task, since the figure varies depending on the diagnostic criteria used, the population studied (i.e., size and selection of sample), and the number of sources required to make the diagnosis [11,12]. Despite these challenges, ADHD is the most common neurobehavioral health condition among school-aged children today [12]. In the first national sample for ADHD prevalence, the National Survey of Children's Health (NSCH) estimated that approximately 4.4 million children aged 4–17 years were reported to have a history of ADHD diagnosis. Males were 2.5 times more likely to receive ADHD diagnosis compared to females and approximately half of children in the United States with reported ADHD diagnoses were being treated with medication at the time of the survey [13].

ADHD diagnosis is most frequently made between 6 and 12 years of age. Behavioral symptoms of ADHD are often identified at school, and the highest prevalence of diagnosis occurs at 9–12 years of age. The child in question is brought in for clinical evaluation due to variety of behavioral symptoms, such as being too distracted, being too talkative, acting younger than their chorological age (i.e., described as "immature" by parents and teachers), and history of repeating a grade [14]. Other common behavioral problems seen in children with ADHD include resistance to environmental reinforcement, little sense of physical safety, aggressive behaviors, oppositional attitude to the environment, poor social skills, and low self-esteem [15]. In addition, recent research has demonstrated that a large number of children with ADHD have challenging behaviors in the preschool years. However, only a small portion of preschool children with ADHD receives treatment. One study estimates that only 19% of children with preschool-onset behavior disorder receive service [16]. Common barriers in receiving treatment include missed diagnosis and parents' belief that symptoms of ADHD would lessen or disappear over time [17].

Not all diagnosed children require medications, and symptoms such as hyperactivity and impulsiveness may decrease with age. However, several studies have shown that inattention and symptoms of learning problems (specific reading, math, and writing disorders), as well as other behavioral disorders associated with ADHD (e.g., anxiety, ODD, and depression) either do not change or actually increase with age. Overall, the progression of ADHD is consistent with life-long chronic neurobehavioral disorders and requires multimodal management strategies that need a framework similar to biopsychosocial techniques used for obesity, asthma, and epilepsy. Approximately 65% of children diagnosed with ADHD continue to have partial symptoms beyond the age 25 years [18,19].

Although there is no single test to diagnose ADHD, guidelines and criteria on the diagnosis are provided by the *Diagnostic and Statistical Manual of Mental Disorders, Fourth Edition (DSM-IV)* [20]. The DSM-IV offers an operational description of 18 behavioral symptoms encompassed by the ADHD diagnosis. These symptoms cluster into three areas – problems with: (1) inattention, (2) hyperactivity, and/or (3) impulsivity.

For children between the ages of 6 and 12, inattention is described by behaviors like "having difficulty sustaining attention" or "not being attentive to details and/or making careless mistakes", "appearing not to listen to instruction", or "failing to finish tasks." Hyperactivity is a physical state noticeable by movement and over-activity. It includes behaviors like "fidgeting", "unable to stay seated", "inappropriate running and/or climbing". These children are often described as always "on the go," or "acting as if driven by a motor." Impulsivity is the tendency to act on impulse rather than thought or considering the consequences of their action. Children or adolescents who are overly impulsive tend often demonstrate behaviors like "blurting answers before questions are finished", "having difficulty waiting turns," or "interrupting or intruding on others." A complete description of the behaviors that are problematic for children with

the diagnosis of ADHD can be found in the DSM-IV diagnostic manual.

Based on the DSM-IV criteria, ADHD can be divided into the following major subtypes: predominately inattentive type, predominately impulsive/hyperactive type, and the combined type (inattention + hyperactivity/impulsivity). Of these, the combined type is most common and individuals with this subtype have "more co-occurring psychiatric and substance use disorders and are the most impaired of all" [8]. The child in question needs to exhibit at least six or more of the behaviors designated by DSM-IV in order to be considered the ADHD diagnosis. In addition, these symptoms (1) need to have been present for at least six months, (2) need to have started before seven years of age, (3) need to cause significant impairment in two or more settings (such as in both classroom and at home as opposed to exhibiting these behaviors only in school), (4) should not be results of another mental disorder, such as anxiety, adjustment disorder, or post-traumatic stress disorder (PTSD), and (5) must result in significant impairment in social, academic, or occupational function [12,20]. It is important to note, however, that a thorough medical and behavioral history and examination needs to be undertaken to eliminate other possibilities, such as age-appropriate high activity, thyroid disorders, hearing loss or vision problem, sleep disorders, sudden change in the child's life (e.g., parents' divorce, death of family member), severe neglect or trauma, presence of learning disabilities, or under-stimulation (e.g., children with high IQs). In addition, there are several disorders that have ADHD as a comorbidity. These include Tourette syndrome (TS), developmental coordination disorders (DCD), prematurity, seizure disorders, and fetal alcohol syndrome.

30.2.1 Comorbidity and ADHD

To ensure optimal treatment response and outcome, it is important to keep in mind that there are several comorbidities of ADHD that can either be present at the time of the diagnosis or develop in later stages of life. These are illustrated in Table 30.1. Approximately two-thirds (64%) of school-aged children

Table 30.1 Comorbidities of ADHD [23–25]

Common ADHD Comorbidity	Symptoms	Frequency in Children with ADHD
Oppositional Defiant Disorder (ODD)	Frequent temper tantrums; Argues with adults; Refusal to obey adult requests; Deliberately annoys other people; Blames others for mistakes; Easily annoyed; Spiteful or vindictive behavior; Aggressiveness toward peers; Difficulty maintaining friendships; Academic problems	40%
Conduct Disorder (CD)	Bullies, threatens or intimidates others; Often initiates physical fights; Has used a weapon that could cause serious harm to others (e.g., a bat, brick, broken bottle, knife or gun); Physically cruel to people or animals; Steals from a victim (e.g., assault); Fire setting with intention to cause damage; Deliberately destroys other's property	14%
Learning Disorder (LD)	Difficulty in reading, math, and writing; Problems with language processing, nonverbal skills or executive function.	25–50%
Anxiety	Excessive worries and tension; Has unrealistic view of problem; Restlessness or feeling of being "edgy;" Tiredness; Trouble falling or staying asleep; Trembling; Being easily startled	31%
Depression	Persistent feelings of sadness; Loss of interest in activities previously enjoyed; Change in weight; Difficulty sleeping or oversleeping; Energy loss; Feelings of worthlessness; Thoughts of death or suicide	4%
Tics Disorder	Excessive blinking; Grimaces of the face; Quick movements of the arms, legs, or other areas; Sounds (grunts, throat clearing, contractions of the abdomen or diaphragm)	5%
Tourette's Disorder	Involuntary, purposeless movements (e.g., head jerk, eye blink, twitching) 50% have obsessive compulsive disorders 50% have ADHD	<1%
Sleep Disorder	Lack of sleep (e.g., insomnia); Disturbed sleep (e.g., obstructive sleep apnea); Excessive sleep (e.g., narcolepsy)	25–50%
Adaptive Dysfunction	Difficulty with self-care, self maintenance, and social skills	25–50%
Developmental Coordination Disorder	Difficulty in sports, balance (e.g., riding a bicycle, gymnastics), and/or handwriting	10–20%
Substance Addiction	Aggressiveness and irritability; Forgetfulness; Disappearing money or valuables; Feeling rundown, hopeless, depressed, or even suicidal; Getting drunk or high on drugs on a regular basis; Lying, particularly about how much alcohol or other drugs being used; Avoiding friends or family in order to get drunk or high; Planning drinking in advance, hiding alcohol, drinking or using other drugs alone; Having to drink more to get the same high	25% if treated, 70% if not treated. (Higher if CD or mood disorders)
Injuries	Fractures, concussions, lacerations	28% (children) 32% (teens) 38% (adults)

diagnosed with ADHD have comorbid conditions, with oppositional defiant disorder (ODD) present in 21%, anxiety in 10%, anxiety and ODD in12%, conduct disorder (CD) in 7%, tic disorder in 10%, and mood disorder (including depression, dysthymia, and bipolar disorder) in 4% [21]. Children with ADHD also have increased rates of developmental delays, developmental coordination disorder, and language disorder compared to their non-ADHD counterparts [17]. A classical study conducted by Hechtman and colleagues demonstrated that children with ADHD are at increased risk for long-term adverse social consequences in adolescence and early adulthood and that the disorder continues in a large number of individuals diagnosed in children [22]. Similarly, follow-up studies of the ADHD population have shown that people with ADHD are more likely to drop out of school (32–40%), not complete college (5–10%), have few or no friends (50–70%), under-perform at work (70–80%), engage in antisocial activities (40–50%), experience teen pregnancy (40%), have sexually transmitted diseases (16%), have multiple car accidents, and experience depression (20–30%) and personality disorders (18–25%) [7]. Addiction and substance misuse in relationship to ADHD and its comorbidities are examined later in this chapter.

Of various psychiatric comorbidities in ADHD, oppositional defiant disorder (ODD) is the most common [26]. In the past ODD was considered to be a precursor to CD. However, recent evidence suggests that the presence of ODD poorly predicts the development of CD, although the majority of individuals with CD have ODD [27]. ODD commonly refers to behaviors of defiance and aggressiveness that are done to protest demands and disrupt structured settings. Children with ODD will often talk back to authority figures, refuse to take responsibility for their actions, are noncompliant to rules and regulations, get easily annoyed and angry, refuse to compromise, and blame others for their behavior. It has also been reported that children with ADHD and ODD have higher rates of unintentional injury [17]. CD is a severe disruptive behavioral disorder with bullying, threatening others, initiating physical fights, physical cruelty to humans

and animals, destroying other's property, stealing, setting fires, running away from home, and using weapons (baseball bat, gun, knife, broken bottle, etc.). Children and adolescents with ADHD and CD fare much more poorly in adulthood compared to those with ADHD and ODD or ADHD alone. The combination of ADHD and CD results in higher rates of delinquency, illegal behavior, and substance addiction [26,28,29]. In addition to increased risk of severe accidents, drug addiction, and serious criminal activities, individuals with CD as comorbidity to their pre-existing ADHD often develop antisocial personality disorder (ASPD) as adults and face adverse outcomes in education, social life, and work life [30].

Mood disorders, especially depression, can be frequently found in children and adolescents with ADHD. Irritability, moodiness, and emotional immaturity are some common characteristics of the ADHD population with mood disorders, which in turn lead to difficulties managing disappointment and frustration effectively [29]. Usually the mood disorders are not the result of ADHD itself (e.g., low self-esteem due to poor academic performance or poor social life), but they co-exist with ADHD and may have different causal pathways. Unlike ODD and CD, which declare themselves by easily observed challenging behaviors, mood disorders (e.g., depression and anxiety) reflect internal feelings which may be harder to detect than conduct problems [31].

Both learning problems and specific learning disabilities (e.g., dyslexia, dyscalculia, dysgraphia, nonverbal learning disability, auditory and visual processing disorders) are also one of many comorbidities affecting children and adolescents with ADHD. If not addressed properly, these disorders can have serious consequences on a child's school life, education, self-esteem, and employment [10,26,32,33]. Learning disabilities are seen as neuropsychological disorders that present significant difficulties in academic achievement and higher order applied cortical functioning [26]. Learning disorders are a measurable difference between different cognitive processes that are critical in learning new information. Some children with above average intelligence may have learning disorders and do quite well if given necessary guidelines and management to deal with their impairment. Learning disability, however, is applied when the learning disorder interferes with attaining success at school and impacts on academic achievement (i.e., passing to the next grade). It is difficult to determine if learning problems among the ADHD population is a byproduct of ADHD (or vice versa), or if learning problems occurs separately from attention deficit hyperactivity disorder. However, there is increasing evidence which suggests children with ADHD, compared to their non-ADHD peers, have higher rates of learning disorders and cognitive impairments that impact on executive functioning, complex language, perceptual and social skills, memory, and information processing [10]. A child with such cognitive inefficiencies in the classroom will experience frustration, boredom, depression, and wide gaps between core intelligence and academic achievement.

Although there are those who believe that ADHD lessens in severity over time, many children diagnosed with ADHD continue to exhibit symptoms that impact on school, home, and community life throughout their adolescent years, in addition to experiencing challenging social behaviors [10]. They often struggle in high school subjects where demand for prolonged attention, patience, attention to detail, organization, and long-term planning are essential to academic success. Adolescents with ADHD face frequent detention, repeating a grade, failing in class, and in severe cases they might be suspended or expelled from school due to lack of attendance, poor academic achievement, or aggressive behavior. Without proper treatment and management, teens with ADHD are likely to not complete all the requirements for a high school degree. Normal teenage stressors such as identity crisis, peer acceptance, and dating can also pose significant challenges and jeapordize social and emotional well-being in adolescents with ADHD. In this regard, the majority of teens with ADHD might be considered "unreliable" or "irresponsible" by adults and will be given less opportunities to perform "adult tasks," such as babysitting, driving, and working part-time jobs [10,34].

30.2.2 Diagnostic limitations

There are several diagnostic limitations to ADHD. Due to the fact that ADHD is a profile of behaviors, diagnosis of this disorder is largely based on observation and clinical history. These can be highly subjective, depending on what teachers, parents, and caregivers consider "easily distracted," "talks excessively," or "careless." At the same time, temperament or individual differences in children are hard to assess and what appears to be symptoms of ADHD can be difficult to distinguish from normal behavior [35].

The fact that DSM-IV is based on a field trial also creates problems in terms of diagnostics. While DSM-IV has a more empirical value than its predecessor DSM-III, the majority of 500 children from multiple clinical sites used in the field study were of European American background. Therefore, clinicians may have to make adjustments when diagnosing children of non-European descent [36].

Two features of the DSM-IV guideline creates diagnostic confusion: (1) by lacking clear criteria for symptoms and by grouping various behaviors under one label, diagnostic specificity is reduced; (2) the DSM-IV recognizes as many diagnoses as symptoms permit. The requirement that some symptoms appear before the age of seven years may not be reasonable for inattentive symptoms, which may manifest only in the context of academic demands. It is also worth pointing out that while DSM-IV can be useful in ADHD diagnosis in children, some of the symptoms are not developmentally appropriate for adults (such as "inappropriate running/climbing" or "difficulty waiting turn") and, therefore, DSM-IV is less effective in diagnosing an adult ADHD [37].

In addition, DSM-IV makes no distinction among various ADHD comorbidities, regardless of the differences in their severity. There is no special category for severe comorbidities like CD, which requires special attention and different prevention and intervention management than that of other comorbidities such as anxiety and depression. However, under DSM-IV no such distinction is made, and all comorbidities are categorized under the same umbrella.

30.3 ADHD AND ADDICTION

In recent years there has been rising concerns regarding the susceptibility of substance use disorders (SUD), alcohol use disorders (AUD), and nicotine dependence disorder among the ADHD population. This fear was fueled in part by the methylphenidate and amphetamine stimulant medication used to treat ADHD. Both chemicals have overlapping structure with street drugs such as speed and cocaine [5,38–40]. Although prescribed stimulant medications improve focus, attention, and learning ability of children with ADHD, and in current doses and formulation have very little possibility of addiction, parents and the public "often worry that giving their child stimulant medication hyperactivity will set him up to be a drug abuser later in life" [5,32,39]. The link between stimulant medication and SUD in the ADHD population will be examined later in this section. But first, the relationship between SUD and ADHD itself is evaluated.

Both legal (e.g., tobacco, alcohol) and illegal (e.g., cannabis, cocaine, heroin, methamphetamine) substance use have been positively linked to psychiatric morbidity, including ADHD [26]. Several studies have observed that ADHD is over-represented in the adolescent SUD population [41]. Children with ADHD have higher rates of SUD in adolescence and adulthood, engage in risky behaviors (illicit drug, alcohol, and tobacco use) at an earlier age, and have a two-year earlier onset of SUD compared to their non-ADHD peers [10,26,42]. Adolescents and adults with ADHD are also more likely to experience relapse of substance misuse compared to their non-ADHD counterparts who are suffering from drug misuse [43]. Retrospective studies also suggest that there is a high prevalence of ADHD among adolescents and adults with SUD; up to 50% of adolescents and 25% of adults with SUD have been found to have ADHD [44–49]. Persistence of ADHD symptoms in adolescence has also been linked to higher risk of alcohol use [50].

One explanation as to why children and adolescents with ADHD engage in risky behaviors and are more prone to SUD in adulthood than their peers without ADHD can be found, in part, by the very nature of the disorder. Impulsivity, or lack of impulse control, makes the ADHD population vulnerable to illicit drugs, alcohol, and tobacco use because they are likely to engage in risky behaviors whenever the opportunity presents itself without contemplating the consequences [10].

Lack of academic success and nonrewarding social life in school can also facilitate drug and alcohol use among children and adolescents with ADHD. Poor academic performance has been linked to "marginal peer affiliation," which in turn can provide more opportunities for drug and alcohol use [51].

The fact that many people with ADHD exhibit thrill-seeking activities can be one additional reason behind the high rate of SUD among the ADHD population. Children and adolescents with ADHD crave excitement and novel stimulation more than their non-ADHD peers. Children with undiagnosed ADHD usually gratify this desire through causing disruption in class, picking fights with siblings or classmates, and constantly taking physical risks (e.g., performing dangerous tricks without adult supervision or permission). This behavior, if ADHD is not properly diagnosed and treated, continues throughout adolescence and young adulthood with added risk of engaging in recreational drugs, tobacco, alcohol, and unprotected sex. Thrill-seeking behaviors among ADHD population have more to do with trying to avoid boredom and under-stimulation than resulting from inattention [33].

Substance use among the ADHD population can also be attributed to "self-medication,". People with undiagnosed ADHD or those who are not receiving treatment might turn to legal (e.g., tobacco, alcohol) as well as illegal (e.g., cocaine, marijuana) substances in order to subdue their symptoms of anxiety, restlessness, hyperactivity, depression, and low self-esteem. Cocaine, for example, will have similar effects to that of Ritalin (such as increased level of focus and clarity of thought) when taken by people with ADHD. To those with undiagnosed ADHD, cocaine can be seen as an effective, but short-term cure to alleviate the painful symptoms of ADHD. Marijuana and alcohol can also serve as short-term calming agents that reduce anxiety although, in the long run, continual use will actually increase levels of depression and anxiety [33].

Externalizing behavioral characteristics that are included in a range of psychiatric diagnoses increase the risk for substance use disorders. In the diagnosis of ADHD, the lack of control is captured primarily by the hyperactive/impulsive symptoms in the DSM-IV. Other psychiatric conditions that include high levels of impulsivity are conduct disorder (CD), oppositional defiant disorder (ODD), and adult antisocial personality disorder. Both antisocial personality disorder and conduct disorder play a well defined and important role in the development of SUD and addiction among children and adolescents diagnosed with ADHD. Diagnosis of conduct disorder alone in childhood has been strongly linked to substance and alcohol addiction in adolescent and adulthood [27,28]. In addition, children with ADHD and subsequent CD suffer a more severe clinical course and earlier onset of more intense antisocial behaviors than might be expected with ADHD alone. In a longitudinal study of 165 offspring of families with a positive history of alcohol use disorder, Schuckit and colleagues found that among children who developed ADHD without the presence of CD, none developed SUD in adulthood [52]. Surprisingly, in those children who developed CD in childhood, they experienced an 18-fold higher risk for a SUD diagnosis over the next 20 years [53–55]. Among 1500 twin siblings followed in the Minnesota Twin Family Study, the appearance of CD between the ages of 11 and 14 was the most powerful predictor of substance use disorders (cannabis, alcohol, and illicit drugs) by 18 years of age [56]. To better understand the relative contributions of ADHD and CD on substance use disorders, Elkins and colleagues reported the magnitude of influence of a CD diagnosis

between 11 and 14 years of age on the later development of an alcohol use disorder was nearly six times the odds associated with having an ADHD diagnosis by 11 years of age. Finally, they found that – categorical diagnoses aside – the hyperactive and impulsive symptoms of the ADHD diagnosis better predicted the adolescent substance initiation over the next four years and substance use disorder outcome at 18 years of age, after controlling for conduct disorder, than the inattentive symptoms of the ADHD diagnosis.

It is worth mentioning that the high rate of addiction and substance use among the ADHD population usually occurs in countries where CD is seen as a comorbidity to ADHD and not a separate disorder. For example, in the DSM-IV used in the United States a child can have both ADHD and CD. In Britain, however, where the International Classification of Diseases (ICD-10) is used, a child can either be diagnosed with ADHD or CD alone. As we have examined above, the correlation between CD and addiction is significantly high, but in countries where CD is not considered as a comorbidity of ADHD, the addiction among ADHD population is lower than that of the United States [57].

30.3.1 Ritalin, ADHD, and addiction manifestation

One of the most debated subjects pertaining to ADHD and addiction has been the use of psychostimulants in treating attention deficit hyperactivity disorder [5,26,32,38–40].

Recent studies, however, discredit this belief. In fact, it has been suggested that children with ADHD treated with psychostimulants have lower levels of substance use compared to other ADHD children not treated with stimulants [38]. Similarly, substance misuse of alcohol and marijuana is more common among adolescents with untreated ADHD [26,29]. Also, there is no evidence indicating that methylphenidate and amphetamine produce feelings of "euphoria," feelings of being "high," or induce tolerance [29]. Unlike other illicit "street drugs," psychostimulants are highly regulated and taken in specific doses at a time during the day under the supervision of caregivers and parents. The fact that these drugs are administered and approved by authority figures reduces the "thrill" of misusing it. Also, oral ingestion of psychostimulants has shown to release dopamine at a slower rate compared to intravenous or intranasal intake.

While psychostimulants are recommended for treatment of ADHD children and adolescents without SUD, caution is required when treating adolescents who are already involved with substances. This is due to the potential risk of misuse by the adolescent's non-ADHD peers. Several nonpsychostimulant drugs (such as Buproprion and Atomoxetine) have been shown to be safe and effective in treating adolescent and adult ADHD populations with SUD [58]. However, ongoing investigations examining how to best manage untreated ADHD in the setting of substance addiction are required. Also needed are studies that explore the impact of early comprehensive interventions for children with ADHD on long-term health, mental health, and SUD.

30.4 TREATING ADDICTION IN ADHD

Untreated ADHD poses a higher risk for substance addiction than ADHD that is appropriately managed. It has been suggested that the risk for SUD declines dramatically for adolescents with ADHD who are being treated for the disorder [59,60]. In this regard, stimulant medications like amoxetine and bupropion have been tried for those adolescents with substance addiction and under-treated ADHD.

Also, ADHD children with conduct disorder have a greater risk for substance addiction compared to children with ADHD alone. These findings illustrate the complexity of addiction within the context of ADHD. However, these results are preliminary and further research is required, especially among adolescents with ADHD, CD, and SUD, on best multimodal practices.

30.5 CONCLUSIONS

Although knowledge of ADHD has expanded dramatically in the past two decades, basic and clinical research is still in its infancy. It can be said with complete confidence that ADHD is a chronic disorder which often is accompanied by one or more comorbidities and, if not treated and managed properly, can have a devastating impact, not only on physical and mental health but also, most notably, in the areas of higher education attainment, employment, and relationship successes. In addition, individuals with CD and ADHD are especially vulnerable to SUD and addiction. However, both ADHD and its comorbidities can be managed effectively with combinations of psychostimulant drugs, behavioral therapy, educational and vocational accommodation, and ongoing counseling. While out knowledge of ADHD and its comorbidities is far from complete, several options have proven effective in treating individuals with this disorder and keeping its disruptive impact to a minimum. For obvious reasons, long-term follow-up study of the ADHD population from diagnosis in preschool to adulthood is exceedingly rare. The current challenge is to ensure that diverse populations of children with ADHD have access to interventions that optimize health, learning, and social competencies. This strategy will also secure the protective factors that lesson vulnerability to substance addiction.

REFERENCES

1. Barbaresi, W.J., Katusic, S.K., Colligan, R.C. *et al.* (2002) How common is attention-deficit/hyperactivity disorder? Incidence in a population-based birth cohort in Rochester. *Minn. Arch. Pediatr. Adolesc. Med.*, **156** (3), 217–224.
2. Cuffe, S.P., McKeown, R.E., Jackson, K.L. *et al.* (2001) Prevalence of attention-deficit/hyperactivity disorder in a community sample of older adolescents. *J. Am. Acad. Child Adolesc. Psychiatry*, **40** (9), 1037–1044.

3. Pelham, W.E., Foster, E.M., and Robb, J.A. (2007) The economic impact of attention-deficit/hyperactivity disorder in children and adolescents. *J. Pediatr. Psychol.*, **32** (6), 711–727.

4. Wolraich, M.L. (2006) Attention-deficit hyperactivity disorder. *Semin. Pediatr. Neurol.*, **13** (4), 279–285.

5. Keane, H. (2008) Pleasure and discipline in the uses of Ritalin. *Int. J. Drug Policy*, **19** (5), 401–409.

6. Zito, J.M., Safer, D.J., dosReis, S. *et al.* (2000) Trends in the prescribing of psychotropic medications to preschoolers. *JAMA*, **283** (8), 1025–1030.

7. Barkley, R.A. (2002) International consensus statement on ADHD. *Clin. Child Fam. Psychol. Rev.*, **5** (2), 89–111.

8. Wilens, T.E., Biederman, J., and Spencer, T.J. (2002) Attention deficit/hyperactivity disorder across the lifespan. *Annu. Rev. Med.*, **53**, 113–131.

9. Barkley, R.A., Shelton, T.L., Crosswait, C. *et al.* (2000) Multi-method psycho-educational intervention for preschool children with disruptive behavior: preliminary results at post-treatment. *J. Child Psychol. Psychiatry*, **41** (3), 319–332.

10. Barkley, R.A. (1995) *Taking Charge of ADHD*, The Guilford Press, NY, New York.

11. Brassett-Harknett, A. and Butler, N. (2005) Attention-deficit/hyperactivity disorder: an overview of the etiology and a review of the literature relating to the correlates and lifecourse outcomes for men and women. *Clin. Psychol. Rev.*, **27** (2), 188–210.

12. Worley, K.A. and Wolraich, M.L. (2003) Attention-deficit hyperactivity disorder, in *Disorders of Development and Learning*, 3rd edn (ed. M.L. Wolraich), BC Decker Inc., Hamilton, ON.

13. Centers for Disease Control and Prevention (CDC) (2005) Mental health in the United States: prevalence of diagnosis and medication treatment for attention-deficit/hyperactivity disorder. *MMWR Morb. Motral. Wkly. Rep.*, **54**, 842–847.

14. Brown, T.E. (2000) *Attention-Deficit Disorders and Comorbidities in Children, Adolescents, and Adults*, 1st edn, American Psychiatric Press, Washington, DC.

15. Parker, S., Zuckerman, B., and Augustyn, M. (2005) *Developmental and Behavioral Pediatrics – A Handbook for Primary Care*, 2nd edn, Lippincott Williams & Wilkins, Philadelphia PA, pp. 114–123.

16. Pavuluri, M.N., Luk, S.L., and McGee, R. (1999) Parent reported preschool attention deficit hyperactivity: measurement and validity. *Eur. Child Adolesc. Psychiatry*, **8** (2), 126–133.

17. Greenhill, L.L., Posner, K., Vaughan, B.S., and Kratochvil, C.J. (2008) Attention deficit hyperactivity disorder in preschool children. *Child Adolesc. Psychiatr Clin. N. Am.*, **17** (2), 347–366, ix.

18. Faraone, S.V., Biederman, J., and Mick, E. (2006) The age-dependent decline of attention deficit hyperactivity disorder: a meta-analysis of follow-up studies. *Psychol. Med.*, **36** (2), 159–165.

19. Mannuzza, S., Klein, R.G., Bessler, A. *et al.* (1998) Adult psychiatric status of hyperactive boys grown up. *Am. J. Psychiatry*, **155** (4), 493–498.

20. American Psychiatric Association (2000) Task Force on DSM-IV, in *Diagnostic and Statistical Manual of Mental Disorders: DSM-IV-TR*, 4th text revision edn, American Psychiatric Association, Washington, DC.

21. Jensen, P.S., Hinshaw, S.P., Kraemer, H.C. *et al.* (2001) ADHD comorbidity findings from the MTA study: comparing comorbid subgroups. *J. Am. Acad. Child Adolesc. Psychiatry*, **40** (2), 147–158.

22. Hechtman, L., Weiss, G., and Perlman, T. (1984) Hyperactives as young adults: past and current substance abuse and antisocial behavior. *Am. J. Orthopsychiatry*, **54** (3), 415–425.

23. Freeman, R.D., and Tourette Syndrome International Database Consortium (2007) Tic disorders and ADHD: answers from a world-wide clinical dataset on Tourette syndrome. *Eur. Child Adolesc. Psychiatry.*, (Suppl. 1), 15–23, Erratum in: *Eur. Child Adolesc. Psychiatry* (2007) **16** (8), 536.

24. Swain, J.E., Scahill, L., Lombroso, P.J. *et al.* (2007) Tourette syndrome and tic disorders: a decade of progress. *J. Am. Acad. Child Adolesc. Psychiatry*, **46** (8), 947–968.

25. Owens, J.A. (2005) The ADHD and sleep conundrum: a review. *J. Dev. Behav. Pediatr.*, **26** (4), 312–322.

26. Atkins, M.S. and Maríñez-Lora, A.M. (2008) Attention-deficit/hyperactivity disorder and psychiatric comorbidity, in *Capute & Accardo's Neurodevelopmental Disabilities in Infancy and Childhood*, vol. **II** (ed. P.J. Accardo), The Spectrum of Neurodevelopmental Disabilities, 3rd edn, pp. Paul H Brookes Publishing Company, Baltimore, MD.

27. Biederman, J., Petty, C.R., Dolan, C. *et al.* (2008) The long-term longitudinal course of oppositional defiant disorder and conduct disorder in ADHD boys: findings from a controlled 10-year prospective longitudinal follow-up study. *Psychol Med.*, **38**, 1027–1036.

28. McMahon, R.J., Wells, K.C., and Kotler, J.S. (2006) Conduct problems, in *Treatment of Childhood Disor-*

ders, 3rd edn (eds E.J. Mashand R.A. Barkley), The Guilford Press, New York, NY.

29. American Academy of Pediatrics (2004) *ADHD: A Complete and Authoritative Guide* (eds M.I. Reiffand S. Tippins), American Academy of Pediatrics.

30. Bernfort, L., Nordfeldt, S., and Persson, J. (2007) ADHD from a socio-economic perspective. *Acta Paediatr.*, **97** (2), 239–245.

31. Stein, M.A. and Shin, D. (2008) Disorders of attention, in *Capute & Accardo's Neurodevelopmental Disabilities in Infancy and Childhood*, 3rd edn, vol. **II** (ed. P.J. Accardo), The Spectrum of Neurodevelopmental Disabilities, Paul H Brookes Publishing Company, Baltimore, MD.

32. Bain, L.J. (1991) *A Parent's Guide to Attention Deficit Disorders*, Dell Trade Paperback, New York, NY.

33. Hallowell, E.M. and Ratey, J.J. (1994) *Driven to distraction: Recognizing and Coping with Attention Deficit Disorder from Childhood through Adulthood*, Touchstone, New York, NY.

34. Robin, A.L. (1999) Attention-deficit/hyperactivity disorder in adolescents: Common pediatric concerns. *Pediatr. Clin. North Am.*, **46** (5), 1027–1038.

35. Carey, W.B. (2002) Is ADHD a Valid Disorder? in *Attention Deficit Hyperactivity Disorder: State of the Science, Best Practices* (eds P.S. Jensenand J.R. Cooper), Civic Research Institute, Kingston, NJ.

36. Smith, B.H., Barkley, R.A., and Shapiro, C.J. (2006) Attention-Deficit/Hyperactivity Disorder, in *Treatment of Childhood Disorders*, 3rd edn (eds E.J. Mashand R.A. Barkley), The Guilford Press, New York, NY.

37. McGough, J.J. and Barkley, R.A. (2004) Diagnostic controversies in adult attention deficit hyperactivity disorder. *Am. J. Psychiatry.*, **161** (11), 1948–1956.

38. Barkley, R.A., Fischer, M., Smallish, L., and Fletcher, K. (2003) Does the treatment of attention-deficit/hyperactivity disorder with stimulants contribute to drug use/abuse? A 13-year prospective study. *Pediatrics*, **111** (1), 97–109.

39. Wise, R.A. (1984) Neural mechanisms of the reinforcing action of cocaine. *NIDA Res. Monogr.*, **50**, 15–33.

40. Wise, R.A. (2002) Brain reward circuitry: insights from unsensed incentives. *Neuron.*, **10**, 36 (2), 229–240.

41. Szobot, C.M. and Bukstein, O. (2008) Attention deficit hyperactivity disorder and substance use disorders. *Child Adolesc. Psychiatr Clin. N. Am.*, **17** (2), 309–323, viii.

42. Wilens, T.E., Biederman, J., Mick, E. *et al.* (1997) Attention deficit hyperactivity disorder (ADHD) is associated with early onset substance use disorders. *J. Nerv. Ment. Dis.*, **185** (8), 475–482.

43. Latimer, W.W., Ernst, J., Hennessey, J. *et al.* (2004) Relapse among adolescent drug abusers following treatment: The role of probable ADHD status. *J. of Child and Adolescent Substance Abuse*, **13** (3), 1–16.

44. Schubiner, H., Tzelepis, A., Milberger, S. *et al.* (2000) Prevalence of attention-deficit/hyperactivity disorder and conduct disorder among substance abusers. *J. Clin. Psychiatry*, **61** (4), 244–251.

45. DeMilio, L. (1989) Psychiatric syndromes in adolescent substance abusers. *Am. J. Psychiatry*, **146** (9), 1212–1214.

46. Eyre, S.L., Rounsaville, B.J., and Kleber, H.D. (1982) History of childhood hyperactivity in a clinic population of opiate addicts. *J. Nerv. Ment. Dis.*, **170** (9), 522–529.

47. Carroll, K.M. and Rounsaville, B.J. (1993) History and significance of childhood attention deficit disorder in treatment-seeking cocaine abusers. *Compr. Psychiatry*, **34** (2), 75–82.

48. Levin, F.R., Evans, S.M., and Kleber, H.D. (1998) Prevalence of adult attention-deficit hyperactivity disorder among cocaine abusers seeking treatment. *Drug Alcohol Depend.*, **52** (1), 15–25.

49. Wilens, T.E., Faraone, S.V., and Biederman, J. (2004) Attention-deficit/hyperactivity disorder in adults. *JAMA*, **292** (5), 619–623.

50. Molina, B.S. and Pelham, W.E.Jr. (2003) Childhood predictors of adolescent substance use in a longitudinal study of children with ADHD. *J. Abnorm. Psychol.*, **112** (3), 497–507.

51. Farrell, M. (2007) Substance use and psychiatric comorbidity in children and adolescents, in *Alcohol, Drugs, and Young People: Clinical Approaches* (eds E. Gilvarryand P. McArdle), MacKeith Press, London.

52. Schuckit, M.A., Smith, T.L., Pierson, J. *et al.* (2007) Externalizing disorders in the offspring from the San Diego prospective study of alcoholism. *J. Psychiatr Res.*, Aug 30; [Epub ahead of print].

53. Aytaclar, S., Tarter, R.E., Kirisci, L., and Lu, C. (1999) Association between hyperactivity and executive cognitive functioning in childhood and substance use in early adolescence. *J. Am. Acad. Child Adolesc. Psychiatry*, **38**, 172–178.

54. Biederman, J., Wilens, T.E., Mick, E. *et al.* (1998) Does attention-deficit hyperactivity disorder impact the developmental course of drug and alcohol abuse and dependence? *Biol. Psychiatry*, **44**, 269–273.

55. Hesselbrock, M. and Hesselbrock, V.M. (1992) Relationship of family history, antisocial personality disorder and personality traits in young men at risk for alcoholism. *J. Stud. Alcohol.*, **53**, 619–625.

56. Elkins, I.J., McGue, M., and Iacono, W.G. (2007) Prospective effects of attention-deficit/hyperactivity disorder, conduct disorder, and sex on adolescent substance use and abuse. *Arch. Gen. Psychiatry.*, **64** (10), 1145–1152.

57. Gibbins, C. and Weiss, M. (2007) Clinical recommendations in current practice guidelines for diagnosis and treatment of ADHD in adults. *Curr. Psychiatry Rep.*, **9** (5), 420–426.

58. Davis, R.D. and Riggs, P.D. (2007) Integrated treatment of substance use disorders and co-occurring psychiatric disorders in adolescents, in *Alcohol, Drugs, and Young People: Clinical Approaches* (eds E. Gilvarryand P. McArdle), MacKeith Press, London.

59. Biederman, J., Wilens, T., Mick, E. *et al.* (1999) Pharmacotherapy of attention-deficit/hyperactivity disorder reduces risk for substance use disorder. *Pediatrics*, **104** (2), e20.

60. Simkin, D.R. (2002) Adolescent substance use disorders and comorbidity. *Pediatr. Clin. North Am.*, **49** (2), 463–477.

31

Addictive disorders in the elderly

Andrea Bial

Department of Medicine, Section of Geriatrics, University of Chicago Medical Center, Chicago, IL, USA

31.1 DEMOGRAPHICS OF AGING

Most physicians and healthcare providers are aware that the United States population is aging. Not only are more Americans reaching the age of 65 years, but more are reaching into the "oldest" old category of 85 years and above. In 2006, the number of persons aged 65 years or older was 37.3 million. They represent approximately 12.4% of the population, or approximately one in eight Americans. This percentage has tripled since 1900 and the number has increased 12-fold. By 2030 they will represent 20% of the population. Compared to 1900, the number of elderly persons 75–84 years of age is 17 times larger and the number of persons 85 years of age and older is 43 times larger. Because of the "Baby Boom" generation (those born at the end of World War II, usually considered 1946), the number of persons 65 years of age and older will increase by 15% between 2000 and 2010, and by 36% between 2010 and 2020.

Given this growth in the number of older patients, it is not surprising that there will too few geriatricians to care for all of the elderly. All physicians, almost regardless of specialty, will be seeing increasing numbers of elderly patients and will need to be familiar with geriatric issues, including issues around alcohol and other substance addictions. This chapter will help healthcare providers of all medical and surgical specialties care for their older patients who may be using alcohol or illicit drugs, or misusing prescription drugs. Throughout this chapter, "elderly" or "older" will refer to patients 65 years of age or older unless otherwise designated. While this is often the age used to define "elderly" due to Medicare benefits, researchers have not always consistently used this cut-off, making reviews of the literature somewhat challenging. Therefore, throughout this chapter it is noted whenever different age minimums were used.

31.2 OVERVIEW: IDENTIFYING ADDICTIVE DISORDERS IN THE ELDERLY

For a multitude of reasons that will be discussed, it can be very difficult to identify problem drinking or drug use in older patients. First and foremost, it should be understood that there may be a

Addictive Disorders in Medical Populations   Edited by Norman S. Miller and Mark S. Gold

predisposition to the adverse affects of alcohol or drugs as patients age. While there is no clinically significant decline in liver function with normal aging, there is a decrease in muscle mass and total body water. This, combined with an increase in adipose tissue mass, may predispose patients to have toxicity at lower levels of alcohol or other drugs. In other words, older patients may still be able to metabolize the alcohol in the same way as when they were younger, but they can feel its affects at an earlier point due to the decrease in total body water (e.g., they lose the dilution effect). There is a decline in renal function as patients age, although the rate of decline is highly variable and unpredictable. It is particularly important to measure creatinine clearance or glomerular filtration rates (GFRs in older patients to obtain an accurate measure of their kidney function and not rely on the creatinine alone, which may be inaccurate in older patients with reduced muscle mass. For example, drugs such as many benzodiazepines may have prolonged affects in older patients due to kidney disease that is unrecognized due to a "normal" creatinine of 1.0 mg/dl, when in reality the glomerular filtration rate is 30 mg/min.

The majority of this chapter will focus on alcohol, as it has the greatest amount of research in older patients. Illicit drugs and prescription drug addiction will be discussed as well, but in less detail, due to the fact that there is much less research done in these areas.

31.2.1 Identifying alcohol use and addiction in the elderly

Research in the field of alcohol use and addiction can be very confusing, as there is no specific definition or consensus as to what defines "problem drinking." According to the *Diagnostic and Statistical Manual of Mental Disorders, Fourth Edition* (DSM-IV) [1], alcohol dependence is present when there is a maladaptive pattern of substance use, leading to clinically significant impairment or distress, with three or more of the following over 12 months: tolerance (the need for increased amounts of alcohol for the same effect or a diminished effect

with the same amount); withdrawal; taking continually larger amounts or using for longer than intended; persistent desire for alcohol or unsuccessful efforts to cut down or control its use; great deal of time spent acquiring alcohol, using it, or recovering from it; social/occupation/recreational activities curtailed due to alcohol; and continued use despite knowledge of having a persistent or recurrent problem associated with alcohol use. Alcohol abuse is defined as a maladaptive pattern of substance use leading to clinically significant impairment or distress, with one or more of the following over 12 months: failure to fulfill obligations at works, school, or home; use of substance in hazardous situations; legal problems; and continued use despite persistent or recurrent social or interpersonal problems caused or exacerbated by the alcohol. By these criteria, the 2001–2002 estimated prevalence of alcohol abuse in those 65 years of age and older was 2.36% for men and 0.38% for women. However, these statistics likely underestimate the amount of problem drinking significantly. Older patients may not follow DSM-IV criteria which, in fact, were based on lifestyles and habits of younger drinkers. For example, older patients may not be working due to retirement or may not be driving due to arthritis; they will, therefore, not fail to fulfill occupational obligations nor be involved in hazardous situations, such as Driving Under the Influence (DUI) convictions. As a result, their problem drinking could easily be missed if only using DSM-IV criteria. The elderly may be more likely to live alone, or be alone for long periods when other family members are at work, and drinking can easily be hidden or the amount of drinking be underestimated in this setting. They may be less inclined to report, or at least report accurately, their alcohol intake. Families may either not be aware of their older loved one's drinking or believe it not to be harmful. There may be a subtle feeling of, "They've reached this age; they deserve a little drink now and then." Further, as will be discussed in more detail below, healthcare providers often assume older patients do not drink, or do not have a problem with drinking (or other drugs), and fail to ask the patient when getting a history.

The National Institute on Alcohol Abuse and Alcoholism (NIAAA) recommends no more than one drink per day for persons 65 years of age and older. Of course, how people define "drink" can be quite variable. According to the NIAAA, 12 ounces of beer = 8–9 ounces malt liquor = 5 ounces table wine = 3–4 ounces fortified wine (i.e., sherry or port) = 2–3 ounces of cordial/liqueur/aperitif = 1.5 ounces brandy = 1.5 ounces spirits (i.e., gin, vodka, whiskey, etc.). Up to 20% of older adults drink more than seven alcoholic beverages per week [2]. It is important when taking the history in an older patient to ask not only how many drinks per day they have, but what their drink of choice is and how much. Breslow [3] used three cross-sectional surveys in the years 2000–2001 and found that approximately one-third of the United States elderly population consumed alcohol of any amount. According to the American Geriatrics Society [4], up to 50% of elderly Americans may drink alcohol, with up to 15% experiencing health risks due to the alcohol they drink or the combination of alcohol and their other comorbidities or medications. Therefore, these statistics underscore the point that older Americans are in fact drinking alcohol; clearly healthcare providers must obtain alcohol histories from older patients.

Complicating the picture of alcohol use is the fact that many older Americans believe that there may be some benefit to mild or moderate drinking, in particular on heart disease and dementia. There have been several studies suggesting this, and the media frequently brings attention to the reports. Abramson *et al.* [5] found that heart failure rates declined with increasing amounts of alcohol consumption (either no alcohol, 1–20 ounces, or 21–70 ounces); this was independent of confounding factors and not entirely explained by the reduction in myocardial infarction risk. Mukamal *et al.* [6] found that consumption of 1–6 drinks per week was associated with a lower risk of incident dementia than abstention of all alcohol. Thun *et al.* [7] followed 490 000 men and women over nine years and found that middle-aged and older patients with moderate alcohol consumption had slightly reduced overall mortality (however, note should be made that mortality did increase with increasing use of

alcohol). As a result of these and other studies, some elderly might either start drinking alcohol in the belief that it will help them, or at least not cut back or recognize problems associated with their drinking.

Older patients are often not asked about alcohol or other drug use when seeing healthcare providers. Studies show that regardless of the setting – emergency department, inpatient units, outpatient clinics – healthcare providers often do not ask about substance addiction. In fact, it appears they may use preconceived ideas as to decide whether or not to ask a particular patient about substance addiction. In a study of a large sample of adult patients attending their primary care provider (PCP) clinic over a three-year period, only 16% of the patients were asked about alcohol use at all. Men were asked more than women. Interestingly, non-Caucasian patients were asked more frequently than Caucasian patients, when in fact the Caucasian patients drank more, on average, than the non-Caucasian patients. Those in the lowest income range were asked more than those in the highest income range but, again, there was actually more drinking in the highest income range. Many studies have shown that there is an increased likelihood of unhealthy drinking in Caucasian, "younger-old," and divorced or separated male patients who smoke and have a higher education, greater income, and better health. While these characteristics are important to know, it is also clearly important to make no assumptions when obtaining social histories from older patients.

31.2.2 Statistics on alcohol use and addiction in the elderly

While it appears that overall use of alcohol declines with aging, the reasons for this trend are not exactly known. Most likely it is due to a combination of factors, including actual reduced intake (due to any number of reasons as well, including the fact that lower amounts of alcohol produce the same effect). In addition, younger patients with heavy alcohol use may die prior to reaching "older" age. Approximately 10–20% of older adults drink more than the recommended limit of seven drinks per week.

However, the percentage of elderly who actually have a drinking problem (whether defined by DSM-IV or other criteria), may range from 4–15% for men and 2–3% for women. Merrick *et al.* [8] studied over 12 000 community-dwelling older patients and found that 9% of the patients reported drinking more than 30 drinks in a month or more than four drinks in one setting. Prevalence was fourfold higher in men than women. Approximately one-third of elderly persons begin drinking in later life. Those who do tend to have more social supports, and they do better in alcohol treatment than early-onset drinkers. The early-onset drinkers are likely those who started drinking early in life and managed to survive into older age. However, the "early-onset" and "late-onset" categories as a way to define older drinkers are not used consistently in the literature and are not clearly defined (for example, it is not universal as to what age defines "early" and "late").

As mentioned in the last section, men drink more than women at all ages, although the statistics may not be completely accurate due to the fact that women may be closet-drinkers and most statistics on alcohol use are obtained from patient self-report. Also, women are more likely to start later in life. As stated previously, men who are single (especially if divorced or separated), well-educated, smokers and have a history of substance use or addiction are also more likely to be problem drinkers. Retirement is not a consistent predictor of alcohol use or addiction. Like other stressful life events (for example, death of a spouse), retirement may trigger some later-in-life drinking but not consistently or predictably. However, healthcare providers should consider losses or changes (especially those which were unexpected or undesired) as potential risk factors and ask about alcohol use, even if it has been addressed in the past.

Depression is also associated with alcohol use and addiction. The presence of (or suspicion of) new depression in an older patient should prompt healthcare providers to investigate alcohol use, just as finding alcohol use should prompt providers to rule out coexisting depression (see Table 31.1 as well as Section 31.3 for more discussion of depression and

Table 31.1 Warning signs of addiction of alcohol or drugs in older patients

Sign/Symptom	Example
Excessive attachment to a particular drug or resistant to tapering/discontinuing	Not willing to consider a selective serotonin reuptake inhibitor (SSRI) instead of the benzodiazepine to treat continued anxiety
Excessive worry about supply and timing of drug	Frequent requests for "emergency" prescriptions because mail-order has not yet arrived
Continued use of drug even after condition for which it was prescribed has resolved	Continued requests for an opioid after knee replacement surgery many weeks after discharge
Complaints about providers who do not prescribe as the patient requests	Especially if patient wants greater number of pills or higher doses
Changes in appearance	Decline in grooming and hygiene
Changes in relationships	Greater isolation from family members or other social supports; more arguments or reports of strife; reluctance to elaborate on these issues
Changes in personality	Appearing more irritable, anxious, or depressed
Changes in cognition	Reduced ability to handle medications, missing appointments or not remembering what was discussed at previous visits; also consider withdrawal in post-operative patients who develop delirium
New vague physical complaints	New gastrointestinal complaints, arthralgias or myalgias, changes in sleep (insomnia or hypersomnia)
Changes in control of medial conditions	Newly poor control of blood sugar or blood pressure
Changes in mobility	New falls, accidents, or traumas.

Adapted from Simoni-Wastila [9], Widlitz [10], and American Geriatrics Society [4].

alcohol use). Older patients are at risk for this "dual diagnosis," and yet can still benefit from treatment, just as in younger patients.

As noted previously, the "Baby Boomer" generation is aging and will affect many aspects of the healthcare system. Gfroerer *et al.* [11] used data from the National Household Survey on Drug Abuse to create regression models and applied these to the projected population in 2020. They found that the number of older adults in need of substance addiction treatment will increase from 1.7 million in 2000 to 4.4 million in 2020. Further, where this generation lives may affect its drinking behavior. One cannot assume that living in a facility means no risk of alcohol addiction. Brennan [12] found that men and women in nursing homes with alcohol use disorders were more functional than those without such disorders (in basic activities of daily living (ADL) and instrumental activities of daily living (IADL)). The men tended to be younger than the women, and both genders had lived alone prior to admission. Some authors have suggested that as many as one-quarter of nursing home patients have some form of an alcohol disorder. Therefore, regardless of a patient's living situation, healthcare providers must consider alcohol use.

31.2.3   Statistics on illicit drug use in the elderly

Statistics for the use of illicit drugs in older patients are often difficult to find. Case reports exist in the literature of the occasional elderly patient with new-onset illegal drug use or the initially-young drug user who has aged, but otherwise there is very little research in this area. It is assumed to be rare for older patients to begin in later life to use "street" drugs (like cocaine, methamphetamine, etc.). Of likely greater risk is their misuse of prescription drugs, which is addressed in the next section. Older patients who use street drugs are most likely those who started when younger and were able to live long enough to become "elderly". Many believe that the onset of illegal drug use in those 65 years of age and older is nearly nonexistent.

A recent study by Rivers *et al.* [13] of urine drug screens on patients 60 years of age or older presenting in an inner-city academic emergency department found the rate of cocaine-positive samples to be 2.0% (17/852 patients). Patients with positive samples were more likely to be of the "young" old (mean age 66.4 years vs. 76.0 years for negative samples), and male, and more likely to be diagnosed with drug or alcohol addiction. According to the Substance Abuse and Mental Health Services Administration's (SAMHSA) National Survey on Drug Use and Health [14], between the years of 2002 and 2005, the rate of illicit drug use increased for adults aged 50–59. However, looking more specifically at those aged 55–59, the trend was mixed without significant difference between the two years. This may reflect that the younger patients (50–54 years) are the aging baby boomers. It will be important to follow these trends and see whether and how their use of illicit drugs changes as they age.

31.2.4   Statistics on prescription drug addiction in the elderly

Although only approximately 12% of the population, older patients use 25–30% of the prescription medications. Up to 11% of women aged 50 years of age or older misuse prescription drugs. Misuse is defined as any of the following: using someone else's prescription; requesting one without appropriate need; taking higher-than-prescribed doses; using the drug for purposes other than the indication; hoarding drugs; or using the drugs with alcohol. Factors associated with misuse of prescription drugs include female sex, social isolation, history of substance addiction or mental health disorder, chronic physical illness, multiple comorbid illnesses, and medical exposure to prescription drugs with addiction potential. Approximately one-quarter of older adults use psychoactive medications with addiction potential, such as benzodiazepines or opioids. Benzodiazepine dependency can develop after just two months of regular use in some patients. It has been associated with increased falls, motor vehicle accidents, and delirium.

Withdrawal from benzodiazepines is uncomfortable and potentially life threatening; it can include tremulousness, anxiety, nausea, vomiting, insomnia, and even seizures. Opioid addiction is rare in older adults unless they have had a history of opioid or alcohol addiction. Like any medications which can cause sedation or central nervous system (CNS) side effects, opioids can be associated with sedation, falls, and delirium. Holroyd and Duryee [15] examined the prevalence of substance use disorders among patients 60 years of age and older presenting to the University of Virginia's geriatric psychiatry outpatient clinic over approximately a three and one-half year period. Twenty-eight (20%) of the 140 patients had some type of substance addiction. 16 (11.4%) had benzodiazepine dependence and 2 (1.4%) had opioid dependence (12 or 8.6% had alcohol dependence). These statistics may worsen as the "Baby Boomers" age; with their familiarity with the Internet and medical savvy, they may begin requesting and/or receiving more potentially-addictive prescription medications. However, it is important that providers not under-prescribe them for fear of addiction potential, as under-treated pain is a much greater problem in older adults than opioid addiction. When prescribing potentially addictive medications to older patients, it is important to make the indication for the medication clear to the patient, explain the expected course of use, and begin at the lowest dose.

Complicating this issue of prescription drug addiction further is the difficulty in identifying these patients. Perhaps even more so than alcohol, patients are unlikely to admit, or perhaps even to recognize, that they are misusing a prescription medication. As discussed previously, the DSM-IV is not very sensitive to the older population. Providers must be aware of the potential for addiction of the drugs they prescribe. Table 31.1 lists in detail the signs and symptoms that should alert healthcare providers to the potential for drug or alcohol addiction in an older patient.

31.3 ROLE OF ADDICTIVE DISORDERS IN THE DISEASES OF THE ELDERLY

Almost all of the geriatric "syndromes" (including depression, delirium, dementia, incontinence, falls, and gait disturbances) can be caused or worsened by alcohol and substance use. In fact, it may be difficult to differentiate these conditions from alcohol use and addiction. Healthcare providers should consider screening questions (discussed in greater detail in the next section) on older patients with new or unexplained confusion or delirium, falls, sleep disorders, incontinence, hygiene issues, and depression (Table 31.1). The following section addresses specific diseases in older patients that may be affected by or related to alcohol or other substance use.

31.3.1 Falls and/or trauma

There is an increased risk of falls and other forms of trauma with alcohol use or other drugs that cause sedation (or other central nervous system (CNS) side effects, including dizziness, drowsiness, vertigo, and confusion). There is also an increased prevalence of osteoporosis with aging alone; when this risk is combined with alcohol (which affects gait and coordination), there is an increase in hip fracture rates. Finkelstein [16] found in men with alcohol addiction a 4.5 greater increased risk of a fall-related injury and in women a 3.7 increased risk. For other drug addiction, the odds ratio for men with a fall-related injury was 2.5 and for women 2.2. Onen et al. [17] prospectively evaluated patients 60 years of age and older presenting to the emergency department over a three-month period. The prevalence of alcohol use disorders in this population was approx 5%, and a little less than half (42%) had falls as their reason for admission, compared to 21% of the nonalcohol-using elderly control patients. In a fascinating study, Zautcke et al. [18] looked at level I and II trauma centers in Illinois over a three-year period. Of the 130 000 + traumas, almost one-quarter (24%) involved patients 65 years and older. Of those, only about 5% were even tested for alcohol use, and of those tested almost 50% were positive. Of those who were positive, almost 72% had blood alcohol levels above the legal driving limit for Illinois (80 mg/dl). Urine toxicology screens were done on only 5.5% of older victims. Almost 90% did not have drugs present on the screen, but of those who were positive the most common drugs were benzodiazepines and opioids, alone and/or mixed. Almost half of the older patients with alcohol in their blood presented with falls (as their trauma), whereas only one-quarter of older patients without alcohol had falls as their trauma. The message from this study is clear and supports the points made earlier: older patients are not being tested for alcohol and other drug use, and healthcare providers should have high suspicion of alcohol or drug addiction in the setting of new onset or worsening falls, accidents, or other traumas.

31.3.2   Cardiac

Despite some of the more recent research suggesting that mild to moderate alcohol consumption may be cardioprotective in certain settings, it is still felt by most that there is an increased risk of cardiomyopathy, congestive heart failure, myocardial infarction, hypertension, and cardiac arrhythmias with alcohol misuse (often referred to as the "holiday heart" syndrome).

31.3.3   Cognitive impairment

Alcohol may have directly toxic effects on the brain leading to an alcohol-related dementia and the absence of alcohol can lead to delirium as a patient withdraws. During admissions for alcohol withdrawal, patients 60 years of age and older have an almost fivefold greater risk for delirium. Just as in younger patients, older patients may experience Wernicke's encephalopathy or Korsakoff's psychosis. Patients referred to psychiatric services for substance addiction treatment often have a dual diagnosis of either depression (see below) or dementia (approximately 10–50%).

31.3.4   Gastrointestinal (GI) system

Most healthcare providers are aware of the increased risk of liver disease and cirrhosis, pancreatitis, and GI bleeding with chronic alcohol use and addiction.

31.3.5   Hematology/oncology

There is an increased risk of neoplasms with alcohol addiction, especially of the head and neck, liver, and breast cancer in women. Providers may see macrocytic anemia in chronic alcohol use even in the absence of thiamine and folate deficiency. The presence of an elevated mean corpuscular volume (MCV) should prompt providers to investigate alcohol use if not already done.

31.3.6   Malnutrition

Multiple vitamin deficiencies may occur in chronic alcohol use, including vitamin D, thiamine, and folate deficiencies. These can occur from poor nutritional intake, compromised vitamin metabolism, and reduced sun exposure (in vitamin D deficiency). Older patients may also be at risk for malnourishment if they are on fixed incomes and are using their limited resources to obtain alcohol. They are unlikely to be eating well in this circumstance.

31.3.7   Insomnia

Older patients may have difficulty sleeping from any number of reasons (many years of poor sleeping habits, depression, medication side effects, medical problems such as incontinence, sleep apnea, congestive heart failure (CHF), etc.). It is important not only to investigate potential causes of insomnia but also to determine if a patient is self-medicating by drinking alcohol prior to bedtime in order to hasten sleep onset. While patients may fall asleep earlier than they would have otherwise, their sleep will be more fragmented and less restorative, potentially leading to a vicious cycle of alcohol use and possible addiction. Over time with continued use of alcohol, its helpful affect in diminishing sleep latency is decreased while its disruptive affect to sleep later in the night continues. Even alcohol drunk at "happy hour" or with dinner can affect an older person's sleep many hours later.

31.3.8 Depression

Although not well studied, there is a correlation with alcohol use and depression or other mental health disorder in older patients, leading to a "dual diagnosis." The numbers range from 20–70% depending on the study and the population used (mostly psychiatric settings). As mentioned previously, the identification of either alcohol use or depression in an older patient should prompt providers to investigate the presence of the other. However, the treatment of these "dual diagnosis" patients is likely best done by those with training and experience in treating these patients.

31.4 ROLE OF ADDICTIVE DISORDERS IN MEDICATION USE IN THE ELDERLY

As mentioned previously, the elderly frequently use prescription and over-the-counter medications. In fact, "polypharmacy" is frequently considered a geriatric syndrome. Polypharmacy can be defined as taking a large number of medications (often five or more), taking medications due to side effects of other medications (for example, needing potassium due to the use of furosemide), or taking medications for unclear indications (for example, continuing to take colchicine despite the lack of a gout flare for decades). In addition, they may not consider over-the-counter medications as actual "medications," and therefore may not report their use to their providers. There is a very complicated relationship between alcohol and medications. Alcohol can inhibit the metabolism of some drugs, causing toxic levels of the medication, or it can activate the metabolism and decrease the medication's availability and effect. It can also interact directly with some drugs and transform them into toxic chemicals. Some of the effects can continue to be an issue even for several weeks after cessation of the alcohol. Finally, some drugs can affect how alcohol gets metabolized and potentially increase the risk for intoxication.

Medications with potentially deleterious interactions with alcohol and examples of these medications are listed in Table 31.2. While every effort was made to include the drugs most commonly prescribed to older patients, it is certainly not exhaustive. Healthcare providers need to consider a patient's alcohol intake prior to prescribing any new medication and be aware of a drug's potential interaction with alcohol prior to prescribing it to their patients who drink. It is also important to note that any medication with central nervous system side effects (such as sedation, dizziness, drowsiness, confusion, etc.) has the potential to be worsened by alcohol use.

Acetaminophen becomes toxic to the liver when used with chronic alcohol use, even when only small amounts of acetaminophen (<4 grams/day) are used. Patients who drink >3 drinks/day are especially at increased risk of liver damage with acetaminophen use.

Antibiotics: some antibiotics can cause side effects such as nausea, vomiting, and headache when combined with alcohol; examples of these include metronidazole, some sulfonamides and griseofulvin. Isoniazid and rifampin can both be rendered less effective due to reduced availability caused by alcohol use. Isoniazid and ketoconazole can cause liver damage when taken with chronic alcohol use.

Anticoagulants such as warfarin have increased availability in the presence of acute alcohol consumption and thus increase the patient's risk for bleeding; for chronic alcohol use, the availability is decreased, thus putting the patient at risk for thrombosis.

Antidepressants like tricyclic antidepressants (TCAs) and monoamine oxidase inhibitors (MAOIs) are currently used less frequently for depression in older patients; however, both have increased risk of side effects, including drowsiness and dizziness if used in acute and chronic alcohol consumption.

Table 31.2 Medications with potentially deleterious interactions with alcohol

Medication Class	Examples
Acetaminophen	Tylenol
Antibiotics	Metronidazole, sulfonamides, griseolfulvin, insoniazid, rifampin, ketoconazole
Anticoagulants	Warfarin
Antidepressants	Tricyclic antidepressants (TCAs) such as amitriptyline; Monoamine oxidase inhibitors (MAOIs) such as phenelzine
Antidiabetic	Chlorpropamide, glyburide, metformin
Antihistamines	Diphenhydramine, cetirizine, others
Antiseizure	Dilantin, clonazepam
Benzodiazepines	Diazepam, lorazepam, others
Cardiovascular drugs	Nitroglycerin, propranolol, hydralazine, angiotensin receptor blockers, calcium channel blockers; atorvastatin, lovastatin, others
Gastrointestinal (GI) drugs	H2 blockers such as ranitidine and others
Narcotics	Propoxyphene, oxycodone, others
Nonsteroidal anti-inflammatory drugs (NSAIDs)	Ibuprofen, aspirin, others

Adapted from NIAAA [19], AGS [4].

Antidiabetic drugs, such as chlorpropamide, glyburide, and glucophage may cause nausea, vomiting, and headaches similar to the antibiotics.

Antihistamines: diphenhydramine is available over-the-counter (OTC) as are others in this class, while some are still by prescription only. However, as with any drug with central nervous system side effects, the use of alcohol with antihistamines increases the risk of sedation, confusion, and falls.

Antiseizure medications like dilantin can have their availability increased by acute alcohol consumption and decreased by chronic consumption. Clonazepam use can potentiate the central nervous system side effects, including drowsiness and dizziness.

Benzodiazepines: As with narcotics, there is an increased risk of potentiating the central nervous system side effects. There may also be a greater risk for respiratory depression when used in combination with alcohol.

Cardiovascular drugs: Many classes of drugs in this category may interact with alcohol. Examples include nitroglycerin, propranolol, hydralazine, angiotensin receptor blockers, and calcium channel blockers; these and others may contribute to hypotension, dizziness, and syncope when used with alcohol. There is an increased risk of liver damage if the "statin" drugs (e.g., lovastatin, atorvastatin, etc.) are used with alcohol.

Gastrointestinal drugs: Histamine-2 blockers may raise alcohol levels and can affect liver enzymes. In addition, some may have drowsiness as a side effect, which can be exacerbated in the presence of alcohol.

Narcotics: There is an increased risk of potentiating the central nervous system side effects with alcohol use as well as an increased risk of respiratory depression.

*Nonsteroidal anti-inflammatory drugs (NSAID)*s can increase the risk of bleeding alone and this risk is exacerbated by alcohol use.

Pringle *et al.* [20] examined the use of alcohol with medications that had potentially adverse reactions in a large sample (>83 000) older patients (aged 65–106 years). They used a mailed survey to assess alcohol habits and accessed prescription medication use by using a state-funded program that gives prescription benefits to lower income elderly (Pennsylvania Pharmaceutical Assistance Contract for the Elderly; PA-PACE). The overall prevalence of alcohol use was 20.3%. 7% of the sample drank every day or nearly every day, 8% drank several times a week, 13% drank several times a month, and 72% drank once a month or less. Of the drinkers who used at least one potentially interacting drug, approximately 45% used only one drug, approximately 29% used two drugs, approximately 14% used three drugs, and approximately 13% used four or more drugs. The most common category of drug used was NSAIDs (although NSAID users were less likely to drink heavily), followed by antihistamines and antihypertensives. The reasons for these combinations were not obtained and were likely multifactorial. One can imagine that patients may not have known of any potential interaction of the drug(s) they were taking and alcohol use. This study underscores the importance of assessing older patients' drinking habits and knowing which medications may be affected by the alcohol use. The range of effects must also be considered. For some drugs, like the antibiotics, one might recommend a reduction in alcohol; whereas other drugs, like NSAIDs, providers may want to avoid altogether in those patients with heavy alcohol use.

31.5   ASSESSMENT OF ALCOHOL USE IN OLDER PATIENTS

There is much debate in the literature as to the best tool to use to assess an older patient's drinking habits. Each tool or survey has its advantages and disadvantages. Unfortunately, as of yet there is no short, easily-administered, validated tool available to those healthcare providers seeing older patients. However, four common tools will be discussed briefly, with some final recommendations for assessment at the end. Firstly, the CAGE questionnaire [21] has the advantage of being taught widely in medical schools and being easy to remember. It consists of four questions: (1) Have you ever tried to *C*ut down on your drinking? (2) Have people *A*nnoyed you by criticizing your drinking? (3) Have you ever felt bad or *G*uilty about your drinking? (4) Have you ever had a drink first thing in the morning/*E*ye-opener? Secondly, the Short Michigan Alcohol Screening Test–Geriatric Version (SMAST–G) [22] is a self-administered 10-item screening questionnaire with yes/no questions examining attitudes and behaviors of individuals towards their alcohol intake. Thirdly, the Alcohol-Related Problem Survey (ARPS) is a self-administered questionnaire on medical and psychiatric conditions, medication use, functional status, and alcohol use. Its scoring rules categorize patients according to the World Health Organization (WHO) criteria of harmful drinking (the use of alcohol that causes physical or psychological complications), hazardous drinking (the use of alcohol that places a person at risk for physical or psychological complications), or nonhazardous drinking. Finally, the Alcohol Use Disorders Identification Test (AUDIT) [23] was developed by the WHO to identify hazardous drinking, harmful drinking, or alcohol dependence. This test takes into account quantity and frequency of consumption, unlike the others, but this may limit its sensitivity and specificity in older patients whose drinking may be harmful or hazardous not because of the amounts of alcohol they drink but also due to their coexisting comorbidities or potentially-interactive medications. The CAGE and SMAST–G do not detect binge drinking, may not be sensitive to earlier stages of drinking disorders, and do not distinguish between current and past drinking. All of the tools rely on self-report. Culberson [21] recommends starting with the question: "Have you had a drink containing alcohol within the past three months?" If the patient answers positively, then providers can follow it up with one of the screening tests. The American Geriatrics Society (AGS) [4] recommends starting with, "How often do you have a drink containing alcohol, including any beer, wine, or liquor/spirits?" For those who have had any alcohol in the last year, ask the following questions: (1) On average, how many days per week do you drink alcohol? (2) On a typical day when you drink, how many drinks do you have? (In asking this, it is important to remember to review amounts: 12ounces beer = 4–6 ounces wine etc., in order to be certain what the patient means by "a" drink.) (3) How often do you have three or more drinks on one occasion? Regardless of the questions chosen, the most important point is that drinking habits in older patients should be assessed. Healthcare providers should familiarize themselves with a tool or set of questions with which they are most comfortable so that they remember to address alcohol use in their older patients.

Other than the tools discussed, there are unfortunately few other tests available to assess whether or not an older patient is drinking in an unhealthy manner. In particular, there are no definitive laboratory recommendations. Liver transaminase levels (e.g., AST and ALT) should be obtained, but these may be elevated due to any number of diseases. Alcohol use is certainly in the differential if a patient's mean corpuscular volume or gamma-glutamyl transferase (GGT) are elevated, but these tests are also not definitive. They can, however, be used to question a patient further once found.

Healthcare providers can also check blood alcohol levels or urine toxicology screens if they are suspicious that patient has recently used or is under the influence.

31.6 INTERVENTION AND REFERRAL

Unfortunately, there has historically been poor referral of elderly to substance addiction treatment. Brennan *et al.* [24] used Medicare data to evaluate the mental health outpatient care received by older adults with substance use disorders up to four years after discharge from the hospital. Less than one-third (28.6%) received mental health outpatient care over the four years. Mulinga [25] found that of the 176 patients 60 years of age and older admitted to the hospital with diagnoses of alcohol dependence or addiction, 29% went to psychiatric wards (vs. 78% of younger patients admitted with the same diagnoses) and only 15% were referred to alcohol rehabilitation (either inpatient or outpatient). These are abysmal rates of referral. Further, evidence suggests that older patients may do just as well as, if not better than, younger patients when in treatment. In fact, women in particular may have better outcomes if treated in elderly-specific programs. However, there are major limitations in the treatment-compliance literature and fewer women than men enter treatment programs. In general, older patients are more likely to complete treatment programs than younger patients and have better outcomes (in terms of alcohol or drug abstinence). Snowden *et al.* [26] found that geriatric patients were only 5% of the 5900 admissions to a general adult psychiatric unit over a six-year period, but they fared the same as younger patients at discharge on the Psychiatric Symptom Assessment Scale and on the risk for readmission. They did, however, have a slightly longer length of stay than the younger patients (median 16 days vs. 10 days).

Unfortunately, the difficulty can be in finding elderly-specific programs. For those with later-onset drinking, it may be helpful to identify the stresses or triggers that prompted the drinking, diagnose and treat any underlying psychiatric issue

(especially depression or early dementia), and help determine activities or interests that can keep the patient engaged and socializing. While much of this can be done by primary care providers, it may require a psychiatrist experienced in substance addiction issues in older patients. There are also a number of medications available that have been used in alcohol treatment, such as disulfiram and naltrexone. Their use is beyond the scope of this chapter. These medications are best prescribed and managed by those with experience in treating older patients with alcohol addiction. Further, patients ideally should be referred to an alcohol treatment program, such as Alcoholics Anonymous (AA), especially one that has older members in its group.

It is important to reiterate that while elderly-specific treatment programs are the ideal, primary care providers and other healthcare providers can be integral in helping older patients achieve reduction or elimination of their substance addiction. Heavy alcohol users or chronic, long-term benzodiazepine users may need inpatient detoxification, but many older patients can be managed in the outpatient setting. As part of Project GOAL (Guiding Older Adult Lifestyles), Fleming *et al.* [27] screened over 6000 older patients in community-based clinics for problem drinking. One hundred fifty-eight patients screened positive. The intervention group received two 10-to-15-minute physician-delivered counseling sessions. Those who received this intervention had significant reductions in alcohol use, including binge drinking, at 3, 6, and 12 months after the intervention.

An important issue especially for primary care providers who may be counseling older patients regarding alcohol or substance use is the issue of driving. Clearly, providers need to recommend abstinence if a patient admits to driving while under the influence. This can create a difficult situation, as providers will want the patient to be honest, but the patient may realize that their driving privileges may be revoked if they admit to using alcohol or other substances while driving.

States vary in their requirements regarding reporting. Some states have mandatory reporting, while others only suggest reporting if the provider suspects that drinking is affecting the patient's driving. Readers are advised to check their state's requirements.

31.7 CONCLUSIONS

Older patients do use alcohol and illicit drugs, and they do misuse prescription medications. While the actual numbers of patients involved in these activities may currently be small (especially for illicit drug use), that number will likely grow as the Baby Boomers age. Further, these older patients are frequently not recognized despite their frequent use of the healthcare system. Patients may be socially isolated and thus able to drink without detection, or family members may choose to overlook the behavior for a variety of reasons. Alcohol and drug addiction can complicate many geriatric conditions and can interact with many of the medications older patients are taking. It is imperative that all healthcare providers at least consider substance use in

their older patients, especially those presenting with the symptoms and behaviors listed in Table 32.1. Once identified, patients should be counseled regarding the national recommendations for drinking (no more than one per day or seven per week) and assessed for the level of treatment they might need (whether inpatient, outpatient with a primary care provider, or referral to an addiction specialist). Further research in the area of illicit and prescription drug use in older patients is clearly needed, as well as providers who maintain a high index of suspicion for alcohol or other substance addiction in their older patients, so that they may appropriately treat not only their potential addiction issue but their comorbid conditions as well.

REFERENCES

1. American Psychiatric Association (2000) *Diagnostic and Statistical Manual of Mental Disorders*, 4th edn, American Psychiatric Association, Washington, DC.
2. National Institute on Alcohol Abuse and Alcoholism (1998) Alcohol Alert, 40. http://pubs.niaaa.nih.gov/publications/aa40.htm (accessed 26 February 2008).
3. Breslow, R.A., Faden, V.B., and Smothers, B. (2003) Alcohol consumption by elderly Americans. *J. Stud. Alcohol*, **64**, 884–892.
4. American Geriatrics Society (2003) Clinical guidelines for alcohol use disorders in older adults. http://www.americangeriatrics.org/products/positionpapers/alcoholPF.shtml (accessed 12 March 2008).
5. Abramson, J.L., Williams, S.A., Krumholz, H.M. *et al.* (2001) Moderate alcohol consumption and risk of heart failure among older person. *JAMA*, **285**, 1971–1977.
6. Ludwick, R.E., Sedlak, C.A., Doheny, M. *et al.* (2000) Alcohol use in elderly women: nursing considerations in community settings. *J. Geron. Nursing*, **26**, 44–49.
7. Thun, M.J., Peto, R., Lopez, A.D. *et al.* (1997) Alcohol consumption and mortality among middle-aged and elderly U.S. adults. *N Engl J Med*, **337**, 1705–1714.
8. Merrick, E.L., Horgan, C.M., Hodgkin, D. *et al.* (2008) Unhealthy drinking patterns in older adults: prevalence and associated characteristics. *J. Am. Geriatr. Soc.*, **56**, 214–223.
9. Simoni-Wastila, L. and Yang, H.K. (2006) Psychoactive drug abuse in older adults. *Am. J. Geriatr. Pharmacother.*, **4**, 380–394.
10. Widlitz, M. and Marin, D. (2002) Substance abuse in older adults: an overview. *Geriatrics*, **57**, 29–34.
11. Gfroerer, J., Penne, M., Pemberton, M. *et al.* (2003) Substance abuse treatment need among older adults in 2020: the impact of the aging baby-boom cohort. *Drug Alcohol Depen.*, **69**, 127–135.
12. Brennan, P.L. and Moos, Rh. (1996) Late-life drinking behavior. *Alcohol Health Res. W.*, **20**, 197–205.
13. Rivers, E., Shirazi, E., Aurora, T. *et al.* (2004) Cocaine use in elder patients presenting to an inner-city emergency department. *Acad. Emer. Med.*, **11**, 874–877.

14. United States Department of Health and Human Services. Substance Abuse and Mental Health Services Administration's national survey on drug use and health. http://oas.samhsa.gov/nsduhLatest.htm (accessed 12 March 2008).

15. Holroyd, S. and Duryee, J.J. (1997) Substance use disorders in a geriatric psychiatry outpatient clinic: prevalence and epidemiologic characteristics. *J. Nerv. Mental Health*, **185**, 627–632.

16. Finkelstein, E., Prabhu, M., and Chen, H. (2007) Increased prevalence of falls among elderly individuals with mental health and substance abuse conditions. *Am. J. Geriatr. Psychiatry*, **15**, 611–619.

17. Onen, S.H., Onen, F., Mangeon, J.P. *et al.* (2005) Alcohol abuse and dependence in elderly emergency department patients. *Arch. Geron. Geriatrics*, **41**, 191–200.

18. Zautcke, J.L., Coker, S.B., Morris, R.W., and Stein-Spencer, L. (2002) Geriatric trauma in the state of Illinois: substance use and injury patterns. *Am. J. Emerg. Med.*, **20**, 14–17.

19. National Institute on Alcohol Abuse and Alcoholism (2007) Harmful interactions: mixing alcohol with medicines. http://pubs.niaaa.nih.gov/publications/Medicine/medicine.htm (accessed 27 February 2008).

20. Pringle, K.E., Ahern, F.M., Heller, D.A. *et al.* (2005) Potential for alcohol and prescription drug interactions in older people. *J. Am. Geriatr. Soc.*, **53**, 1930–1936.

21. Culberson, J.W. (2006) Alcohol use in the elderly: beyond the CAGE. Part 2: Screening instruments and treatment strategies. *Geriatrics*, **61**, 20–26.

22. Hirata, E., Almeida, O., Funari, R. *et al.* (2001) Validity of the Michigan Alcoholism Screening Test (MAST) for the detection of alcohol-related problems among geriatric outpatients. *Am. J. Geriatr. Psychiatry*, **9**, 30–34.

23. World Health Organization (2001) The alcohol use disorders identification test: guidelines for use in primary care. 2nd ed. http://whqlibdoc.who.int/hq/2001/WHO_MSD_MSB_01.6a.pdf (accessed 20 February 2008).

24. Brennan, P.L., Kagay, C.R., Geppert, J.J., and Moos, R. H. (2001) Predictors and outcomes of outpatient mental health care: a 4-year prospective study of elderly medicare patients with substance use disorders. *Med. Care*, **39**, 39–49.

25. Mulinga, J.D. (1999) Elderly people with alcohol-related problems: where do they go? *Int. J. Geriat. Psychiatry*, **14**, 564–566.

26. Snowden, M.B., Walaszek, A., Russo, J.E. *et al.* (2004) Geriatric patients improve as much as younger patients from hospitalization on genera psychiatric units. *J. Am. Geriatr. Soc.*, **52**, 1676–1680.

27. Fleming, M.F., Manwell, L.B., Barry, K.L. *et al.* (1999) Brief physician advice for alcohol problems in older adults: a randomized community-based trial. *J. Fam. Pract.*, **48**, 378–384.

Part Five

Treatment of addictive disorders

32

Pharmacological therapeutics for detoxification in addictive disorders

Firas H. Kobeissy [1,3*] **Carolina F. Braga,** [1] **Noni A. Graham,** [1] **and Mark S. Gold** [1,2]

[1] *Department of Psychiatry, University of Florida College of Medicine and McKnight Brain Institute, Gainesville, FL, 32611, USA*
[2] *Departments of Psychiatry, Neuroscience, Anesthesiology, Community Health & Family Medicine, University of Florida College of Medicine and McKnight Brain Institute, Gainesville, FL, 32611, USA*
[3] *Center for Neuroproteomics and Biomarkers Research*

32.1 INTRODUCTION

With the growing rates of drug abuse and dependence in the population, there is increasing recognition that all physicians should be able to identify and treat various forms of substance addictions and misuse. However, for some substances, pharmacological strategies and efficacious treatment are still being researched. Among the several options available for treatment, detoxification represents an integral step towards achieving a sound treatment. Detoxification refers to the abrupt cessation or rapid decrease in the administration of a substance of abuse and dependence. Detoxification may cause unpleasant physical and/or psychological withdrawal symptoms. Thus, it is characterized as the main challenge for an individual who is transitioning from substance misuse to nonuse. Detoxification is a necessary step towards long-term treatment and recovery. The goal of detoxification is to provide a safe withdrawal setting while motivating the patient to continue with treatment. Pharmacological management of withdrawal is sometimes necessary for effective recovery and treatment. This chapter addresses the best pharmacological therapeutics currently available for detoxification of alcohol, sedative/hypnotics, nicotine, cannabis, cocaine and other stimulants, opiates, inhalants, and hallucinogens.

32.2 ALCOHOL

Alcohol addiction costs the United States billions of dollars each year in lost production, health and medical care, motor vehicle accidents, violent crime and social programs for alcohol problems [1].

*Corresponding Author: Dr. Firas Kobeissy (e-mail: firasko@gmail.com); Department of Psychiatry, University of Florida, L4-100F (P.O. Box 100256) Gainesville, FL, 32611 Fax: (352) 392-2579

Addictive Disorders in Medical Populations   Edited by Norman S. Miller and Mark S. Gold
© 2010 John Wiley & Sons, Ltd.

Thus, there is an urgent need for comprehensive treatment for alcohol addiction. The first step is usually detoxification and management of withdrawal symptoms. When someone who has become chemically dependent upon alcohol decides to stop drinking, he/she will experience physical discomfort or withdrawal. Symptoms can range from mild (i.e., shakes, sweats, nausea and/or headache) to severe (i.e., hallucinations and/or seizures). The more severe withdrawal symptoms can become fatal if not medically treated.

The revised Clinical Institute Withdrawal Assessment for Alcohol (CIWA-Ar) scale is a tool for quantifying the risk and severity of alcohol withdrawal. The CIWA-Ar is widely used in assessing alcohol withdrawal due to its efficiency, clinical usefulness, validity, and credibility [2,3]. The use of an objective clinical scale is important in order to identify patients who need immediate sedation in order to prevent further complications [4]. Reassessment of the withdrawal symptoms should be performed at regular intervals. There are both subjective and objective criteria contained within the scale, which allow the clinician to make an informed decision concerning the use of pharmacological medication.

The CIWA-Ar is characterized as a symptom-triggered therapy and is an assessment for monitoring withdrawal symptoms. This 10-item scale measures the severity of alcohol withdrawal by the observation of signs and symptoms, such as: nausea and vomiting; tremor; tactile, visual and auditory disturbances; paroxysmal sweats; anxiety; headache and fullness in the head; agitation; and orientation and cloudiness of sensorium of the patient. Each criterion is rated on a scale from zero to seven, except for "orientation and clouding of sensorium," which is rated on a scale from zero to four. The assessment requires approximately five minutes to administer and the maximum score is 67. Mild withdrawals correspond to CIWA-Ar scores of eight or less, scores in the range of 9–15 represent moderate withdrawal symptoms and scores greater than 15 indicate severe withdrawal with a higher risk of seizures and confusion [3–5]. It is important to note that some patients (6.4%) still suffer complications despite low scores if left untreated [4].

As for treatment protocols, the appropriate treatment usually is determined based on the patient's CIWA-Ar score. Patients scoring less than 10 and with no increased risk for seizures can be managed without additional medication for withdrawal [3,6]. These patients should be recommended to nondrug therapy in a quiet and reassuring environment where signs and symptoms of withdrawal will continue to be monitored. Patients with CIWA-Ar scores that are equal to or higher than 10 should be entered into a treatment program and receive pharmacotherapy to treat their symptoms and reduce their risk of seizures and delirium tremens [3,6]. A follow-up of the CIWA-Ar should be repeated every one or two hours until withdrawal symptoms resolve [2]. The CIWA-Ar score has a direct correlation with the amount of medication prescribed and the duration of the treatment assigned: increasing scores on the CIWA-Ar indicate the need for increased dosage of the medication or a more intensive level of treatment, while a decrease on the CIWA-Ar scores dictates reducing the quantity of medication used and duration of treatment.

Benzodiazepines are widely prescribed for the management of alcohol withdrawal symptoms [3,7]. This class of drugs contains the best efficacy and safest results when compared to placebos [8]. Benzodiazepines present a low potential for physical dependency and have a wide safety margin; therefore, administration over several hours is possible. In addition, benzodiazepines present with minimal side effects. Benzodiazepines enhance the effects of GABA-A receptors on the brain, thus mimicking the effects of alcohol. Therefore, benzodiazepines are cross-tolerant with alcohol, thereby easing withdrawal symptoms. These agents not only improve the symptoms of alcohol withdrawal but also significantly reduce the risks for seizures and delirium tremens [8].

The two primary methods of therapy used to administer benzodiazepines during alcohol withdrawal treatment are fixed-dosage therapy and symptom-triggered therapy. For the fixed-dosage approach, the patient receives a scheduled amount of medication during regular intervals regardless of presence and/or severity of symptoms and whenever necessary. The amount of medication is then tapered once the withdrawal symptom is controlled. This method is usually recommended as the first-line pharmacological approach [9]. In contrast, for the symptom-triggered approach, the patient's CIWA-Ar score is monitored at regular intervals and the medication is administered only when the patient's score is elevated. Thus, the latter approach prevents the over-use of medication, as it is only administered when symptoms are present [9].

In a randomized double-blind study comparing fixed-dosage regimen therapy and symptom-triggered therapy, 117 patients with alcohol dependence were admitted to an alcohol treatment program. Fifty-six patients were treated with oxazepam only when alcohol withdrawal symptoms were present (symptom-triggered) and sixty-one patients received fixed dosages every six hours and as needed (fixed-schedule). The results showed that treatment duration for the symptom-triggered group was significantly lower: 20 hours, as opposed to 62.7 hours for the fixed-dose group [9]. In addition, the symptom-triggered group received 37.5 mg of oxazepam as opposed to 231.4 mg received in the fixed-dose group [9]. In both treatments, there was no difference found in the severity of withdrawal, incidence of seizure, and/or delirium tremens. Symptom-triggered therapy is as effective, if not more effective, than the fixed-dosage regimen [9]. The same results were attained when comparing symptom-triggered and fixed-dosage lorazepam in a Veteran's Hospital [10]. Thus, this approach leads to more rapid detoxification while reducing the total dosage of benzodiazepines given to a patient, which decreases the incidence of over-sedation. In addition, more rapid detoxification leads to shorter hospital stays and lower overall treatment costs. However, studies using symptom-triggered therapy on patients who are at high risk for seizures despite exhibiting no or only mild withdrawals or whose withdrawal symptoms cannot be equally assessed, have not been done [11]. For these patients, the fixed-dosage regimen therapy may be more effective.

Patients who are considered at high risk for alcohol withdrawal should receive benzodiazepines, especially diazepam and chlordiazepoxide [12]. These long-acting agents are considered the "gold-standard" in alcohol withdrawal treatment because of their well-documented efficacy profile; they provide a smoother withdrawal course, decreasing the risk of rebound symptoms [13,14]. In addition, these agents are self-tapering because of their long half-life. However, for patients who are elderly and/or with severe liver dysfunction, a short-acting benzodiazepine [either oxazepam (20–40 mg every three or four hours for 3–5 days) or lorazepam (1–4 mg for every three or four hours for 3–5 days)], should be used to avoid the risk for over-sedation [15]. Because these agents are short acting, although not shown, it is believed they may be less effective in preventing seizures and delirium and require proper tapering before the medication can be discontinued [15].

Other medications, such as beta-blockers, clonidine and haloperidol, may be used as adjunctive agents to treat symptoms not controlled by benzodiazepines [15]. By themselves, these medications alleviate withdrawal symptoms, but there is not enough significant evidence to determine their effect on delirium and seizures [16]. Beta-blockers should be used as an adjunct treatment in patients with coronary artery disease [5]. Clonidine has been effective in improving the autonomic symptoms of withdrawal [16]. Atenolol has been shown to reduce cravings [17]. Haloperidol is used in adjunction to benzodiazepines to treat agitation and hallucinations that are unresponsive to adequate doses of benzodiazepines [18,19]. Because antipsychotic agents such as haloperidol decrease the seizure threshold, they should only be administered in combination with benzodiazepines [18].

Additional supportive medication may be advisable in patients who are undergoing alcohol detoxification. Thiamine (50–100 mg per day) can be used to avoid the development of Wernicke's Encephalopathy [20]. Multivitamins and folate are also useful to prevent alcohol-related deficiencies.

A promising new approach for managing alcohol withdrawal is the tricyclic anticonvulsant carbamazepine. It has proven to be highly effective, preventing seizure disorder while simultaneously presenting some advantages over benzodiazepines, especially in patients with a history of multiple treated withdrawals receiving pharmacological treatments [21]. Carbamazepine does not interact with alcohol, nor does it interfere with mental processes or have the potential for abuse [21]. In a randomized, double-blinded trial comparing the effectiveness of carbamazepine versus the short-acting benzodiazepine lorazepam, one hundred and thirty six patients were randomly assigned to receive 600–800 mg of carbamazepine or 6–8 mg of lorazepam in divided doses on day 1, tapering to 200 mg of carbamazepine or 2 mg of lorazepam. The CIWA-Ar was used to assess alcohol withdrawal symptoms on the first five days and post-medication on days 7 and 12. Self-reporting of daily drinking was recorded by each participant in a daily drinking log and breath alcohol level was measured at each visit. Side effects were also recorded daily. Carbamazepine and lorazepam were equally effective at decreasing the symptoms of alcohol withdrawal; however, carbamazepine was shown to be more effective in preventing rebound withdrawal symptoms and reducing post-treatment drinking, especially for those with a history of multiple treated withdrawals [22]. Previous trials comparing carbamazepine with oxazepam found similar results [23]. Patients with significant hepatic or hematological abnormalities and patients using medications that could alter withdrawal symptoms were not included in this study.

Alcohol withdrawal is a result of a physical dependence on alcohol and abrupt cessation of drinking. Severe withdrawal symptoms can be avoided by full assessment of the patient with the CIWA-Ar scale. Benzodiazepines are the most efficacious drugs to prevent severe withdrawal symptoms, especially the risk of seizures. Alternative medications can be used with benzodiazepines as adjunct therapy. The treatment of alcoholic intoxication and withdrawal is only the first step toward full recovery. Further research addressing issues such as the specific mechanism responsible for withdrawal symptoms will enable clinicians to provide a more efficient and improved detoxification treatment for patients who are experiencing or are at risk for alcohol-induced withdrawals.

32.3   SEDATIVE-HYPNOTICS

Although benzodiazepines are commonly used in the management of alcohol withdrawal, these substances may present a high-risk potential for chronic abuse. According to the Drug Abuse Warning Network (DAWN), in 2005 an estimated 34% of visits associated with nonmedical use of pharmaceuticals were due to sedative-hypnotics [24].

The most common sedative-hypnotics are benzodiazepines and barbiturates, which act as central nervous system depressants, increasing gamma-aminobutyric acid (GABA) activity and thus producing a relaxing affect. Although alcohol is also a depressant, alcohol abuse is so common and its literature so extensive that its analysis will be presented separately. Continuous chronic use of sedative-hypnotics can cause physical dependence and withdrawal affects. Withdrawal from sedative-hypnotic substances includes restlessness, insomnia, anxiety, seizures, and even death. The first step of treatment is detoxification followed by long-term rehabilitation. Medical help is required for detoxification as this process is life threatening. Polydrug addiction, especially alcohol and cocaine, is a concern among patients who misuse sedative-hypnotics and in this case treatment must address multiple addictions.

Two different strategies are commonly used during the withdrawal phase of treatment: (1) gradually tapering off the substance of abuse and (2) use of a medication with the loading dose titrated to clinical effect. The strategy selected by the clinician should take into account the particular sedative-hypnotic (short-acting or long-acting sedatives), the duration and severity of dependence and the dosage of abuse. Short-acting medications – pentobarbital (Nembutal), secobarbital (Seconal), alprazolam (Xanax), meprobamate (Miltown, Equanil), methaqualone (Quaalude) – require a detoxification period of 7–10 days, whereas long-acting medications – phenobarbital, diazepam (Valium), chlordiazepoxide (Librium) – require a period of two weeks for detoxification [25].

Although sharing many characteristics with alcohol withdrawal syndromes, barbiturate withdrawal symptoms generally appear somewhat later and are characterized by its clinically variable reactions, including seizures and delirium. The convulsions have been shown to appear 24 and 115 hours after the last dose administration. On the other hand, the seizures are variable in occurrence, about two-thirds of the patients having more than one seizure. More than 50% of the patients may exhibit psychotic symptoms resembling alcohol delirium tremens characterized by disorientation relevant to time and place and by mostly visual hallucinations [26]. Deaths have resulted in association with barbiturate withdrawal [26]. Hospitalization and pharmacotherapy with phenobarbital is recommended for patients who have previous history of ingesting more than 0.4 g of secobarbital or its equivalent for 90 or more days or of 0.6 g for 30 or more days or a previously experienced barbiturate-induced seizure or delirium during withdrawal periods [26,27].

While any cross-tolerant drug can be used, phenobarbital substitution has shown to be more efficacious than other methods of detoxifying patients while presenting the least adverse side effects. Furthermore, slower rates of phenobarbital elimination result in less manipulative drug-seeking behavior [26,27]. Robinson, Sellers and Janecek (1981) measured the safety of oral phenobarbital in twenty-one barbiturate addicts by administering oral phenobarbital at a rate of 120 mg/h until a clinical endpoint was achieved. The endpoint was marked by the presence of at least three of the following conditions: nystagmus, drowsiness, ataxia, dysarthria or emotional lability. None of the patients in the study developed seizures or barbiturate withdrawal symptoms [28]. These results were supported by similar studies, which found phenobarbital to be a safe method of barbiturate and nonbarbiturate hypnosedative withdrawal regardless of its half-life [26,27,29].

The patient is prescribed an equivalent dosage of phenobarbital, which is divided into three of four dosages; the initial dosage is usually 60–90 mg taken orally [3]. Monitoring of the patient is necessary so that doses can be adjusted if the patient develops symptoms of sedative-hypnotic withdrawals or phenobarbital toxicity. Signs of phenobarbital toxicity include sustained nystagmus, slurred speech, and ataxia. Once the patient is stabilized, gradual tapering by 30 mg per day is recommended. Gradual tapering of phenobarbital depends on severity of symptoms and sedative-hypnotic substance abused. If the patient demonstrates severe withdrawal symptoms, such as seizures and delirium, treatment with a rapid onset medication, such as intravenous diazepam and lorazepam, is adequate for immediate alleviation. After stabilization, the patient can be safely switched to an equivalent dose of phenobarbital.

Medical management is also necessary for the management of benzodiazepine withdrawal. However, prior to the commencement of treatment, clinicians must distinguish between natural dependence and addiction. Dependence is a predictable phenomenon that may occur in patients taking therapeutic dosages of benzodiazepines [30,31]. Several studies found that benzodiazepine addiction is commonly observed among patients with history of alcohol and drug misuse rather than patients with anxiety disorders [31–34]. This is due to benzodiazepines' reinforcing effects that intensify one's "high." Gradual tapering of the current benzodiazepine dosage, substitution of a long-acting benzodiazepine, and phenobarbital substitution are different approaches used in the withdrawal treatment phase [33,35,36]. Studies show that gradually tapering off benzodiazepines is an effective method for withdrawing patients from long-term benzodiazepine use [37–39]. Additionally, studies found the management of benzodiazepine cessation to be further facilitated by a regimen of imipramine before and during the benzodiazepine taper [40,41]. These studies found that imipramine allows for a significant decrease in symptoms of anxiety and depression [40,41].

Rebound depression and insomnia may result from the discontinuation of hypnotic medications [42]. The role of adjunct psychotherapy in alleviating such withdrawal symptoms still remains unclear. Cognitive therapy was found to alleviate insomnia when combined with benzodiazepine tapering [39,43]. However, benzodiazepine tapering without adjunct psychotherapy was found to result in significantly higher longitudinal abstinence rates in long-term benzodiazepine users [44].

Medical intervention is necessary in the management of sedative-hypnotic withdrawal symptoms. Studies have shown phenobarbital to be safe and effective in the management of barbiturate withdrawal, while tapering off is preferred for the treatment of benzodiazepine withdrawal symptoms. It is important to note that medical management of

benzodiazepine dependence and abuse is only the first step towards recovery.

The detoxification of chronic sedative-hypnotic substances can usually be done in an outpatient setting with the help of the clinician. Gradual reduction of the abused substance is usually the first step in treatment in order to prevent the risk of withdrawal and seizures. After successful completion of the detoxification phase, the patient enters the prolonged phase of recovery in which the person attempts to stay drug-free.

32.4 NICOTINE

Cigarettes and other smoked tobacco products contain an exorbitant amount of chemicals and substances that the body becomes accustomed to over time. Thus, despite the clear health benefits of smoking cessation, it is very difficult to abruptly become smoke-free. Nicotine is the principle component of tobacco products and recovery from its addiction alone takes time. Nicotine creates a chemical dependency that causes the body to have physical and psychological withdrawals when a certain level of nicotine is not maintained in the system. "Quitter's flu" is a common term used to describe the nicotine withdrawal period in which nicotine withdrawal symptoms mimic a case of the cold or flu. Although short-lived, symptoms of withdrawal can be unpleasant and stressful. Those include headache, anxiety, nausea, and a craving for more tobacco. The duration and intensity of withdrawal symptoms vary from person to person. On average, nicotine withdrawal symptoms peak between 48 and 72 hours after last use. The intense negative side effects associated with nicotine withdrawal contribute to its high relapse rate. Thus, pharmacotherapy may be beneficial to relieve the severity of these symptoms.

Several pharmacological approaches exist to aid those who are trying to be nicotine-free. Assessing the extent of the patient's addiction may be helpful when choosing the most effective treatment. Since many smokers attempt to quit several times before they are successful, the clinician should take into consideration previous attempts at becoming

nicotine-free. In addition, information on the intensity of previously experienced withdrawal symptoms (if ever present) can be very valuable to the development of a rational approach to treatment. Because cravings are short-lived, exercising, relaxing, and engaging in other activities for a few minutes are alternatives to help patients through a craving period. However, if the patient has previously failed at quitting abruptly or does not feel comfortable, pharmacotherapy approaches may be used to alleviate withdrawal symptoms.

A pharmacotherapy approach approved by the US Food and Drug Administration is nicotine replacement therapy (NRT), which uses gum, lozenges, and patches to ease the severity of withdrawal symptoms. The nicotine gum, which requires a "chew and park" method of chewing, is available in 2 mg or 4 mg dosages. It quickly delivers nicotine to the brain; however, the nicotine gum must be chewed properly in order to be effective in reducing nicotine withdrawals. Similar to the gum, nicotine lozenges come in the form of hard candy. It slowly releases nicotine as it dissolves in the mouth. For proper results, the lozenge should not be bitten or chewed. The patch works by releasing a constant amount of nicotine into the body. Some patches may be required to be worn all day. These medications are all sold over-the-counter in the United States.

Prescription-only nicotine replacement therapies include the nicotine nasal spray and inhaler. Two squirts of the nasal spray comprise a dose, releasing a total of 1.0 mg of nicotine into the body

(0.5 mg per squirt). The nicotine released from the nasal spray is absorbed relatively faster than other nicotine replacement therapy methods [45]. The nasal spray has also proven efficacy in alleviating nicotine withdrawal symptoms and has shown a year cessation rate of 15–25% [46–48]. Use of the inhaler resembles smoking through its "hand-to-mouth" rituals as observed in habitual smokers. Each inhaler contains 500 mg of nicotine and a puff contains 13 µg of nicotine. However, very little nicotine actually reaches the lung because the nicotine-containing vapor is actually deposited and absorbed inside the mouth [45]. Success rates of 11–18% are shown in one-year cessation studies with the inhaler [49,50]. It is important to consider that cold weather might diminish the absorption of nicotine when using the inhaler.

In all nicotine replacement therapy treatment, options the amount of nicotine is gradually decreased until a dose of zero is reached and the patient is completely freed from nicotine addiction. These therapies effectively suppress cravings for nicotine. Studies found that nicotine replacement therapy is statistically more effective than placebos in treating patients who doubt their ability to abruptly stop use of tobacco. However, there has been no definite study in regards to which method of nicotine replacement therapy is more efficient.

In one study, examining the effectiveness of nicotine replacement therapy during a 12-month period, the sustained abstinence success rate of the population using nicotine replacement therapy was 5.3% as opposed to 2.6% with placebo [51]. Similarly, a meta-analysis of the efficaciousness of over-the-counter nicotine replacement therapy and its long-term (greater than six months) abstinence rates in comparison with other prescription therapies, found that nicotine replacement therapy has similar success rates in comparison [52]. Another study examined the effectiveness of nicotine patches – in terms of smoking cessation and suppression of withdrawal severity with two different counseling treatments. It was concluded that the nicotine patch treatment approximately doubles the cessation rate, which was maintained six months after initiation of treatment [53]. Additionally, it alleviates symptoms of nicotine withdrawal.

Nonnicotine therapies for the treatment of nicotine withdrawal have also shown to increase the probability of smoking cessation. One nonicotine therapy approved by the Food and Drug Administration is the nontricyclic antidepressant bupropion. Zyban, the form which was specifically developed for smoking cessation, is an easy-to-use tablet. Like nicotine replacement therapy, bupropion has been shown to double cessation rates when compared with a placebo. In a study with more than 600 participants, patients were randomized to placebo or placed on a 50 mg, 100 mg, or 150 mg bupropion regimen for six weeks [54]. Most importantly, previous diagnosis of major depression was an exclusion criterion in this study. The cessation rates were 10.5%, 13.7%, 18.3% and 24.4%, respectively. In addition, bupropion reduced weight gain and had minimal side effects including insomnia and dry mouth.

Varenicline, a nicotine receptor partial agonist, is the newest pharmacotherapy for nicotine cessation approved by the Food and Drug Administration. Varenicline has been proven to reduce cravings and withdrawal symptoms. Treatment begins a week prior to the date set for the patient to stop use of tobacco. During the first week, the drug is gradually increased 0.5 mg per day during the first three days. During days 4 through 7, the drug is increased 0.5 mg twice a day and on day 8 the recommended dosage of 1 mg twice a day is implemented. Studies have found varenicline to be twice more effective than bupropion and four times more effective than placebo after a 12-week treatment program [55,56]. At a 52-week follow-up, varenicline had more effective continuous abstinence rates [55,56]. Thus, varenicline is more effective than placebo and bupropion therapy in long-term and short-term comparisons [55,56].

Clonidine is a therapy that may be used in those who have been unsuccessful with nicotine replacement therapy, bupropion or varenicline. Approved by the Food and Drug Administration for use as an antihypertensive medication, it has been shown to increase smoking cessation by 11%. Side effects of clonidine include dizziness, dry mouth, sedation, and orthostatic hypotension [57]. Nortriptyline is another possible second-line therapy for smoking cessation. A tricyclic antidepressant, nortriptyline showed a 12% improvement over controls in short-term smoking cessation [58]. Finally, methoxsalen, although not created for smoking cessation, has been shown to reduce the CYP2A6 enzyme that metabolizes nicotine. This allows for nicotine to remain in the blood for longer periods, thereby reducing the craving for nicotine. Methoxsalan is a compound used to treat psoriasis and other skin disorders and side effects include sensitivity to light, premature skin aging, cataracts. and skin cancer [59,60]

32.5 CANNABIS

The increasing demand for treatment of cannabis dependence has led to the validity and clinical significance of cannabis-induced withdrawal symptoms [61,62]. Although significant withdrawal reactions from cannabis are rare, the detoxification of marijuana still causes uncomfortable physical symptoms, which increases the difficulty of overcoming cannabis addiction. Anxiety, irritability, restlessness, insomnia, weight loss, nausea, and sweating are the most frequently reported adverse side effects of cannabis withdrawal [61,63–66]. Symptoms are manifested in as little as 1–2 days after the last delta-9-tetrahydrocannabinol (THC) administration and resolve within 10 days [63,67–69]. Cannabis-induced withdrawal symptoms are subtle due to its long half-life [70]. Cannabis-dependent individuals report resuming cannabis use in order to avoid and/or alleviate withdrawal symptoms [71]. Thus, decreasing withdrawal symptoms will reduce relapse rates and allow for a more successful recovery program.

The most promising pharmacological treatment for the management of cannabis withdrawal is oral THC substitution. Oral THC is a long-acting agent with slow onset. Using THC capsules to alleviate withdrawal symptoms, and possibly to treat cannabis dependence, uses the same principles as in other effective drug treatment programs: for example, methadone substitution treatment and nicotine replacement treatments.

An inpatient study found oral THC capsules (50 mg/day) administered on the first day of marijuana abstinence significantly decrease cravings and withdrawal symptoms while producing no intoxication when compared to placebo [61]. In another study [72], lower doses of oral THC (30 mg/day) reduced discomfort of withdrawal symptoms while the higher THC doses (90 mg/day) completely alleviated withdrawal symptoms with minimum adverse side effects. Thus, clinicians can adjust the dose regimen of oral THC in order to alleviate a patient's withdrawal symptoms based on the severity of their dependence. It is important to note that the high doses of THC produced euphoria in some patients, which can be associated with potential abuse in patients seeking that feeling [72]. The latter study [72] extended on the previous study by Haney finding oral THC to be as effective in an outpatient setting [73].

Another study [74] analyzing the acute and residual cognitive effects of 7.5 and 15 mg of delta-9-THC in infrequent cannabis users, found that use leads to impairment of episodic memory and learning two hours after administration (peak plasma concentration), while perceptual priming and the working memory were unaffected. Furthermore, these effects were not found 24–48 hours after the administration of delta-9-THC, which indicates the residual effects are minimal [74].

Lofexidine is an antihypertensive that has been used as a treatment option for opiate withdrawal. Clinical trials are underway for its use in treating marijuana withdrawal and relapse. In a small study of nontreatment-seeking volunteers, lofexidine in combination with THC was shown to improve sleep and decrease marijuana withdrawal, craving, and relapse in daily marijuana smokers better than either monotherapy [73].

Other potential medications have shown to have no positive effects in alleviating withdrawal symptoms. Divalproex and bupropion worsened the negative mood symptoms associated with cannabis withdrawals [61,75]. Nefazodone alleviated certain withdrawal symptoms, but had no effect on the majority of the symptoms [76]. The present data clearly suggest the role of oral THC as an effective treatment of cannabis withdrawal symptoms.

32.6   COCAINE AND OTHER STIMULANTS

Until recently, treatment for stimulant addiction was mainly nonpharmacological due to the belief that it created a psychological dependency. Due to recent advances regarding the mechanism involved in stimulant addiction, it is now known that chronic stimulant abuse leads to neurophysiological adaptation [77]. This finding has paved the way for the research and discovery of several targets for stimulant pharmacotherapy: antidepressant, anticonvulsant, and dopaminergic medications [77]. Despite these findings, however, there is still no proven effective medication for cocaine dependence. Since the ultimate goal of treatment is to achieve ceased stimulant abuse by drastically reducing and controlling the inevitable cravings experienced during the period of withdrawal treatment, current research is focused on anticraving pharmacological agents.

The first study published on pharmacological methods for cocaine dependence focused on relieving withdrawal symptoms, such as cravings and post-addiction dysphoria, with medication that affected the dopamine receptors [78]. Gawin and Kleber showed a decrease in these symptoms with the use of the tricyclic antidepressant desipramine [78]. Giannini and colleagues achieved the same results in a larger open field study [79]. Subsequently, low doses of bromocriptine, a dopaminergic agonist, were shown to be effective in cocaine detoxification [80]. Futhermore, Giannini and Billet found bromocriptine to be slightly more effective than placebo in managing stimulant withdrawal symptoms and bromocriptine-desipramine treatment to be even more effective than monotherapy [81].

Although promising, recent evidence is inconsistent with the findings above. Handelsman and colleagues found no significant difference between bromocriptine and placebo in reducing cocaine use or cravings [82]. Several other studies did not support the role of bromocriptine in relieving stimulant-induced withdrawal symptoms [83–85].

During withdrawal from stimulants and other drugs, intense cravings are the trademark symptom. These cravings may play a major role in relapse rates and some studies suggest a relationship between the severity of cravings and stimulant dependence relapse rates as well as treatment outcome [86–91]. However, other studies found no association between the variables mentioned above [92,93]. This inconsistency may be due to the lack of reliable and valid instruments to measure "craving" in a patient.

A valid measure of "craving" in stimulant-dependent patients is the Cocaine Craving Questionnaire-Now (CCQ-Now) or its abbreviated format, CCQ-Brief. Findings from different studies have shown these questionnaires to be reliable and valid instruments in the comprehensive assessment of cocaine cravings and in assessing relapse susceptibility as well as treatment outcome [88,94,95]. The administration of the CCQ-Now and CCQ-Brief may be beneficial in increasing treatment retention and in the overall recovery from stimulant addiction.

Stimulant withdrawal management deals with a wide range of physiological and psychological symptoms [96]. Despite early beliefs that stimulant withdrawal followed a three-phase sequence – crash, withdrawal, and extinction [97] – more recent studies have shown no classic pattern of stimulant-induced withdrawal [98–101]. In these studies, symptoms of withdrawal in cocaine-dependent patients were mild and gradually improved with the continuation of the study. Weddington's examination of cocaine withdrawal showed a linear decrease in symptoms such as craving and dysphoria [101]. Because of the steady linear reduction in symptoms, these authors concluded symptoms such as cravings, sleeping disturbance, fatigue, restlessness, and depression should be characterized as "short-term abstinence" rather than withdrawal symptoms [99–101].

Similar results were found when analyzing the symptoms of methamphetamine abstinence [102,103]. The most prominent symptoms – depression, irritability, and poor concentration – are shown to be mild and to linearly decline from a high initial peak [102,103]. McGregor *et al.* found evidence of a phasic withdrawal pattern in methamphetamine-induced withdrawal [103]. He further distinguished the initial 7–10 days of symptoms present as the acute phase and the subsequent two weeks as the subacute phase [103].

Due to the transient characteristics of these mild abstinence-induced symptoms, no pharmacological treatment is indicated unless severe symptoms, such as acute psychotic disorders or other medical emergencies, are present. Recent advances regarding the mechanisms involved in cocaine addiction have led the way for the discovery of several targets for stimulant pharmacotherapy. Treatment with disulfiram has shown to reduce cocaine use in a number of clinical trials [1,104–114]. Other pharmacotherapies showing promise in reducing cocaine dependency include GABA medications: tiagabine and topiramate, beta-adrenergic blocker and propranolol [113,115–118], stimulant medication [110,111,119,120], modafinil and a cocaine vaccine [112,113,117,118,120]. However, these pharmacotherapies are still experimental and not yet approved by the Food and Drug Administration [112,113]. Thus, larger controlled clinical trials must be performed in order to validate the efficacy of these promising treatments.

The literature concerning stimulant withdrawal remains controversial. Mood and cognitive skills improve gradually and linearly during short-term abstinence from stimulants. Currently, there is no proven effective pharmacotherapy for stimulant dependence [114], although considerable advances on the neurobiological mechanisms of this addiction could pave the way for future effective pharmacotherapy development.

32.7 OPIATES

Unlike stimulants, opiates produce physical symptoms as a result of detoxification. Opiate withdrawal occurs when a chronic opiate addict abruptly stops or dramatically reduces opiate use. Although withdrawal from opiates causes physical discomfort, it is not life threatening. The most common clinical characteristics of opiate withdrawal include dilated pupils, diarrhea, runny nose, goose bumps, abdominal pain, sweating, agitation, nausea, and vomiting. The symptoms and severity of withdrawal varies according to the specific opiate used and the length and amount of regular use. The faster metabolizing opiates are associated with shorter and more severe withdrawal symptoms [3]. Heroin withdrawal symptoms usually peak at 36–72 hours after the last dose and usually last five days [3], whereas opiates that bind tightly to receptors and/or are slowly metabolized have longer yet more mild withdrawal symptoms [3]. Methadone withdrawal reaches its peak within 4–6 days of the last dose and usually last 10–12 days [3]. In addition, duration and dose of regular use is directly related to the severity of withdrawal symptoms.

A physical examination and an analysis of the clinical history are sufficient in order to evaluate the severity of withdrawal symptoms. These should include an analysis of the individual's psychological, psychosocial, and physical status. In addition, a physical examination of cutaneous signs may be advantageous in the diagnostic process. Due to the medical complications associated with opiate addiction, several laboratory tests, such as a urine screening for drugs, complete blood count (CBC) with differential analysis, HIV test, chest X ray, PPD (purified protein derivative, also known as tuberculin skin test) plus antigen testing, hepatitis antigen and antibody tests, are all recommended prior to determining an adequate treatment plan for withdrawal [3].

The most common treatment for opiate withdrawal is methadone substitution, in which methadone is substituted for the addicted opiate and then slowly tapered once the patient is stabilized [121–123]. Because methadone has a longer half-life than other opiates, the withdrawal and risks of complications are minimized, producing a smoother treatment [3]. In addition, methadone can be orally given and is a long-acting agent. A dose of 10–20 mg of methadone is the recommended initial dosage and should reduce withdrawal symptoms, if initially present, in 30–60 minutes. In this case, the patient should be kept under observation in order to evaluate the effectiveness of the dose. If withdrawal symptoms continue, an additional 5–10 mg of methadone can be prescribed. If there were originally no withdrawal symptoms, the patient should be observed for drowsiness and/or depressed respiration [3]. This process is repeated every 12 hours until the cessation of withdrawal symptoms. An initial dose should not exceed 30 mg and the patient should not be given more than 40 mg in a 24-hour period during the first few days of treatment. The revised dose that adequately suppressed withdrawal symptoms on the first day of treatment is repeated until the patient is stabilized. Methadone is then gradually withdrawn either by decreasing the dosage by 5 mg/day until zero dose is reached or by 5 mg/day until a dose of 10 mg is reached in which 2–3 mg is withdrawn a day until zero dose is reached [3]. However, problems have been found with this treatment protocol, in particular concerning residual withdrawal symptoms [124,125]. Currently, there is no consensus on the most efficacious treatment procedure for the management of opiate withdrawal [126].

Also administered by opioid substitution, levo-alpha-acetyl-methadol (LAAM) can suppress opiate withdrawal for longer periods than methadone, thus should be administered no more than every other day. Induction onto LAAM to relieve opiate withdrawal symptoms begins with a dose of 20–40 mg. Doses are adjusted up or down to approximate the patient's tolerance threshold in order to reduce and/or eliminate craving for opiates.

If relief is not felt within 48 hours, patients need to be made aware that time rather than more medication is required for LAAM's effects to manifest. Thus, this is not considered a first-line therapy for opiate withdrawal [127].

An alternative nonopioid approach is to directly treat the withdrawal symptoms with clonidine, a α_2-agonist approved by the Food and Drug Administration for the treatment of high blood pressure. The discovery of the efficacy of clonidine in alleviating opiate-induced withdrawal symptoms lead to widespread use of this medication [128]. However, when compared to methadone substitution, there was no significant difference between the two treatments [129]. Clonidine had a lower retention in treatment than methadone substitution [129,130]. Furthermore, clonidine was linked with many adverse side effects, such as hypotension and sedation [129].

Dissatisfaction with clonidine's adverse side effects has opened doors to newer and more efficient approaches in the detoxification of opiates. Lofexidine is an analog of clonidine (with fewer side effects) used preferably in outpatient settings. Still, in a review of detoxification treatment trials, if given the choice of clonidine, lofexidine or methadone, patients preferred methadone over other medications [131].

Buprenorphine, a partial agonist of the mu receptor and an agonist at the kappa receptor, has been shown to be more effective with less adverse side effects than clonidine [126,129,132–135]. Participants stay in treatment longer with buprenorphine than clonidine regardless of the treatment setting [129,134–136]. Furthermore, buprenorphine has a low risk for addiction, low physical dependence, and its slow rate of dissociation from opioid receptors allows for flexibility in the dose regimen [136,137]. The efficiency of buprenorphine is also associated with its long duration of action, due to its long plasma half-life [125,138]. Due to the latter characteristic, the sublingual solution of buprenorphine has been equally effective in the precipitation of opiate-induced withdrawal whether administered daily, twice a week, or thrice weekly [139–142]. In comparison with methadone, Johnson [136] found buprenorphine, 8 mg/d, to be as effective as methadone, 60 mg/d, and superior to methadone, 20 mg/d, in treatment retention and reduction of illicit use. In addition, Gowing *et al.* found buprenorphine to alleviate withdrawal symptoms faster than methadone and to provide less severe withdrawals [125,128]. Buprenorphine is also safer than methadone in overdose [143]. In a blinded study, an erroneous administration of 32 mg of buprenorphine (32 times greater than the prescribed 1 mg) only caused the patient to experience insomnia, pressure headache, and vomiting [144]. Other studies found the monotherapy of buprenorphine to be as effective as methadone treatment [134,145,146].

Naloxone has been effectively combined with buprenorphine by tablet to further decrease its potential for abuse compared with that associated with methadone [139,147–149]. This sublingual combination was created to hinder people from crushing the pills and dissolving the powder for injection in attempt to get high off of the buprenorphine (an opioid). Intramuscular injection of buprenorphine/naloxone would cause immediate withdrawal symptoms and the agonist properties of buprenorphine would likely kick in, extending this period of withdrawal [147,148]. However, in the sublingual form buprenorphine/naloxone is well tolerated with no major adverse side effects –

neither precipitation of withdrawal nor high potential for abuse – in opioid-dependent individuals [147]. However, Strain [150] found the sublingual administration of buprenorphine/naloxone to have the potential for addiction in nondependent opioid addicts.

Recently, the number of opiate addicts with multiple drugs of abuse has increased, complicating the detoxification process [151,152]. When comparing the efficacy of methadone and buprenorphine in the treatment of benzodiazepine/opiate co-dependents, Reed [125] found buprenorphine to be more effective than methadone in alleviating withdrawal symptoms. In addition, patients were more likely to complete treatment when buprenorphine was used [125]. Another study found a buprenorphine/carbamazepine combination to significantly decrease withdrawal symptoms when compared to methadone/carbamazepine [151]. Although buprenorphine/carbamazepine was more effective in the detoxification process for opioid dependents with polydrug addiction, neither group presented severe side effects [151]. Furthermore, when compared with clonidine/carbamazepine, the combination of valproate with buprenorphine has been shown to be safer and more effective for minimizing withdrawal symptoms during polydrug detoxification [152].

32.8 INHALANTS

Inhalant addiction encompasses a variety of agents that are volatile at room temperature [153]. Unlike other addictive substances, these agents are grouped together by having a common route of misuse [153]. The misuse of these volatile substances creates a rapid onset of intoxication marked by a "high." Chronic abuses of inhalants who abruptly decide to stop may experience withdrawal symptoms for several weeks. Symptoms include hand tremors, excessive sweating, constant headaches, and irritation. The lack of research on inhalant abuse and dependence prevents effective treatment. A supportive environment is the mainstay treatment as there are no reversal agents for inhalant intoxication. With

the exception of nitrites, inhalants are depressants directly affecting the central nervous system [153–155] Nitrites primarily cause "vasodilation and smooth muscle relaxation" [153,155–157]. The immediate effects of inhalants only last a few minutes [153]. Therefore, repeated use of inhalants may be common in order to extend intoxication. Chronic use may lead to a psychotic disorder characterized by deliriums, hallucinations and disorientation [153,154,158,159]. In the case of continued chronic misuse of inhalants, neurological damage can become permanent [160–162].

Abrupt cessation of volatile substance misuse can lead to mild withdrawal symptoms, such as anxiety, depression, loss of appetite, irritation, aggressive behavior, dizziness, tremors, and nausea. These withdrawal symptoms are infrequent [162] and, due to their transient nature, acutely intoxicated patients barely seek medical help, unless the condition becomes life threatening. Severe withdrawal symptoms may include seizures, coma, cardiopulmonary arrest or death. Intoxication from volatile substance abuse may also lead to "sudden sniffing death syndrome" [163–166]. Shepherd describes this syndrome as "unpredictable, unpreventable and resuscitation is rarely successful" [163]. A study found as many as half of inhalant-related deaths to be attributed to sudden sniffing death syndrome [164]. The risk of "sudden sniffing death syndrome" has no bearing on whether or not the patient previously had a history of chronic abuse. In a study, 22% of deaths that occurred from "sudden sniffing death syndrome" happened during initial experimentation [165].

Since there is little literature on the effectiveness of different treatment programs for inhalant abuse and/or dependence, management of acute intoxication primarily relies on assessing acute injury or toxicity and stabilizing the patient in a calm and supportive environment. It is also important to closely monitor hydration and cardiorespiratory status [153,162,167]. Thus, the first step towards recovery is to detoxify the patient [153,160,162]. After stabilization, a complete physical and mental examination should be performed to assess the patient's need for intervention [153,154,158,159]. Currently, intervention for volatile substance addiction is primarily directed towards counseling and abstinence. A survey of drug treatment program directors concluded that drug treatment programs have inadequate resources and trained staff for inhalant user treatment [168]. Further research on the treatment of inhalant addiction is needed in order to improve current therapies available, and to develop new approaches. Studies should focus on detoxification and relief of withdrawal symptoms, as these are the first steps into recovery.

32.9 HALLUCINOGENS

Hallucinogens, also known as psychedelic drugs, affect the brain, causing intense sensory experiences. Unlike other addictive drugs, adverse side effects of hallucinogens are not dose-related but related to personal predisposition and the setting in which the drug was administered. A "bad trip" occurs when negative side effects occur due to administration of hallucinogens. These are characterized by extreme anxiety, fearful hallucinations, panic, paranoia, and even suicide. There are only a few studies on the long-term effects of hallucinogens. Furthermore, there is little evidence that dependence or withdrawal symptoms occur for hallucinogens.

Hallucinogen episodes usually wear off within 12 hours [25]. "Talking down" an individual experiencing mild adverse reactions from hallucinogens is sufficient therapy [169]. This should be done in a quiet and calm environment to reduce stimuli.

If the patient's adverse side effects intensify and the patient becomes violent, 1–2 mg of intramuscular alprazolam (Xanax) is adequate treatment [25]. The effects of hallucinogens are not easy to predict. Since psychedelic drugs do not seem to cause physical addiction, they are not associated with true withdrawal symptoms.

32.10 CONCLUSIONS

There are several pharmacotherapies available to treat intoxication and withdrawal and it is important for providers to embrace and incorporate them into standard care. Thus far, benzodiazepines are the mainstay for alcohol withdrawal and barbiturates for sedative-hypnotic withdrawal. Bupropion, nicotine replacement therapy or varenicline are top treatment options for control of nicotine withdrawal symptoms. Oral THC capsules have been shown to effectively reduce cravings and cannabis-induced withdrawal symptoms. Methadone substitution and withdrawal is the most common treatment for opiate detoxification. New research has found buprenorphine and the buprenorphine/naloxone combination to be as effective, if not more effective, than methadone in alleviating withdrawal symptoms. Options are few and far between in treatment of stimulant, inhalant, and hallucinogen intoxication and withdrawal. More research is needed in the area of addiction pharmacotherapies to give patients a fighting chance at full recovery.

REFERENCES

1. National Institute on Alcohol Abuse and Alcoholism (2001) Alcohol Alert 51. http://pubs.niaaa.nih.gov/publications/aa51.htm (accessed 31 January 2010).

2. Sullivan, J.T., Sykora, K., Schneiderman, J. *et al.* (1989) Assessment of alcohol withdrawal: the revised clinical institute withdrawal assessment for alcohol scale (CIWA-Ar). *Br. J. Addict.*, **84** (11), 1353–1357.

3. Marc Galanter, M.D. and Herbert D. Kleber, M.D. (eds) (1994) *The American Psychiatric Press Textbook of Substance Abuse Treatment*, American Psychiatric Press, Washington.

4. Foy, A., March, S., and Drinkwater, V. (1988) Use of an objective clinical scale in the assessment and management of alcohol withdrawal in a large general hospital. *Alcohol. Clin. Exp. Res.*, **12** (3), 360–364.

5. Bayard, M., McIntyre, J., Hill, K.R., and Woodside, J. Jr. (2004) Alcohol withdrawal syndrome. *Am. Fam. Physician.*, **69** (6), 1443–1450.

6. Nuss, M.A., Elnicki, D.M., Dunsworth, T.S., and Makela, E.H. (2004) Utilizing CIWA-Ar to assess use of benzodiazepines in patients vulnerable to alcohol withdrawal syndrome. *W. V. Med. J.*, **100** (1), 21–25.

7. Denis, C., Fatseas, M., Lavie, E., and Auriacombe, M. (2006) Pharmacological interventions for benzodiazepine mono-dependence management in outpatient settings. *Cochrane Database Syst. Rev.*3 (Art. No.: CD005194). doi: 10.1002/14651858.CD005194.pub2.

8. Ntais, C., Pakos, E., Kyzas, P., and Ioannidis, J.P. (2005) Benzodiazepines for alcohol withdrawal. *Cochrane Database Syst. Rev.*3 (Art. No.: CD005063). doi: 10.1002/14651858.CD005063.pub2.

9. Daeppen, J.B., Gache, P., Landry, U. *et al.* (2002) Symptom-triggered vs fixed-schedule doses of benzodiazepine for alcohol withdrawal: a randomized

10. DeCarolis, D.D., Rice, K.L., Ho, L. *et al.* (2007) Symptom-driven lorazepam protocol for treatment of severe alcohol withdrawal delirium in the intensive care unit. *Pharmacotherapy*, **27** (4), 510–518.

11. Saitz, R., Mayo-Smith, M.F., Roberts, M.S. *et al.* (1994) Individualized treatment for alcohol withdrawal. A randomized double-blind controlled trial. *JAMA*, **272** (7), 519–523.

12. Saitz, R. and O'Malley, S.S. (1997) Pharmacotherapies for alcohol abuse. Withdrawal and treatment. *Med. Clin. North Am.*, **81** (4), 881–907.

13. Addolorato, G., Leggio, L., Abenavoli, L. *et al.* (2006) Baclofen in the treatment of alcohol withdrawal syndrome: a comparative study vs diazepam. *Am. J. Med.*, **119** (3), 276, e213–e278.

14. Erstad, B.L. and Cotugno, C.L. (1995) Management of alcohol withdrawal. *Am. J. Health Syst. Pharm.*, **52** (7), 697–709.

15. Kraemer, K.L., Conigliaro, J., and Saitz, R. (1999) Managing alcohol withdrawal in the elderly. *Drugs Aging*, **14** (6), 409–425.

16. Mayo-Smith, M.F. (1997) Pharmacological management of alcohol withdrawal. A meta-analysis and evidence-based practice guideline. American Society of Addiction Medicine Working Group on Pharmacological Management of Alcohol Withdrawal. *JAMA*, **278** (2), 144–151.

17. Horwitz, R.I., Gottlieb, L.D., and Kraus, M.L. (1989) The efficacy of atenolol in the outpatient management of the alcohol withdrawal syndrome. Results of a randomized clinical trial. *Arch. Intern. Med.*, **149** (5), 1089–1093.

18. Johnsen, J. and Morland, J. (1990) Alcohol withdrawal – biological background, diagnosis and treatment. *Tidsskr Nor. Laegeforen*, **110** (12), 1528–1532.

19. Naranjo, C.A. and Sellers, E.M. (1986) Clinical assessment and pharmacotherapy of the alcohol withdrawal syndrome. *Recent Dev. Alcohol.*, **4**, 265–281.

20. McKeon, A., Frye, M.A., and Delanty, N. (2008) The Alcohol Withdrawal Syndrome. *J. Neurol. Neurosurg Psychiatry*, **79**, 854–862.

21. Leggio, L., Kenna, G.A., and Swift, R.M. (2008) New developments for the pharmacological treatment of alcohol withdrawal syndrome. A focus on non-benzodiazepine GABAergic medications. *Prog. Neuropsychopharmacol. Biol. Psychiatry*, **32** (5), 1106–1117.

treatment trial. *Arch. Intern. Med.*, **162** (10), 1117–1121.

22. Malcolm, R., Myrick, H., Roberts, J. *et al.* (2002) The effects of carbamazepine and lorazepam on single versus multiple previous alcohol withdrawals in an outpatient randomized trial. *J. Gen. Intern. Med.*, **17** (5), 349–355.

23. Stuppaeck, C.H., Pycha, R., Miller, C. *et al.* (1992) Carbamazepine versus oxazepam in the treatment of alcohol withdrawal: a double-blind study. *Alcohol. Alcohol.*, **27** (2), 153–158.

24. Drug Abuse Warning Network (DAWN) (2007) 2005: National Estimates of Drug-Related Emergency Department Visit. DAWN Series D-29, DHHS Publication No. (SMA) 07-4256, Rockville, MD.

25. Giannini, A.J. (2000) An approach to drug abuse, intoxication and withdrawal. *Am. Fam. Physician*, **61** (9), 2763–2774.

26. Sellers, E.M. (1988) Alcohol, barbiturate and benzodiazepine withdrawal syndromes: clinical management. *Cmaj*, **139** (2), 113–120.

27. Sullivan, J.T. and Sellers, E.M. (1986) Treatment of the barbiturate abstinence syndrome. *Med. J. Aust.*, **145** (9), 456–458.

28. Robinson, G.M., Sellers, E.M., and Janecek, E. (1981) Barbiturate and hypnosedative withdrawal by a multiple oral phenobarbital loading dose technique. *Clin. Pharmacol. Ther.*, **30** (1), 71–76.

29. Janecek, E., Kapur, B.M., and Devenyi, P. (1987) Oral phenobarbital loading: a safe method of barbiturate and nonbarbiturate hypnosedative withdrawal. *Cmaj*, **137** (5), 410–412.

30. Salzman, C. (1998) Addiction to benzodiazepines. *Psychiatr. Q.*, **69** (4), 251–261.

31. O'Brien, C.P. (2005) Benzodiazepine use, abuse, and dependence. *J. Clin. Psychiatry*, **66** (Suppl. 2), 28–33.

32. (1988) Abuse of benzodiazepines: the problems and the solutions. A report of a Committee of the Institute for Behavior and Health, Inc. *Am. J. Drug Alcohol. Abuse*, **14** (Suppl. 1), 1–69.

33. Smith, D.E. and Landry, M.J. (1990) Benzodiazepine dependency discontinuation: focus on the chemical dependency detoxification setting and benzodiazepine-polydrug abuse. *J. Psychiatr. Res.*, **24** (Suppl. 2), 145–156.

34. DuPont, R.L. (1990) A practical approach to benzodiazepine discontinuation. *J. Psychiatr. Res.*, **24** (Suppl. 2), 81–90.

35. Landry, M.J., Smith, D.E., McDuff, D.R., and Baughman, O.L. 3rd (1992) Benzodiazepine dependence and withdrawal: identification and medical management. *J. Am. Board Fam. Pract.*, **5** (2), 167–175.

36. Ashton, H. (1994) The treatment of benzodiazepine dependence. *Addiction*, **89** (11), 1535–1541.

37. Vicens, C., Fiol, F., Llobera, J. *et al.* (2006) Withdrawal from long-term benzodiazepine use: randomised trial in family practice. *Br. J. Gen. Pract.*, **56** (533), 958–963.

38. Voshaar, R.C., Gorgels, W.J., Mol, A.J. *et al.* (2003) Tapering off long-term benzodiazepine use with or without group cognitive-behavioural therapy: three-condition, randomised controlled trial. *Br. J. Psychiatry*, **182**, 498–504.

39. Baillargeon, L., Landreville, P., Verreault, R. *et al.* (2003) Discontinuation of benzodiazepines among older insomniac adults treated with cognitive-behavioural therapy combined with gradual tapering: a randomized trial. *Cmaj*, **169** (10), 1015–1020.

40. Rickels, K., DeMartinis, N., Garcia-Espana, F. *et al.* (2000) Imipramine and buspirone in treatment of patients with generalized anxiety disorder who are discontinuing long-term benzodiazepine therapy. *Am. J. Psychiatry*, **157** (12), 1973–1979.

41. Rynn, M., Garcia-Espana, F., Greenblatt, D.J. *et al.* (2003) Imipramine and buspirone in patients with panic disorder who are discontinuing long-term benzodiazepine therapy. *J. Clin. Psychopharmacol.*, **23** (5), 505–508.

42. Loder, E. and Biondi, D. (2003) Oral phenobarbital loading: a safe and effective method of withdrawing patients with headache from butalbital compounds. *Headache*, **43** (8), 904–909.

43. Morin, C.M., Bastien, C., Guay, B. *et al.* (2004) Randomized clinical trial of supervised tapering and cognitive behavior therapy to facilitate benzodiazepine discontinuation in older adults with chronic insomnia. *Am. J. Psychiatry*, **161** (2), 332–342.

44. Oude Voshaar, R.C., Gorgels, W.J., Mol, A.J. *et al.* (2006) Long-term outcome of two forms of randomised benzodiazepine discontinuation. *Br. J. Psychiatry*, **188**, 188–189.

45. Henningfield, J.E., Fant, R.V., Buchhalter, A.R., and Stitzer, M.L. (2005) Pharmacotherapy for nicotine dependence. *CA Cancer J. Clin.*, **55** (5), 281–299, quiz 322–283, 325.

46. Sutherland, G., Stapleton, J.A., Russell, M.A. *et al.* (1992) Randomised controlled trial of nasal nicotine spray in smoking cessation. *Lancet*, **340** (8815), 324–329.

47. Hjalmarson, A., Franzon, M., Westin, A., and Wiklund, O. (1994) Effect of nicotine nasal spray on smoking cessation. A randomized, placebo-

controlled, double-blind study. *Arch. Intern. Med.*, **154** (22), 2567–2572.

48. Schneider, N.G., Terrace, S., Koury, M.A. *et al.* (2005) Comparison of three nicotine treatments: initial reactions and preferences with guided use. *Psychopharmacology (Berl.)*, **182** (4), 545–550.

49. Schneider, N.G., Olmstead, R., Nilsson, F. *et al.* (1996) Efficacy of a nicotine inhaler in smoking cessation: a double-blind, placebo-controlled trial. *Addiction*, **91** (9), 1293–1306.

50. Hjalmarson, A., Nilsson, F., Sjostrom, L., and Wiklund, O. (1997) The nicotine inhaler in smoking cessation. *Arch. Intern. Med.*, **157** (15), 1721–1728.

51. Wang, D., Connock, M., Barton, P. *et al.* (2008) Cut down to quit' with nicotine replacement therapies in smoking cessation: a systematic review of effectiveness and economic analysis. *Health Technol. Assess*, **12** (2), 1–156.

52. Hughes, J.R., Shiffman, S., Callas, P., and Zhang, J. (2003) A meta-analysis of the efficacy of over-the-counter nicotine replacement. *Tob. Control*, **12** (1), 21–27.

53. Fiore, M.C., Kenford, S.L., Jorenby, D.E. *et al.* (1994) Two studies of the clinical effectiveness of the nicotine patch with different counseling treatments. *Chest*, **105** (2), 524–533.

54. Hurt, R.D., Sachs, D.P., Glover, E.D. *et al.* (1997) A comparison of sustained-release bupropion and placebo for smoking cessation. *N. Engl. J. Med.*, **337** (17), 1195–1202.

55. Gonzales, D., Rennard, S.I., Nides, M. *et al.* (2006) Varenicline, an alpha4beta2 nicotinic acetylcholine receptor partial agonist, vs sustained-release bupropion and placebo for smoking cessation: a randomized controlled trial. *JAMA*, **296** (1), 47–55.

56. Jorenby, D.E., Hays, J.T., Rigotti, N.A. *et al.* (2006) Efficacy of varenicline, an alpha4beta2 nicotinic acetylcholine receptor partial agonist, vs placebo or sustained-release bupropion for smoking cessation: a randomized controlled trial. *JAMA*, **296** (1), 56–63.

57. Gourlay, S.G., Stead, L.F., and Benowitz, N.L. (2004) Clonidine for smoking cessation. *Cochrane Database Syst. Rev.*3 (Art. No.: CD000058). doi: 10.1002/14651858.CD000058.pub2.

58. Marlow, S.P. and Stoller, J.K. (2003) Smoking cessation. *Respiratory Care*, **48** (12), 1238–1254, discussion 1254–1236.

59. Sellers, E.M., Kaplan, H.L., and Tyndale, R.F. (2000) Inhibition of cytochrome P450 2A6 increases nicotine's oral bioavailability and decreases smoking. *Clin. Pharmacol. Ther.*, **68** (1), 35–43.

60. Yano, J.K., Hsu, M.H., Griffin, K.J. *et al.* (2005) Structures of human microsomal cytochrome P450 2A6 complexed with coumarin and methoxsalen. *Nature Structural & Molecular Biology*, **12** (9), 822–823.

61. Haney, M., Hart, C.L., Vosburg, S.K. *et al.* (2004) Marijuana withdrawal in humans: effects of oral THC or divalproex. *Neuropsychopharmacology*, **29** (1), 158–170.

62. Copeland, J., Swift, W., Roffman, R., and Stephens, R. (2001) A randomized controlled trial of brief cognitive-behavioral interventions for cannabis use disorder. *J. Subst. Abuse Treat.*, **21** (2), 55–64, discussion 65–56.

63. Jones, R.T., Benowitz, N.L., and Herning, R.I. (1981) Clinical relevance of cannabis tolerance and dependence. *J. Clin. Pharmacol.*, **21** (8–9 Suppl.), 143S–152S.

64. Watson, S.J., Benson, J.A. Jr., and Joy, J.E. (2000) Marijuana and medicine: assessing the science base: a summary of the 1999 Institute of Medicine report. *Arch. Gen. Psychiatry*, **57** (6), 547–552.

65. Crowley, T.J., Macdonald, M.J., Whitmore, E.A., and Mikulich, S.K. (1998) Cannabis dependence, withdrawal, and reinforcing effects among adolescents with conduct symptoms and substance use disorders. *Drug Alcohol. Depend.*, **50** (1), 27–37.

66. Mendelson, J.H., Mello, N.K., Lex, B.W., and Bavli, S. (1984) Marijuana withdrawal syndrome in a woman. *Am. J. Psychiatry*, **141** (10), 1289–1290.

67. Stephens, R.S., Roffman, R.A., and Simpson, E.E. (1993) Adult marijuana users seeking treatment. *J. Consult Clin. Psychol.*, **61** (6), 1100–1104.

68. Budney, A.J., Moore, B.A., Vandrey, R.G., and Hughes, J.R. (2003) The time course and significance of cannabis withdrawal. *J. Abnorm. Psychol.*, **112** (3), 393–402.

69. Copersino, M.L., Boyd, S.J., Tashkin, D.P. *et al.* (2006) Cannabis withdrawal among non-treatment-seeking adult cannabis users. *Am. J. Addict.*, **15** (1), 8–14.

70. Miller, N.S. and Gold, M.S. (1989) The diagnosis of marijuana (cannabis) dependence. *J. Subst. Abuse Treat.*, **6** (3), 183–192.

71. Budney, A.J., Hughes, J.R., Moore, B.A., and Vandrey, R. (2004) Review of the validity and significance of cannabis withdrawal syndrome. *Am. J. Psychiatry*, **161** (11), 1967–1977.

72. Budney, A.J., Vandrey, R.G., Hughes, J.R. *et al.* (2007) Oral delta-9-tetrahydrocannabinol suppresses cannabis withdrawal symptoms. *Drug Alcohol Depend.*, **86** (1), 22–29.

73. Haney, M., Hart, C.L., Vosburg, S.K. *et al.* (2008) Effects of THC and lofexidine in a human laboratory model of marijuana withdrawal and relapse. *Psychopharmacology (Berl.)*, **197** (1), 157–168.

74. Curran, H.V., Brignell, C., Fletcher, S. *et al.* (2002) Cognitive and subjective dose-response effects of acute oral Delta 9-tetrahydrocannabinol (THC) in infrequent cannabis users. *Psychopharmacology (Berl.)*, **164** (1), 61–70.

75. Haney, M., Ward, A.S., Comer, S.D. *et al.* (2001) Bupropion SR worsens mood during marijuana withdrawal in humans. *Psychopharmacology (Berl.)*, **155** (2), 171–179.

76. Haney, M., Hart, C.L., Ward, A.S., and Foltin, R.W. (2003) Nefazodone decreases anxiety during marijuana withdrawal in humans. *Psychopharmacology (Berl.)*, **165** (2), 157–165.

77. Kleber, H.D. (1992) Treatment of cocaine abuse: pharmacotherapy. *Ciba. Found Symp.*, **166**, 195–200, discussion 200–196.

78. Gawin, F.H. and Kleber, H.D. (1984) Cocaine abuse treatment. Open pilot trial with desipramine and lithium carbonate. *Arch. Gen. Psychiatry*, **41** (9), 903–909.

79. Giannini, A.J., Malone, D.A., Giannini, M.C. *et al.* (1986) Treatment of depression in chronic cocaine and phencyclidine abuse with desipramine. *J. Clin. Pharmacol.*, **26** (3), 211–214.

80. Dackis, C.A., Gold, M.S., Sweeney, D.R. *et al.* (1987) Single-dose bromocriptine reverses cocaine craving. *Psychiatry Res.*, **20** (4), 261–264.

81. Giannini, A.J. and Billett, W. (1987) Bromocriptine-desipramine protocol in treatment of cocaine addiction. *J. Clin. Pharmacol.*, **27** (8), 549–554.

82. Handelsman, L., Rosenblum, A., Palij, M. *et al.* (1997) Bromocriptine for cocaine dependence. A controlled clinical trial. *Am. J. Addict.*, **6** (1), 54–64.

83. Teller, D.W. and Devenyi, P. (1988) Bromocriptine in cocaine withdrawal – does it work? *Int. J. Addict.*, **23** (11), 1197–1205.

84. Gorelick, D.A. and Wilkins, J.N. (2006) Bromocriptine treatment for cocaine addiction: association with plasma prolactin levels. *Drug Alcohol Depend.*, **81** (2), 189–195.

85. Kranzler, H.R. and Bauer, L.O. (1992) Bromocriptine and cocaine cue reactivity in cocaine-dependent patients. *Br. J. Addict.*, **87** (11), 1537–1548.

86. Weiss, R.D., Griffin, M.L., Hufford, C. *et al.* (1997) Early prediction of initiation of abstinence from cocaine. Use of a craving questionnaire. *Am. J. Addict.*, **6** (3), 224–231.

87. Weiss, R.D., Griffin, M.L., Mazurick, C. *et al.* (2003) The relationship between cocaine craving, psychosocial treatment, and subsequent cocaine use. *Am. J. Psychiatry*, **160** (7), 1320–1325.

88. Paliwal, P., Hyman, S.M., and Sinha, R. (2008) Craving predicts time to cocaine relapse: Further validation of the Now and Brief versions of the cocaine craving questionnaire. *Drug Alcohol. Depend.*, **93** (3), 252–259.

89. Bordnick, P.S. and Schmitz, J.M. (1998) Cocaine craving: an evaluation across treatment phases. *J. Subst. Abuse*, **10** (1), 9–17.

90. Rohsenow, D.J., Martin, R.A., Eaton, C.A., and Monti, P.M. (2007) Cocaine craving as a predictor of treatment attrition and outcomes after residential treatment for cocaine dependence. *J. Stud. Alcohol Drugs*, **68** (5), 641–648.

91. Robbins, S.J. and Ehrman, R.N. (1998) Cocaine use is associated with increased craving in outpatient cocaine abusers. *Exp. Clin. Psychopharmacol.*, **6** (2), 217–224.

92. Miller, N.S. and Gold, M.S. (1994) Dissociation of "conscious desire" (craving) from and relapse in alcohol and cocaine dependence. *Ann. Clin. Psychiatry*, **6** (2), 99–106.

93. Weiss, R.D., Griffin, M.L., and Hufford, C. (1995) Craving in hospitalized cocaine abusers as a predictor of outcome. *Am. J. Drug Alcohol Abuse*, **21** (3), 289–301.

94. Sussner, B.D., Smelson, D.A., Rodrigues, S. *et al.* (2006) The validity and reliability of a brief measure of cocaine craving. *Drug Alcohol Depend*, **83** (3), 233–237.

95. Tiffany, S.T., Singleton, E., Haertzen, C.A., and Henningfield, J.E. (1993) The development of a cocaine craving questionnaire. *Drug Alcohol Depend*, **34** (1), 19–28.

96. Crosby, R.D., Halikas, J.A., and Carlson, G. (1991) Pharmacotherapeutic interventions for cocaine abuse: present practices and future directions. *J. Addict. Dis.*, **10** (4), 13–30.

97. Gawin, F.H. and Kleber, H.D. (1986) Abstinence symptomatology and psychiatric diagnosis in cocaine abusers. Clinical observations. *Arch. Gen. Psychiatry*, **43** (2), 107–113.

98. Miller, N.S., Summers, G.L., and Gold, M.S. (1993) Cocaine dependence: alcohol and other drug dependence and withdrawal characteristics. *J. Addict. Dis.*, **12** (1), 25–35.

99. Satel, S.L., Price, L.H., Palumbo, J.M. *et al.* (1991) Clinical phenomenology and neurobiology of cocaine

abstinence: a prospective inpatient study. *Am. J. Psychiatry*, **148** (12), 1712–1716.

100. Coffey, S.F., Dansky, B.S., Carrigan, M.H., and Brady, K.T. (2000) Acute and protracted cocaine abstinence in an outpatient population: a prospective study of mood, sleep and withdrawal symptoms. *Drug Alcohol. Depend*, **59** (3), 277–286.

101. Weddington, W.W., Brown, B.S., Haertzen, C.A. *et al.* (1990) Changes in mood, craving, and sleep during short-term abstinence reported by male cocaine addicts. A controlled, residential study. *Arch Gen Psychiatry*, **47** (9), 861–868.

102. Newton, T.F., Kalechstein, A.D., Duran, S. *et al.* (2004) Methamphetamine abstinence syndrome: preliminary findings. *Am. J. Addict.*, **13** (3), 248–255.

103. McGregor, C., Srisurapanont, M., Jittiwutikarn, J. *et al.* (2005) The nature, time course and severity of methamphetamine withdrawal. *Addiction*, **100** (9), 1320–1329.

104. Carroll, K.M., Fenton, L.R., Ball, S.A. *et al.* (2004) Efficacy of disulfiram and cognitive behavior therapy in cocaine-dependent outpatients: a randomized placebo-controlled trial. *Arch. Gen. Psychiatry*, **61** (3), 264–272.

105. George, T.P., Chawarski, M.C., Pakes, J. *et al.* (2000) Disulfiram versus placebo for cocaine dependence in buprenorphine-maintained subjects: a preliminary trial. *Biol. Psychiatry*, **47** (12), 1080–1086.

106. Petrakis, I.L., Carroll, K.M., Nich, C. *et al.* (2000) Disulfiram treatment for cocaine dependence in methadone-maintained opioid addicts. *Addiction*, **95** (2), 219–228.

107. McCance-Katz, E.F., Kosten, T.R., and Jatlow, P. (1998) Chronic disulfiram treatment effects on intranasal cocaine administration: initial results. *Biol. Psychiatry*, **43** (7), 540–543.

108. McCance-Katz, E.F., Kosten, T.R., and Jatlow, P. (1998) Disulfiram effects on acute cocaine administration. *Drug Alcohol. Depend*, **52** (1), 27–39.

109. Hameedi, F.A., Rosen, M.I., McCance-Katz, E.F. *et al.* (1995) Behavioral, physiological, and pharmacological interaction of cocaine and disulfiram in humans. *Biol. Psychiatry*, **37** (8), 560–563.

110. Vocci, F. and Ling, W. (2005) Medications development: successes and challenges. *Pharmacol. Ther.*, **108** (1), 94–108.

111. Vocci, F.J. and Elkashef, A. (2005) Pharmacotherapy and other treatments for cocaine abuse and dependence. *Curr. Opin. Psychiatry*, **18** (3), 265–270.

112. Karila, L., Gorelick, D., Weinstein, A. *et al.* (2008) New treatments for cocaine dependence: a focused review. *Int. J. Neuropsychopharmacol*, **11**, 425–438.

113. Sofuoglu, M. and Kosten, T.R. (2005) Novel approaches to the treatment of cocaine addiction. *CNS Drugs*, **19** (1), 13–25.

114. Gorelick, D.A., Gardner, E.L., and Xi, Z.X. (2004) Agents in development for the management of cocaine abuse. *Drugs*, **64** (14), 1547–1573.

115. Kampman, K.M., Dackis, C., Lynch, K.G. *et al.* (2006) A double-blind, placebo-controlled trial of amantadine, propranolol, and their combination for the treatment of cocaine dependence in patients with severe cocaine withdrawal symptoms. *Drug Alcohol Depend*, **85** (2), 129–137.

116. Kampman, K.M., Volpicelli, J.R., Mulvaney, F. *et al.* (2001) Effectiveness of propranolol for cocaine dependence treatment may depend on cocaine withdrawal symptom severity. *Drug Alcohol. Depend*, **63** (1), 69–78.

117. Saitz, R. (1998) Introduction to alcohol withdrawal. *Alcohol Health Res. World*, **22** (1), 5–12.

118. Sofuoglu, M. and Kosten, T.R. (2006) Emerging pharmacological strategies in the fight against cocaine addiction. *Expert Opin. Emerg. Drugs*, **11** (1), 91–98.

119. Dackis, C.A., Kampman, K.M., Lynch, K.G. *et al.* (2005) A double-blind, placebo-controlled trial of modafinil for cocaine dependence. *Neuropsychopharmacology*, **30** (1), 205–211.

120. Preti, A. (2007) New developments in the pharmacotherapy of cocaine abuse. *Addict. Biol.*, **12** (2), 133–151.

121. Kaye, A.D., Gevirtz, C., Bosscher, H.A. *et al.* (2003) Ultrarapid opiate detoxification: a review. *Can J. Anaesth*, **50** (7), 663–671.

122. Kleber, H.D. and Riordan, C.E. (1982) The treatment of narcotic withdrawal: a historical review. *J. Clin. Psychiatry*, **43** (6 Pt 2), 30–34.

123. Kreek, M.J. (2000) Methadone-related opioid agonist pharmacotherapy for heroin addiction. History, recent molecular and neurochemical research and future in mainstream medicine. *Ann. NY Acad. Sci.*, **909**, 186–216.

124. Gossop, M., Griffiths, P., Bradley, B., and Strang, J. (1989) Opiate withdrawal symptoms in response to 10-day and 21-day methadone withdrawal programmes. *Br. J. Psychiatry*, **154**, 360–363.

125. Reed, L.J., Glasper, A., de Wet, C.J. *et al.* (2007) Comparison of buprenorphine and methadone in the treatment of opiate withdrawal: possible advantages of buprenorphine for the treatment of opiate-benzodia-

zepine codependent patients? *J. Clin. Psychopharmacol.*, **27** (2), 188–192.

126. White, R., Alcorn, R., and Feinmann, C. (2001) Two methods of community detoxification from opiates: an open-label comparison of lofexidine and buprenorphine. *Drug Alcohol Depend*, **65** (1), 77–83.

127. Marion, I. (1995) LAAM in the treatment of opiate addiction. Treatment Improvement Protocol (TIP) Series 22, DHHS Publication No. (SMA) 95-3052, US Department of Health and Human Services, Public Health Service, Substance Abuse and Mental Health Services Administration/Center for Substance Abuse Treatment (SAMHSA/CSAT), Rockville, MD.

128. Gowing, L.R. and Ali, R.L. (2006) The place of detoxification in treatment of opioid dependence. *Curr. Opin. Psychiatry*, **19** (3), 266–270.

129. Gowing, L., Ali, R., and White, J. (2009) Buprenorphine for the management of opioid withdrawal. *Cochrane Database Syst. Rev.* 3 (Art. No.: CD002025). doi: 10.1002/14651858.CD002025.pub4.

130. Amato, L., Davoli, M., Ferri, M. *et al.* (2004) Effectiveness of interventions on opiate withdrawal treatment: an overview of systematic reviews. *Drug Alcohol Depend*, **73** (3), 219–226.

131. Strang, J., Bearn, J., and Gossop, M. (1999) Lofexidine for opiate detoxification: review of recent randomised and open controlled trials. *Am. J. Addict.*, **8** (4), 337–348.

132. O'Connor, P.G., Carroll, K.M., Shi, J.M. *et al.* (1997) Three methods of opioid detoxification in a primary care setting. A randomized trial. *Ann. Intern. Med.*, **127** (7), 526–530.

133. Janiri, L., Mannelli, P., Persico, A.M. *et al.* (1994) Opiate detoxification of methadone maintenance patients using lefetamine, clonidine and buprenorphine. *Drug Alcohol Depend*, **36** (2), 139–145.

134. Ling, W. and Wesson, D.R. (2003) Clinical efficacy of buprenorphine: comparisons to methadone and placebo. *Drug Alcohol Depend.*, **70** (2 Suppl.), S49–S57.

135. Collins, E.D., Kleber, H.D., Whittington, R.A., and Heitler, N.E. (2005) Anesthesia-assisted vs buprenorphine- or clonidine-assisted heroin detoxification and naltrexone induction: a randomized trial. *JAMA*, **294** (8), 903–913.

136. Johnson, R.E., Jaffe, J.H., and Fudala, P.J. (1992) A controlled trial of buprenorphine treatment for opioid dependence. *JAMA*, **267** (20), 2750–2755.

137. Manlandro, J.J. Jr. (2007) Using buprenorphine for outpatient opioid detoxification. *J. Am. Osteopath Assoc.*, **107** (Suppl. 5), ES11–ES16.

138. Bullingham, R.E., McQuay, H.J., Moore, A., and Bennett, M.R. (1980) Buprenorphine kinetics. *Clin. Pharmacol. Ther.*, **28** (5), 667–672.

139. Robinson, S.E. (2006) Buprenorphine-containing treatments: place in the management of opioid addiction. *CNS Drugs*, **20** (9), 697–712.

140. Marsch, L.A., Bickel, W.K., Badger, G.J., and Jacobs, E.A. (2005) Buprenorphine treatment for opioid dependence: the relative efficacy of daily, twice and thrice weekly dosing. *Drug Alcohol Depend*, **77** (2), 195–204.

141. Chawarski, M.C., Schottenfeld, R.S., O'Connor, P.G., and Pakes, J. (1999) Plasma concentrations of buprenorphine 24 to 72 hours after dosing. *Drug Alcohol Depend*, **55** (1–2), 157–163.

142. Schottenfeld, R.S., Pakes, J., O'Connor, P. *et al.* (2000) Thrice-weekly versus daily buprenorphine maintenance. *Biol. Psychiatry*, **47** (12), 1072–1079.

143. Ling, W., Charuvastra, C., Collins, J.F. *et al.* (1998) Buprenorphine maintenance treatment of opiate dependence: a multicenter, randomized clinical trial. *Addiction*, **93** (4), 475–486.

144. Raisch, D.W., Fye, C.L., Boardman, K.D., and Sather, M.R. (2002) Opioid dependence treatment, including buprenorphine/naloxone. *Ann. Pharmacother*, **36** (2), 312–321.

145. Bickel, W.K., Stitzer, M.L., Bigelow, G.E. *et al.* (1988) A clinical trial of buprenorphine: comparison with methadone in the detoxification of heroin addicts. *Clin. Pharmacol. Ther.*, **43** (1), 72–78.

146. Umbricht, A., Hoover, D.R., Tucker, M.J. *et al.* (2003) Opioid detoxification with buprenorphine, clonidine, or methadone in hospitalized heroin-dependent patients with HIV infection. *Drug Alcohol Depend*, **69** (3), 263–272.

147. Stoller, K.B., Bigelow, G.E., Walsh, S.L., and Strain, E.C. (2001) Effects of buprenorphine/naloxone in opioid-dependent humans. *Psychopharmacology (Berl.)*, **154** (3), 230–242.

148. Fiellin, D.A., Friedland, G.H., and Gourevitch, M.N. (2006) Opioid dependence: rationale for and efficacy of existing and new treatments. *Clin. Infect. Dis.*, **43** (Suppl. 4), S173–S177.

149. Mendelson, J., Jones, R.T., Fernandez, I. *et al.* (1996) Buprenorphine and naloxone interactions in opiate-dependent volunteers. *Clin. Pharmacol. Ther.*, **60** (1), 105–114.

150. Strain, E.C., Stoller, K., Walsh, S.L., and Bigelow, G.E. (2000) Effects of buprenorphine versus buprenorphine/naloxone tablets in non-dependent opioid abusers. *Psychopharmacology (Berl.)*, **148** (4), 374–383.

151. Seifert, J., Metzner, C., Paetzold, W. *et al.* (2002) Detoxification of opiate addicts with multiple drug abuse: a comparison of buprenorphine vs. methadone. *Pharmacopsychiatry*, **35** (5), 159–164.

152. Kristensen, O., Lolandsmo, T., Isaksen, A. *et al.* (2006) Treatment of polydrug-using opiate dependents during withdrawal: towards a standardisation of treatment. *BMC Psychiatry*, **6**, 54.

153. Williams, J.F. and Storck, M. (2007) Inhalant abuse. *Pediatrics*, **119** (5), 1009–1017.

154. Lorenc, J.D. (2003) Inhalant abuse in the pediatric population: a persistent challenge. *Curr. Opin. Pediatr.*, **15** (2), 204–209.

155. Balster, R.L. (1998) Neural basis of inhalant abuse. *Drug Alcohol Depend*, **51** (1–2), 207–214.

156. Sigell, L.T., Kapp, F.T., Fusaro, G.A. *et al.* (1978) Popping and snorting volatile nitrites: a current fad for getting high. *Am. J. Psychiatry*, **135** (10), 1216–1218.

157. Haverkos, H.W., Kopstein, A.N., Wilson, H., and Drotman, P. (1994) Nitrite inhalants: history, epidemiology, and possible links to AIDS. *Environ. Health Perspect*, **102** (10), 858–861.

158. Meredith, T.J., Ruprah, M., Liddle, A., and Flanagan, R.J. (1989) Diagnosis and treatment of acute poisoning with volatile substances. *Hum. Toxicol.*, **8** (4), 277–286.

159. Brouette, T. and Anton, R. (2001) Clinical review of inhalants. *Am. J. Addict.*, **10** (1), 79–94.

160. Gautschi, O.P., Cadosch, D., and Zellweger, R. (2007) Postural tremor induced by paint sniffing. *Neurol. India*, **55** (4), 393–395.

161. Maruff, P., Burns, C.B., Tyler, P. *et al.* (1998) Neurological and cognitive abnormalities associated with chronic petrol sniffing. *Brain*, **121** (Pt 10), 1903–1917.

162. Anderson, C.E. and Loomis, G.A. (2003) Recognition and prevention of inhalant abuse. *Am. Fam. Physician*, **68** (5), 869–874.

163. Shepherd, R.T. (1989) Mechanism of sudden death associated with volatile substance abuse. *Hum. Toxicol.*, **8** (4), 287–291.

164. Bass, M. (1970) Sudden sniffing death. *JAMA*, **212** (12), 2075–2079.

165. Ramsey, J., Anderson, H.R., Bloor, K., and Flanagan, R.J. (1989) An introduction to the practice, prevalence and chemical toxicology of volatile substance abuse. *Hum. Toxicol.*, **8** (4), 261–269.

166. Flanagan, R.J., Ruprah, M., Meredith, T.J., and Ramsey, J.D. (1990) An introduction to the clinical toxicology of volatile substances. *Drug Saf.*, **5** (5), 359–383.

167. Broussard, L.A. (2000) The role of the laboratory in detecting inhalant abuse. *Clin. Lab. Sci.*, **13** (4), 205–209.

168. Beauvais, F., Jumper-Thurman, P., Plested, B., and Helm, H. (2002) A survey of attitudes among drug user treatment providers toward the treatment of inhalant users. *Subst. Use Misuse*, **37** (11), 1391–1410.

169. Haddad, L.M. (1976) Management of hallucinogen abuse. *Am. Fam. Physician*, **14** (1), 82–87.

33

Pharmacological therapeutics for relapse reduction in addictive disorders

Lisa J. Merlo,[1] Kimberly G. Blumenthal,[2] Kendall Campbell,[3] Morrow Omli,[1] and Mark S. Gold[4]

[1] Department of Psychiatry, Division of Addiction Medicine, University of Florida, Gainesville, FL 32611, USA
[2] Yale University School of Medicine, New Haven, CT 06510, USA
[3] Department of Community Health and Family Medicine, University of Florida, Gainesville, FL 32611, USA
[4] Departments of Psychiatry, Neuroscience, Anesthesiology, Community Health & Family Medicine, University of Florida College of Medicine and McKnight Brain Institute, Gainesville, FL 32611, USA

33.1   SIGNIFICANCE TO THE CLINICIAN

Relapse, which is generally considered the return to active use of a substance after a period of intentional abstinence [1], was previously interpreted as a failure of treatment or catastrophic loss of "recovery" status. Though no consensus has yet been reached in the field regarding the markers of relapse, lapses (i.e., temporary "slips" back to active use that do not meet criteria for abuse or dependence) are now generally understood to be an expected part of the addiction cycle. However, the most desirable outcome, and a key marker of recovery according to the prevailing definition [2], is for individuals with addictive diseases to maintain long-term abstinence from addictive substances. Indeed, research has demonstrated that the length of abstinence achieved during treatment is predictive of successful outcome [3]. Psychotherapeutic relapse prevention techniques encompass an important component of care [4].

In addition, pharmacological therapeutic interventions (PTIs) may assist with relapse prevention. For example, PTIs may cause an immediate reduction of alcohol/drug craving [5]. As a result, patients may benefit from the prescription of PTIs, which are readily available for many addictive substances, and may increase the likelihood of achieving abstinence and sobriety. Unfortunately, many clinicians do not feel comfortable managing the treatment of addictive disorders, and may not understand the clinical utility of PTIs in the standard of care. Given the potential advantages of using PTIs to assist with treatment for addictive disorders, more work is needed to disseminate the research findings and promote clinician competence in this area.

This chapter discusses issues related to the implementation of pharmacological therapeutics for relapse reduction in addictive disorders. Specifically,

Addictive Disorders in Medical Populations   Edited by Norman S. Miller and Mark S. Gold
© 2010 John Wiley & Sons, Ltd.

it addresses the scope of the problem (i.e., prevalence of relapse), describes the clinical relevance of relapse, and discusses the types of PTIs currently available for relapse reduction. It offers a guide for clinicians who wish to learn more about the incorporation of PTIs in the care of patients recovering from addiction.

The over-arching goal of this chapter is to make clinicians aware of the state of the art in pharmacological intervention for relapse prevention in patients with addictive diseases. Upon completion of this chapter, the reader will be familiar with the major advances in the treatment of relapse to alcohol, opiates, cocaine and other stimulants, cannabis, sedative-hypnotics, hallucinogens, nicotine, and inhalants. Specifically, the reader will:

1. Understand the prevalence and course of relapse in patients with substance use disorders

2. Be aware of available pharmacological therapeutic interventions (PTIs)

3. Recognize which PTIs are appropriate for each addictive substance

4. Possess a user-friendly guide for the use of PTIs in patients at risk for experiencing relapse.

33.2 CLINICAL PREVALENCE

Relapse typically occurs in over half of the addicted population. In general, long-term administration of addictive substances increases the likelihood of relapse, even years after successful detoxification. Several factors may influence the onset of relapse. For example, priming (e.g., new exposure to a formerly misused substance), environmental cues (e.g., people, places, or things associated with past drug use), and stress can all trigger intense craving and cause relapse [6]. The prevalence of relapse in addictive disorders varies by patient demographics as well as the addictive substance.

33.2.1 Prevalence of relapse to specific addictive drugs

33.2.1.1 Alcohol

Patients recovering from alcohol addiction or dependence display varying rates of relapse. Most studies show that relapse occurs among 40–60% of patients within the first few months, and that relapse prevalence climbs to 70–80% by the end of year one. Longer-term studies have proven somewhat more optimistic. In a two-year longitudinal study of 199 individuals after treatment, Booth *et al.* found that 9.1% of individuals remained substance-dependent at all interviews, 69.4% abstained once remission was achieved, and only 17.5% had a relapsing and remitting course [7]. Evidence from a population-based study demonstrated that only 25.9% experienced recurrence of alcohol use disorder symptoms at three-year follow-up, and only 5.1% experienced the recurrence of dependence [8]. This rate is much lower than that seen in most treatment samples; however, this is expected, given that those entering treatment generally display greater severity of disease and/or other comorbidities. Research has also identified some prognostic factors for successful abstinence from alcohol, including (1) the absence of a pre-existing antisocial personality disorder or additional substance use disorder, (2) evidence of general life stability, and (3) completion of a full two-to-four week course of initial rehabilitation [7]. The presence of these three factors predicts abstinence for at least one or more years. Conversely, the absence of these factors is associated with a much higher likelihood of relapse. For example, alcoholics with other drug problems and those who are homeless are thought to have an 85–90% chance of relapse within one year. Common reasons given for relapse include depression, boredom, loneliness, stopping Alcoholics Anonymous, and anxiety.

The High-Risk Alcoholism Relapse (HRAR) Scale, was developed during a study of relapse following inpatient alcoholism treatment in a cohort of male United States Veterans. Predictive validity was confirmed using other populations. For example, DeGottardi and colleagues [9] showed that a High-Risk Alcoholism Relapse score higher than three was associated with a 10.7 times greater likelihood of relapse following liver transplantation. Interestingly, a recent study showed that the highest rates of relapse among alcohol addicts are in those aged 18–24 years [10]. It is also noteworthy that there is evidence to suggest that smoking is associated with a better outcome in recovering alcoholics. One recent study found abstinence rates of 38% for smoking alcoholics, compared to only 28% for nonsmoking alcoholics [11].

33.2.1.2 Opiates

In opiate addiction, as with other illicit drugs, the longer the duration of the treatment program, the less likely that relapse will occur [12]. Unfortunately, rates of absolute abstinence from opiates are low. For example, though long-term treatment for heroin dependence generally includes abstinence-based treatments (e.g., detoxification, participation in Narcotics Anonymous), many patients abstain from heroin via maintenance therapy with opioid agonists, opioid antagonists, or heroin injected in a controlled setting (maintenance therapies will be further discussed later in this chapter). In addition, results of a 12-year follow-up study of opiate addicts by the Drug Abuse Reporting Program demonstrated that 75% of patients had relapsed to daily use of opiates one or more times following treatment. However, it is noteworthy that 63% of the sample went at least three years without relapsing to daily opiate use [13].

33.2.1.3 Cocaine and other stimulants

In most studies, long-term abstinence rates for patients recovering from addiction to cocaine or other stimulants rarely approach 50%. There are exceptions in some specialized patient populations. For example, healthcare professionals with stimulant addictions have demonstrated abstinence rates approaching 70% [14]. In general, treatment prognosis for individuals with cocaine addiction depends on both the degree of physical dependence and many psychosocial factors (e.g., fewer medical or psychiatric comorbidities, better psychosocial functioning, and a supportive social network). These factors are associated with improved prognosis, regardless of the treatment modality. However, the most important factor in predicting abstinence from cocaine is treatment retention. Prognosis improves with both increased frequency/intensity and duration of treatment. Shorter stays in treatment (i.e., less than 90 days) have been associated with increased risk of relapse [13]. As mentioned previously, 12-step programs, including Cocaine Anonymous, improve treatment outcome. Relapse rates are also lower when substance addiction treatment is combined with primary medical care intervention, psychiatric care (when appropriate), and vocational rehabilitation.

33.2.1.4 Cannabis

Unfortunately, cannabis use is also associated with a high rate of relapse. For example, Moore and colleagues [15] found that 71% of individuals who achieved at least two weeks of abstinence during an outpatient treatment program for cannabis dependence lapsed at least once within six months of their abstinence. Of those who lapsed, 71% relapsed into heavier use, which was defined as at least four days of marijuana use in a week. Additionally, early lapse was strongly associated with relapse [15]. Reason for relapse has been studied in adolescent and adult outpatients. Among teens, the most common reasons for relapse include social pressure, cannabis withdrawal, and negative affect [16]. On the other hand, adult marijuana smokers cite boredom/stress/anxiety (58%), enjoyed/missed the high (39%), relaxation (18%), and cannabis craving (16%) as the most common reasons for relapse [17].

Withdrawal symptoms from cannabis are generally mild and have not consistently been predictive of relapse [18]. However, it is important to note that spontaneous quitting of marijuana is associated with increased use of legal substances such as alcohol, tobacco, and sleep aids. Cessation of marijuana use has not been associated with initiation of new substance use [17], but marijuana use does play a role in relapse to cocaine and alcohol. Patients who used cannabis were three times more likely to relapse after extended abstinence from cocaine and nearly five times more likely to relapse after abstinence from alcohol [19]. Fortunately, social support and participation in psychosocial interventions are related to successful abstinence from marijuana. In a meta-analysis of psychosocial interventions for substance use disorders, Dutra and colleagues found that psychosocial interventions are more efficacious for cannabis use disorders than all other substance use disorders [20].

33.2.1.5 Nicotine

Though it is apparent that many smokers wish to quit, rates of abstinence from nicotine are quite low. Forty percent of smokers stop smoking for at least one day in an effort to quit each year, but 70–80% of those seeking treatment for nicotine dependence relapse [21]. In addition, most research has focused upon assessing abstinence after only one year; whereas other studies using long-term tracking of participants reveal that 35–40% of patients who achieve one year of abstinence may relapse between years 1 and 5 after quitting [22]. The level of nicotine dependence exhibited by a patient appears to be a particularly important factor in predicting relapse. For example, two prospective studies, which included over 13 000 smokers, found that the amount of time lapsed before a patient's first cigarette of the day and the number of cigarettes smoked per day were key predictors of treatment outcome and relapse. Although there is evidence to suggest that women have higher relapse rates than men, a systematic review by Singleton and colleagues showed no differences between genders with respect to quit rates [23].

33.2.1.6 Inhalants

Though inhalant addicts would likely benefit from participation in conventional treatment programs

for substance addicts, a survey of substance addiction treatment programs revealed that most do not feel they are adequately equipped to address inhalant abuse or dependence. Findings showed that program directors perceive a great deal of neurological damage among inhalant users, and they are markedly pessimistic about treatment effectiveness and recovery. The survey respondents also felt that there were insufficient resources for inhalant user treatment and that special staff training in this area is needed [24].

33.2.1.7 Polysubstance addiction

There is a demonstrated lack of research regarding relapse to the use of sedative-hypnotics or hallucinogens; however, when assessing abstinence or relapse in any substance user, it is important to recognize the pervasiveness of polysubstance addiction. Drug use is often opportunistic, and many drug users will deviate from their drug of choice due to availability. In addition, individuals who use one substance may be more willing to try others. For example, cigarette smokers and heavy alcohol drinkers are 10 times more likely than others to use cocaine. Of individuals who misuse alcohol, 21% have a lifetime history of another drug use disorder. Similarly, of those who misuse illicit drugs, 47% have a lifetime history of alcohol addiction, and 75–95% of them smoke cigarettes. In the 2004 National Survey on Drug Use and Health, 92% of individuals who had used cocaine in the past month also used alcohol, 79% smoked cigarettes, and 73% used both alcohol and cigarettes [25].

33.2.2 Factors affecting relapse: all substances

Despite the high rates of relapse noted among various groups of substance addicts, not all individuals have the same chance of experiencing relapse. For example, low socioeconomic status, comorbid conditions, and lack of family or social supports are associated with increased risk of relapse [21].

In addition, studies have repeatedly demonstrated that patients who comply with recommended education, counseling, and/or medication have more favorable prognoses and lower incidence of relapse. For example, Alcoholics Anonymous affiliation and/or attendance are associated with increased rates of abstinence and decreased likelihood of relapse [10,26,27]. Many other 12-step programs (e.g., Narcotics Anonymous and Cocaine Anonymous) boast similar results, including increased abstinence, decreased substance use, and better psychological health. Similarly, the evidence shows improved outcomes after completion of a residential treatment program. After a first serious treatment course, 10–20% of patients never relapse. Unfortunately, there is a high rate of relapse immediately after leaving treatment. Within the first three months post-treatment (described as the "critical period"), over 50% of patients will relapse. It has been suggested that attendance at programs like Alcoholics Anonymous or Narcotics Anonymous following residential treatment ("90 meetings in 90 days") produces a more favorable prognosis and can ensure that the patient has adequate support to maintain abstinence past this critical period. However, a five-year follow-up study of patients discharged from residential treatment for drug dependence found that attendance at Alcoholics Anonymous or Narcotics Anonymous did not affect abstinence from alcohol or cocaine, but did increase the likelihood that a person would be abstinent from opiates [28]. With each year of attempted abstinence, an additional 2–3% of substance addicts will achieve long-term sobriety [29].

33.3 CLINICAL RELEVANCE OF RELAPSE

About 25–40% of hospital admissions are related to substance addiction and its sequelae. Additionally, 10–16% of outpatients seen in general practice suffer from problems related to addiction [30]. Substance dependence is a chronic disease, and substance use and relapse are clinically relevant in virtually all medical disciplines. Therefore, clinicians should be aware of and routinely monitor for substance use disorders. Attention to this health concern is particularly important for patients who have medical comorbidities. Managing medical problems within the context of addiction can be quite challenging and frustrating. As described in other chapters, there is significant evidence demonstrating that substance addiction can both cause and exacerbate medical problems. As a result, relapse to substance use may have serious medical ramifications in addition to the financial, legal, and interpersonal consequences of addiction. Treatment for substance addiction and relapse prevention may be a crucial component of medical care for individuals with certain medical conditions.

33.4 CLINICAL DIAGNOSIS OF RELAPSE

It is very important for healthcare providers to diagnose relapse as quickly as possible. This allows for quick intervention and more expedient restoration to sobriety/recovery, which may mitigate the return of some psychosocial and interpersonal stressors associated with addiction. Research has shown that many relapses can be predictable and preventable, as long as the recovering addict is well supported [31]. Perhaps the most important aspect of diagnosing relapse is identifying relapse triggering cues. There is a strong relationship between contact with substance-related cues and subsequent relapse [32]. Examples include renewing relationships with drug using friends, participating in rituals of drug use, and returning to the location where the drug use occurred. Understanding the influence of these cues may be related to tolerance. Tolerance can be defined as adaptation to a drug or the ability of the body to compensate for the effects of the drug. Changes occur within the body whenever drugs are used. Once a user has developed tolerance to a substance, his brain begins to "crave" the drug as a way to return to homeostasis. Indeed, exposure to drug-related cues may reinstate such neurobiological changes, even in the absence of the drug. Thus, observing for relapse triggering cues is important to prevent a lapse from resulting in the return to full blown addiction. Some research even suggests that neuro imaging data may be used to predict the likelihood of relapse in certain patients [33].

Medical indications that relapse have occurred may not be glaringly apparent. For example, there may be no abnormal physical examination findings that were not recorded during a previous visit. Despite this, it is important to perform a careful and complete physical examination, as there may be anatomical or physiological changes that would suggest ongoing substance addiction. Laboratory data may offer more information than the physical examination, especially with regard to alcohol relapse. For example, liver tests that indicate hepatocyte damage from alcohol may be used. Biological markers such as gamma glutamyl transferase (GGT), carbohydrate-deficient transferrin (CDT), and mean corpuscular volume (MCV) may also have utility as indicators of alcohol relapse. Sensitivity for detecting relapse is 55% for CDT, 50% for GGT and 20% for MCV [34]. In addition, there are data

to suggest that when these tests are used in combination with careful history taking, the specificity improves. Though carbohydrate-deficient transferrin is arguably the most sensitive marker for alcohol relapse [34], there are limitations to its specificity. For example, women must consume larger volumes of alcohol to produce a positive test. In general, a woman would have to consume 4–5 alcoholic beverages within two-to-four weeks in order to produce a positive test [35]. As a result, use of breathalyzer testing may have some utility, and screening for ethyl glucuronide may improve urine testing for alcohol [36], as it allows for detection of alcohol metabolites in urine up to five days after last use.

With regard to other addictive substances, random drug screening through urinalysis is the preferred method for identifying relapse. In general, urine screening is more accurate than self-report [37,38], and is more sensitive and less invasive than blood testing [39,40]. Although drug testing cannot distinguish whether substance use is indicative of addiction, it can identify whether the substance has been used. For individuals in recovery who are abstaining from substance use, any substance use is considered a "lapse" and may be clinically important.

33.5 PHARMACOLOGIC THERAPEUTIC INTERVENTIONS FOR RELAPSE PREVENTION AND TREATMENT

When considering treatment for addictive behavior and relapse, it is important to note that pharmacotherapy alone is usually not recommended. Rather, treatment outcome is enhanced by combining psychosocial treatment (e.g., motivational interviewing, cognitive behavioral therapy, contingency management, family/marital therapy, and/or participation in a 12-step program) with medication. Psychosocial treatment is covered in other sections of this book, so this chapter focuses on drug-specific pharmacologic therapeutic interventions (PTIs) used in treating addiction and preventing relapse.

Over the past few decades, significant progress has been made in the development of pharmacological

interventions for drug and alcohol addiction [5]. Pharmacological treatments for intoxication, overdose, and detoxification/withdrawal are covered in another chapter, but several additional PTIs have been identified or developed to prevent relapse to active substance use. In general, the goals of these PTIs are to reduce drug craving, block the euphoric effects associated with use, or produce aversive experiences following use. Research has demonstrated that these medications are most effective when administered within the context of concurrent psychotherapy [5]. This section covers PTIs for the prevention of relapse in the misuse of alcohol, opiates, cocaine, cannabis, sedative/hypnotics, hallucinogens, nicotine, and inhalants.

33.5.1 Alcohol

Much research has been conducted to identify, develop, and assess the efficacy of various medications in preventing relapse to alcohol abuse and dependence. Though there are no endogenous "alcohol" receptors in the human brain, alcohol has demonstrated effects on several neurotransmitter systems. As a result, several medications, which target different neurotransmitters and receptors, have been developed to prevent relapse among alcohol addicts [41]. As mentioned previously, the risk for relapse to alcohol is quite high, particularly in the first 6–12 months. As a result, it is recommended that an initial course of pharmacotherapy extends at least three months. Research has not yet demonstrated a preferred sequence in terms of choosing which medication to try first; however, if one medication is not effective, it is reasonable to consider others. Results of published studies have demonstrated no additive benefit of combining medications for concurrent administration [42,43]. But, as with all pharmacotherapy for relapse prevention, research has shown that medications are most effective when used in conjunction with psychological and behavioral therapies.

33.5.1.1 Disulfiram

This drug, commonly known as Antabuse, was the first medication to be offered for the treatment of alcohol dependence. The US Food and Drug Administration (FDA) first approved disulfiram in 1951, and it has been used safely and somewhat effectively in clinical settings since that time. The mechanism of action in disulfiram is to block the enzyme, aldehyde dehydrogenase, which helps to metabolize alcohol. As a result, consumption of alcohol after pretreatment with disulfiram causes acetaldehyde to accumulate in the bloodstream. The consequences of this accumulation can include nausea, vomiting, sweating, flushing, palpitations, and difficulty breathing [44], making alcohol consumption an extremely aversive experience for the user. Disulfiram is administered orally once per day

and can be effective for individuals who are committed to sobriety; however, medication compliance is frequently problematic. Results of clinical trials have demonstrated limited support for its efficacy, generally due to low compliance [45,46]. Some research suggests that compliance may be increased if disulfiram administration is supervised by a spouse or employer [47]. More recent advances in PTIs for the prevention of relapse to alcohol have rendered disulfiram less popular. Indeed, many providers currently use disulfiram as a "last resort" intervention.

33.5.1.2 Naltrexone

Naltrexone is an opioid antagonist that blocks access to the endogenous opioid receptors [48,49]. It was FDA approved for the treatment of alcohol dependence in December 1994. When used as a treatment for individuals who misuse alcohol, naltrexone reduces craving and is believed to interfere with alcohol-induced brain reward by inhibiting the release of dopamine. Naltrexone can be administered orally in once-daily tablet form or in extended-release form via intramuscular injection once per month. The latter method may be particularly useful when medication compliance is a problem.

After a complete history, physical examination, and laboratory testing, most patients are started on 50 mg orally per day. However, a recent large, randomized controlled trial indicated that a therapeutic dose of 100 mg per day may be more effective [42]. Some clinicians provide patients with a naltrexone ID card or ask them to order a Medic Alert bracelet that clearly indicates that they are maintained on an opioid antagonist. This can be useful if opiate medication for pain relief is needed, as the dose would need to be adjusted accordingly. Common side effects of naltrexone include lightheadedness, diarrhea, dizziness, and nausea; however, these effects are transient for most patients and naltrexone is generally well-tolerated. Weight loss and increased interest in sex have also been reported by some patients. In addition, patients maintained on opioid antagonists should be treated with non-opioid cough, antidiarrheal, headache, and pain medications.

Research has demonstrated that naltrexone pre-treatment results in decreased alcohol self-administration in nonhuman primates [50]. Studies using human subjects have demonstrated that treatment with naltrexone is associated with lower relapse rate, fewer drinking episodes, decreased "heavy drinking" days, longer time to relapse, and reduced tendency for a slip to become a relapse [51–53]. It is also associated with lower rates of treatment dropout than placebo [53]. Oral naltrexone appears to be most effective for individuals who experience "slips" to heavy drinking, and may not be as helpful in the maintenance of abstinence [54,55]. Injectable naltrexone appears to be particularly efficacious among men and individuals who have already achieved a period of abstinence [56]. In addition, naltrexone has demonstrated efficacy in treating individuals with high levels of depression and/or high levels of somatic distress [57]. Indeed, recent studies suggest that naltrexone may be most effective for alcohol dependent individuals with a family history of alcohol dependence [58].

33.5.1.3 Acamprosate

In July 2004, after many years of safe use in Europe and around the world, the FDA approved the use of acamprosate for the maintenance of alcohol abstinence. Acamprosate is a synthetic compound that has a chemical structure similar to that of the amino acid neurotransmitters homotaurine and GABA. Chronic alcohol use is associated with decreased GABA and glutamate activity, and glutamate systems may become unstable for up to 12 months after a person stops drinking.

Acamprosate is administered orally, generally three times per day. Similar to naltrexone, acamprosate reduces the reinforcing (pleasurable) effects of alcohol to reduce craving. Common side effects include diarrhea, anxiety, insomnia, nausea, dizziness, and weakness. Some research indicates that acamprosate may worsen depression and/or suicidal ideation, so patients with a history of major

depression should be monitored closely or prescribed a different medication. In addition, a recent study has suggested that acamprosate is more efficacious among patients with low levels of somatic distress [57].

Numerous European studies and a review of published double-blind, placebo-controlled clinical trials evaluating the safety and efficacy of acamprosate for the treatment of alcohol dependence, indicated that acamprosate was associated with improved treatment completion rates, abstinence rates and/or cumulative abstinence during treatment, and time to first drink [59]. In addition, results of a later meta-analysis of 17 studies comparing acamprosate to placebo indicated a six-month abstinence rate of 36% for patients taking acamprosate, versus 23% for those taking a placebo [60]. This positive treatment effect, combined with an excellent safety profile, initially suggested great hope for the use of acamprosate across a broad range of patients with alcohol dependence. Unfortunately, two large-scale studies in the United States failed to support the efficacy of acamprosate [42,61], at least among patients who were not motivated to abstain completely from alcohol [61]. Comparison with the European studies suggests that acamprosate may be most effective for patients who have already achieved a longer period of abstinence [62]. As a result, clinicians may wish to delay initiation of acamprosate medication until the patient has achieved more stable sobriety.

33.5.1.4 Topiramate

Topiramate was FDA approved as an antiepilectic drug. However, recent research has demonstrated the efficacy of topiramate in decreasing binge drinking and assisting with relapse prevention in patients with alcohol dependence. Though the mechanism of action remains unclear, the results of preliminary outcome studies for topiramate in this population are promising. It appears that topiramiate may exert its effect by increasing or facilitating GABA transmission while decreasing transmission of glutamate.

Topiramate is administered orally. Common side effects include difficulty concentrating, paresthesias, taste distortion, and decreased eating. These side effects may have contributed to the significantly greater drop-out among patients treated with topiramate versus placebo [63]. Side effects (e.g., nausea, dizziness, somnolence/fatigue, ataxia, concentration problems, confusion, paresthesias, and speech difficulties) may be limited by gradually titrating patients up to the minimum therapeutic dose, which may enhance treatment compliance.

Preliminary research demonstrated that treatment with topiramate is associated with several positive drinking outcomes when compared to placebo, including decreased episodes of binge drinking, prolonged abstinence, and fewer drinking-related consequences [64,65]. Results of a recent multisite randomized trial comparing topiramate plus brief behavioral therapy to placebo plus brief behavioral therapy indicated that patients in the topiramate condition displayed fewer binge drinking episodes and achieved more days abstinent, fewer drinks per day, and lower levels of plasma gamma glutamyl transferase [63]. It is noteworthy that abstinence was not required for treatment entry and these group differences were apparent by the fourth week of the study.

33.5.1.5 Serotonin reuptake inhibitors

Examples of serotonin reuptake inhibitors (SRIs) include fluoxetine, fluvoxamine, sertraline, citalopram, escitalopram oxidate, paroxetine, and so on. Serotonin reuptake inhibitors are a class of medications which exert their mechanism of action by blocking reuptake of the neurotransmitter serotonin. Alcohol is believed to affect the serotonin system, so research has been conducted to examine whether serotonin reuptake inhibitors, which are most commonly used to treat depression and anxiety, would demonstrate efficacy in reducing quantity of drinking, frequency of drinking, and frequency of binge drinking among individuals with alcohol dependence. Serotonin reuptake inhibitors are generally well-tolerated, but common side effects include nausea, headache, sedation, and sexual dysfunction [66].

Though not yet FDA approved for the treatment of alcohol dependence or relapse prevention, serotonin reuptake inhibitors display limited efficacy in reducing alcohol consumption [67]. They appear to be most efficacious in reducing symptoms of alcohol dependence in patients with comorbid depression [68,69]. The use of serotonin reuptake inhibitors may be indicated in cases of early-onset alcohol dependence among individuals with a biological predisposition to alcohol dependence as well [70].

33.5.2 Opiates

Like endogenous opioids, the opiate drugs produce their primary effects at the mu-opioid receptors within the brain. Though many addicts use an illicit opiate (e.g., heroin), a growing number of opiate addicts use prescription pain killers (e.g., codeine, fentanyl, morphine, hydrocodone, and oxycodone). The opiates are highly addictive, in part due to the fact that tolerance develops relatively quickly, and also because of the significant withdrawal symptoms that can occur. These drugs are extremely potent and can cause sedation, euphoria, confusion, and respiratory depression. There are several methods of pharamcological intervention for relapse prevention in opiate users. Opiate agonists, partial agonists, and antagonists have all demonstrated some efficacy in improving rates of abstention among individuals in recovery. The following is a description of PTIs currently being used for relapse prevention in opiate users.

33.5.2.1 Methadone

Methadone is a lipid-soluble, long-acting synthetic opioid agonist that was FDA approved as a pharmacologic maintenance treatment for opiate dependence in 1960 [71]. Maintenance therapy involves administration of an agonist medication in order to relieve withdrawal symptoms and craving, without producing the same degree of euphoria associated with the addictive drug. At adequate doses, methadone can prevent opiate withdrawal and craving [72]. It also reduces the euphoric effects of concurrent heroin or other opiate use, due to cross-tolerance. Methadone is administered orally either in liquid or tablet form. It is well absorbed and has a long half-life and duration of action [72]. Side effects include hypotension, bradycardia, peripheral dilation, palpitations, drowsiness, dizziness, tiredness, nausea/vomiting, constipation, and weakness.

Despite these potential side effects, in 2000 the Office of National Drug Control Policy declared methadone a safe drug [73]. The FDA has since reported that methadone misuse is associated with several negative consequences, including slowed or stopped breathing, life-threatening cardiac arrhythmias, narcotic overdose, and even death. In addition, methadone is included as a Schedule II drug (i.e., high addiction potential), and the therapeutic dose is quite high (generally above 40mg). In opiate-naïve individuals, even this therapeutic dose can lead to a fatal overdose [74,75]. As a result, methadone maintenance therapy (MMT) is generally managed within specialized treatment centers that are federally regulated. These programs can be highly efficacious in increasing abstinence from heroin when monitored and combined with counseling and contingency management [76,77]. Methadone has been shown to reduce opiate-related mortality and morbidity as it relates to infectious disease. In fact, in one prospective study, a seven-fold reduction in HIV was noted in the methadone treated group versus the untreated cohort [78].

33.5.2.2 LAAM

Levo-alpha-acetylmethadol (LAAM) was approved by the FDA in 1993, but has since been removed from the market due to the side effect of cardiotoxicity. LAAM is an opioid agonist, like methadone, and was used for similar patients. However, LAAM differed from methadone in terms of its pharmacologic properties. Whereas methadone requires daily administration, LAAM was administered only once every three days [71]. Unfortunately, time to initial stabilization was longer, and there were reports of ECG changes with LAAM, which include prolongation of the QTc interval and ventricular arrhythmia [78].

33.5.2.3 Buprenorphine

The compound referred to as buprenorphine is a semi-synthetic, mixed opioid agonist-antagonist. Its mechanism of action is twofold, operating as a partial agonist at the muopioid receptor and an antagonist at the kappa opioid receptor [71]. Though buprenorphine was originally developed and marketed as an analgesic, it has demonstrated efficacy in reducing opiate use and blocking the physiological and subjective effects of opiate drugs. Buprenorphine was FDA approved for the management of opiate dependence in 2002. However, oral administration is generally not recommended due to significant first-pass hepatic metabolism [79]. Thus, buprenorphine is commonly administered sublingually or via intramuscular injection. When injected subcutaneously, buprenorphine demonstrated decreased addiction potential compared to morphine, as well as decreased withdrawal symptoms [78].

Buprenorphine is generally well tolerated and has a low risk of physiological dependence. Although considered to be much less addictive than pure mu agonists, it does have significant addiction potential. As a result, buprenorphine can be combined with naloxone to create a less abusable tablet [80]. In one study comparing subjects who were taking either buprenorphine or the buprenorphine/naloxone combination, results indicated reduced opiate use and craving for both groups when compared to the placebo group [78]. No significant differences emerged between the two active treatment groups. Multiple studies have demonstrated the efficacy of buprenorphine in reducing opiate use [81–84], even in the case of comorbid cocaine use [85].

Currently, clinicians who prescribe buprenorphine must obtain specific education on the use of buprenorphine as a maintenance medication. Most are board certified in Addiction Psychiatry or certified by the American Society of Addiction Medicine. However, given these parameters, it is possible that buprenorphine can be used for office-based treatment in primary care [86]. Preliminary data show that 70–80% of patients who were administered buprenorphine in a primary care setting were retained in treatment, and about half of them produced opiate-negative urine samples for at least three weeks in a row [87,88].

33.5.2.4   Naltrexone

As mentioned previously, naltrexone is an opioid antagonist that completely blocks access to the endogenous opioid receptors. In patients recovering from opiate addiction, naltrexone administration prevents the euphoric effects of opiate drugs (e.g., heroin, morphine, oxycodone). Unfortunately, naltrexone has not demonstrated comparable efficacy in reducing craving, as compared to agonist therapies. Potential side effects include nausea, headaches, dizziness, fatigue, insomnia, anxiety/nervousness, and sleepiness. Compliance remains a problem as well, with research demonstrating only 20–30% retention rates after six months [71]. Regardless, naltrexone does show some efficacy among individuals who are highly motivated to maintain abstinence. In addition, the injectable one-month dosing of naltrexone has demonstrated efficacy in decreasing opiate use [89,90]. Naltrexone may also be particularly useful for patients who misuse both opiates and alcohol.

33.5.3   Cocaine and other stimulants

Unfortunately, the treatment of dependence on cocaine and other stimulants, as well as the prevention of relapse to these drugs, is very challenging. To date, no pharmacological agents have been identified that consistently demonstrate efficacy for patients with cocaine or other stimulant addiction [71,91], and there are no FDA approved medications for this population. As a result, this section discusses medications that are currently being explored and/or have shown limited efficacy with this population.

33.5.3.1   Cocaine vaccine

Recent research has examined the feasibility and efficacy of immunizing individuals against the effects of cocaine. The "cocaine vaccine," which has demonstrated positive outcomes in animals [92,93], was developed to prevent cocaine from crossing the blood–brain barrier. The mechanism of action involves injecting a cocaine-protein conjugate into the bloodstream, which causes the body to produce antibodies. Once the antibodies adhere to the cocaine molecules, the resulting compound is too large to cross from the circulatory system to the brain. This prevents cocaine from exerting its effects within the brain [94], resulting in a significant decrease in the euphoria generally associated with use.

The cocaine vaccine has demonstrated promising outcomes in preliminary trials. In one study, cocaine antibodies were produced in cocaine-misusing subjects, as expected, based on timing and dosing of the vaccine. A later trial demonstrated that five out of nine subjects achieved abstinence from cocaine during the study (i.e., 12 weeks), and the other four subjects noted significant reductions in their experience of a euphoric high [95]. Finally, an open-label trial demonstrated decreases in cocaine-associated euphoria among patients who relapsed [96].

The cocaine vaccine has virtually no negative side effects and is well tolerated [94]. In addition, there is no addiction potential and the effects are sustained for several months [97]. However, there may be a significant length of time following treatment before the vaccine takes effect (e.g., enough antibodies are produced). Additionally, its efficacy appears to vary greatly among individuals [95]

33.5.3.2   Stimulant therapy

Given that treatment with an opioid agonist has demonstrated efficacy for patients with opiate addiction, research has been conducted to assess whether using stimulant therapy for cocaine/stimulant addiction would produce similar results. However, the data have not uniformly supported this hypothesis. Indeed, one study actually showed that methylphenidate treatment was associated with increased cocaine use [98], though another provided preliminary data that it may be effective for patients with comorbid attention deficit hyperactivity disorder [99]. Treatment with pemoline resulted in both positive and negative effects [100]; and cocaine tea has been associated with reduced cocaine use [101].

Recent research has focused on modafinil, a newer stimulant medication. Preliminary research has shown that modafinil decreases the euphoric high from cocaine use, and may also decrease cravings [102,103]. It appears to be well tolerated by patients, but does not result in a high. As a result, it has not demonstrated a significant addiction liability [103].

33.5.3.3 Disulfiram

As noted earlier, disulfiram is currently approved for the treatment of alcohol dependence and relapse prevention. In research examining patients with comorbid alcohol and cocaine use [104], treatment with disulfiram was associated with decreases in use of both alcohol and cocaine. Disulfiram has demonstrated efficacy in reducing cocaine use following a reduction in alcohol use [78]. In addition, studies involving patients with opiate dependence who misused cocaine also demonstrated significant positive effects of disulfiram treatment on the reduction of cocaine use [105,106]. Pharmacological studies have examined the interaction among cocaine and disulfiram [107]. It appears that disulfiram may cause adverse effects of cocaine use by significantly increasing plasma concentrations of cocaine [108] and inhibiting dopamine beta hydroxylase [109].

33.5.3.4 Naltrexone

Naltrexone has demonstrated dose-dependent efficacy in reducing cocaine-seeking behavior in rats [110]. However, human studies have been inconclusive [111,112]. It appears that naltrexone may have some efficacy when combined with relapse prevention psychotherapy [112].

33.5.3.5 Topiramate

As with alcohol topiramate has also been applied to the treatment of cocaine dependence. The preliminary study indicated that individuals who received cognitive behavioral therapy plus topiramate had higher rates of abstinence for at least three weeks and used significantly less cocaine than individuals who received cognitive behavioral therapy plus placebo [113]. Later studies supported the efficacy of topiramate as a treatment for cocaine dependence in animal models as well as among human subjects with comorbid alcohol dependence [114]. No large-scale studies have been conducted, so more research is needed to replicate and extend these findings.

33.5.3.6 Baclofen

The drug, baclofen, is a GABA-B receptor agonist. It exerts its mechanism of influence by inhibiting synaptic reflexes in the spinal cord, and serves as a dopamine antagonist in the nucleus accumbens [115]. Numerous studies have been conducted that support the use of baclofen for reduction of cocaine-seeking behaviors [116], cocaine self-administration [117], and "relapse" following extinction [118] in rat models. In addition, preliminary human studies have demonstrated its efficacy in reduction of craving for cocaine [119,120], as well as reduction of cocaine use [121], particularly among heavy users [122].

33.5.4 Cannabis

Although research continues to accumulate on the topic, at this time there are no medications approved to assist with relapse prevention for cannabis addiction or dependence [72]. One study assessing the potential efficacy of naltrexone in treating heavy cannabis users demonstrated that pretreatment with naltrexone actually *increased* subjective ratings of the cannabis-induced high [123]. As a result, current research has switched to a focus on endogenous cannabinoid receptors. For example, a CB-1 selective antagonist (Rimonabant) has been shown to decrease the pleasurable effects of cannabis in a dose-dependent fashion [124]. However, the effects of Rimonabant on self-administration of cannabis (if any) are not yet known. Use of oral THC (tetrahydrocannabinol, i.e., cannabinoid agonist maintenance therapy) has also been evaluated in one study. Results indicated that cannabis self-administration rates were not affected, though participants' subjective reports of the pleasurable effects of the drug decreased after three days on maintenance therapy [125]. Finally, a randomized controlled trial assessing the efficacy of bupropion and nefazodone demonstrated that neither drug was more effective than placebo in helping the patient to achieve abstinence or avoid withdrawal symptoms [126].

33.5.5 Sedative-hypnotics

The sedative-hypnotics include a broad class of medications. Benzodiazepines, barbiturates, and several other compounds are included in this category. In general, it is believed that these substances exert their effects through modulation of the GABA-A receptor [72]. No pharmacological treatments have been developed to reduce relapse in patients who are addicted to sedative-hypnotics. Instead, prevention remains the most effective intervention. Given that these drugs are frequently prescribed for the treatment of anxiety, clinicians should monitor carefully for signs of misuse in order to prevent the development of an iatrogenic addiction.

33.5.6 Hallucinogens

Hallucinogens are potent psychoactive substances that cause altered states of perception and feeling. They are divided into two primary classes: indole alkylamines, which have effects that are somewhat similar to serotonin, and phenylalkylamines, which have effects that are more similar to dopamine and norepinephrine [72]. Examples of the indole compounds include LSD, DMT (N,N-Dimethyl-tryptamine), and psilocybin. Examples of the phenylalkylamines include mescaline and DOM (2,5-Dimethoxy-4-methylamphetamin). Unfortunately, no pharmacological treatments have yet

been identified to prevent relapse to hallucinogen addiction or dependence. Antidepressant medications (e.g., monoamine oxidase inhibitors or serotonin reuptake inhibitors) may be helpful in managing mood or anxiety symptoms that could contribute to use of hallucinogens [72].

33.5.7 Nicotine

Smoking is one of the leading preventable causes of death. However, quitting is very difficult, and even individuals who attempt to quit many times may experience relapse. As a result, there is great need for treatments to assist with quitting and prevent relapse. Behavioral interventions have demonstrated some success, and significant advances in pharmacotherapeutic interventions have contributed to higher quit rates. In general, the three main types of pharmacotherapy to prevent relapse in tobacco users include nicotine replacement therapy, bupropion, and varenicline.

33.5.7.1 Nicotine replacement therapy

Over the past two decades, various forms of nicotine replacement therapy (NRT) have been developed to help prevent relapse to smoking. They are believed to exert their effect by partially replacing the nicotine that was previously obtained through use of tobacco products. This helps to alleviate nicotine withdrawal symptoms and cravings, in order to remove a significant motivation for smoking [127]. Some NRT products (e.g., gum, inhaler, lozenge) also include a mechanism of oral behavioral stimulation, which may assist individuals who experience a strong behavioral "addiction" to smoking. The first NRT product to be FDA approved was nicotine gum, followed shortly by the transdermal nicotine patch. Since then, nicotine nasal spray, the nicotine inhaler, and nicotine lozenges have been developed. The nicotine patch is arguably the easiest to use, though the NRT product of choice depends more on the individual's habits, needs, and smoking history.

Nicotine replacement therapy products are well tolerated by most individuals [128,129] and have an excellent safety profile [130,131]. However, there is some evidence that NRT is associated with increased mortality among patients in the medical intensive care unit [132]. In addition, use of NRT while smoking is not recommended. The addiction potential is low [133], but patients can exhibit withdrawal symptoms when they discontinue use. Common side effects vary by product type but include skin irritation (patch), jaw pain (gum), mouth/throat irritation (gum, inhaler, lozenge, nasal spray), dyspepsia (gum), cough (inhaler, nasal spray), hiccups (gum, lozenge), and runny nose/nasal irritation (nasal spray) [134].

In general, each NRT product has demonstrated efficacy in helping individuals to quit smoking and maintain abstinence from tobacco products. Several studies have demonstrated that use of any of the various forms of NRT can double an individual's chances at successfully quitting smoking [128]. Other research has provided support for the various NRT products in terms of reducing intensity, frequency, and duration of craving episodes [129]. None of the products has emerged as more effective than the others, but it is recommended that NRT be used in combination with a comprehensive behavioral treatment program to improve success.

33.5.7.2   Bupropion

Bupropion was initially approved in as an antidepressant. After clinical accounts of patients with depression who quit smoking while taking bupropion [135], it was studied [136] and in 1997 became the first non-NRT medication to be FDA approved for smoking cessation [137]. Though the exact mechanism of action remains unclear, it is believed that bupropion assists with smoking cessation by inhibiting dopamine and norepinephrine reuptake [138], and blocking nicotinic receptors [139].

Bupropion is generally administered in sustained release formulation and is well tolerated by most patients. Patients are typically titrated to a therapeutic dose of 300 mg/day. The most common side effects include headache, dry mouth, and insomnia. Given that bupropion has been associated with

seizures in a very small number of patients, it is not recommended for patients with a history of seizure disorder. Bupropion is also contraindicated for patients with eating disorders and those at risk for head trauma [72].

Several studies assessing the efficacy of bupropion have demonstrated that it can add considerably to rates of success among individuals motivated to quit smoking [140–142]. It can also be used to help decrease nicotine cravings [143]. More recently, bupropion has been studied specifically as an intervention to prevent relapse to smoking, with similar findings [144]. Results are improved when bupropion is combined with behavioral therapy/counseling [141], and also may be improved when combined with NRT [142].

33.5.7.3   Varenicline

Most recently, the pharmacological agent, varenicline, was FDA approved as a treatment for smoking cessation. Unlike NRT or bupropion, varenicline is a partial nicotine agonist that exerts its effects on a specific nicotinic acetylcholine receptor subtype [145,146]. It assists with smoking cessation by combating withdrawal symptoms and blocking the effects of nicotine from smoking. As a result, even individuals who relapse while taking varenicline do not experience the pleasure typically associated with smoking [145,146]. Varenicline is also associated with reduced craving for tobacco products. In general, varenicline is believed to be very safe for patients. However, some evidence suggests that it may be associated with increased psychiatric symptoms, and the FDA has issued a public health advisory addressing this concern.

In recent studies, varenicline has demonstrated efficacy (compared to placebo) for assisting smoking cessation at all time points. In addition, it has demonstrated greater efficacy (compared to bupropion) at both 12 weeks and 24 weeks [147,148]. These results have been replicated in Asian trials [149,150]. At one-year follow-up, abstinence rates for individuals treated with varenicline were approximately 2.5 times greater than placebo and 1.7 times greater than bupropion [147,148].

33.5.8 Inhalants

The inhalants include a diverse group of compounds which are generally not well understood. However, the current belief is that inhalants exert their effects through GABA- and dopamine-mediated mechanisms [151]. No medications have consistently demonstrated efficacy in relapse reduction for inhalant abuse or dependence. However, lamotrigine (an anticonvulsant that affects GABA intake) has recently shown promise in reducing symptoms of inhalant dependence [152]. More research is needed on this topic.

33.6 CONCLUSIONS

Drug and alcohol addiction are significant public health concerns. Many pharmacological treatments have been developed to assist with detoxification and withdrawal. In addition, recent advances in pharmacotherapy for relapse prevention have improved the likelihood that individuals will achieve sustained sobriety and recovery. Choice of medication frequently differs depending on the addictive substance, though there are some medications that appear to be effective for several drug classes. Pharmacotherapy is most effective when combined with behavioral therapy or other psychosocial interventions, such as participation in a 12-step program. This combined treatment offers hope to many individuals who are struggling to overcome an addictive disorder.

REFERENCES

1. American Psychiatric Association (2000) *Diagnostic and Statistical Manual of Mental Disorders*, 4th edn, American Psychiatric Association.

2. Betty Ford Institute Consensus Panel (2007) What is recovery? a working definition from the Betty Ford Institute. *J. Subst. Abuse Treat.*, **33**, 221–228.

3. Klingemann, H. and Sobell, L.C. (eds) (2007) *Promoting Self-Change from Addictive Behaviors: Practical Implications for Policy, Prevention, and Treatment*, Springer, New York.

4. Marlatt, G.A. and Gordon, J.R. (eds) (1985) *Relapse Prevention: Maintenance Strategies in the Treatment of Addictive Behaviors*, Guilford Press, New York.

5. O'Brien, C.P. (2005) Anticraving medications for relapse prevention: A possible new class of psychoactive medications. *Am. J. Psychiatry*, **162**, 1423–1431.

6. Cami, J. and Farre, M. (2003) Drug addiction. *N. Engl. J. Med.*, **349**, 975–986.

7. Booth, B.M., Fortney, S.M., Fortney, J.C. *et al.* (2001) Short-term course of drinking in an untreated sample of at-risk drinkers. *J. Stud. Alcohol.*, **62**, 580–588.

8. Dawson, D.A., Rise, B., and Grant, B.F. (2007) Rates and correlates of relapse among individuals in remission from DSM IV alcohol dependance: a 3-year follow up. *Alcohol. Clin. Exp. Res.*, **31**, 2036–2045.

9. DeGottardi, A. and Spahr, L. (2007) A simple score for predicting alcohol relapse after liver transplantation. *Arch. Intern. Med.*, **167**, 1183–1188.

10. Kaskutas, L., Ammon, L., and Delucchi, K. (2005) Alcoholics anonymous careers: Patterns of AA involvement five years after treatment entry. *Alcohol. Clin. Exp. Res.*, **29**, 1983–1990.

11. Schmidt, L. and Smolka, M. (2007) Results from two pharmacotherapy trials show alcoholic smokers were more severely alcohol dependent but less prone to relapse that alcoholic non-smokers. *Alcohol. Alcohol.*, **42**, 241–246.

12. Zhang, Z., Friedmann, P.D., and Gerstein, D.R. (2003) Relapse in opioid dependence does retention matter? Treatment duration and improvement in drug use. *Addiction*, **98**, 673–684.

13. Simpson, D.D., Joe, G.W., and Fletcher, B.W. (1999) A national evaluation of treatment outcomes for cocaine dependence. *Arch. Gen. Psych.*, **56**, 507–514.

14. Domino, K.B. *et al.* (2005) Risk factors for relapse in health care professionals with substance use disorders. *JAMA*, **293**, 1453–1460.

15. Moore, B.A. and Budney, A.J. (2003) Relapse in outpatient treatment for marijuana dependence. *J. Subst. Abuse Treat.*, **25**, 85–89.

16. Cornelius, J.R., Maisto, S.A., Pollock, N.K. *et al.* (2003) Rapid release generally follows treatment for substance use disorders among adolescents. *Addict. Behav.*, **28**, 381–386.

17. Copersino, M.L., Boyd, S.J., Tashkin, D.P. *et al.* (2006) Quitting among non-treatment seeking marijuana users: reasons and changes in other substance use. *Am. J. Addict.*, **15**, 297–302.

18. Arendt, M., Rosenberg, R., Foldager, L. *et al.* (2007) Withdrawal symptoms do not predict relapse among subjects treated for cannabis dependence. *Am. J. Addict.*, **16**, 461–467.

19. Aharonovich, E., Liu, X., Samet, S. *et al.* (2005) Postdischarge cannabis use and its relationship to cocaine, alcohol, and heroin use: a prospective study. *Am. J. Psychiatry*, **162**, 1507–1514.

20. Dutra, L., Stathopoulou, G., Basden, S.L. *et al.* (2007) A meta-analytic review of psychosocial interventions for substance use disorders. *Am. J. Addict.*, **16**, 461–467.

21. O'Brien, C. and McLellan, A. (1996) Myths about the treatment of addiction. *Lancet*, **347**, 237–240.

22. Hajek, P., Stead, L.F., West, R. *et al.* (2005) Relapse prevention interventions for smoking cessation. *Cochrane Database Syst. Rev.* 1 (Art. No.: CD003999). doi: 10.1002/14651858.CD003999.pub3.

23. Singleton, J.K., Levin, R.F., Feldman, H.R., and Truglio-Londrigan, M. (2005) Evidence for smoking cessation: Implications for gender-specific strategies. *Worldviews Evid. Based Nurs.*, **2**, 63–74.

24. Beauvais, F., Jumper-Thurman, P., Plested, B., and Helm, H.A. (2002) A survey of attitudes among drug user treatment providers toward the treatment of inhalant users. *Subst. Use Misuse*, **37**, 1391–1410.

25. SAMHSA (2005) Results from the 2004 National Survey on Drug Use and Health: National findings. Office of Applied Studies, NSDUH Series H-28. DHHS Publication No. SMA 05-4062, Rockville, MD.

26. Humphreys, K., Moos, R.H., and Cohen, C. (1997) Social and community resources and long-term recovery from treated and untreated alcoholism. *J. Stud. Alcohol*, **58**, 231–238.

27. Gossop, M., Harris, J., and Best, D. (2003) Is attendance at alcoholics anonymous meetings after inpatient treatment related to improved outcomes? A 6 month follow-up study. *Alcohol. Alcohol.*, **38**, 421–426.

28. Gossop, M., Stewart, D., and Marsden, J. (2007) Attendance at Narcotics Anonymous and Alcoholic Anonymous meetings, frequency of attendance and substance use outcomes after residential treatment for drug dependence: a five year follow-up study. *Addiction*, **103**, 199–125.

29. Vaillant, G.E. (1995) *The Natural History of Alcoholism Revisited*, Harvard University Press, Cambridge, MA.

30. Kissen, B. (1997) Medical management of alcoholic patients, in *Treatment and Rehabilitation of the Chronic Alcoholic*, Plenum, New York.

31. Shaw, B.R. (2006) Can new technologies prevent relapse? "Body monitoring" technologies hold promise for helping people in recovery. *Behav. HealthC.*, **26**, 30–32.

32. Johnson, A. (1998) Understanding relapse the key to recovery. *J. Addiction and Ment. Health*, **27**, 5.

33. Paulus, M.P., Tapert, S.F., and CShuckit, M.A. (2005) Neural activation patterns of methamphetamine-dependent subjects. *Neuropsychopharm*, **26**, 53–63.

34. Mundle, G., Ackermann, K., and Mann, K. (1999) Biological markers as indicators for relapse in alcohol-dependent patients. *Addict. Biol.*, **4**, 209–214.

35. Elliott, V.S. (2000) Lab test offers new way to spot alcoholism. *American Medical News*, **43**, 28.

36. Skipper, G.E., Weingmann, W., Thierauf, A. *et al.* (2004) Ethyl glucoronide: a biomarker to identify alcohol use by health professionals recovering from substance use disorders. *Alcohol.*, **39**, 445–449.

37. Preston, K.L., Silverman, K., Schuster, C.R., and Cone, E.J. (1997) Comparison of self-reported drug use with quantitative and qualitative urinalysis for assessment of drug use in treatment studies. *NIDA Res. Monogr.*, **167**, 130–145.

38. Harrison, L.D., Martin, S.S., Eney, T., and Harrington, D. (2007) Comparing drug testing and self-report drug use among youth and young adults in the general population, in *Methodology Series M-7*, SAMHSA Office of Applied Studies, Rockville, MD.

39. Huestis, M.A. and Cone, E.J. (1998) Differentiating new marijuana use from residual drug excretion in occasional marijuana users. *J. Anal. Toxicol.*, **22**, 445–454.

40. Cone, E.J., Sampson-Cone, A.H., Darwin, W.D. *et al.* (2003) Urine testing for cocaine abuse: metabolic and excretion patterns following different routes of administration and methods for detection of false-negative results. *J. Anal. Toxicol.*, **27**, 386–401.

41. Kranzler, H.R. (2000) Pharmacotherapy of alcoholism: Gaps in knowledge and opportunities for research. *Alcohol. Alcohol.*, **35**, 537–547.

42. Anton, R.F., O'Malley, S.S., Ciraulo, D.A. *et al.* (2006) Combined pharmacotherapies and behavioral interventions for alcohol dependence: the COMBINE study: a randomized controlled trial. *JAMA*, **295**, 2003–2017.

43. Petrakis, L., Poling, L., Levinson, C. *et al.* (2005) Naltrexone and disulfiram in patients with alcohol

dependence and comorbid psychiatric disorders. *Biol. Psychiatry*, **57**, 1128–1137.

44. Miller, N.S. and Gold, M.S. (1991) *Drugs of Abuse: a Comprehensive Series*, Plenum Medical Book Co., New York.

45. Fuller, R.K. and Gordis, E. (2004) Does disulfiram have a role in alcoholism treatment today? *Addiction*, **99**, 21–24.

46. Garbutt, J.C., West, S.L., Carey, T.S. *et al.* (1999) Pharmacological treatment of alcohol dependence: A review of the evidence. *JAMA*, **281**, 1318–1325.

47. Allen, J.P. and Litten, R.Z. (1992) Techniques to enhance compliance with disulfiram. *Alcohol. Clin. Exp. Res.*, **16**, 1035–1041.

48. Volpicelli, J.R., Volpicelli, L.A., and O'Brien, C.P. (1995) Medical management of alcohol dependence: Clinical use and limitations of naltrexone treatment. *Alcohol. Alcohol.*, **30**, 789–798.

49. AHCPR (1999) Pharmacotherapy for alcohol dependence, in *Evidence Report/Technology Assessment 3*, AHCPR.

50. Altshuler, H.L., Phillips, P.E., and Feinhandler, D.A. (1980) Alteration of ethanol self-administration by naltrexone. *Life Sci.*, **26**, 679–688.

51. O'Malley, S.S. *et al.* (1996) Six-month follow-up of naltrexone and psychotherapy for alcohol dependence. *Arch. Gen. Psych.*, **53**, 217–224.

52. Volpicelli, J.R. *et al.* (1992) Naltrexone in the treatment of alcohol dependence. *Arch. Gen. Psych.*, **49**, 876–880.

53. O'Malley, S.S., Jaffe, A.J., Chang, G. *et al.* (1992) Naltrexone and coping skills therapy for alcohol dependence. A controlled study. *Arch. Gen. Psych.*, **49**, 881–887.

54. Srisurapanont, M. and Jarusuraisin, N. (2005) Naltrexone for the treatment of alcoholism: a meta-analysis of randomized controlled trials. *Int. J. Neuropsychopharmacol.*, **8**, 267–280.

55. Bouza, C., Angeles, M., Munoz, A., and Amate, J.M. (2004) Efficacy and safety of naltrexone and acamprosate in the treatment of alcohol dependence: A systematic review. *Addiction*, **99**, 811–828.

56. Garbutt, J.C., Kranzler, H.R., O'Malley, S.S. *et al.* (2005) Efficacy and tolerability of long-acting injectable naltrexone for alcohol dependence: a randomized controlled trial. *JAMA*, **293**, 1617–1625.

57. Kiefer, F., Helwig, H., Tarnaske, T. *et al.* (2005) Pharmacological relapse prevention of alcoholism: clinical predictors of outcome. *Eur. Addict. Res.*, **11**, 83–91.

58. Monterosso, J.R. *et al.* (2001) Predicting treatment response to naltrexone: the influence of craving and family history. *Am. J. Addict.*, **10**, 258–268.

59. Mason, B.J. (2001) Treatment of alcohol-dependent outpatients with acamprosate: a clinical review. *J. Clin. Psychiatry*, **62**, 42–48.

60. Mann, K., Lehert, P., and Morgan, M.Y. (2004) The efficacy of acamprosate in the maintenance of abstinence in alcohol-dependent individuals: results of a metaanalysis. *Alcohol. Clin. Exp. Res.*, **28**, 51–63.

61. Mason, B.J., Goodman, A.M., Chabac, S., and Lehert, P. (2006) Effect of oral acamprosate on abstinence in patients with alcohol dependence in a double-blind, placebo-controlled trial: the role of patient motivation. *J. Psychiat. Res.*, **40**, 383–393.

62. Mason, B.J. and Ownby, R.L. (2000) Acamprosate for the treatment of alcohol dependence: a review of double-blind, placebo-controlled trials. *CNS Spectrums*, **5**, 58–69.

63. Johnson, B.A., Rosenthal, N., Capece, J.A. *et al.* (2007) Topiramate for treating alcohol dependence: a randomized controlled trial. *JAMA*, **298**, 1641–1651.

64. Johnson, B.A., Ait-Daoud, N., Bowden, C. *et al.* (2003) Oral topiramate for treatment of alcohol dependence: a randomised controlled trial. *Lancet*, **361**, 1677–1685.

65. Johnson, B.A., Ait-Daoud, N., Akhtar, F.Z., and Ma, J.Z. (2004) Oral topiramate reduces the consequences of drinking and improves the quality of life of alcohol-dependent individuals: a randomized controlled trial. *Arch. Gen. Psych.*, **61**, 905–912.

66. Bezchlibnyk-Butler, K.Z., Jeffries, J.J., and Martin, B.A. (2000) *Clinical Handbook of Psychotropic Drugs*, 10th edn, Hogrefe & Huber, Seattle.

67. Naranjo, C.A., Poulos, C., Bremner, K. *et al.* (1994) Fluoxetine attenuates alcohol intake and desire to drink. *Int. Clin. Psychopharmacol.*, **9**, 163–172.

68. Cornelius, J.R., Salloum, I.M., Ehler, J.G. *et al.* (1997) Fluoxetine in depressed alcoholics: a double-blind placebo-controlled trial. *Arch. Gen. Psych.*, **54**, 700–705.

69. Naranjo, C.A. and Knoke, D.M. (2001) The role of selective serotonin reuptake inhibitors in reducing alcohol consumption. *J. Clin. Psychiatry*, **62**, 18–25.

70. Johnson, B.A., Ait-Daoud, N., Bowden, C.L. *et al.* (2000) Ondansetron for reduction of drinking among biologically predisposed alcoholic patients: a randomized controlled trial. *JAMA*, **284**, 963–971.

71. Litten, R.Z. and Allen, J.P. (1999) Medications for alcohol, illicit drug, and tobacco dependence: An

update of research findings. *J. Subst. Abuse Treat.*, **16**, 105–112.

72. Welsh, C.J. and Liberto, J. (2001) The use of medication for relapse prevention in substance dependence disorders. *J. Psychiatr. Pract.*, **7**, 15–31.

73. Broekhuysen, E.S. (2000) Methadone, in White House ONDCP Drug Policy Information Clearinghouse Fact Sheet. National Criminal Justice Reference Service, National Criminal Justice Reference Service, Washington DC, Available at http://www.whitehousedrugpolicy.gov/publications/factsht/methadone/index.html.

74. Chugh, S.S., Socoteanu, C., Reinier, K. *et al.* (2008) A community-based evaluation of sudden death associated with therapeutic levels of methadone. *Am. J. Med.*, **121**, 66–71.

75. Calman, L., Finch, R., Powis, B., and Strang, J. (1996) Only half of patients store methadone in safe place [letter]. *Br. Med. J.*, **313**, 1481.

76. Calsyn, D.A. and Saxon, A.J. (1987) A system for uniform application of contingencies for illicit drug use. *J. Subst. Abuse Treat.*, **4**, 41–47.

77. McLellan, A.T., Arndt, I.O., Metzger, D.S. *et al.* (1993) The effects of psychosocial services in substance abuse treatment. *JAMA*, **269**, 1953–1959.

78. Vocci, F.J., Acri, J., and Elkashef, A. (2005) Medication development for addictive disorders: the state of science. *Am. J. Psychiatry*, **162**, 1432–1440.

79. Jasinski, D.R., Fudala, P.J., and Johnson, R.E. (1989) Sublingual versus subcutaneous buprenorphine in opiate abusers. *Clin. Pharmacol. Ther.*, **45**, 513–519.

80. Robinson, G.M., Dukes, P.D., Robinson, B.J. *et al.* (1993) The misuse of buprenorphine and a buprenorphine-naloxone comination in Wellington, New Zealand. *Drug Alcohol. Depend.*, **33**, 81–86.

81. Johnson, R., Jaffe, J., and Fudala, P. (1992) A controlled trial of buprenorphine treatment for opioid dependence. *JAMA*, **267**, 2750–2755.

82. Kosten, T.R., Schottenfeld, R., Ziedonis, D. *et al.* (1993) Buprenorphine versus methadone maintenance for opioid dependence. *J. Nerv. Ment. Dis.*, **181**, 358–364.

83. Resnick, R., Galanter, M., Pycha, C. *et al.* (1992) Buprenorphine: an alternative to methadone for heroin dependence treatment. *Psychopharmacol. Bull.*, **28**, 109–113.

84. Ling, W., Charuvatra, C., Collins, J.F. *et al.* (1998) Buprenorphine maintenance treatment of opiate dependence: a multicenter, randomized clinical trial. *Addiction*, **93**, 475–486.

85. Strain, E., Stitzer, M., Liebson, I. *et al.* (1994) Buprenorphine versus methadone in the treatment of opioid-dependent cocaine users. *Psychopharmacol.*, **116**, 401–406.

86. van den Brink, W. and van Reen, J.M. (2003) Pharmacological treatments for heroin and cocaine addiction. *Eur. Neuropsychopharmacol.*, **13**, 476–487.

87. O'Connor, P.G., Oliveto, A.H., Shi, J.M. *et al.* (1996) A pilot study of primary-care-based buprenorphine maintenance for heroin dependence. *Am. J. Drug Alcohol. Abuse*, **22**, 523–531.

88. Fiellin, D.A. and O'Connor, P.G. (2002) Office-based treatment of opioid-dependent patients. *N. Engl. J. Med.*, **347**, 817–823.

89. Hulse, G.K., O'Neil, G., Hatton, M., and Paech, M.J. (2003) Use of oral and implantable naltrexone in the management of the opioid impaired physician. *Anaesth Intensive Care*, **31**, 196–201.

90. Foster, J., Brewer, C., and Steele, T. (2003) Naltrexone implants can completely prevent early (1-month) relapse after opiate detoxification: a pilot study of two cohorts totalling 101 patients with a note on naltrexone blood levels. *Addict. Biol.*, **8**, 211–217.

91. Heidbreder, C. (2005) Recent advances in the pharmacotherapeutic management of drug dependence and addiction. *Curr. Psychiatry Rev.*, **1**, 45–67.

92. Fox, B.S., Kantak, K.M., Edwards, M.A. *et al.* (1996) Efficacy of a therapeutic cocaine vaccine in rodent models. *Nat. Med.*, **2**, 1129–1132.

93. Kantak, K.M., Collins, S.L., Lipman, E.G. *et al.* (2000) Evaluation of anti-cocaine antibodies and a cocaine vaccine in a rat self-administration model. *Psychopharmacol.*, **148**, 251–262.

94. Kosten, T.R. and Biegel, D. (2002) Therapeutic vaccines for substance dependence. *Expert Rev. Vaccines*, **1**, 363–371.

95. Kantak, K.M. (2003) Vaccines against drugs of abuse: a viable treatment option? *Drugs*, **63**, 341–352.

96. Martell, B.A., Mitchell, E., Poling, J. *et al.* (2005) Vaccine pharmacotherapy for the treatment of cocaine dependence. *Biol. Psychiatry*, **58**, 158–164.

97. Kosten, T. and Owens, S.M. (2005) Immunotherapy for the treatment of drug abuse. *Pharmacol. Ther.*, **108**, 76–85.

98. Gorelick, D.A. (1998) Pharmacologic therapies for cocaine and other stimulant addiction, in *Principles of Addiction Medicine*, 2nd edn (eds A.W. Graham and T.K. Schultz), American Society of Addiction Medicine, Chevy Chase, MD, pp. 531–544.

99. Levin, F.R., Evans, S., McDowell, D. *et al.* (1998) Methylphenidate treatment for cocaine abusers with adult attention deficit/hyperactivity disorder: a pilot study. *J. Clin. Psychiatry*, **59**, 300–305.

100. Margolin, A., Avants, S., and Kosten, T.R. (1996) Pemoline for the treatment of cocaine dependence in methadone-maintained patients. *J. Psychoactive Drugs*, **28**, 301–304.

101. Llosa, T. (1994) The standard low dose of oral cocaine used for the treatment of cocaine dependence. *Subst. Abuse*, **15**, 215–220.

102. Dackis, C.A. and O'Brien, C.P. (2003) Glutamatergic agents for cocaine dependence. *Ann. NY Acad. Sci.*, **1003**, 1–18.

103. Dackis, C.A., Kampman, K.M., Lynch, K.G. *et al.* (2005) A double-blind, placebo-controlled trial of modafinil for cocaine dependence. *Neuropharmacology*, **30**, 205–211.

104. Carrol, K.M., Fenton, L.R., Ball, S.A. *et al.* (2004) Efficacy of disulfiram and cognitive behavior therapy in cocaine-dependent outpatients: a randomized placebo-controlled trial. *Arch. Gen. Psych.*, **61**, 264–272.

105. George, T.P., Chawarski, M.C., Pakes, J. *et al.* (2000) Disulfiram versus placebo for cocaine dependence in buprenorphine-maintained subjects: a preliminary trial. *Biol. Psychiatry*, **47**, 1080–1086.

106. Petrakis, I.L., Carroll, K.M., Nich, C. *et al.* (2000) Disulfiram treatment for cocaine dependence in methadone-maintained subjects. *Addiction*, **95**, 219–228.

107. Hameedi, F.A., Rosen, M.I., McCance-Katz, E.F. *et al.* (1995) Behavioral, physiological, and pharmacological interaction of cocaine and disulfiram in humans. *Biol. Psychiatry*, **37**, 560–563.

108. McCance-Katz, E.F., Kosten, T.R., and Jatlow, P. (1998) Disulfiram effects on acute cocaine administration. *Drug Alcohol. Depend.*, **52**, 27–39.

109. Vaccari, A., Saba, P.L., Ruiu, S. *et al.* (1996) Disulfiram and diethyldithiocarbamate intoxication affects the storage and release of striatal dopamine. *Toxicol. Appl. Pharmacol.*, **139**, 102–108.

110. Burattini, C., Burbassi, S., Aicardi, G., and Cervo, L. (2008) Effects of naltrexone on cocaine- and sucrose-seeking behaviour in response to associated stimuli in rats. *Int. J. Neuropsychopharm.*, **11**, 103–109.

111. Somoza, E., Carter, J., Upadhyaya, H. *et al.* (1998) A double-blind, placebo-controlled clinical trial of naltrexone as a treatment for cocaine dependence, in *Problems of Drug Dependence 1998: Proceedings of the 60th Annual Scientific Meeting, The College on Problems of Drug Dependence* (ed. L.D. Harris), National Institute of Drug Abuse, Bethesda, MD, p. 295.

112. Schmidtz, J.M., Stotts, A.L., Rhoades, H.M., and Grabowski, J. (2001) Naltrexone and relapse prevention treatment for cocaine-dependent patients. *Addict. Behav.*, **26**, 167–180.

113. Kampman, K.M., Pettinati, H.M., Lynch, K.G. *et al.* (2004) A pilot trial of topiramate for the treatment of cocaine dependence. *Drug Alcohol. Depend.*, **75** (3), 233–240.

114. Johnson, B.A. (2005) Recent advances in the development of treatments for alcohol and cocaine dependence: focus on topiramate and other modulators of GABA or glutamate. *CNS Drugs*, **19**, 873–896.

115. Fadda, P., Scherma, M., Fresu, A. *et al.* (2003) Baclofen antagonizes nicotine-, cocaine-, and morphine-induced dopamine release in the nucleus accumbens of rat. *Synapse*, **50**, 1–6.

116. Di Ciano, P. and Everitt, B.J. (2003) The GABA(B) receptor agonist baclofen attenuates cocaine- and heroin-seeking behavior by rats. *Neuropharmacology*, **28**, 510–518.

117. Roberts, D.C. (2005) Preclinical evidence for GABAB agonists as a pharmacotherapy for cocaine addiction. *Physiol. Behav.*, **86**, 18–20.

118. Campbell, U.C., Lac, S.T., and Carroll, M.E. (1999) Effects of baclofen on maintenance and reinstatement of intravenous cocaine self-administration in rats. *Psychopharmacol.*, **143**, 209–214.

119. Brebner, K., Childress, A.R., and Roberts, D.C. (2002) A potential role for GABA (B) agonists in the treatment of psychostimulant addiction. *Alcohol. Alcohol.*, **37**, 478–484.

120. Ling, W., Shoptaw, S., and Majewska, D. (1998) Baclofen as a cocaine anti-craving medication: a preliminary clinical study. *Neuropharmacology*, **18**, 403–404.

121. Haney, M., Hart, C.L., and Foltin, R.W. (2006) Effects of baclofen on cocaine self-administration: opioid- and nonopioid-dependent volunteers. *Neuropharmacology*, **31**, 1814–1821.

122. Shoptaw, S., Yang, X., Rotheram-Fuller, E.J. *et al.* (2003) Randomized placebo-controlled trial of baclofen for cocaine dependence: preliminary effects for individuals with chronic patterns of cocaine use. *J. Clin. Psychiatry*, **64**, 1440–1448.

123. Haney, M., Bisaga, A., and Foltin, R.W. (2003) Interaction between naltrexone and oral THC in heavy marijuana smokers. *Psychopharmacol.*, **166**, 77–85.

124. Huestis, M.A., Gorelick, D.A., Heishman, S.J. *et al.* (2001) Blockade of effects of smoked marijuana by the CB1-selective cannabinoid receptor antagonist SR141716. *Arch. Gen. Psych.*, **58**, 322–328.

125. Hart, C.L., Haney, M., Ward, A.S. *et al.* (2002) Effects of oral THC maintenance on smoked

marijuana self-administration. *Drug Alcohol. Depend.*, **67**, 301–309.

126. McDowell, D., Levin, F.R., Brooks, D.J. *et al.* (2006) Treatment of cannabis-dependent treatment seekers: A double-blind comparison of nefazodone, bupropion and placebo. College on Problems of Drug Dependence 68th Annual Scientific Meeting. Scottsdale, AZ.

127. Gross, J. and Stitzer, M.L. (1998) Nicotine replacement: ten-week effects on tobacco withdrawal symptoms. *Psychopharmacol.*, **98**, 334–341.

128. Silagy, C., Lancaster, T., Stead, L. *et al.* (2004) Nicotine replacement therapy for smoking cessation. *Cochrane Database Syst. Rev.* 3 (Art. No.: CD000146). doi: 10.1002/14651858.CD000146.pub2.

129. Hajek, P., West, R., Foulds, J. *et al.* (1999) Randomized comparative trial of nicotine polacrilex, a transdermal patch, nasal spray, and an inhaler. *Arch. Intern. Med.*, **159**, 2033–2038.

130. Joseph, A.M., Norman, S.M., Ferry, L.H. *et al.* (1996) The safety of transdermal nicotine as an aid to smoking cessation in patients with cardiac disease. *N. Engl. J. Med.*, **335**, 1792–1798.

131. Murray, R.P., Bailey, W.C., Daniels, K. *et al.* (1996) Safety of nicotine polacrilex gum used by 3,094 participants in the Lung Health Study, Lung Health Study Research Group. *Chest*, **109**, 438–445.

132. Lee, A.H. and Afessa, B. (2007) The association of nicotine replacement therapy with mortality in a medical intensive care unit. *Crit. Care Med.*, **35**, 1517–1521.

133. West, R., Hajek, P., Foulds, J. *et al.* (2000) A comparison of the abuse liability and dependence potential of nicotine patch, gum, spray and inhaler. *Psychopharmacol.*, **149**, 198–202.

134. Nides, M. (2008) Update on pharmacologic options for smoking cessation treatment. *Am. J. Med.*, **121**, S20–S31.

135. Ferry, L.H., Pettis, J.L., Loma, L., and Burchette, R.J. (1994) Evaluation of bupropion versus placebo for treatment of nicotine dependence. American Psychiatric Association Annual Meeting New Research Program and Abstracts. American Psychiatric Association, Washington, DC, pp. 199–200.

136. Ferry, L.H. and Burchette, R.J. (1994) Efficacy of bupropion for smoking cessation in non depressed smokers. *J. Addict. Dis.*, **13**, 249.

137. Foulds, J., Burke, M., Steinberg, M. *et al.* (2004) Advances in pharmacotherapy for tobacco dependence. *Expert Opin. Emerg. Drugs*, **9**, 39–53.

138. Dani, J.A. and Heinemann, S. (1996) Molecular and cellular aspects of nicotine abuse. *Neuron.*, **16**, 905–908.

139. Slemmer, J.E., Martin, B.R., and Damaj, M.I. (2000) Bupropion is a nicotinic anatagonist. *J. Pharmacol. Exp. Ther.*, **295**, 321–327.

140. Hurt, R.D., Glover, E.D., Sachs, D.P.L. *et al.* (1996) Bupropion for smoking cessation: a double-blind, placebo-controlled dose response trial. *J. Addict. Dis.*, **15**, 137.

141. Hurt, R.D., Sachs, D.P.L., Glover, E.D. *et al.* (1997) A comparison of sustained release bupropion and placebo for smoking cessation. *N. Engl. J. Med.*, **337**, 1195–1202.

142. Jorenby, D.E., Leischow, S.J., Nides, M.A. *et al.* (1999) A controlled trial of sustained-release bupropion, a nicotine patch, or both for smoking cessation. *N. Engl. J. Med.*, **340**, 685–691.

143. Jorenby, D. (2002) Clinical efficacy of bupropion in the management of smoking cessation. *Drugs*, **62** (Suppl. 2), 25–35.

144. Hays, J.T., Hurt, R.D., Rigotti, N.A. *et al.* (2001) Sustained-release bupropion for pharmacologic relapse prevention after smoking cessation: a randomized, controlled trial. *Ann. Intern. Med.*, **135**, 423–433.

145. Coe, J.W., Brooks, P.R., Vetelino, M.G. *et al.* (2005) Varenicline: an alpha-4 beta-2 nicotinic receptor partial agonist for smoking cessation. *J. Med. Chem.*, **48**, 3474–3477.

146. Rollema, H., Chambers, L.K., Coe, J.W. *et al.* (2007) Pharmacological profile of the alpha-4 beta-2 nicotinic acetylcholine receptor partial agonist varenicline, an effective smoking cessation aid. *Neuropharmacology*, **52**, 985–994.

147. Gonzales, D., Rennard, S.I., Nides, M. *et al.* (2006) Varenicline, an alpha4beta2 nicotinic acetylcholine receptor partial agonist, vs sustained-release bupropion and placebo for smoking cessation: a randomized controlled trial. *JAMA*, **296**, 47–55.

148. Jorenby, D.E., Hays, J.T., Rigotti, N.A. *et al.* (2006) Efficacy of varenicline, an alpha-4 beta-2 nicotinic acetylcholine receptor partial agonist, vs placebo or sustained-release bupropion for smoking cessation: a randomized controlled trial. *JAMA*, **296**, 56–63.

149. Tsai, S.T., Cho, H.J., Cheng, H.S. *et al.* (2007) A randomized, placebo-controlled trial of varenicline, a selective alpha-4 beta-2 nicotinic acetylcholine receptor partial agonist, as a new therapy for smoking

cessation in Asian smokers. *Clin. Ther.*, **29**, 1027–1039.

150. Nakamura, M., Oshima, A., Fuijmoto, Y. *et al.* (2007) Efficacy and tolerability of varenicline, an alpha-4 beta-2 nicotinic acetylcholine receptor partial agonist, in a 12-week, randomized, placebo-controlled, dose-response study with 40-week follow-up for smoking cessation in Japanese smokers. *Clin. Ther.*, **29**, 1040–1056.

151. Ridenour, T.A. (2005) Inhalants: not to be taken lightly anymore. *Curr. Opin. Psychiatry*, **18**, 243–247.

152. Shen, Y. (2007) Treatment of inhalant dependence with lamotrigine. *Prog. Neuropsychopharmacol. Biol. Psychiatry*, **31**, 769–771.

34

Psychosocial treatments for addictive disorders: models, settings, and important roles for referring physicians

John McKellar, John Finney, and Rudolf Moos

Veterans Affairs Palo Alto Health Care System and Stanford University School of Medicine, Menlo Park, CA, 94025, USA

34.1   INTRODUCTION

Current guidelines recommend routine screening of all adult medical patients for alcohol use disorders [1] and drug use [2]. The goal is to identify patients who engage in excessive drinking, are dependent on alcohol, and misuse drugs. Brief interventions delivered within primary care are recommended for patients who drink excessively but do not have major psychosocial problems [3], whereas it is recommended that patients with more serious drinking problems or drug disorders be referred to specialty substance use disorder (SUD) services [2].

Despite recent attention to issues such as screening and the delivery of brief advice, relatively little attention has been paid to other services, such as making referrals to alcohol and drug specialty treatment. With better understanding of how to encourage patients to seek treatment, as well as knowledge of the nature, settings, and effectiveness of such treatments, primary care providers who care for patients with chronic medical disorders may be more willing to make such referrals.

This chapter attempts to fill this knowledge gap. The course of addictive disorders is briefly reviewed and then empirically-supported suggestions are provided for use of screening instruments to determine optimal interventions for patients and techniques primary care providers can use to encourage patients to enter SUD treatment. Some of the most common psychosocial approaches to SUD treatment are then described and evidence for their effectiveness identified. Discussed next is a recent change in the view of SUDs, from a condition that can be managed in an acute episode of treatment to that of a potentially chronic relapsing and remitting disorder that often requires intermittent long-term care. The chapter concludes with a discussion of how to manage treatment-resistant patients and again highlights the role that referring physicians can play in the SUD treatment process.

Addictive Disorders in Medical Populations   Edited by Norman S. Miller and Mark S. Gold
© 2010 John Wiley & Sons, Ltd.

34.2 THE COURSE OF ADDICTIVE DISORDERS

Addictive disorders range from binge drinking to the diagnostic category of alcohol or drug dependence. Accordingly, the course of these disorders when treated varies widely, as some individuals respond to brief interventions and recover quickly, some experience a fluctuating course of remission and relapse, and still others follow a more recurring and chronic course.

Long-term evaluations of SUD treatment indicate a number of different post-treatment trajectories [4]. For some, treatment brings about life changes similar to that of a religious conversion, in which a period of abstinence can lead to enhanced hope and self-esteem and the development of new social networks that are supportive of abstinence. For others, however, the effects of treatment decay after weeks or months as the individual slides back into old patterns of substance use and social behavior. For many in the latter group, the course of their disorder waxes and wanes with periods of self- or treatment-initiated abstinence followed by relapse into substance use and eventual re-entry into treatment, and then, hopefully, recovery.

Increasingly, management of chronic illness is seen as a central focus in primary care settings. The adoption of models of chronic illness management marks one of the biggest shifts in care provided by primary care physicians [5]. This shift does not reflect increased diagnosis of chronic illnesses but, instead, reflects a reconceptualization of how care should be managed. Changes in clinical management of chronic illnesses include increased engagement of patients in management of their disorders, increases in patient-targeted education, and more efforts to ensure continuous follow-up of the course of a disorder (e.g., Hba1c to monitor patients with diabetes). Concordant with these changes, there is growing recognition that SUDs can be chronic and that systems of care should better reflect this reality [6].

Although the cycling of remission, relapse, remission of some patients may seem an indictment of psychosocial treatments for SUD, a number of researchers have taken a more optimistic perspective [7,8]. As is the case with other chronic disorders, treatment reduces the severity of SUD symptoms *while it is being administered*. It should not be surprising, then, that symptoms often re-emerge after discontinuation of treatment. Thus, similar to management of chronic medical illnesses in primary care, effective care for SUD should focus not only on acute management of emergent symptoms of SUD, but also should adopt a continuing care perspective.

34.3 SCREENING AND INITIAL REFERRAL OF PATIENTS

Routine screening of alcohol and drug use in medical settings offers one of the most effective methods for reducing the harm associated with SUDs. The screening tools available are discussed in Chapter 6. The goals of this section are to provide primary care providers with empirically-supported methods for the use of screening tools to initiate discussions about substance use, and information on how to use screening tools to determine optimal interventions for those who screen positive.

34.3.1 Screening tools and discussions of substance use

Widespread screening of substance use in primary care settings has the potential to normalize discussion of substance use between the provider and patient and reduce potential for stigma and discomfort [9]. Unfortunately, however, screening for SUD in primary care is not currently widespread and physicians often report difficulty raising the topic of substance use when patients do not see it as a problem.

Motivational Interviewing [10] techniques provide one useful guide to structure discussion of a patient's drinking or drug problems, once the patient has completed a screening instrument. A convenient method for remembering the central components to motivational interviewing is through use of the acronym FRAMES. Feedback involves providing objective information about the patient's current level of substance use, including frequency of substance use and associated problems with use. Responsibility emphasizes that the patient is responsible to make changes or to determine a course of action (e.g., "It's up to you to decide what to do with this information"). Advice is also an element of the intervention; it may be suggested that the individual try to abstain from drinking, cut down on drinking, or seek formal treatment. Providing a Menu of choices (e.g., self-help group, self-help book, specialized treatment program) at the "advice" stage may increase the acceptability of solutions and allow the patient to choose an option that meets particular needs and situations. Empathy may be the most important facet of motivational interviewing, as the provider indicates an understanding that changing any health behavior can be difficult. Finally, reinforcing the patient's feelings of Self-efficacy about his or her ability to change the course of their substance use can help instill optimism and efforts towards change.

Because the FRAMES approach primarily involves exploration of levels of substance use problems, assessment can occur in much the same manner that other health behaviors, such as diet or level of exercise, are assessed. Once a patient's level of use and problems have been assessed, the provider can use the patient's information and reactions as a guide for referral. A patient's initial disinterest in either changing drinking or in enrolling in treatment should not be seen as a permanent state or as a signal to increase persuasion efforts. Treating drinking or drug use as a medical concern that negatively impacts the patient's health can serve to decrease defensiveness and allow for more careful consideration on the patient's part. Although a patient may not indicate immediate interest in moderating substance use or in enrolling in treatment, this does not mean that the provider should never raise the topic again. A physician's advice to enter treatment is one of the most commonly stated reasons for entry into SUD treatment [11]. The next section provides suggestions for using the FRAMES technique with a specific screening instrument: the AUDIT-C.

34.3.2 Determining an optimal initial intervention

One of the explicit goals in creating the Alcohol Use Disorders Identification Test (AUDIT) was that the instrument provides information to guide referral decisions. Scores from the 10-item full AUDIT range from 0–40 and comprise three levels of risk with specific recommendations for each level [12]. Recommendations include that: (1) patients scoring in the 0–7 range are considered to be *no-risk* and are encouraged to continue drinking in the same manner; (2) patients scoring 8–15 should be given advice focusing on reduction of hazardous drinking; (3) patients scoring 16–19 should be given brief counseling plus continued monitoring; and (4) patients who score 20 and higher should be referred to specialized providers for evaluation of alcohol dependence.

A recent study offers similar guidelines, but bases the guidelines on use of the 3-item AUDIT-C [13] and one question about previous alcohol treatment (Have you ever been in alcohol treatment or Alcoholics Anonymous?). The AUDIT-C and the question about previous treatment strongly predicted the past-year severity of drinking problems, adverse consequences of drinking, and presence of dependence symptoms. The algorithm for use of the brief screening tool can be seen in Figure 34.1. Individuals reporting no past history of treatment, scores on the AUDIT below eight, and drinking within recommended levels (less than five drinks per occasion for men or four drinks for women, and less than 14 drinks per week) should be advised to maintain drinking at current levels. Individuals who report no past history of treatment, score below eight on the AUDIT-C, but currently have hazardous levels

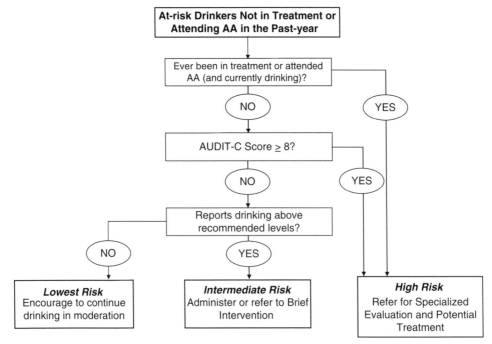

Figure 34.1 Alcohol screening algorithm using AUDIT-C [13]

of drinking should be referred for brief intervention plus continued monitoring. Individuals who report a previous history of treatment (with current drinking) or scores greater than or equal to eight on the AUDIT-C should be referred to specialized treatment for additional assessment and appropriate treatment. In situations where specialized SUD treatment options are not available and the patient's screening indicates a high level of risk, physicians should consider referral to self-help organizations, such as Alcoholics Anonymous (Section 34.5.2).

The algorithm in Figure 34.1 helps to fill in some of the specific elements of the FRAMES approach, such as when to issue advice and what might be involved with providing a menu of options. However, the option in the algorithm to refer patients to specialty care might be followed more often if providers had better information about specialty care. Information about specific aspects of specialty care or self-help organizations is essential for three primary reasons: (1) to increase a provider's confidence that effective treatments are available; (2) to help providers prepare the patient for SUD treatment and increase the likelihood of follow-through; and (3) to increase the ability of the physician or primary care provider to support the patient during acute SUD treatment and, if necessary, continuing SUD care.

34.4 DESCRIPTIONS OF PSYCHOSOCIAL TREATMENTS FOR SUD

The primary goals of this section are to (a) describe some of the most common forms of professional psychosocial treatment for SUD and consider the body of empirical evidence supporting these approaches, (b) describe the most common settings (e.g., inpatient, intensive outpatient) for professional psychosocial treatments, and, finally, (c) discuss direct referral to mutual help organizations (e.g., Alcoholics Anonymous, Narcotics Anonymous, Smart Recovery). Pharmacologic treatments for SUD (e.g., methadone, naltrexone, acomprosate) are covered in separate chapter (Chapter 33).

34.4.1 Common forms of psychosocial treatment

34.4.1.1 12-Step substance use disorder treatment programs

The most common form of psychosocial treatment in the United States is 12-step oriented treatment [14]. Traditional 12-step treatment combines the 12-step approach of Alcoholics Anonymous (AA), Narcotics Anonymous (NA), and Cocaine Anonymous (CA) with the disease model of addiction. It assumes that, as a result of biological or psychological vulnerability, patients have lost control over the addicted substance. Treatment attempts to bring about the patient's acceptance of the disease model of addiction, of an "alcoholic" or "addict" identity, and of abstinence as a treatment goal, as well as involvement in 12-step activities (e.g., attending meetings, getting a sponsor, working the steps).

Although acceptance of an alcoholic or addict identity and the treatment goal of abstinence figure prominently within 12-step treatment, other important aspects of this approach include honest self-examination, atonement for past wrongs, spiritual reflection, and service to other individuals with alcohol or drug problems. The concept of "fellowship" is also central to many 12-step treatment programs. In the early stage of treatment patients are often encouraged to obtain a sponsor and to attend 12-step meetings frequently (e.g., 90 meetings in 90 days). Such involvement extends the supportive aspects of treatment outside program hours or meeting times, forming a new social network supportive of sobriety.

Alcoholics Anonymous and 12-step oriented treatment are sometimes referred to as if they were interchangeable. However, they differ in a number of important respects. Alcoholics Anonymous (and Narcotics Anonymous or Cocaine Anonymous) is a nonprofessional organization that is operated by alcoholic peers, is free of charge to members, and may be attended indefinitely. In contrast, 12-step oriented treatment programs have paid professional staff, charge fees, and are typically licensed or accredited.

Two recent studies support the effectiveness of 12-step treatment approaches. One such study is Project MATCH [15], a randomized, multisite trial that examined the relative efficacy of 12-step facilitation treatment, cognitive-behavioral treatment, and motivational enhancement treatment. Over 900 patients received one of these three treatments as outpatient "aftercare" following inpatient or day hospital treatment; the other arm of the study focused on over 700 individuals who had presented at outpatient clinics or had been recruited through advertisements. Patients in all three treatments demonstrated comparable significant increases in percent of days abstinent and decreases in number of drinks consumed on drinking days both at one-year and three-year follow-ups [16,17]. When the outcome focus was total abstinence, 12-step facilitation treatment had somewhat better results than the other two therapies.

A naturalistic, multisite evaluation focused on over 3000 Department of Veterans Affairs (VA) SUD patients who received traditional 12-step, cognitive-behavioral, or eclectic (mixed 12-step and cognitive-behavioral) treatment under "normal" conditions of treatment delivery. At a one-year follow-up, there were no differences among the three groups on 9 of 11 outcome criteria [18]. However, patients in 12-step programs were significantly more likely than cognitive-behavioral patients to abstain from alcohol and other drugs in the three months prior to follow-up, and eclectic-program patients were more likely to be unemployed than patients in the other two groups. Because of prior empirical support for cognitive-behavioral treatment, the fact that 12-step patients fared as well as or better than those receiving cognitive-behavioral treatment in two large-scale treatment evaluations is important evidence supporting the effectiveness of 12-step approaches and should give healthcare providers confidence about making referrals to such programs.

34.4.1.2 Cognitive-behavioral treatment programs

Cognitive-behavioral (CB) treatment programs assume that substance use is a learned behavior, whose onset and perpetuation is influenced by distorted beliefs about the effects of the addicted substance and by reliance on substance use as a (maladaptive) coping behavior. To achieve the goal of improved coping, cognitive-behavioral treatment typically involves several tasks. The first task is to determine with the patient the functional course of the disorder in terms of precipitating and maintaining factors. This functional analysis focuses on identifying specific personal factors (e.g., depression, interpersonal distress) and environmental factors (e.g., peer pressure) that are associated with, or trigger, substance use.

Once problem areas and situations are better understood, patients are taught cognitive coping techniques, such as challenging negative thoughts as they occur, or behavioral techniques, such as how to effectively negotiate problematic social situations that may lead to drinking. The final task of cognitive-behavioral treatments involves implementing new coping techniques and refining them to suit the needs of the individual patient. Because a heavy emphasis is placed on tailoring cognitive-behavioral interventions to the specific needs of patients (in terms of the pattern of precipitating or maintaining events) there is considerable flexibility in terms of goals of treatment for the patient. For instance, although abstinence goals are encouraged they are not typically a prerequisite for treatment entry.

Three general reviews of psychosocial treatments for SUD provide evidence for the effectiveness of cognitive-behavioral interventions [19–21]. The relevant studies included in these reviews generally were methodologically strong. For the most part, the interventions identified as highly effective in these reviews focus primarily on enhancing patients' skills in coping with everyday circumstances and on improving the match between patients' abilities and environmental demands. In addition to helping enhance the patient's coping skills, several of the cognitive behavioral therapies, such as behavioral couples therapy and community reinforcement, seek to improve the patient's social support system. Of the 15 modalities examined in all three reviews, eight of the top ten modalities were forms of cognitive-behavioral therapy. A noteworthy finding of these studies is the generally low effectiveness of prevalent treatments such as educational films, confrontational interventions, and general alcoholism counseling (Table 34.1).

34.4.2   Treatment settings

Like much of medicine, care for SUD patients has shifted from inpatient to ambulatory care settings. This section describes the most common settings of SUD treatment and reviews literature on the comparative effectiveness of different settings. Arranged in terms of increasing intensity of services provided, the general settings for SUD treatment include outpatient treatment, day treatment (intensive outpatient), residential treatment, and inpatient treatment. Although these categories suggest a continuum of care, it is rare that a given treatment system incorporates more than one or two of these settings of treatment.

34.4.2.1   Outpatient settings

The vast majority of SUD patients is treated in outpatient settings that provide services of varying intensity and duration. Outpatient services generally offer counseling sessions once or twice a week. The format of the counseling sessions may range from individual therapy, to couples therapy, to group therapy, with group therapy being the most prevalent. Day hospital or intensive outpatient programs provide treatment for several hours per day or during evening hours for 4–6 weeks and were originally developed as an alternative to inpatient care.

34.4.2.2   Residential and inpatient settings

Residential treatment programs also range greatly in terms of level of structure, the role of professionals, and the degree to which they are guided by particular psychosocial treatment orientations. At one end of the continuum are residential programs that include on-site addiction counseling, on-site 12-step meetings, employment training, and 24-hour supervision. At the other end of the continuum are much less structured programs known as "sober living houses" that provide no treatment services or supervision and only require that residents remain sober. The length of time in residential treatment also varies considerably. Structured treatment facilities typically have projected lengths of stay ran-

Table 34.1 Theoretical orientations to common substance use disorder treatments

Motivational Interviewing	12-step Oriented Treatment	Cognitive-Behavioral Therapy	Relapse Prevention
F – Give information/feedback about issue at hand.	1. Disease model of addiction.	1. Substance use is, at least partly, a learned behavior.	1. Identify high-risk situations for relapse.
R – Reinforce the client's responsibility to change his or her own behavior.	2. Acceptance of "alcoholic" or "addict" identity.	2. Focus on understanding factors that precipitate or maintain substance use (e.g., depression, negative thoughts).	2. Avoid high-risk situations through evaluation of "seemingly irrelevant" decisions.
A – Give clear advice about what options are.	3. Focus on goal of abstinence.	3. Focus on teaching alternative forms of coping (e.g., altering negative thoughts).	3. Distinction between "lapses" (return to substance use) and "relapse" (return to uncontrolled substance use).
M – Offer a menu of solutions and assist the client to choose.	4. Treatment involves "working" the 12-steps.	4. Abstinence often encouraged, but not required.	
E – Show empathetic response to client's situation and the difficulty of making behavior/lifestyle changes.			
S – Reinforce the client's ability to handle the situation and make good choices (self-efficacy).			

ging from 1–6 months, whereas less structured facilities allow residents to stay as long as they pay rent.

Inpatient treatment for SUDs may involve detoxification, rehabilitation, a combination of the two or one followed by the other. However, inpatient treatment, even detoxification, is becoming increasingly rare. For example, the Department of Veterans Affairs went from having 180 inpatient facilities in 1991 to just 20 inpatient facilities in 2001 [22]. Most inpatient programs traditionally last 21–28 days and provide services similar to those described above for structured residential programs (e.g., individual, group, and couples therapy). It is also common practice for patients to be referred to outpatient and or 12-step oriented continuing care after completion of an inpatient episode.

The effectiveness of inpatient treatment versus outpatient treatment is controversial. Finney and colleagues [23] analyzed a number of studies and concluded that outpatient treatment is most appropriate for patients with strong social networks of friends and/or family and those who do not have serious psychiatric or medical comorbidities. Concordantly, inpatient services are most appropriate for patients with few social resources and those who have serious co-occurring medical or psychiatric conditions.

34.5 SELF-HELP FOR SUBSTANCE USE DISORDER

Some providers may find themselves in a setting where professional psychosocial treatment options are nonexistent, distant from a patient's home, or are otherwise perceived to be unacceptable to the patient. One viable alternative to referral to specialty treatment programs is referral to a self-help organization. The following section provides some guidance on referring patients to self-help. As the largest and best-studied self-help organization, AA is the major focus. However, this section concludes with a discussion of other non-12-step self-help organizations that are accessible in some areas of the United States.

34.5.1 For whom are self-help groups particularly helpful

Clinical concerns are often raised about the fit of particular patients with certain self-help organizations. For example, are 12-step programs appropriate for patients with both a SUD and a mental health disorder, or, does a person need to be "religious" to benefit? The following section focuses on three areas of concern: psychiatric comorbidity, religious orientation, and gender.

34.5.1.1 Patients with psychiatric disorders

Many patients with SUD [24] also have psychiatric comorbidities. Clinical concerns are sometimes raised about referring these dual diagnosis patients to self-help groups, such as AA. One concern is that, because of the abstinence-orientated nature of the program, 12-step members will discourage other members from taking psychotropic medications. Empirical evidence supporting this assumption is lacking, however, as surveys of AA participants find that a substantial majority believes psychotropic medications to be beneficial [25]. Another concern is that is that dual diagnosis patients will not be able to integrate socially with others in AA and will drop out. A number of studies of dual diagnosis patients with a wide range of psychiatric disorders from depression, anxiety disorders and even schizophrenia and post-traumatic stress disorder, suggest equivalent attendance rates for those with and without psychiatric comorbidities [26–28]. In general, dual diagnosis of psychiatric and SUD does not appear to be a contraindication for referral to 12-step programs such as AA.

In the case where a patient with a dual diagnosis refuses traditional AA, another 12-step option available in some areas is Double-Trouble. This 12-step oriented program is only available to individuals with both a substance use and a psychiatric disorder and has an additional emphasis on medication adherence.

34.5.1.2 Patient's religious orientation

Explicit use of terms such as "higher power" and "spirituality" in the literature of 12-step programs has led some clinicians to suggest that religious background should be taken into account when referring patients to these programs. Practice guidelines from the American Psychiatric Association extended the concern about religious background further by recommending that clinicians refrain from referring nonreligious patients to 12-step organizations. One study of more than 3000 men tested this assumption empirically and found that not having a religious orientation did not impact 12-step attendance rates [29]. Another randomized trial tested the hypothesis that more religious patients would fare better in 12-step facilitation therapy than in the other two arms of the study. However, degree of religious involvement did not interact with treatment orientation in predicting drinking outcomes (Project Match, 1997). Thus, degree of religious affiliation does not appear to predict either 12-step attendance rates or the effectiveness of 12-step facilitation treatment.

34.5.1.3 Gender

One final concern relates to the question of how much women benefit from AA. In general, women's attendance has been less well studied, despite the fact that women make up roughly one-third of AA members [30]. Some clinicians have raised concerns about the 12-step emphasis on "powerlessness" and that the minority status of women in most 12-step groups may make it more difficult to discuss women-specific issues. However, the general picture painted by studies of AA attendance by women is very positive [31]. Women

benefit at least as much from attendance as men, and tend to attend more frequently [32].

34.5.2 Tips to facilitate referral to self-help

The most crucial component of making referrals to self-help organizations is knowledge of local programs. The easiest way to learn about such resources is by searching online. Most self-help organizations have listings that indicate whether or not meetings are taking place in a give locale. Information numbers for Alcoholics Anonymous are available in almost every telephone book in the United States.

Once a clinic has determined the location of local self-help groups, the next step is to have the resource information on hand. Alcoholics Anonymous provides "meeting guides" for most localities that can be obtained for free. In addition, clinics can order brochures that acquaint patients with the philosophy of AA and the structure of different meetings. Similar information is available for online self-help groups listed in the next section. The key is to have information readily available for distribution when a patient is either identified with a SUD or brings up the topic independently.

One final suggestion is important to increase the likelihood of longer term self-help attendance. Patients should be encouraged to attend meetings in at least three different locations to explore which meeting seems to be the best fit for them. Meetings vary greatly in terms of the demographic characteristics of participants, such as age, gender, economic status, and ethnic group membership. Thus, patients' experiences at different groups meetings can also vary greatly, and patients should be encouraged to "shop around" for a group that feels right to them.

34.5.3 Self-help groups other than AA

Although non-12-step self-help organizations constitute only a fraction of all self-help programs for SUD, their growing representation in some metropolitan areas (e.g., New York, San Francisco, Milwaukee) warrants some attention and description.

- *Secular Organization for Sobriety* embraces rationality and scientific knowledge and does not include spiritual content. The organization believes that abstinence can be achieved through group support and through making sobriety one's priority in life.

- *Smart Recovery* views excessive use of alcohol and other drugs as a maladaptive behavior rather than a disease. Its goal is to use behavioral techniques to enhance members' capacity to abstain from alcohol and cope with craving.

- *Women for Sobriety* was founded to help women alcoholics recover through a positive, feminist program that encourages increased self-worth and enhances emotional and spiritual growth. It emphasizes the value of having all-female groups to improve members' self-esteem and to facilitate recovery.

- *Moderation Management* is the only self-help organization aimed at nondependent problem drinkers. This group operates under the premise that problem drinking is a learned habit that can be brought under control without the necessity for abstinence.

34.6   ROLE OF REFERRING PHYSICIAN DURING SELF-HELP AND/OR PROFESSIONAL SUD TREATMENT

Primary care providers can play an important role in supporting their patient's efforts to manage a SUD. Continued monitoring of a patient's substance use and attendance in treatment can occur in the same fashion as monitoring of progress with any referral to specialty treatment. If a patient is referred to gastroenterology for an evaluation, it is expected that, on return to primary care, the physician will ask about the results of the prescribed course of care and monitor the effectiveness of treatment. A patient who is referred for brief intervention or SUD specialty care can be monitored in a similar manner with attention to adherence to prescribed treatment and ongoing evaluation of the patient's functioning.

Providing support and encouragement during a period when the patient is successfully managing their SUD helps to reinforce treatment gains achieved by the patient and provides valuable information about what "works" for the specific patient. The easiest way to gain this valuable information is to simply ask: "What seems to be different for you?" or "What is working for you right now?" Should the patient return to substance use, information on what "works" can serve as the "Advice" part of a FRAMES assessment. Based on what has been effective or ineffective, a patient can be re-linked to specialty care or self-help.

34.7   CONTINUING CARE

Due to the relapsing nature of the disorder for some, patients who receive treatment for an SUD are urged to participate in continuing care. Continuing care usually consists of outpatient "aftercare" groups and/or attendance at 12-step meetings. The goals of such care may include: (1) reducing the likelihood of relapse by learning how to cope with urges and/or high risk situations; (2) consolidating the gains achieved in the initial period of treatment; and (3) ongoing case monitoring of substance use to provide support and, if needed, re-engagement with more intensive treatment. One of the most common approaches used for continuing care is relapse prevention. The following section describes continuing care in the form of relapse prevention and discusses the empirical support for continuing care and the use of self-help programs.

34.7.1   Relapse prevention

Relapse prevention [33] represents a variant of cognitive-behavioral therapy that specifically focuses on helping the patient to learn skills and strategies to either prevent or limit relapse episodes. Similarly to cognitive-behavioral treatment, relapse prevention helps patients to identify high-risk situations that might lead to a return to substance use, analyzes how they have coped with these situations in the past, and then teaches new coping strategies, as needed. Patients are also encouraged to examine the pattern of decisions that lead to high-risk situations. For example, an individual does not end up in front of a bar at 9 p.m. by happenstance. This destination is a result of a number of smaller "seemingly irrelevant" decisions, such as deciding that it would be better to fill-up the car with gas at night than in the morning, deciding that it would be cheaper to get gas across town, and suddenly finding that the cheaper gas station is right next to one's favorite bar.

The relapse prevention framework makes an important distinction between a "lapse" and "relapse." Within this model, a "lapse," or return to substance use does not necessarily imply a return to a full-blown SUD, or "relapse" into uncontrolled substance use. This distinction is particularly helpful for patients who feel guilty about their lapse or who feel particularly strongly about their need for complete abstinence. The relapse prevention model focuses on the fact that lapses often occur and that their occurrence represents an opportunity for the patient to either use or learn new coping skills [34]. Lapses are seen as part of a learning process by building better confidence in the patient's ability to cope with situations that might inhibit long-term sobriety.

A meta-analysis by Irvin and colleagues [35] reviewed the results of 26 controlled trials of relapse prevention for SUDs. Most of the studies included in this review evaluated relapse prevention immediately following another primary intervention. The effectiveness of relapse prevention in decreasing substance use for all SUD(s) was significant and even stronger effects were found for alcohol use disorders and for psychosocial problems associated with substance use. These results persisted after controlling for factors such as treatment setting (inpatients vs. outpatient) and method of treatment (individual, group, couples therapy).

Several studies support the effectiveness of outpatient aftercare groups. Ito and Donovan's [36] review of studies conducted prior to 1985 suggests a link between "aftercare" participation and positive outcomes. A large study following patients treated in the Navy found that the single best predictor of positive outcomes at one-year follow-up was months of aftercare attendance [37]. Within the VA, duration of attendance in follow-up outpatient sessions was related to positive outcomes at one-year [38] and at two-year follow-ups [39]. A recent review of randomized continuing care studies found mixed support for continuing care [7], as three of seven studies comparing continuing care to minimal care or no care supported the efficacy of continuing care. One factor complicating interpretation of randomized continuing care studies is that the randomization procedure may attenuate the influence that motivation exerts on long-term outcomes. This is particularly the case is if attendance in continuing care reflects a positive outcome of initial treatment.

Support also exists for the effectiveness of 12-step self-help group attendance in enhancing long-term outcomes after an episode of SUD treatment. For instance, in a randomized trial of alcohol treatment (Project MATCH, 1997, 1998) post-treatment 12-step self-help group attendance was related to better drinking outcomes at one and three years [40], irrespective of the type of treatment. In fact, the amount of self-help group attendance "explained" the positive effect of 12-step facilitation on abstinence. In research in the VA, patients with alcohol and/or drug use disorders who attended more 12-step self-help groups in the first year after acute treatment were more likely to be in remission at two years [39] and five years [41]. Level of post-treatment self-help group attendance accounted for the positive effect of 12-step treatment (relative to cognitive-behavioral treatment) on patient's abstinence at one-year follow-up.

More extended treatment may improve patient outcomes because it provides patients with ongoing support and the potential to discuss and resolve problems prior to the occurrence of a full-blown relapse. In this vein, brief interventions may be most effective for relatively healthy patients who have intact community support systems. Patients who fail to respond to less intensive interventions, have concomitant psychiatric disorder, and/or deficient social resources appear to be better candidates for more intensive treatment [42,43].

34.8 MANAGING TREATMENT-RESISTANT PATIENTS

One of the primary goals of screening and referral is to increase identification of patients with a SUD and the patient's access to appropriate treatment services. In the process of screening, however, clinicians will inevitably encounter patients who screen positive for drinking or drug problems, and are unwilling to accept any form of treatment. The traditional understanding of why a patient refuses treatment is that the patient is unwilling to admit to, or "denies", the existence of problems. More recent conceptualizations of why patients refuse treatment view refusal as an inability to see, in the moment, a connection between substance use and medical or social problems. The goal of the clinician, then, is to help the patient better understand the link between substance use and current or future problems.

Monitoring of substance use can occur in a manner similar to the monitoring of any lifestyle behavior. Ongoing monitoring of drinking or drug use conveys to a patient that such behavior is of concern to his or her physician. Such monitoring also allows for the opportunity to tie substance use to the emergence or exacerbation of medical conditions, such as hypertension or gastrointestinal upset. Such occurrences provide the primary care provider with an opportunity to link substance use to medical problems and, potentially, encourage either efforts to cut-down on drinking or to enter treatment.

34.9 CONCLUSIONS

Primary care and (non-SUD) specialty care physicians can play pivotal roles in the care of patients with SUD. The first and most obvious role for front-line medical providers is in identifying patients with an SUD and initiating the treatment process. The FRAMES method from Motivational Interviewing

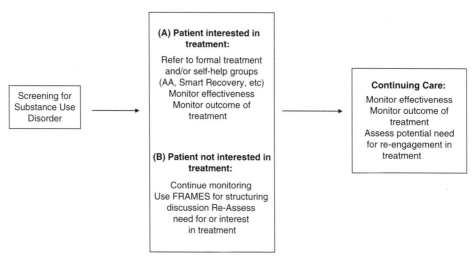

Figure 34.2 Providers role in ongoing care

provides a useful guide to structure discussion of a patient's drinking or drug problems and to urge him or her to seek treatment.

Another important role that physicians can play in their patients' SUD treatment is in monitoring of the course of the disorder. Monitoring a patient's success in maintaining substance use goals by a personal physician reminds the patient of the link between substance use and their health. Also, if indicated, such monitoring can lead to considering more intensive SUD care, or enrollment in or re-engagement with continuing care services. An overall algorithm for primary care provider's role in supporting patients with a SUD can be seen in Figure 34.2.

The authors believe that an effective approach to patient referral and treatment should include the following: (1) uncomplicated substance using patients (no dependence symptoms, good social resources, no psychiatric comorbidity) should be referred to, or supplied with, brief interventions; (2) patients whose problems are more serious or who do not improve after a brief intervention should be referred for outpatient treatment; (3) patients with few social resources or in a living environment that would impede recovery should be referred to residential treatment; (4) inpatient referral should be reserved for patients with serious psychiatric and/or medical comorbidity; and (5) patients referred to treatment should be continuously monitored by their referring physician in order to significantly augment the long-term effectiveness of psychosocial treatments.

ACKNOWLEDGMENT

This work was supported by the Department of Veterans Affairs Quality Enhancement Research Initiative, Mental Health Strategic Healthcare Group, and Health Services Research and Development Service. The views expressed are those of the authors and do not necessarily represent the views of the Department of Veterans Affairs.

REFERENCES

1. US Preventive Services Task Force (1996) *Guide to Clinical Preventive Services: Report of the U.S. Preventive Services Task Force*, 2nd edn, Williams and Wilkins, Baltimore.

2. VA/DoD Evidence-based Clinical Practice Guideline Working Group (2001) Management of Substance Use Disorder in a Primary Care Setting (No. Office of Quality and Performance 10Q-CPG/SUD-01), Veterans Health Administration, Department of Veterans Affairs, Health Affairs, Department of Defense, Washington, DC.

3. Bradley, K.A., Kivlahan, D.R., Bush, K.R. *et al.* (2001) Variations on the CAGE alcohol screening questionnaire: strengths and limitations in VA general medical patients. *Alcohol. Clin. Exp. Res.*, **25** (10), 1472–1478.

4. Vaillant, G.E. (2003) Natural history of addiction and pathways to recovery, in *Principles of Addiction Medicine* (eds A.W. Graham, T.K. Schultz, M.F. Mayo-Smith *et al.*), American Society of Addiction Medicine, Inc., Chevy Chase, Maryland, pp. 1–16.

5. Shoor, S. and Lorig, K.R. (2002) Self-care and the doctor-patient relationship. *Med. Care*, **40** (4 Suppl.), II40–II44.

6. McLellan, A.T., Lewis, D.C., O'Brien, C.P., and Kleber, H.D. (2000) Drug dependence, a chronic medical illness: implications for treatment, insurance, and outcomes evaluation. *JAMA*, **284** (13), 1689–1695.

7. McKay, J.R. (2001) Effectiveness of continuing care interventions for substance abusers: Implications for the study of long-term treatment effects. *Evaluation Rev.*, **25** (2), 211–232.

8. McLellan, A.T. (2002) Have we evaluated addiction treatment correctly? Implications from a chronic care perspective. *Addiction*, **97** (3), 249–252.

9. Fiellin, D.A., Reid, M.C., and O'Connor, P.G. (2000) Screening for alcohol problems in primary care: a systematic review. *Arch. Intern. Med.*, **160**, 1977–1989.

10. Miller, W.R. and Rollnick, S. (2002) *Motivational Interviewing: Preparing People to Change Addictive Behavior*, 2nd edn, Guilford, New York.

11. Simpson, C.A. and Tucker, J.A. (2002) Temporal sequencing of alcohol-related problems, problem

recognition, and help-seeking episodes. *Addict. Behav.*, **27** (5), 659–674.

12. Babor, T.F., Higgins-Biddle, J.C., Saunders, J.B., and Monteiro, M. (2001) AUDIT – The Alcohol Use Disorders Identification Test: guidelines for use in primary health care (No. WHO/MSD/MSB/01.6a): World Health Organization, Department of Mental Health and Substance Abuse.

13. Bradley, K.A., Kivlahan, D.R., Zhou, X. *et al.* (2004) Using alcohol screening results and treatment history to assess the severity of at-risk drinking in Veterans Affairs primary care patients. *Alcohol. Clin. Exp. Res.*, **28** (3), 448–455.

14. Brown, H.P., Peterson, J.H., and Cunningham, O. (1988) Rationale and theoretical basis of a behavioral/cognitive approach to spirituality. *Alcoholism Treat. Q.*, **5** (2), 47–59.

15. Babor, T.F. and Del Boca F.K. (eds) (2003) *Treatment Matching in Alcoholism*, Cambridge University Press, New York, NY.

16. Project MATCH Research Group (1997) Matching Alcoholism Treatments to Client Heterogeneity: Project MATCH posttreatment drinking outcomes. *J. Stud. Alcohol.*, **58** (1), 7–29.

17. Project MATCH Research Group (1998) Matching alcoholism treatments to client heterogeneity: treatment main effects and matching effects on drinking during treatment. *J. Stud. Alcohol.*, **59** (6), 631–639.

18. Ouimette, P.C., Finney, J.W., and Moos, R.H. (1997) Twelve-step and cognitive-behavioral treatment for substance abuse: a comparison of treatment effectiveness. *J. Consult. Clin. Psychol.*, **65** (2), 230–240.

19. Finney, J.W. and Monahan, S.C. (1996) The cost-effectiveness of treatment for alcoholism: a second approximation. *J. Stud. Alcohol.*, **57** (3), 229–243.

20. Holder, H., Longabaugh, R., Miller, W.R., and Rubonis, A.V. (1991) The cost effectiveness of treatment for alcoholism: A first approximation. *J. Stud. Alcohol.*, **52**, 517–540.

21. Miller, W.R. and Wilbourne, P.L. (2002) Mesa Grande: a methodological analysis of clinical trials of treatments for alcohol use disorders. *Addiction*, **97** (3), 265–277.

22. Humphreys, K. and Horst, D. (2001) Results of the 2000 Drug and Alcohol Program Survey. Department of Veterans Affairs, Palo Alto, CA.

23. Finney, J.W., Hahn, A.C., and Moos, R.H. (1996) The effectiveness of inpatient and outpatient treatment for alcohol abuse: the need to focus on mediators and moderators of setting effects. *Addiction*, **91** (12), 1773–1796; discussion 1803-1720.

24. Kessler, R.C., Nelson, C.B., McGonagle, K.A. *et al.* (1996) The epidemiology of co-occurring addictive and mental disorders: implications for prevention and service utilization. *Am. J. Orthopsychiat.*, **66** (1), 17–31.

25. Rychtarik, R.G., Connors, G.J., Dermen, K.H., and Stasiewicz, P.R. (2000) Alcoholics Anonymous and the use of medications to prevent relapse: an anonymous survey of member attitudes. *J. Stud. Alcohol.*, **61** (1), 134–138.

26. Kelly, J.F., McKellar, J.D., and Moos, R. (2003) Major depression in patients with substance use disorders: relationship to 12-Step self-help involvement and substance use outcomes. *Addiction*, **98** (4), 499–508.

27. Ouimette, P., Humphreys, K., Moos, R.H. *et al.* (2001) Self-help group participation among substance use disorder patients with posttraumatic stress disorder. *J. Subst. Abuse Treat.*, **20** (1), 25–32.

28. Tomasson, K. and Vaglum, P. (1998) Psychiatric co-morbidity and aftercare among alcoholics: a prospective study of a nationwide representative sample. *Addiction*, **93** (3), 423–431.

29. Winzelberg, A. and Humphreys, K. (1999) Should patients' religiosity influence clinicians' referral to 12-step self-help groups? Evidence from a study of 3,018 male substance abuse patients. *J. Consult. Clin. Psychol.*, **67** (5), 790–794.

30. Alcoholics Anonymous (1999) 1998 Membership Survey: A Snapshot of A.A Membership, AA World Services, New York, NY.

31. Kelly, J.F. (2003) Self-help for substance-use disorders: History, effectiveness, knowledge gaps and research opportunities. *Clin. Psychol. Rev.*, **23** (5), 639–663.

32. Timko, C., Moos, R.H., Finney, J.W., and Connell, E.G. (2002) Gender differences in help-utilization and the 8-year course of alcohol abuse. *Addiction*, **97** (7), 877–889.

33. Parks, G.A., Anderson, B.K., and Marlatt, G. (2001) Relapse prevention therapy, in *International Handbook of Alcohol Dependence and Problems* (eds N. Heather and T.J. Timothy *et al.*), John Wiley & Sons Ltd, pp. 575–592.

34. Larimer, M.E., Palmer, R.S., and Marlatt, G.A. (1999) Relapse prevention. An overview of Marlatt's cognitive-behavioral model. *Alcohol Res. Health*, **23** (2), 151–160.

35. Irvin, J.E., Bowers, C.A., Dunn, M.E., and Wang, M.C. (1999) Efficacy of relapse prevention: a meta-analytic review. *J. Consult. Clin. Psych.*, **67** (4), 563–570.

36. Ito, J. and Donovan, D.M. (1986) Aftercare in alcoholism treatment: A review, in *Treating Addictive Beha-*

viors: Processes of Change (eds W.R. Miller and N. Heather), Plenum Press, New York, NY.

37. Trent, L.K. (1998) Evaluation of a four- versus six-week length of stay in the Navy's alcohol treatment program. *J. Stud. Alcohol.*, **59** (3), 270–279.

38. Ouimette, P.C., Moos, R.H., and Finney, J.W. (1998) Influence of outpatient treatment and 12-step group involvement on one- year substance abuse treatment outcomes. *J. Stud. Alcohol.*, **59** (5), 513–522.

39. Ritsher, J.B., Moos, R.H., and Finney, J.W. (2002) Relationship of treatment orientation and continuing care to remission among substance abuse patients. *Psychiatr. Serv.*, **53** (5), 595–601.

40. Tonigan, J., Connors, G.J., and Miller, W.R. (2003) Participation and involvement in Alcoholics Anon-ymous, in *Matching alcoholism treatments to client heterogeneity: The results of Project MATCH* (eds T.F. Babor and F.K. Del Boca), Cambridge University Press, New York, NY, pp. 184–204.

41. Ritsher, J.B., McKellar, J.D., Finney, J.W. *et al.* (2002) Psychiatric comorbidity, continuing care and mutual help as predictors of five-year remission from substance use disorders. *J. Stud. Alcohol.*, **63** (6), 709–715.

42. Crits-Christoph, P. and Siqueland, L. (1996) Psycho-social treatment for drug abuse. Selected review and recommendations for national health care. *Arch. Gen. Psychiatry*, **53** (8), 749–756.

43. Higgins, S.T., Budney, A.J., Bickel, W.K. *et al.* (1993) Achieving cocaine abstinence with a behavioral approach. *Am. J. Psychiatry*, **150** (5), 763–769.

35

Treatment models for comorbid psychiatric and addictive disorders

Jon D. Kassel, Adrienne J. Heinz, Daniel P. Evatt, and Ashley R. Braun
University of Illinois, Chicago, IL, USA

35.1 INTRODUCTION

As exemplified throughout this volume, the devastating toll exacted by substance use disorders (SUDs) is incalculable in terms of lost work productivity, interpersonal strife, detrimental health consequences, and, perhaps most importantly, human suffering. Moreover, it is now well established that SUDs frequently present themselves in conjunction with other psychiatric conditions [1,2]. Whereas substance use occurs more often alongside externalizing disorders (i.e., antisocial personality disorder) relative to disorders of affect (e.g., depression and anxiety; [1]), rates of anxiety and depression (at both clinical and subclinical presentation levels) remain far greater in substance users compared to the general population [3].

It is important to note that the precise nature of the relationship between psychiatric disorders and substance addiction – and, for that matter, other addictions like compulsive gambling and sexual behavior – is far from well understood. For instance, associations between psychiatric disorders and drug use appear to change over time, such that rates of comorbidity are far higher for drug and alcohol dependence than for addiction [2,4]. Correspondingly, the prevalence of anxiety and depression is significantly higher among substance addicts relative to those who use, but do not misuse, drugs and alcohol [5]. Importantly, issues regarding causality – that is, the extent to which substance disorders precede or follow other psychiatric problems, or are both caused by a third, common factor – remain unanswered (a conceptual review can be found elsewhere [6]).

In their recent excellent review of the comorbidity literature, Hall *et al.* [7] point to a number of observations supported by the current database regarding psychiatric comorbidity and SUDs. Indeed, these observations hold important implications regarding the treatment of these disorders. Firstly, and as already noted, comorbidity between anxiety, depression, and substance use is common. Secondly, comorbidity rates are highest between: anxiety and mood disorders, and between alcohol and other SUDs. Thirdly, comorbidity rates are high

Addictive Disorders in Medical Populations   Edited by Norman S. Miller and Mark S. Gold
© 2010 John Wiley & Sons, Ltd.

between substance use disorders and anxiety and mood disorders, as well as between conduct disorders, antisocial personality disorder and addictive disorders. Fourthly, all of these disorders are typically manifested during adolescence, pointing to the importance of early intervention. Fifthly, rates of treatment seeking for substance misuse and addiction are generally low. Finally, despite advances in pharmacotherapy and behavioral interventions, extant treatments for substance misuse and addiction are often inadequate.

Steeped in the belief that treatment of substance use disorders cannot ignore issues pertinent to comorbidity (e.g., externalizing problems, emotional distress), several influential treatments for addiction are described, all of which either implicitly or explicitly address psychiatric comorbidity. It is noted that a discussion of treatment models of comorbid psychiatric and addictive disorder could readily fill a book itself. As such, this overview is brief and, hopefully, will serve to motivate the clinician to seek further information and guidance regarding the treatment of these difficult and emotionally painful disorders. The chapter is begun with an overview of what might arguably be viewed as the most enduring and influential perspective on why substance addiction so frequently co-occurs with other psychiatric disorders.

35.2 STRESS COPING AND SELF-MEDICATION MODELS

According to stress coping [8] and self-medication [9] models of substance addiction, drugs are thought to serve a coping function whereby they facilitate attempts at mood regulation. Across a diverse array of psychoactive drugs, including alcohol, cocaine, marijuana, and tobacco, there is reason to believe that many people use these substances as a means of regulating their mood and coping with stress and negative affect. Hence, it is conceivable that those individuals who present with psychiatric disorders – that are almost always accompanied by, and often defined in terms of, psychological distress – are most vulnerable to misuse drugs because drugs confer affective benefits, at least in the short run.

At the same time, and as articulated in neurobiological models of addiction [10], repeated use of drugs can result in the emergence of a withdrawal syndrome comprised of negative affect. As such, over time, drug use becomes negatively reinforced via reduction of these aversive withdrawal symptoms. Such a phenomenon may also go some way towards to clarifying the previously noted bidirectional relationship between substance addiction and psychiatric disorders. That is, whereas disorders marked by affective distress may genuinely heighten vulnerability to drug use, over time drug use itself results in emotionally unpleasant withdrawal symptoms that heighten vulnerability to developing psychiatric disorders epitomized by affective distress (e.g., depression, anxiety).

In summation, there is a robust and consistent relationship between SUDs and a variety of other psychiatric disorders. Whereas the precise causal mechanisms linking these disorders remain unclear, there is burgeoning reason to believe that most drug addicts self-administer drugs, in great part, as a means of affect regulation. Correspondingly, emergent withdrawal syndromes – typified by the presence of various manifestations of negative affect [11] – serve to both negatively reinforce further drug use and heighten vulnerability for the development of psychiatric disorders.

35.3 TREATMENT IN THE COMMUNITY

Over the last three decades, community-focused treatment has been forwarded as a cost-effective alternative to inpatient treatment of the severely mentally ill. Several community-based approaches have emerged including Assertive Community Treatment (ACT), intensive case management, and integrated models. Whereas intensive case management and integrated models have received increasing attention in recent years, the majority of empirical scrutiny has been directed toward ACT. ACT is not a clinical intervention *per se*, but rather a community-based approach to providing psychological care and referral directed towards people who do not have the means, capacity, or willingness to seek out traditional treatment on their own.

35.3.1 What is ACT?

The ACT model was developed on the premise that treatment should be individualized, continuous, and readily available. The initial goals of ACT included provision of basic needs, reduction of psychiatric symptoms, and decreased institutionalization rates [12,13]. Hence, six basic tenets of ACT are: (1) low patient-to-staff ratios; (2) provision of services in the community; (3) caseloads shared across clinicians; (4) 24-hour coverage; (5) services provided directly by the ACT team; and (6) time-unlimited service [14].

35.3.2 ACT and comorbid substance use and psychiatric disorders

ACT was developed in order to offer a community treatment alternative to inpatient institutionalized treatment of severe mental illness, such as schizophrenia. Numerous studies have investigated the effectiveness of ACT in the treatment of severe mental illness. Whereas some findings suggest ACT may reduce symptom severity, a meta-analysis of ACT treatment studies from 1980 to 1998 found that the most consistent benefit of ACT over standard case management was improved (reduced) hospitalization rates [15]. Moreover, a more recent meta-analysis revealed that such reductions in hospitalization are most frequent in patients who already use a great deal of hospital resources [16]. In other words, while ACT may prove beneficial in communities with high rates of hospitalization, it may yield marginal effects in communities that have already achieved a low rate of bed use.

Relative to the substantial body of literature devoted to ACT and treatment of severe mental illness, much less research has focused on the effectiveness of ACT specifically in the treatment of co-occurring substance use and psychiatric disorders. Overall, such investigations have yielded inconclusive findings. On one hand, there is some evidence that ACT may improve treatment engagement [17], decrease substance addiction, and increase quality of life [18,19]. On the other hand, investigations have consistently failed to demonstrate significant therapeutic advantages of ACT over treatment-as-usual on co-occurring psychiatric and SUDs [18,20,21]. Furthermore, one investigation found that ACT was no more cost effective than standard case management in the treatment of co-occurring severe mental illness and SUDs [21].

In a recent comparison of ACT and standard case management for the integrated treatment of co-occurring substance use and psychiatric disorders, Essock *et al.* [22] found improved institutionalization rates in the ACT group. However, similar to results from studies examining the effects of ACT on severe mental illness (without comorbid SUDs), findings suggested that improved institutionalization rates for comorbid patients were only observed in communities with relatively high pre-existing rates of institutionalization. One explanation offered by the authors for the similar performance of ACT and standard case management was that case management has, in fact, begun to incorporate many of the strategies of ACT. As such, many of the advantages that ACT presumably held over standard case management in the treatment of co-occurring disorders may have diminished in recent years.

35.3.3 Integrated treatments and intense case management models

Several integrated and intense case management models have been proposed for the treatment of comorbid SUDs and severe mental illness [23,24]. These models are largely based on the notion that separate evidence-based interventions can be effectively combined to treat comorbid substance use and psychiatric disorders [23]. A recent comprehensive review of case management for substance misusing populations found that, whereas case management proves to be an overall effective treatment, few studies have revealed significant advantages of case management over other standard treatments [25]. There was some evidence that intensive case management may be particularly effective among substance misusing populations, but more research is necessary to replicate these findings.

A review of 10 comprehensive outpatient integrated programs suggested that integrated treatments are effective in engaging dually diagnosed patients and reducing substance addiction [26]. In this investigation, consistent effects of integrated treatment on hospital use and psychiatric symptoms were not observed. A difficulty in assessing the effectiveness of integrated programs is that such programs vary greatly in the inclusion and implementation of standardized treatment strategies. Nevertheless, those integrated models that have demonstrated positive outcomes appear to share the following common features: (1) programs developed within outpatient mental health programs; (2) awareness of SUDs is integrated into all aspects of the program; (3) provide continuous outreach and monitoring to dually diagnosed patients; (4) recognize that recovery takes time (months to years); and (5) include motivational interviewing strategies to help patients identify drug use as a problem [27].

35.3.4   ACT among diverse and special populations

ACT programs may be particularly beneficial for ethnic minority groups. Due to language and cultural barriers, ethnic minority groups may not be likely to seek out treatment for psychiatric illnesses. A recent outcome study of the effectiveness of ACT for ethnic minorities found that ACT improved hospitalization rates, symptoms severity, and patient satisfaction [28]. In this investigation, outcome comparisons between groups were not provided.

A recent meta-analysis of the effectiveness of ACT for homeless populations found that ACT resulted in a greater reduction in homelessness and greater improvement in symptom severity, relative to standard case management [29]. A significant difference in hospitalization was not observed between ACT and standard case management for homeless patients. These findings are in contrast to those from ACT studies (not specifying homeless populations) that tend to find reduced hospitalization rates, but no relative benefit of ACT on symptom severity.

There is some initial evidence that ACT in its current form may not be particularly effective in treating individuals with intellectual disabilities. Recent investigations suggest that traditional empirical approaches (randomized controlled trials) may not be appropriate for study of ACT in intellectually disabled populations [30], and that ACT fails to demonstrate a relative advantage over traditional standard community treatment in outcomes for the intellectually disabled [31]. Further study is necessary to determine if ACT is appropriate for the intellectually disabled (recommendations for further study can be found elsewhere [32,33]).

35.3.5   Limitations and criticisms of ACT

Dewa *et al.* [34] investigated the time (direct and indirect) required to implement an ACT program. Findings suggested that ACT teams spent the largest amount of time and resources on medically-orientated activities at the expense of psychosocial activities. This result is consistent with outcome data suggesting that whereas ACT may effectively reduce hospitalization (a medically-orientated outcome), it may not significantly influence psychosocial outcomes. Another finding from the study was that case workers spent approximately one half hour of indirect time (travel and preparation) to every hour of direct time with patients. The authors note that case workers may have to dedicate even more indirect time in larger service areas (necessitating more travel).

Gomory [35] has been particularly critical of the ACT model. Paramount among these concerns is the claim that ACT is fundamentally coercive and unethical. Gomory [35] argues that the prime mechanism of ACT is coercion and that staff members frequently act coercively to maintain medication compliance and implement programmatic interventions, often against patients' wishes. The claim that ACT reduces hospitalization rates was also sharply questioned. Gomory [35] contends that the frequently cited reductions in hospitalization rates in ACT treatment groups are a natural, yet unremarkable (and inevitable) result of an administration rule not to admit ACT participants into the hospital for any reason, while control group patients are admitted without such constraints.

In a review of the ethical concerns of ACT, Williamson [36] echoes many of the same apprehensions put forth by Gomory. However, Williamson argues that there are limitations in using traditional principles of ethical treatment to deal with the dilemmas of treating a resistant, but severely mentally ill population. Hence, Williamson proposes that ACT programs should shift their focus to areas of assistance that patients value. In doing so, outreach efforts are likely to be more effective and patients more likely to express greater appreciation and satisfaction with treatment.

35.3.6 Recommendations for community-based treatment in practice

In summary, community-based treatments have shown some positive outcomes in the treatment of comorbid substance use and psychiatric disorders. It is noteworthy that whereas many investigations cited above failed to find relative benefits of ACT, intensive case management, or integrated treatments, these investigations typically compared such treatments with other intensive community-based treatments (frequently the three treatment approaches were compared to one another). In other words, while

it is true that none of the intensive community-based programs discussed here demonstrate a clear advantage over other approaches, they all tend to fare well against standard treatment programs.

Community diversity and treatment populations should be considered when implementing intensive community-based treatment programs. ACT appears to be particularly effective in reducing hospitalization rates in communities with relatively high rates of hospitalization and institutionalization. ACT also appears to effectively improve clinical and social outcomes in homeless populations. When implementing ACT, communities should take care to avoid coercion and unethical strategies to engage patients and influence treatment behaviors. On a practical note, a recent investigation estimated that communities should ideally develop enough ACT teams to serve approximately 50% of their adult population with severe mental illness [37].

In comparative studies of ACT and intensive case management, case management has typically performed about as well as ACT. Case management is constantly evolving and it has been suggested that case management has proven effective because it has naturally adopted many of the strategies of ACT and integrated treatment. As an overall recommendation, it would be useful for case management programs to actively adopt effective strategies from ACT and integrated treatment, such as assertive engagement and empirically supported treatments.

In summary, findings suggest that integrated treatments are particularly effective in reducing substance addiction and engaging patients. A review of the literature also reveals that integrated treatments may not be as effective as ACT for reducing hospitalization rates. At the same time, ACT appears to be most effective in reducing rates in communities with pre-existing high levels of bed use. As such, integrated treatments might be most beneficial in communities with low levels of hospitalization where the relative benefit of ACT is less.

35.4 12-STEP APPROACHES

A form of mutual help, 12-step groups provide a well-organized structure for individuals with SUDs

to collectively support one another in achieving and maintaining sobriety. Following the inception of

Alcoholics Anonymous (AA) in 1935, several specialized groups within the 12-step tradition have since emerged to address the unique challenges and needs specific to certain addictions (e.g., Narcotics Anonymous, NA; Gamblers Anonymous, GA). Today, 12-step programs are the most widely used treatment resource among individuals with SUDs. In the United States alone, AA membership is estimated at over 1.2 million people [38]. On an international level, NA membership has risen dramatically, such that the number of regularly held groups increased from 21,500 in 2005 to 25,065 in 2007 [39]. Moreover, these programs are extremely cost effective because, unlike other forms of treatment, 12-step groups do not employ the services of professionally trained care providers.

In essence, the 12-step philosophy espouses that addiction is a disease over which one is powerless. Therefore, surrender to a higher power is deemed necessary to recovery. Another basic tenet of the program is that abstinence, not harm-reduction (e.g., moderation management), is the only viable option for maintaining sobriety. These tenets, along with other 12-step principles have been increasingly integrated into formalized treatment for SUDs [40]. In support of this paradigm shift, a burgeoning literature indicates that 12-step involvement is useful in maintaining abstinence from substances [41,42], and is at least as effective as other available treatments for SUDs [43–45]). Although the 12-step approach is firmly established as an empirically validated psychosocial treatment for SUDs, less research is available regarding its effectiveness for individuals with comorbid SUDs and psychiatric disorders.

35.4.1 12-Step programs and comorbidity

As noted earlier, over 50% of individuals with mental illness are known to have a co-occurring problem with substance misuse [46,47]. Given the serious and persistent nature of problems associated with a dual diagnosis [48], coupled with a need for treatment cost containment, researchers have sought to better understand how dually diagnosed

individuals (DDIs) could benefit from participation in self help groups. A handful of studies have approached this particular question by assessing attitudes towards participation by DDIs in 12-step groups. According to one survey [49], DDIs report feeling comfortable in a 12-step setting and also with the program's philosophy. Further, negative attitudes towards taking psychotropic medication (in accordance with the program's total abstinence model) are much less pronounced than before joining [50]. However, other studies have identified some barriers for comorbid 12-step participants. For example, a review by Noordsy *et al.* [51] revealed that seriously mentally ill patients had a lower rate of consistent, long-term 12-step attendance. The authors enumerated several potential explanations for this finding, one being that DDIs may not feel they share enough in common with other group members. Other noted obstacles, including but not limited to, paranoia in meetings and believing that other group members do not understand mental illness, have been correlated with lower 12-step attendance among patients with a psychotic diagnosis [52].

Despite some of these perceived obstacles, most studies have found 12-step attendance among DDIs similar to that of individuals with a SUD only [49,52,53]. Some studies, however, have linked certain subsets of mental illness with lower 12-step participation. Specifically, individuals with social phobia and psychotic disorders (e.g., schizophrenia, schizoaffective disorder) attend fewer 12-step meetings compared to individuals with other psychiatric disorders [52–54]. Twelve-step participation by specific diagnostic groups indicated no overall participation differences between individuals with only a SUD and those with a comorbid SUD and major depressive disorder (MDD [55]) or post-traumatic stress disorder (PTSD [56]).

Studies investigating the relationship between 12-step attendance and relevant outcomes among DDIs have been largely conducted with male VA populations. Nevertheless, the available literature demonstrates a positive relationship between 12-step attendance and improved clinical outcomes [57–61], and that the degree of benefit does not appear to differ from individuals with a SUD only [62,63]. Further, one non-VA study found that homeless DDIs whose alcohol use disorder had remitted at 18 months had more frequent contact with AA and NA members at baseline [64]. However, some variability in this widely observed relationship, unique to MDD, was highlighted in a comparison of veterans with SUDs alone to veterans with comorbid SUDs and MDD [55]. Specifically, the effect of 12-step involvement on abstinence and remission status was the same one year out but was significantly weaker for the MDD-SUD group at two years out (compared to SUD alone). Despite mixed findings as to whether 12-step groups are equally beneficial to all subsets of DDIs (as compared to SUD-only patients), the preponderance of evidence suggests that benefits derived from 12-step participation do extend to this high-risk population.

More recently, researchers have sought to compare the effectiveness of various SUD treatments for DDIs. This initiative was likely sparked when the authors of Project MATCH identified a client attribute by treatment interaction, in the outpatient arm, such that individuals low in psychiatric severity experienced more days abstinent after 12-step facilitation (TSF) than cognitive-behavioral therapy (CBT); as psychiatric severity increased, the advantage of 12-step facilitation disappeared [44]. Ouimette *et al.* [43] and colleagues, however, were not able to replicate these findings in a VA sample with more variable psychiatric severity. Moreover, the same team of researchers found no difference in improvement among DDIs as a function of treatment condition (i.e., CBT, TSF [65]). Other studies have arrived at the same conclusion [46,66]. By contrast, evidence for a treatment matching effect was reported in a study comparing the efficacy of CBT and 12-step facilitation for urban crack cocaine users [67]. Specifically, among patients with a previous or current diagnosis of MDD, those assigned to CBT were significantly more likely to achieve more consecutive weeks of abstinence during treatment compared to those in the 12-step facilitation group. A number of studies have found other psychosocial interventions to yield significantly better outcomes than 12-step facilitation for certain populations of DDIs. Such treatments

include behavioral skills training and intensive case management for severely mentally ill substance addicts [68], group CBT for personality disorders in an inpatient setting [69], and Dual Focus Schema Therapy for methadone-maintained individuals with personality disorders [70]. The heterogeneity of these findings underscores the need for more clinical trials to further assess the relative effectiveness of treatments for subgroups of DDIs.

Both anecdotal evidence and survey findings indicate the need for, and potential advantages of, specialized 12-step programs for DDIs. For example, ratings by DDIs of statements comparing a regular 12-step group to a 12-step group specially designed for DDIs suggested that the latter setting allowed them to feel more comfortable and safe discussing dual recovery needs [53]. Echoing this finding, it was reported that 54% of a sample of 125 AA contact persons felt that participation (by DDIs) in a 12-step group intended for DDIs would be more desirable than a mainstream 12-step group [50]. To address these sentiments, and to counter reported difficulties of comorbid 12-step participants, specialized 12-step groups have been introduced in an effort to create a community in which DDIs can openly discuss issues related to both battle fronts of their recovery. Among them are Double Trouble in Recovery (DTR), Dual Recovery Anonymous (DRA), and Self Management and Recovery Training (SMART; see [71]).

Double Trouble in Recovery programs have been particularly well received [72,73] and are generally viewed by DDIs as helpful in maintaining abstinence and facilitating recovery. Initial research on the efficacy of this nascent program is also promising. Regular Double Trouble in Recovery attendance has been associated with decreases in substance use during treatment [74,75] and better medication compliance over time [76]. A cross-sectional examination of DDIs participating in either a Double Trouble in Recovery program or a traditional 12-step program found that Double Trouble in Recovery participation, but not traditional 12-step participation, was associated with less substance addiction and psychiatric distress along with greater well-being [77]. Two analyses of the same sample of DDIs have attempted to elucidate the active ingredients or mechanisms of change in Double Trouble in Recovery. Specifically, internal locus of control and sociability mediated both abstinence and health promoting behavior, although spirituality and hope only mediated the latter outcome [78]. Further, two of three mutual aide processes including the helper therapy process and the reciprocal learning process but not emotional support, mediated Double Trouble in Recovery outcomes [79]. Although a more systematic examination of process variables for modified 12-step programs for DDIs is required, it is likely they are similar to the mechanisms of change identified among nonmentally ill 12-step participants [80,81].

In summary, 12-step groups remain a cost effective and effective treatment option for those with SUDs. Moreover, burgeoning evidence suggests that 12-step participation is beneficial to those with comorbid psychiatric disorders as well. It is also important to note that as recently as 20 years ago, data on the effectiveness of Alcoholics Anonymous and similar programs were scant, due, in great part, to the tenet of anonymity central to 12-step programs. Nonetheless, this obstacle appears to have been overcome as evidenced by the publication of numerous studies examining the effectiveness of 12-step programs. Given their profound influence on the SUDs treatment community, this development is construed most positively, and goes some way toward providing the empirical support necessary to guide therapists when considering treatment options for clients.

35.5   COGNITIVE AND BEHAVIORAL THERAPIES

This last section addresses a very different, albeit no less influential, approach to treating substance addiction in the context of other psychiatric disorders. As such, CBT, mindfulness training, and acceptance and commitment therapy are briefly addressed.

35.5.1   Cognitive-behavioral therapy (CBT)

CBT has been frequently used to treat substance use disorders that co-occur with other psychiatric disorders, including bipolar disorder, post-traumatic stress disorder (PTSD), depression, anxiety, and personality disorders. Specific treatments that are designed to target both conditions throughout the course of the intervention have been developed. Simply put, CBT emphasizes the role played by cognition (e.g., dysfunctional attitudes, automatic negative thoughts) and behavior in promoting affective distress and psychiatric disorders. As such, the primary objective of CBT is to heighten clients' awareness of their underlying, core belief systems and modify them in a way that facilitates positive and enduring change. Change is also promoted through behavioral prescription and positive reinforcement of desired behavioral outcomes.

Thus, CBT is well suited as a therapeutic approach to treating comorbid substance addiction across a host of psychiatric disorders. One such example is a 20-session manualized, group therapy, designed to target comorbid bipolar disorder and substance addiction [82]. Throughout the 20 weeks, topics that are relevant and common to both disorders are addressed, placing particular importance on issues of recovery and relapse. Similarly, a 12-week randomized study was conducted in 46 outpatients diagnosed with both bipolar disorder and SUD, comparing medication management alone and medication management combined with individualized CBT [83]. Whereas substance addiction outcomes failed to differ across groups, the medication management with CBT group resulted in a higher completion rate, and showed greater improvements in mood compared to the medication management only group. CBT has been used to treat comorbid PTSD and SUDs as well. For example, results of a twelve-session, individual CBT therapy for Alcohol Dependence (AD) and PTSD study revealed improvement in PTSD symptoms as well as decreased alcohol use [84]. Participants also exhibited improvements in other areas, such as psychiatric distress, social relationships, and physical health.

Another CBT option for PTSD and SUD, entitled "Seeking Safety," involved 24-session manualized CBT [85,86]. As its name suggests, the key element of this treatment is safety, which refers both to safety, or abstinence, from substances, as well as from trauma. Other important treatment factors included reaching out for help and surrounding oneself with supportive people. A total of 27 women with comorbid PTSD and SUD participated in the initial trial. At the conclusion of treatment, significant increases in abstinence rates over time were found. Moreover, significant decreases in drug and alcohol use, subtle trauma symptoms, and depression were observed. Seeking Safety has since been evaluated further, with initial promising results, with other populations, including adolescent girls [87], incarcerated women [88], and civilian men [89].

Cohen and Hien [90] assessed the utility of using traditional CBT in a group of 107 women with comorbid PTSD and SUD. A total of 75 received CBT compared with 32 in a control condition. All participants received a referral list of community resources. At the conclusion of the three-month treatment period, participants in the CBT group showed significant decreases in PTSD symptoms and alcohol use symptoms compared to the control group. However, in other outcome measures, including drug use disorder symptoms, depression, dissociation, and social and sexual functioning, no significant differences were observed between groups.

CBT has also been used to treat comorbid depression and SUDs. One interesting study specifically examined the effectiveness of two forms of CBT in treating patients with comorbid depression and substance abuse: high-structure behaviorally-oriented (HSB) counseling and low-structured, facilitative (LSF) counseling [91]. Perhaps not surprisingly, results showed that participants with more severe depression benefited more from high-structure behaviorally-oriented counseling, while those with fewer depressive symptoms benefited to a greater extent from low-structured, facilitative counseling. An important finding from this study – and one that the field continues to try and address – is the potential for treatment matching, that is, matching specific treatments with particular client characteristics.

With respect to the treatment of comorbid depression and SUD, Life Enhancement Treatment for Substance Use Treatment (LETS ACT!) [92] has recently been employed to promising effect. The rationale for this treatment is that by increasing enjoyable activities (a strategy long advocated by behavior therapy), negative affect will decrease. A total of 44 individuals residing at an inpatient substance addiction treatment facility with SUD and elevated depressive symptoms participated in this six-session, manualized group treatment. Participants were randomly assigned to the treatment group or to treatment-as-usual (TAU), which consisted of stress and anger management groups, spirituality, relapse prevention, basic education and job training, as well as 12-step groups. At the post-treatment assessment, the treatment group showed significant improvements in depressive symptoms, anxiety symptoms, as well as greater enjoyment of activities compared to treatment-as-usual. Given the strength (in terms of its many active components) of the "control" group, the demonstrated efficacy of the LETS ACT approach is certainly promising. Of course, the extent to which this treatment also proves effective in reducing substance addiction rates needs yet to be addressed.

Lastly, CBT has been investigated as a treatment option for comorbid personality disorders and SUDs as well. Fisher and Bentley [69] compared three treatment groups in inpatient and outpatient settings: the disease and recovery group (steeped in a medical model view of substance addiction), a group employing CBT, and a treatment-as-usual comparison group. The two experimental groups met three times a week for four weeks, while the comparison group received the usual treatment mandated at the center. A total of 19 participants in each center were included in the final analyses. Results showed that in the outpatient center, the CBT group evidenced greater improvements in alcohol use, social and familial relationships, and psychological problems. In the inpatient setting, whereas the two active treatment groups yielded similar outcomes, they both proved more effective than the control group.

35.5.2 Mindfulness

Individuals with comorbid mood and substance disorders may benefit from mindfulness techniques as an adjunct to standard CBT [93]. It has been proposed that repeated drug use may impair one's ability to regulate affect (in the absence of using drugs toward that same end). In such instances, affect regulation components of mindfulness – that draw upon diverse influences, ranging from cognitive therapy to Zen Buddhism – may be particularly useful. Treatment protocols are being developed to test the utility of mindulfness as an adjunct to CBT for addiction in treating deficits in affect regulation [93].

Mindfulness has also been employed as part of a broader treatment plan to help treat sleep disorders in adolescents who have been treated for a SUD [94]. It was predicted that when sleep disturbances improved, the likelihood of relapse to substance addiction would decrease. Mindfulness-based stress reduction was one component of the six-week treatment, which also involved cognitive restructuring of maladaptive beliefs concerning sleep and sleep disturbance, stimulus control instructions to help the individual use bedtime cues to induce sleep, and sleep education. Post-treatment sleep improved significantly. However, throughout the sleep treatment, substance use increased. For those who completed the program, a decreasing trend in substance use was observed across the 12-month follow-up period. This trend was not seen for noncompleters. Hence, although still in its early stages, the application of mindfulness training to those suffering from comorbid SUDS and psychiatric disorders certainly appears promising.

35.5.3 Acceptance and commitment therapy

Acceptance and commitment therapy is a relatively new entry in the treatment armamentarium that, although steeped in radical behaviorism, draws upon other diverse influences, including dialectical behavior therapy, mindfulness, and Buddhism. Simply put, it involves six major components, including acceptance of private events (as opposed to experiential avoidance), cognitive defusion, being present, self as context, values, and committed action [95]. Although acceptance and commitment therapy has been tested with respect to its efficacy in treating a host of psychiatric disorders and SUDs, little research has been conducted in which acceptance and commitment therapy has been applied to individual with such comorbid disorders.

An intriguing case study was conducted with a 19-year-old Caucasian female with comorbid PTSD and substance addiction [96]. The treatment protocol consisted of basic acceptance and commitment therapy principles, including experiential avoidance, acceptance of events, and commitment to behavior change. After 12-months of treatment, depression, psychological distress, and avoidance symptom ratings had decreased to the point where they were subthreshold for clinical diagnosis. Importantly, the client also maintained abstinence from all drugs subsequent to seven months of active treatment. As such, acceptance and commitment therapy appears promising and warrants further research to assess its utility in treating comorbid psychiatric disorders and substance addiction.

In summary, CBT and its derivatives, including mindfulness and acceptance and commitment therapy, are being increasingly assessed with respect to their effectiveness in treatment SUDs in conjunction with other psychiatric disorders. Given the long history of CBT, and its strong empirical support, there is reason to be optimistic that these approaches offer much in the way of treating this difficult population.

35.6 CONCLUSIONS

It has become increasingly clear that SUDs rarely occur in a diagnostic vacuum. That is, substance addicts frequently present with other psychiatric disorders. While this reality complicates the clinical picture, and resultant treatment, it simply cannot be ignored. Indeed, we recently observed ([97], p. 282): "It is important to remember that any observed associations between drug use behavior and emotion ultimately reveal relationships that reflect the severe emotional pain experienced by the vast majority of substance abusers. Indeed, the personification of the "happy drunk," or the addict as a hedonist run amok, is rarely exhibited by individuals truly in the throes of addiction. Instead, the clinician is witness to individuals with marked affective distress. Hence, the observations derived from epidemiological studies that consistently point to strong associations between disordered emotion and substance abuse reflect important experiential phenomena."

In this chapter, a number of approaches to the treatment of comorbid psychiatric disoders and SUDS have been reviewed. Although these approaches are certainly diverse, they all possess the capability of addressing issues inherent to such complex clinical presentations. And there are certainly other treatment options available to the clinician that have not been discussed in this chapter. Foremost among these would be pharmacotherapy targeted at treating the affective distress accompanying substance use disorders. By way of example, bupropion (an antidepressant) has been used to good effect in the treatment of nicotine dependence. Interestingly, it appears that bupropion facilitates smoking cessation regardless of whether the smoker is depressed or not. As such, it is believed that this drug likely works through its lessening of negative affect [98].

To end with one last observation: Although throughout this chapter the importance of assessing for the presence of other psychiatric disorders (e.g., depression) has been emphasized when treating substance addicts, the converse is also true. That is, when clients present with primary conditions other than SUDs, it is imperative that the clinician assesses for the possible presence of substance use, addiction, and dependence. It is our view (and one shared by many others) that in order to effectively treat any psychiatric disorder, issues pertinent to substance use must be addressed up front. The good news is that there are now a host of empirically supported treatments available for intervening with this difficult population.

ACKNOWLEDGMENT

Preparation of this chapter was supported by grant 1PO1CA98262 from the National Cancer Institute.

REFERENCES

1. Compton, W.M., Thomas, Y.F., Stinson, F.S., and Grant, B.F. (2007) Prevalence, correlates, disability, and comorbidity of *DSM-IV* drug abuse and dependence in the United States. *Arch. Gen. Psychiatry*, **64**, 566–578.

2. Grant, B.F., Stinson, F.S., Dawson, D.A. *et al.* (2004) Prevalence and co-occurrence of substance use disorders and independent mood and anxiety disorders. *Arch. Gen. Psychiatry*, **61**, 807–816.

3. Lasser, K., Boyd, J.W., Woolhandler, S. *et al.* (2000) Smoking and mental illness: A population-based prevalence study. *JAMA*, **284**, 2606–2610.

4. Conway, K.P., Compton, W., Stinson, F.S., and Grant, B.F. (2006) Lifetime comorbidity of DSM-IV mood and anxiety disorders and specific drug use disorders: Results from the National Epidemiologic Survey on Alcohol and Related Conditions. *J. Clin. Psychiat.*, **67**, 247–257.

5. Merikangas, K.R., Mehta, R.L., Molnar, B.E. *et al.* (1998) Comorbidity of substance use disorders with mood and anxiety disorders: Results of the International Consortium in Psychiatric Epidemiology. *Addict. Behav.*, **23**, 893–907.

6. Kassel, J.D. and Hankin, B.L. (2006) Smoking and depression, in *Depression and Physical Illness* (ed. A. Steptoe), Cambridge University Press, Cambridge, England.

7. Hall, W., Degenhardt, L., and Teesson, M. (2009) Reprint of "Understanding comorbidity between substance use, anxiety and affective disorders: Broadening the research base". *Addict. Behav.*, **14**, 795–799.

8. Wills, T.A. and Shiffman, S. (1985) Coping and substance use: A conceptual framework, in *Coping and Substance Use* (eds S. Shiffman and T.A. Wills), Academic Press, New York, pp. 3–24.

9. Khantzian, E.J. (1997) The self-medication hypothesis of substance use disorders: A reconsideration and

recent applications. *Harvard Rev. Psychiat.*, **4**, 231–244.

10. Koob, G. and Le Moal, S. (2001) Drug abuse, dysregulation of reward, and allostasis. *Neuropsychopharmacology*, **24**, 97–129.

11. Baker, T.B., Piper, M.E., McCarthy, D.E. *et al.* (2004) Addiction motivation reformulated: an affective processing model of negative reinforcement. *Psychol. Rev.*, **111**, 33–51.

12. Stein, L.I. and Test, M.A. (1980) Alternative to mental health treatment. I: Conceptual model, treatment program, and clinical evaluation. *Arch. Gen. Psychiatry*, **37**, 392–397.

13. Test, M.A. (1981) Effective community treatment of the chronically ill: What is necessary? *J. Soc. Issues*, **73**, 71–86.

14. Mueser, K., Bond, G.R., Drake, R.E., and Resnick, S.G. (1998) Models of community care for severe mental illness. A review of research on use management. *Schizophr. Bull.*, **24**, 37–74.

15. Ziguras, S. and Stuart, G. (2000) A meta-analysis of the effectiveness of mental health case management over 20 years. *Psychiatr. Serv.*, **51**, 1410–1421.

16. Burns, T., Catty, J., Dash, M. *et al.* (2007) Use of intensive case management to reduce time in hospital in people with severe mental illness: systematic review and meta-regression. *Br. Med. J.*, **335**, 336–342.

17. Passetti, F., Jones, G., Chawla, K. *et al.* (2008) Pilot Study of Assertive Community Treatment Methods to Engage Alcohol-Dependent Individuals. *Alcohol Alcohol.*, **43**, 451–455.

18. Drake, R.E., McHugo, G.M., Clark, R.E. *et al.* (1998) Assertive community treatment for patients with co-occurring severe mental illness and substance use disorder: a clinical trial. *Am. J. Orthopsychiat.*, **68**, 201–215.

19. Peterson, L., Jeppesen, P., and Thorup, A. *et al.* (2005) A randomised multicentre trial of integrated versus standard treatment for patients with a first episode of psychotic illness. *Br. Med. J.*, **331**, 602–608.

20. Bond, G.R., McDonel, E.C., Miller, L.D., and Pensec, M. (1991) Assertive community treatment and reference groups: An evaluation of their effectiveness for young adults with serious mental illness and substance abuse problems. *Psychosoc. Rehabil. J.*, **15**, 31–43.

21. Clark, R.E., Teague, G.B., and Ricketts, S.J. *et al.* (1998) Cost-effectiveness of assertive community treatment versus standard case management for persons with co-occurring severe mental illness and substance use disorders. *Health Serv. Res.*, **33**, 1285–1308.

22. Essock, S.M., Mueser, K.T., Drake, R.E. *et al.* (2006) Comparison of ACT and standard case management for delivering integrated treatment for co-occurring disorders. *Psychiatr. Serv.*, **57**, 185–196.

23. Blakely, T.J. and Dziadosz, G.M. (2007) Creating an agency integrated treatment program for co-occurring disorders. *Am. J. Psychiatr. Rehabil.*, **10**, 1–18.

24. Miller, N.S. (1994) *Treating Coexisting Psychiatric and Addictive Disorders*, Hazelden Educational Materials, Center City, MN.

25. Vanderplasschen, W., Wolf, J.R., Rapp, R.C., and Broekaert, E. (2007) Effectiveness of different models of case management for substance-abusing populations. *J. Psychoactive Drugs*, **39**, 81–95.

26. Drake, R.E., Mercer-McFadden, C., Mueser, K.T. *et al.* (1998) Review of integrated mental health and substance abuse treatment for patients with dual disorders. *Schizophrenia Bull.*, **24**, 589–608.

27. Drake, R.E. and Mueser, K.T. (2000) Psychosocial approaches to dual diagnosis. *Schizophrenia Bull.*, **26**, 105–118.

28. Yang, J., Law, S., Chow, W. *et al.* (2005) Assertive community treatment for persons with severe and persistent mental illness in ethnic minority groups. *Psychiatr. Serv.*, **56**, 1053–1055.

29. Coldwell, C.M. and Bender, W.S. (2007) The effectiveness of assertive community treatment for homeless populations with severe mental illness: a meta-analysis. *Am. J. Psychiatry*, **164**, 393–399.

30. Oliver, P.C., Piachaud, J., Done, J. *et al.* (2002) Difficulties in conducting a randomized controlled trial of health service interventions in intellectual disability: implications for evidence-based practice. *J. Intell. Disabil. Res.*, **46**, 340–345.

31. Martin, G., Costello, H., Leese, M. *et al.* (2005) An exploratory study of assertive community treatment for people with intellectual disability and psychiatric disorders: conceptual, clinical, and service issues. *J. Intell. Disabil. Res.*, **49**, 516–524.

32. Hemmings, C., Underwood, L., and Bouras, N. (2008) ACT for People With Intellectual Disabilities and Mental Health Problems. *Psychiatr. Serv.*, **59**, 936–937.

33. Prakash, J., Andrews, T., and Porter, I. (2007) Service innovation: assertive outreach teams for adults with learning disability. *Psychiatr. Bull.*, **31**, 138–141.

34. Dewa, C.S., Horgan, S., McIntyre, D. *et al.* (2003) Direct and indirect time inputs and assertive community treatment. *Community Ment. Health J.*, **39**, 17–32.

35. Gomory, T. (2001) A critique of the effectiveness of assertive community treatment. *Psychiatr. Serv.*, **52**, 1394–1395.

36. Williamson, T. (2002) Ethics of assertive outreach (assertive community treatment teams). *Curr. Opin. Psychiatry*, **15**, 543–547.

37. Cuddeback, G.S., Morrissey, J.P., and Meyer, P.S. (2006) How many assertive community treatment teams do we need? *Psychiatr. Serv.*, **57**, 1803–1806.

38. Alcoholics Anonymous World Services (2008) Retrieved from http://www.alcoholics-anonymous. org/en_media_resources.cfm?PageID=74 (accessed 1 August 2008).

39. Narcotics Anonymous World Services (2007) Retrieved from http://www.na.org/basic.htm#Membershipdemographics (accessed 1 August 2008).

40. Roman, P.M., and Blum, T.C. (1998) National treatment center study Summary report (no. 3): Second wave on-site results. Unpublished manuscript, University of Georgia.

41. Fiorentine, R. (1999) After drug treatment: Are 12-step programs effective in maintaining abstinence? *Am. J. Drug Alcohol Ab.*, **25** (1), 93–116.

42. Timko, C., Moos, R.H., Finney, J.W., and Lesar, M.D. (2000) Long-term outcomes of alcohol use disorders: Comparing untreated individuals with those in alcoholics anonymous and formal treatment. *J. Stud. Alcohol*, **61**, 529–540.

43. Ouimette, P.C., Finney, J.W., Gima, K., and Moos, R.H. (1999) A comparative evaluation of substance abuse treatment – iii. Examining mechanisms underlying patient-treatment matching hypotheses for 12-step and cognitive-behavioral treatments for substance abuse. *Alcohol. Clin. Exp. Res.*, **23**, 545–551.

44. G. Project Match Research (1997) Matching alcoholism treatments to client heterogeneity: Project match posttreatment drinking outcomes. *J. Stud. Alcohol*, **58**, 7–29.

45. G. Project Match Research (1998) Matching alcoholism treatments to client heterogeneity: Treatment main effects and matching effects on drinking during treatment. *J. Stud. Alcohol*, **59**, 631–639.

46. Cleary, M., Hunt, G., Matheson, S. *et al.* (2008) Psychosocial interventions for people with both severe mental illness and substance misuse. *Cochrane Database Syst. Rev.* (1).

47. Kessler, R.C., Nelson, C.B., McGonagle, K.A. *et al.* (1996) The epidemiology of co-occurring addictive and mental disorders: Implications for prevention and service utilization. *Am. J. Orthopsychiat.*, **66**, 17–31.

48. Laudet, A.B., Magura, S., Vogel, H.S., and Knight, E. (2000) Recovery challenges among dually diagnosed individuals. *J. Subst. Abuse Treat.*, **18**, 321–329.

49. Pristach, C.A. and Smith, C.M. (1999) Attitudes towards alcoholics anonymous by dually diagnosed psychiatric inpatients. *J. Addict. Dis.*, **18**, 69–76.

50. Meissen, G., Powell, T.J., Wituk, S.A. *et al.* (1999) Attitudes of AA contact persons toward group participation by persons with a mental illness. *Psychiatr. Serv.*, **50**, 1079–1081.

51. Noordsy, D.L., Schwab, B., Fox, L., and Drake, R.E. (1996) The role of self-help programs in the rehabilitation of persons with severe mental illness and substance use disorders. *Community Ment. Health J.*, **32**, 71–81.

52. Bogenschutz, M.P. and Akin, S.J. (2000) 12-step participation and attitudes towards 12-step programs in dual diagnosis patients. *Alcohol. Treat. Q.*, **18**, 31–46.

53. Jordan, L.C., Davidson, W.S., Herman, S.E., and BootsMiller, B.J. (2002) Involvement in 12-step programs among persons with dual diagnoses. *Psychiatr. Serv.*, **53**, 894–896.

54. Myrick, H. and Brady, K.T. (1997) Social phobia in cocaine dependent individuals. *Am. J. Addiction*, **6**, 99–104.

55. Kelly, J.F., McKellar, J.D., and Moos, R. (2003) Major depression in patients with substance use disorders: Relationship to 12-step self-help involvement and substance use outcomes. *Addiction*, **98**, 499–508.

56. Ouimette, P., Humphreys, K., Moos, R.H. *et al.* (2001) Self-help group participation among substance use disorder patients with posttraumatic stress disorder. *J. Subst. Abuse Treat.*, **20**, 25–32.

57. Moggi, F., Ouimette, P.C., Finney, J.W., and Moos, R.H. (1999) Effectiveness of treatment for substance abuse and dependence for dual diagnosis patients: A model of treatment factors associated with one-year outcomes. *J. Stud. Alcohol*, **60**, 856–866.

58. Moos, R.H., Finney, J.W., Ouimette, P.C., and Suchinsky, R.T. (1999) A comparative evaluation of substance abuse treatment: I. Treatment orientation, amount of care, and 1-year outcomes. *Alcohol. Clin. Exp. Res.*, **23**, 529–536.

59. Ouimette, P., Moos, R.H., and Finney, J.W. (2003) PTSD treatment and 5-year remission among patients with substance use and posttraumatic stress disorders. *J. Consult. Clin. Psych.*, **71**, 410–414.

60. Ouimette, P.C., Moos, R.H., and Finney, J.W. (2000) Two-year mental health service use and course of remission in patients with substance use and posttraumatic stress disorders. *J. Stud. Alcohol*, **61**, 247–253.

61. Timko, C. and Sempel, J.M. (2004) Intensity of acute services, self-help attendance and one-year outcomes among dual diagnosis patients. *J. Stud. Alcohol*, **65**, 274–282.

62. Ouimette, P.C., Moos, R.H., and Finney, J.W. (1998) Influence of outpatient treatment and 12-step group involvement on one-year substance abuse treatment outcomes. *J. Stud. Alcohol*, **59**, 513–522.

63. Ritsher, J.B., McKellar, J.D., Finney, J.W. *et al.* (2002) Psychiatric comorbidity, continuing care and mutual help as predictors of five-year remission from substance use disorders. *J. Stud. Alcohol*, **63**, 709–715.

64. Trumbetta, S.L., Mueser, K.T., Quimby, E. *et al.* (1999) Social networks and clinical outcomes of dually diagnosed homeless persons. *Behav. Ther.*, **30**, 407–430.

65. Ouimette, P.C., Gima, K., Moos, R.H., and Finney, J.W. (1999) A comparative evaluation of substance abuse treatment – iv. The effect of comorbid psychiatric diagnoses on amount of treatment, continuing care, and 1-year outcomes. *Alcohol. Clin. Exp. Res.*, **23**, 552–557.

66. Tate, S.R., Wu, J., McQuaid, J.R. *et al.* (2008) Comorbidity of substance dependence and depression: Role of life stress and self-efficacy in sustaining abstinence. *Psychol. Addict. Behav.*, **22**, 47–57.

67. Maude-Griffin, P.M., Hohenstein, J.M., Humfleet, G.L. *et al.* (1998) Superior efficacy of cognitive-behavioral therapy for urban crack cocaine abusers: Main and matching effects. *J. Consult. Clin. Psych.*, **66**, 832–837.

68. Jerrell, J.M. and Ridgely, M.S. (1995) Comparative effectiveness of 3 approaches to serving people with severe mental-illness and substance-abuse disorders. *J. Nerv. Ment. Dis.*, **183**, 566–576.

69. Fisher, M.-S. and Bentley, K.-J. (1996) Two group therapy models for clients with a dual diagnosis of substance abuse and personality disorder. *Psychiatr. Serv.*, **47**, 1244–1250.

70. Ball, S.A. (2007) Comparing individual therapies for personality disordered opioid dependent patients. *J. Pers. Disord.*, **21**, 305–321.

71. Brooks, A.J. and Penn, P.E. (2003) Comparing treatments for dual diagnosis: Twelve-step and self-management and recovery training. *Am. J. Drug Alcohol Ab.*, **29**, 359–383.

72. Bogenschutz, M.P., Vigil, J., and Arenella, P. (2002) Attitudes of dually diagnosed patients towards double trouble in recovery and traditional 12-step programs. American Academy of Addiction Psychiatry Annual Meeting. Las Vegas, NV.

73. Vogel, H.S., Knight, E., Laudet, A.B., and Magura, S. (1998) Double trouble in recovery: Self-help for people with dual diagnoses. *Psychiatr. Rehabil. J.*, **21**, 356–364.

74. Bogenschutz, M.P. (2005) Specialized 12-step programs and 12-step facilitation for the dually diagnosed. *Community Ment. Health J.*, **41**, 7–20.

75. Magura, S., Rosenblum, A., Villano, C.L. *et al.* (2008) Dual-focus mutual aid for co-occurring disorders: A quasi-experimental outcome evaluation study. *Am. J. Drug Alcohol Ab.*, **34**, 61–74.

76. Magura, S., Laudet, A.B., Mahmood, D. *et al.* (2002) Adherence to medication regimens and participation in dual focus self-help groups. *Psychiatr. Serv.*, **53**, 310–316.

77. Laudet, A.B., Magura, S., Vogel, H.S., and Knight, E. (2000) Support, mutual aid and recovery from dual diagnosis. *Community Ment. Health J.*, **36**, 457–476.

78. Magura, S., Knight, E.L., Vogel, H.S. *et al.* (2003) Mediators of effectiveness in dual-focus self-help groups. *Am. J. Drug Alcohol Ab.*, **29**, 301–322.

79. Magura, S., Laudet, A.B., Mahmood, D. *et al.* (2003) Role of self-help processes in achieving abstinence among dually diagnosed persons. *Addict. Behav.*, **28**, 399–413.

80. Kassel, J.D. and Wagner, E.F. (1993) Processes of change in Alcoholics Anonymous: A review of possible mechanisms. *Psychotherapy*, **30**, 222–234.

81. Bogenschutz, M.P. (2007) 12-step approaches for the dually diagnosed: Mechanisms of change. *Alcohol. Clin. Exp. Res.*, **31**, 64S–66.

82. Weiss, R.D., Najavits, L.M., and Greenfield, S.F. (1999) A relapse prevention group for patients with bipolar and substance use disorders. *J. Subst. Abuse Treat.*, **16**, 47–54.

83. Schmitz, J.M., Averill, P., Sayre, S. *et al.* (2002) Cognitive-behavioral treatment of bipolar disorder and substance abuse: A preliminary randomized study. *Addict. Disord. Their Treat.*, **1**, 17–24.

84. Back, S.E., Jackson, J.L., Sonne, S., and Brady, K.T. (2005) Alcohol dependence and posttraumatic stress disorder: Differences in clinical presentation and response to cognitive-behavioral therapy by order of onset. *J. Subst. Abuse Treat.*, **2**, 29–37.

85. Najavits, L.M., Weiss, R.D., and Liese, B.S. (1996) Group cognitive-behavioral therapy for women with PTSD and substance use disorder. *J. Subst. Abuse Treat.*, **13**, 13–22.

86. Najavits, L.M., Weiss, R.D., Shaw, S.R., and Muenz, L.R. (1998) "Seeking safety": Outcome of a new cognitive-behavioral psychotherapy for women with posttraumatic stress disorder and substance dependence. *J. Trauma. Stress*, **11**, 437–456.

87. Najavits, L.M., Gallop, R.J., and Weiss, R.D. (2006) Seeking safety therapy for adolescent girls with PTSD and substance use disorder: A randomized controlled trial. *J. Behav. Health Ser. R.*, **33**, 453–463.

88. Zlotnick, C., Najavits, L.M., Rohsenow, D.J., and Johnson, D.M. (2003) A cognitive-behavioral treatment for incarcerated women with substance abuse disorder and posttraumatic stress disorder: findings from a pilot study. *J. Subst. Abuse Treat.*, **25**, 99–105.

89. Najavits, L.M., Schmitz, M., Gotthardt, S., and Weiss, R.D. (2005) Seeking safety plus exposure therapy: An outcome study on dual diagnosis men. *J. Psychoactive Drugs*, **37**, 425–435.

90. Cohen, L.R. and Hien, D.A. (2006) Treatment outcomes for women with substance abuse and PTSD who have experienced complex trauma. *Psychiatr. Serv.*, **57**, 100–106.

91. Gottheil, E., Thornton, C., and Weinstein, S. (2002) Effectiveness of high versus low structure individual counseling for substance abuse. *Am. J. Addiction*, **11**, 279–290.

92. Daughters, S.B., Braun, A.R., Sargeant, M.N. *et al.* (2008) Effectiveness of a brief behavioral treatment for inner-city illicit drug users with elevated depressive symptoms: the life enhancement treatment for substance use (LETS Act!). *J. Clin. Psychiat.*, **69**, 122–129.

93. Hoppes, K. (2006) The Application of Mindfulness-Based Cognitive Interventions in the Treatment of Co-occurring Addictive and Mood Disorders. *CNS Spectr.*, **11**, 829–851.

94. Bootzin, R.-R. and Stevens, S.-J. (2005) Adolescents, substance abuse, and the treatment of insomnia and daytime sleepiness. *Clin. Psychol. Rev.*, **25**, 629–644.

95. Hayes, S.C., Luoma, J.B., Bond, F.W. *et al.* (2006) Acceptance and commitment therapy: Model, processes and outcomes. *Behav. Res. Ther.*, **4**, 1–25.

96. Batten, S.V. and Hayes, S.C. (2005) Acceptance and Commitment Therapy in the Treatment of Comorbid Substance Abuse and Post-Traumatic Stress Disorder: A Case Study. *Clinical Case Studies*, **4**, 246–262.

97. Kassel, J.D. and Evatt, D.P. (2009) Afterword: new frontiers in substance abuse and emotion, in *Substance Abuse and Emotion* (ed. J.D. Kassel), American Psychological Association, Washington, DC, pp. 281–286.

98. Lerman, C., Roth, D., Kaufman, V. *et al.* (2002) Mediating mechanisms for the impact of bupropion in smoking cessation treatment. *Drug Alcohol Depen.*, **67**, 219–223.

36

Brief interventions for alcohol and drug problems

Kristen L. Barry,[1] Laurie Brockmann,[2] and Frederic C. Blow[1]

[1] University of Michigan Department of Psychiatry and Department of Veterans Affairs Serious Mental Illness Treatment Research and Evaluation Center (SMITREC), Ann Arbor, MI 48109, USA
[2] University of Michigan Department of Psychiatry, Ann Arbor, MI 48109, USA

36.1 INTRODUCTION

Alcohol and drug misuse/addiction are common occurrences in the United States. Few individuals, however, who would be appropriate for brief interventions, brief treatments, and/or specialized substance addiction treatment actually receive the appropriate care that they need. Substance use is associated with a number of physical health, mental health, social, and legal consequences, including higher HIV risk, as described throughout this book [1–12].

One of the early goals of the Healthy People 2000 [13] guidelines was to increase the proportion of physical and mental health providers who screen and provide advice for alcohol and drug problems. Practitioners from a variety of disciplines, including primary and emergency medical care, can play a crucial role in detecting and treating at-risk and problem substance use. Because providers and other staff in most medical settings have limited time and a large numbers of patients, the use of brief effective techniques to change problematic behaviors related to substance use are imperative. The seriousness of the problems related to alcohol and drugs and the potential for changing patient behaviors led to the development of efficient and effective screening and intervention methods that can be implemented in fast-paced medical and other healthcare-related settings.

This chapter focuses on the theoretical, research, and practical basis for the use of screening and brief interventions for alcohol and drug misuse/addiction.

Addictive Disorders in Medical Populations Edited by Norman S. Miller and Mark S. Gold
© 2010 John Wiley & Sons, Ltd.

36.2   BRIEF MOTIVATIONAL INTERVENTIONS

There is a spectrum of intervention techniques that can be used across the range of drinking patterns (Figure 36.1) from prevention strategies for individuals who do not have problems related to use to those who have severe dependence. Brief interventions are techniques that can have the goal of: (1) reducing or stopping use; or (2) providing a test of "cutting down" to determine if a patient has higher tolerance and if cutting down is problematic.

Brief motivational interventions such as motivational interviewing [14] and motivational enhancement therapy are designed to increase motivation to change behaviors. Brief interventions for alcohol and drug problems are defined as time-limited, patient-centered approaches focused on reducing or eliminating drinking and drug use. Brief interventions are characterized by few sessions (five or fewer; often one or two) of relatively brief duration (a few minutes to an hour) [15]. Research has shown the efficacy and effectiveness of a variety of brief interventions across treatment settings, populations, and providers. Often used to reduce alcohol consumption among individuals with at-risk or hazardous drinking, brief interventions can often also motivate patients to seek and engage in additional treatment as needed. Brief interventions can provide immediate attention to individuals at risk and help facilitate the level of care needed to address substance use problems and prevent or

minimize potential consequences. Brief interventions are also attractive as a cost-effective, efficient way to prevent and treat substance use problems.

36.2.1   Theoretical background

Cognitive and social psychology are the theoretical foundations for brief motivational interventions, within a specific framework of the transtheoretical model of change [16]. This model conceptualizes health behavior change as a progression through a series of stages: precontemplation, contemplation, preparation, action, and maintenance [17].

Precontemplation is the stage at which there is no intention to change behavior in the foreseeable future. Many individuals in this stage are unaware or underaware of their problems. *Contemplation* is the stage in which people are aware that a problem exists and are seriously thinking about overcoming it but have not yet made a commitment to take action. *Preparation* is a stage that combines intention and behavioral criteria. Individuals in this stage are intending to take action in the next month and have unsuccessfully taken action in the past year. *Action* is the stage in which individuals modify their behavior, experiences, or environment to overcome their problems. Action involves the most overt behavioral changes and requires considerable commitment of time and energy. *Maintenance* is

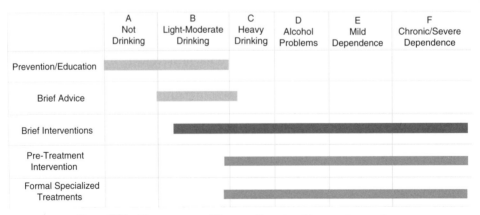

Figure 36.1   The spectrum of interventions to address patterns of use

the stage in which people work to prevent relapse and consolidate the gains attained during action.

The goal of brief motivational interventions is to help individuals progress through the stages of change. The practitioner seeks to develop a discrepancy in the client's perceptions between current behavior and significant personal goals and priorities. The client's motivation for change comes from intrinsic personal desire for and commitment to change. Typically, the practitioner uses open-ended questions to explore perceived positive and negative aspects of substance use and to elicit client expression. The practitioner also paraphrases the key motivational points, "reflecting back" to the client what they have articulated. Then time is devoted to providing feedback to the client, developing a plan for change, and anticipating the challenges to instituting and maintaining the plan.

36.3 USE OF SCREENING AND ASSESSMENT IN INTERVENTION PROCESS

There are recommended levels of alcohol consumption to minimize risky or problematic drinking and to prevent alcohol-related problems. For example, the National Institute for Alcoholism and Alcohol Abuse (NIAAA) [18] defines moderate alcohol use guidelines for most adult women as 3–7 drinks per week or up to one drink per day. Guidelines for most adult men are 4–14 drinks per week or up to two drinks per day. Drinking at these levels is usually not associated with health risks [19]. The NIAAA and the Center for Substance Abuse Treatment's Treatment Improvement Protocol (TIP) on older adults [20] recommends that persons age 65 and older consume no more than one standard drink per day or seven standard drinks per week. In addition, older adults should consume no more than 2 standard drinks on any drinking day.

A drink is 12 grams of alcohol (e.g., 12 ounces of beer or wine cooler; 5 ounces of wine; or 1.5 ounces of 80-proof distilled spirits).

Some individuals, however, should not consume alcohol at all. These include women who are pregnant or trying to become pregnant, individuals taking certain over-the-counter or prescription medications, those with medical conditions that can be made worse by drinking, individuals planning to drive a car or engage in other activities requiring alertness and skill, recovering alcoholics, and people younger than age 21 [21].

Screening for problem substance use is a critical first step in identifying patients who may need further in-depth assessment and those who may be suitable candidates for brief interventions. Screening generally identifies at-risk and harmful substance use, while more extensive assessment measures the severity of the substance use, problems and consequences associated with use, factors that may be contributing to substance addiction, and other characteristics of the problem. The screening and assessment process should help determine if a patient's substance use is appropriate for brief intervention or warrant a different approach.

Although screening and assessment are addressed in further detail elsewhere in this book, two brief approaches bear mentioning [18]. Simple questions about heavy substance use days can be used during a clinical interview or before a patient is seen, followed up with further questions as indicated.

Prescreening question: Do you drink beer, wine, or other alcoholic beverages?

Follow-up questions: If yes, how many times in the <past year; past three months; past 6 months> have you had five or more drinks in a day (for men)/four or more drinks in a day (for women)?

An average, how many days/week do you drink alcoholic beverages? *If weekly or more*: On a day when you drink alcohol, how many drinks do you have?

Prescreening question: Do you sometimes use illegal drugs or prescription drugs in a way different than prescribed?

Follow-up question: If yes, follow up with additional questions regarding which substances, frequency and quantity of use.

A useful validated screening instrument is the Alcohol Use Disorders Identification Test (AUDIT), which was developed by the World Health Organization (WHO) as a brief screening tool for excessive drinking [22–26]. It can also be helpful in developing a framework for brief interventions for individuals drinking at hazardous or harmful levels. The AUDIT (http://www.niaaa.nih.gov/NR/rdonlyres/287137A9-62BF-4EDE-A752-4A351C57A0B8/0/Audit.pdf) is well validated in adults under 65 in primary care settings. The AUDIT is comprised of two sections: a ten-item scale with alcohol-related information for the *previous year only*, and a "Clinical Screening Procedure," which includes a trauma history and a clinical examination. The questionnaire is introduced by a section explaining to the respondent that questions about alcohol use in the *previous year only* are included. The questionnaire is often used as a screener without the clinical examination. The recommended cut-off score for the AUDIT has been eight.

Screening opportunities include during routine appointments, new patient intake forms, before prescribing medications (particularly those that interact with alcohol or other drugs), in emergency departments/urgent care centers, patients who may be pregnant or trying to conceive, patients with health conditions that may be alcohol related, patients with illnesses that are not responding to treatment as expected, populations of patients who may be more likely to drink heavily, such as adolescents or young adults.

36.4   RESEARCH ON BRIEF INTERVENTIONS

36.4.1   Alcohol: primary care

Although traditional approaches to alcohol and other drug problems have focused on long-term counseling, there is increasing evidence that brief interventions delivered in healthcare settings can effectively reduce drinking in at-risk and problem drinkers, in particular. The clinical trials of brief advice with at-risk drinkers have been based, in part, on the original "stop smoking" trials. Early studies in Europe and other countries demonstrated a significant (10–20%) reduction in the drinking by persons in the experimental groups when compared to control groups who did not receive the advice [27–29]. Since these early studies, there have been many clinical trials testing the efficacy of brief interventions for at-risk and problem use in medical settings.

The majority of intervention studies have been conducted in primary care and emergency medicine settings and most have focused on alcohol, with fewer focused on illicit drugs. From a public health perspective, because of the large numbers of patients seen in these venues, the development of easy-to-use quickly administered screening and intervention materials has been an important concern. Brief interventions have been studied and implemented in many primary care settings. In primary care, brief interventions for alcohol misuse have ranged from a few simple, straightforward comments from the clinician to the patient to several short counseling sessions followed by phone contact. Brief comments to a patient with at-risk or problem drinking might include the clinician stating concerns about the patient's drinking, informing the patient that their current consumption levels are above recommended limits, and recommended the patient reduce or stop drinking [30].

The preponderance of brief intervention trials from the 1980s to present has focused on primary care settings [28,31–34]. One of the largest clinical trials conducted in primary care practices, Project TrEAT (Trial for Early Alcohol Treatment), involved two brief in-person sessions conducted one month apart with each session followed up by a two-week follow-up phone call [34]. Those patients receiving the intervention reduced alcohol use and had fewer hospital days and emergency department visits compared to controls. The effectiveness of the intervention was still significant after four years.

There have been meta-analytic reviews in this subject [35,36]. The general form of the interventions in these studies has included personalized feedback based on the patients' responses to screening questions and untailored (generic) messages to cut down or stop drinking. Meta-analyses of randomized controlled studies have found that these techniques generally reduce drinking in the intervention versus control conditions. Results indicate that, across studies, participants reduced their average number of drinks per week by 13–34% compared to controls. The proportion of participants in intervention condition drinking at moderate or safe levels was 10–19% greater than controls over 12 months.

Brief interventions may also be useful with primary care patients who report symptoms of substance addiction or dependence. Motivational interviewing techniques may help patients accept the need for and become motivated to pursue more intensive treatment for substance addiction. The primary care clinician helps facilitate the referral process to specialized treatment [30].

36.4.2 Alcohol: emergency departments

In addition, a number of brief alcohol intervention trials have been conducted in emergency settings [37–40]. The Emergency Department (ED) is an ideal venue for substance use screening and brief interventions for patients seen for medical conditions and/or injuries. Much of the brief intervention research in the ED has focused on injured patients. This population has often been the chosen focus because studies have found that up to 36% percent of injured patients presenting to the ED had positive blood alcohol concentrations [41,42]. Positive blood alcohol tests have been found in up to 47% of hospital inpatients that have been admitted for trauma [43,44]. Alcohol use is implicated in nearly 50% of all motor vehicle crash (MVC) deaths, suicides, and homicides. An ED study of injured vehicular crash occupants using standard criteria revealed that 23% had a diagnosis of either alcohol addiction or dependence [45], while

a trauma center study demonstrated that 17% of crash victims were alcohol dependent at the time of injury [42]. In addition, rates of driving under the influence of alcohol are increasing, particularly among young adults [46].

The rates of alcohol use and misuse led the American Academy of Emergency Medicine to develop guidelines for the collection of blood alcohol concentrations (BACs) and for alcohol screening in EDs (http://www.aaem.org/). Given the rates of alcohol and drug problems seen in this setting and the strong recommendations to identify these individuals when they present to the ED, there is a need to bridge the gap between screening and assistance with problems including entry into treatment, where appropriate.

Brief interventions in the ED can motivate patients with substance misuse, addiction, and dependence to seek addictions treatment. Taking advantage of a "teachable moment" in which a patient has needed medical care for a substance use-related injury, ED clinicians will provide a brief intervention in the acute care setting, often including referrals and/or follow-up for further treatment. One study found that patients who received a brief intervention in the ED, plus a booster session 7–10 days later, had fewer alcohol-related injuries and problems after one year compared to patients receiving standard ED care [47]. Innovative and time-efficient methods for screening and brief interventions have been developed specifically for use in ED settings [48].

Brief intervention approaches have been used among ED patients admitted to hospital [49,50], and on injured patients in the ED [37,51–55]. A recent meta-analysis of ED studies concluded that ED-based interventions significantly reduce alcohol-related injury but do not necessarily decrease alcohol consumption [40].

36.4.3 Illicit drug use/misuse across medical settings

Although a number of studies address the need for and use of brief interventions for illicit drug use [56–61], there are few published randomized controlled brief intervention trials with illicit substance users. Despite some differences, such as duration of the interventions, promising results have been shown in studies investigating the effectiveness of brief interventions among cocaine, heroin, and amphetamine users from a variety of non-ED based settings [62–65]. For example, Bernstein *et al.* [63], reported that a brief intervention for heroin and/or cocaine users recruited from several walk-in nonemergent clinics (urgent care, women's clinic, and a homeless clinic) that included a motivational intervention session delivered by trained peer educators and a subsequent booster call ten days later, led to a reduction in heroin and cocaine use, and an increased likelihood of abstinence from these drugs at a six-month follow-up visit.

Stotts *et al.* [65] found positive results from a brief motivational intervention delivered to cocaine users in an outpatient detoxification treatment program. Baker *et al.* [62] found an increased likelihood of abstinence from amphetamines among individuals who received either a two- or a four-session brief, cognitive-behavioral therapy-based, intervention. Bashir *et al.* [66] found positive results from a brief intervention delivered by primary care in a small study (n = ∼100). Similarly, positive results have been reported from brief motivational interventions by among community cannabis-dependent adults the Marijuana Treatment Project Research Group [67–69]. Positive outcomes have been reported to persist through the follow-up period, ranging from 3 to 15 months [69]. Bernstein *et al.* [64] found that an ED-based brief "negotiated" interview and an active referral process resulted in a 45% reduction in severity of drug problem among patients who kept their follow-up treatment appointments.

Taken as a whole, the available evidence consistently supports the effectiveness of brief interventions to reduce drug use, however, the research in drug users is still preliminary.

36.5 SPECIAL POPULATIONS

36.5.1 Alcohol: prenatal care

For pregnant women who may be consuming alcohol or have mild to moderate alcohol problems, brief interventions are recommended as an initial step to change drinking behavior. A majority of pregnant women seek prenatal care during the first trimester and brief interventions to reduce or stop alcohol consumption can be well received among the other recommendations for healthy behaviors during pregnancy. Prenatal brief interventions have also been shown to reduce drinking levels among pregnant women most effectively when a partner (generally the father of the unborn child) also participated in the intervention [30]. Brief interventions have been conducted with women who have been identified as drinking during their last pregnancy to motivate reductions in alcohol use for subsequent pregnancies. Women receiving this brief intervention drank significantly less than the control group during later pregnancies [21].

36.5.2 Alcohol: older adults

To date, there have been two brief alcohol intervention trials with older adults. Fleming *et al.* [70] and Blow and colleagues [71] have conducted randomized clinical brief intervention trials to reduce hazardous drinking in older adults using advice protocols in primary care settings. These studies have shown that older adults can be engaged in brief intervention protocols, the protocols are acceptable in this population, and there is a substantial reduction in drinking among the at-risk drinkers receiving the interventions compared to a control group.

The first, Project GOAL: Guiding Older Adult Lifestyles withdrawal [70] was a randomized, controlled clinical trial. The intervention consisted of two, 10–15 minute, physician-delivered counseling visits that included advice, education, and contracting using a scripted workbook. No significant differences were found between groups at baseline on alcohol use, age, socioeconomic status, smoking status, rates of depression or anxiety, frequency of conduct disorders, lifetime drug use, or healthcare utilization. At baseline, both groups consumed an average of 15–16 drinks/week. At 12-month follow-up, the intervention group drank significantly less than the control group (p < .001).

The second elder-specific intervention study, the Health Profile Project [71], contained both brief advice/discussion by either a psychologist or a social worker, as used in the WHO studies, and motivational interviewing techniques including feedback. A total of 452 subjects were randomized in this trial, with over 26% being African American. Follow-up rates of 92% were obtained at the 12-month follow-up. Blow and colleagues found results similar to those of Fleming *et al.* [70] in terms of seven-day alcohol use and binge drinking over the course of the study. These randomized, controlled clinical trials extend the potential of brief interventions from younger at-risk drinkers to even more vulnerable populations of older adults.

36.6   SUMMARY OF BRIEF INTERVENTION TRIALS

Brief motivational interventions have been used successfully in a variety of treatment settings. To summarize the results of brief intervention research, in the 12 studies that met review criteria for the US Preventive Services Task Force (English-language; multicontact behavioral intervention; primary care-based; 6- to 12-month follow-up; nondependent drinkers) [36], participants reduced average number of drinks per week by 13–34% compared to controls. The proportion of participants in intervention condition drinking at moderate or safe levels was 10–19% greater than controls after 12 months.

Brief interventions in the ED also have the potential to reduce costs associated with injury and other alcohol-related health consequences, with research suggesting a savings of $3.81 for every $1 spent [72], with similar findings for primary care samples (i.e., $4.30 for every $1 spent; [73]).

In the primary care trial [34], cost analysis also found that the total cost/patient of the brief intervention was $205 (both clinic and patient costs). The cost advantage between intervention and control group was significant for subsequent medical (p = .02) and motor vehicle (p = .03) events. Overall, this suggested a $43 000 reduction in future health costs for every $10 000 invested in early intervention.

36.7   SBIRT MODEL

Out of all of the research on alcohol and drug screening and brief interventions a comprehensive model for addressing alcohol and drug use in medical settings, SBIRT, has been developed. SBIRT includes screening, brief intervention, and referral to treatment. *Screening* quickly assesses the severity of substance use and identifies the appropriate level of intervention/treatment. *Brief intervention* focuses on increasing insight and awareness regarding substance use and motivation for behavioral change. *Referral to treatment* provides those identified as needing more extensive treatment with access to specialty care, where appropriate [74]. Referral to treatment can take place at any point in this continuum and is based on severity (Figure 36.2).

Screening, brief interventions, and referral to treatment for substance use offers opportunities for early detection, focused motivational enhancement, and targeted encouragement to seek needed substance addiction treatment. This chapter focuses on the use of brief interventions to assist individuals to reduce or discontinue their use of alcohol or drugs or to seek specialized treatment, if needed.

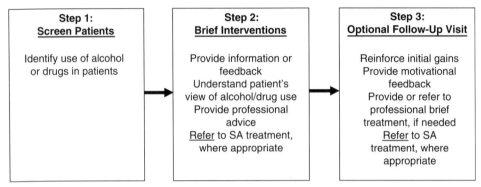

Figure 36.2   The basic steps in conducting SBIRT. *Adapted from: SAMHSA, Committee on Trauma Quick Guide [48]*

36.8   RESEARCH TO PRACTICE: GOALS AND COMPONENTS OF BRIEF INTERVENTIONS FOR CLINICIANS

36.8.1   Goals

The primary goal of a brief motivational intervention is to lessen the potential harm of continued use and misuse of alcohol and drugs. Specific goals will vary by individual characteristics and context, including risky substance use behaviors, consumption patterns, problems related to substance use, and the individual's unique set of circumstances and motivations. Often simple, immediate or intermediate goals are important with brief interventions to help individuals with substance misuse or addiction identify attainable goals and experience success in setting and achieving a goal. Examples include contacting a treatment agency and attending an assessment appointment, decreasing frequency of substance use, participating in a meeting, or stopping use of one substance.

36.8.2   Components and steps of brief interventions

Six key elements have been identified as critical for effective brief interventions. The acronym FRAMES summarizes these six components [15].

- *Feedback* is given to the individual about personal risk or impairment.

- *Responsibility* for change is placed on the participant.

- *Advice* to change is given by the clinician.

- *Menu* of alternative self-help or treatment options is offered to the participant.

- *Empathic* style is used by the counselor.

- *Self-efficacy* or optimistic empowerment is engendered in the participant.

A brief intervention consists of basic components that incorporate FRAMES and remain consistent regardless of the number of sessions or the length of the intervention. These include: introducing the issues in the context of the client's health; screening, evaluating, and assessing; providing feedback; talking about change and setting goals; and summarizing and reaching closure.

Brief intervention protocols often use a workbook containing the steps listed below. Workbooks provide opportunities for the patient and practitioner to discuss sections on drinking cues, reasons for drinking, reasons to cut down or quit, a drinking agreement in the form of a prescription, and drinking diary cards for self-monitoring. Providers can be easily trained to administer the intervention protocol through role-playing and general skills training techniques in educational programs. This approach is nonconfrontational and generally follows motivational interviewing principles as described by Miller and Rollnick [14].

There are nine basic steps in most manualized brief interventions (adapted from [75]).

1. *Identification of future goals for health, work, school, activities, hobbies, relationships, and financial stability.* This step is important because it provides information on what the patient is interested in achieving and can help to target goals of the intervention.

2. *Summary of health habits.* Customized feedback on screening questions relating to drinking patterns and other health habits (may also include smoking, nutrition, tobacco use, seat belt use, safe sex, etc.). This health behaviors information can be derived from screening and pre-assessment questionnaires or from the patient during this session.

3. *Discuss the types of drinkers in the population, where the patient's drinking patterns fits into the population norms for their age group.* The purpose of this is to introduce drinking guidelines (women under 65: no more than one drink/day; men under 65: nor more than two drinks/day; women and men 65 and over: no more than one drink/day or seven drinks/week), the idea that the patient's alcohol use can be related to their physical and emotional health, and that their level of drinking can put them at risk for more health-related problems. This brief discussion may evoke a number of strong reactions from patients (argumentation, minimizing, acceptance, concern, tearfulness, embarrassment, hostility, etc.). It is important to avoid creating additional resistance. It is very important to "roll with the patient's resistance" or reluctance to further examine their drinking behavior in an empathetic manner.

4. *Consequences of at-risk and problem drinking.* Relate this to any potential or ongoing health problem that is currently important in the person's care (e.g., hypertension, gastrointestinal problems, etc.). It should be noted that some patients might also begin to recognize that their drinking is problematic. This may facilitate a change in drinking behavior.

"I'm concerned about your (high blood pressure, sleep problem, abdominal pain) and I think your alcohol use may be a part of the problem".

5. *Reasons to quit or cut down on drinking.* This is a very brief discussion of how changing drinking levels could have important benefits for the individual.

6. *Introduce the concept of standard drinks.* This discussion focuses on the equivalence of alcohol content across various beverage types. This concept provides the context for a discussion of sensible drinking limits.

   Key Point
   One standard drink = 12 ounces Beer or ale; 1.5 ounces shot of distilled spirits; 4–5 ounces wine; 4 ounces sherry; 4 ounces liqueur).
   - When pouring wine, sherry, or distilled spirits, *measuring* is important to ensure that the patient is consuming standard drinks.
   - Alcohol is alcohol. Some patients may think that they do not use alcohol because they "only drink beer or wine". Some view "hard" and "soft" alcoholic beverages as different in their effects.
   - Review standard drinks briefly. Avoid disputes about details regarding the alcohol content of specific beverages.

7. *Negotiated drinking agreement.* Agreed upon drinking limits in the form of an agreement or "prescription" can be negotiated and signed by the patient and the clinician. *Patients take this "prescription" with them when they leave the office.* This "formal" agreement is a particularly effective tool in changing drinking patterns.

A follow-up visit or phone call can help the patient stay on track with any changes in drinking patterns. It also useful for the patient to record any alcohol use on a calendar as a method to keep track of progress and pitfalls for discussion at a follow-up phone call or visit.

Key Points:

- Give guidance on abstinence vs. cutting down. Patients who have a serious health problem or take medications that interact with alcohol should be advised to abstain. Others may be appropriate candidates to cut down on drinking to below recommended limits. Based on clinical judgment regarding the seriousness of the alcohol problem, the clinician will decide if the patient should cut down on use or be abstinent. The provider may say,

"I want you to stop drinking any alcohol for the next month so we can see if your abdominal pain decreases".

OR

"I want you to cut back your drinking to no more than one drink every other day. How do you feel about that?"

This last statement provides the opportunity to negotiate and empowers the patient to be a part of the decision making process. These approaches can also be tests to determine the seriousness of the patient's alcohol problem. If the patient cannot abstain or cut down, it suggests a more serious problem that requires referral and follow-up.

- Complete the *negotiated* agreement/prescription.
- Provide guidance by recommending a low level of alcohol use or abstinence. Remember, you may have to negotiate "up" so start low.
- The prescription-type form contains a space to write what you have negotiated with the patient: (1) stop or cut down on drinking; (2) when to begin; (3) how frequently to drink

- If the patient is reluctant to sign the agreement, try to determine the reason for their reluctance and alleviate their concerns if possible. If they still do not wish to sign, the clinician can sign and give it to the patient for consideration over the next two weeks prior to the follow-up phone call.

- Be sensitive to the patients' reactions including concern, embarrassment, defensiveness, minimization of drinking problems, or hostility. It is very important to "roll with the patient's resistance" or reluctance to further examine their drinking behavior in a matter-of-fact and empathic manner. Avoid disputes over these guidelines and suggest that whether they agree with them or not, ask their patience to continue on to see how alcohol could affect their life.

DRINKING AGREEMENT
Date_____

Start date::_____
Agreement_____
Patient signature_____
Clinician signature_____

---

8. *Coping with risky situations.* Social isolation, boredom, and negative family interactions can present special problems. The patient will need to identify situations and moods that are related to drinking too much alcohol, and to identify some individualized cognitive and behavioral coping alternatives.

9. *Summary of the session.* The summary should include a review of the agreed upon drinking goals and a discussion of the drinking diary calendar to be completed.

36.8.3 Essential knowledge and skills for brief interventions

Providing effective brief interventions requires the clinician to possess certain knowledge, skills, and

Table 36.1 Differences between motivational and confrontational approaches

Confrontational Approach	Motivational Interviewing Approach
• Accept self as alcoholic	• De-emphasis on labels
• Personal pathology – reduces personal choice, judgment, control	• Emphasis on personal choice and responsibility
• Present evidence of problems	• Elicit concern/evidence
• Resistance = "denial"	• Resistance influenced/induced by interviewer
• Meet resistance with argumentation and correction	• Meet resistance with reflection
• Goals and strategies prescribed	• Goals and Strategies negotiated – involvement and acceptance of goals are vital

abilities. Essential skills include: (1) an understanding of the "stages of change" that patients generally move through when contemplating and altering behavior patterns, as well as trying to maintain behavior changes; (2) an attitude of understanding and acceptance; (3) active listening and helping patients address ambivalence; and (4) a focus on intermediate goals.

Five main interactive processes are useful in applying the techniques of motivational intervention and helping patients progress through the stages of change, as described by Miller and Rollnick in their book on principles of motivational interviewing [14]:

• Expressing empathy

• Developing discrepancy

• Avoiding argumentation

• Rolling with resistance

• Supporting self-efficacy

The differences between the motivational approach and more traditional confrontational substance addiction approaches can be seen in Table 36.1.

Through all these processes, the practitioner communicates interest in and acceptance for what the patient is communicating. It is important to avoid behaviors that are not part of active, supportive listening and reflection. These include lecturing, criticizing, labeling, moralizing, or distracting.

To help providers intervene effectively in time-sensitive settings, the NIAAA has developed a booklet and guidelines for intervening [18].

36.9 BRIEF THERAPIES FOR SUBSTANCE USE PROBLEMS

Brief therapies are often used with either patients who are experiencing more consequences from their use, have difficulty changing their substance use behavior, or to promote relapse prevention [76]. The most common brief therapies used in these situations are cognitive-behavioral therapies.

36.10 COGNITIVE-BEHAVIORAL THERAPIES: COPING SKILLS AND RELAPSE PREVENTION

36.10.1 Cognitive-behavior therapy

Cognitive-Behavior Therapy (CBT) is a form of therapy that is centered in the present and focused on the problem at hand. CBT is an integration of principles derived from behavioral theory, cognitive social learning theory, and cognitive therapy. It can be uniquely appropriate for treating substance misuse and addiction, representing a more comprehensive approach that pays particular attention to the behavioral aspects of substance use.

CBT can be used as a primary approach or in conjunction with other therapies, including brief motivational interventions. Modification of both cognitive processes and behaviors is a principal focus. Positive behaviors and thoughts are reinforced, while altering maladaptive behaviors and thoughts is encouraged. Skills training, discussion, and operant conditioning techniques can be used to help clients recognize and change maladaptive behaviors, thoughts, attitudes, and beliefs. With substance addiction clients, identifying "triggers" or cues for substance use, constructing potential alternative courses of action, role-playing or practicing those alternative choices, and other relapse prevention strategies are key parts of cognitive behavioral therapy for alcohol and drug addiction.

Within a cognitive-behavioral theoretical model, individuals who misuse drugs or alcohol lack coping skills or for some reason choose not to use the coping skills they do have. They also generally will develop a set of "expectancies" over time, both based on their own perceived positive experiences of substance use as well as the observations they have made of others using substances in certain circumstances or to cope with difficult emotions.

CBT helps patients identify the situations that are the most likely in which they will drink or use drugs, plan strategies to avoid or cope with these situations, and address more constructively the situations, emotions, and thoughts that contribute to substance addiction.

36.10.1.1   Core elements of CBT

Functional analysis is the process by which clients gain an understanding of the antecedents and consequences of their own substance use. The goal is to increase personal awareness of these factors, provide focus to the cognitive-behavioral interventions designed to address these factors, and promote more beneficial behaviors and decisions in the future. The clinician may help the client identify substance use triggers (places, people, activities, times of day, other situational aspects of use), the thoughts and feelings that are involved in substance use (i.e., boredom, stress, anger, anticipation, sadness), and what behaviors the client engages in when those triggers and/or thoughts and feelings are present (binge drinking, smoking marijuana alone, etc.). A functional analysis will also examine both the positive and negative results of using drugs or alcohol.

Coping skills training takes the functional analysis of both the situations as well as the thoughts and feelings that most commonly precipitate substance use, and helps the client develop skills to cope with these more effectively. Skills and cognitive strategies are taught and practiced, ideally with role-playing and other types of "real-life" skill-building exercises. Positive, constructive feedback helps clients develop self-efficacy and confidence to change substance use behaviors. Examples of specific coping skills include refusal skills, enhancing social supports, increasing pleasant activities, problem solving, anger management, effective communication, and coping with cravings.

Relapse prevention extends client-centered functional analysis and coping skills training to specifically address the concept of anticipating relapse, identifying risky relapse situations, the cognitions and emotions that may occur in the relapse process, and provide clients with strategies to prevent initial lapses and provide relapse management skills if and when a lapse occurs.

36.11   RELAPSE PREVENTION STRATEGIES

(Adapted from Witkiewitz and Marlatt, ed. 2007).

1. *Stop, look and listen.* When a lapse occurs, stop the flow of events (leave the situation, call a supporter on the phone, etc.). Look and listen to what is happening in the situation and how one is responding to the events at hand.

2. *Keep calm.* A lapse can be a mistake or a "slip-up", but does not represent total failure. Think of it as a learning experience, a one-time event that can be used to better avoid similar situations and cope more effectively in the future.

3. *Renew commitment.* Motivation after a lapse can be a challenge. Patients may focus on the negative aspects of the current set-back and need to encouragement to remember past successes, personal goals, and the long-term priorities that led to stopping or decreasing substance use.

4. *Review the situation that led to the relapse.* A functional analysis of the situation that led to the lapse is very useful, including identifying the specific circumstances, people involved, thoughts and feelings preceding and during the lapse, and the positive and negative aspects of the substance use. Targeting the specific circumstantial, cognitive and emotional, and behavioral aspects of the lapse will help the client be more prepared to cope more successfully the next time.

5. *Make immediate recovery plan.* Patients need to have a set of steps to follow immediately after a lapse. Identifying a person to contact, a safe alternative activity, a crisis hotline to call, and/or other "safety nets" will help patients be prepared to keep lapses to one-time events, rather than returning to a pattern of regular alcohol or drug abuse.

6. *Addressing the "Abstinence Violation Effect."* A lapse after a period of successful abstinence or reduced substance use can cause patients to experience a range of negative emotions and thoughts, including guilt, shame, and a sense of failure. Practitioners need to help patients view the experience as one to learn from, examining the factors and feelings that accompanied it, and feel empowered to address similar situations in the future.

36.12 ADDITIONAL BRIEF THERAPIES FOR ADDRESSING SUBSTANCE ADDICTION

(Adapted from SAMHSA Treatment Improvement Protocol Series No. 34: Brief Interventions and Brief Treatments for Substance Abuse [15].

Most brief therapies focus primarily on the individual. There is a growing awareness in substance addiction treatment, however, regarding the importance of family and other significant relationships in terms of motivation and support for behavior change.

36.12.1 Family systems therapy

Family systems therapy applies the principles of general systems theory to families, with specific attention paid to the ways in which family interactions may revolve around alcohol or drug use, how family dynamics may contribute to or interact with substance use, and how family functioning is both influenced by and influences substance use. The goals of this therapeutic approach include identifying the role of substance use in the family and modifying family dynamics and interactions to decrease or eliminate substance use as a critical part of family functioning.

36.12.2 Behavioral couples therapy

Behavioral couples therapy is a therapeutic approach which draws upon a family systems approach, but also has roots in a family disease model (in which substance addiction is viewed as an illness affecting not only the substance addict but also the family system) and behavioral approaches (in which family interactions are viewed as potentially reinforcing substance addiction). The goals of behavioral couples therapy include eliminating alcohol and drug misuse and addiction, engaging the partner/family's support for the patient's efforts to change, and restructuring couple/family's interaction patterns in ways to support long-term behavior change and reducing or abstaining from drug and alcohol use.

36.12.3 Strategic/interactional therapies

Strategic/interactional therapies attempt to identify the patient's strengths and actively create personal and environmental situations in which success can be achieved. Strategic/interactional approaches shift the focus from the patient's weaknesses to strengths. Most commonly implemented with individuals with serious mental illnesses, this type of intervention has utility for individuals with substance addiction.

Strategic/interactional therapeutic approaches often primarily address how a patient's relationships may deter or contribute to substance addiction, shifting power dynamics in relationships,

helping family or other important relationship systems change to support change, maintaining behaviors that control substance use, and addressing relapse factors.

36.12.4 Humanistic and existential therapies

Humanistic and existential psychotherapies use a wide range of approaches to the planning and treatment of substance use disorders. These approaches are built on a belief that individuals have a capacity for choice and self-awareness. Aspects of humanistic and existential approaches include empathy, reflective listening, encouragement of affect, and acceptance of the patient's subjective experiences.

36.13 CONCLUSIONS

The results of research on brief interventions for alcohol problems (and newer work on illicit drug use) indicate that brief interventions can reduce use and/or consequences over at least a one-year period, and in some studies, much longer. The nonconfrontational, respectful approach used in motivational brief interventions and brief therapies is acceptable and generally effective with both younger and older adults. There are research questions that remain regarding the "active ingredients" that are needed in across clinical settings and the appropriate length and complexity of the intervention needed.

Brief interventions are one of a spectrum of approaches to address alcohol and drug use/misuse/addiction. "Real world" implementation strategies to address time and logistical barriers will be the key to their adaptation. The use of screening, brief interventions, brief therapies, and referral to substance addiction treatment, where appropriate provides a state-of-the-art constellation of short, targeted approaches for use by provider and other healthcare staff that form an evidence-based practice for working with a vulnerable population to improve outcomes and manage costs.

REFERENCES

1. Adrian, M. and Barry, S.J. (2003) Physical and mental health problems associated with the use of alcohol and drugs. *Subst. Use Misuse*, **38**, 1575–1614.
2. Barry, K.L., Milner, K., Blow, F.C. *et al.* (2006) Screening for psychiatric emergency department patients with major mental illnesses and at-risk drinking. *Psychiatr. Serv.*, **57**, 1039–1042.
3. Booth, B.M., Kwiatkowski, C.F., and Chitwood, D.D. (2000) Sex-related HIV risk behaviors: Differential risks among injection drug users, crack smokers, and injection drug users who smoke crack. *Drug Alcohol Depen.*, **58**, 219–226.
4. Chen, K., Scheier, L., and Kandel, D.B. (1995) Effects of chronic cocaine use on physical health: a prospective study in a general population sample. *Drug Alcohol Depen.*, **43**, 23–37.
5. Centers for Disease Control and Prevention (2005) Basic statistics. http://www.cdc.gov/hiv/topics/surveillance/basic.htm (accessed 28 February 2008).
6. Johnson, M., Brems, C., and Burke, S. (2002) Recognizing comorbidity among drug users in treatment. *Am. J. Drug Alcohol Ab.*, **28**, 243–261.
7. Grant, B.F. (1995) Comorbidity between DSM-IV drug use disorders and major depression: Results of a national survey of adults. *J. Subst. Abuse*, **7**, 481–497.

8. Kandel, D.B., Huang, F.Y., and Davies, M. (2001) Comorbidity between patterns of substance use dependence and psychiatric syndromes. *Drug Alcohol Depen.*, **64**, 233–241.

9. Vincent, N., Shoobridge, J., Ask, A. *et al.* (1998) Physical and mental health problems in amphetamine users from metropolitan Adelaide, Australia. *Drug Alcohol Rev.*, **17**, 187–195.

10. Garrity, T.F., Leukefeld, C.G., Carlson, R.G. *et al.* (2007) Physical health, illicit drug use, and demographic characteristics in rural stimulant users. *J. Rural Health*, **23**, 99–107.

11. Sanchez, J., Comerford, M., Chitwood, D.D. *et al.* (2002) High risk sexual behaviors among heroin sniffers who have no history of injection drug use: Implications for HIV risk reduction. *AIDS Care*, **14**, 391–398.

12. Zule, W.A., Costenbader, E., Coomes, C.M. *et al.* (2007) Stimulant use and sexual risk behaviors for HIV in rural North Carolina. *J. Rural Health*, **23** (Suppl.), 73–78.

13. US Department of Health and Human Services (1990) Healthy People 2000. National promotion and disease prevention objectives. US Department of Health and Human Services, Public Health Services, 64-183; DHHS Publication no. (PHS) 91-50212, Washington, DC.

14. Miller, W.R. and Rollnick, S. (2002) *Motivational Interviewing: Preparing People to Change Addictive Behavior*, 2nd edn, The Guilford Press, New York.

15. Barry, K.L. (1999) Brief interventions and brief therapies for substance abuse, Treatment Improvement Protocol (TIP) Series No. 34.: US Department of Health and Human Services, Public Health Service, Substance Abuse and Mental Health Services Administration (SAMSHA), Center for Substance Abuse Treatment (CSAT), Rockville, MD.

16. Prochaska, J.O. and Di Clemente, C.C. (1984) *The Transtheoretical Approach: Crossing the Traditional Boundaries of Therapy*, Dorsey/Dow Jones-Irwin, Homewood, IL.

17. Prochaska, J.O. and Di Clemente, C.C. (1992) Stages of change in the modification of problem behavior, in *Progress in Behavior Modification*, vol. **28** (eds M. Hersen, R. Eisler and P.M. Miller), Sycamore Publishing Company, Sycamore, Il.

18. NIAAA (2005) Helping Patients Who Drink Too Much: A Clinician's Guide, Updated Edition; http://pubs.niaaa.nih.gov/publications/Practitioner/CliniciansGuide2005/clinicians_guide.htm (accessed 2 February 2010).

19. US Department of Health & Human Services and US Department of Agriculture (2005) Dietary Guidelines for Americans, 6th edn, US Government Printing Office, Washington, DC.

20. Blow, F.C., Gillespie, B.W., Barry, K.L. *et al.* (1998) Brief screening for alcohol problems in an elderly population using the Short Michigan Alcoholism Screening Test-Geriatric Version (SMAST-G), *Alcohol. Clin. Exp. Res.*, **24**, 1820–1825.

21. Barry, K.L., Caetano, R., DeJoseph, M.C. *et al.* (January 2008) Reducing Alcohol-Exposed Pregnancies. A report of the National Task Force on Fetal Alcohol Syndrome and Fetal Alcohol Effects.

22. Babor, T.F., Kranzler, H.R., and Lauerman, R.J. (1989) Early detection of harmful alcohol consumption: Comparison of clinical, laboratory, and self-report screening procedures. *Addict Behav.*, **14** (2), 139–157.

23. Fleming, M.F., Barry, K.L., and MacDonald, R. (1991) The Alcohol Use Disorders Identification Test (AUDIT) in a college sample. *Int. J. Addict.*, **26**, 1173–1185.

24. Schmidt, A., Barry, K.L., and Fleming M.F. (1995) Detection of problem drinkers: The Alcohol Use Disorders Identification Test (AUDIT). *South Med. Journal*, **88** (1), 52–59.

25. Barry, K.L. and Fleming, M.F. (1993) The alcohol use disorders identification test (AUDIT) and the SMAST-13: predictive validity in a rural primary care sample. *Alcohol Alcohol.*, **2** (1), 33–42.

26. Fiellin, D.A., Reid, M.C., and O'Connor, P.G. (2000) Screening for alcohol problems in primary care: A systematic review. *Arch Intern. Med.*, **160** (13), 1777–1989.

27. Kristenson, H., Ohlin, H., Hulten-Nosslin, M. *et al.* (1983) Identification and intervention of heavy drinking in middle-aged men: Results and follow-up of 24–60 months of long-term study with randomized controls. *Alcohol. Clin. Exp. Res.*, **7** (2), 203–209.

28. Wallace, P., Cutler, S., and Haines, A. (1988) Randomized control trial of general intervention in patients with excessive alcohol consumption. *Br. Med. J.*, **297**, 663–668.

29. Saunders, J.B., Aasland, O.G., Babor, T.F. *et al.* (1993) Development of the Alcohol Use Disorders identification Test (AUDIT): WHO collaborative project on early detection of persons with harmful alcohol consumption - II. *Addiction*, **88**, 791–804.

30. National Institute on Alcohol Abuse and Alcoholism (2005) Brief Interventions. Alcohol Alert No. 66.

31. Chick, J., Lloyd, G., and Crombie, E. (1985) Counseling problem drinkers in medical wards: a controlled study. *Br. Med. J.*, **290**, 965–967.

32. Harris, K.B. and Miller, W.R. (1990) Behavioural self-control training for problem drinkers: Components of efficacy. *Psychol. Addict. Behav.*, **4** (2), 90–92.

33. Babor, T.F. and Grant, M. (1992) Project on Identification and Management of Alcohol-Related Problems. Report on Phase II: A Randomized Clinical Trial of Brief Interventions in Primary Health Care, World Health Organization, Geneva.

34. Fleming, M.F., Barry, K.L., Manwell, L.B. *et al.* (1997) Brief physician advice for problem alcohol drinkers: A randomized controlled trial in community-based primary care practices. *JAMA*, **277** (13), 1039–1045; editorial pp. 1079–1080.

35. Ballesteros, J., Gonzalez-Pinto, A., Querejeta, I., and Arino, J. (2003) Brief interventions for hazardous drinkers delivered in primary care are equally effective in men and women. *Health Psychol.*, **22** (2), 156–165.

36. Whitlock, E.P., Polen, M.R., Green, C.A. *et al.* (2004) Behavioral counseling interventions in primary care to reduce risky/harmful alcohol use by adults: a summary of the evidence for the U.S. Preventive Services Task Force. Clinical Guidelines, American College of Physicians.

37. Blow, F.C., Barry, K.L., Walton, M.A. *et al.* (2006) The efficacy of two brief intervention strategies among injured, at-risk drinkers in the emergency department: impact of tailored messaging and brief advice. *J. Stud. Alcohol.*, **67**, 568–578.

38. Maio, R.F., Shope, J.T., Blow, F.C. *et al.* (2005) A Randomized controlled trial of an ED-based interactive computer program to prevent alcohol misuse among injured adolescents. *Ann. Emerg. Med.*, **45**, 420–429.

39. Monti, P.M., Colby, S.M., Barnett, N. P. *et al.* (1999) Brief interventions for harm reduction with alcohol-positive older adolescents in a hospital emergency department. *J. Consult. Clin. Psychol.*, **67** (6), 989–994.

40. Harvard, A., Shakesshaft, A., and Sanson-Fisher, R. (2008) Systematic review and meta-analyses of strategies targeting alcohol problems in emergency departments: interventions reduce alcohol-related injuries. *Addiction*, **103**, 368–376.

41. Macdonald, S., Wells, S., Giesbrecht, N., and Cherpitel, C.J. (1999) Demographic and substance use factors related to violent and accidental injuries: results from an emergency room study. *Drug Alcohol Depen.*, **55**, 53–61.

42. Soderstrom, C.A., Smith, G.S., Dischinger, P.C. *et al.* (1997) Psychoactive substance use disorders among seriously injured trauma center patients. *JAMA*, **277**, 1769–1774.

43. Soderstrom, C.A., Dailey, J.T., and Kerns, T.J. (1994) Alcohol and other drugs: an assessment of testing and clinical practices in U.S. trauma centers. *J. Trauma*, **36**, 68–73.

44. Rivara, F.P., Mueller, B.A., Fligner, C.L. *et al.* (1989) Drug use in trauma victims. *J. Trauma*, **29**, 462–470.

45. Maio, R.F., Waller, P., Blow, F.C. *et al.* (1997) Alcohol abuse/dependence in motor vehicle crash victims presenting to the emergency department. *Acad. Emerg. Med.*, **4**, 256–262.

46. Blow, F. (1998) Substance abuse among older adults. Treatment Improvement Protocol (TIP) Series No. 26, US Department of Health and Human Services, Public Health Service, Substance Abuse and Mental Health Services Administration (SAMHSA), Center for Substance Abuse Treatment (CSAT), Rockville, MD.

47. National Institute on Alcohol Abuse and Alcoholism (1995) Alcohol Alert 30, http://pubs.niaaa.nih.gov/publications/aa30.htm (accessed 2 February 2010).

48. SAMHSA Committee on Trauma Quick Guide (2007) Alcohol screening and brief interventions (SBI) for trauma patients. DHHS Publications No. (SMA) 07-4266.

49. Dyehouse, J.M. and Sommers, M.S. (1995) Brief intervention as an advanced practice strategy for seriously injured victims of multiple trauma. *AACN Clinical Issues*, **6**, 53–62.

50. Welte, J.W., Perry, P., Longabaugh, R., and Clifford, P.R. (1998) An outcome evaluation of a hospital-based early intervention program. *Addiction*, **93**, 573–581.

51. Gentilello, L.M., Rivara, F.P., Donovan, D.M. *et al.* (1999) Alcohol interventions in a trauma center as a means of reducing the risk of injury recurrence. *Ann. Surg.*, **230**, 473–480.

52. Neumann, T., Neuner, B., Weiss-Gerlach, E. *et al.* (2006) The effect of computerized tailored brief advice on at-risk drinking in sub-critically injured trauma patients. *J. Trauma*, **61**, 805–814.

53. Johnston, B.D., Rivera, F.P., Droesch, R.M. *et al.* (2002) Behavior change counseling in the emergency department to reduce injury risk: a randomized, controlled trial. *Pediatrics*, **110**, 267–274.

54. Longabaugh, R., Woolard, R.E., Nirenberg, T.D. *et al.* (2001) Evaluating the effects of a brief motivational intervention for injured drinkers in the emergency department. *J. Stud. Alcohol.*, **62**, 806–816.

55. Mello, M.J., Nirenberg, T.D., Longabaugh, R. *et al.* (2005) Emergency department brief motivational interventions for alcohol with motor vehicle crash patients. *Ann. Emerg. Med.*, **45**, 620–625.

56. Lang, E., Engelander, M., and Brooke, T. (2007) Report of an integrated brief intervention with self-defined problem cannabis users. *J. Subst. Abuse Treat.*, **19**, 111–116.

57. Compton, P., Monahan, G., and Simmons-Cody, H. (1999) Motivational interviewing: an effective brief intervention for alcohol and drug abuse patients. *Nurse Pract.*, **24**, 27–28; 31–34; 37–38 passim; quiz 48–49.

58. Weaver, M.F., Jarvis, M.A., and Schnoll, S.H. (1999) Role of the primary care physician in problems of substance abuse. *Arch. Intern. Med.*, **159**, 913–924.

59. Greber, R.A., Allen, K.M., Soeken, K.L., and Solounias, B.L. (1997) Outcome of trauma patients after brief intervention by a substance abuse consultation service. *Am. J. Add.*, **6**, 38–47.

60. Samet, J.H., Libman, H., LaBelle, C. *et al.* (1995) A model clinic for the initial evaluation and establishment of primary care for persons infected with human immunodeficiency virus. *Arch. Intern. Med.*, **55**, 1629–1633.

61. Baker, A., Kochan, N., Dixon, J. *et al.* (1994) Controlled evaluation of a brief intervention for HIV prevention among injecting drug users not in treatment. *AIDS Care*, **6**, 559–570.

62. Baker, A., Lee, N.K., Claire, M. *et al.* (2005) Brief cognitive-behavioral interventions for regular amphetamine users: a step in the right direction. *Addiction*, **100**, 367–378.

63. Bernstein, J., Bernstein, E., Tassiopoulos, K. *et al.* (2005) Brief motivational intervention at a clinic visit reduces cocaine and heroin use. *Drug Alcohol Depen.*, **77**, 49–59.

64. Bernstein, E., Bernstein, J., and Levenson, S. (1997) Project ASSERT: an ED-based intervention to increase access to primary care, preventive services, and the substance abuse treatment system. *Ann. Emerg. Med.*, **30**, 181–189.

65. Stotts, A.L., Schmitz, J.M., Rhoades, H.M., and Grabowski, J. (2001) Motivational interviewing with cocaine-dependent patients: A pilot study. *J. Consult. Clin. Psych.*, **69**, 858–862.

66. Bashir, K., King, M., and Ashworth, M. (1994) Controlled evaluation of brief intervention by general practitioners to reduce chronic use of benzodiazepines. *Br. J. Gen. Pract.*, **44** (386), 408–412.

67. Copeland, J., Swift, W., Roffman, R., and Stephens, R. (2001) A randomized controlled trial of brief cognitive–behavioral interventions for cannabis use disorder. *J. Subst. Abuse Treat.*, **21**, 55–64.

68. Stephens, R.S. and Roffman, R.A. (2000) Comparison of extended versus brief treatments for marijuana use. *J. Consult. Clin. Psych.*, **68**, 898–908.

69. Marijuana Treatment Project Research Group (2004) Brief treatments for cannabis dependence: findings from a randomized multisite trial. *J. Consult. Clin. Psych.*, **72**, 455–466.

70. Fleming, M.F., Manwell, L.B., Barry, K.L. *et al.* (1999) Brief physician advice for alcohol problems in older adults: A randomized community-based trial. *J. Fam. Pract.*, **48** (5), 378–384.

71. Blow, F.C. and Barry, K.L. (2000) Older Patients with at-risk and problem drinking patterns: New developments in brief interventions. *J. Geriatr. Psych. Neur.*, **13** (3), 115–123.

72. Gentilello, L., Ebel, B., Wickizer, T. *et al.* (2005) Alcohol intervention for trauma patients treated in emergency departments and hospitals: A cost benefit analysis. *Ann. Surg.*, **241** (4), 541–550.

73. Fleming, M.F., Mundt, M.P., French, M.T., *et al.* (2002) Brief physician advice for problem drinkers: long-term efficacy and benefit-cost ratio. *Alcohol. Clin. Exp. Res.*, **26**, 36–43.

74. SAMHSA (Substance Abuse and Mental Health Services Administration) (2008) http://www.sbirt.samhsa.gov/ (accessed 18 february 2010).

75. Barry, K.L. (2002) Alcohol and drug abuse, *Fundamentals of Clinical Practice*, 2nd edn (eds M. Mengeland W. Holleman), Plenum Medical Book Company, New York, NY, pp. 689–716.

76. Barry, K.L., Oslin, D., and Blow, F.C. (2001) *Alcohol problems in Older Adults: Prevention and Management*, Springer Publishing Co., New York.

37

Treatment outcomes for addictive disorders

Erin L. Winstanley,[1] Shannon K. Bolon,[2] and Marc Fishman[3]

[1] Lindner Center of HOPE, Mason, OH, 45040, USA and Department of Psychiatry and Behavioral Neuroscience, University of Cincinnati College of Medicine, Cincinnati, OH 45221, USA
[2] Department of Family and Community Medicine, University of Cincinnati College of Medicine, Cincinnati OH, 45221, USA
[3] Mountain Manor Treatment Center, Baltimore, MD, 21229, USA and Department of Psychiatry and Behavioral Sciences, Johns Hopkins University School of Medicine, Baltimore, MD 21205, USA

37.1 INTRODUCTION

Drug addiction is essentially a brain disease, but of course drugs' destructive health effects extend beyond the intricate chemical pathways of the brain.

Dr. Nora Volkow,
Director of the National Institute on Drug Abuse

The consequences of untreated addictive disorders are often devastating, like many other chronic multisystem disorders. Treatment, however, is effective and increasingly so as the field advances. While some addiction patients may be frustratingly refractory, addiction patients generally respond well to treatment, with considerable improvements in their functioning and overall health. While the main message is that treatment works, addiction is a complex, heterogeneous condition. Examining the multidimensional outcomes of addiction treatment helps us to understand what works, for whom and under what conditions. It is also important to understand the outcomes of treatment as more than the unidimensional measurement of abstinence alone. A multidimensional approach to outcomes measurement may include: drug use, symptoms, functional impairment, quality of life, and patient satisfaction. Furthermore, the escalating costs of healthcare combined with ongoing economic conditions make it essential to know not only what works, but also what is cost effective. Research on treatment outcomes, cost effectiveness, and real-world implementation should allow clinicians, administrators, and policy makers to identify empirically demonstrated treatments that work and are *practical*.

In this chapter the empirical evidence on the outcomes of alcohol and/or drug treatment are reviewed, as well as cost analysis of the respective treatments. The focus is on treatment and secondary prevention strategies that target individuals that are using, misusing, or addicted to alcohol and/or drugs (excluding tobacco use). Not covered is the effectiveness of primary prevention strategies that target the initiation of alcohol and/or drug use, which is covered elsewhere in this book. The chapter begins with a general overview of addiction treatment outcomes and then discusses outcomes associated with pharmacological and psychosocial treatment. The description of treatments is limited, so as to not be repetitive of other chapters in this book. The chapter concludes with a discussion of treatment outcomes in special patient populations and important factors that can mediate the effectiveness of treatment outcomes.

37.2 DOES TREATMENT WORK?

Just say no.

Nancy Regan

In the past, the effectiveness of addiction treatment was criticized because of perceptions that not enough people achieved lasting abstinence, considered as the only benchmark of success. Under this paradigm, an individual should be cured for the rest of their life after receiving a discrete index episode of addiction treatment. But this paradigm sets a false standard both for clinical practice and for outcomes research. The benchmark for assessing treatment outcomes needs to be more than a unidimensional measure of total abstinence from alcohol and/or drugs, since both dimensional reductions in use short of abstinence and increasing duration of intermittent abstinence are associated with clinically meaningful improvements. Furthermore, defining treatment success as only the achievement of enduring abstinence

following a discrete time-limited intervention is *inconsistent* with our understanding of addiction as a chronic, remitting-relapsing disorder [1].

A unidimensional perspective of addiction treatment outcomes also obscures the importance of the functional impairments that occur as consequences of addiction, and the dimensional improvements following treatment that should be central in defining success. Understanding addiction as a chronic disorder is important because treatment success can now be benchmarked against other chronic conditions, such as asthma and diabetes. And, in fact, addiction treatment does achieve rates of success that are comparable to other chronic diseases [1]. Examples of the low and high range of treatment success are shown in Figure 37.1. Reported effect sizes vary based on definition of success and whether the comparison group was either no treatment or another treatment demonstrated to be efficacious.

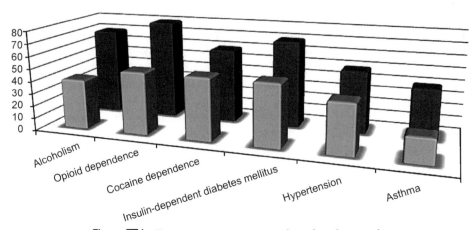

Figure 37.1 Treatment success rates at six and twelve months

37.3 WHAT ARE THE OUTCOMES OF TREATMENT?

A person with mental illness can recover even though the illness is not "cured" …. [Recovery] is a way of living a satisfying, hopeful, and contributing life even with the limitations caused by the illness.

1999 Surgeon General's Report on Mental Health

A health services perspective on treatment outcomes is displayed in Figure 37.2 and incorporates how factors at the organizational and individual levels inform our understanding of how the structure and process of care impact intermediate outcomes (efficacy) and the ultimate goal of improving patient well being. The generally accepted primary outcome of addiction treatment is substantial reduction in alcohol and/or drug use (and abstinence is certainly subsumed as a subset of that outcome), although the field does not yet have consensus on a standard threshold or set of measures. Some examples of dimensional outcomes from the alcohol literature, where there is perhaps better agreement, include: reduction of drinking days, reduction in heavy drinking days (where heavy drinking is defined as more than four drinks per day for men, more than three drinks per day for women), or increased time to major relapse. Another approach is to use more categorical measures, for example, patients addicted to cocaine are more treatment resistant and, therefore, two weeks

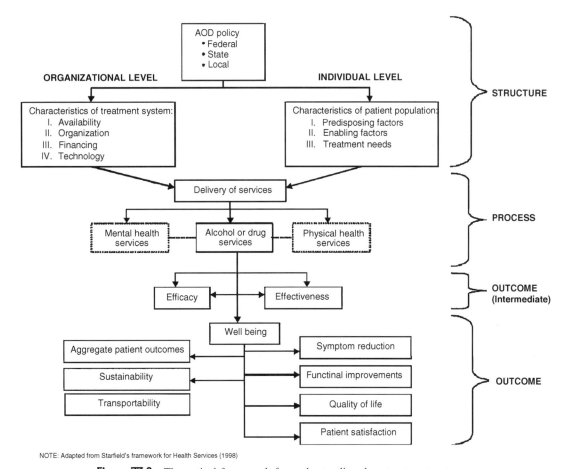

NOTE: Adapted from Starfield's framework for Health Services (1998)

Figure 37.2 Theoretical framework for understanding drug treatment outcomes

of continuous cocaine abstinence is often a primary outcome.

The secondary outcomes of addiction treatment include reduction of symptoms consistent with the Diagnostic and Statistical Manual of Mental Disorders (DSM-IV) alcohol and/or drug abuse or dependence criteria and often include functional impairments that occur as consequences of addiction. These secondary outcomes include improvements in the following functional domains: psychiatric status (e.g., depressive symptoms), employment (e.g., number of days worked in past month), physical health (e.g., comorbid medical conditions or medical consequences of prolonged drug use), legal involvement (e.g., driving under the influence, criminal recidivism), family relationships, and stable housing. In treatment seeking populations, rates of co-occurring alcohol and/or drug and mental health problems range from 70 to 90% [2,3] and these patients generally have lower rates of treatment success [4]. Intravenous drug use is one of the primary modes of HIV transmission in the United States [5]. Drug users, in general, are more likely to engage in risky sexual behaviors that put them at risk for HIV/AIDS, hepatitis, and other sexually transmitted diseases [6]. Treatment effectiveness is demonstrated not only by reductions in direct measures of drug use and primary symptoms of addiction, but also by reductions in co-occurring physical and mental health problems, and improvement in functional domains.

Tertiary outcome measures are more subjective in nature and may include health-related quality of life measures and patient satisfaction. Health-related quality of life (HR-QOL) measures are common across a variety of health conditions and often the same measurement instruments (i.e., Short-Form 12 [7]) are applied to different disease states. Health-related quality of life measures, in general, are subjective measures of how disease states impact an individual's ability to perform the activities of daily living, as well as satisfaction with life [8]. Finally, patient satisfaction is an important outcome measure not only because of how it may relate to patients' willingness to use services and adhere to clinical recommendations,

but also as an integral component of patient-centered care, which was recognized by the Institute of Medicine as one of the six aims of high-quality healthcare [9].

Other important factors that influence treatment outcomes include: (1) stage of disease progression, (2) degree of impairment, (3) substance of choice (including route of administration), (4) target population, and (5) the treatment modality, dose, and setting. Early onset of alcohol and/or drug use, severe impairment resulting from alcohol and/or drug use, and IV route of administration have been associated with poorer treatment outcomes. Often outcomes are tailored to the specific patient population of interest. For example, some treatment interventions may target impairment particularly in alcohol-dependent persons, and an outcome variable of interest could be decreased rates of driving while under the influence. Another example is an intervention for pregnant women with heroin or cocaine dependence with the outcome of increased mean delivery birth weight. Examples of special treatment populations in specific settings that may influence outcomes include criminal justice populations in drug courts, professionals in employee assistance programs, and HIV patients in infectious disease clinics.

Often it can be difficult to compare addiction treatment outcomes across studies because of differences in how outcomes are defined, measured, and follow-up periods. One important example is that some studies may report outcomes for *only* the primary substance of choice rather than other substances. This is an important distinction because the majority of persons with alcohol and/or drug dependence are polysubstance users. In terms of measurement, the gold standard to assess alcohol and/or drug use is a physiologic measure, such as urine analysis, hair testing or breathalyzer. The greater the severity of alcohol and/or drug addiction/dependence in the population of interest, the more likely measurement will need to incorporate strategies to ensure that the physiologic samples are not adulterated (i.e., observed urine samples). However, the costs of physiologic measurement of alcohol and/or drug use can be prohibitive and the clinical research setting may present collection feasibility issues, such as access to a laboratory to validate positive urine analysis test results. On the other hand, self-reports of alcohol and/or drug use have been extensively validated, correlate well with physiologic measures, and are usually acceptable as a reasonable indicator of actual use [10–12].

The gold standard for the ascertainment of categorical diagnosis of alcohol and/or drug abuse or dependence are structured interviews (such as is the Structured Clinical Interview for DSM-IV (SCID) [13]), but, in general, checklists derived from such instruments serve as suitable, simpler substitutes. There are numerous instruments (e.g., Addiction Severity Index, [14]) to assess addiction/dependence symptoms and related functional impairment

applicable to a wide variety of patient populations. More information on screening, clinical and research instruments is provided in Chapter 2.

Another important consideration in evaluating addiction treatment outcomes is the type and intensity of services provided. For example, greater reductions in alcohol and/or drug use are observed in higher levels of care such as inpatient settings and other controlled settings such as prisons or jails. This may be due to the intensity of services provided in these settings, as well as practical constraints, such as patients' limited access to alcohol and/or drugs. The next section expands upon the core components of treatment that are associated with positive outcomes.

37.4   GENERAL EFFECTIVENESS

If we burn ourselves out with drugs or alcohol, we won't have long to go in this business.

John Belushi (comedian, actor, musician)

There are a handful of large-scale studies that include multiple mixed treatment modalities and components, attempting to capture standard clinical care in community-based treatment settings. One of the largest such studies is the Drug Abuse Treatment Outcome Studies (DATOS). The sample included over 10 000 patients across 11 cities in the United States and included inpatient, residential, outpatient, and methadone services. The DATOS study found that treatment reduced drug use irrespective of treatment setting and drug of choice; and the magnitude of the reductions in use were correlated with the length of treatment [15]. A meta-analysis of drug treatment outcome studies estimated the mean effect size of 0.33 for drug use and an effect size of 0.13 for crime when compared to either no drug treatment or minimal drug treatment [16]. Effect size is a standardized mean difference between the treatment and comparison groups that ranges from 0 (no treatment effect) to 1 (high treatment effect). Data from the Drug Abuse Reporting Program (DARP), Treatment Outcome Prospective Study (TOPS), DATOS, and multiple other

studies have found that patients retained in treatment for at least three months have substantially better outcomes. Additional studies have confirmed that reductions in drug use persist long-term [17] and these findings are also applicable to adolescents [18]. A subset of subjects in the DATOS study was followed up five years post-treatment. These subjects continued to show improvement across multiple indicators including decreased substance use, decreased involvement in illegal activities, and increased employment [19]. In this study, positive five-year post-treatment outcomes were again associated with longer treatment duration [19], suggesting a persistent dose-dependent relationship.

The effectiveness of alcohol and/or drug treatment extends beyond drug use and includes improvement in related functional domains. Receipt of alcohol and/or drug treatment is associated with reductions in criminal behavior [15,20], improvements in co-occurring psychiatric and physical health symptoms, improvements in employment [15] or school performance [20], and family/social interactions. Improvements in functional domains do vary significantly depending on the extent to which treatment integrates tertiary services at the facility or uses clinical care managers to coordinate external social services.

As with all chronic diseases, alcohol and/or drugs disorders require comprehensive, coordinated, continuous, patient-centered care. The Chronic Care Model (CCM) for improving chronic disease management, originally created for and adopted in primary care settings, emphasizes the coordination of patient care services from multiple healthcare providers and uses resources at the clinic, health system, and community levels to optimize treatment success [21]. The implementation of CCM principles in a variety of chronic illnesses has been shown to reduce healthcare costs and use of healthcare services in patients with chronic illness [22]. The efficacy of CCM elements have also been evaluated in mental health and alcohol and/or drug treatment and are effective. Extended rehabilitation services [23], individualized counseling [24], long-term medication management strategies [1], and case management [25] improve alcohol and/or drug outcomes. The impact of implementing the complete CCM on alcohol and/or drug treatment remains unknown, but evaluation of individual model elements and emerging clinical consensus suggest that the complete model has potential for even greater benefit.

37.5   SYSTEM-LEVEL FACTORS THAT INFLUENCE OUTCOMES

Although substance abuse is prevalent in most schools, primary care practices, mental health clinics, and criminal justice agencies, there is insufficient training, organization, or reimbursement to screen, assess, and refer those with dependence or abuse disorders to appropriate services.

McLellan and Meyers [26]

There are several system-level barriers to demonstrating the effectiveness of addiction treatment. First, only a very small percentage of those in need of treatment receive it. It is estimated that only 10–33% of people in need of addiction treatment receive services (not enough services, or the right services, but *any* services.) [27–29]. Even if services are available, patients need to be able to pay for those services. In 2009, 48 million Americans lacked any form of health insurance [30] and 25 million Americans were under-insured [31]. Parity legislation became effective in October 2009; it requires that health insurance companies offer the same coverage for behavioral healthcare as medical healthcare. At this time, its impact on use of alcohol and/or drug services is unknown. Secondly, there are high rates of drop out from treatment, both in clinical trials and in real-world clinical settings. Approximately 35% patients complete outpatient publicly-funded treatment [32]. The high rates of drop out from clinical trials can limit the generalizability of findings to only patients who are retained, which further limits our ability to move therapies from bench to bedside. At the systems level, improvement in access to and retention in treatment is vital to ensuring that the effectiveness of treatments are realized by patients suffering from addictions.

As has been demonstrated for other physical health diseases, the coordination of care across multiple treatment systems is associated with better outcomes. For example, treating co-occurring mental health problems and alcohol and/or drug problems is more effective in reducing drug use [33]. Not only can the coordination of care improve treatment outcomes, but there is also evidence that the geographic proximity of services matters. The availability of addiction treatment varies geographically and patients may not be aware of treatment locations. Kessler *et al.* [34] found, in an epidemiological study using a nationally representative sample, that 41% of subjects reported that they did not get behavioral treatment because they did not know where to go for services.

However, not all treatments are as effective as others and in the next three sections the most effective pharmacological and psychosocial treatments are highlighted, as are interventions that target special populations.

37.6   PHARMACOLOGICAL TREATMENT OUTCOMES

It is easy to get a thousand prescriptions but hard to get one single remedy.

Chinese Proverb

Medications are used widely to improve the safety and comfort of detoxification, and hopefully increasing the rates of engagement into ongoing treatment following detoxification. Additionally, anti-addiction medications are being more widely adopted as maintenance therapy for opiate dependence and alcohol dependence, and have been very effective in substantially reducing drug use and improving function. Methadone and buprenorphine are available for treatment of opioid dependence, and the US Food and Drug Administration (FDA) has approved naltrexone (oral and extended-release formulations), disulfiram, and acamprosate for the treatment of alcohol dependence [35]. Unfortunately, medications are not yet available for all drugs of addiction. While there are no FDA-approved pharmacological treatments for cocaine, methamphetamine, or marijuana dependence; there are exciting possibilities under investigation. It is also important to keep in mind that the ability of these efficacious treatments to be fully realized in the community is limited by the availability of clinical staff that are both able and willing to prescribe the pharmacotherapies, as well as limited by the stigma associated with addictions that may make patients reluctant to seek care in these specialty care settings.

37.6.1   Methadone

Agonist replacement therapy with methadone has been widely available for over 40 years, has been repeatedly confirmed as effective, and has become the standard of care for heroin addiction. The outcomes associated with methadone treatment are substantially improved when provided in conjunction with psychosocial counseling and access to other social services (e.g., medical and psychiatric care) [36]. The outcomes of methadone treatment include reduced criminal behaviors and reduced risk of HIV infection [37] and it is highly cost beneficial in respect to reducing criminal costs and the medical costs associated with treating HIV [38,39].

37.6.2   Buprenorphine

The partial agonist buprenorphine has some potential pharmacological advantages over the pure agonist methadone, including lower toxicity in overdose, somewhat less addiction liability, and greater ease of taper. The most commonly used formulation has the antagonist naloxone added (active parenterally, but inactive when used sublingually as intended) to help prevent diversion for injection use. Buprenorphine is effective for opioid dependence and comparable to at least mid-range doses of methadone.

Perhaps more important than its pharmacologic properties, buprenorphine can be prescribed in general medical settings, unlike methadone, which requires complex regulatory licensure in specialized settings. The Drug Addiction Treatment Act of 2000 made pharmacotherapy for opiate addiction available in general substance addiction treatment programs (in contrast to methadone centers) and primary care settings. Physicians are now able to prescribe buprenorphine on a limited basis with the appropriate, simple training and certification [40]. However, some research suggests that the beneficial impact of expanding buprenorphine availability may be limited by physicians' reluctance to serve this patient population [41].

37.6.3   Naltrexone

Studies have demonstrated that naltrexone is a highly efficacious for the treatment of opioid dependence [42–46], but while naltrexone is an effective blockade of the euphoric effects of the drug, the effectiveness is often reduced by patient noncompliance or treatment drop-out. A meta-analysis of naltrexone for opioid dependence found that the effect size varied given treatment retention from 0.13 in studies with low treatment retention to 0.60 in studies with high treatment retention based on specialized compliance enhancement procedures [45]. Extended release naltrexone may have promise for addressing the issue of poor adherence to the oral formulation [47].

For alcohol dependence, multiple studies [42] have shown the effectiveness of oral and injectable extended release naltrexone. The COMBINE study found that naltrexone reduced the number of drinking days (effect size 0.22) and increased time to relapse (hazard ratio 0.72). It also provided evidence that naltrexone can be effective in nonspecialty care settings when combined with medical management [42]. Although the evidence has been more mixed, physicians are also able to prescribe other effective phar-macological treatments for alcohol dependence, such as disulfiram and acamprosate [48].

37.6.4 Promising medications in development

Investigations of potential new medications for addiction is an exciting area of research, both because of the possibility of effecting fundamental biological mechanisms, as well as the prospect of wider dissemination in medical care settings. Promising pharmacotherapies include extended release naltrexone for opiates [47], long acting preparations of buprenorphine (including an implant) for opiates [49,50], topiramate for alcohol [51], immunotherapy vaccination for cocaine [52], slow-release methylphenidate for methamphetamine [53], vigabatrin for methamphetamine [54,55], and dronabinol (THC) for marijuana [56].

37.7   PSYCHOSOCIAL AND BEHAVIORAL TREATMENT OUTCOMES

For me, an area of moral clarity is: you're in front of someone who's suffering and you have the tools at your disposal to alleviate that suffering or even eradicate it, and you act.

Paul Farmer

Various forms of counseling and other psychosocial and behavioral treatments have been confirmed as effective. A recent meta-analysis of 34 clinical trials found that "the average patient undergoing psychosocial interventions achieves acute outcomes better than approximately 67% of the patients in the control conditions"[57]. This study also found that contingency management (CM), cognitive-behavioral therapy (CBT) plus contingency management, cognitive-behavior therapy, and relapse prevention (RP) were effective treatments and specific both to the primary drugs of addiction, as well as polysubstance addiction [57]. The effect sizes of these treatments are displayed in Figure 37.3 and the observed rates of treatment

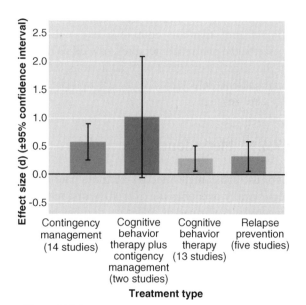

Figure 37.3   Mean effect sizes across treatment types

effectiveness are comparable to other psychiatric treatments [57].

A variety of other "brand-name" manualized psychotherapies have been found to be effective, some of which are based on cognitive-behavioral therapy or relapse prevention. The Substance Abuse and Mental Health Services Administration (SAMHSA) has a registry of evidence-based programs and practices (http://www.nrepp.samhsa.gov/); many of these have been integrated into specialty addiction treatment, and a summary is provided in Table 37.A.1 in Appendix 37.A.

Given that patients with addiction have problems in multiple domains, clinical case management can be an adjunctive intervention to facilitate patients' access to a variety of social services. Case management is associated with reduced drug use, as well as improvement in medical and psychiatric status [58,59]. While clinicians in addiction specialty treatment frequently recommend continuing care counseling or "aftercare" post-treatment discharge (e.g., participation in Alcoholics Anonymous), there is mixed evidence to support its effectiveness [60].

Contingency management, also known as motivational incentives, is a behavioral intervention with very strong empirical support of effectiveness (Figure 37.3), although it has not been extensively integrated into routine alcohol and/or drug treatment. Motivational incentives use positive reinforcement to elicit desired behaviors. The positive reinforcement is frequently a monetary award and the targeted behavior is negative urine test for drug use or treatment attendance. Variants may also add negative consequences as reinforcers, as in motivated stepped care, most frequently used in the context of methadone maintenance treatment [61,62]. In this example, motivated stepped care uses two negative consequences (methadone taper and increased required psychotherapy attendance) in response to either treatment noncompliance or a drug-positive urine test. Unfortunately, motivational incentives have not been widely adopted despite the fact that it may very well be one of the best interventions because it is hard to establish the infrastructure to fund these incentives. Additionally, it can be a difficult from a public

policy perspective to explain why alcohol and/or drug patients should be "paid to get sober" [45].

Information from clinical trials is often difficult to translate into expectations for standard clinical care. Results under artificial research conditions may be better than usual clinical care because of increased resources, exclusion of complex patients from trials, smaller case loads, specialized training and fidelity to standardized protocols. Standard clinical care, however, may be superior because it uses multiple modalities concurrently or sequentially, blending of modalities, multiple treatment episodes or levels of care, and extended durations of treatment.

Attempts to compare modalities of care head to head, as in the prototypical Project MATCH Study for alcohol (Motivational Enhancement Therapy (MET) vs. CBT vs. Twelve Step Facilitation; [63]) and also the Cannabis Youth Treatment study (MET/CBT vs. Adolescent Community Reinforcement Approach vs. Multidimensional Family Therapy for adolescent cannabis use disorders [64]) typically show that patients improve substantially with all high quality treatments examined, without gross differences by modality. Presumably the message is that treatment works, that practitioners should have access to a variety of evidence informed modalities, and that we do not yet have the ability to adequately differentiate the applicability of "pure" types of treatment in what are assuredly heterogeneous treatment populations.

In summary, there are a variety of psychosocial and pharmacotherapy treatments that are effective in the treatment of alcohol and/or drug disorders. There is increasing evidence that the *combination* of psychosocial and pharmacological treatments (if available) is associated with improved outcomes [36,65]. However, there is limited information on how best to combine these treatments. Additional research is needed to better understand how pharmacotherapies and psychosocial treatments impact outcomes, in particular, the sequencing of treatment approaches.

A more comprehensive list of effective treatments, as well as the National Institute on Drug Abuse (NIDA) principles of effective treatment, are included in Appendix 37.A (Table 37.A.2).

The NIDA Clinical Trials Network (NIDA CTN) which conducts clinical trials of both pharmacological and psychosocial treatments in community-based addiction treatment centers to expand our evidence based real-world treatment outcomes, provides an online dissemination library at http://ctndisseminationlibrary.org/.

37.8   OUTCOMES IN NON-SPECIALTY SETTINGS

There's no wrong door to treatment.

Substance Abuse and Mental Health Services Agency
(SAMHSA)

Approximately 41% of behavioral health (mental health and substance addiction) services are received in settings other than addiction specialty care [66]. In recent years, there has been an emphasis on improving the identification and management of alcohol and/or drug problems in medical care settings. Figure 37.4 shows why this is so critical, in that the emergency room has essentially become a behavioral health setting, with patients having substantial rates of substance problems, though unfortunately under-recognized, and even more so under-treated.

Expanding alcohol and/or drug services in medical care settings is advantageous because it allows the opportunity for early identification of problematic patterns of alcohol and/or drug use and it is a venue to deliver services to those who may be less likely to seek care from the addiction specialty care system. For example, there is evidence that the availability of buprenorphine in primary care settings has made pharmacological drug treatment available to patients that were *not* seeking care in specialty addiction settings [67]. Given the stigma associated with addiction, primary care facilities may provide a more discrete opportunity for patients to seek addiction services.

The National Institute on Drug Abuse (NIDA) recommends the "Five As of Intervention" in general medical settings:

ASK – Screening is the first *A* because it asks one or more questions related to drug use.

ADVISE – The second *A* involves strong direct personal advice by the provider to the patient to make a change, if it is clinically indicated.

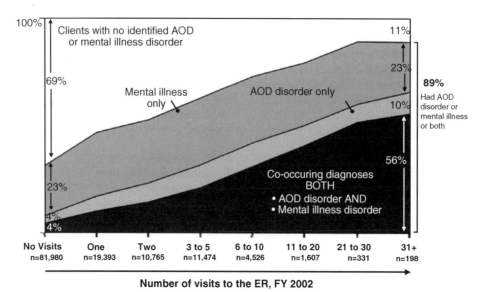

Figure 37.4 Percentage of emergency room patients with behavioral health problems

ASSESS – The third *A* refers to determining how willing a patient is to change his or her behavior after hearing the provider's advise.

ASSIST – The fourth *A* refers to helping the patient make a change if he/she appears ready.

ARRANGE – The final *A* is to refer the patient for further assessment and treatment, if appropriate, and to set up follow-up appointments.

Additional information on how to implement this intervention (including recommended screening questionnaire, brief intervention and supporting documents) into medical settings is available in the resource guide entitled "Screening for Drug Use in General Medical Settings" (available at http://www.drugabuse.gov/nidamed/resguide/).

There are a limited number of interventions that focus on the delivery of addiction services in medical settings. Effective interventions in primary care settings include: screening and brief interventions, relapse prevention, and coordination of multiple specialty services [68]. The majority of these interventions focus on reducing alcohol use and harm-related behaviors associated with alcohol use and misuse. Brief interventions, usually a single 5–10 minute psychoeducation session, can reduce frequency or amounts of alcohol use by 20 to 30% [69]. Screening and brief interventions often also target harmful drinking below the threshold of full DSM-IV criteria for abuse or dependence, while individuals who meet diagnostic criteria should be referred to specialty addiction care. The emergency room should be another opportunistic setting for screening and intervention. The evidence for interventions in the emergency room is mixed, with a meta-analysis of emergency room based interventions showing that brief interventions are not effective in reducing alcohol consumption, although there is some evidence that these interventions reduced alcohol-related injuries [69]. Additionally, there is evidence that brief interventions may not be effective in reducing alcohol use or improving linkages with alcohol and/or drug treatment in medical inpatient settings [70].

37.9 OUTCOMES ASSOCIATED WITH MEDICAL TREATMENT

Health is a state of complete physical, mental and social well-being and not merely the absence of disease or infirmity.

World Health Organization

Medical care settings are not only an alternative venue for the provision of alcohol and/or drug services, but also important in terms of addressing the medical co-morbidities that may be exacerbated by or the consequences of continued alcohol and/or drug misuse and addiction. A study among privately insured patients seeking alcohol and/or drug treatment found that 57% of the patients had a substance addiction related health condition and among those: 27% were psychiatric, 36% were medical, and 37% were both medical and psychiatric conditions [71]. Common medical conditions associated with alcohol and/or drug addiction include: alcoholic liver disease, hypertension, psychiatric problems, and viral hepatitis [71]. These, as well as other medical conditions, have been extensively addressed in previous chapters. In general, outcomes are better when addiction treatment and medical care are integrated [71,72]. Integrated Outpatient Treatment is an intervention that integrates psychosocial services for alcohol dependence in primary care settings and has demonstrated increased rates of alcohol abstinence two years post-treatment initiation [72]. For patients in alcohol and/or drug treatment without a usual source of medical care, receipt of at least two visits with a primary care physician is associated with reductions in alcohol and/or drug use and alcohol and/or drug problem severity [68]. Patients who trusted their primary care physicians and thought they had a comprehensive understanding of themselves had better alcohol and/or drug outcomes [48]. Additionally, research has found that medical care provided onsite at alcohol and/or drug treatment settings or transportation to medical care settings improves rates of medical utilization [73,74].

Much of this type of research has been done in respect to alcohol consumption and highlights both the salutary and deleterious effects of consumption, and the establishment of healthy drinking guidelines. Modest alcohol use can be protective or a risk factor for different disease states depending upon the level of use. For example, a meta-analysis of the effect of alcohol use on diabetes mellitus found that moderate alcohol consumption (less than four drinks/per day) was associated with a lower incidence of diabetes and heavy consumption (more than three drinks per day) was associated with an increased risk [75]. However, even minimal alcohol consumption was associated with an increased risk of breast cancer although this effect was moderated by Body Mass Index (BMI) [76].

The pharmacologic management of pain is of special interest given the risk of dependence associated with opioid medications and the overlap of chronic pain conditions with addiction. A recent meta-analysis of the use of opioids to manage pain found inconclusive evidence to support use of opioids to manage long-term pain and that rates of current substance use disorders in this population (patients with chronic pain) was as high as 43% [77].

In summary, the provision of medical care for patients with alcohol and/or drug disorders has the potential to improve outcomes. As our healthcare infrastructure struggles to better integrate medical and addiction treatment, advances in healthcare information technologies may provide a new mechanism to enhance a coordinated approach to care.

37.10 IS TREATMENT COST EFFECTIVE?

According to several conservative estimates, every $1 invested in addiction treatment programs yields a return of between $4 and $7 in reduced drug-related crime, criminal justice costs, and theft. When savings related to health care are included, total savings can exceed costs by a ratio of 12 to 1.

NIDA, Principles of Drug Addiction Treatment

In the determination of whether a health intervention is cost effective, it is necessary to consider both the analytic approach and define the recipients of the potential cost savings. There are two primary analytic approaches to economic analyses: cost benefit and cost effectiveness. Cost-effectiveness analysis (CEA) relies on one indicator of outcome, which is assumed to be correlated with other potential outcomes [78]. The cost-effectiveness analysis approach has been widely embraced internationally because of the ability to convert cost-effectiveness analysis into an analysis of cost utility or quality-adjusted life years (QALYs). As a general rule of thumb, a cost of $50 000–60 000 per quality-adjusted life year is considered to be a cost effective health intervention [79]. However, this threshold may be significantly lower in low- and middle-

income countries. From a global public health perspective, quality-adjusted life years have been a mechanism to hierarchically categorize the global burden of diseases and incorporate mortality, morbidity, and disability into a single measure [80]. Using this method, alcohol use disorders were identified as a leading cause of disability in middle- and high-income countries around the world [81]. While the cost-effectiveness analysis approach has numerous advantages, some economists have argued that it is problematic because it generally reduces alcohol and/or drug treatment outcomes into a singular measure and the cost effectiveness of a given treatment can yield conflicting results due to which outcome measures were used [78].

The negative consequences associated with addiction can be translated into costs at the individual, family, community and societal levels. The cost savings realized by addiction treatment are largely driven by reductions in: risky sexual behaviors, IV drug use, and criminal behaviors. A California-based study found that on average substance addiction treatment costs $1583 and saves the community $11 487 (costs of incarceration, unemployment, comorbid medical and psychiatric treatments) [82]. Pharmacologic opiate treatment can reduce the risk of HIV/AIDS [37] and health economists have estimated that the average annual cost to treat one HIV-infected person is $157 811 compared to $4000 to provide methadone treatment [38]. Studies suggest that treatment, in general, is cost effective/beneficial. However, there is little data available to compare the cost effectiveness of various treatment approaches. Studies that take a societal perspective on cost and treatments that target patients with cocaine or opioid dependence are more likely to be cost effective/beneficial.

37.11 SPECIAL POPULATIONS

My makeup wasn't smeared, I wasn't disheveled, I behaved politely, and I never finished off a bottle, so how could I be alcoholic?

Betty Ford

37.11.1 Gender

There is some evidence that addiction treatment is equally effective for men and woman [83], however treatment needs and the availability of services may vary. For example, the special needs of pregnant women and the need for childcare for mothers with young children may be significant barriers to receiving services. There is some evidence that women-only treatment programs may be associated with better outcomes when compared to mixed-gender treatment programs [84,85].

37.11.2 Adolescents

Alcohol and/or drug treatment is effective for adolescents and the most established psychotherapies for adolescents include Cognitive-Behavioral Therapy, Motivational Enhancement Therapy, and functional family therapies [86]. Rates of abstinence at one year after treatment initiation were 25 to 62%, depending on the level of care and drug of choice [87]. Family factors may play a more prominent role in moderating treatment outcomes compared to adults, and adolescents who receive drug treatment may experience greater reductions in criminal problems compared to adults [16]. In the authors' anecdotal experience treating adolescents, parental involvement in the treatment process can be an important ingredient in both retaining adolescents in treatment and improving outcomes.

37.11.3 Homeless

Patients that are either homeless or lack a stable residence are particularly difficult to treat. Stable housing may be a prerequisite of abstinence, however many housing shelters prohibit alcohol and/or drug use and even use of addiction pharmacotherapies (e.g., methadone). Furthermore, the homeless patient is more likely to have co-occurring psychiatric and medical disorders that require treatment. Treatments that target homeless populations may have lower rates of success in reducing drug use and may emphasize the achievement of secondary outcomes, such as stable housing or employment.

37.11.4 Minorities

Racial and ethnic disparities in access to alcohol and/or drug services have been well documented [29,88], however the reasons for this disparity are not entirely clear. Treatment needs to be culturally competent in terms of race, ethnicity, sexual identity, and religion. Treatment interventions that address and tailor their programming to the sociocultural needs of their patient population will likely experience better outcomes. For example, the lack of multilingual clinical staff may be a treatment barrier for patients with English as a second language and the involvement of families may vary culturally.

37.11.5 Criminal justice populations

Treatment outcomes for patients involved in the criminal justice system usually incorporate reductions in criminal behaviors as a primary outcome measure, for example decreased rates of re-arrest or return to prison while on probation. Specialized interventions that may improve effectiveness in this population include tight linkage of criminal justice sanctions and reprieves to treatment progress in such settings as drug courts, treatment in controlled criminal justice environments "behind the walls," and close coordination and linkages to community treatment and resources that support community re-integration on release from prison.

37.12 CONCLUSIONS

....it would seem appropriate to cease asking whether treatment for drug abuse is effective and begin asking instead how treatment can be improved and how it can be tailored to the needs of different types of clients.

Prendergast, Podus, Chang and Urada [16]

The outcomes of alcohol and/or drug treatment are more than the achievement of abstinence and incorporate a multidimensional approach that is consistent with our understanding of addiction as a chronic, remitting-relapsing disorder. The most frequently used outcome measures include: drug use, treatment retention, symptoms, functional impairment, quality of life and patient satisfaction.

Treatment outcomes are moderated by a variety of individual, organizational, and systems-level factors. Individual-level factors include: (1) stage of disease progression, (2) degree of impairment, (3) substance of choice (including route of administration), and (4) target population. Organizational-level factors such as treatment modality, dose, setting, and the coordination of tertiary services are also important. And, finally, federal and state policies impact outcomes, for example through prescription regulations that promote the broad availability of buprenorphine treatment, insurance regulations that encourage treatment access (for example through mandating coverage parity), reimbursement strategies that encourage screening and treatment in primary care settings, and overall allocation of resources to expand treatment capacity.

At the population level, the effectiveness of empirically-demonstrated interventions are not fully realized because of the low rates of treatment access and retention in treatment. Less than two in three adults who may need alcohol and/or drug treatment access treatment [26] and approximately one-third of patients drop out of treatment early [57]. A significant number of patients receive treatment outside of the addiction specialty system. Through better identification of alcohol and/or drug problems in medical settings, clinicians have the potential to reduce the significant unmet need for addiction services and provide an alternative "door" to treatment. Effective interventions in primary care settings include: screening and brief interventions, relapse prevention, and coordination of multiple specialty services.

Overall, treatment works and it is cost-effective/ beneficial. The efficacy of numerous pharmacological and psychotherapies are comparable to treatments for chronic medical conditions and other nonalcohol and/or drug psychiatric disorders. Additional research is needed to better understand the optimal sequence of delivering and combining these therapies, as well as to establish the incremental cost effectiveness of specific therapies. Therapeutic optimism is certainly warranted, as clinical improvement is the rule rather than the exception when substance use disorders are identified and treated, and the field is in a period of exciting new investigation and discovery.

APPENDIX 37.A NIDA PRINCIPLES OF EFFECTIVE TREATMENT

No single treatment is appropriate for all individuals. Matching treatment settings, interventions, and services to each individual's particular problems and needs is critical to his or her ultimate success in returning to productive functioning in the family, workplace, and society.

Treatment needs to be readily available. Because individuals who are addicted to drugs may be uncertain about entering treatment, taking advantage of opportunities when they are ready for treatment is crucial. Potential treatment applicants can be lost if treatment is not immediately available or is not readily accessible.

Effective treatment attends to multiple needs of the individual, not just his or her drug use. To be effective, treatment must address the individual's drug use and any associated medical, psychological, social, vocational, and legal problems.

An individual's treatment and services plan must be assessed continually and modified as necessary to ensure that the plan meets the person's changing needs. A patient may require varying combinations of services and treatment components during the course of treatment and recovery. In addition to counseling or psychotherapy, a patient at times may require medication, other medical services, family therapy, parenting instruction, vocational rehabilitation, and social and legal services. It is critical that the treatment approach be appropriate to the individual's age, gender, ethnicity, and culture.

Remaining in treatment for an adequate length of time is critical for treatment effectiveness. The appropriate duration for an individual depends on his or her problems and needs. Research indicates that for most patients, the threshold of significant improvement is reached at about three months in treatment. After this threshold is reached, additional treatment can produce further progress toward recovery. Because people often leave treatment prematurely, programs should include strategies to engage and keep patients in treatment.

Counseling (individual and/or group) and other behavioral therapies are critical components of effective treatment for addiction. In therapy, patients address issues of motivation, build skills to resist drug use, replace drug-using activities with constructive and rewarding nondrug-using activities, and improve problem solving abilities. Behavioral therapy also facilitates interpersonal relationships and the individual's ability to function in the family and community.

Medications are an important element of treatment for many patients, especially when combined with counseling and other behavioral therapies. Methadone and levo-alpha-acetylmethadol (LAAM) are very effective in helping individuals addicted to heroin or other opiates stabilize their lives and reduce their illicit drug use. Naltrexone is also an effective medication for some opiate addicts and some patients with co-occurring alcohol dependence. For persons addicted to nicotine, a nicotine replacement product (such as patches or gum) or an oral medication (such as bupropion) can be an effective component of treatment. For patients with mental disorders, both behavioral treatments and medications can be critically important.

Addicted or drug-abusing individuals with coexisting mental disorders should have both disorders treated in an integrated way. Because addictive disorders and mental disorders often occur in the same individual, patients presenting for either condition should be assessed and treated for the co-occurrence of the other type of disorder.

Medical detoxification is only the first stage of addiction treatment and by itself does little to change long-term drug use. Medical detoxification safely manages the acute physical symptoms of withdrawal associated with stopping drug use. While detoxification alone is rarely sufficient to help addicts achieve long-term abstinence, for some individuals it is a strongly indicated precursor to effective drug addiction treatment.

Treatment does not need to be voluntary to be effective. Strong motivation can facilitate the treatment process. Sanctions or enticements in the family, employment setting, or criminal justice system can increase significantly both treatment entry and retention rates and the success of drug treatment interventions.

Possible drug use during treatment must be monitored continuously. Lapses to drug use can occur during treatment. The objective monitoring of a patient's drug and alcohol use during treatment, such as through urinalysis or other tests, can help the patient withstand urges to use drugs. Such monitoring also can provide early evidence of drug use so that the individual's treatment plan can be adjusted. Feedback to patients who test positive for illicit drug use is an important element of monitoring.

Treatment programs should provide assessment for HIV/AIDS, hepatitis B and C, tuberculosis, and other infectious diseases, and counseling to help patients modify or change behaviors that place themselves or others at risk of infection. Counseling can help patients avoid high-risk behavior. Counseling also can help people who are already infected manage their illness.

Recovery from drug addiction can be a long-term process and frequently requires multiple episodes of treatment. As with other chronic illnesses, relapses to drug use can occur during or after successful treatment episodes. Addicted individuals may require prolonged treatment and multiple episodes of treatment to achieve long-term abstinence and fully restored functioning. Participation in self-help support programs during and following treatment often is helpful in maintaining abstinence.

Table 37.A.1 SAMHSA's evidence-based programs and practices

Intervention	Description	Target Population
A Woman's Path to Recovery	12 group sessions, 90-minute session durations	Women with substance use disorders
Adolescent Community Reinforcement Approach	Individual behavioral intervention	Adolescents and their family members
Alcohol Behavioral Couples Therapy	Outpatient therapy based on cognitive-behavioral therapy	Individual's with alcohol use disorder and their intimate partners
Behavioral Couples Therapy for Alcoholism and Drug Addiction	Outpatient therapy based on cognitive-behavioral therapy	Individual's with substance use disorder and their intimate partners
Brief Marijuana Dependence Counseling	12-weeks	Individuals with marijuana dependence
Brief Strategic Family Therapy	12–16 family sessions	Adolescents with substance use disorders and their family members
Brief Strengths-Based Case Management for Substance Addiction	One-to-one social service intervention, 90 min sessions, maximum 5 visits	All
Chestnut Health Systems–Bloomington Adolescents Outpatient and Intensive Outpatient Treatment Model	Blended theoretical framework (Rogerian, behavioral, cognitive and reality)	Adolescents
Cocaine-Specific Coping Skills Training	8 individual or group, 45-minute session duration	Individuals with cocaine dependence
Customized Employment Supports	Vocational services, individual sessions with vocational rehabilitation counselor	Unemployed individuals with substance use disorders
Drinker's Check-up	Computer-based brief intervention to reduce alcohol use and negative consequences of use	Individuals using alcohol
Family Behavior Therapy	Based on Community Reinforcement Approach, 15 sessions over 6 mo	Individuals with substance use disorders and their families
Forever Free	Blended approach including counseling, 12-step programs, and educational seminars	Incarcerated women with substance use disorders
Friends Care	Aftercare program	Individuals who are mandated to outpatient treatment as part of their parole or probation
Healthy Workplace	Prevention of alcohol and/or drug dependence, based in workplace, small group sessions with videos and educational materials	Individuals using substances
Interim Methadone Maintenance	Methadone plus emergency counseling	Individual's on a waiting list (>14 d) for methadone treatment
Living in Balance	Emphasizes relapse prevention, 1.5–2 h psychoeducational and experiential training sessions	All

(continued)

Table 37.A.1 (*Continued*)

Intervention	Description	Target Population
Matrix Model	Mixed approach incorporates relapse prevention groups, individual counseling, and urine testing, usually 16 weeks	Individuals with stimulant dependence
Moral Reconation Therapy	Cognitive-behavioral approach to reduce criminal recidivism, 1–2 group session per week for 6 mo	Adolescent and adult criminal offenders
Motivational Enhancement Therapy (MET)	Based on Motivational Interviewing, nonconfrontational manner to elicit behavior change, address patients' ambivalence about achieving abstinence	All
Motivational Interviewing (MI)	Goal-directed, client-centered approach to resolve patients' ambivalence about treatment	All
Multidimensional Family Therapy (MFT)	Comprehensive and multisystemic family-based approach, 12–16 session, 60–90 min duration per session	Adolescents
Network Therapy	Incorporates members of patients' social support network, incorporates CBT and community reinforcement techniques, twice weekly for 12–14 wk	All
Parenting with Love and Limits	Combined group and family therapy	Children and adolescents with co-occurring mental health and substance use disorders
Pathways' Housing First Program	Needs-based approach that uses an assertive community treatment team, does not require sobriety nor psychiatric treatment	Homeless individuals with severe mental illness and substance use disorders
Phoenix Academy	Therapeutic Community, residential treatment program integrated with on-site school	Adolescents with co-occurring mental health and substance use disorders
Prize Incentives Contingency Management for Substance Addiction	Awards abstinence and treatment compliance, usually incorporates urine testing	All
Project SUCCESS	Prevent and reduce substance use among students	Adolescents in school
Recovery Training and Self-Help	Group aftercare program, incorporates vocational training	Individuals with opioid dependence
Reinforcement-Based Therapeutic Workplace	Voucher-based abstinence reinforcement therapy, incorporates urine screening and occurs within a therapeutic workplace	Individuals on methadone maintenance therapy

Relapse Prevention Therapy	Behavioral self-control program that enhances coping skills to prevent relapse	All
Seeking Safety	Flexible approach focusing on coping skills and psychoeducation	Patients with a history of trauma and substance use disorders
Service Outreach and Recovery Program	Multicomponent program usually at soup kitchens and incorporates peer advocates	Indigent and residentially unstable individuals with substance use disorders
Supportive-Expressive Psychotherapy	Form of focal psychotherapy	Individuals with opioid and cocaine use disorders
Texas Christian University Mapping-Enhanced Counseling	Incorporates graphic visualization tools to improve patient/counselor communication	All
Teen Intervene	Early intervention program that integrates MET and CBT	Adolescents that are using substances, but not dependent
Trauma Recovery and Empowerment Model	Group-based manual-driven, 24–29 sessions	Women with a history of physical or sexual abuse
Twelve-Step Facilitation Therapy	Brief counseling sessions based on principles of the 12-step fellowships, manualized	All

Table 37.A.2   Summary of Cochrane reviews on alcohol and/or drug treatments

Therapy	Description	Year	Sample Size	Conclusion
Alcohol				
Pharmacological (Detoxification)	Anticonvulsants	2005	48	Inconclusive; trend towards efficacy
Pharmacological (Detoxification)	Benzodiazepines	2005	57	Effective treatment, particularly in respect to reducing alcohol withdrawal seizures
Pharmacological	Opioid antagonists (naltrexone, nalmefene)	2005	29	Efficacy demonstrated for naltrexone, but not for nalmefene; naltrexone plus psychosocial treatment may be superior
Pharmacological	Psychotropic analgesic nitrous oxide (PAN)	2005	5	Same effectiveness as sedatives for managing acute alcohol withdrawal; more trials needed
Pharmacological	Topiramate	2008	3	Effective in improving drinking outcomes, quality of life and safety
Pharmacological	Pregnant woman	2009	0	No studies met inclusion criteria
Psychosocial	12-step programs (e.g., Alcoholics Anonymous)	2006	8	Inconclusive due to the limited number of efficacy studies
Psychosocial	Brief interventions in primary care settings	2007	21	Significant reduction in alcohol consumption in men, not in women.
Psychosocial	Primary prevention programs	2002	56	Strengthening Families Program (SFP) showed promise; further research needed
Psychosocial	Psychosocial interventions for pregnant women	2008	0	No studies met inclusion criteria
Psychosocial	Brief interventions in general hospital wards	2009	11	Inconclusive, trend towards reduction in alcohol use
Psychosocial	Social norms interventions	2009	22	Web/computer feedback and individual face-to-face probably effective
Psychosocial or Educational Intervention	Pregnant women or women planning to become pregnant	2009	4	Trend towards reduction in alcohol use, however insufficient data
Alcohol and Drugs				
Psychosocial	Case management	2007	15	Increased linkage to services shown in 10 studies; inconclusive regarding substance use reduction
Psychosocial	Therapeutic communities	2005	7	Inconclusive

Home Visits	Home visits for women who are pregnant or postpartum and using alcohol and/or drugs	2005	6	Insufficient evidence
Amphetamines				
Pharmacological	Fluoxetine, amlodipine, imipramine and desipramine	2001	4	Insufficient evidence
Pharmacological	Antipsychotic drug injections	2001	0	No trials found
Pharmacological	Variety of treatments	2001	2	Some benefits with amineptine to treat withdrawal; amineptine has been withdrawn from the market; more research needed
Pharmacological	Amineptine, mirtazapine	2009	4	Not effective
Pharmacological (Amphetamine psychosis)	Antipsychotic drugs (olanzapine, haloperidol)	2009	1	Evidence of efficacy, olanapine may be superior to haloperidol, more research needed
Benzodiazepines				
Pharmacological	Benzodiazepine dependence management	2006	8	Benzodiazepines used for pharmacological purposes should be decreased gradually; possible indication of carbamazepine for withdrawal treatment
Cannabis				
Psychosocial	Psychosocial interventions in outpatient settings	2006	6	Reductions in cannabis use and dependence symptoms, more research needed
Cocaine				
Alternative	Auricular acupuncture	2006	7	No evidence of efficacy, although additional research may be warranted
Pharmacological	Anticonvulsants	2008	15	Inconclusive
Pharmacological	Antidepressants	2007	18	No reduction in use; poor med compliance
Pharmacological	Antipsychotics	2007	7	Inconclusive; small trials
Pharmacological	Dopamine agonists (amantadine, bromocriptine, pergolide)	2003	17	No demonstrated effectiveness
Pharmacological	Carbamazepire	2002	5	No current evidence of efficacy
Cocaine and Amphetamines				
Psychosocial	Various psychosocial interventions	2007	27	Inconclusive overall; possible indication of contingency management in reduction of cocaine use and treatment retention

(continued)

Table 37.A. 2 (*Continued*)

Therapy	Description	Year	Sample Size	Conclusion
Drugs (un-specified)				
Psychosocial	Interventions in nonschool settings	2005	17	Inconclusive; more research needed
Psychosocial	Psychosocial interventions for pregnant women	2007	9	Contingency management increased retention; not enough evidence to support Motivational Interviewing
Psychosocial	School-based prevention	2005	32	Skills-based programs deter marijuana and heroin use
Treatment Setting	Interventions in the courts, secure establishments, and the community	2006	24	Limited evidence that therapeutic communities with aftercare reduced use and criminal activity
Heroin				
Pharmacological	Heroin maintenance	2005	4	Inconclusive
Pharmacological	LAAM versus methadone maintenance	2002	18	LAAM better than methadone in lessening use; evidence regarding safety inconclusive
Methaqualone				
Pharmacological or Psychosocial	Variety of treatments	2005	0	No suitable trials identified
Opioids				
Pharmacological (Detoxification)	Alpha2 adrenergic agonists (lofexidine, clonidine, methadone)	2009	24	Efficacy equivalent to methadone, fewer side effects with methadone
Pharmacological	Buprenorphine, clonidine, methadone	2006	18	Increased retention with buprenorphine when compared with clonidine; only slightly better symptom management when compared with methadone
Pharmacological	Buprenorphine, methadone	2007	24	Methadone more effective in reducing heroin use
Pharmacological	Methadone versus buprenorphine versus oral slow morphine for pregnant women	2008	3	None superior; more research needed
Pharmacological	Tapered doses of methadone	2005	16	Decreased withdrawal severity
Pharmacological (Maintenance)	Methadone comparing high (60–100 mg/day) to low (<60 mg/day)	2003	21	Higher dose associated with decreased opioid use, cocaine use, and better treatment retention
Pharmacological (Maintenance)	Methadone versus no replacement therapy	2009	11	Decrease in heroin use and increase in treatment retention

Category	Treatment	Year	N	Finding
Pharmacological (Detoxification)	Opioid antagonists under heavy sedation	2006	6	No support for this treatment; significant risk of adverse events
Pharmacological (Detoxification)	Opioid antagonists with minimal sedation	2006	9	Feasible with a high level of medical monitoring, additional research needed
Pharmacological (Maintenance)	Naltrexone	2003	11	Trend towards efficacy, however more research needed
Pharmacological (Detoxification)	Oral substitution treatment	2007	33	Lowers injection-related HIV risk, but not sex-related risk
Pharmacological	Sustained-release naltrexone	2008	1	Insufficient evidence, however high dose increased days in treatment; adverse events at injection site frequent
Pharmacological (Maintenance)	Buprenorphine versus methadone	2008	24	Buprenorphine is effective, but methadone at adequate dosage is superior
Pharmacological (Maintenance)	Oral naltrexone	2006	10	Trend towards reduction in heroin use, more research needed
Psychosocial and Pharmacological (Detoxification)	Psychosocial + pharmacological detoxification	2008	9	Decreased rates of opiate use and improved treatment compliance
Psychosocial and Pharmacological (Maintenance)	Psychosocial treatment + methadone	2004	12	Adding psychosocial therapy to methadone maintenance has greater reductions in opiate use than methadone maintenance alone
Psychosocial and Pharmacological (Maintenance)	Psychosocial treatment + agonist maintenance (comparing methadone, buprenorphine, clonidine and lofexidine)	2008	28	Greater reductions in use when combined
Pharmacotherapy (Detoxification)	Comparing methadone, buprenorphine, clonidine and lofexidine	2009	22	Buprenorphine more effective than clonidine and lofexidine; buprenorphine has some advantageous over methadone
Psychosocial	Psychosocial treatment without pharmacological treatment	2004	5	Insufficient evidence
Treatment Setting	Inpatient versus Outpatient settings for detoxification	2005	1	Inconclusive

REFERENCES

1. McLellan, A.T., Lewis, D.C., O'Brien, C.P., and Kleber, H.D. (2000) Drug dependence, a chronic medical illness: implications for treatment, insurance, and outcomes evaluation. *JAMA*, **284** (13), 1689–1695.

2. Grilo, C.M., Becker, D.F., Fehon, D.C. *et al.* (1996) Conduct disorder, substance use disorders, and coexisting conduct and substance use disorders in adolescent inpatients. *Am. J. Psychiatry*, **153** (7), 914–920.

3. Roehrich, H. and Gold, M.S. (1986) Diagnosis of substance abuse in an adolescent psychiatric population. *Int. J. Psychiat. Med.*, **16** (2), 137–143.

4. King, R.D., Gaines, L.S., Lambert, E.W. *et al.* (2000) The co-occurrence of psychiatric and substance use diagnoses in adolescents in different service systems: frequency, recognition, cost, and outcomes. *J. Behav. Health Serv. Res.*, **27** (4), 417–430.

5. Dondero, T., Allen, D.M., McCray, E. *et al.* (1991) Injected drug abuse: the driving force for much of the US HIV epidemic. Int Conf. AIDS, 7, 385.

6. Winstanley, E.L., Gust, S.W., and Strathdee, S.A. (2006) Drug abuse and HIV/AIDS: international research lessons and imperatives. *Drug Alcohol Depend.*, **82** (Suppl. 1), S1–S5.

7. Ware, J. Jr., Kosinski, M., and Keller, S.D. (1996) A 12-Item Short-Form Health Survey: construction of scales and preliminary tests of reliability and validity. *Med. Care*, **34** (3), 220–233.

8. Fayers, P.M. (2000) *Quality of Life: Assessment, Analysis and Interpretation*, John Wiley & Sons, Ltd, Chichester.

9. Institute of Medicine (US). Committee on Crossing the Quality Chasm: Adaptation to Mental Health and Addictive Disorders (2006) *Improving the Quality of Health Care for Mental and Substance-Use Conditions*, National Academies Press, Washington, DC.

10. Ensminger, M.E., Anthony, J.C., and McCord, J. (1997) The inner city and drug use: initial findings from an epidemiological study. *Drug Alcohol Depend.*, **48** (3), 175–184.

11. Gfroerer, J. (1985) Influence of privacy on self-reported drug use by youths. *NIDA Res. Monogr.*, **57**, 22–30.

12. Gfroerer, J., Eyerman, J., and Chromy, J. (2002) Redesigning an Ongoing National Household Survey: Methodological Issues, Substance Abuse and Mental Health Services Administration. Rockville, MD.

13. First, M., Spitzer, R.L., Gibbon, M., and Williams, J. (2002) Structured Clinical Interview for DSM-IV Axis I Disorders, Patient Edition (Version 2.0 edn) Biometrics Department, New York State Pscyhiatric Institute, New York, NY.

14. McLellan, A.T., Luborsky, L., Woody, G.E., and O'Brien, C.P. (1980) An improved diagnostic evaluation instrument for substance abuse patients. The Addiction Severity Index. *J. Nerv. Ment. Dis.*, **168** (1), 26–33.

15. Hubbard, R.L., Craddock, S.G., Flynn, P.M. *et al.* (1997) Overview of 1-year follow-up outcomes in the drug abuse treatment outcome study (DATOS). *Psychol. Addict. Behav.*, **11** (4), 261–278.

16. Prendergast, M.L., Podus, D., Chang, E., and Urada, D. (2002) The effectiveness of drug abuse treatment: a meta-analysis of comparison group studies. *Drug Alcohol Depend.*, **67** (1), 53–72.

17. Gossop, M., Marsden, J., Stewart, D., and Rolfe, A. (1999) Treatment retention and 1 year outcomes for residential programmes in England. *Drug Alcohol Depend.*, **57** (2), 89–98.

18. Brown, S.A., D'Amico, E.J., McCarthy, D.M., and Tapert, S.F. (2001) Four-year outcomes from adolescent alcohol and drug treatment. *J. Stud. Alcohol.*, **62** (3), 381–388.

19. Hubbard, R.L., Craddock, S.G., and Anderson, J. (2003) Overview of 5-year follow-up outcomes in the drug abuse treatment outcome studies (DATOS). *J. Subst. Abuse Treat.*, **25** (3), 125–134.

20. Hser, Y.I., Grella, C.E., Hubbard, R.L. *et al.* (2001) An evaluation of drug treatments for adolescents in 4 US cities. *Arch. Gen. Psychiatry*, **58** (7), 689–695.

21. Bodenheimer, T., Wagner, E.H., and Grumbach, K. (2002) Improving primary care for patients with chronic illness. *JAMA*, **288** (14), 1775–1779.

22. Bodenheimer, T., Wagner, E.H., and Grumbach, K. (2002) Improving primary care for patients with chronic illness: the chronic care model, Part 2. *JAMA*, **288** (15), 1909–1914.

23. McKay, J.R. (2005) Is there a case for extended interventions for alcohol and drug use disorders? *Addiction*, **100** (11), 1594–1610.

24. McKay, J.R., Alterman, A.I., Cacciola, J.S. *et al.* (1999) Continuing care for cocaine dependence: comprehensive 2-year outcomes. *J. Consult. Clin. Psychol.*, **67** (3), 420–427.

25. McLellan, A.T., Weinstein, R.L., Shen, Q. *et al.* (2005) Improving continuity of care in a public addiction treatment system with clinical case management. *Am. J. Addict.*, **14** (5), 426–440.

26. McLellan, A.T. and Meyers, K. (2004) Contemporary addiction treatment: a review of systems problems for

adults and adolescents. *Biol. Psychiatry*, **56** (10), 764–770.

27. Epstein, J.F. (2002) Substance Dependence, Abuse and Treatment: Findings from the 2000 National Household Survey on Drug Abuse, NHSDA Series A-16, DHHS Publ No SMA 02-3642, US Department of Health and Human Services, Rockville, MD.

28. Kessler, R.C., Demler, O., Frank, R.G. *et al.* (2005) Prevalence and treatment of mental disorders, 1990 to 2003. *N. Engl. J. Med.*, **352** (24), 2515–2523.

29. Winstanley, E.L., Steinwachs, D.M., Ensminger, M.E. *et al.* (2008) The association of self-reported neighborhood disorganization and social capital with adolescent alcohol and drug use, dependence, and access to treatment. *Drug Alcohol Depend.*, **92** (1–3), 173–182.

30. Commonwealth Fund Commission (2009) Executive Summary: The Path to a High Performance, US Health System.

31. Schoen, C., Collins, S.R., Kriss, J.L., and Doty, M.M. (2008) How many are underinsured? Trends among U. S. adults, 2003 and 2007. *Health Aff. (Millwood)*, **27** (4), w298–w309.

32. Substance Abuse and Mental Health Services Administration (2009) The TEDS Report: Treatment Outcomes among Clients Discharged from Outpatient Substance Abuse Treatment, Rockville, MD.

33. Weiss, R.D., Kolodziej, M., Griffin, M.L. *et al.* (2004) Substance use and perceived symptom improvement among patients with bipolar disorder and substance dependence. *J. Affect. Disord.*, **79** (1–3), 279–283.

34. Kessler, R.C., Aguilar-Gaxiola, S., Berglund, P.A. *et al.* (2001) Patterns and predictors of treatment seeking after onset of a substance use disorder. *Arch. Gen. Psychiatry*, **58** (11), 1065–1071.

35. Garbutt, J.C. (2009) The state of pharmacotherapy for the treatment of alcohol dependence. *J. Subst. Abuse Treat.*, **36** (1), S15–S23. quiz S24–S15.

36. McLellan, A.T., Arndt, I.O., Metzger, D.S. *et al.* (1993) The effects of psychosocial services in substance abuse treatment. *JAMA*, **269** (15), 1953–1959.

37. Ward, J., Hall, W., and Mattick, R.P. (1999) Role of maintenance treatment in opioid dependence. *Lancet*, **353** (9148), 221–226.

38. French, M.T., Mauskopf, J.A., Teague, J.L., and Roland, E.J. (1996) Estimating the dollar value of health outcomes from drug-abuse interventions. *Med. Care*, **34** (9), 890–910.

39. Zaric, G.S., Barnett, P.G., and Brandeau, M.L. (2000) HIV transmission and the cost-effectiveness of metha-

done maintenance. *Am. J. Public Health*, **90** (7), 1100–1111.

40. Fiellin, D.A. and O'Connor, P.G. (2002) New federal initiatives to enhance the medical treatment of opioid dependence. *Ann. Intern. Med.*, **137** (8), 688–692.

41. Kissin, W., McLeod, C., Sonnefeld, J., and Stanton, A. (2006) Experiences of a national sample of qualified addiction specialists who have and have not prescribed buprenorphine for opioid dependence. *J. Addict. Dis.*, **25** (4), 91–103.

42. Anton, R.F., O'Malley, S.S., Ciraulo, D.A. *et al.* (2006) Combined pharmacotherapies and behavioral interventions for alcohol dependence: the COMBINE study: a randomized controlled trial. *JAMA*, **295** (17), 2003–2017.

43. Cornish, J.W., Metzger, D., Woody, G.E. *et al.* (1997) Naltrexone pharmacotherapy for opioid dependent federal probationers. *J. Subst. Abuse Treat.*, **14** (6), 529–534.

44. Hollister, L.E., Schwin, R.L., and Kasper, P. (1977) Naltrexone treatment of opiate-dependent persons. *Drug Alcohol Depend.*, **2** (3), 203–209.

45. Johansson, B.A., Berglund, M., and Lindgren, A. (2006) Efficacy of maintenance treatment with naltrexone for opioid dependence: a meta-analytical review. *Addiction*, **101** (4), 491–503.

46. Martin, W.R., Jasinski, D.R., and Mansky, P.A. (1973) Naltrexone, an antagonist for the treatment of heroin dependence. Effects in man. *Arch. Gen. Psychiatry*, **28** (6), 784–791.

47. Comer, S.D., Sullivan, M.A., Yu, E. *et al.* (2006) Injectable, sustained-release naltrexone for the treatment of opioid dependence: a randomized, placebo-controlled trial. *Arch. Gen. Psychiatry*, **63** (2), 210–218.

48. Kim, T.W., Samet, J.H., Cheng, D.M. *et al.* (2007) Primary care quality and addiction severity: a prospective cohort study. *Health Serv. Res.*, **42** (2), 755–772.

49. Lanier, R.K., Umbricht, A., Harrison, J.A. *et al.* (2008) Opioid detoxification via single 7-day application of a buprenorphine transdermal patch: an open-label evaluation. *Psychopharmacology (Berl.)*, **198** (2), 149–158.

50. Sigmon, S.C., Moody, D.E., Nuwayser, E.S., and Bigelow, G.E. (2006) An injection depot formulation of buprenorphine: extended bio-delivery and effects. *Addiction*, **101** (3), 420–432.

51. Johnson, B.A., Rosenthal, N., Capece, J.A. *et al.* (2007) Topiramate for treating alcohol dependence: a randomized controlled trial. *JAMA*, **298** (14), 1641–1651.

52. Orson, F.M., Kinsey, B.M., Singh, R.A. *et al.* (2009) Vaccines for cocaine abuse. *Hum. Vaccin*, **5** (4), 194–199.

53. Elkashef, A., Vocci, F., Hanson, G. *et al.* (2008) Pharmacotherapy of methamphetamine addiction: an update. *Subst. Abus.*, **29** (3), 31–49.

54. Brodie, J.D., Figueroa, E., Laska, E.M., and Dewey, S.L. (2005) Safety and efficacy of gamma-vinyl GABA (GVG) for the treatment of methamphetamine and/or cocaine addiction. *Synapse*, **55** (2), 122–125.

55. DeMarco, A., Dalal, R.M., Pai, J. *et al.* (2009) Racemic gamma vinyl-GABA (R,S-GVG) blocks methamphetamine-triggered reinstatement of conditioned place preference. *Synapse*, **63** (2), 87–94.

56. Budney, A.J., Vandrey, R.G., Hughes, J.R. *et al.* (2007) Oral delta-9-tetrahydrocannabinol suppresses cannabis withdrawal symptoms. *Drug Alcohol Depend.*, **86** (1), 22–29.

57. Dutra, L., Stathopoulou, G., Basden, S.L. *et al.* (2008) A meta-analytic review of psychosocial interventions for substance use disorders. *Am. J. Psychiatry*, **165** (2), 179–187.

58. McLellan, A.T., Hagan, T.A., Levine, M. *et al.* (1998) Supplemental social services improve outcomes in public addiction treatment. *Addiction*, **93** (10), 1489–1499.

59. McLellan, A.T., Hagan, T.A., Levine, M. *et al.* (1999) Does clinical case management improve outpatient addiction treatment. *Drug Alcohol Depend.*, **55** (1–2), 91–103.

60. McKay, J.R. (2008) Effectiveness of continuing care interventions for substance abusers: Implications for the study of long-term treatment effects. *Eval. Rev.*, **25**, 211–232.

61. Brooner, R.K., Kidorf, M.S., King, V.L. *et al.* (2007) Comparing adaptive stepped care and monetary-based voucher interventions for opioid dependence. *Drug Alcohol Depend.*, **88** (Suppl. 2), S14–S23.

62. Brooner, R.K., Kidorf, M.S., King, V.L. *et al.* (2004) Behavioral contingencies improve counseling attendance in an adaptive treatment model. *J. Subst. Abuse Treat.*, **27** (3), 223–232.

63. (1997) Matching Alcoholism Treatments to Client Heterogeneity: Project MATCH posttreatment drinking outcomes. *J. Stud. Alcohol.*, **58** (1), 7–29.

64. Dennis, M., Godley, S.H., Diamond, G. *et al.* (2004) The Cannabis Youth Treatment (CYT) Study: main findings from two randomized trials. *J. Subst. Abuse Treat.*, **27** (3), 197–213.

65. Montoya, I.D., Schroeder, J.R., Preston, K.L. *et al.* (2005) Influence of psychotherapy attendance on buprenorphine treatment outcome. *J. Subst. Abuse Treat.*, **28** (3), 247–254.

66. McKusick, D., Mark, T.L., King, E. *et al.* (1998) Spending for mental health and substance abuse treatment, 1996. *Health Aff. (Millwood)*, **17** (5), 147–157.

67. Sullivan, L.E., Barry, D., Moore, B.A. *et al.* (2006) A trial of integrated buprenorphine/naloxone and HIV clinical care. *Clin. Infect. Dis.*, **43** (Suppl. 4), S184–S190.

68. Saitz, R., Horton, N.J., Larson, M.J. *et al.* (2005) Primary medical care and reductions in addiction severity: a prospective cohort study. *Addiction*, **100** (1), 70–78.

69. Havard, A., Shakeshaft, A., and Sanson-Fisher, R. (2008) Systematic review and meta-analyses of strategies targeting alcohol problems in emergency departments: interventions reduce alcohol-related injuries. *Addiction*, **103** (3), 368–376 discussion 377–368.

70. Saitz, R., Palfai, T.P., Cheng, D.M. *et al.* (2007) Brief intervention for medical inpatients with unhealthy alcohol use: a randomized, controlled trial. *Ann. Intern. Med.*, **146** (3), 167–176.

71. Weisner, C., Mertens, J., Parthasarathy, S. *et al.* (2001) Integrating primary medical care with addiction treatment: a randomized controlled trial. *JAMA*, **286** (14), 1715–1723.

72. Willenbring, M.L. and Olson, D.H. (1999) A randomized trial of integrated outpatient treatment for medically ill alcoholic men. *Arch. Intern. Med.*, **159** (16), 1946–1952.

73. Friedmann, P.D., Lemon, S.C., Stein, M.D. *et al.* (2001) Linkage to medical services in the Drug Abuse Treatment Outcome Study. *Med. Care*, **39** (3), 284–295.

74. Umbricht-Schneiter, A., Ginn, D.H., Pabst, K.M., and Bigelow, G.E. (1994) Providing medical care to methadone clinic patients: referral vs on-site care. *Am. J. Public Health*, **84** (2), 207–210.

75. Howard, A.A., Arnsten, J.H., and Gourevitch, M.N. (2004) Effect of alcohol consumption on diabetes mellitus: a systematic review. *Ann. Intern. Med.*, **140** (3), 211–219.

76. Terry, M.B., Zhang, F.F., Kabat, G. *et al.* (2006) Lifetime alcohol intake and breast cancer risk. *Ann. Epidemiol.*, **16** (3), 230–240.

77. Martell, B.A., O'Connor, P.G., Kerns, R.D. *et al.* (2007) Systematic review: opioid treatment for chronic back pain: prevalence, efficacy, and association with addiction. *Ann. Intern. Med.*, **146** (2), 116–127.

78. Sindelar, J.L., Jofre-Bonet, M., French, M.T., and McLellan, A.T. (2004) Cost-effectiveness analysis of addiction treatment: paradoxes of multiple outcomes. *Drug Alcohol Depend.*, **73** (1), 41–50.

79. Owens, D.K. (1998) Interpretation of cost-effectiveness analyses. *J. Gen. Intern. Med.*, **13** (10), 716–717.

80. Degenhardt, L., Whiteford, H., Hall, W., and Vos, T. (2009) Estimating the burden of disease attributable to illicit drug use and mental disorders: what is "Global Burden of Disease 2005" and why does it matter? *Addiction*, **104**, 1466–1471.

81. World Health Organization (2008) Global Burden of Disease 2004 Update, World Health Organization, Switzerland.

82. Ettner, S.L., Huang, D., Evans, E. *et al.* (2006) Benefit-cost in the California treatment outcome project: does substance abuse treatment "pay for itself"? *Health Serv. Res.*, **41** (1), 192–213.

83. Hser, Y.I., Huang, D., Teruya, C., and Douglas Anglin, M. (2003) Gender comparisons of drug abuse treatment outcomes and predictors. *Drug Alcohol Depend.*, **72** (3), 255–264.

84. Niv, N. and Hser, Y.I. (2007) Women-only and mixed-gender drug abuse treatment programs: service needs, utilization and outcomes. *Drug Alcohol Depend.*, **87** (2–3), 194–201.

85. Sun, A.P. (2006) Program factors related to women's substance abuse treatment retention and other outcomes: a review and critique. *J. Subst. Abuse Treat.*, **30** (1), 1–20.

86. Waldron, H.B. and Turner, C.W. (2008) Evidence-based psychosocial treatments for adolescent substance abuse. *J. Clin. Child Adolesc. Psychol.*, **37** (1), 238–261.

87. Winters, K.C. (1999) Treating adolescents with substance use disorders: An overview of practice issues and treatment outcome. *Subst. Abus.*, **20** (4), 203–225.

88. Wu, P., Hoven, C.W., Tiet, Q. *et al.* (2002) Factors associated with adolescent utilization of alcohol treatment services. *Am. J. Drug Alcohol Abuse*, **28** (2), 353–369.

38

Biopsychosocial recovery from addictive disorders

Sara Jo Nixon[1] and Robert A. Prather[2]

[1] Division of Addiction Research, Department of Psychiatry, University of Florida, Gainesville, FL, 32610, USA
[2] Department of Psychiatry, University of Florida, Gainesville, FL, 32610, USA

38.1   OVERVIEW: SIGNIFICANCE TO THE CLINICIAN

The complexity of addictive behaviors has been referenced by innumerable researchers and clinicians. Crews and his colleagues [1] developed a visual model to illustrate the complicated, interactive variables influencing the etiology and maintenance of addiction. A generalized version of this model is shown in Figure 38.1. This diagram illustrates the interaction of genetic predispositions, exposure variables and other environmental factors which jointly interface to create not a linear descent (as shown by the center arrow), but rather one that encircles the fundamental process (i.e., addiction) through a process of intertwined biopsychosocial variables.

To fully address recovery is to necessarily address factors beyond the physiological cravings and perturbations associated with initial withdrawal. In addition to dealing with comorbid physical disease, such as hepatic and cardiovascular function, physicians must frequently determine the appropriateness of other medications, particularly those which have psychoactive dimensions. The use of anxiolytics and antidepressants and related medications is addressed in other chapters. However, it should be recognized that a growing body of medications directed to facilitating early/continued abstinence is available [2]. Medications, particularly those developed for alcohol addiction, may be useful in reducing craving, prolonging time to first use, and reducing consumption during a "slip" or "lapse" [3–5].

However, studies of pharmacotherapies have produced inconsistent results [6]. A likely contributor to this confusion is the highly variable definition for "successful outcomes". Even the fundamental construct of "recovery" has been inconsistently defined and applied in research as well as clinical practice [7–9]. For example, as illustrated in Table 38.1, the DSM-IV [10] criteria fail to use the word "recovery", choosing instead the term "remission." Furthermore, the nosology classifies the degree of success in outcome on the basis of

Addictive Disorders in Medical Populations   Edited by Norman S. Miller and Mark S. Gold
© 2010 John Wiley & Sons, Ltd.

Figure 38.1 Interactive variables influencing the etiology and maintenance of addiction. *Modified from [1]*

negative consequences rather than consumption and, therefore, avoids direct confrontation with philosophical and treatment questions regarding abstinence requirements. Thus, the term "full remission" is applied to individuals achieving 12 months without any criteria for addiction or dependence without regard to actual use. The implications of these gradations are, however, poorly understood when evaluating long-term physical and mental health.

Generally, "recovery" is considered to be a process or state engaging a daily commitment and proactive steps to deter use. Some writers have suggested that at least for a subgroup of former misusers/addicts, return to moderate/nonproblematic use may be possible. This potential outcome appears to be reflected in the DSM-IV criteria discussed above. The issue remains controversial among professional and recovering groups. Two studies conducted by different research teams in different geographic areas and evaluating participants from different treatment modalities suggest that if nonproblematic use is possible, it is unlikely for the majority of former problem users. Data from these studies are summarized in Table 38.2. While

Table 38.1 Remission specifiers [10]

	DSM-IV Categories of Remission
Early Full Remission	This specifier is used if, for at least 1 mo, but less than 12 mo, no criteria for Dependence or Abuse have been met.
Early Partial Remission	This specifier is used if, for at least 1 mo, but less than 12 mo, one or more criteria for Dependence or Abuse have been met (but the full criteria for Dependence have not been met).
Sustained Full Remission	This specifier is used if none of the criteria for Dependence or Abuse have been met any time during a period of 12 mo or longer.
Sustained Partial Remission	This specifier is used if full criteria for Dependence have not been met for a period of 12 mo or longer; however, one or more criteria for Dependence or Abuse have been met.

Considerations of agonist/antagonist therapy and/or residence within a controlled environment (e.g., half-way house, jail, etc.) serve as qualifiers.

Table 38.2 Long-term outcomes: % each category

	I	II	III	IV
Cisler and Zweben [11] N = 1605	36%	12%	20%	32%
Hallford *et al.* [12] N = 61	34%	13%	26%	27%

I = Abstainers.

II = Moderate intake: <4 (female), <6 (male) drinks per drinking day and <12 (female), <15 (male) drinks per drinking week OR 1 or 2 occasions of drinking more than the limits set above.

III = Heavy intake: 3 or more occasions of drinking more than the limits set above with nonrecurrent problems.

IV = Heavy intake and recurrent problems [11–13].

these data are not generally supportive of sustained moderate use, it should be noted that participants in these studies met criteria for substance *dependence* as opposed to *addiction*. That is, it is unclear whether individuals with the less severe substance use disorder, that is, addiction, would be more likely to successfully engage in post-treatment moderate drinking. The distinction between addiction and dependence is gaining recognition but remains under-appreciated among the nonaddiction professionals and the public.

Recognizing the absence of a common or shared definition for "recovery" as a basic construct, a workgroup of experts in the field was convened by the Betty Ford Center [7] to attempt to provide clarification. This definition is provided in Table 38.3.

Although not intended to be a "final" but rather a "working" definition, it is noteworthy in several ways. Firstly, it emphasizes an *ongoing* commitment by its reference to "*maintained lifestyle*". Secondly, it identifies the *individual responsibility*

for recovery by defining it as being "*voluntarily maintained*". Thirdly, it embraces a *broader definition* than one that refers only to the presence/absence of substance use (i.e., abstinence) by referring to the importance of *personal health and citizenship*. Clearly, it invokes the importance of biopsychosocial factors in the process of recovery.

Accepting this definition for working purposes, dictates that attention be extended beyond physiological measures of health to broader constructs associated with successful living. The panel is not alone in this recommendation, as other experts have also recognized improvement in relationships, social support, and employment as an essential component of "recovery" [16–19].

Furthermore, the definition posits that *abstinence* from alcohol and nonprescription drugs is *necessary although not sufficient* to constitute "recovery".[1] As will be discussed later, abstinence is typically defined as a dichotomous variable, that is, present/absent: yes/no. However, application of a categorical variable is complicated by the patterns of use following treatment and philosophical issues regarding the process of recovery. These issues are more fully explored in Section 39.3.

The goals/objectives of the chapter are to: (a) provide on overview of the complex nature of recovery from addictive disorders; (b) enhance physician knowledge and comfort level when treating patients with addictive disorders; (c) increase understanding of the pertinence of physician awareness and engagement in the recovery process; and (d) provide a brief overview of physician involvement in more common types of treatment and support. The various addictions diverge greatly in the maturity of their research bases. Because of this inequity, much of the available literature focuses on alcohol. Addiction and substance misuse research does, however, appear to be developing into a more inclusive realm [20]. To provide additional direction, also included are references to brief interventions and assessments that can be reasonably administered in a clinic or private office setting.

Table 38.3 Defining recovery: the Betty Ford Institute consensus panel [7]

Definition: Recovery from substance dependence is a voluntarily maintained lifestyle characterized by (1) sobriety, (2) personal health, and (3) citizenship.

Component Explanation:
1. *Sobriety* is considered to be primary and necessary for a recovery lifestyle. The group contends that sobriety is most readily achieved through abstinence. Early sobriety = 1–11 mo; Sustained sobriety = 1–5 yr; Stable sobriety = 5 yr or more.
2. *Personal health* refers to improved quality of personal life as defined and measured by validated instruments, such as the physical health, psychological health, independence, and spirituality scales of the World Health Organization quality-of-life instrument [14, 15].
3. *Citizenship* refers to living with regard and respect for those around you as defined and measured by validated instruments such as the social function and environment scales of the WHO quality-of-life instrument [14, 15].

---

[1] The panel desired to include tobacco products in the prohibited list of substances. However, given traditional concepts of recovery and sobriety, it elected to remain silent on this issue for the present time.

38.2 PROTRACTED WITHDRAWAL SYNDROMES AND INITIAL RECOVERY

The physiological and psychological distress accompanying the early hours and days of abstinence is alarming. Depending on the drug(s) of addiction, the pattern of consumption, and a number of individual risk variables, it may constitute a medical emergency. Hospitalization and medications in addition to a supportive environment may be needed. The subsiding of these early physical symptoms represents the termination of the inaugural phase of withdrawal. The next weeks and months are accompanied by significant shifts in the allostatic load across physical and psychological domains.

One aspect of this protracted withdrawal is affective and mood disruption, characterized by mixed states vacillating between depressive symptoms to euthymic and sometimes manic states. Differentiating these withdrawal-related mood changes from underlying, primary mood disorders is critical. The association between alcohol and stimulants and depression has long been known. However, a growing literature suggests that certain commonly used drugs, such as marijuana and the stimulants, may increase the probability of more severe psychiatric presentation, such as symptomatology associated with schizophrenic or bipolar disorders, respectively [21–23]. It is not clear whether these symptoms are evoked directly by the drugs or whether the drugs serve to trigger or release these symptoms in at-risk users, such as those with positive family histories for certain psychiatric disorders. Regardless of the mechanism, these correlations reinforce the importance of obtaining family histories of psychiatric disorders other than substance addiction and in careful observation of those patients with positive family histories.

38.2.1 Psychosocial factors

Fortunately, most newly recovering persons do not experience psychotic or bipolar episodes. However, the large majority do report increases in negative affect, as reflected in elevated scores on measures of depression and/or anxiety. Often these elevations do not reach severe levels and often they dissipate in the first 3–6 weeks of abstinence, although they may remain elevated relative to unaffected community comparison groups for some time. The prolonged nature of these elevations is illustrated in a classic study conducted by De Soto and colleagues [24, 25].

These data (Figure 38.2) illustrate two highly relevant points. Firstly, the decline toward "community" levels is initially quite steep, followed by consistent, but less dramatic declines. That is, abstinence is accompanied by a steep decline in negative symptoms of mood and life distress in the first two years. The rate of improvement slows substantially after this point. It may be frustrating and disappointing to recovering patients to experience this leveling effect. At this point, it may be critical to ensure that adequate psychosocial support continues to be engaged not only to encourage sustained recovery but also to provide reassurance that continued improvement can be anticipated.

Secondly, the trajectories, at least in these samples, were remarkably similar for men and women. Despite well-recognized gender differences in substance addiction, the similarity in the pattern of recovery among men and women suggests a not-dissimilar process of distress and recovery over time.

The early months of recovery are accompanied by changing demands/expectations across psychosocial domains. Intimate relationships are often challenged as partners strive to re-establish and/or re-define their interactions. Parents and children face conflict as roles are re-defined. Friends and colleagues are confronted with determining their attitudes regarding addiction, the process of recovery, and their own use. Those persons newly in recovery may be trying to obtain essential support for their sobriety while living or working in environments which explicitly or implicitly discourage sobriety. Finally, even if family, friends, and employers are supportive of recovery, the stress

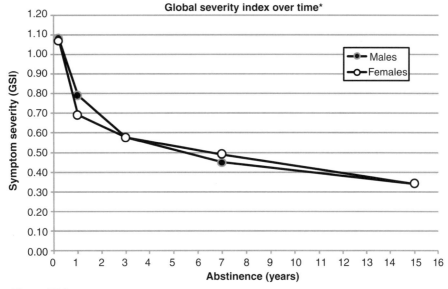

Figure 38.2   Global Severity Index (GSI) of the Brief Symptom Inventory (BSI) [25–27]

associated with sober living and confronting actual or perceived expectations regarding sobriety can be overwhelming. The outcome can be increased anxiety, depression, anger, and decreased self-esteem. It is important that physicians be aware of this process and its potential impact on physical and biopsychosocial recovery.

38.2.2   Cognitive factors

Psychosocial adaptation may be further complicated by neurocognitive deficits frequently observed in recently recovering individuals. These deficits are evidenced in both neuropsychological and neuroimaging studies [28–32]. The prevalence of these deficits among individuals in early recovery is quite high, with some estimates approaching 85% among detoxified, non-Korsakoff alcoholics [33]. The breadth of the deficits is illustrated in Table 38.4.

It should be noted that the term "deficits" typically refers not to clinically defined impairment (i.e., ≥1.5 standard deviations below normalized scores). Rather, it refers to lower performance or altered structure/function relative to age, gender, and education matched community comparison groups. Thus, although individuals fail to meet clinical diagnoses, their level of function places them at an

obvious disadvantage when compared to the functioning level of those with whom they seek to socialize and work. Furthermore, the impact of substance use disorders on neurobehavior is modulated by a number of other factors, including family history, the presence of certain childhood behavior disorders, age, and the specific drug or drugs of addiction. Disentangling the relative impact of each of these factors continues to be a critical area for both clinical and basic researchers [34].

Given the widespread neurobehavioral deficits, it is not surprising that clarifying the path of recovery is difficult. The question of its recovery has been addressed repeatedly over 25 years [51–57]. Studying recovery of function is complicated by the high rates of relapse which confound recovery, reducing sample sizes and statistical validity. Despite the challenges, certain patterns can be predicted. For example, the first skills to recover appear to be those associated with verbal functions, such as basic verbal learning (e.g., list learning) and memory (e.g., memory for short stories). For some individuals, these skills recover within the first 3–4 weeks of sustained sobriety. For others, additional time may be needed. Recovery of the most complex functions, those associated with problem solving, introspection, and abstraction appears to occur much later (months to years) and may not, at least

Table 38.4 Compromised neurobehavioral domains

Cognitive-Behavioral [30, 31, 36–38]	Specific impairments include deficits in both verbal and visual-spatial learning and memory; perceptual motor skills, balance (heel-to-toe walking), abstraction/problem solving, executive cognitive function, attention, impaired ability appropriate emotion in auditory or visual stimuli.

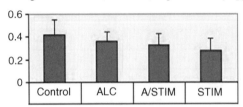

"ALC" = alcohol dependent, "A/STIM" = alcohol and stimulant dependent, "STIM" = stimulant dependent. Shared letters denote nonsignificant differences. This study found that community controls were only statistically significantly better in relation to the A/STIM and STIM groups. Individual comparisons show the ALC group performed significantly better than the STIM group, but did not differ significantly from either the Control or A/STIM groups. This pattern of results was relatively consistent across the subtests of problem-solving/abstraction, short-term memory, and cognitive flexibility and reflects drug group differences. [35, 36]

Function [39–43]	Aberrations in distribution of alpha and beta brain waves; reduction in amplitude and/or increased latency in event-related potentials (ERPs) associated with attentional functions, working memory and target detection, and detection of semantic incongruity; differential activation patterns between addicted and nonaddicted on a variety of stimuli ranging from drug related to those associated with universal emotions.

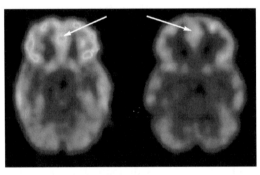

PET: Cocaine addicts have reduced metabolism in the orbitofrontal cortex. In this comparison of a healthy subject (left) and a cocaine abuser (right), the highest and the lowest level of metabolic activity, as measured by [18]FDG, can be seen. [20]

Structural [44–50]	Increased size of lateral ventricles, cortical and cerebellar shrinkage, decreased white matter integrity, compromise in corpus callosum (may be qualified by gender and specific area of the corpus callosum).

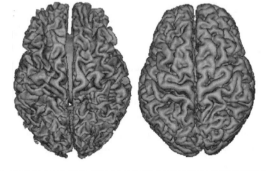

in some individuals, achieve full recovery [51, 55, 58]. This last statement must be qualified, however, by referencing a statement made earlier; just as initial deficits are affected by a variety of familial, genetic, and childhood factors, so is the process of recovery.

The role of neurocognitive deficits on sustained recovery (i.e., abstinence) has also been examined. Despite the anticipated negative association (increasing deficits being associated with decreasing abstinence, increasing use), studies have typically found weak, inconsistent associations [59, 60]. It is likely that these negative findings may be related to a variety of factors including, as noted earlier, the finding that most participants do not meet criteria for clinical impairment and the variability or range of normal scores may obscure the association of interest.

Recently, Bates and colleagues [61] reconsidered data obtained through the large, longitudinal NIAAA funded study entitled Project Matching Alcoholism Treatment to Client Heterogeneity (MATCH). Using data from this longitudinal study, they reviewed performance on the neuropsychological tests and classified performance on each as either impaired, with scores ≥ 1.5 Standard Deviations below age stratified normative data, or unimpaired. They then derived composite impairment indices by summing the number of tests on which an individual was impaired. (Consistent with earlier research, a large majority of participants failed to meet clinical impairment criteria on any of the tests.) In addition to conducting a more sophisticated data analysis than often employed, Bates and colleagues also used more sensitive outcome variables by including drinks per drinking day and percentage days abstinent rather then gross measures of "abstinent" or "relapsed", for example. These analyses supported the investigators' prediction that there is an association between deficits and recovery trajectories but that it is indirect. Consistent with other literature, poorer self-efficacy and treatment compliance were associated with increased drinking. Alcoholics Anonymous involvement across groups was associated with reduced drinking. However, this association was moderated by group, with the impaired group benefiting significantly less than the unimpaired group. These findings, suggesting differential effectiveness of mutual self-help, are highly relevant to physician referral, which is further discussed in Section 39.4.

38.2.3   Summary

Biological, psychological, and social factors play a significant role in sustaining recovery over time. Significant variables include self-efficacy, treatment compliance, social support, and participation in leisure activities not associated with substance use [61–63]. Thus, contacts with programs and activities which will enhance these efforts are imperative. Physician awareness of individuals skilled in providing substance addiction treatment and community programs directed to enhancing sobriety should be greatly encouraged. Information regarding some of these groups is provided in Section 39.4.

38.3   THE COMPLEXITY OF DEFINING RELAPSE

In medicine, the primary intent is to prevent, cure, and/or control disease. For the addictive disorders, reconciling the issues of curing and/or controlling is difficult; it is complicated by varying beliefs regarding personal responsibility for onset, sustainability of remission, and the availability of appropriate pharmacotherapies. Given the complexity of the etiology and maintenance of substance use disorders, it should be expected, as noted in Section 39.1, that defining a "best" outcome has not been without controversy. Our "gold standard" outcome has been and remains abstinence. However, most outcome studies have found that a minority of treated individuals maintain abstinence. Relapse rates often lie between 40 and 60% within the first post-treatment months and rise to between 70 and 80% by the end of the first year [64–66]. Longitudinal studies have also revealed considerable shifting of individuals between drinking categories across time [16, 67]. It is an understatement to refer to these data as disheartening.

It has been argued that relying on a strict application of the categorical system (i.e., use/no use) denies the essence of human behavioral change; that is process. Shifting from a "using" to "nonusing" existence requires an interplay of biological, psychological, and social influences in a process of acquiring more effective coping skills and successfully engaging social support, as well as the adaptation of neurobiological systems. As a process, recovery may be accompanied by both success and failure with failures providing the opportunity to practice newly developing skills as well as reevaluate the need for additional intervention [68]. Within this more liberal framework, an individual does not necessarily "relapse" in the clinical application of the term with the consumption of a single or perhaps a few drinks [16].

Traditional views (as well as the definition broadly accepted here) create an expectation of continuous abstinence, that is, perfection in the behavior of not using. However, as illustrated above and throughout the literature, perfection is almost never achieved and particularly not in the initial phases of sobriety. Marlatt and others [16, 69] have suggested that this expectation results in the "abstinence violation effect," which combined with

lowered self-esteem and self-efficacy may propel "lapses" toward reinstatement of problem drinking (i.e., relapse).

A related issue centers on the fact that some users want to reduce potential harm to themselves and others without necessarily being abstinent. Harm reduction [70–74] may include the possibility of use but within certain limitations, such as in a way which avoids law violations, maintains normal physiological indicators, and/or sustains a marriage. It has been suggested, as shown in Table 38.2, that few individuals with significant substance use problems are likely to be able to sustain these reduced levels over time [12, 16, 63, 69, 75]. However, harm reduction initiatives may be more effective for those who are addicts without meeting dependence criteria. Furthermore, setting limits for individuals who are not currently contemplating or initiating a sober lifestyle, may reduce use and encourage additional reductions.

In summary, using the traditional dichotomous definition of relapse/recovery simplifies classification. It, simultaneously, however, discounts the efforts of those striving toward healthy living and, perhaps, ultimate abstinence. Although continued drinking among dependent individuals cannot be condoned, the context surrounding the drinking and the drinker's response to the episode must be evaluated in making clinical recommendations.

38.4 PHYSICIAN SUPPORT: ASSESSMENT, REFERRAL, AWARENESS AND FOLLOW-UP

From the shear number of chapters in this book, it is obvious that addiction plays a substantive role in the practice of medicine. Despite its ubiquitous impact, many physicians remain uncomfortable and/or under-trained in approaching and treating substance addiction among their patients. Unfortunately, many psychiatrists and mental health professionals also have little direct training or experience. Given the prevalence of substance use disorders and their impact on health, the lack of available training is extremely unfortunate and costly.

Appropriate use of brief interventions and motivational interviewing conducted by physicians and/or medical staff can effectively lower use when

properly used. These approaches focus on enhancing clients' motivation to engage in healthier behaviors and, thereby, assess willingness to change not on the basis of the presence or degree of denial, but rather the level of motivation and readiness to change. The change in language reflects more than just one of semantics, as it places the attention of the interaction not on "breaking down" or "through" defenses, but rather identifying a starting point of forward positive change. Individuals are made aware of their physical risk, (e.g., elevated liver function tests or increased blood pressure), provided with information regarding potential outcomes and direct advice emphasizing personal responsibility in the context of supportive messages directed to enhancing self-efficacy is shared. These interventions require only a minimum time commitment but should provide timely feedback derived from the same domains judged to be compromised in the initial intervention (i.e., if liver function test results were elevated, they should be retested and these results should be shared with the client) [76–78]. Obviously, care must be taken in applying these techniques with individuals who have alcohol/drug dependency and in whom abrupt cessation might result in physical withdrawal. Furthermore, follow-up with these patients is essential, not only to provide feedback, but to assess continued use patterns and evaluate for other disease states. A detailed overview of these techniques is beyond the scope of the present chapter. However, interested readers are invited to consult the additional literature given in the References, including Miller and Heather [79].

There are also a number of paper/pencil questionnaires which require little time and can be re-administered. Although these questionnaires do not substitute for clinical acumen, they may serve to focus attention to critical concerns and increase office visit efficiency. Available instruments include assessments for depressive symptoms which include ratings for change in sleep, appetite, and fatigue [80], calendars for recent drug and/or alcohol use and meeting/counseling attendance [81] as well as a variety of quality of life inventories [14, 15].

Given the documented importance of social support in sustaining recovery, it is important that individuals desiring abstinence-based recovery identify and engage such support. Referral to individual counseling and/or psychotherapy with therapists trained in treating substance addiction may be necessary to identify address psychiatric and/or behavioral issues and identify a long-term treatment plan.

Many clients will benefit from participating in community-based mutual self-help programs. These programs do not provide therapy. However, the shared experiences and support and help of others who have also experienced the ravages of addictive disorders can serve as a critical source of social support. There are now a variety of community-based support-driven programs. The most common ones remain those associated with the 12-Step orientation. The first, Alcoholics Anonymous (AA) was formed in 1935 and enjoys a rich history and effective worldwide outreach [82]. It is difficult to determine AA's effectiveness in sustaining recovery as measured by abstinence. Part of this difficulty lies in the anonymous nature of the AA membership as well as additional restriction associated with the traditions [83].

Other challenges arise from inconsistent definitions regarding AA membership versus "newcomer" status. For example, Lloyd [84], citing the comments published by AA associated with the 1989/1990 triennial survey [85], indicated a steep decline in attendance with 50% of first contact no longer attending at three months and 90% dropping out by 12 months. McIntire, citing these same comments reports, based on a figure in that report, that 81% of those who "came to AA reported "dropped out" within 30 days; that 90% were gone by the end of three months or 90 days and that 95% were no longer attending at one year. Regardless of the specific differences, such data ostensibly suggest that AA is efficacious to only a minority of alcoholics. However, before drawing this conclusion, a nuance in the traditions of AA should be noted. Membership in the Fellowship of AA is defined by only one criterion, the "desire to stop drinking" [86]. Newcomers are not commonly seen as "new members" until they have had the opportunity to experience the traditions of AA. Often this is assumed to occur over approximately 90 days and some writers [87, 88] have suggested that approximately 50% of newcomers discontinue by this time. The distinction between newcomer and new member may be subtle, but is certainly more than one of semantics. It emphasizes the fact that individuals vary in their readiness to change (and perhaps their need to, since visitors often attend meetings) as well as their fit within the AA fellowship.

AA was conceived and continues on the basis of its ability to meet the needs of alcoholics. However, the success of this approach, grounded in the foundation of powerlessness over a drug or behavior and the 12 traditions has been expanded. Twelve-step based programs now exist for a variety of disorders, including cocaine dependence, gambling, nicotine use, and eating disorders.

The outreach of 12-step programs is sufficiently widespread that it is rare to find individuals who do not at least recognize the name. However, many are not aware of the traditions or the fact that the groups are independent and have distinct personalities and expectations. For example, some groups are nonsmoking while others allow it. Some have a predominance of younger or older participants. Some areas have gender-specific groups and others have identified groups for gay/lesbian/bisexual/transgender persons. Furthermore, the groups vary in their acceptance of medications used to enhance or sustain recovery. Therefore, where pharmacotherapy is an appropriate component of the treatment plan, physicians should discuss this issue with their patients.

Regardless of the disorder or drug, most 12-step programs adhere to a fundamental belief that the addicted individual is powerless over the drug/activity and seek the aid of a higher power in being released from this subjugation. These concepts and beliefs are difficult or unacceptable for some people with addictive disorders. For these individuals, other avenues are available. Many communities now have recovery support groups emphasizing individual choice, rational decision making, and behavioral consequences. These groups may be found under names such as "Rational Recovery", "Women for Sobriety", and "Secular Organizations for Sobriety". Given the variations in form and expectations, physicians should make referrals to specific groups only after clarifying existing social supports, previous exposure to self-help groups, attitudes toward medication (as appropriate), presence of dual diagnosis, and attitudes toward powerlessness and a higher power [79, 89].

Despite the fact that one of the founding members of AA was a physician, medical professionals have typically remained dissociated from these community-based, mutual self-help groups. Regardless of the rationale, this distancing has reinforced concepts of the separation of addiction from general medicine and separated those who may need medical treatment from those who might provide it. As the neurobiological mechanisms, including gene and gene X environment interactions [90, 91], underlying addiction are better understood, this chasm will undoubtedly be reduced.

Another transition that will mitigate the distance is the growing recognition of the problem of addiction and process of recovery among medical professionals. Widely accepted estimates of physician recovery remain unavailable. Some programs report recovery rates as high as 94–100% [92, 93]. Although these exceptional outcomes may be biased in their mode of recruitment and/or exclusion criteria (i.e., failing to use an intent to treatment analysis where appropriate), physician treatment programs are accompanied by exceptionally high recovery rates. Lloyd [84] reports a 21-year follow-up of 100 alcoholic doctors and reports a 73% recovery rate of an average period of 17.3 years (range 12–28 years).

It should be noted, however, that recovery in this context does not necessarily refer to sustained abstinence. In this report, duration of abstinence is defined as a period of uninterrupted abstinence, whereas recovery is defined as a period of abstinence which may be interrupted by relapse and "re-recovery". Ten of the 51 participants who are noted as being in recovery (currently abstinent) reported periods of drinking over the study period and another three reported to have returned to unaffected drinking. Of the 54 physicians who were either abstinent or normal drinkers, 54% reported currently practicing medicine and the remainder had retired. As demonstrated in other settings, social support and personal accountability associated with mutual self-help groups was a critical component early in recovery. Interestingly, 29% of those currently abstinent reported continued involvement with AA.

38.5   CONCLUSIONS

Attention to the physiological components of addictive disorders, such as withdrawal, craving and organ system compromise, is an important aspect of treatment. However, this level of intervention is likely inadequate to address the multisystem compromise associated with addictions. As reflected in the Betty Ford Consensus Panel report [7], recovery from addictive disorders is a process engaging physiological, psychological, and social systems. Furthermore, psychosocial systems, although compromised in addiction, are critical to sustained recovery. That is, the very systems (family, friends, employment) essential for recovery are typically significantly damaged at the point of initiating recovery efforts. Therefore, newly recovering individuals should be strongly encouraged to seek psychosocial support through the most appropriate means.

Neurocognitive compromise is also common among addicts and those in recovery. These deficits can negatively affect the psychosocial support as well as feelings of self-efficacy, key components of effective recovery. Fortunately, many of the deficits do appear to improve with time; however, the degree to which they recovery varies greatly between individuals and among specific cognitive domains. There are inadequate data to fully address deficits associated with polydrug addiction, although the outcome likely varies as a result of the specific addicted drugs and measures taken [30, 94–96]. Currently there are a number of studies directed to the evaluation of the effects of cigarette smoking and/or nicotine use among substance addicts on brain structure and function.

Finally, many newly recovering addicts find community-based mutual-self help groups to be extremely helpful or even necessary. However, the personalities and expectations of these groups varies substantially. It is essential that the physician be aware of the groups' characteristics as well as the client's needs and past history before making a referral to a specific group. Physicians, and other healthcare providers, who are informed regarding the biopsychosocial aspects of recovery can be strong advocates and allies in the process.

REFERENCES

1. Crews, F.T., Buckley, T., Dodd, P.R. *et al.* (2005) Alcoholic neurobiology: changes in dependence and recovery. *Alcohol. Clin. Exp. Res.*, **29** (8), 1504–1513.

2. McLellan, A.T., Lewis, D.C., O'Brien, C.P., and Kleber, H.D. (2000) Drug dependence, a chronic medical illness: implications for treatment, insurance, and outcomes evaluation. *JAMA*, **284** (13), 1689–1695.

3. Anton, R.F., O'Malley, S.S., Ciraulo, D.A. *et al.* (2006) Combined pharmacotherapies and behavioral interventions for alcohol dependence: the COMBINE study: a randomized controlled trial. *JAMA*, **295** (17), 2003–2017.

4. Kranzler, H.R. and Van Kirk, J. (2001) Efficacy of naltrexone and acamprosate for alcoholism treatment: a meta-analysis. *Alcohol. Clin. Exp. Res.*, **25** (9), 1335–1341.

5. O'Malley, S.S., Jaffe, A.J., Rode, S., and Rounsaville, B.J. (1996) Experience of a "slip" among alcoholics treated with naltrexone or placebo. *Am. J. Psychiatry*, **153** (2), 281–283.

6. Rohsenow, D.J., Miranda, R. Jr., McGeary, J.E., and Monti, P.M. (2007) Family history and antisocial traits moderate naltrexone's effects on heavy drinking in alcoholics. *Exp. Clin. Psychopharm.*, **15** (3), 272–281.

7. Betty Ford Institute Consensus Panel (2007) What is recovery? A working definition from the Betty Ford Institute. *J. Subst. Abuse Treat.*, **33**, 221–228.

8. Laudet, A.B. (2007) What does recovery mean to you? Lessons from the recovery experience for research and practice. *J. Subst. Abuse Treat.*, **33** (3), 243–256.

9. Laudet, A.B., Morgen, K., and White, W.L. (2006) The role of social supports, spirituality, religiousness, life meaning and affiliation with 12-step fellowships in quality of life satisfaction among individuals in recovery from alcohol and drug problems. *Alcohol. Treat. Q.*, **24** (1–2), 33–73.

10. American Psychiatric Association Task Force on DSM-IV (1994) *Diagnostic and Statistical Manual of Mental Disorders*, 4th edn, American Psychiatric Association, Washington, DC.

11. Zweben, A. and Cisler, R. (1996) Composite outcome measures in alcoholism treatment research: problems and potentialities. *Subst. Use Misuse*, **31** (13), 1783–1805.

12. Cisler, R.A. and Zweben, A. (1999) Development of a composite measure for assessing alcohol treatment outcome: operationalization and validation. *Alcohol. Clin. Exp. Res.*, **23** (2), 263–271.

13. Hallford, H.G., Tivis, R.D., and Nixon, S.J. (2003) An empirical assessment of post-treatment alcohol consumption. *Psychiatry Res.*, **121** (2), 197–205.

14. WHO-QOL Group (1998) Development of the World Health Organization WHOQOL-BREF quality of life assessment. *Psychol. Med.*, **28** (3), 551–558.

15. WHO-QOL Group (1998) The World Health Organization Quality of Life Assessment (WHOQOL): development and general psychometric properties. *Soc. Sci. Med.*, **46** (12), 1569–1585.

16. Miller, W.R. (1996) What is a relapse? Fifty ways to leave the wagon. *Addiction*, **91** (Suppl.), S15–S27.

17. Miller, W.R., Brown, J.M., Simpson, T.L. *et al.* (1995) What works? A methodological analysis of the alcohol treatment outcome literature, in *Handbook of Alcoholism Treatment Approaches: Effective Alternatives*, 2nd edn (eds R.K. Hesterand W.R. Miller), Allyn and Bacon, Boston, pp. 12–44.

18. Meyers, R.J. and Smith, J.E. (1995) *Clinical Guide to Alcohol Treatment: The Community Reinforcement Approach*, Guilford Press, New York.

19. McKay, J.R. and Weiss, R.V. (2001) A review of temporal effects and outcome predictors in substance abuse treatment studies with long-term follow-ups. Preliminary results and methodological issues. *Evaluation Rev.*, **25** (2), 113–161.

20. Fowler, J.S., Volkow, N.D., Kassed, C.A., and Chang, L. (2007) Imaging the addicted human brain. *Sci. Pract. Perspect.*, **3** (2), 4–16.

21. Camacho, A. and Akiskal, H.S. (2005) Proposal for a bipolar-stimulant spectrum: temperament, diagnostic validation and therapeutic outcomes with mood stabilizers. *J. Affect. Disord.*, **85** (1–2), 217–230.

22. D'Souza, D.C., Abi-Saab, W.M., Madonick, S. *et al.* (2005) Delta-9-tetrahydrocannabinol effects in schizophrenia: implications for cognition, psychosis, and addiction. *Biol. Psychiatry*, **57** (6), 594–608.

23. D'Souza, D.C., Perry, E., MacDougall, L. *et al.* (2004) The psychotomimetic effects of intravenous delta-9-tetrahydrocannabinol in healthy individuals: implications for psychosis. *Neuropsychopharmacology*, **29** (8), 1558–1572.

24. De Soto, C.B., O'Donnell, W.E., Allred, L.J., and Lopes, C.E. (1985) Symptomatology in alcoholics at various stages of abstinence. *Alcohol. Clin. Exp. Res.*, **9** (6), 505–512.

25. De Soto, C.B., O'Donnell, W.E., and De Soto, J.L. (1989) Long-term recovery in alcoholics. *Alcohol. Clin. Exp. Res.*, **13** (5), 693–697.

26. Derogatis, L.R. (1977) SCL-90-R: Administration, Scoring and Procedures Manual I, Johns Hopkins University School of Medicine, Clinical Psychometrics Research Unit, Baltimore.

27. Derogatis, L.R. (1982) The Brief Symptom Inventory (BSI): Administration, Scoring & Procedure Manual I, Johns Hopkins University School of Medicine, Clinical Psychometrics Research Unit, Baltimore.

28. Rourke, S.B. and Loberg, T. (1996) The neurobehavioral correlates of alcoholism, in *Neuropsychological Assessment of Neuropsychiatric Disorders*, 2nd edn (eds I. Grantand K.M. Adams), Oxford University Press, New York, pp. 423–487.

29. Volkow, N.D., Fowler, J.S., and Wang, G.J. (2003) The addicted human brain: insights from imaging studies. *J. Clin. Invest.*, **111** (10), 1444–1451.

30. Ceballos, N.A., Tivis, R., Lawton-Craddock, A., and Nixon, S.J. (2005) Visual-spatial attention in alcoholics and illicit stimulant abusers: effects of nicotine replacement. *Prog. Neuropsychopharmacol. Biol. Psychiatry*, **29** (1), 97–107.

31. Ceballos, N.A. (2006) Tobacco use, alcohol dependence, and cognitive performance. *J. Gen. Psychol.*, **133** (4), 375–388.

32. Nixon, S.J., Lawton-Craddock, A., Tivis, R.D., and Ceballos, N.A. (2007) Nicotine's effects on attentional efficiency in alcoholics. *Alcohol. Clin. Exp. Res.*, **31** (12), 2083–2091.

33. Parsons, O.A. (1986) Alcoholics' neuropsychological impairment: Current findings and conclusions. *Ann. Behav. Med.*, **8** (2–3), 13–19.

34. Chen, A.C., Porjesz, B., Rangaswamy, M. *et al.* (2007) Reduced frontal lobe activity in subjects with high impulsivity and alcoholism. *Alcohol. Clin. Exp. Res.*, **31** (1), 156–165.

35. Lawton, A.J. (1999) Cognitive efficiency in stimulant abusers with and without alcohol use disorders. Unpublished master's thesis, University of Oklahoma, Oklahoma City, OK.

36. Lawton-Craddock, A., Nixon, S.J., and Tivis, R. (2003) Cognitive efficiency in stimulant abusers with and without alcohol dependence. *Alcohol. Clin. Exp. Res.*, **27** (3), 457–464.

37. Oscar-Berman, M. and Marinkovic, K. (2007) Alcohol: effects on neurobehavioral functions and the brain. *Neuropsychol. Rev.*, **17** (3), 239–257.

38. Oscar-Berman, M. (2000) Neuropsychological vulnerabilities in chronic alcoholism, in *Review of NIAAA's Neuroscience and Behavioral Research Portfolio*, NIAAA Research Monograph No. 34 (eds A. Noronha, M. Eckardt,and K. Warren), National Institutes of Health, Bethesda, MD, pp. 437–471.

39. Bauer, L.O. (2001) Electroencephalographic studies of substance use and abuse, in *Brain Imaging in Substance Abuse: Research, Clinical, and Forensic Applications* (ed. M.J. Kaufman), Humana Press, Totowa, NJ, pp. 77–112.

40. Ceballos, N.A., Nixon, S.J., and Tivis, R. (2003) Substance abuse-related P300 differences in response to an

implicit memory task. *Prog. Neuropsychopharmacol. Biol. Psychiatry*, **27** (1), 157–164.

41. Nixon, S.J., Tivis, R., Ceballos, N. *et al.* (2002) Neurophysiological efficiency in male and female alcoholics. *Prog. Neuropsychopharmacol. Biol. Psychiatry*, **26** (5), 919–927.

42. Pfefferbaum, A., Desmond, J.E., Galloway, C. *et al.* (2001) Reorganization of frontal systems used by alcoholics for spatial working memory: an fMRI study. *Neuroimage*, **14** (1 Pt 1), 7–20.

43. Porjesz, B., and Begleiter, H. (1993) Neurophysiological factors associated with alcoholism, in *Alcohol-Induced Brain Damage*, vol. **22** (eds W.A. Hunt and S.J. Nixon), National Institutes of Health, Rockville, MD, pp. 89–120.

44. Harper, C., Matsumoto, I., Pfefferbaum, A. *et al.* (2005) The pathophysiology of 'Brain Shrinkage' in alcoholics – structural and molecular changes and clinical implications. *Alcohol. Clin. Exp. Res.*, **29** (6), 1106–1115.

45. Harper, C. (2007) The neurotoxicity of alcohol. *Hum. Exp. Toxicol.*, **26** (3), 251–257.

46. Mann, K., Agartz, I., Harper, C. *et al.* (2001) Neuroimaging in alcoholism: ethanol and brain damage. *Alcohol. Clin. Exp. Res.*, **25** (5 Suppl. ISBRA), 104S–109S.

47. Pfefferbaum, A., Rosenbloom, M.J., Serventi, K.L., and Sullivan, E.V. (2004) Brain volumes, RBC status, and hepatic function in alcoholics after 1 and 4 weeks of sobriety: predictors of outcome. *Am. J. Psychiatry*, **161** (7), 1190–1196.

48. Schulte, T., Sullivan, E.V., Muller-Oehring, E.M. *et al.* (2005) Corpus callosal microstructural integrity influences interhemispheric processing: a diffusion tensor imaging study. *Cereb. Cortex*, **15** (9), 1384–1392.

49. Sullivan, E.V. (2000) Human brain vulnerability to alcoholism: Evidence from neuroimaging studies, in *Review of NIAAA's Neuroscience and Behavioral Research Portfolio*, NIAAA Research Monograph No. 34 (eds A. Noronha, M., Eckardt, and K. Warren), National Institutes of Health, Bethesda, MD, pp. 473–508.

50. Hommer, D., Momenan, R., Rawlings, R. *et al.* (1996) Decreased corpus callosum size among alcoholic women. *Arch. Neurol.*, **53** (4), 359–363.

51. Ersche, K.D., Fletcher, P.C., Lewis, S.J. *et al.* (2005) Abnormal frontal activations related to decision-making in current and former amphetamine and opiate dependent individuals. *Psychopharmacology (Berl.)*, **180** (4), 612–623.

52. Fabian, M.S. and Parsons, O.A. (1983) Differential improvement of cognitive functions in recovering alcoholic women. *J. Abnorm. Psychol.*, **92** (1), 87–95.

53. Parsons, O.A. (1987) Do neuropsychological deficits predict alcoholics' treatment course and posttreatment recovery? in *Neuropsychology of Alcoholism: Implications for Diagnosis and Treatment* (eds O.A. Parsons, N. Butters, and P.E. Nathan), Guilford Press, New York, pp. 273–290.

54. Pfefferbaum, A., Sullivan, E.V., Mathalon, D.H. *et al.* (1995) Longitudinal changes in magnetic resonance imaging brain volumes in abstinent and relapsed alcoholics. *Alcohol. Clin. Exp. Res.*, **19** (5), 1177–1191.

55. Rosenbloom, M.J., Pfefferbaum, A., and Sullivan, E.V. (2004) Recovery of short-term memory and psychomotor speed but not postural stability with long-term sobriety in alcoholic women. *Neuropsychology*, **18** (3), 589–597.

56. Sullivan, E.V., Rosenbloom, M.J., Lim, K.O., and Pfefferbaum, A. (2000) Longitudinal changes in cognition, gait, and balance in abstinent and relapsed alcoholic men: relationships to changes in brain structure. *Neuropsychology*, **14** (2), 178–188.

57. Wang, G.J., Volkow, N.D., Chang, L. *et al.* (2004) Partial recovery of brain metabolism in methamphetamine abusers after protracted abstinence. *Am. J. Psychiatry*, **161** (2), 242–248.

58. Ersche, K.D., Clark, L., London, M. *et al.* (2006) Profile of executive and memory function associated with amphetamine and opiate dependence. *Neuropsychopharmacology*, **31** (5), 1036–1047.

59. Aharonovich, E., Hasin, D.S., Brooks, A.C. *et al.* (2006) Cognitive deficits predict low treatment retention in cocaine dependent patients. *Drug Alcohol Depend.*, **81** (3), 313–322.

60. Parsons, O.A. (1994) Neuropsychological measures and event-related potentials in alcoholics: interrelationships, long-term reliabilities, and prediction of resumption of drinking. *J. Clin. Psychol.*, **50** (1), 37–46.

61. Bates, M.E., Pawlak, A.P., Tonigan, J.S., and Buckman, J.F. (2006) Cognitive impairment influences drinking outcome by altering therapeutic mechanisms of change. *Psychol. Addict. Behav.*, **20** (3), 241–253.

62. Walton, M.A., Blow, F.C., Bingham, C.R., and Chermack, S.T. (2003) Individual and social/environmental predictors of alcohol and drug use 2 years following substance abuse treatment. *Addict. Behav.*, **28** (4), 627–642.

63. Weisner, C., Ray, G.T., Mertens, J.R. *et al.* (2003) Short-term alcohol and drug treatment outcomes predict long-term outcome. *Drug Alcohol Depend.*, **71** (3), 281–294.

64. Bradizza, C.M., Stasiewicz, P.R., and Paas, N.D. (2006) Relapse to alcohol and drug use among individuals

diagnosed with co-occurring mental health and substance use disorders: a review. *Clin. Psychol. Rev.*, **26** (2), 162–178.

65. McKay, J.R., Franklin, T.R., Patapis, N., and Lynch, K. G. (2006) Conceptual, methodological, and analytical issues in the study of relapse. *Clin. Psychol. Rev.*, **26** (2), 109–127.

66. Walitzer, K.S. and Dearing, R.L. (2006) Gender differences in alcohol and substance use relapse. *Clin. Psychol. Rev.*, **26** (2), 128–148.

67. Mann, K., Schafer, D.R., Langle, G. *et al.* (2005) The long-term course of alcoholism, 5, 10 and 16 years after treatment. *Addiction*, **100** (6), 797–805.

68. Connors, G.J., Maisto, S.A., and Donovan, D.M. (1996) Conceptualizations of relapse: a summary of psychological and psychobiological models. *Addiction*, **91** (Suppl.), S5–S13.

69. Marlatt, G.A. and Donovan, D.M. (2005) *Relapse Prevention: Maintenance Strategies in the Treatment of Addictive Behaviors*, 2nd edn, Guilford Press, New York.

70. Marlatt, G.A. (1998) *Harm Reduction: Pragmatic Strategies for Managing High Risk Behaviors*, Guilford Press, New York.

71. Marlatt, G.A., Larimer, M.E., Baer, J.S., and Quigley, L.A. (1993) Harm reduction for alcohol problems: Moving beyond the controlled drinking controversy. *Behav. Therapy*, **24** (4), 461–503.

72. Marlatt, G.A., Somers, J.M., and Tapert, S.F. (1993) Harm reduction: application to alcohol abuse problems. *NIDA Res. Monogr.*, **137**, 147–166.

73. Marlatt, G.A. and Witkiewitz, K. (2002) Harm reduction approaches to alcohol use: health promotion, prevention, and treatment. *Addict. Behav.*, **27** (6), 867–886.

74. Witkiewitz, K. and Marlatt, G.A. (2006) Overview of harm reduction treatments for alcohol problems. *Int. J. Drug Policy*, **17** (4), 285–294.

75. Dawson, D.A., Goldstein, R.B., and Grant, B.F. (2007) Rates and correlates of relapse among individuals in remission from DSM-IV alcohol dependence: a 3-year follow-up. *Alcohol. Clin. Exp. Res.*, **31** (12), 2036–2045.

76. Miller, W.R. (1998) Why do people change addictive behavior? The 1996 H. David Archibald Lecture. *Addiction*, **93** (2), 163–172.

77. Tevyaw, T.O. and Monti, P.M. (2004) Motivational enhancement and other brief interventions for adolescent substance abuse: foundations, applications and evaluations. *Addiction*, **99** (Suppl. 2), 63–75.

78. Monti, P.M., Tevyaw, T.O.L., and Borsari, B. (2004/2005) Drinking among young adults: screening, brief intervention, and outcome. *Alcohol Res. Health*, **28** (4), 236–244.

79. Miller, W.R. and Heather, N. (1998) *Treating Addictive Behaviors*, 2nd edn, Plenum Press, New York.

80. Beck, A.T., Steer, R.A., and Brown, G.K. (1996) *Beck Depression Inventory*, 2nd edn, The Psychological Corporation, San Antonio.

81. National Institute on Alcohol Abuse and Alcoholism (1995) Alcohol Timeline Followback (TLFB), in *Assessing Alcohol Problems: A Guide for Clinicians and Researchers* (eds J.P. Allen, M. Columbus, and National Institute on Alcohol Abuse and Alcoholism (US)), US Department of Health and Human Services, Public Health Service, National Institutes of Health, National Institute on Alcohol Abuse and Alcoholism, Bethesda, MD, pp. 241–252.

82. Vaillant, G.E. (2005) Alcoholics Anonymous: cult or cure? *Aust. N.Z. J. Psychiat.*, **39** (6), 431–436.

83. McIntire, D. (2000) How well does A.A. work? An analysis of published A.A. surveys (1968–1996). *Alcohol. Treat. Q.*, **18** (4), 1–18.

84. Lloyd, G. (2002) One hundred alcoholic doctors: a 21-year follow-up. *Alcohol Alcohol.*, **37** (4), 370–374.

85. Alcoholics Anonymous (1990) Comments on AA's Triennial Survey, Alcoholics Anonymous World Services Inc., New York.

86. Alcoholics Anonymous (1955) Alcoholics Anonymous, 2nd edn, Alcoholics Anonymous World Services Inc., New York.

87. Norris, J.L. (1978) Analysis of the 1977 survey of the membership of A.A. Paper presented at the 32nd International Congress on Alcoholism and Drug Dependence, September, 1978, Warsaw, Poland.

88. Alcoholics Anonymous (1981) Analysis of the 1980 Survey of the Membership of A.A., Alcoholics Anonymous World Services Inc., New York.

89. Tonigan, J.S. and Toscova, R.T. (1998) Mutual-help groups: Research and clinical implications, in *Treating Addictive Behaviors*, 2nd edn (eds W.R. Miller and N. Heather), Plenum Press, New York, pp. 285–298.

90. Agrawal, A., Prescott, C.A., and Kendler, K.S. (2004) Forms of cannabis and cocaine: a twin study. *Am. J. Med. Genet. B Neuropsychiatr. Genet.*, **129** (1), 125–128.

91. Kendler, K.S., Gardner, C., Jacobson, K.C. *et al.* (2005) Genetic and environmental influences on illicit drug use and tobacco use across birth cohorts. *Psychol. Med.*, **35** (9), 1349–1356.

92. Bohigian, G.M., Croughan, J.L., Sanders, K. *et al.* (1996) Substance abuse and dependence in physicians:

the Missouri Physicians' Health Program. *South Med. J.*, **89** (11), 1078–1080.

93. Galanter, M., Talbott, D., Gallegos, K., and Rubenstone, E. (1990) Combined Alcoholics Anonymous and professional care for addicted physicians. *Am. J. Psychiatry*, **147** (1), 64–68.

94. Nixon, S.J., Paul, R., and Phillips, M. (1998) Cognitive efficiency in alcoholics and polysubstance abusers. *Alcohol. Clin. Exp. Res.*, **22** (7), 1414–1420.

95. Meyerhoff, D.J., Tizabi, Y., Staley, J.K. *et al.* (2006) Smoking comorbidity in alcoholism: neurobiological and neurocognitive consequences. *Alcohol. Clin. Exp. Res.*, **30** (2), 253–264.

96. Durazzo, T.C., Rothlind, J.C., Gazdzinski, S. *et al.* (2007) Chronic smoking is associated with differential neurocognitive recovery in abstinent alcoholic patients: a preliminary investigation. *Alcohol. Clin. Exp. Res.*, **31** (7), 1114–1127.

Index

References to tables are given in bold type.